# NOTABLE AMERICAN WOMEN 1607–1950

## A Biographical Dictionary

Edward T. James   EDITOR

Janet Wilson James   ASSOCIATE EDITOR

Paul S. Boyer   ASSISTANT EDITOR

## VOLUME III
## P–Z

The Belknap Press of Harvard University Press
Cambridge, Massachusetts

# NOTABLE AMERICAN WOMEN

## VOLUME III
### P–Z
Classified List of Selected Biographies

# P

**PACKARD, Elizabeth Parsons Ware** (Dec. 28, 1816–July 25, 1897), reformer, whose experience in a mental hospital launched her on a career as advocate of married women's rights and protective legislation for the insane, was born in Ware, Mass. Originally named Betsy, she was the eldest of three children and only daughter of Samuel and Lucy (Parsons) Ware. Her father, a leading Congregational minister in the Connecticut Valley, saw that his daughter received a superior education, and at the age of nineteen she became the principal teacher in a girls' school. Her mother had a long history of mental illness, and just after her twentieth birthday Betsy herself became mentally ill. After five weeks her father took her to the state hospital at Worcester, and in a little over two months this "interesting and intelligent girl," as the hospital record described her, was discharged, recovered.

In 1839 she was married to Theophilus Packard, a clergyman fourteen years her senior. They had six children: Theophilus, born in 1842, Isaac Ware (1844), Samuel (1847), Elizabeth Ware (1850), George Hastings (1853), and Arthur Dwight (1858). During these years they moved several times until they reached Manteno, Ill., where Packard became pastor of the local Presbyterian church. Apparently each of the removals was caused by trouble that Mrs. Packard made in her husband's church. In 1860 she went to the extreme of openly opposing him in matters of religion within his own congregation. Her beliefs were mystical as opposed to his orthodox Calvinism, and behind her theology and disruptive behavior lay a conviction—which she concealed very ably—that she was in part divine: that the Holy Ghost, embodied in herself, was the female counterpart to God the Father. His family also being torn by dissension, Packard finally had her committed to the state hospital in Jacksonville, Ill., under a law giving a man commitment power over his wife provided that the superintendent agreed.

The superintendent at Jacksonville was a highly respected physician, Andrew McFarland. Mrs. Packard was in his hospital for three years. He found her a most interesting case. She had great charm and showed no intellectual disability; yet she was the source of almost intolerable annoyance. Mrs. Packard for her part found her fellow patients "a very pleasant source of social enjoyment"; many of the women confined, she felt, were actually prophetesses, who shared with her their "visions, trances and prophecies" about the Civil War. In 1863 she was discharged into the care of her husband, who, she later testified, intended to have her committed in Massachusetts as hopelessly insane. By early 1864 she was able to enlist the support of friends and neighbors and to obtain a jury trial on a writ of habeas corpus directed to her husband. The trial caused great excitement in the area, and the jury vindicated her as sane. Before the proceedings were over, Packard took his minor children and moved to Massachusetts.

Seeing herself as another HARRIET BEECHER STOWE, Mrs. Packard now took up her pen to launch a crusade for married women's rights, endeavoring thereby to support herself as well. She personally sold tickets entitling the possessors to copies of a book she was writing; when she had raised sufficient money, she had the necessary copies printed. Her first production, combining her favorite themes, was *The Exposure on Board the Atlantic & Pacific Car of the Emancipation for the Slaves of Old Columbia, . . . or, Christianity and Calvinism Compared. With an Appeal to the Government to Emancipate the Slaves of the Marriage Union* (1864). After this volume was published successfully, she several times repeated the process of selling subscriptions to her writings. In 1865 appeared a *Great Disclosure of Spiritual Wickedness!! In High Places. With an Appeal to the Government to Protect the Inalienable Rights of Married Women,* and the next year *Marital Power Exemplified in Mrs. Packard's Trial, . . . or, Three Years' Imprisonment for Religious Belief.* By 1869 she was able to buy a house in Chicago and had compelled her husband to give their minor children into her custody. By 1873 she claimed to have sold 28,000 copies of her books.

Meanwhile she was actively lobbying in state legislatures. The law under which she had been committed was amended in 1865, presumably because her "imprisonment" became a cause célèbre in Illinois. She spent some time in Massachusetts attempting to have the law there changed so as to free her from the potential legal power of her husband, and in 1866 she lobbied unsuccessfully in Connecticut for a woman's rights bill she had drawn up. In 1869 she aided in the passage of an Illinois law (framed by MYRA BRADWELL) giving married women the right to control their own property.

Mrs. Packard found, however, that people were less interested in married women's rights than in exposés of insane asylum abuses. Her later books, therefore, emphasized sensational charges against mental hospital administrators, especially McFarland, who resigned as a result of a hostile legislative investigation which she set off. Her account of *The Prisoner's Hidden Life* (1868) was republished in 1871 and reissued in 1873 as *Modern Persecution, or Insane Asylums Unveiled*. Her basic assumption was that those caring for the mentally ill did so in order to enjoy unrestrained power over the patients and to reap profits from their labor.

Through her lobbying Mrs. Packard was responsible, during the decade following her release, for securing the passage of laws in four states—Massachusetts, Illinois (1867), Iowa (1872), and Maine (1874)—dealing with mental patients. The Illinois law required a jury trial before a patient could be committed, as had been necessary since 1865, but now with the patient present; he was thus in effect "accused of insanity," often a very cruel procedure. The Massachusetts law required only that a number of relatives of a person committed be notified. (Mrs. Packard mistakenly believed that the law contained other safeguards that she had advocated.) Both the Iowa and Maine laws provided for a permanent visiting committee to investigate possible abuse of patients in the state hospitals.

Mrs. Packard's influence on popular attitudes toward mental hospitals was more important than the laws for which she was responsible. She not only solicited newspaper publicity, but she talked—presumably at length —to virtually everyone who bought one of her books and to many more besides. Psychiatrists and reformers of the day were striving for the recognition of "insanity" as an illness that might be cured by proper treatment in hospitals. Mrs. Packard helped reinforce old stereotypes and suspicions, undermining public confidence—at best not great—in the motives of

physicians and in the desirability of hospitalization except for purposes of restraint. Since psychiatrists wanted hospitalization to be a purely medical matter, with both commitment and treatment in the hands of experts free from lay interference, they viewed Mrs. Packard's efforts as retrogressive; to combat them they tried to undermine her influence with legislators by producing evidence of her own mental illness. She attributed such opposition to "the conspiracy" aimed at her personally.

After the 1870's Mrs. Packard fell from the public eye. She died in Chicago in 1897 of paralysis (undoubtedly following a stroke) and was buried there in Rose Hill Cemetery.

[Mrs. Packard's books give her version of her life and struggles; they should be used with caution. On her life up to 1860, the best source on disputed points is her psychiatric case history in *Am. Jour. of Insanity*, July 1863, pp. 89–92. For her family, see John Montague Smith, *Hist. of the Town of Sunderland, Mass.* (1899), p. 563. There are case notes in the records of Worcester (Mass.) State Hospital. Relevant printed documents are reports of the Ill. State Hospital for the Insane in the 1860's and the report of the investigating committee printed in the *Jour. of the Ill. House of Representatives*, Jan. 4, 1869, pp. 43–101. Obituaries appear in the *Chicago Tribune* and the *Boston Transcript* of July 28, 1897. Standard secondary sources are W. R. Dunton, Jr., "Mrs. Packard and Her Influence upon Laws for the Commitment of the Insane," *Johns Hopkins Hospital Bull.*, Oct. 1907, and "Further Note on Mrs. Packard," *ibid.*, July 1908; Richard Dewey, "The Jury Law for Commitment of the Insane in Ill. (1867–1893), and Mrs. E. P. W. Packard, Its Author," *Am. Jour. of Insanity*, Jan. 1913.]

JOHN CHYNOWETH BURNHAM

**PACKARD, Sophia B.** (Jan. 3, 1824–June 21, 1891), teacher and church worker, founder of Spelman College in Atlanta, Ga., was born in New Salem, Mass., the third daughter and fifth child of Winslow Packard, a farmer, and Rachel (Freeman) Packard. Her father, a descendant of Samuel Packard, who came to Massachusetts Bay from Wymondham, England, in 1638, was a man of strong religious conviction. He also believed in the value of education, though Betsey Sophia—as she was known throughout her childhood—was to get her own schooling only by persistent effort. After attending the local district school she began at the age of fourteen to teach in rural schools, and thereafter studied and taught in alternate years. In 1845 she attended New Salem Academy for at least a term, and in 1850 she received a diploma from the Charlestown (Mass.) Female Seminary, becoming an assistant teacher there the following year. After teaching in schools on Cape Cod, in 1855

Miss Packard returned to New Salem Academy as preceptress and teacher.

At New Salem she met Harriet E. Giles (1833–1909), then a senior in the classical and "ornamentals" departments. The two women became devoted friends, beginning a lifelong association. Together they taught at Orange, Mass., for three years, and then briefly opened a school of their own in Fitchburg, Mass., before accepting positions at the Connecticut Literary Institution in Suffield, Conn., in the fall of 1859. There they remained five years, until Miss Packard in the fall of 1864 became co-principal of the Oread Collegiate Institute in Worcester, Mass. Her fellow principal, John Shepardson, was also pastor of the Petersham (Mass.) Baptist Church, and the main administrative responsibilities at the Oread Institute fell to Miss Packard. She also taught classes in metaphysics and literature; Miss Giles taught music and ornamentals. After Dr. Shepardson's resignation in 1866, Miss Packard continued at the Institute, but her association with his successor was less successful, and in 1867 Miss Packard and Miss Giles—according to a student's later account—"closed their connection with the school under trying circumstances."

They spent the next twelve years in Boston, where Miss Packard first took a position with the Empire Life Insurance Company. Though commended for her clear and accurate mind, sound judgment, and integrity, she found business unsatisfying, and in 1870 she became assistant to the Rev. George C. Lorimer of the Shawmut Avenue Baptist Church. It was unusual for a woman to hold such a position, but Dr. Lorimer had early come to consider her "a woman with a great lifework before her," and when he became pastor at Tremont Temple in Boston in 1873, Miss Packard went with him as pastor's assistant. Her duties included conducting the women's prayer meeting, teaching Bible class in the Sunday school, and visiting the sick.

In 1877, as a leader in a group of some two hundred New England women concerned with the plight of the freedmen in the South, Miss Packard helped organize the Woman's American Baptist Home Mission Society, auxiliary to the American Baptist Home Mission Society, which had been building mission schools since 1832. She presided at its first meeting, became its first treasurer, served on virtually every committee, and in 1878 accepted the executive post of corresponding secretary. In February 1880 she traveled to the South to determine what help was most urgently needed. She returned to Boston that spring determined to dedicate herself to establishing a school for Negro women and girls in Georgia. After al-most a year's hesitation the society in March 1881 reluctantly endorsed the plan, and Miss Packard and Miss Giles departed at once for Atlanta.

Ten days after their arrival, on Apr. 11, 1881, they opened their school in the basement of Friendship Church, whose pastor, the Rev. Frank Quarles, a leader in the Negro community, gave invaluable assistance and encouragement in the first difficult months. The basement room was dark, damp, and cold, with straight benches and no desks, but students, eleven the first day, "of all ages and attainments," came in increasing numbers. By midsummer the enrollment had reached eighty. At this juncture the women's mission society withdrew its support. It was not until the following January that it made a firm commitment to the school and reinstated Miss Packard and Miss Giles in salaried positions. The two women had meanwhile gone ahead with their work, teaching ten or eleven daily classes, holding prayer meetings, visiting Negro families, organizing Sunday schools, and giving sewing classes. By February there were 150 pupils, and a third teacher, Sarah Champney, was dispatched to the school.

Miss Packard next undertook a fund-raising campaign to secure suitable quarters for the school. In December the American Baptist Home Mission Society made a down payment on nine acres of land and five buildings, four wooden barracks and an army hospital formerly occupied by Union troops. After hearing Miss Packard speak in Cleveland, Ohio, John D. Rockefeller became interested in her work, and with his aid she managed to complete payment on the property in 1884. That year the school was given the name Spelman Seminary, in honor of Mrs. Rockefeller and her parents, who had been ardent abolitionists.

In February 1883 the school had moved into its new quarters, at the same time instituting a teacher training program, a model school, and industrial and boarding departments. So fast did it grow—there were four hundred pupils by the end of 1883—that soliciting money became Miss Packard's perpetual concern. In 1886 many small contributions, capped by gifts from John D. Rockefeller, built Rockefeller Hall, housing a chapel, offices, and dormitory rooms. The loss by fire the next year of Union Hall, the former army hospital, was a setback, but Miss Packard persevered, and slowly enough money was collected to start another building, completed in 1888, which the trustees voted to name Packard Hall. That year the seminary was granted a charter by the State of Georgia, and Miss Packard became treasurer of the board of trustees.

Sophia B. Packard became ill in 1890 and at the request of the trustees took a vacation, traveling with another Spelman teacher to Egypt and the Holy Land. She returned to the seminary seemingly with health renewed, but the following June, while en route to New England for the summer, she died of a cerebral hemorrhage at the St. James Hotel in Washington, D.C., at the age of sixty-seven. She was buried in Silver Lake Cemetery, Athol, Mass.

With little initial backing, Miss Packard and Miss Giles, who succeeded her as Spelman's president, had seen the school grow in ten years to an enrollment of 464 students, coming from twelve states, and a faculty of thirty-four. They enjoyed the wholehearted support of the Negro community, and had won influential friends, especially from the North. Any social ostracism from Southern white people was endured without bitterness. Tall, with blue eyes, light brown hair, and a "generous figure," Miss Packard stood erect and walked briskly all her days. Both her associates and the early Spelman graduates speak of her "irrepressibly buoyant spirit," her "inimitable way of mingling fun and pathos, warning and entreaty." The spirit of her undertaking was perhaps best described by Samuel Graves, president of Morehouse College, the neighboring Baptist college for Negro men: "There was a divine and noble contagion in her. The old basement of the Friendship Church was full of it. It pervaded the Seminary . . . and with its growth the enthusiasm grew." Spelman Seminary in 1924 became Spelman College, and in 1929 joined with Morehouse College and Atlanta University in a broader university affiliation.

[Florence M. Read, *The Story of Spelman College* (1961), which includes a full bibliography. See also: Martha B. Wright and Anna M. Bancroft, eds., *Hist. of the Oread Collegiate Institute* (1905); and references to Spelman College in Ridgely Torrence, *The Story of John Hope* (1948); and Raymond B. Fosdick, *Adventure in Giving: The Story of the Gen. Education Board* (1962) and *John D. Rockefeller, Jr.* (1956). Death record from D.C. Dept. of Public Health.]

FLORENCE MATILDA READ

**PALMER, Alice Elvira Freeman** (Feb. 21, 1855–Dec. 6, 1902), educator, second president of Wellesley College, was born in Colesville in the Susquehanna Valley of upstate New York, the oldest of four children of James Warren Freeman and Elizabeth Josephine (Higley) Freeman. Of English and Scottish origins, the family bore the character of generations of God-fearing New England farmers. Alice's mother, like her maternal grandmother, Elvira Frost, had taught school before marrying. At her daughter's birth Mrs. Freeman was only seventeen, and Alice always felt that she grew up with her mother. Independent and mature, she took responsibility for her younger sisters and brother; with her mother she shared the sacrifices made when James Freeman gave up farming to become a doctor, studying first with a physician in a nearby town and then, between Alice's seventh and ninth years, at Albany Medical College. His medical practice never proved financially rewarding, but his daughter remembered home as the place "where the daily interests of every member of the family centered in caring for the sick, the poor, the aged" ("Why I Am an Optimist," 1902, MS. at Wellesley College). Her mother also devoted public effort to temperance and protective legislation for women and children; in her later years in Saginaw, Mich., she raised the money to build a women's hospital there.

From early childhood Alice absorbed her parents' devotion to Christian orthodoxy, their respect for education, and their tenacious urge for self-improvement. Learning to read at three, she entered the district school at Colesville at five. When she was ten the family moved to Windsor, N.Y., where she attended the coeducational Windsor Academy. At this excellent school she enjoyed an introduction to Greek, Latin, French, and mathematics and awakened to new ambitions for her future. In 1869, at fourteen, she joined the local Presbyterian church, of which her father was an elder. The same year she became engaged to one of her teachers, Thomas D. Barclay, a recent college graduate; he directed her reading, gave her books, and informed her of the new notions about higher education for women. When, however, he departed for Yale Divinity School and urged Alice to marry him upon her graduation from the academy, she declined in favor of going to college.

Initially the Freemans opposed this extraordinary ambition of their daughter and contended that their modest means should be saved for the education of their son. Alice's determination became persuasive, however, when she promised not to marry until she had repaid her parents for her own college expenses and had seen her brother and sisters through whatever education they chose. Rejecting Elmira College, which was nearest home, and Vassar, which was also in her own state, Alice decided to apply to the University of Michigan, which had begun to accept women in 1870 and was clearly the best institution available to her sex. In 1872 Dr. Freeman traveled the thousand miles to Ann Arbor with his daughter for her entrance examinations and interview with President James B. Angell. Although he did not find the applicant admissible on the basis of her academic preparation, Angell, a vigorous supporter of co-education, recognized Alice's promise and recommended that she be permitted to enter on six weeks' trial. Studying intensively over the summer, Alice made up her deficiencies by the end of the first term.

At Michigan, Alice Freeman held her own in the classes with men students and made lasting friendships with the few women undergraduates. She taught Sunday school and took a leading part in the students' Christian Association, as well as in the debating club. (Later these activities influenced her approach to extracurricular clubs for Wellesley students.) Slender and a little below average height, with large hazel eyes and a mass of curly brown hair, she continued to attract suitors. She was mindful, however, of her obligations to her family and decided not to fall in love. In her junior year, because of her father's worsening financial difficulties, she arranged without informing her parents to take a temporary job as principal of the Ottawa, Ill., high school for twenty weeks, the duration of the school term, thereby earning enough to relieve her family and finish her college course. She managed to complete her senior year on schedule, graduating in 1876 as one of eleven women in a class of seventy-five. One of the two women chosen for the first time to receive a commencement part, she spoke on "The Relations of Science and Poetry."

The next year she taught at a girls' seminary in Lake Geneva, Wis., taking part of her salary in tuition for her sister Ella. That summer she began graduate work in history at Ann Arbor. President Angell had recommended her to Henry F. Durant, the founder of Wellesley College, who offered her an instructorship in mathematics, but in view of the condition of her beloved sister Stella, ill with tuberculosis, and her father's financial straits she accepted instead a better-paying position as preceptress (principal) of the Saginaw, Mich., high school, securing a teaching post for Ella in one of the town's grammar schools. The two girls then moved their family to Saginaw. In December 1878 Alice Freeman refused another offer from Wellesley, this time in Greek. By the following June, however, Stella had died, and Dr. Freeman's practice was growing. Alice now felt free to accept a third offer from Durant and become head of the history department at Wellesley. She continued to spend summers in Ann Arbor, and although she was not able to complete a doctoral thesis, Michi-

gan awarded her an honorary Ph.D. degree in 1882.

As Angell had earlier, Durant soon recognized the intellectual commitment and strength of purpose underlying Alice Freeman's charm and grace. She in turn was inspired by his concern with shaping an institution to impart the virtues of "a noble, white unselfish Christian womanhood." In addition to a heavy teaching schedule in history, she conducted a daily Bible class, supervised a portion of the domestic work, and in her dormitory room devoted long hours to the guidance of students. Meanwhile her small resources were strained to pay her brother's expenses at the University of Michigan medical school. Midway through her first year at Wellesley her health gave way. Her chronic cough grew worse, and she suffered a lung hemorrhage, but after a period of rest she was able to return to work on a reduced schedule in the spring.

Upon Henry Durant's death in the fall of 1881 Wellesley's first president, Ada L. Howard, resigned, and Alice Freeman was appointed vice-president and acting president for the year. In 1882, at the age of twenty-seven, she succeeded to the presidency. Her six-year administration was crucial in the early growth of Wellesley College. Her predecessor is forgotten because she had been president in name only, an executive officer carrying out Durant's directives. In an institutional sense, Alice Freeman was Wellesley's real first president.

At the outset of her tenure, President Freeman's private parlor was her office; she was her own secretary as well as her own dean, writing letters by hand and seeing students on academic, social, and disciplinary matters. In handling crises she was energetic and resourceful. When two Wellesley graduates were refused appointments as missionaries because they did not adhere to the theological doctrines of Dr. Edmund K. Alden, the secretary of the American Board of Commissioners for Foreign Missions, she enlisted the aid of her friend the Rev. Lyman Abbott, who brought the issue before the public through the columns of his journal, the *Outlook*. The candidates were reinstated. Of Alice Freeman's part in the episode, Abbott wrote in his *Reminiscences* (1915, p. 474): "She combined in an extraordinary degree intensity of feeling with absolute self-control."

By the end of six years Alice Freeman had established basic patterns for the college. Most importantly, her structure of administrative organization involved the direct participation of the faculty. Unlike Durant, President Freeman consulted the heads of departments in a systematic way, thus laying the groundwork for Wellesley's Academic Council. She initiated the first standing committees on such matters as graduate work, entrance examinations, and the library. On the faculty she had the support of several graduates of the University of Michigan, including KATHARINE COMAN. Jointly they fostered the student Christian Association, comparable to the one they had known at Michigan, to amalgamate the college's earlier missionary and temperance societies. By raising the standards of admission Alice Freeman transformed what had been essentially a boarding school into a college. Her only published *President's Report* (1883) indicates the kinds of changes in curriculum which she promoted: improvement in the four-year Bible study course and the introduction of Dr. ELIZA M. MOSHER's lectures in practical physiology, preceding the anticipated appointment of a professor of biology. Above all, the report emphasized the progress derived from the establishment of Wellesley preparatory schools. By 1887 there were fifteen such "feeder" schools throughout the United States, which she had helped bring into being. At the start of her presidency the college had 450 students; when she retired there were 600.

Alice Freeman early sought to encourage the educated women of her generation through collective association. She was a leading spirit among the seventeen women from eight different colleges who in 1882 formed the Association of Collegiate Alumnae (later the American Association of University Women), dedicated to the promotion of women's educational interests, and was its president in 1885–86. In 1884, as one of the three American delegates to the International Conference on Education in London, she took her first trip abroad, accompanied by her father, spending a week at Newnham College of Cambridge University.

President Freeman, unlike the founder of Wellesley, made it her business to relate the college to the surrounding community and to other academic institutions. Through Prof. Eben N. Horsford of Harvard, a trustee and loyal donor to Wellesley, she was introduced to the academic and social milieu of Cambridge, Mass., and at Horsford's home in 1884 she met George Herbert Palmer (1842–1933), professor of philosophy at Harvard. Two years later Palmer gave a course at Wellesley, and in February 1887 they were secretly engaged. News of Miss Freeman's intention to marry and to resign from Wellesley, made public after the college closed in June, alarmed the trustees and quickly became a public issue. Antifeminists gained ammunition for their argument that women were undependable in po-

sitions of public responsibility, while militants for woman's rights lamented that the first woman college president (more accurately, the first to make her mark) had given up their battle and accepted the security of marriage. Devotees of the college suggested that Palmer come to Wellesley in whatever capacity he would, either as professor or as joint president. Or, they asked, would he not be willing to live in Wellesley and commute to Harvard in order that Wellesley might keep its president? Retrospectively, Palmer wrote that he and Alice agreed that her pioneering and creative work at Wellesley was done and that the institution needed a quiet period of consolidation. He also felt that her health, strained by years of overwork, could not stand further pressure. They were married on Dec. 23, 1887, at the Boston home of former Gov. William Claflin and his wife, both Wellesley trustees.

Alice Freeman Palmer understood what she had given up in marrying and had no conflict about her decision. Later she wrote about it in a collection of poems for her husband, published posthumously:

> . . . At a crisis hour
> Of strength and struggle on the heights of life
> He came, and bidding me abandon power,
> Called me to take the quiet name of wife.

She had always felt that marriage "includes all that is best in life," and in her schoolteaching days had conveyed her own conception of it in a letter to a friend: to "feel always that you are *bound* up together—that everything you each do is *full* of the other." In their marriage the Palmers supported and complemented each other at home and in the world. With little previous experience in household management Mrs. Palmer quickly came to excel in the domestic arts. To her disappointment there were no children, but their Cambridge home became a hospitable center for relatives, friends, students, visiting educators, young women seeking advice, and Mrs. Palmer's co-workers in a host of educational causes. Marriage to a distinguished member of the Harvard faculty enhanced her stature and visibility in academic circles throughout the United States. In an era of educational expansion, her experience and insight now brought her into a position of even broader influence in the higher education of women, exerted through leadership in a series of key committees. In his remarkable biography of his wife George Herbert Palmer recorded her gain in "new buoyancy and a wider power," and rightly concluded that their years together brought about the full expression of this woman in a public as well as in a private sense.

Any institution that promised to promote or improve women's education could be sure of Alice Freeman Palmer's quick response and unstinting aid. Soon after her marriage she joined Wellesley's board of trustees, and as a member of its executive committee she served the college well until her death, particularly in helping to select, personnel and raise funds. When the University of Chicago opened in 1892 with coeducation and a residential college plan, President William Rainey Harper prevailed upon Mrs. Palmer to be the first dean of women, with an obligation to be in residence no more than twelve weeks a year. She arranged the women's housing, supervised their studies, and organized a fund-raising committee; when the position of women students was secure she relinquished the deanship in 1895 to her assistant, MARION TALBOT.

During the same period, Mrs. Palmer was identified closely with the struggle of the Harvard Annex to achieve institutional identity as Radcliffe College. She was one of the major supporters of ELIZABETH CARY AGASSIZ (see Alice Freeman Palmer to C. W. Eliot, undated, Harvard University Archives) in working for a legal arrangement by which Radcliffe graduates would receive Harvard A.B.'s. When it was suggested that Harvard might agree if Radcliffe had a minimum endowment of $100,-000, Mrs. Palmer as president of the Woman's Education Association of Boston, with a committee under her charge, raised $90,000 in the winter of 1893–94. The Harvard Corporation, however, voted by a majority of one to require Radcliffe to grant its own degrees, and the money was returned to the donors. In 1900 Mrs. Palmer agreed to become a trustee of Bradford Academy (later Bradford Junior College). This oldest private school for girls in New England had fallen into a state of decline, but with her aid it was modernized and soundly reestablished. She also continued as a leader in the councils of the Association of Collegiate Alumnae, serving as president for a second term in 1889–90 and shaping its programs to secure better physical education for women and fellowship funds for graduate study.

In 1889 Mrs. Palmer accepted appointment to the Massachusetts State Board of Education, which supervised the normal schools, where most of the state's primary and elementary school teachers were trained, and exercised an important influence on the public schools. As the board's most effective advocate before the legislature, she played a leading part in the notable upgrading of the normal schools achieved during the 1890's—a work which President Charles W. Eliot of Harvard declared equal to that of their founder, Horace Mann.

Like her husband, Mrs. Palmer was known for her judgment and her acute perception of people, and was consulted regarding appointments by college and school administrators all over the country. Concerned at her prodigal expenditure of herself in committee work, interviews, and speeches, Palmer once suggested that instead she write books which would leave a permanent impress. "It is people that count," she replied. A few magazine essays preserve her favorite themes. Women, she believed, needed even more than men the enrichment of life that a college education could bring, because they had more leisure and because their home occupations were disconnected and of little educational value. Able, seriously motivated girls, she felt, should attend coeducational institutions, which offered the highest standards in teaching and curriculum. Women's colleges would further the education of students whose parents were skeptical or fearful of coeducation. Coordinate colleges for women, associated with men's colleges, were devised, she wrote, to protect the men's institutions; but even these "second tables" were better than none at all.

Mrs. Palmer never subscribed to the egalitarian view that all men and women would benefit from a college education. She had no tolerance for students who lacked intelligence and character, or for those without ideals of service and industry. The orthodox Protestantism in which she had been reared remained central in her life. She was a member of the American Board of Commissioners for Foreign Missions and president for several years of the Woman's Home Missionary Association of the Congregational Church, one of her few departures from educational work. One of her last responsibilities was the presidency of the board of directors of the International Institute for Girls in Spain, founded by the noted missionary ALICE GORDON GULICK. In the pattern of her mother, Alice Palmer worked for the temperance cause. It was characteristic, however, that her co-worker in annual campaigns against the licensing of bars in Cambridge was a Catholic priest, and that as a member of the State Board of Education she defeated a bill to introduce into the schools temperance literature which she considered exaggerated and unscientific.

Mrs. Palmer always idealized the simple, rural, impoverished life of her childhood and youth, yet she was well aware of the shift of population to the cities, and one of her arguments for college education was that exposure to the new subjects of economics and sociology would draw girls into the "absorbing work of modern city life" in settlement houses and charitable aid societies. She did not concern herself directly with the aspirations of Negroes or immigrant groups, but the disadvantaged individual who roused her interest received her full attention. Many young women without resources turned to her for help, and if they had the qualities she valued she guided them to their goals. A chance meeting with Charlotte Hawkins, a young Negro girl in Cambridge, resulted in the financing of Miss Hawkins' education at the state normal school in Salem; Charlotte Hawkins Brown later founded a school for girls in North Carolina which she named Palmer Memorial Institute. On another occasion Mrs. Palmer resigned as trustee of a women's college when she learned that a girl had been refused admission because she was "colored"; her action brought a swift reversal of the school's decision (George Herbert Palmer, talk at Palmer Institute, Charlotte Hawkins Brown Papers, Schlesinger Library).

Mrs. Palmer, like her husband, was a supporter of woman suffrage, but she did not speak or lobby for the cause, believing that it was her obligation to prepare women through education for their responsibilities as voters of the future. Through their work in organizing the Woman's Building at the Chicago World's Fair of 1893 she felt that women had demonstrated their ability as "a banded sex"; in the future she believed that their self-consciousness would lessen and their productivity be measured on an individual human basis.

During the Palmers' married life Professor Palmer had three sabbatical leaves, which they spent in Europe, setting up housekeeping for several months at a time in favorite cities and taking bicycling trips through the countryside. Summers and college vacations were spent at Palmer's ancestral farm in Boxford, Mass., where Mrs. Palmer enjoyed bird watching, making preserves, sewing, and experimenting with photography. On their last trip abroad in 1902 she fell ill in Paris and, following an operation for an obstruction of the intestine, died in a French hospital of heart failure at the age of forty-seven. Her ashes were eventually placed in the Wellesley College Chapel with those of her husband, who survived her by thirty-one years.

Alice Freeman Palmer became a symbol both for those who believed in new roles for women and for those who held to the old expectations for the sex. For her generation, in her combination of intellectual interests, ideals

of service, and happy domesticity, she had been the representative college woman.

[The basic sources are George Herbert Palmer, *The Life of Alice Freeman Palmer* (1908), and the published collection of their letters, *An Academic Courtship* (1940), with an introduction by Caroline Hazard; see in addition Palmer's introduction to the volume of his wife's verse, *A Marriage Cycle* (1915). Also of value are the Palmers' *The Teacher: Essays and Addresses on Education* (1908), and two memorial publications: *A Service in Memory of Alice Freeman Palmer Held by Her Friends and Associates in Appleton Chapel, Harvard Univ.* (1903) and *Alice Freeman Palmer. In Memoriam* (Assoc. of Collegiate Alumnae, 1903). An important part of her work is recorded in the *Annual Reports* of the Woman's Education Assoc. of Boston, 1891–1900. There are letters and MSS. of Mrs. Palmer at the Wellesley College Library and Houghton Library at Harvard.]

BARBARA MILLER SOLOMON

**PALMER, Bertha Honoré** (May 22, 1849–May 5, 1918), Chicago society leader, was born in Louisville, Ky., the elder of two daughters and the second, apparently, of the six children of Eliza Jane (Carr) and Henry Hamilton Honoré. Her ancestry, predominantly Huguenot, also contained Scottish, Irish, and Welsh strains. Her paternal great-grandfather, Jean Antoine Honoré, a friend of Lafayette, had settled in Maryland in 1781, moving later to Louisville, where he founded a family hardware and cutlery importing business. Her mother, from Oldham County, Ky., was descended from Edward D'Arcy (later Dorsey), who had come to Maryland in the seventeenth century.

When Bertha was six the family moved to Chicago, where her father invested in real estate and became one of the expansionists of the young city on Lake Michigan. Bertha attended St. Xavier's Academy and Dearborn Seminary in Chicago and in 1867 graduated from the fashionable Visitation Convent school in Georgetown, D.C. On July 29, 1870, she was married to Potter Palmer, of New England Quaker origins, who had moved to Chicago from upstate New York in 1852 and had made a fortune in dry goods, real estate, and cotton trading during the Civil War; she was twenty-one, he forty-four. With support from his energetic young wife, Palmer took a leading role in rebuilding Chicago after the great fire of 1871; his Palmer House, where he and Bertha were magnificently quartered, became one of America's celebrated hotels. Here were born their two sons: Honoré in 1874 and Potter, Jr., in 1875.

As the wife of one of Chicago's financial

giants, Mrs. Palmer inevitably occupied a position of social prominence. Though the city's social life was notably fluid and open, distinctions were fine enough to place the Palmers among the "old rich," the prefire aristocracy. The marriage of Bertha's younger sister, Ida, in 1874 to Frederick Dent Grant, oldest son of the President, confirmed her hegemony over the city's incipient elite. In her role as social arbiter she came to embody what the novelist Henry Blake Fuller in 1897 termed Chicago's "upward movement," a concerted effort by influential women to elevate the taste and cultural tone of a raw city preoccupied with the getting of riches. (In 1895 Fuller used Mrs. Palmer as the prototype of Mrs. Granger Bates in *With the Procession*, a novel about Chicago society.) Bertha Palmer joined the Fortnightly, a fashionable club devoted to the discussion of intellectual and artistic topics, and with her husband she belonged to the Contributors' Club, an association of writers and patrons which had its own magazine for members' literary productions. She and her husband also contributed to the Chicago Academy of Design, focus of the city's artistic life. As an art collector Mrs. Palmer pioneered in introducing the French Impressionists to America. In the late 1880's, advised by the painter MARY CASSATT, whom she had met in Paris, she began acquiring works of Degas, Renoir, Monet, and Pissarro. At her death she left $100,000 in paintings and objets d'art to Chicago's Art Institute; her younger son, also a collector, later became president of its board. The Palmers' own mansion, an elaborate battlemented castle on Lake Shore Drive completed in 1885, epitomized the best contemporary standards. Its lavishly eclectic interior included, besides a Louis XVI salon and rooms in Japanese and Moorish styles, a seventy-five-foot-long gallery holding three tiers of contemporary paintings.

Mrs. Palmer also possessed an interest in social and economic reform; she was the best known of the wealthy Chicago women of the period who combined social display with hardheaded civic effort. In association with women like Louise de Koven Bowen (d. 1953) and ELLEN MARTIN HENROTIN, and backed by the philanthropic spirit of the Chicago Woman's Club, she established a new hurdle for socially ambitious Chicago women: active participation in practical undertakings for the public welfare. Although the annual Charity Ball which she popularized did not win the approval of most reformers, her social conscience was far from casual. In the 1890's she became a familiar sight at JANE ADDAMS' Hull House,

swathed in furs and feathers, attending meetings or organizing reformist crusades. A supporter of the Women's Trade Union League, she was largely responsible for the successful organization of the Chicago millinery workers. She was interested in better educational opportunities for women and served (1892–96) as a trustee of the coeducational Northwestern University. While mildly favoring woman suffrage, she deplored militant feminism and in one lecture on the subject urged women not to neglect their femininity in the struggle for equality.

The World's Columbian Exposition held in Chicago in 1893 gave Bertha Honoré Palmer her most spectacular opportunity for civic and social leadership and brought to a triumphant culmination her career as "the Mrs. Astor of the Middle West." As chairman of the exposition's Board of Lady Managers she made the Woman's Building one of the exposition's most memorable achievements by seeing to it that the exhibits from forty-seven nations—many secured through her personal approaches to government leaders and European royalty—illuminated women's emergence as a social and economic force and created sympathy for the handicaps under which they still labored. Although some of her co-workers thought her high-handed and inclined to take more credit than was her due, most praised her as a brilliant and imaginative executive. On the social side, all the distinguished foreign visitors to the exposition were entertained by the Palmers, usually to a full accompaniment of newspaper publicity. One celebrated contretemps occurred when the cigarette-smoking Infanta Eulalia of Spain refused to meet "an innkeeper's wife" socially. Mrs. Palmer, remaining silent in accordance with her lifelong policy of avoiding public controversy, was generally thought to have had the best of the incident. After 1893 "Mrs. Potter Palmer of Chicago," with her diminutive but regal figure, her elegantly coiffed silver hair, and her seven-strand necklace of 2,268 pearls, became legendary across the nation.

The World's Fair brought Chicago shame as well as glory when William T. Stead, the British editor and reformer, in 1893–94 exposed the city's wide-open vice conditions. Mrs. Palmer supported Stead's evangelistic clean-up campaign and seconded his endorsement of a plan (originally put forward by a local newspaperman, Ralph M. Easley) to organize a citizens' league to work for improved municipal conditions and industrial conciliation. When the Chicago Civic Federation (forerunner of the National Civic Federation) was organized in December 1893, Mrs. Palmer was persuaded by its president, Lyman J. Gage, to accept the first vice-presidency. The new organization quickly became a rallying point for civic renewal, but Mrs. Palmer's confidence in it diminished in 1894 when, during the famous Pullman strike, her appeals on behalf of the federation to George M. Pullman to adopt a more conciliatory attitude toward his workers had no effect. An ardent Democrat, she was on the platform when William Jennings Bryan delivered his "Cross of Gold" speech before the Democratic convention of 1896. Unsuccessful in her efforts to secure an ambassadorship for her husband—Potter Palmer had little taste for politics—she campaigned to better effect when her son Honoré won election as city alderman in 1901 and again in 1903.

The undisputed queen of Chicago society, Mrs. Palmer invaded Newport in 1896, renting a "cottage" that season and for several years thereafter. Although that bastion of the Eastern aristocracy was notoriously cool to Midwesterners, she won friends through her tact, her friendships with much-sought-after European royalty, and a timely appointment by President McKinley as the only woman among the United States Commissioners to the Paris Exposition of 1900. The high point of her. Newport period came in September 1899 with the marriage there of her niece Julia Grant to Prince Michel Cantacuzène of the Russian nobility.

Potter Palmer's admiration for his wife's achievements was unflagging, but with advancing years he retired into the background. After his death in 1902, Mrs. Palmer passed much of her time in Europe, at Hampden House in London or at her Paris residence on the Rue Fabèrt. With her "abdication," Chicago social leadership fell to EDITH ROCKEFELLER MC CORMICK. In 1910 Mrs. Palmer acquired extensive acreage around Sarasota and Tampa, Fla., establishing a country home, The Oaks, at Osprey. Energetic as always, she ranched and farmed on an elaborate scale, clearing large tracts, cultivating citrus fruit, breeding cattle, and generally contributing to the early development of Florida's west coast. She died of cancer at The Oaks in 1918 and was interred in the family mausoleum at Graceland Cemetery, Chicago. A member of the Disciples of Christ Church in her early years, she later became an Episcopalian. Her sons survived and inherited the family fortune; by wise management she had more than doubled the $8,000,000 left by her husband.

[Ishbel Ross, *Silhouette in Diamonds: The Life of Mrs. Potter Palmer* (1960), draws upon Mrs. Palmer's papers in the Chicago Hist. Soc., the Sarasota County (Fla.) Hist. Commission, and the Chicago offices of the Palmer Fla. Realty Co., among other sources. *Addresses and Reports of Mrs. Potter Palmer* (1894) records her activities in connection with the World's Columbian Exposition. On the Chicago background see: Henry B. Fuller, "The Upward Movement in Chicago," *Atlantic*, Oct. 1897; Emmett Dedmon, *Fabulous Chicago* (1953); Bessie L. Pierce, *Hist. of Chicago*, vol. III (1957); Hugh D. Duncan, *Culture and Democracy* (1965); Bernard Duffey, *The Chicago Renaissance in Am. Letters* (1954); and Dixon Wecter, *The Saga of Am. Society* (1937). Genealogical information from Mrs. Dorothy T. Cullen, The Filson Club, Louisville, Ky.]

ISHBEL ROSS

**PALMER, Frances Flora Bond** (June 26, 1812–Aug. 20, 1876), better known as Fanny Palmer, draftsman and lithographer, one of the most productive staff artists of the firm of Currier & Ives, was born at Leicester, England, the eldest of three known children of Robert and Elizabeth Bond. Her father was a successful attorney in London and left ample legacies to his children. Frances and her sister, Maria Parker, attended Miss Linwood's School in London; her brother, Robert, was educated at Eton. In the early 1830's Frances was married to Edmund Seymour Palmer, described as a "gentleman" but apparently a poor provider. They had two children, Flora E. and Edmund Seymour, both born about 1834 and possibly twins. Financial reverses apparently beset the Bond family, however. Frances and her brother and sister had been well trained in art and music, and in the early 1840's, deciding to turn this talent to a means of support, the Palmers and Bonds emigrated to the United States. Contemporary directories show the Palmers living in New York City in 1844; after 1848 they made their home in Brooklyn.

With her husband, Fanny Palmer set up a lithographic printing and publishing business, called F. & S. Palmer, with the principal address at 43 Ann Street, New York. Her early work, published by other printers as well as by her own firm, consisted of landscapes, flower prints, music sheet covers, and architectural elevations; the latter were copies on stone of original drawings by Alexander J. Davis and William H. Ranlett. In 1847 Ranlett wrote that Mrs. Palmer "stands at the head of the art" of lithography. The Palmer firm failed about 1851; Seymour Palmer then became keeper of The Woodcock, a tavern in Brooklyn. He died ignominiously in 1859 by falling down stairs in a Brooklyn hotel.

By 1849 Fanny Palmer had become a staff artist of the firm of Nathaniel Currier; in that year were published her two well-known views of Manhattan, one from Brooklyn Heights and the other from Weehawken, N.J. Her most important original work is the watercolor which Currier lithographed with a few additions of his own and published as "The High Bridge at Harlem, N.Y." the same year. With the exception of a few copies of paintings of clipper ships by J. E. Butterworth in the early 1850's, Fanny Palmer was a creative lithographer, doing her own drawings directly on the stone. The only woman in her field, she was one of the best American lithographers; she also achieved success in working with Charles Currier to perfect the lithographic crayon. Trained as a draftsman in England, she was familiar with lithographic art when she came to the United States; she introduced to American printers the skill of printing a background tint. She is not known to have painted in oil, although oil copies of her prints exist.

Mrs. Palmer's most creative work was done in the 1850's when she produced scores of medium and large folio country landscapes and farm scenes. She possessed the ability to create atmospheric landscape on stone, a talent which her colleagues lacked, though they in turn assisted in drawing some of the human figures for her pictures. Her best work of this period can be seen in ten large folios: two sets of four prints—"American Farm Scenes" (1853) and "American Country Life" (1855)—and the pair "American Winter Scenes," "Morning" and "Evening" (1854). After James M. Ives joined the Currier firm in 1857, Fanny Palmer's style became more varied and dramatic. In the 1860's she produced "The 'Lightning Express' Train, Leaving the Junction" (1863); "American Express Train" (1864); "A Midnight Race on the Mississippi" (1860); and "The Champions of the Mississippi, A Race for the Buckhorns" (1866). In her last years with Currier & Ives she collaborated with Ives, who drew the figures in her prints; this collaboration was unsuccessful, however, Ives' figures proving incompatible with her work. Fanny Palmer nonetheless did achieve an epic style in "The Rocky Mountains, Emigrants Crossing the Plains" (1866), and in "Across the Continent, Westward the Course of Empire Takes Its Way" (1868), the latter published in her final year with the Currier & Ives firm. Of the approximately two hundred lithographs Fanny Palmer made for N. Currier and, after 1857, for Currier & Ives, the titles mentioned remain popular through hundreds of reproductions on calendars and greeting cards and in advertising. Unfortunately, the artist-lithographer rarely receives a credit line today.

Mrs. Palmer was a small, cheerful woman with dark hair and an English complexion. Apparently long hours of work over the lithographic stones at home caused her to stoop as if she were a hunchback. Always the chief support of her family, she remained charitable to those in need. She died of tuberculosis at the age of sixty-four; a parishioner of the Church of the Holy Trinity (Episcopal), Brooklyn, she was buried in Greenwood Cemetery.

[Mary Bartlett Cowdrey, "Fanny Palmer, An Am. Lithographer," in Carl Zigrosser, ed., *Prints* (1962); Harry T. Peters, *Currier & Ives: Printmakers to the Am. People* (2 vols., 1929–31), which reproduces (I, 111) a photograph of Fanny Palmer; obituary notice in *Brooklyn Eagle*, Aug. 22, 1876. Unpublished sources include: Parish Register records for St. Margaret's, Leicester, England, and the Church of the Holy Trinity, Brooklyn; Bond and Palmer family death and interment records, Greenwood Cemetery, Brooklyn; Harriet Endicott Waite Papers, Archives of Am. Art, Smithsonian Institution, Washington, D.C. Many of F. F. Palmer's lithographs have been reproduced in two volumes edited by Colin Simkin, *Currier and Ives' America* (1952) and *A Currier & Ives Treasury* (1955).]

MARY BARTLETT COWDREY

**PALMER, Lizzie Pitts Merrill** (Oct. 8, 1838–July 28, 1916), philanthropist, whose bequest founded the Merrill-Palmer Institute in Detroit, was born in Portland, Maine, the only child of Charles and Frances (Pitts) Merrill. Her father, descended from the Winslow family of Plymouth Colony, made a fortune in the lumber business, first in Maine and later in the pineries of central Michigan, to which state he moved his family in the 1850's.

On Oct. 16, 1855, at seventeen, Lizzie was married to a young Detroit businessman, Thomas Witherell Palmer, who afterward became a partner of her father. Lizzie Palmer's health was delicate throughout her life. She nevertheless accompanied her husband to Washington in 1883 when he was elected United States Senator and proved herself a popular hostess. She also went with him to Spain upon his appointment as United States minister in 1889. Palmer resigned this position the following year, and he and his wife returned to Detroit, bringing with them the young son of a Spanish military officer who subsequently became their ward, with the name of Harold Palmer. The Palmers, childless themselves, took several other children into their home and provided for their education.

Thomas Palmer, an advocate of woman suffrage and prohibition, was active with his wife in philanthropy. They gave support to the Detroit Institute of Art and were responsible for founding the Michigan branch of the Society for the Prevention of Cruelty to Animals. Other benefactions went to hospitals, the Y.M.C.A., and the University of Michigan. At the conclusion of her husband's public life, Mrs. Palmer was content to live quietly at their country estate, a 600-acre farm a few miles outside the city which Palmer had inherited from his mother. At his wife's request he built a four-room log cabin on the property (1887), which she furnished with authentic pioneer family heirlooms. This remains a principal attraction of Palmer Park, which the Palmers gave to the City of Detroit for public use about 1893.

Concern for her health was the primary factor in Mrs. Palmer's removal to the East Coast for long intervals in her later years. News of her husband's death in June 1913 reached her at her residence, Larchmont Manor, on Long Island Sound in New York. Wealthy in her own right and without close relatives, she now found herself in possession of a considerable fortune. Its ultimate disposition was her most notable achievement. She died of pneumonia in 1916, at Great Neck, Long Island, and was buried at Elmwood Cemetery, Detroit.

It seems probable that Mrs. Palmer's own childlessness, as well as her husband's earlier interest in establishing an institution for delinquent girls, influenced the form of her plan for disposing of her estate. As she put it in her will: "I hold profoundly the conviction that the welfare of any community is divinely, and hence inseparably, dependent upon the quality of its motherhood." She therefore left the bulk of her estate—more than $3,000,000—"for the founding, endowment and maintenance of a school to be known as the Merrill-Palmer Motherhood and Home Training School," leaving the "plan and system" of the school to the judgment of its administrators. The trustees appointed a board of directors, composed entirely of women, who in turn chose as the first director of the school Edna Noble White (d. 1954), head of the home economics department at Ohio State University and president of the American Home Economics Association. Under Dr. White's guidance the school opened its doors in 1922 to girls at the college level, with a curriculum centered on a nursery school, where little children could be studied and observed, and residence units where students could learn the principles of homemaking from experience. Besides benefiting the Detroit community directly through an infant laboratory, nursery school, play group, summer camp, and guidance service, the Merrill-Palmer Institute of Human Development and Family Life, as it has since become known, has through its research and its training of teachers exerted a continuing influence both in this country and abroad.

[Mrs. Pauline Park Wilson Knapp, President of the Merrill-Palmer Institute, and Allan J. Schuster, Editor of Publications, were generous with information about Mrs. Palmer. The historical library and archives at the institute hold her will, newspaper clippings, and account books, diaries kept by her father, and other material. Additional information was provided by the Burton Hist. Collection of the Detroit Public Library, and the Detroit Hist. Soc. The only specific published account of Mrs. Palmer is "Historic Citizen: Lizzie Merrill Palmer," *Detroit Hist. Soc. Bull.*, Dec. 1960. Other material may be found in biographical sketches of her husband, such as those in the *Dict. Am. Biog.* and *Biog. Directory Am. Cong.*; of special importance is M. Agnes Burton, "Thomas Witherell Palmer," *Mich. Hist. Collections*, XXXIX (1915), 207–17. See also references to Mrs. Palmer in Friend Palmer, *Early Days in Detroit* (1960), pp. 584, 586, 823 ff.; and *The Merrill-Palmer School: An Account of Its First Twenty Years, 1920–1940* (1940) and subsequent annual and triennial reports. Obituaries of Mrs. Palmer appeared in the *Detroit News* and the *Detroit Free Press* for July 29, 1916. Other newspaper accounts of interest may be found in the *Detroit News,* Aug. 18, 1901, Nov. 28, 1927, Feb. 26, 1950, and the *Detroit Free Press,* Aug. 11, 1916. Mrs. Palmer's date of birth is taken from her death certificate, N.Y. State Dept. of Health, Albany.]

RODERICK NASH

**PALMER, Phoebe Worrall** (Dec. 18, 1807– Nov. 2, 1874), evangelist and religious author, was born in New York City, the fourth of ten children of Henry Worrall, proprietor of an iron foundry and machine shop, and his wife, Dorothea Wade. Phoebe's father, born in Yorkshire, England, had been converted to Methodism in his youth by John Wesley; seeking greater religious and political freedom, he came to the United States, where he married an American Methodist. Phoebe's mother was noted for the good order and discipline she maintained in her large family. It was the father, however, who "commanded" the household (Wheatley, p. 16), and Phoebe was reared on a strict regimen of daily family worship.

In her youth she gave indications of literary ability, writing poems as early as the age of ten. Her youthful diary records her great admiration for her parents and for Methodist ministers. On Sept. 28, 1827, at nineteen, she was married to Walter Clark Palmer, a young homeopathic physician and a fellow Methodist who, like Phoebe, had been "powerfully converted" at the early age of thirteen.

Although the religious career of Phoebe Palmer can be specifically dated from her experience of "entire sanctification" on July 26, 1837, several events had prepared the way. Early in her marriage two sons, Alexander and Samuel, died within weeks after birth; their deaths were interpreted by the Palmers as a heavenly sign to concentrate their energies upon religious activities. In 1832 they attended the famous great revival in New York's Allen Street Methodist Episcopal Church, with which they were connected, and both went forward to kneel at the altar to dedicate themselves to the work of spiritual holiness. In 1835 Phoebe Palmer's sister, Mrs. Sarah Lankford (who at Phoebe's death was to become the second Mrs. Walter C. Palmer), instituted a weekly afternoon prayer meeting for women of the Allen Street and Mulberry Street Methodist churches. Though the two sisters at first shared the leadership, this soon fell solely to Mrs. Palmer. Either she or a visiting minister would conduct the meeting, which began with reading of the Scriptures, singing, and prayer, followed by the giving of personal testimony. The gathering soon became known as the Tuesday Meeting for the Promotion of Holiness, thus reflecting its dedication to the seeking of entire sanctification according to the doctrine of Christian perfection—a doctrine originally advanced by the Methodist founder John Wesley but by the 1830's shared by some of the leading evangelists of other denominations, notably Charles G. Finney.

Around Mrs. Palmer's Tuesday Meeting, which continued at her home for thirty-seven years, centered much of the development of the perfectionist movement. In 1839 the Meeting began to include men as well as women, under the leadership of an influential recruit, Prof. Thomas Coggeshall Upham of Bowdoin College, whose wife had been a member. It soon drew such crowds that the Palmers had to move to larger quarters. To Mrs. Palmer's parlors came many Methodists who became leaders in the movement, among them Bishop Leonidas L. Hamline, who was sanctified under her guidance in the early 1840's; John Dempster, founder of the Concord (later Boston) and Garrett seminaries; Bishop Edmund S. Janes; and Nathan Bangs, presiding elder in New York City. Hamline and Bangs

remained close friends of Mrs. Palmer and her husband for many years, despite their disagreement, during the 1850's, with some aspects of her teachings. By 1858, however, the Tuesday Meeting had become broadly evangelical, drawing laymen and ministers from many denominations.

Phoebe Palmer's published writings and her work as a traveling evangelist made a still wider impact. She contributed frequently to the principal journal of the perfectionist movement, the *Guide to Holiness*, and wrote a succession of books. The first, *The Way of Holiness* (1845), a narrative of her own religious experience, reportedly sold 24,000 copies in six years and was frequently reissued. Seven other volumes followed, the last, *Pioneer Experiences* (1868), being a collection of personal testimonies. All did much to popularize the perfectionist revival. In 1862 Dr. Palmer purchased the monthly *Guide to Holiness* and installed his wife as editor-in-chief. Circulation rose immediately from 13,000 to 30,000, and Mrs. Palmer remained as editor until her death.

In Mrs. Palmer's evangelist preaching her husband was an active partner. About 1850 they began to spend half of each year attending Methodist camp meetings and conducting holiness revivals in the eastern United States and Canada. Their tours ultimately extended to other sections of the country and to camp meetings of the interdenominational National Association for the Promotion of Holiness, organized in 1867. During the winter and spring they normally returned to New York, where Dr. Palmer resumed his medical practice. In 1859, however, they went to England and remained for four years, conducting extended revivals in the British Isles. "Thousands on thousands are born again," read a contemporary report, "through listening to the appeals of the Doctor and his lady."

For Phoebe Palmer, sanctification led naturally to service to one's fellow man. Early in the 1840's she had enrolled as a distributor of tracts in New York slums and as a visitor to the city prison, the Tombs. For eleven years, beginning in 1847, she was corresponding secretary of the New York Female Assistance Society for the Relief and Religious Instruction of the Sick Poor. Her best-known charitable work was the founding, in 1850, of the Five Points Mission in one of the city's most squalid neighborhoods. Undertaken, through her leadership, by the Methodist Ladies' Home Missionary Society, this precursor of later settlement houses and institutional churches contained a chapel, schoolroom, baths, and twenty rent-free apartments for the indigent.

In matters of social reform Mrs. Palmer was a moderate. During the 1850's and '60's she and her Methodist associates followed a policy of public neutrality on the slavery question. She also eschewed the cause of woman's rights and sought to avoid public prominence; only after much persuasion did she allow her name to be listed on the title pages of her books. Although her modesty, personal charm, and lack of any feminist fanaticism saved her from conservative criticism, her very example did signalize and popularize the larger role for women that was a feature of the holiness movement. The wives of some of its leaders took an active part in camp meetings and revivals; and women in many cities organized weekday gatherings in their homes on the model of Mrs. Palmer's. She herself in her *Promise of the Father* (1859) cited Biblical authority for the right of women to participate in church work.

Phoebe Palmer remained active in holiness ministry until her final years. A third child, Eliza, had died in infancy, but her three later children all lived to maturity: Sarah, Phoebe, and Walter Clark Palmer, Jr., the publisher of many of her works. She died of "immediate suffocation" (pneumonia?) in New York City in 1874, at the age of sixty-six. At her funeral the Rev. T. DeWitt Talmage of the Brooklyn Tabernacle hailed the "Twenty-five thousand souls saved under the instrumentality of Phoebe Palmer!" She was buried in Greenwood Cemetery, Brooklyn.

Theologically, mid-nineteenth-century America was an era of romanticism and transcendentalism, of which one facet was the revivalism popularly identified with Charles G. Finney. Phoebe Palmer's career paralleled that of Finney, although she worked in different fields and her message carried different stresses. Closely associated in her endeavors with her husband, she nevertheless made a distinctive contribution in four areas: the Tuesday Meeting, holiness writings, revivalism, and social welfare. Her career exemplifies two developments in the American society of her time: the growth of city life, which fostered the doctrine of perfectionism, and the enlarged role of women in religious affairs.

[Richard Wheatley, *The Life and Letters of Mrs. Phoebe Palmer* (1876); John L. Peters, *Christian Perfection and Am. Methodism* (1956); Timothy L. Smith, *Revivalism and Social Reform* (1957). See also J. A. Roche, "Mrs. Phœbe Palmer," *Ladies' Repository*, Feb. 1866, a good contemporary description; George Hughes, *The Beloved Physician, Walter C. Palmer* (1884); *N.-Y. City Directory*, 1847–48, on Henry Worrall; and, on the Five Points Mission, *The Old Brewery, and the New Mission House at the Five Points* (1854) and Carroll S. Rosenberg, "Protestants and Five Pointers," *N.-Y. Hist. Soc. Quart.*, Oct. 1964.]

w. j. mc cutcheon

**PALMER, Mrs. Potter.** *See* PALMER, Bertha Honoré.

**PALMER, Sophia French** (May 26, 1853–Apr. 27, 1920), professional nurse, was born in Milton, Mass., the fifth daughter and seventh among the ten children of Simeon and Maria Burdell (Spencer) Palmer, natives, respectively, of Boston and of Hartford, Conn., whose ancestors had been among the first colonists to settle in New England. Simeon Palmer attended Yale University and graduated from the Harvard Medical School (1837). Teele's *History of Milton* records that he practiced medicine "as occasion required" but engaged chiefly in literary pursuits.

The details of Sophia Palmer's early education are unknown. On May 1, 1876, at the age of twenty-two, she was admitted to the Boston Training School for Nurses (now the Massachusetts General Hospital School of Nursing) by its superintendent, LINDA RICHARDS. In Miss Palmer's time many parents looked askance at nursing as a vocation for their daughters. This may have been true in her case, for the history of the training school comments that no relatives visited her while she was there. However, her youngest sister, Ida Russell Palmer, also became a nurse (Newport, R.I., Training School, 1891). During the last eleven months of the two-year training course, Sophia Palmer was placed in charge of the wards. After graduating on July 15, 1878, she spent more than a year in Philadelphia, caring for patients of Dr. S. Weir Mitchell, and for several years more she was occupied with private nursing, chiefly of patients with nervous or mental illnesses.

In 1884 Miss Palmer became superintendent of the newly organized St. Luke's Hospital, New Bedford, Mass., where she laid the foundations for its training school; but she resigned after a year when, for reasons of economy, the hospital reduced the number of nurses. Returning to private nursing, she also spent nine months in what she considered extremely profitable postgraduate experience at the Massachusetts General Hospital (1888). Moving to Washington, D.C., in 1889, she became the founder and administrator of the training school for nurses at the Garfield Memorial Hospital. The medical staff at first were openly hostile to the idea of such a school, but Miss

Palmer's venture was so successful that, at the graduation of the first class, the former leader of the opposition gave the address and presented the diplomas. In 1896 Miss Palmer became the superintendent of the Rochester (N.Y.) City (General) Hospital and Training School, where she remained for four years.

Sophia Palmer's administrative talents were further displayed during the crucial years when nurses were endeavoring to develop professional organizations, to set standards of training and practice, to promote regulatory legislation, and to establish a professional journal. During the period 1893 to 1895 Miss Palmer helped edit the *Trained Nurse and Hospital Review*, published by the training school of the Buffalo General Hospital. She was a founding member of the American Society of Superintendents of Training Schools for Nurses (1893), helped draft its constitution and bylaws, and was one of its representatives in organizing the national Nurses' Associated Alumnae of the United States and Canada, later the American Nurses' Association. Miss Palmer's common sense and diplomacy saved more than one tense situation.

In the summer of 1900 she was chosen by the Associated Alumnae to be editor-in-chief of the official publication it was launching, the *American Journal of Nursing*. The *Journal* published its first issue, of 2,500 copies, that October. Miss Palmer, who for more than a decade used her own home as an office, also assumed full responsibility for the business management of the new periodical and remained its editor until her death. She had a gift for logical analysis and expressed her ideas concisely. Known for her outspoken editorials, she made the magazine a powerful influence in promoting needed reforms in nursing education, encouraging unity of purpose and establishing communication between nurses as well as keeping them informed on vital social issues.

In November 1899 Miss Palmer had enlisted the help of the New York State Federation of Women's Clubs in seeking legislation to regulate the training and practice of nurses in that state. This was the first step in an educational campaign, conducted through the pages of the *American Journal of Nursing* and through her visits to state associations, which gave impetus to the countrywide movement for state supervision of nursing schools and state registration of trained nurses. When the New York law, one of the first, was passed in 1903, Miss Palmer was one of five nurses appointed as members of the Board of Nurse Examiners, and she was elected its first chairman.

Miss Palmer was an attractive woman, above average in height. Although she was a militant leader in the cause of nursing reform and was sometimes impatient at its slow progress, her friends describe her as sympathetic and generous, with a deep concern for people. She was especially interested in the young, and in 1906 adopted an eight-year-old girl, who died in her twentieth year. Active until the end, Sophia Palmer died at sixty-six at Forest Lawn, N.Y., near Rochester, in 1920 following a cerebral hemorrhage. Her ashes were buried in the family plot in Forest Hills Cemetery, Boston. The Sophia F. Palmer Library of the *American Journal of Nursing* and the Palmer-Davis Library of the Massachusetts General Hospital School of Nursing honor her memory.

[Files of *Am. Jour. of Nursing*, 1900-20, especially obituary of Miss Palmer, Apr. 1920, tributes to her, June 1920, and Mary M. Riddle, "Twenty Years of the Jour.," Oct. 1920; see also Katharine DeWitt, "The Jour.'s First Fifty Years," Oct. 1950. Other information from: Miss Palmer's school record, Mass. Gen. Hospital School of Nursing; Sara E. Parsons, *Hist. of the Mass. Gen. Hospital Training School for Nurses* (1922); information from records of St. Luke's Hospital, New Bedford, Mass., and Garfield Memorial Hospital, Washington, D.C.; Meta R. Pennock, ed., *Makers of Nursing Hist.* (1940); Mary M. Roberts, *Am. Nursing: Hist. and Interpretation* (1954); Am. Soc. of Superintendents of Training Schools for Nurses, *Annual Reports of Conventions;* Nat. League of Nursing Education, 21st *Annual Report*, 1915. Family information from Albert K. Teele, ed., *The Hist. of Milton, Mass., 1640 to 1887* (1887), p. 531, and from Mrs. Willard Selleck, Wenatchee, Wash., a niece.]

STELLA GOOSTRAY

**PANSY.** *See* ALDEN, Isabella Macdonald.

**PARKER, Cynthia Ann** (1827?-1864?), Indian captive, mother of the Comanche chief Quanah Parker, was born in Crawford County, Ill., where her parents, Silas M. and Lucy (Duty) Parker, were then farming. Her paternal grandfather, Elder John Parker, a Baptist patriarch, had led his numerous clan from the Virginia frontier to break land in newer pioneering ventures in Georgia, Tennessee, and Illinois. Moving ultimately to Texas, these related families settled near the present Groesbeck, in Limestone County, then on the exposed frontier, and grouped their cabins inside a blockhouse known as Fort Parker. The men became leaders in the Texas government.

On May 19, 1836, Indians attacked the settlement, killed five men, and took off several captives, including Cynthia Ann. The nine-year-old girl was adopted by the Quahadas of the Staked Plains, wildest of Comanche bands. She learned to set up a tepee, to preserve buffalo meat, to tan and decorate skins for clothing. She married a noted war chief, Nocona, and became the mother of two sons, Quanah (Fragrance) and Pecos, and a baby daughter, Topsannah (Prairie Flower). Twice she was seen by white men, but she rejected all efforts to free her. The story of the "White Comanche" became a Southwestern legend.

On Dec. 18, 1860, she and some other women went out to get a supply of buffalo meat. To help in the killing and butchering she took along José, a Mexican captive. On her pony she carried Topsannah, then about eighteen months old. Meanwhile a force of Texas rangers, dragoons, and volunteer settlers were out to punish the Comanches for a recent raid. They discovered the work party and mistook it for the entire hostile village. The women were shot down as they fled, and José was killed fighting as bravely as a Comanche. Sul Ross, the ranger captain, believed he had annihilated Nocona's band and killed the chief; and this version still appears in many histories. Cynthia Ann was captured. The ranger accounts differ as to why she was not shot, whether it was the child in her arms or a glimpse of her blond hair. She was "very dirty" from the butchering and her fair skin was burned as dark as an Indian's, but her eyes were blue. She remembered no English word except her name.

The rangers treated her sympathetically, but she cried incessantly. She was restored to her white relatives, and her brother built a separate cabin for her near his house in a settlement north of Tyler. She recovered her use of English and learned the arts of white housekeeping. Topsannah even attended a school in the settlement. "She looked to be stout and weighed about 140 pounds, well-made, and liked to work," said a man who remembered Cynthia Parker. "She had a wild expression and"—in accordance with Indian etiquette— "would look down when people looked at her. . . . She was an open-hearted, good woman, and always ready to help somebody." In her only known photograph she has a gentle, troubled expression and regular, even pretty, features. But she tried several times to escape and join the Comanches. Then her little girl died, and she soon followed her, dying as an Indian dies when hope is gone. She was buried in the Fosterville cemetery in Henderson County.

Apparently Nocona never remarried. He continued to raid the settlements until he died from an infected wound. Pecos died of small-

pox. Quanah, Cynthia Parker's other son, grew up to be the greatest war chief of the Comanches and the last to surrender when they were finally subdued in 1875. Then he settled down near Fort Sill in present-day Oklahoma, acquired a big house, and became a leader of progress. Here he learned for the first time of his mother's death. He questioned everyone he could find who had known her during her white captivity. He had a painting made from her photograph and hung it over the reed organ in his parlor. He adopted her name as the surname of his family. Finally, in 1910, granted a $1,000 appropriation from Congress for the purpose, he had her body brought from Texas and reburied in the mission cemetery near his home. At the funeral he made a short speech in his halting English: "Forty years ago my mother died. She captured by Comanche, nine years old. Love Indian and wild life so well no want to go back to white folks. All same people anyway, God say. I love my mother. I like white people. . . . When end come then they all be together again."

When the end came for him the next year he was buried beside her. But in 1957 Fort Sill acquired the site for its missile range, and the two bodies were removed to the post cemetery. Six of the "White Comanche's" seven surviving grandchildren were present at the reburial; the pallbearers were her great-grandsons; and the little great-great-granddaughter chosen to place a wreath on her grave bore the name of Cynthia Ann. Eight years later the body of Topsannah, whose original burial place at Asbury, near Tyler, had been found after years of searching, was buried beside her mother.

[Grace Jackson, *Cynthia Ann Parker* (San Antonio, 1959); Norman B. Wood, *Lives of Famous Indian Chiefs* (1906); J. Evetts Haley, *Charles Goodnight: Cowman & Plainsman* (1936); Howard H. Peckham, *Captured by Indians* (1954); Paul I. Wellman, "Cynthia Ann Parker," *Chronicles of Okla.*, June 1934; William Moses Jones, *Texas Hist. Carved in Stone* (1958); [Daniel A. Becker,] "Comanche Civilization with Hist. of Quanah Parker," *Chronicles of Okla.*, June 1923; *Daily Oklahoman*, Aug. 10, 1957; Angie Debo, "Quanah Parker," *Am. Heritage*, Summer 1953, and "Two Graves in Okla.," *Harper's Mag.*, Dec. 1956; interviews with Rev. and Mrs. White Parker, July 13, 1947, and Mar. 8, 1952; interview with Mrs. Neda Parker Birdsong, June 23, 1956.]

ANGIE DEBO

PARLOA, Maria (Sept. 25, 1843–Aug. 21, 1909), pioneer in home economics teaching, was born in Massachusetts, but nothing further is known of her origins and early life. When she enrolled at the Maine Central Institute, Pittsfield, Maine, she was already in her twenty-eighth year, orphaned, and long self-supporting. At that time (1871) she gave her home address as Portsmouth, N.H.; her first work, *The Appledore Cook Book*, published the next year, revealed that she had worked as a cook in private families and as pastry cook in several New Hampshire hotels, principally at summer resorts and including the Appledore House on the Isles of Shoals. During the first of her two years at the Maine school she had studied in the normal department, and she accordingly went into teaching, taking a position in Mandarin, Fla. (where HARRIET BEECHER STOWE had a home), which she held for several seasons.

An experience in Mandarin led to her becoming a teacher of cooking. Always warmly generous, especially toward young people, she wished to help buy an organ for the Mandarin Sunday school; to raise funds she gave her first lecture on cooking at New London, Conn., in the summer of 1876. Her performance was so well received that friends advised her to open a cooking school, which she chose to do in Boston. After giving four lectures there in May 1877, she opened her school the following October in the former Tremont Street studio of the artist William M. Hunt. She was an immediate success. Before the school year was over she had pioneered by giving a series of lectures at a private school in Portsmouth and before the pupils of Lasell Seminary, Auburndale, Mass., in addition to assisting with charity cooking classes. In 1878 she publicly demonstrated outdoor cooking in Boston and published a pocket-sized book, *Camp Cookery*.

The adventuresome spirit that had taken her to Florida, combined with her lifelong eagerness to observe and learn, carried her to England that summer to study methods of cookery teaching, particularly at the National Training School for Cookery in London, and to France, where she learned something of French cooking. In March 1879 she became one of the two teachers at the newly opened Boston Cooking School. Though pressed to take charge of this school, she continued to run her own, consenting, however, to inaugurate a normal class at the Boston Cooking School in November 1880. Meanwhile, she had published a textbook, *First Principles of Household Management and Cookery* (1879), a work which included a discussion of the chemical elements of food and of the human body, and her activities had attracted the attention of JULIET CORSON, who publicized them in her *Training Schools of Cookery* (1879). In August 1879 Miss Parloa gave a series of lectures at the summer assembly in Lake Chautauqua, N.Y. Her later audiences included Harvard medical students and groups in Chicago and other Western cities. Her rapidly expanding interests eventually extended to the role of science in the home and the community. It was at her request and for her classes that ELLEN H. RICHARDS developed the chemistry of cooking and cleaning, material that was to become standard in home economics training. It was also Miss Parloa's suggestion that led Mrs. Richards and others to work for the introduction of such topics into public school curricula.

At about the time she published *Miss Parloa's New Cook Book and Marketing Guide* (1881), which, like her *Appledore Cook Book*, went through numerous editions, she began to wish for a location offering greater scope. By 1883 she had opened a school in New York City, in a house which she leased near Stuyvesant Square. In the evenings she gave free classes to girls at city mission schools. Her *Practical Cookery* was published in 1884. But New England called her back, and her considerable earnings enabled her to remove in 1887 to Roxbury, Mass., and concentrate on writing and lecturing. From 1891 until her death she contributed regularly to the *Ladies' Home Journal*, of which she was also part owner. Her field study of European family life, beginning in 1894, resulted particularly in articles on the French. By 1898 she had returned to New York, where she continued to be influential in teacher training. She was a charter member the next year of the small conference that Mrs. Richards started at Lake Placid, N.Y., and afterward of the American Home Economics Association into which that group developed. Though informally trained herself, she always advocated scientific education. Her numerous later works included two Farmers' Bulletins prepared for the United States Department of Agriculture: *Canned Fruits, Preserves, and Jellies* (1904; also issued in translation by the Mexican government, 1911) and *Preparation of Vegetables for the Table* (1906).

For the last six years of her life she lived in Bethel, Conn., near an old friend, where she indulged her passion for flower gardening and became engrossed in community life. She was the chief instigator of the Village Improvement Society, which landscaped the school grounds the year before her death. In Bethel she shared her home with two orphan girls, among the many young persons she had befriended. She died there of acute nephritis, as she was preparing for another extended visit to Europe. Her ashes were buried, after Episcopal services, at Forest Hills Cemetery, Boston. Maria Parloa's infectious enthusiasm had so inspired others that her influence in home economics went far beyond what she herself contributed through her sound judgment and broad grasp of problems.

[William V. Alexander, "Maria Parloa," *Good Housekeeping*, May 1885; alumni records of Maine Central Institute, Pittsfield; Juliet Corson, *Training Schools of Cookery* (U.S. Bureau of Education Circular of Information No. 4–1879, 1879); minutes of meetings of Boston Cooking School Committee, 1872–82, Simmons College Archives; "A Pioneer School of Domestic Science," *Am. Kitchen Mag.*, Mar. 1898; Mary J. B. Lincoln, "The Pioneers of Scientific Cookery," *Good Housekeeping*, Oct. 1910; appreciation and tributes, *Jour. of Home Economics*, Oct. 1909; *Who's Who in America*, 1899–1900 through 1906–07; *N.Y. Times*, Aug. 23, 1909; *Danbury* (Conn.) *Evening News*, Aug. 23, 30, 31, 1909; *Danbury News*, Aug. 25, 1909; death certificate from town records, Bethel, Conn.; recollections of Katherine La Valla of Bethel, Conn. See also Caroline L. Hunt, *The Life of Ellen H. Richards* (1912).]

MARY TOLFORD WILSON

**PARRISH, Celestia Susannah** (Sept. 12, 1853–Sept. 7, 1918), Southern educator, was born on her father's plantation near Swansonville, in Pittsylvania County, Va. She was the eldest of the three children, two daughters and a son, of William Perkins Parrish and his second wife, Lucinda Jane Walker. Little is known of Celestia's early years except that she possessed a precocious intellect and a burning desire to excel. Parrish, apparently a man of some wealth and position, encouraged her intellectual ambitions, but the Civil War swept away the local schools, and in the course of that holocaust both he and his wife died. Their children passed into the care of an uncle and two maiden aunts. The uncle died when Celeste (as she was commonly known) was fifteen, whereupon she discovered that her aunts wished to be relieved of the burden of her support. After only a sporadic acquaintance with formal schooling, she began a lifelong career of teaching in 1869.

At first, Miss Parrish later recalled, she was an utter failure in the classroom, but after discovering a book on pedagogy, she experienced something akin to a religious conversion and promised God that she would become a better teacher. Working in the rural schools of Pittsylvania County for five years, she acquired an excellent reputation and in 1874 won an invitation from the schools of Danville, Va. Here she was able to join her sister, whom she

was now supporting, as a student at the Roanoke Female Institute (later Averett College). The institute awarded Celestia Parrish a diploma in 1876, but she yearned for a degree from an authentic college. The six weeks she spent the next summer at an institute for teachers at the University of Virginia heightened her ambition to become, in her words, "a cultivated woman," but the doors of the university's regular session were closed to women.

Miss Parrish resigned from the Danville schools in 1883, taught a variety of courses at the Roanoke Female Institute for a year, enrolled in 1884 as a student in the Virginia State Normal School (later Longwood College) in Farmville, and so impressed the faculty that immediately after her graduation, in June 1886, she was invited to teach the lower branches of mathematics. Thereafter she involved herself actively in problems of teacher training, but she had also settled on the plan of attending "a great university" in the North. Securing a year's leave of absence, she enrolled at the University of Michigan in 1891 to study mathematics and astronomy. On her return to Virginia she accepted a position teaching mathematics, philosophy, psychology, and pedagogy at Randolph-Macon Woman's College, recently founded at Lynchburg and dedicated to the proposition that Southern women were entitled to higher learning. Unfamiliar with modern psychology, yet determined to give her students the best, Miss Parrish spent the summer of 1893 at Cornell University, where she met the famed experimental psychologist Edward Bradford Titchener. That fall she established a crude psychological laboratory at Randolph-Macon—probably the first south of Baltimore—returning to Cornell during the summer sessions of 1894 and 1895 to pursue work on a degree. In January 1895 the *American Journal of Psychology* published some results of her experimental work, "The Cutaneous Estimation of Open and Filled Spaces," a solid, though minor, contribution to a large body of research produced in the 1890's on cutaneous sensibility. In June 1896 she received a Ph.B. degree from Cornell.

With the cherished college diploma in hand at the age of forty-two, Miss Parrish devoted increasing energy to making a bachelor's degree more accessible to other Southern women. She argued, in a series of published writings, for the admission of women to Southern colleges and universities, for the conversion of female seminaries into colleges, and for the strengthening of the few existing women's colleges. She did not hesitate to make exacting demands of her students at Randolph-Macon, and she took pride in marshaling the young ladies before skeptics to demonstrate that hard work had not impaired their health. Turning from argument to organization, she founded an alumnae association at Randolph-Macon, served as vice-president of the Association of Collegiate Alumnae, presided over its Virginia branch, and, in 1903, became a founder and first president of the Southern Association of College Women (see ELIZABETH AVERY COLTON), a group dedicated to raising standards of women's education.

It was her work on behalf of the public schools in the South, however, which brought Miss Parrish greatest distinction, earning her a reputation as one of the pioneers of progressive education. In 1897, the year after completing her degree at Cornell, she had attended the summer session at the University of Chicago, then a center of progressive ferment. Returning for the following two summers, she studied under John Dewey and acquainted herself with his Laboratory School. Seeking an opportunity to duplicate Dewey's experimental work, Miss Parrish left Randolph-Macon early in 1902 to become professor of pedagogic psychology and head of the department of pedagogy at the Georgia State Normal School in Athens. There she impressed the philanthropist George Foster Peabody, who provided $10,000 for a building to house experimental classrooms and $3,500 for equipment.

The Muscogee Elementary School (named for Peabody's home county in Georgia) opened in Athens during the fall of 1903, one of the first schools in the nation explicitly founded on progressive ideas and most certainly the first in the South. Adhering closely to Dewey's program and rhetoric, Miss Parrish gathered about her a dedicated band of young disciples, urging them to throw away textbooks, ignore traditional subject divisions, and devote their skills to developing "units" of work that would be interesting to the children and relevant to the life of the rural community. This radical and demanding program aroused opposition, but by Peabody's wish Miss Parrish had been granted a free hand, and she brooked no interference. The student-teachers were suitably impressed, although some testified to the difficulty of reproducing Muscogee's ideal features when they scattered to the hinterlands of Georgia. During these years Miss Parrish took the lead in introducing the parent-teacher association movement into Georgia, founding the state's first Mothers and Teachers Cooperative Club and becoming the first president of the statewide organization.

Her tenure at Athens ended in 1911, when she accepted an appointment as state supervisor of rural schools for the North Georgia District. (Most of the Muscogee staff left at the same time, and the school became merely one of many good, but unexceptional, centers for the training of teachers.) This last assignment proved perhaps the most difficult of Celestia Parrish's career. Overseeing more than 2,400 rural schools and more than 3,800 teachers in forty-eight mountainous counties, she discovered that only one-fifth of the teachers possessed as much as normal-school training, and some could claim only a fourth-grade education. Only a few counties taxed themselves for support of the schools, most relying instead on inadequate funds from the state. The problem here was not to produce an ideal education, but to encourage any kind of education at all, and the fundamental barriers—poverty and indifference—were probably beyond the powers of anyone to surmount. Nevertheless, this dedicated reformer managed to visit each county annually, traveling by rail, buggy, and wagon. She conducted summer institutes, demonstrated the art of teaching to neophytes, and exhorted county superintendents, patrons, and teachers to give the rural schools the support they needed. Miss Parrish continued her relentless and sometimes unpopular campaign until her death in 1918.

Outside of her work, Celestia Parrish, a Baptist, took part in missionary societies, in the Young Women's Christian Association (she is said to have organized the first college Y.W.C.A. in the South), and in the Woman's Christian Temperance Union. About the time of her move to Georgia she adopted a young girl and took over the care of two nephews, sons of her brother. She died a few days before her sixty-fifth birthday in a cottage she had built in Clayton, Ga., and was buried at the Clayton Baptist Church, under a monument that bears the inscription "Georgia's Greatest Woman."

[The best source on the early life of Miss Parrish is her own sketch, *My Experience in Self-Culture* (pamphlet, Special Collections Division, Univ. of Ga. Libraries). The *Woman's Who's Who of America*, 1914–15, and *Who Was Who in America*, vol. I (1942), contain brief entries, probably prepared by the subject herself. The records of Longwood College, the "Record Minutes of the Ga. State Board of Education," 1870–1923, the catalogues and yearbooks of Randolph-Macon Woman's College and Ga. State Normal School, and the records of Cornell Univ., the Univ. of Mich., and the Univ. of Chicago provide confirmation of biographical data. The most useful writings about Miss Parrish are articles by Dr.

Gillie A. Larew and Dr. Meta Glass in the *Va. Jour. of Education*, May 1942; a brief portrait by Elise Gibbs in *Some Ga. Hist. Sketches* (1943); a typescript by Mary E. Creswell, "Personal Recollections of Celeste Parrish" (in the possession of Prof. Anne F. Scott, Duke Univ.); and obituaries in the *Atlanta Jour.* and *Atlanta Constitution* for Sept. 9, 1918. Other material from interviews and correspondence with the following friends of Miss Parrish: Dr. Gillie A. Larew, Lynchburg, Va.; Mrs. Charles W. Banner, Greensboro, N.C.; and Miss Elise Gibbs and Miss Mary Edwards Mitchell of Atlanta, Ga. Writings by Miss Parrish include two books: *The Lesson* (1909) and *Course of Study: Muscogee Elementary School of the Ga. State Normal School, Athens* (n.d.), the latter written in collaboration with two of her colleagues. Articles by Miss Parrish may be found in the *Independent*, Apr. 1901 and Oct. 1901; *Educational Rev.*, Nov. 1901; *Elementary School Teacher*, Nov. 1905; and Southern Educational Assoc., *Jour. of Proc. and Addresses*, 1899, 1900. Particularly informative about her work in the rural schools of Georgia are her reports, which appeared in the *Annual Report of the* (Ga.) *Dept. of Education* for the years 1912–18.]

CHARLES E. STRICKLAND

**PARSONS, Elsie Clews** (Nov. 27, 1875–Dec. 19, 1941), sociologist, anthropologist, and folklorist, was born in New York City, the eldest of three children and only daughter of Henry Clews, a Staffordshire potter's son who had left England as a young man to found in New York the banking firm bearing his name. Her mother was Lucy Madison (Worthington) Clews of Kentucky, twenty-five years younger than her husband. Mrs. Clews, a woman of strong Southern sympathies, was a descendant of President Madison and a granddaughter of an early governor of Kentucky, Gabriel Slaughter.

Elsie's mother would have preferred that she enter society, but Elsie, after study with private tutors and at Miss Ruel's school in New York, went on to the newly founded Barnard College. After receiving her A.B. in 1896, she stayed on for graduate study at Columbia; the anthropologist A. L. Kroeber later recalled how "her statuesque figure floated through the seminar alcoves of the Low Library on Morningside Heights as a memorably astonishing sight." She received her A.M. in 1897, taught history briefly at Columbia's Horace Mann High School, and completed her Ph.D. in 1899. Her doctoral dissertation, a compilation of colonial legislation on education, which Columbia University published that year, reflected the influence both of her adviser, the colonial historian Herbert L. Osgood, and of Franklin H. Giddings, the Columbia sociologist.

On Sept. 1, 1900, at Newport, R.I., she was married to Herbert Parsons, a New York lawyer five years her senior. A graduate of St. Paul's School, Harvard College, and the Yale Law School, Parsons was a New York City alderman who went on to become a Republican member of Congress (1905–11), Republican National Committeeman (1916–20), and long-time delegate to Republican conventions. During his tenure in Congress she and her husband lived in Washington, and thereafter in the New York City area. Of their six children, four survived childhood: Elsie ("Lissa"), born in 1901, John Edward (1903), Herbert (1909), and McIlvaine (1911).

With marriage and motherhood Mrs. Parsons continued an active academic career. From 1899 to 1902 she was Hartley House Fellow at Barnard and from 1902 to 1905 lecturer in sociology; she also taught a graduate course at Columbia University on the family, in which students were required to work with underprivileged New York families. Her first book, *The Family* (1906), grew from these lectures. Though a textbook, it is also a feminist tract, asserting that if women are to be fit wives and mothers they must enjoy the opportunities for development open to men. *The Family* brought persuasive sociological arguments to the feminist cause, explaining the modern subordinate state of women as a residue from earlier cultures which regarded menstruation, pregnancy, and childbirth with mingled awe and revulsion.

Despite its scholarly tone *The Family* attracted wide attention when ministers—and political opponents of Herbert Parsons—denounced its advocacy of trial marriage. To avoid such notoriety Elsie Parsons employed a pseudonym ("John Main") for her next work, *Religious Chastity* (1913), a study of sexual practices associated with various religions. There followed in short order (and under her own name) a spate of popularly written books—*The Old-Fashioned Woman* (1913), *Fear and Conventionality* (1914), *Social Freedom* (1915), and *Social Rule* (1916)—relating the attitudes and conventions of modern society to the folkways of simpler cultures and pleading for a mitigation of the excessive conformity that had characterized her own upbringing. In the last two books she treated age, sex, "caste" and locality as "categories" which "imprison" personality and from which "the mind as it matures seeks escape."

Perhaps the most original of these early works was *The Old-Fashioned Woman*. Mrs. Parsons argued that the sex taboos underlying female subordination are subtly expressed in modern times in an exaggerated distinction between the sexes, beginning with the toys and games of the nursery and continuing in adult life in invidious contrasts of dress, speech, work, and reading habits. Too many women, she charged spiritedly, submit to the meaningless ritual of parties and dinners and the elaborate process of "coming out" that is often but a prelude to a marriage in which "the wedding ring is a token of inadequacy as well as of 'respectability.'" She ridiculed the chivalric code whereby men "*will* have a woman go first—through a door or into a lifeboat—whatever inconvenience or tragedy such precedence may cause her." Full of witty anecdotes and epigrams ("Women try hard to live down to what is expected of them"), *The Old-Fashioned Woman* was a powerful solvent of ingrained ideas and prejudices.

Elsie Clews Parsons' nonconformist temper shaped her life as well as her books. She attended the salon of Mrs. Mabel Dodge, where young intellectuals and radicals congregated, wrote occasionally for Max Eastman's *Masses*, and enjoyed the friendship of Walter Lippmann and other founders of the liberal *New Republic* in 1914. During World War I, while her husband served in the intelligence branch of the A.E.F., she espoused pacifism, a position that cost her many friends. In 1919 she lectured on anthropology at the first session of the New School for Social Research, founded in New York City by Alvin Johnson and others who were troubled by the restrictions on academic freedom at older institutions. One of her students at the New School was RUTH BENEDICT, then at the threshold of her career in anthropology.

Such a life was singular indeed for a woman who by birth and marriage belonged to the wealthy, social, and generally conservative circles of Manhattan and Newport. Her father, Henry Clews, himself a self-made man and casual author, grudgingly admired his daughter's brilliance and independence, but her mother found Elsie's iconoclasm a severe trial. Elsie's marriage to Herbert Parsons was a happy one, despite their apparent differences. They shared a love of the outdoors and spent many summers hiking, riding, and swimming at a family farm in Lenox, Mass., where Mrs. Parsons appropriated a small hillside cabin for her writing. Since Herbert Parsons was himself a person of independent mind he could accept his wife's ways with equanimity. His interest in politics and hers in ethnology were nicely combined in 1903 when they were members of a delegation accompanying Wil-

liam Howard Taft, then president of the Philippine Commission, on a Far Eastern tour. When the group was presented to the Chinese Empress it was Mrs. Parsons who sewed the required black headdresses for the ladies in the party.

A turning point in Elsie Parsons' life came in 1915 when on a Southwestern trip with her husband she first saw Indians in their environment. She rapidly shifted her allegiance from the speculative, deductive sociology of Giddings to the anthropology of her Columbia friend Franz Boas—two men whose rivalry led to a rift that still divides their respective disciplines. Her first published reports on the Zuñi in 1915 and 1916 clearly show the influence of Boas in their meticulous recording of data, attention to folklore, and preference for empirical fact over speculative theory.

At the conclusion of *Social Rule* in 1916 Mrs. Parsons suggested that a life devoted to science was a possible escape from the restrictions of sex and "caste," and it was this course that she herself now chose. Leaving her daughter Elsie to care for the household and the younger children, she began a series of annual extended field trips to the pueblos of Arizona and New Mexico, where she lived with and interviewed Zuñi, Hopi, Taos, Tewa, Laguna, and other tribal peoples. After her husband's death in 1925 her travels became even more frequent and extensive. These researches bore fruit in such solid treatises as *The Social Organization of the Tewa of New Mexico* (1929), *Hopi and Zuñi Ceremonialism* (1933), and the exhaustive two-volume *Pueblo Indian Religion* (1939). Buttressing these works are over a hundred articles in scholarly journals like the *American Anthropologist*, the *Journal of American Folklore*, *Scientific Monthly*, and *Man* (London). The anecdotal style of her earlier books gave way in her anthropological studies to a rigorously spare scientific approach with a heavy accumulation of data on secret societies, ritual practices, and kinship. Despite the stylistic change, the major concern of her earlier speculative works—the effect of society's pressures upon the individual—remains central in her later writings. Some of her most original and valuable contributions appear in footnotes and parenthetical asides noting deviations and rebellions against the accepted practices and rituals.

She had always been interested in folklore, and her growing belief that folktales revealed tribal values and views led her into new fields of study, among the Portuguese-speaking Cape Verde Negroes in Massachusetts coastal towns, the Gullahs of the Carolina coastal islands, and the mixed populations of a dozen Caribbean isles. The results appeared in a number of volumes published by the American Folklore Society, including *Folk-Lore from the Cape Verde Islands* (1923), *Folk-Lore of the Sea Islands, S.C.* (1923), *Folk-Lore of the Antilles, French and English* (3 vols., 1933–43), and other collections of scrupulously transcribed folktales.

Once having abandoned the generalizations of her early period, Elsie Parsons remained skeptical of anthropologists like Edward Sapir and her own former pupil Ruth Benedict whose work was more speculative and interpretative. One question which did engage her attention toward the end of her career concerned the degree of Spanish influence on twentieth-century Indian cultures. In pursuit of an answer she visited Central and South American towns gathering material for her final ethnographies, *Mitla, Town of the Souls* (1936), a Mexican village study, and the posthumous *Peguche* (1945), describing an Ecuadorean community. In *Mitla* she enlivened her account with vignettes of conversation and gossip illustrating the blend of various traditions.

Her colleagues acknowledged her contributions by electing her to the presidency of the American Folklore Society (1918–20), the American Ethnological Association (1923–25), and the American Anthropological Association (1940–41). She was associate editor of the *Journal of American Folklore* from 1918 until her death. In addition, she gave financial support to these groups, particularly the American Folklore Society, and quietly financed many field trips by young scholars. In one instance she subsidized an Indian artist of New Mexico for five years while he painted scenes of tribal life, published in 1962 by the Smithsonian Institution as *Isleta Paintings*.

To the end Elsie Clews Parsons retained her scorn for social convention. She hated weddings and funerals, even refusing to attend services for her husband in 1925. Conventional greetings like "hello" and "goodbye" annoyed her and she usually avoided them. After returning to her New York apartment from a field trip she invariably delayed meeting her friends until she had been visited by her hairdresser, her manicurist, and her cosmetician, but such concessions to society were grudging, and her more usual appearance was in the rough khaki of her field trips, her hair tied in a bandanna and her notes, manuscripts, and other possessions stuffed in a succession of duffel bags, shopping bags, and string bags. Her associates valued not only this refreshing

unconventionality but also her firmness, tenacity of purpose, and generosity. A. L. Kroeber has described "her erect carriage, chiseled features, level look, and slow direct smile."

In 1940 Mrs. Parsons endorsed Norman Thomas for the presidency and announced that she was still a pacifist. In December of the following year, three weeks after completing the manuscript of *Peguche*, she died in New York City of complications following an appendectomy. At her request her remains were cremated.

[Appreciations and evaluations by professional colleagues are in *Am. Anthropologist*, Apr.–June 1943 (by Leslie Spier and A. L. Kroeber); *Jour. Am. Folklore*, Jan.–Mar. 1943 (by Gladys F. Reichard), which includes a photograph; and *Scientific Monthly*, May 1942 (by Franz Boas); see also references in Margaret Mead, *An Anthropologist at Work: Writings of Ruth Benedict* (1959). The memoir of Mrs. John D. Kennedy (Elsie Parsons Kennedy) in the Oral History Collection, Columbia Univ., pictures her mother vividly. On Herbert Parsons see *Who's Who in N.Y.*, 1924. See also *N.Y. Times*, Dec. 20, 1941, and *Who Was Who in America*, vol. II (1950). The Am. Philosophical Soc. library holds the bulk of Elsie Clews Parsons' papers, including extensive correspondence from 1938 to 1941, field notebooks, and MSS. John T. McCutcheon, *Drawn from Memory* (1950), chap. xxxviii, "The Pirate Cruise," is a sprightly account by a journalist who accompanied her on a field trip.]

PAUL S. BOYER

**PARSONS, Emily Elizabeth** (Mar. 8, 1824–May 19, 1880), Civil War nurse, was born at Taunton, Mass., the eldest of the three sons and four daughters of Theophilus and Catherine Amory (Chandler) Parsons. Her father, son of Theophilus Parsons (1750–1813), chief justice of the Massachusetts supreme judicial court, was a lawyer and later Dane Professor of Law at Harvard. A leading supporter of President Lincoln during the Civil War, he championed the constitutional interpretations of the Radical Republicans in the Reconstruction period.

From childhood Emily labored under a series of physical handicaps. A household accident when she was five blinded her right eye and impaired her vision in the left. Scarlet fever at seven left her totally deaf for a time and permanently damaged her hearing, so that she could never join freely in general conversation. In 1843 she suffered a serious ankle injury which made walking painful and occasionally sent her to bed throughout the rest of her life. Despite these difficulties she early manifested "a disposition to earnest and persistent activity," and a strong desire to help relieve suffering. After graduating from Cambridge High School she assisted her mother in the management of the household and busied herself in the charitable activities of the Church of the New Jerusalem (Swedenborgian), to which the family belonged. For a well-bred young woman, occupational opportunities were limited.

She was thirty-seven years old when the Civil War broke out and had never been away from home, but she immediately determined to volunteer as a nurse. Overcoming her father's objections on the score of her handicaps, she first gained admittance, through the recommendation of Dr. Jeffries Wyman of Cambridge, to the Massachusetts General Hospital as a student and volunteer nurse. During the next eighteen months she was able not only to learn at first hand how to dress wounds and prepare invalid diets but also to observe the operation of a well-run hospital. This preparation, coupled with her own executive gifts, gave her a professional competence almost unique among Civil War nurses.

In October 1862 she began work at the Fort Schuyler military hospital on Long Island Sound near New York City. Given charge of a ward of some fifty patients, she assisted the surgeon, supervised four orderlies, administered medicine and diets, managed supplies, and yet found time for personal attention to each patient. Though working sixteen hours a day, she quickly decided that she had found her vocation. "To have a ward full of sick men under my care is all I ask; I should like to live so all the rest of my life," she wrote her mother. Her health suffered in the dank, barnlike hospital, however, and in December she was forced to leave Fort Schuyler. While recuperating at the home of a friend in New York City she met JESSIE BENTON FRÉMONT, then recruiting nurses for a Western Sanitary Commission hospital in St. Louis. Believing that her health would improve in the West, she secured her father's still reluctant permission and accepted Mrs. Frémont's invitation.

In January 1863 Emily Parsons began nursing at Lawson Hospital, St. Louis. The next month she was appointed head nurse of the *City of Alton,* a Sanitary Commission hospital transport. Steaming down the Mississippi to within sight of the Confederate stronghold at Vicksburg, the boat took on about four hundred sick and wounded soldiers for transportation to Memphis hospitals. "I feel now as if I had really entered into the inner spirit of the times,—the feeling which counts danger as nothing," she wrote. She returned to St. Louis suffering from "malarial fever contracted on

the river," a disease which would long plague her. By April, however, she was sufficiently recovered to become supervisor of nurses at the newly established Benton Barracks Hospital on a fairground near St. Louis. With 2,500 beds, Benton Barracks was the largest military hospital in the West, and Miss Parsons' appointment was one of the most important given to a woman in the Civil War. For sixteen months, with periodic time off because of illness, she worked immediately under the director, Dr. Ira Russell, selecting and supervising the female nurses and overseeing the male nurses through ward masters. Her warm sympathy and innate good sense made her an outstanding administrator as well as a good nurse. Her efficient management was reflected in the low mortality rate at Benton Barracks Hospital, and her good humor and friendly ways made her popular not only with the patients but also with the surgeons and attendants—an achievement few woman volunteers of the Civil War could claim.

As the war moved eastward and Benton Barracks Hospital turned its facilities to the aid of Negro refugees, Miss Parsons' interest did not diminish. When an attack of malaria sent her home to Cambridge in August 1864, she continued to gather clothing and other provisions for the St. Louis freedmen. In a wartime letter she had written: "I wonder what I shall do with myself when the war is over; I never can sit down and do nothing." Her choice was to continue hospital work, and in 1865 she began collecting money for a general hospital in Cambridge. Two years later she opened her hospital in a rented house, where she lived as matron and nurse. Assisted by two local doctors, she treated many destitute women and children. By 1871, when a charter was secured and a board of trustees organized, it was planned to receive male patients as well. This institution was forced to close in 1872, but the fund raising Miss Parsons had begun continued after her death, and the Cambridge Hospital (later renamed Mount Auburn Hospital) was established on a permanent basis in 1886. Emily Elizabeth Parsons died of "apoplexy" at her parents' Cambridge home in 1880, at the age of fifty-six, and was buried in Mount Auburn Cemetery in that city.

[The basic source, *Memoir of Emily Elizabeth Parsons* (1880), contains many of her wartime letters as compiled and edited by her father. See also L. P. Brockett and Mary C. Vaughan, *Woman's Work in the Civil War* (1867), pp. 273–78; [Jacob G. Forman,] *The Western Sanitary Commission* (1864); *Dedication of the Cambridge*

*Hospital* (1886); William R. Cutter and William F. Adams, eds., *Genealogical and Personal Memoirs Relating to the Families of the State of Mass.* (1910). Death record from Mass. Registrar of Vital Statistics.]

GEORGE W. ADAMS

PARTON, Sara Payson Willis (July 9, 1811–Oct. 10, 1872), author and newspaper columnist, better known as Fanny Fern, was born in Portland, Maine. Originally named Grata (soon changed to Sara) Payson, after the mother of the Congregational minister Edward Payson, whose sermons had influenced her father, she was the fifth of the nine children of Nathaniel and Hannah (Parker) Willis. Her ancestors had come from England to Massachusetts in the early seventeenth century. Her paternal grandfather, Nathaniel Willis, edited a Whig journal in Boston during the Revolutionary War, and her father published an anti-Federalist organ, the *Eastern Argus,* in Portland. Objections to his excessive religious fervor and an unfortunate libel suit caused him to return the year after Sara's birth to Boston, where he set up a printing business and in 1816 established the Boston *Recorder,* one of America's first religious newspapers. He is best remembered, however, as the founder (1827) of the *Youth's Companion.* Of her mother, Sara once wrote that "she made everyone who came near her better and happier." Her older brother Nathaniel Parker won fame as a poet and as an editor of the *New York Mirror.* A younger brother, Richard Storrs, was a composer and editor of the *Musical World and Times.*

Sara's schoolgirl nickname, "Sal Volatile," characterized her personality, which fizzed, foamed, and sparkled throughout her life. She was educated in Boston and at the seminary of CATHARINE BEECHER in Hartford, Conn., where her wit impressed her classmates. On her return to Boston she contributed occasionally to her father's *Youth's Companion.* In May 1837, at twenty-six, she was married to Charles H. Eldredge, a well-to-do bank cashier. They had three children: Mary, born in 1839, Grace Harrington (1840), and Ellen Willis (1844). A series of personal tragedies ended this happy period of Sara's life; the death of her beloved mother was followed by that of her daughter Mary, and in 1846 she was left a widow. Unable to find employment and only grudgingly supported by her father and the Eldredges, she married Samuel P. Farrington, a Boston merchant and a widower, in 1849, an unhappy venture which ended three years later in divorce. Thrown on

her own resources again, she tried teaching and sewing, but her earnings were so meager that she was forced to give up her daughter Grace to the Eldredge grandparents. Sara finally turned to her pen, shielding her identity under the name "Fanny Fern." The *Mother's Assistant,* the *True Flag,* and the *Olive Branch,* small Boston magazines, accepted some of her pieces in 1851, and soon many newspapers reprinted these amusing paragraphs.

Thus launched upon a journalistic career, Sara Farrington attracted the attention of an astute publisher, James C. Derby of Auburn, N.Y., who collected her writings in *Fern Leaves from Fanny's Port-Folio* (1853), which became an immediate best seller, adorning thousands of parlor tables both in America and England. A second series of *Fern Leaves* appeared in 1854 as well as a juvenile, *Little Ferns for Fanny's Little Friends.* The three books brought her sales up to 132,000 copies in the United States and 48,000 abroad; within two years she had received more than $10,000 in royalties. This astounding success inspired Robert Bonner, owner of the *New York Ledger,* to add her in 1855 to his galaxy of contributors at the unheard-of sum of $100 for a regular weekly column, thus making her one of America's first women columnists. Having moved to New York, she remained with the *Ledger* for the rest of her life, never missing an issue and reaching a weekly audience of half a million readers. In the next fifteen years she published a series of her collected *Ledger* pieces: *Fresh Leaves* (1857), *Folly as It Flies* (1868), *Ginger-Snaps* (1870), and *Caper-Sauce* (1872), as well as two more juveniles. In addition she wrote two novels, *Ruth Hall* (1855) and *Rose Clark* (1856). The former, a roman à clef depicting her relatives in an unpleasant light, particularly her brother Nathaniel (who had opposed her journalistic career), created a minor literary scandal.

As literature Fanny Fern's books have little merit except as revealing popular taste. As social history, however, they cast considerable light on American home life of the period. Her chatty pieces, spiced with wit and impudence, dealt sympathetically with domestic problems in terms which women could understand and did something to prepare her sex for a larger role in society. She championed intellectual equality between the sexes and condemned the double standard of morality, deplored excessive housework and too large families, encouraged women to seek wider fields of endeavor, and poked fun at the august male. She had warm sympathy for children, urging parents to respect their individuality and making a special plea for the willful and the tomboy. Critical of conventional religion, she demanded messages of help and comfort from the pulpit in place of dry theological discourse. Her review of *Leaves of Grass* in the *Ledger* for May 1856 challenged the prudish Victorian concept of sex and gave her a place in literary history as the first woman to express publicly her appreciation of Walt Whitman's genius. Though at first she held aloof from the suffrage movement, suggesting that it was "better policy to play possum, and wear the mask of submission," she came by 1858 to support the cause. With JANE C. CROLY she was one of the founders, in 1868, of New York City's pioneer woman's club, Sorosis.

A large woman, with "light brown hair, florid complexion, and large, blue eyes," Fanny Fern made a striking appearance. Even a malicious critic, while stating candidly that "Fanny isn't handsome, and never was," admitted that she had "a splendid form, a charming foot and ankle, a fascinating expression, and the manners of a queen" (*Life and Beauties of Fanny Fern*, p. 53). On Jan. 5, 1856, she was married to the biographer James Parton, eleven years her junior. Her daughter Ellen lived with them. The early years of the marriage were stormy, but the addition of a baby grandchild, Ethel, daughter of Fanny's daughter Grace, who died in 1861, helped unite the household. After a six-year struggle with cancer Mrs. Parton died in New York City at sixty-one, in 1872. She was buried in Mount Auburn Cemetery, Cambridge, Mass. In 1876 Ellen Eldredge became Parton's second wife.

[James Parton, *Fanny Fern: A Memorial Volume* (1874); James C. Derby, *Fifty Years among Authors, Books and Publishers* (1884); sketch by Grace Greenwood in *Eminent Women of the Age* (1869); *The Life and Beauties of Fanny Fern* (1855); John S. Hart, *The Female Prose Writers of America* (1851 and later editions); Mary Clemmer Ames, *Outlines of Men, Women, and Things* (1873); Henry A. Beers, *Nathaniel P. Willis* (1885); Milton E. Flower, *James Parton* (1951); files of N.Y. *Ledger*, 1856–72; obituary in N.Y. *Evening Post*, Oct. 11, 1872; Elizabeth B. Schlesinger, "Fanny Fern: Our Grandmothers' Mentor," *N.-Y. Hist. Soc. Quart.*, Oct. 1954. See also: Robert P. Eckert, Jr., "Friendly, Fragrant Fanny Ferns," *Colophon*, Part 18 (1934); Florence B. Adams, *Fanny Fern* (pamphlet, privately printed, 1966); Emory Holloway and Ralph Adimari, eds., *N.Y. Dissected* (1936)—a collection of Whitman's newspaper articles with editorial commentary—pp. 146–54, 162–65. The Sophia Smith Collection, Smith College, has letters, clippings, and an informal MS. biography of Fanny Fern by Ethel Parton.]

ELIZABETH BANCROFT SCHLESINGER

**PATRICK, Mary Mills** (Mar. 10, 1850–Feb. 25, 1940), missionary educator, first president of the American College for Girls in Istanbul, Turkey, was born in Canterbury, N.H., the oldest of the six children of John and Harriet (White) Patrick. Her mother's family traced its ancestry to the Plymouth Colony. Her father, a descendant of Matthew Patrick who emigrated from Ireland to Warren, Mass., in 1724, was the son of William Patrick (1773–1862), a graduate of Williams College in its first class (1799) and pastor of the Congregational church in Canterbury from 1803 to 1843. During most of Mary's childhood the family home was in North Boscawen, N.H., where her father was a farmer. In 1865 the Patricks moved to Lyons (later part of Clinton), Iowa, to a farm on the banks of the Mississippi. The family had an intellectual bent. After morning prayers the children sometimes took turns translating a verse from the New Testament into Greek, Latin, French, or German. One of Miss Patrick's three brothers, George Thomas White Patrick, became a professor of philosophy and psychology at the University of Iowa, and an aunt, Frances Emily White, became professor of physiology at the Woman's Medical College of Pennsylvania.

Mary Patrick attended the local Lyons Collegiate Institute, graduating in 1869. Two years later the American Board of Commissioners for Foreign Missions offered her an appointment as teacher in a mission school in Erzurum, in the eastern highlands of the Ottoman Empire. This opportunity, as she later wrote, "appealed to my love of adventure as well as to the altruism engendered by the atmosphere of my home" (*Under Five Sultans*, p. 3), and she promptly accepted. In Erzurum she taught Armenian girls, learned ancient and modern Armenian, and covered some 3,000 vacation miles on horseback in the countryside.

In 1875 Miss Patrick was transferred to Üsküdar (Scutari), the principal Asian suburb of Istanbul, to the American High School for Girls (also known as The Home), founded by the Woman's Board of the A.B.C.F.M. in 1871. In 1883 she became co-principal, and about 1889, sole principal. She learned Turkish and, by living in nearby Greek villages in the summers, modern Greek. She also learned, probably later, French and German. In 1888–89 she was in the United States, evidently studying, for she received the M.A. from Iowa in 1890. But she was also planning to convert the high school into a college. Miss Caroline Borden of Boston, for years her vigorous backer among the trustees, secured in March 1890 a college charter from the Commonwealth of Massachusetts. Miss Patrick was appointed president at the standard mission salary of $440 a year.

Until 1914 the American College for Girls, more commonly known as Constantinople Woman's College, or by its close friends as "C.C.," remained in Üsküdar, while enrollment of Armenian, Greek, and Bulgarian girls climbed to over 250, including the preparatory department. Only a few Turkish girls attended before the revolution of 1908 because of the opposition of Sultan Abdülhamid II. One of these, Halidé Edib (Adivar), the college's best-known Turkish graduate, has contrasted Miss Patrick with another teacher, a devout Christian evangelist, whom she also admired: "Dr. Patrick seemed more universal in spirit; she had wide sympathies and represented altogether a freer line of education based on a human international understanding" (*Memoirs of Halidé Edib*, 1926, p. 193).

Miss Patrick received the Ph.D. degree in 1897 from the University of Bern, after summer study in various European universities and a thesis published as *Sextus Empiricus and Greek Scepticism* (1899). Her interest in Greek culture and philosophy, which possibly reflected the influence of her brother, continued throughout her life. In 1912 she published *Sappho and the Island of Lesbos*, in which she speaks admiringly of "the free life of the past, surrounded by that beauty of nature which in the souls of the Greeks was transformed into beauty of thought and mind." At the age of seventy-nine she published another scholarly study, *The Greek Skeptics* (1929). The life of the mind was her constant emphasis to students and colleagues, though she was not above showing students that a long-handled broom swept more efficiently than the short Turkish twig-broom. A feminist and a believer in woman suffrage, in her earlier days she sometimes shocked Near Easterners, her biographer reports, both by her advanced views and by riding a bicycle.

Miss Patrick succeeded in freeing the college from all mission ties with the issuance of a new Massachusetts charter in 1908. Soon thereafter a new site was purchased at Arnavutköyü (Arnautkeui) on the European shore of the Bosporus. To the fine new buildings there erected the college moved in April 1914. At the dedication ceremonies on June 3 Miss Patrick was decorated with the Third Order of Shefakat by Sultan Mehmed V and awarded an honorary LL.D. by Smith College; she received a Litt.D. from Columbia in 1922.

Under Miss Patrick's guidance the college survived the vicissitudes of the Balkan Wars and World War I, never closing despite the rupture in American-Turkish relations. Though the college's earlier service had been largely to the Christian minorities of the Ottoman Empire, after 1908, and especially after the Turkish Republic was established in 1923, the college became a significant force in educating Turkish women. Only one Turkish higher school, a normal school for girls established in 1869, antedated the college. But the student body was always international. By the time of Miss Patrick's retirement there were some twenty nationalities represented among 400 students. Her dreams of adding full-fledged schools of medicine and education went unrealized. The college remains, however, as her monument, now (1971) essentially on a lycée level, administered as part of Robert College, the nearby American institution for men.

Miss Patrick retired in 1924. She lived in New York City until 1932, and thereafter in Palo Alto, Calif., until her death of coronary occlusion in her ninetieth year. Her ashes were buried in Canterbury, N.H.

[Miss Patrick's writings include *Under Five Sultans* (1929), a mediocre book of reminiscence interlarded with secondhand history, and *A Bosporus Adventure* (1934), a rather spotty history of the college; a good biography and a good history remain to be written. Her books may be supplemented by the rather eulogistic biography by a colleague, Hester D. Jenkins, *An Educational Ambassador to the Near East* (1925). *George Thomas White Patrick, An Autobiog.* (1947), by Miss Patrick's brother, gives family details.]

RODERIC H. DAVISON

PATTERSON, Eleanor Medill (Nov. 7, 1881–July 24, 1948), newspaper editor and publisher, was born in Chicago, the second of two children and only daughter of Elinor (Medill) and Robert Wilson Patterson, Jr., both of Scotch-Irish stock. She was a granddaughter of Joseph Medill, builder of the *Chicago Tribune* and a founder of the Republican party; after Medill's death in 1899 her father succeeded him as editor and head of the *Tribune*. All four of Medill's grandchildren gained prominence: Eleanor's brother, Joseph Medill Patterson, founded the New York *Daily News*, while her cousins Medill McCormick and Robert Rutherford McCormick—the sons of her aunt Katherine Medill and Robert Sanderson McCormick of the farm-equipment family—became respectively a United States Senator and head of the *Tribune*.

Christened Elinor Josephine, she adopted the name Eleanor Medill Patterson while still in her youth. The nickname Cissy, acquired in girlhood, remained with her all her life. Educated at home under a domineering mother intent on social eminence in Chicago, Newport, and Washington, Cissy first tasted freedom at fifteen as a student at Miss Hersey's School in Boston; she later attended Miss Porter's School in Farmington, Conn. A slender, tall (five feet seven and one-half inches) young woman with long coppery hair, a perfect white complexion, and a carriage and walk ("like a tigress") so graceful that people ignored her pug nose and too-large eyes, she was a superb horsewoman who occasionally achieved feats of endurance. Like her mother she was also susceptible to neurotic breakdowns and found love and friendship difficult to achieve.

At the age of twenty-one she joined the Robert S. McCormicks in Europe, where her uncle was the American envoy in Vienna and then St. Petersburg. She scintillated in the pomp of Hapsburg and Romanov balls, and was courted by Count Josef Gizycki, a Polish nobleman perhaps twice her age. A charming and handsome cavalryman with a passion for gambling and women, Gizycki finally won her parents' consent to the match, and they were married on Apr. 14, 1904, in the mansion on Dupont Circle in Washington, D.C., which Stanford White had designed for the Pattersons. It was immediately clear that Gizycki had married for money. Blansko, his "castle" in Moravia, Russian Poland, proved to be a shabby wooden building in a muddy village, and in Cissy's suite there were traces of her husband's most recent mistress. But she endured and even bore him a daughter, Felicia Gizycka, on Sept. 3, 1905. In January 1908, however, at Pau, the French resort, when Gizycki beat Cissy for her protests over his attentions to another woman, she fled to London with Felicia. The count's agents snatched the child away a couple of months later, but Cissy's father induced President-elect Taft to intercede directly with Czar Nicholas II, and in August 1909 Cissy was able to return to the United States with her daughter. Her divorce from Gizycki was granted in June 1917 after an eight-year court fight. One of the tragedies of her life was her failure to achieve rapport with Felicia, whose marriage in 1925 to the journalist Drew Pearson, arranged by Cissy, ended in divorce three years later. Pearson remained on good terms with his former mother-in-law until the early 1940's, but Felicia became permanently estranged and attacked her mother in one of her two novels.

The years after 1909 were empty ones for Cissy Patterson, back under her mother's thumb. In August 1916 she sought relief from a series of nervous illnesses in the Jackson Hole country of Wyoming. This led to a lifelong attachment to the area and to one of her few friendships—with Mrs. Rose Crabtree, proprietor of a hotel in the town of Jackson. She bought a remote ranch, went camping as far as the Canadian Rockies, and in 1921 was the first woman to make the perilous 163-mile boat trip through the Salmon River rapids. Until her later years she spent almost every summer in Wyoming. In the mid-1920's, having written some features for the Hearst press, she employed her lively, individual style in two novels. Glass Houses, published first in French (Paris, 1923) and in English in the United States three years later, was an "inside" story of Washington life, involving a "hick senator" and two rival society hostesses whom readers identified as William E. Borah, Mrs. Alice Roosevelt Longworth, and Countess Gizycka herself. After Gizycki's death in 1926 she wrote Fall Flight (1928), a fictionalized account of their marriage.

Meanwhile, on Apr. 11, 1925, in a simple civil ceremony in New York City, she was married to Elmer Schlesinger, a Harvard-educated Manhattan corporation lawyer. They leased an apartment on Fifth Avenue and for the summer months bought Vincent Astor's Harbor Acres estate at Sands Point, Long Island. During stays in Washington, Cissy Schlesinger reigned at the Dupont Circle mansion as one of the capital's most dazzling hostesses. This marriage also cooled, but Schlesinger's death in February 1929 left her badly shaken, and she gave him an elaborate funeral.

Again at loose ends, Mrs. Eleanor Patterson —the name she used after 1929—gained little satisfaction from an annual income of $600,000 to $800,000 (from her Medill-Patterson inheritance), despite spectacular spending on jewels, clothes, and travel about the country in her elegant private railroad car. She had toyed with the idea of going into journalism, and now her friend Arthur Brisbane, William Randolph Hearst's right-hand man, persuaded Hearst to hire Cissy as editor and publisher of his morning Washington Herald, fourth in circulation among the capital's five dailies. On Aug. 1, 1930, she took over with great fanfare.

Mrs. Patterson knew almost nothing about running a newspaper and seemed at first merely to be seeking attention, as, for example, in her personal attacks on Mrs. Longworth. (Over the years she was to exercise her slashing wit in feuds with Drew Pearson, Walter Winchell, Harold Ickes, and many others.) But it soon became apparent that she was in earnest about her new profession. She goaded her reporters on to new feats, built a strong staff of women writers, fought hard for circulation and advertising, and gained respect for her news sense, including an instinct for good writing, photography, and typography. She disguised herself as a destitute woman to report on the plight of the jobless in the depression; campaigned for hot lunches for District of Columbia schoolchildren (typically underwriting the program herself, anonymously, until Congress acted); and, in a series called "Dixie's Dead End," discovered Appalachian poverty before the New Deal did. A mercurial executive, she alternated moments of impulsive generosity—such as inviting women employees to help themselves from her tremendous wardrobe—with ruthless and capricious firings. When she lost a two-year battle to take a group of comic strips away from the rival *Washington Post,* owned by her one-time friend Eugene Meyer, she sent Meyer a pound of raw meat.

In the later 1930's, with Hearst in financial difficulties, Mrs. Patterson was at last able to gain control of his Washington papers, both of which were losing money. On Aug. 7, 1937, she leased the *Herald* and the evening *Times* with an option to purchase. This she exercised on Jan. 28, 1939, and three days later combined the papers into the around-the-clock *Times-Herald,* a paper so lively that even Washingtonians who disliked its owner felt compelled to read it. By 1943 the *Times-Herald* had the largest circulation in the city and had earned its first profit in years. By 1945 the net had climbed to a million dollars; Mrs. Patterson had made good financially in a city known as a graveyard of newspapers.

Frankly more interested in personalities than in politics (in which she tended to follow the lead of her beloved brother Joe, publisher of the New York *Daily News*), Mrs. Patterson retained an early admiration for Franklin D. and Eleanor Roosevelt, and in 1940 joined her brother in supporting Roosevelt for a third term. But there was a strong Midwestern isolationist strain in the Pattersons. Roosevelt's lend-lease bill of December 1940 convinced them that the President was seeking to take the United States into war, and they went into opposition. Although they affirmed their support of the war after Pearl Harbor, Roosevelt never forgave them, and they sniped at him until his death. The patriotism of the Pattersons and of their cousin Col. Robert R. McCormick, publisher of the *Chicago Tribune,* was called into question by the President and

others during the war, but, as Mrs. Patterson's biographers point out, the family's mistrust of foreign nations and its unwavering loyalty to the United States were both of long standing. Cissy Patterson herself was remarkably free of racial and religious bigotry (having, in an intolerant decade, taken a Jew as her second husband), but the cousins were fighters, accustomed to speaking their minds in print, and their opposition to Roosevelt did at times carry them to extremes.

Soon after World War II, Mrs. Patterson's world began to come apart. Her brother died in May 1946, and she quarreled with Colonel McCormick about the management of the family holdings. As her energies ebbed, her interest in the *Times-Herald* slackened. Increasingly suspicious of those about her, she took to carrying a pistol after receiving some threatening letters. In July 1948 she was found dead in the bedroom of her Dower House estate near Marlboro, Md., evidently of a heart attack. Her age was sixty-six. She had taken instruction in Roman Catholicism, but an Episcopal clergyman presided at her funeral in the Dupont Circle mansion and at her burial in the Medill plot in Chicago's Graceland Cemetery. Her will, disposing of an estate of more than $16,000,000, left the *Times-Herald* to seven of its executives, who in 1949 sold the paper to Colonel McCormick's *Chicago Tribune.* But the *Times-Herald* ran into the red again, and in 1954 McCormick sold it to Eugene Meyer, who merged it into his *Washington Post.*

Called "the most powerful woman in America" by *Collier's* magazine and "the most hated woman in America" by *Time,* Eleanor Medill Patterson had an intense and personal impact on her era. A gadfly and a fearless controversialist, she was also an erratic, lonely woman whose impulsive cruelties are remembered more than her many acts of kindness. In eighteen years as an editor she amply proved her abilities as a journalist and an executive, yet the newspaper she had helped build survived her death by only six years.

[Of the two popular biographies—Alice Albright Hoge, *Cissy Patterson* (1966), and Paul F. Healy, *Cissy* (1966)—the first, by a grandniece, is more useful on the personal and family background, and the second, by a *Daily News* reporter, is more perceptive on the journalistic aspects of her career. See also: Felicia Gizycka, *House of Violence* (1932) and *Flower of Smoke* (1939).]

DAVID DENKER

PATTERSON, Hannah Jane (Nov. 5, 1879–Aug. 21, 1937), suffragist, defense official in

World War I, was born in Smithton, Pa., on the Youghiogheny River some twenty miles south of Pittsburgh, one of seven children of John Gilfillan Patterson, a prominent banker in nearby West Newton, and Harriet (Mc-Cune) Patterson. She was educated in the public schools of West Newton and at Wilson College in Chambersburg, Pa., from which she received an A.B. degree in 1901. Following graduation, she studied finance at Columbia University and law at the University of Pennsylvania.

After leaving school Miss Patterson settled in Pittsburgh, where she worked actively with the Consumers' League of Western Pennsylvania and the Allegheny County Committee on School Legislation, and helped launch, through the Civic Club of Allegheny County, the movement that secured a county juvenile court. She particularly developed a keen desire to assist in the emancipation of women, and from 1910 until World War I gave her principal energies to the campaign for woman suffrage. Beginning in Allegheny County, she soon turned to statewide activity. In 1915 she joined her close Pittsburgh friend Mrs. Jennie (Bradley) Roessing, president of the Pennsylvania Woman Suffrage Association, in conducting a concerted drive for a suffrage amendment to the state constitution. Miss Patterson helped lobby the measure through the legislature in 1915 and organized and headed a state Woman Suffrage Party designed to mobilize voting strength at the precinct and township level for the coming referendum, a form of organization she had begun three years earlier in Allegheny County. Though the amendment was defeated that fall at the polls, the substantial vote it received, carrying all of the state but Philadelphia, reflected credit on Miss Patterson's organizing skill, as well as on her quiet, rather easygoing disposition, which enabled her to win friends readily. When CARRIE CHAPMAN CATT, with some reluctance, resumed the presidency of the National American Woman Suffrage Association in December 1915, she successfully urged the election of Hannah Patterson as corresponding secretary (an office which took her to New York City for a year). Though Miss Patterson declined reelection in 1916, she gave significant service that summer when she joined Mrs. Roessing in an effort to secure suffrage planks in the national platforms of the two major parties. The Republicans, meeting first, rejected endorsement of a federal amendment, but Miss Patterson, in conjunction with Senator William E. Borah, maneuvered a tactical victory by obtaining a compromise plank declaring for state action

on behalf of woman suffrage. This prompted the Democrats to adopt a similar proposal, and thus an important milestone was reached in recognizing women's right to vote. Mrs. Roessing later remarked that without Miss Patterson's assistance and tactful lobbying the two suffrage planks would not have been obtained.

When war broke out, Miss Patterson, like many of the other suffrage leaders, directed her attention to national defense. In 1917 President Woodrow Wilson selected her as one of the eleven members of the Woman's Committee of the Council of National Defense, a group, headed by ANNA HOWARD SHAW, designed to organize and coordinate the war work of American women. Miss Patterson was chosen resident director of the Woman's Committee and, in September 1918, associate director of the field division of the entire Council. For her war services she was awarded the Distinguished Service Medal, one of the few women to receive the distinction.

In the 1920's Miss Patterson utilized her earlier training in finance to head the women's department of a leading brokerage firm in Pittsburgh, J. Y. Holmes & Company, for five years. Later she became the first woman director of the bank in West Newton that her father had served as president. Her interest and activity in the financial world well reflected her belief that, given equal opportunity for education and training, women were capable of operating in all fields on a par with men. During her final years Miss Patterson again entered political life. A lifelong Republican and an active member of the Pennsylvania Federation of Republican Women, she managed the successful election campaign of her friend Sara Soffel to a local judgeship in 1931. Four years later Miss Patterson was asked to run for Congress, but, uncharacteristically, she refused on the ground that Pennsylvania was not prepared to elect a woman at that time. She died in Pittsburgh of acute meningoencephalitis in 1937 at the age of fifty-seven and was buried in the family plot in West Newton. "Women have been my major interest all my life," Hannah Patterson once remarked. Her chief contribution was in making her own life and career in varied fields an example of success and worthwhile achievement.

[Ida H. Harper, ed., *Hist. of Woman Suffrage*, vols. V and VI (1922); Henrietta Louise Krone, "Dauntless Women: The Story of the Woman Suffrage Movement in Pa., 1910–20" (unpublished doctoral dissertation, Univ. of Pa., 1946); Emily Newell Blair, *The Woman's Committee, U.S.*

Council of Nat. Defense: An Interpretative Report (1920); Who's Who in America, 1930–31; Wilson Alumnae Quart., Nov. 1937; Pittsburgh Post-Gazette, Dec. 16, 1927, Aug. 23, 1937; Pittsburgh Press, May 25, 1931; N.Y. Times, Aug. 22, 1937; Mrs. Jennie B. Roessing to author, Oct. 10, 1961; cause of death from Pa. Dept. of Health.]

STANLEY I. KUTLER

PATTI, Adelina (Feb. 10, 1843–Sept. 27, 1919), operatic soprano, christened Adela Juana Maria, was born in Madrid, Spain, the third daughter and fourth and youngest child of Salvatore and Caterina (Chiesa) Barili Patti, Italian opera singers on tour there. Her father was a Sicilian; her mother, a native of Rome, had three sons and a daughter by a previous marriage. The entire family was musically inclined, Adelina's sister Carlotta becoming a well-known concert singer. Shortly after Adelina's birth the Pattis returned to Italy and then, at the suggestion of an old friend, migrated to New York City, where her father joined in the management of Palmo's Opera House and later of the Astor Place Opera House, and her mother sang in the companies which flourished in New York at the time. Young Adelina was thus brought up in the musical world of Italian New York of the mid-nineteenth century. Her schooling was sporadic. According to her brother-in-law, the impresario Maurice Strakosch, the vivacious, dark-eyed child when only four could "sing many of the most difficult operatic airs almost to perfection." At eight she performed publicly for the first time at Tripler Hall on Nov. 22, 1851, executing the "Rondo" from La Sonnambula and Jenny Lind's "Echo Song." She was an instant success. Strakosch organized a tour for her with Ole Bull, the Norwegian violinist, which lasted three years and extended to Canada, Mexico, and Cuba. On its completion she ceased singing publicly for a time, but studied under the direction of her half brother Ettore Barili. At the age of sixteen she made her operatic debut at the Academy of Music in New York on Nov. 24, 1859, in Lucia di Lammermoor. "The qualities for this rôle," wrote the New York Tribune the next day, "are full soprano voice, with absolute facility in the upper notes, thorough volatility of tone, or rapid execution, great power of holding tones . . . a gentle ladylike demeanor, and to some extent clearness of dramatic action. All these Miss Adeline Patti possesses unequivocally." She followed her debut with coloratura roles in La Sonnambula, The Barber of Seville, Martha, and I Puritani. Then came a year's tour of the leading cities in the United States, including several months of opera in New Orleans, during which her acclaim grew.

In 1861 Strakosch arranged for Patti to appear in London. In her debut at the Royal Italian Opera at Covent Garden on May 14 in La Sonnambula she created a sensation not equaled since the height of the "Jenny Lind fever." For the next twenty-five years she was the undisputed queen of London opera and the favorite as well in all the major cities of Europe. In writing of her Vienna debut to the Musical World (London), Mar. 17, 1863, Dr. Julius Wagner described her as a young girl with a "delicately chiselled head, . . . fine mobile features, and the guileless eyes of a doe—white marble turned into flesh, surrounded by a dark frame of hair, and daintily intersected by black brows, eyes, and lashes. . . . We have heard singers possessed of more boldness and virtuosity than Mlle. Patti, but this singing child is a charming individuality, with which no other is to be compared." The world's most noted authorities joined in the praise. Giuseppe Verdi called her the greatest singer he had ever heard. Jenny Lind wept in admiration. Daniel Auber, the octogenarian French composer, said after hearing her for the first time, "I was twenty years old throughout the entire performance. . . ." It was the custom for European rulers to give presents to operatic favorites. They outdid themselves in heaping diamonds, emeralds, and rubies on Patti. Queen Victoria invited her to Windsor Castle repeatedly and wept openly when she sang "Home, Sweet Home."

Year after year she made the European circuit—London, Paris, Milan, St. Petersburg, Moscow, Vienna, Monte Carlo, Madrid, Brussels. Her repertoire of forty-two operas remained the same, including, in addition to those of Verdi and Rossini, Donizetti's Lucia, Linda di Chamounix, Don Pasquale, L'Elisir d'Amore, and Figlia del Reggimento; Meyerbeer's Dinorah and L'Africaine; Flotow's Martha; Gounod's Faust and Romeo and Juliet; and Delibes' Lakmé. Her greatest success was as Rosina in Rossini's Barber of Seville. One of her best characterizations was that of Zerlina in Don Giovanni, her only Mozart role. She made some effort to enlarge her repertoire, including a few disastrous appearances as Carmen in Bizet's opera. Wagner's music tempted her, but she wisely realized that its demands would be too great for her light soprano.

Following two decades of unparalleled success in Europe, Patti returned to America in 1881 and embarked upon a series of annual tours which won her equal fame and affection in this country and a fee of $5,000 a concert, a record for the time. The epitome of the prima donna, she traveled the world like a queen: her elaborate private railroad car was the only one ever seen in countless American communities where she sang. At first she appeared with opera companies organized especially for her, but they were soon found wanting artistically, and she turned to conventional concert programs. The format was the same: the assisting artists carried the burden of the numbers; Patti sang two arias from her operatic repertoire, a few simple ballads (she leaned toward "Kathleen Mavourneen" and "Comin' Thro' the Rye"), and ended with "Home, Sweet Home," which became closely identified with her in the public's mind. After postseason performances at the Metropolitan Opera House in New York in 1892, she appeared seldom in opera, though demands for concerts grew. Her last American tour was in 1903–04. Dec. 1, 1906, supposedly marked the end of her professional career, with a "farewell" concert at the Royal Albert Hall in London, but others followed, and her last public appearance was not until Oct. 20, 1914, when she sang in that hall for the benefit of the Red Cross War Fund, with King George V and Queen Mary among the packed audience. Her voice, at seventy-one, showed the passing of time; it had been sixty-four years since she sang as a child in New York's music halls.

For several years after her London debut Patti had maintained a home in nearby Clapham, where she completed her neglected education through reading and improved her knowledge of languages and her technical musicianship. It was in the Roman Catholic church on Clapham Common on July 29, 1868, that she was married to the first of three husbands, a French nobleman, the Marquis de Caux, from whom she was separated in 1877 and divorced in 1885. On June 10, 1886, in a Protestant church near Swansea, Wales, she was wed to the tenor Ernest Nicolini, who had often sung with her; they made their home in a beautiful estate she had purchased on the northern slope of Swansea Valley, a Victorian castle known as Craig-y-Nos. Here Patti built a private theatre and, through her generosity, became known as the Lady Bountiful of Craig-y-Nos. And it was here that she finally retired with her third husband, Swedish Baron Rolf Cederström, thirty years her junior, to whom she was married in the Roman Catholic church at Brecon, Wales, on Jan. 25, 1899, a year after Nicolini's death. She had no children. Her health began to fail in 1918 owing to a heart ailment. She died the following September at Craig-y-Nos and was buried,

after Catholic services, in the cemetery of Père Lachaise in Paris.

Completely Italian by lineage, Patti considered herself a citizen of the world. Though the demands of her career made Great Britain a convenient place to live, the fact that she spent the most impressionable years of her life in America caused her to refer to her return to New York as a homecoming. Her strength as a singer was a voice of great purity of tone and unusual sweetness. She had, seemingly by nature, perfect technique. She adhered to a strict and scientific regimen for protecting her voice. Whether her acting ability kept pace with her singing was a matter of controversy. Some critics felt that she was always her arch self in any role, and that she ignored the composer's wishes in order to show off her voice. Her dazzling runs and trills, her range, and her ease in difficult bravura music kept the public bewitched. She blazed no new trails in introducing music of deserving composers. She stuck, rather, to the beaten paths in familiar music; but history does not record a singer who was so idolized by so large a public for so long a time.

[The most complete biography is Herman Klein, *The Reign of Patti* (1920), which reprints in an appendix a number of reviews and comments. Other biographies are G. M. Dalmazzo, *Adelina Patti's Life* (1877), a brief account; Louisa Lauw, *Fourteen Years with Adelina Patti* (1884); and Theodore Grave, *Le Biographie d'Adelina Patti* (Paris, 1865). The date of her first concert, in Tripler Hall, is from George C. D. Odell, *Annals of the N.Y. Stage*, VI (1931), 181.]

EDWIN TRIBBLE

**PATTON, Abby Hutchinson.** *See* HUTCHINSON, Abigail Jemima.

**PEABODY, Elizabeth Palmer** (May 16, 1804– Jan. 3, 1894), Transcendentalist, teacher, author, and educational reformer, was born at Billerica, Mass., the eldest of seven children, four of them girls, of Nathaniel and Elizabeth (Palmer) Peabody. Her father, once a teacher at Phillips Andover Academy, but in Elizabeth's childhood a dentist at Salem, Mass., to which the family moved after her birth, taught her Latin and inspired her eventual mastering of ten languages. Her mother, who conducted a school in Salem on the principle that every child should receive the training appropriate to genius, was, however, the more decisive influence. Through her school and much private tutoring she developed in Elizabeth a precocious interest in theology, philosophy, history, and literature; her unusual approach to the education of the very young furnishes an important clue to Elizabeth's future involvement in education reform. Elizabeth herself became a teacher in her teens, first at her mother's Salem school. In 1823, after a short and unsuccessful schoolkeeping venture in Boston, she went to Maine, where for two years she was a teacher or governess in wealthy households in Hallowell and Gardiner. With her sister and lifelong collaborator Mary (see MARY PEABODY MANN), she then opened a school in Brookline, a Boston suburb.

It was Elizabeth Peabody's role as a teacher which made possible her early independence from her family and led to her acquaintance with William Ellery Channing, Bronson Alcott, and other New England intellectuals. Her admiration for Channing had begun in her childhood when she heard him preach at Salem, and she had corresponded with him from Maine, but her intimacy with him dates from 1826 when he enrolled his only daughter, Mary, in her Brookline school. Mary furnished a reason for long conferences with Channing on the purposes and methods of education, and these conferences soon expanded into discussions of theology, philosophy, and literature in which Channing as Unitarian-Transcendental Socrates confronted Miss Peabody with the fundamental issues of their mutually liberal faith. She could have received no finer education in New England. Thanks to Channing, she was not only stimulated morally and intellectually, but she became thoughtfully aware of Plato, Swedenborg, Coleridge, Wordsworth, and Goethe, whose *Wilhelm Meister* she and Channing spent a winter reading and discussing. Her reading and speculation under Channing's guidance in the 1820's and 1830's paralleled that being done in more lonely fashion by Emerson, Alcott, Frederic Henry Hedge, and other future Transcendentalists, with the result that almost inevitably she took her place with MARGARET FULLER as the other female charter member of the Transcendentalist Club in 1837.

The relation with Channing was important in other ways. Discovering that his admirers desired printed copies of his sermons, she became his copyist, readying for the printer between 1826 and 1842 some fifty of his sermons, which otherwise would not have made their immediate impact on the development of American Unitarianism and Transcendentalism. Elizabeth Peabody also served Channing as a trial ground for his ideas, modifying with her queries and objections the scope and emphasis in many of his sermons.

Meanwhile, however, her financial situation, always precarious, had worsened. Her school had closed in 1832, and for a time she subsisted on a scant income pieced together from private tutoring, from historical classes, for which young matrons paid subscriptions, and from the meager proceeds of her *First Steps to the Study of History* (1832) and several subsequent textbooks. During this period she became acquainted with the educator Horace Mann, who lived in the same boardinghouse as the Peabody sisters. For a time a romantic attachment seemed about to develop between Mann and Elizabeth, but it was her sister Mary whom he eventually married.

In 1834 a new intellectual adventure began. Bronson Alcott had sensed the depth of Elizabeth Peabody's concern with education soon after their first meeting in 1830. It was natural, therefore, that he should consult her when he arrived in Boston for a fresh start after his Germantown, Pa., school had closed. With the idealism and generosity which characterized her career, she encouraged him to establish another school, transferred to him the students she had gathered for a new school of her own, collected yet other children, and installed herself as his assistant. Her agreement with him called for two and a half hours per day teaching Latin, but she was soon devoting the whole day to his Platonic-Transcendentalist experiment, keeping a record of his Socratic questioning of the young, who he and Miss Peabody believed had had spiritual preexistence, and often participating herself in the definition of words and explication of poems.

Elizabeth Peabody's *Record of a School* (1835), her journal with comments, established Alcott as an important and controversial figure in avant-garde intellectual circles, and this role he himself expanded in 1836–37 with his *Conversations with Children on the Gospels*, which contained further installments of Elizabeth's journal and other records by her sister (see SOPHIA PEABODY HAWTHORNE). These books brought Alcott under severe criticism for some remarks he had made on pregnancy and childbirth in a discussion of Christ's nativity, but it was all-important to the future course of Transcendentalism that Miss Peabody should thus have brought her friend before the public. Emerson's public defense of Alcott brought the two men together in a marriage of minds, with results apparent in Emerson's first book, *Nature* (1836), and in his subsequent poems and essays, with their far-reaching influence. Elizabeth Peabody, although distressed by Alcott's indiscretion, also came to his defense with a long piece, "Mr. Alcott's Book and

School," an article in the *Christian Register and Boston Observer* (Apr. 29, 1837). The episode made her, too, a controversial figure, and its effect upon her prospects was disastrous. Severing her connection with Alcott's school in 1836, she returned to Salem, where for four years she lived with her family, without income or employment.

Her friendship with Emerson, dating from 1822 when he had tutored her in Greek, now deepened. On her frequent trips to Concord she shared with him her discovery of the mystic and poet Jones Very, thus preparing the way for Emerson's acting as editor and publisher in 1839 of Very's *Poems and Essays*. Her other discovery in Salem was Nathaniel Hawthorne, whose family she had known since childhood. Through her friend George Bancroft she secured Hawthorne's appointment at the Boston Custom House. Again rumors of romance proved unfounded, for it was Elizabeth's sister Sophia who in 1842 became Hawthorne's wife.

Hawthorne and Very were not enough to hold Elizabeth Peabody in Salem, and she next moved her family to 13 West Street, Boston, where in the front parlor she opened in 1840 one of the most unusual and influential bookstores in American history. This store made available by purchase or loan foreign books and periodicals and, inevitably, the native documents in radicalism, and soon became the city headquarters of the Transcendentalists. Here on Wednesday evenings Margaret Fuller held her famous Conversations, and here George and SOPHIA RIPLEY, Theodore Parker, Emerson, and others discussed and helped to shape the *Dial* and Brook Farm. Here also Miss Peabody established herself as the first woman publisher in Boston and, it seems likely, in the nation. Her publications included a Channing pamphlet on emancipation and other antislavery literature, three of Hawthorne's books for children, and, briefly, the *Dial*, when the original publisher failed in 1842. In May 1849 appeared the single issue of her own Transcendentalist periodical, *Aesthetic Papers*, where with editorial boldness she published Thoreau's "Civil Disobedience," destined to become a scripture for Gandhi and Martin Luther King.

Elizabeth Peabody was, however, a Transcendentalist of a different variety from Thoreau and Emerson. In "A Glimpse of Christ's Idea of Society" and "Plan of the West Roxbury Community" in the *Dial* she marked as errors both "the isolated cultivation of the soul," in essence the program of Emerson and Thoreau, and the loss of the individual in or-

ganization, the potential danger she saw in George Ripley's Brook Farm and other Fourieristic communities. She believed that "The final cause of human society is the unfolding of the individual man into every form of perfection, without let or hindrance, according to the inward nature of each" (*Dial*, October 1841, p. 226), but she believed this possible only in a society which accepted Christ as its social architect. In "The Dorian Measure, with a Modern Application" (*Aesthetic Papers*) she returned to this thesis. Indicating her admiration for the Spartan state where a lofty religion dominated and shaped every aspect of life, she asserted that the great issue in modern times was "whether there may not be a social organization which does as much justice to the Christian religion and philosophy, as the Dorian state did to Apollo."

In "A Glimpse of Christ's Idea of Society" (*Dial*, October 1841) Miss Peabody contended that the essential reform needed to bring about the ideal society was mankind's "educating its children truly." After 1850 the cause of Christian-Transcendental education for the young became the dominant passion of her life. Transcendentalism as an organized movement had ended by the mid-1840's, and she closed her bookshop about 1850, when she moved with her ailing parents to West Newton, Mass. She then taught briefly in a Boston boys' school conducted by an émigré Hungarian, nursed her mother through her final illness in 1853, and in the latter part of the decade threw herself into promoting, in the public and normal schools of Massachusetts and elsewhere, the chronological history charts invented by the Polish general Józef Bem. After teaching for a time in the Eagleswood School near Perth Amboy, N.J. (see SARAH and ANGELINA GRIMKÉ), she went in 1859 to live in Concord with her recently widowed sister Mary. A staunch abolitionist, Elizabeth Peabody traveled to Virginia the next year to intercede for a man condemned to hang for complicity in John Brown's raid on Harpers Ferry.

But most of her energies went into writing and lecturing on education; between 1850 and 1884 she produced ten books and fifty articles. The pivotal year was 1859, when, while teaching in an infant school conducted in Concord by Mary Mann, she learned from MARGARETHE MEYER SCHURZ of the kindergarten movement founded in Germany by Friedrich Froebel. A year later she started in Boston the first formally organized kindergarten in the United States. The school attracted admiring attention; and Miss Peabody's *Moral Culture of Infancy, and Kindergarten Guide* (1863, written with Mrs. Mann) sold well, but she soon became convinced that she had not truly grasped Froebel's principles. In 1867–68, with money from a series of lectures on history, she traveled in Europe visiting kindergartens conducted on the true Froebel pattern, and on her return devoted herself to promoting the movement. She established and edited in 1873 the *Kindergarten Messenger* and in 1877 organized the American Froebel Union, of which she became the first president.

In her advocacy of kindergartens Elizabeth Peabody had her most widespread impact on American life, although the kindergarten movement soon abandoned her emphasis on spiritual education. Her most significant achievement, however, was her contribution to American Transcendentalism, and appropriately she concluded her teaching career in the 1880's as a faculty member of Bronson Alcott's Concord School of Philosophy. Her *Reminiscences of Rev. Wm. Ellery Channing, D.D.* (1880) is a work of rare charm as well as a key document in New England intellectual history. In *Last Evening with Allston* (1886) she recounted her friendship with the celebrated artist Washington Allston and collected her essays from the *Dial* and *Aesthetic Papers*, together with later pieces, including her penetrating essay on Hawthorne contributed to the *Atlantic Monthly* in 1868. Vigorous to the end, she was unfailingly generous in her enthusiasms; in her eighties, aroused over Indian wrongs, she raised considerable sums of money for the Piute leader SARAH WINNEMUCCA.

Elizabeth Peabody has passed to posterity largely through the reminiscences of those who knew her in extreme old age. From these reports we see her as a colorful eccentric, her notorious indifference to personal appearance made worse by failing eyesight, stoutness, and a chronic lack of money, while her lifelong delight in conversation betrayed her into mere garrulity. Tales have been told of Miss Peabody on her travels, toothbrush in her handbag, nightgown under her dress, discoursing interminably upon kindergartens, immortality, or Chinese grammar. Henry James, despite his denial, may have had her in mind when he created Miss Birdseye in *The Bostonians*. She died at her home in Jamaica Plain, Boston, in 1894, in her ninetieth year. After a funeral at Boston's Church of the Disciples, she was buried in Sleepy Hollow Cemetery, Concord. The Elizabeth Peabody House, a Boston social settlement, was established by her friends in her memory in 1896. Her achievement lies not so much in her own intellectual gifts, though these were considerable, as in her ability to

appreciate original thinking in others, draw it forth, publicize it, and transmit it. The range and stature of the men whose work she championed—Channing, Alcott, Very, Hawthorne, Froebel—is impressive. In educational reform she forms a link between isolated visionaries like Alcott and her own mother, and the organized kindergarten movement of the later nineteenth century. Her contribution to American Transcendentalism was best suggested by Bronson Alcott, who in *Sonnets and Canzonets* placed a sonnet to Elizabeth Peabody between one addressed to the Unitarian Channing and another to the Transcendentalist Emerson.

[The only extensive published biographical account, Louise Hall Tharp, *The Peabody Sisters of Salem* (1950), is largely undocumented and not always trustworthy in detail. On Miss Peabody's kindergarten work, see her own articles in *Education*, May–June 1882, especially pp. 522–25, in Henry Barnard's *Am. Jour. of Education*, XXXII (1882 [1902]), 721–42, and in *Papers on Froebel's Kindergarten . . . Republished from the Am. Jour. of Education* (rev. ed., 1890), pp. 5–16; and Internat. Kindergarten Union, *Pioneers of the Kindergarten in America* (1924), pp. 19–38, including reminiscences by Lucy Wheelock. On the Temple School: Elizabeth Palmer Peabody, *Record of Mr. Alcott's School* (3rd ed., 1874); Josephine E. Roberts, "Elizabeth Peabody and the Temple School," *New England Quart.*, Sept. 1942; and Franklin B. Sanborn and William T. Harris, *A. Bronson Alcott: His Life and Philosophy* (2 vols., 1893). See also Norman H. Pearson, *Hawthorne's Two "Engagements"* (pamphlet, Sophia Smith Collection, Smith College, 1963); Queenie N. Bilbo, "Elizabeth Palmer Peabody, Transcendentalist" (unpublished Ph.D. dissertation, N.Y. Univ., 1932); Josephine E. Roberts, "A New England Family" [the Peabody sisters] (unpublished Ph.D. dissertation, Western Reserve Univ., 1937); George W. Cooke, *An Hist. and Biog. Introduction to Accompany The Dial* (1902); Clarence L. F. Gohdes, *The Periodicals of Am. Transcendentalism* (1931); memorial tributes in *Woman's Jour.*, May 7, 1904.]

CHARLES H. FOSTER

**PEABODY, Josephine Preston** (May 30, 1874– Dec. 4, 1922), poet and dramatist, was born in Brooklyn, N.Y., the second of three daughters who survived infancy. Her father, Charles Kilham Peabody, a merchant, was a native of Wenham, Mass., and a descendant of Francis Peabody, who arrived in Massachusetts from England in the 1630's. Her mother, Susan Josephine (Morrill) Peabody, was from Boston. Both parents were intelligent and sensitive, with a strong literary and artistic bent. Inveterate playgoers, they encouraged their daughters in an early love of the arts, teaching them to paint, providing them with children's editions of literary masterpieces, and acting out informal family plays.

This happy idyll was shaken by the death of Josephine's younger sister, Florence, in 1882, and ended with the death of her father in 1884, which left the family in grave financial difficulties and her mother broken and spiritless. Mrs. Peabody, with Josephine and her older sister, Marion, went to live with the maternal grandmother in Dorchester, Mass., outside Boston. A serious and precocious child, Josephine found no companion but her sister to share her interests and steadily became more shy and withdrawn, depending upon her own imaginative resources for entertainment. Finding the public school in Dorchester unstimulating, she spent most of her spare time writing verses, short stories, and plays, and reading widely and voraciously. The last few years of her early education, from 1889 to 1892, were spent more happily in the Girls' Latin School in Boston, where she studied Latin and Greek classics, but she was forced by ill health to leave after her junior year.

Since the age of thirteen or fourteen Josephine Peabody had been mailing verses to editors of various magazines, and some of them had been accepted for publication. In 1893 she began sending poems to Horace Scudder, editor of the *Atlantic Monthly,* who at her earnest request gave her helpful criticism. In February 1894, when she was nineteen, Scudder accepted one of her poems for publication in the *Atlantic,* and soon after, *Scribner's Magazine,* the other literary giant of the period, followed suit. In the summer of 1894 Scudder and another friend solicited the aid of a local philanthropist and that September enrolled Josephine in Radcliffe College, where for two years she studied as a special student.

She returned to her solitary life in 1896 and settled down to write in earnest. Her reading was a direct influence not only on her style, but also on her choice of genre. She had always loved Keats, and Scudder had introduced her to the Pre-Raphaelite lyrics of Christina Rossetti; both of these poets influenced her early lyric verse. Since she had been brought up on Shakespeare and had developed an admiration for the dramatic monologues of Browning, her simple lyrics evolved naturally into dramatic verse. She began a verse play on Christopher Marlowe early in 1897, and in 1898, when she was twenty-three, Copeland and Day, Boston publishers of the aesthetic and the avant-garde, issued her first book of poems, *The Wayfarers. Fortune and Men's Eyes* followed in 1900, a one-act play built around

Shakespeare's sonnets, with new verse of her own filling out the volume. With these publications her literary reputation began to rise, her frail beauty and youth (HARRIET MONROE recalled her as "exquisite and remote from earth") increasing popular interest in her work. In 1901 she finally finished *Marlowe,* her first full-length drama, which was published by Houghton, Mifflin & Company in the same year. Its style shows a curious mixture of influences, with a Pre-Raphaelite delicacy and wealth of detail superimposed on a framework of Marlovian and Shakespearean blank verse.

From 1901 to 1903 Miss Peabody held a lectureship in poetry and literature at Wellesley College, which helped relieve her continuing financial stringency. A friend, Lillian Shuman, gave her money for a trip abroad in 1902, and she spent the summer in England, Scotland, Holland, and Belgium. Another book of her poetry, *The Singing Leaves,* appeared in 1903. Her *Pan,* a choric idyl set to music, was performed in Ottawa in 1904.

On June 21, 1906, Josephine Peabody was married to Lionel Simeon Marks, professor of mechanical engineering at Harvard, who took her abroad for a year, traveling extensively on the Continent and in his native England. While in Europe she wrote the first draft of *The Piper,* a verse drama employing the old Hamelin legend. She returned to live in Cambridge, Mass., in the fall of 1907. Her daughter, Alison Peabody Marks, was born the following year, which also saw the publication of a volume of poems for and about children, *The Book of the Little Past.* In 1909 *The Piper* was published and entered in the Stratford Prize Competition; just after the birth of her son, Lionel Peabody Marks, the next year, she learned that it had won the prize, out of a field of 315 competitors; and on July 26 she saw it performed with great success at the Stratford Memorial Theatre in England. It later played to equally enthusiastic audiences in London and New York. *The Piper* was the high point of Josephine Peabody's career, bringing her wide literary recognition both abroad and at home.

In her later years she began to take a strong interest in liberal and radical reform movements, probably influenced by the writings of William Morris, and certainly by her husband and her radical sister-in-law, Amy Marks. She joined the Fabian Society in 1909, and in 1911 published *The Singing Man,* a book of poems dealing with the right of all men, including the poor, to know the "joy of living." She also interested herself in woman suffrage and, when war came, in pacifism and refugee relief. Her other literary interests continued, giving rise to a new volume of poems, *Harvest Moon* (1916), and three more published plays: *The Wolf of Gubbio* (1913), on St. Francis of Assisi; *The Chameleon* (1917), a comedy; and *Portrait of Mrs. W.* (1922), a prose play on the eighteenth-century English feminist Mary Wollstonecraft. But the last decade of her life was an increasingly desperate struggle against illness: a hardening of the arteries leading to the brain which did not cloud her mind but overwhelmed her with weariness. She was twice operated upon, in 1912 and 1915. She suffered a two weeks' coma in January 1922 and died that December in Cambridge, at the age of forty-eight. Although Josephine Peabody's best writing is found in her books of poetry, her chief contribution to American letters was through her plays in verse, which helped keep alive a tenuous tradition of this genre in a period when it seemed to be dying out.

[The most inclusive source is Christina Hopkinson Baker, ed., *Diary and Letters of Josephine Preston Peabody* (1925). There is a good evaluation of her in the foreword by KATHARINE LEE BATES to *The Collected Poems of Josephine Preston Peabody* (1927); see also *The Collected Plays* (1927), with a foreword by George P. Baker. Appraisals of her life and work may be found in: *Poetry*, Feb. 1923, pp. 262–67; *Bookman*, May 1923, pp. 263–66; *Saturday Rev. of Literature*, Mar. 20, 1926, p. 650; *Atlantic Monthly*, Dec. 1927, pp. 856–57; Jessie B. Rittenhouse, *My House of Life* (1934); Horace Gregory and Marya Zaturenska, *Hist. of Am. Poetry, 1900–1940* (1942); and David Dickason, *The Daring Young Men* (1953), a study of the American Pre-Raphaelites. See also *Nat. Cyc. Am. Biog.*, XIX, 95–96; *Biog. Cyc. Am. Women*, II (1925), 269–73; *Woman's Who's Who of America*, 1914–15; and obituary in *N.Y. Times*, Dec. 5, 1922. Other information from the Boston Girls' Latin School and the Mass. Registrar of Vital Statistics. There are large holdings of Josephine Peabody's letters and MSS. at Harvard Univ. and Wellesley College.]

JULIAN T. BAIRD, JR.

**PEABODY, Kate Nichols Trask.** *See* TRASK, Kate Nichols.

**PEABODY, Lucy Whitehead McGill Waterbury** (Mar. 2, 1861–Feb. 26, 1949), Baptist lay leader, pioneer in ecumenical foreign missions programs, was born at Belmont, Kans., the second child and first daughter of John and Sarah Jane (Hart) McGill. John McGill, a native of Canada, is listed in the 1860 census as a merchant. His ancestors had originally settled in Ontario, and one of his relatives was the chief benefactor of McGill University in

Montreal. When Belmont, a ferry point on the Missouri River opposite St. Joseph, Mo., was destroyed during the Civil War, Lucy's family went for a few years to Pittsford, N.Y., her mother's birthplace; in 1873 they relocated in nearby Rochester, where McGill became a produce dealer. Five years later Lucy graduated from the Rochester Academy as valedictorian of her class. From 1878 to 1881 she taught at the local State School for the Deaf and occasionally took a course at the University of Rochester.

On Aug. 18, 1881, at the age of twenty, she was married to Norman Mather Waterbury, a Baptist minister and graduate of the University of Rochester (1878) and Rochester Theological Seminary (1881). Within two months the young couple sailed for India under missionary appointment, arriving in early November at Perambore, Madras Presidency, where for five years they worked with the outcaste Telugus. Waterbury, plagued by poor health from the start of the mission, died in November 1886, leaving his wife with three small children, one of whom died during the journey back to the United States. After her return to Rochester, Mrs. Waterbury taught for a while. In 1890 she became corresponding secretary of the home department of the Woman's Baptist Foreign Missionary Society and moved to its headquarters in Boston, where she served for sixteen years.

When her children had graduated from college (Norma Rose from Vassar and Howard Ernest from the Biltmore Forest School after two years at Harvard), Mrs. Waterbury resigned her Missionary Society post and on June 16, 1906, was married to Henry Wayland Peabody, a wealthy and prominent Baptist who had founded Henry W. Peabody and Company, a Boston importing and exporting firm, and was a frequent writer on tariff and currency questions. They made their home on Peabody's estate in Beverly Cove, Mass. Peabody died in 1908, leaving his widow with independent means, free to devote herself to religious and philanthropic work. Her memorial of him was published in 1909.

As early as 1890, long before her second marriage, Lucy Waterbury had begun advocating an ecumenical approach to foreign missions. In that year she and her friend Mrs. HELEN BARRETT MONTGOMERY, later the first woman president of the Northern Baptist Convention (1921), promoted the idea of setting aside a day each year for united prayer for missions, an observance popularly known today as the World Day of Prayer. In 1900 an ecumenical missionary conference held in New

York City, attended by 2,300 women delegates from all parts of the world, established a Central Committee on the United Study of Foreign Missions, and in 1902 Mrs. Waterbury was appointed chairman, a position she filled until 1929. In this capacity she helped produce a series of textbooks for women's study groups, whose distribution reached the millions during her twenty-seven-year tenure. She also helped organize and promote summer schools for mission study, such as those at Northfield, Mass., Chambersburg, Pa., and Chautauqua, N.Y. Her abilities received wide recognition, and at the ecumenical conference of 1910 in Edinburgh, Scotland, she was appointed the sole representative for American women on the important Committee of Reference and Counsel.

Mrs. Peabody's ecumenical interests gained new impetus when in 1913 the Woman's American Baptist Foreign Mission Society was created through a merger of the Boston-based Woman's Baptist Foreign Missionary Society with the Woman's Baptist Foreign Missionary Society of the West. Mrs. Montgomery became president of the new organization, MARTHA HILLARD MAC LEISH vice-president for home administration, and Mrs. Peabody vice-president for the foreign department. In 1913–14 Mrs. Peabody and Mrs. Montgomery made a tour of missionary centers in the Orient, financing it themselves and carrying credentials not from any one board but from the interdenominational Federation of Women's Boards of Foreign Missions. Lucy Peabody's observations convinced her that to help raise the status of women in Eastern countries, women's colleges should be established. On her return she appealed to various mission boards to consider founding interdenominational Christian women's colleges in India, China, and Japan. For a time she hoped for aid from the Interchurch World Movement, a dramatic attempt to revitalize the church at home and abroad inaugurated in 1918 with the sponsorship of John D. Rockefeller and others, but this movement collapsed within two years. Rockefeller, however, then pledged the sum of $1,000,000 in memory of his mother, as an endowment fund to establish seven women's colleges in the Orient (three each in India and China, and one in Japan), if Mrs. Peabody could raise an additional $2,000,000 in cash and subscriptions by Jan. 1, 1923. Accepting the challenge, she "lived oriental colleges" for the next three years. She traveled and lectured from coast to coast, utilized all available news media, including the radio, and enlisted the support of many influential Americans, as well as the cooperation of sixteen denominational mission

boards in this country and two in Canada. After the trustees of the Laura Spelman Rockefeller Fund had extended the expiration date one month, she was finally able to raise the required money. She remained close to the colleges after their establishment by serving on the board of directors of three of them: the Women's Christian College in Madras, India; the Women's Christian Medical College in Vellore, India; and the Shanghai Medical College.

While engaged in this crusade, Mrs. Peabody had grown increasingly disillusioned about her own denomination's approach to foreign missions; she particularly lamented the rancor that divided Baptists over the Interchurch Movement, whose enthusiasm for ecumenicity she shared. As a result she resigned as vice-president of the Woman's American Baptist Foreign Mission Society in June 1921. At the same time, caught up in the fundamentalist-modernist tensions of the 1920's, she criticized the selection of missionary personnel and advocated the recall of all modernists from foreign fields. Charging that "institutionalism and big business have taken the place of evangelism and dependence upon God" (*Message*, April 1949, p. 7), she deplored a system that placed education before conversion and baptism. When the Foreign Board of the Northern Baptist Convention, for administrative reasons, restricted the evangelistic activities of her son-in-law, Dr. Raphael C. Thomas, for twenty-four years a medical missionary in the Philippines, she took the issue to the floor of the 1927 annual convention. Defeated, she walked out of the convention and resigned from every denominational office. A group of sympathetic Baptist missionaries in the Philippines, led by her son-in-law, followed her example and withdrew from Northern Baptist support. This separation led to the formation of the Association of Baptists for World Evangelism, which concentrated its efforts in new mission fields in the Philippines. Mrs. Peabody headed this "Adventure of Faith," as she called it, for seven years, and in 1928 began publishing the *Message* to describe the association's work.

During the 1920's, believing that "my first duty now is to my country," Mrs. Peabody concentrated her efforts on the defense of prohibition. In 1922, when organized opposition to the Eighteenth Amendment and the Volstead Act first began, she helped form the Woman's National Committee for Law Enforcement, of which she was president for more than a decade. Unsalaried and working out of Boston, Mrs. Peabody wrote and spoke frequently on law enforcement, organized state and national conventions, supervised the preparation of textbooks, and helped publish a monthly paper, *Spotlight.* She was disappointed in the conclusions of the Wickersham Commission, appointed by President Hoover in 1929 to survey the problem of enforcing the prohibition and other laws, because they largely ignored the role of women. "Men think logically," she argued, "women biologically. . . . Prohibition will not be enforced until women are recognized as the natural leaders in such education and enforcement" (William C. Durant, ed., *Law Observance,* 1929, p. 396). By 1931 she had moved to Orlando, Fla., because she refused to "live in an outlaw state."

A woman of plain but pleasant features, with a tendency toward stoutness, Mrs. Peabody possessed unusual energy and administrative skills. Gracious and considerate, she shunned acrimony, and even after leaving the Northern Baptist Convention continued to write numerous articles for Baptist publications. Her gentleness especially endeared her to children, who came to know her through the pages of *Everyland,* a missionary magazine for children which she started in 1908, edited for twelve years, and generously supported out of her own funds. "My chief recreations in life," she wrote in 1921, "are grandchildren and gardens." One prayer booklet she wrote for her grandson was translated into Chinese, Japanese, and Indian languages. Mrs. Peabody died of arteriosclerotic heart disease in 1949 in Danvers, Mass., where she had been spending the winter, and was buried in the McGill family plot in Pittsford, N.Y. The rise of women's missionary societies in the late nineteenth century she saw as a manifestation of the new freedom for women, and her devotion to missionary work was based largely on the conviction that only a Christian civilization offered hope to the women of the world.

[There is a eulogistic obituary of Mrs. Peabody in the *Watchman-Examiner,* Mar. 17, 1949; see also, for a summary of her career, *Who Was Who in America,* vol. III (1960). For the most part, however, biographical information has been assembled from a variety of scattered sources, including files of the *Watchman-Examiner* and other material at the Am. Baptist Hist. Soc., Rochester, N.Y. Information on her father and the family background from: 1860 U.S. census schedule for Washington Township, Doniphan County, Kans. (courtesy of Kans. State Hist. Soc.); Rochester (N.Y.) city directories (courtesy of Dr. Blake McKelvey); Fred E. Crawford, *Your Grandmother: A Memoir of Mattie Coolidge Crawford* (privately printed, 1945), pp. 72, 77–79. For her first marriage: *Annual Reports* of Am. Baptist Telugu Mission, 1882–

88. For her second: Mrs. Peabody's *Henry Wayland Peabody, Merchant* (1909). There are brief references to her role in Baptist foreign mission societies in Robert G. Torbet's history of these societies: *Venture of Faith* (1955). Her tour of the Orient is described in Helen Barrett Montgomery, *The King's Highway* (1915). The fullest account of the campaign for the women's union Christian colleges is given by Mrs. Peabody in *Watchman-Examiner,* Mar. 15, 1923, pp. 341–42; see also article by Abby Gunn Baker in *ibid.,* Nov. 30, 1923, pp. 1526–27. On the Woman's Nat. Committee for Law Enforcement, see *Baptist Missionary Rev.,* Oct. 1931, pp. 467–68; Fletcher Dobyns, *The Amazing Story of Repeal* (1940), p. 104; *Union Signal,* Oct. 10, 1931, p. 610; *Watchman-Examiner,* Mar. 27, 1930, p. 399. Mrs. Peabody's *Kidnaping the Constitution* (1934) is a protest against the repeal of the Eighteenth Amendment. Death record from Mass. Registrar of Vital Statistics.]

EARL C. KAYLOR, JR.

**PEALE, Anna Claypoole** (Mar. 6, 1791–Dec. 25, 1878), **Margaretta Angelica** (Oct. 1, 1795–Jan. 17, 1882), and **Sarah Miriam** (May 19, 1800–Feb. 4, 1885), painters of portraits and still lifes, were the youngest of the six children (all but one of them girls) of James Peale (1749–1831), a portrait painter and brother of the better-known artist Charles Willson Peale (1741–1827). The girls' paternal grandfather, Charles Peale, was a schoolmaster who had come from England to Maryland. Their father, who under his brother's guidance had given up the trade of saddler to learn painting, had served under Washington as an officer in the Continental Army from 1776 to 1779, an experience that left his health permanently impaired. He settled in Philadelphia and in 1782 married Mary Claypoole, daughter of James Claypoole, a house painter, and sister of James Claypoole, Jr., a painter of portraits. James Peale worked for a time as assistant in his brother Charles' studio, one of his tasks being the historical backgrounds of the latter's full-length portraits of Washington. As Charles Willson Peale's eyesight became inadequate for the fine precision required in miniature painting, James took over that branch of the art.

The careers of James Peale's daughters in a measure echo their father's. There was the same close family association with the other painting Peales. As James' eyesight changed, Anna in turn entered the painting of miniatures. The young women also assisted their father with his backgrounds after he had returned to work on canvas, and many of the later James Peale portraits contain embroidered shawls, laces, and other fine fabrics quite beyond the old soldier's hand and revealing a purely feminine delight in rich materials. These may be seen again in Sarah's work of later years.

Anna Claypoole Peale, the miniaturist, was born in Philadelphia. She was represented in the first exhibition of the Pennsylvania Academy of the Fine Arts in 1811 with a "Fruit Piece (first attempt)" and in 1814 with a "Frame containing three miniatures." On Nov. 15, 1817, Charles Willson Peale wrote that "Anna in Miniature is becoming excellent," praise which would not have been lightly accorded. In the autumn of the next year her uncle took her with him to Washington to share his studio and paint miniatures on ivory where these were desired. "Her merrit in miniature painting," he reported, "brings her into high estimation, and so many Ladies and Gentlemen desire to sit to her that she frequently is obliged to raise her prices" (to Angelica Peale Robinson, Sept. 23, 1818). Her subjects at this time included President Monroe, Andrew Jackson, and Henry Clay. In the course of her career she also painted miniatures in Baltimore and Boston.

Anna Peale's success was largely owing to a variation of her own upon the pleasant style of portraiture developed within the family. Interest in her subjects was intensified by a darker background, and she brought to them that warmth and intimacy so important in the private art of the miniature, but which had too often been lacking in her father's rather stylized ivories. Her eminence in the profession was acknowledged by her election as an Academician of the Pennsylvania Academy of the Fine Arts in 1824. She exhibited regularly at the academy until 1842, when, following her second marriage, she retired from professional portrait painting. She had earlier, on Aug. 27, 1829, been married to the Rev. William Staughton, Baptist minister and educator, but he died in December of the same year. On June 10, 1841, she became the third wife of Gen. William Duncan. There were no children by either marriage.

Margaretta Angelica Peale, born in Philadelphia four years after Anna, followed a career in art which was essentially that of an amateur, although many of her fruit pieces shown at the academy from 1828 to 1837 are listed as being for sale. She painted a few portraits of good quality, four of which are in the collection of George Washington University. Her obituary in the *Philadelphia Inquirer* cites her as one "whose superior talent in painting fruit has given her a high reputation in Philadelphia." "Miss Peale," the *Inquirer* added,

"possessed a remarkable memory, and was noted for the simplicity and loveliness of her character." She never married.

Sarah Miriam Peale, the last sister, born in Philadelphia in 1800, achieved a career of independent success in the arts such as no woman had attained in America before. Though she painted some miniatures and some still lifes, she was primarily a painter of portraits in oils. Her first work in this medium was a self-portrait painted at the age of eighteen. Her father, after mixing the colors for her and giving explicit directions, left her alone in the studio with a mirror. She depicted herself draped in loose folds of crimson, leaning forward and smiling archly under her curls. James Peale's comment when he saw the work was, "Damn it! Why didn't you do as I told you?" In relating the incident she adds that it was the only time her father ever used profanity in her presence. Her uncle, on the other hand, praised the piece as "wonderfully like." In the Pennsylvania Academy show of that year, 1818, Sarah had a "Portrait of a Lady (second attempt)."

On his visit to Washington in the autumn of 1818 Charles Willson Peale also had "Sally" with him for a while. He found her more intent on breaking hearts than painting portraits, but the old man watched her progress through the social life of the capital with undiminished pride. By 1822 she was actively established in the profession, traveling in search of patronage as so many painters were then obliged to do, dividing her time mostly between Philadelphia and Baltimore. With her sister Anna, she was elected an Academician of the Pennsylvania Academy in 1824. Her representation in the academy exhibits continued from 1817 to 1831. In that year, with the death of her father, she removed to Baltimore, where she was for fifteen years the city's most popular portrait painter. Her portraits are characterized by that air of pleasure and intelligence which is common to so much of the Peale work, and, as her style matured, by a more romantic and thoughtful mood. They are distinguished also by the fine painting of fabrics and furs. Never marrying, she continued to work frequently in conjunction with Anna—the painter in miniature and the painter in large sharing their patronage as others in the family had done before so successfully. Her sitters include many famous persons: Commodore William Bainbridge, Henry A. Wise, Thomas Hart Benton, Daniel Webster, Lafayette.

In 1846 Senator Trusten Polk and other residents of St. Louis persuaded Sarah to settle in that city. There she remained for thirty-two years, the leading portrait painter of the Western metropolis. As age advanced she gave up most of her portrait work and turned to still life. In July 1878 she returned to Philadelphia to share the home of her sister Anna, widowed since the death of General Duncan in 1864. All three sisters lived well into their eighties, and all three died in Philadelphia. They were buried in the James Peale vault in Ronaldson Cemetery, which had been laid out in 1831 for persons with no particular religious affiliation.

From earliest colonial times, women have figured in the history of American art, but Anna and Sarah Peale, and particularly the ebullient Sally, were the first to achieve full professional standing and recognition, achieving it early and maintaining it for more than fifty years. The credit belongs not only to their own energy and talent but also to the background of a large family deeply immersed in art and in liberal thinking and to Charles Willson Peale's insistence upon the equality of the sexes. The successful careers of both Anna and Sarah date from that Washington season of 1818–19, when their uncle, then the oldest and to many the most famous American painter, introduced the two girls to the nation's most sophisticated patronage as associates and compeers.

[Peale Papers, Am. Philosophical Soc., Phila.; Archives of the Peale Museum, Baltimore, courtesy of Wilbur H. Hunter, Director; Wilbur H. Hunter and John Mahey, *Miss Sarah Miriam Peale* (exhibition catalogue, Peale Museum, 1967); C. C. Sellers, *Charles Willson Peale: Later Life* (1947); Anna Wells Rutledge, *Cumulative Record of Exhibition Catalogues, Pa. Academy of the Fine Arts* (1953); John T. Scharf, *Hist. of Saint Louis* (1883); Wolfgang Born, "The Female Peales, Their Art and Its Tradition," *Am. Collector*, Aug. 1946; Harry B. Wehle and Theodore Bolton, *Am. Miniatures* (1927).]

CHARLES COLEMAN SELLERS

**PECK, Annie Smith** (Oct. 19, 1850–July 18, 1935), mountain climber, teacher, and lecturer, was born in Providence, R.I., the youngest of five children and only surviving daughter of George Bacheler Peck, a lawyer and dealer in anthracite coal, and Ann Power (Smith) Peck. Her father, descended from early seventeenth-century English settlers of Hingham, Mass., was a graduate of Brown University; her mother was a descendant of Roger Williams, founder of the Rhode Island colony. Conventional, somewhat austere people, members of the Baptist Church, the Pecks were opposed to Annie's later pursuits; only her brother George gave her sympathy and

support. All three of her brothers, however, were in part responsible for her later accomplishments as a mountaineer. Vowing to outdo them in sports when they refused to let her join their play, she developed the physical stamina, endurance, and fearlessness which, with perfect health, enabled her to surmount the hardships of mountain climbing. Her militant espousal of woman's rights grew naturally from her insistence on equal ·status with her brothers.

The Pecks' respect for classical education assured Annie of good schooling at Dr. Stockbridge's School for Young Ladies in Providence, followed by attendance at the Providence High School and two years at the Rhode Island State Normal School, from which she graduated in 1872. After teaching for two terms in the Providence public schools, she accepted a position as preceptress of the Saginaw, Mich., high school. In 1874 she enrolled at the University of Michigan, which offered women an education on an equal basis with men. She majored in Greek and received her A.B. degree in 1878, earning honors in every subject; she took an A.M. degree by examination in 1881. Continuing her teaching career meanwhile, she briefly held positions as mathematics instructor at Bartholomew's School for Girls in Cincinnati, Ohio, and preceptress of a Montclair, N.J., high school. From 1881 to 1883 she taught Latin and elocution at Purdue University; the following year she studied German and music in Hanover, Germany. In 1885 she became the first woman student admitted to the American School of Classical Studies at Athens. She taught Latin at Smith College in 1886–87. To augment her salary so that she could afford to travel, Miss Peck gave parlor lectures on Greek and Roman archaeology, making stereopticon slides from her own photographs; by 1892 she had made lecturing her vocation.

By her own account Miss Peck's enthusiasm for mountain climbing dated from 1885 when, en route from Germany to Greece, she first saw the "frowning walls" of the Matterhorn. After ascending several smaller mountains while in Europe, she made her first important climb in 1888: Mount Shasta (14,380 feet) in California. In 1895 she climbed the Matterhorn, a feat that brought her instant fame, accompanied by a certain amount of notoriety. Almost as daring as the ascent itself was her climbing costume—knickerbockers, hip-length tunic, stout boots and woolen hose, and a soft felt hat tied with a veil. In Mexico in 1897 she climbed the live volcano Popocatepetl and Mount Orizaba (18,314 feet), the latter peak the highest point in the Americas reached by a woman at that time.

She found mountain climbing exhilarating; her pleasure in the "everchanging vistas" was intensified by the accompanying risks and obstacles. Her exploits as a woman mountain climber, too, were admirably suited to the lecture circuit. By 1900 she was giving public lectures from coast to coast under professional management, and lecturing was to be the main source of her income for the rest of her life. She had a pleasing stage presence and a good speaking voice. Her appearance—she was slight and feminine in her dress—was often surprising to audiences which expected a woman mountain climber to be an Amazon.

While in Europe in 1900 as the United States delegate to the Congrès Internationale de l'Alpinisme in Paris, she climbed the Fünffingerspitze in the Tyrol, Monte Cristallo in the Dolomites, and the Jungfrau. Driven by ambition and a desire to conquer "some height where no *man* had previously stood," she next turned to the relatively unexplored regions of South America and, despite her fifty years, undertook a search for a virgin peak in the Andes, one higher than the already ascended Aconcagua (22,835 feet) in Argentina. Choosing Mount Sorata (Illampu) in Bolivia as a possibility, she broke her own record in 1904 when she reached its summit of 21,300 feet. She next surveyed the approaches to twin-peaked Huascarán (said to be 25,000 feet) in Peru, returning in 1906 to make two attempts that fell short of the summit for lack of experienced help. Accepting defeat for the moment, she explored the Raura Range, climbing its highest peak of 18,000 feet, making a first ascent of a rock mountain at 16,300 feet, and ascending the glacier above Lake Santa Ana, one source of the Amazon. Finally, in 1908, with two expert Swiss guides, she succeeded in climbing the north peak of Huascarán, though her satisfaction in her accomplishment was marred by the fact that one of the guides was actually the first to set foot on the summit.

Unable to measure the altitude of Huascarán scientifically because of strong gales, Miss Peck and the guides estimated the height at about 24,000 feet. This figure, offered in good faith, placed Huascarán at the apex of South America. Annie Peck received international acclaim, a gold medal from the Peruvian government, and a silver stirrup in the form of a slipper from the Lima Geographical Society. Somewhat later FANNY BULLOCK WORKMAN, who had reached an altitude of 23,300 feet in the Himalayas, challenged Miss Peck's claim and sent French engineers to measure Huascarán by triangulation, proving it 21,812 feet. Even so, Annie Peck had climbed higher in the Western Hemisphere than any other American, man or woman. In 1927 the Lima Geographical Society named the north peak of Huascarán Cumbre Aña Peck in her honor.

Miss Peck's success as a mountain climber was achieved in the face of inadequate financing, too little equipment, and inexperienced assistants and porters. Her book *A Search for the Apex of South America* (1911) is a chronicle of near disasters. She exposed herself and others to needless danger and suffering by making do with what she could afford: her financing came from the contributions of friends and from magazines such as *Harper's* which paid in advance for her articles, and was often less than her minimum projected expenses. Lacking accurate information on the terrain, oxygen for high altitudes, and, often, adequate clothing for her native porters, she drove her men relentlessly, impatient with their inexperience and unwillingness to follow her judgment in all matters. The less than full acceptance of her leadership she attributed to resentment against her as a woman. For her the desire to succeed overcame concern for personal danger, lost packs, altitude sickness, and other hazards of mountain climbing, and she had little sympathy for those who did not share her ambition. Certainly there was a steely element in her nature that inspired grudging admiration rather than affection.

Unmarried, rootless—her home was where her trunks were—Miss Peck continued her travels and her explorations until the end of her life. At the age of sixty-one she was the first to climb Mount Coropuna (21,250 feet) in Peru; an active suffragist, she planted a "Votes for Women" pennant at its summit. Her interest in furthering good relations between North and South America provided the material for two books, *The South American Tour* (1913), a descriptive guidebook, and *Industrial and Commercial South America* (1922), a statistical handbook, and for lectures before both North and South American audiences. In 1929–30 she made an extensive tour of the southern continent to demonstrate the availability of commercial aviation and its potentiality as a means of facilitating contacts between the Americas and reported on her trip in *Flying over South America* (1932).

A founder of the American Alpine Club (1902), a Fellow of the Royal Geographical Society (1917), and a member of the Society of Woman Geographers (1928), Annie Smith Peck climbed her last mountain, Mount Madison (5,380 feet) in New Hampshire, at the age of eighty-two. Two years later she began a world tour, but halted at Athens, where she climbed the steep road to the Acropolis, "a humanist who could not leave the world without one more glimpse of the Parthenon" (*New York Times*, July 20, 1935). She died in her apartment in a New York hotel several months later of bronchial pneumonia. After cremation her ashes were buried in North Burial Ground in Providence, R.I.

[Besides Miss Peck's own books, see Frances E. Willard and Mary A. Livermore, eds., *A Woman of the Century* (1893), which covers her pre-mountain-climbing career; *Nat. Cyc. Am. Biog.*, XV, 152; *Woman's Who's Who of America*, 1914–15; *Who Was Who in America*, vol. I (1942); *Annals of the Am. Alpine Club* (Thorington's), 1902–18; *N.Y. Times*, July 19 (obituary), 20 (editorial), 1935. See also *Who's Who in America*, 1930–31, on her brothers George and William; *Scientific American*, Feb. 12, 26, 1910, on her controversy with Fanny Bullock Workman. The Archives of the Soc. of Woman Geographers, Washington, D.C., include several letters by Miss Peck to Harriet Chalmers Adams, 1928–32, and her MS. notes for the Soc.'s *Bulletin*. Information on particular points from Providence Public Library, R.I. College, the Univ. of Mich., Purdue Univ., and Smith College.]

BERTA N. BRIGGS

PEIXOTTO, Jessica Blanche (Oct. 9, 1864–Oct. 19, 1941), social economist and university professor, was born in New York City, the only daughter and eldest of five children of Raphael and Myrtilla Jessica (Davis) Peixotto. Her father, of early American Portuguese Jewish descent, had come to New York from his native Ohio; he became a prosperous merchant engaged in trade with the South and married a Virginian. In 1870 he moved his family to San Francisco, Calif., where his business continued to prosper and where he was active in religious and philanthropic affairs. His four sons also achieved prominence, Edgar (1867–1925) as a San Francisco attorney, Ernest Clifford (1869–1940) as artist and author, Eustace as director of public school athletics in San Francisco, and Sidney Salzado (1866–1925) as a social worker.

Following graduation from the Girls' High School of San Francisco in 1880, Jessica Peixotto, accepting her father's disapproval of her going on to college, remained at home for over a decade, participating in the family's cultural and social life and studying or being tutored in foreign languages, music, household management, decoration, and design. In 1891 she boldly broke the pattern of her existence by enrolling at the University of California in

Berkeley across the Bay. There she developed serious academic interests, in part at least through her friendship with the author Frank Norris, who, she recalled in later life, was particularly delighted when she "led a movement to shorten skirts to shoes' tops to [the] scandal [of the] faculty." Her studies in English, political science, and economics led her, after a bachelor's degree in 1894, to graduate work at the university. After a year's independent research at the Sorbonne (1896–97) she wrote a doctoral dissertation which was published in 1901 under the title *The French Revolution and Modern French Socialism*.

At loose ends again following the award of her doctor's degree in 1900—the second ever given to a woman at the University of California—she cheerfully accepted the invitation of President Benjamin Ide Wheeler to join the faculty of her alma mater as a lecturer in sociology in 1904. Her appointment was soon shifted to the economics department, where she taught until her retirement in 1935; she earned the rank of full professor in 1918 and served briefly as chairman. In the classroom she was a lively and demanding teacher who sought out brilliant students and encouraged them to do their best. Although her own printed studies were critical and incisive, her courses (which ranged over such subjects as "Poverty and Modern Constructive Philanthropy," "Historical and Contemporary Theories of Social Reform," "The Household as an Economic Agent," and "The Child and the State") were often diffuse. In time her graduate seminar in the history of economic thought became renowned, her students being as likely to read Isaiah and Plato as classical and contemporary economists. Though she wrote popular articles on child welfare and coeducation, her major scholarly work lay in the field of cost-of-living studies. A founder and chairman of the Heller Committee for Research in Social Economics, she stimulated many significant investigations.

In her early academic career Jessica Peixotto was profoundly influenced toward social service by her brother Sidney, the founder and director of the Columbia Park Boys' Club in San Francisco, and by her association with Katharine Felton, head of that city's Associated Charities. She was appointed to the California State Board of Charities and Correction by Gov. Hiram Johnson in 1912 and served for twelve years, insisting always upon extensive and sound research preliminary to policy decision. In 1917 as war approached she established a special course for Red Cross and home service workers, but she was called to

Washington the next year to serve first as executive chairman of the child welfare department of the Woman's Committee of the Council of National Defense and then as chief of the council's child conservation section. Here she worked closely with JULIA LATHROP, head of the federal Children's Bureau. At the University of California, Miss Peixotto's interest in both research and social service and her commitment to the principle that sound welfare work required disciplined and trained personnel led her to initiate (1917–18) a special program within the economics department that in time led to the establishment of a separate professional school of social work.

For all these interests and concerns, Jessica Peixotto was never a crusader. Though an advocate of woman suffrage, she was not a "suffragette." Research and experience demonstrated to her the social costs of poverty, and by 1930 she had come to endorse regularity of employment, a living wage, social insurance for old age and unemployment, and social casework for special family needs; but these were objectives she put forward modestly and more out of intellectual conviction than out of compassion. Blue-eyed and dark-haired, dressed always in exquisite and modest taste, Miss Peixotto was strong-minded, self-sufficient, and a polished hostess. Neither solemn nor witty, she was open and free with those she chose to make her intimate associates; but a patrician, if gracious, reserve marked her relations with most others. Although she was devoted to the theatre, she preferred books to music and the visual arts; partisan politics interested her but slightly. She cherished her Jewish heritage, but religion was not an active concern; she was at home primarily in the world of facts and ideas.

In 1928 Jessica Peixotto was elected vice-president of the American Economic Association. In 1933 she served briefly as a member of the Consumers' Advisory Board of the federal National Recovery Administration. Retiring from the University of California faculty in 1935, she was awarded an honorary doctorate in law that year by Mills College and another the following year by the university she had served so long and with such distinction. She died at her home in Berkeley of arteriosclerosis at the age of seventy-seven. Cremation followed her funeral services, which were conducted by Robert F. Leavens of the Unitarian Society and by Monroe E. Deutsch, vice-president and provost of the University of California.

[Besides her doctoral dissertation, Jessica Peixotto's publications include: *Getting and Spending at the Professional Standard of Living: A Study of the Costs of Living an Academic Life* (1927); *Cost of Living Studies*. II: *How Workers Spend a Living Wage. A Study of the Incomes and Expenditures of Eighty-two Typographers' Families in San Francisco* (1929); and various articles in *Survey* and other periodicals. For comments on her life and career see: *Essays in Social Economics in Honor of Jessica Blanche Peixotto* (1935), particularly the biographical sketch by Henry Rand Hatfield (pp. 5–14) and the list of her published writings (pp. 361–63); and Lucy Sprague Mitchell, *Two Lives: The Story of Wesley Clair Mitchell and Myself* (1953). Other sources include: *Sunset*, Apr. 1919; Franklin Walker, "Interview with Jessica B. Peixotto," May 28, 1930 (one-page typescript on her recollections of Frank Norris, in Walker Papers, Bancroft Library, Univ. of Calif.); obituary clippings of Jessica, Edgar, Ernest, and Sidney Peixotto in Bancroft Library; *N.Y. Times*, Oct. 21, 1941; Univ. of Calif., *In Memoriam*, 1941; death record from Calif. Dept. of Public Health; interviews with Prof. Ira B. Cross, Dept. of Economics, and Miss Emily Huntington, director of the Heller Committee for Research in Social Economics, both at the Univ. of Calif.]

CLARKE A. CHAMBERS

PELHAM, Mary Singleton Copley (c. 1710–Apr. 29, 1789), colonial shopkeeper, mother of the artist John Singleton Copley, was one of three children of John and Jane (Bruffe) Singleton, of Quinville Abbey, County Clare, Ireland. The Singletons were descended from a Lancashire family that had settled in Ireland in 1661. Little is known of Mary Singleton's early life. Her first husband, Richard Copley, was probably the son of Charles Copley, alderman, one of the sheriffs of Limerick, and thus like the Singletons one of the smaller landed gentry. Richard and Mary Copley left Ireland for Boston after their marriage, but it is uncertain whether they emigrated before or after the birth of their son, John Singleton Copley, on July 26, 1738. (The possibility persists that young Copley was born in 1737, but a substantial weight of evidence favors the later date.) In Boston, Richard Copley ran a tobacco shop on Long Wharf. According to tradition he died in the West Indies shortly after his son John was born, but this is unlikely since there is evidence that he was involved in a lawsuit to recover a bad debt in 1741, and the inventory of his estate is dated May 6, 1748.

The widow Copley continued her husband's business as a tobacconist, even after she became the third wife, on May 22, 1748, of Peter Pelham, mezzotint engraver, portrait painter, and schoolmaster. They were married at Trinity Church, both being Anglican as well as Irish. Shortly thereafter, on July 11, 1748, there appeared in the *Boston News-Letter* an announcement that affords the chief record of her business career: "Mrs. Mary Pelham (formerly the widow Copley, on the Long Wharf, Tobacconist) is removed from [to] Lindel's Row, against the Quaker's Meeting-House, near the upper End of King Street Boston, where she continues to sell the best Virginia Tobacco, Cut, Pigtail and spun, of all Sorts, by Wholesale, or Retail, at the cheapest Rates." Mary Pelham bore Peter Pelham, who had four sons and a daughter by his previous marriages, a son, Henry, on Feb. 14, 1749 (New Style). Two years later she was once again left a widow with Peter Pelham's death in December 1751.

By her marriage to Peter Pelham, Mary Pelham had afforded her talented first son, John Singleton Copley, a remarkable opportunity. For a boy who was to become colonial America's greatest painter, and one of the leading American artists of all time, the influence of Pelham and an artistic home environment complete with equipment for painting and engraving and a collection of prints and books must have been seminal. There is little evidence of what her own influence might have been upon her son, though her few surviving letters suggest that she was intelligent and reasonably well educated. Young Copley's first paintings and a unique mezzotint appeared less than two years after Pelham's death. During the ensuing years his superbly crafted, realistic portraits of members of a prosperous and materialistic colonial society won him esteem and prosperity. With the disruption of patronage during the turbulent period before the outbreak of the Revolution, Copley left his family in 1774 to take a long-planned study trip to Europe, spending a year in Italy. After the outbreak of hostilities at Concord and Lexington the following year, Mrs. Copley (Susanna Clarke) left Boston with her three oldest children, Elizabeth, John, and Mary, leaving an infant, Clarke Copley, in the care of her mother-in-law, Mary Pelham. The infant died of consumption on Jan. 19, 1776, a few days after his first birthday. Soon afterward Henry Pelham, more outspokenly loyalist than his artist half brother, whose sympathies were divided, also left Boston, eventually joining the Copleys in London. Mary Pelham never saw either son again. She delighted, however, in her elder son's success. Aged and in poor health, she wrote to him on Feb. 6, 1788, "Your fame, my dear son, is sounded by all who are lovers of the art you bid fair to excel in. May God prosper and cause you to succeed in all your undertakings, and enroll your name

among the first in your profession." She died the next year in Boston at the age of seventy-nine after a long illness.

[The basic sources for Copley family information are Martha Babcock Amory, *The Domestic and Artistic Life of John Singleton Copley, R.A.* (1882), and Guernsey Jones, ed., *Letters & Papers of John Singleton Copley and Henry Pelham*, vol. LXXI (1914) of the 7th series of the Mass. Hist. Soc. *Collections*. See also Denison R. Slade, "Henry Pelham, the Half-Brother of John Singleton Copley," Colonial Soc. of Mass., *Publications*, 1902, pp. 193–211. Certain errors in the Amory book are corrected in Barbara Neville Parker and Anne Bolling Wheeler, *John Singleton Copley: Am. Portraits* (1938). The most recent body of information may be found in Jules David Prown, *John Singleton Copley* (2 vols., 1966). Basic genealogical information, not entirely free from error, is available in Sir Bernard Burke, *A Genealogical and Heraldic Hist. of the Landed Gentry of Ireland*, revised by A. C. Fox-Davies (1912), p. 641 (Singleton). Other information may be found in the Early Court Records and Probate Records in the Suffolk County Courthouse, Boston, and in the Genealogical Office, the Public Record Office, and the Registry of Deeds in Dublin.]

JULES DAVID PROWN

**PEMBER, Phoebe Yates Levy** (Aug. 18, 1823–Mar. 4, 1913), Confederate hospital administrator, was born in Charleston, S.C., the fourth of seven children, six of them girls, of Jacob Clavius Levy and Fanny (Yates) Levy. Her father, the son of a Pole who had emigrated to Charleston at the close of the American Revolution, was a prosperous and cultured businessman and an early advocate of Reformed Judaism. Her mother was a native of Liverpool, England. One of Phoebe's elder sisters, Eugenia, married Philip Phillips, a lawyer of Mobile, Ala., and Washington, D.C., who served for one term (1853–55) in Congress. In the 1850's the Levys moved to Savannah, Ga. Nothing is known of Phoebe's schooling, but her wartime letters and reminiscences show that she was well educated. Sometime before the Civil War she was married to Thomas Pember of Boston, of whom little is known other than that he died of tuberculosis in Aiken, S.C., on July 9, 1861, at the age of thirty-six. After his death Phoebe resided with her parents, moving with them to live with relatives in Marietta, Ga., when Federal forces threatened to occupy Savannah shortly after the outbreak of the Civil War.

Family friction made life in the Marietta household difficult, and when in November 1862 Mrs. Pember received through her acquaintance with Mrs. George W. Randolph, wife of the Confederate Secretary of War, the offer of a post as a matron at Chimborazo, an army hospital on the outskirts of Richmond, she quickly accepted. Before the end of the war Chimborazo was to become the largest military hospital in the world up to that time. Mrs. Pember, under the general supervision of the surgeon-in-charge, was responsible for the housekeeping and for patient diet in one of its five divisions, including thirty-one wards, each housed in a separate one-story building and with a capacity of about fifty patients; some 15,200 soldiers probably came under the care of Mrs. Pember and her assistants during the course of the war. The first woman administrator appointed at Chimborazo, she encountered considerable opposition upon entering army life, then generally regarded as man's domain. Though not insensitive to criticism and gossip, she did not permit it to deter her. In a time of crisis, she later wrote, "a woman *must* soar beyond the conventional modesty considered correct under different circumstances" (*A Southern Woman's Story*, 1959 ed., p. 146). Doctors and stewards resented especially the control which she had as matron over the dispensing of whiskey. Some of them tried to make her life intolerable by petty annoyances, but this strong-willed woman, aided on one occasion by a pistol which she kept in readiness, successfully maintained her authority.

Other responsibilities were also strenuous. "I have not been able to get a cook and everything for seven hundred sick men has to be cooked under my eyes by two black imps of fourteen," she wrote a sister in January 1863. Matrons received a salary of forty dollars a month, but this proved so inadequate for her personal expenses that "at night I either write for the magazines or copy writing for the [War] Department." Overworked and without companionship, she fell ill that summer; the surgeon general then encouraged her to board in the city, returning to the hospital each morning in an ambulance sent in to market. She now occasionally mingled in Richmond society, where her wit, charm, and petite beauty made her a welcome guest. One observer of life in the Confederate capital found her "brisk and brilliant" with a "will of steel" beneath her "suave refinement" and "pretty, almost Creole accent" (Thomas C. De Leon, *Belles, Beaux and Brains of the 60's*, 1907, p. 385). As the war dragged on she went less and less into society, finding its reckless gaiety distasteful.

Phoebe Pember remained at her post during the Confederate evacuation of the capital and its occupation by Union forces early in April 1865. After the conclusion of hostilities she returned to Georgia. Little is known of her post-war life beyond the fact that she did considerable traveling in Europe and America. She died in her ninetieth year, in 1913, in Pittsburgh, Pa., of "septic arthritis" of a knee. Her remains were taken to Savannah and buried beside those of her husband in Laurel Grove Cemetery.

Sometime after the Civil War, Phoebe Pember had begun the writing of her wartime reminiscences. These were published in 1879 under the title *A Southern Woman's Story*. Reflecting her own forthright temperament, the book is written in a good-humored anecdotal vein, without sentimentality. The author's strongest words are reserved for the drunken surgeons she encountered, but her story in general does not reflect great credit on those charged with the care of Confederate sick and wounded. Composed after the event, and with an eye to literary effect, Mrs. Pember's book lacks the rough immediacy of KATE CUMMING's war journal. It nonetheless stands as a valuable account of conditions in a major Confederate hospital and an interesting record of one woman's service to the Confederate cause.

[A new edition of Mrs. Pember's book, edited by Bell I. Wiley, appeared in 1959; it contains a biographical sketch and nine of her wartime letters from the Philip Phillips Papers in the Library of Congress and the Pember-Phillips-Myers Collection at the Univ. of N.C. Her grandnieces—Fanny, Georgina, and Daisy Phillips—of Savannah, Ga., have in their possession genealogical and other information about the Jacob Clavius Levy family. Records of the Chimborazo Hospital in the Nat. Archives bear on Mrs. Pember's activities as matron. On her father and grandfather, see Charles Reznikoff and Uriah Z. Engelman, *The Jews of Charleston* (1950), pp. 282, 293–94; and Joseph R. Rosenbloom, *A Biog. Dict. of Early Am. Jews* (1960), p. 92. Death record from Pa. Dept. of Health.]

BELL I. WILEY

**PENDLETON, Ellen Fitz** (Aug. 7, 1864–July 26, 1936), college president, was born in Westerly, R.I., the youngest of the nine children of Mary Ette (Chapman) and Enoch Burrows Pendleton, both natives of Connecticut. Her father, whose Pendleton forebears had settled in Watertown, Mass., about 1635, had moved in 1847 to Westerly, where he became a successful merchant and a supporter of the new Republican party. With Lincoln's election in 1860 he was appointed postmaster, a place he held until his death in 1875. Growing up in comfortable circumstances, with two brothers who went to college (Brown and West Point), Ellen apparently met no objection from her parents when, inspired by a favorite teacher, an early graduate of Wellesley, she herself sought a college education. After graduating as valedictorian of her class at the Westerly High School, Ellen entered Wellesley College in 1882, seven years after it opened. For the next fifty-three years her life was bound up with that institution.

Upon graduation in 1886 Ellen Pendleton was asked to return as a temporary tutor in mathematics, Latin, and Greek; in 1888 she was appointed instructor in mathematics. The following year she studied at Newnham College, Cambridge, one of the first Americans to do so, before returning to Wellesley, where she earned the M.A. in 1891. She became secretary of the college in 1897 and head of College Hall, dean, and associate professor of mathematics in 1901. It was Miss Pendleton who as dean proposed the scholarship for Chinese students established by the trustees following a visit to the college by the Chinese minister of education in 1906. She was acting president during the illness of President CAROLINE HAZARD (1910), and after Miss Hazard's resignation, although many alumnae believed the office should be held by a man (an argument carefully weighed by the trustees), Miss Pendleton was elected to succeed her, in 1911. She was the first alumna to hold the post.

Ellen Pendleton believed firmly in the value of women's colleges. Wedded to the ideal that a liberal arts education in a residential college was preparation for both scholarship and citizenship, she took up her duties at the end of a decade of rapid expansion in the size of the college. During her twenty-five years in office, succeeding crises of fire, war, and economic depression required extraordinary efforts in business administration and fund raising. In March 1914 fire destroyed College Hall, a vast structure which contained most of the classrooms, laboratories, and administrative and faculty offices, as well as the library, chapel, and dormitory quarters for more than two hundred students. The following morning President Pendleton announced an early spring vacation; three weeks later, temporary facilities having been constructed, classes resumed and a major campaign to raise $3,000,000 had begun. Within a decade seven new buildings had been erected, to be followed by eight more before Miss Pendleton's retirement in 1936. Between 1915 and 1935, the physical plant had increased in value from $3,000,000 to more than $10,000,000, and a reserve fund of nearly $1,000,000 for repair and maintenance had been raised. The endowment rose from $1,268,937 in 1911 to $9,795,844.

Although her work as an educator was less dramatic, she effected a liberalization of the entrance requirements and in the college curriculum. The introduction of honors work and independent research, as well as much freedom in the choice of electives, were accompanied by a growth in the size of the faculty. Miss Pendleton insisted on excellence of teaching and high academic standards and vigorously rejected any effort to introduce vocational training or narrow specialization. Not an educational theorist, she displayed her great strengths in practical matters. "No one knew better than she," commented President William Allan Neilson of Smith in the year of her retirement, "how things really worked, and this practical experience in the actual operation of the curriculum must have saved the College many mistakes and much futile experiment." The same practicality marked her close relations with preparatory schools. In Neilson's judgment, she was "a leader in the growing tendency to consider as one process the four years of preparation and the four years of study in college" (*Wellesley Magazine*, June 1936, p. 8). Miss Pendleton was elected president of the New England Association of Colleges and Secondary Schools in 1917.

She never faltered in her strong conviction that academic freedom is a fundamental of college education. She endeavored, though unsuccessfully, to dissuade the board of trustees from their decision not to reappoint the distinguished pacifist Prof. Emily Greene Balch (d. 1961), who fell victim to the loyalty mania of 1918–19. In 1935 when the Massachusetts legislature passed a law requiring a loyalty oath of all teachers, President Pendleton and representatives of the Wellesley faculty, together with others from neighboring institutions, appeared at hearings and spoke against the bill.

An indefatigable worker, Miss Pendleton had interests that extended well beyond her own campus. She served as vice-president of Phi Beta Kappa, president of the College Entrance Examination Board, and vice-president of the Associated Boards for Christian Colleges in China. In 1919 she served on an examining board sent to study institutions of higher learning in Japan and China. In 1923 when Edward Bok founded the American Peace Prize, he named Miss Pendleton as the sole woman on the jury to determine the award. She was a prominent member of the Baptist Church.

Reserved and dignified in manner, "Pres. Pen" evoked admiration and respect from faculty, students, and alumnae. In her determination that Wellesley should uphold the highest intellectual and moral standards, she became a symbol for that serious conception of excellence for women. Miss Pendleton retired in 1936 on the occasion of the fiftieth anniversary of her graduation from Wellesley and the twenty-fifth year of her presidency. A month later she suffered a cerebral hemorrhage and died at the home of a niece in Newton, Mass. She was buried in River Bend Cemetery, Westerly, R.I. Her estate was left to Wellesley to further the academic work of the college.

[Florence Converse, *Wellesley College: A Chronicle of the Years* (1939); Alice P. Hackett, *Wellesley: Part of the Am. Story* (1949); Mercedes M. Randall, *Improper Bostonian: Emily Greene Balch* (1964); *Wellesley Mag.*, June 1936; MSS. and clippings, Wellesley College Library; death record from Mass. Registrar of Vital Statistics.]

KATHRYN PREYER

PENN, Hannah Callowhill (Feb. 11, 1671–Dec. 20, 1726), second wife and executrix of William Penn (1644–1718), founder and first proprietor of the Province of Pennsylvania, was born in Bristol, England. She was the fourth daughter and sixth of nine children of Thomas Callowhill, a prosperous Quaker button manufacturer, linen draper, and merchant, and his wife, Anna (Hannah) Hollister. Anna's father, Dennis Hollister, a grocer by trade, had been a member of Parliament under Cromwell and was a Baptist preacher until he became one of George Fox's first converts to Quakerism in Bristol. By the time Hannah was fifteen, she was her parents' only surviving child and heir. Knowing her to be of a serious turn of mind, they taught her to keep accounts and to understand the various aspects of the Callowhill merchandising ventures. She thus gained a knowledge of business which later proved extremely useful.

When she finally consented to be Penn's wife after almost a year's persistent courtship, he was fifty-two, a widower with teen-age children. Their marriage took place on Mar. 5, 1696, at the old Broadhead Meeting in Bristol; in the next twelve years she bore Penn eight children (not seven as commonly stated). Of these, the first did not live long enough to be named. The succeeding children were John, called "the American" because he was born in Philadelphia (1700); Thomas (1702), later chief proprietor of Pennsylvania; Hannah Margarita (1703); Margaret (1704); Richard (1706); Dennis (1707); and Hannah (1708). Both Hannahs died in early childhood. In this first period of her married life Hannah Penn

made her only trip to Pennsylvania, with her husband and stepdaughter Letitia. They remained in the province just twenty-three months (1699–1701), but during that time she came to know Penn's associates in the provincial government and gained their respect by her common sense, prudence, and dignity. Though she became aware of the economic problems and developing factionalism in the young province, she was concerned primarily with managing the farm at Pennsbury in Bucks County while her husband was engaged in the business of government. Penn had hoped to settle permanently in the province, but political and financial problems that arose in England required them to return.

In the years following Hannah saw her husband pressured by debts and imprisoned, and watched him grow disillusioned with his contentious Assembly and eventually realize that William, Jr., his eldest son by his first marriage, was unsuitable as the future heir to the proprietorship and province of Pennsylvania. She was in full accord when Penn, as a result, in 1703 initiated his first proposal to surrender the government of his province to the Crown for a cash settlement, while retaining title to the land, and when, in order to pay off his debts, he arranged to mortgage the land to English Quaker trustees.

The second period of Hannah Penn's married life began in 1712, when her parents died and when Penn suffered incapacitating strokes. In addition to caring for her own five surviving children, maintaining a large household at Ruscombe in the country near Reading (where they had settled after Penn's release from prison), combating the importunities of her stepchildren, and attending an invalid husband, Hannah now had the double responsibility of administering her parents' estate and managing all her husband's affairs. Always hoping that Penn would recover, she and the councilmen in Philadelphia handled the business of the province by correspondence, Hannah relying heavily on the advice and support of James Logan, Penn's agent there. On the question of surrendering the government, however, she tended to follow the advice of her husband's friends at Court and of her own uncle, Simon Clement.

William Penn died in 1718. In his will, written in 1712 after his first stroke, he had demonstrated his confidence in Hannah by naming her sole executrix and leaving to her and her children the greater part of his Pennsylvania land. But by vesting the government of the province in the hands of English trustees he had laid the foundation for a claim to both soil and government by his eldest son, William, Jr., the de jure heir. That claim, initiated immediately after Penn's death, complicated the last period of Hannah's life with tedious and expensive litigation over the will.

In 1721, now aged fifty, Hannah suffered what was called a "fit of the dead palsy" which, though it left her mind unimpaired, weakened her physically. From then until her death much of the proprietary business was left to the discretion of the devoted Simon Clement and of her eldest son, John, now of age. Never fully relinquishing her right of stewardship, she continued to keep in touch with events in the province and in 1724 concluded a temporary agreement with Lord Baltimore over the long-vexed question of the Pennsylvania-Maryland boundary. By then the mortgage was nearly all paid, and she had come to view the surrender of government with less enthusiasm. She knew that the people of Pennsylvania thought it "inconsistent with the Proprietor's first engagement" with them; moreover, if the will was confirmed in favor of her family, divorcing the soil from the proprietorship and its perquisites would deprive her sons of their full inheritance. She lived just long enough to learn that she had won by default, and that Penn's will would be upheld. A week later she died at the home of her son John in London, following another stroke. She was buried at Jordans Friends Meeting in Buckinghamshire; her coffin reputedly reposes on that of her husband. By her dedication to her husband's policies and her ability through all her trials to act, as Isaac Norris wrote, "with a wonderful evenness, humility and freedom," she had succeeded in keeping the Province of Pennsylvania intact and the people contented. Pennsylvania was held by her branch of the Penn family as a proprietary colony until the Revolution.

[The basic primary sources for Hannah Penn's life are her own letters, those of her husband and children, and those of her contemporaries, chiefly James Logan, Isaac Norris, and Simon Clement. The great majority of these are in the Hist. Soc. of Pa. at Phila. Here also among the enormous collection of Penn MSS. are her Recipe Book and Cash Book (1712–20), as well as many papers containing references to her. Some genealogical data are to be found in the records of English Friends Meetings; transcripts of the earlier records are in the Genealogical Soc. Collections at the Hist. Soc. of Pa.; microfilm copies of the originals are in Friends Hist. Library at Swarthmore College. Henry J. Cadbury has corrected the hitherto accepted date of Hannah's birth and the number of her children in *Pa. Mag. of Hist. and Biog.*, Jan. 1957, pp. 76–82. There is no full-length, critical biography. The fullest and most recent account is Sophie H. Drinker, *Hannah Penn and the Proprietorship of Pa.* (1958), an interpretive presentation of a portion of Hannah's correspondence with her husband, relations, and associates dealing mainly with the second and last periods of her life; the appended chronological listing of "Documents concerning Hannah Penn," which includes the English State Papers relating to her affairs, forms a useful guide to source material. A number of her earliest letters have appeared in *Pa. Mag. of Hist. and Biog.* and in *Correspondence between William Penn and James Logan*, ed. by Edward Armstrong (1872).]

HANNAH BENNER ROACH

PENNELL, Elizabeth Robins (Feb. 21, 1855– Feb. 7, 1936), author and art critic, wife of the artist Joseph Pennell, was born in Philadelphia, Pa., to Edward and Margaret (Holmes) Robins. Her grandfather Thomas Robins, a Virginian of English stock, was the first member of the family to settle in Philadelphia, where for many years he was president of the Philadelphia National Bank. Edward Robins, her father, was a broker. Though he came of an Episcopalian family, he became a convert to Catholicism when Elizabeth was eight, and the children were brought up in that faith. Elizabeth was educated at Sacred Heart convents, first at Conflans, near Paris, where she spent a year when she was six, and, from 1863 to 1872, at Eden Hall in Torresdale, Pa., where she was a classmate of the author AGNES REPPLIER, later a close friend. Since her mother died when Elizabeth was very young, she and her sister spent many of their holidays and summer vacations at the Torresdale convent, with occasional visits to their paternal grandparents' home in Philadelphia. Elizabeth was an able student, though by her own admission not always well behaved; her long years at the convent, however, did little to prepare her for Philadelphia society, and her debut after graduation was the beginning of a rather dull and aimless period in her life. Her father had remarried, and Elizabeth now made her home with him and her stepmother. It was, however, her uncle Charles Godfrey Leland, a well-known humorist and essayist, who became her mentor, after his return to Philadelphia from abroad in 1880, and who was most responsible for Elizabeth's finding her métier as a writer and critic.

Currently interested in introducing the minor arts (handicrafts, drawing, and design) into the curriculum of the public schools, Leland enlisted his niece as his assistant. He tried as well to have her take up the decorative arts, and when she showed little talent, prodded her into beginning to write. In July 1881 her first article, "Mischief in the Middle Ages," appeared in the *Atlantic Monthly*. The magazine published other of her articles, chiefly on history and mythology, and Elizabeth Robins began also, through Leland's good offices, to write for Philadelphia newspapers and a weekly Philadelphia magazine, the *American*. In 1881 Richard Watson Gilder, the editor of *Scribner's Magazine* (soon to become the *Century*), asked Leland to write the text to accompany eight etchings of Philadelphia by Joseph Pennell, a young Philadelphia artist. Leland, too busy himself, suggested his niece instead, and "A Ramble in Old Philadelphia," published in March 1882, was the first of many collaborations. With Pennell's assistance, Elizabeth soon became art critic for the *American* and the Philadelphia *Press*. They were married early in June 1884, the same year that Elizabeth Pennell's first book, the *Life of Mary Wollstonecraft*, was published in the Roberts Brothers' Famous Women Series.

The *Century* had commissioned Pennell to do further illustrations for William Dean Howells' *Tuscan Cities*, and within a few weeks of their marriage the Pennells sailed for England. After a summer cycling trip to Canterbury, which resulted in their first joint book, *A Canterbury Pilgrimage* (1885), they went to Italy before settling in London. Commissions from the *Century, Harper's Magazine*, and other periodicals continued, making it feasible for the Pennells to remain abroad. Their life took on a pattern of work in London during the winters and travel throughout Europe during the summers, at first on a tandem tricycle, later on bicycles, and sometimes on foot. In addition to the many articles which appeared in British and American periodicals between 1884 and 1898, their adventures were published in nine books for which Mrs. Pennell wrote the text and Pennell did the illustrations, among them *Our Sentimental Journey through France and Italy* (1888), *Our Journey to the Hebrides* (1889), *The Stream of Pleasure* (1891), *To Gipsyland* (1893), and *Over the Alps on a Bicycle* (1898).

In 1888 Pennell succeeded George Bernard Shaw as art critic of the London *Star*. Elizabeth Pennell wrote the column when her husband could not do the work, or when his *Century* commitments kept him away from London for long periods, and eventually took it over altogether when he tired of it. Although she did not consider herself an expert, she gained a firm reputation as an art critic, and she contributed articles on art to the London *Chronicle*, the New York *Nation*, and many

other journals. For twenty-five years she visited Paris every spring, after the openings of the annual National Academy and New Gallery exhibitions in London, to review the salons. A lesser interest was the field of cookery, begun when she was invited to do a weekly column on the subject for the *Pall Mall Gazette*, a column she continued for five years. Her culinary essays were collected in 1896 under the title *Feasts of Autolycus, the Diary of a Greedy Woman*, with later editions in 1900 (*Delights of Delicate Eating*) and 1923 (*A Guide for the Greedy*).

The Pennells' marriage, which was childless, was a happy one, her serene nature complementing his tempestuous one. "When work was in question," she wrote, "he could ill adapt himself to the habits and movements of others. With me it was different. . . . Early or late as he might be, however he might alter his day's programme, I was prepared to fit in my engagements and movements to suit his convenience, knowing that artists are not like other men, he least of all." In the early days in London, Pennell's method of writing was to dictate to his wife, who took the text down in longhand, trying to round it out as she wrote. Besides running the household, she kept the accounts and attended to much of the business with publishers and others. Yet their "working partnership" always respected the resolution they had formed before their marriage: "not to allow anything to interfere with his drawing and my writing."

At their London flat "Mrs. Pennell's tact, charm and genius for sympathetic listening, and Mr. Pennell's picturesque frankness made them both popular," wrote Edward Laroque Tinker. Their circle of friends was wide, embracing artists, writers, journalists, and publishers. Aubrey Beardsley, George Bernard Shaw, Phil May, Henry Harland, and William Ernest Henley were among those who frequented the Pennells' Thursday evening "at homes"; their most famous friendship, however, which began in 1892, was with the artist James McNeill Whistler. With Whistler's consent, in 1900 the publisher William Heinemann asked Pennell to write the artist's biography; Pennell agreed on condition that his wife collaborate. *The Life of James McNeill Whistler* (1908) was an immediate success and went through three printings; a fifth and sixth edition (1911 and 1919) were completely revised with the addition of new material. After Whistler's death in 1903 the Pennells gave much of their time to the perpetuation of his fame, helping prepare the memorial exhibition held by the International Society of

Sculptors, Painters, and Gravers in London in 1905, and developing their collection of Whistleriana, which they gave to the Library of Congress in 1921.

Mrs. Pennell traveled less frequently with her husband as she devoted more and more of her time to her writing. After the publication in 1906 of her biography of Charles Godfrey Leland, however, they visited the cathedrals in northern France in preparation for their *French Cathedrals, Monasteries and Abbeys, and Sacred Sites of France* (1909) and made a trip to the United States in 1908—her first in twenty-four years. *Our Philadelphia* (1914), a descriptive recollection of that city during the Victorian era, was followed by *Nights: Rome, Venice in the Aesthetic Eighties; London, Paris in the Fighting Nineties* (1916) and a novel, *The Lovers* (1917).

In 1917, because of the war, the Pennells decided to return to the United States. They went first to Philadelphia, but the city they had known and loved had changed, and in June 1921 they settled in New York, at the Hotel Margaret in Brooklyn. After Joseph Pennell's death in 1926, Mrs. Pennell assembled and published his pictures of New York and Philadelphia, supervised the preparation of *catalogues raisonées* of his watercolors, drawings, etchings, and lithographs, and wrote a two-volume *Life and Letters of Joseph Pennell* (1929), one of her most distinguished works. Elizabeth Robins Pennell died of chronic myocarditis in New York City two weeks before her eighty-first birthday. She was buried beside her husband in the Friends Burial Ground in Germantown, Pa. "She with her books and he with his drawings," wrote their friend Edward Tinker, "have done more than any other two people I know to spread in America a popular knowledge of the art of the old world, of the everyday life of its people, of the beauty of its countryside and of the architectural loveliness of its cities: and all the while they were just as industrious in making known in Europe the work of American artists."

[Elizabeth Robins Pennell, *Our Philadelphia* (1914), *The Life and Letters of Joseph Pennell* (1929), and *Nights* (1916); Edward Laroque Tinker, *The Pennells* (pamphlet, privately printed, 1951); *Nat. Cyc. Am. Biog.*, X, 377; Gertrude B. Biddle and Sarah D. Lowrie, eds., *Notable Women of Pa.* (1942); *Who Was Who in America*, vol. I (1942); *N.Y. Times*, Feb. 8, 9, 1936, July 17, 1936, Feb. 2, 1937. See also the article on Joseph Pennell in *Dict. Am. Biog.* Death record from N.Y. City Dept. of Health (which gives her mother's maiden name as Harriet Holmes). There are 572 letters of Elizabeth Pennell at the Univ. of Pa.; other papers are at the Hist. Soc. of Pa. and the Print Collection of the Library of Congress.]

ALICE LEE PARKER

**PENNINGTON, Patience.** *See* PRINGLE, Elizabeth Waties Allston.

**PERCY, Florence.** *See* ALLEN, Elizabeth Anne Chase Akers.

**PERKINS, Elizabeth Peck** (Feb. 14, 1735/36–May 24, 1807), Boston businesswoman and philanthropist, was born in that city, the eldest of five children of Elizabeth (Spurrier?) and Thomas Handasyd Peck. Her parents had emigrated from England shortly before her birth and had settled in Boston, where Peck became a successful fur trader and hatter. Something of a liberal in religion as well as in politics, he was a friend and frequent host of John Murray, the founder of Universalism in America, and, in his later years at least, an outspoken Whig.

Of his daughter Elizabeth's early life nothing is known. She was married on Dec. 24, 1754, to James Perkins (1733–1773), an employee in her father's countinghouse. He later served as bookkeeper for the noted merchant John Rowe and in time set up in business for himself as a general-store merchant. A man of grave courtesy, he was a strong patriot and according to family accounts a friend of Paul Revere. In 1770 his house and place of business was on King (now State) Street, the leading thoroughfare of the town. His early death, on May 11, 1773, left his wife with eight children, a ninth having died as an infant.

Elizabeth Perkins, with characteristic independence, resolved to establish her own business. Utilizing some of her father's commercial contacts, she opened a "grossary" shop where she sold chinaware, glass, wine, and a wide variety of other imported items. During the siege of Boston and shortly before the battle of Bunker Hill, she moved with her children to Barnstable, Mass., where they found refuge at the home of Squire Edward Bacon, a mild loyalist but an old friend of her husband's. Following the British evacuation the next spring, she returned to Boston and apparently reopened her business. Her father died in 1777 and her mother a year or two later, leaving her, as the sole surviving child, with a respectable inheritance in real estate but only a modest income.

Now completely on her own, Mrs. Perkins succeeded during the difficult wartime years in supporting her family, even managing in 1780 to subscribe $1,000 for the Continental Army. She reared her children with remembered firmness and solicitude, imparting to each a strong sense of duty, industry, and integrity. Her three sons went to work at an early age and in the period of trade revival after 1790 became leading maritime merchants. The two eldest, James (born 1761) and Thomas Handasyd (1764), formed the noted firm of J. & T. H. Perkins; the youngest, Samuel (1767), joined in business with his father-in-law, Stephen Higginson. All three became well known for their extensive philanthropy and civic interest. Thomas, perhaps the most famous of the great China trade merchants of the nineteenth century, was a benefactor of the Massachusetts General Hospital, the Boston Athenæum, and the Perkins School for the Blind (which bears his name).

Her five daughters married well. The eldest, Elizabeth (born 1756), became the wife of Russell Sturgis, a fur merchant who also had learned his trade under Thomas Handasyd Peck. The second, Ann Maynard (1759), married Robert Cushing and was the mother of John Perkins Cushing, a China trade merchant and noted horticulturist. Mary (1769) married Benjamin Abbot, headmaster for many years of Phillips Exeter Academy in Exeter, N.H., and Esther (1771) married first Thomas Doubleday and after his death the merchant Josiah Sturgis, a brother of Russell Sturgis. Margaret Mitchell (1773), the youngest, was married to Ralph Bennet Forbes of Milton; her three sons, Robert Bennet, Thomas Tunno, and John Murray, following in the footsteps of their uncles, became well-known maritime merchants, the last also a noted pioneer in Western railroad expansion.

With her children married and independent, Elizabeth Perkins turned much of her energy to various civic and philanthropic endeavors. Like her father, she was sympathetic to the Universalist doctrines, primarily, it is said, because of her refusal to believe in damnation. Her friendship extended, however, to other religious leaders in the community, including Jean de Cheverus, the first Roman Catholic bishop in Boston, whom she permitted to preach in a building she owned on School Street and to whose work among the poor she made generous contributions. She was deeply concerned with mental illness and in 1800 helped found the Boston Female Asylum, the first charitable institution in Boston established by women. She served the asylum as a director and treasurer and supported it financially both during her lifetime and through a bequest in her will. For many years she continued to own considerable real estate in Boston, largely in the business district.

Toward the end of her life Madame Perkins, as she was often called, resided on Purchase Street in a handsome West Indian-styled house overlooking the harbor. She continued to live with accustomed simplicity, doing most of her own housework and habitually wearing plain dresses of brown calico in the morning and brown silk in the afternoon. A granddaughter remembered her as a stern, reserved woman of impressive dignity and strength of character, greatly honored and respected by her children, somewhat feared by her grandchildren.

Elizabeth Perkins died in her Boston home at the age of seventy-one, after several years of gradual enfeeblement. Her burial place is unknown, but is probably the Old Granary Burial Ground to the east of Boston Common. Although a figure of no unusual historical importance, she is noteworthy as having played an active part in the business and charitable life of her community and in supporting unassisted a family of eight children, all of whom became useful and respected citizens. Something of her remarkable character seems, indeed, to have passed down through successive generations of descendants who to the present day are numbered among the business, political, and civic leaders of Massachusetts.

[The principal sources of information on Elizabeth Perkins are the unpublished reminiscences of her granddaughter Mrs. Samuel Cabot, in the Boston Athenæum, and a brief autobiographical sketch written in 1846 by her son Thomas Handasyd Perkins, in the T. H. Perkins Papers in the Mass. Hist. Soc. Both accounts were written at an advanced age and must be read with caution as to names and dates. Additional material may be found among the letters and documents in the T. H. Perkins Papers. The wills of Thomas H. Peck and Elizabeth Perkins are among the Suffolk Probate Records; the birth and marriage dates of Elizabeth and James Perkins and of their children are in the Boston Town Records. Elizabeth Perkins' obituary notice appeared in the *Columbian Centinel*, May 27, 1807. For her business, see advertisements in the *Boston Gazette*, July 12, 1773, and subsequent dates. A useful letterbook of T. H. Peck covering the years 1760–76 is in the Mass. Hist. Soc. His assistance to John Murray is recounted in Murray's *Records of the Life of the Rev. John Murray* (1816), pp. 180, 183–84. An account of James Perkins and his forebears is contained in Augustus T. Perkins, *A Private Proof* (1890). General coverage of the Perkins family may also be found in Thomas G. Cary, *Memoir of Thomas Handasyd Perkins* (1856), and L. Vernon Briggs, *Hist. and Genealogy of the Cabot Family* (2 vols., 1927). Additional information has been obtained from material to appear in a forthcoming biography of T. H. Perkins by Carl Seaburg and Stanley Patterson.]

HENRY LEE

**PERKINS, Lucy Fitch** (July 12, 1865–Mar. 18, 1937), children's author, was born in Maples, Ind., the second of five daughters. Her father, Appleton Howe Fitch, an Amherst College graduate of a Massachusetts farm background, had been a teacher in Chicago and Peoria, Ill., before serving briefly in the Civil War; afterward he joined relatives in setting up a barrel-stave factory in Maples. Lucy's mother, Elizabeth (Bennett) Fitch, had grown up in Stowe, Vt., and had taught school. She and her husband gave their daughters much of their early education at home, in an atmosphere of hard work, thrift, and Puritan respect for learning. Lucy, "the warrior of the family" according to her daughter, first attended school in 1873 in Hopkinton, Mass., where her father sent his wife and children to live with his parents for three years while he struggled to recover from business losses. In 1879, in search of better schools, the family moved to Kalamazoo, Mich., where Fitch opened a woodworking factory.

From her earliest years Lucy had loved to draw; at sixteen some of her cartoons appeared in the *Kalamazoo Gazette*. Following her graduation from the Kalamazoo high school in 1883 (at the head of her class), relatives banded together to send her to the Museum of Fine Arts School in Boston. Spirited, quick-tempered, and fun-loving, though with a lifelong abhorrence of dancing, drinking, and cardplaying, she found herself very popular with boys. During her third year in Boston she met a young architectural student at the Massachusetts Institute of Technology, Dwight Heald Perkins. They were immediately attracted to each other, but religious differences —she was a strict Congregationalist and he a Unitarian—for a time made marriage seem out of the question to her. Meanwhile she had some success doing free-lance work for *Young Folks Magazine*. In 1886, after graduation from the museum school, she worked as an illustrator for the Prang Educational Company of Boston. Having seen her work there, Walter Scott Perry asked her to be his assistant when, in 1887, he became director of the school of fine and applied arts at Pratt Institute, the new college for manual arts and engineering in Brooklyn, N.Y. After four years of teaching at Pratt, Lucy Fitch left to marry Dwight Perkins on Aug. 18, 1891. They made their home in Chicago.

Although she herself unquestioningly accepted the Victorian code which prescribed that married women should renounce any economic independence, her husband, not wishing her to deny her talents, designed a studio room for her in their home. Not, however, until he became seriously ill during the depression of 1893 did Mrs. Perkins actually resume her career as an artist. The Chicago office of the Prang company promptly gave her work, and for the next ten years she taught, lectured, illustrated, and painted mural decorations in schoolrooms. Her husband became an architect of note and a specialist in school buildings. In 1904 they moved to Evanston, a Chicago suburb, their home for the rest of their lives. Two children were born to them: Eleanor Ellis (1893), who became a writer, and Lawrence Bradford (1908), an architect.

Although Mrs. Perkins had illustrated books for other writers and had published *The Goose Girl* (1906), a collection of children's rhymes, and *A Book of Joys: A Story of a New England Summer* (1907), she considered *The Dutch Twins* (1911) the real beginning of her writing. The idea for the book came about when a publisher friend, Edwin O. Grover, arriving for dinner, saw some drawings she had made of Dutch children and persuaded her to write a series of geographical readers, using twin characters, a boy and a girl. The twenty-six "Twin books," published by the Houghton Mifflin Company over the next two and a half decades, were the result. According to her daughter, Mrs. Perkins did not depend on literary sources for her material, but "sought out and became intimately friendly with someone who had been a child in the place she wanted to write about." When this was impossible, she did research in the public library. Immigration was then at its height, and a visit to Ellis Island had impressed Mrs. Perkins with the necessity for understanding between people of different nations. She hoped that books giving glimpses of a child's life in other countries might serve this end. Later stories, such as *The Puritan Twins* (1921) and *The American Twins of the Revolution* (1926), gave an idea of the founding and early history of the United States.

When once asked how to write for children, Mrs. Perkins replied, "Learn to draw." She did the lively, playful illustrations for her own books before she wrote them, often while kneeling on the floor so that she could see everyday objects from a child's perspective. She always tried out her stories first on a group of neighborhood children ("the poison squad," as she called them), a procedure which may have contributed to the freshness and never-failing childlike humor of her books. The "Twin books" marked the end of the pedantic travelogue type of children's story. Widely read, translated into Japanese and many European languages, their sales totaled over two million copies and made Mrs. Perkins for a time Houghton Mifflin's most profitable author.

Her last book, *The Dutch Twins and Little Brother* (1938), in which she returned to her favorite characters, was published the year after her death. For some years she had suffered from arteriosclerosis. She died of a coronary thrombosis at the age of seventy-one in Pasadena, Calif., where she and her husband had gone in hopes of restoring her health.

[Eleanor Ellis Perkins, *Eve among the Puritans: A Biog. of Lucy Fitch Perkins* (1956), is the principal source. See also autobiographical sketch in Stanley J. Kunitz and Howard Haycraft, eds., *The Junior Book of Authors* (1934); *Nat. Cyc. Am. Biog.*, XXXIII, 524; Durward Howes, ed., *Am. Women*, 1935–36; *Who Was Who in America*, vol. I (1942). Death record from Calif. Dept. of Public Health.]

RUTH HILL VIGUERS

PERRY, Agnes. *See* BOOTH, Agnes.

PERRY, Antoinette (June 27, 1888–June 28, 1946), actress and theatrical director, originally named Mary Antoinette, was born in Denver, Colo., the only child of William Russell Perry, an attorney, and Minnie Betsy (Hall) Perry. Her maternal grandfather, Charles L. Hall, born in New York state of Puritan and Pilgrim forebears, had gone west from Iowa in 1859 in the "Pike's Peak or Bust" wagon train; making a fortune in mining, he served in the territorial legislature and later in the state senate. Antoinette's mother and her grandmother, Mary Melissa (Hill) Hall, introduced the Christian Science faith into Colorado in 1886. An aunt, however, determined Antoinette's career. Mildred Hall and her husband, George Wessells (who first played Moriarty to William Gillette's Sherlock Holmes), toured as an acting team throughout the East and West, and the young Antoinette often traveled with them during her holidays from Miss Wolcott's School in Denver, where she received her education through high school.

She made her own debut as an actress at Powers' Theatre, Chicago, on June 26, 1905— the day before her seventeenth birthday—in *Mrs. Temple's Telegram*. Her first New York appearance was reportedly in the same play at the Madison Square Theatre later that year. The next season, after supporting Hilda Spong in *Lady Jim* (August 1906), she appeared,

under the aegis of David Belasco, with David Warfield in *The Music Master,* and in October 1907 she joined Warfield again as Hallie in *A Grand Army Man.* In 1906–07 and again in 1908–09 she toured in *The Music Master.*

Antoinette Perry gave up the stage on Nov. 30, 1909, to marry Frank Wheatcroft Frueauff (1874–1922), then president of the Denver Gas & Electric Company. They had three daughters: Margaret Hall, born in 1913, Virginia Day (1917), who died in infancy, and Elaine Storrs (1921). They made their home in New York, where Frueauff was a junior partner of the public utilities executive Henry L. Doherty. Antoinette Frueauff became deeply involved in the Liberty Bond drives for World War I. She also aided several rising talents in the arts, among them the composer Deems Taylor, for whom she sponsored the only production of his early experiment in musical theatre, *What Next!* The marriage came to a sudden end with Frueauff's death in July 1922.

In 1924 Antoinette Perry returned to the stage as Rachel Arrowsmith in *Mr. Pitt,* with Walter Huston. Her producer was Brock Pemberton, and this marked the beginning of a lifelong professional and personal association. She next appeared in 1924 as Lil Corey in *Minick;* in 1925 as Ma Huckle in *The Dunce Boy,* Belinda Treherne in a revival of W. S. Gilbert's *Engaged,* and Judy Ross in *Caught;* in 1926 as Sophia Weir in *The Masque of Venice* and Margaret in *The Ladder,* a drama of reincarnation that its dogged sponsor kept running by dropping all admission charges; and in 1927 as Clytemnestra in *Electra,* with Margaret Anglin. She was a small, fair woman with a patrician profile, her gentle, feminine manner complemented by a beautiful speaking voice and spiced by a wicked sense of humor.

In 1928 Miss Perry took up the directing of actors, the field in which she was to make her reputation and her greatest contribution to the stage. Her initial effort (with Brock Pemberton as producer) was Ransom Rideout's *Goin' Home.* Her first great success came the next year with *Strictly Dishonorable,* a comedy of youth in the speakeasy era by Preston Sturges. In eighteen years, working closely with Pemberton, she directed nearly thirty plays, including some of the notable successes of the era. Among the most memorable were *Christopher Comes Across* (1932), *Personal Appearance* (1934), *Ceiling Zero* (1935), *Red Harvest* (1937), *Kiss the Boys Goodbye* (1938) by Clare Boothe (Luce), *Lady in Waiting* (1940), *Cuckoos on the Hearth* (1941), *Janie* (1942), and *Harvey* (1944). Although she was at her best with breezy comedy, she could also respond sensitively to the whimsical and sentimental. Unlike many of the directors of her day, she was no mere drillmaster or coach. The director, she said, "has to think in terms of architecture—which is movement—of ballet, of music, of emphasis." She advised actors to master the tools of their craft, strive for perfection, and "Think clearly, feel deeply, and know the strength of spiritual understanding" (Sobel, pp. 862–64).

Miss Perry took vigorous part in many professional theatrical organizations. She was chairman of the committee of the Apprentice Theatre (an adjunct of the American Theatre Council) in 1937–39, and in 1941 president of the Experimental Theatre, sponsored by the Actors Equity Association and one of the first showcases for young talent. She was also a trustee of the Actors' Fund of America and active on behalf of the Musicians Emergency Fund. With the coming of World War II she helped establish the American Theatre Wing, which provided entertainment and hospitality for servicemen on leave at Stage Door Canteens in New York, Boston, and Washington, as well as hospital entertainment for the wounded; she was its chairman from 1941 to 1944. She was responsible for its first full-scale production: *The Barretts of Wimpole Street*, with a cast headed by Katharine Cornell and Brian Aherne, which played to Allied troops in Europe in 1944–45. In religion, Miss Perry remained a Christian Scientist. She died at her Park Avenue home in New York of a heart attack and overwork in June 1946, at fifty-eight, and was buried beside her husband in New York's Woodlawn Cemetery. Her two daughters, Margaret and Elaine Perry, followed their mother's career as actresses and directors.

Because of Miss Perry's interest in all aspects of the theatre and her selfless assistance to young artists, the American Theatre Wing in 1947 instituted the Antoinette Perry Awards in her memory. These medals, affectionately known as "Tonys" after her nickname, are annually given to actors, directors, writers, composers, producers, and designers who have made significant contributions during a theatrical season.

[*N.Y. Times*, Aug. 1, 1922 (on Frueauff), June 29, July 7, 1946; *Who Was Who in America*, vol. II (1950); *Nat. Cyc. Am. Biog.*, XXXVII, 107; clippings in Theatre Collection, N.Y. Public Library at Lincoln Center; Bernard Sobel, ed., *The Theatre Handbook* (1940), pp. 862–64; information from Margaret and Elaine Perry. On her mother and grandparents, see Wilbur F. Stone,

*Hist. of Colo.*, IV (1919), 206–12 (courtesy of State Hist. Soc. of Colo.).]

ALAN S. DOWNER

**PETER, Sarah Anne Worthington King** (May 10, 1800–Feb. 6, 1877), leader in charitable and church work in Cincinnati and Philadelphia, Catholic convert, was born near Chillicothe, Ohio, the second daughter and second of ten children of Thomas and Eleanor (Van Swearingen) Worthington. Both parents came of well-to-do Virginia families, her mother being of seventeenth-century Dutch ancestry, her father a descendant of Robert Worthington, who migrated from England to New Jersey in 1714. Freeing his slaves, Thomas Worthington had moved in 1797 from Virginia to Chillicothe, where he became active in the movement for Ohio statehood and served his adopted state as governor and United States Senator.

In the Worthingtons' mansion, Adena, designed by the noted architect Benjamin Henry Latrobe, Sarah met Aaron Burr, Henry Clay, and many other notables. At the age of eight she was sent to Mrs. Louise Keats' school near Frankfort, Ky. This English lady imbued her pupil with a strong sense of duty, order, and respect for tradition. When the school was closed in 1811 Sarah went to Mrs. Hayward's Academy in Baltimore, a fashionable finishing school, where she developed a love of music, art, and French and became an accomplished pianist. Unsatisfied, however, by the conventional female curriculum, she read independently in history and literature. She returned to Chillicothe in 1815, a graceful, energetic girl of medium height with blue-gray eyes, dark lashes, and golden hair. At Adena she met young Edward King, a son of the distinguished Federalist statesman Rufus King, who had come to Chillicothe to begin the practice of law. They were married on May 15, 1816. The couple had five children: Rufus (1817), Thomas Worthington (1820), Mary Alsop (1821), Edward (1822), and James (1828), though only the two eldest survived childhood. Stimulated, perhaps, by her husband's accomplishments as a linguist, Mrs. King continued her interest in French language and literature and began to study medieval art and the natural and physical sciences. The larger city of Cincinnati offered greater opportunities for King's law practice, and the family moved there in 1831. They entered the social and civic life of the city at once. Both were ardent workers in St. Paul's Episcopal Church; King was active in organizing the Cincinnati Law School, of which his son Rufus was later dean; and Mrs. King was one of the founders of the Cincinnati Protestant Orphan Asylum (1833), now the Children's Convalescent Home.

King died in February 1836, at forty, and that fall his widow moved to Cambridge, Mass., where she maintained a home for her two sons while they were students at Harvard. She was welcomed into Cambridge intellectual society. There she continued her study of languages, reading German, it is said, with Henry W. Longfellow, who found her a "very attractive woman with an intellectual style of beauty which quite leads one captive." Her account of her struggle for education impressed the young Thomas Wentworth Higginson, later a leader in the woman suffrage movement. Mrs. King's feminism, however, was more moderate. She believed that women should be allowed to study all branches of learning, but thought their interests should complement, not rival, those of men. When her second son graduated from Harvard in 1840 she began a period of travel, visiting in Philadelphia, Washington, Ohio, New Orleans, Havana, and Virginia. In Philadelphia, where her son Thomas was living, she met William Peter, a widower who was the British consul in that city; they were married in Chillicothe on Oct. 21, 1844. An Oxford graduate, a former Whig member of the House of Commons, and an able scholar, Peter shared many of his wife's interests. At her request he published an anthology of Greek and Latin poetry, using his own translations.

Mrs. Peter had long been concerned for those less fortunate than herself. As a young woman she had worked in Chillicothe to relieve distress and poverty among the townspeople. Now, in Philadelphia, she raised money for the Rosine House for Magdalens and organized an association for the protection of seamstresses. Understanding how serious was the plight of women left without means of support, she thought they might be taught to create the decorative designs that American manufacturers then purchased from abroad—patterns for wallpaper and carpets, designs for household utensils, and the like— as well as to practice such practical arts as wood engraving and lithography. In 1848 she began the Philadelphia School of Design in a room of her home, with a teacher whom she herself employed. Publicized by her friend SARAH JOSEPHA HALE, editor of *Godey's Lady's Book*, the school gained support and in 1850 was affiliated with the Franklin Institute. The pioneer school for industrial art in America, it gave women for the first time an adequately paid commercial employment; it proved a long-

lived institution, continuing successfully until 1932, when it was merged into the Moore Institute of Art, Science, and Industry.

The death of her second husband in 1853, added to the loss of her son Thomas in 1851, led Mrs. Peter to return to Cincinnati, where her only remaining son lived. Here she purchased a large home and resumed her many social and artistic interests. She was the benefactress of a number of young artists and was the moving spirit and first president (1853) of the Cincinnati Academy of Fine Arts (sometimes called the Ladies Academy of Fine Arts), which assembled a set of paintings and casts that was for many years the only public art collection in Ohio. By this time, however, religion had begun to occupy most of her attention. Like her two husbands, Mrs. Peter had been a devout Episcopalian and an active parish worker in each city where she had lived. Already inclined to stress the sacramental aspect of the Episcopal Church, in Philadelphia she had become a warm friend of Bishop George W. Doane and, through his influence, a supporter of the American Tractarian movement. She was, however, troubled by a feeling of "deadness" in prayer and an uneasiness which arose "from my own self-accusations, because I was not convinced of the soundness of our doctrine." During a European trip in 1851–52 she had visited Rome and the Holy Land. Impressed by the warmth and certainty of the Roman Catholic Church, she was converted during her second visit in 1853–55 and was received into that communion at Trinità dei Monte in Rome on Mar. 25, 1855.

Mrs. Peter thereafter channeled her learning, her interest in art, and her sympathy for the unfortunate into the work of the Catholic Church. She was especially interested in establishing sisterhoods in the archdiocese of Cincinnati, but this was a larger project than even her means could provide. In 1857 she started on a quest for funds, visiting members of the nobility and wealthy Catholics in Italy, Austria-Hungary, the German states, France, and Holland. Her knowledge of languages, her fine presence, and her social graces, combined with the zeal of a convert, contributed much to her success. She was directly responsible for bringing into the archdiocese the Sisters of the Good Shepherd (1857), who worked with female prisoners; the Sisters of Mercy (1858), who did Christian education and social work; and two charitable groups, the Order of the Poor of St. Francis (1858) and the Little Sisters of the Poor (1868). Through her friendship with Mother MARY ALOYSIA HARDEY she was also influential in establishing in Cincinnati a convent and school of the Order of the Sacred Heart (1869). All of these foundations shared in her patronage and interest, but the Franciscans were especially favored. In fact, she asked permission to enter that order in 1861. Discouraged because of her age, she gave her Cincinnati home to the order and sold her collection of art and Georgian furniture for their benefit, living thereafter in an apartment attached to the convent house and attending convent services regularly.

Throughout the Civil War, Mrs. Peter was a frequent visitor to the military prisons in and around Cincinnati. After the battle of Shiloh in 1862 she accompanied several nursing sisters of St. Francis on a hospital ship to minister to the wounded at Pittsburgh Landing. After the war she maintained an asylum for war orphans for several years. Her charitable work continued unabated to the end of her life. Owing partly to her influence, the city authorities of Cincinnati in 1863 placed their new women's prison for a time under the administration of a member of the Order of the Good Shepherd. She also used her literary accomplishments on behalf of the church, translating Louis Aimé-Martin's *De l'Education des Mères de Famille* and part of Joseph Épiphane Darras' monumental *Histoire Générale de l'Eglise* into English. In 1869 Mrs. Peter suffered a slight stroke, but she retained her regal appearance. She died in Cincinnati eight years later from a coronary thrombosis and was buried in her mortuary chapel in St. Joseph's Cemetery there.

[Letters from Mrs. Peter to members of her family are in the Rufus King Papers, Cincinnati Hist. Soc. There are two biographies: *Memoirs of the Life of Mrs. Sarah Peter* (1889), written by an admiring daughter-in-law, Margaret R. King; and Anna Shannon McAllister, *In Winter We Flourish: Life and Letters of Sarah Worthington King Peter* (1939).]

JOSEPH E. HOLLIDAY

PETTIT, Katherine (Feb. 23, 1868–Sept. 3, 1936), settlement worker in the Kentucky mountains, was born near Lexington, Ky., the daughter of Benjamin F. Pettit, a prosperous farmer, and Clara Mason (Barbee) Pettit, both descendants of pioneer settlers in the state. She was named Katherine Rhoda but disliked her middle name and never used it. She received her early education in Lexington and Louisville, and her later schooling at the Sayre Female Institute of Lexington. In her youth she became a member of the Presbyterian Church.

From childhood she took an interest in the people of the Cumberland plateau of eastern Kentucky, a maze of sharp valleys and steep slopes, with no navigable streams, where isolated families continued to live much as had their Scotch-Irish ancestors 150 years before. Her interest was heightened when a family friend, the Rev. Edward O. Guerrant, told her: "They are an independent, high-spirited folk whose poverty and location have isolated them from the advantages of education and religion." In her twenties she became an active worker in the Woman's Christian Temperance Union, which was carrying on work in the mountains, and in the rural library service of the State Federation of Women's Clubs, but she did not realize how narrow was life's outlook in the hills until the summer of 1895 when she toured the feud-ridden mountains of Perry and Harlan counties and saw the poorly equipped one-room schools, the bare homes, and the hard lives of the women. For five years she made summer trips, taking along flower seeds and pictures to share with the women who treated her so kindly, and promising that she might return someday to help them.

When in 1899, at the convention of the State Federation of Women's Clubs, a letter was read from the Rev. J. T. Mitchell of Hazard, Ky., suggesting that the federation send someone into his county to help mothers with their home problems, Katherine Pettit agreed to hold a homemakers' "camp-meeting" that summer in the country near Hazard to help the mountain women with their domestic and social needs. Miss May Stone of Louisville, a graduate of Wellesley College, agreed to join in this pioneering venture, which was called an "Industrial," after similar all-day gatherings of the W.C.T.U. Leaving the railroad in eastern Kentucky in early August, they rode by wagon to Hazard, bumping forty-five miles over rocky trails and along creek beds. On the edge of town they set up a gaily trimmed tent, and soon inquisitive passersby were asking about these "queer" women who entertained children with games and stories. Before long, both in the camp and in nearby homes, they were showing the mothers how to provide their families with good raised bread, beaten biscuits, cottage cheese, green vegetables, and meat that was not greasy. For almost six weeks they taught cooking and sewing and new games and songs, and gave simple instruction in health, as well as daily Bible and temperance readings. On the closing night of the camp over a hundred people gathered around a huge bonfire to sing together and to bid the visitors goodbye.

The next summer, at the request of local residents, Miss Pettit and Miss Stone, with some helpers, held a ten-week "Industrial" in Hindman, on Troublesome Creek in Knott County, and in 1901 another, lasting nearly fourteen weeks, near Sassafras, beyond Hindman. During each of these three summers the two women kept a diary (now treasured in the Berea College Library) in which Miss Pettit frequently remarked upon the quickness of mountain children in learning new things and the eagerness of the Hindman people to have them settle permanently in their community.

Each of these summer projects had cost the clubwomen less than $300; but a permanent institution would be much more expensive. Both Miss Pettit and Miss Stone shuddered at the thought of the publicity required for raising money, but they had read much about the settlement work of JANE ADDAMS and ELLEN STARR in Chicago and resolved to try the same approach in a rural setting. In the winter of 1901–02 they traveled in the East soliciting funds, and with these, together with contributions from the State Federation of Women's Clubs, the W.C.T.U., and the local residents, they purchased land and in August 1902 opened the Hindman Settlement School, under W.C.T.U. auspices. Bad luck plagued them the first few years; in 1905–06 and 1910 fire raged through the new wooden buildings. Bravely the Hindman community helped the women rebuild and raised $5,000 to purchase a sixty-five-acre farm where greater space would lessen the fire risk. The school survived its early misfortunes and by 1911 had two hundred students and a resident staff of thirteen. Reflecting Miss Pettit's belief that crafts and manual skills were as important in the Cumberland hills as academic subjects, courses were offered in sewing, cooking, basketry, woodworking, and various handicrafts.

Katherine Pettit's dedication was infectious. In 1907 Linda Neville, a Lexington friend and Bryn Mawr graduate, visited the school and became interested in trachoma, a contagious eye disease, common in the mountains, which often led to blindness if not treated. As a result of this visit Miss Neville devoted her life to combating the ailment, accompanying more than 3,000 sufferers to Lexington for treatment and persuading city doctors to hold clinics in the mountains. Beginning in April 1911 a Lexington specialist, Dr. J. A. Stucky, conducted a series of clinics at Hindman where many trachoma patients were treated. They insisted on paying, and as money was scarce, they often brought chickens, eggs, buckets of honey, and bushels of apples. By 1912 suffi-cient interest had been generated to lead the United States Public Health Service to make a medical survey of the area.

In 1913 Miss Pettit left Hindman in the care of Miss Stone in order to fulfill a promise to the people of Pine Mountain in Harlan County to open a settlement there. With her went Miss Ethel de Long (1878–1928), a New Jersey native and Smith College graduate who had taught at Hindman for two years. By the side of these two intrepid women stood William Creech, a remarkable mountaineer who contributed 250 acres of land to the new Pine Mountain Settlement School, writing, "I have heart and cravin that our people may grow better. I have deeded my land to the Pine Mountain Settlement School to be used for school purposes as long as the Constitution of the United States stands" (*One Man's Cravin'*, p. 28). Transforming the virgin forest into habitable land was a demanding task, and for a year and a half the two women and William Creech oversaw the cutting of trees and the making of boards on a sawmill transported forty miles by oxen, along with the clearing of streams, the planting of fruit trees, and the construction of buildings. The school prospered, and by 1915 forty students were in residence.

Working together, these three recast the Hindman pattern to meet local needs. They set up an extension program to benefit isolated one-room schools; founded health centers in remote Big Laurel and Line Fork; pressed for the construction of a road over the mountains to reach outside markets and the railroad; and set up trachoma, hookworm, and dental clinics. Katherine Pettit, herself brought up on a large farm, held farmers' institutes at which she urged the raising of poultry for market as well as for the home table. She emphasized home dyeing and handweaving and encouraged ballad singing and folk dancing, to the delight of the English ballad master Cecil Sharp, who found that many Elizabethan tunes and words survived among the highlanders. Ballads collected by Miss Pettit were published in 1907 in the *Journal of American Folk-Lore*.

The success of the Hindman and Pine Mountain schools was owing in a large measure to the trust the mountain people felt in Miss Pettit and her co-workers. Her strong face revealed her personality; a firm planner and manager, yet outgoing, patient, and kind, she was beloved by children and overworked mothers for her suggestions and personal advice, in which (in the words of Lucy Furman) she was "frank, free-spoken as the highlanders themselves." Shy of publicity, she performed her services quietly, avoiding public speeches and printed articles. In 1930, after seventeen years as co-director of the Pine Mountain Settlement School, she resigned and gave herself over to what she called "free lance work" in the Harlan County area around Pine Mountain, where many small farmers, having sold their plots for a song to take jobs in the coal mines, now found themselves in the depression of the early 1930's both jobless and landless. For five years she tramped the hills, urging men to leave the "dole" and return to the land, teaching them better farming techniques, and transmitting orders from gift shops for handicrafts. In 1932 the University of Kentucky awarded her the Algernon Sidney Sullivan Medal in recognition of her contributions to the state. She died in Lexington of cancer in 1936 at the age of sixty-eight and was buried in the Lexington Cemetery. "This has been a glorious world to work in," she had written to an old friend shortly before. "I am eager to see what the next will be." Though their programs have altered to meet changing circumstances, the two schools she founded still serve the highlanders she loved.

[Diaries and letters of Miss Pettit in Berea College Library; *Notes from Pine Mountain School,* 1919–24, 1926, 1928, 1933; *One Man's Cravin'* (pamphlet, Pine Mountain Settlement School, 1945); articles in *Mountain Life and Work,* Apr. 1928 (pp. 17–18), Apr. 1934 (pp. 1–5), and Summer 1948 (pp. 15–18); Lucy Furman, "Katherine Pettit," Ky. State Hist. Soc., *Register,* Jan. 1937; Ky. Works Progress Administration, *A Dict. of Prominent Women of Louisville and Ky.* (1940), pp. 192–96 (the source for her birth year). Miss Furman has written of Miss Pettit also in *Hindman News,* May 1, 1952, and in her novel, *The Quare Women* (1923). See also Edward O. Guerrant, *The Soul Winner* (1896), pp. 97–99, 210–14; Robert A. Woods and Albert J. Kennedy, eds., *Handbook of Settlements* (1911), pp. 87–88; "Social Settlement Work in the Ky. Mountains," *The Commons,* May 1902; Henderson Daingerfield, "Social Settlement and Educational Work in the Ky. Mountains," *Jour. of Social Science,* Nov. 1901; "A New Departure in Social Settlements," *Annals of the Am. Academy of Political and Social Science,* Mar. 1900, pp. 301–04. Other information from Mrs. Attilla Norman (Henderson Daingerfield Norman) and from death record, Ky. State Dept. of Health.]

ELIZABETH S. PECK

**PHELPS, Almira Hart Lincoln** (July 15, 1793– July 15, 1884), educator, was born at Berlin, Conn., the last of the seventeen children of Samuel Hart and the tenth by his second wife,

Lydia Hinsdale. The American progenitor of her father's family, Stephen Hart, had left England for America in the first quarter of the seventeenth century, becoming an original proprietor of the town of Hartford and later a pioneer settler at Farmington, Conn. Her mother was descended from Robert Hinsdale, who emigrated in 1637 from England to Dedham, Mass., where he was a proprietor before taking part in the settlement of Deerfield in 1667. The family farm in the Mattabesett River valley offered a growing girl all the usual opportunities of New England rural life, but Samuel Hart gave it a special quality that was impressed upon both Almira and her famous sister, EMMA WILLARD. Their home was a center of Jeffersonian sympathy and religious dissent, an oasis in the vast preserve of New England Federalism and Congregationalism.

Almira's first schooling probably began in 1804 under the tutelage of her sister Emma in the Berlin district school. These formal lessons supplemented family discussions of literary classics, current political issues, and the weekly newspaper. She also had access to a storehouse of books in the home of a neighbor whose son had been a bookseller in New York. Almira continued her lessons at the Berlin Academy and in 1809 taught in a rural district school near Hartford. For the next two years she lived in the household of her sister Emma and the latter's husband, Dr. John Willard, in Middlebury, Vt., where she studied with Emma and with Willard's nephew, a student at Middlebury College. In 1812 she attended her cousin Nancy Hinsdale's academy for girls at Pittsfield, Mass., returning the following year to teach in the Berlin Academy and in the winter district school. At about this time, probably in 1814, she opened a small boarding school for young ladies in the family home in Berlin, and in 1816 she accepted charge of an academy at Sandy Hill, N.Y.

On Oct. 4, 1817, she was married to Simeon Lincoln, a Hartford newspaper editor. Their first child, James Hart Lincoln, born in April 1820, lived less than a year. Lincoln himself died of yellow fever in 1823, leaving his thirty-year-old widow with two daughters, Emma Willard and Jane Porter, aged two and one. The insolvency of her husband's estate dictated her return to teaching, this time at the Troy (N.Y.) Female Seminary, where her sister was developing a model boarding school for girls. At Troy, Almira Lincoln was able to participate, with skill and enthusiasm, in broadening the education of American women. There she came under the influence of the naturalist Amos Eaton, a professor at nearby Rensselaer

Institute, began work on her first science textbooks, and shared with Emma Willard the seminary's teaching and administrative responsibilities.

The publication in 1829 of Mrs. Lincoln's *Familiar Lectures on Botany* launched her career as a writer of popular texts. Books on chemistry, geology, and natural philosophy followed, but none equaled in popularity and usefulness her *Botany:* in less than ten years it went into nine editions, selling 275,000 copies by 1872. Because she wished to use texts that would lend themselves to inductive, objective teaching, she had to write them, and in doing so she supplied American schools with some of the tools that brought the sciences into the standard course of study. Poetry, moral observations, imagination, and history were combined with sound science to make of botany, for example, an exercise in personal, intellectual, and philosophic growth. Her service as acting principal of the Troy Seminary in 1830, during Mrs. Willard's absence in Europe, gave her further prominence in the educational world.

On Aug. 17, 1831, Almira Lincoln became the wife of John Phelps, whose daughter Lucy was a student at Troy Seminary, A widower with six children, four of whom were grown, Phelps was a lawyer and politician of Guilford, Vt. Moving there with her husband, Almira Phelps looked after her own children as well as her two stepdaughters, Lucy and Regina Ann. This second marriage produced two children, Charles Edward (1833) and Almira Lincoln (1836). During the period 1831–38, in Guilford and Brattleboro, Vt., Mrs. Phelps revised her botany texts, edited a set of *Lectures to Young Ladies* (1833), and prepared new scientific texts. In 1838, when she was offered the principalship of a new seminary for young ladies in West Chester, Pa., her husband encouraged her to accept and moved his own practice there. The school, however, was a financial failure, and in 1839 Mrs. Phelps accepted an invitation to head another new school, the Rahway (N.J.) Female Institute, of which Phelps the next year became "superintendent." In 1841, at the invitation of the Episcopal bishop of Maryland, the couple took charge of the Patapsco Female Institute at Ellicott's Mills, Md., Mrs. Phelps serving as principal and her husband, until his death in 1849, as business manager.

Patapsco gave Almira Phelps an opportunity to express the ideals that she shared with her sister Emma. Like the seminary at Troy, Patapsco was the kind of school that might have become a college (as did Mount Holyoke), for much of the course of study, especially in the sciences, was of collegiate quality. The school trained young women to become homemakers and teachers, careers to which American society assigned most of them, and, as was usual in this period, supplemented classical and scientific studies with such "accomplishments" as music, languages, and art. To turn out "good women rather than fine ladies" was her goal, an aim that she nurtured with wise talks at weekly assemblies, with a systematic regimen calculated to take "away from females their helplessness," and by encouraging a student group known as the "Doing Good Society."

The death of her daughter Jane in a railroad accident in 1855 influenced Almira Phelps' decision to leave Patapsco and retire to Baltimore in 1856, at the age of sixty-three. Forty years earlier she had written in her journal: "I have preferred a life of usefulness, to exercise the talents which God has given me, to one of indolence." She carried this resolve into retirement, writing for national journals, exploring the fine arts for the first time, producing new volumes until more than twenty had come from her pen. Though she supported educational equality for women, Mrs. Phelps, like her sister Emma, strongly opposed woman suffrage. Soon after the formation of the National Woman Suffrage Association, she joined the Woman's Anti-Suffrage Association for Washington City and, as its corresponding secretary, helped circulate a petition to Congress (1871) protesting the extension of the vote to women and wrote a number of articles supporting the protest.

Portly and commanding in old age, Almira Phelps continued to reveal those qualities ascribed to her in 1831 by her stepdaughter Lucy, who described their new mother to John Phelps' children in Vermont: "A soaring mind, a benevolent disposition, an investigating judgment, and devout piety, patience the most untiring." Her science textbooks led to her election in 1859 as the second woman member of the American Association for the Advancement of Science, the first being MARIA MITCHELL. She died in Baltimore on her ninety-first birthday, the cause of death being listed as "extreme age." She was buried in Baltimore's Greenmount Cemetery. Although she was to some degree overshadowed by the greater fame and achievement of her sister Emma Willard, Almira Phelps nevertheless made the Patapsco Female Institute a respectable Southern version of Troy Female Seminary, and her *Familiar Lectures on Botany* was widely adopted as a school text.

[Emma Lydia Bolzau, *Almira Hart Lincoln Phelps: Her Life and Work* (1936), a definitive biography with an extensive bibliography; Thomas Woody, *A Hist. of Women's Education in the U.S.* (2 vols., 1929), the standard study on the subject; death record from Baltimore City Health Dept.]

FREDERICK RUDOLPH

**PHELPS, Elizabeth Stuart** (1844–1911). *See* WARD, Elizabeth Stuart Phelps.

**PHELPS, Elizabeth Wooster Stuart** (Aug. 13, 1815–Nov. 30, 1852), novelist, was born in Andover, Mass., the second of the five daughters and fifth of the nine children of Moses and Abigail (Clark) Stuart. Both parents were of seventeenth-century Connecticut ancestry. Her father, the son of a Connecticut farmer and educated at Yale, was a Congregational minister and professor of sacred literature at Andover Theological Seminary, where he became the first American Hebrew scholar and proponent of German Biblical scholarship.

Elizabeth's childhood and early girlhood were spent in Andover. Her mother was an invalid, and from the age of three Elizabeth is said to have been obsessed with the idea of death. She early developed "a passionate taste for painting and statuary" and an interest in music; by the time she was ten her skill in storytelling was remarked in the little volumes of stories she was writing for the entertainment of her younger brothers and sisters. At sixteen she left the seclusion of Andover to attend the Mount Vernon School in Boston, under the direction of the Rev. Jacob Abbott, later the author of the *Rollo* books. Living in Abbott's family, she enjoyed the advantages of the city and began to write for a religious magazine which he edited. She signed these contributions "H. Trusta," an anagram of her name which she used for her writing throughout her life. At the same time she entered a period of intense religious inquiry, culminating in July 1834 in the then customary public profession of faith—for her a severe ordeal—in the seminary church at Andover. She now determined to lead a life of Christian duty, from which she rigorously excluded drawing and painting and the writing of poetry and fiction. The onset of a "cerebral disease" had forced her to return home in 1834, and for several years she suffered severe headaches, partial blindness, and paralysis, her illness reaching a crisis in an attack of typhus fever. When she ventured once again to indulge her artistic tastes, however, her health rapidly improved, although she remained subject to fits of despondency.

In September 1842, at twenty-seven, Elizabeth Stuart was married to the Rev. Austin Phelps, born in West Brookfield, Mass., the son of a peripatetic Presbyterian clergyman and teacher. A graduate of the University of Pennsylvania who had studied at Union Theological Seminary and Yale Divinity School, at the time of their marriage Phelps was minister of the Pine Street Congregational Church in Boston. The next six years, filled with the busy social duties of a pastor's wife, were the happiest of Elizabeth's life. Daily rambles around the city furnished ideas for more stories, and she began to try her hand at writing for adults. The Phelpses had three children, Mary Gray (see ELIZABETH STUART PHELPS WARD), born in 1844, Moses Stuart (1849), and Amos Lawrence (1852). Phelps' decision, in 1848, to accept the chair of sacred rhetoric and homilectics at Andover Seminary was a severe trial to his wife, who found the Andover atmosphere oppressive. After their return, however, despite what her daughter later called "the relentless drudgery of domestic toil," Mrs. Phelps managed to devote part of every day to her writing, besides keeping journals of her children's lives and a "Family Journal."

The publication of *The Sunny Side; or, The Country Minister's Wife* in 1851 made her widely known as an author. Rewritten from an earlier manuscript, this family chronicle, in part third-person narrative, in part excerpts labeled "Journal," details the domestic scene in a minister's home from his young manhood to his death. Five publishers had rejected the story before it achieved publication, but within four months 40,000 copies had been sold, and before the end of the year, 100,000. Republished in Edinburgh under the title *The Manse of Sunnyside*, translated into French and German, it sold widely in Europe also. The interest of this homely tale to a churchgoing public presents no enigma. The 1850's were the heyday of the religious novel, and this one was comfortably short in reading time, having only 135 pages. Yet there is skill born of long practice in the easy flow of the story and the natural idiom of the conversation. These are real people, and the circumstantial detail of their daily lives is authentic. Obviously it is in good part a transcript of life in the Phelps home, and some of the "Journal" extracts may be from her own "Family Journal." The author is emotionally involved in the story, which she tells without detachment or the point of view of an artist. To an uncritical audience, its simplicity was its winning merit.

The success of *The Sunny Side* encouraged Mrs. Phelps to increased literary effort, and the next year saw the publication of *A Peep at "Number Five"; or, A Chapter in the Life of a City Pastor*, which she thought her best book, and *The Angel over the Right Shoulder, or the Beginning of a New Year*. At the same time, however, her health was giving way. Her father's death early in 1852 came as a severe shock, and following the birth of her third child in August her old "disease of the brain" recurred; she died that November in Boston, aged thirty-seven. By his mother's wish her infant son was baptized beside her coffin at her funeral. Mrs. Phelps left much work in manuscript. *The Tell-tale; or, Home Secrets Told by Old Travellers* was published in 1853, as was a collection of stories titled *The Last Leaf from Sunny Side* and prefaced by a memoir of the author by her husband. *Little Mary; or, Talks and Tales for Children* appeared in 1854. Elizabeth Stuart Phelps' daughter, who upon her mother's death adopted her name, became a popular novelist of the next generation.

[Memorial by Austin Phelps in Mrs. Phelps' *The Last Leaf from Sunny Side;* Elizabeth Stuart Phelps Ward, *Austin Phelps, a Memoir* (1891) and *Chapters from a Life* (1896); *Vital Records of Andover, Mass., to the End of the Year 1849* (1912); William B. Sprague, *Annals of the Am. Pulpit*, II (1857), 477 (on her father); Sarah Loring Bailey, *Hist. Sketches of Andover* (1880); death record, Mass. Registrar of Vital Statistics.]

OLA ELIZABETH WINSLOW

**PHILIPSE, Margaret Hardenbrook** (fl. 1659–90), colonial merchant and shipowner, was born in the community of Elberfeld in the Rhine Valley, the daughter of Adolph Hardenbrook, or Hardenbroeck. Time has beclouded her early life, but it is known that she was in the Dutch colony of New Netherland by 1659. In that year her brother Abel signed an indenture to serve the Ten Eyck family in New Amsterdam, and she may have accompanied him across the seas. On Oct. 10, 1659, the marriage banns were published between Margaret and Peter Rudolphus (de Vries), a merchant trader and a man of substance in New Amsterdam. They had a daughter, Maria, baptized Oct. 3, 1660.

As of 1660 Margaret was already carrying on mercantile activities, and doing so in her maiden name, as she did throughout her career. She apparently was a business agent for Wouter Valck, Daniel des Messieres, and other Dutch merchants trading with New Netherland. When her first husband died in May or June of 1661, she immediately assumed his role as a merchant and trader, shipping furs to Holland in exchange for Dutch merchandise which she then sold in New Amsterdam. Prob-

ably at this time also, she became a shipowner as well. Legal records of the next two years show that she became embroiled in many suits arising from her late husband's mercantile pursuits. Whether these legal entanglements had anything to do with her next decision is not clear, but she accepted a proposal of marriage from Frederick Philipse, once a carpenter in Peter Stuyvesant's employ but now a rising figure in the economic and political life of New Amsterdam. Banns of marriage were published in October 1662, at the same time that the Court of Orphan Masters requested her to present an inventory of her child's paternal inheritance. She was not able to do so, but the court then accepted the antenuptial agreement between Philipse and herself in lieu of the inventory, and Philipse thereupon adopted her daughter and renamed her Eva (she later married Jacobus Van Cortlandt).

With his wife's inheritance from her late husband, Frederick Philipse was able to expand his mercantile endeavors until he soon was recognized as one of the wealthiest individuals in New Netherland. Margaret, meanwhile, continued her own general overseas trading activities, which frequently necessitated traveling between the mother country and New Amsterdam. A Dutch deposition of 1660 had stated that the merchant Wouter Valck had entered into a financial arrangement with "Margaret Hardenbroeck, living in the Manhattans in New Netherland who is at present married to Pieter Adolphus [Rudolphus], merchant there." Other depositions repeat the same concept of a businesswoman who happens to be married. From similar legal records, it is also determined that she was in Amsterdam in January 1664 and in the period December 1668 to January 1669. On the latter occasion she was one among many merchants of what had now become New York who petitioned the King of England to permit the sailing of the ship *King Charles* from Amsterdam to New York, special authorization being needed because of new privy council orders permitting only one ship to sail to New York annually rather than three. The request was granted after many delays.

A decade later two Labadist missionaries, Jaspar Danckaerts and Peter Sluyter, found Margaret serving as supercargo on board her vessel the *Charles*, on which they sailed from Amsterdam to New York. These devoutly religious men referred in their journal to her "unblushing avarice" and "excessive covetousness," and related an occasion when she ordered the crew to search the seas for a mop which had fallen overboard: "we, with all the rest," they recorded, "must work fruitlessly for an hour or an hour and a half, and all that merely to satisfy and please the miserable covetousness of Margaret" (Murphy, p. 53).

Accompanying Margaret Philipse on this voyage was her daughter Annetje, who eventually married the influential merchant Philip French. Margaret and Frederick Philipse also had three other children: Philip, Adolph, and Rombout. Adolph became his father's partner and later assumed control of his overseas trading operations. Little is known of the other two sons other than that they were engaged in shipping.

Margaret Hardenbrook Philipse seems to have retired from business after her voyage on the *Charles*. She died about 1690. In 1692 Philipse married a second wealthy widow, Catherine (Van Cortlandt) Dervall (1652–1731), and the following year became proprietor of the 96,000-acre Manor of Philipsburg. The Dutch wives of New Netherland were proverbially good at business, but it was most unusual for a woman to engage in international mercantile affairs as had Margaret Philipse.

[Henry C. Murphy, ed., "Jour. of a Voyage to N.Y. in 1679–80," in Long Island Hist. Soc., *Memoirs*, vol. I (1867); I. N. Phelps Stokes, *The Iconography of Manhattan Island*, II (1916), 245–46; Edmund B. O'Callaghan, ed., *Documents Relative to the Colonial Hist. of the State of N.-Y.*, III (1853), 178, 247; Berthold Fernow, ed., *The Minutes of the Orphanmasters of New Amsterdam, 1655–1663* (2 vols., 1902–07); Notarial Records, Gemeente Archief of Amsterdam.]

JACOB JUDD

**PHILLIPPS, Adelaide** (Oct. 26, 1833–Oct. 3, 1882), actress, opera singer, and one of America's first prima donnas, was born in Bristol, England, where her English father, Alfred Phillipps, was an attorney and her Welsh mother, Mary (Rees) Phillipps, a "professor of dancing." Adelaide was one of a family of four boys and two girls with whom she always retained close ties. After first emigrating to Canada, the family settled in Boston, Mass., where Phillipps worked as a druggist and his wife continued to teach dancing. Adelaide attended primary school in Boston's South End. She made her first stage appearance at the age of eight at the Tremont Theatre, Boston (Jan. 12, 1842), in the comedy *Old and Young*, playing five different characters and introducing songs and dances. The next fall, at the Boston Museum (Sept. 26, 1843), she played Little Pickle in *The Spoiled Child*. The *Transcript* the following day hailed her as "a

prodigy" and said that the almost-ten-year-old trouper had "surprised and delighted a crowded audience, by her acting, singing, and dancing." The success of her initial role prompted the museum to bill her in *Old and Young* two days later, though for the most part she appeared as a dancer between the acts of regular shows. A talented child performer, she continued with Boston's only long-lived stock company for a decade or more.

Thomas Comer, who arranged, composed, and directed all the music for the Boston Museum, was the first to take a professional interest in the child's vocal abilities. Later she studied in Boston with Mme. Émile Arnoult, who evidently placed her voice in the contralto range. In 1851, reportedly with the financial aid of the famous singer Jenny Lind, who had been in Boston on tour, and the piano manufacturer Jonas Chickering, among others, Adelaide Phillipps left her theatrical-vaudevillian life for London and vocal training with Manuel Garcia, the most celebrated singing master of the nineteenth century. Her father accompanied her abroad, and was with her when, in the autumn of 1853, she went to Italy for coaching in operatic acting, in Italian diction, and in specific roles. That November she obtained an engagement in Brescia, where she made her operatic debut under the name of "Signorina Fillippi" as Arsace in Rossini's *Semiramide*. She remained in Italy for two years, but her engagements, though well received, were not frequent enough or well enough paid to support her, and she returned to the United States. Back in her adopted country, she made a few appearances in light and Italian opera in Boston, New York, and Philadelphia; but her first important performance was as Azucena in Verdi's *Il Trovatore* in New York, under Max Maretzek, director of the Italian Opera Troupe, at the Academy of Music on Mar. 17, 1856. The young singer's debut was eagerly awaited by a proud press who mistakenly thought she was a native American, but her portrayal of the gypsy mother brought mixed reviews. Though the *Tribune* carried a favorable notice, the *Times* critic (Mar. 18), while generously attributing any shortcomings to "nervousness," bluntly stated that "she has much to learn and many serious defects to correct, not only in the delivery of the voice, but in preserving a correct intonation."

Remaining a member of the Maretzek troupe, Adelaide Phillipps sang in Havana (November 1857), where, according to the singer's own words, she achieved her "greatest artistic success" and received "true appreciation." Unfortunately, at this midpoint in her life, with her operatic career at its height, she contracted yellow fever, which may have been responsible for her later sporadic illnesses and her death at the early age of forty-eight. Before leaving for her second and final professional European tour, she sang with the Handel and Haydn Society, Boston, in Handel's *Messiah* (Dec. 30, 1860) and in Rossini's *Stabat Mater* (Mar. 17, 1861).

In Europe she made a successful debut before the critical Parisian public in October 1861 as Azucena, and went on to sing in Madrid, Barcelona, Prague, Budapest, and Warsaw. Returning to America the next spring, she settled down to the relatively routine life of a traveling opera and concert singer, taking engagements as far south as Havana and as far west as California. Boston—and Marshfield, Mass., where she purchased a farm in 1860—became her permanent homes, and it was in Boston that she made her greatest mark as an oratorio singer, particularly at the triennial festivals of the Handel and Haydn Society (1868, 1871, 1874) and at the Peace Jubilee of June 1869. Appearing with her own "quartette" company, she sang in the Midwest in 1874. Her reception encouraged her to form the Adelaide Phillipps Opera Company, with her younger sister, Mathilde, as one of the group; but this one-season venture was not a financial success. In 1879 Miss Phillipps joined the Boston Ideal Opera Company, with which she sang until her last operatic appearance in December 1881 at Cincinnati. The following year, after recurrences of illness, she traveled to Karlsbad, Germany, to "take the waters," and while there suddenly died. After funeral services at King's Chapel (Unitarian) in Boston, she was buried in Winslow Cemetery, Marshfield, Mass.

Adelaide Phillipps never married, nor was she, apparently, ever romantically attached. Whether this was because of personal inclination or the result of obligations to her family, to whose support she contributed, is difficult to say; photographs show her to have been an attractive young woman. She never reached the heights of stardom to which she aspired as an opera singer. Like many other child prodigies who continued their careers into maturity, she seems to have been unable to surpass the impact of her earliest performances, which were, perhaps, the origin of her fame and, together with her exemplary private life, the source of her admirers' sentimental devotion.

[The chief printed source is the laudatory biography by Mrs. R. C. (Anna Cabot Lowell Quincy)

Waterston, *Adelaide Phillipps: A Record* (1883), which should be supplemented by contemporary newspaper and periodical accounts. Since American critics were often brutally frank, reviews of Miss Phillipps' appearances can be accepted as close to the truth, unlike many notices in foreign papers. References, largely collected from newspapers, to Miss Phillipps' early theatrical career can be found in Claire McGlinchee's *The First Decade of the Boston Museum* (1940). The town clerk of Marshfield, Mass., supplied Miss Phillipps' place of burial and the names of her parents; data on their occupations from city directories of Bristol, England, and Boston, Mass.]

VICTOR FELL YELLIN

**PIATT, Sarah Morgan Bryan** (Aug. 11, 1836– Dec. 22, 1919), poet, was born in Lexington, Ky., the elder of two daughters of Mary (Spiers) and Talbot Nelson Bryan. She was a descendant of Morgan Bryan, father-in-law of Daniel Boone, with whom Bryan had moved from North Carolina to Kentucky in the 1770's; his sons founded Bryan's Station, a pioneer outpost made famous in the old Indian wars. When Sarah Bryan was three years old her family moved from Lexington to Versailles, Woodford County, Ky., where her mother died in 1844. This loss and the subsequent insecurity of her childhood are said to have been responsible for Sarah's sadness and reserve, which remained characteristic traits. She lived for a time with her maternal grandmother, later with friends near Versailles, and then with her wealthy stepmother there, until finally her father placed her with his sister Mrs. Annie Boone at New Castle, Ky. There she graduated from the fashionable Henry Female College.

From early childhood Sarah had been an avid reader, and as a young girl she was thoroughly familiar with the chief English poets of the time, among them Coleridge, Byron, and Shelley, whose work inspired her to start writing verses of her own. Her first poem was published by accident when a cousin showed it to a Texas editor who printed it in his paper, the *Galveston News*. Her work then came to the attention of George D. Prentice, the influential editor of the *Louisville Journal*. Convinced that the young author would one day be the leading woman poet in America, Prentice published her poems in his paper and helped lay the foundations for her career. Her early verses also appeared in the *New York Ledger*, and by 1860 she was a popular and well-known poet in Kentucky, the South, and throughout the United States.

On June 18, 1861, Sarah Bryan, a delicate and graceful girl with hazel eyes and auburn hair, was married to John James Piatt, whom she had met at New Castle. A fellow author, Piatt had written a book of poems with William Dean Howells, his boyhood friend from Ohio. The Piatts had seven children: Marian, Victor, Guy, Cecil, Dougall, Fred, and Donald. For six years they lived in Washington, D.C., where Secretary of the Treasury Salmon P. Chase of Ohio had given Piatt a post in the Treasury Department. They then settled in North Bend, Ohio, near Cincinnati. From 1870 to 1876 Piatt was back in Washington as librarian of the House of Representatives, his family joining him in the winters. In 1882 they began an extended residence in Ireland, where Piatt served as United States consul at Cork until 1893. During this period Mrs. Piatt was a member of a literary circle which included such notable figures as Edmund Gosse, Lady Wilde, Austin Dobson, Edward Dowden, and Katharine Tynan, one of her most sympathetic critics.

A prolific writer, Sarah Piatt published seventeen volumes of poetry, two of which (*The Nests at Washington,* 1864; *The Children Out-of-Doors,* 1885) were written in collaboration with her husband. Although her earlier poems won greater popularity, her best work is represented in such volumes as *An Irish Wild-Flower* (1891), *An Enchanted Castle, and Other Poems* (1893), and *Pictures, Portraits, and People in Ireland* (1893). These were written with the stimulus and critical advice of her husband, who was responsible for the publication of her work in book form. Her collected *Poems* was printed in 1894.

Mrs. Piatt experimented freely and successfully with a wide variety of verse forms. Her rhythms are light and lyrical, brightening the prevalent tone of sadness. Her more individual characteristics, particularly a developing dramatic element, appear in the verses written after her marriage, which reflect joy in her home and family and deep devotion between husband and wife. Her poems for and about her children, often playful and humorous, exhibit a growing sympathy with and knowledge of child life. The tragic loss of two sons, one by drowning and a second in a Fourth of July fireworks explosion, is reflected in her strong religious awareness and preoccupation with the theme of death.

Although nearly forgotten today, Sarah Piatt was accorded high praise during her lifetime by notable critics on both sides of the Atlantic. Her later books were published simultaneously in London, Edinburgh, and Boston. English critics, more appreciative than their American counterparts, often compared her to Christina Rossetti and Elizabeth Barrett Browning. In America, Bayard Taylor, William Dean Howells, John Burroughs, and Hamilton Wright Mabie paid high tribute to her work. Taylor's sympathetic notice in his book *The Echo Club* of *A Woman's Poems* (1871) probably helped make this, her first independent book and issued anonymously, her best-known work.

Financial difficulties plagued the Piatts in their last years, which were spent in North Bend, Ohio; on the initiative of Howells they received aid from the Authors' Club Fund. After her husband's death in February 1917, Mrs. Piatt lived with her son Cecil in Caldwell, N.J., where she died two years later of pneumonia, at the age of eighty-three. She was buried near her husband at Spring Grove Cemetery in Cincinnati.

[Emerson Venable in *Library of Southern Literature,* IX (1909), 4003–05; Frances E. Willard and Mary A. Livermore, eds., *A Woman of the Century* (1893); Katharine Tynan, *Twenty-five Years: Reminiscences* (1913), pp. 274–78; John W. Townsend, *Kentucky in Am. Letters,* I (1913), 303–04; Richard H. Stoddard et al., *Poets' Homes* (1877), pp. 63–70; Clare Dowler, "John James Piatt," *Ohio State Archaeological and Hist. Quart.,* Jan. 1936; Mildred Howells, ed., *Life in Letters of William Dean Howells* (1928), II, 346–47; information from Cincinnati Hist. Soc.; death record from N.J. State Dept. of Health.]

JAMES B. COLVERT

**PICKENS, Lucy Petway Holcombe** (June 11, 1832–Aug. 8, 1899), Confederate hostess, was born at La Grange, Fayette County, Tenn., on the cotton plantation of her distinguished Virginia parents, Eugenia Dorothea (Hunt) and Beverly Lafayette Holcombe; she was the second daughter and second of their five children. The Holcombes moved farther west following the rising fortunes of cotton culture and settled in Marshall, Texas, at Wyalucing, a mansion surrounded by cotton fields and slaves. There Lucy Holcombe grew into a woman of "classic features, titian hair, pansy eyes, and graceful figure." She was a belle of the Deep South, figuring at balls in Jackson, Vicksburg, and New Orleans and inspiring the Mississippi legislature to recess in her honor. Her intellectual activities consisted of two years' schooling at the Bethlehem (Pa.) Female Seminary and the writing of a booklet advocating the liberation of Cuba. Her mother accompanied her to the White Sulphur Springs in Virginia, a matchmaking center for the aristocracy of the Old South, where Francis Wilkinson Pickens of South Carolina, political leader and former Congressman, determined to make her his third wife. She was twenty-five, and he was twenty-seven years her senior. She consented to marry Pickens, it is said, if he would accept the position of minister to Russia offered him by President James Buchanan.

Married at Wyalucing on Apr. 26, 1858, the couple left immediately for Russia. At the court of the czars Lucy Holcombe Pickens displayed her beauty, her black servants, and her Southern viands. She made such an impression that she was showered with expensive gifts by members of the imperial household. Her only child was born in St. Petersburg on Mar. 14, 1859, a daughter who was grandiloquently christened Francesca Eugenia Olga Neva but was ever afterward called Douschka (Russian for "Darling"). While in Russia, Lucy Pickens gave up her Presbyterian affiliation for her husband's Episcopalianism.

Resigning his diplomatic post in the fall of 1860 as the secession crisis developed in South Carolina, Pickens was on Dec. 17 elected governor of his state. As wife of the secession governor, Lucy Holcombe Pickens played a conspicuous part in the festivities of the Confederacy's salad days. She was waited upon by slaves in livery acquired in Europe. Attired in black velvet with an ostrich plume in her hat and riding a spirited horse, she appeared before a regiment called in her honor the Holcombe Legion. Her likeness was engraved upon the hundred-dollar bill of the Confederacy. She was described by MARY BOYKIN CHESNUT—a hostile critic—as "the lovely Lucy Holcombe," who spoke in a "slow, graceful, impressive way, her beautiful eyes eloquent with feeling."

Pickens died in January 1869, leaving his spacious estate of Edgewood at Edgefield, S.C., to his widow. "Lady Pick," as she was familiarly known, kept open house there for the thirty years of her widowhood, entertaining all important comers including the more attractive carpetbaggers. Careless management led to the decline of her farms, but she held on to her property through loans from friends. She was vice-regent for South Carolina of ANN PAMELA CUNNINGHAM's Mount Vernon Ladies' Association and raised money for the erection of the Confederate monument at Edgefield. Her daughter, Douschka, was more interested in horses and the chase than in the social pleasures her mother loved. After being pushed by her mother into an unhappy marriage to George Dugas of a distinguished Georgia family of physicians, Douschka died at the age of twenty-five. The mother delivered a poignant funeral address over the daughter's coffin and had her body carried by ex-slaves to a grave beside her father in the Edgefield Cemetery. Mrs. Pickens, aged sixty-seven, died at Edgewood in 1899 of a cerebral embolism and was buried beside her husband and daughter. As symbolic of the passing of the civilization she so charmingly represented, her house and garden were torn up after her death and reestablished, twenty-three miles away, at Aiken, a resort town of Northern tourists.

[Obituary notices in *Charleston* (S.C.) *News and Courier* and *Columbia* (S.C.) *State*, Aug. 9, 1899; scrapbooks in private possession of Sarah L. Simkins, Lucy Frances Dugas, and Ellen I. Butler. See also Mary Boykin Chesnut, *A Diary from Dixie* (Ben Ames Williams, ed., 1949), pp. 32, 193, 206, 210; William C. Reichel, *A Hist. of . . . the Bethlehem Female Seminary* (1858), p. 367.]

FRANCIS B. SIMKINS

PICOTTE, Susan La Flesche (June 17, 1865–Sept. 15, 1915), Indian physician, was born on the Omaha reservation, which closely approximated the later Thurston County in northeastern Nebraska. The fourth daughter and fifth and youngest child of Chief Joseph La Flesche (Iron Eye) and his wife Mary (One Woman), she was born into a remarkable Indian family (see article on SUSETTE LA FLESCHE TIBBLES). Her father was a vigorous leader striving to make the Omahas a sober and progressive people, and his children carried forward his ideals. Growing up in the Indian culture, Susan did not learn English until she went to the mission and government schools on the reservation. Her real education began at fourteen when, following in the steps of her older sister Susette, she entered the Elizabeth (N.J.) Institute for Young Ladies. After three years there she spent two years at Hampton Institute in Virginia, graduating in May 1886 as salutatorian and receiving a gold medal for high scholastic achievement.

The Women's National Indian Association, founded in 1880 by MARY LUCINDA BONNEY and AMELIA STONE QUINTON, had begun a program of financing professional training for talented Indians. With its aid, Susan La Flesche now entered the Woman's Medical College of Pennsylvania in Philadelphia. Completing the three-year course in two years, she graduated with the M.D. degree in 1889 at the head of a class of thirty-six. She was not quite twenty-four. After a year as an interne in the Woman's Hospital in Philadelphia, she went back to her tribe as physician at the government school for Omaha children. For a time she served also as a medical missionary for the Women's National Indian Association. Later her government services were extended to the rest of the tribe. This was an arduous task, for the 1,300 Omahas were widely scattered and the principal means of transportation was by horseback. The slender young doctor was often nurse as well as physician, and always teacher of new rules for health and sanitation. Even in bitter storms she never considered the way impassable; but the work was too heavy, and after four years she resigned. In 1894 she was married to Henry Picotte, half Sioux and half French in ancestry, and settled in Bancroft, Nebr. There she carried on a growing medical practice among both Indians and whites, meanwhile bringing up two children and nursing her husband during a long illness that ended in his death in 1905. Her two sons, Caryl and Pierre, attended college; Caryl, who served in the army in both world wars, was in the "death march" from Bataan and became a lieutenant colonel.

Soon after the town of Walthill was founded (1906) on the Omaha reservation, Dr. Susan Picotte, following her father's principles, led a delegation to Washington and obtained the stipulation that every deed for property in towns established on the Omaha and Winnebago reservations should forever prohibit the sale of liquor. One of the earliest residents of Walthill, she was a leading spirit in the community, active in church affairs and the women's club, one of the organizers of the County Medical Society, and chairman of the local board of health. She became in effect the real leader of the Omahas, although traditionally they never followed a woman. Having meanwhile become a medical missionary of the Presbyterian Board of Home Missions, under its auspices she established, in 1913, a hospital at Walthill; after her death it was given her name. It was estimated that in twenty-five years she had treated every member of the Omaha tribe and saved the lives of many.

Modest and unselfish, she had humor and a broad tolerance for human frailty. Although for years she suffered extreme pain from an infection of the facial bones, which finally proved fatal, she never lessened her activities. She died in Walthill in 1915 and was buried at Bancroft. Born in one culture, she became part of a far different one, but never lost touch with those who lived according to tribal values; fittingly, Presbyterian clergymen officiated at her funeral, but the closing prayer was made by an aged Indian in the Omaha language.

[Addison E. Sheldon, *Hist. and Stories of Nebr.* (1913); Alice C. Fletcher, *Hist. Sketch of the Omaha Tribe of Indians in Nebr.* (1885); Fannie Reed Giffen, *Oo-Mah-Ha Ta-Wa-Tha* (*Omaha City*) (1898), with illustrations by Susette La Flesche Tibbles; Women's Nat. Indian Assoc., *Sketches of Delightful Work* (1893), pp. 46–52, 81; Julius F. Schwarz, *Hist. of the Presbyterian Church in Nebr.* (1924); *Walthill* (Nebr.) *Times*, Feb. 1915 through June 1916; La Flesche Family Papers at Nebr. State Hist. Soc.; interviews with La Flesche descendants, including Dr. Rosalie Farley, Univ. of Nebr.; Mrs. Marguerite Diddock Langenberg of Walthill, Nebr.; Mrs. Caryl Farley of Lincoln, Nebr.; Mr. Charles Conn of Bancroft, Nebr.; Mrs. Winnie Farley of Grand Island, Nebr.; Mrs. La Flesche Farley of Sioux City, Iowa; and the late Marguerite Farley (Mrs. Charles) Conn. See also the author's "Four Sisters: Daughters of Joseph La Flesche," *Nebr. Hist.*, June 1964, and *Iron Eye's Family: The Children of Joseph La Flesche* (1969).]

NORMA KIDD GREEN

**PIERCE, Jane Means Appleton** (Mar. 12, 1806–Dec. 2, 1863), wife of Franklin Pierce, fourteenth president of the United States, was born at Hampton, N.H., the youngest of three daughters and third of six children of Jesse and Elizabeth (Means) Appleton. Her father, a prominent Congregational minister, became president of Bowdoin College in 1807. Growing up in an atmosphere of inflexible Calvinism, Jane spent her childhood in Brunswick, Maine, and in Amherst, N.H., her mother's home, to which the family returned after Jesse Appleton's death in 1819. Jane received a thorough general education and showed a marked aptitude for study, particularly for literature. In 1826 she met Franklin Pierce, two years after his graduation from Bowdoin. The attractive but frail and introspective girl was drawn to the handsome, mildly convivial young lawyer, and they became engaged. Pierce was elected to Congress in 1833. Despite strong opposition to the match—Mrs. Appleton objecting for social reasons, while her prominent Means and Mason relatives disliked Pierce's affiliation with the Democratic party—they were married on Nov. 19, 1834.

From the start Mrs. Pierce found political life agonizing. Terrified by social functions, she nevertheless struggled to fulfill her obligations as a Congressman's and then a Senator's wife in Washington. The birth of Frank Robert in 1840 and of Benjamin, known as Benny, in 1841, brought her the long-sought joys of motherhood (a first son had died in infancy) and convinced her Calvinist conscience that Washington, tainted by the evils of politics, was no place in which to rear her sons. In 1842 she at last persuaded Pierce to resign from the Senate and retire to Concord, N.H.

Unusually happy in Concord, Mrs. Pierce failed to detect her husband's growing restlessness, for despite a successful law practice, he missed the stimulus of Washington. The death of their son Frank in 1844 widened the gulf between them. Blinded by her own grief to her husband's deeply felt sorrow, Jane lavished all her affection on Benny. With the outbreak of the Mexican War in 1846, Pierce, to his wife's distress, volunteered for service. He received a commission as colonel, acquitted himself creditably, and was promoted to brigadier general. The four years following his return to Concord in 1848 were the most satisfying of their marriage.

But this happy interlude did not prepare Jane Pierce for her husband's return to public life. When Pierce received the Democratic nomination for the presidency in 1852, she fainted away; in succeeding months she prayed fervently for his defeat. She seemed to have become resigned to his victory by the time of a Christmas visit to Boston. On the return journey, however, their train jumped the track and lunged over a fifteen-foot embankment; when the car settled, Mrs. Pierce saw the crushed and lifeless body of eleven-year-old Benny before her, a horror from which she never fully recovered. In the weeks following, she was cared for by her sister Mary Aiken in the Aikens' home at Andover, Mass.

Always solicitous for her welfare, Pierce arranged for his wife to have a devoted, understanding companion at the White House, her old friend Abby Kent Means, her late uncle's second wife. For two years Mrs. Pierce attempted to assume some of the duties of First Lady. Although she avoided large parties, she entertained regularly at small teas and receptions, where her graciousness won much admiration. But her delicate constitution broke under the strain. Convinced that Benny's fate was a divine punishment meted out for Pierce's political ambition, she came to spend much of her time in her sitting room scribbling notes to the dead child. At the close of the presidential term in 1857, the Pierces retired to Concord. A trip to Europe and then to the Bahamas with her husband for a time revived Mrs. Pierce's spirits, but back in Concord memories of Benny returned to haunt her. She found some comfort in long visits to the Aikens at Andover, but withdrew more and more into a fantasy world shared with her children. She died in Andover, of "consumption," at the age of fifty-seven and was buried in the Concord (N.H.) Cemetery.

[The largest single group of Jane Pierce's letters is in the Amos Lawrence and Amos A. Lawrence Papers at the Mass. Hist. Soc. The White House diary of Abby Means and some letters of Mrs. Pierce and her family (including a letter from Alpheus S. Packard, Mrs. Pierce's brother-in-law, concerning the train accident) are in the private possession of Mrs. William Appleton Aiken of N.Y. City. Laura C. Holloway, *The Ladies of the White House* (1880), contains a biographical sketch based upon contemporary accounts; there is a brief sketch also in Mary O. Whitton, *First First Ladies* (1948). Annie M. Means, *Amherst and Our Family Tree* (1921), reprints a number of family letters relating to Mrs. Pierce. Roy F. Nichols, *Franklin Pierce* (2nd ed., 1958), has the fullest account of Mrs. Pierce's married life and is more complete than the earlier (1931) edition. See also Lloyd C. Taylor, Jr., "A Wife for Mr. Pierce," *New England Quart.*, Sept. 1955; and, for genealogy, Isaac A. Jewett, *Memorial of Samuel Appleton, of Ipswich, Mass.* (1850), pp. 43–44. Death record from Mass. Registrar of Vital Statistics.]

LLOYD C. TAYLOR, JR.

**PIERCE, Sarah** (June 26, 1767–Jan. 19, 1852), educator, was the youngest of seven children, all girls but the eldest, born at Litchfield, Conn., to John Pierce, a farmer and potter, and his first wife, Mary Paterson. At least three more children were born of his second marriage, to Mary Goodman. When Sarah was fourteen her father died, and the responsibility for the family was assumed by her brother, Col. John Pierce, paymaster general of the Continental Army. Pierce sent Sarah and her older sister Nancy to New York City to be educated so that they might conduct a school. He died in 1788, but in 1792 Sarah started to teach at Litchfield, beginning, according to tradition, with only two or three pupils in the dining room of her home.

The town at that time was not only a commercial center, some of whose businessmen engaged in the China trade, but also enjoyed an active cultural life, enhanced by the noted law school which another Litchfield citizen, Tapping Reeve, had established a decade earlier. As the fame of Miss Pierce's school grew, the number of pupils increased, and in 1798 public-spirited citizens provided a building; in 1827 this was enlarged and the school incorporated as the Litchfield Female Academy. The excellence of its academic instruction and of Miss Pierce's training in manners and conduct, together with the attractions of its location, gave the school a national reputation for nearly forty years. The pupils, whose ages ranged from seven or eight to the early twenties (and who later included a few boys), came from all over the United States and from Canada; at one time the enrollment numbered 130.

Lodging among approved families of the town, the young ladies studied reading, writing, spelling, grammar, composition, arithmetic, geography, and history, the last Miss Pierce's favorite subject. When her students found the existing textbooks dull, she undertook to write her own, in the form of questions and answers; four volumes were published between 1811 and 1818 under the title *Sketches of Universal History Compiled from Several Authors. For the Use of Schools.* The curriculum also emphasized the feminine arts of needlework and watercolor painting. Dancing classes were held, and the girls sixteen and older attended balls with the law students. The young men of the town also joined in the dramatic performances given at the end of school terms. For these occasions Miss Pierce composed the scripts, often playlets on Biblical themes or domestic dramas pointing up principles of conduct. Religious instruction was given by the Rev. Lyman Beecher, in return for the tuition of his children CATHARINE BEECHER, Henry Ward Beecher, and HARRIET BEECHER (STOWE); on Saturdays the girls were "reminded of their faults which Miss Pierce had discovered during the week" (*Chronicles of a Pioneer School*, p. 67). One unusual feature of the school was the emphasis on healthful exercise; Miss Pierce is said frequently to have led the entire student body on morning and evening walks through the town.

One of her pupils, who became the wife of the distinguished Harvard botanist Asa Gray, described Miss Sarah Pierce as "a small woman, slender & fragile," with "a fair complexion & blue eyes" and a "manner which was decided & firm" (*ibid.*, p. 321). She took a lively interest in literary and political questions, enjoyed intelligent talk, and had an unfailing sense of humor. She conducted her school almost single-handed until 1814, when her nephew, John Pierce Brace, whom she had educated at Williams College, came to assist her. Brace introduced more advanced courses, including logic, moral philosophy, botany, and mineralogy. About 1825 he became principal of the school, although Miss Pierce continued to teach her course in universal history until her retirement in 1833. The school had begun to decline the previous year when Brace left to become principal of the Hartford Female Seminary, and it lasted little more than a decade longer. Sarah Pierce lived to hear the chief justice of Connecticut declare at Litchfield's centennial celebration in 1851 that through her academy she had given "a new tone to female education" in the United States. She died in Litchfield the next year, after an illness ending in "a slight paralysis," and was presumably buried there.

[Emily N. Vanderpoel, *Chronicles of a Pioneer School from 1792 to 1833* (1903) and *More Chronicles of a Pioneer School* (1927), are the fullest sources. See also: Alain C. White, *The Hist. of the Town of Litchfield, Conn.* (1920); Harriet Webster Marr, "Miss Sarah Pierce and Her School for Girls at Litchfield, Conn.," *Old-Time New England,* Apr.–June 1955; Barbara P. Atwood, "Miss Pierce of Litchfield," *New-England Galaxy,* Summer 1967; Probate Records, Conn. State Library. The Litchfield Hist. Soc. has many of the journals and some of the correspondence published by Miss Vanderpoel, as well as other mementos of the academy.]

CATHERINE FENNELLY

**PIKE, Mary Hayden Green** (Nov. 30, 1824–Jan. 15, 1908), author, was born in Eastport, Maine, on the Bay of Passamaquoddy. She was the first of the six children of Elijah Dix Green of North Yarmouth, Maine, and Hannah Claflin (Hayden) Green of Eastport. On both sides she was descended from Massachusetts pioneers; her grandfather Aaron Hayden had come from Hopkinton, Mass., to become a leading citizen of Eastport. Early in Mary's life, her parents moved to Calais, then a small village on the St. Croix River, where her father was to become a figure of some prominence—a Baptist deacon, director of the Washington County Bank, and colonel of militia. She attended the local schools.

Religion had a large place in her early life, particularly after her eleventh year, when a revival under the preaching of the Rev. Samuel Robinson resulted in the formation of the town's first Baptist church. When she joined it a year later her winter baptism in the icy river was remembered in testimony to her twelve-year-old zeal and courage. Her sympathy with the antislavery cause, which was to engage her mature powers, may have been first aroused during a tumult in the town over an abolitionist lecture delivered in the Baptist church in 1838. Feeling ran high on this occasion, and the minister, who had opposed the use of the church for the lecture, resigned as a result of the tempest his stand had caused. At this time Mary Green was fourteen years old.

Two years later, in 1840, she enrolled for the three-year course in the Female Seminary of Charlestown, Mass., an institution acknowledging the Bible as "the standard of government and morals." On Sept. 28, 1845, Mary Green was married to Frederick Augustus Pike, a native of Calais and a graduate of Bowdoin College, who later became mayor of Calais, representative to the state legislature, and, from 1861 to 1869, a member of Congress. They seem to have had no children of their own, but they adopted a daughter.

Mrs. Pike's first novel, *Ida May*, the tale of a white child kidnapped into slavery, appeared in 1854 under the pen name "Mary Langdon." Popularity was immediate, both in America and in Europe. An illustrated edition was published in England during the same year and four later editions before 1882. German translations were also published. Sixty thousand copies were sold in America within two years, and Ida May is said to have become a popular name for girls. The novel's vogue owed something to the recent sensational success of HARRIET BEECHER STOWE's *Uncle Tom's Cabin* (1852), but more to its own melodramatic action. A winter spent in South Carolina had given Mrs. Pike some background for the story. Her second novel, *Caste: A Story of Republican Equality*, followed in 1856 under the pseudonym "Sydney A. Story, Jr." It concerned a quadroon girl forbidden to marry a white man. The London *Athenaeum* found Mrs. Pike's subject of "social slave-life" of more interest to Europeans than "any negro wrongs" and commented favorably on the author's "temperateness" in handling a social question and her "wise and discerning spirit." She was also the author of *Agnes* (1858), a story about an Indian in Revolutionary times, and she contributed to *Graham's* and *Harper's* magazines and to the *Atlantic Monthly*. The destruction by fire in Boston of the plates for *Ida May* and *Caste* prevented reissue in America of these popular books after 1858.

Sometime before moving to Washington, D.C., during her husband's service in Congress, Mrs. Pike had apparently turned from writing to landscape painting. Her chief claim to remembrance as a writer is as one of the crusading novelists, many of them women, for whom Mrs. Stowe had prepared the way. What tracts and impassioned speeches could not do for many thousands, these melodramatic stories accomplished, giving momentum to a great cause by presenting a humanitarian protest in human terms. Readers in the 1850's and 1860's were ready to accept these highly colored protests uncritically for the sake of the cause for which their authors pleaded.

After the Civil War, Mrs. Pike lived for several years in Europe. Following her husband's death in 1886, she made her home with her adopted daughter in Plainfield, N.J., and later with a sister in Baltimore. She died in Baltimore, at the age of eighty-three, and was buried beside her husband in Calais, Maine.

[Isaac C. Knowlton, *Annals of Calais, Maine* (1875); Jonathan D. Weston, *The Hist. of Eastport, and Vicinity* (1834); William Henry Kilby, comp., *Eastport and Passamaquoddy* (1888); *Athenaeum* (London), Jan. 12, 1856, p. 40, Aug. 25, 1860, p. 255; S. Austin Allibone, *A Critical Dict. of English Literature and British and Am. Authors*, II (1870), 1595; John W. Chadwick, *A Life for Liberty* (1899), p. 173; obituary in Baltimore *Sun*, Jan. 16, 1908; information about Elijah Dix Green from Calais (Maine) Free Library. Though other novels have been attributed to Mrs. Pike, she herself asserted that she wrote only *Ida May, Caste*, and *Agnes* (*Boston Transcript*, Jan. 12, 1889).]

OLA ELIZABETH WINSLOW

**PINCKNEY, Elizabeth Lucas** (Dec. 28, 1722?– May 26, 1793), better known as Eliza Pinckney, plantation manager distinguished for her success in the cultivation of indigo in South Carolina, and mother of two leaders of the newly independent United States, was born in the West Indies, probably in 1722. She was the oldest of the four children of George Lucas, a lieutenant colonel in the British army who was later to become lieutenant governor of the island colony of Antigua; her mother's name is not known. In 1738 Lucas, seeking better health for his ailing wife, brought her and their two daughters to a plantation he had inherited on Wappoo Creek in South Carolina, "17 mile by land and 6 by water from Charles Town." When the maritime conflict between England and Spain known as the War of Jenkins' Ear forced him to return to his military post in Antigua in 1739, the management of Wappoo, and of Lucas' two other plantations in the low country, fell to Eliza.

This enterprising teenager, who had spent several years in England completing her education, brought a cosmopolitan perspective to her life at Wappoo. She was accomplished in music and could "tumble over one little tune" on the flute. She quoted Milton, read Richardson's *Pamela*, and spoke French. "I have a little library well furnished for my papa has left me most of his books," she recorded in her journal, and her lively intellect took her into John Locke, Virgil, Plutarch, and the legal authority Thomas Wood. She tutored her sister Polly and taught reading to "two black girls" whom she intended to make "school mistress's for the rest of the Negroe children" if her father approved. In 1741 she sighted a comet whose appearance Sir Isaac Newton had predicted. Eliza enjoyed her brief visits in society-minded Charleston, but gave her considerable energies largely to the plantation routine. Her letters indicate that within the frame of eighteenth-century convention she could turn a phrase with originality and charm; her valuable letterbook is one of the largest surviving collections of letters of a colonial lady.

Colonel Lucas urged his daughter to experiment with diversified crops at Wappoo; and after a year of trial she entered in her copybook, May 20, 1739: "Wrote my Father . . . On the pains I had taken to bring the Indigo, Ginger, Cotton and Lucerne and Casada to perfection and had greater hopes from the Indigo (if I could have the seed earlier next year from the West India's) than any of the rest of the things I had tryd." Indeed, if only a fine grade of blue dye-cakes from indigo grown in Carolina could be prepared for cloth manufacturers in England, two important problems would be solved; for the British begrudged the necessity of purchasing this item from French islands, and the advent of the war had sharply diminished the European market for rice, South Carolina's one staple. "I was ignorant both of the proper season for sowing it [indigo] and the soil best adapted to it," Eliza recalled. Yet it was her perseverance which brought to success experiments in growing this crop which had been tried and discarded near Charleston some seventy years earlier. Knowing how complex was the process of producing the dye from the fresh-cut plants, Colonel Lucas sent an experienced indigo maker from the French island of Montserrat in the summer of 1741. Optimistically, Eliza wrote her father that October "informing him we made 20 weight of Indigo . . . 'Tis not quite dry or I should have sent him some. Now desire he will send us a hundred weight of seed to plant in the spring." The dyemaker, Nicholas Cromwell, proved, however, to be a scoundrel. He feared the indigo trade of his own island would be ruined by Carolina competition and "threw in so large a quantity of Lime water as to spoil the colour."

Experiments continued annually, and the 1744 crop was a true success under the guidance of a second imported professional, Patrick Cromwell, who proved more reliable than his brother. Six pounds from Wappoo were sent to England and "found better than the French Indigo." Seed from this same crop was distributed to many planters, who soon were growing and profiting from the new export product. In 1746 Carolina planters shipped almost 40,000 pounds to England; the next year the total exported was almost 100,000 pounds, and Parliament voted a bounty for indigo from the colony. Indigo sales sustained the Carolina economy for three decades, until the Revolution cut off the trade.

On May 27, 1744, Eliza Lucas was married to Charles Pinckney, a childless widower more than twenty years her senior; Pinckney and his first wife had been her close friends, and he had often lent her books. English-educated, he was Carolina's first native lawyer; he had served as speaker of the Commons House of Assembly (1736–40) and was later (1752) named chief justice of the colony, though the appointment failed of royal confirmation. The marriage was a happy one. Pinckney built a handsome house on Charleston's waterfront for his young bride. And at his fine plantation on the Cooper River, Eliza initiated the culture of silkworms and established a private "silk manufacture."

Four children were born to the couple within five years: Charles Cotesworth (1746), George Lucas (born and died in June 1747), Harriott (1748), and Thomas (1750). Methodical Eliza wrote down her resolution: "to be a good Mother to my children . . . to instill piety, Virtue and true religion into them; to correct their Errors whatever uneasiness it may give myself. . . ." When her firstborn was still only a few months old she sent to London for "the new toy . . . to teach him according to Mr. Lock's method (w$^{ch}$ I have carefully studied) to play himself into learning" and planned to "teach him his letters by the time he can speak." Continuing her guidance in later years, she advised the fifteen-year-old Charles, an ocean away and about to enter Westminster School: "Be particularly watchful against heat of temper; it makes constant work for repentance and chagrine."

Her husband's appointment as commissioner for the colony in London took the family in April 1753 to England, where Eliza Pinckney enjoyed the gaiety of the capital. They had intended to live in England until their sons finished their education; but when war with France broke out she and her husband returned in May 1758 to Carolina, leaving the boys at school. Pinckney contracted malaria and died in July of that year. Again Eliza turned to plantation business as she directed her husband's seven separate land holdings in the low country. Her sons, devoted to the American cause in spite of their long years in England, returned to Charleston before the outbreak of the Revolution. Young Charles had posed for his portrait in the posture of declaiming against the Stamp Act; and Thomas, who had left his native province before he was three, had been nicknamed "the Rebel" at Westminster. On the question of colony versus King, Mrs. Pinckney, according to a granddaughter, had "given no advice and attempted no influence; for having done her best while they were boys to make them wise and good men, she now thankfully acknowledged that they surpassed her in wisdom as in stature." Both sons served in the American army, Charles as Washington's aide in 1777. After the war he represented South Carolina at the Constitutional Convention, served on a special mission to France, and was the candidate of the Federalist party for president in 1804 and 1808. Thomas, also in public service, was governor of the state in 1787 and later minister to Great Britain and special commissioner to Spain. Both the sons inherited their mother's interest in agriculture, initiating improved methods on their own plantations.

During the later years of her life Mrs. Pinckney spent much time with her widowed daughter, Harriott Horry, at her plantation, Hampton, on the Santee River. Here she was surrounded by her grandchildren, as the young families of the two diplomat brothers often joined the hospitable ménage. Mrs. Pinckney helped rear the three daughters of her son Charles, whose wife had died. At Hampton she greeted President Washington on his Southern tour in May 1791. The following year she was stricken with cancer, and early in 1793 she sought the cures of a highly recommended physician in Philadelphia. She died in that city and was buried in St. Peter's churchyard there. By his own request, President Washington served as one of her pallbearers.

[Letters of Eliza Lucas Pinckney in the S.C. Hist. Soc., Charleston, including her letterbook, 1739–62, now being prepared for publication; Harriott Horry Ravenel, *Eliza Pinckney* (1896); Harriet R. Holbrook, ed., *Jour. and Letters of Eliza Lucas Pinckney* (1850); Beatrice St. J. Ravenel, "Notes on John and George Lucas," *S.C. Hist. and Genealogical Mag.*, Oct. 1945; Mabel Webber, "Thomas Pinckney Family of S.C.," *ibid.*, Jan. 1938; Eliza Pinckney to C. C. Pinckney, Sept. 10, 1785, Charleston Library Soc.; *S.C. Gazette* (Charleston), Apr. 1, 1745, Sept. 7, 1747, Oct. 24, 1748; *City Gazette* (Charleston), July 17, 1793. See also Edward Nicholas, *The Hours and the Ages* (1949), and Frances Leigh Williams, *Plantation Patriot* (1967). No portrait of Mrs. Pinckney exists.]

ELISE PINCKNEY

PINKHAM, Lydia Estes (Feb. 9, 1819–May 17, 1883), patent medicine proprietor, was born near Lynn, Mass., the tenth of the twelve children of William Estes, cordwainer and farmer, and his second wife, Rebecca (Chase) Estes. Both parents, of English Quaker stock long resident in America, were strong-minded reformers who, when Lydia was a girl, left the local Friends meeting in a conflict over the slavery issue. In grammar school she was taught by Alonzo Lewis, local poet, antiquarian, and abolitionist. Later, after her graduation from Lynn Academy, Lydia helped organize and served as secretary of the Freeman's Institute, a group devoted to unhampered discussion of all social issues. Abolition was its major concern, and Lydia became acquainted not only with William Lloyd Garrison, Wendell Phillips, and Frederick Douglass, but also with such pioneer feminists as Abby Kelley (later ABBY KELLEY FOSTER) and SARAH and ANGELINA GRIMKÉ. Other causes winning her favor included temperance, Grahamism, and phrenology.

On Sept. 8, 1843, after several years of teaching school, Lydia Estes was married to Isaac Pinkham, a widower with a small daughter. They had five children: Charles Hacker (born 1844), Daniel Rogers (1849), William Henry (1852), Aroline Chase (1857), and a son who died in infancy. For three decades Mrs. Pinkham tried to support the family on her husband's great expectations, never realized, of a fortune through real estate promotion and other business ventures. When the panic of 1873 reduced them to actual destitution, it was the sons who stepped into the breach. Mrs. Pinkham, like many women of her day, had long nursed her family and neighbors with favorite home remedies. Her mixtures were botanical, because she shared a prevailing prejudice against the orthodox medical practitioners of the day, a prejudice in part justified by their harsh medication and other inadequacies in an age when true curative agents were few and knowledge of disease causation scanty. One of her remedies, evidently adapted from *The American Dispensatory* of the Eclectic physician John King, consisted mainly of *Aletris farinosa* (unicorn root) and *Asclepius tuberosa* (pleurisy root), which King thought useful for disorders of the female reproductive system. It had won favor among Mrs. Pinkham's neighbors, who, like her, were reluctant to bring "female complaints" to the attention of a male physician, and her sons now suggested that it be bottled and sold commercially. Mrs. Pinkham prepared a batch in her cellar kitchen, adding about 18 per cent alcohol as a "solvent and preservative," and the first sales were made in 1875.

Lydia E. Pinkham's Vegetable Compound soon won remarkable success in the highly competitive proprietary medicine field. One reason was the diligence of the sons (Isaac

Pinkham was never a significant factor in the venture), who through the starving period of the enterprise's early years peddled the product and indefatigably distributed handbills and pamphlets, first in Lynn and then throughout New England. Daniel, the most imaginative, introduced the compound in Brooklyn and New York, persuading the city's major patent medicine broker, Charles N. Crittenton, to take a cash order. Newspaper advertising, begun in the *Boston Herald* in 1876, led to rapid expansion, profits being poured back into further advertising. The use of Mrs. Pinkham's own dignified, benign countenance as a trademark on labels and advertisements, first tried at Daniel's suggestion in 1879, proved of incalculable effectiveness; hers may well have been the best-known American female face of the nineteenth century. The testimonials of satisfied customers, among them W.C.T.U. leaders, were also widely used.

Mrs. Pinkham, leaving merchandising and finance largely to her sons, supervised production and wrote the advertising copy. Her persuasively vivid messages ranged over various themes, including the evils of fashion, the lot of the working girl, and fiscal reform (her son Daniel was elected to the state legislature in 1878 as a Greenbacker), but always concluded with a reference to the family product. The advertising was extremely bold in the compass of its curative claims, extending even to male kidney problems. (Medical science, though granting the compound a psychological impact, and acknowledging the possible effect of the alcohol upon the user's mood, has discovered no specific, verifiable therapeutic merit in its ingredients.) Mrs. Pinkham's own belief in the efficacy of her product, and in botanic medicine generally, is attested by the large scrapbook of herbal remedies which she indiscriminately compiled and, touchingly, by the various quaint herbal preparations which she prescribed for her own two mortally ill sons, Daniel and William, both of whom died of tuberculosis in 1881.

To her, the company's business side was no more important than the "Department of Advice" which she supervised. Countless women, moved by her constant reiteration that only a woman could understand a woman's problems, wrote with utter candor seeking medical counsel, and each letter received a personal reply. Mrs. Pinkham had no compunctions about prescribing by mail, and many women were doubtless led by her letters to put off securing needed professional attention. Yet in urging good diet, exercise, and cleanliness—along with her Vegetable Compound—she promoted better hygienic practice among women often ignorant of such fundamental principles. The confident tone of her advertisements and the genuine concern evident in her letters were in themselves therapy for some. She was also the author of a booklet about sex and reproduction, frank but in good taste, which received wide circulation. Under Mrs. Pinkham's daughter-in-law and numerous female successors, the "Department of Advice" survived well into the twentieth century.

Eclectic in her religious as in her medical views, Lydia Pinkham after the death of her sons turned increasingly to Spiritualism, which had long interested her. She was above average height, but a reporter once found her "far more delicate and spiritual" than he would have expected in a woman "who has accomplished so much on the material plane of life." She died in Lynn in May 1883, five months after suffering a paralytic stroke, and six years before her husband. Both are buried in that city's Pine Grove Cemetery. At the time of her death the company, incorporated shortly before, was grossing about $300,000 a year. Despite the patent medicine exposures of the muckraking period of the 1900's, a monumental battle for control between two rival family factions, and tightened federal regulations which forced modification of its advertising claims, the company continued to grow, reaching its heyday in the 1920's. The name of Lydia Pinkham, immortalized in song, story, and jest, had long since become a household word.

[Robert C. Washburn, *The Life and Times of Lydia E. Pinkham* (1931), and Jean Burton, *Lydia Pinkham Is Her Name* (1949), are undocumented biographies, the second especially sympathetic, both citing family correspondence. See also Charles Estes, *Estes Genealogies* (1894); John King, *The Am. Dispensatory* (8th ed., 1870); Am. Medical Assoc., *Nostrums and Quackery* (1921), vol. II; E. Lee Strohl in *Surgery, Gynecology & Obstetrics*, Dec. 1957; and advertising material in the Bella C. Landauer Collection, N.-Y. Hist. Soc. The records, through 1925, of the Lydia E. Pinkham Medicine Co., including some family letters, are in the Schlesinger Library, Radcliffe College.]

JAMES HARVEY YOUNG

**PINNEY, Eunice Griswold** (Feb. 9, 1770–1849), folk artist, was born in Simsbury, Conn., the oldest daughter and fourth of eight children of Elisha and Eunice (Viets) Griswold. She was descended from Edward Griswold of Kenilworth in Warwickshire, who came from England to Windsor, Conn., in 1639. Her grandfather Samuel Griswold was apparently the first of the family to move to Simsbury, where he bought a large and prosperous farm later cultivated by her father. Her maternal great-grandfather, John Viets, had come as a young physician to America from Germany shortly before 1700. As staunch Episcopalians, presumably with loyalist sympathies, the Griswold and Viets families suffered during the Revolution; Eunice's father, though he remained neutral, was constantly questioned by the Committee of Vigilance, and the taxes and fines imposed on him depleted his fortune. Mrs. Griswold taught her children at home. Her emphasis on their religious education probably determined the career of Eunice's elder brother Alexander, who became an Episcopal bishop. Mrs. Griswold also instilled in her children "habits of persevering industry." As they reached their fifth birthdays they were given small farm chores to do and taught to knit. In spite of strict discipline, they enjoyed playacting; this may have accounted for the sense of drama subsequently evidenced in Eunice's watercolors.

Late in the eighteenth century Eunice Griswold, like her mother an energetic, religious, well-read woman, was married to Oliver Holcombe of nearby Granby. He drowned before she was twenty-seven, leaving her with two small children, Hector and Sophia. In 1797 she married Butler Pinney, four years her senior and a resident of Windsor, where the couple settled. They had three children: Norman, who became a clergyman, Viets Griswold, who died at the age of fifteen, and Minerva Emeline, who, after teaching art in a Virginia school, married Henry Bright of Northampton, Mass.

Eunice Pinney was almost forty before she took up painting. She developed her talent not with the halting and tentative strokes of the schoolgirl, but with the sure vigor of a mature woman, illustrating her own wide-ranging interests through a variety of subjects, including genre scenes, landscapes, and figure pieces. The figures in her paintings are two-dimensional, with form subordinated to composition and bold pattern. In her several mourning pictures, faces are often hidden with large and artfully draped handkerchiefs—a device, one suspects, for getting around the troublesome task of painting features. But difficulties with features, anatomy, and perspective are overshadowed by fresh, vigorous color and skillful composition. One of her finest watercolors is a tableau of "Two Women," portraying two rigid, seated figures which appear arrested in space against a background designed to heighten the dramatic effect of each detail. Some of her paintings reflect her literary interests: Minerva hovers in a cloud over the victorious Achilles outside the walls of Troy; Charlotte is seen weeping at the grave of young Werther; Valencourt and Emily, chief figures in the *Mysteries of Udolpho*, are illustrated in a composition set within a painted oval and surrounded with quotations from Mrs. Ann Radcliffe's Gothic novel. Mrs. Pinney had the self-taught artist's penchant for modeling from the best source at hand. Both "Mrs. Yorke" and "Children Playing" are close in idea and form to woodcuts from eighteenth-century children's books; the source for "The Cotter's Saturday Night," in pastel shades against a soft gray background, is almost certainly an English aquatint.

Eunice Pinney's primitive watercolors stand out from those of most nineteenth-century artists and are easily recognized as the work of one individual. Marked by tidy craftsmanship and careful organization, they combine mature elegance with naive, and often strangely unrelated, design elements. Today more than fifty paintings signed or attributed to her are owned by descendants, museums, and private collectors, the datable ones ranging from 1809 to 1826. She died in 1849, presumably in Simsbury, where she and her husband had moved sometime before 1844.

[An account of Mrs. Pinney's career as an artist (based on family letters) and a critical estimate of her style are contained in Jean Lipman, "Eunice Pinney," in Jean Lipman and Alice Winchester, eds., *Primitive Painters in America* (1950). For genealogy see Edwin Viets Griswold, *The Griswolds on the Olentangy* (privately printed pamphlet, 1939); John Viets, *A Genealogy of the Viets Family* (1902); and Laura Young Pinney, *Genealogy of the Pinney Family in America* (1924). Brief autobiographical and biographical notes concerning Bishop Griswold are quoted in John S. Stone, *Memoir of Alexander Viets Griswold* (1854).]

MARY BLACK

**PIPER, Leonore Evelina Simonds** (June 27, 1859–July 3, 1950), celebrated medium, was born in Nashua, N.H., the fourth of the six children of Stillman and Hannah (Stevens) Simonds. Of English descent, both parents were devout Congregationalists, as was Leonore until, on a visit to England in 1910, she was baptized and confirmed as an Anglican. The Simonds family early moved to Methuen, Mass., where Leonore grew up. She was married on Oct. 6, 1881, to William R. Piper of Boston, by turns a manufacturer, salesman, and clerk (or superintendent), by whom she had two daughters, Alta Laurette, born in 1884, and Minerva Leonora (1885). They soon moved to the Boston area, which remained her home for the rest of her life.

In an otherwise normal childhood Leonore Simonds occasionally suffered episodes that involved the loss of consciousness and had visionlike experiences suggesting a knowledge of distant events. A few years after her marriage she visited a spiritualistic medium and received help in regard to an injury she had sustained. Later, in a group meeting with this same medium, she fell into a full trance and delivered to a member of the circle a message which he believed to be from his dead son. Among others who now began to request sittings was Mrs. Elizabeth Gibbens, the mother-in-law of the Harvard professor William James, who obtained what she regarded as extraordinary statements of fact that Mrs. Piper could not normally have known. James was at first inclined to belittle the reports, but sittings arranged for him and his wife quickly convinced him of Mrs. Piper's "supernormal" powers. Thereafter he did everything possible to encourage serious investigation of her gifts and for eighteen months personally arranged her sittings.

Through James the American Society for Psychical Research, founded in 1884 (two years after its English prototype), became interested in the Piper case. In the spring of 1887 Dr. Richard Hodgson, an English investigator of psychic phenomena, arrived in Boston, where, made secretary of the society, he took over the arrangements for the sittings and began an investigation which he continued intermittently until his death eighteen years later. Having earlier exposed the fraudulent techniques used by Mme. HELENA BLAVATSKY, Hodgson carefully supervised the Piper investigations, even after he had abandoned his original skepticism. The genuineness of Mrs. Piper's trances was established by a variety of sensory tests, and elaborate precautions were taken to conceal from her the identity of those who attended the sittings, which for a time were scheduled two or three times a day several days a week. At one point she was even shadowed by a detective.

During the first two years of Hodgson's investigations many sitters received what they regarded as personal messages from deceased relatives, delivered through a controlling spirit who claimed to be a French physician named Phinuit (whose previous earthly existence could not be verified). Hodgson soon became convinced that in her trances Mrs. Piper displayed knowledge that she could not have possessed in her normal state, but for several years he could not decide whether the informa-

tion actually came from the dead or from telepathic communication among the living. In 1889 Mrs. Piper visited England, where the three researchers in charge of her sittings affirmed her integrity but rejected the hypothesis of spirit communication, the most skeptical concluding that Phinuit was "only a name for Mrs. Piper's secondary personality," and that her feats were accomplished through reading the minds of her sitters. Hodgson was inclined to agree, though insisting that certain of Mrs. Piper's achievements demonstrated "thought-transference from the minds of distant living persons" (Society for Psychical Research, *Proceedings*, VI, 1890, p. 567, VIII, 1892, p. 56).

Hodgson's skepticism was shaken when in 1892 "Phinuit" was supplanted by a new control purporting to be George Pelham, a young man who had died only recently, from whom Mrs. Piper seemed to communicate personal information that she could not normally have obtained. Reversing his earlier view, Hodgson in February 1898 published a long study affirming the survival of consciousness after death, drawing his evidence from the Pelham case and others. In this report, regarded as a milestone in psychic research, Hodgson stated that "out of a large number of sitters who went as strangers to Mrs. Piper, the communicating G. P. has picked out the friends of G. P. living, precisely as the G. P. living might have been expected to do, and has exhibited memories in connection with these and other friends which are such as would naturally be associated as part of the G. P. personality . . ." (*ibid.*, XIII, 1898, p. 330).

"George Pelham" gradually began relinquishing control, in Mrs. Piper's trances, to a group of religious personages known as the "Imperator Group." Their messages, sometimes expressed through Mrs. Piper's voice (the usual mode of communication up to that time) but more often through automatic writing, remained clear and striking. On a trip to England in 1906, her powers undiminished by the shock of Hodgson's death the year before, Mrs. Piper took a leading part in a new type of communication known as "cross-correspondences," in which several automatists (persons who delivered communications by automatic writing or some other involuntary process) simultaneously produced messages which bore no apparent relation to one another but which contained complementary allusions that suggested a common source, not one of the automatists. (This method had been devised to test the argument that the information given in trances is derived from normal knowledge, or from telepathy with the living, and hence offers no evidence for spirit communication.) In the most remarkable of the Piper cross-correspondences, an investigator, through Mrs. Piper, put to the deceased communicator the question: "What does the word 'Lethe' suggest to you?" Although she had no classical education, Mrs. Piper produced a long series of Latin references well known to the decedent during his lifetime. When the same question was put to a second medium, she also responded with relevant Latin sources, which did not duplicate those communicated by Mrs. Piper.

After Richard Hodgson's death in 1905, messages suggesting his personality began to appear in Mrs. Piper's communications. These, however, offered little firm evidence for survival after death and are of interest chiefly because William James himself made a detailed evaluation and psychological study of them (*ibid.*, vol. XXIII, 1909); he concluded that they *could* reasonably be interpreted as coming from Hodgson but drew no firm conclusions. James' broader analysis of Mrs. Piper's work had earlier appeared in the essay "What Psychical Research Has Accomplished," in *The Will to Believe and Other Essays* (1897). Further sittings of Mrs. Piper in the United States in 1908–09 were of no great importance, except that experiments conducted by the psychologist G. Stanley Hall showed that some "trance personalities" were more suggestible and less confidently knowledgeable about their earthly lives than would have been expected on the basis of their known personalities before death. Mrs. Piper was again in England in 1909–10, but her powers appeared to have waned. A remarkable later episode, which apparently included a warning to Sir Oliver Lodge of the impending death of his son in the First World War, aroused wide popular attention, but provided little evidence for the surviving personality of his son.

Leonore Piper died of bronchopneumonia in 1950, at the age of ninety-one, at her home in Brookline, Mass. She was buried in Mount Pleasant Cemetery, Arlington, Mass. Her secure place in the history of psychic research rests in part upon the rare and extraordinary quality of her gifts, and in part upon the courage with which she quietly pursued a much-ridiculed profession for the sake of its potential value to humanity.

[The *Proc.* of the Soc. for Psychical Research (London) contain many references to Mrs. Piper; see especially: Richard Hodgson, "A Record of Observations of Certain Phenomena of Trance," VIII (1892), 1–167; Mrs. Henry Sidgwick, "Discussion of the Trance Phenomena of Mrs. Piper," XV (1900), 16–38; William James, "Report on Mrs. Piper's Hodgson-Control," XXIII (1909), 2–121; and Mrs. Henry Sidgwick, "A Contribution to the Study of the Psychology of Mrs. Piper's Trance Phenomena," a 657-page paper which comprises the whole of vol. XXVIII (1915). See also: Alta L. Piper, *The Life and Work of Mrs. Piper* (1929); William H. Salter, *Trance Mediumship: An Introductory Study of Mrs. Piper and Mrs. Leonard* (1950); Gardner Murphy and Laura A. Dale, eds., *Challenge of Psychical Research* (1961); Murphy and Robert O. Ballou, eds., *William James on Psychical Research* (1960); Nandor Fodor, *Encyc. of Psychic Science* (1933?); Murray T. Bloom, "America's Most Famous Medium," *Am. Mercury*, May 1950. Mrs. Piper's marriage record and the birth records of her daughters (Mass. Registrar of Vital Statistics) spell her first name "Leonora"; later sources, including her death record, give "Leonore."]

GARDNER MURPHY

**PITCHER, Molly.** *See* MC CAULEY, Mary Ludwig Hays.

**PLACIDE, Suzanne.** *See* DOUVILLIER, Suzanne Theodore Vaillande.

**PLATT, Sarah Sophia Chase.** *See* DECKER, Sarah Sophia Chase Platt.

**PLEASANT, Mary Ellen** (Aug. 19, 1814?– Jan. 11, 1904), sometimes called "Mammy" Pleasant, California pioneer and boardinghouse keeper, well known in San Francisco for over half a century, lived a life that is largely veiled in mystery. Legend and hearsay have depicted her in various guises: as a procuress, and as the "mother of civil rights in California"; as a blackmailer, and as an important financial backer of John Brown's raid. Probably little of her real story will ever be known, but it seems clear that she was a woman of more than ordinary force and ability.

By her own account she was born in Philadelphia on Aug. 19, 1814, to a mother who was a full-blooded Negro; her father, she said, was Louis Alexander Williams, a well-educated merchant and a native of the Sandwich (Hawaiian) Islands. The more common report is that she was born a slave in Virginia or Georgia. Most accounts agree that she lived for a time in Boston. One version has it that a planter named Price bought her freedom and sent her to Boston to be educated (Beasley, pp. 96–97). In Boston she reportedly became acquainted with William Lloyd Garrison and other abolitionists. Her first husband seems to have been Alexander Smith, sometimes described as a Cuban planter; they were apparently living in Boston when he died. By most accounts he left her a substantial legacy, some $45,000, urging her to use it to aid the abolitionist cause. Her second husband, John Pleasant or Pleasants, was reportedly the overseer on Smith's plantation; though he apparently came to California with her, he played little part in her later life.

In or about 1849 Mrs. Pleasant moved west to the new city of San Francisco, where she promptly opened a boardinghouse. She was, it is said, an excellent cook and, with labor and accommodations scarce in these early, booming days, her boardinghouse prospered. Among her boarders were a number of men who later rose to prominence in California business and political circles. It seems likely that she engaged in other business ventures as well. One account has her lending money at 10 per cent interest (Beasley, p. 97). Another suggests that she branched out from boardinghouses to houses of assignation (Dobie, pp. 318–19). According to later reports, she was soon giving financial advice to some of her clients (Beasley, p. 96).

During the 1850's and '60's, according to recollections handed down in California's Negro community, Mrs. Pleasant often assisted members of her race. She sometimes went out into rural areas to rescue slaves who were being illegally held by masters newly come to California. She aided the Negroes' fight to secure the right of testimony in the courts, a right gained by a legislative act of 1863. She was particularly active in establishing the right of Negroes to ride on the city's streetcars. Contemporary newspapers and court reports record her as bringing action against two companies whose conductors refused to give her passage.

The most persistent story about Mammy Pleasant deals with her alleged part in John Brown's raid. In 1858, so the account goes, she sailed for the East, made her way to Chatham, Canada, and there turned over to Brown the sum of $30,000 to finance a blow for the freedom of the slave. When Brown was captured at Harpers Ferry, it is said, a note was found among his belongings reading: "The ax is laid at the foot of the tree. When the first blow is struck there will be more money to help. (signed) W.E.P." Partisans of the legend interpret this as a note from Mrs. Pleasant, her first initial having been misread as "W." Although there is evidence that she did indeed visit the East in 1858 and even purchased real estate in Chatham in September 1858, there is no good evidence that she met Brown (he had left Canada in May 1858)

or turned any money over to him. Oswald Garrison Villard, grandson of William Lloyd Garrison and biographer of John Brown, knew of the Pleasant story and rejected it as apocryphal; at best it is unproven.

Mrs. Pleasant's most important associate of the post–Civil War period was the San Francisco banker Thomas Bell. For years she served as his housekeeper, in his three-story mansard-roofed mansion on Octavia Street—known to a later generation of San Franciscans as the "House of Mystery." Gossip credited her with dominating the household, and after Bell's death in 1892 it was alleged that she had for years drawn heavily on his funds (Young, II, 811).

The personal affairs of one of Bell's business rivals, William Sharon, brought Mammy Pleasant her greatest notoriety. In 1881 Sharon—who had at one time lived at Mrs. Pleasant's boardinghouse and had later gone to Nevada, grown wealthy in mining, and won election to the United States Senate—was sued for divorce and a division of property by Sarah Althea Hill, who claimed to be Sharon's wife and produced as evidence a marriage contract. The first trial, in a state court, ended in a verdict for Miss Hill, but a federal circuit court subsequently overturned the decision, ruling the contract a forgery. Sarah Hill, testifying in court, ultimately confessed that she had acted under the instruction of Mrs. Pleasant, and Mrs. Pleasant herself reluctantly admitted that she had advanced $5,000 to Sarah Hill and subsequently a "great deal" more. The federal judge, in his decision, expressed his opinion that "this case, and the forgeries and perjuries committed in its support, have their origin largely in the brain of this scheming, trafficking, crafty old woman."

A photograph of Mammy Pleasant in her prime shows a handsome, determined face. She has been described as "very black, with thin lips," habitually dressed in a simple black dress and wearing a poke bonnet and a plaid shawl. Living alone in her last years, apparently impoverished, she died in the home of a San Francisco acquaintance who had given her asylum. She was buried in Tulocay Cemetery, Napa, Calif. She had once told a Negro friend "that she had no respect for white people because of the way they had treated her when she was a slave, and that she proposed to rule them with an iron hand" (Beasley, p. 95). Perhaps she had done so. Yet, as a sympathetic commentator has suggested, some of the same tolerance accorded the transgressions of California's early empire builders might well also be given to this black pioneer.

[Mammy Pleasant's "Memoirs and Autobiog.," prepared by Sam P. Davis, in *Pandex of the Press* (San Francisco), Jan. 1902; Delilah L. Beasley, *The Negro Trail Blazers of Calif.* (1919), pp. 95–97; Sue Bailey Thurman, *Pioneers of Negro Origin in Calif.* (1952), pp. 47–50; Charles C. Dobie, *San Francisco: A Pageant* (1934), chap. xxix; John P. Young, *San Francisco: A Hist. of the Pacific Coast Metropolis* (1912), II, 811; Oscar Lewis and Carroll D. Hall, *Bonanza Inn* (1939); Stephen J. Field, *Personal Reminiscences of Early Days in Calif.* (1893), p. 282; various newspaper accounts, especially San Francisco *Call*, May 7, 1899, *San Francisco Chronicle*, July 9, 1899, Jan. 12, 1904, *San Francisco Examiner*, Oct. 13, 1895, Jan. 12, 1904, *Oakland Tribune*, Sept. 3, 1916, *San Francisco Call-Bulletin*, Oct. 30, 1933. Information about the John Brown episode from Mr. Boyd B. Stutler, Charleston, W.Va. On the streetcar cases, see *Daily Alta Calif.* (San Francisco), Oct. 18, 1866, p. 1; San Francisco *Call*, Feb. 15, 1867, p. 2; and Charles H. Parker, *Digest of Calif. Reports and Statutes* (1869), I, 235. For the Sharon-Hill verdict see L. S. B. Sawyer, *Reports of Cases Decided in the Circuit and District Courts of the U.S. for the Ninth Circuit*, XI (1887), 338. Helen Holdredge, *Mammy Pleasant* (1953), though purportedly based in part on unpublished primary sources, is undocumented and at least partly fictionalized.]

W. SHERMAN SAVAGE

**PLUMMER, Mary Wright** (Mar. 8, 1856–Sept. 21, 1916), librarian, was born in Richmond, Ind., of old Quaker stock. She was the oldest of the six children of Jonathan Wright Plummer and Hannah Ann (Ballard) Plummer, respectively of Maryland and Virginia background. Her paternal grandfather, a physician and a Yale graduate, had moved west to Indiana in 1823. Jonathan Plummer, her father, was a wholesale druggist, at first in Richmond and later in Chicago; he was also an approved minister in the Hicksite branch of the Society of Friends.

Mary graduated from the Friends Academy in Richmond and in 1881 enrolled at Wellesley College for a year of special study. She spent the following four years with her family in Chicago, where she taught school. She also read widely, as she had since childhood, and wrote poems, some of which appeared in such eminent journals as *Scribner's Magazine* and the *Atlantic Monthly*. Her interest in library work was aroused when she saw in a Chicago paper an advertisement for a "School of Library Economy" soon to be opened at Columbia College in New York. Mary Plummer was one of the seventeen women and three men who comprised the first class of this pioneering American school for the training of librarians. Founded and directed by Columbia's librarian,

Melvil Dewey, the school, which opened in January 1887, set high standards for library procedures and for the education of professional librarians. Miss Plummer showed such aptitude that in November 1887, during her second term in the two-year program, she was appointed an instructor in cataloguing.

After graduating, in 1888, she served for two years as cataloguer in the St. Louis Public Library, which was headed by Frederick M. Crunden, one of the leaders of the new library profession. She spent the summer of 1890 in Europe; that fall she returned to accept a position on the staff of the recently established Free Library of Pratt Institute in Brooklyn, N.Y. In 1894 she was made head librarian and put in charge of the library school, which had begun classes at Pratt Institute under her direction in 1890; her principal assistant was JOSEPHINE A. RATHBONE. After a year's leave of absence to travel and study in Europe, primarily in Italy, Miss Plummer returned in September 1895 to help finish planning the Free Library's new building, which opened the following spring. It included two innovations that she had suggested: an art reference department for general use, and a special children's room furnished with child-size tables and chairs, the first of its kind to be architecturally planned in a public library. A firm believer in a child's right to intelligent library service, she advocated special training for children's librarians. She was the author of three volumes for children: *Roy and Ray in Mexico* (1907), *Roy and Ray in Canada* (1908), and *Stories from the Chronicle of the Cid* (1910). In 1904 Miss Plummer resigned as librarian of Pratt Institute in order to devote full time to the Pratt Library School, which flourished under her leadership. Her concern extended to the social life of the students. whom she sought to bring in touch with the varied cultural opportunities of New York City.

Holding a deeply idealistic view of the role of the library and the professional librarian in a democracy, Miss Plummer was a leader among those who sought a more strenuous and exacting training for librarians, and her resourcefulness generally enabled her to put her theories into practice. Perhaps her most significant contribution was her report as chairman of the Committee on Library Training of the American Library Association (1903). This report aroused strong opposition, not only from the staffs of smaller schools that could not provide all the courses recommended, but also from those who believed that library work did not require professional training. Henry L. Elmendorf, superintendent of the Buffalo

Public Library, declared that men "did not need, and were not willing to undergo, two years' instruction in library methods, which after all were neither particularly abstruse or difficult" (quoted in Vann, p. 116). Subsequent reports of 1905 and 1906 also met opposition, although Miss Plummer gradually pacified many critics by including some of them on her committee. The A.L.A. refused to do more than "accept" the committee's report, and it was not until 1912, when the Association of American Library Schools (a direct outgrowth of the committee) was formed, that any accrediting agency existed for library schools. Mary Plummer's own *Hints to Small Libraries* (1894, reprinted 1914) provided a guide even for libraries without professional personnel.

When in 1911 the New York Public Library obtained funds from Andrew Carnegie to establish a library school, Miss Plummer was appointed its principal, although Edwin H. Anderson was technically the "director." She chose the faculty members, prepared announcements, and organized the school for its opening classes in September 1911. As at Pratt, a two-year program was instituted, the first year providing elementary library training, and the second, which was necessary for a degree, offering advanced courses in bibliography, cataloguing, and library management, in addition to practice work in the Public Library itself. Although the school was meant primarily to "secure and train the best possible material in the way of assistants for the New York Public Library" (Trautman, p. 32), it also gave professional training to a significant number of library workers across the country. Miss Plummer served as principal until her death.

Mary Wright Plummer was president of the New York Library Club in 1896–97 and 1913–14, president of the New York State Library Association in 1906, a delegate to the International Congress of Libraries in Paris in 1906, and, the culmination of her career, president of the American Library Association in 1915–16. Firsthand accounts of her activities describe her as a woman of poise and personality, widely read, fluent in French, German, Italian, and Spanish, and delicately witty in her conversation as in her writing. This last quality is especially evident in her paper "The Seven Joys of Reading," first read at a meeting of the New York State Library Association in 1909 and later printed in the *Sewanee Review* (October 1910). Of modest and gentle femininity, effective as a leader, she was held in great affection by her associates. She died of cancer at the home of a brother in Dixon, Ill.,

in 1916, at the age of sixty, and was buried in the Chicago suburb of Glencoe.

[A collection of Miss Plummer's poems was privately printed in 1896. Of particular interest are her articles "The Columbia College School of Library Economy from a Student's Standpoint," *Library Jour.*, Sept.–Oct. 1887, and "The Public Library and the Pursuit of Truth," *ibid.*, Aug. 1916. Biographical sources include: N.Y. Library Club, *Meeting in Memory of Mary Wright Plummer* (1916); obituaries in *Library Jour.*, Oct., Nov., and Dec. 1916; Anne Carroll Moore, "Mary Wright Plummer," *Bull. of Bibliog.*, Jan.–Apr. 1930; Josephine A. Rathbone, "Pioneers of the Library Profession," *Wilson Library Bull.*, June 1949; sketch in *Public Libraries*, Oct. 1915; *Nat. Cyc. Am. Biog.*, XXI, 107–08; *Who's Who in America*, 1916–17; and *N.Y. Times*, Sept. 22, 1916. On her role in library education see Mary W. Plummer et al., "Report of the Committee on Library Training," Am. Library Assoc., *Papers and Proc.*, June 1903; Carl M. White, *The Origins of the Am. Library School* (1961); Sarah K. Vann, *Training for Librarianship before 1923* (1961); Ray Trautman, *A Hist. of the School of Library Service, Columbia Univ.* (1954); and Harry M. Lydenberg, *Hist. of the N.Y. Public Library* (1923). On her father and grandfather, see Andrew W. Young, *Hist. of Wayne County, Ind.* (1872), pp. 428–30; and *Am. Ancestry*, XII (1899), 179. Death record from Ill. Dept. of Public Health.]

RUTH HEWITT HAMILTON

**POCAHONTAS** (1595/96?–March 1616/17), legendary Indian heroine, was presumably born in Virginia, the daughter of Powhatan, great chief of Tidewater Virginia. Her true name was Matoaka, which apparently contains an Algonkian root meaning "to play, playful." "Pocahontas" was a descriptive pet name which possibly meant something like "frolicsome."

Nearly half of Pocahontas' real life can be fairly accurately reconstructed from references in contemporary English sources. Her first appearance in recorded history was on the occasion of her intervention on behalf of Capt. John Smith, a leader of the newly founded English colony at Jamestown, when she was the "means to deliver" him from death, on or about Dec. 30, 1607. Smith, on an exploring expedition, strayed much too near to Powhatan's hereditary stronghold between the Pamunkey River and present-day Richmond. His small party was ambushed, and two men were killed. Smith was taken prisoner, his Indian guide having revealed his status as a *werowance*, or petty chief, of the "strangers." Perhaps already known to his captors as both just and fearless, Smith cleverly revealed a bag of such powerful and mysterious "medicine" as a pocket compass, and was soon led before Powhatan, overlord of all Virginia's werowances.

Nearly ten years later, Smith first wrote down what happened, in "A relation to Queene Anne, of Pocahontas": ". . . taken prisoner by the power of *Powhatan* their chiefe King, I receiued from this great Saluage exceeding great courtesie, especially from his sonne Nantaquaus, . . . and his sister *Pocahontas*, the Kings most deare and wel-beloued daughter, being but a childe of twelue or thirteene yeeres of age, whose compassionate pitifull heart, of my desperate estate, gaue me much cause to respect her: I being the first Christian this proud King and his grim attendants euer saw: . . . After some six [correctly, three] weeks fatting amongst those Saluage Courtiers, at the minute of my execution, she [Pocahontas] hazarded the beating out of her owne braines to saue mine, and not onely that, but so preuailed with her father, that I was safely conducted to *Iames*towne . . ." (*Generall Historie*, p. 121). Later, in 1624, the account was vividly expanded, with what regard for the truth is not known.

In any event, soon after Smith's return to Jamestown on Jan. 2, 1608, Powhatan's Indians began to supply the colony with food, "and this reliefe . . . was commonly brought vs by this Lady *Pocahontas*." Smith described her at that time as a child, "which . . . for wit, and spirit, [was] the only Nonpariel" of the country (*True Relation*). To show how he thought of her that year, the last sentence in Smith's brief word list of the Powhatan language may be quoted: "*Kekaten pokahontas patiaquagh niugh* [for *ningh*] *tanks manotyens neer mowchick rawrenock audowgh*. Bid Pokahontas bring hither two little baskets, & I wil giue her white beads to make her a chaine" (*Map of Virginia*).

In addition to these casual visits, Pocahontas went to Jamestown as her father's emissary in May 1608, seeking the release of some Indian prisoners, and not long thereafter, when Smith and a handful of companions visited Powhatan's residence and were entertained with a wild "Mascarado," she ran out to assure the edgy Englishmen that the frenzied dance was all pure fun. Once, in 1609, she seems even to have warned Smith of a surprise attack planned by her father (*Proceedings*, p. 103). But these ministrations virtually came to an end when Smith was forced to return to England the following October, owing to the combination of a serious injury and incipient mutiny.

Smith's appreciation of Pocahontas as a little girl was shared by William Strachey, who landed in Jamestown in 1610 and remained as Secretary of the colony until late in 1611. Strachey called her "wanton," undoubtedly in the sense of frisky or naughty, and reported stories of her cartwheeling "all the Fort over" before his arrival, naked as any other Indian girl or boy, adding that she was married (about 1609) to a "private Captaine called Kocoum," otherwise unidentified. Meanwhile, she is said to have saved the life of young Henry Spelman early in 1610.

Nothing more is known about Pocahontas until the spring of 1613, when Capt. Samuel Argall of Jamestown went trading up the Potomac at the same time that Pocahontas was visiting an ally or tributary of her father's in that region. Learning that she wished to see the English settlers again, Argall, a practical man, quickly decided to lure her aboard his ship and hold her hostage, for the release of English personnel and matériel and the betterment of general Anglo-Indian relations. With the aid of wiles and the gift of a copper pot, Argall soon sailed back to Jamestown with Pocahontas handsomely lodged aboard. The governor, Sir Thomas Gates, received her kindly, treated her as a guest rather than as a prisoner, and placed her under the care of Sir Thomas Dale, Marshal of Virginia. Since she was eager to learn English ways, including religion, Dale in turn seems to have entrusted her to the Rev. Alexander Whitaker, the minister at Henrico, fifty-odd miles up the James River from Jamestown.

Somehow during the summer of 1613 Pocahontas met John Rolfe, a colonist whose experiments with tobacco seed imported from the West Indies were to be of far-reaching importance for Virginia. A widower some ten years her senior, Rolfe was at once drawn to Pocahontas, and in a lengthy letter to Dale he sought permission to marry her. He was aware, he wrote, that she was "an unbelieving creature," but he was willing to act for England's good, and in the service of Jamestown. Pocahontas, as yet without benefit of Christian rationale, may have foreseen peace for her people, and she may have been in love with Rolfe. Whatever the facts, with Dale's approval she was instructed in Christianity, baptized Rebecca, and, about Apr. 5, 1614, married to Rolfe. Although Powhatan granted a tract of land to the couple, it is not certain where they lived or where their only child, Thomas, was born. Certainly, the marriage ushered in a period of far more peaceful relations between the colonists and the Indians.

In 1616 Dale invited Rolfe and his wife and

son to sail with him for England, where they arrived early in June, accompanied by "some ten or twelve old and younge of that countrie [Virginia]" (Chamberlain, II, 12). Tradition has it that they visited Rolfe's mother in Heacham Hall, Norfolk, and it is known that they stayed for a while in London and that the Virginia Company granted a £4 weekly allowance to Pocahontas personally. Later, because of the "bad air" in the city, the family moved to nearby Brentford. Some elements in London society made much of the "Indian Princess," who by then, Smith writes, had been "taught to speake such *English* as might well bee vnderstood, . . . and was become very formall and ciuill after our *English* manner" (*Generall Historie,* p. 121). Others, however, murmured about her "tricking up and high stile and titles" (Chamberlain, II, 57). John, Smith meanwhile wrote his "Relation to Queene Anne" and visited Pocahontas in Brentford. Eventually, she was presented to King James I and Queen Anne and on Jan. 6, 1617, attended Ben Jonson's masque *The Vision of Delight* with them, her father's councillor Uttamatomakkin beside her in native garb.

The following March, Rolfe had to return to Virginia with his family, over Pocahontas' protests. The same Captain Argall who had kidnapped Pocahontas four years earlier commanded the ship, but contrary winds delayed their departure. Before they could leave the Thames, Pocahontas died, probably a victim of a wet, blustery winter. She was buried in the parish church of St. George at Gravesend on Mar. 21. Though she was apparently far from beautiful, she possessed natural dignity, and no one has gainsaid her nobility of character. Her son, Thomas Rolfe, was to bequeath her heritage to a long line of descendants in America (some say in England as well). But the Pocahontas of history lay all but forgotten for nearly a century.

The Pocahontas legend, which eventually came to engulf the facts, has had a long literary life, though it has never taken root in folk tales or songs. Its germ can be found in the planter Robert Beverley's *The History and Present State of Virginia* (1705). *The Female American* (1767), by "Unca Eliza Winkfield," an unidentified English writer, was the first fictional work on the subject. A British sailor named John Davis took full advantage of the romantic potential of the episode in writing a novelette, *Captain Smith and Princess Pocahontas,* and a historical novel, *The First Settlers of Virginia,* both published in 1805. In these, the full-blown legend was born, although the American Wil-

liam Wirt had already eulogized Pocahontas in *The Letters of the British Spy* (1803). James Nelson Barker of Philadelphia produced the first Smith-Pocahontas drama, *The Indian Princess,* in 1808, to be followed by George Washington Parke Custis' better play, *Pocahontas,* in 1830. In general, however, playwrights and novelists have not been successful with the story. The legend of the beautiful Indian maiden who saves the dashing captain for love was forged primarily in verse, and appropriately in Virginia. Almost every nineteenth-century Virginian versifier except Poe made his contribution to it. In the twentieth century, poets of greater fame have found in Pocahontas a symbol of America. Carl Sandburg's "Cool Tombs," Vachel Lindsay's "Our Mother, Pocahontas," Hart Crane's "Powhatan's Daughter" (part of his longer poem *The Bridge*), and Stephen Vincent Benét's *Western Star,* an unfinished epic published posthumously in 1943, all bear witness to the continuing evocative power of the Pocahontas story.

[Primary sources: John Smith, *A True Relation* (1608), *A Map of Virginia* and *Proceedings* (1612), and *The Generall Historie of Virginia* (1624), of which the 1608 and 1612 works appear *literatim* and annotated in *The Jamestown Voyages under the First Charter, 1606–1609* (Philip L. Barbour, ed., 2 vols., 1969), and all three in the collected *Works* (Edward Arber, ed., 1884; reprinted with a new introduction by A. G. Bradley, 2 vols., 1910); William Strachey, *The Historie of Travell into Virginia Britania* (Louis B. Wright and Virginia Freund, eds., 1953); Ralph Hamor, *A True Discourse of the Present State of Virginia* (reprinted with an introduction by A. L. Rowse, 1957); Samuel Purchas, *Hakluytus Posthumus, or Purchas His Pilgrimes* (reprinted, 20 vols., 1905–07; see vol. XIX); *The Letters of John Chamberlain* (Norman E. McClure, ed., 2 vols., 1939). Secondary sources: Philip L. Barbour, *The Three Worlds of Captain John Smith* (1964) and *Pocahontas and Her World* (1970), which contains John Rolfe's letter to Sir Thomas Dale in complete *literatim* transcription; Philip Young, "The Mother of Us All: Pocahontas Reconsidered," *Kenyon Rev.,* Summer 1962; Richard Beale Davis, *Intellectual Life in Jefferson's Virginia* (1964); Jay B. Hubbell, "The Smith-Pocahontas Story in Literature," *Va. Mag. of Hist. and Biog.,* July 1957; Wyndham Robertson, *Pocahontas, Alias Matoaka, and Her Descendants* (1887). The only clearly contemporary likeness of Pocahontas is the engraving by Simon van de Passe, made during her stay in England. The oil portrait now in the National Portrait Gallery, Smithsonian Institution, Washington, D.C., seems to be a later work, made from the engraving. There is an idealized Pocahontas statue in Jamestown, by the sculptor William Ordway Partridge, and a purely imaginary painting, "Baptism of Pocahontas," by John

Gatsby Chapman, in the rotunda of the U.S. Capitol.]

PHILIP L. BARBOUR

POE, Elizabeth Arnold Hopkins (1787?–Dec. 8, 1811), actress, mother of Edgar Allan Poe, was probably the daughter of Henry (William Henry?) Arnold and Elizabeth Smith, who were married at St. George's Church, Hanover Square, London, on May 18, 1784. Both parents were actors at Covent Garden, and there is much information concerning her mother's acting and singing roles there; her father seems to have died about 1790. Mrs. Arnold continued to play engagements at Covent Garden until late 1795. She then set sail for the United States with her daughter and an actor named Charles Tubbs; they arrived in Boston on Jan. 3, 1796. Either before leaving England or just after arrival, she and Tubbs were married, and the two went to Portland, Maine, in an unsuccessful attempt to organize a theatre there. They then joined a troupe which played in Charleston, S.C., where they probably succumbed to yellow fever, for by mid-1798 they disappear from the records. Accompanied by two of her parents' friends, Elizabeth then joined a company in Philadelphia.

Elizabeth Arnold had made her first stage appearance at the age of nine in the old Boston Theatre on Apr. 15, 1796, at the end of the second act of *The Mysteries of the Castle.* From then until the end of her brief life she sang, danced, and acted numerous roles in many theatres along the Eastern seaboard, almost always to warm approbation. Her earliest parts were often boys, such as the Duke of York in *Richard III* and Little Pickle in *The Spoiled Child;* then followed rustic maids like Phoebe in the opera *Rosina,* young gentlewomen like Sophia in the popular *Road to Ruin,* and light farcical roles like Biddy Bellair in Garrick's *Miss in Her Teens.*

In Philadelphia in the spring of 1800 she met her first husband, Charles D. Hopkins, who made his debut on Mar. 14 of that year as Tony Lumpkin. He appears to have been a successful comedian. They were married sometime between June 12 and Aug. 11, 1802, and joined another company of actors, the Virginia Players. Not long afterward, however, in October 1805, Hopkins died, and the next spring (between Mar. 14 and Apr. 9, 1806) the young actress became the wife of a fellow player, David Poe. Her early remarriage has caused Hervey Allen and other Poe biographers to raise a critical eyebrow, but Arthur Hobson Quinn in his *Edgar Allan Poe* (p. 24) points out that "the conditions of the-

atrical life at that time made the lot of a widowed girl of eighteen difficult if not impossible." Her new husband, born in Baltimore in 1784, had deserted the study of law for the stage in 1803. An attractive man, he occasionally suffered from a defect in pronunciation which caused biting comment from newspaper critics.

After their marriage the couple acted together in Richmond, Philadelphia, and New York, and then for three years at the Federal Street Theatre, Boston. Here two of their children were born: William Henry (Leonard?) on Jan. 30, 1807, and Edgar on Jan. 19, 1809. Their last child, Rosalie, was probably born in Richmond on Dec. 20, 1810, though both the place and the date are in doubt. Perhaps the three years in Boston were Mrs. Poe's happiest. In 1807 and again in 1808 she played Cordelia to James Fennell's Lear, and in 1809 she acted Juliet to John Howard Payne's youthful Romeo and Ophelia to his Hamlet. It is probable that the famous actor Thomas Abthorpe Cooper, with whom she had acted in Boston, brought the Poes to the Park Theatre, New York, in 1809, where she supported Cooper as Ophelia and Desdemona, among other roles. Here, as frequently occurred during his career, David Poe was violently and unfairly censured by a critic, and after that October he drops from sight. If he did not desert his wife, he was either unemployed or an invalid and, in addition to her two small children, a drain upon her resources. Several appeals for help for the destitute Elizabeth Poe were printed in the newspapers in the course of the following year. In the fall of 1811 she joined a theatrical company in Richmond, Va. She died there that December, perhaps from pneumonia, and was buried in St. John's churchyard. Her children were brought up by three separate families, Edgar by John Allan, a Richmond merchant, and his wife.

Arthur Quinn's solid research reveals that upon her death, at the age of twenty-four, Mrs. Poe had enacted, besides numerous singing and dancing parts, 201 varied roles, both heavy and light. Often she portrayed two or three characters on the same evening. She was a pleasing, handsome, versatile actress. Her popularity, though minor, was nevertheless pronounced among both audiences and critics. Moreover, her life and career poignantly, yet accurately, reflect the theatrical picture of her time.

[The definitive source is Arthur Hobson Quinn's *Edgar Allan Poe* (1941). See also Hervey Allen, *Israfel: The Life and Times of Edgar Allan Poe*

(2 vols., 1926); George C. D. Odell, *Annals of the N.Y. Stage*, vol. II (1927).]

ALBERT E. JOHNSON

**POITEVENT, Eliza Jane.** *See* NICHOLSON, Eliza Jane Poitevent Holbrook.

**POLK, Sarah Childress** (Sept. 4, 1803–Aug. 14, 1891), wife of James K. Polk, eleventh president of the United States, was born near Murfreesboro in Rutherford County, Tenn., the younger of two daughters and third of four children. Her father, Joel Childress, a native of Campbell County, Va., had settled by the 1790's in Sumner County, Tenn., where he married Elizabeth Whitsitt. Moving to Rutherford County, he became a prosperous planter, merchant, tavern keeper, land speculator, and militia major, frequently entertaining Gen. Andrew Jackson and other prominent Tennesseans during sessions of the state legislature at Murfreesboro. Sarah Childress was thus born into the upper stratum of Tennessee's pioneer society. After private lessons from the teacher of a creditable boys' academy at Murfreesboro and a season at a girls' school in Nashville, the thirteen-year-old Sarah was sent to the best girls' school in the South, the Female Academy conducted by the Moravians at Salem, N.C. She was, however, called home before completing the course by the illness and death of her father. Though he left a splendid estate, much of it was soon lost as a result of the panic of 1819 and poor management by the executor.

Sarah Childress first met her future husband when James Knox Polk was a student with her brother at the Murfreesboro Academy. They did not become well acquainted, however, until some years later when he began coming to Murfreesboro as clerk of the state senate. They became engaged following his election to the legislature in 1823 and were married Jan. 1, 1824. Settling down among her husband's numerous kin in Columbia, Tenn., Sarah took a keen interest in his political career, which led from the legislature to fourteen years' service in Congress (1825–39), the last four as Speaker of the House. As the Polks were childless, she was free to accompany her husband to Washington for the annual sessions of Congress.

Sarah Polk's clustering black curls, handsome dress, and vivacity went far to relieve the severity of her plain, tight-lipped face; and her contemporaries found in her a charm that more than made up for any lack of physical beauty. Ready conversation and a vigorous intellect made her a favorite in Washington drawing rooms, despite the stubbornness with which she observed her Presbyterian scruples against horse racing and the theatre. To her physically frail, hard-driving, introverted husband she became increasingly indispensable, as secretary, political counselor, nurse, and emotional resource. This was particularly true after he left Congress in 1839 to battle uphill and single-handedly to restore Andrew Jackson's Tennessee to Democratic control. Although he won his first race for governor, he lost two bids for reelection before the stunning reversal of his nomination and election to the presidency in 1844.

Mrs. Polk's social grace and her long experience in official circles made her a superbly qualified First Lady; and though she instituted strict Sabbath observance in the White House and an unpopular ban on dancing at presidential functions, she was warmly praised even by her husband's political opponents. She failed, however, in her most difficult task—keeping her husband from overwork; Polk left the White House completely worn out at fifty-four, to die three months later.

For the next forty-two years Mrs. Polk lived on in the handsome Nashville mansion, Polk Place, that her husband had provided for their retirement. There she brought up a great-niece, Sarah Polk Jetton, who, with her husband and their daughter, Saidee, lived with her until her death. Over the years Mrs. Polk became a national monument and relic. During the Civil War, as battle lines swept back and forth through Nashville, Union and Confederate commanders in turn paid their respects. The Tennessee legislature called on her at each session, and every prominent personage and group that came to Nashville did the same. Except to attend the Presbyterian church on Sundays, however, she rarely left the house. She died there in her eighty-eighth year and was buried beside her husband in the handsome vault she had erected at Polk Place; the tomb was later removed to the grounds of the Tennessee state capitol.

[The fullest account of Sarah Polk is found in Anson and Fanny Nelson, *Memorials of Sarah Childress Polk* (1892). Additional detail is contained in Charles G. Sellers, Jr., *James K. Polk, Jacksonian: 1795–1843* (1957) and *James K. Polk, Continentalist: 1843–1848* (1966). The James K. Polk Papers, Library of Congress, contain many letters between Mrs. Polk and her husband and much other material on their common life; a selection of her letters to Polk, 1839–43, has been published in the *Tenn. Hist. Quart.*, June and Sept. 1952.]

CHARLES SELLERS

POLYBLANK, Ellen Albertina. *See* ROGERS, Elizabeth Ann.

PORTER, Charlotte Endymion (Jan. 6, 1857–Jan. 16, 1942), co-founder, with **Helen Archibald CLARKE** (Nov. 13, 1860–Feb. 8, 1926), of *Poet Lore* magazine, was born in Towanda, Pa., one of the three children and the only daughter of Dr. Henry Clinton Porter, a native of Connecticut, and his wife, Elisa Eleanor Betts. Christened Helen Charlotte, she later added the more poetic "Endymion." After graduating from Wells College, Aurora, N.Y., in 1875, she briefly studied Shakespeare and French drama at the Sorbonne. In 1883, having settled in Philadelphia, she became editor of *Shakespeariana*, a periodical launched that year by the Shakespeare Society of New York. In this undertaking she had the warm encouragement and support of Horace Howard Furness, the eminent Philadelphia Shakespeare scholar.

Among the articles published by Miss Porter in *Shakespeariana* was one by Helen Clarke of Philadelphia, a young lady several years her junior. The article, a discussion of Shakespeare's music, reflected Miss Clarke's deep musical interest. Her Scottish grandfather had received a doctorate in music from Edinburgh University; her father, Hugh Archibald Clarke, a native of Toronto, Canada, was an organist, conductor, and composer. He moved to Philadelphia with his London-born wife, Jane Searle, shortly before Helen's birth, eventually to become a professor of music at the University of Pennsylvania. An only child, Helen was educated privately. In 1881, before the University of Pennsylvania was officially opened to women, she entered as a special student, earning a certificate of proficiency in music two years later. Drawn to Miss Porter by their mutual interest in Shakespeare, she discovered another common bond in the Browning Society of Philadelphia, of which both were founding members. Soon an inseparable friendship had been formed.

Charlotte Porter, meanwhile, was finding her *Shakespeariana* position constricting, and in 1887, when her plans for broadening the scope of the magazine were rejected, she resigned. Throughout 1888, during a brief tenure as editor of the *Ethical Record,* she planned, with Miss Clarke, a new literary venture. The result was *Poet Lore,* launched in January 1889 as a monthly magazine "devoted to Shakespeare, Browning, and the Comparative Study of Literature." In 1891 the two editors moved to Boston at the invitation of Dana Estes, an enterprising publisher who offered free office space in return for advertising. Encountering publishing difficulties in 1896, the editors transformed their magazine into a quarterly.

For its first thirteen years *Poet Lore* mirrored the taste and editorial standards of its founders. They selected the contents and frequently wrote articles of opinion and criticism, sometimes signing them "H.A.C.," for "Helen and Charlotte." Partisans alike of Browning and Shakespeare, they announced in the first issue that what Shakespeare had been to the sixteenth century Browning was to the nineteenth —the seminal figure who would determine the future course of literary history. (Helen Clarke, who had been attracted to physics and philosophy through studying the mathematics of musical harmony, was fascinated by the speculations of Herbert Spencer and John Fiske and believed firmly that literary development followed incontrovertible evolutionary laws.) Typical early issues of *Poet Lore* featured essays about Shakespeare and Browning, literary club news, notices of Shakespearean revivals, reviews of books related to Elizabethan or Victorian literature, and outlines for home and group study. The first three volumes contained more than forty articles on Browning and a similar number on Shakespeare. In this heyday of the literary society, and particularly of Shakespeare and Browning clubs, *Poet Lore* adroitly tapped an already keen interest and quickly built a substantial subscription list.

Indeed, the Misses Porter and Clarke became notable entrepreneurs in the flourishing Browning industry. The two-volume selection of the poet's work which they jointly edited in 1896 was followed in rapid succession by an edition of *The Ring and the Book* (1898); a twelve-volume pocket set of Browning's complete works (1898); and, in 1900, *Browning Study Programmes* and a six-volume edition of Elizabeth Barrett Browning. The two women were pillars of the Boston Browning Society, Miss Porter as a long-time (1903–36) vice-president and Miss Clarke in a variety of offices. In 1899 the society staged Helen Clarke's dramatization of *Pippa Passes,* and in 1902–03 Charlotte Porter's stage adaptation of *The Return of the Druses* was performed in Boston and elsewhere. Standing high in Brahmin literary circles, they became charter members of JULIA WARD HOWE's Boston Authors' Club.

Although the founders' regard for Browning and Shakespeare never diminished, *Poet Lore* increasingly reflected their broadening literary interests. By the mid-1890's the Shakespeare-Browning axis had been dismantled, news of the literary societies was disappearing, and the editors were heralding the new world literature they had confidently predicted. Almost alone among American literary journals, *Poet Lore* paid consistent and serious attention not only to contemporary European writing—including that of Scandinavia, Armenia, Greece, Iberia, and Russia—but also to the literature of the Middle East, India, and the Orient. Seeking European writers little known in the United States, they reprinted works by Björnstjerne Björnson, Selma Lagerlöf, Anatole France, Paul Bourget, Gerhart Hauptmann, and Hermann Sudermann. Miss Porter's translation of Maurice Maeterlinck's *Les Aveugles* (*The Sightless*) was published in 1893, a scant two years after the first French performances of his plays. *Clever Tales*, an anthology of European short stories culled from the pages of *Poet Lore* (most of them the editors' own translations), appeared in 1897. Except for the essays of Gamaliel Bradford, Jr., the two editors gave little space to American authors, although in reviews they praised Bliss Carman, Paul Laurence Dunbar, and Edward Rowland Sill. Miss Porter and Miss Clarke did, however, found the American Music Society and the American Drama Society—later the Drama League of America—with the intent of encouraging native artistic expression. Miss Clarke became president of the former organization, Miss Porter of the latter.

In 1903, as the founders' outside literary work multiplied, *Poet Lore* was sold to Richard G. Badger. Though no longer enjoying the undivided attention of either woman, nor so clearly bearing their individual stamp, *Poet Lore* still reflected their cosmopolitan editorial influence and their enthusiasm for such authors as Arthur Schnitzler, Maxim Gorki, Gabriele D'Annunzio, and Rabindranath Tagore. During the First World War they published Greek and Ukrainian folk songs, Japanese hokku verse and Noh plays, and translations of Rainer Maria Rilke and Paul Verlaine without regard to national rivalries. The two women were obviously tiring, however. Their liberalism remained apparent with the publication of Russian and Yiddish writers and of works by W. E. B. Du Bois and Paul Green, but they allowed others to guide *Poet Lore* through the demanding 1920's, when a host of "little magazines" competed for the attention of the avantgarde.

As their involvement with *Poet Lore* diminished, the careers of Charlotte Porter and Helen Clarke, hitherto so closely intertwined, diverged somewhat. Miss Clarke, a gifted amateur, pursued a variety of interests. As early as 1892 she had published *Apparitions*, a volume of songs with piano accompaniment. This was followed by several children's operettas and, in 1912, by *Gethsemane*, a "symbolic rhapsody in verse" for which Gustav Strube composed a musical score. Her dramatization of two Browning poems, for which her father wrote the music, was produced in Boston's Plymouth Theatre in April 1915. Miss Clarke was also the author of numerous works of literary popularization, including *A Child's Guide to Mythology* (1908), *Browning's England* (1908), and *Hawthorne's Country* (1910). In 1915 she organized a weekly "Philosophy Class" (renamed "The Symposium" in 1920) at which Boston ladies discussed art, literature, music, and social questions. Charlotte Porter, by contrast, favoring more scholarly and secluded pursuits, continued to translate the works of various modern poets and dramatists. (A niece, Helen Tracy Lowe-Porter, was later to achieve distinction as Thomas Mann's English translator.) Her most ambitious undertaking was a forty-volume *First Folio Edition of Shakespeare* which appeared between 1903 and 1913.

The long editorial intimacy of the two friends was mirrored in their personal lives. They exchanged rings, lived together in Boston and Cambridge, and spent their summers at Ardensea, Charlotte Porter's cottage on the Isle au Haut in Maine's Penobscot Bay. Miss Porter's *Lips of Music* (1919) is a collection of Sapphic love lyrics originally published in various periodicals, some under a masculine pseudonym. The friendship ended only with the death of Helen Clarke, who succumbed to angina pectoris in Boston in 1926, at the age of sixty-five. Charlotte Porter, surviving until 1942, spent increasing periods of time at Isle au Haut, which gradually became her all-absorbing interest. Reduced in circumstances as she grew older, she eventually became dependent upon the generosity of friends. She entered a Melrose, Mass., nursing home in 1941 and died there some months later, at eighty-five, of cardiovascular disease. Her ashes, like those of Miss Clarke, were scattered at Isle au Haut.

[Melvin H. Bernstein, "The Early Years of Poet Lore, 1889–1929," *Poet Lore*, Spring 1966; Charlotte E. Porter, "A Story of Poet Lore," *ibid.*, Autumn 1926; Frank L. Mott, *A Hist. of Am. Magazines*, vols. III and IV (1938–57); Boston Browning Soc., *The Year Book of the Golden Anniversary* (1937); *Woman's Who's Who of America*, 1914–15, entries on both Miss Porter and Miss Clarke; letters and MSS. of the Boston Authors' Club, Boston Public Library; death records from Mass. Registrar of Vital Statistics. See also, on

Miss Clarke: *Who Was Who in America*, vol. I (1942); *Boston Transcript*, Feb. 9, 1926; alumni records and archives of the Univ. of Pa. On Miss Porter: *Who's Who in America*, 1926–27; *Boston Herald*, Jan. 19, 1942; Wells College archives; information from Mrs. Arthur H. Tully, Cambridge, Mass. Though Miss Porter's birth year is commonly given as 1859, her death certificate lists her age as 85 years, 10 days.]

MELVIN H. BERNSTEIN

**PORTER, Eleanor Hodgman** (Dec. 19, 1868– May 21, 1920), author, is immortalized in the American language by the name of her chief literary creation, Pollyanna, a little girl of dauntless optimism whose "game" of looking for the "glad" side of all misfortunes reformed innumerable misanthropes, snobs, and handicapped children in fiction, and apparently in real life as well. *Pollyanna* entirely dominates any evaluation of Mrs. Porter, and rightly so, for Mrs. Porter's biography is of consequence only in that the materials for all of her sixteen novels and eight collections of short stories are more or less drawn from her youthful experiences.

Eleanor Emily Hodgman was born and grew up in the White Mountain village of Littleton, N.H., the younger of two children and only daughter of Francis Fletcher Hodgman and Llewella French (Woolson) Hodgman, both natives of Littleton. Her father was a druggist; her sickly mother, as Eleanor was fond of repeating, was a direct descendant of Gov. William Bradford of the Plymouth Colony. Like her forebears, Eleanor was a Congregationalist. She attended public schools until ill health forced her to give up high school and live in the outdoors; when well enough she resumed studies under private tutors. As a child she showed some talent for writing but still more for music. She studied voice in Boston privately and at the New England Conservatory of Music, and subsequently gained a local reputation singing in church choirs and at concerts and giving private lessons. On May 3, 1892, she was married to John Lyman Porter of Corinth, Vt., a businessman who became president of the National Separator and Machine Company. After sojourns, over the next ten years, in Chattanooga, Tenn., New York City, and Springfield, Vt., they settled in Cambridge, Mass., where she and her husband lived in an apartment with her invalid mother; they evidently had no children.

In 1901 Mrs. Porter gave up music and devoted herself to writing; by 1915 she claimed to have published some two hundred short stories in various magazines and newspapers. Her initial novel, *Cross Currents*

(1907), was fairly well received, but her first major success was *Miss Billy* (1911), in which a little girl comes to live with three bachelor brothers, revolutionizing their lives. This was followed in 1913 by *Pollyanna*. The critics and the public were at once enthusiastic. *Pollyanna* was eighth on the best-seller list that year; in 1914 it was second, and in 1915 the newly published sequel, *Pollyanna Grows Up*, was in fourth place. For four more years Mrs. Porter's books were to be found among the annual ten best-selling works of fiction: *Just David* (1916), *The Road to Understanding* (1917), *Oh, Money! Money!* (1918), and *Mary Marie* (1920). As for *Pollyanna*, the novel was translated into at least eight languages; was adapted to the stage and had a successful run on Broadway in 1916; and was made into a motion picture by Mary Pickford in 1920 and again by Walt Disney as late as 1960. Her name was given to commercial products and to a game. By 1917 Mrs. Porter's publishers had trademarked the words "Pollyanna" and "Glad," had issued a "Glad Calendar" for recording good deeds, and had published a collection of juvenilia in the *Pollyanna Annual: The Yearly Glad Book* (1917). After Mrs. Porter's death they continued the series as juvenile literature written by Harriet Lummis Smith and Elizabeth Borton until over two million Pollyanna books had been sold.

The reason for the popularity of *Pollyanna* among supposedly literate adults is puzzling to a later generation. No strong-minded woman could identify herself with Mrs. Porter's little heroines, who drop out of school at the slightest illness or social reverse. Her novels are filled with invalids, not-so-good female story writers, music lovers, and village types. But rural goodness and cheery optimism commanded a wide readership in the early twentieth century, as ALICE HEGAN RICE, KATE DOUGLAS WIGGIN, and GENE STRATTON-PORTER had already demonstrated. Despite critics' agreement about lack of artistry, depth, and range, moreover, Mrs. Porter remains an excellent storyteller. Furthermore, she keeps her ear to the ground, incorporating contemporary muckraking themes in what are essentially sentimental novels: *Cross Currents* deals with child labor, *Pollyanna* with insincere and overorganized women's charity associations, *Pollyanna Grows Up* with slum landlordship, and *Mary Marie* with divorce. She also writes with humor, acknowledging that Pollyanna is something of a social nuisance among adults and freely noting when one of her characters drops into the style of the romantic novel. This last trait camouflages her essential sentimentality.

Mrs. Porter had devised a formula according to which an author could, without preaching or moralizing, reinforce the American reader's native optimism, his faith in Christian virtues, and his democratic belief in social leveling. In Mrs. Porter's hands the formula was Pollyanna and her "glad game," whereby innocence and purity brought people with artificial reserve, with hypocritical social consciences, and with legitimate complaints about the bleakness of life all to one simple, uneducated, childish level. A compromise between reform and gentility, between gentility and democratic leveling, is Mrs. Porter's peculiar achievement.

Eleanor H. Porter was much the sort of person her books reflect. An interviewer in 1918 found her "a little woman, blonde, youthful looking, her light and fluffy hair neatly combed, her blue eyes—'laughing eyes'—changing expression rapidly with her thoughts." She earnestly defended her emphasis on "the agreeable, decent qualities of life" (Overton, pp. 108, 117). Her literary career was cut short at the age of fifty-one by pulmonary tuberculosis. She died at her Cambridge home and was buried in Mount Auburn Cemetery, Cambridge. Some of her short stories were collected and published during the five years following her death.

[For contemporary apologetics and Mrs. Porter's literary theory, see Grant Overton, *The Women Who Make Our Novels* (1918), and Grace I. Colbron, "The Popularity of Pollyanna," *Bookman*, May 1915; for an ironic nostalgic view, Robert Shankland, "She Was Glad, Glad, Glad!" *Good Housekeeping*, July 1947; for an indication of the validity of Mrs. Porter's "formula," see movie review in *America*, May 28, 1960, p. 320. Biographical sources: *Who Was Who in America*, vol. I (1942); *Nat. Cyc. Am. Biog.*, XVIII, 382; *Boston Transcript*, May 22, 1920 (sec. 2); and Overton, above. See also, on her total sales and her literary context, James D. Hart, *The Popular Book* (1950). Birth and family information from Town Clerk, Littleton, N.H., and Boston city directories; death record from Mass. Registrar of Vital Statistics.]

FRED E. H. SCHROEDER

PORTER, Eliza Emily Chappell (Nov. 5, 1807–Jan. 1, 1888), teacher and Civil War relief worker, was born in Geneseo, N.Y., the fourth daughter and eighth of the nine children of Robert and Elizabeth (Kneeland) Chappell, who had moved west from Connecticut. After the death in 1811 of her father, a farmer of French and English ancestry, Eliza spent several homesick years with well-to-do relatives in Franklin, N.Y., returning to Geneseo when she was twelve. At fourteen she joined the Presbyterian Church, to which her intensely religious mother belonged, but not until six years later, in the midst of a grave illness, did she experience a long-hoped-for sense of salvation. Recovering, she moved with her mother to Rochester, N.Y., where in 1828 she participated as a children's worker in the revivals of the Rev. Charles G. Finney, who later recalled her as "the most Christlike spirit I ever met" (Porter, *Eliza Chappell Porter*, p. 28).

Though her own schooling had been meager, Eliza had begun teaching at sixteen. Now, in Rochester, she opened an "infant school" patterned on the Pestalozzian schools being started in New York City by JOANNA GRAHAM BETHUNE to bring religiously oriented instruction to young children of the poor. In 1831, after her mother's death, she traveled to the frontier outpost of Mackinac Island as teacher to the children of Robert Stuart, a devout Presbyterian and resident partner of the American Fur Company. Teaching the children of local Indian half-breeds as well as those of Stuart and his associates, Miss Chappell became convinced more firmly than ever that the infant school movement had been "designed by God to open the way for the missionary of the cross" (*ibid.*, p. 62). Stomach hemorrhages forced her to leave Mackinac in September 1832; she spent that winter traveling in New York, visiting the schools of Mrs. Bethune and others, and enlisting teachers and support for infant schools in the Northwest.

In July 1833, after returning to the Northwest long enough to open and staff another school in the French and Indian settlement of St. Ignace, near Mackinac, she moved on to Chicago, then a churchless frontier settlement adjoining Fort Dearborn. Here she soon inaugurated a school in a log cabin owned by John Stephen Wright, real estate promoter and one of the "praying men" of the town. By December the school had won praise from the *Chicago Democrat*, and the following year it received an appropriation of public funds. Transferring her school in January 1834 to the Presbyterian church newly erected by the Rev. Jeremiah Porter, a missionary from Hadley, Mass., whom she had known at Mackinac, Miss Chappell soon began to enroll older girls from the outlying communities as well, hoping to train them as teachers. By the end of the year, however, exhausted by her labors, she again fell seriously ill.

Upon her recovery, she and Porter were married, on June 15, 1835, in Rochester, N.Y. They had nine children, six of whom survived infancy: James Wolcott, Charlotte, Edwards, Henry Dwight, Mary Harriet, and Robert

Otto, though the last, born in 1852, died at seven. In November 1835 Porter accepted a pastorate in Peoria, Ill., and, two years later, in Farmington. In 1840 he moved with his family to Green Bay, Wis., where he remained for the next eighteen years as pastor of its Presbyterian church. Managing a large and cheerful household, Mrs. Porter was tireless in good works and in 1857 established a New England-style academy from which the first graded schools in Green Bay later developed. In 1858 the Porters returned to Chicago, where Jeremiah Porter assumed charge of Edwards Congregational Chapel, a city mission.

In October 1861, soon after the outbreak of the Civil War, Eliza Porter became "directress," or office manager, of the Chicago (later the Northwestern) Sanitary Commission, a voluntary wartime agency founded to solicit contributions of food, medical dressings, and other supplies for use in military hospitals and at the front. By the following spring, however, she had become convinced that she could be more useful in the field. The battle of Shiloh (Apr. 6–7, 1862) found Mrs. Porter in Cairo, Ill., to which she had escorted a group of Chicago women volunteers for hospital duty. With her husband (who had entered the army as a chaplain) and MARY JANE SAFFORD, a young Cairo volunteer, she at once went to nearby Mound City, where together they met the incoming hospital ships and helped transfer the wounded to local hospitals. After a first-hand view of the battlefield, Mrs. Porter returned to Chicago to recruit more volunteer nurses. These she escorted to Savannah, Tenn., where a number of army field hospitals had been established.

From Savannah she proceeded in the early summer of 1862 to Memphis, where her husband had been assigned as chaplain at the Fort Pickering convalescent camp. Here she established a special diet kitchen (an innovation later introduced on a broad scale by ANNIE T. WITTENMYER), making several trips through the farm country of southern Illinois to solicit eggs, butter, and other foodstuffs. While at Memphis she was also instrumental in the establishment of a school among the city's large population of Negro refugees.

In July 1863 Mrs. Porter returned to Chicago, where for three months she again took charge of the Sanitary Commission offices during the temporary absence of the regular directors, JANE C. HOGE and MARY A. LIVERMORE. Traveling south once more in October, she distributed Sanitary Commission supplies at Corinth and Vicksburg and for a month relieved the matron of the Soldiers' Home in Cairo. On Jan. 1, 1864, in the midst of a biting winter rainstorm, she arrived at the field hospital near Chattanooga, where the intrepid MARY ANN BICKERDYKE was already at work caring for the wounded of the battles of Lookout Mountain and Missionary Ridge. Mrs. Porter and Mrs. Bickerdyke had worked together before; indeed, it was Eliza Porter who in April 1862 had secured Mrs. Bickerdyke's appointment as a field agent of the Sanitary Commission. Reunited now at Chattanooga, the two women for the next nine months ministered to Sherman's army during its advance toward Atlanta. Resourceful and indefatigable, they did all manner of work in the field hospitals—cooking, laundering, distributing relief supplies, and in emergencies nursing the wounded. Mrs. Porter, tactful and refined, brought a valuable moderating influence to bear upon the impulsive, rough-spoken, and somewhat domineering "Mother" Bickerdyke, who affectionately called the tiny auburn-haired Eliza her "little brown bird."

The battle at Resaca, Ga., in May 1864, an ordeal for both women, was rendered especially difficult for Mrs. Porter by the knowledge that her eldest son, James, was in the thick of the fighting. For several exhausting days and nights Mrs. Porter and Mrs. Bickerdyke furnished what aid they could to hundreds of wounded men awaiting transfer from the battlefield to field hospitals hastily set up in the neaby town. Mrs. Porter's graphic letters describing these experiences, published in the bulletin of the United States Sanitary Commission in New York, served to heighten public appreciation of the commission's work.

With the fall of Atlanta in September 1864, Mrs. Porter returned to Chicago, to leave almost at once on an inspection tour of military hospitals in Little Rock, Ark., and other towns. In December, with the news that Sherman had reached the sea, she and her husband set out by coastal steamer from New York for Savannah, Ga. They labored for a time in military hospitals there, and then, accompanied by Mrs. Bickerdyke, joined Sherman's army for the victorious northward march upon which it was engaged when the war ended.

In October 1865, after a final summer spent with Mrs. Bickerdyke in hospital work in Kentucky and Alabama, Mrs. Porter traveled with her husband to Texas, where they distributed Sanitary Commission supplies to Union troops stationed along the Mexican border and visited military hospitals in Brownsville and Brazos. Two years in a Congregational pastorate in Prairie du Chien, Wis., followed. They returned in 1868 to Brownsville, where Porter first assumed charge of a local church and then, in 1870, rejoined the regular army as chaplain at nearby Fort Brown. Mrs. Porter, meanwhile, reopened the Rio Grande Seminary, a coeducational school she had founded during her earlier stay in Brownsville.

In 1873 Porter was transferred to Fort Sill, Okla., and a few years later to Fort D. A. Russell near Cheyenne, Wyo. Except for periodic visits to the East owing to ill health, Mrs. Porter lived with her husband at these stations, assisting in his religious labors and conducting schools for the children in the vicinity. After his retirement in 1882, the couple spent their summers with married children in Beloit, Wis., and Detroit, Mich., and wintered with friends in Florida, Texas, or California. Eliza Chappell Porter died of pneumonia in Santa Barbara, Calif., on New Year's Day, 1888, at eighty years of age. After services there and in the New England Congregational Church in Chicago, she was buried in Chicago's Rosehill Cemetery. Her husband survived her by five years. Two of their children became ministers and two went as missionaries to China.

[Mary H. Porter, *Eliza Chappell Porter* (1892); Sarah E. Henshaw, *Our Branch and Its Tributaries* (1868), a history of the Northwestern Sanitary Commission; L. P. Brockett and Mary C. Vaughan, *Woman's Work in the Civil War* (1867); Mary A. Livermore, *My Story of the War* (1887); Mrs. A. H. [Jane C.] Hoge, *The Boys in Blue* (1867); Porter Papers, Beloit College Archives, Beloit, Wis.; Jeremiah Porter, Journals, 1831–48, and "The Earliest Religious Hist. of Chicago" (MSS.), Chicago Hist. Soc.; Muster and Descriptive Rolls, Ill. State Archives; records of Rosehill Cemetery, Chicago; *Chicago Democrat*, Dec. 24, 1833, Sept. 2, 1835; *Rochester* (N.Y.) *Daily Democrat*, June 16, 1835; *Sangamo Jour.* (Springfield, Ill.), Sept. 3, 1836; *Chicago Tribune*, Oct. 18, Nov. 5, 9, 1861, July 10, 1862, Jan. 2, 18, 1888; *Chicago Times*, Jan. 18, 1888; *Chicago Inter Ocean*, Jan. 18, 1888; and, on Jeremiah Porter, *Beloit* (Wis.) *Free Press*, July 25, 27, 1893; *Home Missionary*, Nov. 1893.]

WAYNE C. TEMPLE

**PORTER, Gene Stratton.** *See* STRATTON-PORTER, Gene.

**PORTER, Sarah** (Aug. 16, 1813–Feb. 17, 1900), educator, founder of Miss Porter's School in Farmington, Conn., was the first daughter and third of seven children of the Rev. Noah Porter and his wife, Mehetabel (Meigs) Porter. Born in Farmington, of which her ancestor Robert Porter had been one of the original settlers in 1640, she was heir to a strong Congregational tradition. Her father, pastor of the Farmington Congregational

Church for over sixty years, was the son of a farmer who had been for many years a deacon of the same church; and it was in the Porter house on Main Street in Farmington that the American Board of Commissioners for Foreign Missions was organized in 1810. Dr. Porter, who had graduated from Yale with highest honors, encouraged his children's intellectual pursuits. Miss Porter was permitted to receive the same instruction as her brothers at the Farmington Academy, until then exclusively for boys, and at the age of sixteen she became an assistant teacher there. She was especially devoted to her older brother Noah, later a philosopher and president of Yale. When she was nineteen she joined him in New Haven and, living in the home of a Yale professor, studied for a year with Ethan Allen Andrews, Latinist and lexicographer, who had recently founded a "young ladies' institute" in New Haven.

During the next decade Miss Porter taught in schools at Springfield, Mass., Philadelphia, Pa., and Buffalo, N.Y. In 1841 she returned briefly to Farmington and took fifteen day pupils, but the financial burden of this enterprise upon her family proved too great. Two years later, however, she returned permanently to Farmington and opened a day school in an upper room of the "old stone store." Soon afterward she rented a few rooms in a private home and, at her father's suggestion, established what eventually became one of the best-known boarding schools for girls in the United States. Thereafter, until a few years before her death at the age of eighty-seven, she devoted herself completely to the school, teaching, administering, presiding in the dining room "without preaching," and making herself available to her students at all times.

Miss Porter's concern for the welfare of the school was closely tied to her devotion to the lovely New England village of her birth. Twice she rescued Farmington from the ugly intrusions of modern life: first when railroad tracks between New Haven and Northampton threatened to cross the center of the village, and later when the installation of a trolley line to the neighboring village of Plainville would have required substitution of poles and wires for stately old trees. The graciousness of these natural surroundings had its counterpart in the atmosphere of the school she nurtured. Possessing a broad-ranging intellectual curiosity and a scholarly temperament, she herself for many years was able to teach most of the subjects in the curriculum, which included, in addition to the basic skills, Latin, French, German, chemistry, natural philosophy and rhetoric, mathematics through trigonometry, history, geography, and music. Yet she declined to give a heavily academic orientation to the school. Specific scholarly attainments were secondary to the acquisition of general culture, with emphasis on the development of character and religious training. In addition to daily Bible reading, students were exposed to an hour of doctrine from the pulpit on Sundays, and it was Miss Porter's custom, on all occasions calling for an expression of gratitude, to read aloud the 103rd Psalm. Physical activities, such as rowing, horseback riding, and tennis, were encouraged, and Miss Porter's own interest in local geography and her appreciation of the natural beauties of the Farmington Valley were transmitted on frequent picnics and excursions. She promoted a number of special activities designed to broaden the experience of her students: concerts given by eminent visiting musicians, lectures by luminaries such as Mark Twain and John Fiske, and her own frequent readings from English authors in the study halls.

Miss Porter's personal example is said to have had a forceful effect. An early riser who dispatched her correspondence and read extensively before breakfast, she would often pursue her own work side by side with the girls during study hours. Intellectually adventuresome to a degree unusual for a woman of her time, she undertook the study of Greek when past middle age, and of Hebrew at sixty-five. She early acquired an intense love of German literature and was keenly interested in philosophical matters; indeed, her proficiency in philosophy inspired visits from distinguished scholars who came to Farmington to share their ideas with her and to seek the stimulation of her mind.

Miss Porter's pedagogical principles kept her from requiring of her students the rigorous dedication to learning she herself found congenial: she was inclined rather to see them pursue their studies according to their own capacities and at their own pace; for this reason some have regarded her as a forerunner of "progressivism." But it was a lack of competitiveness, rather than any large measure of permissiveness, that characterized the spirit of the school. Miss Porter disliked rules, grades, and examinations, feeling that such external pressures dampened the spontaneous desire to learn. In keeping with this ideal, it was her custom always to encourage and seldom to reprove. Her manner was firm yet democratic, and her strong New England features suggested kindliness and sagacity in an unruffled temperament.

Miss Porter saw the future role of her students as homemakers rather than as practitioners of a vocation. Accordingly, the school was not oriented toward college preparation during her lifetime. Nevertheless, she vigilantly maintained a high quality of instruction, securing a native Frenchwoman to assist in teaching modern languages and a trained science teacher in the 1880's shortly after colleges had introduced science into their curricula. She herself continued to teach until the last few years of her life. She died in Farmington and was buried there in Riverside Cemetery.

[Sarah Porter kept few records and requested that no biography be written. The excellent local history collection of the Farmington Public Library is the principal source of information on Miss Porter and her school. Especially helpful are George S. Merriam, ed., *Noah Porter: A Memorial by Friends* (1893); *Addresses Delivered at the Opening Services of the Parish House* (Farmington, Conn., 1902); *Farmington, Conn.: The Village of Beautiful Homes* (1906); Lydia Hewes, *A Short Hist. of Farmington, Conn.* (1935). Clippings from the *Hartford Daily Courant* and the *West Hartford News* ("Farmington News" section) in the library's collection offer useful information. Of considerable importance are the files of the *Farmington Bull.*, formerly the *Alumnae Bull.* of Miss Porter's School, containing recollections by several generations of students, excerpts from Miss Porter's correspondence with townspeople, and records of the school's development. The persistence of Miss Porter's image throughout its pages, even during later years when few remained who could personally recall her, is a revealing measure of the extent to which its founder left her impress upon the school. Mr. Robert Porter Keep, a collateral descendant of Sarah Porter, freely shared in conversation his scholarship, his personal memories of Miss Porter, and his intimate knowledge of the school's history.]

ANNETTE K. BAXTER

POWELL, Louise Mathilde (Mar. 12, 1871– Oct. 6, 1943), nursing educator, was born in Staunton, Va., the second of the three children of Hugh Lee Powell and Ella (Stribling) Powell. Both parents were native Virginians; Powell prided himself upon sharing the ancestry of Robert E. Lee. Louise's maternal grandfather, Dr. Francis T. Stribling, was for many years head of the Virginia State (now Western State) Hospital for the Insane and became well known for his reforms in the treatment of the mentally ill.

Reared in a family which held a tradition of gentility and a sense of scrupulous social responsibility in equal value, Louise Powell developed into a gracious, humorous, self-disciplined young woman with a commanding impulse toward service in the field of education. An excellent student, she attended a private school in Staunton, where she showed a special aptitude for mathematics and Latin. After graduation she was persuaded by a former teacher to help establish a new progressive school for girls at Norfolk, Va., and for three years she taught primary subjects there. Prompted in part by admiration for the work of her grandfather, she then enrolled as a student of nursing at St. Luke's Hospital in Richmond. Her ability as an administrator declared itself early, and a few months after graduation from the training course in 1899 she was made superintendent of nurses at St. Luke's, a position she held until 1904. Feeling the need for broader experience, Miss Powell in 1905 took a position at the Baldwin School in Bryn Mawr, Pa., where she served as infirmary nurse for the next three years. In 1908 she entered Teachers College, Columbia University, as a graduate student in nursing.

At Teachers College she found herself in a congenial atmosphere of orderly revolution. The nursing program there, designed to prepare graduate nurses for teaching and administrative posts in hospitals and training schools, was headed by ADELAIDE NUTTING, who as principal of the Johns Hopkins Training School had given leadership to major reforms in American nursing education. When in 1910 the University of Minnesota School of Nursing —the first such school in any college or university, established in 1909—needed a new superintendent, its dedicated friend Dr. Richard Olding Beard of the university's medical faculty sought the advice of Miss Nutting. On her recommendation, he offered the position to Miss Powell, who immediately took up the task. Working under conditions of almost primitive rigor, she used her admirable training, judiciously combined with personal qualities of energy, imagination, and charm, to establish the foundation for a distinguished school. She screened candidates for admission with a conscientiousness which managed to be at once sympathetic and exacting in its academic standards, and in her first year at the university she brought together a company of students who were seeking not merely employment but careers in nursing. A majority of the graduates of that small first class became nationally recognized leaders in their profession.

During her fourteen years at the University of Minnesota, Miss Powell provided steadily broadening opportunities for experience on a professional level, supported throughout by

Elias Lyon, dean of the medical school, and Dr. Louis Baldwin, superintendent of the university hospital, as well as by Dr. Beard. (For the busy war year of 1918–19 she doubled as acting superintendent of the hospital while Dr. Baldwin was absent on military duty.) Important advances included the introduction of the first course in sociology offered to student nurses (1916); a course in public health nursing (1918); a five-year program (as against the regular three-year course) which included instruction in the humanities as well as in the biological and social sciences and which led to the bachelor of science degree (1919); and the so-called "Central School" (1921), which enabled students to have clinical experience of the broadest possible kind in three hospitals of Minneapolis and St. Paul as well as in the hospitals of the university itself. Never satisfied that her own education was complete, Miss Powell spent each of her leaves and most of her vacations in graduate work at such specialized institutions as the Hospital for Sick Children, Mt. Wilson, Md., the Municipal Hospital for Contagious Diseases in Philadelphia, the University of Virginia, and Smith College; she earned the B.S. degree from Teachers College in 1922.

In 1924 Miss Powell went to Cleveland, Ohio, to become dean of the newly founded Western Reserve University School of Nursing. She organized the curriculum along lines pioneered at Minnesota in order to fit it into a newly established medical center, but ill health forced her resignation in March 1927. She retired to Staunton, where she continued her philanthropic work, learning Braille and transcribing much material for the blind, including a biology textbook. She died of a coronary occlusion in 1943, at the age of seventy-two, at the home of her brother near Brownsburg, Va., and was buried in Thornrose Cemetery in Staunton.

[James Gray, *Education for Nursing: A Hist. of the Univ. of Minn. School* (1960); Margene Faddis, *The Hist. of the Frances Payne Bolton School of Nursing* (1948); Mary Marvin Wayland, *Louise M. Powell* (Nat. League of Nursing Education, 1937); Katharine J. Densford (Dreves), "Louise M. Powell," Univ. of Minn. School of Nursing, *Alumnae Quart.*, Jan. 1944; *Am. Jour. of Nursing*, Jan. 1924, p. 298, Dec. 1943, p. 1159; death record from Va. Dept. of Health.]

JAMES GRAY

POWELL, Maud (Aug. 22, 1868–Jan. 8, 1920), violinist, was born in Peru, Ill., the elder of two children and only daughter of Minnie (Paul) and William Bramwell Powell.

Her mother, born Minnie Bengelstater, had been brought to America in 1849 by her German and Hungarian parents; after their death of yellow fever that same year, she was adopted by a family named Paul. Powell, born in upstate New York, the son of a Methodist minister who had emigrated with his wife from England, was the brother of Major John Wesley Powell, explorer of the Grand Canyon and director of the United States Geological Survey. A sister, Juliet Powell Rice, was a pioneer teacher of folk music and transcriber of Indian songs. At Maud's birth William Bramwell Powell was superintendent of schools in Peru, Ill. Two years later he moved to the same post in Aurora, Ill., and then, in 1885, to the District of Columbia, where he instituted a vigorous experimental program that aroused antagonism and led to his eventual dismissal.

If Maud Powell shared the dynamism of her father, it was her mother, an accomplished musician and amateur composer, who guided the development of her musical talent, evident by her fourth year. While attending the public schools in Aurora, she took music lessons from William Fickenscher and his daughter. At eight she was playing Mozart violin sonatas with her mother. At nine she began to travel by herself each Saturday the forty miles to Chicago, to study violin with William Lewis and piano with Agnes Ingersoll; that same year she made a six weeks' tour of the Midwest with the Chicago Ladies' Quartet.

At twelve Maud went to Europe to study, supported at least in part by a purse contributed by Aurora townspeople. Going first to Leipzig, she studied for one year with Henry Schradieck and was awarded a diploma at the examinations given at the Gewandhaus in 1881. It was at this time, during her initial rehearsal with orchestral accompaniment, that she first suffered "the torments of nervousness" that were always to plague her before public appearances. From Leipzig she moved on to Paris, where she was one of six students selected from a group of eighty for a course at the Paris Conservatory with Charles Dancla, whom she was to consider her greatest teacher. In 1883, on the advice of the violinist Hubert Leonard, she went to London, playing there, in the provinces, and before the royal family. While in London she met the noted violinist Joseph Joachim, who invited her to the Royal High School of Music in Berlin, where she studied with him for two years. "The French methods," she later recorded, "taught me to become an artist. . . . I learned in Germany to become a musician."

After a debut with the Berlin Philharmonic in 1885, Maud Powell returned to the United States to make her American debut on Nov. 14 with the New York Philharmonic Society under Theodore Thomas' direction, playing the First Concerto of Bruch. At seventeen she thus found herself on her own as a professional concert violinist. The years following, she later admitted, were the unhappiest of her life. She missed the student life and artistic atmosphere of Europe and even doubted her own talents. She also had to combat contemporary prejudice against women violinists. Strong inner resources brought her through this crisis. During the seven years following her American debut, she made an annual concert tour of the United States with the Thomas orchestra. She was the soloist with the New York Arion Society when it toured Germany and Austria in 1892 under the direction of Frank van der Stucken. In 1893 she was honored by an invitation to play at the Chicago World's Fair. She also read a paper on "Women and Music" at one of a series of musical congresses held in conjunction with the fair. Her interest in chamber music resulted in 1894 in the formation of the Maud Powell String Quartet, which toured widely in the United States until it disbanded in 1898. She then returned to Europe, appearing in London with the Philharmonic and at the Saturday Popular Concerts, and with the Hallé and the Scottish orchestras. She lived for a time in London, touring in Germany, France, Russia, Denmark, and South Africa, as well as annually in the United States.

Maud Powell's vigor and sense of responsibility to the music of her time is demonstrated by the number of first performances in the United States she gave of a wide variety of violin concerti. These were the Saint-Saëns in C major, Harry Rowe Shelley's in G minor, Dvořák's in A minor, Huss' in D minor, Arensky's in A minor, Bruch's *Konzertstück*, and the Sibelius in D minor. The last she played with the New York Philharmonic on Nov. 30, 1906, and her performance of the Tchaikovsky Concerto in New York as early as Jan. 19, 1889, was one of the first American presentations of that masterpiece. Her playing was marked by a large tone and breadth of musical style; she was in the front rank of the violinists of her generation. In the final decades of her career she favored, first, a Joseph Guarnerius instrument, and then, after 1907, a large-model Giovanni Battista Guadagnini. At a time when many performers relied on tricks and virtuoso feats alone, Maud Powell stressed the prime importance of experience in ensemble music and the comprehension of theory and form. In an interview with Frederick H.

Martens about 1919 she emphasized that "mastery of the instrument is a life study" involving more than tone and technique; she felt that for the full development of talent musical surroundings were necessary, as well as a knowledge of many types of music.

On Sept. 21, 1904, Miss Powell was married to the English manager H. Godfrey Turner, who continued to arrange her tours and handle her business affairs. They made their home in Great Neck, Long Island, summering in Whitefield, N.H., where Miss Powell pursued an interest in botany. In her later years she sought to reach a wider audience outside the major musical centers, traveling to schools, colleges, and smaller cities. She was the first violinist to record with the Victor Talking Machine Company. During World War I she entertained troops in training camps and cantonments, preceding her performances with brief talks on the compositions. She was an initial member of the board of the Music Service League of America, which worked to provide hospitals, prisons, and other institutions with phonographs and records. She served on the board of the Brooklyn Music School Settlement and found time and opportunity to encourage aspiring talent in many other ways. Miss Powell's health gave way in her early fifties. In January 1920 she collapsed in Uniontown, Pa., while on a concert tour and died in a hotel there of a heart attack (acute dilatation). A private funeral was held at her home in Great Neck, and her body was cremated.

[Frederick H. Martens, *Violin Mastery* (1919), chap. xvi; autobiographical sketch in *Etude*, Oct. 1911, p. 666; articles on Miss Powell in *Musical Observer*, Feb. 1908, Aug. 1913, and Mar. 1920; obituaries in *Musical America*, Jan. 17, 1920, and *N.Y. Times*, Jan. 9, 1920; clippings in Music Division, N.Y. Public Library at Lincoln Center; death record from Pa. Dept. of Health. See also Nicolas Slonimsky, ed., *Baker's Biog. Dict. of Musicians* (5th ed., 1958); and references in Henry C. Lahee, *Annals of Music in America* (1922). On her family background, see William C. Darrah, *Powell of the Colorado* (1951), and *Dict. Am. Biog.* article on her father.]

ARLAN R. COOLIDGE

**PRANG, Mary Amelia Dana Hicks** (Oct. 7, 1836–Nov. 7, 1927), art educator, played an important role in transmitting to American primary school art teachers the principles of the German educator Friedrich Froebel. Precisely when she first became familiar with German romantic philosophy is hard to determine, for she was born of old New England stock in Syracuse, N.Y., the only daughter of Major (his given name) and Agnes Amelia

Livingston (Johnson) Dana, and a direct descendant of Richard Dana, who settled in Cambridge, Mass., about 1640. Her father was a prosperous merchant; her mother has been described as "a brilliant woman, a poet and artist," and "a leader in the literary society of Syracuse" (Howe, p. 40). An observant little girl, Mary is said to have learned her letters at the age of two. She attended Mary B. Allen's Female Seminary, continuing with the school when it moved from Syracuse to Rochester in 1847 and graduating in 1852. On her twentieth birthday she was married to Charles Spencer Hicks, a young Syracuse lawyer. He was drowned two years later, leaving her with a baby daughter, Margaret.

To support herself, the young widow began taking private pupils, chiefly in drawing. She was soon called to teach art in the Syracuse public high school and in 1868 was appointed supervisor of drawing for all the city schools. Her "remarkable physique and excellent health" gave her unusual energy, and she combined strong convictions on the educational value of art instruction with a "joyousness of spirit" that inspired her pupils (Howe, p. 41). She was always on the lookout for new methods. Thus it was that only two years after Walter Smith, a Boston art teacher, had published his *Art Education* (1872), the school board was applauding the exhibition which Mrs. Hicks presented in order to show the work her students had done according to Smith's system of drawing. In 1875–76 she was a student at Smith's Massachusetts Normal Art School in Boston. Smith's system, primarily concerned with industrial drawing, did not contribute much to her later philosophy. The Syracuse school board and teachers, however, also shared an ardent interest in the "New Education" of Col. Francis W. Parker, and it may well have been at this period that Mrs. Hicks was first influenced by German educational philosophy, with its combination of a child-centered curriculum and Hegelian idealism. She later (1883) taught at Parker's summer school on Martha's Vineyard.

It was likely through Walter Smith that Mary Dana Hicks came to the attention of Louis Prang. A German lithographer who had emigrated to Boston after the abortive revolution of 1848, Prang had popularized the Christmas card in this country and brought fine art to the masses with his famous "chromos," or colored reproductions, of paintings. By the late 1870's he had become interested in art education and was manufacturing not only artists' supplies but wooden models of the "type forms" Froebel prescribed for children's drawing classes, forms which, when combined and varied, would lead, in Froebel's view, to nature and, ultimately, to the spiritual Ideal. Called to Boston by Prang, Mrs. Hicks joined the Prang Educational Company in 1879 and became director of its new correspondence normal school in 1884. An important member of the Prang establishment, she was described as "stately as a duchess" in her office and in her home (Eleanor Ellis Perkins, *Eve among the Puritans*, 1956, pp. 162–63). During her twenty-one years with the company she exercised a considerable influence through the many manuals for Prang's correspondence courses, on which she collaborated from 1887, and through a number of articles in such "new" educational journals as the *Kindergarten Magazine* and *Common School Education*, where they appeared along with essays by such progressive educators as SUSAN BLOW, Parker, and John Dewey. Her teaching manuals are competent but hardly display originality, and though the magazine articles effectively transmit Froebel's ideas, they contain no notable additions.

The same mildness marks her public activities during the retirement which followed her marriage to Louis Prang, on Apr. 15, 1900. Although Mrs. Prang belonged to a large number of organizations—among them the National Education Association, the Eastern Kindergarten Teachers Association, the Eastern Drawing Teachers Association, and the Public School Art League—it seems significant that she held no offices, and that not until after Louis Prang's death (June 14, 1909), when she was in her seventies, did she begin active participation in such progressive and pacifist groups as the Civic Club of Ward 19 of Boston (president, 1909–12), the Roxbury Woman's Suffrage League (president, 1911–12), the Massachusetts Peace Society, the Massachusetts Prison Association, the Massachusetts Single Tax Association, the Boston League for Democratic Control, and the People's Council of the Women's International League for Peace and Freedom. Her religious affiliation, in her later years at least, was Unitarian. Mrs. Prang culminated her years of self-education by earning the degree of Associate in Arts at Radcliffe College in 1916, and in 1921, at the age of eighty-four, a Master of Education degree from Harvard. She died six years later, of apoplexy, in the New England Sanitarium and Hospital, Stoneham, Mass., and was buried in Mount Auburn Cemetery, Cambridge.

[Mary Dana Hicks was the author of *Art Instruction for Children in Primary Schools* (2 vols.,

1899), among other Prang manuals. For her educational theory, the best sources are a series of articles published in *Kindergarten Mag.* in 1889 and 1893–94 and in *Common School Education* in 1889. Biographical sources: Julia Ward Howe, ed., *Representative Women of New England* (1904), pp. 40–43; *New England Hist. and Genealogical Register*, Oct. 1928; obituary in *Boston Transcript*, Nov. 8, 1927. Mrs. Prang's entry in the *Woman's Who's Who of America*, 1914–15, suggests a more militant liberalism—including Fabian socialism, and philosophical anarchism—than other sources seem to bear out. See also Frances E. Willard and Mary A. Livermore, eds., *A Woman of the Century* (1893), under Hicks; and Edward Smith, *A Hist. of the Schools of Syracuse* (1893), pp. 156, 172. Death record from Mass. Registrar of Vital Statistics. For Prang's professional and liberal activities, see *Dict. Am. Biog.* and Carl Wittke, *Refugees of Revolution* (1952).]

FRED E. H. SCHROEDER

**PRATT, Anna Beach** (June 5, 1867–Jan. 3, 1932), social worker, was born in Elmira, N.Y., the oldest of three children of Timothy Smith Pratt and Catherine Elizabeth (Beach) Pratt. Her father, a dry goods merchant, was a native of upstate New York and claimed a *Mayflower* ancestry. Her mother, born in Connecticut, was of French Huguenot descent. Miss Pratt attended local public schools and earned a B.A. degree from Elmira College in 1886. Although her paternal grandfather, a minister, initially aroused what became a lifelong interest in education, and although she taught briefly at a private girls' school and at Elmira College, Miss Pratt adopted social work as a career following an informal philanthropic experiment which she undertook in the 1890's.

Concerned over the welfare of country girls flocking to Elmira for employment in local knitting mills, she formed the Alpha Club, designed to provide them with a wholesome milieu for relaxation and recreation. Along with other Elmira residents whom she enlisted in the project, she waited outside the factory gates to invite the girls to the club for conversation, reading, games, and similar diversions. An intense, deeply spiritual woman in search of a mission, yet serene and composed, with a warm smile which softened her tall, stately dignity, Miss Pratt eventually moved from the amateur benevolence represented by the Alpha Club to a more systematic involvement with problems of poverty and social maladjustment.

She launched her social work career in 1906, when she attended the summer course offered by the New York School of Philanthropy and became overseer of the poor in Elmira, as well as secretary of the newly formed Bureau of Associated Relief. Technically, Miss Pratt's father had been appointed overseer, as it was not considered seemly for a woman to hold the office, but it was understood that she would perform the duties. As secretary of the Bureau of Associated Relief (which became the Social Service League in 1909 and merged, at Miss Pratt's instigation, with the Women's Federation in 1912 to form the Elmira Federation for Social Service), she introduced charity organization methods into local philanthropy. Interviewing as many as sixty-seven clients in a day, she instituted a system of investigation and registration of clients in order to ascertain their "real need" and prevent waste, duplication, and fraud. Few other organized welfare agencies existed in Elmira, and Miss Pratt became the dominant influence in local relief policy, seeking always to subordinate indiscriminate relief to the client's permanent rehabilitation.

Miss Pratt left Elmira to earn a master's degree at the University of Pennsylvania in 1916. She was to remain in Philadelphia for the rest of her life. That fall she accepted an invitation from the trustees of the venerable but moribund Magdalen Society of Philadelphia (renamed the White-Williams Foundation for Girls in 1918 and the White-Williams Foundation in 1920) to become its executive and redirect its work. She hoped to combine social work with her unrelinquished interest in education but at first had no clear-cut notion of how to proceed. A visit to the Bureau of Compulsory Education in Philadelphia, responsible for the issuance of working certificates, revealed that many young girls quit school although neither they nor their parents had really considered the consequences of the step in relation to employment opportunities or the child's health and aptitudes. Assured by educators and social workers in New York, Boston, and Chicago that vocational counseling represented a new and useful field of service, Miss Pratt established a junior employment department in the Foundation.

Barely had the work begun, however, before it was evident that the most effective counseling, aimed at keeping the student in school until graduation, had to begin in the early grades, long before the decision was made to leave school, and that a full understanding of the child could not be obtained without insight into the environmental circumstances which shaped her personality. Thus by 1920, when the Foundation began to include boys in its social work program, Miss Pratt had supplemented the original employment counseling and scholarship grants with casework services in various Philadelphia public schools. School social work was a relative novelty at the time, existing in few communities on either a voluntary or an official basis. As a consequence of Miss Pratt's successful demonstration of its value to school and child alike, it ultimately became, along with vocational guidance, an official component of the Philadelphia educational system.

During the 1920's Miss Pratt became one of the most influential interpreters of theory, practice, and training in school social work. At a time when few facilities for training in the field were available, she organized an elaborate teaching and supervisory program in cooperation with college departments of education and sociology, schools of social work, and social agencies. She upheld school social work as a professional specialty distinct from teaching and requiring an advanced technical preparation. And, most important, she justified the need for school social work to educators and the public as a means of individualizing the child—understanding his unique problems and personality—in face of the pressures for standardization exerted by a system of mass public education. Intellectually alert, attuned to progressive ideas emanating from social work, education, and the behavioral sciences, Miss Pratt emphasized that the child's school performance was not a self-contained intellectual affair, but was associated with his health, the influence of home and social environment, and his emotional needs.

Anna Pratt's contributions to Philadelphia's public school system were increased by an appointment to the Board of Education in 1929 and service as president of the Philadelphia County Council of Home and School Associations from 1925 to 1929. She served as a delegate to the White House Conference on Child Welfare in 1931. For relaxation Miss Pratt enjoyed strolling in fields and woods, identifying birds, mushrooms, and toadstools. A Presbyterian turned Quaker, she died of cancer at Pennsylvania Hospital in Philadelphia at the age of sixty-four and was buried in Woodlawn Cemetery, Elmira, N.Y. A Philadelphia public school was named for her in 1955.

One of many women in the early twentieth century who used social work as a means of forging a creative professional career, Anna Pratt introduced charity organization methods in a small upstate New York town at a time when country philanthropy in general had hardly progressed beyond the Lady Bountiful stage. Her major achievement lay in the planting of casework and counseling services in the

Philadelphia public school system through the White-Williams Foundation. Although pioneering efforts in school social work had begun in New York, Boston, Rochester, and a few other communities before she came to Philadelphia, Miss Pratt directed an unusually comprehensive and systematic experiment in the field, closely related to a program for training and supervising teachers and social workers.

[Useful summaries of the development of the White-Williams Foundation under Miss Pratt's leadership appear in two of the Foundation's publications: *Five Years' Review for the Period Ending Dec. 31, 1921* (1922); and *School Children as Social Workers See Them* (1927). Articles by Miss Pratt explaining her views on school social work include: "The Relation of the Teacher and the Social Worker," *Am. Academy of Political and Social Sci., Annals,* Nov. 1921; "Social Work in the First Grade of a Public School," *Am. Jour. of Sociology,* Jan. 1923; "Should the Visiting Teacher Be a New Official?" *Jour. of Social Forces,* Mar. 1923; "Courses of Training for Visiting Teachers," *Nat. Conference of Social Work, Proc.,* 1923, pp. 425–28; (with Edith M. Everett) "Vocational, Educational and Social Guidance," *School and Soc.,* Aug. 1, 1925; "Training for Educational and Vocational Counselors from the Standpoint of the Field Worker," *Vocational Guidance Mag.,* Apr. 1927. For biographical data see *Woman's Who's Who of America,* 1914–15, and obituary in *N.Y. Times,* Jan. 4, 1932. Several relatives of Miss Pratt, including Mrs. Margaret P. Allen, Miss Alice Gregg, and Mr. Edward H. Pratt, provided assistance on personal and family background. Mr. William M. Cooper, who was personally acquainted with Miss Pratt before she left Elmira, was also most helpful. Additional information was supplied by the Elmira College Alumnae Assoc., the White–Williams Foundation, the Elmira Child and Family Service, and the Steele Memorial Library, Elmira.]

ROY LUBOVE

**PRAY, Malvina.** *See* FLORENCE, Malvina Pray.

**PRENTISS, Elizabeth Payson** (Oct. 26, 1818–Aug. 13, 1878), writer of children's stories, religious fiction, and verse, was born in Portland, Maine. She was the fifth of eight children (the second daughter among the six children who survived infancy) of the Rev. Edward Payson, a native of Rindge, N.H., and Ann Louisa (Shipman) Payson of New Haven, Conn. Her American ancestry reached back to Edward Payson, who had come from Essex County, England, to Roxbury, Mass., in the 1630's. It included three generations of Congregational ministers: her great-grandfather, Phillips Payson of Walpole, Mass., her grandfather, Seth Payson of Rindge, N.H., and her father, an intense revivalist preacher whose sermons, published after his early death, were widely read. Her father, a Harvard graduate, was the strongest influence in Elizabeth's life, and though he died when she was only nine years old, he had already shaped her thought toward religious goals above all others. Highstrung, introspective, strict in self-discipline, she was haunted in her early years by "the depressing sense of inferiority which was born with me." So frail was she physically, subject to "pains in the side," headaches, and fainting, that she could write, at twenty-two, "I never knew what it is to feel well." The persistent theme of perfection of character through suffering, even in her children's books, owed much to her own ill health, which continued throughout her life.

Except for one year (1830) in New York City, where her older sister Louisa had opened a school, Elizabeth Payson spent her childhood and youth in Portland and was educated in local schools. In her twentieth year she opened a school for young children in her mother's house, and for two years (1840–41 and 1842–43) she taught in Mr. Persico's school for girls in Richmond, Va., despite periods of religious brooding and "severe nervous excitement." Her sister Louisa's success as a magazine writer was a spur to her own early ambition to write, and from childhood she composed verses, wrote stories, and kept journals. Her first printed work appeared in 1834 in the recently established *Youth's Companion,* to which she had been encouraged to contribute by Nathaniel P. Willis, the editor's son and a guest in her mother's home. Many of the pieces appearing under the title *Only a Dandelion, and Other Stories* (1854) belong to this early period.

On Apr. 16, 1845, she was married to George Lewis Prentiss, newly ordained as a Congregational minister, and moved to New Bedford, Mass., his first pastorate, thence briefly to Newark, N.J., and in 1851 to New York City, where he thereafter held Presbyterian pastorates. Except for two years abroad (1858–60) and a brief residence in Chicago (1871), New York was her home for the remainder of her life. The marriage was a happy one, though shadowed by her husband's ill health, her own chronic weakness and fatigue, and the death in infancy of two of their six children. Those who survived were Anna Louise, Mary Williams, George Lewis, and Henry Smith.

Mrs. Prentiss' first marked success as a writer for children came in 1853 with *Little Susy's Six Birthdays,* followed in 1856 by *Little*

Susy's Six Teachers and *Little Susy's Little Servants*. Half story, half allegory, these books caught both parental and child interest and were widely read in America, republished in England, and translated into French. *The Flower of the Family: A Book for Girls* (1853), *Henry and Bessie; or, What They Did in the Country* (1855), *Peterchen and Gretchen, Tales of Early Childhood*, a translation from the German (1860), and *Fred, and Maria, and Me* (1867) continued to satisfy the demand and also to increase it. These and later stories of childhood owed their popularity chiefly to the naturalness of the dialogue and the prankishness of the child characters. In making storybook children real in their mischiefs and weekday pleasures, Mrs. Prentiss was following one of the newer mid-century paths for children's stories. Her example influenced other writers.

Her greatest success, *Stepping Heavenward* (1869)—like all her stories thinly veiled autobiography—first appeared serially in the *Chicago Advance*. The public response to this record of a young girl's emotional life was immediate and widespread. American sales reached 100,000; English editions and French and German translations quickly followed. Such popularity is no enigma. Mrs. Prentiss' friend SUSAN WARNER had prepared the way nearly twenty years earlier with *The Wide, Wide World* and *Queechy*. Moreover, Mrs. Prentiss and her readers were squarely in the center of a stream of evangelical preaching which made her interpretation of the daily Christian life utterly familiar to a large section of churchgoing America. In this familiarity lay its power. The verdict of many readers, "I felt that I had written it myself," testifies also to the author's ability to make religious emotion articulate. Literary comment passed her by, and understandably; this book belongs not to literature but to religious and social history.

None of her later books enjoyed a corresponding popularity. Notable among them were *Aunt Jane's Hero* (1871), *Pemaquid: A Story of Old Times in New England* (1877), and *Religious Poems* (1873), reprinted the following year under the title *Golden Hours: Hymns and Songs of the Christian Life*. One of the hymns, "More Love to Thee, O Christ," is included in many modern hymnals. Elizabeth Prentiss died in Dorset, Vt., her summer home for the last ten years of her life, and was buried there in Maplewood Cemetery.

[The principal source is her husband's *The Life and Letters of Elizabeth Prentiss* (1882), which includes extracts from a journal kept from her twentieth year to the end of her life. See also Marion Harland, "Elizabeth Prentiss," in *Our Famous Women* (1884), chap. xxiii.]

OLA ELIZABETH WINSLOW

**PRESTON, Ann** (Dec. 1, 1813–Apr. 18, 1872), physician, dean of the Female (Woman's) Medical College of Pennsylvania, was born in West Grove, Pa., the second of nine children of Amos Preston, a Quaker minister said to have been a man of unusual intellectual gifts, and Margaret (Smith) Preston. She was the oldest of three daughters, but one of her sisters died in infancy, the other in girlhood. West Grove, a Quaker village near Philadelphia, was an intellectual and religious community; the Prestons were active abolitionists and early supporters of the woman's rights movement. Ann attended the Quaker school in West Grove and, later, a Friends boarding school in Chester, Pa., but the growing invalidism of her mother soon brought her home, where she took on the responsibility of running the household and caring for her younger brothers. In addition to these duties she was a member of the local Clarkson Anti-Slavery Society and wrote reports, addresses, and petitions for it; she was also active in the temperance movement. After her brothers grew up she taught school; a volume of rhymed tales for children was published as *Cousin Ann's Stories* in 1849. She had continued her own education informally through the local literary association and lyceum, whose speakers included James Russell Lowell and John Greenleaf Whittier, Wendell Phillips and William Lloyd Garrison, LUCY STONE, ELIZABETH CADY STANTON, and SUSAN B. ANTHONY.

Increasingly, however, Ann Preston found herself concerned with the need for enlightened attitudes toward female physiology, and by the early 1840's she began teaching physiology and hygiene to local classes of women and girls. Encouraged by Philadelphia Quakers, many of them doctors, who already believed in medical education for women—LUCRETIA MOTT had been a friend since childhood—she enrolled in 1847 as a medical apprentice in Dr. Nathaniel R. Moseley's office in Philadelphia. After the completion of the two years' apprenticeship she applied for admission to four of the medical colleges in Philadelphia, but, like ELIZABETH BLACKWELL three years earlier, was refused because she was a woman.

With a steadily growing number of women seeking medical training and meeting such opposition, the Female (later Woman's) Medical College of Pennsylvania was founded in March 1850 by a group of Quakers led by

William T. Mullen, a young businessman who had studied medicine. The following October, shortly before her thirty-seventh birthday, Ann Preston entered the first class with seven other candidates for the M.D. degree, including HANNAH LONGSHORE. She was graduated Dec. 31, 1851, and the next year returned for post-graduate study. She was appointed professor of physiology and hygiene in 1853, thus beginning her lifelong involvement with the college as teacher, administrator, and physician.

In 1858 the Board of Censors of the Philadelphia Medical Society formally ostracized the Woman's Medical College, making impossible the admission of women to the public teaching clinics in Philadelphia or membership in any medical society. The college was also beset by dissension within its own faculty and by public as well as professional antagonism to the idea of women doctors. Undaunted, Dr. Preston organized a board of lady managers to help found a Woman's Hospital in connection with the college to provide bedside clinical instruction; she herself did much of the fund raising. In 1861, at the outbreak of the Civil War, the college closed, but Dr. Preston went on with her preparations for the hospital and her plan to send Dr. EMELINE HORTON CLEVELAND, then demonstrator of anatomy at the college, to the School of Obstetrics at the Maternité of Paris for surgical study. Staffed with men from the original faculty and with four women graduates of the college, the Woman's Hospital was founded in 1861 and ready for occupancy when Dr. Cleveland returned from Paris to become its chief resident. The college itself reopened in 1862; the following year Dr. Preston started a training school for nurses.

In 1866 Dr. Preston was made dean of the Woman's Medical College—the first woman to hold the post—and the following year she was elected to the Board of Corporators. Serene, unwavering, and womanly, her slight figure belying the strength of her determination, she applied successfully in 1868 for her students to attend the general clinics at the Philadelphia Hospital, "Blockley"; the following year she was granted the same privilege at the Pennsylvania Hospital. Acceptance within the profession was not easily won, however. The first women to attend the Pennsylvania Hospital clinic were the objects of a rude demonstration by the male medical students. Shortly afterward a remonstrance protesting the immodesty, even immorality, of educating men and women in medicine together, signed not only by boards of colleges and hospitals but also by a long list of individual doctors, was presented

to Dr. Preston. Her reply, published in Philadelphia newspapers Nov. 15, 1869, has become a classic argument in favor of women in the medical profession, articulating a steadfast, reasonable belief that "wherever it is proper to introduce women as patients, there also it is but just and in accordance with the instincts of the truest womanhood for women to appear as physicians and students."

Dr. Preston continued her work as dean and as professor of physiology until her death; she was also consulting physician to the Woman's Hospital. Her private practice was restricted to office consultations because of her frail health. For many years she suffered from articular rheumatism, a second and serious attack occurring in 1871. She died the next year at the age of fifty-eight at her home in Philadelphia. In her will she left her medical instruments and books to the college plus an endowment of $4,000 for a scholarship. She was buried in the Fair Hill Burial Ground in Philadelphia, but her body was later removed to Friends Burial Ground at West Grove, Pa. Her close friend, former student, and colleague, Dr. Cleveland, succeeded her as dean of the college.

[Materials in the library of the Woman's Medical College, including lectures and articles by Ann Preston, correspondence, clippings, and other records of the college; Eliza E. Judson, *Address in Memory of Ann Preston, M.D.* (1873); Clara Marshall, "Ann Preston, M.D.," Woman's Medical College of Pa., *Bull.*, Mar. 1915; Clara Marshall, *The Woman's Medical College of Pa.: An Hist. Outline* (1897); Gulielma F. Alsop, *Hist. of the Woman's Medical College, Phila., Pa.* (1950); Frances E. Willard and Mary A. Livermore, eds., *A Woman of the Century* (1893); *Eminent Women of the Age* (1869), pp. 544–50. Anna Davis Hallowell, ed., *James and Lucretia Mott: Life and Letters* (1884), prints a letter from Ann Preston to Mrs. Mott. The Phila. County Medical Soc. resolution and Dr. Preston's reply are in the *Medical and Surgical Reporter*, Apr. 6, May 4, 1867.]

GULIELMA F. ALSOP

**PRESTON, Frances Folsom Cleveland.** *See* CLEVELAND, Frances Folsom.

**PRESTON, Margaret Junkin** (May 19, 1820–Mar. 28, 1897), Southern poet, was born at Milton, Pa., the first child of the Rev. George Junkin, Presbyterian minister and educator, and Julia Rush (Miller) Junkin. Both parents were native Pennsylvanians of Scottish descent; eight of their children reached maturity. When Margaret was ten the family moved to Germantown, where Junkin became principal of the Manual Labor Academy of Pennsylvania. In 1832 he became the first president of Lafayette College at Easton, Pa., where the family lived until 1848, except for the period 1841–44 when he served as president of Miami University at Oxford, Ohio. Margaret received most of her schooling at home, where her father, known as a strict disciplinarian, taught her Latin and Greek, as well as English literature and theology. Her lessons were continued by some of the faculty and students of Lafayette. Eye trouble, said to have developed after a girlhood illness, often interfered with her studies and recurred throughout her life; at times she had to have someone write for her or use a writing device made for the blind. She nevertheless began an active writing career while still in her youth. Some of her early stories and verses appeared in magazines and newspapers and occasionally won prizes.

When in 1848 George Junkin was chosen as president of Washington College (later Washington and Lee), the family moved to Lexington, Va. There Margaret, a small woman with auburn curls, found congenial friends and continued her literary work. Her only novel, *Silverwood*, a simple story of Southern life that taught "the lesson of resignation" (Davidson, p. 432), was issued anonymously in 1856, although her publisher had offered to pay an extra sum if she would permit the use of her name.

On Aug. 3, 1857, Margaret Junkin was married to Major (later Col.) John T. L. Preston, professor of Latin at Virginia Military Institute in Lexington and a widower whose seven children ranged in age from five to twenty-two. (Her sister Eleanor had also married a V.M.I. professor, the later Gen. Thomas "Stonewall" Jackson, but had died a year after her marriage.) Now the mistress of a large establishment, for a time she did little writing. She had two sons of her own, George Junkin and Herbert Rush. At the outbreak of the Civil War her father and a sister returned to Pennsylvania and a brother joined the Union Army, but Mrs. Preston remained loyal to her Virginia husband and to the Confederacy. The hidden anguish of this family split was recorded in a remarkable diary, printed in Elizabeth Preston Allan's memoir in 1903. Such conflicts were not, however, the theme of her wartime poetry. In her second book, *Beechenbrook: A Rhyme of the War*, she depicted the suffering and heroism of a Southern wife whose husband dies while fighting for the Confederacy. Written at her husband's suggestion and published in wartime Richmond in 1865 in an edition he had commissioned, the volume sold rapidly

after its republication by a Baltimore firm in 1866 and 1867 and created a considerable literary reputation for her throughout the South. *Old Song and New* followed in 1870, a collection of verse composed, as she wrote the Charleston poet Paul Hamilton Hayne (July 11, 1869), amid a "thousand petty housewifely distractions."

Despite her popularity, Mrs. Preston had no illusions about the extent of her poetic gifts. In *Cartoons* (1875) she compared herself to "one cricket chirping in the grass." Many of her verses reflect the influence of the contemporary American and British poets she most admired, and the echoes of Browning are particularly strong. A book of religious verse, *For Love's Sake*, appeared in 1886. *Colonial Ballads, Sonnets, and Other Verse* (1887) featured narrative poems of early American life. The Prestons journeyed to Europe in the summer of 1884, and the result was a book of travel sketches entitled *A Handful of Monographs* (1886).

In Lexington, where in 1862 her husband had returned to teaching, Mrs. Preston knew well many leaders of the Confederacy, including Robert E. Lee, who served as president of Washington College from 1865 until his death five years later. For the *Century* magazine she wrote her "Personal Reminiscences of Stonewall Jackson" (October 1886) and "General Lee after the War" (June 1889). Commemorative odes made her the "Poet Laureate" of Lexington's two institutions of higher learning. After her husband died in 1890, she moved to Baltimore to live with her eldest son, Dr. George Preston. She died there of "apoplexy" in her seventy-seventh year and was buried in Lexington, Va. She had made a lasting reputation only as a regional poet.

[Elizabeth Preston Allan, comp., *The Life and Letters of Margaret Junkin Preston* (1903), by a stepdaughter, is the only biography. The best critique is a sketch in Jay B. Hubbell, *The South in Am. Literature, 1607–1900* (1954). See also: James W. Davidson, *The Living Writers of the South* (1869); Frances E. Willard and Mary A. Livermore, eds., *A Woman of the Century* (1893); obituary in the Baltimore *Sun*, Mar. 29, 1897; Marshall W. Fishwick, "Margaret Junkin Preston: Va. Poetess," *Commonwealth*, July 1951; *Dict. Am. Biog.* on George Junkin. Death record from Baltimore City Health Dept. There are letters of Mrs. Preston to Paul H. Hayne in the Hayne MSS. at Duke Univ.; the Univ. of N.C. has a collection of her papers numbering 150 pieces.]

                                        ROBERT H. LAND

**PRESTON, May Wilson** (Aug. 11, 1873–May 18, 1949), illustrator, was born in New York

City, the only daughter of Ann (Taylor) and John J. Wilson. Her substantial, conservative, middle-class parents adored their spirited daughter but were disconcerted by her early and purposeful artistic bent. Although dutifully attending public school through high school, she had by sixteen developed into an accomplished self-taught artist and was a founding member (1889) of the Women's Art Club (later the National Association of Women Artists). Her parents, hoping to divert her talent into channels they considered more acceptable for a young lady, sent her that fall to Oberlin College in Ohio, where she enrolled at first in the preparatory school and afterward in the conservatory of music. Bored by her studies, she became the college tennis champion and the star of theatricals, while devoting most of her time to sketching landscapes or portraits of her fellow students.

After three years at Oberlin, aided by a teacher who appreciated her talent, May Wilson persuaded her family to let her return to New York to enter the Art Students' League. She began her work there in October 1892, although the school refused to admit her to the life classes, a disappointment she felt keenly, for she had been encouraged to enlarge her scope of study by such eminent artists and friends as William M. Chase, Robert Henri, and John H. Twachtman. She continued her studies at the League until January 1897, though protesting that she was engulfed in old-fashioned ideas. In the spring of 1898 she was married to Thomas Henry Watkins. The next year she went to Paris under the wing of an English relative and studied under James McNeill Whistler. After scarcely a year she returned to New York. Her husband died in 1900. Soon afterward she began her career as an illustrator, selling her first drawing—so the story goes—to the editor of a third-rate magazine after frankly telling him that she thought a beginner might be able to sell something to "the worst magazine I had ever seen." In 1901 she illustrated her first story for Harper's Bazar.

She also resumed her studies in New York, enrolling in classes presided over by her friend William M. Chase at the New York School of Art. There she met Edith Dimock, with whom she moved into the Sherwood Studios at 58 West 57th Street. Joined shortly by another art student, Lou Seyme, they soon became known as the "Sherwood Sisters" and issued prized invitations to their weekly open house, which offered work, conversation, and games to friends and fellow artists. James Moore Preston, a rising young painter whom May had

met in Paris, was a constant visitor and soon clearly her suitor; he also was responsible for introducing the artist William J. Glackens to his future wife, Miss Dimock. James Preston and May Wilson (Watkins) were married on Dec. 19, 1903, and soon settled at 22 East 9th Street. There they were part of an artistic coterie which became known as the "Ashcan School" because of its predilection for common subjects drawn from city life. Besides Preston and Glackens, the group included Robert Henri, John Sloan, George B. Luks, and Everett Shinn, and it soon expanded to include writers and editors, among them Irvin Cobb, Charles Fitzgerald, Wallace Irwin, and Frank Crowninshield. Deadly serious about the new art they were creating, they found themselves at odds with the National Academy of Design. In 1901 they had formed the Society of Illustrators, and after her marriage May Wilson Preston was for several years its only woman member. In 1912 they organized the Association of American Painters and Sculptors, which the next year sponsored the famous Armory Show, at which she was one of the exhibitors. The group had its lighter aspects as well: its costume balls and beaux-arts balls were gala affairs, and as the Waverly Place Players they performed for audiences large or small, moving from one studio to another for special stage or lighting effects.

During these years Mrs. Preston was becoming increasingly successful as an illustrator, particularly for magazines. Her pictures accompanied the stories of such writers as Mary Roberts Rinehart (for whom she illustrated the famous Tish series), Owen Johnson (whose novel The Salamander she also illustrated, in 1913), Vincent Sheean, Ring Lardner, Joseph Hergesheimer, F. Scott Fitzgerald, P. G. Wodehouse, ALICE DUER MILLER, and I. A. R. Wylie in such popular periodicals as the Saturday Evening Post, McClure's, the Metropolitan, the Woman's Home Companion, the Delineator, and Harper's Bazar. She exhibited at art shows in New York, London, and Paris, frequently winning prizes; in 1915 she was awarded a bronze medal at the San Francisco Panama–Pacific Exposition. A strong believer in woman's rights, she was an active member of the National Woman's Party and marched in suffrage parades.

The Prestons prospered until the depression of the 1930's, when, discouraged and weary, they moved to a barn they had remodeled on the estate of Mrs. George Gould in East Hampton, Long Island. May Preston developed a serious skin infection which finally caused her to give up drawing. Undaunted, she turned to growing flowers and vegetables, combining them for their color effects, and her garden became a showplace of the countryside. She died of a coronary occlusion in 1949 at East Hampton and was buried there. She is remembered as a star of the golden age of American illustration.

[Ira Glackens, *William Glackens and the Ashcan Group* (1957); Walt Kuhn, *The Story of the Armory Show* (pamphlet, 1938); *Craftsman*, July 1910, p. 472; *Woman's Who's Who of America*, 1914–15; *Who's Who in America*, 1924–25; obituary in *N.Y. Times*, May 19, 1949; records of Oberlin College and of Art Students' League; death record from N.Y. State Dept. of Health.]

JANE GRANT

**PRINGLE, Elizabeth Waties Allston** (May 29, 1845–Dec. 5, 1921), South Carolina rice planter and author, was the second daughter of Robert Francis Withers Allston and Adele (Petigru) Allston and the third of their five children who survived childhood. She was born at Canaan Seashore, the family summer home near Pawley's Island in South Carolina. Her father, whose forebears had held extensive grants in the Georgetown District as early as 1763, cultivated thousands of acres of rice lands; a most capable organizer of plantation economy, he wrote an authoritative treatise on rice culture. He also served in the state legislature and as governor, and gave much time to Episcopal Church affairs, the establishment of free schools, and the reform of the poor laws. Elizabeth was named for Allston's "Aunt Blythe," a figure of romance in the family because of her love for a Waties first cousin who, not permitted to marry her, at his early death willed her a fortune in rice lands. Mrs. Blythe's reputation for able management of her plantations and wise care of her people became a legend in the area. On her mother's side Elizabeth Allston descended from an outstanding Huguenot family, the Giberts, and could claim as uncle James Louis Petigru, the brilliant lawyer and Unionist leader.

At Chicora Wood, her family's home on the Peedee River fourteen miles north of Georgetown, she noted her parents' roles as heads of a large establishment with its flow of visitors and growing population of slaves. With her older sister Adele, she received excellent instruction from an English governess until her tenth year, when she was sent to Madame Togno's Charleston boarding school, where French and music were stressed. Of a passionate nature, Elizabeth had her moments of rebellion and uncertainty. In 1862, when the school moved and combined with the remnants of the distinguished academy at Barhamville, an Italian music master, praising her singing voice, instilled a lasting self-confidence by assuring her that she possessed *le feu sacré*.

After the disastrous war years Elizabeth Allston taught in the Charleston school started by her widowed mother. Although she liked teaching, in 1868 she moved back with her mother, her younger brother Charles, and her sister Jane to Chicora Wood, the only one remaining of her father's seven plantations. She was married there on Apr. 26, 1870, to John Julius Pringle of the White House, a plantation eight miles down the Peedee. Of a New York family on his mother's side, Pringle had attended Northern and Swiss schools and studied law at Berlin and Heidelberg. After six years shadowed only by debt and the loss of their infant son, Pringle's sudden death cut short the marriage.

The young widow, who never entirely recovered from her loss, returned to her mother's household and took up the nearest duties, caring for the motherless children of her older brother, sharing in the informal but incessant hospitality of the plantation and island houses. A bequest enabled her early in 1880 to buy the White House plantation from her husband's heirs, and in 1885, despite her family's skepticism, she decided to manage it herself. Her task would have been halved had she lived at the White House—an hour and a half distant— but the close tie between mother and daughter, as well as the unconventionality of choosing a life alone in the country, precluded this. She nevertheless managed the hands and even on occasion shared the field work. In addition to raising rice she kept livestock and poultry, planted for fodder, and cultivated local fruits: peaches, strawberries, and scuppernongs. She herself could perform almost any farm task from making mattresses of the wool of her flock to improvising a method for the delivery of a stillborn calf. She had a scientific approach to agriculture and applied new techniques such as the use of an incubator and the inoculation of alfalfa seed. Mrs. Pringle experienced deep joy in the work and, until the turn of the century, usually showed a profit. With all her arduous activities, including frequent periods of nursing neighbors and family, she found time for much reading and music and a little sketching and translating.

After her mother's death in 1896, Mrs. Pringle, with the financial help of her younger sister, acquired Chicora and, at fifty-one, took on its management as well. She had only a small capital, however, and the labor supply was dwindling and becoming more unreliable;

the next eighteen years were a ceaseless effort to make enough for taxes, wages, and the small deeds of generosity and charity necessary to her nature. Often only the lucky appearance of a buyer for one of her prize animals enabled her to meet the tax deadline. By 1906 storm damage to the rice banks, demoralization of the hands, and, most important of all, the emergence of mechanized rice cultivation in the Southwest had spelled the doom of the low country Carolina plantations and involved Mrs. Pringle in financial failure.

Throughout her busy years as plantation manager she also aspired to authorship, though at first with little success. Save for a translation published in a Charleston paper in 1879 and a short section of her girlhood diary she contributed to a newspaper series in 1884, her early literary efforts (mostly stories and plays) were regularly rejected. She was fifty-eight before she found a market for her writing. In 1903 the New York *Sun* accepted a series of excerpts from her diary which she had submitted at the urging of friends. Published between 1904 and 1907 under the name "Patience Pennington," these were collected in 1913, with additions and charming illustrations by Alice R. Huger Smith, as *A Woman Rice Planter*. The book, which was widely and favorably reviewed, is a collection of humorous, whimsical accounts of the people and simple events at Chicora and in the summer community of Plantersville. Its lasting value, well expressed by its most recent editor, lies in "the story not only of her trials, vexations, and triumphs, but also the death of an old and significant industry, and the end of an era in our social and economic history." Mrs. Pringle's second book, *Chronicles of Chicora Wood*, published posthumously in 1922, depicts life at that plantation in the days of her father. Its detailed description of the intricate workings of a rice plantation has made it valuable to historians of the Old South.

In the last decade of her life Mrs. Pringle restricted the farm work at Chicora to livestock, fodder, and vegetable crops. She was the moving spirit in the extensive repair of old Prince Frederick Church near Chicora, raising the money and supervising the work. She attended to a voluminous correspondence for the Mount Vernon Ladies Association of the Union (founded by ANN PAMELA CUNNINGHAM), which she had wholeheartedly served since 1903 as state vice-regent. In 1915 and 1918 she paid long visits in California to her friend PHOEBE APPERSON HEARST; it was Mrs. Hearst who induced her to set down the childhood recollections that later became *Chronicles*

*of Chicora Wood*. During her long residence at Chicora she stood as friend, guardian, and teacher to the simple folk of the neighborhood, black and white. In her cultivated yet strenuous life there she furnished to such discerning friends as the author Owen Wister, the editor Ellery Sedgwick, and the historian Frederic Bancroft a living example of the best traditions of the region. She died at Chicora at the age of seventy-six after a heart attack and was buried beside her husband at Magnolia Cemetery, Charleston.

[Two manuscript collections in the S.C. Hist. Soc. Library, the Letters and Papers of the Family of Robert F. W. Allston and the Allston-Pringle-Hill Collection, contain letters, extensive diaries, plantation records, clippings, and unpublished writings. Other manuscript sources are in the Frederic Bancroft Collection, Columbia Univ. Library (Letters, Southern Notebook VI); the Alice R. Huger Smith Papers (privately owned); and the Owen Wister Papers, Library of Congress. Cornelius O. Cathey's introduction to the John Harvard Library edition of *A Woman Rice Planter* (1961) is the best account and evaluation of Mrs. Pringle. See also: introduction to J. H. Easterby, ed., *The S.C. Rice Plantation as Revealed in the Papers of Robert F. W. Allston* (1945); Mt. Vernon Ladies Association of the Union, *Annual Reports*, 1903–22; Susan L. Allston, "White House Plantation," *News and Courier* (Charleston, S.C.), Nov. 16, 1930; Lucy H. M. Soulsby, *The America I Saw in 1916–1918* (1920); obituary notice in *Georgetown* (S.C.) *Times*, Dec. 9, 1921. Information was also supplied by Susan L. Allston and Louise L. Logan. Mrs. Pringle's publications include "Fun in the Fort" (by "Esther Alden") in *Our Women in the War* (1885); and "Rab and Dab" (by "Patience Pennington"), *Atlantic Monthly*, Nov. and Dec. 1914, Jan. 1915.]

MARGARETTA P. CHILDS

**PRIOR, Margaret Barrett Allen** (1773–Apr. 7, 1842), charitable worker, was born in Fredericksburg, Va., the daughter of William Barrett, a farmer. Her mother died when Margaret was young, and she was reared by a stepmother and taught "a trade." At sixteen she was married to William Allen, a linen merchant of Baltimore. They had several children, all but one of whom died early. When Allen, now the commander of a merchant ship, was lost at sea about 1808 his widow moved to New York City with her year-and-a-half-old son to be near an older sister. In 1814 she became the wife of William Prior, a merchant and member of the Society of Friends. From 1819 until shortly before his death in 1829 they lived next door to her sister on Bowery Hill in a commodious house with pleasant grounds.

Margaret Prior had joined the Baptist Church about 1800. A religious experience which she had in 1815, however, led her to unite with a Methodist Episcopal congregation and turn to charitable work. During the severe winter of 1818–19 she established a soup kitchen for the poor of the Ninth Ward, her husband paying for the supplies. In 1822 she hired a teacher and started a local school for the children of the poor.

The Priors' own children apparently died young, and it is said that after the death of her seventh child Mrs. Prior determined to become a "mother to the motherless." She took several children into her home for periods of time, and with her husband's approval she deliberately adopted a baby, Adeline, whom no one else wanted because she was crippled by a broken back. Mrs. Prior eventually contrived a brace so that the child could sit up and learn to walk, but she needed constant care for the ten years she lived. Before Adeline's death the Priors adopted another infant daughter, Mary. A highly efficient housekeeper, Mrs. Prior managed with one servant to run her affairs economically, stinting on clothes and sleep to get more time and money for work with other unfortunate children. She was a member of the board of managers of the New York Orphan Asylum (founded by JOANNA GRAHAM BETHUNE and others), was instrumental in establishing an asylum for half-orphans, and was an official visitor at the House of Refuge for delinquent children.

Her greatest interest, however, was in the New York Female Moral Reform Society, an outgrowth of the work of John R. McDowall, spurred by the great revival of 1830–31 in New York initiated by the preaching of Charles Finney. The society hoped for the reclamation of "depraved and abandoned females" but worked primarily for "the preservation of the virtuous." Mrs. Prior, a member of its first board of managers in 1834, was three years later commissioned its first woman missionary, a post which she filled until her death. Her work lay in the poorer parts of the city and involved her in a number of what would now be called social service activities. These were recorded with the assistance of a younger colleague, Sarah R. Ingraham, and appeared regularly in the society's journal, the *Advocate of Moral Reform*. Despite their pious and evangelistic phraseology, the reports are of interest as early case studies and firsthand accounts of slum conditions. Mrs. Prior and her co-workers aided the sick, reported extreme need to ward committees, found employment for deserving girls and women, vis-

ited houses of ill fame, factories, prisons, and the Bellevue Hospital, and occasionally, though not always effectively, invoked police intervention for social problems. She also worked vigorously for temperance, giving up her lifelong use of snuff to persuade a drinker to sign the pledge. She is said in addition to have effected some one hundred religious conversions.

Mrs. Prior discovered those in need of spiritual or temporal help by going from door to door distributing tracts. Originally a lover of fine clothes, she wore Quaker dress at first, but finding this too conspicuous, she adopted the plainest garb, on one occasion assuming the disguise of a washerwoman in order to rescue a girl unwillingly detained in a brothel. The crime and wretchedness she witnessed often kept her from sleeping at night, and the criticism of friends hostile to the moral reform movement tried her "acute sensibility, too easily wounded," but her evangelistic faith strengthened her to continue her work. She often bought food and fuel for the needy, found friends and neighbors to help with money and supplies, secured interpreters for new immigrants, located missing relatives, arranged funerals, and even took the most desperate cases into her own home. To those beyond help—advanced cases of "consumption" and alcoholism and badly diseased prostitutes —she offered prayer and sympathy from a "friend to the friendless." Not always were her ministrations welcome; often she was frightened; but she managed to talk or pray her way out of difficulty, protected from physical violence by her age and sex. She continued to go about her work in all weather, visiting about fifty families a week, until an attack of pleurisy caused "inflammation of the lungs" with general complications. Devotedly cared for by her daughter Mary and by her daughter-in-law, she died at her home in New York in her seventieth year. A biography of Mrs. Prior, *Walks of Usefulness*, published the year after her death by the American Female Moral Reform Society (soon renamed the American Female Guardian Society), went through many editions and was widely cited as an example to women.

[Sarah R. Ingraham, *Walks of Usefulness, or Reminiscences of Mrs. Margaret Prior* (1843); Flora L. Northrup, *The Record of a Century, 1834–1934* (Am. Female Guardian Soc., 1934); files of the *Advocate of Moral Reform* (N.Y.), 1841–43; Mrs. S. R. I. (Sarah Ingraham) Bennett, *Woman's Work among the Lowly* (1877), a record of the work of the Female Guardian Soc. For the founding and purposes of the society, see Robert S.

Fletcher, *Hist. of Oberlin College* (1943), I, 296–314.]

MARY SUMNER BENSON

**PROVOOST, Mary Spratt.** *See* ALEXANDER, Mary Spratt Provoost.

**PRYOR, Sara Agnes Rice** (Feb. 19, 1830–Feb. 15, 1912), author and Southern social leader in postwar New York, was born in Halifax County, Va., to Samuel Blair Rice, a physician turned Baptist minister, and Lucinda Walton (Leftwich) Rice. Among her forebears were Nathaniel Bacon, the seventeenth-century Virginia political leader, and the Rev. David Rice, a founder of Hampden-Sydney College and well known for his labors in establishing Presbyterianism in Kentucky. At the age of three Sara was adopted by a childless uncle and aunt, Dr. and Mrs. Samuel Pleasants Hargrave of Hanover, Va.; in later years she would recall her girlhood with them as a time of "absolute serenity and happiness" (*My Day*, p. 39). When she was nine the Hargraves moved to Charlottesville. Here Sara briefly attended a female seminary conducted by a Presbyterian clergyman, but her principal education came from her aunt, from an irresponsible but gifted German music teacher, and from her friends among the students at the University of Virginia. She early demonstrated literary talent, writing at fifteen a love story which was accepted, though never published, by the *Saturday Evening Post*.

On Nov. 8, 1848, Sara Rice, an attractive brown-eyed, auburn-haired girl of eighteen, was married to Roger Atkinson Pryor, a twenty-year-old law student. They had seven children, born between 1850 and 1868: Marie Gordon, Theodorick Bland, William Rice, Roger Atkinson, Mary Blair, Lucy Atkinson, and Frances Theodora Bland. Of their sons, Roger became an attorney and William a prominent New York gynecologist; Theodorick, a brilliant young man of great promise, was accidentally drowned in 1871 while a student at Columbia Law School.

The early years of Mrs. Pryor's marriage were unsettled. Her husband was admitted to the bar in 1849 and practiced briefly in Charlottesville, but he found Democratic politics and journalism more to his taste. In the 1850's she loyally followed his fortunes as he successively founded and edited a newspaper in his native Petersburg, Va.; assisted John W. Forney in editing the Washington (D.C.) *Union;* became an editor of the *Richmond Enquirer;* returned to Washington in 1857 to establish a fiercely sectional newspaper, *The South;* and in 1859 won election to Congress, filling the seat of an incumbent who had died. Sara Pryor found Washington's social life richly exciting, and her published reminiscences dwell at length on the politicians and belles who filled the capital during the Buchanan administration.

This interlude ended abruptly in March 1861 when her husband, a fire-eating secessionist, resigned his Congressional seat to devote all his energies to bringing Virginia into the Confederacy. When hostilities began he rose rapidly to brigadier general, seeing duty in 1862 in the Seven Days' battles and at Antietam. Mrs. Pryor, placing the children with relatives, visited him in camp when possible and remained with him during lengthy periods of inactivity in Richmond. In November 1862, after a summer as a hospital volunteer in Richmond, she followed her husband to the Blackwater River, a quiet part of the front to which he had been assigned with a small force for foraging duty. In July 1863 he resigned his general's commission in disgust, reenlisted as a private, and was assigned to duty near Petersburg. Here Mrs. Pryor lived for the rest of the war with her children, enduring with fortitude the Union siege of the city. To compound her anxiety, her husband was captured in November 1864 and held prisoner in Washington, D.C., until March 1865.

For two years after the war, Sara Pryor remained with her children in near destitution in occupied Petersburg while her husband, without prospects in Reconstruction Virginia, sought to establish himself as a lawyer in New York City. When in 1867 he won his first important case she joined him there, to remain for the rest of her life. They lived very modestly, first in Brooklyn and then in Manhattan, Mrs. Pryor teaching music to eke out the family income. But influential New Yorkers saw advantages to the Democratic party in winning the friendship of prominent Virginians, and Pryor's career prospered accordingly. Appointed judge of the court of common pleas in 1890, he later (1896–99) served on the state supreme court. Mrs. Pryor, conscious that her husband's decision to cast his lot with former enemies had aroused resentment in the South and some suspicion in the North, identified herself prominently with a number of patriotic societies and philanthropic activities. A founder of the National Society of the Daughters of the American Revolution, she was the first regent of its New York City chapter. She was also a charter member of the

Colonial Dames of America, a vice-president of the Association for the Preservation of Virginia Antiquities, an officer of the Virginia Historical Society, and a leader in the movement to preserve the grave of George Washington's mother. Her gracious manner, distinguished appearance, and gifts as a raconteur soon won her a place in a city learning to be hospitable to charming Southerners. During the Florida yellow fever epidemic of 1888 and the Galveston flood of 1900 she organized society benefits to aid the sufferers.

Through her friend ANNE LYNCH BOTTA, mistress of a celebrated literary salon, Mrs. Pryor came to know MARY MAPES DODGE, KATE FIELD, MARY E. SHERWOOD, and other authors, and was herself encouraged to write. She began by contributing occasional pieces to the *Cosmopolitan,* the *Delineator,* and other magazines, and in 1899, when her husband retired from the bench, she took up the pen in earnest. Her first book, *The Mother of Washington and Her Times,* appeared four years later, when Mrs. Pryor was seventy-three. There followed *Reminiscences of Peace and War* (1904); *The Birth of the Nation* (1907), a history of Jamestown; and *My Day: Reminiscences of a Long Life* (1909). Though quickly forgotten, these works of popular history and highly colored autobiography enjoyed a certain success in their day. They stand now as relics of the upsurge of sentimental interest in the Old South and the Civil War which occurred at the turn of the century as the bitterness of the war and Reconstruction days began to fade.

Sara Pryor died at her home in New York City in February 1912 of chronic pernicious anemia, shortly before her eighty-second birthday. She was buried in Princeton, N.J. Her husband survived her by seven years.

[In addition to Mrs. Pryor's own works, see Walter L. Hopkins, *Leftwich-Turner Familes of Va. and Their Connections* (1931), pp. 60–61; the eulogistic biographical sketch by Marie Pryor Rice in Edwin A. Alderman and Joel Chandler Harris, eds., *Library of Southern Literature* (1907), X, 4273–77; *Who Was Who in America,* vol. I (1942), entries on Sara, Roger, and William Pryor; George B. Taylor, *Va. Baptist Ministers. 3rd Series* (1912), pp. 397–401 (on Samuel Blair Rice); Louise C. Willcox's fulsome "A Light Is Out," *Harper's Weekly,* Feb. 24, 1912; Frank L. Mott, *A Hist. of Am. Magazines,* III (1938), 483; *Dict. Am. Biog.* on Roger A. Pryor; *Richmond Times-Dispatch,* Feb. 16, 1912; *N.Y. Times,* Nov. 6, 1898 ("Illustrated Mag.," p. 4), July 19, 1908, Feb. 16, 1912; death record from N.Y. City Dept. of Health.]

MARGARET LAWRENCE SIMKINS

PUGH, Sarah (Oct. 6, 1800–Aug. 1, 1884), teacher, abolitionist, and woman suffragist, was born in Alexandria, Va., of Quaker parents, the second of two children and only daughter of Jesse and Catharine (Jackson) Pugh. Her father died when Sarah was only three, and her mother moved to Philadelphia, where she and a sister established a dressmaking business. Sarah's education included two years at the Westtown (Pa.) Boarding School, directed by the Quakers. In 1821 she began teaching in the Friends' school of the Twelfth Street Meeting House in Philadelphia, but she resigned her position in 1828 following a split between the Orthodox and the more liberal, or Hicksite, Quakers. This rift in Quakerism started a process of religious questioning within her which eventually led her to accept a unitarian faith with an emphasis on good deeds. In 1829 she established her own elementary school, where she taught for more than a decade, even after the antislavery movement became her major interest.

Hearing the English abolitionist George Thompson speak in 1835 stirred Sarah Pugh into accepting the doctrine of immediate and unconditional emancipation associated with William Lloyd Garrison and his followers. She joined the Philadelphia Female Anti-Slavery Society, of which she was for many years presiding officer, and the American Anti-Slavery Society. When a mob burned Pennsylvania Hall, where the Anti-Slavery Convention of American Women was meeting in 1838, the women finished their deliberations in Sarah Pugh's schoolhouse. Miss Pugh remained loyal to the Garrisonians when the abolitionists in 1840 split into two factions. She faithfully continued to attend antislavery conventions and canvassed her neighborhood with petitions to Congress and the state legislature urging the abolition of slavery. For years the Pennsylvania Anti-Slavery Society met in her home.

In 1840 Sarah Pugh, resigning her school to her co-workers, traveled with LUCRETIA MOTT, MARY GREW, Abby Kimber, and several others as American delegates to the London meeting of the British and Foreign Anti-Slavery Society; and it was she who wrote the strong protest the Pennsylvania women delegates presented when denied active participation. After the convention she toured the British Isles and the Continent and visited with a number of antislavery advocates. Back home, she continued to work for the movement, although most of her time over the next ten years was spent caring for her elderly mother, who died in 1851. Late that year she again went to Europe, with her brother and sister-in-law, remaining in England at the insistence of friends who wanted her help with antislavery work. For seventeen months she visited important cities, explaining American antislavery ideas and goals to groups of British intellectuals, and advising administrative committees and women's groups on organization. Returning to Philadelphia, she carried on the endless detail of the local movement. A small woman, delicately formed, Miss Pugh presided over meetings with calmness and dignity, most noticeably in 1859 when an Anti-Slavery Fair the women were conducting was suddenly denied the use of the building and had to secure a new location and move all its paraphernalia.

After the Civil War, which strengthened Sarah Pugh's faith in the peace testimony of her Quaker forebears, she turned her attention to the plight of the freedmen and the rights of women, for the Pennsylvania Anti-Slavery Association agreed to work for both causes. With Lucretia Mott, she traveled to woman's rights conventions and meetings, her care and companionship making the aged Mrs. Mott's continued attendance possible. Sympathetic to the suffrage cause, she regretted the split in the movement that began in 1869 and took no side in the argument, attending meetings of both groups. She also took an active part in the Moral Education Society, founded in Philadelphia in 1873, circulating petitions against a proposed law to license prostitution in Pennsylvania. She lived to the age of eighty-three, in good health until the last two years of her life, when lumbago made her a semi-invalid. The shock resulting from a bad fall was the immediate cause of her death. She died in Germantown, Pa., where since 1864 she had lived with her brother Isaac and his wife, and was buried in the Friends Fair Hill Burial Ground in Philadelphia. Though never in the forefront of reform leadership, she was an intellectually minded companion of the outstanding reform leaders and devoted her time to the quiet but necessary tasks required to keep their movements active. "I have no fear of her talents rusting for want of use," Lucretia Mott once wrote of Sarah Pugh (Cromwell, p. 112).

[The Memorial of Sarah Pugh: A Tribute of Respect from Her Cousins (1888), is extremely useful, since much of it consists of quotations from her journal and correspondence. Her early work with the suffrage movement is mentioned in Elizabeth C. Stanton et al., Hist. of Woman Suffrage, vol. I (1881). See also the references to her in Otelia Cromwell, Lucretia Mott (1958); and obituary by Mary Grew in Woman's Jour., Aug. 16, 1884. There are some Sarah Pugh letters in the Weston and Garrison Papers in the Boston Public Library.]

LARRY GARA

**PUTNAM, Alice Harvey Whiting** (Jan. 18, 1841–Jan. 19, 1919), pioneer kindergartner, was born in the fledgling settlement of Chicago, a city whose social, cultural, and educational progress was close to her heart all her life. She was the youngest of the three daughters of William Loring Whiting, a commission merchant and a founder of the Chicago Board of Trade (1848), and his wife, Mary Starr, both natives of Connecticut. Like most girls from well-to-do Chicago families at that time, Alice was educated privately, first in a school run by her mother and sister and then at the local Dearborn Seminary. On May 20, 1868, she was married to Joseph Robie Putnam, a native of Groton, Mass., who had come to Chicago and entered the real estate business. Mrs. Putnam had been reared an Episcopalian but on her marriage became a member of the New Jerusalem Church, perhaps because her husband belonged to that denomination or perhaps because the doctrines of Swedenborg appealed to the mysticism and idealism which were strong elements in her own nature.

Her interest in the kindergarten was originally aroused by a concern for the proper education of the two eldest of her four children, Charlotte, Alice, Helen, and Henry Sibley. In 1874 she formed a parents' class of ten or twelve persons to discuss Friedrich Froebel's Mother Play and Songs. Wishing to improve her understanding of the German educator's theories, she enrolled in Mrs. Anna J. Ogden's training school in Columbus, Ohio, and after graduation returned to Chicago and opened a kindergarten in her home. Her parents' class and her kindergarten, said to have been among the first such organizations in Chicago, were the source of the kindergarten movement in that city. By 1880 the movement had attracted sufficient attention and support to warrant the formation of two societies, one of which, the Chicago Froebel Association, sponsored a training school for kindergartners that Mrs. Putnam supervised from 1880 to 1910, for part of this time at Hull House. During the thirty years of its existence the school prepared more than eight hundred kindergarten teachers, and its graduates brought the kindergarten philosophy into many communities in this country and abroad.

Always eager for new ideas, Mrs. Putnam attended SUSAN E. BLOW's kindergarten classes in St. Louis, Mme. MARIE KRAUS-BOELTÉ's in New York, and Col. Francis W. Parker's summer school at Martha's Vineyard. Parker's classes were a revelation to her, for he took Froebel's concepts of freedom, self-expression, and social participation and used them as guides for teaching and learning throughout the elementary school. Mrs. Putnam played a leading role in securing Parker's appointment as principal of the Cook County Normal School in 1882, and, while directing the Froebel Association Training School, she joined his staff as a part-time lecturer and director of his demonstration kindergarten. An equally important step in gaining recognition of the kindergarten's value occurred in 1886 when the Froebel Association persuaded the Chicago Board of Education to allow it to conduct a kindergarten in a public school. By 1892 ten private kindergartens under various auspices were occupying rooms in public schools, and in that year the Froebel Association petitioned the Board of Education to incorporate these into the city system. The petition was granted, and the board began of its own volition to establish public school kindergartens. Thus the kindergarten movement which had been initiated by a dozen parents in Mrs. Putnam's parlor eighteen years before had now achieved the status of a county and municipal enterprise. Although the combined efforts of many people had won this signal victory, Mrs. Putnam's enthusiasm, personal charm, humor, and sound sense, her connections with influential society, business, and professional clubs (she was a leader in the Chicago Woman's Club), her friendship with Parker, JANE ADDAMS, and other prominent citizens, and her tireless work with parents and teachers had contributed in no small measure to the outcome.

Mrs. Putnam carried on a voluminous correspondence with parents and teachers and was active in the affairs of the Chicago Kindergarten Club, which she and ELIZABETH HARRISON had founded in 1883, and the International Kindergarten Union. She was elected president of each of these organizations (in 1890 and 1901) and served regularly on their committees and programs. In 1906 she was appointed nonresident reader in education in the correspondence department of the University of Chicago and offered two courses, "The Training of Children (A Course for Mothers)" and "An Introduction to Kindergarten Theory and Practice." Of medium height and slender in youth, she became increasingly stout and nearsighted with age, and her infirmities led her to give up the superintendency of the Froebel Association Training School in 1910 and her University of Chicago courses in 1916–17. Her remaining years she spent with

her children and grandchildren in Pennsylvania and New York, but several weeks before her death she returned to her beloved native city. She died there of nephritis and was buried in Oak Woods Cemetery, Chicago.

Much of Mrs. Putnam's success as a teacher and as a champion of the kindergarten movement was the result of her open-mindedness and her maternal attitude toward children and students. In her teaching she drew upon a broad range of experience in home and community and upon a lively interest in music, art, and literature. Her first allegiance was to children, not to Froebelian doctrine in the narrow or literal sense. She sought inspiration, assistance, and ideas wherever they could be found, and accepted them so long as they gave promise of enriching child life and of expanding and deepening the sympathies of those who would teach children.

[Biographical material from: *Kindergarten and First Grade*, Mar. 1919, pp. 111–15; Internat. Kindergarten Union, *Pioneers of the Kindergarten in America* (1924), pp. 204–22; *Kindergarten Mag.*, June 1893, pp. 729–33; death record from Ill. Dept. of Public Health; correspondence with Mrs. Putnam's son, Henry Sibley Putnam, Sarasota, Fla. Many of Mrs. Putnam's reports, addresses, and articles appeared in the *Kindergarten Rev.* (e.g., vols. VIII, IX, XII, XIV, XVI) and the Nat. Education Assoc., *Jour. of Proc. and Addresses* (1889, 1893, 1901, 1902, 1908). See also articles by Mrs. Putnam in *The Kindergarten and the School* (1886), pp. 94–107; and *Outlook*, June 13, 1896.]
ROBERT L. MC CAUL

**PUTNAM, Emily James Smith** (Apr. 15, 1865–Sept. 7, 1944), author and teacher, first dean of Barnard College, was born in Canandaigua, N.Y., the second daughter and youngest of five children of James Cosslett Smith, a judge of the New York State supreme court, and his wife, Emily Ward Adams. Both parents traced their ancestry to early Welsh settlers. Emily was born much later than her older sister and brothers; her junior position in a family of adults, she felt, was responsible for her youthful rebelliousness and drive. As a young girl she came under the influence of a neighbor, an enthusiastic Hellenist, who introduced her to the field that became a permanent scholarly interest. In spite of her parents' preference that she pursue the interests appropriate to a young woman of her period, she determined to secure a superior education and prepared with tutors for entrance to college. After graduating with the first class at Bryn Mawr in 1889, she went to England and became one of the first American women to study at Girton College, Cambridge. After her return, she taught at the

Packer Collegiate Institute in Brooklyn, N.Y. (1891–93), and then became a fellow in Greek at the University of Chicago (1893–94). By the age of twenty-nine she was launched on a promising career as a Greek scholar.

In 1894 Miss Smith was appointed dean of Barnard College, the women's college recently founded in association with Columbia University. At Barnard she taught required courses in Homer to freshmen and in Plato to sophomores. Virginia Gildersleeve, a student of hers who later became dean, recalled her "rapier-like mind and satiric wit." Like her predecessor as head of the college, ELLA WEED, Miss Smith held no doctrinaire views of woman's proper role but favored the opening of all educational opportunities so that women might be equipped to pursue their interests freely. Her work as dean was crucial in defining and stabilizing Barnard's relationship to Columbia. She was a strong opponent of what was then a customary pattern for such a women's "annex," a pattern which required that women take examinations for which they were ill-prepared because of exclusion from lectures open only to male students. Consequently, she intensified efforts to open more Columbia courses to Barnard students and to secure for the Barnard faculty scholars of equal standing with those at Columbia. Miss Smith scrupulously consulted President Seth Low and Dean John Van Amringe of Columbia on all questions regarding academic policy and thus averted the growth of separate standards for the two institutions. In 1895 her success in drawing to the Barnard faculty such able scholars as John B. Clark, James Harvey Robinson, and Frank N. Cole initiated a regular exchange of faculty time between Barnard and Columbia, and under her aegis Barnard in 1897 joined Columbia in moving its location from Madison Avenue to Morningside Heights. Miss Smith's most significant achievement as dean was her negotiation in 1900 of a formal agreement between Barnard and Columbia giving the women's college representation on the university council, official appointment by Columbia University for its faculty, broader access for women to graduate study at Columbia, and equal privileges in the university library. Thus Barnard retained its valued independence while continuing to have its degrees granted by Columbia and enjoying even closer association with the university. It was an arrangement unique among women's colleges.

On Apr. 27, 1899, Miss Smith became the second wife of the noted publisher George Haven Putnam, who was twenty-one years her senior. After some debate the trustees accepted the novelty of a married dean, but when she became pregnant she offered her resignation. Palmer Cosslett Putnam, her only child, later an author of scientific and technical works, was born July 13, 1900. Thereafter Mrs. Putnam subordinated her own concerns to her husband's career in publishing and civic affairs. In the latter realm she herself served as president of the League for Political Education from 1901 to 1904. While assisting Putnam devotedly in his many activities she was able to return to Barnard in 1914 as associate in history, and in 1920 she tranferred to the Greek department, remaining until her retirement in 1930, the year of her husband's death. In this period she also continued to publish books, translations, and articles. Her most notable work, *The Lady: Studies of Certain Significant Phases of Her History* (1910), was widely read in women's colleges. A perceptive analysis, it ranged from ancient, medieval, and Renaissance ladies to the bluestocking of the eighteenth century and the mistress of the Southern plantation. *Candaules' Wife and Other Old Stories* (1926) imaginatively expands certain provocative passages from Herodotus. Partly as the outcome of a Columbia friendship with James Harvey Robinson, an early supporter of the idea, Mrs. Putnam in 1919 helped found the New School for Social Research, a New York institution established to promote adult education. She became a member of its board, offered vital encouragement and counsel to its director, Alvin S. Johnson, during its uncertain early years, and lectured at the New School during the period from 1920 to 1932.

Mrs. Putnam had golden hair, bright blue eyes, attractively strong features, and a commanding presence; her penetrating mind and often literary humor invariably drew an appreciative circle at social gatherings and delighted scores of her contemporaries. Among her achievements might be noted her ascent in a basket, in masculine disguise and equipped with her Greek, into one of the monastic sanctuaries of Mount Athos. After her husband's death Mrs. Putnam lived with her sister Alice in Spain until they were forced to leave by the revolution of the mid-1930's. Thereafter they made their home in Jamaica, West Indies, where Mrs. Putnam died in Kingston in 1944, of double pneumonia following exposure in a tropical rainstorm. A lifelong Episcopalian, she was buried in the St. Andrew Parish cemetery in Kingston.

[Besides her books, which include translations of Lucian and of French social thinkers, Mrs. Putnam wrote frequent articles and reviews in journals like the *Outlook,* the *Nation,* and the *Columbia Univ. Quart.* Manuscripts in the Barnard College archives give a detailed record of her activities as dean. The most useful Barnard histories for Mrs. Putnam are Alice Duer Miller and Susan Myers, *Barnard College: The First Fifty Years* (1939), and Marian C. White, *A Hist. of Barnard College* (1954). Virginia C. Gildersleeve, *Many a Good Crusade* (1954), and Alvin S. Johnson, *Pioneer's Progress* (1952), together with William T. Brewster, "Barnard College, 1889–1909," *Colum-*

*bia Univ. Quart.,* Mar. 1910, give some background material by participants. George Haven Putnam, *Memories of a Publisher* (1915), is disappointingly meager. The best sources of information about Mrs. Putnam's life and personality are surviving friends and relatives. Conversations with the following were particularly helpful: Palmer Cosslett Putnam of Venice, Calif., her son; Mrs. Joseph Lindon Smith of N.Y. City, her stepdaughter; Alvin S. Johnson of N.Y. City, former director of the New School.]

ANNETTE K. BAXTER

# Q

**QUINTON, Amelia Stone** (July 31, 1833–June 23, 1926), organizer of Indian reform, was born in Jamesville, N.Y., near Syracuse, one of at least four children of Jacob Thompson Stone and Mary (Bennett) Stone. Growing up in nearby Homer, where her grandfather Asa Bennett (originally from Connecticut) had, as a Baptist deacon during years of revivalism, gone from household to household praying and exhorting, Amelia acquired the deep religious conviction that guided her later years. After attending the coeducational Cortland Academy in Homer, she became "preceptress" of an academy near Syracuse. She next taught a year in a Madison, Ga., seminary and then was married to the Rev. James Franklin Swanson of that state. Upon his death she returned to the North, teaching for a year at Philadelphia's Chestnut Street Female Seminary. A period of volunteer work among the inmates of charitable and correctional institutions in New York City followed. When the temperance crusade sprang into being in 1874, Mrs. Swanson was an early member of the Woman's Christian Temperance Union in Brooklyn. She soon found herself organizing other local unions and then became state organizer for the W.C.T.U. In 1877, her health strained from overwork, she traveled to Europe. After recuperating on the Continent she gave temperance talks in English churches and homes. While in England she was married to the Rev. Richard L. Quinton of London, a lecturer in history and astronomy whom she had met on the voyage over; in the autumn of 1878 they settled in Philadelphia.

Calling the next spring upon her friend MARY L. BONNEY, principal of the Chestnut Street Female Seminary and a fellow member of the First Baptist Church, Mrs. Quinton

found her greatly troubled over newspaper accounts of the continuing pressure on Congress to open the Indian Territory to white settlement. The two women determined on a campaign to arouse an indifferent public on the Indians' behalf. Armed with a petition calling for the honoring of Indian treaties, they circulated copies among prominent Pennsylvania citizens, especially women active in church and charitable work; 13,000 signatures were presented to President Hayes and to the House of Representatives in February 1880. They then formed an interdenominational women's committee in Philadelphia, with Mrs. Quinton as secretary and organizer. A second popular petition, representing 50,000 men and women, was brought before the Senate in January 1881. Later that year Mrs. Quinton began to organize outside Pennsylvania, meeting in different cities with representatives of the local churches; thirteen new committees helped her collect signatures for a third and still more impressive petition, representing 100,000 adherents, presented in the Senate by Henry L. Dawes of Massachusetts, a friend of Indian reform, early in 1882. Written by Amelia Quinton herself, it called for a new federal Indian policy of education, legal equality, and, most important, the allotment of tribal lands in farm-size parcels to individual Indians, looking toward an eventual end of reservations and the absorption of the red man into white society.

With the public conscience now awakening, other citizens' groups began to form: the Indian Rights Association, under men's leadership, took up the call for allotment late in 1882, joined the next year by the Lake Mohonk Conference of Friends of the Indian. Mrs. Quinton's organization, now called the

Women's National Indian Association, in 1883 launched a program of missionary and educational work among the Indians, thus hoping "to hasten . . . their civilization, christianization, and enfranchisement." After discussing plans with a sympathetic Secretary of the Interior in Washington, Amelia Quinton set out in 1884 on her first trip west, touring Indian reservations and speaking to groups of Indian women, while organizing sympathetic white women in Kansas, Nebraska, and Dakota into auxiliaries of her association and urging the men to support the Indian Rights Association. Upon her return she concentrated her efforts on a full-scale campaign by the three reform groups to secure the passage of federal allotment legislation. With other members of a Mohonk committee, she personally presented a plea for Indian allotment, education, and citizenship to President Cleveland in 1885. By late 1886, thanks to her organizing work, the Women's Association alone had eighty-three branches in twenty-eight states and territories. During the previous year its Philadelphia headquarters and branches had contributed articles to some 800 periodicals, presented sixty-five petitions to Congress, held public meetings, and inspired countless individual letters to Congressmen. Headquarters had sent out 49,-000 copies of fifteen new publications, five of them written by Amelia Quinton, who had also delivered fifty speeches and continued to organize while carrying a heavy burden of administration and correspondence. February of 1887 saw the passage of the Dawes Severalty Act, providing for allotment and citizenship. One prominent member of the Indian Rights Association credited "the greater part" of this achievement to "the women of this country," especially through their influence on clergymen, their devising of political strategy, and their letters to Congressmen (*Proceedings* of Lake Mohonk Conference, 1890, p. 101). Allotment was to remain official Indian policy for nearly half a century; only in the 1930's did grave social and economic consequences which the friends of the Indian had not foreseen and a changed climate of opinion lead to the formation of a new policy.

In the year of the Dawes Act the Women's Association made Mrs. Quinton president; for the next eighteen years, usually in this capacity, she was to lead its persisting efforts for Indian welfare. Continuing to attend the Lake Mohonk conferences, as she had since 1885, she served on important committees, reported on her association's work and her extensive travels in Indian country, and urged further reforms like the prohibition of liquor, compul-

sory education, and the extension of civil service to the Indian Bureau. She also worked with the United States Board of Indian Commissioners, a group of unpaid advisers to the bureau, attending its annual meetings with representatives of reform and missionary groups.

Having realized that, with a Democratic administration in power, "we need a Southern constituency," Mrs. Quinton traveled south in 1887, organizing auxiliaries in seven states. Her husband, who in his later years had given much time to the Indian cause, died about this time. In 1888, with Honorary President Bonney, she attended an international missionary convention in London. Her next major organizing tour, in 1891, enrolled ten more branches in the South and twenty-four in the Far West. She also made lobbying trips to Washington, where the association helped push through Congress larger appropriations for Indian education, an antiliquor bill (1897), and measures to protect the lands of threatened tribes.

In the association's steadily growing missionary work Amelia Quinton found her "crowning joy." She supervised the establishment of fifty missions among the Indians, which were eventually transferred to various denominations. Dedicated to rooting out "savagery and sin," Mrs. Quinton saw her group's duty to the Indian as "helping him to cease being an Indian that he may wholly become a man." To this end the association loaned money interest-free for "neat, civilized homes" (a program originated by ALICE CUNNINGHAM FLETCHER among the Omahas) and supported the federal government's efforts to stamp out polygamy and "immoral dances and customs"; she was particularly pleased when one tribe in her presence celebrated its first Fourth of July. The Women's Association also provided teachers and established libraries on the reservations, subsidized the education of Indians like Dr. SUSAN LA FLESCHE PICOTTE, helped students returning from Eastern schools find trades, and developed markets for Indian goods.

With Amelia Quinton's hearty approval her group became the National Indian Association in 1901, its auxiliaries now free to admit men. About 1904 headquarters and president moved to New York. Declining health caused her to refuse reelection as president the next year, but she remained chairman of the missionary department and continued to organize and travel. In 1907 she began several years of work in southern California, presenting the association's program, especially in Los Angeles and Long Beach, and joining in the state auxiliary's drive to bring relief to California's landless Indians. She was back in the East again by 1910, later settling in Ridgefield Park, N.J. Until her eighty-ninth year she occasionally attended meetings of Indian welfare groups. After developing arteriosclerosis, she suffered a cerebral hemorrhage and died in Ridgefield Park in her ninety-third year. She was buried in Homer, N.Y. To the end she had remained confident that "the *right* thing . . . *can* be done; for the right is God's way." A humanitarian innocent of any sense of cultural relativism, she had in long, hard, unpaid service demonstrated her belief that "barbarism has no claim upon us, but barbarians have." Seeing "no *per se* dependent races," recognizing that all races, "with opportunity, witness the same results," she had striven to give Indians a chance to become like everyone else.

[The *Annual Reports*, 1883–1926, of the (Women's) Nat. Indian Assoc. cover Mrs. Quinton's work in detail and contain expressions of her philosophy; the 1883 *Report* reviews the earlier work of the organization under its various names. Her article "Women's Work for Indians," in Lydia H. Farmer, ed., *The Nat. Exposition Souvenir: What America Owes to Women* (1893), surveys the movement to that date. Mary E. Dewey, *Hist. Sketch . . . of the Women's Nat. Indian Assoc.* (1900), the annual *Proc.* of the Lake Mohonk Conference of Friends of the Indian, and the *Reports* of the Board of Indian Commissioners are also useful on her activities. Of the booklets she wrote, an especially interesting one is *Suggestions to the Friends of the Women's Nat. Indian Assoc.* (c. 1886), since it gives her hints on obtaining local publicity. For her pre-Indian career, see Frances E. Willard and Mary A. Livermore, eds., *A Woman of the Century* (1893). Her date of birth comes from her death record (copy from N.J. Dept. of Health). On Deacon Asa Bennett, see the Rev. Alfred Bennett, *Hist. of the Baptist Church of Christ in Homer, N.Y.* (1844); other family data from the entry on Mrs. Quinton in *Lamb's Biog. Dict. of the U.S.*, VI, 389; and Susan W. Dimock, comp., *Births, Baptisms, Marriages and Deaths, from the Records of the Town and Churches in Mansfield, Conn., 1703–1850* (1898). On her temperance work, see brief references in J. Samuel Vandersloot, *The True Path* (1878), p. 576 (as "Mrs. Swanson"), and Annie Wittenmyer, *Hist. of the Woman's Temperance Crusade* (1882), p. 552. There are references to her also in William W. Keen, ed., *The Bi-Centennial Celebration of the Founding of the First Baptist Church of the City of Phila.* (1899).]

IRENE JOANNE WESTING

# R

**RAINEY, Gertrude Pridgett** (Apr. 26, 1886–Dec. 22, 1939), blues singer, better known as "Ma" Rainey, was one of the last of the great entertainers of Negro minstrels and one of the first to feature the distinctive folk-evolved type of song known as "the blues." Though documentation is sparse and not always reliable, enough is now known to verify important details of her life and background. She was born in Columbus, Ga., the second of five children of Thomas and Ella (Allen) Pridgett, both natives of Alabama. Her father's occupation is not known, but after his death, in 1896, her mother worked for the Central Railway of Georgia. A grandmother, who has been described as "a very stately lady," is said to have been on the stage after Emancipation.

Gertrude Pridgett made her first public appearance about 1900 at Springer Opera House in Columbus in a local talent show called "Bunch of Blackberries." On Feb. 2, 1904, she was married to Will ("Pa") Rainey, and for many years they did a song-and-dance act in Negro minstrel troupes, traveling throughout the South. Perhaps as early as 1902, however, she had added blues to her repertoire (Work, p. 32), and these songs quickly became the high points of her performances. In later theatre appearances she was billed as "Madame Rainey," but in the intimacy of early carnival or "tent" shows and to Southern audiences—who warmed to the squat, heavy-featured woman, with her flamboyant dress, flaring hair, and necklace and ear pendants of gold coins—she was known affectionately, if not always to her face, as "Ma." In the tent show, with Coleman (gasoline mantle) lanterns for footlights and music supplied by "jug" bands or jazz bands, she sang her homely songs of everyday life in a small, at times harsh, voice of unusual timbre and haunting pathos.

Over the years she starred in a variety of show troupes—Wolcott's "Rabbit Foot Minstrels," Tolliver's Circus and Musical Extravaganza (during a time when BESSIE SMITH was also with the company briefly), and others—and for such managers or owners as C. W.

Parks, Al Gaines, and Silas Green. When shows wintered in New Orleans she sometimes appeared in tent performances with local jazz musicians. Some of her song lyrics she wrote herself; others were written for her by the Rev. Thomas A. Dorsey (before his retirement from secular music). She was rumored to have retired to Mexico around 1921 but was soon active again. Paul Oliver has established that she continued to work, off and on, until the mid-1930's, when she returned to Columbus and the home she had had built there for her family after the death of her sister Malissa in 1935. A few months later her mother died. Thereafter Ma Rainey spent most of her time in Columbus and in Rome, Ga., where she operated two theatres, the Lyric and the Airdrome. Upon retirement she joined the Congregation of Friendship Baptist Church, of which her brother, Thomas Pridgett, Jr., was a deacon. She died in Columbus in 1939 of coronary heart disease and was buried in the family plot in Porterdale Cemetery.

Until 1923 Ma Rainey had been virtually unknown outside the Negro South. In that year, however, she made the first of a series of phonograph records for the Paramount company that won her a following among Northern Negroes as well. She continued to record until late 1928, when Paramount, believing that her "down home" songs had gone out of fashion, let her go; her known recordings number ninety-two. She never became as popular in the North as Bessie Smith. The latter's songs, even when from the Rainey repertoire, had a decidedly urban flavor, whereas Ma Rainey always reflected the original country background of the blues. But like Bessie Smith, Ma Rainey maintained an integrity of style that helped preserve a continuity from early forms of Afro-American music to jazz. Her importance as a figure in this development, only just beginning to be appreciated at the time of her death, has since been widely recognized.

[Family information was provided by Thomas Pridgett, Jr.; this corrects earlier biographical accounts in important details, notably her given name, which has sometimes erroneously included that of her younger sister, Malissa, who married Frank Nix. Other information from Ma Rainey's marriage certificate (Muscogee County Court, Columbus, Ga.) and death certificate (Ga. Dept. of Public Health), though the former misspells her maiden name and the latter gives her birth year incorrectly as 1892; from the Schomburg Collection of the N.Y. Public Library and from the Institute for Jazz Studies, N.Y. City; and from Miss Artiebelle McGinty (who appeared with Ma Rainey), Prof. Sterling A. Brown, Prof. Marshall W. Stearns, Frederic Ramsey, Jr., Paul Oliver,

Ralph J. Gleason, William Russell, and Zutty Singleton. Published materials include: John W. Work, *Am. Negro Songs* (1940), pp. 32–33; Thomas Pridgett, "The Life of Ma Rainey," *Jazz Information*, Sept. 6, 1940; article in *Jazz Music* (London), Aug. 1943; Charles Edward Smith, "Ma Rainey and the Minstrels," *Record Changer,* June 1955; Thomas Fulbright, "Ma Rainey and I," *Jazz Jour.* (London), Mar. 1956; Sterling Brown's poem on Ma Rainey in his *Southern Road* (1932); Charles Edward Smith et al., eds., *The Jazz Record Book* (1942); Nat Shapiro and Nat Hentoff, eds., *Hear Me Talkin' to Ya* (1955); and Paul Oliver, ed., *Conversation with the Blues* (1965). Reissues of some of Ma Rainey's recordings are included in the following albums: "The Young Louis Armstrong," "Ma Rainey," and "Great Blues Singers" (Riverside records).]

CHARLES EDWARD SMITH

**RAMBAUT, Mary Lucinda Bonney.** *See* BONNEY, Mary Lucinda.

**RAMSAY, Martha Laurens** (Nov. 3, 1759– June 10, 1811), South Carolina bluestocking and exemplar of dutiful womanhood, was born in Charleston. Her father, Henry Laurens, was of French Huguenot descent, the grandson of André Laurens, a saddler, who had arrived in Carolina during the 1690's. Her mother was Eleanor Ball, daughter of Elias Ball, a planter, who had come from Devonshire, England. Active in the rice and slave trades after 1747, Henry Laurens had accumulated one of the largest Carolina fortunes by 1762, when he turned planter, buying plantations totaling some twenty thousand acres and preparing to live off his invested wealth. Martha was the fifth daughter and the eighth of his thirteen children. By the time of their mother's death in 1770, however, only five children survived. Martha herself, it is said, was thought to have succumbed to smallpox as a baby and had been laid out for burial when an ocean breeze revived her.

As a child Martha Laurens showed great eagerness for learning. She could read easily at three and soon learned French, English grammar, geography, arithmetic, and some geometry. Her father approved her studious habits but cautioned her that a knowledge of housewifery was the first requisite in female education. In her twelfth year she "began to be the subject of serious religious impressions." After her mother's death her upbringing fell largely to her aunt and uncle, Mary and James Laurens. Left in their care in 1771, along with a younger sister, when her father took her brothers abroad for schooling, she lived with them for eleven years, at first in Charleston, and then abroad, where James Laurens had gone for his health. They spent several years at watering places in England, from 1775 to 1778, and then went to live at Vigan in the south of France. Much of this time Martha served as nurse for her ailing uncle. She continued an earnest course of reading. First came the Bible and then the old divines of the seventeenth and eighteenth centuries, especially Philip Doddridge; in divinity, her husband later wrote approvingly, she read "much of what was practical, but rarely looked into any thing that was controversial." Of historians she knew Plutarch, Charles Rollin, and William Robertson; of philosophy, not more than Locke's *Essay on Human Understanding*. She read the modern English and French works of genius, taste, and imagination. In a lighter vein she studied botany, dipped into the Archbishop of Cambray's *Dissertation on Pure Love*, committed most of Edward Young's *Night Thoughts* to memory, and learned to sing Dr. Isaac Watts' "divine songs" by heart. Education and religion remained her twin concerns, for when her uncle willed her 500 guineas, she provided for the distribution of Bibles to the people of Vigan and then set up a school for the young which she endowed with a teacher. Both gestures were typical examples of eighteenth-century charity.

In the fall of 1782, to her great joy, her father joined them in France, after his service as president of the Continental Congress, diplomat, and prisoner of war. Though reluctant to leave her dying uncle, she considered at this point marrying a French suitor (a M. de Vernes), but her father thought him an aged fortune hunter, and in obedience she gave up the match. She spent most of 1783 and 1784 with her father, who hoped to cure his gout at Bath—in a sense she had merely exchanged one patient for another. Laurens sailed home in the summer of 1784; Martha and her sister followed early in 1785. Her father's ill health brought Martha in touch with the Charleston physician David Ramsay (1749–1815), a former member of the Continental Congress; and on Jan. 23, 1787, she became his third wife.

With her husband in the state legislature, her sister married to another public figure, Charles Pinckney, and her brother Henry to a daughter of John Rutledge, Martha Ramsay lived at the center of public affairs. It was, however, in the private sphere that she excelled. In her conception, woman's proper role was to provide strength for the men in her life to perform on the public stage. In sixteen years she bore her husband eleven children,

suckling them all: Eleanor Henry Laurens (1787), Martha H. L. (1789), Frances H. L. (1790), Katharine H. L. (1792), Sabine Elliot (1794, who became the second wife of her first cousin Henry Laurens Pinckney), David (1795), Jane Montgomery (1796), James (1797), a second Jane Montgomery (1799), Nathaniel (1801), and William (1802). A letter of 1797 to his wife gives David Ramsay's view of this childbearing: "C. W. Wilson one of our backcountry senators assures me that one couple in his neighborhood have 23 children all alive. This I fear is beyond our mark. May God bless these he has given us and as many more as he in his kind providence pleases and also give you strength and health to bring them up which if done by you I am sure will be well done." Eight of her eleven children survived childhood.

Martha Ramsay was an eighteenth-century woman with the staying powers of a Roman matron. She had read Rousseau on the care of the young, but she preferred the teachings of Locke and the Presbyterian divine Dr. John Witherspoon, combined with "the prudent use of the rod." She taught herself Latin and Greek so that she could educate her sons, whom she prepared for college; she "carried her daughters at home through the several studies taught in boarding schools." Nor was the training of the young Negro slaves neglected. Her children learned to read their Bibles in conjunction with Mrs. Sarah Trimmer's prints of scripture history, Watts' short view of the whole scripture history, and later Newton on the prophecies, thus using books that connected sacred with profane history.

Mrs. Ramsay had grown up in the Church of England, of which her father was an active communicant. Her private "covenant with God," first made at the age of fourteen, she renewed many times. All of her children, with one exception, received baptism publicly. This commitment to religion was important, but it was not a commitment to any one denomination. A quotation appended to the *Memoirs* by David Ramsay reflects the views of husband and wife: "The experimental part of religion has generally a greater influence than its theory." Through persons such as the Countess of Huntingdon, whom she knew, and other figures in England's evangelical revival, she adopted evangelical views; and through the influence of the Charleston ministers William Hollinshead and Isaac Stockton Keith, she became and remained a member of the Congregational Church. But her religion was always "the warm, vital, active, unaffected religion of the Bible." She died in Charleston in 1811, at the age of fifty-one, and was buried in the Congregational churchyard there.

Her historical importance rests primarily upon her husband's *Memoirs of the Life of Martha Laurens Ramsay,* published the year after her death, which sold widely and portrayed her as a model of proper womanhood. Mrs. Ramsay's learning added point to the moral, for even with it she was still the dutiful daughter, wife, and mother. She had read Mary Wollstonecraft's fiery *Vindication of the Rights of Woman,* but "in conformity to the positive declarations of holy writ" she "yielded all pretensions" to equality with men. Yet there may have been a tension between her questioning mind and her firm adherence to woman's traditional place. Did she hate slavery (her husband was known to sympathize with emancipation), yet remain silent out of deference to local society? Did she desire to write, yet out of devotion to her husband spend hours copying the historical writings which engaged his later years? Could these nagging questions have been the "besetting sin" with which she felt a recurrent concern? In the next generation she might have been a SARAH GRIMKÉ. In the estimate of one author, there ran through her character "that strong and vigorous style of thinking" to which we apply the "name of republican virtue" (*American Biography,* p. 339).

[Besides her husband's *Memoirs,* contemporary sources include: "Eulogy of Martha Laurens Ramsay," *Carolina Gazette,* June 22, 1811, reprinted in *S.C. Hist. and Genealogical Mag.,* Oct. 1935; letters by and to Martha Laurens Ramsay in the private collection of Mrs. Henry P. Kendall and in the libraries of the S.C. Hist. Soc., Am. Philosophical Soc., Pa. Hist. Soc., and Chicago Hist. Soc.; will of James Laurens, item #577, Ward-Boughton-Leigh of Brownsover Collection, Warwick County Record Office, England; will of Henry Laurens, Record of Wills, Charleston County, S.C., XXIV, Book C (1786–93), pp. 1152–58. Secondary sources: *Am. Biog.; or, Memoirs of Mrs. A. Judson and Mrs. M. L. Ramsay* (Edinburgh, 1831); David D. Wallace, *The Life of Henry Laurens* (1915); Julia C. Spruill, *Women's Life and Work in the Southern Colonies* (1938); George C. Rogers, Jr., *Evolution of a Federalist: William Loughton Smith of Charleston* (1962).]

GEORGE C. ROGERS, JR.

**RAND, Caroline Amanda Sherfey** (Feb. 4, 1828–July 23, 1905), philanthropist, and, with her daughter, **Carrie Rand HERRON** (Mar. 17, 1867–Jan. 11, 1914), a patron of socialist causes, was born in Hagerstown, Md. She was the first child and only daughter among the four children of Solomon and Catherine (Mc-

Neil) Sherfey, both descendants of German immigrants of 1740. In 1834 her family moved west, at first to Lafayette, Ind., and then three years later to Burlington, Iowa, where Sherfey became in turn a prosperous and highly respected merchant, sawmill operator, and farmer. Active in the Burlington Methodist church, he was noted for his benevolence, which strongly influenced his daughter.

After a brief marriage to J. W. Roberts, Carrie, as she was known, was widowed in April 1851. The following year, on June 13, she became the wife of a prominent Burlington businessman, Elbridge Dexter Rand. A widower with two children, Rand had come to Burlington from New England and had accumulated a sizable fortune in livestock raising and meat packing and then in lumber development in the Mississippi Valley. He was later active in banking and railroad construction. During their thirty-five years of married life Mrs. Rand took a leading part in the local Congregational church, which her husband had helped organize in 1844, aided the abolitionist movement, and shared in her husband's civic and political career. A Whig leader and a founder of the Republican party, Rand served four terms on the city council and one in the state legislature. The couple had four children: Elbridge Dwight (born 1853), Charles Wellington (1855), Horace S. (1861), and Carrie.

In 1891—four years after the death of E. D. Rand—the Rev. George Davis Herron arrived in Burlington as assistant minister of the Congregational church. A young self-taught minister, he had achieved national prominence through his sermon of 1890, "The Message of Jesus to Men of Wealth," appealing to the rich for a sense of responsibility toward social problems. When his support of labor and liberal causes soon threatened his standing with some of his wealthy Burlington parishioners, Mrs. Rand, favorably impressed by Herron's personality and message, decided to give him an opportunity for a wider audience. In 1893, by her gift of $35,000, she created expressly for Herron a unique new Department of Applied Christianity at Iowa College in Grinnell (after 1909 Grinnell College). She and her daughter promptly moved to Grinnell, and with their financial support the college became a center of the social gospel and Christian socialist movements. In addition to undergraduate and graduate courses, a small settlement house was begun, retreats and conventions were held for Congregational ministers, and an annual E. D. Rand Foundation lectureship in applied Christianity was established which brought to the campus between 1894 and 1899 such nationally known ministers and social workers as Washington Gladden, ELLEN G. STARR and JANE ADDAMS of Hull House, and Robert A. Woods of Boston's South End Settlement. Mrs. Rand's daughter, Carrie, meanwhile contributed to women's physical education at the college, serving from 1893 to 1899 as instructor in social and physical culture and adding the duties of "principal for women" (roughly analogous to dean of women) in 1894. At her own expense she secured specialized training in physical education for herself and for an assistant, and in 1897 she gave $8,000 of the $9,470 cost of the new E. D. Rand Gymnasium for women. Both the Rands also supported Herron personally, financing the sixteen-month European tour he made for his health in 1896–97.

Upon his return, Herron turned to nationwide lecturing on an increasingly socialistic theme, leaving much of the routine instruction at the college to his assistant. In October 1899, yielding to pressure from the college trustees, who complained that his radical pronouncements were preventing donations to the college, he resigned his position. The next year, in the course of an eight-month trip abroad together, Herron and his Rand patronesses came to an explicit support of socialism. Herron was one of the main speakers for Eugene Debs in Chicago in the election of 1900; and Herron and young Carrie in January 1901 both joined the Social Apostolate, a group of earnest young ministers working in the Chicago area to achieve Christ's Kingdom through persuasion and the establishment of various cooperative enterprises. Carrie served as treasurer and Mrs. Rand as one of the half-dozen financial supporters of the group.

Ever since Burlington there had been rumors of domestic strife in the Herron household, and during the Grinnell years Herron spent much time with the Rands and frequently took meals with them. In March 1901 Mrs. Herron, charging cruelty and desertion, was granted a divorce and custody of their four children. Two months later, on May 25, 1901, Herron and Carrie Rand were married. The divorce and remarriage ended Herron's career in the church; a committee of Iowa Congregationalists in June deposed him from the ministry. He and Carrie then turned completely to service with the Socialist party. On July 29, 1901, both served as delegates to the Indianapolis convention which created the new Socialist Party of America. Their apartment in New York City and a farm retreat near Metuchen, N.J. (bought for them by Mrs. Rand), became

favorite haunts for their Socialist friends. In 1904 Herron made the nominating speech for Debs and wrote the Socialist party platform. Throughout these years, however, the newspapers never ceased to hound the couple, nearly every report of their activities being prefaced by an inaccurate rehashing of the "barter of wives" and charges that they advocated free love and the abolition of the family. Finally, in 1904, to escape this publicity, the Herrons and Mrs. Rand moved to Florence, Italy; there Mrs. Rand died in 1905.

The Herrons brought her ashes back to the United States for burial at Burlington and then proceeded to carry out the terms of her will. This provided $200,000 for Carrie and placed the bulk of the remainder in a trust fund which the six grandchildren were to receive as they reached twenty-eight. In the interim, half of the income was to be used "to carry on and further the work to which I have devoted the later years of my life." Carrie and the socialist leader Morris Hillquit, as co-trustees of the fund, decided that the bequest could best be used to help establish a socialist school, and in 1906, with this income (slightly over $6,000 a year) as the nucleus of its budget, the Rand School of Social Science in New York City came into being. Designed primarily to train workers for positions of socialist and trade union leadership by offering courses not only in economics, politics, history, and sociology but also in a wide range of liberal and fine arts, it continued for fifty years, going out of existence in 1956.

Returning to Florence, Carrie Herron spent the rest of her life there, with her husband and their two sons, Elbridge and George Davis (born in 1902 and 1909). At their Italian villa she and Herron entertained over the years many American and European socialist leaders and made the wide contacts which enabled Herron to serve the United States government in peace negotiations at the close of World War I. Carrie Herron died of cancer in Florence in 1914, at forty-six. Her body was cremated.

[The principal sources of material about Caroline A. Rand and Carrie Rand Herron are biographical accounts of their fathers and husbands. The two editions of *The Des Moines County Portrait and Biog. Album* (1888 and 1905) are good on Sherfey and Rand; other relevant newspaper clippings, obituaries, photographs, and local histories may be found at the libraries of Burlington, Iowa; Grinnell College, Grinnell, Iowa; and the Tamiment Institute, N.Y. City. Herron has been treated extensively in three unpublished doctoral dissertations: Robert T. Handy, "George D. Herron and the Social Gospel in Am. Protestantism, 1890–1901" (Univ. of Chicago, 1949); Phyllis Ann Nelson, "George D. Herron and the Socialist Clergy" (Univ. of Iowa, 1953); and Herbert R. Dieterich, Jr., "Patterns of Dissent: The Reform Ideas and Activities of George D. Herron" (Univ. of N.Mex., 1957). The best published account of the formation of the Rand School is in Morris Hillquit's *Loose Leaves from a Busy Life* (1934). The Herron Papers at the Hoover Institution of War, Revolution, and Peace, Stanford, Calif.; the Hillquit Papers at the State Hist. Soc., Madison, Wis.; and the Algernon Lee Papers at Tamiment Institute are also helpful.]

PHYLLIS NELSON YUHAS

**RAND, Ellen Gertrude Emmet** (Mar. 4, 1875–Dec. 18, 1941), portrait painter, was born in San Francisco, Calif., the third daughter and third of the six children of Christopher Temple Emmet, a medical graduate of the University of Virginia who went west in the gold rush year of 1849 and became a lawyer, and Ellen James (Temple) Emmet. Her paternal great-grandfather, Thomas Addis Emmet, was an Irish nationalist who emigrated to America in 1804 following the execution and political martyrdom of his famous brother, Robert Emmet; settling in New York City, he resumed his practice of law and in 1812 became attorney general of New York State. On her mother's side, Mrs. Rand was related to the brilliant James family; the collected letters of Henry James contain several teasing and affectionate notes to his young cousin "Bay," as she was known in the family. Also among her relatives were several female painters, including her first cousins Rosina (Emmet) Sherwood (1854–1948)—mother of the playwright Robert E. Sherwood—and Lydia Field Emmet (1866–1952), a member of the National Academy of Design.

Growing up in San Francisco and neighboring San Rafael and, after her father's death (c. 1884), in the New York City area, Ellen received her formal education chiefly from tutors. Her consuming interest, however, was sketching and painting. Having early demonstrated her native ability in drawing, she was permitted to study under Dennis Bunker in Boston and, from 1889 to 1893, at the Art Students' League in New York, where her work was criticized by Robert Reid and William M. Chase. In her eighteenth year she became a contributor of fashion sketches to *Vogue* magazine, and she later provided material for *Harper's Weekly*. A trip abroad with her family at the age of twenty-one brought her into contact with the famous portrait painter John Singer Sargent in London and,

through the architect Stanford White, a friend of the Emmets, with the sculptor Frederick MacMonnies, then living in Paris. She remained in Paris for three years as a student of MacMonnies, who was also highly regarded as a teacher of painting. During this period she developed the skill at firm articulation and vital coloring which quickly brought her recognition.

Following this apprenticeship in Paris, she returned to New York, in 1900, and established herself in a studio in Washington Square South. In 1902 the Durand-Ruel Galleries on Fifth Avenue presented a show exclusively of her works, at a time when solo shows were still something of a novelty. In 1906 she exhibited a group of over ninety paintings at Boston's Copley Hall; only Whistler, Sargent, and Monet had been given one-man shows at Copley Hall before Miss Emmet.

On May 6, 1911, at thirty-six, she was married to William Blanchard Rand, of Salisbury, Conn. Rand managed his family's large farm at Salisbury and also participated in public affairs, both as a selectman of the town and, for two terms, as a state legislator. They had three sons: Christopher Temple Emmet (born 1912), William Blanchard, Jr. (1913), and John Alsop (1914). Mrs. Rand spent the summer months on the farm, where she particularly enjoyed horseback riding and hunting; during the remainder of the year she and the children lived at her studio in New York, where most of her commissions were executed.

Although her fame, like her clientele, seldom spread beyond the circle of the social elite in which she was born and married, she was, like her distinguished contemporary CECILIA BEAUX, always more than a slick society portraitist. Her work, which is scattered throughout prominent schools, universities, and private estates of the Northeast, bears quiet testimony to the qualities of empathy, vitality, and craftsmanship for which she was admired. Her paintings of Franklin Delano Roosevelt, Elihu Root, and Augustus Saint-Gaudens became the official portraits of these historic figures. Her commissions extended through a long list of statesmen, educators, clergymen, captains of industry, and society matrons, including William James, Henry L. Stimson, Bishops William Lawrence and Henry C. Potter, Mrs. Alfred G. Vanderbilt, Anna Roosevelt Cowles, and Daniel Willard, president of the Baltimore & Ohio Railroad. In 1904 at the St. Louis World's Fair she was awarded a silver medal; in 1910 at Buenos Aires a bronze medal; in 1915 at the Panama-Pacific Exposition a gold medal; and in 1922 she won the Beck Gold Medal from the Pennsylvania Academy of the Fine Arts. She was elected an Associate of the National Academy of Design in 1926 and an Academician in 1934. Two of her portraits, those of Saint-Gaudens and of Benjamin Altman, were purchased by the Metropolitan Museum of Art for its permanent collection.

A retrospective exhibit in Pittsfield, Mass., in 1954, more than a decade after her death, brought to public attention a previously unrecognized side of Mrs. Rand's talent. These womanly, spontaneous canvases caught, with easy splashes of color, candid views of family and friends and a sense of intimacy and mood totally lacking in her formal portraiture, and invited comparison with the work of MARY CASSATT. During her later life, following the crash of 1929 which wiped out the family capital, Ellen Rand found such personal expression a luxury she could not afford. Intent upon providing the best schooling for her three sons, and attempting to help in some way everyone with whom she came in contact, she concentrated her energies almost wholly upon her moneymaking commissions. As her draftsmanship became more and more deft, and as her fees reached the level of $5,000 for each painting, she worked at a furious pace; in a peak year (1930) she is said to have earned $74,000. She died of a heart attack in a New York City hospital at the age of sixty-six. Her husband and sons survived her. Funeral services were held at St. John's Episcopal Church, which she had regularly attended while in Salisbury, and she was buried in the Protestant Cemetery there.

[The chief published sources of information on Mrs. Rand are the biographical sketch in *Nat. Cyc. Am. Biog.*, XL, 261–62, and a critical article by Grace W. Curran in *Am. Mag. of Art*, Sept. 1928. See also Christian Brinton, "Miss Ellen Emmet," *Century*, May 1909, for an early appraisal. Critical responses to her posthumous show in Pittsfield may be found in *Time*, Aug. 23, 1954, *Newsweek*, Aug. 30, and the *Hartford Courant*, Aug. 29. The authority for the birth date given here, official records in San Francisco having been destroyed, is the family genealogy by Thomas Addis Emmet, *The Emmet Family* (1898). On her father, see John E. Parsons, ed., "Nine Cousins in the Calif. Gold Rush," *N.-Y. Hist. Soc. Quart.*, Oct. 1963. For the relationship with Henry James, see Percy Lubbock, ed., *The Letters of Henry James* (1920). The Art Students' League provided a record of her dates of enrollment there. Mr. John A. Rand, Salisbury, Conn., and Mrs. Ellen Turner, Cape Porpoise, Maine, possess considerable information about, as well as original works by, Mrs. Rand. A 1960 report by Karin Sandvik, Univ.

of Wis. Library School, provided a useful summary of source materials.]

ALBERT F. MC LEAN, JR.

**RANDOLPH, Martha Jefferson** (Sept. 27, 1772–Oct. 10, 1836), eldest child and close companion of Thomas Jefferson, was born at Monticello in Albemarle County, Va., and was not quite ten when her mother, MARTHA (WAYLES) JEFFERSON, died. While the other surviving children (Mary, then known as Polly and afterward as Maria, and an infant girl who lived little more than two years) remained with relatives in Southside Virginia, Martha accompanied her father, first to Philadelphia, where he attended the Continental Congress, and then, in 1784, to France. Polly reluctantly joined them in 1787, and they remained in Paris until the end of Jefferson's diplomatic mission in the autumn of 1789.

Although he had no advanced ideas about women, he took great interest in the education of his daughters and, subsequently, his granddaughters. The education of Martha (known in her youth as Patsy) was under his direction to a greater extent than Polly's, and she was the more studious of the two. The small private schools she attended emphasized traditional feminine accomplishments. In Philadelphia and at the Abbaye Royale de Panthémont in Paris she gained an acquaintance with the arts, and unquestionably became a cultivated young lady. Tall, reddish-haired, and very much like her father, she was never described as beautiful, though her sister, who may be presumed to have looked like their mother, often was. Her cheerfulness and amiability were frequently remarked upon. Her father expressed the desire that, besides literature, she should have some knowledge of the "graver sciences," but it is uncertain that she was ever much exposed to these. He does not appear to have discussed public affairs with her, but he made sure that she was well acquainted with the classics; and, with the advantage of youth, she surpassed her redoubtable father in French. While at school in Paris she regularly spent weekends with him at his residence, the Hôtel de Longeac; and during extended separations, as when he traveled in the south of France, they carried on considerable correspondence. His letters from that period now seem excessively didactic and moralistic, but she took admonitions with good grace and was in all respects a dutiful daughter. The bond between them grew stronger with the passing years.

A few weeks after the Jeffersons returned to Virginia, and before the head of the family went to New York to become Washington's

Secretary of State, Martha was married at Monticello (Feb. 23, 1790) to her cousin Thomas Mann Randolph, Jr. Young Randolph became alienated from his own father after that gentleman's remarriage, and the young couple were increasingly dependent on Jefferson. Largely through his efforts, Randolph acquired Edgehill, a few miles from Monticello. This remained the family home, but Martha and her increasing flock of children were generally at Monticello when her father was there. Anne Carey, born in 1791, was the eldest of twelve, followed by Thomas Jefferson (1792), Ellen (1794, died in 1795), Ellen Wayles (1796), Cornelia Jefferson (1799), Virginia Jefferson (1801), Mary Jefferson (1803), James Madison (1806), Benjamin Franklin (1808), Meriwether Lewis (1810), Septimia Anne (1814), and George Wythe (1818). During her father's presidency of the United States, Martha Randolph visited him only twice: for a few weeks in 1802–03 with her sister Maria; and for a longer period in 1805–06 during which her eighth child, James Madison, was born in the President's House. Her husband as a Congressman (1803–07) lived there while she was caring for the children in the country.

Although a man of superior intelligence, Randolph was erratic and had an undistinguished career in Congress. He later (1819–22) served as governor of Virginia. Though he pioneered in scientific agriculture, he was not a good manager, and his affairs went from bad to worse. Martha was always loyal to him, but in her affections he never supplanted her father; she became more than ever the personal center of Jefferson's life after Maria's death in 1804, and after his retirement in 1809 she was at Monticello nearly all the time. During this period her husband, whose financial situation continued to deteriorate, became more and more remote from his family; he died in 1828.

From the beginning Jefferson appears to have assumed major responsibility for the education of the Randolph children. This was particularly true of his namesake, Thomas Jefferson Randolph, who took over the management of Jefferson's affairs in the last decade of the ex-president's life. Edgehill came into the possession of this son, who had assumed the debts of his father. After Jefferson's death in 1826, Martha Randolph's financial need became acute. Monticello had to be sold, and she considered opening a school, but the actions of the legislatures of South Carolina and Louisiana, each of which appropriated $10,-000 for her, saved her from impoverishment. She spent her last years with her daughters

in Boston and Washington, D.C., and with her son at Edgehill, where she died of apoplexy at the age of sixty-four. It is chiefly owing to her that Thomas Jefferson has more descendants than any other president. The most prolific of her children was her father's namesake, but mention must also be made of Ellen Wayles Randolph, another great favorite of his, who married Joseph Coolidge, Jr., of Boston and became the progenitor of the extensive New England branch of the family. Martha Jefferson Randolph was buried in the graveyard at Monticello, which she and her son had wisely retained and which has remained through the years a family possession.

["Martha Jefferson and Thomas Mann Randolph, Jr.," chap. iv in *Collected Papers of the Monticello Assoc.* (1965), ed. by G. G. Shackelford, and other articles and genealogies in that volume; *Family Letters of Thomas Jefferson* (1966), ed. by Edwin M. Betts and James A. Bear, Jr.; Sarah N. Randolph, *The Domestic Life of Thomas Jefferson* (1871); Henry S. Randall, *The Life of Thomas Jefferson* (3 vols., 1858), containing family reminiscences; *The Monticello Family: Catalogue of an Exhibition . . . Apr. 12–May 13, 1960* (Thomas Jefferson Memorial Foundation), giving detailed information about portraits. For an earlier account, see Mrs. O. J. Wister and Agnes Irwin, eds., *Worthy Women of Our First Century* (1877), pp. 9–70.]

DUMAS MALONE

**RANDOLPH, Mary Randolph** (Aug. 9, 1762–Jan. 23, 1828), early Southern cookbook author, was born in Virginia at either Tuckahoe, her father's plantation in Goochland County, or Ampthill, that of her mother's family in Chesterfield County. Both parents were members of the planter aristocracy. Mary's father, Thomas Mann Randolph (1741–1793), served Virginia in the colonial house of burgesses, in the Revolutionary conventions of 1775 and 1776, and later in the state legislature; her mother, Anne (Cary) Randolph, was a daughter of Archibald Cary (1721–1787), planter and statesman. Mary was the oldest of thirteen children. Her brother Thomas Mann Randolph (1768–1828) became a Congressman and governor of Virginia and married Martha Jefferson (see MARTHA JEFFERSON RANDOLPH), daughter of his kinsman Thomas Jefferson.

Growing up in this close-knit clan, Molly Randolph, as she was known, was married in December 1780 to a first cousin once removed, David Meade Randolph (1760–1830), of Presque Isle, Chesterfield County. Of their eight children, four lived to maturity: Richard (born 1782), William Beverley (1789), David Meade, and Burwell Starke (1800). Her husband, after serving as a captain in the Revolutionary War, was appointed by President Washington United States marshal (a federal court official) for Virginia, making his home in Richmond. There, at the turn of the century, he built Moldavia, a handsome residence on South 5th Street. But his Federalist politics brought his removal from this post by President Jefferson. To support their growing family the Randolphs sold Moldavia and moved to more modest quarters, where Mrs. Randolph conducted a fashionable boardinghouse. Soon dubbed "the Queen," she attracted, says a Richmond chronicler, "as many subjects as her dominions could accommodate. . . . There were few more festive boards. . . . Wit, humor and good-fellowship prevailed, but excess rarely" (Mordecai, pp. 96–98).

Mary Randolph had been noted for her knowledge of cooking even before her boardinghouse days. From her practical experience as keeper of a large establishment, and perhaps in the hope of further augmenting the family income, she compiled the book of recipes which was published (under her own name) in 1824 in Washington as *The Virginia Housewife*. As her preface indicated, it was written to meet the need she had encountered, on entering housekeeping, for a book "sufficiently clear and concise to impart knowledge to a Tyro." The work was well received; a second edition followed in 1825, and it was often republished—in Baltimore in 1831 and 1838, in Philadelphia in 1850. The recipes were practical in details and specific as to weights and measures, much simpler than those in the eighteenth-century English cookbooks which had previously supplied the American market. The regional emphasis made the work especially popular in the South. "Every Virginia housewife," a later writer (Letitia Burwell) recalled of the antebellum period, "knew how to compound all the various dishes in Mrs. Randolph's cookery book."

But Mrs. Randolph lived for less than four years after the first edition of her cookbook. Little is known of her then save that she was living in Washington, D.C., at the time of her death. Possibly the care of an invalid son hastened her end, for the stone on her grave terms her "a victim of maternal love and duty." By her own wish she was buried at Arlington, the residence of her cousin George Washington Parke Custis, stepson of George Washington and father of Mary Custis (Mrs. Robert E.) Lee.

[There are brief references to Mrs. Randolph in Samuel Mordecai, *Richmond in By-gone Days*

(1856), pp. 96–98; William H. Safford, ed., *The Blennerhasset Papers* (1864), pp. 457–58, 484; Elias Dexter, comp., *The St. Memin Collection of Portraits* (1862); and Fillmore Norfleet, *Saint Memin in Va.: Portraits and Biogs.* (1942), pp. 121, 201–02. On the Randolph genealogy, see W. G. Stanard, "The Randolph Family," *William and Mary College Quart.*, Jan., Oct. 1899; and Robert I. Randolph, *The Randolphs of Va.* (1936). Obituary notices appeared in the Washington *Nat. Jour.* and *Nat. Intelligencer* for Jan. 24, 1828, and the *Richmond Enquirer,* Jan. 29, 1828. On her tombstone, see Enoch Aquila Chase, "Arlington Mystery Solved," Washington *Sunday Star,* Jan. 19, 1930, sec. 3. See also Waldo Lincoln, *Bibliog. of Am. Cookery Books* (1954); *Va. Cookery Past and Present* (Woman's Auxiliary, Olivet Episcopal Church, Franconia, Va., 1957), pp. 425–26; Mary Wingfield Scott, *Houses of Old Richmond* (1941). Norfleet, above, gives her birthplace as Tuckahoe; her gravestone says Ampthill.]

ANNA WELLS RUTLEDGE

**RATHBONE, Josephine Adams** (Sept. 10, 1864–May 17, 1941), librarian, was born at Jamestown, N.Y. Her father, Joshua Henry Rathbone, a physician, was of an old New England family; her mother, Elizabeth Bacon Adams, was from Georgia. Josephine Rathbone attended Wellesley College (1882–83) and the liberal arts college of the University of Michigan (1884–85, 1890–91) without earning a degree.

In 1891, having been attracted to the newly emerging profession of librarianship, she enrolled in the New York State Library School at Albany, N.Y.—the first in the nation, founded only four years before by Melvil Dewey. She received the B.L.S. degree in 1893, having meanwhile (October 1892–June 1893) worked as assistant librarian of the Diocesan Lending Library, All Saints Cathedral, Albany. In September 1893 she joined the staff of the Pratt Institute Free Library in Brooklyn, N.Y., the first free public library in the New York City area, founded in 1887 by Charles Pratt, a wealthy Brooklyn oil manufacturer, along with his school for training in the practical arts, Pratt Institute. Miss Rathbone was hired as an assistant cataloguer, but the position also involved teaching in the institute's library school, opened in 1890 to train assistants primarily for service in the Free Library. When in 1895 it was reorganized as a full-fledged library school with a regular faculty, Miss Rathbone was appointed assistant in charge under MARY WRIGHT PLUMMER, the director of the school and of the library; in 1904, when Miss Plummer relinquished her library office and took complete charge of the school, Miss Rathbone became the chief instructor. Since both were graduates of the pioneer Dewey school, it is hardly surprising that the Pratt curriculum largely followed that of the Albany institution. The Pratt school, however, concerned itself less than the Albany school with training college and university librarians, stressing instead public library service, especially in small- and medium-size libraries. Its emphasis on giving students experience with practical problems (including the mending of books) in the operations of the Free Library necessitated small classes. Though copying the Albany practice of requiring an entrance examination, both Miss Plummer and Miss Rathbone absolutely refused to accept a college diploma in lieu of it, favoring any applicant who showed exceptional aptitude for librarianship. In later years, however, Miss Rathbone urged colleges to encourage undergraduates to aspire to the profession.

In 1911 Miss Plummer left Pratt Institute to direct the New York Public Library School, and the authorities decided once again to combine the directorship of the institute's Free Library and its library school. The position was given to Edward F. Stevens, an expert in "graphic arts"; Miss Rathbone was placed in immediate charge of the school with the title of vice-director. Although no student regarded Stevens as head of the school, the relationship and her title must have disappointed her. She and Stevens gave each other a wide berth, and their contacts, confined to business matters, were conducted with the usual proprieties, only strained voices occasionally betraying their true feelings.

Small and trim, usually dressed in tailored suits, Miss Rathbone was brisk and executive-like in her conduct and gait. She did much teaching, and did it well. Though maintaining an indisputable classroom distance between the students and herself, she offered courses that were lively and not without humor. All that she urged hinged upon her cardinal belief that the essence of librarianship was "to know books and to understand the book needs of people," and to bring books and readers together in "a vital relationship" (*American Library Association Bulletin*, May 1932, pp. 306–07). An avid reader, whose own interests centered about the theatre, political affairs, and literature, she expected students, while mastering technicalities and living with books, to be aware of current events and cultural happenings. She brought Pratt forward to a top position among library schools.

In professional activities, too, Miss Rathbone acquired a wide reputation. She contributed to library periodicals, the American Library Association *Manual,* and the *Cyclopedia of Education,* and published a small volume, *Viewpoints of Travel* (1919). In addition to membership in the American Library Institute, she served the New York State Library Association as secretary (1908) and the New York Library Club as secretary (1895–97, 1909–10) and president (1918–19). The American Library Association profited from her work on innumerable committees, as organizer of personnel for its camp library service during World War I, and as a member of its council (1912–29); and it elected her president (1931–32). A believer in the strenuous life, she delighted in canoe trips, mountain climbing, tree planting, and travel. Among her social clubs were the Cosmopolitan, Trail Riders of the Canadian Rockies, and the Adirondack Mountain Club.

In 1938, at seventy-three, she retired from the Pratt library school and moved to Augusta, Ga., her mother's home, to live with a cousin. Showing little tendency to vegetate, she joined the local chapter of the Colonial Dames of America and the Philomathic Club, and even purchased and learned to drive an automobile. She attended the Church of the Good Shepherd (Episcopal). She died in Augusta of a coronary thrombosis at the age of seventy-six and was buried there in Summerville Cemetery.

[For biographical information see Nordica Fenneman in *Wilson Library Bull.,* June 1949, and Wayne Shirley in *ibid.,* Nov. 1959; Harry M. Lydenberg in *A.L.A. Bull.,* June 1941; *N.Y. State Library School Register, 1887–1926* (1959); *Nat. Cyc. Am. Biog.,* Current Vol. D, p. 411; *N.Y. Times,* May 19, 1941; Durward Howes, ed., *Am. Women,* 1937–38; *Who's Who in America,* various years. Among her significant writings are "Cooperation between Libraries and Schools: An Hist. Sketch," *Library Jour.,* Apr. 1901; "Some Aspects of Our Personal Life," *Public Libraries,* Feb. 1916; "Pioneers of the Library Profession," *Wilson Library Bull.,* June 1949; "Pratt Graduates in Library Work," *Library Jour.,* Feb. 1929; and "Creative Librarianship," *A.L.A. Bull.,* May 1932. Her work is also touched upon in Sarah Vann, *Training for Librarianship before 1923* (1961). Her death certificate is in the Richmond County Health Dept., Augusta, Ga.]

JOSEPH A. BOROMÉ

**RATHBUN, Mary Jane** (June 11, 1860–Apr. 4, 1943), marine zoologist and carcinologist, was born in Buffalo, N.Y., the second daughter and youngest of the five children of Charles Howland Rathbun and Jane (Furey) Rathbun. Her Howland and Rathbun (originally Rathbone) forebears had come to Massachusetts from England early in the seventeenth century. Her grandfather Thomas Rathbun, a stonemason, moved in 1836 from Connecticut to Buffalo, where he became a principal in the firm of Whitmore, Rathbun & Company, which owned and operated several large and productive stone quarries. Charles Rathbun succeeded his father in the business, and both Mary Jane and her oldest brother, Richard, who became assistant secretary of the Smithsonian Institution and director of the United States National Museum, developed their careers in zoology out of early curiosity about fossils they discovered in the family quarries. Mrs. Rathbun, the daughter of an Irishman who had emigrated from King's (later Offaly) County to Quebec in the 1820's, died when Mary Jane was a year old; brought up by an elderly nurse, she was a formal, reserved child. She was educated in the Buffalo public schools, completing high school at the Central School in 1878. She received no further formal education, although she later was given an honorary M.A. degree by the University of Pittsburgh (1916) and was awarded a Ph.D. by George Washington University in 1917.

The most important influence in shaping Miss Rathbun's career was her brother Richard, who had since 1873 worked as an assistant to Spencer F. Baird, head of the United States Fish Commission, and in 1880 became in addition curator of marine invertebrates at the National Museum in Washington. In 1881, at twenty-one, Miss Rathbun spent the summer with her brother at Woods Hole, Mass., a center of marine research. Fascinated by this first contact with the seashore and its fauna, she returned regularly for the next few summers, assisting her brother in the sorting and study of the great and varied collections of marine animals of all kinds that the Fish Commission's survey ships were bringing in to Woods Hole. Dr. Baird, impressed by her keen interest in marine biology and her volunteer work, in 1884 took her on as a full-time employee of the commission and assigned her to the National Museum in Washington to help organize, care for, and catalogue the commission's extensive collections. In November 1886 Baird (who was also secretary of the Smithsonian Institution, of which the museum was a part) transferred Miss Rathbun to the museum staff as a clerk and copyist in the department (later division) of marine invertebrates. She was to remain in the division until her retirement fifty-three years later.

The department was new, and from the start Miss Rathbun carried much of the responsibility for its operations. Although her brother was, as curator, the official head of the department, duties with the Fish Commission and elsewhere took virtually all his time; as early as 1889 his report acknowledged that upon Miss Rathbun had devolved "not only the care and preservation of the collections, but also, for the most part, the general supervision of the department" (Smithsonian Institution, *Annual Report of the Board of Regents, 1889*: U.S. National Museum Report, p. 382). With vast energy she performed the department's clerical duties, drafting and copying (in a neat Spencerian hand) letters and reports, keeping ledger catalogues and card files for all identified crustaceans and other invertebrates in the National Collections, and maintaining the catalogue of the department's library. Yet she found time to carry on her extensive self-education in zoology and marine biology and to begin, as early as 1891, her scientific publications. In 1898 she became second assistant curator of the department, and in 1907 she took formal charge as assistant curator. This position she retained until the end of 1914, when she resigned in order to release her salary to permit the hiring of an assistant. She continued to work at the division, however, as an honorary associate in zoology, with her time now freed for research.

The scientific studies upon which Miss Rathbun's preeminence as a zoologist rests are primarily concerned with the decapod Crustacea: shrimps and crabs and their near relatives, recent as well as fossil. Her bibliography comprises 158 titles dealing largely with the crustacean faunas of the major oceans and most of the countries of the world. Among her more comprehensive treatises are *Les Crabes d'Eau Douce* (published in the *Nouvelle Archives* of the Paris Museum of Natural History, nos. 6 and 8, 1904–06); four monographic studies concerned with the marine crabs (Brachyura) of the Western Hemisphere, published by the United States National Museum: *The Grapsoid Crabs of America* (Bulletin 97, 1918–the study for which she received her doctorate), *The Spider Crabs of America* (Bulletin 129, 1925), *The Cancroid Crabs of America* (Bulletin 152, 1930), and *The Oxystomatous and Allied Crabs of America* (Bulletin 166, 1937); and two fundamental paleontological works dealing with the then available North American fossil decapods —*The Fossil Stalk-eyed Crustacea of the Pacific Slope of North America* (U.S. National Museum Bulletin 138, 1926) and *The Fossil Crustacea of the Atlantic and Gulf Coastal Plain* (Special Paper No. 2, Geological Society of America, 1935). Like her other publications, these were systematic-taxonomic studies, concerned primarily with description and classification. Her findings clarified and brought up to date the classification of many groups and produced significant new taxonomic information. An early advocate of priority as a basis of stability in zoological nomenclature, she made one of her most significant contributions in fixing the nomenclature of many of the decapod Crustacea. Her published works have inspired a later generation of students of Crustacea, and the extensive data she assembled, not only in her research papers but also in her personally compiled records, notes, and card files at the National Museum, have been extensively used by ecologists and students in other fields of zoology. In her own lifetime she was widely consulted by carcinologists the world over.

Small, neat, and plain-featured, Miss Rathbun impressed those who came to know her by her kindliness, her interesting conversation, and her extensive knowledge of her field and of the researchers engaged in it. She never married. Miss Rathbun was an active member of All Souls Unitarian Church. She served as a dedicated "gray lady" in the Washington chapter of the American Red Cross during World War I, and also sent packages of food and clothing to the families of her foreign correspondents; for many years she contributed to the support of the daughter of an Austrian scientist. She died at her home in Washington as a result of a fractured hip and was buried in Buffalo. In her will she left $10,000 to the Smithsonian Institution as a memorial to her brother to further the work on Crustacea.

[The fullest published accounts are the obituaries in *Science*, May 14, 1943, and the *Jour. of the Washington Acad. of Sci.*, Nov. 15, 1943. See also John C. Cooley, *Rathbone Genealogy* (1898), pp. 26–27; *Am. Men of Sci.* (1st ed., 1906, and later editions); feature articles on Miss Rathbun in the *Washington Post*, July 3, 1935, and Jan. 26, 1939; and obituary in Washington *Evening Star*, Apr. 6, 1943. Other data from death record at D.C. Dept. of Public Health and files of U.S. Nat. Museum.]

WALDO L. SCHMITT

RAY, Charlotte E. (Jan. 13, 1850–Jan. 4, 1911), lawyer, was born in New York City, one of the seven children of the Rev. Charles Bennett Ray, of early New England Negro, Indian, and white ancestry, and his second wife, Charlotte Augusta Burroughs, a native of Savannah, Ga. Charles Ray, editor of the *Colored American* and pastor of the Bethesda Congregational Church in New York, was one of the distinguished Negro leaders of his day,

known for his fearless work helping slaves fleeing by means of the Underground Railroad. His daughter Charlotte, described as "a dusky mulatto," attended the Institution for the Education of Colored Youth, in Washington, D.C., founded by MYRTILLA MINER. By 1869 she was a teacher in the normal and preparatory department of Howard University, chartered by Congress two years earlier.

At the same time Miss Ray had begun the study of law at the university. A classmate years later remembered her as "an apt scholar"; a contemporary visitor to the law school was impressed by "a colored woman who read us a thesis on corporations, not copied from the books but from her brain, a clear incisive analysis of one of the most delicate legal questions" (Howard University, President's Report, 1870). She graduated from the law department of Howard in February 1872, reading an essay on "Chancery," which was well received (*New National Era*, Feb. 20, 1872). The following month she was admitted to the District of Columbia bar. The District's legal code had recently been revised and the word "male" in connection with admission to the bar stricken out; her application apparently caused no debate. She seems to have been not only the first Negro woman lawyer in the United States, but the first woman admitted to the bar in the District of Columbia.

Charlotte Ray opened a law office in Washington. Reminiscing in 1897, the Wisconsin lawyer Kate Kane Rossi recalled that "Miss Ray . . . although a lawyer of decided ability, on account of prejudice was not able to obtain sufficient legal business and had to give up . . . active practice" (*Chicago Legal News*, Oct. 23, 1897). She is known to have attended the annual convention of the National Woman Suffrage Association in New York City in 1876. By 1879 she had returned to New York to live. For a time, like her two younger sisters, she taught in the Brooklyn public schools. Sometime after 1886 she was married to a man with the surname of Fraim, of whom nothing is known. By 1897 she was living in Woodside, Long Island. Charlotte Ray Fraim died of acute bronchitis at her Woodside home in 1911, at the age of sixty. She was buried in the Ray family plot in Cypress Hills Cemetery, Brooklyn.

[F. T. Ray, *Sketch of the Life of Rev. Charles B. Ray* (1887); Howard Univ., *Catalogue*, 1869–72, and *Annual Report*, 1870; *Woman's Jour.*, May 25, 1872, p. 161; *Chicago Legal News*, Oct. 23, 1897, p. 80; Sadie T. M. Alexander, "Women as Practitioners of Law in the U.S.," *Nat. Bar Jour.*, July 1941; Elizabeth C. Stanton et al., *Hist. of Woman*

*Suffrage,* III (1886), 19n.; death record from N.Y. City Dept. of Health (Queens Borough). A fuller treatment will appear in the author's forthcoming study, "Women, the Bench, and the Bar." Though her death record lists her married name as "Traim," on her tombstone it is given as "Fraim."]

DOROTHY THOMAS

REAM, Vinnie (Sept. 25, 1847–Nov. 20, 1914), sculptor, was born in Madison, Wis., one of three children, two of them girls, of Robert Lee Ream and Lavinia (McDonald) Ream. Her father, a government surveyor and recorder of deeds, was a native of Center County, Pa.; her mother, of Scottish descent, was from Hagerstown, Md. When Vinnie was ten her family moved to western Missouri, where Ream had been sent on a surveying assignment. Here Vinnie briefly (1857–58) attended the academy section of Christian College, Columbia, Mo., where she showed skill in music and art. The outbreak of the Civil War found Ream with his family in Fort Smith, Ark., engaged in the real estate business. Making their way with difficulty through the Confederate lines, they went to Washington, D.C., where Ream, now partially incapacitated by rheumatism, secured a government position. Vinnie obtained a clerkship in the Post Office Department.

A new vista opened for her in 1863 when she visited the studio of the sculptor Clark Mills in a wing of the Capitol. "As soon as I saw the sculptor handle the clay," she later wrote, "I felt at once that I, too, could model and, taking the clay, in a few hours I produced a medallion of an Indian chief's head . . ." (Eagle, p. 603). Her performance so impressed Mills that he at once accepted her as a part-time pupil. Soon she was making busts of Congressmen and distinguished Washington visitors, including Senator John Sherman, Thaddeus Stevens, General Custer, Horace Greeley, and Francis Preston Blair. Her work found such favor that late in 1864 Congressional friends arranged for her to model a bust of President Lincoln. The President had at first refused, but on hearing that she was a poor girl making her own way he granted her half-hour daily sittings for five months; she was thus, as she recalled, "still under the spell of his kind eyes and genial presence" when he was assassinated.

Her bust of the martyred President pleased her admirers, and in the summer of 1866 Congress authorized a $10,000 contract with Vinnie Ream for a full-scale marble statue of Lincoln to stand in the Capitol rotunda. She was the first woman to win such a federal commis-

sion. That so important an assignment had gone to an eighteen-year-old girl aroused both criticism and incredulity. MARY TODD LINCOLN strongly disapproved, and the journalist JANE GREY SWISSHELM (who had favored HARRIET HOSMER for the commission) suggested in print that Miss Ream's success had been owing solely to her feminine wiles. Though susceptible Congressmen had doubtless been influenced by her petite and girlish charm, her brown eyes, and her flowing dark curls, their action was also a rather touching expression of confidence in a gifted unknown who, like Lincoln himself, seemed to fulfill the long-cherished national hope that the American frontier could be a seedbed of genius.

After completing her plaster model in an improvised studio in the Capitol, Miss Ream decided to go to Rome to turn it into marble. Accompanied by her parents, who were now dependent on her for support, and fortified with a letter of introduction from Secretary of State William H. Seward, she sailed in 1869 for a two-year stay abroad. In Paris she studied briefly under Léon J. F. Bonnat and did busts of Père Hyacinthe and Gustave Doré; in Munich the romantic painter Wilhelm von Kaulbach sat for her. Her Roman studio, next to that of the American portraitist George P. A. Healy, became a popular meeting place for the city's international art community. Vinnie Ream was painted by Healy and by George Caleb Bingham, and herself did busts of Franz Liszt and Giacomo Cardinal Antonelli, the papal secretary of state. One of her friends, the young Danish critic Georg Brandes, was nearly overwhelmed by the force of her personality. "She had a mind of many colours," he later wrote. "And there was the very devil of a rush and Forward! March! about her, *always in a hurry.*" Though deploring her vanity and her habit of becoming "ingratiatingly coquettish towards anyone whose affection she wished to win," Brandes was impressed by her earnestness, her acts of spontaneous generosity, and her total dedication to her work; at last he could only marvel at "her ingenuousness, her ignorance, her thorough goodness, in short, all her simple healthiness of soul" (*Reminiscences,* pp. 319–23).

Choosing marble of the purest white from the quarries of Carrara, Vinnie Ream proceeded under the guidance of her teacher, Luigi Majoli, to transform her model of Abraham Lincoln into stone. In January 1871, with impressive ceremony, the finished statue was unveiled in the Capitol. The President's head was seen bending slightly forward, as though his eyes were fixed on someone—no doubt a newly freed slave—to whom he extended the Proclamation in his right hand. It was an impressive production from an essentially untrained artist, and Wisconsin's Senator Matthew H. Carpenter summed up the prevailing reaction: "Of this statue, as a mere work of art, I am no judge. What Praxiteles might have thought of such a work, I neither know nor care; but I am able to say, in the presence of this vast and brilliant assembly (most of whom knew him well), that it is Abraham Lincoln all over." Although the statue has been severely criticized—a later sculptor, Lorado Taft, called it "a monument to the gallantry of our statesmen" and found that on close examination it "reveals an absence of body within the garments"—it has over the years held its own with the other statuary in the rotunda. Even Taft conceded that for all its flaws it conveys both the artist's sense of awe in the presence of her subject and a certain "melancholy expressiveness."

In 1875, competing with such sculptors as William Wetmore Story and J. Q. A. Ward, Vinnie Ream won a $20,000 federal commission for a heroic bronze of Adm. David G. Farragut. Her statue, cast from the propeller of Farragut's flagship, the *Hartford*, and portraying the Admiral with telescope in hand, his right foot resting on a tackle box, was unveiled in Washington's Farragut Square in April 1881, President Garfield accepting for the nation. Earlier, on May 28, 1878, at thirty, Vinnie Ream had been married to Lieut. (later Brigadier General) Richard Leveridge Hoxie of the army engineers, a friend of the Farragut family. They had one son, Richard Ream Hoxie, born in 1883. When not absent on army assignments or summering in Iowa City, Iowa, Richard Hoxie's hometown, the couple maintained a residence on Farragut Square which became a center of music and conversation. Here Mrs. Hoxie, resuming a youthful avocation, often played the harp for informal gatherings of friends. Giving up her professional artistic career in deference to her husband's wishes, she became active in charities, especially in aid to the blind. She returned to sculpture briefly in 1906 when the State of Iowa commissioned her to make a statue of its Civil War governor, Samuel Kirkwood, for Statuary Hall in the national Capitol. Nearly incapacitated by a chronic kidney ailment, she completed this assignment by means of a rope hoist and boatswain's chair rigged for her by her husband. The model of her last work, a statue of the Cherokee savant Sequoyah, commissioned by the State of Oklahoma and completed shortly before her death, was cast in bronze by the sculptor George Zolnay. In the late summer of 1914, in Iowa City, Vinnie Ream was stricken by an acute attack of uremic poisoning. She was returned by special railway car to Washington for treatment, but died there that November at the age of sixty-seven. After Episcopal services at St. John's Church on Lafayette Square, she was buried in Arlington National Cemetery, where her grave is marked by a bronze replica of her ideal statue "Sappho."

[*Vinnie Ream* (1908), a memoir edited by her husband, contains documents and newspaper stories relating to her career and is illustrated with photographs of some of her works. Gordon Langley Hall, *Vinnie Ream* (1963), a biography for young people, is undocumented but contains new material based on fresh research. Details may also be found in: Georg Brandes, *Reminiscences of My Childhood and Youth* (English translation, 1906); her own autobiographical statement in Mary K. O. Eagle, ed., *The Congress of Women* (1894), pp. 603–08; Charles E. Fairman, *Art and Artists of the Capitol* (1927); Marie Haefner, "From Plastic Clay," *Palimpsest*, Nov. 1930; Lorado Taft, *The Hist. of Am. Sculpture* (1903); Frances E. Willard and Mary A. Livermore, eds., *A Woman of the Century* (1893); *Who Was Who in America*, vol. I (1942); and obituaries in *La Follette's Mag.*, Dec. 1914, Washington *Evening Star*, Nov. 20, 1914, and *Washington Post*, Nov. 21, 1914. The Vinnie Ream Papers are in the Library of Congress. Her works, in addition to those mentioned above, include busts of Generals Grant, Frémont, and McClellan; Peter Cooper; the explorer Albert Pike; Ezra Cornell; Chief Justice Morrison R. Waite; and the British evangelist Charles H. Spurgeon. Cornell Univ. possesses a bust of Lincoln, and her bust of Mayor Samuel T. Powell stands in the Brooklyn City Hall. Her ideal figures include "Miriam," "America," "The West," "The Spirit of Carnival," and "The Indian Girl."]

THURMAN WILKINS

**REED, Elizabeth Armstrong.** *See* REED, Myrtle.

**REED, Esther De Berdt** (Oct. 22, 1746–Sept. 18, 1780), leader of women's relief work during the American Revolution, was born in London, England, one of two children and the only daughter of Dennys De Berdt, a devout Congregationalist descended from Flemish religious refugees, and Martha (Symons) De Berdt. Her father, a merchant in the colonial trade, later served as agent for the colonies of Massachusetts and Delaware and in that capacity helped secure repeal of the Stamp Act. He was host to many Americans at his London home and his country house at Enfield. Several of these visitors courted his daughter, a studious, pious young woman, delicate in appearance yet animated in speech and manner. The one who won her love was Joseph Reed, a young lawyer from New Jersey whom she first met in 1763. But their marriage was delayed, first by the opposition of her father and then by Reed's absence in America for five years. Reed returned to England in 1770, and the wedding took place in London on May 31. The couple had planned to remain in England, but De Berdt's death seven weeks before the wedding left his family financially distressed, and the Reeds, accompanied by Mrs. De Berdt, sailed to America and settled in Philadelphia.

Joseph Reed quickly became a leader of the patriot movement in the growing controversy with England, and his wife also identified herself fully with the American cause. During the meeting of the First Continental Congress in 1774 she was hostess to Washington, John and Samuel Adams, and other delegates. She was glowingly referred to by a Connecticut member as "a Daughter of Liberty, zealously affected in a good Cause." Amid growing tension in early 1775 Mrs. Reed wrote to her brother, Dennis, in England that "if these great affairs must be brought to a crisis and decided, it had better be in our time than in our childrens." Her own children were then three in number: Martha, Joseph, and Esther. Three others were born during the Revolution: Theodosia, Dennis De Berdt, and George Washington; Theodosia died in infancy of smallpox in 1778.

During the first three years of the war Esther Reed's husband was often away with the army as Washington's aide. The family itself was forced to flee Philadelphia on three different occasions, as the city became a military focal point. After the British left Philadelphia, and with the subsequent election of Joseph Reed as president (governor) of Pennsylvania, the Reeds settled again in that city.

In 1780, during the bleakest period of the war, Mrs. Reed, only recently recovered from an attack of smallpox, served with vigor as chairman of a campaign among the women of Philadelphia and Germantown to raise funds for Washington's soldiers. Organizing a committee of thirty-nine women, she was able to report to Washington on July 4 that the equivalent of $7,500 in specie had been contributed. When the General asked that the money be used for linen shirts for his men, the women's committee purchased the linen and cut and sewed the shirts themselves. Over two thousand shirts were delivered to the army at the year's end. Mrs. Reed also tried with some success to spread the work elsewhere, but though her letters brought into being local committees of women in other Pennsylvania towns, in Trenton, N.J., and in Maryland, the Philadelphia endeavor was nowhere equaled in extent and results.

Esther Reed did not live to see her work completed. She died suddenly in Philadelphia in September 1780, at the age of thirty-three, the victim of an acute dysentery. The relief committee was carried forward under the direction of SARAH FRANKLIN BACHE, daughter of Benjamin Franklin. Mrs. Reed was buried at Philadelphia's Second Presbyterian (Arch Street) Church. In 1868 her remains, together with those of her husband, were moved to Laurel Hill Cemetery.

[The Reed Papers, at the N.-Y. Hist. Soc., contain, in vol. I, 77 letters between Esther De Berdt and Joseph Reed during their engagement; some 40 additional letters to or from Esther Reed are scattered through vols. II through VIII; subscription lists for the Phila. women's relief committee are in vol. VII. William B. Reed, *The Life of Esther De Berdt, Afterwards Esther Reed, of Pa.* (1853), is poorly organized and heavily eulogistic, but useful for its many excerpts from her letters. See also Reed's *Life and Correspondence of Joseph Reed* (2 vols., 1847); John F. Roche, *Joseph Reed* (1957); and Albert Matthews, ed., *The Letters of Dennys De Berdt, 1757–1770* (1911).]

JOHN F. ROCHE

**REED, Mary** (Dec. 4, 1854–Apr. 8, 1943), Methodist missionary to lepers in India, was born at Lowell, Washington County, Ohio, the second of the eleven children and first daughter of Wesley W. and Sarah Ann (Henderson) Reed. Her father's family had come from New Jersey; her mother had been born in Ohio of Virginia forebears. Mary's childhood was spent at Crooked Tree in adjacent Noble County. She grew up in a deeply religious home atmosphere. At the age of sixteen she experienced conversion and thereafter took an active part in the work of her local Methodist church. For ten years she taught in a district school in Kenton, Ohio.

At about the age of thirty Mary Reed determined to become a missionary. The Cincinnati branch of the Methodist Woman's Foreign Missionary Society undertook her support, and she sailed for India in November 1884. The following January the society's North India Conference assigned her to Cawnpore to work among Hindu women in the zenanas, but illness prevented her from taking up her post immediately, and she was sent for a time to Pithoragarh in the foothills of the Himalayas to recoup her health, study Hindustani, and observe missionary work in the area. The local population included an unusually large number of lepers, and Miss Reed is believed during this stay to have visited a colony of these outcasts in the vicinity known as Chandag.

Four years of evangelical work at Cawnpore followed. Miss Reed then taught for a year at the Girls' Boarding School maintained by the Woman's Foreign Missionary Society at Gonda. At this time her health gave way again, and in January 1890 she was sent to the United States on furlough. Rest and treatment, including surgery, at the Methodist hospital and deaconess home in Cincinnati failed, however, to relieve her condition. Her symptoms included a constant tingling pain in the right forefinger and a strange spot on one cheek, and she gradually became convinced that she had contracted leprosy and that this was a sign of a divine calling to minister to the victims of this dread disease. The diagnosis was confirmed by Dr. Prince A. Morrow of New York, a skin specialist who had worked with lepers in Hawaii. Concealing news of her condition from family and friends, Miss Reed returned to India, traveling by way of London, where Sir Joseph Frayer, leading authority on Indian diseases, concurred in the diagnosis.

To find Miss Reed a sphere of service among her fellow lepers Bishop James M. Thoburn, the Methodist Church's executive officer in India, in September 1891 approached the Mission to Lepers in India and the East, a British organization founded in 1874 which maintained leper asylums in India and Burma. Early in 1892 Mary Reed was appointed superintendent of the asylum which the mission had established in 1887 near Pithoragarh, located on a mountain ridge above Chandag, and took up her work there. Besides supporting the asylum, the mission responded to Miss Reed's appeals for funds to provide better housing for her charges, and within eight years she had replaced the huts and stables found upon her arrival by a group of substantial houses, a chapel, and a small hospital for the extreme cases, with a dispensary attached. The Indian government gave forty-eight acres of additional land, which was used for grazing and garden plots for the inmates. Miss Reed dealt with legal problems, let building contracts, supervised native workmen, and managed the asylum's finances, besides providing food for the whole community, teaching some of the girls and women to read, dressing the disfiguring sores of her patients, comforting them as best she could, and attempting to bring them the consolations of the Christian faith. Among local Hindus stricken with leprosy there was some reluctance to seek refuge in the asylum "because of the Christian influence exercised," but the numbers sheltered

there doubled in the course of the decade to about ninety, and a majority under Mary Reed's loving tutelage became baptized Christians.

For seven years Miss Reed sought to carry on both her work with the lepers and missionary duties for the Methodist Church. She supervised six village schools and three Sunday schools within a two- to five-mile radius of the asylum, enrolling some two hundred pupils. Native "Bible women" served as teachers and had some success as well in reaching Hindu women in their homes, where Miss Reed's own attempts mostly met with "rebuffs and rude speeches."

In spite of this dual load of responsibilities, Mary Reed's general health remained good, a fact to which her rare European visitors gave wondering testimony. She refused any medical treatment for herself, preferring to leave her case to God's will. Her symptoms had virtually disappeared by 1895. In 1897 she left her mountain ridge for a fifty-mile camping trip through the hills to a gathering of fellow Woman's Foreign Missionary Society workers near Almora; in 1899, her health seemingly completely restored, she made an eight-day journey to Lucknow for the annual Methodist missionary conference and was called to the platform for a tribute by Bishop Thoburn. She was permitted to take an eighteen-month furlough in 1903, part of which she spent in Palestine, and three years later she was able to make a visit to the United States to see her family. After this she did not leave the asylum at Chandag except for a fifty-mile trip in 1924 for dental work. With the aid of Indian assistants she administered the asylum until 1938. Five years later, an accident resulting from failing eyesight caused her death at the age of eighty-eight. She was buried near the chapel she had built. The government of India had awarded her the Kaisar-i-Hind Medal in 1917, and in 1941, upon the fiftieth anniversary of her service in Chandag, she was honored by the American Mission to Lepers, an interdenominational organization founded in 1906 as an offshoot of the Mission to Lepers in India and the East. The American Mission, now known as American Leprosy Missions, Inc., built the Mary Reed Memorial Hospital at Chandag in 1949. Both organizations continue to support the asylum, now under the direction of an Indian physician.

[John Jackson, *Mary Reed: Missionary to the Lepers* (1900), is the basic source. See also: Annie R. Gracey, ed., *Eminent Missionary Women* (1898), pp. 121–31; Lee S. Huizenga, *Mary Reed of Chandag* (pamphlet, 1939); Julia Lake Kellersberger, *Mary Reed, My Jewel* (pamphlet, Am. Leprosy Missions, Inc., n.d.); *Time*, Oct. 27, 1941, p. 70; *N.Y. Times*, May 21, 1943; *Cincinnati Post*, Apr. 22, 1943. On her ancestry see Martin R. Andrews, ed., *Hist. of Marietta and Wash. County, Ohio, and Representative Citizens* (1902), pp. 1340–41.]

JAMES H. PYKE

REED, Myrtle (Sept. 27, 1874–Aug. 17, 1911), popular novelist, was born in the Chicago suburb of Norwood Park, Ill., the youngest of three children and only daughter of Hiram Von Reed and Elizabeth (Armstrong) Reed (1842–1915). Her brothers both achieved distinction in Chicago circles, Charles Bert as a surgeon and obstetrician, Earl Howell as an author and etcher. Her father, a Campbellite preacher from Harvard, Ill., made a precarious living by establishing the first literary magazine in Chicago, the *Lakeside Monthly*, editing another periodical, the *Millenarian*, and lecturing on religion. Her mother, a native of Winthrop, Maine, was a zealous Christian and self-made scholar in comparative religion and Oriental literatures whose books on the Bible, Buddhism, and Hindu and Persian literature won her election to learned societies in England. A member of the Illinois Woman's Press Association, she served as its president for four terms. Elizabeth Reed was a woman of strong character and driving energies who led a rigorously organized life; her traits appeared, with significant modifications, in her daughter's personality.

From her earliest childhood Myrtle Reed's parents encouraged her to emulate her mother and become an author; even her name, it is said, had been chosen by her father with an eye to its appearance in print. She published her first story in a juvenile periodical, the *Acorn*, at the age of ten. As a student at West Division High School in Chicago, she edited the school paper, the *Voice*, to which she contributed a number of her own verses and short stories. Rejecting, however, her mother's example of scholarship, she received at best a superficial education, though she liked to fancy herself a student of philosophy and accounted Carlyle a particular influence on her thought. During her high school years she was troubled by emotional disturbances; a breakdown, attributed to overwork, prevented her from attending college. Working with intermittent but violent bursts of creativity, she channeled her energies into the writing of poetry and fiction presenting a sugary picture of ideal romance.

While editing the *Voice*, she first began corresponding with her future husband, James Sydney McCullough, a young Irish-Canadian then editing a school paper in Toronto with which her paper exchanged. After her graduation in 1893 she started work as a free-lance journalist, contributing poetry, short stories, and sketches to *Bookman*, the *National*, and *Munsey's* magazines. Eventually her pieces would appear in *Harper's Bazar*, *Putnam's Magazine*, and the *Critic*, but at this time she was almost unknown. The manuscript of her first novel, *Love Letters of a Musician*, came back with a scathing rejection from a leading Chicago publisher. Encouraged by McCullough, she offered it to George H. Putnam, who published it in 1899; by 1904 the book was in its fifteenth printing. In 1901 she brought out *The Spinster Book*, a series of light essays on love and courtship, and in 1902 her second novel, *Lavender and Old Lace*, an instantaneous success which went through forty printings during the next nine years. Transferred into print, her elaborate daydreams were a sure formula for popular success, and in rapid order she published five more novels.

During this period McCullough, in order to be near Myrtle Reed, moved to Chicago and set up a real estate business. His frequent visits caused her to supplant her previous ideal of completely helpless femininity, as outlined in *The Spinster Book*, with a concept of the sublime role of the homemaking woman, and she began to publish a series of cookbooks under the pseudonym "Olive Green." She and McCullough were married on Oct. 22, 1906, after a courtship of almost fifteen years. By this time fantasy had become inextricably confused with reality in her mind. Attempting to create the perfect marriage, she began to try to reshape McCullough to fit the role of "model husband" in which she portrayed him in her conversation and writing. When he arrived late at the station for their wedding trip to Washington, he discovered that, to teach him punctuality, she had gleefully taken their combined luggage, tickets, and money and gone on without him. She displayed McCullough to her family and friends at a series of parties, much like a prize exhibit at a fair. He was pliable, but it was patently impossible for him to fit the pattern of her dreamworld, and her attempts to remold him drove him to heavy drinking and frequent business trips. During this period she took the management of her own real estate out of his hands. Divorce was out of the question; from childhood, sensational news stories on divorce had caused her severe distress; and she was still representing her marriage to friends and a vast reading public as a blissful example. Her writings now increasingly came to reflect a preoccupation with death and suicide. She started using the sedative Veronal; the drug heightened the pattern of feverish activity alternating with depression and insomnia which had always troubled her when writing. In August 1911, having just completed her somber novel *A Weaver of Dreams*, she took her own life by swallowing half a bottle of Veronal. She was thirty-six.

In twelve years Myrtle Reed had produced thirteen sentimental romances, one book of short stories, two biographies, one historical novel, ten cookbooks, and various magazine articles on household matters (under the pseudonym "Katherine LaFarge Norton"). She left an estate valued at $100,000 and royalties estimated at $25,000 per year. In accordance with her wishes, her funeral was conducted in an Episcopal chapel and her body cremated. The *Chicago Tribune* aptly headlined her tragedy: "Dies in Bondage to Her Own Fancy."

[The principal biographical sources are: Ethel S. Colson and Norma B. Carson, *Myrtle Reed* (1911), a brief pamphlet issued by G. P. Putnam's Sons which reprints two articles originally published in *Book News Monthly*, Jan. 1911; the forewords by her friend Mary B. Powell in Myrtle Reed's *Happy Women* (1913) and *The Myrtle Reed Year Book* (1911); and newspaper accounts in the *Chicago Daily News*, Aug. 18, 19, 1911, and *Chicago Tribune*, Aug. 19, 20, 21, 1911. See also *Reader Mag.*, Nov. 1904, pp. 709–10; and articles in the *Dict. Am. Biog.* on Elizabeth Armstrong Reed and Earl Howell Reed.]

HOWARD B. CHRISTENSON

REESE, Lizette Woodworth (Jan. 9, 1856–Dec. 17, 1935), poet, was born in the village of Huntingdon, Md., later called Waverly, two miles from Baltimore by the Old York Road. Her father, David Reese, the son of a Welsh immigrant who had come to America about 1832, was a man of restless, roving disposition, given to long absences from home, once going as far as Chile. During the Civil War he served on the Confederate side. Her mother, Louisa Sophia (Gabler) Reese, was the daughter of Carl Friedrich Gabler, a German immigrant, who with his wife and ten children had come as a political refugee from Saxony in the 1840's and established himself as a wheelwright and carriage maker in Huntingdon. A man of dignity and piety, he became a personage in the Waverly neighborhood and in the life of his granddaughter.

Lizette and her twin sister, Sophia Louisa, were born shortly after the death of a two-year-old brother, Friedrich; later there were three other children. The Reese cottage, one story in front and two behind, was set amid dark trees, flowering shrubs, and trailing vines. There were wide spaces, distant views, and few passersby. Lizette Reese's entire life was lived within a few miles of this one-time rural spot, which decade by decade lost its remoteness and became part of a large city. For her, however, the remembered beauty and quietness of its earlier unhurried days, particularly in the spring season, had made an impression deep enough to last a lifetime and to determine one of the most persistent and characteristic themes of her verse. Two of her prose works, *A Victorian Village* (1929) and *The York Road* (1931), recall this childhood setting in days of the omnibus and tollgate.

Her first schooling was in St. John's (Episcopal) Parish School, also close by. Except for this beginning and for a brief period in a school in Birmingham, Pa., where her father, a Civil War prisoner, was recuperating from illness, her entire grammar and high school education was received in the Baltimore public schools. Her teachers remembered her for her delight in telling imaginative stories and making rhymes. "Schoolday joys and hopes are done," she wrote as the last line to the "Parting Ode" she had composed for her high school graduation. A false prophecy it proved to be for her, as she was to spend forty-eight of her adult years in Baltimore schoolrooms. Beginning at seventeen, she taught for two years at St. John's Parish School, for twenty-two years at one of the city's German-English schools, where instruction was given in both languages, for four years at the colored high school, and from 1901 until her retirement in 1921 at the Western High School for girls. In her last two posts she taught English literature and composition. She often chafed under the burden of a heavy teaching routine and was openly critical of what she called the "System," but through it all the poetic impulse not only remained alive and articulate but deepened and grew stronger with the years.

Her first published poem was "The Deserted House," inspired by one of her walks to school. She spent weeks writing it and, with encouragement from a former teacher, presented it in person to the editor of the *Southern Magazine*, where it was published in June 1874. She was eighteen years old. From that time until the year of her death she dedicated her scant leisure to writing. She wrote sparingly and slowly, but there was always a manuscript in progress on her desk. Her first volume of verse, *A Branch of May*, appeared in 1887, thirteen years after her first published poem. Except for the period from 1896 to 1916, her nine later volumes were published at intervals of four or five years, each containing magazine contributions belonging to the intervening period.

Her subject matter was traditional, with scarcely a hint of the tumultuous times through which she was living. In her thought the province of poetry is universal human experience; the "common lot," she called it, but with her it is the common lot intensely perceived and individually experienced. She wrote of grief, contentment, ecstasy, love, death, renunciation; her best poetry is often tempered with a strain of nostalgic sadness. Nearly always nature is her background and setting. But she wrote not always literally, for she, too, could see "a world in a grain of sand, / And a heaven in a wild flower." Her range was limited, but within it she could make a mere atom sharply significant. Her verse form was also traditional. She had come to maturity at a time when Victorian poets both of England and America were shaping poetic taste, and their standards remained her own for life, though she liked to think that she occupied something of a middle ground between the traditionalists and the proponents of "free verse." Temperamentally she was the child of her singing German mother and her silent, brooding Welsh father. Her verse is not powerful, but it communicates, and with a melody that is often flawless. For the singing quality of her brief lyrics Herrick is her poetic ancestor.

Outside of Baltimore, Lizette Woodworth Reese became known slowly and never widely. In 1890 Edmund Clarence Stedman included three of her poems in his *Anthology*. Forty-six years later Louis Untermeyer included twelve in his *Modern American Poetry*. The sonnet "Tears," by which she is most widely known, first appeared in *Scribner's Magazine* in November 1899. During her fourteen years of retirement Miss Reese was active in various community projects and enjoyed the affectionate esteem of her fellow townsmen. Her seventy-fifth birthday was the occasion of a large gathering in her honor, presided over by Henry L. Mencken, who for many years had been her stout champion. On this occasion he eulogized her for her poetic integrity and her refusal to follow fashions in verse. Other honors included election to Phi Beta Kappa by the College of William and Mary, the honorary degree of Doctor of Letters from Goucher College, and the Mary P. L. Keats Memorial Prize. She died in Baltimore shortly before her eightieth birthday and was buried in St.

John's Churchyard, near her childhood home. On her stone are four of her own lines,

> The long day sped,
> A roof, a bed;
> No years,
> No tears.

[Miss Reese's own reminiscences in *A Victorian Village;* Carlin T. Kindilien, "The Village World of Lizette Woodworth Reese," *South Atlantic Quart.*, Jan. 1957; Laura Ruth M. Klein, "Lizette Woodworth Reese, A Critical Biog." (unpublished Ph.D. thesis, Univ. of Pa., 1943); news items in the *Sun* (Baltimore), Dec. 18, 19, 20, and *Evening Sun*, Dec. 17, 18, 19, 20, 1935. See also Fred B. Millett, *Contemporary Am. Authors* (1940), pp. 536–37, a short biographical sketch with a bibliography of writings by and about Miss Reese; R. P. Harriss, "April Weather: The Poetry of Lizette Woodworth Reese," *South Atlantic Quart.*, Apr. 1934; Jessie B. Rittenhouse, *The Younger Am. Poets* (1906), pp. 27–45; and, for another critical estimate, Horace Gregory and Marya Zaturenska, *A Hist. of Am. Poetry, 1900–1940* (1942), pp. 79–83. The Enoch Pratt Free Library of Baltimore has a small collection of books and manuscripts placed there by the Lizette Woodworth Reese Memorial Soc. and a group of letters and memorabilia given by Warren Wilmer Brown, her literary executor. The large deposit collection of her papers and books is at the library of the Univ. of Va.]

OLA ELIZABETH WINSLOW

**REGAN, Agnes Gertrude** (Mar. 26, 1869–Sept. 30, 1943), Catholic social welfare leader and educator, was born in San Francisco, Calif., the third daughter and fourth in a family of nine children. Her father, James Regan (original name, James of Carmel O'Regan), had been born in Valparaiso, Chile, of an Irish father and an English mother; coming in 1849 to California, he worked in the gold mines, was for ten years private secretary to Joseph S. Alemany, first Catholic archbishop of San Francisco, and was later associated with the Hibernia Bank, one of whose founders was his brother-in-law, Richard Tobin. Agnes' mother, Mary Ann Morrison, came of an Irish family that had migrated to America in 1847. Following their marriage in 1863 the Regans at first lived in Chile but soon returned to San Francisco, thereafter their permanent home. Generous hospitality was traditional in the Regan household, and so was the enjoyment of the best in operas, plays, and concerts. They were devout Catholics, and two of the daughters became nuns.

After completing grade and high school at St. Rose Academy, Agnes Regan attended the San Francisco Normal School, graduating in 1887. For over thirty years she served in the

San Francisco school system as teacher, principal, and, from 1914 to 1919, as a member of the Board of Education (part of the time as president) and of the city Playground Commission. With Hiram Johnson, then governor of California, she was instrumental in securing enactment of the first teachers' pension law in the state. In 1920 Archbishop Edward J. Hanna chose her to represent the archdiocese of San Francisco at the organizational meeting of the National Council of Catholic Women in Washington, D.C. She was elected second vice-president of the board of directors and a few months later was appointed the council's first executive secretary. Moving to Washington, she took up the position she was to hold for twenty years.

Agnes Regan was drawn into Catholic social service at an important formative period. The growing concern of the American Catholic community for matters of social welfare had found expression, under the leadership of such liberal clergymen as William J. Kerby and John J. Burke, in the formation of the National Catholic War Council (1917) and its postwar heir, the National Catholic Welfare Conference. The National Council of Catholic Women, one of its subsidiary groups, functioned (along with a similar group for laymen) as a channel of communication and a coordinating body for the church's various lay organizations. As its executive secretary, Miss Regan traveled widely, interpreting the aims of the new council not only to women but also to bishops and priests and helping Catholic women develop local programs. Through its affiliated organizations the council supported religious vacation schools in rural areas, provided aid to immigrants and training in Americanization, and studied the needs of Catholic working girls for housing and protective care. Miss Regan insisted that Catholic women had obligations beyond their local and diocesan interests and urged them to support social legislation. Often appearing herself before Congressional committees, she favored the proposed child labor amendment and the Sheppard-Towner Act to subsidize maternity and infant care, but spoke against the "Equal Rights" amendment. The council in 1927–28 joined with the Y.W.C.A., the National Council of Jewish Women, and the Women's Industrial League in successful support of a change in restrictive immigration laws. Throughout, Miss Regan fostered the development of leadership among Catholic women. By 1941, when she retired as executive secretary, there were 64 diocesan councils, 18 national organizations of laywomen, and 3,500 local organizations

affiliated with the National Council of Catholic Women.

From the start one of the most important responsibilities of the National Council was the training of laywomen in social work. A wartime school for this purpose had been established in Washington in 1918 on the initiative of Father Burke and Father Kerby. In an effort to place it on a firm peacetime basis, an affiliation was first sought with the Catholic University of America (where Father Kerby chaired the department of sociology). When this proved impossible, since the university enrolled no laywomen, Father Burke turned to the newly formed National Council of Catholic Women. Under its auspices the National Catholic Service School for Women (later renamed the National Catholic School of Social Service) opened its doors in the fall of 1921 with a two-year postgraduate program for which the Catholic University in 1923 agreed to grant a master's degree. Miss Regan, who had taken a warm interest in the school from the beginning, was in 1922 appointed to its faculty as instructor in community organization. Three years later she became assistant director, a post she held until her death; for two difficult years (1935–37) she was acting director. Forming a "triple alliance," Miss Regan, Father Kerby, and Father Burke were the dominant influences during the school's first two decades. While living at the school and bearing many of its administrative burdens, Miss Regan retained her secretaryship of the National Council of Catholic Women, although beginning in 1927 this was officially reduced to half time. Support of the school placed heavy demands on the council, and much of Miss Regan's time and energy went into fund raising; when money was short she refused a salary. Her "granite-like determination," in the words of Father Kerby, carried the school successfully through a disheartening succession of crises.

A handsome, vigorous woman, poised and friendly, Agnes Regan was an able speaker. Not an outstanding classroom teacher, she was nonetheless effective in her relationships with students, many of whom sought her personal counsel. She was deeply and unostentatiously religious. Among the honors conferred on her were the papal decoration Pro Ecclesia et Pontifice (1933), an honorary degree from Rosary College (1937), and the first Siena medal of the Theta Phi Alpha fraternity (1937), given annually to an outstanding Catholic woman. She died of hypertensive heart disease in Washington in 1943, at the age of seventy-four, and was buried in Holy Cross

Cemetery, Daly City, Calif., near San Francisco. The bulk of her modest estate was willed to the school. In 1950 Agnes Regan Hall was dedicated at the Catholic University of America, with whose school of social work the National Catholic School of Social Service had in 1947 been merged.

[Loretto R. Lawler, *Full Circle: The Story of the Nat. Catholic School of Social Service, 1918–1947* (1951), gives the best account of her work. See also Msgr. John A. Ryan, *Eulogy—Agnes G. Regan* (undated pamphlet); *Catholic Action* (Washington), July 1937, Oct. 1943; *N.C.C.W. Monthly Message* (Washington), Nov. 1943; Aaron I. Abell, *Am. Catholicism and Social Action* (1960); Francis L. Broderick, *Right Reverend New Dealer: John A. Ryan* (1963). Other information from Mother M. Justin, O.P. (niece), and Clara V. Bradley (friend and colleague) and from personal acquaintance.]

DOROTHY A. MOHLER

REHAN, Ada (Apr. 22, 1857–Jan. 8, 1916), actress, was born in Limerick, Ireland, the third daughter among five or six children of Thomas and Harriett (Ryan) Crehan. Her father has been described as a shipbuilder or sea captain, but his actual status was probably much more modest. In 1865 the family came to the United States and settled in Brooklyn, N.Y., where Ada was educated. At fourteen she followed her two sisters, Kate and Hattie, onto the stage. The former, known professionally as Kate O'Neil, was married to Oliver Doud Byron, and it was in her brother-in-law's production, in Newark, N.J., of his own play *Across the Continent* that Ada made her first appearance, substituting for one night in a minor role. Mrs. Byron next got her a place in the Philadelphia company of Mrs. John Drew (see LOUISA LANE DREW). There, so the story goes, a printer's error resulted in her being listed as Ada C. Rehan, and because her debut was so successful Mrs. Drew persuaded her to keep the name. After two seasons with Mrs. Drew and a sojourn at Macaulay's Theatre in Louisville, her apprenticeship continued in John W. Albaugh's stock company in Albany and Baltimore. Meanwhile, she had made her New York debut in April 1875, at Wood's Museum, as Kate Furnell in *Thoroughbred*, produced by the Byrons. Supporting roles with such stars as Edwin Booth, Lawrence Barrett, and FANNY DAVENPORT followed, until in 1879 she was engaged by the eminent theatrical producer Augustin Daly, the start of an association that was to last for twenty years. Her first part for Daly was a minor one in his production of Zola's *L'Assommoir* (Olympic

Theatre, New York, Apr. 30, 1879). The following September Daly opened his own theatre, where, after an unsuccessful initial bill, he revived his earlier success, *Divorce* (Sept. 30). In it Ada Rehan first played Lu Ten Eyck, but with her elevation to the role of Fanny Adrianse she became Daly's leading lady.

Daly's special achievement during the next two decades, a time when he ranked as America's foremost theatrical manager, was in the realm of ensemble acting. Dictatorial in his methods, planning every detail of a performance, and insisting that actors follow rigidly his conception of each part, he developed a company so expert and so well harmonized that it won high public and critical acclaim. At the heart of the Daly company were the so-called "Big Four"—Ada Rehan, John Drew, Mrs. G. H. Gilbert (see ANNE HARTLEY GILBERT), and James Lewis—known and loved alike by George Bernard Shaw and the humblest urchin on Broadway. Although Ada Rehan played more than two hundred roles in her twenty-six years on the stage, she was most successful in plays of three types, all of them specialties of the Daly troupe: Shakespearean comedies; the "Old Comedies" of such seventeenth- and eighteenth-century playwrights as Cibber, Garrick, Goldsmith, and Sheridan; and Daly's Americanized versions of German farces. Her finest characterizations were her Shakespearean roles of Katharine in *The Taming of the Shrew*, Rosalind in *As You Like It*, and Viola in *Twelfth Night*. She played the first originally in New York on Jan. 18, 1887, the second on Dec. 17, 1889, with later performances on Daly's coast-to-coast tours and abroad. In 1894 Daly's *Twelfth Night*, with Ada Rehan as Viola, achieved a sensational run of over a hundred performances in London. Her success in Shakespearean comedy was largely responsible for Tennyson's decision to entrust his play *The Foresters*, based on the Robin Hood legend, to Daly; in the New York premiere (June 1892) she created the role of Maid Marian, singing songs especially written for her by Sir Arthur Sullivan. The Old Comedies were, like Shakespeare, a standard part of the repertory of most nineteenth-century stock companies, though in Daly's hands they became lavish productions centering around the personality of Miss Rehan. Here she displayed a talent for comedy similar to that needed for Shakespeare, a bit broader perhaps, a bit more roguish, but in the same general tradition and exploiting the same ability to assume romantic "breeches," or male, roles.

Though opinion sometimes varied about the quality of Miss Rehan's acting, there was universal agreement on her beauty and charm. She was tall, held herself well, wore her hair dressed high on her head, and had a lovely neck and shoulders, as seen in John Singer Sargent's full-length portrait of 1895. The English actress Ellen Terry wrote to Daly after first seeing her perform that she was "the most lovely, humorous darling I have even seen on the stage." Critics praised her "velvet voice," her particular archness of expression; even the sober John Ranken Towse found her "in her element in every variety of piquant, tender, mischievous, high-spirited, alluring, whimsical, and provocative girlhood" (*Sixty Years of the Theatre*, 1916, p. 344). Yet the Daly company, which in its earlier days had stressed the natural style of acting as against the older emphasis on histrionics, had by the 1890's hardened into an artificiality of its own, a limitation shared by Miss Rehan. This was particularly evident in Daly's German farces, such pieces as *Needles and Pins* (1880) and *A Night Off* (1885). Featuring the "Big Four," they were amusing plays, unquestionably "proper," handsomely mounted, and popular with fashionable audiences on two continents. Yet by 1896 the critic William Archer could observe of *The Countess Gucki:* "It is not a play . . . it is simply a contrivance for bringing Miss Rehan on the stage and enabling her to exercise those arts of fascination to which we are all such willing slaves." George Bernard Shaw, too, protested the wasting of this "treasure" on "stale farces," adding (1897) that while he found her "irresistible" in Shakespeare, he had "never seen her create a character."

Central to Ada Rehan's career was her relationship with Augustin Daly, both professional and personal. Some, such as Daly's costume designer, W. Graham Robertson, have seen Miss Rehan as the Trilby to Daly's Svengali. Certain it is that Daly found an outlet for his own histrionic talents in Ada Rehan's acting, and when he died, in 1899, she unquestionably lost both her zest and her ability. Quite consciously, Daly sought to pattern her career after that of the celebrated Irish actress Peg Woffington. He once wrote a glowing biography of Woffington (1888) in which the parallels between the two actresses were clearly indicated: not only the stage parts they shared, but also the similar offstage roles they played vis-à-vis their managers, Garrick and Daly. In stressing the "devotion to duty," the "goodness of heart," and the "faithfulness" of Peg, Daly was in effect praising Ada Rehan for qualities that more than endeared her to her own manager. Not until Cornelia Otis Skinner's *Family Circle* (1948), however, did anyone explicitly state the truth: "Ada Rehan, besides being leading lady, enjoyed the offstage rôle of *grande maîtresse*. . . . To hold the whip handle by keeping a woman of her beauty and prominence in the compromising position an extra-marital liaison involved in those cautious times was a sop to his will to power." Daly's explanation of the Woffington-Garrick affair may be said to offer another viewpoint: "Whatever of love there may have been between them was prudently concealed, and both fared all the better for it in the estimation of a world which prefers to consider its idols as models of propriety, even if they be not so."

Following a year's retirement after Daly's death, Ada Rehan made an attempted comeback in *Sweet Nell of Old Drury,* after which she toured with Otis Skinner through the East, South, and Middle West in such old favorites as *The School for Scandal* and *The Merchant of Venice.* The tour, however, was a failure. Miss Rehan was "tired" and "ill"; without Daly, Skinner recalled, she was "helpless." In her own letters to the critic William Winter, she confessed that she was "indifferent" and "miserable." "My loss no one can understand," she complained. She retired a second time from the stage in 1905, at forty-eight. The rest of her life was divided about equally between her residences in New York City and on the English coast. She died in Roosevelt Hospital, New York, in 1916 of arteriosclerosis and cancer. Following cremation, her ashes were placed in the family vault in Greenwood Cemetery, Brooklyn. Otis Skinner's words characterizing the "most striking feature" of her art as an "abundant joy and vitality" probably best summarize her abilities.

[William Winter, *Ada Rehan* (1891; revised 1898) —a volume commissioned by Daly—and *The Wallet of Time* (1913), vol. II; Lewis C. Strang, *Famous Actresses of the Day in America,* First Series (1899); John B. Clapp and Edwin F. Edgett, *Players of the Present,* Part III (1901); obituary, *N.Y. Times,* Jan. 9, 1916; Otis Skinner, *Footlights and Spotlights* (1924); W. Graham Robertson, *Life Was Worth Living* (1931); John Drew, *My Years on the Stage* (1922); Marvin Felheim, *The Theater of Augustin Daly* (1956). The books by Winter and Strang are not to be fully trusted, since they were written to glorify Miss Rehan; more reliable in their evaluations are the reminiscences of Skinner and Drew. Miss Rehan's death certificate (N.Y. City Dept. of Health) supplied her year of birth and her mother's maiden name.]

MARVIN FELHEIM

REID, Christian. *See* TIERNAN, Frances Christine Fisher.

REID, Elisabeth Mills (Jan. 6, 1858–Apr. 29, 1931), philanthropist, Red Cross worker, and social leader, was born in New York City, the second of the two children and only daughter of Darius Ogden Mills and Jane Templeton (Cunningham) Mills, daughter of James Cunningham of Irvington, N.Y., a prominent shipowner and ship builder. Darius Mills' forebears had migrated from the Scottish border of northern England to colonial New York. After beginning his career in New York banking circles, Mills went to California during the gold rush of 1849 and in the next thirty years amassed a fortune in banking and mining. He frequently traveled east and by 1880 had once again made New York the center of his business activity. Upon his death in 1910 almost his entire fortune of $50,000,000 was divided between Elisabeth and her brother, Ogden Mills (father of the later Secretary of the Treasury, Ogden L. Mills).

Elisabeth Mills' early life was spent in California, in Sacramento or San Mateo, where her father had a country place, and at the Hudson Valley home of her maternal grandparents. Her education was supervised by governesses and later continued at Mlle. Vallette's school in Paris and the New York school of ANNA C. BRACKETT. On Apr. 26, 1881, in New York, she was married to Whitelaw Reid, twenty years her senior. Reid, an Ohioan who had risen to fame as a Civil War reporter and in 1872 had succeeded Horace Greeley as editor and chief owner of the *New York Tribune,* subsequently became minister to France (1889–92), Republican candidate for vice-president in 1892, and ambassador to Great Britain from 1905 until his death in 1912. He and his wife had three children, two of whom survived: Ogden Mills Reid (born 1882), who succeeded his father as editor and president of the *Tribune,* and Jean, who married Sir John Hubert Ward, equerry to Queen Alexandra of England.

Mrs. Reid's father had had a lifelong interest in philanthropy, and this, in the words of the *New York Times,* became the "dominating activity" of her own life. She not only contributed large sums but kept in close touch with the operations of the institutions she supported. Primarily interested in hospitals and nursing, she gave particular attention, after the outbreak of the Spanish-American War, to the Red Cross. As secretary of "Auxiliary No. 3," the Red Cross Society for the Maintenance of Trained Nurses, newly established in New York, she persuaded President McKinley to accept over six hundred of the Society's nurses for service in Cuba, the Philippines, and military hospitals in the United States.

This new function of the Red Cross became the cause of conflict with ANITA NEWCOMB MC GEE, who had earlier been appointed by Surgeon General George M. Sternberg to supply qualified nurses to the army through a D.A.R. Hospital Corps.

The charter meeting of the New York chapter of the American Red Cross, of which she became an active director, was held in Mrs. Reid's home in 1905. In the same year she supported and cooperated with MABEL T. BOARDMAN in the reorganization of the Red Cross which followed the retirement of CLARA BARTON. In 1912 Mrs. Reid's contribution helped make possible the establishment of the Red Cross Rural Nursing Service (later the Town and Country Nursing Service), and she served as chairman of this committee from 1913 to 1915, when the European situation absorbed her attention. During World War I she was chairman of the American Red Cross in London and deputy commissioner of the Red Cross for Great Britain. She was also active in France, endowing hospital rooms, helping organize the American Hospital at Neuilly, outfitting ambulances, and converting the American Art Students' Club in Paris (which she had earlier founded) into an officers' hospital and American Red Cross headquarters. For her wartime activities Mrs. Reid was in 1922 made a chevalier of the Legion of Honor by the French government.

In other areas of philanthropy Mrs. Reid served for many years on the board of the Mills Training School for Male Nurses, founded by her father at Bellevue Hospital in New York City in 1888. She built Mills Memorial Hospital in San Mateo, Calif., and (with her brother and others) St. Luke's Hospital in San Francisco. At her death the largest single charitable bequest in her will was $500,000 to the San Mateo hospital. In 1912 she contributed funds to help build the D. O. Mills Training School for Nurses at the Trudeau Sanatorium, Saranac Lake, N.Y., and in 1930 added Reid House, a nurses' residence hall. A member of the Church of the Incarnation (Episcopal) in New York City for almost fifty years, she was an active supporter of the missionary and charitable work of the Protestant Episcopal Church. She helped build the Episcopal Cathedral of Manila and contributed the central chancel of the Cathedral of St. John the Divine in New York.

A loyal and devoted supporter of her husband's newspaper, Elisabeth Reid inherited a controlling interest in the *Tribune* when he died and thereafter had a powerful, if indirect, influence upon its management, directed by her son. She moved in diplomatic circles with ease. By "ten o'clock every morning," when she was hostess of the American embassy in London, "Mrs. Reid knew what Americans had come to London who were worth attention and had provided that they should receive it" (Martin, p. 254). Edward VII and Queen Alexandra were frequent guests and personal friends. Dorchester House, the ambassador's palatial residence, became, it is said, the scene of "some of the greatest social affairs in Europe" (*New York Times*, Apr. 30, 1931). One of her many American triumphs was a ball given in New York in 1919 for the Prince of Wales, with General Pershing and William Howard Taft among the guests. The Reids were high in Republican circles, and their entertainments often served a political as well as a social function. When the Republicans nominated Warren Harding for the presidency in 1920, "Mrs. Reid sighed, accepted the fact, and said, 'Now we must have him East and have people to meet him at dinner'" (Martin, p. 254).

A short and rather shy person with a kindly manner, she possessed a full awareness of her station in life. "Mrs. Whitelaw Reid in a harness of diamonds and rubies graciously allowed me to do homage," wrote Henry Adams of a White House diplomatic reception (*Letters, 1892–1918*, 1938, p. 418). The Reids maintained a town house on Madison Avenue and an 800-acre country estate, Ophir Hall, near Purchase in Westchester County. The latter was a repository for the art collection for which Mrs. Reid was noted, including paintings by Van Dyck, Raeburn, and Canaletto, Gobelin tapestries, Chinese porcelain, eighteenth-century brocades, and Louis XV furniture. While traveling in France in 1931, Mrs. Reid contracted pneumonia and died at her daughter's villa at Cap Ferrat near Nice. She left an estate appraised at $20,000,000. After a memorial service in the American Cathedral of Paris, her funeral was held at the Cathedral of St. John the Divine in New York with burial in Sleepy Hollow Cemetery, Tarrytown, N.Y. Commented the *New York Times* (editorial, Apr. 30, 1931): "In a day when 'society' had lost its moorings, and even its compass, she carried on the fine old tradition."

[The best accounts are in the *N.Y. Herald Tribune*, Apr. 30, 1931, and *N.Y. Times*, Apr. 30, May 19, 22, 1931. See also *Harper's Weekly*, Oct. 1, 1892, p. 943; *Outlook*, Oct. 28, 1905; *Literary Digest*, July 28, 1934, p. 37; *Nat. Cyc. Am. Biog.*, XXII, 2–3. For her Red Cross activities see Lavinia L. Dock et al., *Hist. of Am. Red Cross Nursing* (1922); Portia B. Kernodle, *The Red Cross Nurse*

in *Action, 1882–1948* (1949); *Public Health Nurse*, June 1931, p. 298. For interesting reminiscences see Edward S. Martin in *Harper's Monthly*, July 1931, pp. 253–56; and William Phillips, "An Ambassadress in the Golden Age," *Atlantic Monthly*, Nov. 1961. On her art collection and home see *Arts & Decoration*, June 1931, pp. 18–21, 76, 81; and *Art Treasures and Furnishings of Ophir Hall* (1935). Brief references may be found in Royal Cortissoz, *The Life of Whitelaw Reid* (2 vols., 1931); Harry W. Baehr, Jr., *The N.Y. Tribune since the Civil War* (1936); and Edward L. Trudeau, *An Autobiog.* (1916), pp. 300, 301.]

RAYMOND S. MILOWSKI

**REID, Mrs. Whitelaw.** *See* REID, Elisabeth Mills.

**REIGNOLDS, Catherine Mary** (May 16, 1836–July 11, 1911), better known as Kate Reignolds, actress, dramatic reader, and teacher, was born near London, England, the eldest of three daughters of Robert Gregory Taylor Reignolds and Emma (Absolon) Reignolds. Her father's family was of German extraction; her grandfather (who was killed at Waterloo), her father, and her uncle were officers in the British army. Robert Reignolds died at an early age, leaving his widow with three children to support. Mrs. Reignolds at first attempted a career as a concert singer. Failing in this, she accepted a theatrical offer from John B. Rice of Chicago and, bringing her daughters with her, came to the United States in 1850. She made her debut in *Cinderella* in Tremont Hall at Chicago on Feb. 24, 1851. In a minor role in this same performance young Kate, at fourteen, made her first appearance on any stage, following it up with another small part in *Rob Roy*. It is not clear just when she left Chicago, but she says that for four years she struggled in vain to make a place for herself. Her mother remained on the stage for many years, and both her sisters, Georgie and Jane, also attempted stage careers, but without notable success.

Finally in 1855 Kate Reignolds turned in desperation to Edwin Forrest, then filling an engagement at the Broadway Theatre in New York, and on Apr. 17 he permitted her to play Virginia in support of his Virginius. She made so favorable an impression that engagements followed with William E. Burton, LAURA KEENE, and John Brougham. In the fall of 1857 she joined the company of Ben De Bar at his Opera House in St. Louis. There, and at the St. Charles Theatre in New Orleans, where De Bar spent the winter seasons, she met many outstanding stars, notably CHAR-

LOTTE CUSHMAN, to whom she was indebted for invaluable advice and coaching. In December 1857 she was married to a fellow member of the company, Henry Farren, who, however, died in St. Louis on Jan. 8, 1860. By that year she had acquired such a reputation that she was selected for the important role of Anne Chute in Dion Boucicault's *The Colleen Bawn* at the farewell appearance of AGNES ROBERTSON at the Winter Garden in New York.

A few months later, in August 1860, Kate Reignolds moved to Boston to accept the position of leading lady with the stock company at the Boston Museum. She soon became a great popular favorite there, playing a wide variety of roles from Shakespeare to Boucicault. On June 28, 1861, she became the wife of (Alfred) Erving Winslow, a rising young Boston commission merchant and a member of an old New England family. Although in 1865 she left the museum to travel as a star, Boston remained her home for the rest of her life. In 1868 she appeared at the Princess' Theatre in London and in important houses in the provinces, but her visit to England was cut short by injuries received in a stage accident at Exeter, when a property bridge gave way; she was compelled to return home for medical treatment. After regaining her health she resumed her professional career, touring the United States at the head of her own company, but after the birth of her son, Charles-Edward Amory Winslow, on Feb. 4, 1877, she quietly withdrew to private life.

Some years later, probably emulating FANNY KEMBLE, Mrs. Winslow began to give dramatic readings from the lecture platform. Her selections were taken from the plays of Shakespeare, and also from the modern and controversial works of Ibsen, Sudermann, Maeterlinck, Björnson, and Echegaray. In the 1890's she gave private lessons in elocution and acting to talented young women, her most successful student being the later celebrated actress Josephine Hull (d. 1957). In 1895 she presented some of her pupils in the first Boston performance of Ibsen's *The Pillars of Society*, receiving later a letter of thanks from the dramatist.

Mrs. Winslow died of sunstroke at the age of seventy-five, following several years of ill health, at her summer home in Concord, Mass. Her ashes were buried in the Springfield (Mass.) Cemetery. She was survived by her husband and her son, who later became professor of public health at Yale. Though not a great actress, Kate Reignolds was a gifted and versatile one, and for a quarter of a century she was a prominent and respected figure in the American theatre. William Winter declared in 1866: "Grace, elegance, vivacity, the true spirit of laughing mischief, and withal a vein of earnest and tender sentiment, underlying archness and glitter, meet and blend in her temperament and manner."

[Writing under her married name, Mrs. Winslow published a rather genteel and sentimental volume of memoirs, *Yesterdays with Actors* (1887), and *Readings from the Old English Dramatists* (1895). Other biographical material in: *Nat. Cyc. Am. Biog.*, XXIII, 258; Mabel Ward Cameron, ed., *Biog. Cyc. Am. Women*, I (1924), 330–32; *Who Was Who in America*, vol. I (1942); John B. Clapp and Edwin F. Edgett, *Players of the Present*, Part III (1901); obituaries in *N.Y. Dramatic Mirror*, July 19, 1911, and *Boston Globe*, July 12, 1911; and clippings in the Harvard Theatre Collection. See also: T. Allston Brown, *Hist. of the Am. Stage* (1870); George C. D. Odell, *Annals of the N.Y. Stage*, vols. VI–VIII (1931–36); John S. Kendall, *The Golden Age of the New Orleans Theater* (1952); Robert L. Sherman, *Chicago Stage* (1947); Kate Ryan, *Old Boston Museum Days* (1915); Eugene Tompkins and Quincy Kilby, *The Hist. of the Boston Theatre* (1908).]

WILLIAM G. B. CARSON

**REINHARDT, Aurelia Isabel Henry** (Apr. 1, 1877–Jan. 28, 1948), college president, the second daughter and second of six children of William Warner Henry and Mollie (Merritt) Henry, was born in San Francisco. Her father had come to California in 1858 from Bennington, Vt., in quest at once of adventure, work, and health; her mother's family, originally Pennsylvanian, had arrived five years later, from Muscatine, Iowa. After his marriage, in 1873, Will Henry opened a wholesale grocery business, but returns were slim, and to aid the family finances his wife operated a boardinghouse and then a small hotel. Aurelia was one of forty girls admitted in the fall of 1888 to San Francisco's "Boys' High School"; among her classmates was the future actress BLANCHE BATES. In 1890 the Henrys moved to booming southern California, establishing a general store in San Jacinto, but Mrs. Henry was dissatisfied with the local schools and local "culture" and after two years sent her two elder daughters back to San Francisco. By 1895 the family had settled in Berkeley, where Aurelia and her sisters became the maids and waitresses in their mother's new boardinghouse.

Meanwhile Aurelia Henry had in 1894 entered the University of California at Berkeley. During her college years she wrote verse for the university magazine, was active in dramatics, and had a crowded social calendar. In February 1898, a semester short of her B.Litt.

degree (which she received that June), she became "Instructor in Physical Culture and Elocution" at the University of Idaho. Here she directed dramatics, did "readings" at university and civic gatherings, and left a lasting imprint on many of her students. A large woman of great vitality and personal force, she gave some thought to going into the professional theatre but decided against it and in 1901 enrolled as a graduate student in English at Yale.

During her two years at Yale she studied principally under Albert Stanburrough Cook. Learning in a Dante class that there was no English rendering of *De Monarchia* generally available, she made a translation which was published by Houghton Mifflin in 1904. She had meanwhile (1903) been installed in the "chair of English" at the State Normal School in Lewiston, Idaho. In 1905 she was granted her Yale Ph.D., with a dissertation (later published) on Ben Jonson's *Epicoene*. She spent the year 1905–06 in Europe, chiefly at Oxford and in Italy, on a fellowship from the Association of Collegiate Alumnae. Two more years at Lewiston followed, but though the time there had begun well, it ended badly. There were jealousies in the town, and there was a projected marriage which her mother blocked; in 1908 Aurelia Henry retreated to Berkeley. On Dec. 4, 1909, she was married to Dr. George Frederick Reinhardt, eight years her senior, a family acquaintance since their San Jacinto days, who had founded the University Health Service in Berkeley and become its director. Two sons, George Frederick and Paul Henry, were born, in 1911 and 1913. But in June of 1914 Dr. Reinhardt died suddenly of blood poisoning. The young widow secured an appointment to teach English in the extension division of the University of California and made a spectacular success with lecture courses on the drama in Stockton, Riverside, and Long Beach. At that point Mills College in Oakland, two years without a president and in very shaky condition, invited Mrs. Reinhardt to become its president, a position which no better-known academician would consider.

She took office in August 1916, after a rapid round of visits to Eastern women's colleges. There were 212 students in her first year; by 1927–28 the enrollment had risen to 624. The faculty numbered 39 in 1916–17, and 101 when she retired in 1943. She found the campus with eleven buildings, and left it with twenty-eight. Mills College in 1916 was unknown outside California. In 1943 it had a national and worldwide reputation. These data are enough to suggest the dynamism of

Aurelia Reinhardt's leadership. Her regime was a highly personal one, and to some it appeared both dictatorial and erratic. The casual approach to the financing of new buildings was a recurring cause of dispute with cautious trustees, and faculty appointments were made without any pattern of consultation. President Reinhardt's friends and admirers, however, greatly outnumbered her detractors. In her students (and they were definitely hers) she inspired intense loyalty, not unmixed with a healthy fear.

Off campus she made innumerable speeches, to groups large and small, important and unimportant, near and far. In her local community she served for many years on the board that determined policy for the county hospitals and was president (1919) of the Oakland City Planning Commission. As a Berkeley housewife she had been active in the College Women's Equal Suffrage League. From 1923 to 1927 she was national president of the American Association of University Women; during that time she conducted the campaign which raised the total amount (over $200,000) necessary for purchase of the headquarters building in Washington, D.C. In 1928–30 she was chairman of the department of education of the General Federation of Women's Clubs. Interested in politics and in international understanding, she broke with the Republicans over the League of Nations issue in the election of 1920. In 1928 she was a Republican elector for California, and she was on the defeated Hoover slate in 1932. A member of the Unitarian Church, in 1934 and 1935 she served on the "commission of enquiry" which proposed a reorganization of the American Unitarian Association. From 1940 to 1942 she was the second (and first woman) moderator of that national body.

Dr. Reinhardt retired as president of Mills in 1943. During the next years she traveled in Latin America and in Europe, on the latter trip visiting her son Fred, then a foreign service officer in Russia, later (1961) ambassador to Italy. She had serious heart trouble during this last tour and was in poor condition when she returned to California in September 1947. She died that winter at the home of her son Paul, an ophthalmologist, in Palo Alto, Calif. Her ashes are entombed at the Oakland Columbarium.

[The library of Mills College has a considerable collection of Reinhardt Papers, including correspondence, clippings, manuscripts of Dr. Reinhardt's public addresses, memoranda, and a day-to-day record compiled from many different sources. These will not be open to the general public until April 1977. A memorial booklet, *In Memoriam: Aurelia Henry Reinhardt,* with tributes by colleagues, students, and friends, was issued in 1948 (Eucalyptus Press, Mills College). A significant appreciation is *The Aurelian Way,* the Founders' Day address of 1956 by Evelyn Steel Little (Eucalyptus Press, 1956). A full-length biography is George Hedley, *Aurelia Henry Reinhardt: Portrait of a Whole Woman* (Mills College, 1961). See also Mildred M. Scouller, *Women Who Man Our Clubs* (1934), pp. 173–76.]

GEORGE HEDLEY

**REMOND, Sarah Parker** (June 6, 1826–post 1887?), antislavery lecturer and physician, was born in Salem, Mass., of Afro-American descent, one of the eight children (six girls and two boys) of John and Nancy (Lenox) Remond. Her maternal grandfather, Cornelius Lenox, a Revolutionary War veteran, had settled about 1783 in Newton, Mass., where he became a freeholder. Sarah's father, a native of Curaçao in the West Indies, had arrived in Salem in 1798; a hairdresser, caterer, and merchant-trader, he became in time one of the town's best-known citizens. Sarah's sisters were successful hairdressers and manufacturers of ornamental wigs.

Sarah Parker Remond received her education in the public schools of Salem, where Negroes were early admitted; she and her sisters, however, encountered much prejudice. The training in domestic skills she received from her mother was supplemented with wide reading of newspapers and books, loaned from the private libraries of friends, and by discussions with visitors to the Remond home, which was for many years a haven for abolitionists, black and white, and for other Negro leaders.

As a young girl Sarah, with other members of her family, attended abolitionist meetings, and as an adult she was an active member of the Salem Female Anti-Slavery Society and the Essex County and Massachusetts antislavery societies. Her brother Charles Lenox Remond, sixteen years her senior, became widely known as an antislavery lecturer in the United States and Great Britain, which he visited as early as 1840. Sarah first appears as a champion of her people in 1853, when she was refused a seat in the Howard Athenaeum in Boston for which she had purchased a ticket and was forcibly ejected from the theatre. Miss Remond took her case to the police court, where she won an opinion sustaining the rights of colored persons. In 1856 she was appointed an agent of the American Anti-Slavery Society and appeared with her brother at meetings throughout New York state and as far west as

Ohio. Two more years of lecturing in the company of Charles Remond and other abolitionists followed, including an appearance at the national woman's rights convention in New York City in May 1858.

Sarah Remond then determined to press the antislavery cause before British audiences. In England she hoped also to further her education and to enjoy greater freedom. Traveling with the Rev. Samuel J. May, she arrived in Liverpool in January 1859 and was welcomed into the Lancashire home of William Robson, a prominent English abolitionist whom she had met in Boston the year before. Her first appearance in Robson's town of Warrington inspired the audience to send $100 to the American Anti-Slavery Society, together with a sympathetic *Address . . . to the Citizens of the United States* signed by the leading citizens and 3,522 other inhabitants. Her lectures elsewhere in England, Scotland, and Ireland, well publicized in the London *Anti-Slavery Advocate* and other papers, also drew large and enthusiastic crowds. A lecture by a woman was in itself a novelty; her "appearance is remarkably feminine and graceful," reported a Dublin paper, and she has "a quiet, dignified manner, a well-toned voice and pleasing style of enunciation" (quoted in the *Liberator,* Apr. 8, 1859). Calmly, but in the strongest terms, she denounced slavery as inhuman and un-Christian. Her earnestness easily won the sympathy of her hearers, her recital of the horrors of slavery often bringing tears to their eyes. Sharing the platform with her on occasion were eminent clergymen, professors, and abolitionists, including the famous Frederick Douglass.

Despite her heavy lecture schedule, Miss Remond in October 1859 enrolled in the Bedford College for Ladies (now part of the University of London). There she attended classes until 1861, studying history, mathematics, geography, French, Latin, English literature, elocution, and vocal music. During this period she boarded at the residence of Mrs. Elisabeth Jesser Reid, founder of the college, an ardent abolitionist and widow of a physician. Here she may have met Dr. ELIZABETH BLACKWELL, who shortly before Miss Remond's arrival had begun a lecture tour in England to win support for the woman's medical movement.

In November 1859 Sarah Remond visited the American legation in London to apply for a visa to travel to France. Her request was denied by Benjamin Moran, legation secretary, on the grounds that she was a person of color and therefore without the rights of an American citizen. Upon inquiry, Moran recorded in his journal, he found that her passport, which described her hair and complexion merely as "dark," had been obtained by a Salem judge, "evidently by fraud." Miss Remond next applied in writing to the American minister to Great Britain, George Mifflin Dallas, but was again refused. In December the London *Morning Star* published "a severe article" condemning the legation for its incivility to Sarah Remond, "as well as for the course adopted here of refusing to recognise negroes as citizens." This was followed by a vigorous account of the incident by Miss Remond in the *Daily News*. The episode ended in February when, as Moran noted, the State Department approved his "course in the visé case of the negress Remond." The lack of a visa did not, however, prevent the resourceful Sarah Remond from visiting the Continent, no doubt with the aid of British friends.

Friends also persuaded her to stay abroad longer than the one year she had planned. At the end of the Civil War, when slavery in the United States had been abolished, she turned to lecturing on behalf of the freedmen and was an active member of the London Emancipation Society and the Freedmen's Aid Association of London, organizations which solicited funds and clothing for the ex-slaves. In 1865 she published a letter in the *Daily News* protesting attacks on the Negro race in the London press following a black insurrection in Jamaica.

Sarah Remond left London for Florence, Italy, in 1866. Here she became a medical student in the Santa Maria Nuova Hospital until 1868. No official record has been found of her enrollment or the completion of her medical work, but she is said to have pursued a regular course of study together with hospital practice and to have received a diploma certifying her for "Professional Medical Practice." The Rhode Island reformer ELIZABETH BUFFUM CHACE, who visited Florence in April 1873, wrote of her: "Sarah Remond is a remarkable woman and by indomitable energy and perserverance is winning a fine position in Florence as a physician, and also socially; although she says Americans have used their influence to prevent her, by bringing their hateful prejudices over here. If one tenth of the American women who travel in Europe were as noble and elegant as she is we shouldn't have to blush for our countrywomen as often as we do."

In a letter of February 1887 from Rome, Frederick Douglass mentions a visit he had made to his "old friends the Remonds," no doubt referring to Sarah and her sister Caroline, who had gone to live with her abroad.

Sarah was at this time in her sixty-first year. A holograph note on the back of a photograph of her indicates that she married a man with the surname of Pintor, but nothing further is known of her later life or of her death. The summaries of her lectures published in newspapers and periodicals are the chief surviving record of her condemnation of slavery, of the hypocritical Christianity which condoned it, of colonization, which she regarded as a crystallization of "hatred to an oppressed race," and of the general state of the freedmen after the Civil War.

[Francis Jackson, *Hist. of the Early Settlement of Newton, . . . Mass.* (1854), p. 362; Sarah P. Remond, *The Negroes & Anglo-Africans as Freedmen and Soldiers* (Ladies' London Emancipation Soc., Tract No. 7, 1864), and her articles "Colonization," *Freed-Man,* Feb. 1, 1866, pp. 162–63, and "The Negroes in the U.S.A.," *Jour. of Negro Hist.,* Apr. 1942; references to Miss Remond in the *Liberator,* Nov. 7, 1856, p. 179; Feb. 11, 1859, pp. 22, 23; Feb. 18, 1859, p. 27; Apr. 8, 1859, p. 54; May 20, 1859, p. 77; Dec. 22, 1865, p. 202; Am. and Foreign Anti-Slavery Soc., *Annual Report,* 1853, p. 154; Elizabeth C. Stanton et al., *Hist. of Woman Suffrage,* I (1881), 668n.; Margaret J. Tuke, *A Hist. of Bedford College for Women* (1939); information from registrar of Bedford College; Sarah A. Wallace and Frances E. Gilespie, eds., *The Jour. of Benjamin Moran, 1857–1865,* vol. I (1948); Lillie B. C. and Arthur C. Wyman, *Elizabeth Buffum Chace* (1914), I, 196, II, 42–43; MS. letter of Frederick Douglass, Feb. 11, 1887, at Howard Univ.; Dorothy B. Porter, "Sarah Parker Remond, Abolitionist and Physician," *Jour. of Negro Hist.,* July 1935.]

DOROTHY B. PORTER

**REPPLIER, Agnes** (Apr. 1, 1855–Dec. 15, 1950), essayist, was born in Philadelphia, Pa., the second of four children and second daughter of John George and Agnes (Mathias) Repplier. Though she liked to think of herself as of French descent, her background was strongly German. Her paternal grandfather had come from Strasbourg, but he settled in the German section of Pennsylvania, where he married a German; and her mother, born in Westminster, Md., was also German. Both parents were Roman Catholics. John Repplier, originally from Reading, Pa., handled the retailing of coal for a mining business in which, with his brothers, he was a partner. A widower of means at the time of his marriage to Agnes Mathias, he left the training of his children to his wife, a strong-willed woman who resented her domestic role and managed the family with a firm hand.

Agnes, who received her elementary education at home, learned very slowly at first and hence was often in conflict with her ambitious mother. The girl resented the infantile tales in what she later called "that hated reader," and had such a remarkable memory for the stories and poems she heard read aloud that she did not find it necessary to learn to read herself until she was nearly ten. She then began to read widely, and was particularly enchanted by the poems of Tennyson and Byron. Her formal schooling was brief. In 1867 she was enrolled at Eden Hall, the Sacred Heart convent school at Torresdale, Pa., but she frequently rebelled against the strict discipline and at the end of her second year was dismissed for insubordination. In the fall of 1869 she was sent to a private school recently opened in Philadelphia by AGNES IRWIN, who later became the first dean of Radcliffe College. Again she was dismissed, after only a year and a half, apparently because she refused to read an assigned book that she thought stupid. Both schools, however, had given her a reward far outweighing the disgrace of expulsion. At Eden Hall, Agnes Repplier met Elizabeth Robins (see ELIZABETH ROBINS PENNELL), later a distinguished essayist and writer on art, who became and remained her closest friend. And Miss Irwin, though she refused to keep the recalcitrant girl as a pupil, also became a lifelong friend.

During these years at school, writing had become a strong interest, which Miss Irwin had encouraged, but not until after the dismissal from the second school did Agnes seriously consider it as a possible career. In 1871 her father suffered grave financial losses. Charged by her mother to help the family finances, she began submitting short stories and sketches to the Philadelphia *Sunday Times,* the *Young Catholic,* and similar periodicals which, over the next ten years, provided a welcome, if irregular, income. Then in 1881 she published a short story in the *Catholic World* which was followed in the same magazine by several more in the next two years.

Agnes Repplier's apprenticeship may be said to have ended in 1884 when, upon the advice of Father Isaac Hecker, founder of the *Catholic World,* who thought her plots "mechanical," she abandoned attempts at fiction in favor of the essay. "Ruskin as a Teacher," the paper he commissioned her to write, as she herself said, turned her feet into the path she trod ever after. Two years later, when she was thirty-one, she first appeared in the *Atlantic Monthly* (April 1886) with "Children, Past and Present," a humorous commentary on the methods used during their childhood to discipline certain well-known figures of the past.

Thereafter she published often in that magazine. In 1888 came her first collection, *Books and Men.* From then on publication became a simple matter; seventeen additional volumes of essays eventually followed the first. Miss Repplier was fortunate in beginning her career at a time when the essay was a popular form. She wrote on subjects that interested her—"On the Benefits of Superstition," "The Decay of Sentiment," "Some Aspects of Pessimism"— and combined entertaining literary and historical anecdote with a delicate mockery of her subjects that delighted her readers.

Not long after her first appearance in the *Atlantic,* at the urging of Miss Irwin, Agnes Repplier made her first trip to Boston, where she was welcomed by Thomas Bailey Aldrich, then editor of the *Atlantic,* and spent ten days of "riotous gaiety." Miss Repplier, by her own admission, much preferred the company and conversation of men to that of women, and on this and later visits to Boston, in travels abroad, and through letters from literary admirers, she gained the friendship of such men as Horace Howard Furness, S. Weir Mitchell, Andrew Lang, Oliver Wendell Holmes, James Russell Lowell, Henry James, Theodore Roosevelt, and Walt Whitman. In 1890—again at Miss Irwin's insistence—she offered her first public lecture. Thereafter lecturing and travel for pleasure (principally abroad, with one journey to the West Coast and Alaska) occupied much of the essayist's time away from her desk. The last of numerous extended trips to Europe came in her seventy-fourth year when she was appointed by President Coolidge to a commission for the Ibero-American International Exposition in Seville.

In 1919 Agnes Repplier published the first of five biographies, *J. William White, M.D.* Twenty-odd years before, she had been operated on for cancer by Dr. White of the University of Pennsylvania. To him she felt she owed her life; the book stood in tribute to this friend. A second offering to friendship, her biography of Agnes Irwin, came in 1934. More important were her three biographies dealing with early figures in the history of the Catholic Church in America: *Père Marquette* (1929), *Mère Marie of the Ursulines* (1931), and *Junípero Serra* (1933). The title essay of her last collection, *Eight Decades* (1937), and *In Our Convent Days* (1905), drawn from her experiences at Eden Hall, constitute her only autobiographical writings.

The University of Pennsylvania granted Agnes Repplier an honorary degree in 1902, and five other universities followed: Temple (1919), Yale (1925), Columbia (1927), Marquette (1929), and Princeton (1935). In 1911 Notre Dame bestowed the Laetare Medal upon her. She was elected to membership in the American Philosophical Society in 1928, and in 1935 she received the gold medal of the National Institute of Arts and Letters; nine years earlier she had been one of the first women (after JULIA WARD HOWE in 1907) to be offered membership. Her last essay appeared in the *Atlantic* in 1940, three months before her eighty-fifth birthday. She died ten years later at her apartment in Philadelphia and was buried in the family vault at the Church of St. John the Evangelist.

Miss Repplier's writing was characterized by sharp, vigorous thought expressed with unerring taste. She defended the traditional in morals and manners, using a constant appeal to common sense. Her most congenial subjects were not drawn from the contemporary scene but rather from English literary history of an earlier day. For her, writing was justified primarily by the pleasure it afforded the reader, and not by open didacticism. Even her Catholic biographies are much closer to ordinary biography than the hagiography which her devout religious feelings might have dictated. The Catholic viewpoint is taken for granted, but never underlined with a heavy hand. Her best work displays stylistic beauty, in a critical approach to life and literature, with a generous seasoning of gentle irony.

[Other works by Miss Repplier include: *Essays in Idleness* (1893), *In the Dozy Hours and Other Papers* (1894), *Varia* (1897), *The Fireside Sphinx* (1901), *Points of Friction* (1920), *Under Dispute* (1924), *Times and Tendencies* (1931), and *In Pursuit of Laughter* (1936). For biographical and critical material see: George S. Stokes, *Agnes Repplier* (1949); Emma Repplier, *Agnes Repplier: A Memoir* (1957); John T. Flanagan in *South Atlantic Quart.*, Apr. 1945; Walter Lecky, *Down at Caxton's* (1895), pp. 166–82; memoir by Arthur H. Quinn in *Am. Philosophical Soc.*, *Year Book*, 1950.]

GEORGE STEWART STOKES

**RESTELL, Madame.** *See* LOHMAN, Ann Trow.

**REYNOLDS, Myra** (Mar. 18, 1853–Aug. 20, 1936), English scholar and teacher, was born in Troupsburg, Steuben County, N.Y., the daughter of Newell Lent Reynolds, a school principal who shortly afterward entered the Baptist ministry, and Emily (Knox) Reynolds. Her father was a native of Troupsburg, her mother of Knoxville, Pa., in neighboring Tioga County. It was in that county that Myra spent most of her childhood, while her father combined pastoral and educational duties (for a

time as county superintendent of schools) in Wellsboro and elsewhere. A graduate of Colgate University, he transmitted to his children his strong love of nature, taking them down river rapids and "traipsing over rough hills to find glacial scratches and terminal moraines" (*Vassar Quarterly*, November 1934, p. 324). After earlier education at Cook Academy, a Baptist school, Myra entered the State Normal School at Mansfield, Pa., in 1867 and graduated in 1870. Little information is available about these years, but she presumably taught school until 1876 when, at twenty-three, she entered Vassar College as a freshman, no doubt influenced by a younger sister, Kate, who graduated that June. She later recalled the excitement of her first contact, that year, with the humanities, her "ravenous" reading in the college library. After graduating, A.B., in 1880, she became head of the English department at Wells College in Aurora, N.Y. (1880–82), and then taught for two years in the Corning (N.Y.) Free Academy. In 1884 she was called back to Vassar as a teacher of English, a position she retained until 1892—save for a year and a half (January 1887 to June 1888) as lady principal of Woodstock College in Canada. In the fall of 1892 this seasoned Easterner ventured west to begin graduate study at the newly founded University of Chicago.

She was to remain at the university for the rest of her career. Appointed one of the first four fellows in English in 1892, she received her Ph.D. in 1895. She had meanwhile, in 1894, become an assistant in English. With her doctorate she rose to instructor, becoming assistant professor in 1897, associate professor in 1903, and professor in 1911. An influential teacher whose students included such later professors as George Sherburn and Napier Wilt, she also took a leading part in other activities of the growing university. She was, for example, chairman of the committee that planned and established, in 1894, the University of Chicago Settlement. For more than thirty years, beginning in 1893, she was the head of one of the university's first three residence halls for women students, Nancy Foster Hall, setting a marked standard of graciousness in its furnishings and social occasions. A love of beauty, an interest in the arts and crafts, was part of her own life, both as a person and as a scholar; her studies of literature were enriched by the insights that a knowledge of the other arts of a period can bring. Her students recalled the humanity and wit which also went with her learning. Prof. Lily Bess Campbell has described her as "short and Mr. Polly-ish. She wasn't grim, and she wasn't taut, and she didn't grind at things. She always seemed to be doing just what she wanted to do and to be having a grand time doing it."

Among Miss Reynolds' scholarly publications, one of the first was *The Poems of Anne, Countess of Winchilsea* (1903), ably edited and annotated, with an introduction that was a distinguished piece of biographical research and criticism. Fullness of care and critical imagination were to be characteristic of all her work. So, too, was her sure balance of judgment and sensitiveness to personal values—a combination rare in the opening years of the twentieth century, when the passion for completeness was likely to engulf the researcher in a mass of partially assimilated data. These qualities are perhaps most apparent in her best-known book, *The Treatment of Nature in English Poetry between Pope and Wordsworth* (1909, an amplified version of her doctoral thesis as published in 1896), which is still useful after two or three critical revolutions. Her last important work, *The Learned Lady in England, 1650–1760*, was published, appropriately, in the Vassar Semi-Centennial in 1920. This series of personal sketches has a liveliness and even picturesqueness of style that make it, though perhaps the most loosely organized of all her works, the most engaging to read.

Miss Reynolds retired from the University of Chicago faculty at the age of seventy, in 1923. After her retirement she made her home in Palos Verdes, Calif., near two of her sisters, where she enjoyed her nieces and nephews and their children. She died in a Los Angeles hospital at the age of eighty-three of bronchopneumonia and uremia.

[Myra Reynolds, "A Freshman of 1876," *Vassar Quart.*, Nov. 1934; *Univ. of Chicago Mag.*, Mar. 1923, Nov. 1936, and especially Jan. 1937 (article by Lily Bess Campbell) and Feb. 1937 (letter by Sophonisba P. Breckinridge); Durward Howes, ed., *Am. Women*, 1935–36; obituaries in *Chicago Tribune* and *N.Y. Times*, Aug. 22, 1936; recollections of Dean Napier Wilt, Univ. of Chicago; information from Vassar College Library, from the librarian of Mansfield (Pa.) State College, and (on her father) from the Am. Baptist Hist. Soc., Rochester, N.Y.; death record from Calif. Dept. of Public Health.]

HELEN C. WHITE

RHODES, Mary (1782?–Feb. 27, 1853), Roman Catholic nun, foundress of the Sisters of Loretto, was born in Maryland to Abraham and Elizabeth Rhodes, one of the younger children in a family of seven, two girls and five boys. Little is known of her background and early life; even her place of birth is uncertain. Her father was apparently a planter, for he owned land and, according to the census of 1790, thirteen slaves. Educated by the Nuns of the Visitation at their school in Georgetown (now Washington, D.C.), she was, according to tradition, a pupil of Mother Teresa Lalor, foundress of the convent.

About 1811, when she was twenty-nine, Mary Rhodes went to Kentucky to visit her brother Bennet, one of a group of Maryland Catholics who had founded a settlement on Hardin's Creek, southeast of Bardstown, in 1786. Concerned because her brother's children were receiving neither schooling nor religious instruction in this frontier community, she began to teach them. Soon the neighbors begged her to teach their children also. She discussed the situation with the Rev. Charles Nerinckx, the missionary priest in charge of the area, and they decided to open a school for the girls of the settlement. An abandoned cabin on a hill between the Rhodes home and the little log church of St. Charles was chosen, and Mary Rhodes began teaching there, undaunted even when the rain poured in and turned her dirt floor to mud. As the number of her pupils increased she was assisted by Christina Stuart, who was also from a family in the neighborhood. The two lived for a short time with Bennet Rhodes; then, finding the gaiety of social life distasteful, they moved to another dilapidated cabin close to their school and began to follow a religious routine. They were joined there by Anne Havern, another local girl.

The three women soon expressed to Father Nerinckx a desire to consecrate their lives entirely to God. Having long dreamed of founding in Kentucky a religious community for women, Nerinckx wrote out a simple but rigorous rule for them and appointed Mary Rhodes as temporary directress, to serve until the group should be large enough to hold an election. The rule was approved by Bishop Benedict J. Flaget, who had arrived in Kentucky less than a year before to organize the first Catholic diocese west of the Alleghenies. On Apr. 25, 1812, Father Nerinckx formally gave the three women the veil in a ceremony at St. Charles Church, naming them the Friends of Mary at the Foot of the Cross. Their founding thus preceded by nearly a year that of a second frontier community, the Sisters of Charity of Nazareth, established at St. Thomas', north of Bardstown, by the Rev. John David, with Mother CATHERINE SPALDING as superior. Mary Rhodes' community soon expanded.

Three other women joined the group that summer, among them Mary's sister Ann; although the youngest, she was elected by the others as their first mother superior. By selling her Negro slave, Mother Ann Rhodes raised money to purchase the land where the cabins stood, but the sisters spent their first winter in the direst poverty. Going barefoot as their rule required, they cut and hauled their own firewood and earned a meager living by spinning and weaving. Mother Ann, already in an advanced state of consumption when she was elected superior, died on her straw pallet Dec. 11, 1812. Mary Rhodes was then elected mother superior, a position she was to hold for the next decade.

Under Mother Mary Rhodes additional land was purchased and new buildings raised to accommodate the growing number of boarding students. The chapel was named "Little Loretto," after the noted shrine in Italy, and the order soon came to be called the Sisters of Loretto at the Foot of the Cross, the name it has since borne. On Aug. 15, 1813, the sisters took perpetual vows and were clothed in habits they had spun and woven themselves. Two years later Father Nerinckx went to Rome; when he returned in 1817, bringing word that the Pope had approved the community and its rule, he found that the sisterhood had increased to twenty-four members. So rapidly did it grow, indeed, that the neighbors became alarmed for their daughters, and Bishop Flaget had to intervene to protect the convent. The first branch house was opened in June 1816 at Calvary, Ky.; other branches followed at Gethsemani (1818) and Bethania (1819). In 1824, two years after Mother Rhodes retired as superior, the community moved some seven miles to the farm which had been headquarters for the Rev. Stephen T. Badin, early vicar general of Kentucky, in Marion County, sixty miles southeast of Louisville, at what is now the town of Loretto. Here the order's motherhouse has since remained.

A woman of culture, piety, and zeal, Mary Rhodes also had determination and vision. Her decade of rule laid firmly the policies and aims of the Sisters of Loretto. She lived to celebrate the forty-first year of her profession. Almost totally blind in her last years, she died at the motherhouse of Loretto and was buried in the sisters' cemetery there. During her lifetime the Sisters of Loretto had established branches in Arkansas, Louisiana, and Missouri. A century after her death Loretto counted seventy houses in the United States. Although Father Nerinckx is venerated as founder, it was Mary Rhodes who, on the Kentucky frontier, gave the impetus to establish this American sisterhood devoted to education, only three years after Mother ELIZABETH BAYLEY SETON had founded, in Baltimore, Md., the first American order of nuns.

[Biographical sources for Mary Rhodes are meager. The basic materials are in the archives of the Sisters of Loretto, Loretto, Ky. A sketch of her life and work appears in Anna Minogue, *Loretto Annals of the Century* (1912). Additional details are to be found in the biographies of the Rev. Charles Nerinckx by Camillus Maes (1880) and W. L. Howlett (1940); Martin J. Spalding, *Sketches of the Early Catholic Missions of Ky.* (1844); B. J. Webb, *The Centenary of Catholicity in Ky.* (1884); Joseph B. Code, *Great Am. Foundresses* (1909); and J. H. Schauinger, *Cathedrals in the Wilderness* (1952).]

J. HERMAN SCHAUINGER

RICE, Alice Caldwell Hegan (Jan. 11, 1870–Feb. 10, 1942), author, was born in Shelbyville, Ky., the only daughter and elder of two children of Samuel Watson Hegan and Sallie P. (Caldwell) Hegan. Her paternal grandfather, of Irish birth and educated at St. Patrick's College in Maynooth, had come to America and settled in Louisville, Ky., where her father entered business. Alice attended Miss Hampton's private school in Louisville, where she first began writing. Under the auspices of the First Christian Church, of which she was a lifelong member, she began at the age of sixteen to teach a boys' Sunday school class in a city mission, and the interest of her church in the city's poor took her into an outlying industrial and slum area of Louisville known as the Cabbage Patch. Here she met the indomitable old lady whom she later celebrated in her best-known novel. Her literary ambitions, first fired when the *Louisville Courier-Journal* printed her schoolgirl parody of Ik Marvel's *Reveries of a Bachelor*, were intensified when she became a member of the Authors Club of Louisville, a group of aspiring young women writers, including ANNIE FELLOWS JOHNSTON, GEORGE MADDEN MARTIN, and ELLEN CHURCHILL SEMPLE, who met regularly to discuss writing and to read aloud from the significant books of the day. From this group Alice Hegan received the encouragement to write her first novel, *Mrs. Wiggs of the Cabbage Patch* (1901), which made her famous. It was followed, over the next four decades, by nearly twenty works of popular light fiction.

On Dec. 18, 1902, she was married to Cale Young Rice, a Louisville poet, whose own first book was soon afterward accepted for publication by S. S. McClure. On a New York visit

in 1903, the young couple impulsively accepted McClure's invitation to join his party
on a European holiday. Two fruits of this trip
were a lifelong friendship with IDA TARBELL,
another McClure author, and the novel *Sandy*
(1905), Mrs. Rice's fictional portrayal of her
host's colorful career and personality.

Meanwhile, *Mrs. Wiggs of the Cabbage
Patch*, aided by Anne Crawford Flexner's successful stage adaptation of 1904, had become
a best seller, widely popular in the United
States and abroad. The book's appeal lay in
the character of its protagonist, Mrs. Wiggs,
a widow with five children, living in bitter
poverty, who faces the crises of life (including
her oldest son's death from tuberculosis) with
indestructible cheerfulness and faith. In a
romantic subplot, a pair of aristocratic lovers,
estranged by a quarrel, are reunited when each
develops a social conscience and works altru-
istically to improve the lot of the Cabbage
Patch family. The story shows the author's
real concern for the problems of poverty, but
her somewhat sentimental view on how easily
they were to be solved is revealed by Mrs.
Wiggs' comment, at the end of the novel,
"Looks like ever'thing in the world comes
right, if we jes' wait long enough!"

In a period when reformers and settlement-
house workers were calling attention to the
deplorable living conditions of the urban poor,
Alice Hegan Rice found a formula for popularizing the problem by investing her slum
dwellers with colorful personalities, amusing
dialects, and her own philosophy of optimism.
She was sincere in her belief that literature
could aid reform, and despite the superficiality
of her portrayals she was closer to the muckraking spirit of her friend Miss Tarbell than
were such light sentimentalists of the period
as GENE STRATTON-PORTER and KATE DOUGLAS
WIGGIN. Her *Calvary Alley* (1917) was written
expressly to stir indignation over slum housing
conditions. The Cabbage Patch Settlement
House, founded in 1910 by Louise Marshall,
won the warm support of Mrs. Rice, who sat
on its board. During the First World War she
was a hospital volunteer at Camp Zachary
Taylor in Louisville, an experience she utilized
in her 1921 novel *Quin*. In after years, following a Mediterranean cruise, she became active
on the National Women's Committee for Near
East Relief.

Of her novels, *Mr. Opp* (1909) was the
most serious in conception and evoked the
warmest critical response. An ineffectual, vain
little man, but devoted to the care of a half-
witted young sister, Mr. Opp resolutely remained blind to his own shortcomings and

saw his life not as the failure it actually was,
but as all that he would have liked it to be.
He thus exemplified Mrs. Rice's own philosophy that refusing to recognize defeat represents the highest courage.

She wrote little in the 1920's; her husband,
by contrast, produced a steady stream of
poetry and drama in the vein of Longfellow
and Browning and collaborated with his wife
on two books of short stories. With an ample
income from her earlier novels and the movies
made from them, they lived comfortably in
Louisville's most staid residential neighborhood, St. James Court. Childless, they summered in Maine, occasionally wintered in
Florida, and traveled widely in Europe. They
felt a particular affinity for London, where
they had many literary friends. Essentially
spectators rather than participants in the
events of their era, they felt little but abhorrence for the disillusioned and realistic school
of fiction which dominated the 1920's and
1930's. "Those of us who learned to write
when taste was a thing to be reckoned with
are under a serious handicap today," Mrs.
Rice observed in 1940 (*The Inky Way*, p. 73).
A supporter of prohibition, she served on the
Kentucky State Committee on Law Enforcement. Her racial views were those of her time
and place, as her limitless fund of "darky"
stories would suggest.

Illness and financial reverses brought serious hardship in the 1930's, and Alice Hegan
Rice's later novels, including *Mr. Pete & Co.*
(1933), a picaresque tale of the Louisville
waterfront, were written under the press of
necessity. She died in Louisville in 1942, at
seventy-two, of a coronary occlusion, and was
buried in Cave Hill Cemetery there. Grief-
stricken, her husband took his own life early
the following year.

[The principal sources are her autobiography, *The
Inky Way* (1940), and that of her husband, *Bridg-
ing the Years* (1939). See also *Louisville Courier-
Jour.*, Feb. 11, 1942; Durward Howes, ed., *Am.
Women*, 1939–40; Laban L. Rice, "Alice Hegan
Rice—Home Maker," *Filson Club Hist. Quart.*,
July 1954; Abby M. Roach, "The Authors Club of
Louisville," *ibid.*, Jan. 1957; William F. Dix in
*Outlook*, Dec. 6, 1902; Peter Lyon, *Success Story:
The Life and Times of S. S. McClure* (1963), p.
255; James D. Hart, *The Popular Book* (1950).
Other information from death record, State Dept.
of Health, Frankfort, Ky.; and interview with Miss
Louise Marshall.]

CHARLES M. NORMAN


**RICHARDS, Cornelia Wells Walter.** *See* WAL-
TER, Cornelia Wells.

RICHARDS, Ellen Henrietta Swallow (Dec. 3, 1842–Mar. 30, 1911), chemist and leader in applied and domestic science, was born in Dunstable, Mass., the only child of Peter Swallow, who came of an old Dunstable family, and Fanny Gould (Taylor) Swallow, also of colonial stock and a native of New Ipswich, N.H. The two had met while attending the New Ipswich Academy. After his marriage Swallow combined farming with schoolteaching; it is said that he took a meticulous interest in the way tasks were performed in his household. Mrs. Swallow, who had also taught school, is described as "deft and dainty." The parents educated their daughter largely at home. Ellen was something of a tomboy and helped with the farm work. At the same time, under her mother's tutelage, she acquired such a mastery of housekeeping that at thirteen she won prizes at a fair for an embroidered handkerchief and the best loaf of bread. After the family moved to Westford, Mass., in 1859, she assisted her father in the village store he opened there and attended Westford Academy, studying a little mathematics and French and more Latin. In Littleton, to which the family moved in 1863, she again worked in her father's store, while attending lectures in Worcester one winter and spending much time in study. Hoping to save money for a higher education, she taught school as well, but her mother was often ill and it was difficult for her to teach steadily. The overwork and frustration of this period led to ill health and a spell of deep depression; as she said, "I lived for over two years in *Purgatory*" (Hunt, p. 34). Finally, in September 1868, at twenty-five, she was able to enter Vassar College; classified at first as a special student, she was admitted to the senior class the next year.

Taking her college work with great seriousness, "Nellie" Swallow did her assignments thoroughly and well, and on a regular schedule. Her health rapidly improved. Her mathematics and Latin stood her in good stead, for she was asked to tutor the younger girls in these subjects, thus earning money for both her years at Vassar. Her greatest enthusiasm at college was for science, especially astronomy, which she studied with MARIA MITCHELL, and chemistry, taught by Professor Charles A. Farrar, whose conviction, advanced for the day, that science should contribute to the solution of practical problems deeply impressed her. When another professor, as she wrote in a letter from Vassar, "told us . . . what we might do for science, thinking of that and of my astronomy and chemistry" she was "fast on my way to the third heaven."

Her first plan, after graduating in 1870, was to teach astronomy in Argentina, but this was thwarted by war there. During the summer she decided instead to pursue her study of chemistry, possibly from a desire to help her father in his new undertaking, the manufacture of building stone. Applying to the Massachusetts Institute of Technology in Boston, then a struggling institution only five years old, she was accepted in December 1870 as a special student in chemistry, the first woman to be admitted "so far as I know, [to] *any scientific* school." She was accepted "without charge," she thought because of her financial need; "but I learned later it was because he [the president] could say I was not a student, should any of the trustees or students make a fuss about my presence. Had I realized upon what basis I was taken, I would not have gone" (Hunt, p. 88). She received a B.S. degree from M.I.T. in 1873, and in the same year an M.A. from Vassar, after submitting a thesis in which she estimated the amount of vanadium in iron ore from a deposit at Cold Spring, N.Y. Although she continued her graduate study at M.I.T. for two years, she never received the doctorate for which she had hoped, reportedly because "the heads of the department did not wish a woman to receive the first D.S. in chemistry" (Robert H. Richards, p. 153).

Conscious of her responsibility as the only woman student at the institute, Ellen Swallow had taken care to avoid criticism. "I hope . . . I am winning a way which others will keep open," she wrote in 1871. "Perhaps the fact that I am not a Radical or a believer in the all powerful ballot for women to right her wrongs and that I do not scorn womanly duties, but claim it as a privilege to clean up and sort of supervise the room and sew things, etc., is winning me stronger allies than anything else" (Hunt, p. 91). During her undergraduate and graduate years she served as assistant to Prof. William R. Nichols, who was then engaged in pioneering analyses of public water supplies for the State Board of Health, and to Prof. John M. Ordway, an industrial chemist with an extensive consulting practice.

She also became acquainted with young Prof. Robert Hallowell Richards (1844–1945), who was then in the process of developing the institute's noted metallurgical and mining engineering laboratories. A native of Gardiner, Maine, Richards was a brother-in-law of LAURA ELIZABETH HOWE RICHARDS. He proposed to Ellen Swallow in the chemistry laboratory shortly after she received her M.I.T. degree; they were married on June 4, 1875, and settled in a house in Jamaica Plain, an outlying section of Boston. There were no children. The two shared a single-minded devotion to science. Richards was interested in and supported his wife's work, and she used her training in chemistry to aid him in his, helping him with his lectures and "keeping up with all the German and French mining and metallurgical periodicals (some twenty papers a week come into our house)" (*Journal of Home Economics*, December 1931). For two summers in the upper peninsula of Michigan (1881 and 1882), while Richards was experimenting with methods of concentrating copper ores, she acted as his chemist, and her election to the American Institute of Mining and Metallurgical Engineers, its first woman member, was a source of great pleasure to them both.

Marriage brought economic security, enabling Ellen Richards to devote most of the next ten years to a cause for which she felt a personal responsibility, the scientific education of women. Aware of the growing demand for laboratory instruction in science in the secondary schools, she had while an M.I.T. undergraduate helped teach an experimental course in chemistry at the Girls' High School in Boston to a class of whom half were already teachers. The course had been financed by the Woman's Education Association of Boston, and in November 1875 Mrs. Richards appealed to this organization for funds to establish a Woman's Laboratory at M.I.T. The laboratory opened a year later, the institute supplying quarters in a small frame building newly erected for a gymnasium, and the Woman's Education Association providing apparatus, books, and scholarships. In charge was Professor Ordway, with Ellen Richards as his assistant. Both gave their services and made gifts of money as well, Mrs. Richards contributing an average of $1,000 annually during the seven years of the laboratory's existence. She also gave the students the individualized instruction necessitated by their uneven preparation, advised them on health and finances, and saw to it that these pioneers did not attract unfavorable attention. Training was offered in chemical analysis, industrial chemistry, mineralogy, and biology.

At the same time she undertook to organize a science section for the Society to Encourage Studies at Home, a correspondence school for women conducted by Anna Eliot Ticknor. Mrs. Richards corresponded individually with the science pupils, forming many friendships and learning much about middle-class women's life and discouragements. Noting that illness seemed to be a constant problem, she prepared

a pamphlet discussing healthful dress and food and the importance of exercise and intellectual interests to balance household routine; this was circulated both within and outside the society. In 1882 Mrs. Richards was one of the founders, in Boston, of the Association of Collegiate Alumnae (later the American Association of University Women). She was a leader in its efforts to improve physical education in colleges and to widen opportunities for women in graduate education.

At the Woman's Laboratory, meanwhile, Mrs. Richards, along with her teaching, carried on consulting work for private industry into which Ordway had introduced her. Over the years this was to include the testing of wallpapers and fabrics for arsenic content; the examination of industrial and household water supplies; and a variety of experiments with commercial oils, in which she worked out tests for impurities and studied the causes of spontaneous combustion. In 1878–79 she conducted an investigation for the State Board of Health into the adulteration of staple groceries. Her students in qualitative analysis assisted in testing articles in common household use, such as soda, vinegars, and washing powders; these findings were the basis of her manual *The Chemistry of Cooking and Cleaning* (1882) and of *Food Materials and Their Adulterations* (1885).

The discreet young women under Mrs. Richards' tutelage were soon admitted to the regular courses at M.I.T., and by 1882 four had received degrees. The next year the Woman's Laboratory was closed, the institute having erected a new building which, thanks to the efforts of Ellen Richards, LUCRETIA CROCKER, and ABBY W. MAY, who had raised $10,000 for the purpose, was equipped with a parlor and reading room for the women who were now full-fledged M.I.T. students. Left without "anything to do or anywhere to work," Ellen Richards confessed to feeling "like a woman whose children are all about to be married and leave her alone."

But her career was halted only briefly. In 1884 M.I.T. set up a chemical laboratory for the study of sanitation, the first of its kind, with William Nichols in charge and Ellen Richards as assistant. She now received an appointment to the institute faculty as instructor in sanitary chemistry; this she held until her death twenty-seven years later. During the two-year survey of Massachusetts inland waters which Nichols' successor, Thomas M. Drown, began for the State Board of Health in 1887, Mrs. Richards was in charge of the laboratory. This undertaking was unprecedented in scale and became a classic in the field; its success was in large measure due to her efforts in supervising the analysis of water samples, developing new laboratory techniques and apparatus, and keeping the records. In 1890 M.I.T. established a program in sanitary engineering, the first in any university. Mrs. Richards taught the analysis of water, sewage, and air to successive generations of students, many of whom became leaders in public sanitation elsewhere in the United States and in other countries. Her text, *Air, Water, and Food for Colleges* (1900), written in collaboration with A. G. Woodman, grew out of these classes.

Robert and Ellen Richards frequently entertained their students and other young people, who long remembered their home with "its plants and flowers, its embracing atmosphere of hospitality, . . . and to hungry boys living in boarding houses, what food!" Enthusiastically applying engineering to the home environment, Mrs. Richards had banished heavy draperies, carpets, the feather duster, and the coal stove, and introduced light curtains, rugs over hardwood floors, a vacuum cleaner, gas for cooking, ventilating devices designed by her husband, a shower bath, a year-round hot water heater, and a telephone. A student or two usually lived in the family, furnishing household help in return for room and board. The family home, she was convinced, was the civilizing center of society; she hoped that college women would take the lead in making it more healthful, comfortable, and efficient, thus freeing womankind from "primitive" drudgery for more challenging and constructive work.

From about 1890 on, Ellen Richards' own interests increasingly concentrated on what came to be known, as it grew under her shaping hand, as the home economics movement. Like many other middle-class Americans, she was disturbed by the way families in industrial cities like Boston seemed to have become discouraged and shiftless, particularly in times of economic depression. The manual skills formerly learned by boys and girls in farm homesteads like the one where she had grown up had been lost, and with them a sense of control over the environment. She realized that the home had changed from a center of production to one of consumption; the schools, she felt, must assume the responsibility for training young people in the new economics. She had been immediately interested in the experimental cooking class which MARY PORTER TILESTON HEMENWAY had introduced into one of the Boston public schools in 1885, and

had lectured in the normal school established by Mrs. Hemenway to train teachers of "domestic economy."

Her first major involvement, however, came when PAULINE AGASSIZ SHAW offered to finance "a thorough study of the food and nutrition of working men and its possible relation to the question of the use of intoxicating liquors," leaving the form of the investigation up to Mrs. Richards. The result was the opening, in Boston in 1890, of the New England Kitchen, patterned on public kitchens in Europe. The kitchen offered for sale, for home consumption, cooked foods scientifically prepared to provide maximum nourishment at low cost, and the cooking area was open to the public for the purpose of demonstrating methods of preparation. The idea was copied by philanthropists in other cities, including JANE ADDAMS at Hull House, but proved a general failure, its proponents not having anticipated that American workingmen, with their diverse ethnic backgrounds, would dislike the Yankee dishes offered. Several outgrowths of the project, however, were remarkably successful. In 1893, as part of the Massachusetts state exhibit at the Chicago World's Fair, Mrs. Richards set up the Rumford Kitchen, which served thirty-cent lunches with food values noted on the menu, in a room lined with exhibits explaining recent scientific work on nutrition—the first attempt at popular education in this new field. She was responsible for another innovation in 1894, when the Boston School Committee contracted with the New England Kitchen to provide nutritious school lunches. Other school systems and hospitals were soon consulting her about institutional diet and asking her to recommend experts in the field; dietetics as a profession for educated women thus began to take shape. Mrs. Richards had a hand also in several of the early bulletins on nutrition issued by the federal Department of Agriculture.

For several years beginning in 1896, as chairman of the Woman's Education Association's Committee on Public Schools, she worked to arouse public support in Boston for systematic domestic science instruction, including the establishment of a "Science and Arts High School" for girls. This, however, did not develop. She helped organize a school of housekeeping at the Woman's Educational and Industrial Union in Boston in 1899, and saw this become the department of home economics in Simmons College after the founding of that institution.

In 1899 Mrs. Richards took the lead in bringing together individuals working "for the betterment of the home" in the first of a series of summer conferences at Lake Placid, N.Y. Under her chairmanship these meetings adopted the name "home economics" for the new field; worked out courses of study for public schools, colleges, and agricultural and extension schools, and syllabi for women's clubs; prescribed standards for the training of teachers; compiled bibliographies; and discussed related aspects of nutrition, sanitation, and hygiene. All who attended agreed that Ellen Richards was largely responsible for establishing the new discipline on a broad base firmly related to economics and sociology. In December 1908 veterans of the Lake Placid conferences organized the American Home Economics Association, dedicated to "the improvement of living conditions in the home, the institutional household and the community." Mrs. Richards was chosen president, a post she held until 1910, when she insisted on retiring. She had been the guiding spirit in the establishment of the association's *Journal of Home Economics*, for which she assumed financial responsibility. Always in demand as a lecturer and adviser to individuals and institutions, she also during this decade wrote ten books applying science to problems of daily living. In 1910—the culmination of her efforts —she was appointed to the council of the National Education Association, with the assignment of supervising the teaching of home economics in schools. That October, Smith College awarded her the honorary degree of doctor of science.

A student described Mrs. Richards in 1908 as "a small woman with a thin face, white hair, very black eyebrows, and eyes that sparkled with life." She was a source of wonder to her friends for her innumerable acts of kindness, the efficient way she managed her time, and the wide range of her interests and information (Laura Richards nicknamed her "Ellencyclopedia"). Although she earned a substantial income through her teaching, writing, and consulting work, she left virtually no estate, having given it all away. She and her husband were fond of traveling, but though they dutifully toured Europe early in their marriage, neither was interested in the monuments of the past. They preferred the American West; if ever she should leave New England, Ellen Richards once declared, she would settle in the West, "where there is a little 'go' in the air." Carrying on her full schedule to the end, she died of heart disease at her Boston home in 1911, at the age of sixty-eight, shortly after finishing the writing of an address on "The Elevation of Applied Science to the Rank of the Learned Professions" for M.I.T.'s approaching semicentennial celebration. After services at Boston's Trinity Church (Episcopal) and the Crematory in Forest Hills, she was buried in the Richards family plot in Christ Church Yard, Gardiner, Maine. More than anyone else, she had opened scientific education and the scientific professions to women. She had in addition created the profession of home economics, having been, as ISABEL BEVIER put it, "for twenty-five years its prophet, its interpreter . . . , its inspirer, and to use her own word, its engineer."

[Something of the range of Mrs. Richards' writings is suggested by the following books, in addition to those already mentioned: *Home Sanitation: A Manual for Housekeepers* (1887); *Domestic Economy as a Factor in Public Education* (1889); *Sanitation in Daily Life* (1907); *Laboratory Notes on Industrial Water Analysis: A Survey Course for Engineers* (1908); *Conservation by Sanitation* (1911); *Euthenics: The Science of Controllable Environment* (1912). For biographical material see: Caroline L. Hunt, *The Life of Ellen H. Richards* (1912); Edna Yost, *Am. Women of Science* (1955); Madeleine Stern, *We the Women* (1963); Robert H. Richards, *Robert Hallowell Richards, His Mark* (1936); obituaries in *Jour. of Industrial and Engineering Chemistry*, May 1911, *Technology Rev.* (Mass. Institute of Technology), June 1911, and *Jour. of Home Economics*, June 1911; memorial issue of *ibid.*, Oct. 1911 (which includes a bibliography of her writings), and other articles about her in issues of June 1929, Dec. 1931, and Dec. 1942. See also Ellen Richards, "The Social Significance of the Home Economics Movement," *ibid.*, Apr. 1911; and, for the founding of the Woman's Laboratory at M.I.T. and other matters, the annual *Reports* of the Woman's Education Assoc., Boston, 1875–1902. A collection of Mrs. Richard's papers is in the Sophia Smith Collection, Smith College Library; there are some letters also at Vassar College, at the Mass. Hist. Soc. (in the Edward Atkinson Papers), and at the Univ. of Chicago.]

JANET WILSON JAMES

**RICHARDS, Laura Elizabeth Howe** (Feb. 27, 1850–Jan. 14, 1943), author, sister of MAUD HOWE ELLIOTT, was born in Boston, Mass., the third daughter and fourth of six children of parents distinguished for their fervent humanitarianism and leadership of public causes. Her father was Samuel Gridley Howe, founder and lifelong director of the Perkins Institution for the Blind and of the Massachusetts School for the Feeble-Minded. Her mother was JULIA WARD HOWE, author of "The Battle Hymn of the Republic." Their third daughter was named for LAURA BRIDGMAN, a blind deafmute who, under Dr. Howe's pioneering guidance, was the first individual ever to surmount this handicap. Laura Howe was educated in the private schoolroom that her father set up for his children at the Perkins Institution and at schools in Boston conducted by Henry Williams, Augusta Curtis, and Caroline I. Wilby. The family was Unitarian in religion. Looking back on her early years in a home devoted to the cultivation of noble ideals and of intellectual excellence, yet irradiated by music and laughter, Mrs. Richards was to write that she had been "cradled . . . in poetry, romance, and philanthropy."

In 1867 the young girl accompanied her parents on a trip to Europe which took them as far as Greece, where Dr. Howe, a veteran of the Greek War of Independence, managed the distribution of supplies to the Cretans, at that time involved in a tragic struggle for freedom. In 1869 she became engaged to Henry Richards (1848–1949), a Harvard graduate and architect descended from old and eminent New England stock. Wedded two years later on Bunker Hill Day, June 17, the couple were to enjoy seventy-one years of married life and to become the parents of seven children: Alice Maud (born in 1872), Rosalind (1874), Henry Howe (1876), Julia Ward (1878), Maud (1881, died 1882), John (1884), and Laura Elizabeth (1886).

In 1876 Henry Richards' growing architectural practice was halted by a financial depression, and he moved his family to his birthplace, Gardiner, Maine, to help manage a family paper mill. Their residence, the Yellow House, overlooking the town and the Kennebec River, was known as the happy home of a growing family, as a center for civic enterprise, and as a headquarters for the literary and artistic activity of northern New England. It may be said to symbolize the three closely interwoven aspects of Laura Richards' career.

From the first, "L.E.R.," as she came affectionately to be known, dedicated herself to the welfare of the community in which she was to pass the rest of her life. She became the moving spirit in the building, in 1881, of the Gardiner Public Library; helped found the District Nurse Association, herself paying weekly visits to the aged and infirm; and with her husband successfully campaigned in behalf of the Gardiner Public Health Association, the Gardiner General Hospital, and a new high school. In 1895 she established the Woman's Philanthropic Union, of which she was for twenty-six years president, which coordinated the service programs of the principal charitable societies of Gardiner. Her social sympathies took her also into the National Child Labor Committee and into the presidency of the Maine Consumers' League. No year passed in which she did not write and, with members of the family, produce tableaux vivants, operettas, and plays to further the many causes for human betterment with which she identified herself. Among her most cherished activities were the Howe Clubs, named for her father, which between 1886 and 1930 gathered successive generations of schoolboys at the Yellow House for weekly readings from her favorite writers.

In 1900 the decline of the paper industry in New England diverted Henry Richards' energies to the foundation on Belgrade Great Pond of a boys' summer camp, the first in Maine and one of the first in the country. Camp Merryweather, so named for a family in Laura Richards' books, was conceived as a family undertaking to extend "the general principles of team play—and truth, and courage, and kindness" which informed the home life of the Richardses in Gardiner. Until his retirement at the age of eighty-four in 1932, Henry Richards filled the strenuous role which won him from generations of campers the title of "Skipper," while his wife, as self-designated "First Mate," presided over the camp's richly diversified cultural activities through readings aloud, songfests, and theatrical entertainments.

Mrs. Richards had begun to write as early as her tenth year, and although she was never robust, her list of published writings includes nearly eighty titles. Her earliest work was produced as much in response to the precocious literary appetites of her children as to help out the family finances. In her autobiography, *Stepping Westward* (1931), she tells how she used the back of her firstborn as a writing desk to compose the jingles which, appearing in 1873 in the newly established *St. Nicholas Magazine*, marked her public debut as a writer. Her first published volume, *Five Mice in a Mouse-Trap* (1881), was a collection of stories "told by the Man in the Moon." In the same year came *Sketches & Scraps*, illustrated by her husband, which was the first book of nonsense rhymes written by an American and published in the United States. Then in 1885 and 1887 appeared the two perennially endearing "Toto" books, in the writing of which she had sought solace for the grief occasioned by the death of her infant daughter Maud.

Happy and fun-loving by nature, "L.E.R." found delight in the writing of nursery and nonsense rhymes, which usually bubbled forth accompanied by melodies. Notable among the collections of these verses, the product of what she modestly called her hurdy-gurdy rather than her lyre, were *In My Nursery* (1890),

*The Hurdy-Gurdy* (1902), *The Piccolo* (1906), and *Tirra Lirra* (1932). As her children grew older, she turned to writing the books for young girls which made her literary reputation, although she was inclined to discount their merit. The most famous of these was *Captain January* (1890), a tale of the devotion between "Star Bright," a ten-year-old girl who as an infant had been the sole survivor of a shipwreck, and the Maine lighthouse keeper who had rescued the child and reared her as his own. The book sold 300,000 copies and has twice been filmed. In the same period *Queen Hildegarde* (1889) and *Three Margarets* (1897) inaugurated two very popular series of stories about youthful heroines.

The writings she called "my best work" were the two volumes of charming and poignant fables entitled *The Golden Windows* (1903) and *The Silver Crown* (1906). She also wrote a number of regional novels which, though slight in content, reveal her familiarity with Maine country ways and her sensitive ear for local speech: among others, *Mrs. Tree* (1902), *Mrs. Tree's Will* (1905), *The Wooing of Calvin Parks* (1908), *"Up to Calvin's"* (1910), and *The Squire* (1923).

Mrs. Richards' most substantial literary achievements were inspired by veneration for her parents. In 1876 she began the editorial work on her father's papers which was eventually to issue in the two-volume edition of *Letters and Journals of Samuel Gridley Howe* (1906–09), the second volume of which the author placed in her mother's hands on the latter's ninetieth birthday. In collaboration with her sister Maud Howe Elliott, she wrote *Julia Ward Howe* (1915), awarded the first Pulitzer Prize for biography.

Laura Richards' literary tastes were conservative, instilled by her early love of Shakespeare, the novels of Scott and Dickens, and the nineteenth-century English poets. That she was not unresponsive to new talent, however, is evidenced by her lasting friendship with the Gardiner poet Edwin Arlington Robinson, whose first writings she encouraged and in tribute to whom she wrote a perceptive little volume, *E.A.R.* (1936). In 1936 the University of Maine awarded her the honorary degree of doctor of letters. She continued to write until the last year of her life, the Second World War calling forth a final resurgence of the compassion for suffering humanity bequeathed by her parents. In 1940 she published a fine poem celebrating the heroism of the British at Dunkirk, and in 1941 she dedicated verses to the modern Greeks in their resistance to fascism on battlegrounds where

nearly a century before her father had fought. Laura E. Richards died at her home of lobar pneumonia in her ninety-third year and was buried in Christ Church Yard in Gardiner. To her can be ascribed the successful fulfillment of the aims in life to which her mother before her had aspired: "To learn, to teach, to serve, to enjoy!"

[Mrs. Richards wrote two autobiographical works: *When I Was Your Age* (1894), a volume of childhood reminiscences, and the charmingly informal and anecdotal story of her life, *Stepping Westward* (1931). Valuable information about her contributions to the communal life of the town in which she passed most of her days may be found in *Laura E. Richards and Gardiner* (1940), privately printed by the Gardiner Public Library Assoc., which has also published an eloquent memorial address by Arthur Dehon Hill (Sept. 6, 1944). Anne T. Eaton's article on Mrs. Richards in the *Horn Book,* July–Aug. 1941, contains an excellent critical estimate of her writings; see also the warm account by Ruth Hill Viguers in *ibid.*, Apr. through Dec. 1956 (the last issue includes a bibliography of her writings). For obituary notices, see especially *N.Y. Times,* Jan. 15, 1943, and *Publishers' Weekly,* Jan. 23, 1943, as well as the memorial by Elizabeth Coatsworth in *Horn Book,* Mar.–Apr. 1943. See also Stanley J. Kunitz and Howard Haycraft, eds., *Twentieth Century Authors* (1942); *Woman's Who's Who of America,* 1914–15; Durward Howes, ed., *Am. Women,* 1939–40; and, for her children, Daniel W. Howe, *Howe Genealogies* (rev. ed., 1929). Death record from City Clerk, Gardiner, Maine.]

E. D. H. JOHNSON

**RICHARDS, Linda** (July 27, 1841–Apr. 16, 1930), pioneer nursing educator, was born near Potsdam, N.Y., the youngest of four daughters of Sanford and Betsy (Sinclair) Richards. She was christened Melinda Ann Judson Richards, her father, in naming her for ANN HASSELTINE JUDSON, hoping that she would become a missionary. Her parents had come from Vermont, where both families had settled before the American Revolution. The Richards ancestry was English; the Sinclairs originated in the Orkney Isles. When Linda was about four the family moved to Wisconsin, where her father bought land on the site of the later Watertown, but he died within a few weeks and her mother took the children back to Vermont. Linda spent her childhood in the towns of Derby and Lyndon. For a time she and her mother and sisters lived with her grandfather Sinclair, a man of strong religious convictions whom she later recalled as her "most intimate friend." She attended the Lyndon common schools and the nearby Barton (Vt.) Academy. At the age of thirteen she joined the Lyndon Center Free-Will Baptist Church in a religious revival; her mother died a few months afterward. Her eldest sister, Laura De Lisle Richards, was later associated with Alexander Graham Bell in pioneer work for the deaf and served on the staff of the Clarke School for the Deaf, Northampton, Mass.

In most New England villages during the time of Linda Richards' girlhood there were so-called "born nurses" whom neighbors called upon to care for the sick, and Miss Richards took pride in being considered such a nurse before she was out of her teens. She also lived for a time, probably after her mother's death, in the household of a Dr. Masta and assisted him in the care of his patients. She had to earn her living, and talk of the need for nurses during the Civil War apparently started her thinking of nursing as an occupation. This idea persisted through seven years of employment at the Union Straw Works in Foxboro, Mass., and finally, in search of training, she went to the Boston City Hospital in 1870 to work as an assistant nurse.

There she was disillusioned upon finding the nurses ignorant, often heartless, and almost unsupervised, their work only that which would later be done by ward maids. Her health failing, she left the hospital after three months, having refused an offer to become head nurse because she felt that she knew too little and under the circumstances was unlikely to learn more. About two years later, having in the meantime read an account of the school to train nurses which Florence Nightingale had founded in 1860 at St. Thomas's Hospital in London, she learned of the training school newly organized under the direction of Dr. SUSAN DIMOCK at the New England Hospital for Women and Children in Boston. She registered in September 1872, the first student in the class of five. A year later, having served in the wards and heard twelve lectures by the hospital's medical staff, she received the first diploma of this first American nursing school.

Immediately upon graduation Miss Richards accepted a position as night superintendent at the Bellevue Training School, New York City, the first of the American nursing schools patterned upon the Nightingale system. After a year she returned to Boston to become the superintendent of another Nightingale school, the Boston Training School, later the Massachusetts General Hospital School of Nursing. The school was then under the direction of an independent committee, which had a contractual arrangement with the hospital to open selected wards for training pupils. In operation only a year, the school had had two previous superintendents and faced strong opposition from the hospital's medical staff, which considered untrained nurses adequate and the training program useless and interfering. Over the next three years, until her resignation in 1877, Miss Richards developed a program of regular classroom instruction and placed the school in a firm position. The wards of the entire hospital were opened to the pupils, and the superintendent of the school was recognized as the superintendent of nurses in the hospital. Miss Richards' success had more than local significance, for it gave confidence and prestige to the entire movement for the professional training of nurses.

In the spring of 1877, in fulfillment of a "long cherished plan," Miss Richards went to England to study the Nightingale system firsthand. Through Miss Nightingale herself it was arranged for her to be received as a visitor in St. Thomas's School. Later she observed the nursing at King's College Hospital, London, and the training school at the Edinburgh Royal Infirmary. She also had the benefit of personal conferences with Miss Nightingale. Upon her return to Boston that fall, she helped Dr. Edward Cowles, superintendent of the Boston City Hospital, develop a training school there, the first Nightingale school in this country to be established as an integral part of a hospital organization, a pattern thereafter widely followed. As matron of the hospital and superintendent of the training school opened at Boston City in 1878, she again disarmed medical opposition through her tact, patience, kindliness, and efficiency. In August 1879 she took a leave of absence, but after a prolonged illness she returned three years later to stay until November 1885.

At the peak of her career, Miss Richards now sacrificed her material prospects for an opportunity to serve in Japan under the sponsorship of the American Board of Commissioners for Foreign Missions (Congregational). Arriving there in January 1886, she began an intensive study of the language and that fall opened Japan's first training school for nurses, at the Doshisha Hospital in Kyoto under the direction of Dr. John C. Berry. The school, the first in any mission field, offered the same two-year program given in the best American schools, using American texts in translation. Linda Richards' five years in Japan, which also included teaching Bible classes for older women in neighboring towns and other evangelical work, were probably the happiest of her life. Ill health again intervened, however, and she returned to the United States in March 1891.

During her absence Miss Richards had lost her leadership in the development of American nursing, which was now beginning an effort to raise professional standards through state and national organization. As the profession passed a series of milestones she was duly honored for her pioneering work, being chosen first president of the American Society of Superintendents of Training Schools (1894), purchasing the first share of stock in the *American Journal of Nursing* (1900), and serving on the committee which succeeded in establishing the hospital economics program, the forerunner of the later division of nursing education, at Teachers College, Columbia University. During her later years, however, she was not entirely in sympathy with the objectives of the nursing organizations, especially those regarding nursing legislation and some of the more progressive ideas about nursing education.

Her devotion to her own ideal of personal dedication and service nevertheless continued unswerving. Through the twenty years following her return from Japan she held a number of posts for short periods of time as her health permitted. Her first position (April–November 1891), as head of the Philadelphia Visiting Nurses Society, overtaxed her strength, but she subsequently founded a training school at Philadelphia's Methodist Episcopal Hospital (1892) and reorganized and strengthened those of the New England Hospital for Women and Children (1893–94), the Brooklyn Homeopathic Hospital (1894–95), and the Hartford (Conn.) Hospital (1895–97). Two years as superintendent of the training school at the University of Pennsylvania Hospital in Philadelphia followed. Thereafter she dedicated herself to a new cause: improving standards of nursing in mental hospitals. She served as director of training schools at the Taunton (Mass.) Insane Hospital (1899–1904), the Worcester (Mass.) Hospital for the Insane (1904–05), where she established the school, and the Michigan Insane Asylum in Kalamazoo (1906–09). She returned to the Taunton school for a year before her retirement, at seventy, in 1911. That year her *Reminiscences,* written at the behest of several of the doctors with whom she had worked in her early years, was privately printed. After retirement she lived for a time on a farm near Lowell, Mass., with a cousin; for the last five years of her life she was an invalid, following a cerebral hemorrhage. She died at the New England Hospital in Boston in 1930, at the age of eighty-eight. Her ashes were placed in the Columbarium at Forest Hills Cemetery, Boston.

Linda Richards became known as "America's First Trained Nurse," but since there had been sporadic earlier attempts to set up training programs she can more correctly be said to have received the earliest American diploma in nursing. She stands out in bold relief in the testing days of the training school movement in this country for her pioneer work in the improvement of nursing care and in the promotion of the Nightingale system of nursing education. In 1962 the National League for Nursing created the Linda Richards Award to be given to a nurse in practice who makes a unique contribution of a pioneering nature.

[*Reminiscences of Linda Richards* (1911); autobiographical articles in *Am. Jour. of Nursing,* Nov. 1901, Jan. 1903, and Dec. 1915; articles about her in *ibid.,* Oct. 1900, Nov. 1920 (by Agnes B. Joynes), and Sept. 1948 (by Helen W. Munson), the last with an excellent bibliography; Alfred Worcester, "Linda A. J. Richards," *New England Jour. of Medicine,* May 29, 1930; Isabelle W. Sloane, *America's First Trained Nurse* (pamphlet, 1941). See also Sara E. Parsons, *Hist. of the Mass. Gen. Hospital Training School for Nurses* (1922); Mary M. Riddle, *Hist. of the Boston City Hospital Training School for Nurses* (1928); Boston City Hospital, *Annual Reports,* 1878–84; Am. Soc. of Superintendents of Training Schools, *Annual Convention Reports,* 1894–1900. Unpublished sources include: biographical questionnaire filled out by Miss Richards, in library of United Church Board for World Ministries, Boston ("Memoranda Concerning Missionaries," vol. IX); letters of Linda Richards in Sophia Smith Collection, Smith College; Boston Training School records, 1873–77, in Archives of Mass. Gen. Hospital, Boston; New England Hospital, Minutes of Board of Directors, 1872–73.]

STELLA GOOSTRAY

**RICHMAN, Julia** (Oct. 12, 1855–June 24, 1912), educator, was born in New York City, the third of five children of Moses and Theresa (Melis) Richman, who were of Bohemian ancestry. Her father, a painter and glazier in moderate circumstances, ruled his family autocratically, and young Julia's quick tongue and quick temper caused much family distress. She attended public schools in Huntington, Long Island, where the family lived from 1861 to 1865, and in Manhattan. In November 1872, after completing a two-year course at the city Normal College (later Hunter College), she overruled her father's objections and became a teacher in the New York City schools. The social concern which characterized her later career was evidenced when she became president (1876–81) of the Young Ladies' Charitable Union. In 1882 she was appointed vice-principal of the school where she was then teaching and, two years later, principal of the girls' department of Public School 77, a position she held for nineteen years. In 1897–98 she pursued advanced studies in her field at the school of pedagogy of New York University.

Counting many rabbis as well as teachers among her Prague ancestors, Miss Richman was deeply interested in religious matters. She was active in the Council of Jewish Women and chairman (1895–99) of its committee on religious school work, a director of the Hebrew Free School Association, first president (1886–90) of the Young Women's Hebrew Association, and a member (1889–98) of the Jewish Chautauqua Society's educational council. Her book *Methods of Teaching Jewish Ethics* (with Eugene H. Lehman) appeared posthumously in 1914. Her most important connection, however, was with the Educational Alliance, an organization formed in 1889 to aid in the Americanization of Jewish immigrants. The Alliance conducted special classes for immigrant children, teaching them English and preparing them for the public schools. Miss Richman was an active member of its board of directors from 1893 and served as a link between the Alliance and the school system.

Her work as a principal had meanwhile attracted attention, and in 1903 she was named a district superintendent by the New York City Board of Education. Offered a choice of districts, she selected the Lower East Side, and at once moved from her uptown residence to this crowded immigrant ghetto. Here, with responsibility for some 600 teachers and 23,-000 pupils, she had the opportunity to apply her maturing educational philosophy. She recognized the importance of curriculum—indeed she was co-author of *Pupils' Arithmetic,* a six-volume textbook series inaugurated in 1911 —but she believed the teacher's prime concern should be the whole development and welfare of the child. In practical terms this meant helping immigrant children in their difficult adjustment to American life, and trying to improve the neighborhoods in which they lived. A forceful, self-disciplined, and somewhat authoritarian woman, Miss Richman worked unceasingly to achieve these goals. Her textbook, *Good Citizenship* (with Isabel Richman Wallach), appeared in 1908, but her approach was usually more concrete. "It is so much easier and so much more picturesque to teach children to wave flags while singing the 'Star-Spangled Banner' than to teach them to separate ashes from garbage, as required by law," she said. "But these latter things must be done" (Proskauer and Altman, p. 11). A strong believer in "child's rights," she opened special schools for delinquents, chronic absentees, and overage pupils, and persuaded the school board to institute classes for the mentally retarded and physically handicapped. She started school optical examinations, set up a limited school lunch program, and secured the services of a job counselor for those whose circumstances forced them to leave school as soon as the law permitted.

In 1906 she converted the building in which she lived into a social center for the teachers in her district and a residence for some of them, as well as for three social workers. Here at "Teachers' House" her principals met for regular conferences on pupils' social needs, from which grew many of the innovations for which Miss Richman was noted, as well as a number of articles in *Outlook, Forum, Educational Review,* and other periodicals. She cooperated fully in the projects for community betterment undertaken by various social welfare agencies and was particularly active in the antiprostitution drive which flourished around 1910. The vigor of her reformism sometimes aroused a feeling among local residents that she, as a second-generation American fully committed to middle-class values, lacked sensitivity for the vibrant and variegated life of the East Side. Indeed, her campaign for the abolition of pushcart peddlers gave rise to an unsuccessful petition demanding the transfer of "this self-constituted censor of our morality" (quoted in Moses Rischin, *The Promised City,* 1962, p. 239).

Julia Richman resigned her school superintendency in the spring of 1912, at the age of fifty-six, hoping to devote herself to lecturing, writing, and social concerns. That summer she became ill on shipboard while crossing the Atlantic; shortly after reaching Paris she died at the American Hospital at Neuilly of complications following an appendectomy. She was buried in Linden Hill Cemetery in New York. Memorial services were held at the school which she had served as principal, and at Temple Ahawath Chesed, of which she had been a faithful member. A girls' high school in Manhattan was subsequently named in her honor.

[Bertha R. Proskauer and Addie R. Altman, *Julia Richman* (pamphlet, 1916); *N.Y. Times,* June 25, 26, July 11, 1912; *Literary Digest,* July 13, 1912, p. 65; *Who's Who in N.Y.,* 1903, 1907; *Jewish Encyc.,* X, 406; *Universal Jewish Encyc.,* IX, 158–59; Robert A. Woods and Albert J. Kennedy, *Handbook of Settlements* (1911), pp. 223–24. See also Selma Cantor Berroll, "Immigrants at School:

N.Y. City, 1898–1914" (unpublished Ph.D. dissertation, City Univ. of N.Y., 1967).]

WILLIAM W. BRICKMAN<br>PAUL S. BOYER

RICHMOND, Mary Ellen (Aug. 5, 1861–Sept. 12, 1928), social worker, was born in Belleville, Ill., where her father, Henry Richmond, a carriage blacksmith, had gone to make gun carriages during the Civil War. He was a nonpracticing Catholic, and Mary is thought to have been baptized in that faith. The family soon returned to Baltimore, Md., its earlier home. When Mary, the only one of four children to survive infancy, was three, her mother, Lavinia (Harris) Richmond, died of tuberculosis, and she was left in the care of her widowed maternal grandmother, Mehitabel Harris, and two maiden aunts. Although Henry Richmond married again, Mary had little contact with her stepmother and two half brothers, or with her father, who died when she was seven. The only masculine influence in her childhood came from two uncles who lived nearby and from eccentric boarders in the rooming house from which her grandmother made a precarious living. Mary was early exposed to discussions of such "radical" topics as woman suffrage. Spiritualist meetings and séances were also a part of her upbringing, her grandmother being an ardent believer. An avid reader who went through Dickens and other classics at a precocious age, Mary had no formal schooling until she was eleven. Two favorite teachers encouraged a critical approach to literature and sharpened her talent for essay writing, and she graduated from Baltimore's Eastern Female High School in 1878.

Through an aunt who worked as a proofreader in a New York publishing house specializing in agnostic and other unorthodox literature, Mary secured a clerical job there. She later recalled the next two years of routine work at starvation wages as the most lonely and frustrating period of her life. A debilitating lung ailment, possibly tuberculosis, together with an attack of malaria in 1880, forced her to return to Baltimore, where she worked as a bookkeeper. Meanwhile she continued her wide reading and took part in the social and educational activities of the Unitarian Church, of which she became a member. She also taught Shakespeare in an afterwork self-improvement program.

Mary Richmond discovered social work by chance. Following the depression of 1873, a reaction against haphazard duplication of charitable efforts had given rise to a "charity organization" movement which in the next decade spread to many cities. Late in 1888 or early in 1889 Miss Richmond answered an advertisement for an assistant treasurer placed by the Baltimore Charity Organization Society. "She looked pathetically young," recalled her interviewer, "and she talked like the Ancient of Days!" She was hired, and as her preparation she spent a week observing the work of the Boston Associated Charities and its director, ZILPHA D. SMITH, who introduced her to the literature and philosophy of the movement and became a lifelong friend. The Baltimore agency had among its leaders Daniel Coit Gilman, president of Johns Hopkins University, Charles Bonaparte, liberal Catholic lawyer and philanthropist, and John Glenn, retired businessman, scholar, and philanthropist. For Mary Richmond, with an outstanding but undeveloped intellect, the opportunity to associate with such men was an unexpected fulfillment, while charity organization, dealing with problems so real in her own youth, had more than intellectual appeal. Her reading was now directed toward a specific end, and to gain firsthand knowledge about charitable methods she volunteered as a "friendly visitor" in addition to her office duties. The administrative promise she showed led to her appointment in 1891 as general secretary of the Baltimore Charity Organization Society, a position previously held only by men with graduate training in political economy.

At first Miss Richmond was impressed by charity organization leaders who clung to the view that the poor would respond only to repressive measures. Gradually, however, she came to believe that a full understanding of the circumstances of problem individuals could indicate means for their rehabilitation. The dogma of thorough investigation to prevent exploitation of wealthy givers gave way to the concept of a complete social study, conducted by systematic methods of assembling and evaluating information and recording the steps taken to deal with the problems uncovered. She became certain that a trained, salaried cadre of full-time workers was required to augment volunteers and, through research, to perfect methods of treatment. After experimenting with training courses for agency workers in Baltimore, by 1897 Miss Richmond was advocating the establishment of professional schools for philanthropic work. She appropriated the term "case work" (originated by the London Charity Organisation Society) to describe her method, which she set forth in concise and practical terms in her slim volume *Friendly Visiting among the Poor*, published in 1899.

In 1900 she was called to Philadelphia to be general secretary of its Society for Organizing Charity. There she formed many close friendships, among musicians and artists as well as social workers. Working almost incessantly, she overhauled the moribund Philadelphia organization and, through persuasive presentation of moving case histories, proved a skilled fund raiser as well. She deplored the confused charitable situation in Pennsylvania, where hundreds of organizations of varying merit were competing for legislative grants. In *The Good Neighbor in the Modern City* (1907) she logically outlined a large city's major social needs and the kinds of organizations meeting them, not concealing her belief that many well-intentioned charities were not deserving of support.

Miss Richmond devoted increasing attention to the meticulous analysis of cases in an effort to discover ways of alleviating family difficulties, concentrating on the judicious use of financial relief to overcome personal disadvantages. Social needs requiring legislative action she believed would be disclosed by the individual cases. She herself interested contributors in initiating such reforms as improved public sanitation and the upgrading of custodial institutions, and she was among the leaders in a campaign to tighten child labor and compulsory education laws in Pennsylvania. She felt, however, that any measures for "mass betterment," seeking to aid all deprived families through taxation, would weaken family solidarity and responsibility. Repeatedly she maintained that the major role of social work was individual and family treatment.

Mary Richmond's national stature grew as through articles, speeches, and books she worked to elevate social work to a profession based on scientific knowledge and proven methods. To promote up-to-date approaches and encourage the founding of new societies, she oversaw an exchange of publicity and case materials among agencies; from 1905 to 1909 this project, under her editorship, was a department of the social work journal *Charities and the Commons*.

In 1909 Mary Richmond was named director of the Charity Organization Department of the much-heralded new Russell Sage Foundation, whose head was John M. Glenn, nephew of her former Baltimore associate. She moved to New York with some reluctance and frequently visited friends in Philadelphia and Baltimore, though as a thoroughly urbanized person she came to enjoy New York's cultural diversity, especially its art, dance, and music.

A persistent bronchial condition enforced long summer absences, at first in the Catskills, later in New Hampshire.

At the foundation Miss Richmond directed research on social problems and improved methodology, the results of which were distributed to charitable organizations using casework methods. Her analysis of case material which she had assembled from different kinds of agencies throughout the country was published in 1917 as *Social Diagnosis*, the best-known product of her career. Grounded in her conviction of the importance of a sound beginning in the casework process, *Social Diagnosis* described the nature of social evidence, the pitfalls in its use, and sources of information available for the skilled study of social difficulties. She also taught in schools of social work in New York, Philadelphia, and Boston. Her influence was most far-reaching, however, through the institutes for caseworkers and supervisors which she conducted from 1910 to 1922 and in which she stimulated creative thinking and experimentation with new ways of improving family life.

Mary Richmond's aversion to any form of public relief to families, absorbed from the social elite in Baltimore and reinforced by scandals she observed in Philadelphia, aligned her with those caseworkers who opposed some of the measures social activists were advocating in the period before World War I, among them widows' and old-age pensions. She also was caustically critical of central fund raising, maintaining that it would enable the very rich to dominate agency policy and would prevent givers from becoming familiar with the problems of the recipients. In World War I she urged that casework agencies carry on as usual, though she helped write the manual for Red Cross service to families, suggesting the title "Home Service." Partly because of the wide influence of Miss Richmond's views, schisms in the social work community deepened, and advocates of social insurance and promoters of the proliferating community chests succeeded in defeating her for president of the National Conference of Social Work in 1922.

From 1922 to 1928 Miss Richmond took leadership in a cause in which she had been interested since 1895—improved marriage laws. Characteristically, she had her staff study existing laws and their enforcement before beginning a campaign for compulsory physical examinations and raising the legal age for marriage. *Child Marriages* (1925) and the posthumous *Marriage and the State* (1929), both written with Fred S. Hall, were used by the League of Women Voters and other groups in waging campaigns which succeeded in changing the laws in most states.

As the number of social workers grew, Mary Richmond had headed an effort to standardize a vocabulary and formulate a code of ethics for the profession. When personality theory emerged as the foundation for rehabilitating individuals, she leaned to the theories of Jung and Adolf Meyer, rather than to those of Freud. She was a charter member in 1920 of the American Association of Social Workers. Smith College granted her an honorary masters degree in 1921. In 1922 she described the place she saw for casework in all of social work in her short, popularized *What Is Social Case Work?*

Miss Richmond's strategic position in the Russell Sage Foundation enabled her to influence significantly many schools of social work in their formative years. She played a major role in the emergence of the unique pattern of graduate social work education, a combination of classroom instruction and field experience in various agencies. Her most long-lasting influence, however, may well have come through her students, notably Jane Hoey, who applied her system to the investigation procedures under the public assistance programs after 1935. Mary Richmond died of cancer in 1928 at the age of sixty-seven and was buried in Loudon Park Cemetery, Baltimore. By any standard she had been the central figure in the emergence of professional social work.

[The Mary E. Richmond Archives, Library of the Columbia Univ. School of Social Work, include personal scrapbooks, correspondence, and interviews with colleagues and friends. Much material is also in the archives and publications of the three organizations for which she worked. Joanna C. Colcord and Ruth Z. S. Mann, eds., *The Long View* (1930), a collection of Miss Richmond's most important speeches and essays, illustrates the evolution of her ideas and includes biographical material and a complete bibliography of her writings. Of the many commentaries on Mary Richmond, the following, taken together, give a rounded perspective on her life: memorial issue of *The Family*, Feb. 1929; Virginia P. Robinson, *A Changing Psychology in Social Case Work* (1930), chaps. v and vi; Margaret Rich, "Mary E. Richmond: Social Worker," *Social Casework*, Nov. 1952; Muriel W. Pumphrey, "Mary Richmond and the Rise of Professional Social Work in Baltimore" (doctoral dissertation, N.Y. School of Social Work, Columbia Univ., 1956; Univ. Microfilms, Publication No. 17,076), which includes a full bibliography; Muriel W. Pumphrey, "The 'First Step'— Mary Richmond's Earliest Professional Reading, 1889–91," *Social Service Rev.*, June 1957; anniversary issue of *Social Casework*, Oct. 1961; and Roy Lubove, *The Professional Altruist: The Emergence of Social Work as a Career, 1880–1930* (1965).]

MURIEL W. PUMPHREY

**RICKER, Marilla Marks Young** (Mar. 18, 1840–Nov. 12, 1920), lawyer, suffragist, and freethinker, was born on her father's farm in New Durham, N.H., the oldest daughter and second of the four children of Jonathan B. and Hannah (Stevens) Young. Both parents were descended from early settlers of New England; her father was reportedly a cousin of the Mormon leader Brigham Young. Her mother, a Free-Will Baptist, taught her to read; her father, a Whig, early woman-suffragist, and outspoken freethinker, gave her a substantial education in politics and philosophy. He encouraged her rebellion against the orthodoxy of the church and took her to town meetings and sessions of the local courts. After being educated in local district schools, Marilla Young began to teach school at the age of sixteen. Tall, vigorous, and enthusiastic, she quickly earned a reputation as a good disciplinarian and a "born teacher." She had completed a year's training at Colby Academy in New London, N.H., when the Civil War broke out. Although she attempted to join the Union cause as a nurse, she failed to meet the requirements of maturity and experience with the sick and hence continued as a teacher. On May 19, 1863, at twenty-three, she was married to fifty-six-year-old John Ricker, an intelligent and wealthy farmer who, like her father, believed in equality regardless of sex. When he died five years later he left Marilla Ricker a childless widow, heir to $50,000.

Going abroad in 1872, Mrs. Ricker spent four years across the Atlantic, during which time she developed a fluency in foreign languages (particularly German) and absorbed the exhortations of Annie Besant, Charles Bradlaugh, and others expounding free thought, birth control, and political equality. On her return, having decided upon the law as her tool to help the weak and unfetter the oppressed, she settled in Washington, D.C., and began to read law with Arthur B. Williams and Albert G. Riddle. She was admitted to the District of Columbia bar on May 12, 1882, having passed the bar examination with the highest grade of all who were admitted at the time. She made her first courtroom appearance as an assistant counsel to her fellow freethinker Col. Robert G. Ingersoll in the Star Route mail fraud cases that year. For many years her practice was devoted primarily to criminal law, later to financial and banking law, and after 1900 to labor reforms. In 1882

she was appointed by President Arthur as a
notary public in the District of Columbia, an
office she put to effective use by enabling prisoners to make depositions before her rather
than before other city notaries whom they
could not afford to pay. In 1884 she was appointed a United States commissioner and
examiner in chancery by the judges of the
District's supreme court and as such was the
first woman in the District of Columbia to
perform the quasi-judicial functions attached
to that office. She was admitted to the bar of
the Supreme Court of the United States on
May 11, 1891. During the 1880's, in a test
case, Mrs. Ricker secured a ruling which
brought an end to the District of Columbia's
"poor convict's law" under which pauper
criminals were held indefinitely for fines they
were unable to pay. For this and for her aid
—moral, financial, and legal—to the prisoners
and prostitutes of the District she was dubbed
by the newspapers the "Prisoner's Friend."
Mrs. Ricker lived in Washington for several
decades, returning each summer to New
Hampshire. In that state, in 1879, she secured
an executive hearing before the governor to
protest conditions in the state prison and instigated new legislation giving prisoners the
right to send sealed letters to the governor and
council without interception by the wardens.
Her petition to the state supreme court for
the right of women to practice law in New
Hampshire was granted in July 1890, though
there is no record that she herself was admitted
to the bar there. She did practice in New
Hampshire by admission on motion for individual cases.

As early as 1870 Mrs. Ricker had aided the
suffrage cause. In that year, in New Durham,
she had upon paying her taxes demanded the
right to vote as an "elector" under the terms
of the Fourteenth Amendment. Though her
ballot was refused, she did vote in 1871—presumably the first woman in the United States
to have done so upon this basis—and until
woman suffrage was gained she continued to
lodge a protest each time she paid her taxes.
Meanwhile she served the movement as a
member of the National Woman Suffrage Association, as the New Hampshire Woman Suffrage Association's delegate to national conventions for many years, as a well-known and
witty lecturer, and as a generous contributor
of funds. She was listed as a life member of
the National American Woman Suffrage Association when that organization was formed,
although she later joined LILLIE DEVEREUX
BLAKE's short-lived National Legislative
League. A close associate of BELVA LOCKWOOD

in Washington for a number of years, Mrs.
Ricker headed the New Hampshire ticket of
electors for the Equal Rights party when Mrs.
Lockwood ran for president of the United
States in 1884. She was otherwise a staunch
Republican and campaigned for that party in
1888 and 1892. During President McKinley's
administration Mrs. Ricker requested an appointment as minister to Colombia or some
other South American republic in an effort to
open diplomatic posts to women, but despite
considerable official support she was unsuccessful. Unalterably opposed to Theodore Roosevelt, Progressive Republicanism, and uncon-
tested primary elections, she announced her
candidacy for the governorship of New Hampshire in 1910. Though her candidacy was
treated with respect, the state attorney general
refused her fee on the ground that without
the right to vote she could not run for office.

Writings on free thought occupied Mrs.
Ricker's last years, including three books published by Elbert Hubbard, who hailed her as
the "high priestess" of that movement in America. *Four Gospels* (1911) contrasted her
heroes, Thomas Paine and Robert Ingersoll,
with John Calvin and Jonathan Edwards; her
volumes of essays *I Don't Know, Do You?*
(1916) and *I Am Not Afraid, Are You?* (1917)
attacked clergy, missionaries, and religious reverence, which she called "mental suicide."
Widely traveled and well informed, Mrs.
Ricker was informal in manner, with a lively
sense of humor. She was modest to the point
of self-deprecation and puritanically moral in
her personal relationships. The last two years
of her life were spent in the home of John W.
Hogan, editor and publisher of the *Dover
Tribune*, in Dover, N.H., where she died of a
stroke at the age of eighty. Although she was
a member of the Thomas Paine Memorial
Church, a Universalist minister conducted her
funeral service. Her body was cremated and
her ashes placed around a favorite apple tree
on the New Durham farm where she had been
born.

[Besides her books, Mrs. Ricker wrote various free-
thought pamphlets and articles in the *Truthseeker*
magazine and contributed political discussions over
the years to the *Dover* (N.H.) *Tribune.* For biographical references, see Frances E. Willard and
Mary A. Livermore, eds., *A Woman of the Century* (1893); *Nat. Cyc. Am. Biog.,* XVII, 19; *Who
Was Who in America,* vol. I (1942); John Scales,
*Hist. of Strafford County and Representative Citi-
zens* (1914), pp. 447–48, 610, 613; Elizabeth
Cady Stanton et al., *Hist. of Woman Suffrage,* II
(1881), 586–87, III (1886), 378–79; Katherine
Devereux Blake and Margaret Louise Wallace,

*Champion of Women: The Life of Lillie Devereux Blake* (1943), pp. 208, 213; obituaries in *Foster's Daily Democrat* (Dover, N.H.), Nov. 12, 1920, and *Dover* (N.H.) *Tribune,* Nov. 18, 1920; letter to Lillie D. Blake, May 31, 1899, Blake Collection, Mo. Hist. Soc.; letter to Emma Hirth, Feb. 8, 1918, Doersheck Material, Schlesinger Library, Radcliffe College. A volume by Dorothy Thomas on "Women, the Bench, and the Bar" is in preparation.]

DOROTHY THOMAS

RICKERT, Edith (July 11, 1871–May 23, 1938), medievalist, professor of English, and author, was born in Dover, Ohio, to Francis E. and Josephine (Newburg) Rickert. Christened Martha Edith, she was the oldest of four daughters who survived infancy. Her ancestry was German, Dutch, and English. Her grandfather Rickert had helped establish a Moravian congregation in Dover in 1844. She herself was taken as a small child to a Methodist church; she was later confirmed as an Episcopalian but did not find full satisfaction in any communion. An artistic strain ran in her family. Her father, a businessman, was greatly interested in art; her mother's letters show literary sensitiveness; and one of her sisters, Margaret, became a professor of art at the University of Chicago.

Edith Rickert grew up in La Grange, Ill., and in Chicago, where she attended public schools. At Vassar College she developed the interests in creative writing and research that were to mark her later career. While in college she won a prize offered by the journal *Kate Field's Washington* for the best short story by an American undergraduate; she received her A.B. degree in 1891. In the summer of 1894 she began graduate work in English literature and philology at the University of Chicago, supporting herself for two years (1894–96) by teaching in the Lyons Township High School near Chicago, then spending a year of study abroad. Her dissertation, for which she was awarded the Ph.D. degree in 1899, was a study, with text and notes, of the Middle English romance *Emaré.* Meanwhile she had returned to Vassar as an instructor in English, a post she held from 1897 to 1900.

Miss Rickert's next years (1900–09) were spent in England, where she exercised her scholarship in editing medieval texts, satisfied her creative energies by publishing five novels and more than fifty short stories, and combined both interests in producing several modern translations of medieval literature. The panic of 1907 having reduced her income from writing, she returned to America and sought supplementary sources of income, which she found chiefly in editorial work (for D. C. Heath &

Company and the *Ladies' Home Journal*) and the writing of textbooks. In 1912 she edited with Jessie Paton a collection of *American Lyrics.* During the First World War she worked in the codes and ciphers division of the War Department (1918–19) with Prof. John M. Manly of the University of Chicago, the famous medieval scholar. The two afterward collaborated on several college textbooks (she herself doing the actual writing) and on handbooks for the study of *Contemporary British Literature* (1921) and *Contemporary American Literature* (1922), the last two growing out of summer teaching at the University of Chicago. Aided by Manly's vast authority, the handbooks helped establish contemporary literature as an academically respectable subject in American universities.

In 1924 Miss Rickert joined the faculty of the University of Chicago as associate professor of English, becoming professor in 1930. A woman of beauty and charm, of medium height, with a wide, somewhat Germanic face, and soft, prematurely white hair, she was a brilliant and dynamic teacher. With characteristic femininity she established close personal relationships with her students, yet at the same time she exacted the highest standards of scholarship. She gave them generous encouragement and, even during her busiest years, guided their progress with unerring taste and wisdom. Distressed by the fact that though the historical background of literature was now being studied in the most scholarly fashion, criticism was still largely impressionistic, she sought to lay the foundations for a scientific analysis of style in *New Methods for the Study of Literature* (1927). Enlightening but very laborious, these methods produced a number of Ph.D. dissertations at the University of Chicago but were not widely taken up elsewhere. She herself was a brilliant interpretive as well as a meticulous textual scholar and did not shrink from setting forth daring hypotheses. In "A New Interpretation of 'The Parlement of Foules'" (*Modern Philology,* May 1920) she sought to overthrow the long-accepted Koch-Emerson-Moore hypothesis; in "Political Propaganda and Satire in 'A Midsummer Night's Dream'" (*ibid.,* August and November 1923) she argued that Bottom was a satirical portrait of King James VI of Scotland!

For all her devotion to scholarship, Miss Rickert maintained her interest in creative writing during her later years. She published three volumes of children's stories: *The Bojabi Tree* (1923), *The Blacksmith and the Blackbirds* (1928), and *The Greedy Goroo* (1929).

Her last novel, *Severn Woods* (in England, *Olwen Growing*), appeared in 1930. Toward the end of her life she was looking forward to a return to creative writing as soon as her scholarly work should have been completed, and she left several novels and a large number of short stories in manuscript. The best of her published novels is *Severn Woods*, the story of an English girl's growth of spirit, less in love than through it; her poorest is *The Beggar in the Heart* (1909), in which she unsuccessfully adopts a style of Barrie-esque coyness. Only the first, *Out of the Cypress Swamp* (1902), a historical novel involving the pirate Jean Lafitte and the battle of New Orleans, has an American setting. *The Reaper* (1904) is an appealing story set in the Shetland Islands; *The Golden Hawk* (1907), dedicated to Frédéric Mistral, is a story of Provence. *Folly* (1906) is a character study. All these exotic locales she studied firsthand.

But it is for her teaching and her Chaucer research that Edith Rickert will be remembered. As early as 1930 she and Professor Manly were spending half their time in England, preparing their definitive edition of *The Text of the Canterbury Tales, Studied on the Basis of All Known Manuscripts* (8 vols., 1940), one of the monuments of American literary scholarship. Miss Rickert had always worked with phenomenal industry, but the intense strain of the Chaucer project seriously affected her health. As early as 1935 she was gravely ill; she died in Chicago of a coronary thrombosis two years before the great work appeared. Her ashes were buried in Oak Woods Cemetery in Chicago. Her *Chaucer's World* (1948), edited by two of her former students after her death, comprises materials she had gathered while the edition of Chaucer was being prepared.

[Information about Edith Rickert has been derived from her published writings and unpublished papers in the possession of her sister, Prof. Margaret Rickert; from personal recollections of Prof. Edward Wagenknecht and letters in his possession; and from Fred B. Millett's privately printed *Edith Rickert: A Memoir* (1944). See also Margaret Rickert's foreword to *Chaucer's World*.]

**RIDER-KELSEY, Corinne** (Feb. 24, 1877–July 10, 1947), concert and oratorio singer, later known as Mme. Rider-Reed, was born near Bergen, N.Y., the youngest in a family of four daughters and three sons. Her father, a farmer, died when she was three, and her mother, Fannie Rider, moved into town for five years before settling in Rockford, Ill., where Corinne attended public schools. The whole family were natural singers, and Corinne was early given the lead in school and church programs. At sixteen she decided to study voice, and in 1895, with ninety dollars borrowed for tuition and a room-and-board job, she entered the Oberlin Conservatory of Music. There she had excellent instruction in voice, piano, and harmony, while concerts by such artists as Leopold Godowski, Edward MacDowell, MAUD POWELL, and the Kneisel Quartet introduced her to the best in music and performance. Lack of money, however, forced her to leave Oberlin after one year. Back in Rockford, she became soprano soloist at the Congregational church, appeared in local concerts, and in July 1897 gave her own recital, winning praise for her clear voice and effortless style. Now financially independent, she studied with L. A. Torrens, who came from Chicago once a week.

On Jan. 1, 1900, Corinne Rider was married to George Russel Kelsey, a fellow student from Oberlin. Moving to his home city of Toledo, Ohio, she made her debut there six weeks later as Mrs. Rider-Kelsey and was immediately acclaimed. She sang in recitals, with the Toledo Symphony Orchestra, and as soloist at the Congregational church until October 1903, when she took a three-month leave from her church job for intensive study in New York City with Theodore Toedt, a concert and oratorio singer. To test herself in competition there, she auditioned for soloist at the First Presbyterian Church in Brooklyn and, to her surprise, was chosen out of ninety-one contestants. At the audition committee's urging, she secured a release from her church commitment in Toledo and moved to New York with her husband (who obtained a business post there). More important to her career, she was offered a contract by Henry Wolfsohn, then the leading American manager for musical artists.

In two years Wolfsohn had made the name Rider-Kelsey known throughout the country. After lesser engagements, she sang in the fall of 1904 with the New York Oratorio Society, directed by Frank Damrosch, in *The Messiah*, and with the New York Symphony Orchestra under Walter Damrosch in *Elijah*. The next spring she scored a success in the famous Bach Festival at Bethlehem, Pa., in the *St. Matthew Passion*, and at the Cincinnati Festival in Beethoven's Ninth Symphony. That summer she continued her studies with Toedt to increase her repertoire and was tutored in French, German, and Italian. Mme. ERNESTINE SCHUMANN-HEINK, with whom she appeared the next season in the Maine Festivals, predicted a great future for her; in later years they often concertized together.

Over the next few seasons Mrs. Rider-Kelsey became much sought after and filled an astonishing number of engagements, in New York and other cities. Three times she was soloist with the New York Philharmonic; in 1908–09 she toured for six weeks with the New York Symphony. Each season included many return engagements. So heavy was her schedule that she once collapsed after an appearance in *The Messiah,* having sung the soprano part eight times in two weeks, traveling from Ohio to Maine; but six weeks later she was back on the concert platform. In 1907, on her first trip to England, she sang before the director of the Royal Opera at Covent Garden and was offered a contract to sing Micaëla in *Carmen,* Mimi in *La Bohème,* and Zerlina in *Don Giovanni.* The first American-trained singer to perform in a major role with the company, she made a successful debut as Micaëla in London on July 2, 1908, but, disliking the artificiality of the medium, she asked after three performances to be released from her contract and returned to oratorio and concert work.

Mme. Rider-Kelsey was now at the height of her career, one of America's top musical artists. Critics praised the purity, delicacy, and rich coloring of her voice, her phrasing, her ease, her interpretation, and her perfect Mozart legato. A perfectionist, she set high standards for herself. She included in her programs works of Schubert, Schumann, Strauss, MacDowell, and Elgar as well as the traditional composers, and she excelled in German *lieder.* In 1913, after many orchestral and oratorio concerts in New York, she gave her first solo recital there.

World War I cut short a year in Europe for travel and teaching and curtailed concert opportunities. After the war her voice was less in demand, and she never resumed her former schedule. Previously she had believed in a wholehearted devotion to art, admiring Jenny Lind, who had had "no diversion of interests" in her life. Now she was gripped by depression, doubting herself both as artist and as woman. Her marriage had been childless and had ended in a separation, about 1908, and subsequent divorce. She had, she felt, sacrificed domestic and personal life for professional success.

This period of uncertainty had begun to end by the summer of 1925 when Mme. Rider-Kelsey met the violinist and composer Lynnel Reed while both were teaching in Toledo. She returned to New York in the fall, and in December, at forty-eight, made her last appearance there in a recital of her own. The critics praised her for her warmth of voice and for bringing back older and finer musical skills. The next summer she returned to Toledo to a heavy teaching schedule. She was married to Reed on Aug. 25, 1926. Their twenty years of marriage were happy, despite the hardships most artists suffered during the depression. She and her husband continued to teach, and two of her best students, Dorothy Shadle and Joyce White, became so close to the couple that they were considered "adopted daughters." The Reeds held regular Sunday musicales in their home; Mrs. Reed occasionally appeared with other musicians in Toledo concerts, and infrequently elsewhere. Through the 1930's she sang in the local Presbyterian church.

A small woman with blue eyes, dark brown hair, and a beautiful complexion, Mme. Rider-Kelsey had a quiet, unassuming manner both on and off stage. She liked to be outdoors, in early years often spending her summers walking in the New England mountains; later she became expert at target shooting with a rifle. When she began to keep house she grew fond of flowers and animals. She sang her last professional concert in 1941, at sixty-four, as contralto soloist in the *St. Matthew Passion* in a performance in Toledo. The next year she developed a bad heart condition, and her husband persuaded her to give up teaching. She died in Toledo of angina pectoris in 1947, in her seventy-first year.

[Lynnel Reed, *Be Not Afraid: Biog. of Madame Rider-Kelsey* (1955), is the principal source. See also: Elizabeth Harbison David, *I Played Their Accompaniments* (1940), pp. 42, 76–79, 93–94; *Baker's Biog. Dict. of Musicians* (5th ed., 1958).]

VIOLA L. SCOTT

**RIDGE, Lola** (Dec. 12, 1873–May 19, 1941), poet, wrote, in the best of her poems, of the "bartering, changing, extorting, dreaming, debating, aspiring, astounding, indestructible life of the Ghetto." Like the impoverished Jews with whom she identified (although she herself was not Jewish), she was an immigrant to America. Born in Dublin, Ireland, she was the only surviving child of Joseph Henry Ridge and Emma (Reilly) Ridge. (A brother died in infancy.) She was christened Rose Emily but preferred, in private life, to be called Rosa Delores [*sic*]. In 1887 she was taken by her mother to New Zealand, where Mrs. Ridge had a married sister. She then moved to Sydney, Australia, where she attended Trinity College and studied art under Julian Ashton at the Academie Julienne. After her mother's death, she came in the spring of 1907 to the United States. Settling in New York City, she supported herself as an illustrator, an artist's model, a factory worker, and a writer of advertisements and popular fiction.

She had begun to write poetry in Australia (she later regretted having destroyed these early efforts). Now, having proved her ability to support herself in America, she moved to Greenwich Village, lived ascetically, and wrote poems in the Imagist tradition. She had published as early as 1908 in San Francisco's *Overland Monthly,* and she contributed often, in these prewar years, to EMMA GOLDMAN's radical monthly, *Mother Earth.* Her reputation, however, dates from 1918, when her poem "The Ghetto" appeared in the *New Republic* and then as the title poem of her first volume in that same year. She was immediately recognized and praised; Stephen Vincent Benét, William Rose Benét, Horace Gregory, and Mary Zaturenska accepted her as a gifted poet whose bent was similar to their own.

Although she was a semi-invalid long before she contracted pulmonary tuberculosis in 1929, her poems show an intense sympathy for the "strong flux of life" that triumphed even over the squalor of Hester Street. She praises, in her first book, the workers who built Manhattan and wonders what would happen if they ceased to labor for their "exploiters." In *Sun-Up and Other Poems* (1920), her second book, she satirized "all the policemen like fat blue mullet," and wrote poems for her anarchist friends Alexander Berkman and Emma Goldman. Her life, like theirs, was dedicated to the radical causes that substituted for traditional religion. In the years following World War I, she revived Alfred Kreymborg's magazine, *Others,* after its editors pronounced it dead; she served as an editor of *Broom* (another of the small radical magazines of the period), and she contributed poems to *The Left* and to *New Masses,* as well as to such unpolitical journals as *Poetry* and the *Saturday Review of Literature.* Long before the great depression made literary radicalism popular, she published *Red Flag and Other Poems* (1927) and saluted underdog heroes from Spartacus to the Bolsheviks. Her lines on Alexander Kerensky suggest her own fascination with the contrast between weakness and strength; she described the toppled Menshevik leader as the "flower the storm spewed white and broken out of its red path." Lola Ridge's friend Harry Salpeter remembered her in comparable images of weakness and power: "Blood-drained, ravaged by illness, she is like

a bright, untarnished double-edged sword in her courage and her integrity." (Because she gave her birth date as 1883 rather than 1873, she appeared more sickly than she was.) In their *History of American Poetry,* Horace Gregory and Marya Zaturenska describe her, less poetically, as "a slender, tall, softly-speaking, thin-featured woman in a dark dress," living in a "large, barely furnished, windswept, cold-water loft."

*Firehead,* her next volume, published in 1929, was the outgrowth of her experiences in the campaign to prevent the execution of Nicola Sacco and Bartolomeo Vanzetti, the Massachusetts anarchists accused of murdering a Brockton paymaster. Like John Dos Passos, EDNA MILLAY, and Dorothy Parker, Lola Ridge went to Boston in August 1927 to demonstrate on their behalf. After the failure of the preexecution vigil, she returned to New York and, after two sleepless nights, began *Firehead;* in 1929 she went to Yaddo, the artists' colony in Saratoga Springs, and brought the epic to an end. Although Sacco and Vanzetti are never mentioned, the poem is a version of the Crucifixion which clearly indicates that Calvary was only one of many martyrdoms. The most successful poem of her last volume, *Dance of Fire* (1935), combines images of the Crucifixion with the angry protests of proletarian poetry: "Three Men Die" is her final hymn to Sacco and Vanzetti, two men who had, as she herself did, the "ancient singleness of heart" that kept them to their course "amid the veering winds." The titles of her last two volumes use her favorite symbol, fire, and in this image she spoke her radically individualist manifesto: "Let anything that burns you come out. . . ."

As early as 1923, Lola Ridge won *Poetry* magazine's Guarantor's Prize. In 1934 and 1935 she received the Shelley Memorial Award, and in the latter year a Guggenheim Fellowship. She died at her home in Brooklyn in 1941 in her seventy-eighth year; the principal causes of death were given as pulmonary tuberculosis and myocardial degeneration. She was buried in Brooklyn's Evergreens Cemetery. She was survived by her husband, David Lawson, whom she had married on Oct. 22, 1919. There were no children. In her memory Samuel A. DeWitt established, in 1941, the Lola Ridge Memorial Award, which was granted through 1950 and then discontinued. Since her death Lola Ridge's reputation, even as a minor poet, has declined. Horace Gregory and Marya Zaturenska commented in 1946 that her "moral courage and her imaginative insights seemed to have reached beyond her strength" so that she never wrote "a wholly memorable poem." Nonetheless, her earlier and shorter poems, through *Red Flag*, are a rare combination of compassion and Imagistic craftsmanship.

[There is no biography or critical study beyond brief notices in periodicals and general studies of the period. Evaluations of her work can be found in William Rose Benét's obituary notices in *Saturday Rev. of Literature*, May 31, 1941, and *N.Y. Times*, May 21, 1941; in Alfred Kreymborg's *Our Singing Strength* (1929), pp. 484–88; and in Horace Gregory and Marya Zaturenska's *Hist. of Am. Poetry: 1900–1940* (1946), pp. 444–47. Lola Ridge's comments on her work and Harry Salpeter's description of her appear in Dilly Tante (Stanley J. Kunitz), ed., *Living Authors: A Book of Biogs.* (1931), pp. 340–41. (A photograph appears as well.) The biographical data in Stanley J. Kunitz and Howard Haycraft's *Twentieth Century Authors* (1942), pp. 1172–73, are often inaccurate.]

ALLEN GUTTMANN

**RIEPP, Mother Benedicta** (June 28, 1825–Mar. 15, 1862), Roman Catholic nun and foundress of the Sisters of Saint Benedict in the United States, was born in Waal, in the province of Swabia, Bavaria, Germany. Christened Maria Sybilla, she was the oldest of three children of Johann Riepp, a glassblower, and Katharina (Mayr) Riepp. At nineteen she entered the Convent of Saint Walburga, a cloistered Benedictine convent in Eichstätt, Bavaria. She was invested with the Benedictine habit on Aug. 4, 1844, and was given the name of Sister Benedicta. In 1849 she made her perpetual vows and during her next three years at the convent was a teacher and mistress of novices.

In 1852 Sister Benedicta was appointed superior of a group of three sisters who were sent to America at the request of Father (later Abbot) Boniface Wimmer, a fellow Bavarian who had established the first American Benedictine monastery, at St. Vincent, Westmoreland County, Pa., and was seeking sisters to teach the children of a colony of German settlers at St. Marys in Elk County. The small group of nuns reached St. Marys in July 1852 and established a girls' school. Conditions were harsh, for the community was isolated and poor, and for financial help Mother Benedicta was dependent on an annual allotment provided by the *Ludwig-missionsverein* in Bavaria. She and another sister also taught in the public school, receiving the combined salary of twenty-five dollars a month. Their first convent was a dilapidated building that gave inadequate protection against the Pennsylvania

winters, and the usual diet consisted of a small portion of bread, potatoes, and buckwheat cakes.

St. Marys seemed to offer little opportunity for the future growth of the Benedictine sisterhood in America, but despite hard times the convent grew in numbers. In October 1853, with the support of Father Wimmer, Mother Benedicta admitted twelve novices, although it had been the intent of the motherhouse at Eichstätt that the American mission should remain in a strictly dependent status. She went on to establish several new foundations in other parts of the country at the invitation of bishops there. As early as the spring of 1856 she sent a group of sisters to Erie, Pa., to open a parish school. Other convents at Newark, N.J., and St. Cloud, Minn., both established in 1857, later became the nuclei of the present independent priories at Elizabeth, N.J., Ridgely, Md., and St. Joseph, Minn. Before Mother Benedicta's death in 1862 seven autonomous convents had been established in America as outgrowths of her original foundation.

The pioneer Benedictine nuns faced special problems in America. Frontier conditions and the nature of their work made it impractical for them to adhere rigidly to the customs and routine of their motherhouse in Germany, such as strict enclosure. From the start, Mother Benedicta recognized the need for adapting to the new environment. Her efforts brought her into conflict both with the prioress of the motherhouse in Bavaria, who wanted the American foundations to retain the German customs and spirit, and with Wimmer, who, while agreeing with the need for adaptation to the American way of life, claimed jurisdiction over Mother Benedicta and her nuns by virtue of his office as abbot-president of the American Assinese Congregation of Benedictine Monks, established in 1855. In 1857, after overseeing the departure of a group of sisters for the new convent at St. Cloud, Mother Benedicta traveled to Europe with the intention of gathering funds and obtaining her independence from the rules of the motherhouse at Eichstätt, on the one hand, and the jurisdiction of Abbot Wimmer, on the other. The outcome of her efforts was a decree from Rome on Dec. 6, 1859, that placed the American Benedictine convents under the jurisdiction of the bishops of the dioceses in which they were established.

She herself, however, never regained her position of leadership. During her absence Abbot Wimmer had deposed her and forbidden her to live in any of the houses she had been instrumental in founding. This order he later retracted and allowed her to stay first at the convent in Erie and later at the St. Cloud, Minn., convent, but only as a member of the community, not as superior. By this time Mother Benedicta was in failing health. In 1862, at the age of thirty-six, she died of tuberculosis at St. Cloud. She was buried in the cemetery of the Convent of Saint Benedict, St. Joseph, Minn. A hundred years after her death thirty-two independent priories of Benedictine sisters in the United States, Canada, and Mexico, established either directly or indirectly from her original foundation in St. Marys, Pa., were carrying on the work of education she had begun, besides maintaining orphanages, hospitals, nursing homes, and homes for the aged.

[Parish records in Waal, Swabia, Germany; archives of the Convent of Saint Benedict, St. Joseph, Minn.; Sister Grace McDonald, *With Lamps Burning* (1957); Sister Mary Regina Baska, *The Benedictine Congregation of Saint Scholastica* (1935); Stephanus Hilpisch, *Hist. of Benedictine Nuns* (1958); *Catalogue of the Nuns and Convents of the Order of Saint Benedict in the U.S.* (1903). See also Colman J. Barry, "Boniface Wimmer," *Catholic Hist. Rev.*, Oct. 1953; and Willibald Mathäser, "Konig Ludwig I von Bayern und die Gründung der ersten bayerischen Benediktinerabtei in Nordamerika," *Studien und Mitteilungen zur Geschichte des Benediktiner-Ordens*, 1926, pp. 123–82.]

SISTER EMMANUEL RENNER, O.S.B.

RIND, Clementina (c. 1740–Sept. 25, 1774), printer and newspaper editor, wife of William Rind, public printer in Maryland and Virginia, is said to have been a native of Maryland, but no record of her birth or marriage has been found. Her husband, born in Annapolis in 1733, was reared there as apprentice to the public printer, Jonas Green. During the seven-year period of his partnership with Green (1758–65) young Rind acquired town property, a home, and a wife, Clementina. To protest the Stamp Act the partners suspended publication of the *Maryland Gazette* in October 1765, and shortly thereafter Rind accepted the invitation of a group of Virginia liberals to publish a "free paper" in Williamsburg. The first issue of Rind's *Virginia Gazette* appeared May 16, 1766, under the motto: "Open to ALL PARTIES, but Influenced by NONE." The press, the paper, and the printer quickly established a good reputation. The fall assembly chose Rind as public printer, and in spite of rising costs of paper and other supplies the business prospered. When the editor died in

August 1773, his family was living on the main street in the present Ludwell-Paradise House and the printing shop was operated in the same handsome brick building.

The widow immediately took over the editorship and business management of the press for her "dear infants"—William, John, Charles, James, and Maria. The household included also a kinsman, John Pinkney, an apprentice, Isaac Collins, and a Negro slave, Dick, who probably worked in the shop as a semiskilled artisan. As editor Mrs. Rind was careful to preserve the integrity of the motto and in other respects followed the program set up by her husband. Reports of foreign and domestic occurrences, shipping news, and advertisements were supplemented by essays, articles, and poems accepted from contributors or selected from her "general correspondence" and from London magazines and newspapers. Her choice of subject reveals special interest in new developments and experiments in science, plans for improving educational opportunities —especially those relating to the College of William and Mary—and designs for philanthropic programs. Apparently women were valued readers of her paper, for it carried an unusual number of poetic tributes to ladies in acrostic or rebus form, literary conceits, and news reports with a feminine slant. As conventional fillers she used sprightly vignettes of life in European high society, in rural England, and in the other colonies.

Mrs. Rind was peculiarly sensitive to the good will of contributors and usually explained why specific offerings were not being published promptly. Sometimes, however, contributions were summarily rejected. Scarcely three months after Rind's death her competitor, Alexander Purdie, published an anonymous open letter criticizing her refusal to print an article exposing the misconduct of some of "the guilty Great." Her dignified reply, published in her own paper the next week, demonstrated independence, good sense, and literary skill. She had rejected the article, she wrote, because it was an anonymous attack on the character of private persons and should be heard in a court of law, not in a newspaper; yet she promised: "When the author gives up his name, it shall, however repugnant to my inclination, have a place in this paper, as the principles upon which I set out will then, I flatter myself, plead my excuse with every party." In later issues of her gazette contributors often expressed healthy respect for her standards and literary judgment.

Her bid for public favor was so well received that she expanded her printing program and in April 1774, after six months as editor, announced the purchase of "an elegant set of types from London." A month later the House of Burgesses appointed her public printer in her own right, and they continued to give her press all the public business in spite of competing petitions from Purdie and Dixon, publishers of a rival *Virginia Gazette*.

At the end of August she was in ill health and finding it difficult to collect payments due her; yet her pride in her work and her optimistic plans for the future were undiminished. She died in Williamsburg a month later and was probably buried beside her husband at Bruton Parish Church. Since her children were minors, Pinkney managed the press for them. Like her husband, she left no will, and the settlement of the two estates dragged on for several years after the Revolution. Rind had been a Freemason, and his brother Masons assumed responsibility for the support of his orphans in 1775 and continued for several years to appropriate money for their expenses. Apparently Mrs. Rind's executors were unable to collect the many small sums her patrons still owed the *Gazette* at the time of her death.

Her readers prepared a number of poetic eulogies and a formal elegy of 150 lines. Beneath extravagant metaphors one can read sincere affection and admiration for a woman who combined wide interests, literary talent, and sound critical judgment with personal piety and serenity, spiritual courage, and no small portion of feminine charm.

[Isaiah Thomas, *Hist. of Printing in America* (1810); files of *Va. Gazette* (Rind); *Md. Gazette,* Apr. 12, 1764, Oct. 10, 1765; *Jours. of the House of Burgesses, 1773–1776* (1905); St. Anne's Parish Register, Md. Hall of Records; Bruton Parish Register, Williamsburg; York County Records, Wills and Inventories, Book 22; Williamsburg Masonic Lodge, Minute Book, 1774–79, and Treasurer's Book, 1773–84.]

JANE D. CARSON

**RIPLEY, Martha George Rogers** (Nov. 30, 1843–Apr. 18, 1912), physician and humanitarian, was born in Lowell, Orleans County, Vt., the first of five children of Francis Rogers and his second wife, Esther Ann George. Her ancestors, of English and Scotch-Irish stock, had long lived in New England. In her infancy the family moved west to stake out a farm near Fort Atkinson in northeastern Iowa. Here Martha grew up in a warm family circle surrounded by the discipline of the frontier. Her mother was a Free-Will Baptist who read through the Bible yearly and inculcated the

Puritan virtues; her farmer father aided escaping slaves and was later remembered for his many litigations. Martha obtained a somewhat fitful public school education, attending but not graduating from the Lansing (Iowa) high school, after which she taught school for seven terms. When her youth prevented her from becoming a nurse in the Civil War, she raised money for the United States Sanitary Commission. During diphtheria epidemics she was a skillful and public-spirited nurse.

On June 25, 1867, Martha Rogers was married in Decorah, Iowa, to William Warren Ripley, a Massachusetts man who had gone west after the war to take up ranching. They soon departed for his home state, settling at first in Lawrence and then in Middleton, where he purchased and operated a paper mill. Her three daughters, Abigail Louise, Clara Esther, and Edna May, were born during these years. While living in Lawrence, it is said, Mrs. Ripley successfully petitioned for the appointment of a police matron and was herself given the job. In 1875 she joined the woman suffrage movement, receiving a place the next year on the executive committees of both the state and the New England associations. Meanwhile, illness in the mill towns so absorbed her energies and rekindled her interest in the sick that she determined to become a physician. One of her sisters had graduated from the Boston University Medical School. Mrs. Ripley entered the school in 1880, demonstrated remarkable aptitude and proficiency, and graduated with the M.D. degree in 1883.

That same year her husband suffered a severe injury in a mill accident which forced him to give up business permanently and threw upon his wife the burden of family support. Moving to Minneapolis, Minn., where her husband had relatives, she began a medical practice. In her many professional and reform activities that followed, she had Ripley's sympathetic support; a daughter recalled that he often drove the buggy for her on her night calls. In Minneapolis, Dr. Ripley was immediately elected president of the Minnesota Woman Suffrage Association, on the recommendation of her Massachusetts co-workers LUCY STONE and Henry B. Blackwell. For six years as executive and thereafter from the ranks she supported this unpopular cause, which she saw as woman's guarantee of justice, though only part of the larger effort to gain equal rights.

Her successful medical practice, specializing in obstetrics and children's diseases, was a vehicle through which she expressed an advanced social consciousness. Always alert to human needs, she became known for her responsiveness to those in distress and her zeal to reduce death in childbirth and infant mortality. Aware of the city's need for a home for unmarried mothers, she provided one for three of her patients in 1886. Within a month a move to larger quarters and plans for a permanent facility were required; this was chartered the next year as Maternity Hospital. In stressing social as well as medical care for mothers both rich and poor, married and unmarried, and also for indigent infants, the hospital reflected its founder's humanitarianism. Subsequently it was the focus of her activity and earned an enviable reputation for high professional standards as well as for community service. This pioneer social agency was her major achievement. In addition she was professor of children's diseases in the Homeopathic Medical College (later incorporated into the state university) and lectured at medical schools in neighboring states.

Martha Ripley also strove in other ways for social betterment, particularly that of women and children. Seeking to improve the public schools, she criticized them for overburdening students and molding a standardized child. She long fought for representation of women on the city school board. She actively supported the Woman's Christian Temperance Union and also the attempt to raise the legal "age of consent" from ten to eighteen years. She was an outspoken advocate of "social purity" and urged a single moral standard for men and women. Early recognizing the problems of urban growth, she strongly recommended the scientific incineration of garbage and labored for playgrounds, pure water, and better quarantine facilities. She urged cremation of the dead.

A handsome woman, Dr. Ripley enjoyed vigorous good health. Although she did not shrink from controversy in her efforts at reform, she enjoyed a position of prestige in and far beyond her community. In religion she was a Congregationalist. She died in Minneapolis of the complications of a rheumatic heart a few months after an illness induced by exposure to severe winter weather. Her ashes were eventually placed within the cornerstone of a building erected in her honor at Maternity Hospital. In the words of the memorial plaque installed in the rotunda of the Minnesota State Capitol in 1939, she was a "champion of righteousness and justice" who served humanity "with farsighted vision and sympathy."

[Newspaper clippings pertaining to Dr. Ripley, together with some letters by and to her, in the possession of her daughter Edna Ripley Page (Mrs. Leroy A. Page) of Santa Barbara, Calif., and Minneapolis, are an important source; Mrs. Page also furnished personal information. Useful references are in the following books: Isaac Atwater, *Hist. of the City of Minneapolis, Minn.* (2 vols., 1893); Mary Dillon Foster, *Who's Who among Minn. Women* (1924); Horace B. Hudson, ed., *A Half Century of Minneapolis* (1908); William H. King, *Hist. of Homeopathy and Its Institutions in America* (4 vols., 1905); Elizabeth Cady Stanton et al., *Hist. of Woman Suffrage* (6 vols., 1881–1922); Warren Upham and Mrs. Rose Barteau Dunlap, comps., *Minn. Biogs., 1655–1912* (Minn. Hist. Soc., *Collections*, vol. XIV, 1912); Frances E. Willard and Mary A. Livermore, eds., *A Woman of the Century* (1893). Pamphlets, brochures, and other information of value, all in the Minn. Hist. Soc., are: *Martha G. Ripley, M.D.* (n.d.); *Maternity Hospital, 1887–1937* (1937); Ariel B. Pomeroy, "A Brief Tribute Presented at a Memorial Service for Dr. Martha George Ripley" (typescript, 1937); Ethel Edgerton Hurd, *Woman Suffrage in Minn.* (1916). On her police matronship, see *Woman's Jour.*, Apr. 22, 1899, p. 122. Alice Stone Blackwell, "The Lesson of a Life," *ibid.*, June 22, 1912, is a full and appreciative obituary article; others are in the *St. Paul Dispatch*, Apr. 18, 1912, and the *Minneapolis Morning Tribune*, Apr. 19, 1912. For a fuller account, see the author's article in *Minn. Hist.*, Spring 1964.]

WINTON U. SOLBERG

**RIPLEY, Sarah Alden Bradford** (July 31, 1793–July 26, 1867), New England learned lady, was born in Boston. Her father, Gamaliel Bradford III, a descendant of Gov. William Bradford of Plymouth and of John and PRISCILLA ALDEN, had not turned thirteen when he followed his father into the Continental Army in 1776. After the war he became a captain of armed merchantmen; more than once he saved his ship in combat with French privateers, losing a leg in one fight. He died while warden of the Charlestown State Prison, a pioneer in penal reform. Sarah was the oldest of his nine children. Of her mother, Elizabeth Hickling, we know only that she was so often ill that Sarah had most of the care of the younger ones. She was a lively little girl, rosy-cheeked and blue-eyed, happiest of all at her Grandfather Bradford's home in the orchards and pinewoods of Duxbury, Mass. On visits there she studied with the local minister, Dr. John Allyn, who taught girls as well as boys; in Boston she attended the school of a Mr. Cummings. Under these two fine teachers Sarah learned to read Latin and Greek almost as easily as English; her father helped her with French and Italian. Her childhood days were busy with household tasks, care of the children, and reading: Sophocles, Theocritus, Tacitus, Seneca, and many others. At sixteen she was suddenly discovered and "enchained" by the vigorous intellect and personality of MARY MOODY EMERSON, aunt of Ralph Waldo Emerson. At first Sarah yielded to this sudden intimacy, but when Mary tried to force her own grim Calvinism on her, she refused to accept a creed that might close her mind "against the light of truth."

It was Mary Emerson's half brother who changed Sarah's life. The Rev. Samuel Ripley was the son of Ezra Ripley, minister of the First Parish Church in Concord, and of Phebe Bliss, widow of Ezra Ripley's predecessor, William Emerson. Samuel, born in 1783, grew up in the "Old Manse" in Concord, went to Harvard and to the Harvard Divinity School, and became the beloved minister of the First Church in Waltham, Mass. Sarah, absorbed in her home and books, consented only at her father's urging to marry him, on Oct. 6, 1818. But theirs was a happy marriage of devotion to each other and to their children. Samuel was thirty-five, Sarah twenty-five, when he brought her to the home where, to eke out his salary of $700, he kept a small boarding school. Sarah's twenty-eight years in Waltham were filled with boarders and babies. Seven of their eight children lived to grow up: Elizabeth, Mary Emerson, Christopher Gore, Phebe Bliss, Ezra, Ann Dunkin, and Sophia Bradford. Besides her constant care of them, Sarah was housemother and teacher to endless boys. She would sit rocking a cradle or shelling peas, with Homer or Vergil in her lap while the boys recited around her. "She was always sweet and serene," one of them recalled. In her rare free moments, noted her nephew Ralph Waldo Emerson, who taught at the Ripleys' school during his Harvard vacations, "you will find her reading a German critic or something of the kind sometimes Reid on Light or Optics" (Rusk, p. 75). She taught "rusticated" college students, too, banished to the country as punishment for some offense; President Edward Everett of Harvard said she could have filled any professor's chair. And late at night she went on studying: botany, chemistry, theology, philosophy.

At last, in the spring of 1846, their long "boy-bondage" over, Samuel and Sarah Ripley returned to the Old Manse. But their hard-earned freedom and happiness ended too soon; Samuel died suddenly on Thanksgiving evening, 1847. "His own affectionate heart," said Sarah, "was spared the pain of parting." After that, death came to her family again and again; Ezra died in the Civil War, leaving a young wife. For respite from grief, Sarah turned again to her timeless books. Frank Sanborn,

Concord schoolmaster, came weekly to read Greek with her. Almost to the last she read Homer and the Greek tragedies. At seventy she taught herself Spanish so that she could read *Don Quixote:* "What a vista! A whole new language!" As the years closed in she held more closely to the friends, children, and grandchildren who were left to her. She wrote to a dear sister-in-law, "I have not your faith to console me . . . yet my will, I trust, is resigned where light is wanting. The sun looks brighter . . . as the evening of life draws near." She died of apoplexy in Concord a few days before her seventy-fourth birthday. She lies beside her husband in Sleepy Hollow Cemetery, Concord.

One thinks of Sarah Ripley, the most diversely learned American woman of her age, as one born before her time. Yet for her, as for the English learned ladies of the seventeenth and eighteenth centuries, learning was an avocation; she had no ambition to write or to lead, she was no reformer like her contemporaries LYDIA MARIA CHILD, ELIZABETH PEABODY, and MARGARET FULLER. In her narrow lot she created a life that embodied the spirit of the classics that she loved. In the grave, serene face that looks from her portrait in the Old Manse, there shines a spirit that was "fearless, liberal, and beautiful."

[A transcript of Bradford letters, including Sarah Ripley's letters and letters of her father, is in the Houghton Library at Harvard Univ.; I am indebted to the late Mrs. Gamaliel Bradford for permission to use this. Next to the letters, the best source is the long essay by Elizabeth Hoar in Sarah B. Wister and Agnes Irwin, eds., *Worthy Women of Our First Century* (1877), though Miss Hoar took some liberties with the words and sentence order of the letters she quotes. See also Frances W. Knickerbocker, "New England Seeker: Sarah Bradford Ripley," *New England Quart.,* Mar. 1957; Gamaliel Bradford, *Portraits of Am. Women* (1919), chap. ii; Alden Bradford, "Memoir of Gamaliel Bradford, Esq.," Mass. Hist. Soc., *Collections,* 3rd ser., I (1825), 202–09, on Sarah's father; James B. Thayer, *Rev. Samuel Ripley of Waltham* (privately printed, 1897); Ralph L. Rusk, *The Life of Ralph Waldo Emerson* (1949).]

FRANCES W. KNICKERBOCKER

**RIPLEY, Sophia Willard Dana** (July 6, 1803–Feb. 4, 1861), Transcendentalist, leading spirit in the Brook Farm experiment, and Catholic convert, was born in Cambridge, Mass., the eldest of the four children (two sons and two daughters) of Francis and Sophia (Willard) Dana. Both parents came of families long distinguished in Massachusetts politics and letters. Her grandfathers were Joseph Willard, president of Harvard College, and Francis Dana, first American minister to Russia and later chief justice of Massachusetts. The painter Washington Allston and the poet Richard Henry Dana were uncles, and Richard Henry Dana the younger, author of *Two Years Before the Mast*, was a cousin. Sophia's father, however, was a wastrel who early abandoned his young family and went abroad, returning only infrequently, if at all, during Sophia's girlhood. About 1822, her husband still absent, Mrs. Dana with her two daughters opened a school in Cambridge. The venture prospered; young Sophia, who had studied in Boston with a Dr. Parks, was the highly esteemed principal instructress, counting the children of many distinguished Cambridge families among her pupils.

On Aug. 22, 1827, Sophia Dana was married to George Ripley, a graduate of the Harvard Divinity School who was then minister of Boston's Purchase Street Church, a newly formed Unitarian congregation. They had no children. For the first decade of her marriage, while her husband served his pastorate with indifferent success, Mrs. Ripley performed her domestic and social duties in relative obscurity. But George Ripley was one of the band of Unitarian ministers early drawn to Transcendentalism, and his wife fully shared this enthusiasm. The first meeting of the philosophical discussion group which came to be called the Transcendental Club, and which eventually included Ralph Waldo Emerson, Bronson Alcott, Frederic Hedge, MARGARET FULLER, and ELIZABETH PEABODY, was held at the Ripleys' home in 1836. In the early 1840's Sophia Ripley was an earnest participant in Miss Fuller's "Conversations" and an occasional contributor to the Transcendentalist magazine the *Dial*. In "Woman," a January 1841 *Dial* article, she rejected the concept that confined her sex to a single sphere of activity; woman's sphere, no less than man's, she contended, should be determined by unique personal endowments and interests, and her individuality should be highly valued.

Through Transcendentalism the Ripleys were led into the venture for which they are best remembered: the Brook Farm association. For three summers, beginning in 1838, they had vacationed at a 170-acre dairy farm owned by wealthy friends in West Roxbury, Mass., about nine miles south of Boston. Convinced that this was the ideal site for a communal venture through which his Transcendentalist friends and others might renew contact with the soil and experience the joy of cooperative labor, George Ripley early in 1841 secured the farm, and by April some fifteen people, including Nathaniel Hawthorne, were in residence. The Brook Farm Institute of Agriculture and Education was formally organized in September, with Ripley, who had now withdrawn from the ministry, as director and chief shareholder. Sophia Ripley, a charter member of the association, proved one of its most ardent advocates and tireless workers. She managed the laundry room, undertook such taxing duties as the care of a young Manilan leper who came as a student to the Farm, and was instructor in history and modern languages at the Brook Farm school, her reputation as a teacher helping to make this the most reliably profitable of the community's "industries." Though her schedule was demanding, she found the life exhilarating. "[P]leasures multiply, good words & kind deeds abound," she wrote to Margaret Fuller, "—some among us are truly noble, all mean to be good—& the few who are not what we wish are improving . . ." (Riggs, p. 164). She was not uncritical of the venture, however, for in 1843 she expressed to Emerson her concern that many Brook Farmers seemed to be "rejecting the human side of life, turning their back upon the world's work . . ." (*ibid.*, p. 172).

Although plain in appearance, Sophia Ripley was tall and imposing, her manner suggesting both good breeding and hauteur. Nearsighted, she occasionally made use of a "gold-bowed eye-glass." George Ripley had noted before their marriage that his regard was not based upon "any romantic or sudden passion," but upon her "intellectual power, moral worth, . . . piety, and peculiar refinement and dignity of character" (Swift, p. 139). Friends found her lacking in warmth—even Emerson wrote of her "somewhat hard nature" (Curtis, p. 215)—but praised her wit and her fortitude. These qualities stood her in good stead during Brook Farm's later years. The venture was economically unsound from the first, and neither increasing numbers nor the transformation into a Fourierist phalanx in 1845 improved matters. The destruction by fire of the nearly completed Phalanstery building in March 1846 proved the final blow, and in the summer of 1847 the association was formally disbanded.

Burdened by its debts, the Ripleys moved to Flatbush, Long Island, where Mrs. Ripley secured a teaching position while her husband struggled in vain to save the *Harbinger*, the Fourierist periodical he had edited since its founding in 1845. Sometime in the winter of 1848–49 they moved to a lodging house in

Manhattan, where that spring Ripley became literary critic of the *New York Tribune* at a salary of five dollars a week.

Amid these trials and disappointments, Sophia Ripley found solace in religion; shortly after the collapse of Brook Farm she had espoused the Roman Catholic faith. Her conversion has been seen as a significant break with Transcendentalist ideas, but in fact her interest in Catholicism was stimulated by her Transcendentalist associates at Brook Farm, at least four of whom, including her niece Sarah Stearns, eventually became Catholics. Although Orestes Brownson, a recent convert and a friend of George Ripley's, brought his relentless logic to bear on both the Ripleys, Sophia seems to have been swayed more by sensibility than by sense. The Catholic liturgy, "intensely solemn, sweet & elevating," she found deeply satisfying. When in 1849 she and her niece visited the convent Miss Stearns was about to enter, it seemed to them "so like Brook Farm, that the whole was more a revival of some familiar experience than anything new and strange."

In March 1848 Mrs. Ripley underwent a spiritual crisis in which she became convinced that the "deathlike coldness" of her heart and her incapacity for warm human relationships had not changed, her conversion having merely produced a "gratified imagination & not a sanctified heart" (Riggs, p. 199). She surmounted this stumbling block through the fatherly counsel of John Joseph Hughes, bishop of New York, and her devotion to Romanism grew steadily in her later years. She immersed herself in benevolent work and liked to imagine herself as "lady Superior of some religious order." In 1858 she became a trustee of a newly established convent of the Sisters of the Good Shepherd, whose mission was the reformation of prostitutes. Her conversion to Catholicism may have strained her marital ties, but she and her husband lived in domestic peace until her death in New York City in 1861 of cancer, at the age of fifty-seven. After services at Boston's Purchase Street Church, which had been sold to a Catholic parish, she was buried in the Dana tomb in the old Cambridge burying ground by the First Parish Church (Unitarian). George Ripley survived her by nineteen years.

Though her literary contribution to New England Transcendentalism was slight, Sophia Dana Ripley figured largely in its social and personal aspects. Her letters provide a valuable insight into the Brook Farm experiment, as well as a link between Transcendentalism and the sentimental Catholicism to which many "free spirits" of the 1840's were eventually drawn.

[Mrs. Ripley is mentioned in all histories and reminiscences of Brook Farm, of which the most useful are: Lindsay Swift, *Brook Farm* (1900); Edith Roelker Curtis, *A Season in Utopia* (1961); Georgiana Bruce Kirby, *Years of Experience* (1887); and John T. Codman, *Brook Farm* (1894). The chief biographical sources are Octavius B. Frothingham, *George Ripley* (1882), and Lisette Riggs, "George and Sophia Ripley" (unpublished Ph.D. dissertation, Univ. of Md., 1942). See also Jane Maloney Johnson (Benardete), "'Through Change and Through Storm': A Study of Federalist-Unitarian Thought, 1800–1860" (unpublished Ph.D. dissertation, Radcliffe College, 1958), chap. vi. There are references to Sophia Ripley in Caroline Healey Dall, *Margaret and Her Friends* (1895); and in Ralph Waldo Emerson's *Journals* (10 vols., 1909–14; Edward Waldo Emerson and Waldo Emerson Forbes, eds.) and *Letters* (6 vols., 1939; Ralph L. Rusk, ed.)—see indexes. On the Dana family, see John Jay Dana, *Memoranda of Some of the Descendants of Richard Dana* (1865), p. 58; and unpublished data in "Source Material for a Hist. of Fay House" (Radcliffe College Archives, Special Collections). The principal collection of Sophia Ripley's letters is at the Mass. Hist. Soc., Boston.]

JANE JOHNSON BENARDETE

**RITCHIE, Anna Cora Mowatt.** *See* MOWATT, Anna Cora Ogden.

**RITTENHOUSE, Jessie Bell** (Dec. 8, 1869– Sept. 28, 1948), poet, critic, and anthologist, was the fifth of seven children and the third daughter of John E. and Mary J. (MacArthur) Rittenhouse. Her father, a farmer, traced his descent from William Rittenhouse, who came to Philadelphia from the Rhineland in 1688. Her mother's family had emigrated in 1800 from Inverness, Scotland, to Canajoharie, N.Y.; her grandfather moved on to the Genesee Valley and took out a farm near the later town of Mount Morris. Here Jessie was born and spent her early life. Between the ages of seven and thirteen she attended the village school in nearby Conesus. Two years in the Nunda (N.Y.) Academy prepared her to enter the Genesee Wesleyan Seminary in Lima, N.Y., as a sophomore. She graduated in 1890, having excelled in literature and languages, and returned to her family, who were now living in Cheboygan, Mich. During these years she read voraciously and intelligently, developing a taste for English Romantic and Victorian poetry and some knowledge of the literary climate which had produced it. Limited family finances precluded further formal education.

She next taught briefly, at a private school in Cairo, Ill., and at Akeley Institute for Girls, Grand Haven, Mich., and began to try her hand at feature stories for newspapers. While seeking a subject for one of these free-lance articles, she happened in 1894 to meet a cousin of Clinton Scollard, professor of English at Hamilton College and a recognized younger poet of merit. The cousin gave her a book of Scollard's to read, and she conceived the idea of reviewing it for the *Buffalo Express*, which had taken several of her articles. The review caught the attention of Scollard's publishers, Copeland and Day, a young Boston firm specializing in contemporary poetry. Alert to the possibilities of further publicity, they began sending her books by other young poets on their list, including ALICE BROWN, Richard Hovey, and Bliss Carman. Other publishers followed suit. On the strength of these reviews and articles sold to Buffalo and Rochester newspapers Miss Rittenhouse gained a position as a reporter for the *Rochester Democrat and Chronicle*. She was successful as a reporter but felt a lack of time for her literary interests, and in 1895 she returned to free-lance writing, moving to Chicago, where she had relatives. In 1899, deciding to devote herself exclusively to literary criticism, she went to live in Boston, which from the time of her early reviews she had regarded as a literary mecca.

At the turn of the century, the state of American poetry seemed generally bleak. With Frost and Sandburg as yet unknown and Whitman forgotten, most contemporary verse was a clichéd and pallid imitation of the English Romantics and Victorians. There were a few poets, however, mostly in New England, who, although fairly conventional, did represent a genuine strain of unhackneyed minor art. This group had a loose nucleus in the literary salon maintained in Boston by the magnetic LOUISE CHANDLER MOULTON, who knew Tennyson, Browning, and the Pre-Raphaelite group personally and had a talent for attracting the friendship of celebrities and artists on both sides of the Atlantic. Since many of the poets whose work Miss Rittenhouse had reviewed moved in this circle, she had a natural entrée into a rich source of literary interviews. Slowly developing a receptive market for her articles, she also found time to edit two volumes of translations of Omar Khayyám. In 1904, inspired by a similar book which had appeared in England, she published *The Younger American Poets*, a volume of critical essays on contemporary poets. As a self-confessed disciple of Walter Pater, Miss Rittenhouse adopted for this work not only a vestige of his elaborate style but also his approach to criticism, with its emphasis on the feelings which the object of art evoked in the individual rather than on the details of the object itself. The book received laudatory reviews in the *New York Times* and other newspapers and sold well, helped by the novelty both of its subject—contemporary poets—and of its impressionistic style. The work was much discussed, and was widely used by English departments of foreign universities.

Moving to New York City in 1905, Miss Rittenhouse became a regular reviewer for the *New York Times Review of Books,* a post she retained until 1915, when her expansive style had ceased to be acceptable. She played an important role in the founding of the Poetry Society of America in 1910, a group conceived as an elaborate literary salon for the dissemination of ideas and techniques. She was chosen as the first secretary of the society and devoted the next ten years to developing it as a center for poets and their work. In 1914 she embarked on a series of popular lecture tours, which she continued for ten years, finally giving them up as too strenuous.

In 1913 Miss Rittenhouse had published the first of her anthologies of American poetry, *The Little Book of Modern Verse*, which included poems of the 1890's and the first decade of the twentieth century. The anthology was unusual in that it included living writers. It was also the first to group poems not by author or by chronological sequence but rather by an impressionistic arrangement of individual poems in thematic succession. The book was a great success and was followed during the next twenty years by six more anthologies. Miss Rittenhouse's many activities left her little time for creative work of her own. It was not until 1918 that a book of her lyrics appeared, *The Door of Dreams*, followed by *The Lifted Cup* (1921) and *The Secret Bird* (1930). Her lyrics were brief and frank in expression, reminiscent of the work of her close friend SARA TEASDALE. In 1934 she published her memoirs, *My House of Life*. The Poetry Society of America awarded her its bronze medal in 1930 for distinguished service to poetry, and in 1940 she received the gold medal of the National Poetry Center for *The Moving Tide: New and Selected Lyrics* (1939).

In 1924, in Carmel, Calif., she had become the second wife of Clinton Scollard, whose book of verse had launched her on her critical career thirty years earlier. Spending their summers in Kent, Conn., they established a winter residence in Winter Park, Fla., where Miss Rittenhouse gave an annual course in poetry at Rollins College. After Scollard's death in 1932 she moved to Grosse Pointe Park, Mich. She died in Detroit in 1948, at the age of seventy-eight, and was buried in Cheboygan, Mich.

Although from the second decade of the century a new and vital spirit marked a renaissance in American poetry, Miss Rittenhouse's work remained conservative in temper. By the time of the First World War she had already fallen behind the vanguard of poetic developments, and although she recognized the existence of the new spirit, she never actively shared in it. Her achievement was to provide an affirmation of the worth of American poetry during its lowest ebb in popularity, conveying through her personal warmth in lectures, criticism, and other activities an enthusiasm which helped establish new poets and a taste for critical writing about poetry in America.

[Louis Untermeyer, *The New Era in Am. Poetry* (1919); Howard Willard Cook, *Our Poets of Today* (1918); Gustav Davidson, ed., *In Fealty to Apollo* (1950); obituaries in *N.Y. Times*, Sept. 30, 1948, *Detroit News*, Sept. 29, 1948, *Saturday Rev. of Literature*, Oct. 30, 1948, and *Fla. Mag. of Verse*, Nov. 1948. Miss Rittenhouse left her extensive library and voluminous correspondence to Rollins College.]

GRACE STUART NUTLEY

RIVÉ-KING, Julie (Oct. 30, 1854–July 24, 1937), pianist, was born in the College Hill section of Cincinnati, Ohio. Her father, Leon Rivé, was a well-known French painter; her mother, Caroline (Staub) Rivé, born in France of German descent, was an excellent soprano singer and teacher who had been at the Paris Conservatory at the same time as Jenny Lind. Emigrating from France to New Orleans, the couple lost three children in a cholera epidemic; they later moved to Baton Rouge, La., then to Louisville, Ky., and finally to Cincinnati about 1854. Julie, as a girl of five, was taken to hear the famous pianist and composer Louis Moreau Gottschalk and amazed her parents afterward by picking out at the piano the melodies she had heard. Her mother was her first teacher, and later Henry Andres took her as a pupil. At age eight, or perhaps even earlier, she played Sigismond Thalberg's transcription of themes from *Don Juan* at one of her mother's concerts. Her mother took her to New York in 1866, where she studied under William Mason and Sebastian Bach Mills.

By 1872 she was judged ready for European training. Her teachers abroad were Karl Reinecke in Leipzig, Adolf J. M. Blassmann and Wilhelm Albert Rischpieter in Dresden,

and Franz Liszt in Weimar. She made her European debut in 1874 at one of the concerts of the popular Euterpe Musical Association of Leipzig, with Karl Reinecke conducting. She played Beethoven's Third Concerto and Liszt's Second Rhapsody, arousing great enthusiasm. A European tour was arranged, but the death of her father in a railroad accident caused her to return home. Her first notable American appearance was with the New York Philharmonic Society on Apr. 24, 1875, when she played Liszt's Concerto in E flat and Schumann's "Faschingsschwank aus Wien." She appeared under the same auspices on Feb. 19 of the following year, playing Beethoven's Fifth Concerto and Chopin's "Rondo," Op. 16. In an era of sharp rivalry among piano manufacturers, who often sponsored artists who performed on their instruments, Miss Rivé gave concerts at the Philadelphia Centennial Exposition of 1876 on the Decker piano. That same year, apparently, she was married to the head of the wholesale business of the Decker firm, Frank H. King, who had been managing her concerts. Much of her early success, it is said, was owing to King's able publicity, which overcame the difficulties of "piano politics and the indifference of journalists" (W. S. B. Mathews in *Music*, March 1900, p. 521).

In the years following, Mme. Rivé-King toured extensively in the United States and Canada, her appearances totaling over four thousand, some five hundred of which were with orchestra. In the 1890's she was soloist in over two hundred concerts conducted by Theodore Thomas and eighty conducted by Anton Seidl. She appeared with the Boston Symphony Orchestra in 1886, 1891, and 1892, and with it on the second occasion gave the first American performance of Paderewski's Concerto in A minor, the *Boston Journal* praising her "very thoughtful and brilliant interpretation."

At the height of her concert career the Chicago pianist and teacher W. S. B. Mathews, writing in the magazine *Music*, of which he was editor, declared that Mme. Rivé-King had established "a new standard of concert playing" in the United States. He felt that in the "variety, length, and difficulty" of her programs, as well as in performance, she was carrying on the tradition of Rubinstein and von Bülow. With an immense repertoire of five hundred compositions, she could command both the virtuoso technique demanded by Liszt and other Romantic composers and the precision and control necessary in Bach and Beethoven. Mathews believed that like Theodore Thomas in his orchestral programs, she had done much to educate American taste, introducing many new works to her audiences. She performed the works of American composers, including William Mason, at a time when some courage was required to do so. Her own compositions, including "Impromptu," "Bubbling Spring," "On Blooming Meadow," and "Polonaise Héroïque," found a place on her programs. She also made transcriptions of works by Scarlatti and Liszt.

Mme. Rivé-King was blond and of medium height. Although nothing is known of her private life, contemporaries remarked on her interesting and unaffected personality, and she won many friends, among them Anton Rubinstein, the poet Longfellow, and President Rutherford B. Hayes and his wife, LUCY WEBB HAYES, who had been a pupil of her mother's. After the death of her husband, in 1900, she made her home in Chicago. She continued to tour, and as late as 1929 she appeared in a successful recital in Chicago, but the later years of her life saw a marked decrease in the number of her performances. It was hinted that she was out of favor because she was restricted to the use of a piano not highly regarded by orchestral conductors. From 1905 through 1936 she taught piano at the Bush Conservatory of Music and its successor, the Chicago Conservatory. She followed Liszt's rather informal method of giving class lessons. Her opinions on pedagogy and performance were expressed in magazine articles, in which she balanced an appreciation of the traditional repertoire with acceptance of newer works and her awareness of the importance of knowledge and training with a sense of the performer's individuality. She continued to teach until a few months before her death. In 1937, at eighty-two, she died of cancer and arteriosclerosis in a nursing home in Indianapolis, where she had been taken by a cousin who lived in that city. Her ashes were buried in her husband's grave in Cincinnati.

[F. O. Jones, ed., *A Handbook of Am. Music and Musicians* (1886), pp. 145–47; William S. B. Mathews, *A Hundred Years of Music in America* (1889), pp. 115–16, 122–23, 126, 142, 532, 664; Arthur Loesser, *Men, Women and Pianos* (1954), p. 534; *Am. Art Jour.*, Feb. 13, 1886, p. 1; *Musical America*, June 13, 1908, p. 13; *Musician*, Mar. 1911 (p. 160), Dec. 1913, July 1914 (on her teaching); obituaries in *N.Y. Times*, July 25, 1937, *Cincinnati Enquirer*, July 29, 1937, and *Musical America*, Aug. 1937. Other clippings are in the Music Division, N.Y. Public Library at Lincoln Center. Mme. Rivé-King's death certificate (Ind. State Board of Health) is the source for her birth date.]

ARLAN R. COOLIDGE

**RIVERS, Pearl.** *See* NICHOLSON, Eliza Jane Poitevent Holbrook.

**RIVES, Amélie Louise** (Aug. 23, 1863–June 15, 1945), author, the oldest of three daughters of Sarah (MacMurdo) and Alfred Landon Rives, was born at Richmond, Va., into a family long distinguished in the history of the state. A maternal great-grandfather, Richard Channing Moore, had come from New York to Virginia upon his election as Protestant Episcopal bishop in 1814. On her father's side she was descended from Col. William Cabell and Dr. Thomas Walker, prominent figures of the Revolutionary period. Her grandfather William Cabell Rives, a Jacksonian Democrat later turned Whig who served as minister to France and as United States Senator, opposed secession but ultimately went with the Confederacy; before his death in 1868 he had completed a three-volume *History of the Life and Times of James Madison*. Amélie Rives spent her early years at Castle Hill, a family estate near Cobham in Albemarle County, Va., inherited by her grandmother Judith Page (Walker) Rives, herself the author of several published books. When Amélie was seven, her father, who had been acting chief of engineers for the Confederacy, left a private practice in Richmond for Mobile, Ala., to become head civil engineer of the Mobile and Birmingham Railroad; he subsequently had charge of the construction of several Southern railroad lines. Though Amélie lived in Mobile until adolescence, the family returned every summer to Castle Hill, which she always considered her home.

The girl had all the advantages which wealth and social position could offer. Her education was entrusted to governesses and tutors. A highly imaginative child, she early displayed a partiality for literature and delighted in composing her own stories; if she found no copybook at hand, she wrote on her starched white petticoats. She developed, too, an early love of the outdoors and of animals. Although she later excelled as a horsewoman, she refused to ride to hounds, believing that the sport inflicted excessive suffering on the fox.

From a pretty, precocious child, Amélie Rives matured into a fascinating woman. Tall, with golden hair, classical features, and deep violet eyes, she captivated everyone by her beauty and clever conversation. Yet she disliked society generally, for she never really outgrew a youthful diffidence. She was, furthermore, determined to have a literary career. In March 1886 the *Atlantic Monthly* published

her first story, "A Brother to Dragons," and
soon her stories and poems began to appear
in the *Century, Harper's,* and *Lippincott's.* Her
real success came with the publication in 1888
of her novel *The Quick or the Dead?* which
created a sensation and enjoyed an enormous
sale. Many critics denounced her treatment of
a young widow's tempestuous romance as too
realistic and overstepping the bounds of good
taste.

During her first season at Newport she met
John Armstrong Chanler of New York and Virginia, a lawyer and great-grandson of John
Jacob Astor. They were married at Castle Hill
on June 14, 1888; after their wedding they
divided their time between Europe and Virginia. In England, Amélie Rives found that
the combination of her literary ability, her
charm, and her horsemanship won her a place
in "The Souls," a brilliant coterie with great
political and social influence led by Margot
Asquith, Arthur Balfour, and George Lord
Curzon. But she soon discovered that she had
made a mistake in her marriage, for she and
Chanler shared few interests. They agreed to
separate, and in 1895 she divorced him on
grounds of incompatibility. On Feb. 18, 1896,
at Castle Hill, she was married to a London
acquaintance, Prince Pierre Troubetzkoy, internationally renowned portrait painter and
son of a Russian nobleman who had married
an American. In her happy second marriage,
Amélie Rives traveled extensively, frequenting
circles of the artistic and social elite on both
sides of the Atlantic, though she and her husband returned regularly to Castle Hill. She
had no children by either husband.

At the turn of the century an extended illness threatened to wreck her marriage and end
her career. When she suffered a severe attack
of rheumatic fever in 1898, her doctors prescribed large quantities of morphine to relieve
the pain, and after a long convalescence she
found herself a drug addict. She attempted at
first to disguise the fact, but, realizing that she
was only destroying herself, she resolved to
overcome it. With newspaper headlines in
1901 reporting her impending death, she withdrew to Castle Hill to undergo the cure. By
1902 she had regained her health. This ordeal
provided a theme for perhaps her best novel,
*Shadows of Flames* (1915), one of the first
realistic accounts of drug addiction in American literature.

During the quarter century following her
illness, Amélie Rives continued a successful
literary career. Her novels received critical
and popular acclaim. She experimented, too,
with writing for the theatre, and several of

her plays appeared on Broadway. Her husband's death, in August 1936, left her incon-
solable, and she retired to Castle Hill, where
she lived quietly until poor health forced her
to enter a nursing home at nearby Charlottesville, Va. She died there of heart disease and
was buried next to her husband in the family
plot at Castle Hill.

Although a nominal Virginia background,
almost invariably a shadowy replica of Castle
Hill, figured in much of Amélie Rives' fiction,
she was not a Southern writer in the richer
social sense of her friend ELLEN GLASGOW. Miss
Glasgow herself counted her, in an article in
*Harper's* in December 1928, among those
writers making up a Southern literary renaissance; and in 1931 Amélie Rives participated
in a Conference of Southern Writers held in
Charlottesville at Ellen Glasgow's instigation.
She had previously championed and contributed to Emily Clark's little magazine, the
*Reviewer,* during its short life in Richmond in
the early 1920's. Among her distant Virginia
cousins were such well-known Southern literary figures as Thomas Nelson Page and James
Branch Cabell, as well as a popular novelist
of more ephemeral reputation, Hallie Erminie
Rives. Amélie Rives' literary affinities, however, were more European than American,
more cosmopolitan than local; in her life and
her writing she was, as one acquaintance remarked, "innocent of community spirit." Yet
while she held aloof for the most part from
the active life of Virginia, she took a deep
interest in the movements headed by LILA
MEADE VALENTINE to promote educational reform and woman suffrage in the state.

Because of her beauty, her eccentricities,
and her international fame, Amélie Rives
Troubetzkoy became something of a popular
legend in her day. She has since been almost
forgotten as a novelist; yet her work has historical significance. One of the first American
authors to be influenced by the advances made
in psychiatry during the late nineteenth and
early twentieth centuries, she gives in her best
novels, such as *Shadows of Flames* and *Fire-
damp* (1930), a vivid account of the psycho-
pathic personality and reveals her keen awareness of mental illness.

[The largest collection of letters of Amélie Rives
is in the Alderman Library at the Univ. of Va.
Emily Clark's *Innocence Abroad* (1931) contains
an excellent personality sketch of her. J. D. Hur-
rell, "Some Days with Amélie Rives," *Lippincott's
Monthly Mag.,* Apr. 1888, and Edgar Fawcett,
"A Few More Words about Miss Rives," *ibid.,*
Sept. 1888, give good impressions of her as an
individual and as an author. See also James Rives

Childs, *Reliques of the Rives* (*Ryves*) (1929); Alexander Brown, *The Cabells and Their Kin* (1939 edition); Frederick P. W. McDowell, *Ellen Glasgow and the Ironic Art of Fiction* (1960), pp. 33–34; obituary in *N.Y. Times*, June 17, 1945; and, on Amélie Rives' father, Paul B. Barringer et al., eds., *Univ. of Va.* (1904), I, 382–83. A biographical source outline compiled by Virginia Jones, Emory Univ. Division of Librarianship, was helpful.]

LLOYD C. TAYLOR, JR.

**ROBB, Isabel Adams Hampton** (1860–Apr. 15, 1910), professional nurse, was born in Welland, Ontario, Canada, the second daughter and fourth of seven children of Samuel James Hampton and Sarah Mary (Lay) Hampton. Her parents were Scottish-born, of Irish and Cornish ancestry. Her father earned a comfortable living running a tailor shop. Her mother efficiently managed the household, bringing up her children with Spartan simplicity and stern discipline. After preparatory schooling in Welland, Isabel attended the Collegiate Institute in nearby St. Catharines and there received a teaching certificate. While teaching in the neighboring town of Merritton, she learned of the recently established Bellevue Hospital Training School for Nurses in New York City—the first school to introduce Florence Nightingale's principles of nursing education into the United States—and impulsively sent in an application.

After graduating from the two-year course in 1883, Miss Hampton joined a group of Bellevue nurses at St. Paul's House in Rome, where nursing care was provided for English and American travelers. Her two years there enabled her to travel in Europe and led her to give up her earlier Presbyterianism for the Church of England. In July 1886—still only twenty-six—she was hired by the Illinois Training School for Nurses at Cook County Hospital in Chicago as superintendent of nurses. A tall, strikingly handsome girl, in glowing good health, she combined, then as later, youthful charm and a remote yet dignified poise. She had, moreover, a natural gift for leadership. Her strong creative imagination clearly grasped the needs of the evolving nursing profession, and her compelling personality— backed when needed by a scrupulous insistence on her sphere of authority—helped her carry out her plans. Drawing upon her experience at Bellevue, during her three years at the Illinois school she began her campaign to raise the educational standards of nursing schools by introducing a systematic course of study, the first graded course for nurses in this country.

Meanwhile plans were taking shape for the new Johns Hopkins Hospital in Baltimore, which was to include a nurses' training school. In 1889, as the hospital prepared to open its doors, the trustees selected Miss Hampton as superintendent of nurses and principal of the school. Taking up her new duties that September, she set high standards for both the practical and the theoretical parts of the training program, emphasizing that the school's primary purpose was to educate nurses rather than to staff the hospital. She thus prepared the way for the accomplishment of three major objectives (although none was achieved during her superintendency): a three-year rather than two-year training program, an eight-hour working day, and the abolition of cash allowances to student nurses, which both enlarged the budget for education and enhanced the school's professional status.

In this period Miss Hampton's sphere of influence also extended beyond Johns Hopkins. Concerned with the lack of uniformity in content and length of course among the programs offered by the many hospital training schools, she began as early as 1891 to work for an organization of nurses which would establish national standards. She was given the opportunity to present this idea to a large audience as chairman of the subsection on nursing at the International Congress of Charities, Correction, and Philanthropy held in Chicago in 1893 during the World's Columbian Exposition. A direct result was the organization the next year, under her leadership, of the American Society of Superintendents of Training Schools for Nurses of the United States and Canada (after 1912 the National League of Nursing Education) for the purpose of establishing and maintaining a uniform standard of training.

In June 1894 Miss Hampton resigned her position at the Johns Hopkins Hospital to marry Dr. Hunter Robb, an associate in gynecology there. After their wedding in London on July 11, they settled in Cleveland, Ohio, where Dr. Robb had been appointed professor of gynecology at Western Reserve University. They had two sons, Hampton and Philip Hunter. While devoting herself to her responsibilities as a wife and mother, Mrs. Robb continued to work for the improvement of nursing through professional organizations. In 1897 she was the major impetus in the founding of the Nurses' Associated Alumnae of the United States and Canada (after 1911 the American Nurses' Association), which worked to secure legal standards of nursing in all states; she served as its first president (1897–

1901). With her successor at Johns Hopkins, M. ADELAIDE NUTTING, she took the first steps toward starting a course in hospital economics at Columbia University's Teachers College. She also found time to continue to write, completing after her marriage the second of her two textbooks: *Nursing: Its Principles and Practice* (1893) and *Nursing Ethics* (1900). In 1908 she was elected president of the Society of Superintendents; the next year she addressed the International Council of Nurses in London on the subject of an international standard of nursing education.

Her dynamic career ended abruptly at the age of fifty. While crossing a street in Cleveland to meet her son Hampton at dancing school, Mrs. Robb was crushed between two streetcars and killed instantly. She was buried in her husband's hometown of Burlington, N.J.

[Ethel Johns and Blanche Pfefferkorn, *The Johns Hopkins Hospital School of Nursing, 1889–1949* (1954); Grace Fay Schryver, *A Hist. of the Ill. Training School for Nurses, 1880–1929* (1930); memorial sketches in *Am. Jour. of Nursing,* Oct. 1910. See also John S. Billings, *The Plans and Purposes of the Johns Hopkins Hospital* (1889); Mary M. Roberts, *Am. Nursing: Hist. and Interpretation* (1954). The historical collections at the Johns Hopkins School of Nursing, Baltimore, include unpublished reports by Miss Hampton as principal, a collection of her letters to Elizabeth Birdseye (1886–1909), and student class notes of Miss Hampton's lectures and examination papers. Her paper and others given at the Internat. Cong. of Charities, Correction, and Philanthropy are reprinted in *Nursing of the Sick, 1893* (1949). Family data from Mrs. Robb's niece, Mrs. E. S. Gardiner.]

MARY JANE RODABAUGH

ROBBINS, Jane Elizabeth (Dec. 28, 1860–Aug. 16, 1946), social worker and physician, was born in Wethersfield, Conn., the first daughter and third of the five children of Richard Austin Robbins and Harriet (Welles) Robbins. Both parents were Wethersfield natives of colonial English descent. The father was a prosperous seed merchant who served the local Congregational church as deacon and Sunday school superintendent. He was elected to the state legislature in 1875.

Jane Robbins attended Smith College for only one year (1879–80), but retained a lifelong loyalty to her college class. After five years as a teacher in New Jersey and Kentucky she went to New York City in 1887 with the intention of becoming a physician and with the "vague idea of being some help to the poor." She enrolled in the Woman's Medical College of the New York Infirmary, meanwhile supplementing her medical studies with volunteer social service. Beginning with a Sunday school class at the Five Points Methodist Mission, she soon joined with Jean Fine (Mrs. Charles B. Spahr), a Smith College friend, in organizing a children's sewing club at the Neighborhood Guild on Forsyth Street (later the University Settlement)—America's pioneer social settlement, established in 1886 by Stanton Coit. Dissatisfied, however, with her biweekly visits to the Guild, Miss Robbins moved into a Forsyth Street tenement in the fall of 1888. The following year she helped organize the New York College Settlement on Rivington Street and became one of the first residents. Thus Miss Robbins not only helped plant the social settlement in America but proved that middle-class women could safely reside in slum districts with profit to themselves and their neighbors. The College Settlement she viewed as "simply several young women" sharing their advantages with the immigrant poor in an effort to approximate a "more Christ-like life."

Following her graduation from medical school in 1890 and a year's internship at the New York Infirmary, Dr. Robbins took up medical practice around Mulberry Street, the nucleus of the city's congested but colorful Italian colony. In 1894 she became head worker at the College Settlement. As a physician she had unusual advantages in gaining the confidence and learning the needs of the immigrant population. Her infectious gaiety and optimism, blended with common sense and an unobtrusive dignity, also invited quick personal rapport. She had not originally expected to participate in public affairs. Like many another settlement worker, however, she found that she could not ignore a social environment in which poverty, substandard housing, and lack of educational opportunity seemed to defy every effort to strengthen family ties, nurture health, and transmit American values to immigrants and their children. Thus under her leadership the College Settlement became a vigorous exponent of neighborhood and local reform in the 1890's. In 1894 it sponsored a meeting to assist striking tenement garment makers in wresting a ten-hour day and a minimum weekly wage from subcontractors and manufacturers; and in the same year Settlement residents testified on behalf of working girls before a state investigating committee. Dr. Robbins, a close personal friend of Jacob Riis, appeared before the New York State Tenement House Committee of 1894 to advocate public parks, playgrounds, and baths as well as more effective enforcement of the tenement-house laws. She consistently urged more and better public schools to promote Americanization. While head worker she was officially connected with the public school system as an inspector, and she eventually became a champion of progressive education in the form of an expanded curriculum which considered each child's special needs and talents; she also called for the wider use of the school plant as a neighborhood civic center.

Particularly fond of the Italians, whose language she learned, Dr. Robbins believed that every immigrant group possessed a "rich variety of gifts" which could contribute to the creation of a unique "Anglo-Celtic-Latin-Slavic country." Everything depended, however, upon a constructive assimilation, or the development of a social atmosphere which protected the immigrant from a "cheap Americanism" while stimulating his most desirable personal and ethnic traits. For this reason Dr. Robbins protested against the corrupting influence of the political machine. She realized that the party boss performed important services for the immigrant, but she also insisted that the politics of "fix" which he personified created a distorted image of the American courts and legal system and the responsibilities of citizenship.

Jane Robbins left her position at the College Settlement in 1897 and resumed medical practice for a time. In the three decades following 1898 she moved from one place to another making friends, adopting causes, placing her medical training at the service of those in need. One finds her nursing typhoid patients at Chickamauga Park, Ga., during the Spanish-American War, and then appearing as head worker at Normal College Alumnae House in New York in 1901, at Alta House in Cleveland in 1902, at Little Italy Settlement in Brooklyn in 1911, at Manhattan's Jacob A. Riis Neighborhood Settlement in 1914. In addition she served from 1905 to 1911 as executive secretary of the influential Public Education Association in New York. The Red Cross sent her to Italy during World War I, and after the war she helped organize temporary hospitals in Greece as a member of the Medical Women's International Association. Returning to the United States, she traversed the West in the 1920's, helping out settlements in Cleveland (Alta House, East End Neighborhood House, Goodrich Social Settlement), Minneapolis (Margaret Barry House), and Denver (Neighborhood House). She found time to attend conventions of the Medical Women's International Association at Prague,

Bologna, and Paris and in 1927 returned to Greece for two years to aid refugees of the uprising against Turkey. Dr. Robbins' pace slowed down in the 1930's, when she reached her seventies, but she retained a lively interest in settlement and women's medical affairs. She died of arteriosclerosis in Hartford, Conn., and was buried in Cedar Hill Cemetery, Hartford. She was a Congregationalist.

Jane Robbins' overarching concern with the immigrant problem and her view of the settlement as an instrument of social investigation and reform as well as a humble gathering place for neighbors mark her as a representative settlement leader of the late nineteenth and early twentieth centuries, though her acquisition of a medical degree sets her in a special category. She embodied the memorable qualities of the early settlement movement: its fervor and dedication tempered by knowledge and understanding, its pragmatic experimentalism, and its naive faith and optimism expressed in the quest for human brotherhood.

[The *Reports* of the College Settlements Assoc., 1893–97, contain a full account of the activities of the N.Y. College Settlement while Dr. Robbins was head worker. See also her article "The First Year at the College Settlement," *Survey*, Feb. 24, 1912. The following articles by Dr. Robbins are useful for her views on the immigrant: "The Bohemian Women in N.Y.," *Charities*, Dec. 3, 1904; "Italian To-day, American To-morrow," *Outlook*, June 10, 1905; "The Foreign-Born American," *ibid.*, Aug. 18, 1906. She outlines her conception of the public school's responsibilities in "The Settlement and the Public School," *ibid.*, Aug. 6, 1910; and "The New School-Boy," *ibid.*, Aug. 17, 1912. She deals with politics in "Bureaucratic and Political Influences in Neighborhood Civic Problems," Nat. Conference of Social Work, *Proc.*, 1925, pp. 391–95. The striking similarities in personality and objectives between Dr. Robbins and Jacob Riis are suggested in her article "A Maker of Americans," *Survey*, June 6, 1914. The "Alumnae Biog. Register Issue" of the *Bull.* of Smith College (Nov. 1935) is useful for biographical data, and a detailed history of the Robbins family is contained in Henry R. Stiles, *The Hist. of Ancient Wethersfield, Conn.* (1904), vol. II. Obituaries appeared in the *N.Y. Times* and *Hartford Times* on Aug. 17, 1946, and in the *Smith Alumnae Quart.*, Nov. 1946. Informal reminiscences by Dr. Robbins appeared in *Outlook*, Oct. 4, 1902, and *Hartford Times*, Oct. 5, 1934. Elisabeth C. Day and Ruth Weber of the Nat. Federation of Settlement and Neighborhood Centers brought some letters and other unpublished material by and about Dr. Robbins to the author's attention, and Frances Copeland of the Smith College Alumnae Assoc. supplied useful biographical data. John C. Willard of Wethersfield, Conn., related his impressions of Dr. Robbins and her family, and Richard W. Robbins, a nephew, was most helpful on matters pertaining to her career, family background, and personality. The date of birth is drawn from the Stiles *Hist.* and information supplied by the Wethersfield Town Clerk.]

ROY LUBOVE

ROBERTS, Elizabeth Madox (Oct. 30, 1881– Mar. 13, 1941), poet and novelist, was born in Perryville, Ky., but grew up in the nearby village of Springfield, her home for the rest of her life. She was the second of eight children of Simpson and Mary Elizabeth (Brent) Roberts, both of pioneer stock. Her father, who kept a grocery store and also worked as a surveyor and civil engineer, enjoyed gathering his children around him after supper to tell them stories from Greek and Roman mythology and tales of the early days in Kentucky. But it was their maternal grandmother who carried the racial memory. Elizabeth was fascinated by her stories of Harrod's Fort and the Wilderness Trace. After early schooling in "Professor" Grant's academy, Miss Roberts attended high school in Covington, Ky., graduating in 1900. She was admitted to the State College (now the University) of Kentucky, but though she longed for a college education, she did not matriculate, possibly because of poor health, possibly for want of money. Not until 1917, when she was thirty-five, was she able at last to fulfill her ambition by attending the University of Chicago.

As things turned out, the years between were fruitful for one who was to become a poet and novelist. From 1900 to 1910 Miss Roberts taught school, at first in Springfield, Ky., later in two villages nearby. Her knowledge of the folkways of her region was greatly increased by the experience. In 1910 she went to stay with relatives in Colorado. While there she contributed seven poems to a little book of photographs of mountain flowers, *In the Great Steep's Garden* (privately printed, 1915), her first published work. About 1912 a sister and a brother entered the University of Kentucky; visiting them frequently, she renewed a childhood acquaintance with Prof. James T. Cotton Noe of the school of education, who read her poetry with interest and wrote to Prof. Robert Morss Lovett of the University of Chicago about her. Lovett encouraged her to enroll there. Making up for lost time by avid study of literature and philosophy, she graduated (Ph.B., 1921) with Phi Beta Kappa honors, but she was also known on campus as a writer with professional ambitions. At the end of her course she was awarded the Fiske Prize for a group of poems

which were soon published (1922) by B. W. Huebsch with the title *Under the Tree.* She made many friends at the university, several of whom also became well-known writers. Her first novel, *The Time of Man,* begun in 1922, was published by the Viking Press in 1926, and the discerning saw that a very fine talent had arrived.

Miss Roberts' novels, it should be noted, cannot be adequately summarized, for her methods are oblique, symbolic, poetic. The uniqueness of her art does not lie in the action but in the interior response of those—usually women—who are acted upon. Though she describes scenes from nature and the activities of farm and village life with great beauty of detail, she is not a realist; she stands nearest to such innovators in fiction as Henry James and Virginia Woolf. A passage in her notes defines the end she had constantly in view. "Somewhere there is a connection between the world of the mind and the outer order. It is the secret of the contact that we are after, the point, the moment of union." This "connection" is sustained throughout *The Time of Man.* The story is "about" Ellen Chesser, the daughter of a tenant farmer always on the move. The early chapters are filled with Ellen's reaching toward life and her anguish over the family's poverty. Later, having married, she is on the verge of prosperity when accusations of barnburning against her husband force them to move. At the end Ellen is still in search of "some better country." The perpetual sadness of youth has seldom been so movingly evoked.

Much more somber in tone, *My Heart and My Flesh* (1927) makes fictional use of old Springfield scandals and local persons. Theodosia Bell's well-born family sinks to utter degradation. The most important action revolves around her discovery that two mulattoes living in the village are her half sisters, but her efforts to establish some kind of relationship with them end in disaster. After nearly losing her mind from illness and despair, Theodosia is rescued by Caleb Burns, an earthbound man. There is a suggestion here of the theme of rebirth, which would appear in later novels. The third novel, *Jingling in the Wind* (1928), is a new departure. It is comedy, fantasy, satire, all in one, with some interspersed stories, told by modern pilgrims on a bus journey. Though most critics have viewed this novel as a mere jeu d'esprit, it should not be taken lightly, for in it Miss Roberts has her say about the follies of her time.

Her next book, *The Great Meadow* (1930), is a historical novel about the settling of middle Kentucky. Diony Hall, living on a farm in western Virginia in the 1770's, listens to news of the rich cane lands beyond the mountains. When a suitor comes, Berk Jarvis, who is determined to settle there, she accepts him. After their hard journey to the Cumberland Gap and along the Wilderness Trace, they join other arrivals at Harrod's Fort. When Berk's mother is scalped by Indians, he goes in search of revenge. Convinced by the women of the fort that he is dead, Diony marries again. When Berk returns, it is for her to choose, in accordance with frontier custom, which husband she will have; she chooses Berk. In this novel there is a happy conjunction of the author's intentions and skills. She knew the region and its history intimately. Its folk speech, which she could reproduce so well, was close to the speech of the pioneers. Diony, ardent, imaginative, able to endure, is the archetypal heroine of her fiction (Miss Roberts herself). In consequence there is nothing stagey in the novel. It stands as one of the few great historical novels America has produced.

From a brief news item in the local paper Miss Roberts constructed in 1931 a delightful prose idyl, *A Buried Treasure,* about a farm couple who discover in a stump a kettle filled with old coins. This is the gayest of her novels, a poetization of folk life achieved without condescension or affected simplicity. The next novel, *He Sent Forth a Raven* (1935), is her most baffling work, possibly because there seems to be little connection between the fragmentary plot and the arguments-in-dialogue of some of the characters, who are clearly meant to stand for different attitudes toward life's mysteries.

In the mid-1930's Miss Roberts' pace slackened, chiefly because of ill health. She had long suffered from general debility; in 1936 a specialist diagnosed her illness as Hodgkin's disease. The blow struck when many kinds of public recognition were coming her way, among them *Poetry's* John Reed Memorial Prize in 1928, the O. Henry short story award in 1930, and the Poetry Society of South Carolina's prize in 1931. In 1937 she began spending the winters in Florida, working as she could until the end.

Her last novel, *Black Is My Truelove's Hair* (1938), though written after she had knowledge of her doom, is filled with the serenity of her best work, along with allegorical overtones. The theme is again rebirth, this time of Dena Janes, who has been deserted by her truckdriver lover. She returns to her village, where her crotchety sister Fronia takes her in, and Cam Elliot, the miller's son, restores her to

life. Miss Roberts collected her short stories in two volumes, *The Haunted Mirror* (1932) and *Not by Strange Gods* (1941). Almost every one is a masterpiece. She also continued to write poetry. Though there are traces of Gerard Manley Hopkins and EMILY DICKINSON in *Song in the Meadow* (1940), she had found her own idiom.

Miss Roberts was shy with strangers and somewhat austere toward her fellow townsmen. When she became famous, she insisted on keeping her private life to herself. Her faith was a stoicism that was partly Christian, in part grounded in the idealism of Bishop Berkeley. Her death came in Orlando, Fla., in 1941. She was buried in the Springfield, Ky., cemetery. Among America's many regional novelists, the best have been women: SARAH ORNE JEWETT, WILLA CATHER, and Elizabeth Madox Roberts.

[There have been three book-length studies of Miss Roberts: Harry M. Campbell and Ruel E. Foster, *Elizabeth Madox Roberts: Am. Novelist* (1956); Earl H. Rovit, *Herald to Chaos: The Novels of Elizabeth Madox Roberts* (1960); and Frederick P. W. McDowell, *Elizabeth Madox Roberts* (1963). See also Woodbridge Spears, "Elizabeth Madox Roberts: A Biog. and Critical Study" (unpublished doctoral dissertation, Univ. of Ky., 1953). Miss Roberts' papers are in the Library of Congress; for a description, see Allen Tate in the library's *Quart. Jour. of Current Acquisitions,* Oct.–Dec. 1943. Other references: Alexander M. Buchan in *Southwest Rev.,* July 1940; F. Lamar Janney in *Sewanee Rev.,* Oct.–Dec. 1937; Mark Van Doren, *The Private Reader* (1942), pp. 97–109; Glenway Wescott in *Bookman,* Mar. 1930; information from a brother, Ivor Roberts.]

WILLARD THORP

**ROBERTSON, Agnes Kelly** (Dec. 25, 1833–Nov. 6, 1916), actress, wife of the playwright Dion Boucicault, was born in Edinburgh, Scotland, the daughter of Thomas Robertson, said to have been a bookseller or art publisher. Nothing else is known of her background or early years except that she was apparently intended for the concert stage. At ten she is supposed to have made her first appearance on the dramatic stage of the Theatre Royal, Aberdeen. Subsequently, it is said, she appeared in Glasgow, Liverpool, Hull, and Manchester, where she may have acted with FANNY KEMBLE and William Charles Macready. At the age of sixteen, in 1850, she appeared at the Princess's Theatre, London, newly under the management of Charles Kean, who with his wife, according to some reports, became her guardian. Here, over the next three years, she acted in several plays, notably *The Vampire* and *The Prima Donna* by Kean's assistant, the rising young Irish dramatist Dionysius Lardner (Dion) Boucicault.

In August 1853 she left for America, Boucicault following a few weeks later. Miss Robertson appeared first at Montreal, Canada, in September and then made her New York debut on Oct. 22 at Burton's Theatre, playing six characters in a Boucicault-adapted musical farce, *The Young Actress*. She was immediately successful and soon became one of America's most popular actresses. It was generally understood that shortly before or after her departure from England she had become Boucicault's second wife. She bore him six children: Dion William, Eva (or Eve), Darley George ("Dot"), who later became known as Dion, Jr., Patrice, Nina, and Aubrey Robertson. Aubrey became an actor and also a dramatic author. Dion, Jr., was a most successful actor, manager, and stage director, who created roles in several of A. A. Milne's plays and himself wrote a few stage adaptations. Nina's long dramatic career, which included the creation of J. M. Barrie's Peter Pan and acting in motion pictures, was also distinguished.

From 1853 to 1860 Miss Robertson played in various cities throughout the United States with unvarying popularity, usually in plays written by her husband to exploit her peculiar charm. Her tiny, *gentil* appearance soon earned her the sobriquet of "the fairy star" (in England she had been known as "the Pocket Venus"). She created the title roles in Boucicault's *Jessie Brown, or The Relief of Lucknow* (1858), *Dot* and *Smike* (1859), and *Jeanie Deans* (*The Heart of Midlothian*) (1860), as well as the leading roles of Zoe in *The Octoroon* (1859) and Eily O'Connor in *The Colleen Bawn* (1860). Jessie, the Scotch servant maid, and Eily are the two characterizations for which she was long remembered. The Boucicaults spent the next twelve years in England, where Miss Robertson continued to act in many plays old and new, among the latter being her husband's *Arrah-na-Pogue* (1865) and *The Long Strike* (1866). On a return visit to America in 1872–73 she repeated many of her favorite roles. Thereafter, although Boucicault was often in the United States, Miss Robertson acted principally in London, with only an occasional engagement in New York.

In the 1870's and early '80's Boucicault apparently proved often unfaithful, and his wife once started a divorce action which she discontinued in 1883. In 1885 he left for an Australian tour with Nina, Dion, Jr., and Louise Thorndyke, a young lady with whom he

had acted for several years. That fall, claiming that he had never legally been married to Agnes Robertson, he married Miss Thorndyke in Sydney. His erstwhile wife sued for divorce, at first in New York, where the suit dragged along under a referee, and finally in London, where she was awarded a decree and costs on June 21, 1888, the action becoming final on Jan. 15, 1889. As might be expected, his proclaiming his six children illegitimate turned the public against him and incurred additional sympathy and esteem for Miss Robertson.

On Nov. 25, 1890, two months after Boucicault's death, a benefit under the patronage of leading actors and citizens was tendered her at the Fifth Avenue Theatre, New York, and netted $2,125. She brought her long career as an actress to a close at the Princess's Theatre in London in 1896, though she lived another twenty years. She died in London and was buried there at Brompton Cemetery.

The testimony of friends, supported by early pictures of Miss Robertson, records her striking beauty: she had "the most beautiful blue eyes with black lashes, quantities of lovely black hair, and spoke with the sweetest voice possible" (Panton, pp. 244–45). As an actress her range of characterization was not large. In her early juvenile comedy and in boys' parts she was "bright and bewitching," as a soubrette "charmingly coquettish, capricious, captivating," and she possessed a pleasing ballad voice which Boucicault judiciously used in several of her roles. But it was in the representation of Scotch and Irish peasant girls—sweet, simple, artless, tender, trusting—in sad and, especially, pathetic situations that she signally won the hearts of audiences on both sides of the Atlantic and in which she has probably never been surpassed. When her loveliness waned, the fine instinct of dramatic art remained, and audiences were content to take the mature art without the freshness. Throughout her long life as woman and actress the one word that habitually described Agnes Robertson in print was "sweetness," and one feels, without any cloying reference, its aptness.

[John Parker, ed., *Who's Who in the Theatre* (3rd ed., 1916); J. B. Matthews and Laurence Hutton, *Life and Art of Edwin Booth and His Contemporaries*, vol. V (1886); George C. D. Odell, *Annals of the N.Y. Stage*, vols. VI–VII (1931), IX (1937), and XIV (1945); *N.Y. Tribune*, Sept. 24, 1872, May 2, 1883, June 22, 1888, Sept. 19, 1890, Nov. 26, 1890; *N.Y. Times*, Nov. 7, 26, 1916; the *Times* (London), Nov. 7, 1916; Robinson Locke Collection of Dramatic Scrapbooks, N.Y. Public Library; clippings at Harvard Theatre Collection; Clement Scott, *The Drama of Yesterday and Today* (1899);

Jane Ellen (Frith) Panton, *Leaves from a Life* (1908).]

ALBERT E. JOHNSON

**ROBERTSON, Alice Mary** (Jan. 2, 1854–July 1, 1931), Indian educator and Congresswoman from Oklahoma, was born at Tullahassee Mission in the Creek Nation, Indian Territory (now Tullahassee, Okla.). Christened Mary Alice, she was the second daughter and second of seven children of William Schenck Robertson and ANN ELIZA (WORCESTER) ROBERTSON. Both parents were missionary educators. Alice's mother was a daughter of the famous Congregational missionary Samuel A. Worcester, who had followed the Cherokees on their removal from Georgia to the Indian Territory. Her father, a native of Long Island and a graduate of Union College, had come in 1849 to head the newly created Tullahassee boarding school, supported jointly by the Creek government and the Presbyterian mission board. Save for a five-year exile in the Middle West during the Civil War, he and his family lived at Tullahassee throughout Alice's childhood.

A slender, blond girl with strong sympathies and a restless, independent spirit, Alice received much of her early education from her parents at the mission. In 1871 she entered Elmira (N.Y.) College, where she worked to help pay her expenses. She left after two years and took a proffered job as copyist in the Indian Office at Washington so that a younger sister could go to college. While in the Indian Office she was responsible for drafting a report and recommendations (1877) which defeated a scheme of Senator John J. Ingalls of Kansas to foment insurrection in the Creek Nation and thereby open it to white settlement. Resigning in 1879, Miss Robertson taught briefly at Tullahassee until a fire in December 1880 destroyed the school. Having arranged for twenty-five of the displaced pupils to enter the Carlisle (Pa.) Indian School, she next served for two years as secretary to the superintendent of the Carlisle School, Capt. Richard H. Pratt. She returned to the Indian Territory to assist her mother in plans for rebuilding the mission school at a new location, Nuyaka, her fund-raising speeches in the East in 1882–83 meeting with marked success. In 1885 she was placed in charge of a Presbyterian mission boarding school for girls at Muskogee, where she also taught domestic science. Under her leadership the school was expanded (1894) into a coeducational college, Henry Kendall College (later moved to Tulsa and renamed the University of Tulsa), at which she taught English, history, and civics until 1899.

For several years (1889–92) Miss Robertson took part in the Lake Mohonk Conference of Friends of the Indian and there formed a friendship with Theodore Roosevelt, a bond that was strengthened when she helped two Creek students join his regiment of Rough Riders during the Spanish-American War. When in 1897 the federal government took over responsibility for Indian education, Miss Robertson worked strenuously for appointment as federal supervisor of Creek schools, winning the post in 1900. It was exhausting work, requiring her to make innumerable reports, to appoint and certify teachers, and, driving her buggy over the execrable roads, to visit the schools in her district. On her initiative, President Roosevelt appointed her postmistress of Muskogee, a position she held from 1905 until the beginning of the Wilson administration in 1913.

Miss Robertson then retired to a farm she had established outside Muskogee, where she lived with her adopted daughter—an Indian girl, Suzanne Barnett—and raised dairy cattle and vegetables. As an offshoot, she opened a cafeteria in Muskogee which became highly popular. From her cafeteria, during World War I, she began meeting every troop train that passed through Muskogee, carrying in her Model-T Ford a supply of coffee and refreshments. The fame of motherly, silver-haired "Miss Alice" spread through the training camps; and from her one-woman canteen grew the Muskogee Red Cross service, which became the model for other cities. She had actively opposed woman suffrage, but in 1920, at sixty-six, she was persuaded to run for Congress as a Republican from the Second Congressional District. Campaigning on the principles of "Christianity, Americanism and Standpattism," she was swept into office by a combination of the national Republican landslide and a factional split within the Oklahoma Democracy, defeating the incumbent, William W. Hastings, a Cherokee leader.

As the sole woman member of Congress (her one predecessor, Jeannette Rankin, had completed her term in 1919) Alice Robertson was the object of much public attention. She was given a gracious welcome to the House and was assigned, appropriately, to the Committee on Indian Affairs, along with two lesser committee posts. Her contributions to legislation and debate were negligible. Deeply conservative, she largely followed the policies of the Harding administration, though she broke with the majority of her party to oppose the Sheppard-Towner Bill (enacted 1921) which provided federal grants-in-aid to support centers for child hygiene and prenatal care. Since this measure was strongly backed by women's organizations, her stand drew sharp comment. She felt it her duty also to oppose the soldier bonus bill. Having alienated both veterans and women's groups, and with Oklahoma returning to its normal Democratic affiliation in 1922, Miss Robertson was defeated for reelection.

Partially through the influence of Mrs. Mary C. Thaw, a Pittsburgh philanthropist and her constant financial supporter, Miss Robertson was in 1923 appointed a welfare worker at the veterans' hospital in Muskogee. Her independent temperament, however, led to her dismissal after a few months. Her last years were eased by donations from Oklahoma citizens and from Mrs. Elizabeth Lowell Putnam of Boston, head of the Women's Coolidge for President Club (and a sister of the poet AMY LOWELL and President A. Lawrence Lowell of Harvard University), whose friendship Miss Robertson had won by her opposition to the Sheppard-Towner Bill. Alice Robertson died at Muskogee in 1931 of cancer of the jaw and was buried there in Greenhill Cemetery.

[The best account is Joe Powell Spaulding, "The Life of Alice Mary Robertson" (unpublished Ph.D. dissertation, Univ. of Okla., 1959), which draws upon printed and manuscript sources, including the extensive Alice M. Robertson Collection at the Univ. of Tulsa Library. See also articles on Alice Robertson by Grant Foreman in *Independent*, Mar. 26, 1921, and *Chronicles of Okla.*, Mar. 1932, and by Tom P. Morgan in *Ladies' Home Jour.*, Mar. 1921; *Collier's*, Sept. 2, 1922; *N.Y. Times* obituary, July 2, 1931; Alice M. Robertson, "The Creek Indian Council in Session," *Chronicles of Okla.*, Sept. 1933; Angie Debo, *The Road to Disappearance* (1941) and *And Still the Waters Run* (1940); Althea Bass, "William Schenck Robertson," and Martin Wenger, "Samuel Worcester Robertson," *Chronicles of Okla.*, Spring 1959. For her participation in the Lake Mohonk Conference and her ideas on Indian education, see its *Proc.*, 1889, 1890, 1892.]

ROBERTSON, Ann Eliza Worcester (Nov. 7, 1826–Nov. 19, 1905), missionary, teacher, and Indian linguist, was born of missionary parents at Brainerd Mission, Cherokee Nation, Tenn., but removed in infancy to the Cherokee capital at New Echota, Ga. She was the oldest of seven children. Her parents were Congregationalists serving under the American Board of Commissioners for Foreign Missions: Samuel Austin Worcester from Vermont, descendant of seven generations of ministers; and lovely, gentle Ann (Orr) Worcester from New Hampshire. Worcester, a brilliant linguist, entered almost immediately after his ordination in 1825

upon a lifetime career of publishing in the Cherokee language. In 1831 he was sent to the Georgia penitentiary for refusing to recognize the state's authority over the Cherokee country; appealing to the Supreme Court of the United States, he won the famous decision for the Indians in the case of *Worcester v. Georgia* (1832). But President Andrew Jackson ignored the court ruling and in 1835–38 the Cherokees were driven to the present Oklahoma. Ann Eliza never forgot her grief over their sufferings. She was educated at home and at the Park Hill mission her parents established in 1836 in the Cherokees' new homeland. Her mother died there in 1840, but a conscientious stepmother succeeded to the care of the family. At sixteen (January 1843) Ann Eliza was sent to the St. Johnsbury (Vt.) Academy, where she excelled in Latin and Greek. Her whole aim in her studies was to assist in her parents' work, and in 1847 she went back to teach at Park Hill.

Two years later, in 1849, she was appointed a teacher at the new Tullahassee Manual Labor Boarding School sponsored jointly by the neighboring Creek Nation and the Presbyterian Board of Foreign Missions, with the Creeks paying the running expenses and the board furnishing the teachers. The school opened in January 1850. On Apr. 16, 1850, Ann Eliza Worcester was married to the principal, William Schenck Robertson, a native of Long Island and a graduate of Union College who had become a Presbyterian missionary; with her marriage she joined her husband's denomination. She taught classes, supervised the school housekeeping, and worked with her husband preparing Creek texts for publication. In 1856 he wrote of her Creek studies, "She is now out of sight of the rest of us." She also became the mother of seven children: Ann Augusta (1851), Mary Alice (see ALICE MARY ROBERTSON), Grace Leeds (1856), Samuel Worcester (1860), and three later children who died in infancy. All three daughters subsequently taught in the tribal-mission boarding schools. Augusta married a leading Creek rancher; Alice became the second woman elected to the United States Congress.

The Creeks were making good progress in the 1850's, but this was disrupted by the Civil War. Abandoned by the United States, they made a treaty with the Confederacy, and on the same day—July 10, 1861—abruptly closed their boarding schools and ordered the missionaries to vacate. For five years the Robertsons lived in the Middle West, while Robertson supported his family by teaching and by mission work in Kansas. They returned to Tullahassee at the request of the Creeks in December 1866. Only the brick walls were standing, but Robertson rebuilt the school and it reopened in March 1868. In the following years the missionaries saw former Tullahassee boys become leaders of their people and girls become teachers in the tribal rural schools and mothers of progressive families, while unschooled Creeks in native churches were singing hymns and reading tracts and portions of the Bible in their own language.

The Tullahassee school burned down in December 1880, and the heart-broken Robertson died the following June. Mrs. Robertson, still working on her translations, went to live with her daughter Alice in the growing railroad town of Muskogee. In 1887 she completed the Creek New Testament. Holding it in her hands, she pronounced it "the crowning joy of my life." She continued to revise it, the fifth edition being almost complete when she died. Also published were her translations of the Psalms and Genesis and a Creek hymnal. She carried on her work with a painstaking scholarship that entered into every shading of a word. The New Testament she translated directly from the Greek; in Old Testament Hebrew she was helped by another missionary.

Mrs. Robertson was a slender, frail-looking woman, with a gentle manner and a sensitive face, painfully conscientious, but very determined in defending her scholarship against superficial translations. In 1892 the University of Wooster in Ohio made her an honorary Ph.D. She died in Muskogee, Okla., at the age of seventy-nine and was buried in the Worcester cemetery at Park Hill.

[Alice M. Robertson Collection, Univ. of Tulsa, and other special collections and manuscript sources at Gilcrease Institute, Tulsa, and Okla. Hist. Soc., Okla. City; Hope Holway, "Ann Eliza Worcester Robertson as a Linguist," and other articles on the Robertson-Worcester family in *Chronicles of Okla.*, Spring 1959; Lilah Denton Lindsey, "Memories of the Indian Territory Mission Field," *ibid.*, Summer 1958; Virginia E. Lauderdale, "Tullahassee Mission," *ibid.*, Autumn 1948; Althea Bass, *The Story of Tullahassee* (1960) and *The Cherokee Messenger* (1936); Carolyn Thomas Foreman, *Park Hill* (1948); James C. Pilling, *Bibliog. of the Muskhogean Languages* (Bureau of Am. Ethnology, Bull. No. 9, 1889); Angie Debo, *The Road to Disappearance* (1941). See also *Dict. Am. Biog.* articles on Samuel Austin Worcester and William Schenck Robertson.]

ANGIE DEBO

**ROBINS, Margaret Dreier** (Sept. 6, 1868–Feb. 21, 1945), labor reformer, was born in Brooklyn, N.Y., the oldest of the five children (four girls and one boy) of Theodor and Dorothea Adelheid (Dreier) Dreier who survived infancy. Of her sisters, Mary Elisabeth became prominent in social reform and labor work, Dorothea a painter, and Katherine Sophie an ardent patron of modern art. Theodor Dreier had emigrated to New York in 1849 from Bremen, Germany; on a return visit in 1864 he married a cousin and brought her to America. Reflecting the interests of his forebears—ministers, merchants, and public servants—he became a successful and wealthy businessman, an active participant in civic affairs, and a loyal supporter of the German Evangelical Church. Growing up in Brooklyn, Margaret, or Gretchen as she was called by her friends, had a happy but disciplined childhood, imbued with a sense of responsibility. She attended George Brackett's private school in Brooklyn Heights, and although she did not go to college, her active and inquisitive mind led her to continue her studies; for several years she read history and philosophy under the direction of the Rev. Richard Salter Storrs of Brooklyn's Church of the Pilgrims.

Though she was attractive and popular, the usual round of parties, concerts, and balls failed to satisfy her, and when only nineteen she joined the women's auxiliary at the Brooklyn Hospital, of which her father was a trustee. This gave her her first glimpse of the conditions of the poor. Later she became a member of the State Charities Aid Association's city visiting committee for institutions for the insane, where she benefited from the guidance of the welfare leader Homer Folks. A more important post was the chairmanship (1903–04) of the legislative committee of the Women's Municipal League, in which, together with a young social worker, Frances Kellor (1873–1952), she successfully lobbied for a bill to regulate employment agencies in New York. Meanwhile, in 1904, two other young friends, William English Walling and LEONORA O'REILLY, persuaded her to join the new Women's Trade Union League, which sought to organize working women into trade unions and secure legislation bettering their working conditions, wages, and hours.

Her marriage, on June 21, 1905, took her from New York to Chicago but did not interrupt her work for social justice. Her husband, Raymond Robins (1873–1954), was a Chicago settlement worker who had earlier been a lawyer, lay preacher, and miner and had made a fortune in the Klondike gold rush; sharing Margaret's concern for working men and women, he had a crusading zeal that was contagious. They had no children. Although both were independently wealthy, they moved into a cold-water flat on the top floor of a dreary tenement on the West Side of Chicago. Here they entertained college professors and anarchists, labor leaders and ministers, and here Margaret Robins met the exciting group of settlement workers—JANE ADDAMS, MARY MC-DOWELL, and many others—who were helping to transform Chicago and the nation. She also became deeply involved in the activities of a growing group of Chicago trade union women, including AGNES NESTOR and Elisabeth Christman of the glove-makers' union, Elizabeth Maloney of the waitresses' union, Mary Anderson of the boot and shoe workers, and MARGARET HALEY of the Chicago Teachers' Federation. In 1907 she was elected president both of the Chicago branch of the Women's Trade Union League (an office she held until 1913) and of the National Women's Trade Union League, the position to which she devoted much of her time and energy for the next fifteen years.

More than any other person, Margaret Dreier Robins made the Women's Trade Union League an effective force for labor reform. With Rose Schneiderman of New York and other W.T.U.L. leaders, she was deeply involved in the great garment workers' strikes of 1909–11 in New York, Philadelphia, and Chicago, raising money, obtaining legal counsel, organizing relief, and enlisting influential support. She also gave heavily of her own substantial inheritance, of which she once said: "I never earned a dollar of it and I recognize that I hold it in trust" (Mary Dreier, p. 31). Although Mrs. Robins supported campaigns for protective legislation, she saw labor organization as initially more important, and she directed a number of W.T.U.L. women into organizational work. (One, Mary Anderson, later became the first head of the Women's Bureau of the Department of Labor.) In 1914, at Mrs. Robins' suggestion, the League founded in Chicago a training program for working women. When this experiment ended in 1926 some forty young women had been prepared for local trade union leadership.

Although for several years she edited *Life and Labor,* the official publication of the W.T.U.L., Mrs. Robins' major influence was a personal one. On the lecture platform and in smaller groups she radiated a compelling sincerity, and she had a great ability to smooth over differences between working women and their middle-class supporters. Ready to perform any needed task, in 1911 she spent many early morning hours on Chicago street corners telling hotel and restaurant employees, as they

went to work, about a recently enacted ten-hour law. By such dedication Margaret Dreier Robins won greater acceptance in labor circles than did many Progressive reformers, and by 1911 her Women's Trade Union League had grown from three to eleven local branches. The League was closely allied with the American Federation of Labor in its early years, and Mrs. Robins, long a friend of Samuel Gompers, served for a time on the A.F. of L.'s industrial education committee. A good friend also of the Chicago labor leader John Fitzpatrick, she sat from 1908 to 1917 on the executive board of the Chicago Federation of Labor. She was active in the state labor federation, and in 1915 was appointed by the governor of Illinois to the state unemployment commission.

Margaret Robins was gentle and deeply religious by nature (in later years a Congregationalist), but she was quickly aroused by injustice or exploitation. In 1906, when "Big Bill" Haywood and two other labor leaders were arrested, forcibly transferred from Colorado to Idaho, and placed on trial for the murder of a former governor of Idaho (a charge of which they were eventually cleared), she led a protest parade of some twenty thousand working men and women through Chicago. Though often accused of being an anarchist and a socialist, she was neither. She favored public control of all natural monopolies, but otherwise believed in free enterprise. Experience had taught her, however, that the government must step in to protect the weak, especially women and children. Convinced that the participation of women in politics would be a major step toward achieving this goal, she marched in many suffrage parades and served on many suffrage committees.

Mrs. Robins backed Bryan and the Democrats in 1908, but four years later, with many other reformers, she became an ardent supporter of the Progressive party. As a member of the party's Illinois state committee she spoke throughout the Midwest. In 1916, unlike many of her friends, she campaigned for Charles Evans Hughes, the Republican presidential candidate, citing his favorable labor record. She remained active in Republican politics after the First World War, serving in 1919–20 in the women's division of the party's National Committee. The conservative reaction of the 1920's to some extent drained the ardor from her efforts to aid working women. Furthermore, her Republican loyalties and her readiness to espouse various causes in which her husband was involved, including the movement to "outlaw" war, diminished her influence in labor circles. The annual A.F. of L.

stipend to the Women's Trade Union League had been withdrawn as early as 1915, leaving the League wholly dependent upon wealthy benefactors. Mrs. Robins resigned the presidency in 1922, hoping to devote herself to the International Federation of Working Women, of which she had been elected president the year before. This organization, largely her personal creation, was the outgrowth of two international congresses of working women which she had convened in 1919 and 1921, the first in Washington, the second in Geneva. She resigned at the Vienna congress in 1923, however, when the European delegates voted to transform the organization into a department of the International Federation of Trade Unions, an Amsterdam-based alliance with which the American labor movement had little contact.

In 1924 Margaret and Raymond Robins moved to Chinsegut Hill, their 2,000-acre estate near Brooksville, Fla., where they had vacationed over the years. Here she became occupied with domestic concerns and with a variety of local, state, and national organizations, including the Young Women's Christian Association, the Red Cross, and the League of Women Voters. A member of the Republican National Committee in 1928, she was in 1929 appointed by President Hoover to the planning committee of the White House Conference on Child Health and Protection. In 1932, however, she reluctantly supported Roosevelt, and by 1936 she and her husband had become enthusiastic backers of the New Deal. In 1934 Mrs. Robins was reelected to the executive board of the Women's Trade Union League (now much diminished in membership and influence), and in 1937 she became chairman of its committee on Southern work. She died at Chinsegut Hill, of pernicious anemia and a heart ailment, at the age of seventy-six, and was buried there.

[Margaret Dreier Robins Papers, Univ. of Fla. Library, Gainesville; Raymond Robins Papers, Wis. State Hist. Soc., Madison; records of the Women's Trade Union League in the Library of Congress and the Schlesinger Library at Radcliffe College. The best published source is Mary E. Dreier, *Margaret Dreier Robins: Her Life, Letters, and Work* (1950). See also Gladys Boone, *The Women's Trade Union Leagues in Great Britain and the U.S.A.* (1942); Agnes Nestor, *Woman's Labor Leader: An Autobiog.* (1954); Mary Anderson, *Woman At Work* (1951); Samuel Gompers, *Seventy Years of Life and Labor* (1925), I, 490; Clarke A. Chambers, *Seedtime of Reform* (1963); Allen F. Davis, *Spearheads for Reform* (1967); Eleanor Flexner, *Century of Struggle* (1959); chapter on Katherine Dreier in Aline B.

Saarinen, *The Proud Possessors* (1958); obituary in *N.Y. Times,* Feb. 22, 1945; *Who Was Who in America,* vols. II (1950), on Margaret Dreier Robins, and III (1960), on Raymond Robins. Death record from Fla. State Board of Health.]

ALLEN F. DAVIS

**ROBINSON, Harriet Jane Hanson** (Feb. 8, 1825–Dec. 22, 1911), Massachusetts mill girl and woman suffrage leader, was born in Boston, the only daughter among four children of William and Harriet (Browne) Hanson. Both her parents were descended from early English migrants to New England, and her maternal grandfather, Seth Ingersoll Browne, fought in the Revolutionary War; her mother was born in Boston. Her father, a native of Dover, N.H., was a carpenter of modest means whose death in 1831 forced the poverty-stricken family to move a year later to the burgeoning mill town of Lowell. There her mother boarded workers for the Tremont Corporation while the children found local employment. Harriet entered the mill at age ten as a bobbin doffer. A year later when older workers struck in anger over a wage cut, Harriet impulsively led her hesitant young companions out with them, and later wrote, "As I looked back at the long line that followed me, I was more proud than I have ever been since at any success I may have achieved . . ." (*Loom and Spindle,* p. 85). The protest was short-lived. Despite long hours, the slow rhythm of the early Lowell factory gave time for reading and play between duties, and in retrospect she would profess to value the habits of manual competence and regularity bred by industrial discipline.

The Lowell mill girls were a self-conscious and earnest lot, heady with the chance to earn money and independence from their status at home, yet eager to cultivate themselves as proper and literate New England women. Through the early 1840's (before the girls began to be replaced by Irish immigrants) a paternal corporate management indulged their desires with schools, churches, and libraries while enforcing sobriety and good conduct. In this close environment Harriet bloomed. She attended school when she could until age fifteen, read omnivorously thereafter, took private lessons in drawing, dancing, and language, attended Whig rallies, dabbled in phrenology and Graham dieting, discussed heaven and hell. In the wake of a Lowell religious revival in 1840 she strayed from orthodoxy to Universalism and was publicly "excommunicated" from the Congregational Church in November 1842. The experience left her with a durable distaste for organized religion, although in 1898 she became a communicant of the Episcopal Church.

Happier results flowed from her part in literary stirrings among the mill girls. Their famous *Lowell Offering*, a monthly magazine of poetry, short fiction, and didactic essays published from 1839 to 1845, won international attention. Although Harriet was not "an early or a constant contributor," one of her poems drew the notice of William Stevens Robinson, a young Free Soil editor of the *Lowell Courier*. She was an attractive and gregarious girl, and if a surviving handmade valentine is testimony, Robinson fancied her "lovely form and eyes of jet" as well as her verse. They were married on Nov. 30, 1848. While her husband struggled from one journalistic post to another in the antislavery cause, Harriet settled into the new chores of editorial assistant, housewife, and mother. Over the next decade four children were born to her: Harriette Lucy, Elizabeth Osborne, William Elbridge (who died of typhoid fever at age five), and Edward Warrington.

Meanwhile her husband's militant columns under the pen name "Warrington" made her home a cell of antislavery talk, and Harriet became a quiet but passionate convert to the cause. Residence in Concord from 1854 to 1857 brought her into neighborly contact with Thoreau and Emerson, and she joined the sewing circle of the local women's antislavery society. The outbreak of war found the family living in Malden, Harriet sewing army mittens for Boston contractors while her husband searched for work. Finally his election as clerk of the state house of representatives in 1862 brought financial ease to the family and political prominence to "Warrington."

Following the war, husband, wife, and eldest daughter together took up the new cause of woman suffrage. After "Warrington's" death in 1876 mother and daughter carried on, speaking, writing, organizing. In 1881 Mrs. Robinson contributed a history, *Massachusetts in the Woman Suffrage Movement*. By then friction over techniques and personalities had already divided her from LUCY STONE and the bulk of the New England suffragists and propelled her into the rival camp of SUSAN B. ANTHONY. Mrs. Robinson's working-class past and her husband's radical influence made the broad-gauged reformism of Miss Anthony's National Woman Suffrage Association more palatable to her than Lucy Stone's pristine and moderate American association. After the 1881 convention of the National association in Boston, where she served as a rather lonely welcoming hostess, Mrs. Robinson openly affiliated

with Miss Anthony. With her daughter Harriette R. Shattuck she organized the National Woman Suffrage Association of Massachusetts, spoke for suffrage before a special Senate committee in Washington (1882), supported Benjamin F. Butler for governor of Massachusetts in a vain effort to stimulate his sympathy for the cause (1882–83), and boldly petitioned Congress for removal of her political disabilities (1889). Neither her tactics nor those of other suffragists bore immediate fruit in Massachusetts, where ethnic and religious rancor in the populace precluded any statutory advance toward woman suffrage between 1879 and the passage of the Nineteenth Amendment in 1920.

Mrs. Robinson was an enthusiastic promoter of women's clubs, helping JULIA WARD HOWE form the New England Women's Club in 1868 and serving on the first board of directors of the General Federation of Women's Clubs in the early 1890's. Among her numerous writings, *"Warrington" Pen Portraits* (1877), a memoir of her husband, and *Loom and Spindle* (1898), a lucid recollection of her years in the Lowell mills, remain valuable historical documents, while her efforts to dramatize the cause of woman, *Captain Mary Miller* (1887), a novel, and *The New Pandora* (1889), a verse play, retain at best an antique interest.

In character and appearance Harriet Robinson carried into her mature years the marks of a hard and vigorous youth. Her life was perhaps more valuable for what she experienced than for what she achieved. In any event there is justice in her pride at being a self-made woman of nineteenth-century New England. Handsome, firm-lipped, square-jawed, and stocky in middle age, she revealed herself in private and published words as a devoted wife and mother as well as a tough, self-sufficient, and sensible fighter for her sex. She died at her home in Malden in her eighty-seventh year of pyelonephritis and was buried in Sleepy Hollow Cemetery at Concord.

[Mrs. Robinson's letters, diaries, and papers in the Schlesinger Library, Radcliffe College, are the richest source for her career. Brief sketches appear in Frances E. Willard and Mary A. Livermore, eds., *A Woman of the Century* (1893); and the *Woman's Jour.*, Dec. 30, 1911. Aside from her own writings, valuable introductions to the milieu of Mrs. Robinson's life are Hannah Josephson, *The Golden Threads* (1949), and Lois B. Merk, "Massachusetts and the Woman-Suffrage Movement" (unpublished doctoral dissertation, Radcliffe College, microfilm copy in Schlesinger Library dated 1961). Death record from Mass. Registrar of Vital Statistics.]

GEOFFREY BLODGETT

ROBINSON, Jane Marie Bancroft (Dec. 24, 1847–May 29, 1932), Methodist educator and deaconess leader, was born in West Stockbridge, Mass., the oldest of the three children of the Rev. George C. Bancroft by his second wife, Caroline J. Orton, and the only one to survive childhood. Of Bancroft's five children by his first marriage, two lived to adulthood. Descended from a Cape May, N.J., family, Bancroft had turned free-lance evangelist in 1837 after ten years in the navy; two years later he entered the ministry of the Methodist Episcopal Church. For the next forty years he served small parishes in New England and New York, and during her early life Jane never lived longer than two years in one place. Her mother, who came from Caldwell, N.Y., traced her ancestry to early settlers of Connecticut and to the Bogardus family of Dutch New York; although she had little formal education, she was a woman of keen intellect who read widely and taught herself French and German. She transmitted her venturesome spirit and firm convictions to both Jane and her half sister, Henrietta Ash Bancroft (1842–1929), who became Jane's close associate.

Jane Bancroft graduated in 1871 from EMMA WILLARD's seminary at Troy, N.Y., and the following year from the New York State Normal School at Albany. While pursuing advanced studies on her own, she served as preceptress at the Fort Edward (N.Y.) Collegiate Institute from 1872 to 1876, when she entered Syracuse University as a member of the senior class, receiving the degree of Ph.B. the following spring. From 1877 to 1885 she was dean of the Woman's College and professor of French language and literature at Northwestern University, Evanston, Ill. Continuing her studies meanwhile, she earned from Syracuse the degrees of Ph.M. (1880) and Ph.D. (1884), her doctoral thesis, A Study of the Parliament of Paris and Other Parliaments of France, being published that same year. At Northwestern she founded in 1883 the Western Association of Collegiate Alumnae, a regional forerunner of the American Association of University Women. When Bryn Mawr College opened in 1885, Miss Bancroft was awarded its first history fellowship. The next two years she spent in Europe, accompanied by her parents. In 1886–87 she studied at the University of Zurich; and in 1887–88 she audited a history conférence at the University of Paris, where she was the first woman to be admitted to the École Pratique des Hautes Études. Among her later academic honors were election to Phi Beta Kappa (1907) and LL.D. degrees from

Syracuse University (1919) and the University of Southern California (1929).

In Europe, Miss Bancroft also became interested in various orders of Protestant laywomen organized for social service. On the advice of Elizabeth Lownes Rust, corresponding secretary of the Woman's Home Missionary Society of the Methodist Episcopal Church, she undertook a careful study of deaconesses, as such women were called, with an eye to launching a similar movement among American Methodists. She examined the Lutheran complex at Kaiserwerth, Germany, the Methodists' Bethany Society at Frankfort, and the Episcopal institutions at Mildmay Park in North London. Upon returning to the United States, she published a report on her findings: Deaconesses in Europe and Their Lessons for America (1889).

The deaconess movement had already found sporadic reception among American Lutherans and Episcopalians; and in 1887 Mrs. LUCY RIDER MEYER, a Methodist, had founded the Chicago Deaconess Home. The next year the Methodist General Conference, recognizing "an idea whose time had come," formally approved the organizing of deaconesses "to minister to the poor, visit the sick, pray with the dying, care for the orphan, . . . save the sinning, and, relinquishing wholly all other pursuits, devote themselves in a general way to such forms of Christian labor as may be suited to their abilities." The women were to receive no regular salary, their support being provided by the Church, and each deaconess home was to be under the direction and control of the annual conference where it was located. The Methodist Woman's Home Missionary Society, already conscious that its most important field of activity lay in the growing cities, speedily formed a committee on deaconess work which within a year expanded into a full-fledged Deaconess Bureau, with Jane Bancroft as chairman. For the next twenty years this movement was to be her main interest. Declining a professorship of history at Ohio Wesleyan University, she traveled, spoke, and wrote on behalf of deaconess work. By the end of the century the bureau was directing thirty-two deaconess homes, schools, and hospitals.

Because of its multiple origins and rapid proliferation, the Methodist deaconess movement fell into some controversy. Miss Bancroft favored centralized control through the Woman's Home Missionary Society, arguing that this would provide most effectively for assignment of new trainees and transfers of experienced ones. Mrs. Meyer and her associates in the "independent" deaconess homes, however, preferred to remain under the annual conferences. Although a General Deaconess Board was established in 1908, it was largely advisory, and not until seven years after Miss Bancroft's death did the Methodist Union of 1939 bring all deaconess work under the supervision of a single bureau.

On May 7, 1891, at Cincinnati, Jane Bancroft was married to George Orville Robinson (1832–1915), a Detroit lawyer and a widower with four children. They had no children of their own. Marriage scarcely diminished Mrs. Robinson's activities. Her husband, an active Methodist layman and founder of the Michigan *Christian Advocate*, gave generously of wealth derived from lumber and mining interests to establish new deaconess institutions and enlarge existing ones. In 1897 Mrs. Robinson's half sister Henrietta left a professorship of English at Albion College to become field secretary of the Deaconess Bureau, and when in 1904 this agency was divided into five regional bureaus, Henrietta Bancroft became general superintendent of deaconess work. Mrs. Robinson, who had been a vice-president of the Woman's Home Missionary Society since 1893, served as president of the society from 1908 to 1913.

"She is a most attractive figure on the platform," wrote one of Mrs. Robinson's associates in 1914, ". . . well gowned, winning, womanly, full of fire and enthusiasm" (*Christian Advocate*, Oct. 14, 1914). She addressed the Methodist Ecumenical Council in London when her husband served as a delegate in 1901, and made her presence felt as a lay delegate to the Methodist General Conferences of 1908 and 1920 and to the Methodist Ecumenical Conference in Toronto in 1911 (the first such meeting to accept woman delegates).

In 1918, three years after her husband's death, Mrs. Robinson established a palatial home in Pasadena, Calif., where she lived with Henrietta Bancroft until the latter's death. This building and its eleven-acre tract she later gave to church agencies for a deaconess retirement home and homes for retired ministers. Among other benefactions she contributed more than $10,000 to the California Institute of Technology in Pasadena. While traveling in 1932 Mrs. Robinson suffered a stroke and was hospitalized in Albuquerque, N.Mex. She died two months later in Pasadena, at the age of eighty-four, and was buried beside her half sister in Mountain View Cemetery, Altadena, Calif.

[Besides the two books cited and frequent articles in the *Christian Advocate* and *Woman's Home Mis-* *sions,* Mrs. Robinson published *A Hist. Sketch of the Robinson Family of the Line of Ebenezer Robinson* (1903). On her own life, published material is limited to sketches in such compendiums as Frances E. Willard and Mary A. Livermore, eds., *A Woman of the Century* (1893); Mabel Ward Cameron, ed., *Biog. Cyc. Am. Women,* I (1924), 361–62; *Woman's Who's Who of America, 1914–15;* and *Who Was Who in America,* vol. I (1942). Among occasional notices in the religious press the most informative are in the *Christian Advocate* (Oct. 14, 1914, pp. 1381–82; and June 9, 1932, p. 613, with picture) and *Woman's Home Missions* (July 1932, p. 12). The most recent history of the W.H.M.S. is Ruth Esther Meeker, *Six Decades of Service, 1880–1940: The Woman's Home Missionary Soc. of the Methodist Episcopal Church* (1969); see especially pp. 91–110. See also Marion Talbot and Lois K. M. Rosenberry, *The Hist. of the Am. Assoc. of Univ. Women* (1931), pp. 17, 40–41.]

C. C. GOEN

**ROBSON, May** (Apr. 19, 1858–Oct. 20, 1942), actress, christened Mary Jeannette Robison, was born of English parents in Australia, where her father, Henry Robison, a retired sea captain, had settled for his health. After his early death, the widowed Julia Robison took her four children to London, where Mary, the youngest, began her education at the Sacred Heart Convent at Highgate, continuing it at Brussels and Paris. At the age of sixteen she ran away from home to marry Charles Livingston Gore, aged eighteen, and settled at Fort Worth, Texas. The couple tried ranching, but after a hard struggle of several years gave up and went to New York City, where Gore died, leaving his family penniless. Mrs. Gore managed to support herself and three small children by embroidery work and by painting china and dinner menus in a manner she had learned as a child at the convent school. She also took pupils in painting. Two of her children, a boy and a girl, died during this period, one of diphtheria, the other of scarlet fever. She turned to acting on a sudden impulse one day when passing a theatrical agency, and presently obtained her first part, that of a typical ingenue in a stock melodrama, *Hoop of Gold*. At her own request, she also took on a character role in the same play: Tilly, a cockney slavey. It was the latter role that won applause when she made her debut at the Brooklyn Grand Opera House on Sept. 17, 1883, and she immediately began to develop her personal style in eccentric parts.

Over the next two decades May Robson, as she came to be known through a printer's error, intently cultivated her line of business as a comic character actress. Instead of offering her pretty, girlish, vivacious self to the public she preferred covering her face with layers of greasepaint and makeup and appearing as the wrinkled, frowzy, freakish figures of stock comedy. She took equal care with her costumes, ransacking the East Side of New York for bits of clothing to gain the necessary effects of comedy and truthfulness. "I can't act unless I'm a fright," she confessed after nearly two decades of such work. "If I appear as May Robson unmolested, I'm so self-conscious that I'm a dead failure."

Her popularity with both critics and audiences is reflected in her long association with first Daniel and then Charles Frohman, in whose stock companies she played over a hundred roles, beginning in 1886, with no other contract than a verbal agreement. In 1901 she withdrew from the Charles Frohman Company in order to find more satisfying parts. As Queen Elizabeth in *Dorothy Vernon of Haddon Hall* (1904), starring Bertha Galland, she played her first serious role. Comedy remained, however, her forte, and she drew acclaim for her work with Francis Wilson from 1905 through 1907 in Clyde Fitch's *Cousin Billy* (once more under the banner of Charles Frohman), where she wore her own face for the first time in eighteen years, and in *The Mountain Climber*, where she "carried off first honors . . . and ran away with the play." With prominence and success of this kind, she finally won stardom in her next vehicle, *The Rejuvenation of Aunt Mary*, which opened at the Scranton (Pa.) Lyceum, Oct. 8, 1907. Although *Aunt Mary* received cool notices in New York, the play drew enough popular support to earn an extended road tour and a twelve-week engagement in London. Miss Robson now determined to write her own plays, but *The Three Lights* (*A Night Out*), written in collaboration with Charles T. Dazey, when produced in 1911 proved no more than an amateurish paraphrase of *Aunt Mary*. She voiced her intention to continue writing, even threatening to retire from the stage for the purpose, but no further work came from her pen. Meanwhile, on May 29, 1889, she had been married for a second time, to Augustus Homer Brown, a New York police surgeon and a graduate of Bowdoin College and the Columbia medical school.

Miss Robson sustained her career in a succession of plays during the ensuing years, but it was not until she turned to motion pictures that she won notable distinction. The death of her second husband in 1920 may have broken her New York ties and made a new step desirable. She made a screen version of *The Re-juvenation of Aunt Mary* in 1927 and took up residence in Beverly Hills, Calif., although told that Hollywood was a land of young women where none over twenty should apply. Past her seventieth year and after half a century of theatre work, she finally won her screen laurels as Apple Annie, the aged depression Cinderella, in Frank Capra's *Lady for a Day* (1933). With picture after picture, she then proceeded to win the hearts of a new generation who now knew May Robson as herself, the sharp-tongued, gray-haired grandmother with a heart of gold. A tireless worker as she had been a perennial trouper, she spent her whole life in her work, often on the set from dawn until past midnight. She fittingly received the news that she had become a great-grandmother while at work on a motion picture. Known to the starlit world of Hollywood as "Muzzey," May Robson won the affection, respect, and gratitude of countless movie people. Her devotion to her career is best reflected by her persistence in acting during her last two years in spite of cataracts in both eyes which almost blinded her. May Robson finally retired after *Joan of Paris* in 1942. She died of cancer soon after at her Beverly Hills home, with her son and daughter-in-law, Mr. and Mrs. Edward Gore, and her secretary-companion of thirty years, Lillian Harmer, at her bedside. Her body was cremated and the ashes placed beside the remains of her second husband in Flushing, N.Y.

[May Robson, "My Beginnings," *Theatre*, Nov. 1907; Lewis C. Strang, *Famous Actresses of the Day in America* (1899), chap. xxxi; obituaries in *N.Y. Times* and *N.Y. Herald Tribune*, Oct. 21, 1942; scrapbooks and miscellaneous clippings, Theatre Collection, N.Y. Public Library at Lincoln Center; death record from Calif. Dept. of Public Health. The Library of Congress has a collection of May Robson's papers, including correspondence, scrapbooks, and photographs. Her original name is given on her death record and in *Who's Who in Australia*, 1941. Though her first husband's name is often cited as Edward H. Gore, in the *Theatre* article above she gives it as Charles Livingston Gore.]

H. L. KLEINFIELD

**ROCKEFELLER, Abby Greene Aldrich** (Oct. 26, 1874–Apr. 5, 1948), philanthropist and art patron, was born in Providence, R.I., the second daughter and third of the eight children, three girls and five boys, of Nelson Wilmarth Aldrich, self-made businessman and later United States Senator, and his wife, Abby Chapman. She was reared in a warm, boisterous family environment dominated by the energy and many interests of her father. After education with a private teacher at home, she attended Miss Abbott's School in Providence, graduating in 1893. As a debutante she led an active social life and traveled frequently to New York and Washington, either on shopping expeditions or to watch Senator Aldrich in action. Her first trip to Europe was taken in 1894; other trips followed, several of them in company with her father, who had a strong interest in art collecting.

During this time Abby Aldrich met John Davison Rockefeller, Jr., son of the founder of the Standard Oil Company. Rockefeller was an undergraduate at Brown. After a courtship of several years, they were married on Oct. 9, 1901, in an elaborate wedding at the Aldrich summer home at Warwick Neck, R.I. Their marriage, unusually happy and satisfying, was the union of two quite different personalities, Mrs. Rockefeller's impulsive gregariousness contrasting strongly with her husband's methodical and reserved nature. They had six children: Abigail (1903), John Davison, 3d (1906), Nelson Aldrich (1908), Laurance Spelman (1910), Winthrop (1912), and David (1915).

In the early years of her marriage Mrs. Rockefeller's activities centered around the rearing of her family, together with the running of a nine-story house on West 54th Street in New York City and homes at Pocantico Hills, N.Y., and Seal Harbor, Maine. Marriage to one of the world's richest men also entailed constant entertaining and being entertained. Even so Mrs. Rockefeller took part in many philanthropies. She continued active participation in the Young Women's Christian Association, an interest which had begun in Providence. Earlier a Congregationalist, she joined her husband's Park Avenue Baptist Church, where she founded the Good Fellowship Council, a neighborhood association which included representatives of the many immigrant and minority groups on New York's East Side.

As her children grew older, Mrs. Rockefeller's activities began to match the diversity of her interests, and she devoted time to the Girl Scouts, the American Red Cross, and the newly built Riverside Church. Besides these, there were her husband's projects: the Rockefeller Foundation, the Rockefeller Institute for Medical Research, and, in later years, the restoration of colonial Williamsburg. In 1919, becoming interested in the living conditions of employees at the Bayway, N.J., site of her husband's Standard Oil Company, she promoted the construction of a workman's model house which later developed into a community center, with a baby clinic, Mothers' Club, and

a Community House sponsoring athletic and social activities. Mrs. Rockefeller also was an active participant in the formation and management of International House, a dormitory and social center for American and foreign students located near Columbia University. Founded by her husband, it was still another institution which had as its objective the development of a close community life, best achieved for these foreign students, she felt, in an environment which gave them a sense of membership. During World War I she served on the housing committee of the Y.W.C.A.; and during World War II, with four sons on active service or in government work, she entertained servicemen, helped the U.S.O., and planned veterans' centers for rehabilitation work after the war's end.

Perhaps her most important contribution grew out of a fascination with art, possibly fostered by her father, which led her to become one of the prime movers, along with LIZZIE BLISS and MARY QUINN SULLIVAN, in the founding of the Museum of Modern Art in 1929. A luncheon meeting in her home that May resulted in the formation of a committee which quickly raised the necessary money and recruited a staff. She served on the board of trustees, as treasurer and later as vice-chairman, and during the museum's first seventeen years she donated more than 2,000 art objects, including some 190 paintings and more than 1,600 prints. With her son Nelson she also set up an unrestricted purchase fund, deliberately refusing to impose her personal tastes in art upon the museum staff. Where her husband—himself a noted patron—was primarily concerned with the art object as a thing of beauty and a product of the past, Mrs. Rockefeller had a greater interest in the creative process and in the creator. During the depression she commissioned work from artists like Ben Shahn and Charles Sheeler; her collection, which depended largely on her own personal funds (since she knew her husband's tastes to be different), consisted mainly of modest items like drawings and watercolors and included the work of Charles Burchfield, John Marin, and Max Weber. Although much of this collection was given outright to the Museum of Modern Art, a good part of it was distributed to colleges throughout the East for use in educating future patrons to a new aesthetic vocabulary. Her delight in American folk art —painting, carved animals, and dolls—resulted in the Abby Aldrich Rockefeller Collection in Williamsburg, Va.

In her last years Mrs. Rockefeller spent much of her time at her home in Williamsburg, and with her seventeen grandchildren. After enjoying good health for most of her life, she suffered a heart attack and died in her New York City apartment in 1948, aged seventy-seven. Her body was cremated and the ashes buried in the family plot at Sleepy Hollow Cemetery, Tarrytown, N.Y.

By all accounts, from family and friends, Mrs. Rockefeller's warm good nature dominated both her personal life and her philanthropies. She demonstrated in her own home her belief in the strength and importance of family life. In her philanthropic work it was actual contact with those she helped which moved her most, whether they were foreign students coming to stay with her during holidays or servicemen in her sons' outfits. Concerned always with the human element in her projects, she devoted her attention to amenities which made the difference between adequacy and comfort: she chose with care the furnishings of International House and insisted upon a beauty parlor and similar conveniences in the Grace Dodge Hotel for women in Washington, D.C., built and operated by the Y.W.C.A. Always eager for new and exciting experiences, Mrs. Rockefeller delighted in meeting people and traveling to strange places, the more exotic the better.

All of this activity and interest was made possible only by a basic self-confidence nurtured on the affection which always suffused her family life. Abby Rockefeller's sense of mission and duty was intensified by the fact that she was not born to the enormous Rockefeller fortune and so was more aware of its power and the problems of adjusting to it. Sensitive to the unfairness of intolerance of all kinds, she also tried to break down the barriers which wealth had created.

[Mary Ellen Chase, *Abby Aldrich Rockefeller* (1950), a warm and informal portrayal; Raymond B. Fosdick, *John D. Rockefeller, Jr.* (1956); Aline B. Saarinen, *The Proud Possessors* (1958); *N.Y. Times* obituary, Apr. 6, 1948. A volume of *Abby Aldrich Rockefeller's Letters to Her Sister Lucy* was published in 1957.]

NEIL HARRIS

**RODGERS, Elizabeth Flynn** (Aug. 25, 1847–Aug. 27, 1939), labor leader and insurance society executive, was born in Woodford, Ireland, the daughter of Robert and Bridget (Campbell) Flynn. Sometime during her early childhood her family emigrated to Canada, settling in London, Ontario. There Elizabeth received her formal education (the exact amount is unknown), and there she married George Rodgers (1844–1920). By 1876 she

and her husband had settled in Chicago, where Rodgers, an iron molder, became active in the labor movement. Encouraged by her husband, who believed that a woman with talent should be more than a housewife, Mrs. Rodgers also participated in the movement. Reportedly the first Chicago woman to join the Knights of Labor, she was head of the all-woman Local Assembly No. 1789, organized in September 1881.

Mrs. Rodgers rose rapidly in the hierarchy of this idealistic effort to organize labor into one great national body. From 1881 to 1886 she served variously as a delegate from her local assembly to the State Trades' Assembly of Illinois, a delegate to the city-wide District Assembly No. 24 of the Knights of Labor, and supreme judge of the District Assembly. In August 1886, following the death of the incumbent, she was appointed Master Workman (president) of District Assembly 24, comprising all the Knights of Labor assemblies in Chicago and its suburbs except for the Stock Yards area. She was the first woman to hold such an office in the Knights.

Mrs. Rodgers reached the peak of her career at the national convention of the Knights of Labor in 1886. Attending as a delegate, along with her husband, she brought with her to the convention floor her two-weeks-old son, who charmed newspaper reporters and fellow delegates; the convention presented the baby with a silver cup and spoon. During the election of national officers, Mrs. Rodgers was nominated for the post of general treasurer of the order. She declined on the not unreasonable ground that being the mother of ten children occupied too much of her time. The temperance leader FRANCES WILLARD described Mrs. Rodgers in 1886 as "about forty years of age; height medium; figure neither stout nor fragile; complexion fair, clear, and healthful; eye an honest gray; mouth sweet and smiling; nose a handsome, masterful Roman; head square and full; profile strong and benignant."

With the decline of the Knights of Labor after 1887, Mrs. Rodgers left the labor movement. From 1889 through 1892 she was a partner in the firm of Leavell and Rodgers, Printers. Her second career really began, however, when, with twelve others, she organized the Women's Catholic Order of Foresters, a fraternal life insurance society. She served the society from its beginning until 1908 as chief executive officer, with the title of High Chief Ranger.

After 1908 Mrs. Rodgers lived in Chicago in relative obscurity. She died of a cerebral hemorrhage at the home of a daughter, Mrs. Harry

McLogan, in Wauwatosa, Wis., at the age of ninety-two. She was survived by two sons, William and Robert E., and two other daughters, Rose and Minnie. Always a devout Catholic, she was buried in Mount Olivet Cemetery in Chicago.

[John B. Andrews and William D. P. Bliss, *Hist. of Women in Trade Unions* (vol. X of *Report on Condition of Woman and Child Wage-Earners in the U.S.*, Senate Doc. No. 645, 61 Cong., 2 Sess., 1911), pp. 115, 127, 129; Frances E. Willard, *Glimpses of Fifty Years* (1889), pp. 522–25; *N.Y. Times*, Aug. 31, Oct. 5, 17, 1886; *Chicago Record-Herald*, Aug. 20, 1904, Oct. 5, 1906, Oct. 4, 1910; *Chicago Tribune* and *Chicago Daily News*, Aug. 28, 1939; *Lakeside Annual Directory of Chicago*, 1876–1909; files of Women's Catholic Order of Foresters, Chicago.]

ARCHIE JONES

**ROGERS, Elizabeth Ann** (Nov. 2, 1829–Feb. 20, 1921), and **Ellen Albertina POLYBLANK** (Sept. 30, 1840–July 20, 1930), Anglican sisters and educators, better known as Sisters Beatrice and Albertina, conducted together for its first thirty-five years St. Andrew's Priory, a school for girls in Hawaii. Both were natives of England. Elizabeth Ann Rogers was born in the parish of St. Erth, Hayle, Cornwall, the eldest child of Ann (Ellis) and James Rogers, a carpenter. She early showed piety and was a friend and visitor at the home of the Rev. Thomas L. Williams, the Tractarian vicar of Porthleven, through whom, apparently, she became acquainted with the Congregation of Religious of the Society of the Most Holy Trinity, a sisterhood founded on nineteenth-century notions of medievalism in 1848 by Priscilla Lydia Sellon (1821–1876). During 1865, while visiting in one of the congregation's houses—perhaps already a novice in the congregation's Third Order—Miss Rogers met Queen EMMA of Hawaii, a devoted Anglican, who was trying to find means to improve educational opportunities for Hawaiian girls. In 1866 Miss Rogers served as nurse in a temporary hospital opened by the Mother Foundress in Spitalfields during a cholera epidemic in London. Early in January of the following year she was clothed, under the name of Sister Beatrice, as a novice in the congregation's First Order, Sisters of Mercy, denominated of the Holy Communion.

Ellen Albertina Polyblank, daughter of Selina (Stocker) and Joseph Polyblank, a linen draper, was born in the parish of St. Saviour, Dartmouth, Devon. Nothing is known of her life before she entered the Congregation of the Society of the Most Holy Trinity except what she wrote in a letter in 1885 saying that since childhood she had found reading the Bible distasteful, as she could not understand it. In January 1867, taking the name Sister Albertina, she became a novice in the congregation's First Order. Though she spent sixty-three years as a religious, Sister Albertina never wholly learned self-discipline; for long periods she absented herself from confession and holy communion.

Three sisters of the congregation had established a house and school at Lahaina, Maui, Hawaii, in November 1864. Queen Emma and Thomas Nettleship Staley, first Anglican bishop in the islands, urged that other sisters be sent to establish a school at Honolulu for native girls of a higher social class. On Jan. 15, 1867, the Mother Foundress, Lydia Sellon, left England with three additional missionaries—Sister Eldress Phoebe (Emma Caroline Taylor, 1821–1890) and Sisters Beatrice and Albertina. They arrived at Honolulu on Mar. 30. After visiting Lahaina they took up residence on Emma Square, Honolulu. There the Mother Foundress had purchased land, on which she erected buildings for a girls' school, St. Andrew's Priory, opened on May 30. After the Mother Superior returned to England, the missionaries spent the rest of their lives conducting the school. Most of the students were boarders, some admitted on condition that they never return to their pagan home surroundings, and the sisters were responsible for their complete care.

In later years, former students remembered Sister Beatrice as gentle, saintly, and motherly and Sister Albertina as bright, beautiful, humorous, quick-tempered, and aristocratic. The school and its students had a close association with the royal family. Queen Emma made various donations and always took tea at the Priory on Friday and Sunday afternoons; in 1874, during riots in connection with election of a sovereign, she took refuge there for a few nights. The sisters also extended courtesies to Queen LILIUOKALANI during her arrest in her house, adjoining the Priory, after the revolution of 1893.

No additional sisters were sent out from England, and no novice was ever admitted to the congregation in Hawaii. In 1877 one of the sisters at Lahaina was elevated to Mother Superior and returned to England; at this time Sisters Beatrice and Albertina were finally professed. The school at Lahaina was closed, the two remaining sisters moving to St. Andrew's. By 1890 the others had died, leaving Sisters Beatrice and Albertina to manage the school alone, between them teaching every subject. When the congregation determined to close its mission in Hawaii, the two religious, who were legal or virtual guardians of several Hawaiian girls, secured permission (1892) to remain in Hawaii, provided they could find their own support. Capitation grants from the kingdom and gifts from friends augmented the meager fees of the Priory.

When, in 1902, the Bishopric of Honolulu became a part of the American Protestant Episcopal Church, Sisters Beatrice and Albertina requested the American bishop to find an American sisterhood to take charge of St. Andrew's Priory. This shift did not occur, however, until 1918 when, after sixteen years of management by lay teachers, the school came under the control of the Community of the Transfiguration of Cleveland, Ohio. Meanwhile, with its continuation assured, the two sisters had in 1902 retired to a cottage on the Priory grounds. In 1907, when the Congregation of the Society of the Most Holy Trinity deeded the Priory premises in trust to the Missionary District of Honolulu, previously informal commitments for the support of the two sisters were embodied in a legal contract. For the remainder of their lives the two lived simply, read their daily offices, attended the Hawaiian services of St. Andrew's Cathedral, visited with former pupils, and corresponded with their congregation's motherhouse in Ascot, Brecknall, Berkshire. Sister Beatrice died in Honolulu in 1921. The shock of finding her dead in bed impaired Sister Albertina's reason. Among other eccentricities that followed was a mild flirtation with Buddhism. She died nine years later, and her cremated ashes were buried in Oahu Cemetery, as had been the remains of Sister Beatrice. Their school, which during the thirty-five years of their active teaching had offered the best education available to Hawaiian girls in the islands, became a distinguished college preparatory school with an enrollment of over six hundred girls of all racial strains.

[Thomas Jay Williams, *Priscilla Lydia Sellon* (1950); letters from Hawaiian missionaries in *Vigilate* (Ascot, England), Michaelmas 1931 and Jan., Feb., and Midsummer 1932; Records of Conveyances of Hawaii (Bureau of Conveyances, Honolulu), vol. 299, pp. 275–88; *Hawaiian Monthly Chronicle* (Honolulu), Mar.–Apr. 1921, p. 1, Aug. 1930, pp. 9–10; *Honolulu Star-Bull.*, Feb. 21, 1921, July 21, 1930; *Honolulu Advertiser*, Feb. 21, 1921, Feb. 24, 1926, July 21, 1930; notes from the archives of Ascot Priory, supplied by the Rev. Thomas Jay Williams of N.Y. City.]

ANDREW FOREST MUIR

ROGERS, Grace Rainey (June 28, 1867–May 9, 1943), art collector and philanthropist, was born in Cleveland, Ohio, the only daughter among the four children of William J. and Eleanor B. (Mitchell) Rainey. Her father, a businessman and civic leader, made his fortune in the coke industry. Her mother was active in art philanthropy; she served as a trustee of the Cleveland School of Art and founded what became the Eleanor B. Rainey Memorial Institute, a combination handicraft school and social settlement for which she provided a building. One of Grace's brothers was Paul J. Rainey, a noted explorer, big-game hunter, and pioneer in motion-picture photography of wild animals. William Rainey Harper, first president of the University of Chicago, was a cousin.

Grace Rainey was educated at Mrs. Mittleburger's School in Cleveland and during her youth seems to have made frequent trips to Europe, where she began her art collection. This consisted mainly of French eighteenth-century paintings and artifacts and Persian art. Very little information is available about her private life; she is said to have been a "shy, retiring person." She was married on Sept. 28, 1907, to Henry Welsh Rogers, a New York businessman and graduate of Princeton University. They had no children and were divorced in 1918. Mrs. Rogers apparently spent most of her time in New York City, Newport, R.I., and Greenwich, Conn., with trips to Europe almost every year. She was a member of several prominent New York clubs.

Her major philanthropic activities were donations and benefactions to art museums, memorials to her explorer brother Paul, who died in 1923, and support for various social and humane causes. She was a member of the advisory council of the Cleveland Museum of Art, an honorary trustee and (from 1926) a fellow for life of the Metropolitan Museum of Art in New York, and one of the original trustees (1929–34) of the Museum of Modern Art. Her most notable art donation was the gift of an eighteenth-century French room, the Rousseau de la Rottière Room, to the Cleveland Museum of Art in 1942. The room, which had been in use in her New York apartment before it was given to the museum, contained doors, wall panels, rugs, sculpture, lighting equipment, and objets d'art designed for the Abbé Terray, comptroller general of finance under Louis XV; it was described as "among the most important acquisitions that the museum has ever received" (*Bulletin*, September 1943, p. 107). Her donations to the Metropolitan Museum included paintings by Daumier, Tiepolo, and Ingres. She also participated in numerous loan exhibitions, particularly of Persian art.

In 1934 Mrs. Rogers commissioned the American sculptor Paul Manship to design the Paul J. Rainey Memorial Gates at New York City's Bronx Zoo. She donated her brother's Louisiana animal farm to the Audubon Society as the Paul J. Rainey Wildlife Sanctuary. At her death, she left a $200,000 endowment fund for the Eleanor B. Rainey Memorial Institute. Her other social philanthropies included The Seeing Eye, founded by DOROTHY HARRISON EUSTIS to provide guide dogs for the blind, the Children's Aid Society, and the Society for the Prevention of Cruelty to Animals.

The two most important gifts associated with her name were created from bequests in her will. The Grace Rainey Rogers Memorial Annex to the Museum of Modern Art, completed in September 1951 at a cost of $400,-000, was an art center for amateurs containing studios and workshops. The Grace Rainey Rogers Auditorium, a concert hall in the Metropolitan Museum, opened in May 1954, was built at a cost of well over a million dollars; the initial contribution, several hundred thousand dollars, came from Mrs. Rogers and the balance from general museum funds.

Mrs. Rogers died in Greenwich, Conn., at the age of seventy-five, of arteriosclerosis with terminal uremia and pneumonia. Funeral services were held at the Central Presbyterian Church in New York City, and she was buried in the family mausoleum at Lakeview Cemetery, Cleveland. Under the terms of her will her residual estate, after other benefactions, personal and charitable, was divided among the three art museums in which she had been interested, the Cleveland Museum receiving $235,000, the Metropolitan $731,000, and the Museum of Modern Art $696,000.

[*Cleveland News*, May 10, 1943; *Cleveland Plain Dealer*, May 10, 1943, May 23, 1945; *Cleveland Press*, May 10, 1943, Mar. 23, 1945; *N.Y. Herald Tribune*, May 11, 1943; *N.Y. Times*, May 11, 1943, June 5, 1943, Sept. 25, 1951, May 2, 1954; Cleveland Museum of Art, *Bull.*, Apr. 1942, pp. 47–68, Sept. 1943, p. 107; Metropolitan Museum of Art, *Bull.*, June 1926, p. 155, June 1930, p. 146, May 1954, pp. 249–55; A. Conger Goodyear, *The Museum of Modern Art: The First Ten Years* (1943), pp. 17, 146; letter from a niece of Mrs. Rainey, Mrs. Mathias Plum; death record from Conn. State Dept. of Health.]

DANIEL M. FOX


**ROGERS, Harriet Burbank** (Apr. 12, 1834–Dec. 12, 1919), educator of the deaf, was born in North Billerica, Mass., the fourth of five daughters of Calvin Rogers, a farmer, and his wife, Ann Faulkner, the daughter of a woolen manufacturer. After local schooling she attended the Massachusetts State Normal School at West Newton, from which she graduated in 1851, and a private school in Lowell, Mass. She taught for some time in country schools and for several years in the Westford (Mass.) Academy. In 1863, through her eldest sister, Elisa Ann, who had taught at the Perkins Institution for the Blind, she was asked to take as a private pupil a little deaf girl, Fanny Cushing. After some hesitation over her fitness for the task she consented, believing that the hand of Providence was leading her in this direction.

Despite the experience of her sister, who had worked with LAURA BRIDGMAN, the first deaf-blind child in the United States to be successfully educated, Harriet Rogers herself had little knowledge of the teaching of the deaf. The Cushings hoped their daughter could be taught to speak, although at this time instruction of the deaf in the United States was almost wholly by the manual alphabet, or sign language. A friend of Miss Rogers gave her a newspaper clipping about a school in Germany where deaf children were taught to reproduce speech sounds by feeling the teacher's breath patterns and the voice vibrations in the teacher's throat and chest and then seeking to create the same effects themselves. Using this as a starting point, Miss Rogers achieved considerable success with her young pupil.

Her work soon became joined with that of a powerful advocate of new teaching methods for the deaf: Gardiner Greene Hubbard. A lawyer, businessman, and member of the Massachusetts State Board of Education, Hubbard had been shocked by his inability, in 1863, to find anyone willing or able to teach his recently deafened young daughter (later the wife of Alexander Graham Bell) to speak. He and Mrs. Hubbard taught the child themselves, and she was thereby enabled to retain the beginnings of speech and language gained before the loss of hearing and to continue her education by means of speech and lipreading. In 1864 Hubbard sought, unsuccessfully, to charter a school for the deaf based on these principles. Meeting Miss Rogers the next year, he encouraged her to advertise for additional pupils and to open a school at Chelmsford, Mass., in June 1866 with five pupils.

Hubbard's efforts to obtain a state-chartered school for the oral teaching of the deaf now gained the support of a Northampton resident, John Clarke, who offered to contribute toward its endowment. On June 1, 1867, the state legislature voted to grant a charter to the Clarke Institution for Deaf Mutes (later the Clarke School for the Deaf) at Northampton. Miss Rogers was chosen as its director, and in October she moved her pupils from Chelmsford to Northampton. Clarke School was then opened as the first in the United States to teach the deaf entirely by means of articulation (speech) and lipreading. To broaden her knowledge, she spent the year 1871–72 in Europe, where she studied German schools operated on the same oral principles. Originally planned for the partially deaf and for those who had lost their hearing when past the age of four, the oral method, under Miss Rogers' direction, quickly proved effective as well for many children born deaf.

Experimental in nature, the Clarke School was founded on a supreme faith that deaf and speechless children need not be permanently set apart from their fellows but could be prepared for a relatively normal position in community life. This faith sharply challenged the prevailing assumptions among educators of the deaf that the only practical method of communication was the manual one. From the start the new oral method attracted followers —at first largely women—who regarded it as almost a holy cause. The teachers of sign language—mostly men—looked down upon the oralists as "visionary enthusiasts." A bitter contest ensued, with Miss Rogers and her group of devoted teachers in the vanguard of the "oralists." As time went on, oral schools multiplied, and the older schools began to adopt the so-called "combined system," under which the pupils were taught speech skills and used speech in the classroom but reverted to sign language outside the classroom. Though the controversy was to continue for another decade, leading to the formation in 1890 of the American Association to Promote the Teaching of Speech to the Deaf, the terms of its eventual resolution were foreshadowed when the older American Instructors of the Deaf, at its 1886 convention, went on record as favoring earnest and persistent efforts in every school for the deaf to teach each pupil to speak and read from the lips.

Meanwhile Miss Rogers continued to direct the Clarke School, aided from 1873 onward by CAROLINE A. YALE as associate principal. Bronchial trouble forced her to leave the school in 1884 for the more salubrious climate of Colorado, and in 1886 she formally resigned. She spent the latter part of her life in North Billerica, where for a time she supervised the local kindergarten. She was a lifelong Unitarian. She died in North Billerica at the age of eighty-five of chronic bronchitis and emphysema and was buried in Billerica.

[Letters and personal papers of Miss Rogers at the Clarke School; *Annual Reports* of the Clarke School; addresses by Miss Rogers in Am. Assoc. to Promote Teaching of Speech to the Deaf, *Report of Proc.*, 1896, pp. 60–65, and 1912, pp. 469–72; obituary article by Caroline A. Yale in *Volta Rev.*, July 1920. See also: *Vital Records of Billerica, Mass., to the Year 1850* (1908), pp. 162, 163; *Hist. Sketches of the Framingham State Normal School* (1914), p. 48. Death certificate from Town of Billerica.]

MARY E. NUMBERS

**ROHLFS, Anna Katharine Green.** *See* GREEN, Anna Katharine.

**ROOSEVELT, Alice Hathaway Lee** (July 29, 1861–Feb. 14, 1884), first wife of Theodore Roosevelt, was the second of the six children, all girls but the youngest, of George Cabot Lee, of the Boston banking firm of Lee, Higginson & Co., and his wife, Caroline Watts Haskell of New Bedford, Mass. Born in the Boston suburb of Chestnut Hill, Alice entered a family whose members had for generations been prominent in the commercial, political, and social life of the Commonwealth. She received a conventional, fashionable education, growing up within the protective shelter of a small and self-assured circle of relatives and old, close friends.

On Oct. 18, 1878, the tranquil course of a Bostonian girlhood was dramatically changed when Theodore Roosevelt first looked upon her and "loved her as soon as I saw her sweet, fair young face" (Roosevelt, *In Memory*, p. 3). At the time she was seventeen and he, just turned twenty, was a junior in Harvard College. There followed a turbulent courtship in which Rooseveltian exuberance collided with maidenly shyness and indecision. "See that girl? I am going to marry her. She won't have me, but I am going to have *her!*" (Pringle, p. 42). And finally, after months of bobsledding, picnics, small dances, bird walks, and drives in dogcarts, the young man achieved his object. The two were married on Oct. 27, 1880, in the First Parish Church (Unitarian) in Brookline.

For three years they lived together in a happiness that has seemed idyllic to those who have looked back upon it. Their home for most of this period was in the house of Roosevelt's mother at 6 West 57th Street in New York City. Some part of the time each year he was in Albany serving in the state legislature, but often he returned to share with Alice their active domestic and social life in New

York. For her part she was constantly busy with her mother-in-law in "many charities." From "visiting hospital wards to dispensing ice-cream at a newsboys' lodging-house, both found pleasure in making this world less of a sorrow to the poor and more of a lesson to the rich" (*New York Herald*, Feb. 15, 1884).

In the course of the year 1883, after the young wife discovered she was to have a baby, the round of pleasure and duty was steadily reduced. When the child, Alice, the later "Princess Alice" Roosevelt Longworth, was born on Feb. 12, 1884, her father was summoned from Albany, where he had been attending committee hearings on pending legislation. On the next day he reached his mother's home expecting to receive a jubilant welcome. Instead he found his mother dying of typhoid fever and his wife, weakened by childbirth and Bright's disease, barely able to recognize him. In the small hours of the next morning his mother died and early in the following afternoon his wife also died. After a joint funeral service they were buried at Greenwood Cemetery in Brooklyn. A few days later Roosevelt returned to Albany to finish the legislative session and then went to bury himself for several years in the Badlands of Dakota.

No record of what Alice Lee was really like comes down to us from the girl herself. Others after her brief life have spoken for her. She was "loving," "demure," "charming," "of quick intelligence," "gay," "exceptionally bright," "the life of the party." That she was five feet seven inches tall, slender, with fair hair, "erect carriage," blue eyes, and "curly locks" is about all in the way of fact, as opposed to evaluation, that remains of her. The rest was spoken in shocked, fond retrospect and has been repeated by others who never knew her but have been moved by her story. Her meaning therefore comes to us most clearly through her effect upon her husband. In the record of their courtship, marked by his dark moments of jealousy and his longer hours of black despair at the thought that he might never win her, he seems as deeply moved as he ever was by anything in his whole career. When she died, he wrote soon after in a privately printed memorial that "the light went from my life for ever." Some kind of light within himself he did put out apparently at that time. Never did he, the most open of men, speak of Alice Lee by name again, even to her daughter.

[Hermann Hagedorn, *The Roosevelt Family of Sagamore Hill* (1954); Elting E. Morison, ed.,

*The Letters of Theodore Roosevelt*, vol. I (1951); Henry F. Pringle, *Theodore Roosevelt: A Biog.* (1931); Carleton Putnam, *Theodore Roosevelt*, vol. I (1958); Theodore Roosevelt, *In Memory of My Darling Wife Alice Hathaway Lee Roosevelt and of My Beloved Mother Martha Bulloch Roosevelt* (1885); family data from Harvard Univ. Archives file on George Cabot Lee.]

ELTING E. MORISON

ROOSEVELT, Edith Kermit Carow (Aug. 6, 1861–Sept. 30, 1948), second wife of Theodore Roosevelt, was born in Norwich, Conn., to Gertrude Elizabeth (Tyler) and Charles Carow. On both sides of her family line were names illustrious in the American past: the soldier Daniel Tyler, the naval officer Benjamin Lee, the great Puritan divine Jonathan Edwards. At the time Edith was born her family was securely fixed in the history and social hierarchy of New York City, but her grandfather's mercantile firm, Kermit and Carow, in which her father seems to have been employed, fell upon hard times, and when Charles Carow died in 1883 he left his wife and two daughters in what were called "reduced circumstances."

As a child Edith lived in a brownstone house on Union Square. Her education was strictly regulated by a thoughtful mother. Besides the Comstock School, there were good books, symphony concerts, the theatre (if it was Shakespeare), and small parties with appropriate children in the neighborhood. Among these children were Theodore Roosevelt and his sister Corinne, who became Edith's most intimate childhood friend. What feelings developed between the growing girl and the young man in this period it is impossible to discover, but there is a little evidence as well as much ex post facto speculation to suggest that Edith was much attracted by, indeed perhaps devoted to, Roosevelt by the time he went off to college in 1876. To such speculations Roosevelt himself contributed by suggesting at a later time that the two had in fact been engaged before his first marriage (Putnam, I, 171, 556; Pringle, p. 107).

Whatever the truth may have been, Roosevelt in his junior year at Harvard fell in love with Alice Lee (see ALICE HATHAWAY LEE ROOSEVELT) and married her in 1880. A little more than three years later she died in childbirth. For the next two and a half years the young widower and Edith Carow saw each other intermittently during what proved to be a hesitant and at times painful courtship. Each had old memories, allegiances, and personal prides to work through before such conflicts of emotion as existed were resolved in 1886.

On Dec. 2 of that year the two were married in London, England, where Mrs. Carow and her daughters had moved in the hope of living more cheaply. The wife of second choice, Edith Carow became the mother of five very energetic children—Theodore, born in 1887, Kermit (1889), Ethel (1891), Archibald (1894), and Quentin (1897). In September 1901 she also became the First Lady of an extraordinary president.

She had certain natural advantages: good looks, good intelligence, a presence of dignity and distinction. She had as well the acquired graces of tact in social situations, informed conversational skill, and trained musicianship. But there was also something puzzling about her—an austerity, an aloof composure, at times "an almost Oriental detachment" (Hagedorn, p. 10). Perhaps, as some observers believed, this came from some deep inner uncertainty, some introspective hypersensitivity. On the other hand, as others noticed, she was also shrewd, forthright, and unsentimental, and she could be ruthless (Putnam, I, 170). Whatever the cause, there was a kind of iron in her soul.

Whether or not these impressive qualities enabled her to modify her husband's course and decisions at critical moments remains still a matter of debate; that they enabled her to remain a person in her own right and thus to strengthen the person she was married to is beyond all doubt. She was one of the very few—perhaps, with Elihu Root, the only one—who never let Theodore Roosevelt fool himself about what he was doing and why he was doing it. Once, for instance, in 1910 when he was speculating about the kind of irresistible pressures that might force him quite against his will to enter the White House once more she remarked, "Put it out of your mind, Theodore, you will never be President of the United States again."

When he was president she was a most impressive First Lady. Her wide reading, lively interest in current events, sense of position, directness of statement, and almost regal poise made her an excellent hostess on public occasions and at private gatherings. Though not warm and gay, she had an inborn sense of taste that gave people confidence if it did not put them fully at ease. All these qualities, together with a tough-minded honesty, she brought not only to her official position but also to the thoughtful administration of her large, bustling, and exacting family. The balance between the public obligation and the private need she always maintained with due understanding and solicitude, reserving a sub-

stantial part of each day for the children. Her greatest contribution to her husband in his work as chief executive, besides the skill she showed in protecting him from all the normal domestic anxieties and irritations, was to assist him, by her frequent forthright assessments of his behavior, in keeping some perspective about himself. From him she received both devotion and great respect.

No doubt her achievement was obtained at some cost, undisclosed, to her own self. After her husband's death in 1919 she traveled continuously, admitting that sometimes in the past she had been "irked by the weight of the always beloved shackles" of family and public life. For the rest she lived a quiet, unassuming existence, based on Sagamore Hill, the Roosevelt home at Oyster Bay, N.Y., following her children and grandchildren with continuous interest and clearly expressed opinions. Living to eighty-seven, she died at Sagamore Hill in 1948 of myocardial insufficiency and congestive failure. She was buried, after Episcopal services, beside her husband in Youngs Memorial Cemetery, Oyster Bay. She was remembered as a woman who had given both distinction and dignity to her position, and as "one of the strongest-minded and strongest-willed presidential wives who ever lived in the White House" (*Life*, Dec. 13, 1948, p. 48).

[Hermann Hagedorn, *The Roosevelt Family of Sagamore Hill* (1954); Elting E. Morison, ed., *The Letters of Theodore Roosevelt* (8 vols., 1951–54); Henry F. Pringle, *Theodore Roosevelt: A Biog.* (1931); Carleton Putnam, *Theodore Roosevelt*, vol. I (1958); William R. Thayer, *Theodore Roosevelt: An Intimate Biog.* (1919); Edward Wagenknecht, *The Seven Worlds of Theodore Roosevelt* (1958); James Morgan in *Bay View Mag.*, Jan. 1908; *Woman's Who's Who of America*, 1914–15; *Time*, Oct. 11, 1948; *N.Y. Times*, Jan. 15, 1933, Sept. 17, 1935, Oct. 26, 1936, Feb. 7, 1937, and Oct. 1, 3, 13, 28, 1948. Edith Roosevelt contributed a chapter on her travels from 1919 to 1927 to a family volume, *Cleared for Strange Ports* (1927).]

ELTING E. MORISON

RORER, Sarah Tyson Heston (Oct. 18, 1849–Dec. 27, 1937), teacher of cooking, cookbook author, and dietitian, was born in Richboro, Bucks County, Pa., the daughter of Charles Tyson Heston, a pharmacist, and Elizabeth (Sagers) Heston. Her father was descended from Zebulon Heston, who came from Heston, England, in 1684 and settled in Bucks County. When Sarah was about a year old, Charles Heston moved his family to Buffalo, N.Y. During the Civil War he served as druggist with a hospital unit and returned home with impaired health. Although few details of Sarah's early life are known with certainty, she apparently attended the East Aurora (N.Y.) Academy, graduating, according to one account, in 1869. Shortly thereafter the family moved to Philadelphia. On Feb. 23, 1871, at the Reformed Church in Philadelphia, she was married to William Albert Rorer, a bookkeeper. They had three children: William Albert (1871); Anne Elizabeth (1874), who lived only two years; and James Birch (1876). The family was not prosperous and for a time lived with relatives or at a series of boardinghouses.

Although the poor health of her first son and her own digestive difficulties had drawn her attention to questions of diet, Mrs. Rorer later remarked that she was "not especially interested in either cooking or housekeeping" before 1879 (*Ladies' Home Journal,* June 1905, p. 38). In that year, however, encouraged by her cousin Mary Coggins and by ELIZA TURNER and LUCRETIA BLANKENBURG, she enrolled in the cooking school organized by these and other members of the recently formed New Century Club, where the clubrooms were sometimes filled "with the aroma of the frying-pan and the odor of the pungent onion and cabbage" (*New Century Club History,* p. 48). The following year she became director of the school, a post she held for three years. She apparently made some study also of physiology, anatomy, and chemistry, probably through private instruction from professors at the University of Pennsylvania Medical School and through attending lectures at the Woman's Medical College of Pennsylvania. When in 1880 the college's dean and professor of chemistry, RACHEL BODLEY, was invited to lecture on "Household Chemistry" before the Franklin Institute, Mrs. Rorer assisted by doing the illustrative cooking.

Mrs. Rorer left the New Century Cooking School in 1883 and opened her own Philadelphia Cooking School, for which she wrote a small handbook of recipes. By 1897 her school was conducting classes for ladies, cooks, and young girls, as well as a two-year normal course to prepare teachers of the domestic arts. Each year a scholarship was provided for a Negro girl, whose training would help her teach her own people. Concerned with the living conditions of the poor, Mrs. Rorer also taught cooking and hygiene to "ragpickers" and other destitute girls at the Bedford Street Mission in a Philadelphia slum. During this same period, at the request of Dr. S. Weir Mitchell and others on the staff of the Medical School of the University of Pennsylvania, she

established a diet kitchen where special dishes were prepared to meet the particular medical needs of certain patients. She also delivered a series of lectures on suitable diets for the sick to students at the Woman's Medical College, nurses at the Woman's Hospital, and fourth-year medical students at the university. An increasing number of graduates of her cooking school, beginning as early as 1893, became hospital dietitians. In all her classes Mrs. Rorer not only taught the principles of wise marketing and the mechanics of preparing food but also emphasized the chemical principles involved in cooking and took as her province "the building and repairing of the human body." She counseled against gluttony and urged the unwisdom of consuming elaborate twelve-course dinners.

Mrs. Rorer's national renown began when she wrote *The Philadelphia Cook Book* (1886), dictating the entire text to her husband in the evenings and often working until midnight. In 1885 she started a monthly publication, *Table Talk,* which she sold seven years later. During a three-month visit to Europe in 1892 she studied methods of teaching domestic science in France and England. In 1893 she became editor and part owner of *Household News,* a new publication which was absorbed by the *Ladies' Home Journal* in January 1897, at which time she began a long association with the *Journal* as its domestic editor. Each month she suggested menus, provided detailed recipes, and conducted a question and answer page to deal with such problems as how to make cut glass shine, how to clean brass, and the duties of servants. She continued to publish cookbooks: *Mrs. Rorer's New Cook Book* (1902) and others ranging over the entire cuisine, from bread and bread making, sandwiches and salads, to candies, new ways to serve oysters, and diets for the sick. She also lectured frequently in cities throughout the United States. At the World's Columbian Exposition in Chicago in 1893, she had charge of a "corn kitchen," where she daily demonstrated recipes using what she felt was a neglected food.

Mrs. Rorer (who had separated from her husband in the later 1890's) closed her Philadelphia Cooking School in 1903. Growing interested, shortly afterward, in the Chautauqua movement in Pennsylvania, she became director of its School of Domestic Science, instituted cooking classes in rural sections of the state, and for several terms served as president of the Women's Auxiliary Board. In 1911 she resigned from the *Ladies' Home Journal,* although she continued to write and lecture.

Three years later, now in her mid-sixties, she assumed charge of the culinary department of *Good Housekeeping* magazine; since she had begun spending her winters in Trinidad, where her son James was a government mycologist, she carried out many of her duties by mail.

A large, handsome woman of strong convictions, noted for her caustic wit, Mrs. Rorer had done much to make cooking a science in the United States. Impoverished in her old age, she received a small pension established by members of the Pennsylvania Dietetic Association, of which she was an honorary member. She attended its meeting of June 1, 1934, at Buck Hill Falls, Pa., and although nearly blind and crippled by a fall the year before, delivered a paper on "Early Dietetics" and was "the life of the party." Three years later, at the age of eighty-eight, she died at the home of her son William in Colebrook, Pa., of bronchial pneumonia following a hip fracture. She was buried in Hill Church Cemetery in nearby Lebanon.

[Mrs. Rorer published two brief reminiscences: "How I Cured My Own Ill-Health," *Ladies' Home Jour.*, June 1905; and "Early Dietetics," reprinted from the *Jour.* of the Am. Dietetic Assoc. in Adelia M. Beeuwkes, E. Neige Todhunter, and Emma Seifrit Weigley, eds., *Essays on Hist. of Nutrition and Dietetics* (1967). Published accounts of her career, often contradictory or inaccurate on her early life, include: Mrs. Talcott Williams, "The Most Famous Cook in America," *Ladies' Home Jour.*, Feb. 1897; Elise Biesel, "The First Cook in the Land," *Good Housekeeping*, Mar. 1914; Mary P. Huddleson, "Sarah Tyson Rorer—Pioneer in Applied Nutrition," in Beeuwkes, Todhunter, and Weigley, above; *Nat. Cyc. Am. Biog.*, XVI, 232; *Who Was Who in America*, vol. I (1942); Gertrude B. Biddle and Sarah D. Lowrie, eds., *Notable Women of Pa.* (1942), pp. 242–43. Death record from Pa. Dept. of Health. Mr. James Birch Rorer of Washington, D.C., provided family information. Additional information was supplied by Mrs. Emma Seifrit Weigley, who is completing a doctoral dissertation on Mrs. Rorer at N.Y. Univ.]

LYLE G. BOYD

**ROSE, Ernestine Louise Siismondi Potowski** (Jan. 13, 1810–Aug. 4, 1892), feminist, reformer, and freethinker, was born in the ghetto of Piotrkow, Russian Poland, the daughter of the town rabbi. Her family name was Potowski; her given name, Ernestine Louise, was acquired after she reached England, possibly an equivalent of or a substitute for other Polish or Hebrew names. An only child, precocious and independent, she grew up with more freedom and more education than was customary for Jewish girls of her background. Her father, to whom she was close, taught her

to read Hebrew, but she early came to question the teachings of the Torah. "I was a rebel at the age of five," she said in later life. At fourteen she rejected all Jewish dogma in regard to the inferiority of women. The death of her mother in 1826, leaving her substantial property, led her father, following prevailing custom, to sign a contract for her marriage to a man of his own age to whom her inheritance was to be given as a dowry. Rebelling against an action in which she had no voice, she went at sixteen to a Polish court to obtain her inheritance and spoke so well in her own defense that she secured a legal document endorsing her claim. The next year, turning over most of her inheritance to her father as a gesture of her freedom, she renounced the Jewish faith and left Poland forever.

After two years in Berlin, where she supported herself by inventing and selling a household deodorant, she moved on to Holland. She was in Paris at the time of the Revolution of 1830. The next year she went to England and at once became acquainted with a group of reformers and philanthropists that included Joseph Gurney, Elizabeth Fry, and Robert Owen. Miss Potowski joined Owen in founding, in 1835, the Association of All Classes of All Nations, which was to work for the salvation of mankind by peaceful means. In this period she met William Ella Rose, jeweler, silversmith, and disciple of Robert Owen; they were married in 1836, leaving at once for the United States. They had no children.

William Rose began work as a silversmith in New York City, and his wife found a cause for which to work in the married women's property bill recently introduced in the state legislature. In 1840, in company with Paulina Wright (later PAULINA WRIGHT DAVIS) and ELIZABETH CADY STANTON, she circulated petitions and spoke for the bill before a legislative committee in Albany. Despite their efforts, however, it did not pass both houses until 1848 and even then failed to include some of the desired provisions, which took twelve more years to achieve. Meanwhile Ernestine Rose had become active in the free-thought movement. She lectured for the Society for Moral Philanthropists, attended free-thought conventions, and contributed for fifty years to a free-thought weekly, the *Boston Investigator*. She joined in the efforts of a group of utopian socialists, led by John Anderson Collins, which in 1843 founded a short-lived colony in Skaneateles, N.Y., modeled on Owen's New Harmony community. In 1845 she sat beside Robert Owen at a "Convention of the Infidels of the United States" in Coliseum Hall in New

York City. Both she and her husband were active in the annual public celebrations of Thomas Paine's birthday; her speech at the banquet of 1850 so impressed James Gordon Bennett that he printed it in its entirety in the *New York Herald.*

During the 1850's Mrs. Rose, though interested also in the temperance and antislavery movements, devoted her principal efforts to the cause of woman's rights. Although not present at the famous Seneca Falls meeting in 1848, she attended the first national woman's rights convention in Worcester, Mass., in 1850, where she introduced a resolution calling for "political, legal, and social equality with man." Between 1850 and 1870 she missed few of the national conventions and spoke at many of the state ones. She lectured in more than twenty states and addressed legislative bodies, skillfully weaving antislavery, temperance, and freedom of thought into her woman's rights speeches. The spring of 1854 she spent in the Washington area with SUSAN B. ANTHONY, speaking incessantly for the cause. Some of the more pious feminists were troubled by Mrs. Rose's irreligion, but Miss Anthony's support and friendship never wavered. All contemporary accounts indicate her popularity and praise her voice, her delivery, and her appearance. One of the leading woman orators of the day, she was sometimes called the "Queen of the Platform."

During the Civil War, Ernestine Rose worked with Mrs. Stanton and Miss Anthony in the Women's Loyal National League, and after the war in the American Equal Rights Association, formed in 1866 as a successor to the earlier woman's rights conventions and dedicated to seeking both Negro suffrage and woman suffrage. In these postwar years Mrs. Rose was also concerned with the difficulties of working women and the cause of universal peace. In 1869, again with Mrs. Stanton and Miss Anthony, she took the lead in transforming the Equal Rights Association into the National Woman Suffrage Association. But more than three decades of reform work had taken its toll, and that year, suffering from neuralgia and rheumatism, Mrs. Rose sailed with her husband for Europe and a long vacation. They traveled in Europe for a year and then settled down in England, where Mrs. Rose occasionally made speeches for various reform movements. Her last public appearance and speech in the United States was at a convention of the National Woman Suffrage Association in 1873 when she and her husband were in the United States liquidating their New York property in order to make England

their permanent home. William Rose died in 1882. His wife survived him by another decade, dying in Brighton in 1892 at the age of eighty-two. She was buried beside her husband in Highgate Cemetery, London. In later years, replying to a query regarding the pioneers of the suffrage movement, Susan B. Anthony wrote: "begin with Mary Wollstonecraft . . . then Frances Wright—then Ernestine L. Rose. . . ."

[Mrs. Rose left no papers. The only biography, Yuri Suhl, *Ernestine Rose and the Battle for Human Rights* (1959), is based on contemporary printed sources. See also Elizabeth C. Stanton et al., *Hist. of Woman Suffrage,* I (1881), 95–100; Sara A. Underwood, *Heroines of Freethought* (1876), pp. 255–81; Ida H. Harper, *The Life and Work of Susan B. Anthony* (2 vols., 1898); and Lillian O'Connor, *Pioneer Women Orators* (1954). There are useful references to Mrs. Rose in Susan B. Anthony's diary for 1854, Schlesinger Library, Radcliffe College.]

ALICE FELT TYLER

**ROSE, Mary Davies Swartz** (Oct. 31, 1874–Feb. 1, 1941), pioneer nutritionist, was born in Newark, Ohio, the first of five children of Hiram Buel Swartz and Martha Jane (Davies) Swartz. Both parents were natives of Ohio, the father of Dutch, German, and Scottish descent, the mother of Welsh. While Mary was still an infant the family moved to Wooster, Ohio, where Swartz, a lawyer and graduate of the University of Michigan, became mayor (1877–81) and later probate judge. After attending Wooster High School, Mary entered (1893) the preparatory department of Shepardson College (later part of Denison University) in Granville, Ohio—her mother's alma mater. She began the college course a year later, but interrupted her studies in 1897 to teach in Wooster High School, enrolling also for a year (1898–99) at the College of Wooster. She returned in 1900 to complete the classical course at Shepardson, graduating with a bachelor of letters degree in 1901. The following year she spent studying home economics at the Mechanics Institute in Rochester, N.Y., after which she taught that subject from 1902 to 1905 at Fond du Lac (Wis.) High School.

In the fall of 1905 Mary Swartz entered Teachers College, Columbia University, as a student in household arts, and upon receiving her B.S. degree the next year, she became an assistant in the department with a special interest in the chemistry of food and nutrition. To further prepare her in this growing field the college granted her a traveling fellowship for advanced study. As it was not then possible to secure graduate training in nutrition, she elected to study physiological chemistry at Yale University under Prof. Lafayette B. Mendel. Completing the Ph.D. degree in 1909, she returned to Teachers College as an instructor.

On Sept. 15, 1910, she was married to Anton Richard Rose, three years her junior, a Yale graduate student in biochemistry. A native of Minnesota, he received his master's degree from Yale in 1911 and his Ph.D. from Columbia in 1912. Their only child, Richard Collin Rose, was born in 1915. Five years later the family moved from Manhattan to Edgewater, N.J., where their home overlooking the Hudson became known as a center of gracious hospitality. In 1924 Anton Rose left the faculty of Fordham University to take a position with the Prudential Insurance Company of Newark, N.J.; at his death in 1948 he was director of its longevity laboratories. A devoted husband, he was a source of encouragement to his wife in her developing professional career.

In 1910 Mary Rose was appointed assistant professor of nutrition at Teachers College, where the year before, under her stimulating guidance, a department of nutrition had been established within the new School of Household Arts. She was made an associate professor in 1918 and three years later became professor of nutrition. With Prof. Henry C. Sherman of Columbia's chemistry department, a pioneer in nutrition research, she organized a program whereby Teachers College students could secure a solid grounding in the scientific aspects of nutrition as well as in the best methods of teaching the subject. She was a gifted teacher, and her department became a leading university center for training in nutrition, drawing able students from all parts of the United States and from abroad.

Professor Rose's own scientific interests were wide-ranging, including such subjects as energy metabolism, the nutritive value of food proteins, and vitamin values, but most of her more than forty scholarly papers, bearing such titles as "Iron Requirement in Early Childhood" and "The Food Consumption of Nursery School Children," emphasized the practical applications of nutrition research. The author of two widely used and frequently reissued textbooks, *A Laboratory Hand-book for Dietetics* (1912) and *The Foundations of Nutrition* (1927), she also wrote articles for general circulation, such as "What Sweets Shall Children Have?" and a popular book for mothers, *Feeding the Family*, first issued in 1916.

The scope of her professional affiliations and interests was similarly broad. A charter member of the American Institute of Nutrition (an honorary society of research scientists) in the late 1920's, she was its president in 1937–38 and associate editor of its publication, the *Journal of Nutrition*, from 1928 to 1936. The American Dietetic Association elected her an honorary member in 1919, and frequently invited her to address its annual conventions. During the First World War she published *Everyday Foods in War Time* (1918) and served as a deputy director for New York City of the Bureau of Conservation of the United States Food Administration. She was one of the three American members of the commission of experts appointed by the Health Committee of the League of Nations in 1935 to study the physiological bases of nutrition, attending its meetings in Geneva and London. In 1940 she was one of five advisers on nutrition to the Council of National Defense. She was also a member (1933–41) of the Council on Foods of the American Medical Association. In her later years she became particularly interested in the development of nutrition programs in the public schools. Her book *Teaching Nutrition to Boys and Girls* (1932) was written for elementary school teachers, and throughout the 1930's, with the assistance of research grants, she conducted experimental studies in the public schools of New York City on ways of introducing nutrition education in all grades.

Mary Swartz Rose retired from Teachers College in June 1940, after thirty-one years of service. She died of cancer in 1941 at her Edgewater home and was buried in Maple Grove Cemetery, Granville, Ohio. Of Baptist background, she was a member of Riverside Church in New York. A scholarship and a lectureship in her name were established respectively by Teachers College and the Greater New York Dietetic Association. The Mary Swartz Rose Fellowship for graduate study in nutrition or allied fields, established in 1948 by the Nutrition Foundation, Inc., is awarded annually by the American Dietetic Association.

[Obituary articles by Henry C. Sherman in *Jour. of Nutrition*, Mar. 1941, pp. 209–11, and *Jour. of Biological Chemistry*, Sept. 1941, pp. 687–88; *Jour. Am. Medical Assoc.*, May 24, 1941, p. 2401; *Jour. of Home Economics*, Apr. 1941, pp. 221–24; Yale Univ., *Obituary Record of Graduates*, 1940–41, pp. 227–28; *Am. Men of Science* (6th ed., 1938) on Mary Swartz Rose and her husband; *Who Was Who in America*, vol. I (1942); *N.Y. Times*, Feb. 2, 1941. See also Mary I. Barber, ed., *Hist. of the Am. Dietetic Assoc., 1917–1959* (1959); Ben Douglass, *Hist. of the Lawyers of Wayne County*,

*Ohio* (1900), p. 87; Mary Swartz Rose, "Univ. Teaching of Nutrition and Dietetics in the U.S.," *Nutrition Abstracts and Revs.*, Jan. 1935, pp. 439–46, especially p. 442; and Clara Mae Taylor, "Recollections of Mary Swartz Rose," *Jour. Am. Dietetic Assoc.*, July 1963. Denison Univ. and the College of Wooster provided enrollment and other data. A portrait by Ivan Olinsky, presented to Teachers College in 1936 by Professor Rose's former students, hangs in the Grace Dodge Room.]

CLARA MAE TAYLOR

ROSS, Betsy (Jan. 1, 1752–Jan. 30, 1836), legendary maker of the first Stars and Stripes, was born Elizabeth Griscom in Philadelphia, Pa., the seventh daughter and eighth of the seventeen children of Samuel and Rebecca (James) Griscom. The basic facts of her life are well established. Her great-grandfather Andrew Griscom, a carpenter, emigrated from England to New Jersey in 1680 and later moved to Philadelphia. Samuel Griscom also followed the building trade and is reputed to have assisted in the construction of Independence Hall. Elizabeth's Quaker parents probably sent her to the Friends' school on South Fourth Street; her mother taught her to do needlework, at which she apparently became skillful.

On Nov. 4, 1773, Elizabeth Griscom was married at Gloucester, N.J., to John Ross, son of the Rev. Aeneas Ross, rector of Emmanuel Church in New Castle, Del., her marriage to an Anglican causing her expulsion from the Society of Friends. For some years afterward she attended Christ Church (Anglican) in Philadelphia; she then became a staunch member of the Society of Free Quakers, commonly known as the "Fighting Quakers." John Ross, who had been apprenticed to an upholsterer, started an upholstery business with his wife on Chestnut Street and later moved to Arch Street. In January 1776, while on militia duty, he was fatally injured in an explosion of gunpowder at the Philadelphia waterfront. Mrs. Ross continued to work with the needle, supplementing her income by making flags for the State of Pennsylvania. It appears from the tax records that she acquired property in Philadelphia and Cumberland counties, a substantial 190 acres and some livestock in the latter.

Elizabeth Ross ended her brief widowhood on June 15, 1777, by marrying Joseph Ashburn, first mate of the brigantine *Patty*. The couple had two children, Zillah, born in 1779, who is said to have died young, and Eliza (1781). Ashburn's ship was captured by the British in 1781 and he was confined to an English prison, where he died in March 1782. A friend and fellow prisoner, John Claypoole, on his return to Philadelphia that sum-

mer, called on Mrs. Ashburn to deliver farewell messages from her late husband. Within less than a year, on May 8, 1783, they were married. They had five daughters: Clarissa Sidney, born in 1785, Susan (1786), Rachel (1789), Jane (1792), and Harriet (1795), the last dying in infancy. Claypoole was employed for a time in the United States Custom House; he suffered from paralysis for a number of years before his death in August 1817. His widow continued to live in Philadelphia until her own death in 1836, at the age of eighty-four. She was buried in the Free Quaker Burying Ground; her remains were reinterred in 1857 in Mount Moriah Cemetery, where her daughter Clarissa had purchased a plot.

The Betsy Ross story, familiar to most Americans, depicts her as being visited in her upholstery shop in June 1776 (or, in some accounts, 1777) by George Washington, Robert Morris, and George Ross, uncle of her late husband, as members of a secret committee of the Continental Congress authorized to design a flag for the nation-to-be. Accepting her suggestion that five-pointed stars be substituted for the six-pointed ones in their rough sketch when she demonstrated the ease with which such a star could be cut with a single snip of the scissors, they entrusted the making of the flag to her. Some versions of the story add that she was given a contract to manufacture flags for the government and continued in the business until her death.

This charming account was first told in a paper read by her grandson William Canby before the Historical Society of Pennsylvania in March 1870. It had been related to him, he reported, as early as 1857 by his aunt Clarissa Sidney (Claypoole) Wilson, who had often heard it from her mother. Canby's search for confirmation in contemporary documents proved essentially fruitless. The story appeared in *Harper's Monthly* in July 1873, was inserted by George H. Preble in the second edition of his *Origin and History of the American Flag* in 1880, and by the mid-1880's had reached school textbooks. The rise of American patriotic societies in the late nineteenth century, with their stress on the flag, gave it further impetus. Charles H. Weisberger's painting, "Birth of Our Nation's Flag," depicting Betsy Ross displaying a finished Stars and Stripes to her distinguished callers, was first exhibited at the World's Columbian Exposition in Chicago in 1893 and did much to stir up interest in the subject. The house where the event is said to have taken place was marked in 1887, and in 1898 a Betsy Ross Memorial Association was organized to convert the "Flag House" into a national shrine. To raise the necessary funds some two million ten-cent subscriptions were sold to schoolchildren and members of patriotic societies, each of whom received a reproduction of the Weisberger painting.

Historical records lend little credence to the story. The only documentary evidence to support it is found in the minutes of the Pennsylvania State Navy Board, which show an order for payments of "14..12..2" to Elizabeth Ross in May 1777 for making "ship's colours, &c." Records of the Continental Congress mention no committee concerned with designing a flag. Betsy Ross and her first Stars and Stripes, however, seem permanently embedded in American legend.

[The Betsy Ross legend is perpetuated in: Lloyd Balderston, *The Evolution of the Am. Flag. From Materials Collected by the Late George Canby* (1909); H. K. W. Wilcox, "National Standards and Emblems," *Harper's Monthly*, July 1873; Edwin S. Parry, *Betsy Ross, Quaker Rebel* (1930); Addie G. Weaver, *The Story of Our Flag, Colonial and National* (1898); 74 Cong., 2 Sess., "Memorial to Betsy Ross," *House Report* 2265 (1936). Opposing the legend are the following: George H. Preble, *Origin and Hist. of the Am. Flag* (new ed., 1917), I, 259–89; Byron McCandless, "The Story of the Am. Flag," *Nat. Geographic Mag.*, Oct. 1917; Theodore D. Gottlieb, comp., *The Origin and Evolution of the Betsy Ross Flag: Legend or Tradition* (1938); Franklin Hanford, *Did Betsy Ross Design the Flag of the U.S.A.?* (1917); William C. Miller, "The Betsy Ross Legend," *Social Studies*, Nov. 1946. See also: *Pa. Archives*, 2nd Ser., I, 164; 3rd Ser., XIV, 709, XV, 151, XX, 231, 364, XXIV, 748; Rebecca I. Graff, *Genealogy of the Claypoole Family of Phila.* (1893); John W. Jordan, ed., *Colonial Families of Phila.* (1911), II, 1250–51; Joseph Jackson, "Washington in Phila.," *Pa. Mag. of Hist. and Biog.*, Apr. 1932; Charles F. Jenkins, "John Claypoole's Memorandum-Book," *ibid.*, July 1892.]

ELIZABETH COMETTI


ROURKE, Constance Mayfield (Nov. 14, 1885–Mar. 23, 1941), student of American culture, was born in Cleveland, Ohio, the only child of Henry Button Rourke, a lawyer, and Constance Elizabeth (Davis) Rourke. Her ancestry was mainly Southern pioneer, Irish on her father's side. One of her Tennessee forebears, George Mayfield, was stolen by the Creeks as a baby and later knew Davy Crockett; but of this Miss Rourke was little aware until her own later research, for she grew up, as she put it, "without much emphasis upon my own ancestry . . . because of a parental revolt against a grandfather who made too much of these matters" (Kunitz and Haycraft,

pp. 1206–07). About 1892 Mrs. Rourke, now a widow, moved to Grand Rapids, Mich., where her Methodist minister father lived. While she earned a livelihood as a schoolteacher and principal, Constance attended the local public schools and then went on to Vassar College, there to develop a keen interest in literary criticism and aesthetics. After taking an A.B. degree in 1907, she spent a year at the Sorbonne in Paris. During the period 1908–10 she was a research reader at the Bibliothèque Nationale and at the British Museum. Called back to Vassar as an instructor in English, she taught there until her resignation in 1915. For the next quarter century of research and writing she lived in Grand Rapids with her mother, with whom she had an extraordinarily close bond. It was appropriate that one whose fame rests on her search for the roots of American culture should have chosen to root her own adult life in the community where she had grown up. Constance Rourke was a citizen of Grand Rapids in the fullest sense of the word, with friendships among a wide range of people throughout the city.

In her apprentice years as a free-lance writer, Miss Rourke confined herself to critical articles for the *New Republic*, the *Freeman*, and other magazines of opinion. Her first book, *Trumpets of Jubilee* (1927), marked out the area of all her later work. Her aim was to define the American character by evoking and interpreting the popular or folk taste of a bygone era, in this case by studying the lives of five Americans of the mid-nineteenth century who had had an enormous popular appeal: Lyman Beecher, HARRIET BEECHER STOWE, Henry Ward Beecher, Horace Greeley, and P. T. Barnum. She dealt with them in an exciting and colorful style, but except for the astute literary analysis of *Uncle Tom's Cabin*, with its suggestive comparison of Mrs. Stowe's talent to Hawthorne's, the book today seems disappointingly superficial. Her key failure is her reduction of Lyman Beecher's religion to a caricature that might have been composed by H. L. Mencken. *Troupers of the Gold Coast, or The Rise of Lotta Crabtree* (1928), her second book, is undistinguished; at this point in her career her enthusiasm for the color and zip of American popular taste seemed to be overwhelming her capacity to judge both its merit and its significance.

Then in 1931 Miss Rourke published *American Humor: A Study of the National Character*. This was at once hailed by the critics as a classic of American literary scholarship—an estimate which has never been challenged. A paperback reprint was widely sold in the

1950's. The first of its two parts studies the various strands in the American comic tradition: the humor of the Yankee and the backwoodsman and the Negro; of the minstrel show and the religious revival and the strolling players; of the explorers and the flatboatmen and the California miners. For years Miss Rourke had patiently accumulated almanacs from New England attics. She had visited Negroes and listened to their anecdotes and jokes, and had read through vast library collections of American humor and folklore. To her prodigious scholarship she added a matured style with all the pictorial qualities of her earlier prose but more precise and judicious, capable of registering the sadness that lies at the base of American humor as well as of delighting in the comic extravagances of the national spirit. Her portrait had certain faults, but these do not mar the main outlines of the image she projected. In the second part of *American Humor*, Miss Rourke studied the relation of such writers as Hawthorne, Poe, Melville, James, and Twain to this popular comic lore. She hoped thus to relate these classic figures more fully to "the materials of the American tradition," and also, like Van Wyck Brooks, to introduce to the alienated "highbrow" writer of her own day the rich, traditional store of his native culture. Though occasionally this approach led to distortion, as in her treatment of Hawthorne, at other times, particularly in her essay on James' *The American*, she emphasized an important aspect of an artist's work that more solemn critics had all but ignored. In full command of a luminous and swiftly moving prose, Miss Rourke set forth some of the finest literary judgments of American writers that have ever been written.

Her next two books, *Davy Crockett* (1934) and *Audubon* (1936), show signs of haste and are deservedly forgotten. A more discerning and careful work is *Charles Sheeler: Artist in the American Trdition* (1938). Dealing here with a painter who, like herself, had found aesthetic pleasure and inspiration in the functional form of Shaker houses, barns, and furniture, she created a memorable example of the modern American artist drawing strength from his native soil.

Intermittently throughout the 1930's, in preparation for a projected multivolume American cultural history, Miss Rourke traveled across the United States unearthing remnants of folk art, craftsmanship, and music, and interviewing "old timers" who responded volubly to her unaffected interest and enthusiasm. From her unfinished manuscript and mass of notes Van Wyck Brooks extracted fragments for posthumous publication as *The Roots of American Culture* (1942). The book includes an account of early American theatricals, an essay on early American music, another on the Shakers, and an article on minstrel shows. Her demonstration that even the most lighthearted Negro songs contained a strong element of protest and rebellion anticipated the discoveries of later authoritative scholarship.

Constance Rourke welcomed and encouraged the increase of respectful interest in popular culture which marked the depression years. She was an organizer of the National Folk Festival held in St. Louis in 1934, and for a brief period in 1937 was editor of the Federal Art Project's Index of American Design. A fall on an icy porch in Grand Rapids early in 1941 brought her life to a premature end. She died there, of complications resulting from a fractured vertebra, at the age of fifty-five, and was buried in Woodlawn Cemetery, Grand Rapids. As a local businessman observed, she was the town's "most distinguished citizen," a tribute to her personality as well as to her scholarship.

[Stanley Edgar Hyman's *The Armed Vision* (1948), pp. 127–41, which relates her work to modern anthropology and perceptively assesses her achievement, and Margaret Marshall's moving and insightful remembrances in the *Nation*, Mar. 29 and June 21, 1941, and Oct. 24, 1942, are the best appraisals. See also: obituaries in the *N.Y. Times* and *N.Y. Herald Tribune* for Mar. 24, 1941, and editorial in the *Times*, Mar. 25; Stanley J. Kunitz and Howard Haycraft, *Twentieth Century Authors* (1942), which contains an autobiographical statement; *Nat. Cyc. Am. Biog.*, XXXII, 100 (with portrait); Van Wyck Brooks' preface to Miss Rourke's *The Roots of Am. Culture* and his *Days of the Phoenix* (1957), pp. 103–05; Fred B. Millett, *Contemporary Am. Authors* (1940), pp. 556–57. A cousin, Mrs. Alice Fore of Carbondale, Ill., provided helpful information.]

KENNETH S. LYNN

ROWLANDSON, Mary White (c. 1635–post 1678), Indian captive, was born in England, one of six daughters and three sons of John and Joane (West) White of South Petherton, Somersetshire. While Mary was still a small child the family migrated to Salem, Mass., and later, in 1653, to the newly founded frontier village of Lancaster. Here, in 1656, she became the wife of Joseph Rowlandson, son of Thomas Rowlandson of Ipswich and Lancaster's first regular minister. Establishing their home on a sloping hill just above Ropers Brook, a site now marked by a commemorative tablet, the Rowlandsons had four children: Mary (born Jan.

15, 1657/58), who died in infancy; Joseph
(Mar. 7, 1661/62); a second Mary (Aug. 12,
1665); and Sarah (Sept. 15, 1669).

The ordeal which lifted Mary Rowlandson
from the obscurity of a frontier parsonage to a
permanent place in history came about during
King Philip's Indian uprising. At dawn on Feb.
10, 1675/76, a war party of Indians attacked
Lancaster, killing settlers and burning their
homes. Laying siege to the Rowlandson house,
where some three dozen villagers had sought
refuge, they killed twelve of them, including
Mrs. Rowlandson's eldest sister and other relatives, and took twenty-four captives, among
them the minister's wife and children. Wrote
Mrs. Rowlandson later: "I had often before
this said, that if the Indians should come, I
should chuse rather to be killed by them then
taken alive but when it came to the tryal my
mind changed; their glittering weapons so
daunted my spirit, that I chose rather to go
along with those (as I may say) ravenous
Bears, then that moment to end my dayes"
(Nourse and Thayer, p. 5.) Rowlandson, being away at the time, returned to find his home
in ashes and has family gone.

At first the plight of the captives, driven
westward into the wintry wilderness by warriors who showed them little pity, was truly
deplorable. Although young Joseph and his sister Mary apparently were uninjured, both
Mrs. Rowlandson and six-year-old Sarah were
suffering from bullet wounds. During the night
of Feb. 18–19, having had no food for a week,
Sarah died in her mother's arms. Mrs. Rowlandson lived as a prisoner and slave among
the Indians, moving with them in frequent mi-
grations which took them as far as the Connecticut River, into southwestern New Hampshire,
and back to Mount Wachusett near Lancaster.
She plodded much of the way on foot, often
with a heavy burden, suffering from hunger
and debility. Gradually, however, her wounds
healed through the application of oak leaves,
and she adjusted to the meager Indian diet of
groundnuts, meal, horsemeat, and occasional
wild game.

During her three-month captivity Mary
Rowlandson was attached to the household of
the proud squaw-sachem Weetamoo. She was
subjected to considerable abuse, for the Indians themselves were hungry and irritable,
but her skill at sewing and knitting won her
favor, and she experienced some kindness. She
occasionally was able to visit with her two surviving children, but more often than not was
separated from them. One of her most memorable experiences occurred early in March
when she had an interview with Philip, the

Wampanoag sachem who had instigated the
war.

Through all her sufferings, intensified by
fears not only for her own safety but for that
of her children, Mary Rowlandson remained
steadfast in her Christian faith, maintaining a
spirit of courage, resilience, and inner dignity.
Comforted by a Bible given her by an Indian
who had seized it in a raid, she looked forward to her redemption in God's own time.
Meanwhile, seizing a likely chance, she asked
the Indians if they would sell her back to her
husband. They agreed on a ransom of £20
and sent word to Boston. Finally, on May 2,
1676, through the efforts of her husband and
others, notably John Hoar of Concord, who
came unarmed to the Indian camp at Mount
Wachusett bearing the ransom, Mary Rowlandson was released. The warmth of the Indians'
farewell suggested that they had developed a
genuine affection for their prisoner. Her two
children reached safety at widely separated
points some weeks later. In August, King
Philip was shot and beheaded by the colonists,
and the war petered out.

The reunited Rowlandson family lived for a
time in Boston in a house rented for them by
the South Church, but Joseph Rowlandson
soon accepted a call as pastor of the church at
Wethersfield, Conn., where he was installed on
Apr. 7, 1677. He died on Nov. 24, 1678,
whereupon the town voted an annual pension
of £30 for his widow. How long she survived
is not recorded.

Mary Rowlandson's fame spread rapidly with
the publication of her own account of her captivity, originally written for her children, at
Boston in 1682. Recognized as a classic of frontier literature and a prime example of the
American captivity narrative, this small volume
has appeared in more than thirty editions,
and portions have been included in numerous
anthologies. Characterized by vivid episodic
narration couched in a vigorous, earthy style,
Mrs. Rowlandson's account of her adventures
has been a favorite of generations of readers.
As a source, it contributes much to our knowledge of conditions among the Indians during
King Philip's War and sharpens our impressions of various Indian leaders. Above all, it
bears eloquent witness to a Puritan woman's
abiding religious faith in a time of supreme
hardship and peril.

[No copy of the first edition of Mary Rowlandson's memoir is known to have survived; a rare
copy of the second edition, published at Cambridge in 1682, with the title *The Soveraignty &
Goodness of God, Together, with the Faithfulness
of His Promises Displayed; Being a Narrative of*

the Captivity and Restauration of Mrs. Mary Rowlandson, is in the Prince Collection of the Boston Public Library. Especially useful is the annotated facsimile edition, edited by Henry S. Nourse and John E. Thayer (1903). A more accessible version is in Charles H. Lincoln, ed., Narratives of the Indian Wars, 1675–1699 (1913), pp. 107–67. Frederick L. Weis, ed., The Narrative of the Captivity and Restoration of Mrs. Mary Rowlandson (1930), derived from the Nourse and Thayer edition, includes (pp. 81–82) a list of the various editions of the work. For contemporary mention of the incident see Increase Mather, A Brief Hist. of the War with the Indians in New-England (1676), and William Hubbard, A Narrative of the Troubles with the Indians in New-England (1677). The best modern retelling is in Howard H. Peckham, Captured by Indians (1954). For background consult Douglas E. Leach, Flintlock and Tomahawk: New England in King Philip's War (1958). For further biographical details see Henry S. Nourse, ed., The Early Records of Lancaster, Mass. (1884); A Digest of the Early Conn. Probate Records, vol. I, Hartford District, 1635–1700 (1904); Almira Larkin White, Genealogy of the Descendants of John White of Wenham and Lancaster, Mass., vol. I (1900); and New England Hist. and Genealogical Register, XVI (1862), 352, 354, 356–57, containing a record of Mary Rowlandson's children. The problem of locating geographically and dating various episodes of the captivity is discussed in Henry S. Nourse, "Mrs. Mary Rowlandson's Removes," Am. Antiquarian Soc., Proc., n.s. XII (1897–98), 401–09; and Douglas E. Leach, "The 'Whens' of Mary Rowlandson's Captivity," New England Quart., Sept. 1961.]

DOUGLAS EDWARD LEACH

ROWSON, Susanna Haswell (c. 1762–Mar. 2, 1824), novelist, actress, and educator, was born in Portsmouth, England, the only child of William Haswell, a lieutenant in the Royal Navy, by his first wife, Susanna Musgrave, daughter of a commissioner of customs. Other members of the Haswell family to achieve eminence include two of Susanna's three half brothers—Robert Haswell, an American naval officer and minor writer, and John Montrésor Haswell, who was cited by Congress for his bravery in the war with Tripoli—and her cousin Anthony Haswell, who came to Boston about 1770 and became a famous editor and balladeer in early Vermont. Since her mother had died in giving her birth, Susanna's early rearing was entrusted to relatives. About four years after her birth her father was assigned to duty in the revenue service in Massachusetts. There he married Rachel Woodward of George's Island in Boston harbor and settled in nearby Nantasket. In 1768 Haswell returned to England for his daughter. In her partly autobiographical novel, Rebecca, or Fille de Chambre

(1792), Susanna recounted the hazards of her voyage to America, ending in shipwreck on an island in Boston harbor, and then the contrasting years of peaceful and simple pleasures of life at Nantasket.

The Haswells circulated easily in the literate and stable aristocracy of the Boston area and enjoyed the best of life in the New World. Susanna's precocious knowledge of the classics at the age of twelve is said to have impelled their eminent summer neighbor, James Otis, to call her "my little scholar." But the quiet harmony of their life was soon shattered by the Revolution. Applying for permission to leave America in the fall of 1775, Haswell (a member of the hated revenue service) was denied his request. His property was confiscated, and he and his family were interned as loyalists. After being held at Hingham for two years, they were moved in the fall of 1777 to Abington, where their sufferings were intensified by their isolation and by the crippling illness of the head of the family. Finally, in the spring of 1778, Haswell was permitted, on giving his parole to Gen. William Heath, to take his family to Halifax, Nova Scotia, and thence to London, where they lived in poverty because of a several years' delay in the granting of Haswell's government pension.

Susanna began job-hunting at once and soon became governess to the children of the Duchess of Devonshire. In this role she not only toured Europe but also saw something of the private lives of the aristocracy, which she later used as material for her fiction. In 1786 she published her first novel, Victoria, with a dedication to the Duchess. She then retired from her job to marry, in 1787, William Rowson, a hardware merchant and a trumpeter in the Royal Horse Guards. A handsome, sociable man, too fond of liquor, too trusting in business enterprises, and sire of an illegitimate child, Rowson was not an ideal husband. There can be little doubt that certain of the trials of female patience recounted in Mrs. Rowson's major novel, Charlotte Temple (1791), had some foundation in her own life. With the failure of Rowson's hardware business in 1792, both husband and wife took to the stage, playing in Edinburgh in 1792–93. Here they were booked by Thomas Wignell to act in his company in the new Chestnut Street Theatre in Philadelphia. After performing in Annapolis, Philadelphia, and Baltimore, in 1796 the Rowsons settled in Boston to play at the Federal Street Theatre. Although not a gifted actress, Mrs. Rowson had a warm personality and versatile talents; she could dance, sing, play the harpsichord and guitar, write plays, and compose both lyrics and librettos. During her five-year career in the theatre she acted 129 different parts in 126 different productions, a number of them written by herself, and some with the collaboration of musicians such as Alexander Reinagle of Philadelphia. The most successful of her theatrical works was the operetta *Slaves in Algiers, or a Struggle for Freedom* (1794), in which a group of American women, captured by North African pirates and held for ransom, eventually make their escape. Other successes were *The Volunteers* (1795), a musical farce based on the Whiskey Rebellion; and *Americans in England, or Lessons for Daughters*, a three-act comedy, first presented in 1797, in which she made her last appearance.

In the spring of that year, now in her mid-thirties, Mrs. Rowson retired from the stage and opened a Young Ladies Academy in Boston. She moved it in 1800 to Medford, in 1803 to Newton, and in 1811 back to Boston, where until her retirement in 1822 she occupied quarters on Hollis Street. One of the first schools established in the United States to offer girls some education above the elementary level, the academy was highly successful. Mrs. Rowson wrote some of her own textbooks, including *An Abridgment of Universal Geography, together with Sketches of History* (1805?), *A Spelling Dictionary* (1807), and *Biblical Dialogues between a Father and His Family* (1822). The school was also unusual in offering its young women formal instruction in public speaking and in providing well-qualified music teachers trained in Europe.

In other contributions to Boston's cultural life, William Rowson played a memorable trumpet in the Handel and Haydn Society's performances of the *Messiah*, while Mrs. Rowson, who counted among her friends such leading musicians as the Graupners and Von Hagens, helped organize concerts. When the *Boston Weekly Magazine* was begun in 1802, Mrs. Rowson became a contributor, as she was to the *Monthly Anthology* and Joseph T. Buckingham's *New England Galaxy*. She had meanwhile published other ventures in the field of the novel, among them *Trials of the Human Heart* (1795), a rather loosely organized four-volume work to which both Benjamin Franklin and MARTHA WASHINGTON were subscribers, and *Reuben and Rachel* (1798), a rambling historical novel dealing with the heirs of Columbus. *Sarah, the Exemplary Wife*, a series of fictionalized moral tracts first published in her *Boston Weekly Magazine*, appeared in 1813.

Varied as were Mrs. Rowson's activities, her main importance is as the author of one book—*Charlotte Temple* (London, 1791; Philadelphia, 1794), the first American best seller, which has seen over two hundred editions to date. (She also wrote a sequel, *Charlotte's Daughter; or, The Three Orphans*, published posthumously in Boston in 1828.) A sentimental novel patterned on the standard seduction story, *Charlotte Temple* tells of a sheltered English schoolgirl possessed of more tenderness than prudence who is seduced, carried off to New York, and abandoned by a British army officer whose villainy is punished, after Charlotte's death, by the torments of remorse. The subtitle of the book, "A Tale of Truth," may well be correct, for some evidence exists that the original of the seducer, Montraville, was Mrs. Rowson's cousin, Col. John Montrésor. Like many another best seller, *Charlotte Temple* is more significant for the historian of popular taste than for the literary critic. Although the contrived plot and wooden characters today invite ridicule, in its own time a book hinting at the power of the sexual impulse and detailing the penalties meted out to women for accepting illicit love under the "double standard" may well have been a useful part of the education of a young girl.

Although Mrs. Rowson had no children, her household was large, for it included her husband's younger sister, Charlotte; his illegitimate son, William; her own niece, Susan Johnston; and her adopted daughter, Fanny Mills. To these last two she turned over her school in 1822, though she apparently still maintained much of the alertness and vivacity that had marked all her life. Mrs. Rowson regularly attended the preaching of the Rev. John S. Gardiner at Trinity Church, and found scope for expressing her humanitarian convictions by serving for some years as president of the Boston Fatherless and Widows' Society. She died at her home in Boston and was buried in the family vault of her friend Gottlieb Graupner in St. Matthew's Church, South Boston. When this church was demolished in 1866, her remains were transferred to Mount Hope Cemetery in Dorchester.

Reared in a loyalist family, Mrs. Rowson became an ardent, articulate American patriot. An active proponent of the theatrical and musical arts in the early years of the United States, a broad-minded and effective teacher, she was also one of the first to express, through her novels, a subtle protest against the dependent status of women in her day.

[The best sources for her life are Elias Nason, *A Memoir of Mrs. Susanna Rowson* (1870), and

Samuel L. Knapp's "Memoir" in the preface to *Charlotte's Daughter* (1828). See also R. W. G. Vail, *Susanna Haswell Rowson, the Author of Charlotte Temple: A Bibliog. Study* (1933); obituary in Boston *Evening Gazette*, Mar. 6, 1824; Joseph T. Buckingham, *Personal Memoirs and Recollections of Editorial Life* (1852), I, 83–85; Francis W. Halsey, editorial introduction to *Charlotte Temple* (1905 edition); John Spargo, *Anthony Haswell, Printer-Patriot-Ballader* (1925), which has a good account of the Haswell family; Constance Rourke, *The Roots of Am. Culture* (1942), pp. 75–87; and Julian Mates, *The Am. Musical Stage before 1800* (1962). The journalist William Cobbett attacked Mrs. Rowson's spread-eagle patriotism in his pamphlet *A Kick for a Bite* (1795).]

RICHARD D. BIRDSALL

**ROYALL, Anne Newport** (June 11, 1769–Oct. 1, 1854), traveler, author, and eccentric, sometimes termed the first American newspaperwoman, was born near Baltimore, Md., the elder of the two daughters of William Newport, a small farmer who was reputed to be the illegitimate son of one of the Maryland Calverts, and his wife, Mary. Little is known of Anne's mother except that she had relatives named Anderson in Virginia, whence she presumably came. In the troubled days before the Revolution, William Newport remained loyal to the King. Ostracized as a Tory by his neighbors, and having lost the modest annuity he had been receiving from the Calvert family and apparently most of his landholdings as well, he moved with his wife and daughters to the western Pennsylvania frontier. By 1775 he had taken up land near Hannastown in Westmoreland County. He apparently taught Anne to read, and she later recalled having attended a "log school" near her home.

About 1775 William Newport seems to have died, perhaps in one of the Indian massacres of the period. His widow married a man named Butler, by whom she had a son, and after Butler's death she moved down the Shenandoah Valley, seeking aid from Virginia friends or relatives. In 1785, when Anne was sixteen, they came to Sweet Springs in Monroe County, now part of West Virginia. Here Mrs. Butler entered the home of Capt. William Royall as a servant. Royall was a wealthy gentleman-farmer who had served in the Revolution, reportedly a personal friend of George Washington, and a well-educated man of wide scholarly interests. His library was among the largest in Virginia. He professed himself a deist, admired Voltaire and Thomas Paine, and was an enthusiastic Freemason. His neighbors considered him something of an eccentric, since he freed his slaves and refused to fence in his cattle.

Royall became interested in Anne, gave her the run of his library, and transferred to her many of his own enthusiasms and ideas about life and society. To the astonishment of the neighborhood, in 1797 he married his protégée, now twenty-eight and some twenty years his junior. They had no children. Upon Royall's death in 1813 Anne determined to leave the "cold, dreary, hard-frozen hills" of western Virginia and traveled luxuriously south to Alabama in her coach with three servants. Here she seems to have lived during most of the next decade. Her enjoyment of means, however, ceased in 1823 when relatives of Royall succeeded in voiding his will on the claim that Anne was an adulteress, leaving her penniless at the age of fifty-four. Since her husband had been a Revolutionary veteran, Mrs. Royall went to Washington to demand a widow's pension. The negotiations dragged on for many years, although she had some influential friends (among them John Quincy Adams) who helped her cause. Finally in 1848, in her old age, she received $2,400 by act of Congress. William Royall's legal heirs took half; of the remainder her debts and legal fees took all but ten dollars.

Meanwhile, as she waited for her pension, Anne Royall began to earn a meager living by journeying through the country and publishing accounts of her impressions. Undaunted by the dangers and discomforts of travel by stage, steamer, and foot in the 1820's, lonely and often penniless, she visited almost every settlement of importance in the United States, taking voluminous shorthand notes. In all she brought out ten volumes, still useful as a source of information about contemporary society: *Sketches of History, Life and Manners in the United States* (1826); *The Black Book; or, A Continuation of Travels in the United States* (3 vols., 1828–29); *Mrs. Royall's Pennsylvania* (2 vols., 1829); *Mrs. Royall's Southern Tour* (3 vols., 1830–31); and *Letters from Alabama* (1830). She also wrote a weak novel, *The Tennessean* (1827), and an awkwardly bad play, *The Cabinet*. Her travel books sold fairly well, for she had a straightforward, readable style and an overweening curiosity about everything she observed. Embittered by her losses and hardships, she had also a termagant's temper and a vitriolic pen, bestowing malice or praise of people and places as the spirit moved her. Between journeys she returned to Washington to press her pension case. There, in 1829, she was brought to trial on a charge of publicly abusing a group of Presbyterians whose place of worship was near her house and was convicted under an old law as a common scold. Because of her age, she was given a fine of ten dollars instead of a ducking, and her fine was paid by Jackson's Secretary of War, John Eaton, one of the witnesses in her defense.

In 1830 Mrs. Royall, now sixty-one, took up permanent residence in Washington, where she obtained an old printing press, hired printers, and, with the help of Mrs. Sarah Stack, thereafter her loyal friend and companion, began to turn out ephemeral pamphlets, sheets, and books for sale to interested Washingtonians. The next year she began publishing a newspaper, *Paul Pry*, a lively weekly in which local gossip and sharp-tongued editorial comment found prominent place. Small, wiry, and energetic in her pursuit of customers, she became a familiar figure in the halls of Congress, wearing her three-dollar plaid coat, carrying a green umbrella, and peddling her publications. Those who did not buy were likely to be subjected to a tongue-lashing, or find themselves pilloried in next week's edition. Washington legend has it that during John Quincy Adams' administration she once caught him swimming in the Potomac and sat on his clothes until he consented to an exclusive interview. Since Adams was one of her friends and supporters, it seems unlikely that she would have so embarrassed him, or needed to, but the tale has persisted.

Mrs. Royall's first newspaper lasted from Dec. 3, 1831, to Nov. 19, 1836. It was succeeded by the aptly named *The Huntress*, which she edited from Dec. 2, 1836, to July 2, 1854, or from her sixty-eighth year through her eighty-fifth. In her papers she defended Sunday transportation of the mails and states' rights, opposed the Bank of the United States, advocated sound money and internal improvements, stood with the Jacksonians against nullification, and campaigned for tolerance for Catholics. Her uncanny ability to nose out graft proved the terror of politicians, and though she was notoriously careless about verifying scandal, her papers served as watchmen of public morality. Public men, she said, were "fair game." Always an aggressive freethinker, Anne Royall did not like ministers or missionaries, and convinced herself that they were plotting to seize control of the government. Suspicious of Britain, she saw another conspiracy in booksellers' heavy stocking of English books. Vociferously championing the Masons at the height of anti-Masonic feeling in America, she once suffered a broken leg when an Anti-Mason she had been berating threw her down a flight of stairs; already prone to see plots against her, she enjoyed the role of martyr. She had a bitter tongue, a keen mind, violent enemies, and, at the same time, reluctant admirers, who respected her for the sincerity of her views and the courage with which she declared them. She was, said John Quincy Adams, "like a virago errant in enchanted armor, redeeming herself from the cramps of indigence by the notoriety of her eccentricities and the forced currency they gave her publications." Three months after *The Huntress* ceased publication, Anne Royall, old and ailing, died a pauper in Washington. She was buried in the Congressional Cemetery.

[The best documented account is George S. Jackson, *Uncommon Scold: The Story of Anne Royall* (1937). See also Sarah Harvey Porter, *The Life and Times of Anne Royall* (1909), and the sketch in Helen Beal Woodward, *The Bold Women* (1953). A new edition of her *Letters from Ala.*, ed. by Lucille Griffith, was published in 1969.]

RUSSEL B NYE

**ROYCE, Sarah Eleanor Bayliss** (Mar. 2, 1819–Nov. 23, 1891), California pioneer, mother of the philosopher Josiah Royce, and author of an autobiographical account of the Gold Rush and early California, was born in Stratford-on-Avon, England, the daughter of Benjamin and Mary T. Bayliss. Soon after her birth her father moved the family to America and established a merchandising business in Rochester, N.Y. Sarah received a "careful, old-style academy education" at the Albion Female Seminary in Rochester. She married a fellow native of England, Josiah Royce, who as a child had come from the tiny town of Ridlington, Rutlandshire, to Canada. The marriage is said to have taken place in 1847. Royce was to prove a restless individual, always moving his family to a new community in pursuit of the business success that ever eluded him.

In 1848 the Royces began their greatest adventure, the overland trip that ultimately carried them to California. They moved slowly westward over a period of months, and on Apr. 30, 1849, started across the Iowa prairies for California. By that time they had a two-year-old daughter, Mary. Mrs. Royce kept an intermittent "Pilgrim's Diary," from which, more than thirty years later, she wrote a vivid and moving autobiographical account intended solely for the use of her son, who was then writing his history of pioneer California. On their journey the Royces suffered the usual dangers and hardships encountered by most Forty-Niners, but in addition had to make most of the journey almost alone because they wished to observe the Sabbath as a day of rest and prayer. Early October found them still plodding across the desert west of Salt Lake, and when they missed a fork in the trail and thus wasted days of toil, water, and food, their chances of survival became slight. In this extremity Mrs. Royce—a member of the Disciples of Christ, or Campbellites—sought strength in her intensely felt faith in God. "I had known what it was to *believe* in God, and to pray that He would never leave us. [But now] He came so near that I no longer simply *believed* in Him, but *knew* His presence." Thereafter her faith had a strong mystical element. Almost miraculously, the little party reached the Carson River, and in mid-October started for the Sierra Nevada mountains. They would never have surmounted this barrier if a government relief expedition had not exceeded its instructions in order to seek them out and help them across before snow closed the passes. Mrs. Royce saw this as an act of "the same rich Providence that had led, and was still so kindly leading us."

In California, Royce unsuccessfully tried his hand at jobs in raw mining camps, in Sacramento and San Francisco, and finally in the mining town of Grass Valley. By that time the Royces had two more daughters, Hattie and Ruth, and at Grass Valley a son, Josiah, was born. In each of these moves Mrs. Royce managed to make a home for her family in whatever tent, cloth house, single room, or real house they happened to occupy for the moment. Her material possessions were few, but they included a Bible, a volume of Milton, writing materials, a child's storybook that she had found in an abandoned wagon on the Plains, and a few other works that ultimately included histories, an encyclopedia, and astronomical charts. When no suitable school was available at Grass Valley, she created one and taught it herself in her home. Similarly, at Grass Valley services for an embryonic congregation were held in the Royces' living room whenever a clergyman was available. In her fortitude and resourcefulness and her determination to preserve spiritual and cultural values, Mrs. Royce illustrated the pioneer wife and mother at her best. Less admirable was the tendency she and her daughters showed to overprotect the only boy in the family, young Josiah, who grew up to be socially awkward and lonely. After twelve years at Grass Valley, the Royces moved to San Francisco so that the children could enjoy better schooling. The elder Josiah Royce died in 1889 at the age of seventy-six. His son had begun his long career at Harvard in 1882. After her husband's death, Mrs. Royce went east for a year, then returned

to live at San Jose, Calif., with her daughter Ruth, who had been librarian of the State Normal School since 1881. She died in San Jose at the age of seventy-two as a result of nervous shock suffered when she was knocked against a wall in the local post office. Her autobiographical account, edited by Ralph H. Gabriel, was published in 1932 as *A Frontier Lady: Recollections of the Gold Rush and Early California.*

[Mrs. Royce's *A Frontier Lady* includes a brief biographical sketch by her daughter-in-law, Katharine Royce. The Calif. Section of the Calif. State Library, Sacramento, has obituary notices that appeared in the *San Francisco Call* on Nov. 24 and 25, 1891, the latter summarizing a long obituary from the *San Jose Mercury.* Information was also supplied by a descendant, Mrs. Robert L. Hacker of Portland, Oreg. Josiah Royce, the philosopher, reminisced about his boyhood in an extemporaneous talk printed in his *The Hope of the Great Community* (1916), pp. 122–32, and summarized his mother's experience in *California, from the Conquest in 1846 to the Second Vigilance Committee in San Francisco* (1886), pp. 241–44. The Royce family papers, which were in the possession of the philosopher's widow, appear to have been scattered since her death.]

RODMAN WILSON PAUL

**RUFFIN, Josephine St. Pierre** (Aug. 31, 1842–Mar. 13, 1924), clubwoman and Negro leader, was born in Boston, Mass., the fifth daughter and youngest of six children of John and Eliza Matilda (Menhenick) St. Pierre. Her mother was a native of Cornwall, England. Her father was the son of Jean Jacques St. Pierre, an early nineteenth-century French immigrant from Martinique, who had married Betsey Hill of Taunton, Mass., of mixed Negro, French, and Indian ancestry—the descendant, according to family tradition, of an African prince who had escaped from a slave ship and found refuge in an Indian settlement near Taunton. John St. Pierre became a clothes dealer, an occupation frequently followed by the Negroes of his day, and was a founder of the Zion Church of Boston. Little is known of his other children, who either died young or disappeared into the white world.

Mrs. Ruffin reflected in her appearance the heterogeneous stock of her ancestors. She was small, of light brown complexion, with soft wavy hair and keen features. Her manner and bearing, even as a young woman, were imposing and self-assured. "She always had the lead in the play," and "you knew when she entered the room," recalled one person who knew her well. She received her early education in Salem, Mass., her parents having refused to send her to Boston's segregated school for Negroes; but when a legislative act broke down this barrier in 1855, she was enrolled in the Bowdoin School in the West End. In 1858, at sixteen, she was married to George Lewis Ruffin (1834–1886), of a prominent Negro family recently moved to Boston from Richmond, Va. Her marriage first brought Mrs. Ruffin into social prominence in the Boston Negro community, offsetting her simple birth and somewhat limited education, and her husband's later career gave her added prestige. Immediately after their marriage the Ruffins went to Liverpool, England, apparently to escape the indignities of the North of their day. Returning after the outbreak of the Civil War, Ruffin worked as a barber but presently attended the Harvard Law School, graduating in 1869, and went on to become a state legislator, a member of the Boston City Council, and, in 1883, Boston's first Negro municipal judge. Meanwhile the Ruffins had become the parents of five children: Hubert St. Pierre, Florida Yates, Stanley, George Lewis, and Robert (who died in infancy). The three sons followed successful careers as, respectively, a lawyer, an inventor and manufacturer, and an organist; Florida taught in the Boston public schools.

Skilled at organizing and interested in people, Mrs. Ruffin took an active part in the crucial causes of her day: Negro rights, the Civil War, welfare work, and the suffrage movement. During the war she recruited soldiers and aided the Sanitary Commission. In 1879, when the mass exodus of Southern Negroes to Kansas strained the resources of that state, she organized the Boston Kansas Relief Association. For some years she was a visitor for the Associated Charities of Boston. She served on the executive board of the Massachusetts Moral Education Association and of the Massachusetts School Suffrage Association, of which she was a charter member. In this way she became acquainted with JULIA WARD HOWE, LUCY STONE, and other local leaders of the woman's movement.

Mrs. Ruffin's particular concern was the development of the Negro woman in the Boston community and throughout the United States. In 1894 she organized, with her daughter, the Woman's Era Club, among the first of the Negro women's civic associations. Mrs. Ruffin served until 1903 as its president and for several years edited its monthly publication, the Woman's Era. As president she called in Boston in 1895 a conference of representatives of other clubs which organized the National Federation of Afro-American Women. Its purpose, as Mrs. Ruffin put it in her address, was to demonstrate the existence of a "large and growing class" of intelligent, cultured Negro women sharing the aims of "all good, aspiring women" and by this "dignified showing" to refute charges of ignorance and immorality. In 1896 the Federation merged with the Colored Women's League of Washington to form the National Association of Colored Women, Mrs. Ruffin serving as the first vice-president.

In 1893, while working on the Boston Courant, a weekly Negro newspaper, Mrs. Ruffin had become a member of the New England Woman's Press Association, in which she remained active for some years. Through her Woman's Era Club she became a member of the Massachusetts State Federation of Women's Clubs, serving on its executive board from 1899 to 1902. In 1900 the Woman's Era Club was accepted for membership in the General Federation of Women's Clubs by the Federation's executive committee; Mrs. Ruffin attended its convention in Milwaukee that year as a representative of all three groups. At the convention, however, strong opposition arose to the membership of a Negro organization, and the board refused to ratify the acceptance of the Woman's Era Club. The credentials committee proposed to seat Mrs. Ruffin as a delegate of either of the other two groups, but she refused on principle. Despite considerable publicity and protests from several state delegations, the General Federation maintained its color bar at this time.

In later years, though the Woman's Era Club ceased to exist, Mrs. Ruffin remained active in community leadership. She was a founder of the Association for the Promotion of Child Training in the South, of the Boston branch of the National Association for the Advancement of Colored People, and of the League of Women for Community Service (see MARIA BALDWIN). In 1902 she helped found the American Mount Coffee School Association to raise funds for the enlargement of Mrs. Jennie (Davis) Sharpe's school at Mount Coffee, Liberia, serving as vice-president, with Edward Everett Hale as president. Mrs. Ruffin died of nephritis in 1924, at the age of eighty-one, at her home on St. Botolph Street in Boston. Funeral services were held in Boston's Trinity Church (Episcopal), of which she was a member, and she was buried at Mount Auburn Cemetery, Cambridge.

[Julia Ward Howe, ed., Representative Women of New England (1904), pp. 335–39; Woman's Who's Who of America, 1914–15; Hallie Q. Brown, Homespun Heroines and Other Women of Distinction (1926), pp. 151–53; Elizabeth Lindsay Davis, ed., Lifting as They Climb: An Hist. Record of the Nat. Assoc. of Colored Women (1933), pp. 17–19, 236–39; Myra B. Lord, *Hist. of the New England Woman's Press Assoc.* (1932); *Progress and Achievement: A Hist. of the Mass. State Federation of Women's Clubs* (1932), p. 27; Emma L. Fields, "The Women's Club Movement in the U.S., 1877–1900" (unpublished master's thesis, Howard Univ., 1948); death record, Mass. Registrar of Vital Statistics. See also Eleanor Flexner, *Century of Struggle: The Woman's Rights Movement in the U.S.* (1959), pp. 189–91; and Alice Dunbar Nelson, *Masterpieces of Negro Eloquence* (1914), which contains an open letter to the Education League of Ga. written by Mrs. Ruffin in 1889. For accounts of the Gen. Federation of Women's Clubs controversy, see *Woman's Jour.*, June 16, 23, 30, 1900; and Mary I. Wood, *Hist. of the Gen. Federation of Women's Clubs* (1912), pp. 129–31. Incomplete files of the *Woman's Era* are in the Moorland Collection, Howard Univ. Library, and in the Boston Public Library.]

ADELAIDE CROMWELL HILL

**RUMSEY, Elida Barker.** *See* FOWLE, Elida Barker Rumsey.

**RUMSEY, Mary Harriman** (Nov. 17, 1881–Dec. 18, 1934), social welfare leader, spokesman for consumer interests in the early New Deal, was born in New York City, the eldest of the six children of Edward Henry Harriman, the railroad financier, and MARY WILLIAMSON (AVERELL) HARRIMAN. She grew up amid material comfort, although it was not until the turn of the century that her father, by gaining control of the Union Pacific and Southern Pacific railroad systems, accumulated his immense fortune. The Harriman family was close-knit; the children had constant parental attention in their schooling, their out-of-school interests, and their Episcopal religious training. Mary grew up in New York City, with a brief interlude in Chicago. She spent vacations with her family at Arden, their country estate in the Ramapo Hills of New York; at the Orange County Hunt Club near Middleburg, Va.; or at one of several Harriman ranches in the West. The whole family enjoyed outdoor life; they all joined the Alaska expedition which E. H. Harriman organized in 1899, chartering a vessel and recruiting a distinguished group of scientists. Mary—slim, dark-eyed, of effervescent personality and volatile mind—became a close companion of her father, and as she grew older he shared with her his plans for railroad expansion. In 1898, with her sister Cornelia, she spent the summer riding a special train with him on his first inspection tour of the Union Pacific system.

Mary Harriman's keen social consciousness found expression as early as 1901 when she led the New York debutantes of that season in founding the Junior League for the Promotion of Settlement Movements (later renamed the Junior League of New York), from which developed the national Junior League movement. Its purpose, as she outlined it, was to encourage girls of social position to take a more active part in work for community welfare and social betterment. With her parents' encouragement she broke with tradition and attended college, graduating from Barnard in 1905. The courses in sociology and eugenics she found particularly stimulating. She became much attached to Barnard, on whose board of trustees she sat from 1911 until her death. After her father's death in 1909 she helped manage the Arden estate, especially its extensive dairy farm. She also encouraged her mother's wide-ranging philanthropic activities, bringing new ideas and projects to her attention. It was in part through her urging that Mrs. Harriman in 1910 agreed to finance the Eugenics Records Office at Cold Spring Harbor, Long Island. The temperaments of the two women were very different, the difference between reticence and exuberance, between formality and casualness; they were at times in conflict, but this did not weaken their close family attachment or the pride of one in the other.

On May 26, 1910, Mary Harriman was married to Charles Cary Rumsey, a Harvard graduate and a Buffalo sculptor who had been one of the artists engaged to decorate Arden House. They had three children: Charles Cary, Jr. (born 1911), Mary Averell Harriman (1913), and Bronson Harriman (1917). Rumsey was devoted to horses and polo, and their home at Sands Point, Long Island, became a center of sporting activity as well as artistic effort, as did the farm which Mary Rumsey acquired near Middleburg, Va. Applying her interest in eugenics, Mrs. Rumsey experimented with cattle breeding. She also developed a lively interest in agricultural cooperation and helped organize the Eastern Livestock Cooperative Marketing Association, one of many such cooperatives founded in this period. During the First World War the family lived in New York City, where Mrs. Rumsey strongly supported the Community Councils being organized under the aegis of the United States Council of National Defense and worked for their perpetuation after the war as local cooperative groups. Her belief in the importance of community action to meet national challenges, rooted in experience with cooperatives in Virginia and in her wartime activities, was crystallized by her reading of *The National Being*

(1916) by the Irish poet, mystic, and social reformer George Russell (Æ).

The death of her husband as the result of an automobile accident in September 1922 turned Mary Rumsey's interest more fully to social issues and public affairs. In 1928 she and her brother Averell (later United States ambassador to the Soviet Union and governor of New York), running counter to the family's Republican tradition, supported the presidential candidacy of Alfred E. Smith. Of this break with her father's past, Mrs. Rumsey said: "His period was a building age, when competition was the order of the day. Today the need is not for a competitive but for a cooperative economic system" (quoted in *New York Times*, Dec. 19, 1934). The financial crisis of 1929 gave her an opportunity to translate her ideas into practical form. She took part in the work of the Emergency Exchange Association, a New York City effort to combat unemployment by substituting an exchange of skilled labor for money wages, and she helped publicize the "block-aid" campaign which sought to mobilize neighborhoods to cope with the hardships of unemployment and other problems.

Mrs. Rumsey had long been a personal friend of Mrs. Franklin D. Roosevelt and Secretary of Labor Frances Perkins. These ties, coupled with her pro-New Deal sympathies, her enthusiasm for community cooperation, and her organizational gifts, led President Roosevelt in June 1933 to appoint her chairman of the Consumers' Advisory Board of the National Recovery Administration. The board, composed mainly of academic economists and representative clubwomen, sought to represent the consumer viewpoint as the N.R.A. drew up its industrial fair practices code. Opposed by both labor and business interests as a disruptive hindrance to the bargaining over the codes, and attacked by N.R.A. officials jealous of their own prerogatives, it had some difficulty getting under way. Under Mrs. Rumsey's leadership, however, the board made its influence felt, particularly in combating price mark-ups and in protecting cooperatives from price discrimination. Looking toward the formation of a national consumer constituency, Mrs. Rumsey hoped to create county consumer councils which would support the efforts of the Consumers' Advisory Board. To this end she established within the board a Bureau of Economic Education under Prof. Paul H. Douglas of the University of Chicago. As head, also, of the Consumers' Division of the National Emergency Council, another New Deal agency, she worked to achieve the same ends.

Mrs. Rumsey was a charming, spirited woman with great driving force, and her friendship with Eleanor Roosevelt and with Frances Perkins, whose Washington house she shared, gave her ideas increasing influence. In November 1934, however, on her fifty-third birthday, she fell from her horse during a fox hunt on her Virginia farm and suffered several broken bones. Pneumonia developed during her convalescence, and she died in December at Washington Emergency Hospital. The funeral, at St. Thomas' Episcopal Church in Washington, was attended by Mrs. Roosevelt and high administration figures. Mary Harriman Rumsey was buried beside her parents in the graveyard of the village church at Arden, N.Y.

[For summaries of Mrs. Rumsey's career see the extensive obituary in the *N.Y. Times*, Dec. 19, 1934; *Nat. Cyc. Am. Biog.*, XXV, 27; and *Who Was Who in America*, vol. I (1942). See also *N.Y. Times*, May 27, 1910 (marriage), Mar. 27, 1932, sec. 2 ("block-aid" movement), Dec. 24, 1932 (Emergency Exchange Assoc), Aug. 6, 1933, sec. 6 (article on her by S. J. Woolf), and Dec. 20, 1934 (editorial); Raymond Moley in *Today*, Dec. 29, 1934. Persia Campbell, *Mary Williamson Harriman* (1960), contains passing references. On her government service, see Persia Campbell, *Consumer Representation in the New Deal* (1940); Arthur M. Schlesinger, Jr., *The Coming of the New Deal* (1958); Frances Perkins, *The Roosevelt I Knew* (1946), p. 206; Rexford G. Tugwell, *The Democratic Roosevelt* (1957), p. 335n; and Sue Shelton White, "The County Consumer Councils and Their Service," *Nat. Consumer News*, Aug. 25, 1935, p. 5. On the founding of the Junior League, see *N.Y. Times*, Mar. 12, 1961.]

PERSIA CAMPBELL

RUSSELL, Annie (Jan. 12, 1864–Jan. 16, 1936), actress, was born in Liverpool, England, the oldest of three children of Joseph and Jane (Mount) Russell. Her father, who is said to have been a civil engineer and to have attended Dublin University, was Irish, her mother English. Joseph Russell died soon after bringing his family to Canada in 1869, leaving them in severe want. After acting in a Christmas pageant and joining a local dramatic club, Annie made her professional debut in 1872 at Montreal, playing Jeanne in *Miss Multon*, though the touring star, ROSE EYTINGE, nearly balked at her inexperience. After singing in a juvenile company of Gilbert and Sullivan's *H.M.S. Pinafore*, in 1878 she joined E. A. McDowell's company to tour South America and the West Indies. Two years of trouping in roles ranging from fresh-faced boys to wrinkled old women brought her to the Madison Square Theatre in New York. Here in October 1881, hiding her age by wearing a long dress, jewelry, and an elaborate coiffure, she won the

title role in *Esmeralda,* a stage adaptation by
FRANCES HODGSON BURNETT and the actor William Gillette of a story by Mrs. Burnett. Soon
a star in this spindly drama about country folk
in Paris saved by true love, Miss Russell was
now embarked on a long succession of sunbonnet heroines who made her name beloved
across the continent. After 350 appearances as
Esmeralda in New York, followed by a year's
tour, she deepened nationwide affection with
two years in the title role of *Hazel Kirke.* At
Albany, N.Y., during this tour, she was married, on Nov. 2, 1884, to Eugene Wiley Presbrey, a stage manager for the A. M. Palmer
Company, in which she was performing.

Miss Russell then played various versions of
the gingham girl in such plays as *Sealed Instructions* (1885) and *Elaine* (1887) until an
illness, perhaps induced by marital strife,
forced her off the stage for three years. Following a testimonial performance by professional friends which netted her $3,000 in 1891,
she fled what one newspaperman called her
"brute of a husband" and sailed for Italy to
restore her wrecked health; she was divorced
in 1897. Returning to the New York stage in
1894, she played several commonplace parts
until Charles Frohman in 1896 starred her in
*Sue,* adapted from a story by Bret Harte. The
first woman to star under Frohman's management, Miss Russell soon won the hearts of
London audiences as well. Having married an
English actor, Oswald Yorke, on Mar. 27, 1904,
she returned to London in 1905 to create the
role of Barbara Underhill in Shaw's *Major
Barbara,* playing under the author's direction.
In 1906 she opened the new Astor Theatre
in New York in *A Midsummer Night's Dream,*
with a surprising portrayal of Puck, "a batwinged, mouse-eared, fawn-like, tricksy sprite,"
as one witness put it, a new Annie Russell
with "flashing animal spirits" instead of tears.
Because of illness she shelved Puck after one
season.

In her Puck, Annie Russell realized part of
a lifelong dream: to raise the standards of
American entertainment and "elevate the playgoer." Although one of America's best-paid
actresses, earning $500 a week and second in
the Frohman galaxy only to Maude Adams
(d. 1954), Miss Russell complained in 1902
that after thirty years on the stage she was not
allowed to play great parts. Audiences had
been spoiled "by too much scenery and not
enough acting"; they sought only to be amused
and ignored "the many splendid plays." By
1912 she had converted enough followers to
present the Annie Russell Old English Comedy
Company, which she directed in three works

of the standard English repertoire, *She Stoops
to Conquer, Much Ado about Nothing,* and
*The Rivals,* herself playing a leading role in
each. Critics hailed the beauty and humor of
these productions. The New York engagement
was maintained through a subscription plan
supported by a number of New York's wealthiest women, after Miss Russell addressed one of
their fashionable clubs with her first public
plea for a theatre of refinement, beauty, and
grace. Here and elsewhere she argued that the
public debased the theatre, that managers considered it safer to give the public "what it
wants than what it ought to have," and that
the theatre was filled with "good millinery,
good looks, high kicking, and low thinking"
rather than ideas. If women supported the
theatre, she believed they could protect the
dignity of the American stage. In a second address she urged parents to keep their daughters away from vulgar plays and instead to
teach them to seek the best the theatre offered.
From Shakespeare's heroines, for example, the
young girl could absorb the high ideals and
learn the grace and charm by which she would
grow lovely.

Although her company drew widespread
praise, Annie Russell disbanded it after one
season. She retired from the stage in 1918
after touring for two seasons in *The Thirteenth
Chair,* a "gruesome" play which shattered her
nerves. Her health was already undermined
by extensive war work for the Red Cross at the
Debarkation Hospital in Grand Central Palace, New York, for the Salvation Army, and
for French war orphans. She acted only once
again, in 1932 at Rollins College in Florida,
playing the Queen in Browning's poetic drama
*In a Balcony* to open the new Annie Russell
Theatre, built with a gift of $100,000 from her
friend of thirty-five years, Mary Louise Curtis
(Mrs. Edward W.) Bok. For the remainder of
her life (her second husband having died in
1931) she taught at Rollins College as professor of theatre arts. She died of myocarditis
at her home in Winter Park, Fla., and was
buried at Short Hills, N.J.

The two phases of Annie Russell's career,
the youthful heroine and the adult moralist,
were closely linked. As described in the period
of her first success, she presented a willowy
figure, expressive eyes, and a vivacious manner. As a "winsome and winning little charmer"
she gave a semblance of life to cardboard
heroines who skipped across the stage and
smiled through tears. Yet she herself soon
grew tired of "Annie Russell parts," which she
named "Anniegenues," and yearned for more
complex roles. Two decades later another in-

terviewer found a charming woman of buoyant personality and mature intellectual stature.
Trained in a theatrical era that held to the traditions of the English stage, she appreciated
the virtues of clear enunciation and intelligent
acting. Molded in the Genteel Tradition, she
also believed that art should be a vehicle for
morality. She therefore dedicated herself to
a noble aim, but her standards remained
wholly conventional. She disliked Ibsen and
"problem plays" because they stressed "ab-
normality." She railed at audiences who went
to the theatre only for diversion and who
boycotted plays that offered "to uplift and rest
the spirit" and cultivate good taste. At the
same time she found excuses for the manager
who, as a businessman, must produce the
frothy dramas she deplored. In this dilemma
she had helplessly turned to American clubwomen to help "elevate the playgoer." Hers
was a touching conflict, and it throws light on
the reasons for the stunted growth of the
American stage in her time.

[Annie Russell voiced her ideas on the theatre in
three articles which appeared in the *Ladies' Home
Jour.*: "What It Really Means to Be an Actress,"
Jan. 1909; "As the Player Sees the Playgoer," Nov.
1912; and "The Tired Business Man at the
Theater," Mar. 1914. Contemporary accounts of
her appear in Gustav Kobbé, *Famous Actors &
Actresses and Their Homes* (1903); Lewis C.
Strang, *Famous Actresses of the Day in America*
(1899) and *Famous Actresses of the Day in America*, Second Series (1901). See also *Who's Who in
the Theatre* (8th ed., 1936); obituary in *N.Y.
Herald Tribune*, Jan. 17, 1936; death record from
Fla. State Board of Health. The fullest data on her
life and work are to be found in the unclassified
material, largely clippings, scrapbooks, photographs, and programs, in the Theatre Collection
of the N.Y. Public Library at Lincoln Center. The
Harvard Theatre Collection abundantly supple-
ments this material.]

                                    H. L. KLEINFIELD

**RUSSELL, Lillian** (Dec. 4, 1861–June 6,
1922), actress, star of musical comedy, was
born in Clinton, Iowa. Christened Helen Louise Leonard, she was the fifth and youngest
daughter of Charles E. and Cynthia Howland
(Van Name) Leonard, natives, respectively, of
Michigan and Buffalo, N.Y. In 1865 Leonard
sold his weekly *Clinton Herald* and opened a
job-printing firm in Chicago. Here Helen attended the Sacred Heart convent school and
Park Institute, a finishing school. A naturally
gifted musician, she also took private voice
lessons and sang in an Episcopal church choir.
Her mother, a feminist, woman suffrage champion, and author, in 1868 helped found the

Chicago Sorosis, the city's first woman's club.
In 1877 or 1878 the strong-minded Mrs. Leon-
ard left her husband and moved with several
of her daughters, including Helen, to New
York City. Here she was soon caught up in new
enthusiasms, including eugenics, homeopathy,
Christian Science, and the Marxist-oriented
Socialist Labor Party.

Helen, meanwhile, hoping for an operatic
career, had resumed her voice lessons under
Dr. Leopold Damrosch. In 1879, to Damrosch's
dismay, she joined the chorus of a Brooklyn
company of Gilbert and Sullivan's *H.M.S.
Pinafore*, only to withdraw two weeks later
after secretly marrying the orchestra leader,
Harry Braham. The death of their infant son
was followed in rapid succession by their
separation and divorce. Meanwhile, Tony
Pastor had heard Helen sing at the theatrical
boardinghouse where she was living, and on
Nov. 22, 1880, having renamed her Lillian
Russell, he placed her on the stage of his
Broadway variety theatre as an "English ballad
singer." The following February she appeared
in *The Pie Rats of Penn Yan*, Pastor's burlesque
of *The Pirates of Penzance*. After a cross-country tour with Pastor's troupe that summer, she
signed with John A. McCaull to appear at New
York's Bijou Opera House in *The Snake
Charmer* (October 1881), a version of Edmond Audran's *Le Grand Mogul*. Her fresh
beauty, pleasing voice, and natural grace
charmed audiences and won acclaim rivaling
that of the show's star. In October 1882, after
restlessly appearing under several managers,
she returned to McCaull in Gilbert and Sullivan's *The Sorcerer* and Jacques Offenbach's
*The Princess of Trebizonde*. The next year,
escaping conflicting contracts she had unwisely
signed, she sailed for England with Edward
Solomon, a composer, to whom she was married on May 10, 1884. She made her debut at
London's Gaiety Theatre soon after her arrival
but first won success in October 1884 in Solomon's *Polly, or, the Pet of the Regiment*. That
winter she returned to New York as the mother
of a baby girl, Dorothy. American audiences
applauded her in *Polly* and other operettas by
Solomon and his librettist Harry Stephens, but
this collaboration ended in the autumn of 1886
with Solomon's arrest for bigamy. Repudiating
the marriage (it was eventually annulled),
Miss Russell departed for the Pacific Coast
with J. C. Duff's Opera Company in a production of *Iolanthe*.

Two seasons on the road with Duff established her reputation, and in 1888 Rudolph
Aronson offered her $20,000 a season to appear
regularly at the Casino, New York's leading

light opera theatre. Now at the crest of her popularity, Miss Russell won particular acclaim for her performance in Offenbach's *The Grand Duchess* (1890). With her lovely features and complexion, statuesque proportions, and opulent gowns, she became the feminine ideal of her generation. One admirer found her "exquisite" voice and "blonde loveliness" a "superb revelation." A symbol of her time, in May 1890 she was the first person to speak over the newly perfected long-distance telephone, as from her New York dressing room she sang a song from *The Grand Duchess* to a group of Washington notables including President Harrison. Although she was now earning $35,000 a year, Miss Russell in 1891 abruptly switched from Aronson to T. Henry French, who had offered her $1,200 a week and a share in the box office receipts. Now the star of "The Lillian Russell Opera Company," she opened at Manhattan's Garden Theatre that autumn in Audran's *La Cigale*. Other productions followed in New York and on tour, but French encountered financial difficulties and in 1893 Miss Russell shifted to the management of Lederer and Canary, returning to the Casino in *The Princess Nicotine*.

On Jan. 24, 1894, in Hoboken, N.J., she was married for a third time, to the tenor John Haley Augustin Chatterton, who under his stage name of Signor Giovanni Perugini was also playing in *The Princess Nicotine*. The marriage soon foundered, and within months the two were attacking each other in the public press, Miss Russell charging that Chatterton had married her simply to advance his career. After their divorce in 1898 rumors linked Miss Russell's name with numerous eligible bachelors, including her good friend and frequent dining companion "Diamond Jim" Brady. When off the stage during these years she divided her time between her lavish Manhattan residence and a summer estate at Far Rockaway, Long Island. She was also a fixture at the Saratoga racing season, where a frequent escort was the copper magnate Jesse Lewisohn.

In 1895 Henry E. Abbey lured Miss Russell to the management of Abbey, Schoeffel, and Grau with promises of securing grand opera bookings, but upon the advice of her friend Nellie Melba she decided not to compete with the established divas. Even in her own medium she seemed to be losing momentum. *The Goddess of Truth* (February 1896) and other Abbey confections failed to please, and a journalist wrote that Miss Russell had "ceased to be a drawing card of pronounced magnetism." Furthermore, she was growing increasingly

stout at a time when the public taste in beauty was shifting from buxom amplitude to the more lithe and delicate femininity of such younger stars as ANNA HELD and Edna Wallace Hopper (d. 1959). In 1896–97, again under new management, she made a comeback in *An American Beauty* and *The Wedding Day,* but early in 1899 she abruptly left the cast of Offenbach's *La Belle Hélène,* in which Miss Hopper was also appearing.

A new avenue opened in 1899, however, when she signed to play at Weber and Fields' Music Hall. Demanding and receiving $1,250 a week, she enjoyed five gay seasons with Joe Weber and Lew Fields in their celebrated troupe, starring in *Whirl-i-gig, Fiddle-dee-dee, Hoity Toity, Twirly Whirly,* and *Whoop-dee-doo* and leaving the company only when the comedians dissolved their partnership in 1904. That December she achieved a memorable success in the title role of *Lady Teazle,* a musical version of *The School for Scandal,* at the Casino, but the 1905–06 season found her touring with F. F. Proctor's vaudeville company.

In 1906, troubled by a deterioration of her voice, complicated by minor throat surgery she had undergone the year before, she contracted with Joseph Brooks to tour in straight comedy roles. Covering thousands of miles in her private Pullman car, "Iolanthe," she was applauded in *The Butterfly* (1907) and *Wildfire* (1908), in which a horseman defeats an automobile buff for the heroine's affections. Her subsequent nonsinging roles drew lukewarm responses, however, and she soon returned to vaudeville, where she could still melt audiences with "Come Down, My Evenin' Star," a hit song from the halcyon Weber and Fields days.

On June 12, 1912, she was married to Alexander Pollock Moore, owner of the *Pittsburgh Leader* and a power in Republican politics. Earlier that year she had briefly rejoined Weber and Fields when they reunited in *Hokey-Pokey,* but as a matron of fifty she was now turning to other pursuits. She wrote a syndicated newspaper column; lectured on health, beauty, and love before vaudeville audiences; advocated woman suffrage; and lent her name to a cosmetic firm which manufactured "Lillian Russell's Own Preparation." A movie version of *Wildfire* (1914), in which she starred with John Barrymore, was not a success. She recruited for the Marine Corps and spoke for bond drives during the First World War and after the Armistice raised money for the American Legion and became active in the Women's Republican Club of Pennsylvania.

Appointed a special investigator on immigration by President Harding, she toured Europe briefly early in 1922 and returned urging isolationism and tighter immigration restrictions. She died at her Pittsburgh home that June, of "cardiac exhaustion" and nephritis, at the age of sixty. Survived by her fourth husband and daughter, she was buried in Allegheny Cemetery near Pittsburgh.

Lillian Russell's life of monumental achievement, robust activity, conspicuous consumption, and flamboyant display reflected the tempo of the plush era in which she flourished. Having won early success in lighter roles, she never realized her hopes for turning her impressive natural talent into more serious channels. Despite the scandals which periodically enveloped her, she remained loyal to her mother, her sisters, and her daughter, whose convent education she carefully supervised. If she drove a hard bargain, she was also unexcelled in her reputation for openhanded generosity. She prolonged her career through an impressive span of years, guarding her voice as tenderly as her complexion and fighting poundage and time's ravages with a martinet's discipline in exercise and diet. When she could no longer succeed in familiar roles she set about finding new ones with unflagging self-confidence and will power. Her beauty remains legendary.

[The principal source is the Robinson Locke Scrapbooks, together with other, unclassified material, in the Theatre Collection of the N.Y. Public Library at Lincoln Center. There are useful clippings also in the Harvard Theatre Collection. Parker Morell, *Lillian Russell: The Era of Plush* (1940), emphasizes the social history of her lifetime. George C. D. Odell, *Annals of the N.Y. Stage*, vols. XI–XV (1939–49), amplifies the record of her performances with personal comment. John Chapman and Garrison P. Sherwood, *The Best Plays of 1894–1899* (1955), and Burns Mantle and Garrison P. Sherwood, *The Best Plays of 1899–1909* (1944), help complete the record. See also Lewis C. Strang, *Prima Donnas and Soubrettes* (1900), chap. iii; and obituaries in *N.Y. Times,* June 7, 1922, and *Literary Digest,* June 24, 1922. Lillian Russell's "Reminiscences," *Cosmopolitan,* Feb.–Sept. 1922, are discursive and disappointing. Dorothy Russell, "My Mother, Lillian Russell," *Liberty,* Oct. 19–Nov. 23, 1929, is of little value. Rudolph Aronson, *Theatrical and Musical Memoirs* (1913), makes brief mention of Miss Russell. Death record from Pa. Dept. of Health. On her mother, see: Moses Rischin, *The Promised City* (1962), p. 225; Bessie L. Pierce, *A Hist. of Chicago,* II (1940), 456–57; and Frances E. Willard and Mary A. Livermore, eds., *A Woman of the Century* (1893).]

H. L. KLEINFIELD

**RUSSELL, Mother Mary Baptist** (Apr. 18, 1829–Aug. 6, 1898), Roman Catholic nun, superior of the Sisters of Mercy in San Francisco, was born in Newry, County Down, Ireland. Christened Katherine Russell, she was the third of four daughters and of the six children of Arthur Russell, a sea captain turned brewer, and his wife, the widowed Margaret (Mullan) Hamill, who also had six children by her first marriage. Of Katherine's two brothers, the elder, Charles, was made Lord Chief Justice of England in 1894, the first Catholic appointed since the Reformation; and the younger, Matthew, became a Jesuit orator and writer. Katherine attended private schools in Newry and was tutored by a governess. Although the Russells were a family of means, the children were not indulged and were made to take their religion seriously. Katherine's dedication to the care of the less fortunate was in part inspired by her mother, who supervised relief to the starving poor of the Newry community during the Great Famine; three of her daughters joined the Sisters of Mercy. Katherine entered the Kinsale convent of that order in November 1848, on the advice of her theologian uncle, Charles William Russell, president of St. Patrick's College in Maynooth. While still a novice she helped care for victims of the cholera epidemic of 1849. She received the habit on July 7, 1849, and with it the name Sister Mary Baptist. She made her final profession in August 1851.

In 1854 Joseph S. Alemany, first archbishop of the newly established San Francisco diocese, sent to Ireland for recruits. Under the guidance of Sister Mary Baptist as superior, eight nuns and novices left Kinsale for California, carefully instructed to follow a program of care of the sick, instruction of the poor, and protection of distressed young women. From the time she arrived in San Francisco, Mother Baptist concerned herself with the needs of the whole community. In 1855 she volunteered the services of the sisters to help the city's single hospital handle an epidemic of Asiatic cholera, for six months leading in nursing the stricken on day and night shifts. As a result the city authorities asked her that year to assume the responsibility of the city's dependent sick on a contract basis; for this purpose she purchased the building of the former State Marine Hospital, which became the city and county hospital. Two years later, however, a controversy involving charges of violation of the separation of church and state caused her to terminate her contract. Immediately she founded St. Mary's Hospital, the first Catholic hospital on the Pacific Coast, housed initially in the former Marine Hospital building and then, four years later, in a new building on San Francisco's Rincon Hill.

Although nursing remained the principal activity of Mother Baptist and her Sisters of Mercy, they were constantly mindful of their other obligations. Within two months of landing on the West Coast they opened a night school for adults. In 1855 the sisters established the House of Mercy, primarily as a shelter for unemployed women. The next year Mother Baptist took in a young prostitute, a Protestant girl who appealed for help, and soon others followed, leading to the establishment in 1861 of a separate Magdalen Asylum; eight years later 187 girls had been admitted, of whom only 9 had left or been sent away as incorrigible. In 1857 Mother Baptist went to Sacramento to organize the first Catholic convent and school in the state capital. St. Mary's Hospital had from the outset offered classes in religious instruction, and in the early 1870's the sisters established Our Lady of Mercy School for girls, St. Joseph's School for boys, and an industrial school for girls on the Rincon Hill property. Mother Baptist's initiative and organization brought together the teachers of the Catholic schools of the archdiocese in 1894, the first meeting of its kind in the United States.

She and the sisters for forty years made regular visits to the city prison, the county jail, and San Quentin state prison, with special calls to death row. A home for the aged and infirm was established in 1872. A pavilion in the hospital yard provided a daily hot meal for the city's poor and unemployed in depression times. In 1882 Mother Baptist purchased a 200-acre ranch near Santa Rosa to serve as a vacation retreat for the sisters and provide farm products for the hospital; this was later replaced by a convent in the Marin County hills north of San Francisco. Such a wide range of activities was costly. As early as 1859 Mother Baptist organized San Francisco's first Sodality of Our Lady, through which Catholic women were recruited to help finance the sisters' undertakings. In 1870 the state legislature voted the Sisters of Mercy $5,000 in gratitude for their volunteer nursing in the city's "pest house" during nine months of smallpox epidemic in 1868. On a visit to the United States in 1883, Lord Russell found his sister a notable figure, but an entry in his diary—"I left poor Kate very sad, poor soul, but greatly pleased at having had the Old Land brought closer to her by my presence"—provides a glimpse of a more private Mother Baptist.

Though respectful of the authority of the archbishop of San Francisco, her canonical superior, and mindful of her obligations to the aims of her order, Mother Baptist on occasion showed an independence of mind that bespoke a woman of character. As early as 1856, despite the urging of Archbishop Alemany, she decided not to have her teaching sisters examined by public school authorities in order to obtain public funds, just as forty years later she turned down the suggestion of his successor that the lay sisters of her community change their apparel. Her determination to meet community needs brought support from Catholics and non-Catholics alike. At the age of sixty-nine Mother Baptist died at St. Mary's Hospital of "clogging of the arteries of the brain." She was buried in St. Michael's Cemetery, next to the Magdalen Asylum. In its obituary the *San Francisco Bulletin* called her the "best-known charitable worker on the Pacific Coast."

[Archives of the Sisters of Mercy, Convent of Our Lady of Mercy, Burlingame, Calif.; Matthew Russell, S.J., *The Life of Mother Mary Baptist Russell, Sister of Mercy* (1901), also reprinted in his *The Three Sisters of Lord Russell of Killowen and Their Convent Life* (1912); Sister Mary Aurelia McArdle, *California's Pioneer Sister of Mercy: Mother Mary Baptist Russell, 1829–1898* (1954); Charles Lord Russell of Killowen, *Diary of a Visit to the U.S.A. in the Year 1883* (1910), p. 146.]

JOHN TRACY ELLIS

**RUTHERFORD, Mildred Lewis** (July 16, 1851–Aug. 15, 1928), educator, apologist for the Old South, was born in Athens, Ga., the third daughter and fourth child in a family of five girls and one boy. Her parents, Williams R. and Laura Battaille Rootes (Cobb) Rutherford, were descended from colonial Virginia forebears who had moved to Georgia after the American Revolution. Miss Rutherford came naturally by her two major interests. Her father ran a boys' school in Athens and became professor of mathematics at the University of Georgia. Two of her uncles, Howell and Thomas Reade Rootes Cobb, helped lead Georgia out of the Union and served as generals in the Confederate Army. During the war her mother worked tirelessly in the Soldiers' Aid Society, and Mildred and her sisters helped roll bandages and pack food for the soldiers.

Growing up in Athens, Mildred Rutherford entered at the age of eight the Lucy Cobb Institute, a local girls' school founded in 1858 by her uncle T. R. R. Cobb and named for his daughter. After graduating in 1868, she taught for several years in the Atlanta public schools. In 1880 she was called back to Lucy Cobb as principal, and for most of the next forty-six years she served the school as administrator and teacher. From 1895 to 1907 her sister Mary Ann (Rutherford) Lipscomb was co-principal with her, and in 1908 Miss Rutherford resigned as principal to give more time to her writing; but she took over again as president from 1917 to 1922 and was director in 1925–26. Antebellum Lucy Cobb Institute had sought, along with a good education, to implant the Old South's principles of gentility and culture in its students, and "Miss Millie" carried this same program on into the twentieth century. If such an education took little account of changing ideas and conditions, the principal's sturdy integrity and gracious manners left their imprint upon several generations of Southern girls.

Miss Rutherford wrote the textbooks for her literature classes: *English Authors* (1890), *American Authors* (1894), and *French Authors* (1906). Her approach to literature was didactic and personal. She was more concerned with censuring immoralities in the life and works of Whitman, Swinburne, and Zola than with considering their art and thought. Her high praise of Dickens, Thackeray, and Macaulay was equally unsupported by thoughtful criticism. In *American Authors,* and later in *The South in Literature and History* (1907), Miss Rutherford demanded a higher place for certain Southern writers in the nation's literature. She contended that Henry Timrod, William Gilmore Simms, and Joel Chandler Harris deserved the recognition given Whitman, Cooper, and Howells. Today her textbooks are useful only for biographical data on a number of obscure writers.

Miss Rutherford carried on her fight for Southern rights in almost every high office of the United Daughters of the Confederacy. She was the first president of its Athens chapter (1890–1928), historian and president (1899–1902) of the Georgia Division, and historian-general (1914–16) and honorary president of the national organization. She helped establish new chapters, conducted fund-raising campaigns, and faithfully attended the reunions of Confederate veterans. Other organizations devoted to the Confederacy also considered her their spokesman. A handsome, stately woman and a fluent orator, she made an impressive defense of Southern motives and institutions before audiences in all parts of the country, sometimes appearing in antebellum costume to create an appropriate atmosphere. She compiled a list of questions by which Southerners could judge the fairness and accuracy of American histories. From 1923 to 1927 she published a series of pamphlets which pressed her two major charges against Northern historians: that they had denied the South its proper place in the nation's history, and that they had misrepresented the Southern side in the War between the States—which she insisted was not a civil war or a war of rebellion. She argued that the North had started the war not to end slavery but to ruin the South economically, and had vilified Jefferson Davis to make Abraham Lincoln into a folk hero. Some of her contentions were based partly upon documentary evidence, such as her defense of Henry Wirz, superintendent of Andersonville Prison; others were wholly without foundation, such as her charge that the famous Gettysburg speech was not the one spoken by Lincoln.

But whatever Miss Rutherford's defects, she was at least consistent. She fought national prohibition, woman suffrage, and child labor laws as violations of states' rights. A few welfare causes did claim her support. Herself a Baptist, she headed the Athens City Mission Board and was active in the Young Women's Christian Association, serving from 1910 on its national board; and she succeeded her sister Bessie as head of an industrial home for girls the latter had founded. Miss Rutherford's honors were local: a Doctor of Literature degree from the University of Georgia (1923) and offices in various women's organizations. Having suffered from Bright's disease and arteriosclerosis, she died in Athens of hypostatic pneumonia at the age of seventy-seven and was buried in Oconee Cemetery in Athens. The Lucy Cobb Institute survived her by only three years.

[Margaret Ann Womack, "Mildred Lewis Rutherford, Exponent of Southern Culture" (master's thesis, Univ. of Ga., 1946); Lucian L. Knight, *Georgia's Bi-centennial Memoirs and Memories,* II (1932), 91–110 (with portrait); Lucian L. Knight, ed., *Library of Southern Literature,* XV (1907), 381; Augustus Longstreet Hull, *Annals of Athens* (1906); *Athens Daily Herald,* Mar. 18, 1914; *Athens Banner Herald,* Apr. 16, 1922; *Woman's Who's Who of America,* 1914–15; death record from Ga. Dept. of Public Health. See also Margaret A. Moss, "Miss Millie Rutherford, Southerner," *Ga. Rev.,* Spring 1953. A biographical source outline prepared by Judith Harrold, Emory Univ. Division of Librarianship, was helpful. Virginia Clare, *Thunder and Stars: The Life of Mildred Rutherford* (1941), is a somewhat sentimental treatment.]

JOHN E. TALMADGE

RUTHERFORD, Minnie Ursula Oliver. *See* FULLER, Minnie Ursula Oliver Scott Rutherford.

RUTLEDGE, Ann May(e)s (Jan. 7, 1813–Aug. 25, 1835), legendary sweetheart of Abraham Lincoln, was born in Kentucky, the third of the nine children of James and Mary (Miller) Rutledge. Her father, a native of South Carolina, had migrated through Georgia and Tennessee to Kentucky, and later moved on to Illinois, where in 1829 he and John M. Camron built a mill on the Sangamon River and thus founded New Salem. Rutledge believed in education and was a leader in the community. As the village grew he converted his home into a tavern. Abraham Lincoln boarded there in 1832 and became well acquainted with Rutledge's daughter, a pretty, amiable, blue-eyed girl with reddish blond hair.

Ann was engaged to a good friend of Lincoln's, John McNamar, a young merchant of New Salem who had come from New York to make his fortune in the West, and they were to be married as soon as he returned from a trip to the East to provide for his parents. Before leaving, he bought a farm about seven miles north of New Salem at Sand Ridge, and in 1833 the Rutledges moved to this farm as a kind of family arrangement in view of the impending marriage. After this move Lincoln saw much less of Ann, though this was the period to which legend assigns their romance.

McNamar's absence was prolonged by an extended illness of his own, his father's illness and death, and the settling of his father's estate. He was still absent in August 1835 when Ann Rutledge died of typhoid or "brain fever." Lincoln, like others who knew the Rutledges well, was greatly distressed. Lincoln's friend James Short, with whom he sometimes stayed at Sand Ridge, noted his grief, and later (in 1865) said he "then supposed" Lincoln must have been in love with Ann, adding, however, that he had seen no evidence of this while she was living. Lincoln's sorrow and this posthumous conjecture were to be the starting point and basis of the legend.

The legend had its origin after Lincoln's death in 1865 when William H. Herndon, who had been his junior law partner, began to collect material for a life of the President. Herndon was an earthy man, overly fond of drink and firmly convinced, as he often asserted, that he could read people's minds and that he knew what was truth by his own power of intuition.

The result was that he usually believed what he wanted to believe. Learning that Lincoln at New Salem thirty years before had grieved over the death of a young woman, Herndon, with his lawyer's skill at suggestion, interviewed the old settlers of that vanished village and collected a mass of long-delayed, vague, and contradictory reminiscence out of which he fashioned the love story of Lincoln and Ann Rutledge. On Nov. 16, 1866, he gave a lecture in Springfield in which he proclaimed that Ann was the only woman Lincoln had ever loved and that his heart was buried in her grave. No doubt Herndon wanted to believe the poetic story, especially as it tore down MARY TODD LINCOLN, with whom he had always been at odds. He went on to describe a scheduled wedding day—nonexistent except in his imagination—on which Lincoln had played the part of a defaulting bridegroom, and to present the Lincoln-Todd marriage as a loveless one and Mary Lincoln as a shrew.

*Herndon's Lincoln,* written by Herndon and Jesse W. Weik and published in 1889, gave the fully embellished love story. It was accepted and incorporated into Lincoln biography and other literature for many years, while access to Herndon's original material, his so-called evidence on the romance, was denied to the historical profession. The Library of Congress finally obtained the Herndon-Weik Manuscripts and opened them to the public in 1942. The verdict of Lincoln scholars, after careful analysis, is that there is not a scrap of reliable evidence to support this long-lived legend.

[A full analysis of the Lincoln-Rutledge material in the Herndon-Weik collection was published with documentation in vol. II of J. G. Randall's *Lincoln the President: Springfield to Gettysburg* (1945), under the heading "Sifting the Ann Rutledge Evidence." The legend is fully discussed, with documentation, in Ruth Painter Randall's *Mary Lincoln: Biog. of a Marriage* (1953). Paul M. Angle treats the romance in his "Editor's Preface" to the 1930 edition of *Herndon's Life of Lincoln.* David Donald's *Lincoln's Herndon* (1948) is indispensable to a study of this subject. Benjamin P. Thomas' *Lincoln's New Salem* (1954) gives an excellent account of the Rutledges. Ann's middle name and the name of her mother were furnished by Rutledge descendants.]

RUTH PAINTER RANDALL

# S

SABIN, Ellen Clara (Nov. 29, 1850–Feb. 2, 1949), school administrator and college president, was born in Sun Prairie, Dane County, Wis., the oldest of the eleven children of Samuel Henry Sabin and Adelia M. (Bordine) Sabin. She grew up chiefly on the 300-acre farm near Windsor, in the same county, that her father bought in 1854 after returning from the California gold rush. There "Ella," as she was called, attended district school. In January 1866, at fifteen, she entered the University of Wisconsin, which she attended for three years. Meanwhile she began teaching at the district school in Sun Prairie township. A new system of visual aids for slow learners in geography that she developed led, in 1868, to her appointment as teacher of the third and fourth grades in the Sun Prairie grade school. A year later she began teaching a seventh-grade class in Madison; within a few months she was appointed principal of the Fourth Ward (later the Doty) School, where she continued until 1872.

In that year Samuel Sabin, once again feeling the lure of the West, moved with his entire family to Eugene, Oreg. Finding the only primary school a "dilapidated building located in a sea of mud," Ellen established a one-room school of her own; she charged fifty cents a week tuition and "was able to salt down $200 in gold" during the winter of 1872–73. That spring a paper on the teaching of history which she presented at the state Teachers' Institute in Salem made such an impression that she was nominated, at twenty-two, for the vacant post of state superintendent of schools. She withdrew her name but accepted a job in the Old North (later Atkinson) School of Portland, where a year later she was appointed principal—the first woman to hold such a position in that city.

The Old North School was located on the waterfront, the roughest section of Portland, but Miss Sabin, undeterred by police warnings, walked unaccompanied through the district to get acquainted with school families. Replacing corporal punishment by conferences with pupils and parents, she achieved a degree of cooperation unknown before. She established a kind of job placement system for her boys through personal visits to factories and businesses along the wharves. To raise the self-respect of able students, she had them tutor those in difficulties, and she continued to try out new teaching methods. Her success attracted attention throughout the state, and in 1887, after a year in Europe studying educational procedures, she became superintendent of schools in Portland, the only large city to employ a woman in such a position at that time.

In 1891 Ellen Sabin returned to her home state to accept the presidency of Downer College, a girls' school at Fox Lake. The salary was half what she had received in Portland, but the trustees promised "to back her plans and in no way hamper her" as she set out to raise standards and increase enrollment. It was obvious, however, that backwoods Fox Lake was not a favorable location. Milwaukee College for Women (see MARY MORTIMER) had an excellent location but poor leadership. A visit to Ellen Sabin by two women trustees of the Milwaukee institution in February 1894 led to the first steps toward merger. In September 1895 Downer College moved to Milwaukee and Miss Sabin assumed control of both institutions; the merger was completed in April 1897, and that same year ground was broken for the first building on a new campus for Milwaukee-Downer College located on the north edge of Milwaukee.

Ellen Sabin believed in moving forward with large plans to "the remoter goal." "Our danger," she declared in a commencement address in 1920, "lies in inadequate vision rather than in extravagant expectations." Under her direction the college won full accreditation, its endowment increased from $138,000 to $666,146, and its new campus expanded to forty-three acres with sixteen red sandstone and brick buildings in "English Domestic Gothic." Miss Sabin's educational policy was much in the tradition of the college's founder, CATHARINE BEECHER. Though maintaining standards in the traditional disciplines, she refused to imitate the exclusively academic program of the Eastern women's colleges. Milwaukee-Downer, she believed, should "meet the needs of its locality" and offer practical training, particularly in "the science and art of home making," as preparation for women's "chief vocation." In addition to the standard course leading to a B.A. degree, therefore, the college offered diplomas in home economics, nursing, and occupational therapy (the last two being innovations of the World War I period). Miss Sabin also stressed gymnastics and the arts; she herself taught the classes in Biblical literature.

Ellen Sabin retired from the presidency in 1921. Her first college degree, an honorary A.M., had come from the University of Wisconsin in 1895; she later received honorary doctorates from Beloit and Grinnell colleges. She was a member of the National Council of

Education from 1886 to 1892, and between 1919 and 1923 served on the Wisconsin State Board of Education. Always active in the American Association of University Women, she was one of the first members of its Milwaukee branch, the College Women's Club, of which she was president, 1900–02. In 1945 the Wisconsin A.A.U.W. gave her name to its national graduate fellowship. She was a leader in the Milwaukee County League of Women Voters and the Women's Club of Wisconsin. Her church affiliation was Congregational, and she was a lifetime member of the Republican party.

During the years of her retirement, Miss Sabin made her home briefly in Milwaukee, then in Lake Mills, Wis., and finally with her sister Mrs. E. Ray Stevens in Madison, Wis., where she died, of chronic endocarditis, at the age of ninety-eight. She was buried in the Windsor (Wis.) Cemetery. In 1964 Milwaukee-Downer College became part of Lawrence University, Appleton, Wis.

[Marie Adams, *Ellen Clara Sabin: A Life Sketch* (1937); Grace Norton Kieckhefer, *The Hist. of Milwaukee-Downer College, 1851–1951* (1950); Ellen C. Sabin, *Twenty-five Years of Milwaukee-Downer College* (leaflet, 1920); *Who Was Who in America*, vol. II (1950); *Milwaukee Jour.*, Feb. 2, 1949; death record from Wis. Dept. of Health and Social Services.]

WALTER F. PETERSON

**SACAJAWEA** (c. 1786–Dec. 20, 1812), Indian interpreter for the Lewis and Clark expedition, has become one of the best-known women in the annals of the American West. Born about 1786, she belonged to the Lemhi band of Shoshoni, or Snake, Indians who inhabited the eastern part of the Salmon River country of present-day central Idaho. When the Lemhis, on an eastward trip in 1800, encountered a war party of the Hidatsa, or Minnetaree, tribe at the three forks of the Missouri, Sacajawea (Sacagawea, Sakakawea) was one of those captured and sold or gambled away as a slave. By 1804 she had become the property of Toussaint Charbonneau, a French Canadian living with the Hidatsas. That year the Lewis and Clark expedition, which had set out in May from St. Louis, reached its winter stopping place at the Mandan villages, close to the Hidatsa tribe, on the Missouri River in present-day North Dakota. When the party set off again the following April, Charbonneau, hired as an interpreter, went along, taking with him Sacajawea and her two-month-old son, Jean Baptiste Charbonneau.

Sacajawea proved a valuable member of the expedition. For one thing, its success hinged upon avoiding Indian hostilities, and she and her infant were a sign to the natives that Lewis and Clark were not bringing out a war party. Her knowledge of the Mandan and Shoshoni languages enabled the explorers to communicate, through her husband and thence through her, with members of those tribes. Through a longer chain of interpreters, she enabled Lewis and Clark to speak with some of the other Pacific Northwest tribes. She also helped by cooking, hunting up edible wild foods, and the like, and once saved valuable instruments and records from being lost overboard in a storm, showing, in the words of William Clark, "equal fortitude and resolution, with any person onboard at the time of the accedent" (Thwaites, II, 39). Sacajawea proved, in particular, the best possible emissary in gaining the favor of the Lemhi Shoshoni, whose help was essential in getting the explorers across the Continental Divide. Upon being reunited with her people, she found to her joy that her brother had become chief of the band; from then on the heretofore suspicious Lemhis gave Lewis and Clark guidance, horses, and other help necessary to get the party to the navigable waters of the Clearwater and the Columbia. There is, however, no substance to the legend that Sacajawea herself directed the explorers across the continent. Though she recognized some of the landmarks of the upper Missouri, she did not travel with the advance party that established contact with the Lemhi band, and an elderly Lemhi Shoshoni served as guide across the difficult Lolo Trail. On the return journey in 1806, she was able to show Clark how to get through Big Hole and to point out Bozeman Pass (Thwaites, V, 250, 260). That was about the extent of her service as guide.

In the years after the expedition, William Clark, who had become attached to Sacajawea's son during the journey, assumed responsibility for his education. The younger Charbonneau's later career included six years in Europe with Prince Paul of Württemberg (who took the eighteen-year-old boy back with him from an American visit), many seasons of trapping in the Rockies, service in the Mexican War, and eighteen years in the California gold fields. Clark also did what he could to help Charbonneau and Sacajawea get established in St. Louis, where they tried to settle down as late as 1810. In the spring of 1811 Sacajawea "had become sickly, and longed to revisit her native country" (Brackenridge, p. 10). Since Charbonneau, who "had become weary of a civilized life," also preferred to return to the fur trade, they moved to Fort Manuel on the Missouri not far below the later North Dakota–South Dakota line. The author Henry Brackenridge, who came up the Missouri that spring with Sacajawea, described her as "a good creature, of a mild and gentle disposition, greatly attached to the whites, whose manners and dress she tries to imitate." The next year John C. Luttig, a clerk at Fort Manuel, noted in his journal, on Dec. 20, 1812, the death of Charbonneau's "Snake Squaw" of a "putrid fever," remarking that she was "a good and the best Women [sic] in the fort." Unlike Brackenridge, Luttig did not specifically indicate that this Snake wife of Charbonneau was Sacajawea. But even if Charbonneau had another Snake wife with him (an unlikely possibility), Sacajawea did not survive past 1828, for in a list of members of the expedition William Clark compiled that year he listed her as "Dead."

The popular legend which pictures Sacajawea as Lewis and Clark's principal guide dates from the early twentieth century. First formulated in the writings of an Oregon author, Eva Emery Dye, it gained added force from the great national interest aroused by the centennial observances of the Louisiana Purchase and the Lewis and Clark expedition and was carried forward by the efforts of Oregon suffragists and the Wyoming historian GRACE RAYMOND HEBARD. Mrs. Dye's novel *The Conquest: The True Story of Lewis and Clark* (1902), with its exaggeration of Sacajawea's role, went through ten editions. Mrs. Dye also headed a women's association that raised funds for a statue of Sacajawea, designed by Alice Cooper, which was unveiled at the Lewis and Clark Exposition of 1905, with speeches by SUSAN B. ANTHONY and ANNA HOWARD SHAW, and subsequently placed in a Portland park. Additional statues and monuments, and the naming of mountain peaks, streams, and other geographic features for Sacajawea, testify to her hold on the American imagination.

[Grace R. Hebard's *Sacajawea* (1933), although based upon extensive research, is tendentious and unfortunately confuses another Sacajawea, who lived on the Wind River Reservation in Wyoming until 1884, with the original Sacajawea of Lewis and Clark. Later evidence concerning Sacajawea, especially William Clark's indication in his cash book for 1825–28 that she was deceased, excludes the Wind River Sacajawea from serious consideration; see Donald Jackson, ed., *Letters of the Lewis and Clark Expedition, with Related Documents, 1783–1854* (1962), pp. 638–39; and Helen Addison Howard, "The Mystery of Sacagawea's Death," *Pacific Northwest Quart.*, Jan. 1967. Similarly, biographical investigation of Sacajawea's

son, Jean Baptiste, has disposed of the claims of a false Baptiste, an Indian who survived on Wind River for two decades beyond the lifetime of the Baptiste who accompanied Lewis and Clark; see LeRoy R. Hafen, ed., *The Mountain Men and the Fur Trade of the Far West*, I (1965), 205–24. See also Reuben Gold Thwaites, ed., *Original Journals of the Lewis and Clark Expedition* (8 vols., 1904–05); Henry M. Brackenridge, *Jour. of a Voyage up the River Missouri* (2nd ed., 1816), p. 10; John C. Luttig, *Jour. of a Fur-Trading Expedition on the Upper Missouri, 1812–1813* (Stella M. Drumm, ed., 1920), p. 106; John E. Rees, "The Shoshoni Contribution to Lewis and Clark," *Idaho Yesterdays*, Summer 1958; Russell Reid, "Sakakawea," *North Dakota Hist.*, Apr.–July 1963. On Mrs. Dye and the Portland statue, see Helen Krebs Smith, ed., *With Her Own Wings* (1948), pp. 229–30; Ida H. Harper, ed., *The Hist. of Woman Suffrage*, VI (1922), 540–41; and Ronald W. Taber, "Sacagawea and the Suffragettes," *Pacific Northwest Quart.*, Jan. 1967.]

MERLE W. WELLS

**SADLIER, Mary Anne Madden** (Dec. 31, 1820–Apr. 5, 1903), Catholic author, was born at Cootehill, County Cavan, Ireland, the daughter of Francis Madden, a prosperous merchant. Reared by her father after the mother's early death, she showed talent as a writer and at the age of eighteen contributed verses to *La Belle Assemblée* (London). Her father suffered business reverses, and after his death she emigrated, in 1844, to New York City. In November 1846 she was married to James Sadlier, who with his brother Denis had established a Catholic publishing house in New York. For the next fourteen years she lived in Montreal, Canada, where her husband was branch manager of the firm. Their family eventually included three daughters, three sons (two of whom died in early manhood), and a foster son.

During the years in Montreal, Mrs. Sadlier began her serious writing, publishing a collection of short stories and several novels, and writing for the *Boston Pilot* and other Catholic journals, including the *New York Tablet* (published by the Sadlier firm), which she later helped edit. By the time the family returned to New York in 1860, she had become widely known as a writer of fiction and poetry supporting the Catholic faith. A leading figure in conservative Catholic circles, she kept up a large acquaintance among literary, clerical, and lay friends, held weekly receptions at her house on East Broadway, and maintained a summer home at Far Rockaway. She also gave active support to New York's Catholic charities. Among her associates were Orestes Brownson, Archbishop Hughes of New York, and the Irish statesman Thomas D'Arcy McGee, whose poems she collected and edited.

Mrs. Sadlier's historical importance rests upon her novels, which first appeared in serial form in Catholic newspapers in Canada and the United States. Although she distrusted literature, believing it subversive of morality, she defended her use of the novel as being the best means for helping young Irish Catholics resist the temptations of American Protestant culture. She wrote out of specific moral concern and frequently upon request. *Bessy Conway* (1862), for example, dealt with the moral hazards suffered by Irish servant girls and was suggested by Isaac Hecker, founder of the Paulist Fathers. Though little more than collections of ill-articulated didactic episodes, the novels were widely read. *Willie Burke: A Tale of the Irish Orphan in America* sold seven thousand copies within the first weeks of publication. James Sadlier was also influential in suggesting themes for her stories, based on his understanding of the Catholic market. After his death in 1869 Mrs. Sadlier turned in her writing increasingly to religious and historical themes. The renewal of mass Irish immigration in the 1880's, however, led to the republication of several of her earlier Irish-American tales.

Mary Anne Sadlier's Irish-American novels are valuable documents of American social history, telling much about mid-nineteenth-century Irish life and honestly revealing the squalor that attended it. But more important, they reveal, and perhaps even contributed to, the tensions of Irish assimilation to American culture. Running through her stories is a strain of irascibility and violence. *The Blakes and the Flanagans* (1855) embodies satisfaction with the beating administered to a fallen-away Catholic turned ruffian. Bloodshed and bitterness characterized the historical novels, such as *De Fromental* (1887), a tale of Catholic suffering at the hands of democrats in the French Revolution.

By encouraging the Irish to adopt Yankee habits of thrift, sobriety, and hard work, Mrs. Sadlier's novels were a force for Americanization; by attacking Protestant domination of American institutions, they were a force for social change. Mrs. Sadlier appears to have closely reflected the dilemmas of Irish assimilation: wanting, on the one hand, to achieve Yankee material success, she nevertheless repudiated the liberalism and individualism that energized American culture. Her novels affirmed the virtues of the traditional Irish patriarchal family and of a hierarchical society. At a time when there was sharp conflict

between liberal and conservative Catholicism, she was a strong voice for the latter.

Sometime in the 1880's Mrs. Sadlier returned to Montreal to be near her married children. In 1895 she received the University of Notre Dame's Laetare Medal for her efforts in behalf of the Catholic faith. She died in Montreal at the age of eighty-three and was buried in Calvary Cemetery, Woodside, N.Y. In the course of her life she had produced nearly sixty books, some fifty of them original novels and stories. At the time of her death many of her translations of religious works from the French, her *Catechism of Sacred History and Doctrine* (1864), and a number of her novels were still being read. Her daughter Anna Theresa also became a prominent Catholic author.

[William D. Kelly, "A Benefactress of Her Race," *Ave Maria*, Apr. 4, 1891; Anna T. Sadlier, "Mrs. Sadlier's Early Life, Her Books and Friends," *Donahoe's Mag.* (Boston), Apr. 1903; *Boston Pilot*, Apr. 11, 1903 (which reprints the Kelly article); Agnes Brady McGuire, "Catholic Women Writers," in Constantine E. McGuire, ed., *Catholic Builders of the Nation* (1923), IV, 184–203; Robert C. Healey, *A Catholic Book Chronicle: The Story of P. J. Kenedy & Sons, 1826–1951* (1951); information from Calvary Cemetery.]

THOMAS N. BROWN

**SAFFORD, Mary Jane** (Dec. 31, 1834–Dec. 8, 1891), Civil War nurse and physician, was born in Hyde Park, Vt., the second daughter and youngest of five children of Joseph and Diantha (Little) Safford and a descendant of Thomas Safford, who emigrated from England in 1630 and was a founder of the Massachusetts Bay Colony. When she was three her family moved to a homestead at Crete, Ill., near Chicago, where her father farmed. In 1849, following the death of her mother, she attended school at Bakersfield, Vt., and, after graduation, spent a year studying French near Montreal. She then lived in the family of an educated German for the purpose of learning that language. Returning to Illinois, she went to live in Joliet with an older brother, Alfred Boardman Safford, who was in the mercantile business. She soon moved with him to Shawneetown, Ill., where she took steps to establish and teach in a public school, while her brother advanced the money to construct the building. Their next move, in 1858, was to nearby Cairo, where Alfred Safford soon became a wealthy banker and community benefactor.

Mary Safford's opportunity for a life of more active usefulness came with the outbreak of the Civil War. A week after the fall of Fort

Sumter, Cairo, strategically located at the confluence of the Ohio and Mississippi rivers, was occupied by a regiment of Chicago volunteers, and the town quickly became a major military supply depot and training center. When sickness broke out in the crowded camps, sprawling in the mud behind the levee, crude hospitals were improvised in tents or sheds, without special supplies or nursing care. Eager to be of help, Mary Safford on her own authority began visiting the sick. Overcoming the opposition of officers and surgeons, she made daily rounds, carrying a memorandum book in one hand and a large basket of delicacies in the other, while a porter followed with an even larger basket. She personally prepared the articles of sick diet, after securing a surgeon's authorization. In addition to food, she supplied handwork, magazines, newspapers, games, and letter-writing materials, all purchased with moneys donated by her brother. Later, because of her careful management, she was permitted to draw upon United States Sanitary Commission supplies. Contemporaries described her as "very frail" and "as *petite* as a girl of twelve summers," with a "sweet, young face . . . pleasant voice, and winning manner" that disarmed opposition. Her patients dubbed her the "Cairo Angel."

By the summer of 1861 Miss Safford had developed a close working relationship with the vigorous and blustery volunteer nurse "Mother" MARY ANN BICKERDYKE, who trained her in actual nursing. That fall the two women helped care for the first battle casualties to come into Cairo. Miss Safford even visited the field after the fighting at Belmont, a short distance downriver on the Missouri shore, to minister to wounded not yet evacuated, improvising a white flag with her handkerchief and a stick when she was fired upon. The following February, after the battle of Fort Donelson, she and Mother Bickerdyke made five trips together on the Sanitary Commission's transport *City of Memphis*, accompanying wounded men to hospitals in Cairo and other nearby towns. Mary Safford combined "a calm dignity and self-poise that never blanched at any sight of horror," wrote a Sanitary Commission executive, Mrs. JANE C. HOGE, "with a quiet energy and gentle authority that commanded willing obedience." Completely exhausted after Fort Donelson, she limited her work for a time, but action at Shiloh in April brought her again into service on the hospital ship *Hazel Dell*. A wounded officer aboard later remembered seeing her "everywhere, doing everything, straightening out affairs, soothing and comforting, and sometimes praying, dressing wounds, cooking and nursing." A complete collapse followed, putting an end to her wartime career.

To recover her health, she joined in the summer of 1862 the party of former Illinois governor Joel A. Matteson, a friend of her Joliet days, on an extended tour of Europe. Her interest in medicine was sharpened when she visited foreign hospitals, and upon her return to the United States she entered Dr. CLEMENCE S. LOZIER's New York Medical College for Women, graduating in 1869. In the summer of 1869 Dr. Safford visited for a time in Chicago, where in September she attended a woman suffrage convention presided over by her friend MARY A. LIVERMORE. That fall she returned to Europe for nearly three years of surgical training, first in the General Hospital of Vienna and then at medical centers in Germany, including the University of Breslau, where she was credited with the first ovariotomy performed by a woman.

Dr. Safford began practice in Chicago in the spring of 1872. By this time she was already well known not only as a physician but as an advocate of dress reform, appearing in her office in a dress of "rich blue cloth, the skirt without hint of flounce, overskirt, or bustle" and an inch above floor level, revealing shoes "broad and square at the toe, with immensely thick soles, and flat, low heels" (*Woman's Journal*, May 18, 1872). That year she was married to James Blake of Boston. In 1873, when the Boston University School of Medicine was organized, she joined its faculty as professor of women's diseases. She also engaged in private practice and served on the staff of the Massachusetts Homeopathic Hospital. She lectured and wrote pamphlets on women's dress, exercise, and hygiene, took a warm interest in efforts to better the condition of working girls, and became one of the first women to serve on the Boston School Committee (1875). Her marriage probably ended in divorce, for she resumed the use of her maiden name in 1880. Failing health forced her retirement in 1886. Soon afterward she moved with her two adopted daughters, Margarita and Gladys Safford, to the resort town of Tarpon Springs, Fla., where her brother Anson P. K. Safford, earlier territorial governor of Arizona (1869–77) and father of that state's public school system, also resided. She died in Tarpon Springs in 1891, shortly before her fifty-seventh birthday, and was buried there in Cycadia Cemetery.

[The standard genealogical source is the typewritten MS. compiled by Edward S. Safford, "The

Saffords in America" (1923), Library of Congress. Miss Safford's pre–Civil War years are treated in William Henry Perrin, ed., *Hist. of Alexander, Union and Pulaski Counties, Ill.* (1883). For her wartime activities, see L. P. Brockett and Mary C. Vaughan, *Woman's Work in the Civil War* (1867); Mary A. Livermore, *My Story of the War* (1887); Mrs. A. H. Hoge, *The Boys in Blue* (1867); Nina Brown Baker, *Cyclone in Calico: The Story of Mary Ann Bickerdyke* (1952); and Agatha Young, *The Women and the Crisis* (1959). For her medical career, see Egbert Cleave, *Biog. Cyc. of Homeopathic Physicians and Surgeons* (1873); N.Y. Medical College for Women, *Seventh Annual Announcement*, 1869–70; Boston Univ. School of Medicine, annual announcements, 1873–86. For other useful biographical material see Elizabeth C. Stanton et al., *Hist. of Woman Suffrage*, III (1886), 570; *Woman's Jour.*, May 18, 1872, Dec. 19, 1891; *Boston Transcript*, Dec. 16, 1891; and *To-Day* (Phila.), June 1894.]

LE ROY H. FISCHER

**SAGE, Margaret Olivia Slocum** (Sept. 8, 1828–Nov. 4, 1918), philanthropist, was the first of two children born to Joseph and Margaret Pierson (Jermain) Slocum at Syracuse, N.Y. Her father claimed descent from Anthony Slocum, who came to Massachusetts from England in the 1630's; her mother, also of colonial lineage, was born at Sag Harbor, Long Island. Joseph Slocum, a prosperous merchant, served as state assemblyman from Onondaga County in 1849 and went twice to Russia as an agent of the Russian government to organize agricultural schools and introduce improved farm implements. Until she was eighteen Olivia, as she was known, lived at home in Syracuse, attending local schools and mastering the genteel domestic arts. In 1846 she set out for Mount Holyoke Seminary, but fell ill at Troy, N.Y., where an uncle persuaded her to enroll in the Troy Female Seminary, founded by EMMA WILLARD, from which she graduated the next year. Because of family financial reverses she turned to teaching, occupying a position at the Chestnut Street Seminary in Philadelphia. Delicate health, however, forced her to resign after two years, and though her interest in the education of women continued, for the next two decades she taught only briefly and irregularly, as her health allowed.

On Nov. 24, 1869, at forty-one, she was married to Russell B. Sage (1816–1906), a widower whose first wife had been one of her close friends at the Troy Seminary. A former Congressman, Sage had risen rapidly in the business world of New York City after moving there from Troy in 1863. He and his wife maintained a city home in New York, a coun-

try house at Lawrence, Long Island, and a retreat at Sag Harbor. There were no children.

Mrs. Sage's education and social position, combined with her energy, self-assurance, and personal force, well fitted her for a public role. Women, she believed, were the intellectual equals and moral superiors of men, and though their first duty was to the home, they had an obligation to work for the improvement of society. A Presbyterian by birth as well as by marriage, she interested herself in home and foreign missions, the Woman's Christian Temperance Union, the rescue of fallen women, the crusade against tobacco and vice, improved police protection, milk inspection, the humane treatment of animals, the woman suffrage movement, and the cause of education. She induced her husband to underwrite the education of forty Indian children, pay for a dormitory at the Troy Seminary (renamed the Emma Willard School in 1895), and give $50,000 to the Woman's Hospital of the State of New York; but during his lifetime she did not succeed in dulling his acquisitive instinct or substantially reducing the fortune which he had built up in railroad, stock market, and money-lending ventures. When he died on July 22, 1906, leaving an estate of more than $63,000,-000, the nation's newspapers noted that Russell Sage had no reputation for generosity.

In the next twelve years Mrs. Sage became America's foremost woman philanthropist. The first and most original of her major gifts was the Russell Sage Foundation, established with a $10,000,000 endowment in 1907 for the purpose of improving social and living conditions in the United States. Robert W. de Forest, her attorney and philanthropic adviser, long-time president of the New York Charity Organization Society, helped her shape the foundation's early program. She gave untold sums in small amounts to conventional charities—to churches, schools, hospitals, homes for the aged, fresh air funds, the Y.M.C.A. and Y.W.C.A., Bible and tract societies, and the American Seaman's Friend Society, over which her younger brother, Col. Joseph J. Slocum, presided. She bought Constitution Island, in the Hudson River off West Point, long the home of SUSAN and ANNA WARNER, for the use of the United States Military Academy, and 70,000 acres on Marsh Island in Louisiana as a refuge for birds. She contributed a dormitory to Harvard, requesting that it be named Standish Hall in token of her conviction that her father was the sixth lineal descendant of Miles Standish. At a cost of $650,000 she purchased the Pierson-Sage campus for Yale University, thereby memorializing the maternal side of her family.

In 1910 Mrs. Sage gave a new campus to the Emma Willard School, and in 1916, at the suggestion of the school's principal, ELIZA KELLAS, she utilized its old campus and buildings to found Russell Sage College, for women's vocational education, to which she had given $1,000,000 by the time of her death. These lifetime gifts foreshadowed even larger outlays in her will.

Education, religion, and welfare claimed the major share of her estate. An unexpected provision in her will, widely discussed at the time of her death, deducted from the amounts designated for a number of institutions her lifetime gifts to them after the will had been drawn up. Russell Sage College, despite Mrs. Sage's oral assurances, was thus left without an expected endowment. There were, however, many large bequests. Syracuse University received $1,600,000. She gave $800,000 each to thirteen leading Eastern men's and women's colleges, to two Negro institutions (Tuskegee and Hampton), and to the New York Public Library. Religious bequests, for missions, Bible and tract societies, and ministerial relief, totaled approximately $7,500,000. In the welfare field Mrs. Sage added $5,600,000 to the endowment of the Russell Sage Foundation, $1,600,000 each to the Children's Aid Society, the Charity Organization Society, and the Woman's Hospital, and half as much to the Presbyterian Hospital, the Infirmary for Women and Children, and the State Charities Aid Association. The arts and sciences benefited through sizable bequests to the Metropolitan Museum of Art, the American Museum of Natural History, the New York Botanical Gardens, and the New York Zoological Society. Mrs. Sage's total gifts for public purposes, roughly estimated at $75,000,000 to $80,000,000, entitle her to rank with Andrew Carnegie, John D. Rockefeller, and J. P. Morgan as a leading benefactor. Because she distributed her largesse mainly in New York and New England, however, she never achieved a truly national reputation.

The wellsprings of Mrs. Sage's charity were her childlessness, a desire to improve her husband's reputation, a passion for memorializing her family (but not herself), a commitment to Christian stewardship, and a sense of class obligation—richesse oblige. Places, institutions, and causes with which she and her family had been intimately associated enjoyed special favor. Her giving was sometimes impulsive, but more often studied. She entrusted the screening of fresh proposals to her secretary, Miss E. L. Todd, and often solicited expert advice; but she tolerated no pressure. She despised begging letters, of which she received thousands, and insisted that giving money to the poor was "the very worst thing to do." Her interest in practical education and uplift reflected her belief that what the poor needed most was instruction in self-help and moral responsibility. Though she talked much of equality, her conception of servants as erring and naughty children, her strictures on the "moral filth" of the poor, and her insistence on the need for missionary work among them betrayed a strong class bias. Her criticisms of the idle rich proceeded from the assumption that their drinking, smoking, gambling, and sexual immorality set a bad example for the lower classes. She admired Queen Victoria and Theodore Roosevelt as moral leaders, and believed that well-bred women, because of their idealism and uncompromising spirit, were best suited to lead in this sphere. Her own career reflected her conviction that "God had a purpose in planting high-toned and good women in American soil."

Mrs. Sage had already attained her ninetieth year when she died in New York City of ailments resulting from her advanced age. She was buried in the family plot at Oakwood Cemetery, Syracuse.

[Mrs. Sage's personal papers are at the Russell Sage Foundation, unorganized and largely unused. Her essay on "Opportunities and Responsibilities of Leisured Women," *North Am. Rev.*, Nov. 1905, offers the best summary of her ideas. For obituaries and bequests see *N.Y. Times*, Nov. 4, 5, 14, 1918; *N.Y. Tribune*, Nov. 5, 1918; *Troy Record*, Nov. 14, 1918. Arthur H. Gleason, "Mrs. Russell Sage and Her Interests," *World's Work*, Nov. 1906, is laudatory and unintentionally revealing. Robert W. de Forest, "Margaret Olivia Sage, Philanthropist," *Survey*, Nov. 9, 1918, offers a concise analysis of her strategy of giving. A sentimental appraisal can be found in Mary Jane Fairbanks, ed., *Emma Willard and Her Pupils* (1908). See also Julia Patton, *Russell Sage College* (1941), and Grace Overmyer, "Hudson River Bluestockings—The Warner Sisters of Constitution Island," *N.Y. Hist.*, Apr. 1959. Charles E. Slocum, *A Short Hist. of the Slocums, Slocumbs, and Slocombs of America*, vol. I (1882), and Henry Whittemore, *Hist. of the Sage and Slocum Families* (1908), are useful for family backgrounds; the latter represents Mrs. Sage's effort to give her deceased husband a more distinguished lineage by advancing the claim that his ancestors marched with William the Conqueror.]

IRVIN G. WYLLIE

**SAGE, Mrs. Russell.** *See* SAGE, Margaret Olivia Slocum.

**SALMON, Lucy Maynard** (July 27, 1853– Feb. 14, 1927), historian, was born in Fulton,

N.Y., a small mill town on the Oswego River. The only daughter of George Salmon and his second wife, Maria Clara Maynard, she had one older brother and three older half brothers. Her father, who owned a flourishing tannery, was a director of the town bank, an active Presbyterian, and a staunch Republican of abolitionist sympathies. Her mother, educated at the Ipswich (Mass.) girls' seminary of MARY LYON and ZILPAH GRANT, had been principal of the Fulton Female Seminary from 1836 until her marriage. Both parents were of Puritan heritage, their forebears having emigrated to Massachusetts from England before the English Civil War.

When Lucy was seven her mother died. Her father remarried a year later, and her stepmother seems to have laid greater stress on the child's spiritual health and ultimate salvation than on her physical well-being and happiness. Lucy attended school in Oswego and later at Falley Seminary, the Fulton Female Seminary reorganized as a coeducational school; shy and sensitive, she was easily discouraged over her schoolwork and her relations with her schoolmates. Alarmed by her thinness and low spirits, her parents sent her to visit relatives in Michigan and Illinois. A Detroit cousin who was preparing to enter the University of Michigan encouraged her also to apply; after a year of preparatory study in the Ann Arbor high school, she enrolled as a freshman in the autumn of 1872—one of about fifty women students at the university. Studying under Charles Kendall Adams, she discovered history to be "the nicest thing we have had yet." After the death of her father in her junior year, she earned her board by acting as steward for a students' eating club and graduated in 1876. In looking back in later years, she singled out three important things she had learned at the university: "the necessity of production, the pleasure to be found in 'enjoying one's mind,' and the inspiration that came from democratic simplicity of thought and action."

For five years after leaving college Lucy Salmon served as assistant principal and then as principal of the high school in McGregor, Iowa, teaching "a little of everything." Disliking the monotony of small-town life, she then resigned and returned to Ann Arbor in the fall of 1882. After a year of graduate work she received an A.M. degree in modern European history and English and American constitutional history. She spent three unhappy years teaching at the Indiana State Normal School at Terre Haute, and then accepted a fellowship at Bryn Mawr College for the year 1886–87, for graduate study in American history. The next year she became the first teacher of history at Vassar College; she was appointed full professor in 1889 and remained there for the rest of her career.

Miss Salmon believed that learning should be a joint enterprise of teacher and student, and conducted her advanced classes as seminars. She urged the importance of keeping up with current affairs and introduced a class on the newspaper to the curriculum. She particularly stressed the need for scholarly research techniques, instituting a course in the use of historical materials, and she tried, without success, to establish a course in the history of science. As the history classes attracted a larger number of students, the faculty of the department gradually increased to seven. Miss Salmon as chairman allowed her colleagues complete freedom in choosing their teaching methods.

Her scholarly writing had begun with a brief monograph on *Education in Michigan during the Territorial Period* (1885). Her master's thesis, *History of the Appointing Power of the President*, appeared the next year in the first volume of the American Historical Association *Papers* and foreshadowed her lifelong interest in civil service reform. Miss Salmon's historical study of *Domestic Service* (1897), in which she had the aid of Carroll D. Wright, commissioner of the federal Bureau of Labor, made a pioneering application of statistical method to this field. The book derived from her basic faith in democracy and from her strong disapproval of the class distinctions that were accepted as a part of the service system at Vassar, a conviction she again voiced in *Progress in the Household* (1906). Her interest in the periodical press was reflected in *The Newspaper and the Historian* and *The Newspaper and Authority*, both published in 1923, which were based on a notable collection of books on journalism assembled at Vassar under her guidance. Two books published posthumously, *Why Is History Rewritten?* (1929) and *Historical Material* (1933), show her dedication to the "New History" of James Harvey Robinson and others.

Miss Salmon's influence upon Vassar extended beyond the history department. She took an active part in the drive to obtain a better library; after the construction of a new building in 1900, she continued to give much of her time to the library's development and was responsible for many fine acquisitions. She joined other members of the faculty in their campaign, eventually successful, for a curriculum with fewer required courses, so that students would be free to spend more time in studies of special interest to them. In 1913 Miss Salmon was instrumental in effecting a liberalization of the college administration which gave greater influence to the faculty and lessened what Miss Salmon considered the monarchical power of the president and trustees.

Despite her discontent with the college's administrative conservatism and with the artificiality of institutional living, after a two-year leave of absence for travel and study in Europe from 1898 to 1900 she returned to Vassar. In the course of the next year she and Adelaide Underhill, Vassar librarian and close friend, moved into a house of their own off the campus. With the move into Poughkeepsie, Miss Salmon assumed the responsibilities of local citizenship, joining the Women's City and County Club and working for such civic improvements as public playgrounds. Also active in professional organizations, she was a member of the American Historical Association from its founding in 1884, for many years attended its annual meetings, and served on some of its important committees, including the executive committee (1915–19). In an effort to promote understanding between teachers of history in elementary and high schools and those in colleges and universities, she helped found the Association of History Teachers of the Middle States and Maryland and served as its first president. She also was an early advocate of uniform college entrance examinations. She participated in the beginnings of the Western Association of Collegiate Alumnae, later encouraging it to unite in a nationwide Association of Collegiate Alumnae. Miss Salmon came to regard woman suffrage as an imperative reform and actively supported the movement, although it was an unpopular cause in Poughkeepsie and agitation in its favor on the Vassar campus was prohibited. A lifelong pacifist, she hoped that the United States would escape involvement in World War I, and later was deeply disappointed when the United States failed to join the League of Nations.

Still active at the compulsory retirement age of seventy, she succeeded in obtaining a reprieve; and in 1926 friends among the alumnae established the Lucy Maynard Salmon Fund for Research, the income from which enabled her to continue her scholarly work. In February 1927 she suffered a severe stroke and died in a Poughkeepsie hospital without regaining consciousness. She was buried in the Poughkeepsie Rural Cemetery. A student's casual tribute to Miss Salmon's teaching, paid several years earlier, perhaps best characterizes her qualities: "It doesn't always seem like his-

tory, and sometimes it's rather dull, but you are never the same person afterwards."

[Louise Fargo Brown, *Apostle of Democracy: The Life of Lucy Maynard Salmon* (1943), is a full-scale biography. See also *Addresses at the Memorial Service for Lucy Maynard Salmon, Held at Vassar College, Mar. 6, 1927* (1927); and two tributes by former students: Elsie M. Rushmore, "In Memory of Lucy Maynard Salmon," *Vassar Quart.*, July 1932; and Rebecca Lowrie, *Lucy Maynard Salmon* (1951). The Vassar College Library has a file of miscellaneous MS. and printed data.]

VIOLET BARBOUR

SAMAROFF, Olga (Aug. 8, 1882–May 17, 1948), concert pianist and teacher, was born in San Antonio, Texas. Christened Lucy Mary Olga Agnes Hickenlooper, she was the older of two children and only daughter of Carlos Hickenlooper, an auditor, and his wife, Jane Loening. Save for a German maternal grandfather, she was of American colonial stock, her father being of Dutch descent. Her great-grandfather on her mother's side, Dr. Eugene Palmer, had moved in the 1840's from Stonington, Conn., to Louisiana, where he and his family joined the local Catholic church; his daughter, Lucie (Palmer) Loening Grünewald, settled with her second husband in Texas.

Olga began her schooling at the Ursuline Convent in Galveston, Texas, and at the same time started music lessons with her Grandmother Grünewald, who taught piano. At her urging, and on the advice of the composer Edward MacDowell and others who had heard the girl play, the family determined to send her abroad for training, though with the genteel assumption that a woman should pursue a professional career only "if she had to." In 1896, accompanied by her grandmother, Olga went to Paris, and after a year of preliminary study became the first American girl to win a scholarship at the Paris Conservatoire. There she studied for two years with Élie M. Delaborde, meanwhile continuing her academic education at the Convent of the Holy Sacrament, where she boarded. Further piano study followed in Berlin with Ernst Jedliczka and Ernest Hutcheson. In 1900, however, she gave up active participation in music to marry Boris Loutzky, a Russian engineer. During the next three and a half years they lived in Berlin and in Petrograd; but the marriage proved unsuccessful and ended in divorce and a papal annulment in 1904. A public career now became not only possible but financially desirable.

Although a previous European debut was then considered essential to success on the

American concert stage, the New York manager Henry Wolfsohn thought she might win sufficient attention by hiring an orchestra for an American debut. "Haunted by the thought of all the sacrifices my family had made for my education," as she wrote in her autobiography, she decided to risk the expense. On Wolfsohn's insistence, she searched the family tree for a European name and came up with Olga Samaroff, which she later adopted legally. On Jan. 18, 1905, she appeared at Carnegie Hall with the New York Symphony under Walter Damrosch; her program, which the critics rated ambitious in its inclusion of concertos by both Schumann and Liszt, received reasonably good notices, with praise for her endurance and skill. Her debut was followed by a series of engagements in private musicales in New York City. In May 1905 she gave her first public performance abroad, at Steinway Hall in London. After an appearance with the Boston Symphony Quartet, her concert career was well established with an invitation to play with the Boston Symphony itself in April 1906. That spring Charles A. Ellis, manager of the Boston Symphony and of such celebrated artists as Nellie Melba, Paderewski, and Fritz Kreisler, offered to undertake her management. In subsequent appearances with all the major American orchestras and in frequent concerts both in the United States and abroad, critics noted qualities of elegance, warmth, verve, subtlety, and brilliance, combined with technical mastery. Four years after her debut the magazine *Musical America,* in an article "Samaroff Praised by the European Critics" (Jan. 2, 1909), placed her in the first rank of the world's pianists.

Her concert career was temporarily subordinated to the demands of private life with her marriage, on Apr. 24, 1911, to Leopold Stokowski, then conductor of the Cincinnati Symphony Orchestra, and the birth of her daughter, Sonya Maria Noël. She gradually resumed concert appearances beginning in 1913, and after her divorce from Stokowski in 1923 she again took up a more active musical role. In the fall of 1925, however, an arm injury forced her to cancel a concert tour. Never enthusiastic about the life of a concert artist, she decided at this point to give it up and devote herself to teaching. That year she joined the staff of the newly formed Juilliard Graduate School of Music, where she taught piano for the rest of her life. According to her own account, she loved teaching from the beginning. Her concern for her students extended beyond music lessons: they were guests at her

summer home in Seal Harbor, Maine; were taken by Mme. Samaroff to Haus Hirth in Untergrainau, near Garmisch, Bavaria, for summers of "cultural enrichment"; and occasionally shared her New York apartment. Her interest was not limited to aspiring professionals, but included also the development of outstanding teachers. In 1929 she succeeded Hendrik Ezerman, on the invitation of his widow, as head of the piano department of the Philadelphia Conservatory of Music, where she continued to teach one day a week, along with her teaching at Juilliard, for more than ten years. Among her pupils were such outstanding pianists as Eugene List, Joseph Battista, William Kapell, and Rosalyn Tureck.

Her teaching obligations did not consume all of her time, however. In 1928, remembering her own difficulties in arranging her debut, she founded the Schubert Memorial, Inc., to provide an impressive debut with a symphony orchestra for gifted young artists in the concert and opera fields. The project, always of intimate concern to her, was financially successful; through competitions sponsored by the National Federation of Music Clubs, it also gained professional esteem. After the Schubert Memorial was well established, Olga Samaroff turned her attention to developing the layman's music courses which she considered complementary to it. Conducted for many years at the David Mannes Music School and Town Hall in New York City, as well as in Philadelphia and Washington, these courses expressed her increasing awareness of nonmusicians' ignorance of music and her interest in educating such people to appreciate music. Mme. Samaroff's *The Layman's Music Book* (1935), which was used as a text, was later reprinted as *The Listener's Music Book* (1947), following presentation of the course on radio in 1944 and on television in 1945. She also wrote *The Magic World of Music* (1936), *A Music Manual* (1937), and an autobiography, *An American Musician's Story* (1939); and for two seasons (1926–27) she was music critic of the New York *Evening Post.*

Olga Samaroff was among the founders in 1931 of the Musicians' Emergency Fund of New York, which distributed aid to needy musicians during the depression years. A guest lecturer at Yale, Harvard, Columbia, Washington University, the University of Minnesota, and the Curtis Institute, she received honorary degrees from the University of Pennsylvania (1931) and the Cincinnati Conservatory of Music (1943). Her position as one of the nation's foremost musicians led to international activities: in 1936 she was one of three delegates from the United States to the International Music Education Congress in Prague; in May 1938 she was chosen by the State Department to represent the United States as one of the judges at the piano contest Concours Eugène Ysaÿe, organized by Queen Mother Elisabeth of Belgium.

First and foremost, though by no means solely, a teacher, Olga Samaroff credited her success to years of observing Stokowski's orchestral rehearsals and to a conversation she once had with the French actor Coquelin, who believed that "If our interpretation rests upon the insight vouchsafed by inspirational flashes and deep understanding combined with sufficient mastery to carry it out . . . we shall always have something worthy to offer the public." Disdainful of "slick" pianists and imitators, she worked to bring out the individual talents of her students; her capacity for developing intense loyalty from those with whom she worked and for changing their lives was both rare and powerful. After her death from a heart attack in New York City, her pupils set up the Olga Samaroff Memorial Fund to establish a home in New York City for music students.

[Olga Samaroff's autobiography, above, is the principal source. See also *Who Was Who in America,* vol. II (1950); *Nat. Cyc. Am. Biog.,* XXXVI, 96; *N.Y. Times,* Jan. 19, 1905; *Musician,* Nov. 1914; and obituaries in *Musical America,* June 1948, *Newsweek,* June 7, 1948, *Etude,* Sept. 1948, and *N.Y. Times,* May 18, 1948. For a pupil's reminiscences, see Claudette Sorel in *Music Jour.,* Mar. 1961.]

WILLIAM DINNEEN

SAMPSON, Deborah (Dec. 17, 1760–Apr. 29, 1827), Revolutionary soldier and early woman lecturer, was born in Plympton, near Plymouth, Mass., the oldest, apparently, of three daughters and three sons of Jonathan Sampson, a farmer, and Deborah (Bradford) Sampson. She came of old Pilgrim stock, her mother being descended from Gov. William Bradford and her father from Miles Standish and John Alden. Jonathan Sampson's disappointment in his share of his father's estate was so corrosive that he fell into intemperate habits, went to sea, and finally abandoned his family, probably losing his life in a shipwreck. Mrs. Sampson, finding it difficult to support her young family, was obliged to disperse her children. Deborah lived for three years with a Miss Fuller and afterward, at about ten, was bound out as a servant in the home of Jeremiah Thomas of Middleborough, where she remained until she was eighteen. Here she developed into a strong, capable young woman, skilled in the domestic arts. Part-time attendance at the Middleborough public school, supplemented by instruction from the Thomas children, enabled her to obtain some education, and when her term of service in the Thomas family expired in 1779, she taught for six months in the same local school. In November 1780 she became a member of the First Baptist Church of Middleborough. Two years later (Sept. 3, 1782) this body excommunicated her on the strong suspicion of "dressing in men's clothes, and enlisting as a Soldier in the Army," after having "for some time before behaved verry loose and unchristian like." By then she had disappeared from Middleborough.

The venturesome young woman had, it seems, walked to Boston and from there to Bellingham, Mass., where on May 20, 1782, she enlisted in the Continental forces under the name of Robert Shurtleff (Shirtliff). A member of the 4th Massachusetts Regiment, Capt. George Webb's company, she was mustered into service at Worcester on May 23. Her height, which was above the average, her strong features, her stamina, and her remarkable adaptability enabled her to conceal her identity and perform her military duties. She participated in several engagements and was wounded in one near Tarrytown, N.Y. Not until she was hospitalized with a fever in Philadelphia was her sex finally discovered. She was discharged by Gen. Henry Knox at West Point on Oct. 25, 1783.

On her return to Massachusetts in November, she went to live with an uncle at Sharon. Here she resumed female attire, met Benjamin Gannett, a farmer, and was married to him on Apr. 7, 1785. Three children were born to them: Earl Bradford, Mary, and Patience. Reports of Deborah Sampson's adventure began to attract attention, and in 1797 Herman Mann, to whom she had told her story, published a romanticized biography under the title *The Female Review.* Mann next prepared a lecture for her which told her story in extravagant phraseology extended beyond the bounds of truth. Beginning with an appearance at the Federal Street Theatre in Boston, on Mar. 22, 1802, she toured various New England and New York towns until Sept. 9, giving her "Address" as advertised in the local press. Besides bringing her some remuneration and considerable personal satisfaction, the trip enabled her to visit one of her former commanding officers, Gen. John Paterson, who probably assisted her in obtaining a pension from the United States government.

Her first pension came from Massachusetts, which in 1792 awarded her the sum of £34 bearing interest from Oct. 23, 1783. In 1804 Paul Revere wrote to a member of Congress in behalf of Deborah Gannett, who was then in poor health and financial difficulties. On Mar. 11, 1805, she was placed on the pension list of the United States at the rate of four dollars per month, beginning Jan. 1, 1803; the amount was afterward increased. After her death her husband petitioned the federal government for a pension, representing himself to be in indigent circumstances, with two daughters dependent on charity; he declared that for many years he had paid heavy medical bills for his wife, whose sickness and suffering were occasioned by her military service. The belated response of Congress was an "Act for the relief of the heirs of Deborah Gannett, a soldier of the Revolution, deceased," approved July 7, 1838, which provided for a payment of $466.66, the equivalent of a full pension of eighty dollars per annum, from Mar. 4, 1831, to the decease of Benjamin Gannett in January 1837. This sum was paid to the three heirs, Earl B. Gannett, Mary Gilbert, and Patience Gay. Deborah herself had died in Sharon in 1827 at the age of sixty-six. Her grave is in Rockridge Cemetery, Sharon.

[The best sources of information are: introduction and notes by John A. Vinton in the 1866 edition of Herman Mann, *The Female Review: Life of Deborah Sampson;* "Military Pension File S32722, Deborah Gannett (alias Robert Shurtleff), Revolutionary War," in Nat. Archives, Washington; introduction by Eugene Tappan to the reprint of Deborah Sampson's "Address" in Sharon Hist. Soc., *Publications,* No. 2 (1905); *Acts and Laws of the Commonwealth of Mass.,* chap. 23, Jan. 20, 1792; Commonwealth of Mass., *Mass. Soldiers and Sailors of the Revolutionary War* (1906), XIV, 185. See also Thomas W. Baldwin, *Vital Records of Sharon, Mass., to the Year 1850* (1909), pp. 97, 166; Esther Forbes, *Paul Revere & the World He Lived in* (1942), pp. 432–35. Sketches of Deborah Sampson, not always accurate, are found also in: Elizabeth F. Ellet, *The Women of the Am. Revolution* (1848), II, 122–35; Hezekiah Niles, *Principles and Acts of the Revolution in America* (1822), p. 417; and Sarah J. Hale, *Woman's Record* (1853), p. 497.]

ELIZABETH COMETTI

SAMPTER, Jessie Ethel (Mar. 22, 1883–Nov. 11, 1938), poet and Zionist, was born in New York City, the younger of the two daughters of Rudolph and Virginia (Kohlberg) Sampter. Jessie's maternal grandfather, Jacob Kohlberg, had left Germany and sailed around the Horn to join in the California gold rush, but had eventually settled in New York as a tobacco merchant. Michael Sampter, her paternal

grandfather, had also emigrated from Germany to New York, where, after starting as a tailor's assistant, he became a prosperous wholesaler of men's clothing. His son Rudolph, Jessie's father, graduated from the Columbia Law School and established his own law firm. The cultured Victorian family in which she grew up had cast off all links with its ancestral Judaism; Jessie did not even realize that she was a Jew until she was about eight. Her father, an avowed atheist, was a friend and disciple of Felix Adler, whom he supported in the founding of the Ethical Culture Society.

Weak and sickly as a child, Jessie was educated at home. She displayed some musical talent and hoped to become a violinist, but an attack of poliomyelitis when she was twelve left her with weakened hands and curvature of the spine, for which she had to wear a brace. During her long convalescence she wrote poems and articles which appeared in *St. Nicholas,* a magazine for children. She completed her education by traveling to England in 1899–1900, in the company of her mother and sister and some cousins. For one year (1902–03) she took courses at Columbia University, including one on story writing. In 1906 her sister, Elvie, was married; her father had died in 1895 and her mother died in 1909. Restless and lonely, Jessie fell in love with a man who did not care for her, and was thus left, in her late twenties, to face a life of emptiness.

Though without religious training, Miss Sampter was concerned with the meaning of life and with the problem of moral and religious teachings for children. To attack these questions she assembled a group of young cousins at weekly intervals to discuss the roles of spiritual force, science, and aesthetics in their lives. These discussions formed the basis of her book *The Seekers,* published in 1910. She also established a friendship with two Jewish girls, MARY ANTIN and Josephine Lazarus (sister of EMMA LAZARUS), which remained important all her life. Through friends in the Poetry Society of America, she met its president, the Rev. Merle St. Croix Wright, a Unitarian minister, and under his influence joined the Unitarian Church.

Wright called her attention to the *Book of Pain and Struggle Called the Prophecy of the Fulfillment* (1911), by a young Jewish poet, Hyman Segal, which embodied the experience and dreams of the masses of Jewish immigrants from Eastern Europe who had been arriving in New York in the years after the Russian pogroms of 1881–82. She had previously attempted to find a spiritual home at both orthodox and reformed Jewish synagogues, but neither provided what she sought. These poems, however, gave Miss Sampter a sense of identity with other Jews, and through Segal she was introduced to HENRIETTA SZOLD, who took her to Rabbi Mordecai M. Kaplan of the Jewish Theological Seminary. These two men, leaders of the younger Jewish intellectuals, taught Jessie Sampter a contemporary, social-activist approach to the Jewish faith, a concern for the misery of the Yiddish-speaking ghetto of New York's East Side, and a faith in Zionism. She lived for a while in a Jewish settlement house, where she tried to adopt the life of a religiously orthodox Jewess. In her unpublished autobiography, "The Speaking Heart," she wrote: "I have a people, a congregation. It is not in the Church nor in the Synagogue. It is in the streets, in the tenements, in the crowded 'Pale' of Russia and Poland, in the little agricultural settlements in Palestine. . . . It is my people, a chosen people. God has called it, has chosen it for suffering and service."

Jessie Sampter was one of the early leaders of Hadassah, the women's Zionist organization that Miss Szold had founded. In 1914–15 she organized a School of Zionism, under the auspices of Hadassah, to educate American Jews in the principles of that movement. One of her students of this period later recalled her as "two brilliant eyes illumined as from within, peering from a startlingly emaciated body." From her teaching came two published manuals, *Course of Zionism* (1916) and *Guide to Zionism* (1920).

After recovering from a nervous breakdown in 1918, Miss Sampter moved the next year to Palestine, where she spent the rest of her life, except for three trips to the United States (1921, 1925, and 1930). Still an invalid when she arrived in Jerusalem, she lay in bed and made toys for children, their first since the war. She soon regained her strength and began relief work among the most deprived group of Jews in the country, those from Yemen, and established evening classes for Yemenite working girls. To satisfy her longing for normal family life, in 1923 she adopted a two-year-old orphan girl, Tamar, and the next year she moved from Jerusalem to Rehoboth, where she worked among a large Yemenite community in that town. She also helped organize the Scout movement in Palestine.

During the 1920's the center of the kibbutz movement, for communal agricultural settlements, was in the Galilee. Miss Sampter's travels there in 1925 inspired a group of prose poems which she published in 1927 in a book called *The Emek*. Now believing that com-

munal life offered the greatest rewards, in 1933 she moved to Givat Brenner, a kibbutz settlement. In the next year she built a rest home for the kibbutz with the money with which she had planned to publish some of her works.

During her years in Palestine, Jessie Sampter learned to write in Hebrew as well as her native English. She wrote prose and poetry, biographical sketches, Zionist essays, and articles about Arab-Jewish relations. She translated into English the children's poems of the Hebrew poet Hayyim Nahman Bialik, as *Far Over the Sea* (1939). Other works include *In the Beginning* (1935), a semiautobiographical novel, and collections of poems in *The Coming of Peace* (1919) and *Brand Plucked from the Fire* (1937). In 1938 she suffered two serious illnesses, first pneumonia, then malaria, and failed to make a full recovery. She died that year at Givat Brenner, at the age of fifty-five.

Jessie Sampter was a minor writer and poet whose personal life is more interesting and important than her works. She was one of a number of German Jews from families long settled in America who, having lost their sense of identity with Hebraism, regained it by committing themselves to the cause of the poor but devout East European Jews who emigrated to the United States in great numbers in the 1880's.

[Bertha Badt-Strauss, *White Fire: The Life and Works of Jessie Sampter* (1956), is the principal source. See also the articles about Jessie Sampter in Fanny Goldstein, comp., *Suggestive Material for the Observance of Jewish Book Week* (mimeographed, 1939); *N.Y. Times,* Nov. 26, 1938.]

ARTHUR HERTZBERG

SANDERS, Elizabeth Elkins (Aug. 12, 1762– Feb. 19, 1851), social critic and pamphleteer, was born in Salem, Mass., the second daughter of Thomas and Elizabeth (White) Elkins. Her father's occupation is unrecorded; he died before her second birthday, at the age of twenty-six. Nothing is known of her education, but presumably she attended one of the dame schools of the day. On Apr. 28, 1782, she was married to Thomas Sanders, the son of a Gloucester merchant. At the time of their marriage Sanders was in the employ of Elizabeth's kinsman Elias Hasket Derby, the leading merchant in Salem, and Sanders in his turn became one of Salem's most prominent and wealthy men. Like most other successful Salem families of the period, the Sanderses lived in a handsome house on Chestnut Street. They were popular and hospitable in a hospitable age.

In these comfortable surroundings Elizabeth

Sanders had six children: Charles (born 1783), Catherine (baptized Aug. 29, 1784), Mary Elizabeth (born 1788), Caroline (born 1793), Lucy (baptized Aug. 8, 1793), and George Thomas (born 1804). Of these, Charles donated Sanders Theatre to Harvard University, his alma mater; George became the father of Thomas Sanders, the telephone financier; Mary Elizabeth married Leverett Saltonstall; and Caroline married Leverett's brother Nathaniel.

An omnivorous reader, Elizabeth Sanders was a person of strong and fixed opinions. Two issues about which she felt most deeply were the plight of the American Indian and the evils of foreign missions. From numerous books written by travelers among the Indians—including the French Jesuit Pierre Charlevoix, the naturalist William Bartram, and the Moravian minister John Heckewelder—she became convinced that the American aborigines were a people of superior morality and culture who had been treated without justice or humanity by the United States government. She was particularly incensed by the expulsion of the Creeks and Cherokees from Georgia, a policy she found personified in Gen. Andrew Jackson. In 1828, following Jackson's nomination for the presidency, she published anonymously in Salem *Conversations, Principally on the Aborigines of North America*, a 179-page expression of admiration for Indian culture, indignation over its destruction, and contempt for the "sanguinary chieftain" Jackson. Similar themes pervade Mrs. Sanders' *The First Settlers of New England* (1829).

She continued in succeeding years to contribute reviews and letters to the press, but her next polemical pamphlet, *Tract on Missions*, did not appear until 1844, when she was eighty-two. This work expresses at length her deep aversion to foreign missions—a distaste already apparent in the *Conversations*. Herself a member of Salem's First Church (Unitarian), she was convinced that most missionaries, particularly those of the evangelical and Calvinist persuasions, were motivated solely by a desire to live opulently at the expense of others. Their preaching, she felt, served principally to degrade peoples whose native religion often compared favorably with the missionaries' own. It was absurd to contribute to foreign missions, she asserted, when the record at home—Indian mistreatment, industrial exploitation, Negro slavery—left so much to be desired.

Mrs. Sanders pursued this theme in two further pamphlets: *Second Part of a Tract on Missions* (1845) and *Remarks on the "Tour around Hawaii," by the Missionaries, Messrs.*

*Ellis, Thurston, Bishop, and Goodrich* (1848), the latter published in her eighty-seventh year. Parts of these essays first appeared as articles in the Unitarian *Christian Register* and *Christian Examiner*. Though one-sided and uncritical in their use of sources, they are clearly the work of a wide-ranging and vigorous mind. All of Mrs. Sanders' writing is characterized by a trenchant, sometimes sarcastic, prose style. A frequent target of her barbs was the missionary to Burma, Adoniram Judson. By contrast, she thought highly of Herman Melville, whose castigation of the Hawaiian missionaries in *Typee* (1846) she fully approved.

Though a generous giver to charities, Elizabeth Elkins Sanders is said to have exercised a careful discrimination in her philanthropy, rejecting any appeal based on "sickly sentimentality" (*Salem Register*, Feb. 27, 1851). She was of a kindly temperament, quick-witted yet tolerant. Children and young people, whose companionship she sought in her lively old age, found her particularly sympathetic. When her eyesight failed, the books in which she was interested were read to her. She died in Salem in 1851, of "infirmity of lungs," at eighty-eight years of age, seven years after her husband's death.

Laudatory local obituaries characterized Mrs. Sanders as a person of influence. She was in reality, however, an atypical and isolated figure, her views running sharply counter to the prevailing current of her day. She sought with but slight success to apply elements of an eighteenth-century world view—deism, rationality, the concept of the "noble savage"—to the issues of a later generation dominated by expansionist fervor, evangelical zeal, and sentimentality. The missionary enterprise she ridiculed and the Indian policies she denounced remained in full favor for decades to come.

[Obituaries in *Salem Gazette*, Feb. 21, 22, 1851, and *Salem Register*, Feb. 27, 1851; Marianne C. D. Silsbee, *A Half Century in Salem* (1887), pp. 95–96; D. Hamilton Hurd, *Hist. of Essex County*, II (1888), 2076–77; *Vital Records of Salem* (3 vols., 1916–24); Leverett Saltonstall, *Ancestry and Descendants of Sir Richard Saltonstall* (1897); death record (under "Saunders") in Mass. Office of Vital Statistics. Mrs. Sanders' published writings, all anonymous, also include *Reviews of a Part of Prescott's 'History of Ferdinand and Isabella,' and of Campbell's 'Lectures on Poetry'* (1841).]

ERNEST S. DODGE

SANDERSON, Sibyl Swift (Dec. 7, 1865–May 15, 1903), operatic soprano, was born in Sacramento, Calif., the eldest in a family of four daughters of Margaret Beatty (Ormsby) and

Silas Woodruff Sanderson. Her father, born in Vermont and educated at Williams and Union colleges, had been admitted to the bar in Albany, N.Y. About 1851 he moved to California, where he served successively as state legislator, justice of the California supreme court, and chief counsel of the Central Pacific and Southern Pacific railroads. Sibyl was educated by governesses and at private schools, where she demonstrated such unusual vocal talent that in 1881 her mother took her to Paris and left her with a French family for two years to study music and languages. After an interval spent in San Francisco, in 1885 she again sailed for France, with her mother and sisters, and in January 1886 entered the Paris Conservatory. The family were called home by the death of Judge Sanderson in June, but in October, Sibyl returned to Paris alone. Again at the conservatory, she studied with Jean-Baptiste Sbriglia, Mathilde Marchesi, and Jean and Édouard de Reszke, but finding the methods of training too rigorous for her rather small voice, she soon withdrew.

An engagement, however, to sing at a Paris salon reportedly took the critics by storm. The composer Jules Massenet after hearing her was "astounded, stupefied, subjugated!" as he wrote in his autobiography (p. 176); her voice "ranged from low G to the counter G—three octaves—in full strength and in pianissimo." When, in 1888, she made her operatic debut (under the stage name "Ada Palmer") in the title role of his Manon at The Hague, he called her "ideal," and her success encouraged him to launch her career in Paris. For her debut there he wrote Esclarmonde, working with her each evening on the scene he had written that day. He sought especially to feature the high register of her voice, and when she first sang the title role, at the Opéra Comique on May 14, 1889, she received acclaim for her "Eiffel Tower Notes," as her high cadenzas were called, the Tower and Esclarmonde both being prime attractions for the Paris Exposition of 1889. Her beauty, too, won attention; when, in her Paris debut, she "removed the veil that covered her face," it is said, "there was a gasp of adoration from one end of the house to another" (Garden, p. 24).

Sibyl Sanderson next sang for two seasons at the Théâtre de la Monnaie in Brussels, and it was reported that a young Belgian prince committed suicide for love of her. She proceeded then to St. Petersburg to appear in Leo Delibes' Lakmé. At this time she met the Crown Prince Nicholas, who, it was said, attended all of her performances and expressed his favor by giving her costly jewels. She now reigned as a leading prima donna. Massenet composed Le Mage for her in 1891 and Thaïs in 1894, and in 1893 Saint-Saëns selected her to create the title role in Phryné. In 1894 she sang leads in Gounod's Romeo et Juliette and Verdi's Rigoletto. Massenet had intended Thaïs for the Opéra Comique, but when Sibyl Sanderson moved to the Paris Grand Opéra, the work followed her; he described her performance in the title role as "never to be forgotten." His infatuation with her voice, indeed, became notorious. According to H. E. Krehbiel: "It was once common gossip in Paris that Massenet composed 'Le Jongleur' to answer the flings of the boulevardiers that his inspiration required the spur of Sibyl Sanderson's charms."

However celebrated on the Continent, she found less favor in England and America. In 1891 at her London debut in Covent Garden her "small, clear tones" were overpowered by the full-bodied voice of the tenor lead in Manon, Ernest Van Dyck; and when she reached the United States and in January 1895 sang at the Metropolitan Opera in the first of four performances of Manon, the critic Henry Krehbiel found that although her voice was true in intonation, it was small, sometimes unsteady, and lacking in warmth (Seltsam, p. 70). On returning to Europe, however, she elicited great applause as Manon and Phryné at Milan in 1896.

Meanwhile, she had fallen in love with Antonio Terry, a millionaire Cuban living in Paris, and they were married on Dec. 1, 1897, after she had been received into the Catholic Church. Persuaded by her husband to retire from the stage, she soon suffered a paralytic stroke, and though she recovered, she never again enjoyed robust health. The couple settled quietly at Terry's château in Chenonceaux, France, where a daughter was born who lived only a short time. In December 1898 Terry himself died, leaving in his widow's care a daughter from his first marriage. After the courts had unsnarled his estate, Sibyl Sanderson found her income curtailed to $20,000 a year and returned to the stage. In 1900 she sang in Berlin, at the Winter Garden, then in Vienna, Budapest, St. Petersburg, and Moscow.

"Should there be a change in public taste in America," wrote one critic in 1901, "by which the operas in which she is queen become fashionable, she can return and score an overwhelming triumph." This she attempted to do that year, in the roles of Manon, Micaela, and Juliette, but the American public remained unresponsive, feeling her voice to be "small" and her acting "cold." Her New York visit was again cut short. After traveling to the West, she sang in Memphis, Tenn., but was unable to finish the performance. Her final appearance in America occurred at the Philadelphia Academy of Music, where she sang Juliette on Jan. 2, 1902. Back in Paris, she achieved another triumph at the Opéra Comique in *La Carmélite* by Reynaldo Hahn.

Rumor now connected her with several suitors, until the announcement of her engagement to Count Paul Tolstoi, cousin of the novelist. The wedding was to take place in the summer of 1903, but that spring Sibyl Sanderson contracted influenza, which developed into pneumonia, and she died in Paris, at thirty-seven. Her ashes were buried at the Cemetery of Père Lachaise. "I have never known anybody with such a divine sense of loyalty," wrote her protégée Mary Garden. "Tragedy of all sorts clouded her short life, but she never lost her innate grace and courtesy."

[Details about Sibyl Sanderson may be found in: Jules Massenet, *My Recollections* (1919); Henry T. Finck, *Massenet and His Operas* (1910); Hobart H. Burr in *Cosmopolitan,* Aug. 1901; Emma Eames, *Some Memories and Reflections* (1927); Mary Garden, *Mary Garden's Story* (1951); H. E. Krehbiel, *More Chapters of Opera* (1919); Henry C. Lahee, *Famous Singers of Today and Yesterday* (1898); Harold Rosenthal, *Two Centuries of Opera at Covent Garden* (1958), p. 240; William H. Seltsam, comp., *Metropolitan Opera Annals* (1947); Oscar Thompson, *The Am. Singer* (1937); *Baker's Biog. Dict. of Musicians* (3rd ed., 1919); Oscar Thompson, ed., *The Internat. Cyc. of Music and Musicians* (1938); obituaries in *Le Guide Musical,* May 31–June 7, 1903 (by Henri de Curzon), *Musical Courier,* May 20, 1903, and *N.Y. Times,* May 17, 1903. Other data from Calif. Section, Calif. State Library, and from clippings in Harvard Theatre Collection.]

THURMAN WILKINS

**SANFORD, Maria Louise** (Dec. 19, 1836–Apr. 21, 1920), teacher and college professor, was born in Saybrook, Conn. (later called Old Saybrook), of hardy New England stock. An early forebear, Thomas Sanford, had reached the colonies in 1639. She was the youngest daughter and third of four children of Henry E. Sanford, a shoemaker, and his wife, Mary Clark. Her father had established a shoe store in Georgia, but shortly before Mary's birth it failed because of hard times and local hostility to Northerners. A thousand dollars in debt, he moved his family to his father's home in Saybrook and then to Meriden, where he took a job in his brother's auger factory and struggled to repay his creditors rather than declare bankruptcy. The atmosphere of the home was one of self-respect and hard work

in the face of poverty. Maria's mother taught her poetry and had her memorize much of the Bible; her tales of Revolutionary heroes and especially of women like Elizabeth Fry, the English prison reformer, and MARY LYON, founder of Mount Holyoke Seminary, instilled in Maria a concern for the values of education and service to others. She entered a country school at the age of four. Always an avid reader, she continued her education at the Meriden academy and at the New Britain Normal School, where she graduated with honors in 1855.

Her first teaching job was in a rural school at Gilead, Conn., forty miles from home. For the next twelve years she taught in various towns in Connecticut, moving closer to home as she lost her fear of failure. Subject during these years to "deep depression," she was distressed by the death of her father in 1859 and, about one year later, when teaching in New Haven, by the termination of her engagement to a theological student. While continuing to teach and to keep house for her mother and her young brother, she now devoted herself to study, following a stiff course of reading in history, logic, and the sciences outlined for her by Prof. John Fiske of Yale. By the time she was thirty her unusual teaching methods, especially her wish to use interest in the subject as a substitute for rigid discipline, had attracted much attention. In 1867 she secured a position in Parkersville, Chester County, Pa., moving the next year to the academy in Unionville. A vigorous campaign in 1869 to elect her county superintendent of schools, a post then unheard-of for a woman, narrowly failed. She was, however, appointed a school principal, and promptly instituted monthly meetings of the four schools in her town to demonstrate new teaching methods. At the same time she began to address teachers' institutes—usually the only woman speaker—urging teachers to bring "moral training" into the classroom, stressing thoroughness, neatness, good manners, and the dignity of work.

In 1869 a new field opened up when she accepted a post as teacher of English and history at the new Quaker college at Swarthmore. Promoted after a year to professor of history, she became, though not the first woman in the United States to achieve this rank, the first to complete a long and active career. A dynamic teacher, Miss Sanford gave her students instruction not only in the classroom but also during long Sunday afternoon walks, and doubled her attention to the backward or unruly. In 1874 her mother died and she assumed responsibility for a niece, the first of many relatives whom she was to help educate. By the mid-1870's she had begun giving public lectures on historical and contemporary topics such as "Honesty in Public and Private Life." A developing enthusiasm for art found an outlet in talks illustrated with slides, then an innovation. Eventually she was giving three days a week to public lecturing, despite criticism from her Swarthmore colleagues and a severe salary cut in 1878. Her last years at Swarthmore were further shadowed by a love affair with a colleague whose status as a married man made a happy outcome impossible. Though both behaved with great moral scruple, Maria Sanford suffered intensely, and in 1879 she resigned her post.

After a year of lecturing she met at Chautauqua William Watts Folwell, president of the young University of Minnesota. He invited her to join his faculty, where, as assistant professor and then as full professor of rhetoric and elocution, she remained from 1880 until she retired in 1909. At Minnesota she communicated her passion for poetry and art to hundreds of students; by the time of her retirement her department had become the largest in the university. Short-haired, dressed severely in black, walking with a long, rapid stride, she was a familiar campus figure, always available to students for help and advice and a constant friend to the needy, many of whom she lodged in her own home. Miss Sanford early became known throughout the state as well; her popular lecture to farm wives on "How to Make Home Happy," delivered as part of a series for farmers organized by the university, did much to save the land-grant institution from dismemberment at a time when the legislature threatened to separate the academic and agricultural colleges.

Miss Sanford's middle and later years were clouded by difficulties. On the advice of a former student, she made heavy investments during a real estate boom in the late 1880's. Borrowing from banks, she also persuaded friends in Connecticut and Pennsylvania to invest. The collapse of the boom left her some $30,000 in debt. Refusing to escape through bankruptcy proceedings, she assumed the full burden, as her father had done. Repayment became the dominating purpose of her life, driving her to new efforts to earn money and to economies which were extreme to the point of eccentricity. Paying back loans in driblets from her savings, she was eighty years old before she cleared the debt. Beginning in the 1880's also, Miss Sanford faced mounting criticism from her colleagues and from some students for her odd habits, her feminist ideas,

and her inspirational teaching methods. Her practice of renting art books to students and of tutoring them for money aroused further protest. But present and former students rallied to her defense, and in 1899 she won third prize in a newspaper "favorite teachers" contest, which, together with contributions from admiring students, financed a summer tour of art centers in Europe. In 1900 the board of regents threatened to dismiss her, but following an upsurge of protest she was retained, though at a salary reduced from $2,400 to $1,800. In 1907, after an appeal to the governor, her salary was raised to $3,000, entitling her to a $1,500 Carnegie pension, and it was announced that she would retire in two years. Her retirement, at seventy-two, stirred an outpouring of tribute from alumni and students for her "moral and artistic upbuilding of both city and state."

During her last decade her pace did not slacken. She traveled throughout the nation giving readings from her favorite poems and lecturing on popular themes in the arts and public affairs and on woman suffrage, to which she was a belated convert. She continued to be active in women's clubs, such as the Minneapolis Improvement League, which she had founded in 1892, and the Woman's Welfare League. During 1910 she spent many months clearing a tract of wilderness land in Florida, hoping to make a retirement home there for the family of one of her nieces, a missionary in Smyrna. In the same year her name was given to the first women's dormitory at the University of Minnesota. In 1916, on her eightieth birthday, the University of Minnesota held a statewide convocation of all its colleges in her honor, and a Minneapolis public school was named for her.

In April 1920 Miss Sanford delivered her famous apostrophe to the flag at the opening session of the assembly of the Daughters of the American Revolution in Washington, D.C. The next day she died in her sleep at the home of Minnesota's senior Senator, Knute Nelson. Her grave is in Mount Vernon Cemetery, near Philadelphia. In 1958 her statue was placed in the national Capitol in Washington as one of Minnesota's two representatives in Statuary Hall.

Maria Sanford was not a scholar or an original thinker. Her temper was conservative and her philosophy that of staunch self-reliance. Her views on such matters as unionization and collective bargaining revealed the reluctance of the nineteenth-century liberal to accept "socialistic principle." But she was as liberal as she was zealous in her service to education, charity, and religion. A Congregationalist by rearing and affiliation, she felt a flexible sympathy with other denominations and on many occasions filled vacant Unitarian pulpits. A teacher who gave generations of Midwestern farm students their first glimpse of the arts, she was to a legion of admirers the embodiment of rural nineteenth-century America and its sturdy values of honesty, hard work, and self-help.

[The principal source is Helen Whitney's biography, *Maria Sanford* (1922), based on the Sanford Papers in the Archives of the Univ. of Minn.; this includes an autobiographical account of Miss Sanford's early life originally serialized in the *Minneapolis Sunday Jour.* (May 2–June 6, 1920). See also: James Gray, *The Univ. of Minn., 1851–1951* (1951); Oscar W. Firkins, *Memoirs and Letters* (1934); Maude S. Shapiro, "A Rhetorical Critical Analysis of the Lecturing of Maria Louise Sanford" (Ph.D. thesis, Univ. of Minn., 1959); *Nat. Cyc. Am. Biog.*, XX, 67; *Minn. Alumni Weekly*, Dec. 25, 1916, May 7, 1920; *Minneapolis Tribune*, Dec. 17, 1916; *Minneapolis Jour.*, Apr. 21, 1920. There is material also in the papers of William Watts Folwell, Ina Firkins, Anne Maude Butmer, Lillian M. Swenson, and Maude H. Thomas, in the Univ. of Minn. Archives.]

JAMES GRAY

**SANGSTER, Margaret Elizabeth Munson** (Feb. 22, 1838–June 3, 1912), magazine editor and author, was the oldest of the two daughters and two sons of John and Margaret R. (Chisholm) Munson, each of whom had been widowed and had a son by the earlier marriage. Born in New Rochelle, N.Y., Margaret grew up in an atmosphere characterized by her parents' emphasis on the pleasures of reading and their devotion to Calvinist principles. Her father, a native of England, had spent most of his youth in Ireland and then migrated first to Canada and later to New York; originally a Wesleyan Methodist, at the time of his second marriage he had accepted his wife's Presbyterianism. He was an amiable, restless man whose life was a search for new starts and who supported his family with a series of clerical jobs and real estate ventures. Mrs. Munson, born in New York of Scotch Covenanter parentage, took charge of the children's early education, and Margaret by the time she was four could read "almost any book." In 1841 the family moved to New York City and, five years later, to Paterson, N.J., where Margaret attended a Baptist school, the Passaic Seminary, and began her lifelong interest in the foreign mission movement. She later graduated from the French and English school of Monsieur Paul Abadie in Brooklyn, where she

learned French and Latin and particularly enjoyed the classes in history, English, and botany. Her father died in 1854, and her uncle, David Chisholm, assumed his role in the family.

In her writing career, Margaret Sangster never experienced the difficulties encountered by most young authors. Throughout her late childhood and her school days she had filled her notebooks with verses and essays that reflected her practical and religious attitudes toward life. When at seventeen she first submitted a story ("Little Janey") for print, to the Presbyterian Board of Publication in Philadelphia, she received an acceptance, a check for forty dollars, and a commission to write a brief children's story for each of a set of a hundred pictures. She completed the assignment, but her writing career was interrupted when in October 1858 she was married to George Sangster, a Scotsman whom she had met at a Sunday school convention where he was one of the speakers. Sangster was a widower with two small daughters, to whom Margaret became devoted. In 1859 she had a son, George Munson, her only child. Her husband served as a Union officer during the Civil War and then took his family to Norfolk, Va.; they returned in 1870 to Brooklyn, N.Y., where he died the next year.

Faced with the responsibility of supporting her family, Mrs. Sangster turned seriously to writing. In Norfolk after the war she had contributed prose and verse to the *Christian Intelligencer*, the *Sunday School Times*, the *Atlantic Monthly*, the *Independent*, and *Hearth and Home*. The editor of *Hearth and Home*, George Cary Eggleston, gave her several writing assignments, and in 1873, when MARY MAPES DODGE left to join the staff of the newly launched *St. Nicholas* magazine, Mrs. Sangster took her place as editor of *Hearth and Home's* children's page and was later made an assistant editor. She now began to focus on what was to be a major activity for the rest of her life: that of a Christian leader of women. Believing that she had a "mission to girlhood," she responded to the questions that reached her desk with a series of letters and short essays addressed to American girls. Through the popular magazines of the late nineteenth century she developed a variety of themes— "The Girl and Her Friends," "Her Innocent Pleasures," "The Girl in Business," "When Her Prince Comes," "The Little Home for Two," "Shall Both Be Wage Earners?" and "Waiting for the Angels." When *Hearth and Home* stopped publication with the Christmas issue of 1875 Mrs. Sangster went to the *Christian*

*Intelligencer* as editor of their family page, became a literary adviser for Harper & Brothers, and edited "The Little Postmistress" department of *Harper's Young People* (1882–89). In 1889 she was appointed editor of *Harper's Bazar,* a position she was to hold for the ten years before the firm failed. During her incumbency she shifted the emphasis of the magazine's content, diminishing the amount of fiction and making it more of a "service" magazine aimed at the feminine reader. During this period she also wrote several novels, but her main effort went into her editorial chores and into supplying articles and verse for such magazines as the *Ladies' Home Journal, Cosmopolitan,* the *Youth's Companion,* the *Christian Herald,* and the *Woman's Home Companion,* whose editorial staff she joined in 1904.

A contemporary critic came close to the present-day estimate of her literary production when he wrote: "Mrs. Sangster's verses are unaffected, kindly in thought and feeling, and are sure to find many readers." Though the modern reader may dislike the didacticism ("If Christ Were Here Tonight"), the sentimentality ("When Daddy Lights the Tree"), and the unrestrained romanticism ("Hurray for the pulses of swift delight"), these qualities merely represent the fashions of the time. Beyond them, her writings contain much common sense and reflect genuine concern for the welfare of children and unprotected young women. During most of her lifetime Mrs. Sangster was openly opposed to the cause of woman suffrage, believing it a threat to the welfare of the family. About 1910, however, when she was in her seventies, her views changed, partly because of the courage shown by English suffragists, and partly because she had come to recognize "the helplessness of woman as a competitor in the labor market when she has no voice in the making of the laws affecting her."

Mrs. Sangster, like her verses, was cheerful, kindly, and unaffected. Widely read, she appreciated good writing—Jane Austen and Charles Dickens, Robert Browning and Christina Rossetti were among her favorites—but she had no illusions about her own achievements ("the gentle reader is not supposed to be a rigid critic, nor to ask a symphony when one plays only a slender pipe"). She was for many years an active member of the Dutch Reformed (Presbyterian) church of Brooklyn Heights. Toward the end of her life she lived in Glen Ridge and Maplewood, N.J. She lost her sight several years before her death, but she continued to write with the aid of secretaries. She died in South Orange, N.J., at the age of seventy-four, of respiratory paralysis following a cerebral thrombosis, and was buried in Cypress Hills Cemetery, Brooklyn, N.Y. She had been the editor of a major magazine, and her writings, which found a large and admiring audience, reflect the American character and interests of her time.

[Margaret Sangster's *An Autobiog.: From My Youth Up* (1909) confirms the cheerful, practical, and religious character that is evident in the published compilations of her magazine work: *Poems of the Household* (1882), *Little Knights and Ladies* (1895), *Cheerful To-days and Trustful To-morrows* (1899), *Winsome Womanhood* (1900), *Good Manners for All Occasions* (1904), *Radiant Motherhood* (1905), *Fairest Girlhood* (1906), *A Little Book of Homespun Verse* (1911), *Eastover Parish* (1912), and *My Garden of Hearts* (1913). See also: Kate Upson Clark, "A Chat about Margaret E. Sangster," *Woman's Home Companion,* Sept. 1904; Margaret Sangster, "My Opinion of Suffrage," *ibid.,* July 1910; Francis W. Halsey, *Women Authors of Our Day in Their Homes* (1903); John G. L. Dowgray, Jr., "A Hist. of Harper's Literary Mags., 1850–1900" (Ph.D. dissertation, Univ. of Wis., 1955), pp. 259, 263; *Who Was Who in America,* vol. I (1942); *N.Y. Times,* June 5, 1912. Death record from N.J. State Dept. of Health.]

CARLIN T. KINDILIEN

**SARTAIN, Emily** (Mar. 17, 1841–June 17, 1927), painter, mezzotint engraver, and art educator, was born in Philadelphia, Pa., one of the eight children and the only daughter of John Sartain, a prominent artist and engraver, and Susannah Longmate (Swaine) Sartain. Her parents had been born in England, coming to the United States shortly after their marriage in 1830. Emily Sartain's mother was a granddaughter of Edward Longmate and a daughter of John Swaine, both noted English engravers. John Sartain traced his ancestry back to the French Sartains of the island of Jersey in the sixteenth century and had been apprenticed to his wife's father. Members of the fourth generation of a talented family, Emily and three of her brothers—Samuel, Henry, and William (the first two older than she)—also became artists.

Emily Sartain was educated in Philadelphia and early showed marked artistic ability, which was encouraged by her father. She studied for six years, 1864–70, at the Pennsylvania Academy of the Fine Arts under Christian Schussele and then went to Europe for four years, during which she was a pupil of Evariste Luminais in Paris and copied paintings in the galleries of Italy and Spain. The

Paris Salon accepted one of her paintings in 1875, and again in 1883. The 1875 picture, "La Pièce de Conviction," was also exhibited (as "The Reproof") in 1876 at the Philadelphia Centennial Exposition, where it was awarded a medal. Upon her return to the United States, she concentrated on mezzotint engraving, an art she had learned from her father. This technique, much admired in the late eighteenth and early nineteenth centuries, is a process of burring a copper or steel plate to produce a very even grain, so that the resulting print is soft and velvety in appearance, containing all degrees of light and shade but no sharp outlines. From 1881 to 1883 Miss Sartain was art editor of the magazine *Our Continent*.

Her longest association was with the Philadelphia School of Design for Women, of which she became the principal in 1886. She held this position with distinction until her retirement in 1920, when she was succeeded by her niece Harriet Sartain. The school, founded by SARAH W. PETER in 1844, was the first in the United States to teach industrial art to women. Emily Sartain made many changes in the curriculum and turned away from the English tradition patterned on the Kensington School of Art, by which students were set to copying the work of the great masters, to the French method, which emphasized the study of perspective and the use of live models. She believed strongly that commercial and noncommercial art demanded the same skills and differed only in purpose; hence the commercial artist should receive the same rigorous training given to other artists and should try to produce work that conformed to the highest aesthetic principles.

Miss Sartain's paintings are of lesser importance, historically, than her teaching. She exhibited at the Pennsylvania Academy in 1867 and during the 1880's; in 1881 and 1883 she won the academy's Mary Smith Prize for the best painting by a woman artist. Although she was reportedly the only woman to do mezzotints, little of her work seems to have been preserved; an example in the Print Room of the New York Public Library suggests that her technical ability outweighed her artistic talent.

Emily Sartain was one of the founders (1877) of the New Century Club, a Philadelphia woman's club; a founder and president (1899–1903, 1904–05) of the Plastic Club, composed of women artists, in the same city; and president (1908–09) of the Browning Society of Philadelphia. In 1891 she started a summer school of art at Natural Bridge, Va. Most of her summers were spent in Europe.

She was the American delegate to international congresses on industrial art in Paris in 1900 and Berne in 1904. After her retirement from the School of Design, she lived in California in the winters. In her last years she suffered from angina pectoris, and she died in 1927, at the age of eighty-six, while visiting a nephew in Philadelphia on her way to Europe for the summer. She was buried in the family plot in Monument Cemetery, Philadelphia.

[*Phila. Record,* June 21, 1927; John Sartain, *Annals of the Sartain Tribe, 1557–1886* (privately printed, 1886?); *Beecher's Illustrated Mag.,* July 1871, p. 287 (with portrait); *Woman's Progress,* Oct. 1893; *Woman's Who's Who of America,* 1914–15; *Nat. Cyc. Am. Biog.,* XIII, 326; *Phila. Evening Public Ledger,* Apr. 13, 1935; death record, Pa. Dept. of Health.]

AGNES ADDISON GILCHRIST

**SAWYER, Caroline Mehitable Fisher** (Dec. 10, 1812–May 19, 1894), author and editor, was born in Newton, Mass., the daughter of Jesse and Anna (Kenrick) Fisher. She had a sister and two brothers; other children in the family died in infancy. Her father apparently died sometime during her childhood, and she grew up in the household of her grandfather John Kenrick, a prominent philanthropist and pioneer abolitionist. At eight she attended a Baptist Sunday school and could recite long passages from the Bible; before she was ten she was reading Shakespeare and Plutarch; before she reached thirteen she was composing poetry, some of which appeared in print. Her invalid uncle, Enoch B. Kenrick, another member of the household and an amateur botanist of note, removed her from the country school and tutored her for ten years, making her proficient in French and German and generally one of the better-educated women of her day. Thomas Jefferson Sawyer, a Universalist pastor and her future husband, described her at eighteen as a "tall, plain-looking girl" who "rather pleased me because she had . . . an amiable disposition, a virtuous heart, and withal a sound head." They were married in Newton on Sept. 21, 1831, and went to New York, where Sawyer was minister of a church first on Grand Street, then on Orchard Street.

Caroline Sawyer devoted herself to her husband's interests. She helped organize and actively participated in the work of the Universalist Ladies' Dorcas Society to aid the poor. A group of Iowa Indians, for her kindness to them on a New York visit in 1843, conferred on her a name meaning "One who holds converse with the Great Spirit." The same helpfulness and understanding endeared her to her husband's pupils when he left the city to become principal of the Clinton (N.Y.) Liberal Institute in 1845. In 1853 he returned for a second pastorate at Orchard Street, resigning in 1861 to retire to a farm in Clinton. They had seven children: Anna Gertrude, born in 1834, who married the landscape painter Jervis McEntee; Thomas Jefferson (1836); Oscar Gerhard (1838), who became known as a war correspondent of the *New York Herald;* Theodore Alvan and Frederick Augustus, twins born in 1841; Mary Angela (1846); and Alice Kenrick (1850). Theodore and Mary died in 1848.

Throughout the busy years Mrs. Sawyer found time for a great deal of writing. She contributed stories, essays, and poems to Universalist magazines such as the *Christian Messenger* and its successor, the *Universalist Union,* whose "Youth's Department" she directed from 1840 to 1845, and to many other periodicals, including the *Democratic Review, Graham's Magazine,* the *Knickerbocker Magazine,* and the *New Yorker.* From 1850 to 1858 she edited the *Rose of Sharon,* an annual gift book, and from 1861 to 1864 the *Ladies' Repository,* a Boston Universalist monthly. The *Repository* described her as "pre-eminent . . . as a literary woman" with "talent, scholarship, taste, and a love of literature." Her first book, *The Merchant's Widow, and Other Tales* (1841), written when she was too ill for more active work, sold out a first edition of 1,000 copies in ten days; Horace Greeley praised it as the "gentle teachings of an earnest and holy spirit." In 1845 she published *The Juvenile Library,* a four-volume collection of her stories. She was best known, however, for her poems, which her contemporaries described as "lyric music" and "inspired thought" evidencing "scholarly finish."

Caroline Sawyer's last twenty-five years were happy and serene. She lived at Tufts College in Medford, Mass., where from 1869 onward her husband was Packard Professor of Theology. There, as elsewhere, she opened her home to all—faculty, students, parents; and there in 1891 she celebrated her sixtieth wedding anniversary. She died three years later, at her home in nearby Somerville, of malarial fever. Her husband survived her by five years. In 1900, at their graves in Mount Auburn Cemetery, Cambridge, Hosea Starr Ballou, president of the Boston Universalist Club, dedicated a monument in the form of a cross as a mark of the "gratitude which Universalists everywhere owe to Thomas J. Sawyer, and scarcely less to his gifted wife, Caroline M. Sawyer."

[The fullest account is in Richard Eddy, *The Life of Thomas J. Sawyer, S.T.F., LL.D., and of Caroline M. Sawyer* (1900). See also Mrs. E. R. Hanson, *Our Women Workers* (1882); and brief notices in *Lamb's Biog. Dict. of the U.S.,* VI, 620, and Sarah J. Hale, *Woman's Record* (1853). Some of Mrs. Sawyer's poems appear in Caroline May, *The Am. Female Poets* (1848), and in T. Buchanan Read, *The Female Poets of America* (1849). Death record from Mass. Registrar of Vital Statistics.]

ELIZABETH F. HOXIE

**SCHOFF, Hannah Kent** (June 3, 1853–Dec. 10, 1940), child welfare worker and juvenile court reformer, was born in Upper Darby, Pa., near Philadelphia, the oldest of five children of Thomas and Fanny (Leonard) Kent. Her father, a woolen manufacturer, was a native of Lancashire, England; her mother, born in Bridgewater, Mass., and a graduate of the Bridgewater Normal School, was descended from Solomon Leonard of Monmouthshire, England, one of the original proprietors of Bridgewater. Growing up in Upper Darby and in nearby Clifton Heights, Hannah Kent was educated by tutors, at the school of Mary Anna Longstreth in Philadelphia, and at the Waltham (Mass.) Church School. On Oct. 23, 1873, she was married to Frederic Schoff, a Massachusetts engineer. After several years in Newtonville, Mass., they moved to Philadelphia, Mrs. Schoff's home for the rest of her life. They had seven children: Wilfred Harvey (born 1874), who became a noted economist, Edith Gertrude (1877), Louise (1880), Leonard Hastings (1884), Harold Kent (1886), Eunice Margaret (1890), and Albert Lawrence (1894).

In 1897 Mrs. Schoff, representing the women's New Century Club of Philadelphia, attended the first National Congress of Mothers, convened in Washington by ALICE MC LELLAN BIRNEY. She immediately rose to prominence in the new movement, first as program chairman and then as vice-president (1898–1902). Her husband, who gave her encouragement and counsel in all her undertakings, served for many years on the Congress' advisory board. In 1899 Mrs. Schoff founded the Pennsylvania Congress of Mothers, the second state branch to be organized; she was its president until 1902. In that year she succeeded Mrs. Birney as president of the National Congress. When she retired in 1920 the number of state branches had grown from eight to thirty-seven and membership had reached 190,000. An able administrator, Mrs. Schoff put the finances of the Mothers' Congress on a firm footing by inaugurating an endowment fund, established a national headquarters in Washington, and, from 1906 until 1920, edited the Congress' journal, *Child Welfare* (renamed in 1934 the *National Parent-Teacher*).

Stressing the need for practical action to complement inspiring oratory, Mrs. Schoff vigorously promoted the establishment of parent-teacher organizations in the schools. Her success in making this a major goal of the Mothers' Congress was signalized in 1908 when the name was changed to National Congress of Mothers and Parent-Teacher Associations (after 1924 the National Congress of Parents and Teachers). A second goal was the mobilization of the national and state mothers' congresses in support of the various child welfare measures introduced in the reforming upsurge of the Progressive period. She made her frequent and widespread lecture tours occasions for alerting audiences to the needs of disadvantaged children, and she utilized committees of the Mothers' Congress (such as the child labor committee set up in 1904 under FLORENCE KELLEY) to marshal support for national and state child labor legislation, uniform marriage and divorce laws, and federal aid for kindergarten and elementary education.

In 1908 Mrs. Schoff organized an International Conference on Child Welfare in Washington. Sponsored by the Mothers' Congress with the assistance of the State Department and the active support of President Theodore Roosevelt, the conference permitted delegates from many states and foreign countries to compare notes on child welfare. Two subsequent conferences were held, in 1911 and 1914. In 1910 Mrs. Schoff was appointed by the State Department as the United States delegate to the Third International Congress for Home Education in Brussels, and from 1913 to 1919 she was a special collaborator in the Home Education Division of the United States Bureau of Education.

Mrs. Schoff's deepest interest was in juvenile court and probation reform, for which she labored long and enthusiastically. She was first attracted to this area in 1899 when the case of an eight-year-old Philadelphia girl arrested and imprisoned for arson was widely publicized. She secured the child's release and observed with gratification her rapid rehabilitation in a foster home. When further study revealed that nearly five hundred children were being held in Philadelphia prisons along with hardened criminals, some after criminal court trials and others merely upon their parents' request, she became convinced that new legislation was needed. In 1900, as head of a social service committee set up at her initia-

tive by the New Century Club, Mrs. Schoff published a compilation of the laws of every state affecting delinquent and dependent children and visited such states as Illinois, where new techniques for treating juvenile offenders were being tried. Securing legal advice, she drafted several bills setting up special juvenile courts distinct from the criminal courts, providing detention homes for children awaiting trial, and initiating a probation system for young offenders. With aid from the educator MARY SMITH GARRETT, she lobbied vigorously for her bills, interviewing the governor and other political leaders, and in 1901 they were enacted into law by the Pennsylvania legislature.

Eager for the success of her creations, Mrs. Schoff now devoted herself to the juvenile court established in Philadelphia, the second in the nation. As president of the Philadelphia Juvenile Court and Probation Association (1901–23) she faithfully attended nearly every session of the new court during its first eight years, studying thousands of cases. She also was chairman of the committee which chose the city's first probation officers. As her reputation grew, Mrs. Schoff led in setting up juvenile court systems in other states, notably Connecticut, Louisiana, and Idaho, and persuaded President Theodore Roosevelt to endorse such legislation in a special message to Congress. She was invited to address the Canadian Parliament on the subject, the first time a woman had been so honored, and subsequently helped train several Canadian probation workers and establish a juvenile court system in that country. Utilizing her position as head of the National Mothers' Congress to promote her court reform interests, she asked Judge Ben B. Lindsey of Denver, a leader in the juvenile court movement, to address the Mothers' Congress in 1904. The following year she led the organization in establishing a committee on juvenile court and probation work under Lindsey's chairmanship.

In 1909 the United States Bureau of Education made Mrs. Schoff chairman of the American Committee on the Causes of Crime in Normal Children. In this capacity she conducted an extensive survey of the origins of criminal behavior among several thousand prisoners in eight states, supplementing her questionnaires by a large number of personal interviews. The findings were published by Mrs. Schoff in *The Wayward Child* (1915), a book which relied on fact and personal observation rather than exhortation to show the need for reform in the legal treatment of children.

A woman of great energy, Hannah Schoff was a director of the National Kindergarten Association and in 1913 founded the Philadelphia Alliance for the Care of Babies. In addition to *The Wayward Child* she published *Wisdom of the Ages in Bringing Up Children* (1933), an anthology, as well as articles in *Good Housekeeping* and other magazines. She was a member of the Daughters of the American Revolution and the Society of Mayflower Descendants; in religion she was a Swedenborgian. Surviving her husband by eighteen years, she died in Philadelphia of a cerebral hemorrhage at the age of eighty-seven. Her ashes were buried in the Schoff plot in the Newton Cemetery, Newton Center, Mass.

[For other writings by Mrs. Schoff see the *Proc.* of the White House Conference on the Care of Dependent Children (1909), pp. 69, 150–51, 163, 170; "Education for Child Nurture and Home Making Outside of Schools," U.S. Bureau of Education, *Report,* 1914, I, 363–74; and Education in the Home" (with Ellen C. Lombard), *ibid.,* 1916, I, 289–302. For biographical data see: Nat. Cong. of Parents and Teachers, *Golden Jubilee Hist., 1897–1947* (1947), pp. 51–76; Pa. Cong. of Parents and Teachers, *Today and Yesterday* (1960); Helen C. Bennett, *Am. Women in Civic Work* (1915), pp. 139–60; *Nat. Cyc. Am. Biog.,* XVIII, 99; *Who Was Who in America,* vol. I (1942); and *Woman's Who's Who of America,* 1914–15. See also obituaries in the *Phila. Inquirer,* the *Phila. Record,* and the *N.Y. Times,* Dec. 12, 1940, and death record in Pa. Dept. of Health. Family data were supplied by Mrs. Schoff's son, Dr. Leonard Hastings Schoff of Atglen, Pa. See also Manning Leonard, *Memorial: Genealogical, Historical and Biographical of Solomon Leonard* (1896), p. 238; and Wilfred H. Schoff, *The Descendants of Jacob Schoff* (1910), pp. 143–44.]

ELVENA B. TILLMAN

SCHOFIELD, Martha (Feb. 1, 1839–Jan. 13, 1916), educator of freedmen, was born near Newton, Bucks County, Pa., the third of five children and one of four daughters of Oliver and Mary (Jackson) Schofield. The Schofields were Hicksite Quakers, Martha's mother serving as "recorded minister" of the local meeting. Ardent abolitionists as well, they often sheltered fugitive slaves on their farm. In 1852, after the death of Oliver Schofield, the family moved to Darby, Pa., where Mrs. Schofield married John Child, a widower with several grown children. Martha, meanwhile, attended a private school conducted by her uncle John Jackson in nearby Sharon, and subsequently taught at a Friends' school in Purchase, N.Y., and in a Philadelphia school for Negroes. She returned about 1860 to Darby after an unhappy romance with a conservative young

Quaker; "The Hicksite was too strong in me," she wrote.

During the Civil War, Martha Schofield served as a visiting nurse at a nearby hospital. In 1865 she volunteered for service with the Pennsylvania Freedmen's Relief Association and was assigned to the Sea Islands of South Carolina, the scene of an intensive wartime educational effort by Northern abolitionists to demonstrate that ex-slaves could become productive free citizens. Reaching Wadmalaw Island in October, she immediately set up the "Garrison School," which she conducted for about a year with the help of Mary A. Sharp, a fellow Pennsylvanian. In 1866–68 she taught at a succession of schools on St. John's, Edisto, and St. Helena islands; on the last she was a neighbor of another Northern educator, LAURA M. TOWNE. Strong in her sympathies for the freedmen, Miss Schofield was so often embroiled in controversies with Union officers and Freedmen's Bureau agents, whom she considered lax or incompetent, that her fellow teachers feared her expulsion. She was bitterly critical, too, of the Southern whites, whose ruin she found "a glorious spectacle."

In 1868, after a grave illness which may have been tuberculosis, she moved to Aiken, S.C., a small town about a hundred miles from the coast noted for both its salubrious climate and its lawlessness. Here, with an assistant— Mary Taylor of Chester County, Pa. (a cousin of the author Bayard Taylor), who had come to South Carolina in 1866 as an assistant to CORNELIA HANCOCK—she began teaching in a Negro school which had been established two years before by the Freedmen's Bureau. In 1870 she persuaded the bureau to replace the inadequate schoolhouse with a new structure on land she donated for the purpose. During the disturbances surrounding the end of Reconstruction in 1876–77 she proved a bold and determined friend of the Negro. After the cessation of Freedmen's Bureau support, Miss Schofield's school was adopted by a group of Friends in Germantown, Pa. Still later, the John F. Slater Fund for Negro education gave valuable aid. On her annual summer pilgrimages to the North, Miss Schofield raised needed money from wealthy Quakers and philanthropists, a number of whom agreed to serve as trustees in 1886 when the institution was incorporated as the Schofield Normal and Industrial School. A brick structure had been built in 1882, and an industrial building was added seven years later. By 1900 the Schofield School had become one of the outstanding and influential Negro schools in the South, offering instruction through the high school level in farming, carpentry, blacksmithing, cooking, sewing, and printing, as well as more traditional subjects. Miss Schofield, who suffered from chronic poor health, placed great emphasis on cleanliness and personal hygiene, proper diet, and good living conditions. Unlike Laura Towne, she fully shared the view of such men as Samuel Chapman Armstrong and Booker T. Washington that vocational training —"education for life"—was the principal mission of Negro schools. She hoped for eventual desegregation, but if that could not be accomplished favored the creation of a separate state for Negroes.

Although she had retired as principal in 1881 to become business manager, Martha Schofield remained throughout her life her school's guiding spirit. She died at Aiken in 1916, having devoted more than half of her seventy-six years to the cause of Negro education in the South. She was buried in the Friends' Burying Ground in Darby, Pa. The Schofield School in time became a public school and was still in existence in 1970.

[Mary S. Patterson, *Martha Schofield* (pamphlet, 1944); Matilda A. Evans, *Martha Schofield, Pioneer Negro Educator* (1916); records of the Bureau of Refugees, Freedmen, and Abandoned Lands, Nat. Archives, Washington; Schofield Papers, Friends Hist. Library, Swarthmore College; letter from Martha Schofield to William L. Garrison, May 23, 1866, Sophia Smith Collection, Smith College; files of *Pa. Freedman's Bull.* and *Am. Freedman* for 1866; Laura M. Towne, *Letters and Diary* (Rupert S. Holland, ed., 1912); Cornelia Hancock, *South after Gettysburg* (Henrietta S. Jaquette, ed., 1956); Katherine Smedley, "The Northern Teacher on the S.C. Sea Islands" (unpublished M.A. thesis, Univ. of N.C., 1932); Luther P. Jackson, "The Educational Efforts of the Freedmen's Bureau and Freedmen's Aid Societies in S.C., 1862–1872," *Jour. of Negro Hist.*, Jan. 1923; Amory D. Mayo, "The Work of Certain Northern Churches in the Education of the Freedmen," U.S. Commissioner of Education, *Report*, 1902, I, 285–314; George B. Tindall, *S.C. Negroes, 1877–1900* (1952).]

HENRY L. SWINT

**SCHUMANN-HEINK, Ernestine** (June 15, 1861–Nov. 17, 1936), opera singer, was born in Lieben, near Prague, Bohemia, the eldest of the four children of Hans Roessler, a lieutenant in the Austrian army, and Charlotte (Goldman) Roessler. Poor and always hungry, she grew up in army posts in Italy, Bohemia, and Poland, sporadically attending convent schools, for the Roesslers were Roman Catholics. Her talent was first recognized by her maternal grandmother, a Hungarian Jew; later Mother Bernardine of the Ursuline convent in Prague,

finding her "blessed with a great voice," encouraged her to study singing. The family's poverty limited her in her choice of an instructor, but in Graz, Austria, where her father was stationed, she took lessons for four years with Marietta von Leclair, the daughter of an army officer and a retired prima donna. While in Graz she made her first professional appearance, at fifteen, as contralto soloist in Beethoven's Ninth Symphony.

Through the influence of Frau Nina Kienzl, the mother of the composer Wilhelm Kienzl, Ernestine auditioned for the Court Opera in Vienna, but was rejected because she was too poor and too homely. Shortly afterward, however, an agent arranged a second audition with the Dresden Royal Opera, which offered her a contract. She made her operatic debut in Dresden on Oct. 13, 1878, as Azucena in *Il Trovatore*, but sang only minor roles thereafter. In 1882 she was dismissed for marrying without the permission of the Opera officials and her husband, Ernst Heink, at the same time lost his position as secretary to the Royal Opera. After three children—August, Charlotte, Henry—in as many years, she was in Hamburg, singing small parts and earning a little money, when Heink left her, burdened with his debts and pregnant with their fourth child. They were subsequently divorced, about 1892. During the summer of 1887 she had a brief success in Berlin, where she made her debut at the Kroll Theatre, and in Hamburg, where she sang in a performance of Brahms' Rhapsody under the direction of Hans von Bülow; but the birth of her fourth child, Hans, prevented her singing in the Mozart cycle that followed, thus alienating von Bülow and relegating her again to small parts in the Hamburg Opera. At a low ebb financially and professionally, she sent her children to her parents for safekeeping and concentrated on her career.

A quarrel between the director of the Hamburg Opera and a temperamental prima donna contralto provided Mme. Heink with the opportunity for better parts; after singing Carmen on short notice, without an orchestral rehearsal, she went on to Fidès in *Le Prophète*, Ortrud in *Lohengrin*, and a ten-year contract. Her major roles during this period included Leonora in *La Favorita*, Adriano in *Rienzi*, Amneris in *Aïda*, and her first appearance as Erda in *Siegfried*. In addition to her work at the Hamburg Opera she studied oratorio singing with Matilda Brandt, the dramatic soprano at the Hamburg Opera, and traveled with the company on summer concert tours to Scandinavia, Dresden, Vienna, Paris, and London, where she made her debut at Covent Garden on June 8, 1892, as Erda. Her marriage in 1893 to Paul Schumann, an actor and stage manager, made possible a reunion with her children and began a period of great domestic happiness. Schumann, a constructive and devoted critic, was an important influence in his wife's career until his death in 1904. They had three children of their own: Ferdinand, Marie, and George Washington, the last her only American-born child. By the time of her second marriage Mme. Schumann-Heink's professional life was firmly established. Beginning in 1896 she sang at the Bayreuth Festivals at the invitation of Cosima Wagner, widow of the composer; she continued to sing there regularly until 1903 and thereafter made occasional appearances until World War I. From 1897 to 1900 she sang at Covent Garden during the summer season, again appearing primarily in Wagnerian roles.

Mme. Schumann-Heink began her American career in 1898 when she signed a contract with Maurice Grau of the Metropolitan Opera. She made her American debut as Ortrud on Nov. 7 in Chicago, a month before the birth of her youngest son. Her five seasons with the Metropolitan she considered the high point of her career. Known primarily as a Wagnerian contralto, particularly for her Ortrud, Erda, and Fricka in *Die Walküre*, she was also noted as Fidès and as Gluck's Orpheus. Out of loyalty to Maurice Grau, however, she left the Metropolitan after Grau's retirement in 1903. A venture in light opera, when she toured in Julian Edwards' *Love's Lottery* (1904–05), proved too tiring for her voice, and the following year she undertook a European tour under the management of the New York impresario Henry Wolfsohn. She became an American citizen in 1905; in Chicago that same year, on May 27, she married William Rapp, her secretary, twelve years her junior, and brought her children to the United States. She and Rapp separated about 1911; they were divorced in 1914.

During the decade preceding World War I, Mme. Schumann-Heink made occasional appearances in opera in New York and in Chicago but devoted herself primarily to concert performances. In January 1909 she created the role of Klytemnestra in Richard Strauss' *Elektra* in Dresden, but never repeated it, considering it too much for her voice. The war years affected her deeply. In 1915 her oldest son, August, loyal to the Fatherland, joined the German navy; he was lost in a submarine. A second son, Hans, died of pneumonia in 1915. Her other sons all fought in the American forces. After the United States en-

tered the war she devoted her energies to war work, giving concerts for the Red Cross, entertaining servicemen at her home, and touring army camps, where she was affectionately called the "Mother of the A.E.F." After the armistice she continued to sing in veterans' hospitals, and until her death the welfare of her "boys" was of first importance to her. Now well past the peak of her operatic career, Mme. Schumann-Heink made infrequent appearances in opera during the 1920's, but she had by no means retired. In December 1926, the fiftieth anniversary of her debut at Graz, she gave a concert at Carnegie Hall, followed by a twenty-thousand-mile "farewell" tour. She gave her last performance in opera as Erda at the Metropolitan Opera House on Mar. 11, 1932.

In 1930, in an attempt to revive her fortune, lost through easy generosity and the depression, she sang in vaudeville at Roxy's Theatre in New York City. Well received during her week's engagement, she later toured with "Roxy and His Gang," appearing in vaudeville as late as 1932. In 1931, in a poll conducted by *Good Housekeeping* magazine, she was chosen as one of America's twelve greatest living women. An ardent American, in 1933 she decreed a self-imposed exile from Nazi Germany, proudly proclaiming her Jewish ancestry, and she continued to speak out against the Hitler regime. In 1935 she made her first appearance in motion pictures, in *Here's to Romance*. She subsequently signed a three-year contract with Metro-Goldwyn-Mayer, but illness prevented her from making any of the projected films. In 1936, at the age of seventy-five, she succumbed to leukemia. She died in Hollywood; her ashes were buried at Greenwood Cemetery, San Diego, Calif.

Acclaimed in her operatic career as probably the world's greatest Wagnerian contralto, Mme. Schumann-Heink was a renowned Erda, an overwhelming Fidès; she could "bring down the house" with the "Brindisi" from *Lucretia Borgia;* her interpretation of Waltraute became tradition at Bayreuth. But she reached the general public as well. Her concerts often included such familiar songs as "The Rosary," and in later years recordings and the radio brought her a still wider following; her annual Christmas Eve broadcast of "Silent Night" became a national tradition. This final popularity stemmed as much from her personality as from her voice. A natural and unpretentious warmth glowed from her immense frame. "In American parlance, she was as big as a house. . . . [Her] countenance possessing motherly charm was singularly homely, rugged as a face from some honest old German print" (*Commonweal*, Dec. 4, 1936). Few singers have so captured the American heart.

[Mary Lawton, *Schumann-Heink: The Last of the Titans* (1928), autobiographical in form; Herman Klein, *Great Women-Singers of My Time* (1931) and *The Golden Age of Opera* (1933); *N.Y. Times*, June 16, 22 (sec. 8), 1930, Feb. 9, 24, 1931, Nov. 18, 22 (sec. 11), 1936; Edward Hogan, "Grandma in the Movies," *Vanity Fair*, Feb. 1936; *Nation*, Nov. 28, 1936, p. 620; marriage record (1905) from County Clerk, Cook County, Ill.; death record from Calif. Dept. of Public Health.]

ANN TOWNSEND ZWART

SCHURZ, Margarethe Meyer (Aug. 27, 1833– Mar. 15, 1876), early kindergarten advocate, wife of the German-American statesman Carl Schurz, was born in Hamburg, Germany. Her father, Heinrich Meyer, a German Jew, was a prosperous merchant-manufacturer and the head of a family known for its interest in music, education, and political liberalism. She had an older sister and two older brothers. Although little is known about her elementary and secondary education, it was sufficient to permit her attendance at lectures by Friedrich Froebel, the founder of the kindergarten movement, in Hamburg when she was sixteen. From these she prepared a set of notes on kindergarten training which later drew his approval.

In 1852 she traveled to London to care for a sick sister, Bertha, the wife of Johann Ronge, a German expatriate and disciple of Froebel. While helping the Ronges maintain their kindergarten, the first in England, Margarethe Meyer met Carl Schurz, recently expelled from both Germany and France for his participation in the German revolution of 1848–49. Schurz was completely captivated by the young girl, whose dark curly hair, large brown eyes, fine features, and intelligent conversation distinguished her from her peers. After a brief courtship the couple was married on July 6 and emigrated that fall to the United States, establishing a residence in a German-speaking community near Philadelphia. Here their first child, Agathe, was born in the summer of 1853. Because she was both homesick and in frail health, Schurz took his wife to England in 1855 for a period of convalescence, returning alone to the United States later in the year and purchasing a tract of land near Watertown, Wis. There the family settled in the autumn of 1856.

For several months during the following winter Margarethe Schurz used one of the rooms in their newly completed house as a simple kindergarten, teaching Agathe, now three, and the children of several nearby relatives according to the Froebelian plan. The school was short-lived, as the family left Watertown the following spring. No doubt Mrs. Schurz continued to teach her daughter, but the nomadic nature of her existence and her chronic ill health precluded the establishment of an effective institution. During a trip to Boston in 1859 she introduced Agathe to ELIZABETH PEABODY, who immediately recognized in the child a maturity and responsiveness not found among her own pupils. Mrs. Schurz explained that the difference was the result of Agathe's Froebelian education. Miss Peabody, an enthusiast for a variety of reforms, quickly became a devotee of the kindergarten movement, founding a school the following year in Boston, an endeavor Mrs. Schurz encouraged by sending her the preface to Froebel's *Education of Man*.

From this episode has stemmed the exaggerated claim that Margarethe Schurz "founded" the first kindergarten in America. If her efforts in 1857 were of a pioneering nature, the fact was missed entirely by her husband, whose letters contain many references to his wife and daughter but make no mention of an incipient kindergarten in his home. That Mrs. Schurz's influence was more inspirational than substantive can be drawn from the fact that only after a subsequent trip to Europe did Miss Peabody comprehend the principles underlying the kindergarten movement.

Although talented and well educated, Margarethe Schurz was never able to capitalize on these assets. Her husband recognized what he called her "gifted nature," but also noted that she had had few opportunities to express herself. Instead, she followed his career as Civil War general, Republican publicist, and United States Senator from Missouri, maintaining a household, often under adverse conditions, rearing their children (Agathe, Marianne, and Carl Lincoln; a third daughter died in infancy), serving as his secretary, and, on one occasion, bearing a letter of his from the Union lines to the White House and reading it to President Lincoln. Although she took a genuine interest in her husband's public activities, she never shared his identification with and love for his adopted country and continued to yearn for her *Vaterland*, a situation causing occasional domestic tension. She preferred a quasi-Germanic life among enclaves of Germans in Watertown, St. Louis, and Bethlehem, Pa., to the intense social life of Washington, D.C. On four occasions she returned to Germany. Ostensibly for her physical health, these trips were essential, if only temporary, antidotes for homesickness. The last of them took her to Hamburg during the winter of 1875. Returning early in 1876 to her husband in New York City, she died at their home there in March of complications following the birth of their fifth child, Herbert. She was forty-two. After temporary interment in Woodlawn Cemetery in New York she was buried in Hamburg, Germany.

[Most of the details of Mrs. Schurz's life must be screened from writings by and about her more illustrious husband. The three most helpful sources are: *The Reminiscences of Carl Schurz* (3 vols., 1907–08); Joseph Schafer, ed. and translator, *Intimate Letters of Carl Schurz, 1841–1869* (1928); and Claude M. Fuess, *Carl Schurz, Reformer* (1932). There are Schurz Papers in the Library of Congress and the Watertown (Wis.) Hist. Soc. Discussions of the involvement of Mrs. Schurz in the kindergarten movement are found in Johann and Bertha Ronge, *A Practical Account of the Kindergarten* (1874); Elizabeth P. Peabody, "The Origin and Growth of the Kindergarten," *Education*, May–June 1882; and Elizabeth Jenkins, "How the Kindergarten Found Its Way to America," *Wis. Mag. of Hist.*, Sept. 1930. Death record from N.Y. City Dept. of Health.]

JONATHAN MESSERLI

**SCHUYLER, Catherine Van Rensselaer** (Nov. 4, 1734–Mar. 7, 1803), colonial hostess and patriot, wife of the Revolutionary War general Philip Schuyler, was born in Claverack, Columbia County, N.Y., about forty miles southeast of Albany. She was the first of six children of Johannes (John) Van Rensselaer and his first wife, Engeltie (Angelica) Livingston. Her father, a great-grandson of Kiliaen Van Rensselaer, the first patroon of the Rensselaerswyck Manor in Dutch New Netherlands, received as his share of the family's holdings a portion of the lower manor at Claverack and the Crailo Estate in Greenbush, N.Y. In an attempt to populate Claverack he encouraged settlers by providing them with perpetual leases and treating leniently those unable to pay their rent. Before the Revolution he served as an officer in the British army, but he became an ardent patriot when the American struggle for independence broke out. Catherine's mother, a daughter of Robert and Margaret (Schuyler) Livingston, died in 1747 at forty-nine, whereupon Johannes Van Rensselaer married Gertrude Van Cortlandt; there were apparently no children by this second marriage.

Young Catherine has been described as an attractive, vivacious girl of medium height, "delicate but perfect in form and feature," and so graceful that admirers often referred to her as "sweet Kitty Van Rensselaer" or "the Morning Star." Born into one of New York's most distinguished Dutch families, she received a good education in comparison with other women of her time. Also from the Dutch aristocracy came her husband, Philip John Schuyler, a distant cousin. At the time of their marriage, on Sept. 7, 1755, in Albany's Dutch Reformed Church, he was on furlough from his duties as a captain in the French and Indian War. Although the marriage linked two of New York's largest landholding families, Catherine and Philip, like many newlyweds, had little money; they therefore lived at first at the Albany home of Schuyler's mother, where the young wife gave birth to two children. When French forces defeated Gen. James Abercromby's army, in which her husband was serving, at Ticonderoga in the critical summer of 1757, young Kitty managed to help nurse wounded soldiers as they were brought into Albany. In 1761, during Schuyler's absence on a mission to England at the close of the war, she is said to have supervised the initial stages of construction on the mansion (then called "the Pastures") they built on the outskirts of Albany.

In the years of peace Philip Schuyler, who had now inherited large landholdings from his father and uncle, developed a busy colony at Saratoga (later Schuylerville), some thirty miles from Albany. Here he settled artisans and tenant farmers, erected saw and grist mills, raised flax and wheat, and shipped his produce to market; and here he built a country house that was the scene of much hospitality. Catherine Schuyler shared fully in these undertakings, directing the household and acting for her husband in his absence.

Her responsibility increased when the Revolutionary War called Philip Schuyler once more into military service as one of the four major-generals appointed in June 1775 under General Washington's command. Two years later, as British forces under Gen. John Burgoyne advanced down the Hudson Valley, Mrs. Schuyler, with but a single guard, set out from Albany for their summer estate, which lay in the path of the invaders, seeking to save its furnishings. Refugees she met on the road, bound for Albany and panic-stricken by the recent Indian murder of JANE MC CREA, begged her not to proceed, but she is said to have replied: "The General's wife must not be afraid." Upon her arrival she received and carried out her husband's orders to burn his extensive wheat fields so that the British could not harvest them; her courage gave others the strength to do the same. That September, after Burgoyne's surrender, Mrs. Schuyler and her husband entertained him and his officers in their Albany home, dismissing his recent destruction of their Saratoga mansion with a graciousness that greatly touched him.

When General Schuyler was elected to Congress, Catherine Schuyler and her two youngest daughters accompanied him to Philadelphia. That winter (1779–80), when Washington called Schuyler to his winter quarters as military adviser, they took a house at Morristown, N.J. During this sojourn their daughter Elizabeth became engaged to Washington's young aide, Alexander Hamilton; they were married at the family home in Albany on Dec. 14, 1780 (see ELIZABETH SCHUYLER HAMILTON). Mrs. Schuyler saw eight of her fifteen children reach maturity: Angelica (born February 1756), who married John Barker Church, later a member of the British Parliament; Elizabeth (1757); Margaret (1758), who married Stephen Van Rensselaer, the patroon; John Bradstreet (1765); Philip Jeremiah (1768); Rensselaer (1773); Cornelia (1775); and Catherine Van Rensselaer (1781).

Advancing years, as her husband followed a career in Federalist politics, brought on a stoutness and illnesses which caused Mrs. Schuyler much discomfort. The end came for the happy couple after nearly forty-eight years of marriage when she died in Albany of a stroke in 1803; her husband survived her by little more than a year. Her remains were probably placed in the burial vault of Abraham Ten Broeck, then transferred to the Van Rensselaer and Schuyler family vaults; years later they were removed to a now unknown resting place.

[The Schuyler Papers in the N.Y. Public Library are excellent for their many references to Catherine's activities and her relationship with Philip; there are items of interest also in the Schuyler Papers in the N.Y. State Library. Katharine S. Baxter, *A Godchild of Washington* (1897), contains a sketch written by Mrs. Schuyler's youngest daughter; Mary Gay Humphreys, *Catherine Schuyler* (1897), is sympathetic but poorly proportioned. Her early married life is touched upon in Don R. Gerlach, *Philip Schuyler and the Am. Revolution in N.Y., 1733–1777* (1964). Florence Van Rensselaer, *The Van Rensselaers in Holland and in America* (1956), is an excellent but incomplete genealogical source; other information is available in the Schuyler Family Bible, Schuyler Mansion, Albany. See also: Anne Grant, *Memoirs of an American Lady* (2 vols., 1808); Franklin Ellis, *Hist. of Columbia County, N.Y.* (1878), useful for information about Johannes Van Rensselaer; Marquis de Chastellux, *Travels in North-America in the Years 1780, 1781, and 1782* (2 vols., 1787), which has a few comments about

Catherine Schuyler in her later years; George W. Schuyler, *Colonial N.Y.: Philip Schuyler and His Family* (2 vols., 1885); Anna K. Cunningham, *Schuyler Mansion: A Critical Catalogue of the Furnishings and Decorations* (1955), excellent for information about the house; Benson J. Lossing, *The Life and Times of Philip Schuyler* (2 vols., 1872–73); Bayard Tuckerman, *Life of Gen. Philip Schuyler* (1903); Joel Munsell, *The Annals of Albany* (10 vols., 1850–59).]

MARTIN H. BUSH

**SCHUYLER, Louisa Lee** (Oct. 26, 1837–Oct. 10, 1926), leader in welfare work, was born in New York City of distinguished lineage. Her father, George Lee Schuyler, an engineer and lawyer, was a grandson of the Revolutionary War general Philip Schuyler; her mother, Eliza (Hamilton) Schuyler, was a granddaughter of Alexander Hamilton. Much of Louisa's childhood was spent, along with her older brother and younger sister, on the Hudson River estate of the Hamiltons near Dobbs Ferry. She was educated by private tutors. With an ample income throughout her life, she made many trips to Europe, summered at Newport and Mount Desert, and maintained a fashionable apartment in New York City as well as a country place upstate.

Her parents had, in the 1850's, supported the work of the newly founded Children's Aid Society of New York, and Miss Schuyler, just before the Civil War, served as a voluntary sewing instructor in an "industrial school" for immigrant children under its management. When the war broke out, her mother was one of the "most respected gentlewomen" of the city who helped found the Woman's Central Association of Relief, an organization which soon became the most important auxiliary of the United States Sanitary Commission. The Rev. Henry W. Bellows, pastor of All Souls Unitarian Church in New York City, which the Schuylers attended, personally asked Louisa to work for the Central; no doubt equally compelling was her mother's willingness to serve on the executive committee.

Promptly made chairman of the committee of correspondence, Miss Schuyler was soon responding to the unprecedented challenge of the Civil War with a personal commitment that went far beyond what had been expected of a young woman of her social position and religious interest. She distinguished herself primarily by the efficiency and orderliness of her methods. Besides systematizing office procedure, negotiating compromises with competing organizations, and sustaining a public information campaign, she undertook in 1863 to establish a network of tributary county and village societies to be kept up to the mark by the constitutions and standard procedures she had devised and by regional supervisors and traveling lecturers she had appointed. "One earnest woman," she wrote, could do more for the soldiers "by enlisting the active sympathy and cooperation of her friends and neighbors than by days and nights of unassisted toil." She chose for herself a role that kept her separated from the "little villages" that produced the supplies and from the soldiers in the hospitals and camps who received them; she thought of herself as a trustee who should combine service to the people with a gently insistent bureaucratic control over them. She proved so successful in managing people that to the end of her life she was often compared to a captain of industry. But her manipulation was never cynical; she never lost faith that the people would do what was right if they were properly informed and properly led. No doubt her family heritage helped her to sympathize with the people without identifying with them —to admire them, yet see that they needed intelligent leadership.

Having driven herself relentlessly during the war, Miss Schuyler found it emotionally shattering to close up the Central; as a result, she suffered a complete collapse. The slightest exertion prostrated her, and she was forced to give up all responsibilities and most personal contacts. For six years she spent much of her time abroad, and her health never fully recovered. Throughout her life, periods of intense activity were always followed by such severe fatigue that an extended vacation was necessary. After the death of her parents, she shared an apartment with her sister, Georgina, who like Louisa never married. A gentle, quiet woman, with interests in art, poetry, and genealogy, Georgina nicely complemented Louisa, whose decisiveness and preoccupation with public affairs were reflected in her direct glance, high cheekbones, and, through middle age, in the almost masculine cut of her hair. Henri Bonnat, whose portrait of her, painted in 1879, is now in the New-York Historical Society, thought her face combined great strength with unusual tenderness; and a doctor who met Miss Schuyler for the first time when she was more than seventy was struck by her erect figure and rather formidable manner— "evidently a great personage," he concluded.

During the early postwar years Miss Schuyler constantly turned over in her mind a plan to harness once again for the public good the power of citizens organized under strong leadership. For a peacetime goal she chose the reform of public institutions of charity and correction—asylums, almshouses, jails, hospitals, schools—to be brought about by a systematic extension of the familiar custom of charitable visiting. The benefits, she thought, would be as great to the visitors as to the institutions. As they had on the Sanitary Commission, men and women would work together, developing a sense of public responsibility and a point of view which would transcend local and sectarian barriers. Having secured the advice and support of the landscape architect and city planner Frederick Law Olmsted and other former Sanitary Commission associates, Louisa Schuyler began in the fall of 1871 by inspecting the Westchester County poorhouse and organizing her neighbors into a visiting committee; she next convened a group of prominent ladies at the Schuylers' New York City home to visit the Bellevue Hospital. In May 1872 she formed the State Charities Aid Association, an organization of such citizen groups, each of which was to visit regularly one public charitable institution, bringing comfort to the inmates, studying the need for administrative or legislative reforms, and educating the public to its interests and responsibilities. So many of the S.C.A.A.'s members were recruited from New York society that the route from the Schuyler home to Bellevue was once described as "the fashionable promenade of the City." The combination of prestige, wealth, and political ability secured a succession of legislative accommodations which guaranteed to S.C.A.A. committees access to charitable institutions without making their findings subject to governmental surveillance. Soon the organization had won a reputation as a friend of the friendless and an expert adviser on social legislation.

The Association's stated purpose—to help children confined in public institutions, to improve hospital care, and to reform the pauper system in the name of "Christianity, Science, and Philanthropy"—involved it in a wide variety of enterprises. But Miss Schuyler devoted most of her time to two. In 1873 she helped establish a training school for nurses at Bellevue Hospital (see ELIZABETH C. HOBSON), the first large school in America to measure up to Florence Nightingale's exacting standards. From its inception it attracted not the demoralized incompetents who traditionally had passed for nurses, but educated young women from middle-class homes who aspired to make nursing their profession. Miss Schuyler's other special concern was the care of the mentally ill, who, largely confined in county poorhouses, were not segregated from either paupers or delinquents. Since 1865 New York law had declared the state responsible for their care, but Albany officials found themselves stymied by niggardly legislators and greedy poorhouse supervisors. Beginning in 1884, Miss Schuyler through the S.C.A.A. conducted a massive publicity and lobbying campaign which resulted in an 1890 law turning the care of the mentally ill over to state institutions. With her usual thoroughness, she returned to Albany the following year to defeat crippling amendments to the law and to secure adequate appropriations. In 1892 she obtained a law segregating epileptics from the mentally ill and providing them with special kinds of treatment.

Although not thereafter a prime mover in the State Charities Aid Association, Miss Schuyler was in 1907 appointed one of the charter trustees of the Russell Sage Foundation. The next year, appalled to learn that many children suffered from preventable blindness, she quickly brought representatives of the Sage Foundation, the S.C.A.A., the American Medical Association, the New York Association for the Blind, and state and city health departments together with influential private citizens. From this nucleus of knowledge and power, she developed an organization which after many difficult years she helped stabilize in 1915 as the National Committee for the Prevention of Blindness.

Miss Schuyler received many honors, among them a Doctorate of Laws in 1915 from Columbia University—its second to a woman—and a medal from the Theodore Roosevelt Memorial Association. She had devoted much of her long life to establishing institutions that would spread the gospel of the "new philanthropy." Her unique contribution, however, had been to reformulate the charitable role to be played by women of social standing. With more confidence than her mother's generation felt in the potential services of the middle classes—whether acting in voluntary groups or through the state—she had endeavored by her own activities and by the advice she gave the daughters of her New York friends to demonstrate that the elite could and should provide the needed leadership. Not that she became a professional welfare worker. Unlike her close friend of Civil War days, JOSEPHINE SHAW LOWELL, whose zeal to coordinate charity enterprises took her all over the United States and made her a leading actor in the National Conference of Charities and Correction, Miss Schuyler, confining herself to New York, remained in close touch with the society in which her family had always figured prominently. Even in New York she took little part in the daily affairs of institutions she had founded. Though not content merely to play the lady bountiful, she elected to become an organizer of victory, rather than a full-time reformer or a settlement house worker. If this decision was in part the result of illness and increasing age, it stemmed also from temperament and social position. Characteristically, she never evinced the slightest interest in "the emancipation of women." Fully in command of her world, she never conceived of women as an underprivileged class.

Her disinterestedness did not flag after 1921 when she suffered an illness which left her paralyzed on one side and virtually blind. Her mind was unimpaired, and at the age of eighty-eight she reported finding it "pleasant" to spend her wakeful hours at night "composing in thought . . . letters to newspapers or articles for magazines." One of the last of these letters requested the Sage Foundation to consider the usefulness of roof gardens atop New York docks as a refuge from summer heat for weary mothers and their children. She died at the country estate of J. P. Morgan in Highland Falls, N.Y.; after a funeral service at All Souls Church, of which she had been a lifelong member, she was buried in Sleepy Hollow Cemetery at Tarrytown, N.Y.

[For details of Miss Schuyler's life, see *Louisa Lee Schuyler* (Nat. Committee for the Prevention of Blindness, 1927); her own *Forty-Three Years Ago*, a pamphlet published by the State Charities Aid Assoc. (1915); *Nat. Cyc. Am. Biog.*, XX, 19; *N.Y. Times*, Oct. 11, 1926; and Francis G. Peabody, *Reminiscences of Present-Day Saints* (1927). Her papers are not collected, but there are important selections in the N.-Y. Hist. Soc., in the U.S. Sanitary Commission Papers in the N.Y. Public Library, in the archives of the State Charities Aid Assoc. and of the Russell Sage Foundation, in the Homer Folks Papers at the Columbia School of Social Work, and in the Sophia Smith Collection at Smith College. Two letters to Frederick Law Olmsted (Aug. 27 and Nov. 8, 1869), in the Olmsted Papers, Library of Congress, throw light on the shaping of her postwar plans. Her most important published writings are to be found in the *Bulletins* of the Sanitary Commission and the reports of the Woman's Central Assoc. of Relief and of the S.C.A.A. See also Robert D. Cross, "The Philanthropic Contribution of Louisa Lee Schuyler," *Social Service Rev.*, Sept. 1961.]

ROBERT D. CROSS

**SCHWIMMER, Rosika** (Sept. 11, 1877–Aug. 3, 1948), feminist and pacifist, was born in Budapest, Hungary, the oldest of three children of Max B. Schwimmer, a dealer in produce and horses, and Bertha (Katscher) Schwimmer. Her family had been distinguished in Hungarian Jewish and literary life. Her maternal uncle, Leopold Katscher, a prominent social reformer and novelist, inspired Rosika's dedication to the causes of woman's rights and peace. Rosika, whose youth was marked by illness, was educated by private tutors, in a convent school in Temesvár, where her father owned a model experimental farm, and in a Budapest high school. An accomplished linguist as well as a pianist and singer, she worked for a time as a "bobbin girl" in a factory to study women's working conditions. Married in January 1911 to a Hungarian journalist named Bédy, she was divorced two years later, and was thereafter known as Mme. Bédy-Schwimmer or Mme. Schwimmer; she had no children.

In June 1904 she attended the Berlin meeting of the International Council of Women at which was founded the International Woman Suffrage Alliance, under the presidency of CARRIE CHAPMAN CATT, the American suffrage leader. Returning home, Mme. Schwimmer helped to found and served as co-leader of the Hungarian feminist and pacifist organization Feministák Egyesülete. She represented Hungary in the International Neo-Malthusian League (a group favoring birth control), served on the board of the Hungarian Peace Society, wrote extensively on home economics, published several short stories and a short novel, edited the feminist-pacifist journal *A Nö*, and translated into Hungarian CHARLOTTE PERKINS GILMAN's feminist classic, *Women and Economics*. In March 1909 she was appointed to the national board governing child welfare. In June 1913 she organized the Seventh Congress of the International Woman Suffrage Alliance in Budapest and was elected a corresponding secretary. A platform orator eloquent in several languages, from 1906 she lectured throughout Europe, settling in London early in 1914 as press secretary for the Alliance and foreign correspondent for several European newspapers, including the *Pester Lloyd* (Budapest).

The First World War split the international suffrage movement and stranded Rosika Schwimmer in Great Britain. She began to rally European pacifist sentiment, circulating petitions among suffrage leaders urging President Woodrow Wilson to initiate efforts to end the war through mediation. In August 1914 she sailed for the United States, where, accompanied by Mrs. Catt, she talked with Secretary of State William Jennings Bryan and, on Sept. 18, with President Wilson, to whom she presented a petition representing some million organized European suffragists.

Wilson, although he was privately exploring the possibility of mediation, was evasive, and Mme. Schwimmer determined to arouse American public opinion. Touring the United States in the fall and winter of 1914–15, often appearing with the British suffragist Emmeline Pethick-Lawrence, she spoke in twenty-two states on behalf of mediation by neutral nations, before suffrage meetings, women's clubs, business associations, and even the Nebraska legislature. A short, rotund, and round-faced woman with thick black hair and brown eyes, Mme. Schwimmer was a persuasive speaker. Some found her theatrical, but to most her vivid descriptions of war's devastation were deeply affecting. "Rare self-forgetfulness and perfect simplicity make her a speaker never to be forgotten," wrote the Missoula (Mont.) *Missoulian* (Feb. 28, 1915), and her appeal before the Chicago Association of Commerce was so moving that the speaker scheduled to follow her declined to do so (*Chicago Tribune*, Nov. 26, 1914). Her most marked characteristic was a "tremendous power of will . . . like a powerfully running current which never paused or slackened night or day" (Emily Greene Balch in *New York Times*, Aug. 13, 1948).

Largely through these efforts, a number of local peace groups sprang up, notably in New York and Chicago, which early in January 1915, in a Washington convention called by Mrs. Catt and JANE ADDAMS, were united as the Woman's Peace Party. Mme. Schwimmer was a leader in this development and became "international secretary" of the new organization. In February she participated in a national Emergency Peace Conference in Chicago, and afterward in the International Congress of Women at The Hague (Apr. 28–May 1, 1915). This congress, which founded the International Committee of Women for Permanent Peace (later the Women's International League for Peace and Freedom), was attended by twenty-four hundred persons and was a high point in the antiwar movement. After an eloquent appeal by Rosika Schwimmer, the congress endorsed a plan for neutral mediation which had been conceived independently by Mme. Schwimmer and by Julia Grace Wales, a Canadian instructor of English at the University of Wisconsin who also was present at the conference. Delegations were dispatched to neutral and belligerent governments to determine the feasibility of mediation. Treated courteously by the cautious statesmen of fourteen countries, the delegates, including Mme. Schwimmer, Miss Addams, Dr. Aletta Jacobs of the Netherlands, and Miss Chrystal

Macmillan of Great Britain, concluded that neutral intervention would be welcomed. American peace organizations and other groups endorsed the mediation plan, but when this was presented to President Wilson by a delegation from the Congress of Women and by David Starr Jordan, chancellor of Stanford University, he remained noncommittal.

On Nov. 17, however, the indefatigable Mme. Schwimmer reached the industrialist Henry Ford, who had recently pledged his fortune to peace. A week later, after long conversations with Mme. Schwimmer and Louis P. Lochner of the Chicago Peace Society, Ford endorsed neutral mediation and announced that he was chartering the Scandinavian-American liner *Oscar II* to carry a group of Americans to Europe as an unofficial mediation commission. Two days later Mme. Schwimmer, accompanied by Mrs. Philip Snowden, wife of the English Labour leader, made a final unavailing appeal to Wilson to organize a conference of neutrals. On Dec. 4, 1915, the *Oscar II*, despite the growing coolness of many leaders of the Woman's Peace Party toward the project, sailed from Hoboken, N.J., with more than a hundred and sixty social reformers, students, and reporters aboard. Ridiculed by the press (including the reporters aboard ship), the odyssey of the *Oscar II* was far from pacific. Mme. Schwimmer, the moving spirit of the enterprise, took a domineering approach that aroused much resentment. The mystery with which she surrounded certain secret "documents" in her possession—actually only rather innocuous and guarded endorsements by various leaders of the idea of mediation—gave the newspapers further opportunity to make light of the venture. Soon rumors were circulating, baseless but widespread and persistent, that Rosika Schwimmer was a sinister enemy sympathizer exercising a Svengali-like influence over the gullible Ford. When the ship landed at Christiania, Norway, the ailing Ford quickly departed for home, leaving his erstwhile followers confused and divided. Following Jane Addams' advice, most European leaders of the International Committee of Women for Permanent Peace declined to support the venture. Though Mme. Schwimmer did help organize the Neutral Conference for Continuous Mediation, which assembled in Stockholm, she resigned late in February 1916 amidst charges that she had been dictatorial. In June, after a period of illness, she established a rival and secret International Committee for Immediate Mediation, which enjoyed no noticeable success.

In October 1918 Rosika Schwimmer was named to the National Council of Fifteen which governed Hungary upon the abdication of King Charles IV. That November the new prime minister, Count Michael Karolyi, appointed her Hungarian minister to Switzerland, reportedly the first woman ambassador of modern times. When Karolyi's government fell in March 1919 she refused to serve his successor, the Communist Béla Kun, and was consequently deprived of her civil rights. In January 1920 she fled Hungary to escape the reactionary and anti-Semitic Horthy regime which succeeded Kun in power. After wandering through Europe as a refugee, she returned to the United States in September 1921, settling in Chicago. Her plans to resume her career as a journalist and lecturer were hindered, however, by a smear campaign which labeled her a swindler of Henry Ford, a German spy, and even a Bolshevik agent. She particularly smarted under the false charge that her behavior in connection with the peace expedition had caused Ford's anti-Semitism, and in September 1927 she openly sought vindication; grudgingly, Ford testified to her sincerity and honesty. Further vindication came in 1929 when she won $17,000 in damages from one of her chief traducers.

In May 1924 it became known that Mme. Schwimmer was seeking United States citizenship. This news heightened the abuse to which she was being subjected, as the American Legion and other groups joined the attack upon her. When her final papers were filed in 1926, she refused to affirm that she would bear arms in defense of the United States. A United States District Court denied her application, but on appeal this opinion was reversed. The case went to the Supreme Court, which on May 27, 1929, ruled against Mme. Schwimmer by a six-to-three decision. Justice Oliver Wendell Holmes, joined by Justices Louis D. Brandeis and Edward T. Sanford in a celebrated dissent, found that Mme. Schwimmer "seems to be a woman of superior character and intelligence, obviously more than ordinarily desirable as a citizen of the United States," and added, ". . . if there is any principle of the Constitution that more imperatively calls for attachment than any other, it is the principle of free thought—not free thought for those who agree with us but freedom for the thought that we hate." For the rest of her life she remained an alien in her adopted land, declining to apply again for citizenship.

Rosika Schwimmer's final years in the United States were devoted to a variety of causes, primarily the advocacy of world government. In 1924, with her close friend Lola

Maverick Lloyd, she published a plan for world federation, and in 1937 the two women founded the Campaign for World Government, whose program, outlined in such pamphlets as *Chaos, War or a New World Order* (1937), called for "an all-inclusive non-military, democratically constituted Federation of Nations." After World War II she advocated a Peoples' World Constitutional Convention to draft a federal constitution. Besides her polemical writing, Mme. Schwimmer produced *Tisza Tales* (1928), a charming collection of Hungarian legends and folk stories. She died of bronchopneumonia complicated by diabetes at Mount Sinai Hospital in New York City at the age of seventy. Her ashes were scattered in Lake Michigan.

[The Schwimmer-Lloyd Collection in the N.Y. Public Library contains Mme. Schwimmer's extensive personal papers, books, clippings, etc. Other manuscript sources are: Rosika Schwimmer Papers, Hoover Institution, Stanford Univ.; Jane Addams and Woman's Peace Party papers, Swarthmore College; and Ford Expedition papers, Library of Congress and the Ford Archives, Dearborn, Mich. Printed sources include: *Rosika Schwimmer, World Patriot* (Internat. Committee for World Peace Prize Award to Rosika Schwimmer, 1937); Edith Wynner, *World Federal Government: Why? What? How?* (1954); Internat. Woman Suffrage Alliance, *Reports*, 1904–13; *Report* of the Internat. Cong. of Women, The Hague, 1915; briefs and court report, *U.S. v. Rosika Schwimmer*, 279 U.S. 644; Rosika Schwimmer, "Citizenship Case," *Report* of Sixth Cong. of Women's Internat. League for Peace and Freedom, 1929, pp. 124–27. Also of value are: Louis P. Lochner, *Henry Ford, America's Don Quixote* (1925); Marie Louise Degen, *Hist. of the Woman's Peace Party* (1939); Gertrude Bussey and Margaret Tims, *Women's Internat. League for Peace and Freedom, 1915–1965* (1965); Allan Nevins and Frank E. Hill, *Ford: Expansion and Challenge, 1915–1932* (1957), chap. ii, "Peace Crusade"; John Bainbridge and Russell Maloney, "Where Are They Now?" *New Yorker*, Mar. 9, 1940; obituary in *N.Y. Times*, Aug. 4, 1948. Information was also received from Miss Edyth Wynner, who is preparing a full-scale biography of Rosika Schwimmer.]

MARTIN DAVID DUBIN

**SCOTT, Charlotte Angas** (June 8, 1858–Nov. 8, 1931), mathematician, was born in Lincoln, England, to the Rev. Caleb and Eliza Ann (Exley) Scott. Her father, the principal of the Lancashire Independent College at Whalley Range, later succeeded the eminent English Congregational minister Joseph Parker at the City Temple in London. From her father's example, it has been suggested, Charlotte Scott acquired the "literary powers [that] added

much to the distinction and influence of her work" (Macaulay, p. 232). Her early education was private. Entering Girton College, Cambridge University, in 1876, she graduated in honors in 1880, a year in which four young women—admitted only informally, as custom decreed, to the examinations for Cambridge men—won "firsts" (honors in the highest of three classes). Two were in history and one in moral science; but it was Miss Scott's attaining of the equivalent of eighth place in mathematics, an unprecedented field for women, that caught public attention. When the Tripos list, ranking the Cambridge winners of firsts, was read in the Senate House, at the eighth name loud cries of "Scott of Girton" rang from the gallery. The next year a public petition secured the formal admission of women to the Tripos, the third-year examinations, though not yet their right to receive Cambridge degrees. Miss Scott remained at Girton as resident lecturer on mathematics (1880–84), meanwhile continuing her studies at the University of London, from which she received the bachelor of science degree in 1882 and, in 1885, the doctorate of science.

That same year she was called to the United States to inaugurate both undergraduate and graduate programs in mathematics at the newly founded Bryn Mawr College. Of the college's initial faculty of six, assembled with a sure eye for quality by Dean (later President) M. CAREY THOMAS, Miss Scott was the one woman member. From the beginning she won admiration for her understanding and intellect. This admiration was rooted in the classroom. As one of her students (Isabel Maddison) has written: "She had the rare gift of lucid explanation combined with an intuitive perception of just what the student could grasp. . . . Nor did she spare any effort to help a stupid student who really tried, though she was ruthless with the lazy or casual." She published a text, *An Introductory Account of Certain Modern Ideas in Plane Analytical Geometry* (1894), in which she treated point and line coordinates simultaneously to expose duality principles, but with characteristic vigor gave up its use in class long before others did because the field was changing rapidly at the research level. Her advanced students spoke of the curiously exciting quality of her lectures; the elegance of her presentation made them conscious, for the first time, of mathematical style. A long succession of her Ph.D.'s joined the faculties of American colleges.

Her scholarship was recognized and respected beyond the bounds of Bryn Mawr. She took an active part in the development of the New

York Mathematical Society, contributing from the beginning to its *Bulletin* (1891–94). When, in 1894–95, the group reorganized as the American Mathematical Society, electing officers and a council, she was the only woman listed, serving a three-year term on the council; she was vice-president in 1906. Miss Scott's friend and fellow Cambridge mathematician, Frank Morley of Haverford, has described her as delighting in the carefree pursuit of knowledge. She published some thirty papers in American, British, and Continental mathematics journals. The range of her contribution to the newly developing field of algebraic geometry is attested by the bibliographies in the National Research Council bulletin on this subject (Bulletin No. 63, 1928). Her particular interest within this field was the difficult problem of analysis of singularities for algebraic curves. In 1922 some seventy members of the American Mathematical Society, with another seventy former students, met at Bryn Mawr in her honor, and the eminent philosopher Alfred North Whitehead came from England to give the main address.

In later years Miss Scott was troubled by increasing deafness and poor health. Advised to seek outdoor exercise, she took up golf and then gardening, until even the casual undergraduate knew her house by the glory of her flowers—scarlet poppies with Canadian phlox, or the tawny spread of chrysanthemums. She continued, also, to take part in faculty deliberations, where her high standards, her imagination, judgment, and capacity for untiring work had made her highly valued. When she retired in 1925 from the department she had directed for forty years, the college's board of directors assessed her influence over those years as being second only to that of President Thomas herself.

Upon her retirement Miss Scott returned to England and made her home in Cambridge, where she died at the age of seventy-three and was buried in St. Giles' Cemetery.

[F. S. Macaulay in *Jour. London Math. Soc.*, July 1932, pp. 230–40; London *Times*, Nov. 10, 1931; Isabel Maddison in *Bryn Mawr Alumnae Bull.*, Jan. 1932; Faculty and Board Minutes, Bryn Mawr College, 1931; *Bull. Am. Math. Soc.*, Jan. 1895, p. 97, Feb. 1896, pp. 224–25, June 1922, p. 274. See also Cornelia Meigs, *What Makes a College?* (1956); *Woman's Who's Who of America*, 1914–15.]

MARGUERITE LEHR

**SCRIPPS, Ellen Browning** (Oct. 18, 1836– Aug. 3, 1932), newspaper writer and publisher, philanthropist, was born in London, England, the second daughter and third of six children of James Mogg Scripps, a skilled bookbinder, and his second wife, Ellen Mary Saunders. Her mother died of cancer when Ellen was only five. When she was eight, in 1844, the father, following the lead of venturesome Scripps cousins, emigrated with his brood (including a daughter by the first marriage) to a family farm near Rushville, Ill. Although Ellen did not marry, she had much of the experience of a family, for throughout her girlhood she helped tend her many brothers and sisters, including the five by her father's third marriage. Reading aloud to a circle of small listeners enabled her to explore eagerly many books from his library. City-bred, perfectionist James Mogg Scripps "failed" at tanning, mining, woodworking, brick and tile making, ice cutting, and farming, but despite these reverses Ellen, after teaching district school, enjoyed the then rare privilege for a girl of a "collegiate education," with two years (1857–59) in the Female Department of Knox College, Galesburg, Ill. On graduation she resumed teaching in Rushville and later taught at Augusta and Hamilton, Ill. During the Civil War she was busy with relief, fund raising, and other activities of the Sanitary Commission and the Freedmen's Association.

The career that was to bring Ellen Scripps fortune and fame commenced quietly in postwar 1867. Her older brother James Edmund Scripps had begun newspaper work in Detroit, Mich., where as part owner he merged the *Daily Advertiser* with the *Tribune*. For coworkers, he summoned the Rushville kin. Ellen answered the call, invested her modest savings, and for several months was a proofreader, until her father's illness called her home. Meantime fire destroyed the *Tribune* plant. Using insurance money, James Scripps launched the *Detroit Evening News* (Aug. 23, 1873) as a two-cent, four-page daily. Returning to Detroit that year, after her father's death, Ellen again read proof, but also did copyreading, as well as writing of her own. From extensive combing of many newspapers, she developed a front-page feature of miscellany, "Matters and Things," aimed to interest a wide range of readers, including women. No member of the Scripps clan worked harder or with more understanding of the journalistic opportunity and how to meet it than did the perceptive, energetic, and always curious sister. A vital service was in keeping the Scripps brothers, particularly James Edmund, George Henry, and their youngest half brother, Edward Wyllis, together at times when they were ready to fly apart.

To the restless, ambitious, brilliant E. W. Scripps, eighteen years her junior, she was particularly close. When he struck out on his own in 1878 with the Cleveland *Penny Press,* aimed primarily at workingmen and their families, Ellen backed him financially and with articles and her compilation of news and comment, producing this material at night after a full day's work on the *Detroit Tribune.* Although she gave up regular journalistic work after returning from a two-year European trip with the ailing E. W. in 1883, she remained an active partner in the family enterprises. Over the next two decades, using funds she accumulated as a stockholder in Detroit, she helped E. W. repeatedly, either in keeping his papers going or in acquiring new ones, as he laid the basis for the Scripps-McRae League, predecessor of the Scripps-Howard chain. By 1900 Ellen was a shareholder in six of his nine newspapers, which had a total circulation of 350,000 and a gross income greater than $1,200,000. Eventually she held stock in sixteen dailies and shared in their mounting profits, which she often put back into producing a better and more attractive newspaper. She favored E. W.'s plan of setting up enterprising editors in promising smaller cities such as Des Moines, Kansas City, Denver, El Paso, and Portland, Oreg., and allowing them a reasonable time in which to make good. She also was a believer in local autonomy for each paper in a kind of federal system of ownership.

When E. W. Scripps built a ranch villa, Miramar, north of San Diego, Calif., in 1891, Ellen joined him and his family there. It was Ellen who had the capital available as funds were needed for the large estate. Thereafter southern California was her home, after 1897 at her own South Molton Villa (named for the London street on which she was born), on a cliff at La Jolla overlooking the ocean. Here she lived modestly with her sister Virginia, doing her own cleaning and cooking. By rising at five o'clock or soon thereafter, she had more hours each day for reading, planning, and writing, always in longhand, including weekly letters over many years to E. W. Scripps, whether from home or abroad.

From 1900 to 1930 Miss Scripps' income grew more than forty times (Britt, p. 86). Since she had a horror of leaving money to be distributed by executors and lawyers, she made it a serious order of business to devote her fortune to worthy causes and institutions of her own choosing. As early as 1903, with funds inherited from her brother George, she joined E. W. Scripps in establishing the Marine Biological Association of San Diego. This pioneering enterprise, located in La Jolla, became in 1912 a part of the University of California,

bearing from 1925 the name of the Scripps Institution of Oceanography. Her deep interest in scientific research led her also to finance at the Scripps Memorial Hospital in La Jolla a clinic for the study of metabolism, afterward the Scripps Clinic and Research Foundation. Long interested in education, she gave $100,-000 to Knox College and assisted the Bishops School for Girls in La Jolla. Her major benefaction, however, was the founding of Scripps College for Women, one of a group of associated but autonomous colleges in Claremont, Calif., built around the nucleus of Pomona College. The general concept came from President James A. Blaisdell of Pomona (to which Ellen Scripps had earlier contributed), but in its stress on a broad core program in the humanities, Scripps College accurately reflected the spirit of its founder. When it opened in 1927 she was just short of her ninety-first birthday; to it she contributed more than $1,515,000 during her lifetime, with a substantial addition under her will. Other gifts before her death created or developed the Torrey Pines Park and the San Diego Zoo. Although Ellen Scripps avoided positions in organizations, she did allow herself in 1917 to be made a director of the National Recreation Association, in whose work she took a deep interest.

Christened a Methodist, Miss Scripps in later life was not affiliated with any denomination. She believed strongly in freedom of judgment. "What is sin in one man," she once wrote, "is righteousness in another; and vice and virtue, right and wrong, are not absolute terms" (Britt, p. 73). Her gift of a recreation center to the town of La Jolla specified that it should be maintained for the discussion of public questions, and that no speaker should be barred because of his opinions. In this same spirit, she opposed the "deportations delirium" under Attorney General A. Mitchell Palmer and was a member of the Amnesty League for release of political prisoners after World War I. She also took an active part in early efforts to abolish the death penalty. In 1924 she contributed to the third-party presidential candidacy of Robert M. La Follette.

Probably Ellen Browning Scripps' most remarkable characteristic was her apparently endless spread of interests, from marine life and the habits of birds and plants around her to the newest political and social ideas and proposals. This lively curiosity increased, if anything, in her later years. A slight woman with an aquiline nose and striking eyes, she possessed excellent health well into her tenth decade. She died of infirmities in her sleep at her La Jolla home in her ninety-sixth year.

Her will provided some $2,000,000 in bequests to new and old institutions and projects. As she had instructed, her body was cremated and the ashes scattered in the Pacific.

[The fullest account is Albert Britt, *Ellen Browning Scripps: Journalist and Idealist* (1960), which largely supersedes such earlier works as J. C. Harper's memorial booklet, *Ellen Browning Scripps* (1936), and the essays by C. B. Anderson and Albert Britt in *The Humanities at Scripps College: Views and Reviews, 1927–1952* (1952). On her role in the Scripps newspapers see the various books on E. W. Scripps, of which the best researched and most balanced is Oliver Knight, ed., *I Protest: Selected Disquisitions of E. W. Scripps* (1966), with an extended biographical introduction. See also: James E. Scripps, *A Genealogical Hist. of the Scripps Family* (1903); Frank L. Mott, *Am. Journalism* (1941); Bruce Barton in *American Mag.*, Sept. 1928; *N.Y. Times*, Aug. 4, 1932; *San Diego Union*, Aug. 4, 1932; *Berkeley* (Calif.) *Gazette*, Aug. 3, 11, 1932; also obituary and portrait in *Recreation*, Oct. 1932.]

IRVING DILLIARD
MARY SUE DILLIARD SCHUSKY

**SCUDDER, Janet** (Oct. 27, 1869–June 9, 1940), sculptor, was born Netta Deweze Frazee Scudder in Terre Haute, Ind. She was the third daughter and fifth child of William Hollingshead Scudder, listed in the 1880 census as a confectioner, and his first wife, Mary Sparks. Her Puritan forebears had settled in Salem, Mass., about 1635. A branch of the family migrated in the 1730's to New Jersey, from which her grandfather moved west to Kentucky. The family line included John Scudder (1793–1855), first American medical missionary to India, and his many missionary descendants, including Dr. Ida S. Scudder. (Her own religious affiliation was Presbyterian.) Nettie Scudder's mother died when she was five, and a few years later she lost the gentle, blind grandmother with whom she associated her early artistic awakening. Her schoolteacher stepmother was uncongenial and her father was silent and withdrawn; her childhood she recalled as "sad and dismal."

Nettie, energetic and something of a tomboy, attended public schools in Terre Haute and Saturday drawing classes at Rose Polytechnic Institute there. At eighteen, despite the burden of the twenty-dollar tuition and five dollars a week for room and board, her father sent her to the Cincinnati Academy of Art. Here she studied anatomy, drawing, and modeling, encouraged by the sculptor Louis Rebisso, and prepared to earn a living by woodcarving. At the academy, finding her name awkward, she changed it to Janet Scudder. Her father died in 1890, but her eldest brother

supported her through a third year at the academy, and in the summer of 1891 she moved to Chicago to live with him. Summarily dismissed from her factory job as a woodcarver because the union did not accept women, Miss Scudder became one of the group of young women hired by the sculptor Lorado Taft to assist him in enlarging, from scale models, works of sculpture for the World's Columbian Exposition of 1893. Through Taft and a Terre Haute benefactor, she also received commissions to do statues for the Illinois and Indiana buildings. In Taft's studio Miss Scudder worked long hours in an intensely creative atmosphere, learning the techniques of her art and the extent of her abilities.

At the Exposition grounds Janet Scudder saw Frederick MacMonnies' fountain being erected in the Court of Honor under his supervision, and though shyness prevented her from speaking to him, she knew then that this was the man with whom she must study. In the fall of 1893, accompanied by Lorado Taft's sister, Zulime, Miss Scudder set off for MacMonnies' studio in Paris. When a letter of introduction to the sculptor from a prominent Chicagoan failed, she knocked on his studio door and persuaded him to let her study life drawing and modeling; within the year she became one of his assistants. She studied drawing further at the Colarossi Academy, and later organized a small class of artists when MacMonnies agreed to act as critic. From MacMonnies she also learned the art of modeling in low relief that later found expression in her medallions.

Lack of money and professional jealousies among MacMonnies' assistants forced Miss Scudder back to New York in the summer of 1894. There she lived out a bleak and impoverished few months before securing through the father of a fellow student in Paris a $750 commission from the New York Bar Association to design a seal. In the next two years she did architectural ornamentation and portrait medallions. By 1896 she had enough commissions to return to Paris to work. It was a triumph when, through MacMonnies, the Luxembourg Museum took some of her medallions. For several years she supported herself by making urns and other cemetery pieces while she cast about for her own special métier. Then a trip to Florence revealed to her the cherubic, youthful figures of Donatello and Verrocchio, recalling her earlier pleasure in MacMonnies' figures of children. As she traveled south to Naples and Pompeii, where a piece of sculpture was often the focus for a house, she realized she wanted to make statues to decorate, to please, and to amuse. Back in Paris she began work immediately on the "Frog Fountain," the first of her famous garden statues.

Janet Scudder returned in 1899 to gain a reputation in New York City. Her first recognition and further commissions came from the architect Stanford White, who bought her "Frog Fountain" and wisely advised her to make only four copies of this major work. Success followed quickly. Commissions for garden fountains came from the Rockefellers, the Pratts, and the McCormicks. The Metropolitan Museum ordered a copy of the "Frog Fountain." Her portrait medallions became a vogue. Her "Young Diana" won honorable mention at the Paris Salon of 1911, and in 1913 she had a one-man show in New York. For a friend she designed an Italian villa in Maine, her only venture into architecture. She also took an active interest in the woman's rights movement through the art committee of the National American Woman Suffrage Association.

About 1909 Janet Scudder chose Paris as the best place to work and returned there to live, with frequent visits to New York. In 1913 she bought a house at Ville d'Avray just outside of Paris, where she could see her works in progress to best advantage in the garden. With the outbreak of war Miss Scudder returned to New York to help organize the Lafayette Fund, raising money to send kits of clothing and other necessaries to French soldiers and for war relief. Between 1914 and 1916 she also found time to do a great deal of her own work, exhibiting ten pieces at the Panama-Pacific Exposition of 1915, where she won a silver medal. With America's entry into the war Miss Scudder served overseas, first with the Y.M.C.A. and then under the Red Cross, managing a friend's singing tour of American camps and then decorating recreation huts. Her house outside of Paris she turned over to the Y.M.C.A.

For the next twenty years Miss Scudder lived mostly at Ville d'Avray. Her friend Mabel Dodge Luhan recalled her as "tall and stooped a little . . . rather sentimental and very generous" (*Intimate Memories*, II, 1935, 217–18). In 1920 she was elected an Associate of the National Academy of Design. A developing interest in color led her to turn to painting, though without giving up sculpture entirely; her paintings were exhibited in New York in 1933. Her later works in sculpture were in a more serious vein and more reserved in style. She returned from France at the outbreak of the Second World War in 1939 and died the following year at Rockport, Mass., of lobar pneumonia at the age of seventy.

Janet Scudder was one of the earliest Americans to concentrate on lighthearted garden sculpture, a field she helped make an art in itself. The style of her spirited figures, as she freely admitted, was strongly influenced by MacMonnies and by the Italian Renaissance. Other women had preceded her in sculpture, some a generation earlier, but none had equaled her professional success.

[The best source for Miss Scudder's work and personality is her autobiography, *Modeling My Life* (1925). Other biographical accounts, not always accurate, include: J. Walker McSpadden, *Famous Sculptors of America* (1927), pp. 351–59; *Nat. Cyc. Am. Biog.*, XV, 346–47; and entries in: *Am. Art Annual*, 1905–06 and later editions; Durward Howes, ed., *Am. Women*, 1939–40; *Woman's Who's Who of America*, 1914–15; and *Who Was Who in America*, vol. I (1942). Emphasis on her work as an artist may be found in Beatrice G. Proske, *Brookgreen Gardens—Sculpture* (1943); Mary Q. Burnet, *Art and Artists in Ind.* (1921); and W. Francklyn Paris, *Hall of Am. Artists*, vol. IX (1954). Of periodical articles, the most informative are: Leila Mechlin in *Internat. Studio*, Feb. 1910; Lorado Taft, "Women Sculptors of America," *Mentor*, Feb. 1, 1919; and obituaries in *N.Y. Times*, June 11, 1940, and *Art Digest*, July 1940. The Ind. State Library supplied her birth date (from Vigo County birth records) and the family listing from the 1880 census. Death record from Mass. Registrar of Vital Statistics.]

LEWIS W. WILLIAMS II

**SEAMAN, Elizabeth Cochrane** (May 5, 1865?–Jan. 27, 1922), journalist, better known as "Nellie Bly," was born in the small town of Cochran's Mills in Armstrong County, Pa., near Pittsburgh. The town was named for her father, Michael Cochran (she herself added the final *e*), a moderately successful mill owner and lawyer. Her mother, Mary Jane Kennedy, was Cochran's second wife. Elizabeth, the third child of this marriage, grew up in a family that eventually totaled ten children, including two older brothers and three older half brothers, and she learned early to hold her own in an intensely competitive environment. Her only recorded formal education was a year (1880–81) at a boarding school in Indiana, Pa. Her father died during her childhood, and his widow moved to Pittsburgh.

In 1885, not yet twenty, Elizabeth Cochrane took her first step into journalism. The *Pittsburgh Dispatch* had published an editorial, "What Girls Are Good For," that strongly opposed the idea of woman suffrage and criticized women who wished to leave the shelter of the home to make careers. The indignant reply she sent in so impressed the editor, George A. Madden, that he tested her on other assignments and then gave her a regular job as a reporter. She chose the by-line "Nellie

Bly"—after the Stephen Foster song—and quickly demonstrated that she was not the kind of woman journalist who wrote with violet ink on scented paper. Spurning the ladylike essays favored by the few newspaperwomen of the day, she insisted on reporting on poor working conditions in factories, the problems of the working girl, slums, and even a subject so taboo as divorce. Nellie Bly was slight in build, with large eyes in a pleasant face; she had exceptional drive and determination.

During the winter of 1886–87 the *Dispatch* sent her to Mexico and published her letters describing the contrasts between the lives of the rich and the poor, the political corruption, and the need for reform. These stories, widely reprinted, led the Mexican government to expel her. Soon after her return she invaded New York City, the nation's journalistic capital. Brashly forcing her way into the office of Joseph Pulitzer, whose *World* was the fastest-growing paper in the city, she persuaded him to let her undertake a dramatic assignment: in order to expose the brutality and neglect which marked the care of the mentally ill, she would feign insanity and have herself committed to the public asylum on Blackwell's Island. So successfully did she carry out this assignment that a public investigation was launched and a number of reforms initiated. Taken on in 1887 as a *World* regular, Miss Cochrane repeatedly employed the same reportorial technique. Disguised, she would allow herself to become the victim of some iniquity and then, casting off the mask, would write her exposé. She took a job in a sweatshop and wrote of the exploitation of the workers; had herself arrested and jailed for theft and wrote of the indignities suffered by women prisoners; assumed the guise of the wife of a patent-medicine manufacturer opposed to a certain reform bill and exposed a bribing lobbyist. For stories in a lighter vein, she posed as bait for a "masher" and danced in a corps de ballet. All this was part of Pulitzer's new journalism, a combination of uplift and circulation-building stunts which entertained the reader and, by exposing malefactors, identified the *World* with the cause of the common man. Although such techniques occasionally degenerated into pure sensationalism, they may have helped pave the way for the more serious, and better documented, exposures of the Progressive muckrakers.

Unlike her earlier ventures, Nellie Bly's most famous exploit was wholly theatrical and devoid of social content. Late in 1889 Pulitzer sent her around the world, by commercial transportation, to challenge the eighty-day record of Jules Verne's fictional hero, Phineas Fogg. Leaving in mid-November with a minimum of baggage, she crossed the Atlantic and the Mediterranean; proceeded to Aden, Colombo, Singapore, Hong Kong, Tokyo, and San Francisco; and returned to New York on Jan. 25, 1890, after a journey of seventy-two days, six hours, and eleven minutes. Giving front-page space to her descriptions of travel by train, steamer, ricksha, and sampan, the *World* had skillfully kept public attention focused on her progress. The trip itself was exotic and exciting, and Nellie Bly seemed to embody the romance of journalism, the lure of travel, and the pluck of the American girl. Songs and dances were dedicated to her, clothes, games, and toys named after her, and parades organized in her honor. Thanks to Pulitzer's powers of publicity, Nellie Bly had become a creation of the sensational press she had helped build.

The rest of her life, by contrast, seems anticlimactic. While returning from an assignment to the Middle West to investigate the plight of ranchers after two summers of drought and prairie fires, she met on the train a New York businessman, Robert L. Seaman, to whom she was married a few days later, on Apr. 5, 1895. He was seventy-two, she still in her twenties. Perhaps, as her biographers have suggested, after her strenuous exploits she wished to be fathered and cared for as a dependent woman. They lived quietly in New York until Seaman's death in 1910. Thereafter Nellie Bly's luck deserted her. She attempted to operate her husband's iron manufacturing company, but disputes, reverses, and litigation ate up her accumulated fortune. Leaving the country, perhaps to escape creditors, she spent some time during the First World War in Austria-Hungary. She transferred certain remaining properties to Austrian ownership for legal reasons, only to lose them when the United States entered the war.

Returning to the United States by 1919, she secured a position on the *New York Journal* through its editor, Arthur Brisbane, an old friend from the *World*. Aging, and out of place in the fervid world of Hearst journalism in the 1920's, she never regained her former celebrity. She died of bronchopneumonia in a New York hospital early in 1922, and after Episcopal services was buried in Woodlawn Cemetery, New York City. Although she was not herself a particularly warm or colorful person, the courage and adventurous spirit she displayed in a short but lively career makes her one of the more vivid figures in the annals of American journalism.

[Elizabeth Cochrane was the author of three books: *Ten Days in a Mad-House* (1887), *Six Months in Mexico* (1888), and *Nellie Bly's Book: Around the World in Seventy-two Days* (1890). Somewhat helpful are two undocumented biographies: Mignon Rittenhouse, *The Amazing Nellie Bly* (1956), and Iris Noble, *Nellie Bly: First Woman Reporter* (1956), a juvenile. (The title claim of the latter is incorrect.) There are sketches in Ishbel Ross, *Ladies of the Press* (1936), and (under "Cochrane") in Frances E. Willard and Mary A. Livermore, eds., *A Woman of the Century* (1893), and some references in James W. Barrett, *The World, the Flesh, and Messrs. Pulitzer* (1931). See also obituaries in the *N.Y. Times* and *World*, Jan. 28, 1922. Her death certificate, obtained through the N.Y. City Dept. of Health, records her age as fifty-six, suggesting a birth date of 1865 rather than the 1867 accepted by her biographers.]

BERNARD A. WEISBERGER

**SEDGWICK, Anne Douglas** (Mar. 28, 1873–July 19, 1935), novelist, oldest of three daughters of Mary (Douglas) and George Stanley Sedgwick, was born in Englewood, N.J., near New York City, where her father was an attorney. Her parents came of prominent New England families whose ancestors had settled in Massachusetts in the seventeenth century; Ellery Sedgwick, editor of the *Atlantic Monthly*, was a distant cousin.

Although Anne Sedgwick spent only a small part of her life in her native country, her American experience left a strong, if somewhat idealized, imprint. For most of her first ten years she lived in the family home at Irvington-on-Hudson, a fashionable suburb of New York City. In this prosperous, genteel environment she was further sheltered by receiving her education at home from a governess. When she was nine her father became financial agent for an English firm and moved the family to London. In her early teens Anne spent two years (from twelve to fourteen) with her maternal grandparents in Chillicothe, Ohio—years she remembered vividly. Her recollection of the Middle West was a characteristic genteel image: "Sobriety, sweetness, tradition, are the things that best fit my memories of my grandfather's and grandmother's Ohio home, an Emersonian flavor, a love of books and of nature" (quoted in *Bookman*, April 1927, p. 126). Her memory of "dear old negro servants" was a further embellishment. Although her tastes and interest in literature, art, interior decoration, and gardening were shaped mostly in the Old World, her letters express a feeling of separation from—and nostalgia for—America.

At eighteen, having completed her education in England, Miss Sedgwick went to Paris, where for five years she studied painting. At least one of her portraits, a study of her sister, was exhibited in the Champs de Mars Salon. She also became interested in the manners and character of the French people, whom she saw in sharp contrast to the Americans she had known and the English. The theme of subtle psychological differences among these peoples was to play an important part in her novels. Her writing career began adventitiously. For the entertainment of her sisters she wrote a Henry Jamesian romance with a picturesque Old World cultural setting, *The Dull Miss Archinard*. Her father, finding the manuscript, showed it to a London publisher, who issued it in 1898. With the popular success of this novel, Miss Sedgwick turned from the brush to the pen. Between 1899 and 1907 she produced five more novels, the most notable of which was *A Fountain Sealed* (1907).

On Dec. 11, 1908, at thirty-five, she was married to Basil de Sélincourt, an English essayist three years younger than she. Their home, called Far End, in the tranquil environment of Oxfordshire on the edge of the Cotswolds, became the center of her existence for the rest of her life, except for the World War I period. Their social circle in the early years consisted largely of political and intellectual leaders of the old Liberal party, among them Prime Minister Herbert Asquith and his wife. A close friend was Max Plowman, poet, critic, and radical journalist. In this period she wrote one of her most successful novels, *Tante* (1911).

World War I took Miss Sedgwick back to France, where, beginning in 1915, she and her husband worked in hospitals caring for civilian war casualties and orphaned French children. Several of Miss Sedgwick's immediate postwar works were based on French persons she knew during this period, among them *The Little French Girl* (1924), which with *Tante* was her best seller in the United States. Early in 1919 the De Sélincourts returned to their home at Far End, where Anne Sedgwick busied herself again with her hobbies of gardening and bird watching and continued her novel writing at a leisurely pace. Idealizing an older, slower past, she was not wholly in accord with the modern skeptical spirit. She did, however, favor such reforms as woman suffrage so long as they contributed to universal brotherhood. In the late 1920's she fell victim to a long, gradual, paralytic illness, and, fearful of the consequences, her husband took her on her last visit to America in 1931. There she attended her induction into the National Institute of Arts and Letters. On her return to England she received further treatment, but she died in 1935 in the London suburb of Hampstead. Her husband survived her.

Most of the twenty books Anne Sedgwick wrote (two of them collections of short stories) may be classified as international novels of manners. A less significant figure than her contemporary EDITH WHARTON, she shared the latter's kinship with the tradition of Henry James, though she disavowed discipleship. Like James and Mrs. Wharton, she wrote "well-bred" fiction which explores problems of social relationships, and she shared James' interest in the American confronting English and Continental ways of life. She differed from James quite basically, however, in making the conflicts between characters explicit and dramatic (and more heavily involved in plot), as well as in her more fixed judgments, which some critics found too obtrusive. Often her novels analyze the effect of egocentric persons on the lives of those drawn to them by their apparent genius or goodness, as in *Tante,* a study of a world-famous pianist who feeds upon the adulation of her followers and does battle with the husband of her protégée for the girl's loyalty. She characteristically pits differing social views against each other: in *Tante,* the individualism of bohemian society against the ordered patterns of English society—always her norm. Her own preference was clearly for "a social system of harmonious people . . . bound together by a highly evolved code" (*Boston Transcript,* Aug. 30, 1924, Book Section, p. 1). *The Little French Girl* contrasts French and English mores; Americans figure prominently in other novels, notably in *Franklin Winslow Kane* (1910) and *Adrienne Toner* (1922). Although her reputation has waned, in her day Anne Douglas Sedgwick was ranked by at least one critic as the ablest follower of Henry James (Joseph Wood Krutch in the *Nation,* Oct. 22, 1924).

[Basil de Sélincourt, *Anne Douglas Sedgwick: A Portrait in Letters* (1936); Esther Forbes, "Anne Douglas Sedgwick and Her Novels," *Bookman,* Aug. 1929, and *Anne Douglas Sedgwick: An Interview* (1927); Fred B. Millett, *Contemporary Am. Authors* (1940); Stanley J. Kunitz and Howard Haycraft, *Twentieth Century Authors* (1942). For consideration of Miss Sedgwick's literary technique, see Grant Overton, *An Hour of the American Novel* (1929) and *The Women Who Make Our Novels* (rev. ed., 1928); and Arthur H. Quinn, *Am. Fiction* (1936). For obituaries, see *Commonweal,* Aug. 2, 1935; London *Times,* July 22, 1935; *N.Y. Times,* July 22, 1935; *Publishers' Weekly,* July 27, 1935. There is an unpublished dissertation by Grace Swanson, "The Novels of Anne Douglas Sedgwick" (N.Y. Univ., 1956).]

JAMES D. ARNQUIST

**SEDGWICK, Catharine Maria** (Dec. 28, 1789–July 31, 1867), author, was born in Stockbridge, Mass., the third daughter and sixth of seven surviving children of Theodore Sedgwick (1746–1813) and his second wife, Pamela (Dwight) Sedgwick. Descended on her mother's side from two of the more famous clans of the Connecticut River aristocracy, the Dwights and the Williamses, she took pride in the fact that her father, if of more modest ancestry, had clearly outdistanced his wife's relations. Theodore Sedgwick saw service in the state legislature, in both houses of Congress, and on the Massachusetts supreme court. Catharine's early years were dominated by his strong personality and by the misfortunes of her mother. Pamela Sedgwick, a delicate woman of great sweetness and charm, fell victim to melancholia and, during Catharine's youth, experienced two brief periods of insanity. To "Young Kate" and a trusted Negro servant, Mumbet, fell the chief care of the household and of Mrs. Sedgwick. Such service accentuated the naturally sympathetic disposition of the young girl and helped create an unusually close bond among the Sedgwick children.

Catharine's formal education was desultory, though superior to that of most girls of her period. She attended the district school, where she "learned to parse glibly" and ran up a large bill at the general store "in mad squanderings for raisins, sweets, and Malaga wine." Subsequently she was enrolled for brief periods at Mrs. Bell's academy in Albany and Miss Paine's finishing school in Boston. Her most effective instruction, however, took place at home, where her father encouraged her to read Shakespeare, Cervantes, and Butler and admired her ability at "reading aloud."

In her girlhood, as later, Catharine was vivacious and gay, but also tenderhearted and innately religious. Her mother died when she was seventeen, and when her father remarried a year later, in 1808, she experienced the classic difficulty in accepting her new stepmother. At this point she began wintering in New York City with her older, married brothers. The shock of her father's death, in 1813, stimulated her concern with matters of the spirit, and her letters at this time began to show a mounting sense of impatience with the stern Calvinist creed in which she had been reared. Catharine's deliberations and struggle lasted eight years. By 1821 she was convinced that for her the Unitarian faith offered the only salvation from hypocrisy, and to the dismay of her sisters, but in company with her brothers Robert and Henry, she formally joined the new Unitarian Meeting House in New York.

She was by this time a friend and devoted disciple of William Ellery Channing, whom she viewed as a saint and who with his doctrines had a great influence on her literary career. This began almost by accident. Increasingly bereft as one after another of her sisters and brothers married, Catharine Sedgwick at the behest of her brother Theodore undertook in 1821 to write a small tract. Its purpose was to describe the unchristian bigotry of a particular type of narrowly orthodox Calvinist. As she wrote, however, her natural gift for romantic invention—previously utilized only to devise bedtime stories for a growing company of nieces and nephews—began to take hold, and the tract became a novel. Published in 1822, *A New-England Tale* was the best work yet produced in America by a woman writer and enjoyed an immediate success. Its faithful description of the people and hills of Miss Sedgwick's native Berkshire County won special acclaim in that artistically imitative era, when a story natively American in setting and characters verged on the experimental.

*A New-England Tale* was followed by *Redwood* (1824) and *Hope Leslie* (1827). With these books Miss Sedgwick firmly established her popularity and reputation. Though the shrewd and winning spinster Debby Lenox in *Redwood* is perhaps Miss Sedgwick's best character portrait, *Hope Leslie*, her first attempt at historical romance, is her finest novel. Laid in seventeenth-century Massachusetts, it reflects considerable research into Mohawk customs and tribal rites and a sincere effort to re-create the past. Despite a needlessly complex plot and overidealized characters, the author's power of vivid narration is clearly evidenced. In *Clarence* (1830) Sedgwick attempted a description of the fashionable New York of her own day, she to the historical romance with *The Linwoods* (1835), depicting the colony of New York in the Revolutionary era. In both books she skillfully combines the pathetic episode and preposterous coincidence—so beloved by the readers of her time—with homely and realistic detail.

Twenty-two years elapsed before Miss Sedgwick offered her sixth and last novel, *Married or Single?* (1857), whose stated purpose was to "lessen the stigma placed on the term, old maid." She had by no means been idle during this period, however, producing a long array of moral tracts and didactic tales which were readily absorbed in the magazines, annuals, and gift books of the day and in which, despite their inferior literary quality, she took great pride. Possessing a strong social con-science, she felt a positive duty to utilize her popularity for the intellectual, moral, and social advancement of her fellow beings. In her stories she quietly championed such reforms as the alleviation of city tenement conditions, the abolition of dueling, and the propagation of religious toleration. The only organized movement in which she played an active role, however, was that of prison reform; from 1848 until her death she was "first director" (president) of the Women's Prison Association in New York. Appalled by the institution of slavery, she nevertheless lost friends by refusing to join the abolitionists, whom she considered far too violent and extreme. Nor was she a member of the early woman's rights movement. She wrote two stories which tacitly called for improved property rights for married women, but in general she felt that if women would but demonstrate their moral and intellectual equality with men, time would gradually bring them social and political gains.

For most of her life alternating between Stockbridge and then Lenox in the summer and New York in the winter, Miss Sedgwick had wherever she lived a circle of devoted admirers. The recipient of some half-dozen marriage proposals, she accepted none, but, perhaps in consequence, lavished ever-mounting affection on relatives and friends. Her breakfast parties in Lenox toward the end of her life were famous for their distinguished company and conversation. With her brisk headlong walk and great corkscrew curls, she was to be seen tramping the Berkshire hills for wild flowers at six, ravaging her personally tended strawberry beds at seven, and greeting company at nine with a natural flow of wit that equally delighted émigrés from Austrian Italy, the actress FANNY KEMBLE, emissaries of Kossuth, and William Cullen Bryant. She died in her seventy-eighth year of "paralysis," after a two-year period of invalidism, at the home of a niece in West Roxbury, Mass. She was buried in the Sedgwick family plot in Stockbridge.

Though Miss Sedgwick's greatest sources of happiness were her family, her religion, and her friends, her fame must rest on her books. She did not produce a single great work, nor even one unmarred by many faults. Yet she is a significant figure in the history of American letters on several counts. A leader in the conscious movement to forge a native literature, she was also one of the leading practitioners of the historical romance in America. She was, moreover, a transitional figure, standing between the Gothic extravagance and romanticism of the past and the genteel realism of the future. If her characters were at times wooden and one-sided, she nevertheless possessed the ability to make unadulterated goodness both attractive and credible. Somewhat imitative in the format of her novels, she was inventive in the depiction of scenes and incidents never before utilized in American fiction. Miss Sedgwick wrote for her time with conscious moral purpose; she was the most popular American female novelist before HARRIET BEECHER STOWE.

[The Catharine M. Sedgwick Collection on loan deposit at the Mass. Hist. Soc. furnishes the chief source for any study of Miss Sedgwick's life and works; it contains personal correspondence, letter books, journals, and notebooks. Valuable secondary sources are: Mary E. Dewey, ed., *Life and Letters of Catharine M. Sedgwick* (1871); Sister Mary Michael Welsh, *Catharine Maria Sedgwick* (1937), a careful, detailed study containing a complete bibliography of Miss Sedgwick's writings; Richard D. Birdsall, "William Cullen Bryant and Catharine Sedgwick—Their Debt to Berkshire," *New England Quart.*, Sept. 1955; H. D. Sedgwick, "The Sedgwicks of Berkshire," Berkshire Hist. and Scientific Soc., *Collections*, vol. III (1900); and Gladys Brooks, *Three Wise Virgins* (1957), pp. 157–244. See also Richard E. Welch, Jr., *Theodore Sedgwick, Federalist* (1965). Death record from Mass. Registrar of Vital Statistics.]

RICHARD E. WELCH, JR.

SEMBRICH, Marcella (Feb. 15, 1858–Jan. 11, 1935), opera singer, was born in Wisnieczyk, Galicia, a part of Austrian Poland. Christened Praxede Marcelline Kochanska, she was one of the thirteen children of Casimir and Juliana (Sembrich) Kochanski. Her father, who had spent his youth in a military band, supported his growing family by teaching and performing on several instruments. Marcella, as she became known, received piano lessons from her father when she was four years old and violin lessons when six. She soon participated in the family's quartet, which was often hired for small entertainments; she also spent long hours copying music. After several years as an itinerant teacher, Kochanski obtained a position as village organist at Bolechów and moved there with his family. Through the efforts of an interested villager Marcella was taken to the conservatory at Lemberg (Lwów) about 1869, where she began serious study of the piano—her preference at this time—with Wilhelm Stengel. She also continued with the violin, began the study of harmony with Charles Mikuli, the conservatory director, and received valuable experience in the conservatory chorus, although her vocal abilities had not yet been discovered. During this time she met some of her expenses by playing for children's dancing classes and for evening dances of the aristocracy.

At sixteen, after some four years of studying piano with Stengel, Marcella was recommended to Julius Epstein in Vienna for further work. After her audition, at which she sang in addition to playing violin and piano, Epstein arranged an interview with the great singer Mathilde Marchesi, who confirmed Marcella's potential vocal talent. Thus encouraged, the girl took voice lessons with Victor Rokitansky of the Vienna Conservatory. During this Vienna education two episodes significantly influenced her future: an interview with the composer Franz Liszt, who advised that her voice was her greatest gift; and a performance at the Vienna opera where she first heard ADELINA PATTI, in whose tradition she would soon follow.

After a year with Rokitansky, Marcella Kochanska went in 1875 to Milan to study the elements of the Italian operatic style with Giovanni Lamperti and his father, Francesco Lamperti. To the latter she afterward attributed the development of her dramatic coloratura voice. At nineteen she went to Athens under a contract for twenty-four performances of *Lucia di Lammermoor, Dinorah,* and *I Puritani.* There, on May 5, 1877, she was married to her former teacher, Wilhelm Stengel, twelve years her senior. A widower with two sons, Stengel now became the young diva's manager, secretary, protector, and most severe critic—a career that lasted through their forty years of marriage. After a brief honeymoon in Athens, she made her operatic debut there in June as Elvira in *I Puritani.* At the end of this engagement she returned to Vienna for coaching in the German repertoire by Richard Lewy and in dramatic interpretation by the actress Marie Seebach.

Adopting her mother's maiden name as her professional name, Mme. Sembrich went to the Saxon Royal Opera in Dresden in 1878 and in October made her German debut, singing Lucia. Occasional programs took her to Milan, Vienna, and Warsaw; at Leipzig in 1879 she performed in a concert directed by Brahms, whose songs she later brought to the American concert stage. An abundance of talent in the Dresden company, however, gave her little opportunity to advance. She had better luck in London. Obtaining an audition before Ernest Gye of Covent Garden, she secured a five-year contract and opened with the Royal Italian Opera in London on June 12, 1880, in *Lucia.* She continued to rise in her genre, the Italian bel canto, through subsequent revivals of Mozart operas. She also came to the concert stage—unusual for an opera singer in this time—in Sir Julius Benedict's annual concerts at Floral Hall, Covent Garden. Two other significant programs took place when Mme. Sembrich shared a command performance at Buckingham Palace with Patti in 1881 and appeared at the Winter Palace of Czar Alexander II in St. Petersburg the following year.

Mme. Sembrich came to New York in 1883, making her American debut before the golden horseshoe of the new Metropolitan Opera House on Oct. 24 as Lucia, in the second program of the season. She was warmly received. That year she appeared in some fifty-five performances in eleven different roles, and at a spring concert in 1884 honoring the manager, Henry E. Abbey, she performed works for violin, piano, and voice before an amazed New York audience. The Metropolitan's first season was a financial disaster, however, and its investors turned to Leopold Damrosch, who began a long series of "all-German" years presenting Wagnerian opera to New York. The florid Italian style of Sembrich and many of her associates was not adaptable to the Bayreuth repertoire, and Mme. Sembrich returned to Europe and further study with Lamperti, making tours which took her to Austria, Germany, France, Russia, and Scandinavia during the next few years. She and her husband made their home in Dresden and had two sons: Marcel, who died in 1901, and William Marcel. Mme. Sembrich rarely mentioned her family during her career.

After a return to Covent Garden in 1895, she made plans for a new attempt at an American career, beginning with a series of New York recitals in the fall of 1897. Although there was no winter season at the Metropolitan that year, the Maurice Grau management offered her a contract for the 1898 season. Her reappearance on the Metropolitan stage on Nov. 30, 1898, as Rosina in *The Barber of Seville,* began ten years of great performances in the disciplined bel canto style of beautiful and sustained tone which has become known as the "Sembrich tradition." Working under the stress which a noted performer endures, she often demonstrated a prima donna temperament. When the reigning star Nellie Melba in 1900 laid exclusive claim to the roles which she and Mme. Sembrich had been sharing, the latter went to Berlin to form her own company. In other publicized incidents Sembrich stormed from a Chicago performance when upstaged by the colorful Fritzi Scheff in *The Magic Flute,* and refused to continue to perform in *La Traviata* when informed that New York's special guest, Prince Henry of Prussia, had already retired with his entourage. At the height of her career in 1905–06, Mme. Sembrich received fees of $1,000 for each of her forty-five performances that season. She often sang with Caruso in his familiar vehicles *Rigoletto* and *Pagliacci* and was touring with him in San Francisco at the time of the great earthquake in 1906.

Mme. Sembrich announced her retirement at the Metropolitan in November 1908; a farewell performance the following February closed an operatic career of thirty-one years. From 1909 to 1917 she was a dominant figure on the concert stage in a repertoire featuring the songs of Brahms, Schumann, and French and Italian composers, and the modern composers Debussy and Ravel. She appeared wearing copies of her famous jewels, with gowns made by Paquin of Paris and her singer's tiny wordbooks covered to match.

Extremely nearsighted from the long sessions of music copying in her youth, and so sensitive about a cast in one eye that her portraits appeared in profile, she followed a routine of five-mile walks, endless games of solitaire, dinners of ham, toast, and tea, and long periods of silence to protect her voice. After the death of Stengel in 1917, Mme. Sembrich made no further appearances but devoted herself to teaching. Besides private lessons, she taught after 1924 in the vocal departments of the Juilliard School in New York and the Curtis Institute in Philadelphia; among her pupils were SOPHIE BRASLAU, ALMA GLUCK, and Maria Jeritza. Though she built a summer retreat and studio on Lake George at Bolton, N.Y., in 1923, she never became an American citizen. She was living in New York City at the time of her death, from emphysema and heart complications, in 1935. Her funeral was held at St. Patrick's Cathedral in New York, with music by the organist Pietro Yon and the cathedral choir; a requiem mass was sung at Dresden, after which Mme. Sembrich was buried in the Stengel family mausoleum there. Hailed by one commentator as "the best-loved singer known to New York" (Odell, XII, 290), Marcella Sembrich won high critical as well as popular acclaim. As an operatic soprano she is generally ranked with such luminaries as Patti, Melba, and Christine Nilsson; through her teaching and concert work she reached the prominence of Lilli Lehmann as well.

[Georg Armin, *Marcella Sembrich und Herr Prof. Julius Hey* (Leipzig, 1898); Henry G. Owen, *A Recollection of Marcella Sembrich* (1950); *An Outline of the Life and Career of Mme. Marcella Sembrich* (Sembrich Memorial Assoc., 1945); Avis B. Charbonnel, "Touring with Sembrich," *Musical Courier,* July 1949; Lawrence Reamer in

*Munsey's Mag.*, Feb. 1909; obituaries in *Musical America*, Jan. 25, 1935, *Musical Courier,* Jan. 19, 1935, and *N.Y. Times,* Jan. 12, 1935; clippings in Music Division and Theatre Collection of N.Y. Public Library at Lincoln Center; personal recollections of Mme. Avis Bliven Charbonnel of Providence, R.I., former accompanist to Mme. Sembrich. See also: Hermann Klein, *Great Women-Singers of My Time* (1931); Irving Kolodin, *The Story of the Metropolitan Opera, 1883–1950* (1953); Gustave Kobbé, *Opera Singers* (1901); Oscar Thompson, ed., *Internat. Cyc. of Music and Musicians* (4th ed., 1946). The Sembrich Memorial Assoc. gave helpful assistance.]

JOYCE MANGLER CARLSON

**SEMPLE, Ellen Churchill** (Jan. 8, 1863–May 8, 1932), geographer, was born in Louisville, Ky., the third daughter and youngest of five children of Alexander Bonner Semple, a prosperous wholesale hardware merchant of Scotch-Irish parentage, who had moved to Louisville from Pittsburgh in 1835. He died when Ellen was twelve. Thereafter her education was guided by her mother, Emerine (Price) Semple, a descendant of old Maryland and Kentucky families, who has been described as "an exceptionally gifted woman of rare charm." One of Ellen's sisters, Patty Blackburn Semple, helped found the Louisville Woman's Club in 1890 and served as its first president.

After preparing for college under private tutors, Ellen Semple followed her sister Patty to Vassar, where she graduated in 1882 as valedictorian and the youngest member of her class. Returning home, she soon tired of conventional social life and began to read widely in history and allied subjects while teaching in a private school. Frequent discussions with professional and cultural leaders of the community awakened her interest in social and economic problems. Her interest in geography was first aroused during a trip abroad with her mother (apparently in 1887), when she met an American student who had worked at the University of Leipzig under the great German anthropogeographer Friedrich Ratzel. The student loaned her a copy of Ratzel's book, and she determined to study with him herself. Back in Louisville she read sociology, economics, and "fragments of geography" at home and upon passing a written examination received an M.A. degree from Vassar in 1891. She then went directly to Leipzig. Miss Semple's study with Ratzel was to provide a foundation for her lifework. Although women were not allowed to enroll at the university, she attended his classes, sitting beside the professor's platform, literally at his feet. Adopting Ratzel's theory that environment determines human development and his method of studying so-

cieties in similar environments for similar patterns of development, she became his most brilliant student and a warm friend of his family. Other professors permitted her to join their courses in economics and statistics. After a year's study in Leipzig she returned to Louisville and with her sister Patty, who had been divorced after an unhappy marriage, in 1893 founded a girls' school, the Semple Collegiate School, where for two years Ellen taught history. She made another journey to study at Leipzig in 1895, and then returned to Louisville, where she settled down to library and field research and practiced the craft of authorship, along with ALICE HEGAN RICE and other fledgling writers, in the Authors Club of Louisville.

One of her first subjects lay close at hand. Always a skilled horsewoman, she rode into the Kentucky highlands and, living among the people there, studied the influence of geographic isolation on their habits of life. Her article "The Anglo-Saxons of the Kentucky Mountains" (*Geographical Journal,* June 1901) established her scholarly reputation. Her first book, *American History and Its Geographic Conditions* (1903), in which she viewed American expansion as the inevitable result of geographic forces, attracted wide attention both among fellow scientists and among a general public that was increasingly conscious, in these years following the Spanish-American War, of the importance of geographical study. In further token of her scholarly standing, she read a paper in 1904 before the International Geographical Congress in Washington and, on a trip abroad in 1905, before the Royal Geographical Society in London, teaching at Oxford during the summer term. She was invited to lecture at the University of Chicago in 1906 and continued to give courses there, with the rank of lecturer, until 1924, coming in alternate years for one term. Her summers she spent in the Catskill mountains, living alone in a tent and working on her writing.

*Influences of Geographic Environment, on the Basis of Ratzel's System of Anthropo-Geography,* her second and most significant work, appeared in 1911. It had been planned, at Ratzel's request, as an interpretation of his system for English-speaking readers, but the finished book embodied so much of her own thought that it was difficult to distinguish between the two fountainheads. Drawing on her knowledge of geography, anthropology, history, and economics, Miss Semple classified the various kinds of geographic influences and described how each affected man at every stage of his historic development. The principal theme she here expounded—briefly, that factors of the physical environment have determined man's choice of settlement, his activities, and his outlook—has perhaps evoked more discussion and argument among geographers than any other single idea in the field. Reviewers hailed the book as "unquestionably the most scholarly contribution to the literature of geography that has yet been produced in America" (*Journal of Geography*, Sept. 1911), and "one of the few products of American contemporary science which may safely challenge the best that has been put forth in this field by any foreign scientist whatsoever. . . . It places Miss Semple among the handful of women the world over who are the peers of the foremost men of science" (*Nation*, Dec. 21, 1911). Much acclaimed also was the author's flowing prose style, which though it today seems somewhat ornate and prolix, yet remains picturesque and readable.

Immediately after the publication of *Influences,* Miss Semple embarked with two friends on a world tour of eighteen months. In Japan she walked two hundred miles to observe Japanese agriculture at different elevations. At the border of the Mongolian desert she studied patterns of desert trade, and in Greece she took the first motor tour that had ever been made through some of its remote mountain areas. Arriving in England in the summer of 1912, she once again taught for a term at Oxford and lectured before the Royal Geographical Society. On her return to America late that year she continued work on a study of Mediterranean geography, teaching also at Wellesley (1914–15), the University of Colorado (1916), and Columbia (1918). During 1918 she served in New York City on "The Inquiry," a governmental group set up during World War I under the supervision of Col. Edward M. House to study problems that might arise at the peace conference. Miss Semple's special area was the Mediterranean region and the Near East, and her manuscripts on "The Austro-Italian Frontier" and "The Turkish Empire, Past and Present" were used by President Wilson at Versailles.

When in 1921 a Graduate School of Geography was established at Clark University, Worcester, Mass., under the direction of Wallace W. Atwood, Miss Semple was called to its faculty as lecturer; she was made professor of anthropogeography in 1923 and held the post until her death nine years later, although she usually alternated semesters of teaching and writing. Tall and distinguished in appearance, she was a person of charm and integrity, and at Clark, as at other times and places, she ac-

quired a wide circle of friends from all walks of life. A serious and demanding teacher, she sometimes found it difficult to communicate readily in the classroom, but she was extraordinarily devoted to her students and in her individual contacts with them won their devotion in return. A severe heart attack in 1929 led friends and colleagues to fear that she would be unable to finish her last book, but her resolute spirit prevailed. *The Geography of the Mediterranean Region: Its Relation to Ancient History* (1931) was published a few months before her death. The culmination of more than twenty years' study and travel in a part of the world she loved and knew intimately, the book set forth the influence of the physical characteristics of the Mediterranean basin on the societies of antiquity and hence upon the whole of Western civilization. Weakened by asthma attacks, Miss Semple was taken to West Palm Beach, Fla., where she died in 1932 of sepsis from lung abscesses. She was buried at Cave Hill Cemetery in Louisville.

Before her death the pendulum of scholarly thought had already begun to swing away from her dominating concept, set forth most forcibly in her *Influences of Geographic Environment.* In the realm of geographical methodology the antideterministic approach (exemplified, for instance, in the "possibilist" school, which holds that man has freedom to choose from among a range and variety of possibilities) came strongly to the fore, and it became fashionable in academic circles to cite passages in *Influences* as shining examples of how not to think. By the very controversy she had aroused, however, as well as by her scholarly research and writing, Ellen Semple had made a major contribution to the twentieth-century development of geography as a true university discipline, with a methodology and literature of its own. Her accomplishments received recognition in several forms. She was awarded an honarary LL.D. by the University of Kentucky (1923); she received the Cullum Medal of the American Geographical Society (1914) and the gold medal of the Geographic Society of Chicago (1932); and in 1921 she was elected president of the Association of American Geographers, the first woman to win this distinction.

[The most important sources on Miss Semple's life are the collection of her papers at the Univ. of Ky. Library, which includes an unpublished biographical study by a former student, Ruth E. Baugh, and a folder of clippings, letters, etc., in the alumnae files of Vassar College. Printed accounts include two appreciative obituary articles, by Charles C. Colby in the *Annals* of the Assoc. of Am. Geographers, Dec. 1933, and by Wallace W. Atwood in *Jour. of Geography*, Sept. 1932; and two recent studies: Lawrence Gelfand, "Ellen Churchill Semple: Her Geographical Approach to Am. Hist.," *ibid.*, Jan. 1954, and John K. Wright, "Miss Semple's 'Influences of Geographic Environment': Notes toward a Bibliography," *Geographical Rev.*, July 1962. Other data from former colleagues and students of Miss Semple and from death certificate supplied by Fla. Bureau of Vital Statistics.]

**SESSIONS, Kate Olivia** (Nov. 8, 1857–Mar. 24, 1940), California horticulturist and nurserywoman, was born in San Francisco, the first of two children and only daughter of Josiah and Harriet (Parker) Sessions. Both parents were natives of Connecticut; they were married in San Francisco, to which Josiah Sessions had moved in 1851. A breeder of fine horses, he received considerable publicity as the importer of a famous Hambletonian trotting stallion by boat from New York in 1864; in 1868 he moved his family across San Francisco Bay to a farm in Oakland. In this rural environment and upper-middle-class Unitarian family Kate grew up. She roamed the Oakland hills on her pony as a child and became familiar with flowers there and in her mother's garden. In 1876, the year after she graduated from the Oakland public schools, she made a trip to Hawaii, where her interest in beautiful plants was stimulated. In 1877 she entered the University of California at nearby Berkeley—where she quickly became known as "the prettiest girl on campus"—and enrolled in the scientific course. She received the Ph.B. degree in 1881, having specialized in chemistry.

After working for a time as a substitute teacher at the primary school in Oakland, Kate Sessions moved in 1883 to San Diego, Calif., as instructor and vice-principal at the Russ School (later San Diego High School). Although she was known as an excellent teacher, her interests were in horticulture, and in 1885 she left to open a nursery in nearby Coronado, with an office and retail flower shop in San Diego. In 1892 she obtained a lease from the city of San Diego for thirty acres of undeveloped land in the city park at Sixth and Upas streets to use as a nursery on condition that she plant one hundred trees there yearly and donate three hundred more to the city. This was the beginning of what became San Diego's Balboa Park and of the introduction of many exotic trees for the gardens and streets of San Diego. Later, in 1903, Miss Sessions transferred her nursery to the Mission Hills section of San Diego, and between 1927 and 1930 she moved it to the town of Pacific Beach, her home after 1923. She gave up her retail

flower shop in San Diego in 1909 but continued to operate a nursery business of modest size until her death.

Miss Sessions' greatest importance lies in the new varieties of plants she introduced into the San Diego area and into the horticultural trade generally. Interested in promoting colorful and drought-resistant varieties, she secured plants through Dr. Francesco Franceschi (Emanuele Orazio Fenzi) and his nursery, the Santa Barbara (Calif.) Acclimatization Association; from La Mortola Gardens in northern Italy; from other gardens and horticulturists all over the world; and from her own travels. In 1902 she made a collecting trip to Baja (Lower) California, in Mexico, with Dr. Townshend Stith Brandegee, from which she brought back seeds, young specimens, and pictures of the palm later described as *Erythea brandegeei*. Now widely distributed in California, this was introduced into the nursery trade by Miss Sessions. Although claims in this field are often conflicting, it seems clear that she first obtained the seed of *Fremontia mexicana*, a large flowering shrub native to San Diego County, and sent it to the nurseryman Theodore Payne, who distributed it in 1916. Her constant search for better selections of cultivated material led also to introductions into horticulture of a fine form of *Romneya coulteri*, the Matilija poppy, and *Ceanothus cyaneus*, a striking native shrub. These three plants of the San Diego area are now widely cultivated in California and are not uncommon in English gardens. It was largely through her efforts that such plants as queen palm (*Arecastrum romanzoffianum*, known locally as *Cocos plumosa*), silk oak (*Grevillea robusta*), flame eucalyptus (*Eucalyptus ficifolia*), Chinese twisted juniper (*Juniperus chinensis torulosa*), bunyabunya tree (*Araucaria bidwillii*), camphor tree (*Cinnamomum camphora*), silver tree (*Leucadendron argenteum*), cork oak (*Quercus suber*), many acacias, bougainvilleas, hibiscus, Pride of Madeira (*Echium fastuosum*), many vines, aloes, mesembryanthemums and other succulents were popularized and introduced into the San Diego landscape. In 1939 she was the first woman to receive the Meyer Medal, awarded by the council of the American Genetic Association for distinguished service in the field of foreign plant introduction, in recognition of "her outstanding contributions to the horticulture of her native state."

Miss Sessions was one of the leaders in the founding, in 1909, of the San Diego Floral Association and for over twenty years served as an officer or board member. To its journal,

*California Garden,* she contributed some 250 popular articles and brief notes in which she discussed the many new plants being introduced, described her travels to Europe in 1925 and to Hawaii in 1926, and promoted interest in horticulture; she also contributed occasional articles to local newspapers. She participated in many flower shows, her exhibits winning recognition for their unusual plant materials. During the years 1915–18 she served as supervisor of agriculture for the San Diego grammar schools, and her classes for children were popular. Interested in seeing that each plant was placed where it would grow best, she drew some plans and elevations for gardens, and she worked with the architect Irving Gill on the landscaping of several country houses. In 1939 she conducted classes for adults in "Gardening Practice and Landscape Design" for the University of California Extension Division. The founder of Arbor Day celebrations in San Diego, she was honored by many tree plantings during her lifetime. A "K. O. Sessions Day" was celebrated at the California-Pacific International Exposition in San Diego in 1935; and an elementary school (1956) and a memorial park (1957) were named in her honor in Pacific Beach.

Early portraits of Kate Olivia Sessions show her as a petite, very feminine young lady; the story is that she arrived in San Diego with a wardrobe of fine dresses. When she turned to nursery business these were laid aside for clothes more appropriate for gardening. Later accounts speak of her heavy working shoes and describe her as weathered and hunched from hours of working out-of-doors with her beloved plants. She died in neighboring La Jolla, Calif., at the age of eighty-two from bronchial pneumonia following a broken hip and was buried in Mount Hope Cemetery, San Diego.

[*Sessions Family in America* (1890); files of *Calif. Garden* (the Autumn 1953 issue is devoted to Kate Sessions); scrapbooks and bibliography file, San Diego Public Library; Clarence A. McGrew, *Hist. of San Diego and San Diego County* (1922), II, 82; C. H. Heilbron, ed., *Hist. of San Diego County* (1936); *Jour. of Heredity,* Dec. 1939, pp. 531–32; T. D. A. Cockerell, "Kate Olivia Sessions and Calif. Floriculture," *Bios,* Dec. 1943; Theodore Payne, "Hist. of the Introduction of Three Calif. Natives," *El Aliso,* Mar. 1950; *Madroño,* July 1952, pp. 258–59; Victoria Padilla, *Southern Calif. Gardens* (1961); personal information from Milton P. Sessions, a nephew of Miss Sessions, and his daughter Marian Sessions Healy, and from Alice M. Rainford, who purchased the retail cut flower business from Miss Sessions in 1909. Miss Sessions did not, as sometimes reported, serve on the San Diego Park Board.]

MILDRED E. MATHIAS

SETON, Elizabeth Ann Bayley (Aug. 28, 1774–Jan. 4, 1821, Roman Catholic convert, foundress and head of the first American sisterhood, was born, probably in New York City, the second of three daughters of Richard Bayley, a physician, by his first wife, Catherine Charlton. Her paternal grandfather was from Hoddeston, Hertfordshire, in England; his wife, Susanne LeCompte of New Rochelle, N.Y., was of French Huguenot stock. On her mother's side Elizabeth was of Anglo-Irish descent, her grandfather, the Rev. Richard Charlton, having come from Ireland to Staten Island, N.Y., where he was an Episcopal rector, by way of England and the Leeward Islands. Of her maternal grandmother, Mary Bayeux, little is known.

After the death of her mother, when Elizabeth was scarcely three years old, her father married Charlotte Amelia Barclay, who instilled in the young girl a deep love for the Psalms. Seven children were born of this second marriage. Elizabeth's childhood was not always happy, being spent sometimes in New York City with her stepmother, sometimes with her father's relatives in New Rochelle, again with her mother's relatives on Staten Island. Her father's profession frequently took him from home. Dr. Richard Bayley was a pioneer in the study of diphtheria and in surgery, performing in 1782 the first successful amputation of an arm at the shoulder joint; he subsequently lectured on anatomy and surgery at Columbia College, helped organize the New York Medical Society, and served as the first city health officer and as first state quarantine officer of the port of New York. Little is known of Elizabeth's education save that with her sister Mary Magdalen she attended a school called "Mama Pompelion's," learning to play the piano and to speak French.

At the age of nineteen, on Jan. 25, 1794, she was married to William Magee Seton, a young merchant of an Anglo-Scottish family that had come to America before the American Revolution. The marriage was a happy one and produced five children: Anna Maria, born in 1795, William (1796), Richard Bayley (1798), Catherine Josephine (1800), and Rebecca (1802). While her husband's business prospered Mrs. Seton enjoyed going to the theatre and balls and took an active part in charitable work. In 1797 she cooperated with ISABELLA MARSHALL GRAHAM in forming a society to aid destitute widowed mothers, and she served as the society's treasurer until 1804. In 1800 she came under the influence of the Rev. John Henry Hobart, an assistant at Trinity (Episcopal) Church of New York, and her spiritual life deepened just as it was to be most sorely tested. Her husband's business never recovered from the effects of the undeclared war with France and by December 1800 went into bankruptcy. The following year her beloved father died of yellow fever contracted during an epidemic while performing his duties as quarantine officer. Then in 1803 her husband's health, never strong, became so critical that an ocean voyage was undertaken as a last resort. Leaving the four younger children with relatives but accompanied by the eldest, Anna Maria, Mrs. Seton and her husband on Oct. 1, 1803, boarded the *Shepherdess* bound for Leghorn, Italy. On their arrival she found to her dismay that because the ship had sailed from New York, where yellow fever had broken out, the *Shepherdess* and its passengers were quarantined. Confined to the damp, cold quarters of a lazaretto (public hospital) on a canal several miles from the city, she had little hope of her husband's survival; when they were released thirty days later, on Dec. 19, she took him to Pisa, where he died on Dec. 27.

While waiting more than three months for passage back to New York she was befriended by two brothers who had been affiliated with her husband's mercantile firm, Antonio and Filippo Filicchi, and their wives Amabilia and Mary (the former Mary Cowper of Boston). At their hands she not only became familiar with the sights of Leghorn and Florence, the museums and churches, but was also introduced to the teachings of the Roman Catholic Church. Influenced by the example of the Filicchis, her reading of the life of St. Francis de Sales, and the explanations of the Rev. Peter Plunkett, an Irish priest in Leghorn, she was drawn to the Church but remained only at the threshold during her sojourn in Italy. She returned to New York accompanied by Antonio Filicchi, arriving June 8, 1804, to enter a period of most painful indecision. Torn between the entreaties and warnings of her pastor, Hobart, and her Protestant friends and relatives on the one hand and the promptings and persuasions of Filicchi and the Catholic clergy he enlisted on the other, she at last on Mar. 14, 1805, became a Catholic.

For the next three years she remained in New York City trying to support her five children in an atmosphere hostile to her new religious affiliation. Disinherited by her godmother, Mrs. Sarah Startin, and criticized by former friends, she tried unsuccessfully to start a school with a Mr. and Mrs. Patrick White from Albany, N.Y. She was reduced to accepting financial aid from her brother-in-law, Dr. Wright Post, and from Charles and John

Wilkes, friends of the Seton family, in order to eke out a living while running a boarding-house for boys who attended an Episcopal school. With financial assistance from Antonio Filicchi, she placed her own sons in the Catholic academy in Georgetown, D.C. By June 1808, the number of her boarders having much diminished, she accepted an invitation from the Rev. William Valentine Dubourg, S.S., then president of St. Mary's College in Baltimore, to come to that city to start a school for Catholic girls. Through her friendship with Archbishop John Carroll (who had confirmed her on May 26, 1806, in New York) she now had access to the leading wealthy Catholic families of Maryland: the Carrolls, Pattersons, Catons, Harpers, and Barrys. In September she began a school on Paca Street in a small house adjacent to the seminary and chapel of the Society of St. Sulpice in Baltimore; here she taught the daughters of leading families and prepared children for their first communion. The next spring she was joined by two of her husband's sisters, Cecilia and Harriet Seton, both of whom, having converted to Catholicism, remained with her for the rest of their lives.

During this year in Baltimore her long-cherished wish to found a religious community began to be realized in the beginnings of a new order which became the Sisters of Charity of St. Joseph. Disappointed in her first hopes—for a Baltimore foundation financed by the Filicchis—she accepted the site offered in Emmitsburg, Md., by Samuel Sutherland Cooper, a wealthy Philadelphia convert who was then preparing for the priesthood at the Sulpician seminary in Baltimore. On Dec. 7, 1808, the first recruit to the new undertaking joined her in Baltimore; on Mar. 25, 1809, Mrs. Seton took her first vows before Archbishop Carroll; and in June, together with four additional candidates, she appeared in public for the first time, on the Feast of Corpus Christi, in the order's habit (a black dress with a shoulder cape and a white cap tied beneath the chin). On June 21, together with two pupils from the Paca Street school, her sisters-in-law, and part of the community, she set out for Emmitsburg.

Mother Seton and her new community first occupied a stone farmhouse of four rooms, where snow drifted over them on occasion as they slept. Water was carried from a spring, and laundry was done at Tom's Creek. Sundays they trudged several miles to mass in the village or climbed a mountainside nearby to the chapel at Mount St. Mary's school for boys, recently founded by the Sulpicians.

Often the sisters had scarcely enough to eat. By February 1810 Mother Seton had moved into a larger building of plastered logs, the "White House." The community now grew rapidly, with postulants and pupils coming from Maryland and New York. Although the sisters nursed the sick and ministered to the poor, St. Joseph's School, for girls from prosperous families, was its central activity. Income from these boarding students provided a sound financial base, enabling Mother Seton to offer free schooling to needy girls of the local parish. This latter work has led to the tradition in some quarters of calling her the "foundress of the parochial school system in the United States." In 1810 Mother Seton received a copy of the rule of the Sisters of Charity of St. Vincent de Paul brought from France by Bishop Benedict Flaget; on Jan. 17, 1812, this set of regulations, somewhat modified to fit the American scene and her own position as mother of five children, was confirmed by Archbishop Carroll.

During the next years Mother Seton witnessed the spread of her community to Philadelphia (1814) and New York (1817); and at the time of her death, plans were nearly complete for a foundation in Baltimore. Amid all these labors she remained a devoted mother, sparing no efforts to ensure both the physical and spiritual welfare of her children. One grandson, Robert Seton (1839–1927), became a Roman Catholic archbishop. Mother Seton's health declined rapidly after 1818, yet she remained active and cheerful, saying, "Afflictions are the steps to heaven." She died at St. Joseph's in Emmitsburg of tuberculosis early in 1821, at the age of forty-six.

There is little doubt that her contemporaries believed Mother Seton to be of extraordinary virtue. Archbishop John Carroll used the word "saint" when referring to her; Bishop John Cheverus of Boston commented on the "miracles of grace and sanctity to which she witnesses." Her confessor Simon Bruté, later Bishop of Vincennes, attested, "I believe her to have been one of those truly chosen souls who, if placed in circumstances similar to those of St. Theresa or St. Frances de Chantal, would be equally remarkable in the scale of sanctity." In 1882 James Cardinal Gibbons suggested that her cause for canonization might be proposed, but it was not until 1907 that the first action was taken, with the creation of an ecclesiastical court of investigation. By 1914 twelve volumes of her writings had been presented to Rome; on Jan. 15, 1936, the formal examination of these writings was completed. On Feb. 28, 1940, a decree of the Congregation of Rites

formally introduced the cause. On Dec. 18, 1959, her virtues were declared heroic and the title "Venerable" bestowed; her remains were then removed from the community's cemetery to the altar of the chapel of St. Joseph Central House at Emmitsburg. On Mar. 17, 1963, she was beatified and the title "Blessed" conferred. The communities of Sisters of Charity who today trace their origins back to Mother Seton's foundation include the New York Sisters of Charity of Mount St. Vincent-on-the-Hudson, the Cincinnati Sisters of Charity of Mount St. Joseph, the New Jersey Sisters of Charity of Convent Station, the Sisters of Charity of Seton Hill, Greensburg, Pa., and the Sisters of Charity of Halifax, Nova Scotia. The Emmitsburg community remains active; St. Joseph's School has become a college for women.

[Annabelle M. Melville, *Elizabeth Bayley Seton* (1951), is the definitive biography. Charles I. White, *Life of Mrs. Eliza A. Seton* (1853), was long the chief source of information. Additional published accounts include: Robert Seton, *Memoir, Letters and Jour. of Elizabeth Seton* (1869), a not always accurate collection of memorabilia by Mrs. Seton's grandson; Hélène Bailly de Barberey and Joseph B. Code, *Elizabeth Seton* (1927), a translated and augmented version of a French work, first printed in 1868, which contains many documents; Joseph B. Code, *Letters of Mother Seton to Mrs. Julianna Scott* (1935), personal glimpses into the friendship of Mrs. Seton and a Protestant friend in Philadelphia; Joseph I. Dirvin, *Mrs. Seton, Foundress of the Am. Sisters of Charity* (1962), an attempt to analyze the spiritual life of Mother Seton with emphasis on her life as religious superior. On her order, see Sister Mary Agnes McCann, *The Hist. of Mother Seton's Daughters* (2 vols., 1917).]

ANNABELLE M. MELVILLE

SEVERANCE, Carolina Maria Seymour (Jan. 12, 1820–Nov. 10, 1914), reformer and woman's club pioneer, was born in Canandaigua, N.Y., the eldest of the five children, three girls and two boys, of Orson Seymour, a bank cashier, and Caroline Maria (Clarke) Seymour. Her father, born in West Hartford, Conn., was a Presbyterian; her mother was a native of New York City and an Episcopalian. After Seymour's death in 1824 the family moved for a time to nearby Auburn, N.Y., where the influence of a devout Presbyterian uncle and guardian, James S. Seymour, combined with the revivalism of Charles G. Finney, made Caroline's childhood a time of religious turmoil. She began her schooling in Canandaigua after her mother's return there and went on to the Upham Female Seminary, Miss Almira Bennett's

Boarding School in Owasco Lake, N.Y., and the female seminary of Mrs. Elizabeth (Stryker) Ricord in Geneva, N.Y., from which she graduated with honors in 1835. After briefly attending the Auburn (N.Y.) Female Seminary as student and teacher, Caroline taught for a time at Mrs. Luther Halsey's boarding school for girls on the Ohio River below Pittsburgh.

Back in Auburn, she was married on Aug. 27, 1840, to Theodoric Cordenio Severance, a young Ohioan of New England birth who was working in her uncle's bank. They moved to Cleveland, where Severance entered the banking business. They had five children: Orson Seymour (born and died in 1841), James Seymour (born 1842), Julia Long (1844), Mark Sibley (1846), and Pierre Clarke (1849).

Mrs. Severance later credited her marriage with freeing her from "bondage to authority, dogmas and conservative ideas" and making a reformer of her (Ruddy, p. 55), for the Severance family was active in liberal causes. Soon her home was a gathering place for abolitionists, literary folk, temperance workers, woman's rights leaders, and advocates of dietary reform. She and her husband left the Presbyterian Church after their marriage to form the Independent Christian Church, a group dedicated to antislavery principles which attracted liberal and reformist parishioners and ministers, including, in 1854, Amory D. Mayo, the noted Unitarian clergyman. Though moving toward religious liberalism, Caroline Severance was at one point so swayed by a local preacher's belief in the imminence of the Second Coming that she visited other Cleveland ministers earnestly seeking to convert them to her view. She was also greatly influenced by Andrew Jackson Davis, a celebrated spiritualist of the period.

Through the touring Hutchinson family singers (see ABBY HUTCHINSON PATTON) she became interested in woman's rights and worked with the pioneer Ohio feminist FRANCES DANA GAGE in lecturing, writing, and organizing meetings for the cause. She attended the second statewide woman's rights convention in Akron in 1851 and reported on it for the Cleveland newspapers. The following year she attended a similar convention in Syracuse, N.Y., where she met ELIZABETH CADY STANTON and other national leaders of the movement. In May 1853 she presided over the first annual meeting of the Ohio Woman's Rights Association. Later that year she attended the national convention in New York City, where her speech was greeted by "shouts and laughter" from hostile males in the crowd (*History of Woman Suffrage*, I, 569). On the same New York visit she joined ANTOINETTE BROWN BLACKWELL and Wendell Phillips in protesting the exclusion of women from the Whole World's Temperance Convention. On May 23, 1854, she presented a memorial to the Ohio senate, written at the request of the Ohio Woman's Rights Association, requesting that women be granted the right to control their inherited property and earnings.

Under the influence of touring New England lecturers like Emerson, Wendell Phillips, and Bronson Alcott, who frequently stayed in the Severance home, she formed a great love of Boston and became convinced, as she said, that Cleveland "did not offer the kind of companionship I craved" (*Woman's Journal*, May 31, 1902, p. 174). The educational needs of her family also weighed upon her, and when in 1855 her husband was offered a position in Boston's North Bank, they seized the opportunity to move. Mrs. Severance soon became a part of Boston's intellectual, religious, and reformist life. She regularly attended sermons by the liberal Unitarian Theodore Parker and joined in organizing the Free Religious Association after Parker's death. She was the first woman to speak in the popular Parker Fraternity Lecture Course, and her discourse, "Humanity: A Definition and a Plea" (delivered earlier before the Young Man's Library Association of Cleveland), was so well received that she was made an officer of the organization. She served on the first board of the New England Hospital for Women and Children, founded in 1862 by her friend of Cleveland days Dr. MARIE ZAKRZEWSKA. Woman's rights remained a central interest as well; on May 27, 1859, she presided over "an enthusiastic convention" in Boston, where James Freeman Clarke, Wendell Phillips, and others endorsed the cause. As the slavery issue grew, Mrs. Severance, a close friend of William Lloyd Garrison and his family, delivered abolitionist lectures in Massachusetts and Rhode Island from 1856 until the outbreak of the war. In 1861 Theodoric Severance, who had moved from the Liberty party into the new Republican party, was appointed customs collector at Union-occupied Port Royal, S.C., and Mrs. Severance spent two war winters with him there.

After the war she lectured for a time on "practical ethics" at the school for young ladies operated in Lexington, Mass., by Dio Lewis, a physical culture innovator, and resumed her woman's rights activities. In 1866 she joined SUSAN B. ANTHONY in opposing inclusion of the word "male" in the Fourteenth Amendment and became with her a founder and corresponding secretary of the American Equal Rights Association. Despite her close ties with Miss Anthony and Mrs. Stanton, however, she joined LUCY STONE and other New England suffragists in 1869 in founding at a Cleveland convention the American Woman Suffrage Association. Lending her support, as well, to the social purity movement, she was a founder (1873) and first president of the Moral Education Association of Boston.

During the winter of 1867–68 Caroline Severance discussed with a group of friends her longstanding idea of a club where women interested in reform could meet for companionship and cultural stimulation. The result was the organization, on Feb. 16, 1868, of the New England Woman's Club—the pioneer, with New York's Sorosis of that same year, among American women's clubs. Mrs. Severance was its president until 1871, when she was succeeded by JULIA WARD HOWE. From the beginning the club was a vehicle for reform, helping to establish the Girls' Latin School and the Co-operative Building Association, securing the election of women to the Boston school board, and sponsoring physiology lectures to local schoolteachers by Dr. Zakrzewska; even dress reform engaged its attention for a time in 1873.

In 1875 Caroline Severance and her husband left Boston for California, where two of their sons were living. Settling in Los Angeles, they founded the city's first Unitarian congregation, Unity Church, which became a center of religious liberalism. While Theodoric Severance engaged in raising oranges, his tireless wife pursued her many civic and reform interests. In 1876 she sponsored a training school for kindergarten workers led by EMMA MARWEDEL, and in 1885 she organized the Los Angeles Free Kindergarten Association, which waged a successful campaign to have kindergartens made a regular part of the Los Angeles school system. The woman's club she began at Unity Church in 1878—the city's first—lapsed in 1880 during her absence in the East. It was revived in 1885 as the Los Angeles Woman's Club but disintegrated in 1888 when family illness had recalled her again to Boston. Mrs. Severance's third such venture, the Friday Morning Club, took permanent root; she served as its first president, 1891–94. Like its Boston prototype, the Friday Morning Club was in the forefront of civic reforms, such as the establishment of a juvenile court system; through such members as KATHERINE P. EDSON it achieved statewide influence.

Mrs. Severance remained active despite advancing years and the death of her husband in 1892. When in December 1900 the Los Angeles County Woman Suffrage League was reorganized after a period of inactivity, she served as its president, a position she held until 1904. In 1897 she inaugurated at her spacious Los Angeles home a weekly discussion group where she championed Christian Socialism, Progressivism, anti-imperialism, and peace—the latter having been close to her heart since 1871 when she had joined Julia Ward Howe in founding a short-lived Women's International Peace Association. In 1911 the aged champion of woman's rights was the first to register under California's new woman suffrage law. In her final years Mrs. Severance loved to reminisce about her friendships with Emerson, Alcott, Parker, Garrison, Whittier, and many others. She was frequently honored by women's organizations for her impressive career in reform, spanning nearly seventy years. She died in 1914 at the age of ninety-four; funeral services were held at the Friday Morning Club, with burial in Rosedale Cemetery.

[Ella G. Ruddy, ed., *The Mother of Clubs: Caroline M. Severance* (1906), contains much valuable material. See also Mary S. Gibson, *Caroline M. Severance, Pioneer* (Friday Morning Club, 1925); Frances E. Willard and Mary A. Livermore, eds., *A Woman of the Century* (1893); *Who Was Who in America*, vol. I (1942); obituary in *Los Angeles Times*, Nov. 11, 1914; James M. Guinn, *Hist. and Biog. Record of Southern Calif.* (1902); *Sunset Mag.*, Aug. 1911, pp. 167–70; *Annals of Cleveland, 1818–1935; A Digest and Index of the Newspaper Record* (multigraphed, 1937–38), 1844, 1851, 1853; George D. Seymour and Donald L. Jacobus, *A Hist. of the Seymour Family* (1939), pp. 310–11; John F. Severance, comp., *The Severans Genealogical Hist.* (1893). Useful references also occur in Elizabeth C. Stanton et al., *Hist. of Woman Suffrage* (6 vols., 1881–1922); Ida H. Harper, *Life and Work of Susan B. Anthony* (3 vols., 1898–1908); Lillie B. C. Wyman and Arthur C. Wyman, *Elizabeth Buffum Chace* (2 vols., 1914); Harriot K. Hunt, *Glances and Glimpses* (1856), p. 323; Marie E. Zakrzewska, *A Woman's Quest* (Agnes E. Vietor, ed., 1924); Kate Douglas Wiggin, *My Garden of Memory* (1923). On her woman's club activity see Julia A. Sprague, *Hist. of the New England Women's Club* (1894); Caroline M. Severance, "The Genesis of the Club Idea," *Woman's Jour.*, May 31, 1902; Mrs. Henry C. Crowther, *Highlights: The Friday Morning Club* (n.d.); Mary D. Spalding, "Madame Severance and the First Woman's Club of Los Angeles, 1878" (unpublished MS. in possession of Florence Kreider, Los Angeles, who, with Bernice Kirkhardt, also of Los Angeles, provided information for this article); and Thelma Lee Hubbell and Gloria R. Lothrop, "The Friday Morning Club," *Southern Calif. Quart.*, Mar. 1969. A few letters may be found in the A. L. Park Papers, Huntington Library, San Marino, Calif.; the Sophia Smith Collection, Smith College; and the Schlesinger Library, Radcliffe College.]

JOAN M. JENSEN

SEVIER, Clara Driscoll. *See* DRISCOLL, Clara.

SEWALL, Lucy Ellen (Apr. 9?, 1837–Feb. 13, 1890), early woman physician, was the elder of two daughters of Samuel Edmund and Louisa Maria (Winslow) Sewall. She was born in Roxbury, Mass., into a family prominent in state and local affairs. Her grandfather Joseph Sewall, a Boston merchant and later treasurer of Massachusetts, was a great-grandson of the famous colonial justice and diarist Samuel Sewall. Her mother came of a well-to-do Quaker family of Portland, Maine. A Harvard-trained Boston lawyer, Samuel E. Sewall, like his cousin Samuel J. May, was in the vanguard of the Massachusetts abolitionists and a firm supporter of William Lloyd Garrison, though unlike Garrison he believed in the use of political and legal means. Thus he was the Liberty party's candidate for governor, 1842 to 1847, and was elected a Free Soil member of the Massachusetts senate in 1851. As early as 1840 he had become involved in agitation for woman's rights, a cause which he continued to serve with legal and financial aid for the rest of his life. His interest in abolition and feminism was endorsed not only by his first wife, who died in 1850, but by her youngest sister, Harriet (Winslow) List, who became his second wife in 1857.

Growing up amidst these advanced ideas perhaps predisposed Lucy Sewall to follow a course, considered arduous and unusual by her contemporaries. Little is known of her childhood or education, though she seems to have had a close bond with her father, and she is said to have learned to read French, German, and Latin by an early age. While still in her teens she is reported to have established a school for small children on the family property in Melrose, Mass. But a visit to the Sewall home in 1856 by Dr. MARIE ZAKRZEWSKA of the New York Infirmary turned her interest to the study of medicine. In July 1859, one month after Dr. Zakrzewska had arrived in Boston to occupy the chair of obstetrics at the New England Female Medical College, Lucy Sewall enrolled as a student; for three years she studied directly under Dr. Zakrzewska and served as her assistant. Samuel E. Sewall, a director of the college from 1850 to 1856 and a trustee from 1856 to 1862, backed his daughter's entry into the medical field with enthusi-

asm. After graduating in the spring of 1862, Lucy Sewall spent a year of successful study in hospitals in London and Paris and then returned to Boston to become resident physician of the New England Hospital for Women and Children, established the previous year by Dr. Zakrzewska (with Samuel Sewall as one of the initial backers and a vice-president).

The New England Hospital was the setting for Dr. Sewall's entire medical career. Serving as resident physician from 1863 to 1869, she handled the day-to-day management of the hospital, the instruction of students, and an exhausting measure of patient care in the dispensary. The example of her zeal, skill, and self-denial as resident converted the wellborn Englishwoman Sophia Jex-Blake to a medical career; Dr. Jex-Blake was later instrumental in opening the medical field in Britain to women. Like most of her female colleagues, Dr. Sewall devoted much of her time to work among poor women, and her reputation rested in part on her success in obstetrics. In 1869 she resigned her position as resident to become one of two attending physicians at the hospital and a director. The change allowed her more time for her increasing private practice, and she continued to hold the two latter positions until her death. Her independent financial position and the social standing of her family aided her in her career, but she was hampered all her life by ill health; during her last few years a worsening heart condition, listed on her death certificate as mitral stenosis, made her a semi-invalid. She died in Boston in 1890 at the age of fifty-two and was buried in Mount Auburn Cemetery, Cambridge. In 1892 a new maternity building at the New England Hospital was dedicated to Lucy Ellen and Samuel E. Sewall.

Few descriptions of Dr. Sewall's appearance are available, but tributes to her humility, grace, charm, and womanliness abound in the writings of her friends. Her correspondence would indicate that she was not immune to the usual feminine interest in clothes and social life. Though her father was a liberal Unitarian who had been profoundly influenced by William Ellery Channing, she apparently had no church affiliation. She was so absorbed by her practice that she did little medical writing, and she was not a member of woman's rights organizations. As a staunch feminist, however, she was one of a group of eight women physicians (including Dr. Zakrzewska, EMILY BLACKWELL, and MARY PUTNAM JACOBI) who unsuccessfully offered Harvard University $50,000 in 1881 to provide medical study for women. Her own social position and her medical competence helped gain acceptance for other women doctors and for the New England Hospital in its formative years.

[Any account of Dr. Sewall's life must be pieced together from a variety of sources. The *Annual Reports* of the New England Hospital for Women and Children, 1863–1890, provide an outline of her career, and extracts from her correspondence with Sophia Jex-Blake, published in Margaret Todd's *The Life of Sophia Jex-Blake* (1918), give the most vivid picture of her personal life. The Mass. Hist. Soc. has several letters written by Samuel E. Sewall and Lucy Sewall which describe her work abroad during the period 1862–63, and the reaction of a French physician to her visit is found in *L'Union Médicale* (Paris), XIX (1863), 289–97. A biography of Dr. Zakrzewska edited by Agnes C. Vietor, *A Woman's Quest* (1924), includes information of value, as does Nina Moore Tiffany's *Samuel E. Sewall* (1898). The latter gives her birth date as Apr. 9, although her death record and newspaper obituaries make it Apr. 26. A general account of her career appears in a pamphlet, *The New England Hospital, 1862–1962* (1962). There are obituary notices of interest in the *Boston Post*, Feb. 19, 1890; *Boston Transcript*, Feb. 17, 1890; and the *Woman's Jour.*, Feb. 22, 1890.]

SHIRLEY PHILLIPS INGEBRITSEN

**SEWALL, May Eliza Wright** (May 27, 1844–July 23, 1920), educator, suffragist, clubwoman, and pacifist, was born in Greenfield, Milwaukee County, Wis., the second daughter and youngest of four children of Philander Montague Wright and Mary Weeks (Brackett) Wright. Her parents were New Englanders of colonial descent who had migrated westward, first to Ohio and then to Wisconsin, where Wright, a former schoolteacher, settled his family on a farm. May, a precocious child who is said to have read Milton at seven, studied at home with her father and at academies in Wauwatosa and Bloomington, Wis. After teaching school for a time at Waukesha, Wis., she entered Northwestern Female College (later absorbed by Northwestern University) in Evanston, Ill., receiving the degrees of Mistress of Science in 1866 and Master of Arts in 1871.

She spent several years as a teacher and school administrator in the small communities of Corinth and Plainwell, Mich., and Franklin, Ind. In 1872 she was married to Edwin W. Thompson, a mathematics teacher from Paw Paw, Mich., and moved with him to Indianapolis, Ind., where they both taught in what later became Shortridge High School. After Thompson's death in 1875 she continued in that institution for five years, teaching German and English literature. On Oct. 30, 1880,

she became the wife of Theodore Lovett Sewall, a graduate of Harvard College who conducted a boys' school in Indianapolis; she had no children by either marriage. In 1882 Mrs. Sewall founded with her husband the Girls' Classical School of Indianapolis. Sewall, always sympathetic toward his wife's career, closed his boys' school in 1889 in order to give more effective assistance to the school for girls; he died in 1895. Mrs. Sewall remained at the head of the girls' school until June 1907. During her twenty-five years as teacher and principal in this well-known Indianapolis institution she introduced dress reforms and physical education and prepared hundreds of young women for college through a rigorous course in ancient and modern languages and mathematics.

May Wright Sewall became most widely known, however, for her work in the organized woman's movement. An ardent suffragist, she was in 1878 a founder, with ZERELDA G. WALLACE, and first secretary of the Indianapolis Equal Suffrage Society. Remaining aloof from the state suffrage organization, formed in 1869 as a branch of LUCY STONE's American Woman Suffrage Association, this Indianapolis group in 1887 called a convention at which was organized a rival state organization, under the presidency of HELEN MAR GOUGAR, affiliated with the National Woman Suffrage Association of ELIZABETH CADY STANTON and SUSAN B. ANTHONY. Mrs. Sewall served as chairman of the executive committee of the new group until 1889, when the two state societies merged and she retired "for personal reasons." A decade later, however, she led in reorganizing the Indiana suffrage association, which had become dormant. She had meanwhile been a prime mover in the near-successful campaign of 1881–83 for a state suffrage amendment. On the national level, she was chairman of the executive committee of the National Woman Suffrage Association for eight years (1882–90) and a frequent witness before Congressional committees.

Mrs. Sewall left her mark in the woman's movement particularly through the National and the International Council of Women. These two organizations grew out of an international assembly of women held in Washington, D.C., in 1888 to honor the fortieth anniversary of the original woman's rights convention. First planned by Mrs. Stanton and Miss Anthony, this meeting evolved, under the leadership of FRANCES WILLARD and Mrs. Sewall, into an attempt (only partially realized) to unite for common purposes representatives of women's organizations of all types, at home and abroad—professional, educational, cultural, religious, welfare, and reform. Mrs. Sewall was the initial recording secretary of the National Council of Women and later served as its president (1897–99) and as president of the International Council (1899–1904). Somewhat similar in scope was another project Mrs. Sewall headed: the World's Congress of Representative Women, held in conjunction with the Columbian Exposition in Chicago in May 1893, at which some 330 women read papers on all aspects of women's concerns. Mrs. Sewall traveled extensively in Europe in 1891–92 to publicize the Congress and secure speakers, and she presided over its sessions. She was also a founder and officer of two other national organizations in these years: the first vice-president of the General Federation of Women's Clubs (1889) and twice president of the Western Association of Collegiate Alumnae (1886, 1888–89), a forerunner of the American Association of University Women.

In addition to lecturing widely in the United States on behalf of woman's rights, Mrs. Sewall was an internationalist and world traveler, visiting almost every European country in the course of her duties as officer and delegate of various women's associations. President McKinley appointed her United States representative at the Paris Exposition of 1900. For the last fifteen years of her life she was especially concerned with world peace. An active member of the American Peace Society, she espoused the cause among women's organizations here and abroad, persuading the National Council of Women in 1907 and the International Council in 1909 to adopt peace programs. Her work in this field reached its climax at the Panama-Pacific Exposition in San Francisco in 1915 when she called and presided over the International Conference of Women Workers to Promote Permanent Peace. In December of that year she sailed with ROSIKA SCHWIMMER and other pacifists on Henry Ford's peace ship, the Oscar II, in a fruitless attempt to halt the European war.

Despite her national and international commitments, Mrs. Sewall found time to participate in local and civic affairs in Indiana. Her home in Indianapolis was a center of club and educational activities where she organized such groups as the Contemporary Club and the Ramabai Circle (one of a number of American societies formed to aid the effort of Pandita Ramabai in India to found a school for child widows as a step toward elevating the position of Indian women). She was one of the founders of the Indianapolis Art Association in 1883 and of the affiliated art school

which became in 1902 the John Herron Art Institute. She was a charter member, in 1875, of the Indianapolis Woman's Club and conceived and planned the building of its clubhouse, the Propylaeum, completed in 1891. For several years she edited a woman's column in the *Indianapolis Times*.

When the Girls' Classical School closed in 1907, Mrs. Sewall left Indianapolis for the East, making Cambridge, Mass., and Eliot, Maine, her headquarters thereafter. Although both she and her husband had been members of the Unitarian Church, after his death she became a convert to spiritualism, an interest she pursued for the rest of her life. In her *Neither Dead Nor Sleeping* (1920) she described her unusual psychical experiences and set down messages allegedly received from her dead husband. She died at the age of seventy-six, of chronic parenchymatous nephritis, at St. Vincent's Hospital, Indianapolis. She was buried in that city's Crown Hill Cemetery.

May Wright Sewall was an effective teacher and platform speaker, but her chief talents lay in organization and administration. One chronicler of the woman's movement found her a "powerful, dominant and queenly personality" who inspired both "tender and loyal friendships and vivid aversions" (Irwin, p. 229). A second-generation leader of the woman's rights crusade, she helped carry the movement into important new areas—women's clubs, internationalism, and world peace.

[Mrs. Sewall edited several volumes dealing with aspects of the woman's movement: *The World's Congress of Representative Women* (2 vols., 1894), an account of its background and an abridged record of its proceedings; *Internat. Council of Women, 1899–1909* (2 vols., 1910); *Genesis of the Internat. Council of Women and the Story of Its Growth* (1914); *Women, World War and Permanent Peace* (1915). The Ind. State Library, Indianapolis, has a few of her letters and several scrapbooks, as well as two short unpublished sketches of her life, by Merica E. Hoagland and Grace Julian Clarke. Brief, eulogistic accounts are found in: Frances E. Willard and Mary A. Livermore, eds., *A Woman of the Century* (1893); *Pictorial and Biog. Memoirs of Indianapolis and Marion County, Ind.* (1893), pp. 322–25; Jacob P. Dunn, *Ind. and Indianans* (1919), IV, 1679; and, by Bertha Damaris Knobe, in *Harper's Bazar*, June 1900. Other references: obituaries in *N.Y. Times*, July 24, 1920, and *Indianapolis News*, July 23, 1920; *Nat. Cyc. Am. Biog.*, XIX, 108; *Woman's Who's Who of America*, 1914–15. There are scattered references in the official *Reports* and *Proceedings* and in the histories of the organizations in which she had an active part, including the Nat. Council of Women, the Internat. Council of Women, the Nat. Woman Suffrage Assoc., and the Gen. Federation of Women's Clubs. See also: Anna Garlin Spencer, *The Council Idea: A Chronicle of Its Prophets and a Tribute to May Wright Sewall* (1929); Elizabeth C. Stanton et al., *Hist. of Woman Suffrage*, vols. III–VI (1886–1922), especially the chapters on Indiana (she herself wrote the one in vol. III); Jane C. Croly, *The Hist. of the Woman's Club Movement in America* (1898), pp. 433–39; Marion Talbot and Lois K. M. Rosenberry, *The Hist. of the Am. Assoc. of Univ. Women* (1931), pp. 40–41, 112–13, 279; Art Assoc. of Indianapolis, *A Record* (1906); Inez H. Irwin, *Angels and Amazons* (1934). Death certificate from Ind. State Board of Health, Indianapolis.]

CLIFTON J. PHILLIPS

**SEYMOUR, Mary Foot** (1846–Mar. 21, 1893), stenographer, businesswoman, and journalist, was born in Aurora, Ill., to Ephraim Sanford Seymour and Rosette (Bestor) Seymour, of Vermont and Connecticut stock. Her father, a graduate of Middlebury (Vt.) College, had studied law before settling in Illinois. While practicing in Galena, he published *The Galena Directory and Miner's Annual Register*. He also wrote an *Emigrant's Guide to the Gold Mines* and *Sketches of Minnesota*. After Seymour's death, in Nevada City, Calif., in 1851, his widow took the children (two girls and two boys) to Wilbraham, Mass., where a married sister lived. Mary was educated at private schools there and in Somerville, N.J., for both families moved to Jersey City in 1858. She completed her education at the Twelfth Street School in New York City in 1864.

Mary Seymour early showed an interest in writing, composing verse and stories for children which she published under a pseudonym. She tried schoolteaching in New York City and in Jersey City, where in 1874–75 she taught the second grade in Public School 13. Her health was not good, and she filled periods of enforced rest by teaching herself shorthand, with a view to becoming a law reporter. With the manufacture and marketing of the first efficient typewriters in the late 1870's, Miss Seymour realized that the device would open up a new field of employment for women, and in 1879 she established the Union School of Stenography at 38 Park Row, New York City. At one time she operated four schools in the city, besides a business (the Union Stenographic Company) employing twenty-five "type-writers," as stenographers were then called, and an employment bureau, the Union Stenographic and Typewriting Association. In 1884 she moved to New York City to be near her work.

Her interest in preparing women for jobs in business, together with her writing ability, led her to start in January 1889 the bimonthly *Business Woman's Journal*. According to the prospectus, each number was to include an account of a successful woman, articles of interest to women in business, and news of women's organizations. In addition to editorials and most of the unsigned items, Mary Seymour herself contributed a series, "Practical Hints to Stenographers and Type-writers," which was later issued separately. Publication of the *Journal* was soon placed in the hands of the Mary F. Seymour Publishing Company, organized by Miss Seymour early in 1889. It was capitalized at $50,000; stock was offered on terms as low as $2.50 per month, and each stockholder was to receive a free subscription to the *Journal* and a discount on advertising therein. All the officers were women. Miss Seymour served as president, and the vice-presidents included Mrs. MAY WRIGHT SEWALL, Mrs. ISABELLA BEECHER HOOKER, FRANCES E. WILLARD, and Miss Willard's friend the English temperance reformer Lady Henry Somerset.

In the type chosen, use of pictures, and general layout, the *Journal* presented an attractive appearance. Its content was, at least much of the time, practical and sprightly. The subscription price was a dollar a year, and in time it attained a regular distribution of some 5,000 copies. In October 1892, hoping to capture a broader audience, Miss Seymour launched the *American Woman's Journal*, of which the *Business Woman's Journal* now became a department. The section on stenography and typewriting was continued; there were also columns on such topics as occupations for women, reliable investments, insurance, the home circle, and advice to housewives.

Mary Seymour put her stenographic and editorial talents to work assisting various women's groups. She prepared the stenographic report of the inaugural meeting of the International Council of Women in Washington, D.C., in 1888. In 1891 she attended the First Triennial Council of the National Council of Women, as a delegate from the Women's Press Club of New York, delivering a speech, "Occupations of Women to Date," which later appeared in the *Journal*. Miss Seymour served as a commissioner of the federal Court of Claims for New York City; in 1884 she is said to have been appointed a commissioner of deeds for the State of New Jersey. She was an advocate of woman suffrage. She died of pneumonia at her New York home in 1893, aged about forty-seven. A Methodist minister conducted her funeral, assisted by the Rev. PHEBE HANAFORD, well known in woman's rights circles. Burial was in the Bay Cemetery. The *Journal* survived its founder by only three years.

[Files of the *Business Woman's Jour.*, 1889–93 (the most complete set is in the Kans. State Hist. Soc.; microfilm in Schlesinger Library, Radcliffe College), including pieces about Miss Seymour in Apr. 1893 and Apr. 1894; Frances E. Willard and Mary A. Livermore, eds., *A Woman of the Century* (1893), with photograph; *Appletons' Annual Cyc.*, 1893, p. 568; *N.Y. Times*, Mar. 22, 1893; *N.Y. Daily Tribune*, Mar. 22–24, 1893; death certificate. See also Internat. Council of Women, *Report*, 1888, pp. 455 and 456n; and, for the family history of her mother, Arthur H. Radasch, *Barstow-Bestor Genealogy* (1964), pp. 181–82.]

ROBERT W. LOVETT

**SHADD, Mary Ann.** *See* CARY, Mary Ann Shadd.

**SHARP, Katharine Lucinda** (May 21, 1865– June 1, 1914), librarian, founder of the Illinois State Library School, was born in Elgin, Ill., the only child of John William and Phebe (Thompson) Sharp. She had one younger half brother, born in 1881 of her father's second marriage. Her maternal grandfather, Thomas Hinckley Thompson, had been an early settler of Dundee, Ill.; her father, a commission merchant, was a native of Arkport, N.Y. By 1869 he had moved his office and his family to Chicago, but in 1872 his wife died, and Katharine, then seven, was left with relatives in Dundee and Elgin. She attended Elgin Academy and at sixteen was admitted to Northwestern University in Evanston, Ill. An energetic and efficient student, active in the affairs of her class, she graduated, Ph.B., in 1885; four years later she received the degree of Ph.M. From 1886 to 1888 she taught Latin, French, and German at Elgin Academy, but she soon found that secondary teaching did not interest her. In October 1888 she took a position as assistant librarian of the new Scoville Institute in Oak Park, Ill., later the Oak Park Public Library.

Her interest in the library profession deeply aroused by this first post, Miss Sharp in the fall of 1890 entered the pioneering New York State Library School at Albany, directed by Melvil Dewey. She graduated with the B.L.S. degree (Bachelor of Library Science) in 1892, at the age of twenty-seven. Already, in the summer of 1891, she had organized one library (the Adams Memorial Library in Wheaton, Ill.); in the ensuing year she set up another (the public library in Xenia, Ohio) and prepared a "Comparative Library Exhibit" on behalf of the New York State Library School for display at the Chicago World's Fair of 1893. As a result of the attention her work received, she was in December 1893 appointed librarian

of the newly established Armour Institute of Technology at Chicago and head of its "department of library economy"—the first library school in the Middle West. During her four years there she trained forty-one librarians, among them such later leaders of the profession as Cornelia Marvin Pierce (d. 1957), ALICE S. TYLER, and Margaret Mann.

During this period Miss Sharp took an active part in state and national library affairs, directing a summer school for the Wisconsin Library Association in 1895 and 1896, promoting the development of libraries in Illinois through the State Teachers' Association and the State Federation of Women's Clubs, and winning election, in 1895, to the council of the American Library Association. She served on the council for ten years, in 1898 and in 1907 as vice-president. These professional activities, combined with the reputation of her school for producing thoroughly trained librarians, called attention to Miss Sharp's abilities, and in the spring of 1897 she had two offers—one from the University of Wisconsin and the other from the University of Illinois—to move her school to a state university where it could be better supported. The Armour authorities were agreeable, and in September 1897 Miss Sharp went to the University of Illinois as professor of library economy, head librarian, and director of the Illinois State Library School.

At the time of its move to the University of Illinois, Miss Sharp's school offered the B.L.S. degree, since its two-year curriculum required two years of college courses for admission. A strong advocate of a full bachelor's degree as a prerequisite for library training, Miss Sharp lived to see that requirement established at Illinois in 1911; and during her own directorship, in 1903, the admission requirement rose to three years. By 1900 seventy-five students were enrolled in the school, which was, from the beginning, one of the foremost library schools in the United States. Meanwhile Miss Sharp, with the close support of President Andrew S. Draper of the University of Illinois, set about building a strong university library, gathering together scattered book collections, weeding out and supplementing them, reclassifying and recataloguing them. She also built up an expert staff of trained librarians to head the library's operating departments and teach in the library school. She herself was an especially able teacher.

Though teaching and administration occupied most of Miss Sharp's time, she was also a clear and convincing writer. Of her published articles and unpublished addresses, the most important is her *Illinois Libraries* (University of Illinois, *University Studies,* vol. II, nos. 1, 3, 6–8, 1906–08), an 800-page history of all libraries in the state, public, academic, and special; for this study Miss Sharp received the M.L.S. degree from the New York State Library School in 1907. She took an active part in the university's social life and was a faithful member of the local Episcopal church. Her tendency to push herself too hard took its toll, and her health, never strong, seriously declined in the years 1905–07. Depressed, too, by her father's death, followed closely by that of her much-loved half brother, she resigned in 1907; the university that year awarded her an honorary Master of Arts degree. In her retirement Miss Sharp went to live with her good friends the librarian Melvil Dewey and his wife at their Lake Placid Club in the Adirondack Mountains of New York. In 1914, shortly after her forty-ninth birthday, she was seriously injured in an automobile accident. She died a few days later in Saranac Lake, N.Y., and was buried in the Dundee, Ill., cemetery.

Tall and fine looking, Katharine Sharp was a woman of distinguished bearing and presence. She possessed administrative skill and a keen mastery of her emerging profession. Her shortcomings were closely related to her virtues: firm and decisive, she seemed pedantic and inflexible to some faculty members; indefatigable in her own work, she sometimes appeared to be a relentless taskmaster. She was naturally self-contained, but despite their awe of her, she won her students' constant admiration (as one of them has written) by "her splendid mind, her dignity, her gracious bearing, and her love of her profession." A bronze bas-relief portrait by the sculptor Lorado Taft, located in the University of Illinois Graduate School of Library Science, perpetuates her memory.

[MS. materials at the Univ. of Ill. Library, including the Sharp letterbooks and papers, 1893–1907, and a collection of memorial letters about her; Laurel Grotzinger, *The Power and the Dignity: Librarianship and Katharine Sharp* (1966); Frances Simpson, *Katharine L. Sharp (An Appreciation)* (pamphlet, 1914); sketch by Harriet E. Howe in Emily M. Danton, ed., *Pioneering Leaders in Librarianship* (1953); obituaries in *Library Jour.,* July 1914, and *Public Libraries,* July 1914; *ibid.,* Nov. 1921, p. 567, and May 1922, pp. 292–93 (on the memorial bas-relief); *Woman's Who's Who of America,* 1914–15; Univ. of Ill. Library School Assoc., *Fifty Years of Education for Librarianship* (1943). See also biographical sketches in *N.Y. State Library School Register, 1887–1926* (1959) and Northwestern Univ., *Alumni Record of the College of Liberal Arts* (1903); Sarah K. Vann, *Training for Librarianship before 1923* (1961); George G. Dawe, *Melvil Dewey* (1932); and Wayne S. Yenawine, "The Influence of Schol-ars on Research Library Development at the Univ. of Ill." (unpublished doctoral thesis, Univ. of Ill., 1955).]

ROSE B. PHELPS

SHATTUCK, Lydia White (June 10, 1822–Nov. 2, 1889), naturalist, botanist, and teacher of science, was born in East Landaff (later Easton), N.H., to Timothy and Betsey (Fletcher) Shattuck, both natives of Massachusetts. Five older children had died before Lydia's birth; she and a younger brother alone survived infancy. Her father, a descendant of William Shattuck, who had come from England to Watertown, Mass., about 1642, was a farmer of sturdy New England stock, intellectual, kindly, and deeply religious. His land near the Franconia Mountains was extensive but not richly productive. From her mother Lydia acquired an aesthetic perception which from her earliest years led to an enjoyment of the wild flowers that she sought in her ramblings.

Lydia's local schooling was soon completed, and at fifteen she was teaching district school. For short periods during the next eleven years she took time out from teaching to study at academies or schools in Haverhill, N.H., Center Harbor, N.H., and Newbury, Vt. At twenty-six she entered Mount Holyoke Seminary at South Hadley, Mass., where she came under the influence of its founder, MARY LYON, in the last months of Miss Lyon's life. She also developed from her love of flowers an absorbing interest in botany as a science. After her graduation with honor in 1851, she stayed on as a teacher.

Lydia Shattuck was the outstanding figure of her generation in carrying forward at Mount Holyoke the tradition of scientific instruction that Mary Lyon had instituted. This she did through her own excellent, scholarly teaching, through indoctrination of younger instructors, and by helping secure various distinguished visiting professors to teach short science courses. Her own scientific background developed largely from her keen observations, intelligent training, wide reading, and association with scientists of other institutions. When the Anderson School of Natural History at Penikese Island, off Woods Hole, Mass., began in the summer of 1873, she was one of the fifty persons (fifteen of them women) carefully chosen as pupils by Louis Agassiz from hundreds of applicants. There she had the valuable experience of exploring the field of marine biology and of making new acquaintances among some of the foremost naturalists of the day. Also richly productive for her work as a naturalist were her various travels, which took her to Europe, Canada, California, and Hawaii.

Her field of research was typical of her generation—the classification of plants and the setting up of collections—and she excelled in both. With the aid of inspired students and graduates as collectors, the Mount Holyoke Seminary herbarium came to contain thousands of carefully analyzed specimens of plants, seeds, and woods from all over the world. Through her efforts the seminary established a botanical garden, and many of its wild treasures she herself collected and transplanted there. Miss Shattuck had few, if any, scientific publications; correspondence with other botanists took their place. She was made a member of the Woods Hole Biological Laboratory Corporation, and at one time was president of the Connecticut Valley Botanical Association. In the estimate of one of her contemporaries (Prof. C. A. Young of Princeton), Miss Shattuck's "attainments as a botanist and student of natural history" were "remarkable for the time, and . . . there were very few women in the country who could be ranked with her in that respect."

The students caught her energetic enthusiasm and recognized her mastery of the material that she taught. Next to botany, chemistry was her favorite subject; others were physics, physiology, and astronomy. While training her students in science she also helped them see the beauty and poetry in nature. Since to her the beauty of nature was an expression of the divine, it was to her great credit as a scientist that she accepted the controversial theory of evolution and promoted it at Mount Holyoke, where conservative religious tradition was strong. Her friendship with Asa Gray, the noted Harvard University botanist and an early exponent of Darwinism, may have helped her adopt this point of view.

Miss Shattuck won the deep affection of students and colleagues. Her gracious, gentle manner was without ostentation; her disposition serene, modest, and friendly. In appearance she was distinguished and singularly attractive, with bright blue eyes, a clear complexion, regular features, and fair, curly hair that became snow white in later years. Throughout her life she remained a member of the Methodist Church, the denomination of her upbringing. In 1888 Mount Holyoke Seminary became a college, and upon her retirement the next year Miss Shattuck received the title of professor emeritus. After several months in poor health she died that fall at Mount Holyoke of "a complication of heart, lung, and kidney difficulties" and was buried in Evergreen Cemetery, South Hadley, Mass. In the 1890's a building erected

to house the college's work in chemistry and physics was named in her memory; when this was demolished in 1954, the name was transferred to a later building for physics.

[*Memorial of Lydia W. Shattuck* (1890), which includes a biographical sketch and tributes; Lemuel Shattuck, *Memorials of the Descendants of William Shattuck* (1855); archives of Mount Holyoke College; Arthur C. Cole, *A Hundred Years of Mount Holyoke College* (1940); death record from Mass. Registrar of Vital Statistics.]

CHARLOTTE HAYWOOD

SHAW, Anna Howard (Feb. 14, 1847–July 2, 1919), minister, lecturer, and suffragist, was born in Newcastle-on-Tyne, England, the youngest of three surviving daughters and sixth of seven surviving children of Thomas Shaw and his wife, Nicolas Stott. Her father was of northern Highland extraction; her mother came of a Scottish family that had settled in Alnwick, Northumberland County. The Stotts were among the earliest English Unitarians; Anna's grandmother stood by each year while some of her furniture was taken to be sold for the Church of England tithes which she refused to pay. Thomas Shaw, a skilled maker of wallpaper, gave up his craft to open a flour and grain business, but when this failed in 1845 the family's situation quickly deteriorated. Three years after Anna's birth he sailed for America, where Mrs. Shaw and the children joined him in the spring of 1851.

After a year in New Bedford, they settled in Lawrence, Mass., where Thomas Shaw became involved with the reform movements of the day (his house was a station on the Underground Railroad). An engaging but impractical man, in 1859 he joined with other Englishmen hoping to establish a frontier colony and took up a 360-acre claim in Michigan. At a site nine miles from the nearest settlement, which later became the town of Big Rapids, he made a clearing in the woods and built a crude log cabin without flooring and with only empty holes for doors and windows. Returning with his second and third sons to Lawrence to resume his old trade, he sent his wife and four youngest children to live on the Michigan claim, under the care of his eldest son, twenty-year-old James. Overwhelmed by the isolation and primitive living conditions, Mrs. Shaw suffered a temporary mental breakdown and became a semi-invalid. When after a few months James became ill and returned to Massachusetts, twelve-year-old Anna and her younger brother Henry were forced to assume the burden of the family's survival. While the older sisters attended to the domestic chores, Anna and Henry learned to cut wood, haul water, make furniture, and plow the land. Thomas Shaw occasionally sent money and boxes of books, and after eighteen months briefly rejoined his family, but at the outbreak of the Civil War he and his older sons enlisted, again leaving his wife and children to fend for themselves. During these years, Anna later remembered, life "degenerated into a treadmill"; she developed both a low opinion of men's abilities and an ambition to excel in a man's world, passions that helped shape her career. About this time she also decided that she would like "to talk to people, to tell them things" and began preaching sermons to the trees in the surrounding forest.

Anna had had some schooling in Lawrence and had become an omnivorous reader. At thirteen she resumed her formal education, in a newly built frontier schoolhouse. Two years later she began teaching in a similar school. She refused an offer of marriage, and after the end of the war she moved to Big Rapids, where she lived with a married sister, in order to learn a trade. There for the first time she heard a woman minister, a Universalist, to whom she confided her desire to preach. When the Rev. Marianna Thompson advised her that the first step was an education, she enrolled in the local high school. Encouraged by the principal, Lucy Foot (a Methodist), she studied debating and elocution. A movement was then under way in Methodist churches to license women ministers, and Miss Foot brought Anna to the attention of the presiding elder of the district. At his urging, Anna Shaw preached her first sermon in 1870. Some thirty-five others followed, one in each town of the district, and in 1871 she was licensed as a preacher.

Her Unitarian family were hostile not only to her "conversion" to Methodism but also to her preaching; they offered to send her to the University of Michigan if she would give up her vocation. In turning down their aid, Anna Shaw made the decision to take the hard way toward her goal whatever the cost, a resolution in which she was strengthened by the active encouragement of MARY A. LIVERMORE, whom she met after a lecture in Big Rapids. Despite inadequate preparation and meager resources, in 1873, at the age of twenty-six, she entered Albion College, a Methodist coeducational institution in Michigan, where she earned money for board by preaching and giving lectures on temperance. After little more than two years she decided not to postpone training for the ministry any longer, and in February 1876 she enrolled in the divinity school of Boston University.

This step proved a hazardous one, for as a woman she was ineligible for the assistance available to young men preparing for ordination. For room and board Miss Shaw was dependent on what she could earn by "substitute preaching," and she very nearly starved before she was rescued by members of the Woman's Foreign Missionary Society. Later she was able to add to that organization's stipend by taking temporary charge of a church in nearby Hingham, Mass. She graduated with a certificate in 1878, the only woman in her class.

After a three-month tour of Europe, made possible by the legacy of a friend, in October 1878 she was called as pastor to a Methodist church at East Dennis on Cape Cod, and was also given temporary charge of a nearby Congregational church. In order to be able to administer the sacraments, she applied for ordination, but the New England Conference of the Methodist Episcopal Church refused to ordain a woman, and when Miss Shaw appealed their decision to the General Conference, it not only sustained the action but also revoked her license to preach. She thereupon applied to the Methodist Protestant Church and, after a sharp debate, was ordained in October 1880, that denomination's first woman minister.

Miss Shaw held her two posts for seven years, but the work proved insufficiently challenging to a woman of her inexhaustible energies. Feeling that as a physician she could perhaps be more useful to women, in 1883 she enrolled in the medical school of Boston University, spending several days a week in Boston to pursue her studies; in addition, she began to speak on the issues of temperance and woman suffrage. She was graduated with the degree of M.D. in 1886, but she had come to believe that both the ministry and medicine were limited in their ability to deal with basic social problems, particularly those of women. Increasingly she was drawn to the conclusion that there was "but one solution for women— the removal of the stigma of disfranchisement" (Story of a Pioneer, p. 151). In 1885 she had resigned both her pastorates and taken a position as lecturer and organizer with the Massachusetts Woman Suffrage Association. Friendship with FRANCES WILLARD led her also to become superintendent of the Franchise (suffrage) Department of the national Woman's Christian Temperance Union, a post she held from 1888 to 1892. Meanwhile, in 1887, she resigned from her work with the state suffrage association to embark on a career as a lecturer. This not only enabled her to earn a living but provided a forum for promoting both of her favorite causes, temperance and suffrage.

The most decisive factor in this development was her friendship with SUSAN B. ANTHONY. Dr. Shaw had preached a striking sermon before the International Council of Women in 1888 which caught Miss Anthony's interest. In the forty-one-year-old minister she recognized a talent for oratory which the suffrage movement sorely needed, as well as qualities of warmth, humor, and devotion, combined in a woman unhampered by domestic responsibilities. Miss Anthony sat up an entire night with Dr. Shaw, persuading her to put her gifts to the service of the suffrage cause. The combination of personal appeal and principled conviction proved decisive, as was always the case with the dynamic but essentially lonely woman preacher. Already active in the American Woman Suffrage Association through her friendship with LUCY STONE and Henry Blackwell, Dr. Shaw was drawn into work for the rival National Association even before the two groups merged in 1890. The following year she was appointed national lecturer of the newly united National American Woman Suffrage Association, and when Susan Anthony became its president in 1892, Anna Howard Shaw became vice-president, a position she held until 1904.

From that time on her life was merged with the suffrage movement. She became a familiar figure at annual conventions and Congressional hearings on the proposed woman suffrage amendment to the Constitution, as well as in the innumerable campaigns held in connection with state referenda on suffrage. An unimpressive five feet tall, she was stocky in build; as she grew older, her white hair swept up in a pompadour lent dignity, and her flashing black eyes and quick smile, added to her compelling eloquence, made her an arresting platform personality. She spoke in every state in the union. The extent of her travels, the hardships imposed by bad weather and poor accommodations, her mounting fatigue, the great number of meetings at which she poured out (in the words of CARRIE CHAPMAN CATT) "her incomparable eloquence on the unregenerate of the land" (letter to Mary G. Peck, Jan. 10, 1913) are documented in her correspondence, especially in her letters to Lucy Anthony, niece of Susan B. Anthony, who was for thirty years her friend and secretary. In 1903 Anna Shaw built a home at Moylan, Pa., which she and Lucy Anthony shared until her death. Other friends included many of the leading women reformers of her day. President M. CAREY

THOMAS of Bryn Mawr College was a close associate in later years.

Dr. Shaw's dearest wish was to succeed to the leadership of the National American Woman Suffrage Association when Susan B. Anthony retired, but when, in 1900, the post went instead to Carrie Chapman Catt, she served loyally under her leadership. When Mrs. Catt resigned in 1904, Dr. Shaw became president. Anna Howard Shaw took up the task of leading the suffrage movement at a time when it needed strong yet flexible guidance, which she was unable to provide. She was a poor administrator, lacked the art of working closely with others, and was inclined to be suspicious of the motives and abilities of those who differed with her. She also antagonized men, whose votes were essential to the success of the suffrage cause. Most serious of all, she lacked judgment, so that during the eleven years of her presidency, though the suffrage movement in general showed increasing vitality, the organization which should have channeled the forces fell more and more into confusion. Lack of any definite strategy, and in particular the abandonment of active work for the federal suffrage amendment, led in 1914 to the formation of a new organization, the Congressional Union, which at first worked within the fold of the N.A.W.S.A. but very shortly came into open conflict with it. Dr. Shaw tried hard to find common ground with the union's energetic young leaders, Alice Paul and Lucy Burns, especially since she had originally encouraged their efforts. Her attempts failed, both because of the widening rift in policy between the two groups and because she could no longer command the support of her own organization, by now rent with dissatisfaction. In November 1915 she announced that she would not stand for reelection at the forthcoming annual convention.

Dr. Shaw was unenthusiastic about Mrs. Catt's return to the presidency of the N.A.W.S.A.—her own choice would have been HARRIET BURTON LAIDLAW. She remained on the association's board, but as Mrs. Catt brought in her own lieutenants Dr. Shaw was somewhat shunted aside. She nevertheless put her best oratory into the closing campaigns of the suffrage struggle. With the entry of the United States into World War I she was asked to serve as chairman of the Woman's Committee of the United States Council of National Defense and threw herself—her energies still phenomenal at seventy—into the job of coordinating women's contributions to the war effort. Her committee had little authority, but she did her stubborn best to keep other government agencies from invading its field of responsibility and to make the voice of women heard. In May 1919 she was awarded the Distinguished Service Medal for her wartime services.

During her war work Dr. Shaw continued to speak and work for suffrage whenever her heavy schedule permitted. She expected to return to full-time effort for the cause, but another urgent plea for her services took precedence—a plea to join ex-President William Howard Taft and President A. Lawrence Lowell of Harvard in a speaking tour, sponsored by the League to Enforce Peace, to rally public support for Woodrow Wilson's projected peace treaty, and especially for the League of Nations. This effort, coming in her seventy-third year on top of her strenuous exertions at the Council of National Defense, proved too much. In June 1919 Dr. Shaw was taken ill with pneumonia, in Springfield, Ill. She rallied enough to return to her home at Moylan, Pa., where she died a few weeks later; her body was cremated. She lived long enough to know that the suffrage amendment had at last passed both houses of Congress and was on its way to ratification.

[Anna Howard Shaw Papers, Schlesinger Library, Radcliffe College; Anna Howard Shaw (with Elizabeth Jordan), *The Story of a Pioneer* (1915); Ida H. Harper, *The Life and Work of Susan B. Anthony*, vols. II–III (1898–1908); Susan B. Anthony and Ida H. Harper, eds., *The Hist. of Woman Suffrage*, vols. IV–VI (1902–22); Eleanor Flexner, *Century of Struggle: The Woman's Rights Movement in the U.S.* (1959); N. Y. *Times* obituary, July 3, 1919. See also: Nat. Am. Woman Suffrage Assoc., *Anna Howard Shaw, A Memorial* (pamphlet, 1919?); Helen C. Bennett, *Am. Women in Civic Work* (1915); Emily N. Blair, *The Woman's Committee, U.S. Council of Nat. Defense* (1920); Wil A. Linkugel, "The Speeches of Anna Howard Shaw" (Ph.D. dissertation, Univ. of Wis., 1960; copy in Schlesinger Library, Radcliffe); Linkugel and Kim Giffin, "The Distinguished War Service of Dr. Anna Howard Shaw," *Pa. Hist.*, Oct. 1961. For recent evaluations of Anna Howard Shaw, see James R. McGovern, "Anna Howard Shaw: New Approaches to Feminism," *Jour. of Social Hist.*, Winter 1969; and William L. O'Neill, *Everyone Was Brave: The Rise and Fall of Feminism in America* (1969).]

ELEANOR FLEXNER

**SHAW, Mary G.** (Jan. 25, 1854–May 18, 1929), actress, was born in Boston, Mass., the daughter of Levi W. and Margaret (Keating) Shaw, natives respectively of Wolfeboro, N.H., and of Ireland. Her father, a carpenter and builder, was for many years assistant inspector of buildings for the city of Boston. Mary Shaw

graduated from the Girls' High and Normal School in Boston in 1871 and then taught in her native city. When her voice gave out because of constant use in the classroom, she studied elocution, which led in turn to her interest in the theatre. Her initial efforts to make a career on the professional stage in New York were fruitless, and she returned to Boston, where she acted intermittently with amateur groups, then joined the Boston Museum stock company in 1879, beginning as a chorus member in the extravaganza *A Robisonade*. With the help of FANNY DAVENPORT, whom she had supported at the Museum, she obtained an engagement with Augustin Daly's company. The next season she played Lady Sneerwell to Miss Davenport's Lady Teazle when the latter's production of Sheridan's *The School for Scandal* opened at the Park Theatre in Brooklyn in October 1881 and at the Grand Opera House in New York the following May. In 1883 she began several seasons with HELENA MODJESKA's repertory company; her roles included Celia in *As You Like It*, Mariana in *Measure for Measure*, and Elizabeth in *Mary Stuart*. From 1888 to 1890 she toured with JULIA MARLOWE.

Modjeska later recalled Miss Shaw as "a studious, intellectual young woman, with a great deal of talent" (*Memories and Impressions*, 1910, p. 463), but for a time her ability gained little recognition. Her first starring venture, in the spring of 1890, as Herthe in a touring production of *A Drop of Poison* (adapted from the German of Oscar Blumenthal), met with indifferent success. For most of the following decade she played in supporting roles and touring companies—among them Joseph Jefferson's *Rip Van Winkle* and MINNIE MADDERN FISKE's *Tess of the D'Urbervilles*. She did, however, portray Mrs. Alving when Ibsen's *Ghosts* opened at the Carnegie Lyceum, New York, on May 29, 1899, and she originated the role of Amrah in William Young's effective dramatization of Lew Wallace's *Ben Hur* at the Broadway Theatre the following November.

Miss Shaw was among the first actresses, along with Modjeska, Mrs. Fiske, ALLA NAZIMOVA, and Beatrice Cameron, to introduce Ibsen to American audiences; and the most significant phase of her career began in 1903 when for thirty-seven weeks she starred in a road production of *Ghosts* which took her as far west as Denver, Colo. During the following years she toured the United States intermittently in *Ghosts* and in *Hedda Gabler*. Of Ibsen, she affirmed: "He is grand, he is unique —the dominating influence, I suppose, upon the drama of our time, and doubtless in the future"

(*Theatre Magazine,* May 1902). At the Garrick Theatre in October 1905 she created the part of Mrs. Warren in the first New York production of Bernard Shaw's *Mrs. Warren's Profession.* To the *New York Times* reviewer (Oct. 31), she "reflected to an astonishingly offensive, natural degree the abandoned creatures after whom she has evidently modeled herself." The play was closed by the police as "revolting, indecent, and nauseating where it was not boring"; but, following a favorable decision by the state supreme court, Miss Shaw returned to New York in a second production (Manhattan Theatre, Mar. 9, 1907), which afterward traveled across the country to California. Her impassioned advocacy of Ibsen and Shaw, and of neglected native plays such as James A. Herne's controversial *Margaret Fleming,* generally met with slight encouragement; yet she was honored, in 1899, by an invitation to speak at St. Martin's Hall, London, on "The Stage as a Means of Livelihood in America." To "hear her speak from the platform," wrote "H. T." in the *Theatre Magazine* (August 1902), ". . . is to confirm the impression of an extraordinary intellectual force, mixed in some strange way with a frankly feminine charm. . . . She has rich bronze hair. . . . Her eyes are intensely blue . . . sparkling, laughing or tender by turns, and again, in moments of earnestness, confronting you with the steady, inscrutable blaze of infinite horizons."

An ardent feminist, Miss Shaw in 1893 portrayed Rosalind in the Professional Women's League's anomalous all-woman *As You Like It* (Palmer's Theatre, New York, Nov. 21). She later promoted the suffrage movement by starring in Elizabeth Robins' *Votes for Women* (Wallack's Theatre, New York, Mar. 15, 1909). She was a member of the Episcopal Actors' Guild. Mary Shaw directed Strindberg's *Countess Julia* (48th Street Theatre, New York, Apr. 28, 1913), and continued into the 1920's to appear on the stage, acting in the season before her death in the Civic Repertory Company's touring production of *The Cradle Song.* She died of heart disease in New York City at the age of seventy-five; her remains were cremated at the Fresh Pond Crematory, Middle Village, N.Y. She was married twice. Little is known of her first husband, by whom she had a son, the actor Arthur Shaw. Her second marriage, about 1885, to a French actor-director of Modjeska's company, the Duc de Brissac, ended in divorce.

[Lewis C. Strang, *Famous Actresses of the Day in America* (1899) and *ibid.,* Second Series (1902); "Mary Shaw—A Woman of Thought and Action," *Theatre Mag.,* Aug. 1902; Mary Shaw, "My 'Immoral' Play: The Story of the First Am. Production of 'Mrs. Warren's Profession,'" *McClure's Mag.,* Apr. 1912; Rose Young, "Suffrage as Seen by Mary Shaw," *Harper's Weekly,* May 8, 1915; *N.Y. Times* obituary, May 19, 1929; clippings in Harvard Theatre Collection; enrollment records of Girls' High School, Boston; Boston city directories, 1854–78.]

PAT M. RYAN

SHAW, Pauline Agassiz (Feb. 6, 1841–Feb. 10, 1917), educational philanthropist, was born in Neuchâtel, Switzerland, the second daughter and youngest of three children. Her father, the famed naturalist Louis (Jean Louis Rodolphe) Agassiz, was the son of a Swiss Protestant minister. He had married Cécile Braun, the delicate, artistically talented daughter of a cultivated German official in Karlsruhe, Baden, early in his career and was in the United. States pursuing scientific investigations when she died of tuberculosis in 1848. Pauline and her older sister Ida lived with relatives in Europe until their father remarried in 1850. Soon thereafter the children joined their father and stepmother—ELIZABETH CABOT CARY AGASSIZ, daughter of a substantial Boston merchant—in Cambridge, Mass., where Agassiz had accepted a Harvard professorship. Mrs. Agassiz, to supplement the family purse, conducted a special school for girls, at which Agassiz and several of his colleagues served as part-time teachers. The great names of the Cambridge intellectual community were familiar visitors to the home; in this circle, and in her stepmother's school, young Pauline acquired a graceful manner and a sparkling liberal education.

On Nov. 13, 1860, at nineteen, she was married to Quincy Adams Shaw, sixteen years her senior. The son of a wealthy, philanthropic Boston businessman, Shaw had graduated from Harvard in 1845 and had accompanied Francis Parkman on the trip to the Rockies described in Parkman's *The Oregon Trail.* He later became interested in Michigan copper mining and, combining his financial resources with the technical skills of Pauline's brother, Alexander Agassiz, organized the Calumet and Hecla Mining Company, whose riches formed the basis of his fortune. In his handsome estate on the brow overlooking Jamaica Pond in Boston, Pauline Shaw raised her five children—Louis Agassiz, Pauline, Marian, Quincy Adams, and Robert Gould. At the time of his death in 1908, Shaw was reputed to be one of New England's richest men. His wealth, which had filled his home with superb French landscape paintings, underwrote his wife's and his own munificent philanthropies.

Mrs. Shaw had a passion for the education of the young. The unorthodox nature of her own childhood training opened her mind to vigorous educational experimentalism. Now that she had acquired the means to encourage other people's innovations she acted with swift, tactful energy. Her interest in the flagging young Boston kindergarten movement, begun by ELIZABETH PEABODY and others in the 1860's, ensured its survival in the face of early public apathy. Mrs. Shaw opened two kindergartens, one in Brookline and the other in Jamaica Plain, in the summer of 1877, and as her interest expanded was by 1883 supporting some thirty-one in greater Boston. Many of these were housed in public school buildings, but she financed their staffs and equipment and guided their supervision through her chief assistant in this work, Laliah B. Pingree. Convinced by her experience of the utility of kindergarten education, Mrs. Shaw urged the Boston School Committee, which had in 1879 discontinued the experimental kindergarten it opened in 1870, to reconsider its position. In 1888 the city accepted from her fourteen of her schools, embarking on a program of publicly financed kindergarten education which has steadily expanded since. The proper rearing of children, Mrs. Shaw believed, was "the great problem of the race." Her initiative in bringing money and expertise to the problem gave an important impulse to the kindergarten movement in the East.

Meanwhile her interest in child education opened her eyes to the larger needs of Boston's congested urban life and prompted an ever-deepening commitment to the welfare of the whole community. Concern for the children of working mothers led her to organize a chain of day nurseries, beginning in 1878, and since she regarded these as an enterprise in community advancement as well as a family convenience, soon her nurseries were filling with evening classes in hygiene, temperance, and sewing for mothers and older children. Through the 1890's those of her nurseries which were located in poorer tenement districts evolved into flourishing neighborhood settlement houses—among the first in the city. Their services were calculated to attract both sexes and all ages and included recreational facilities, libraries, and classes in craft skills and citizenship. Mrs. Shaw felt a special compassion for the rootless immigrant, adapted her houses to his special needs wherever possible, and sought to eliminate from their operation all racial discrimination as harmful to the growth of neighborhood cohesion. In a time when public welfare services were primitive or nonexistent, such places

as the Cambridge Neighborhood House and the Ruggles Street Neighborhood House in Boston (both of which began as nurseries in 1879) were valuable in softening the edge of urban poverty.

In Boston's polyglot North End, Mrs. Shaw launched two educational experiments of special note. In 1881 she founded the North Bennet Street Industrial School to give public school children classes in cooking, printing, and metal and woodworking skills. Such training seemed to serve a valid social function and appealed to Mrs. Shaw's taste for the concrete and empirical in education. Soon her school was generating a variety of new programs in the Boston school system. The closely associated Sloyd Training School, which she founded in 1888 (named for a currently popular Scandinavian system of woodwork teaching), turned out teachers of manual training and practical arts not only for Boston but for other parts of the country. At her second major North End project, the Civic Service House on Salem Street, started in 1901 with the help of a young Harvard-educated immigrant, Meyer Bloomfield, Mrs. Shaw tried to implement her concern for the civic training of the foreign-born. This project attracted Boston University's reformist professor Frank Parsons, who organized a Breadwinners' Institute at the Civic Service House to bring enlightenment in history, English, industrial economics, and practical psychology to North End wage earners. In 1907 Mrs. Shaw approved plans drawn up by Parsons for a vocational guidance center at the Civic Service House, intended to aid young men and women in the choice of satisfying careers. Here was the origin of Boston's Vocation Bureau, directed after Parsons' death by Meyer Bloomfield and supported for years by Mrs. Shaw and other Boston philanthropists. The vocational guidance movement spread rapidly through the public schools and gained sponsorship from the education department of Harvard University. Once again, funds intelligently directed had helped create a seminal educational enterprise.

Mrs. Shaw experienced conversion to the cause of woman suffrage only after the movement had reached relative maturity, in the late 1890's. Thereafter she gave it discreet but ample financial support. In 1901 she founded the Boston Equal Suffrage Association for Good Government, its awkward name reflecting her insistence that women look to the vote as an opportunity for civic service as well as a personal right. She served as president of the organization for sixteen years and, more importantly, subsidized the extensive lobbying activities of its executive secretary, Maud Wood Park (d. 1955). She provided office space for local suffragists, bolstered the finances of ALICE STONE BLACKWELL's weekly suffrage newspaper, the *Woman's Journal*, and contributed large sums to suffrage campaigns in Massachusetts and various Western states. Mrs. Shaw believed that the West, with its new and unfixed political traditions, if properly encouraged, would be the scene of important triumphs for the movement, and her faith was vindicated after 1910. Toward the end of her life she remarked that woman suffrage and world peace were the two great causes of the day, and that the achievement of the first would enhance the prospects for the second. She supported numerous peace organizations.

A woman of august beauty and charm, Mrs. Shaw was plagued throughout her adult life by delicate health and occasional mental depression. Perhaps her private anxieties accentuated the sensitivity for others which is reflected in her letters and work. She rarely displayed her enthusiasms in public, and her pleasure at seeing her projects flower never yielded to paternalistic self-indulgence. In an age when community welfare depended heavily on the conscience of the rich, she brought an air of quiet stewardship to the office of philanthropy. "I had too much," she wrote to her children a few months before her death, "—you will all have too much—and it will require great effort with God's help to determine 'to give' rather than 'to hold,' and to think deeply as you spend; to spend for progress and welfare rather than for 'pleasure'—or mere temporary amusement." Mrs. Shaw concluded simply: "What I had, I chose to spend in asking others to work with me." She died of bronchial pneumonia shortly after her seventy-sixth birthday at her home in Boston's Jamaica Plain section, and after services in the First Parish Church (Unitarian) in Brookline was buried at Forest Hills Cemetery in Boston.

[A small collection of Mrs. Shaw's papers is in the Schlesinger Library, Radcliffe College; the library also has an excellent unpublished study by A. Alexandra Pierce, "Pauline Agassiz Shaw: A Memorial Essay" (1959). Appraisals of Mrs. Shaw's work by appreciative contemporaries appear in *Pauline Agassiz Shaw: Tributes Paid Her Memory at the Memorial Service Held Apr. 8, 1917, at Faneuil Hall, Boston* (1917). See also obituary notices in *Boston Transcript*, June 12, 1908 (on her husband), Feb. 10, 12, 1917; Fanny L. Johnson, "Hist. of the Kindergarten Movement in Boston," *Kindergarten Rev.*, Apr. 1902; "Boston Day Nurseries," *ibid.*, Mar. 1902; Robert A. Woods and Albert J. Kennedy, eds., *Handbook of Settlements* (1911), pp. 107–09, 119–21, 123–24, 135–

36; Frank Parsons, "The Vocation Bureau," *Arena,* July 1908; John M. Brewer, *Hist. of Vocational Guidance* (1942), pp. 53–75.]

GEOFFREY BLODGETT

**SHELDON, Mary Downing.** *See* BARNES, Mary Downing Sheldon.

**SHERMAN, Mary Belle King** (Dec. 11, 1862–Jan. 15, 1935), clubwoman, national parks champion, was born in Albion, N.Y., the second in a family of two daughters of Rufus and Sarah Electa (Whitney) King. Through her mother she was descended from John Whitney, who settled in Watertown, Mass., in 1635. Mary spent her early childhood in modest circumstances on a farm near Rochester, N.Y., where she attended public school. When she was about twelve, her father became a partner in an Illinois publishing firm and the family moved to Chicago. There, at St. Xavier's Academy and Park Institute, she completed her education.

On Feb. 10, 1887, in the Chicago suburb of Hyde Park, Mary Belle King, a slender, attractive young woman with titian hair and blue eyes, was married in an Episcopal service (the family's faith) to twenty-seven-year-old John Dickinson Sherman. A Chicago newspaperman, Sherman ultimately became associate editor of the *Inter Ocean* and an editor of the Western Newspaper Union. The couple had one child, John King.

Mrs. Sherman engaged in little outside activity during her son's childhood. She joined the Chicago Woman's Club at the urging of her socially active mother-in-law, Louise Dickinson Sherman, but an assignment to write a paper on "The Nadir of Shakespeare's Unfaith" nearly ended her career as a clubwoman. When, however, a neighborhood study group in parliamentary law met at her home, she became fascinated by the subject and determined to master it. She put her talent to practical use as recording secretary of the Chicago Woman's Club, parliamentarian for the Illinois Federation of Women's Clubs, and (1904–08) recording secretary of the General Federation of Women's Clubs. In addition, she wrote a widely used handbook, *Parliamentary Law at a Glance* (rev. ed., 1901)—later retitled *Parliamentary Law and Rules of Procedure*—and was for a time an instructor in the subject at Chicago's John Marshall Law School.

She was elected a vice-president of the General Federation of Women's Clubs in 1908, but a tropical disease contracted on a tour of women's clubs in the Canal Zone, coupled with a serious shoulder injury in 1913, forced her into virtual retirement from 1910 to 1914.

While recuperating at the family vacation cabin at Estes Park, Colo. (which after 1914 became the Shermans' permanent home), she was inspired by the beauty of the surrounding Rocky Mountain peaks to devote herself to the preservation of outstanding scenic areas. City people especially, she believed, needed the opportunity to find rest and restoration of spirit in such surroundings. As chairman of the conservation department of the General Federation (1914–20), she lobbied strenuously and successfully in Washington for a National Park Service (established in 1916) and for the creation of national park areas in the Rockies (1915), at the Grand Canyon (1919), and in a number of other localities. She persistently urged the inclusion of nature study in the elementary-school curriculum and worked for the planting of trees and shrubs along the nation's highways. For her efforts she was made a vice-president of the American Forestry Association and a trustee and life member of the National Parks Association. In the First World War she served with the United States Bureau of Education as assistant to the director of the "School Garden Army."

In 1924, after four years as head of the applied education department of the General Federation of Women's Clubs, Mary Sherman was elected president of the organization. A hard worker and a quiet leader, she devoted her efforts mainly to improving efficiency at the Washington headquarters, where she spent much of her time, particularly after her husband's death in 1926. The principal innovation in the Federation's program during her presidency was a series of surveys conducted in 1925–27 to gather data on the use of various laborsaving devices in homes throughout the country, and a subsequent publicity campaign to encourage the purchase of such devices and appliances. This project, financed in large part by public utility interests, generated serious charges that the Federation was permitting its name and prestige to be exploited.

Retiring as president in 1928, Mrs. Sherman continued for four years as chairman of the General Federation's Department of the American Home, which she had inaugurated in 1924. She also served from 1926 until her death on the advisory council of the National Broadcasting Company, and in 1925, in recognition of her club leadership and her Republican sympathies, she was appointed by President Coolidge to the George Washington Bicentennial Commission. Her final years were divided between the national capital and her son's home in Denver. In October 1934 she was struck by a bus in Washington. Cerebral thrombosis developed, and she died in Denver the following January, at seventy-two. Her remains were cremated.

No profound thinker, Mary Belle Sherman held conventional views on the major social issues of her day. As president of the General Federation of Women's Clubs she concentrated on administrative detail, doing little to reverse the conservative drift of that organization in the 1920's. Her more lasting contribution was to the national parks movement, for which she rightly won the sobriquet "National Park Lady."

[The Archives of the Gen. Federation of Women's Clubs in Washington contain the published records of Mrs. Sherman's administration as well as of the others in which she served, and some brief MS. biographies. Her speech at the National Parks Conference of 1917, *Women's Part in National Park Development* (U.S. Dept. of the Interior, National Park Service, 1917), is illuminative. Other information from: Mildred M. Scouller, *Women Who Man Our Clubs* (1934), pp. 43–47; Mildred W. Wells, *Unity in Diversity: The Hist. of the Gen. Federation of Women's Clubs* (1953), pp. 87–93, 184–90, 196; Ida C. Clarke, "Have We Found Our 'Female Moses'?" *Pictorial Rev.*, Oct. 1924; Frances D. McMullen, "The National Park Lady," *Woman Citizen*, May 17, 1924; entries on Mrs. Sherman and her husband in *Who Was Who in America*, vol. I (1942), and earlier volumes of *Who's Who*; Frederick C. Pierce, *Whitney: The Descendants of John Whitney* (1895); obituary in *Rocky Mountain News* (Denver), Jan. 16, 1935. Copies of Mrs. Sherman's marriage license application and marriage record were obtained from the County Clerk, Cook County, Ill., and of her death certificate from the Colo. State Dept. of Health, Denver. John King Sherman provided helpful information about his mother and loaned a collection of newspaper clippings.]

DOROTHY E. JOHNSON

**SHERWOOD, Mrs. John.** *See* SHERWOOD, Mary Elizabeth Wilson.

**SHERWOOD, Katharine Margaret Brownlee** (Sept. 24, 1841–Feb. 15, 1914), journalist, poet, and clubwoman, a leader of the Woman's Relief Corps, was born in Poland, Mahoning County, Ohio, the oldest of the three children of James Brownlee, a Scottish immigrant, and his wife, Rebecca Mullen, a native of Pennsylvania. Her father, listed in successive censuses as a farmer, a drover, and an assessor, later became a judge. Kate, as she was usually known, was educated at the Poland Union Seminary. On Sept. 1, 1859, she was married to Isaac Ruth Sherwood, a journalist in various Ohio towns who, after rising to the rank of brigadier general in the Civil War, went into politics, first as a Republican, then as a Greenbacker, and finally as a Democrat. Settling eventually in Toledo, he represented that district in Congress from 1907 until shortly before his death in 1925.

Mrs. Sherwood became an energetic participant in her husband's activities, as well as developing many interests of her own. After her husband enlisted in the Civil War, she took over managing and editing the *Williams County Gazette* in Bryan, Ohio. For some ten years after 1875 she helped her husband edit the *Toledo Journal*. Later she became Washington correspondent for a newspaper syndicate, paid for European travels by writing for the American Press Association, contributed political satires to Charles A. Dana's *New York Sun*, and served as the first president (1902) of the Ohio Newspaper Women's Association. She also began writing verse for various periodicals, two volumes of which were eventually published. The first, *Camp-Fire, Memorial-Day, and Other Poems* (1885), said to have gone through several editions, consisted primarily of patriotic poems of an occasional nature evoking memories of the Civil War, such as "Thomas at Chickamauga," "Memorial Day at Andersonville, 1884," and "Christmas at the Soldiers' Orphans' Home," but also included sentimental items of a more general character like "The Old Gnarled Apple Tree" and "What Do the Roses Say?" The second volume, *Dream of the Ages: A Poem of Columbia* (1893), was a more pretentious long allegorical historical work, rather didactic in tone, whose themes ranged through the early white-Indian conflict, Negroes and slavery, the Civil War and freedom, and the meaning of the flag. She is said to have been the only Northerner ever invited by ex-Confederates to celebrate the Southern soldiers; her poem, written for the unveiling of a statue of Gen. Albert Sidney Johnston in New Orleans, won praise from both sides. She also did French and German translations, particularly of Heine, Goethe, and Friedrich Bodenstedt. Although her work has not achieved any permanent place in American literature, in her day Kate Brownlee Sherwood became widely known as "the poetess of the Congressional circle."

Her strong interest in anything connected with the Civil War led her into the movement to found a female affiliate of the Union veterans' organization, the Grand Army of the Republic. Such a group in Toledo became the model for a number of similar local bodies throughout the Middle West which in 1883 joined with others in the East to form "the Woman's Relief Corps, Auxiliary to the Grand Army of the Republic," of which Mrs. Sher-

wood became the second national president. The Northern counterpart of the United Daughters of the Confederacy, which it antedated by more than a decade, the W.R.C. was one of the first patriotic organizations for women and also one of the largest, having more than 100,000 adherents at the turn of the century. It supplied charitable aid to needy Union veterans, worked in behalf of soldiers' homes, founded institutions of its own for the wives and mothers of veterans, lobbied for pensions for ex-army nurses, and agitated for patriotic instruction in the schools. For a number of years Mrs. Sherwood also edited the woman's department of the *National Tribune* of Washington, the most prominent of the special papers directed to the former Union soldiers and their families.

Her interest in other club and civic work reflected the degree to which increased leisure had now made such activity possible for the urban middle-class woman. Mrs. Sherwood was prominent also in the Daughters of the American Revolution and the National Council of Women (into which she brought the Woman's Relief Corps); was the first president (1893) of the Sorosis Club of Canton, Ohio (she had become a nonresident member of the original Sorosis in New York City in 1870); was secretary of university extension courses in Toledo; worked for the establishment of children's playgrounds, the teaching of patriotism in schools, and woman suffrage; taught a men's Bible class in a Presbyterian church; and was an honorary member of the Toledo Council of Jewish Women. At her death the *Toledo News-Bee* declared, "No other woman has occupied so important a place in Toledo's public life. Her untiring energy was the force behind many a civic improvement, many a step forward in our communal life."

Pleasing in personality, moderately progressive in her causes, Mrs. Sherwood seems to have won widespread respect and admiration. She died in Washington in 1914, a month after a first stroke of paralysis and a week after the second. Secretary of State William Jennings Bryan read part of his lecture "The Prince of Peace" at her funeral services, and the pallbearers included eight Congressmen. She was buried in Woodlawn Cemetery, Toledo. Besides her husband, she left a daughter, Lenore, and a son, James, who was also a journalist in Ohio. Mrs. Sherwood's career reflects the social and professional opportunities that were opening up for able, energetic women in the late nineteenth century. Both her writings and her club life reveal, too, the tremendous impact the Civil War had upon her generation.

[U.S. census schedules for Poland Township, Mahoning County, Ohio, 1850, 1860, and 1870 (Nat. Archives); Frances E. Willard and Mary A. Livermore, eds., *A Woman of the Century* (1893); Harvey Scribner, *Memoirs of Lucas County and the City of Toledo* (1910); *Who's Who in America*, 1912–13; *Nat. Cyc. Am. Biog.*, II, 201; William Coyle, ed., *Ohio Authors and Their Books* (1962); Jane C. Croly, *The Hist. of the Woman's Club Movement in America* (1898), pp. 981–82; obituaries in *Washington Post, Evening Star* (Washington), and *Toledo News-Bee*, Feb. 16, 1914.]

WALLACE EVAN DAVIES

SHERWOOD, Mary (Mar. 31, 1856–May 24, 1935), physician, was born in Ballston Spa, Saratoga County, N.Y., the second daughter and second of six children of Thomas Burr Sherwood and Mary Frances (Beattie) Sherwood. Her father, a descendant of Thomas Sherwood, who had emigrated from Ipswich, England, to Boston in 1634, had graduated from Union College at Schenectady and been admitted to the bar, but chose to engage in farming rather than the law. The family had a tradition of love of learning. Mary's sister Margaret Pollock Sherwood (1864–1955) became professor of English literature at Wellesley College; a brother, Sidney Sherwood (1860–1901), was associate professor of economics at the Johns Hopkins University when his early death cut short a promising career. Mary Sherwood graduated from the State Normal School at Albany, N.Y., and after teaching school for a few years enrolled in Vassar College, where she received her A.B. degree in 1883. She served as an assistant in chemistry at Vassar, 1883–85, and taught geometry and astronomy at Packer Collegiate Institute in Brooklyn, N.Y., in 1885–86. At this time she decided to study medicine. Determined to find a school where her opportunities would be equal to any man's, she chose the University of Zurich in Switzerland, which had been open to women since 1865. During her four years there she studied bacteriology, in one of the first such courses ever offered. She received her M.D. degree in 1890; her thesis on *Polyneuritis recurrens* was published in *Virchow's Archiv*, a German medical journal, in 1891.

On her return to the United States, Dr. Sherwood settled in Baltimore, where her brother Sidney was completing his doctorate in political economy. The Johns Hopkins Hospital was but newly opened, and she presented letters of introduction from her Zurich professors. Denied a residency because of her sex, she nevertheless was welcomed to the wards and laboratories of Drs. William Osler and William Henry Welch, and Dr. Howard Kelly made her an assistant in his private work. In 1892 she was joined by her friend and former classmate at Zurich, Dr. LILIAN WELSH. The two women opened an office together, beginning what was to be a lifelong personal and professional association. Their first two years of practice were lean, but they persevered, encouraged largely, as Dr. Welsh later recalled, by Mary Sherwood's "unbounded optimism and a kind of characteristic obstinacy."

The direction of Dr. Sherwood's professional career was determined in 1894 when she was appointed to succeed Dr. KATE CAMPBELL HURD-MEAD as medical director of the Bryn Mawr School in Baltimore, one of the first girls' secondary schools to provide medical care for its students. Dr. Sherwood considered it her primary task to prevent disease and correct defects, and she became expert in detecting early signs of contagious disease. The work of Dr. Sherwood, and of Dr. Welsh in a similar post at the Woman's College of Baltimore (later Goucher College), drew the attention of the Baltimore Public School Board, which asked them to give physical examinations to prospective teachers, a responsibility Dr. Sherwood continued until it was taken over by the Health Department in 1923. In 1893, she and Dr. Welsh had taken charge of the recently founded Evening Dispensary for Working Women and Girls of Baltimore, an enterprise which not only served a charitable end but also provided clinical experience for women physicians. Dr. Sherwood's association with the dispensary, where she worked regularly until it was given up in 1910, made her acutely aware of the need for better obstetrical and infant care, and she took every opportunity to urge improvements. When the Bureau of Child Welfare of the Baltimore City Health Department was initiated, she was appointed to organize and develop it and served as its director from 1919 to 1924, the first woman to head a municipal bureau in Baltimore. She also served continuously on various municipal boards, among them the Board of City Charities and the Public Baths Commission, as well as on the executive committee of the Babies' Milk Fund Association.

A member of several medical societies and vice-president (1898–99) of the Medical and Chirurgical Faculty of Maryland (the state medical society), Dr. Sherwood served as the first chairman of the obstetrical section of the American Child Health Association. As a member of the Baltimore Association for the Promotion of the University Education of Women, she helped secure the admission of women to graduate schools of the Johns Hopkins University. She also took a prominent part in the woman's club movement in Baltimore. She was a charter member (1894) and one of the original board of managers of the Arundell Club and was active in its subsidiary, the Arundell Good Government Club, which was succeeded by the Women's Civic League. A strong advocate of woman suffrage, she served in February 1906 as physician to the ailing SUSAN B. ANTHONY, who was in Baltimore for a convention of the National American Woman Suffrage Association. From 1923 to 1925 she was a trustee of Goucher College.

A handsome, dignified woman, Mary Sherwood was serious but gracious, forthright but tactful. She attended the Unitarian church. All her life she worked toward securing equal educational, professional, and civic rights for women. Probably her greatest contributions to these goals were her example as a dedicated physician and her major achievements in preventive medicine and child welfare, in a day when women in medicine were handicapped by prejudice. In her last years she limited her practice to work at the Bryn Mawr School, where she was active until the day of her death. She died in Baltimore at the age of seventy-nine following a coronary occlusion, and was buried in London Park Cemetery, Baltimore.

[Lilian Welsh, *Reminiscences of Thirty Years in Baltimore* (1925); *The Sun* (Baltimore), May 26, 1935; Florence R. Sabin, "Doctor Mary Sherwood," *Goucher Alumnae Quart.*, July 1935; Vassar College alumnae records; death record from Baltimore City Health Dept.]

JANET BROCK KOUDELKA

SHERWOOD, Mary Elizabeth Wilson (Oct. 27, 1826–Sept. 12, 1903), author of etiquette books and novels of manners, was born in Keene, N.H., the eldest of seven children, three of them girls, of James and Mary Lord (Richardson) Wilson. The Wilsons, of Scotch-Irish extraction, were a distinguished New Hampshire family. Mary Elizabeth's great-grandfather had fought in the Revolution; her grandfather James Wilson was a member of Congress, as was in later years her father, a lawyer and Whig politician whom Daniel Webster called "the first of the stump speakers." Her mother, who died in 1848, she described as a "beautiful and quiet person" with a "soul made for renunciation."

After earlier schooling in Keene, Mary Elizabeth became a boarder in George B. Emerson's school in Boston. Here, as she later put it, "We learned to be ladies, I hope, for we certainly learned very little else." She was painfully aware of her classmates' fashionable dress and cultivated "Boston pronunciation." "Do you think we attend to *clothes* quite enough, at Keene?" she enquired of her mother (*Epistle*, pp. 12, 14). In 1842 she accompanied her father, then surveyor general of public lands in Iowa and Wisconsin, on a trip to Dubuque, and the sight of tired and sick women, coupled with the horror of finding a snake in her cabin, made her determine "never to undertake frontier life." Much more to her taste was the social whirl of Washington, where she acted as her father's hostess during his three years in Congress (1847–50).

On Nov. 12, 1851, in Keene, she was married to John Sherwood, a New York lawyer, and after a wedding trip to the West Indies they settled in Manhattan. Of their four sons, James Wilson, the eldest, died as a boy, and John Philip, the youngest, in 1883; Samuel (born in 1853) and Arthur Murray (1856) survived. Mrs. Sherwood became a frequent visitor to the salon of ANNE CHARLOTTE LYNCH BOTTA, and soon began giving "literary afternoons" herself to raise money for the restoration of Mount Vernon. With other society ladies she helped organize the great Metropolitan Fair of 1864 for the benefit of the wartime Sanitary Commission. In 1869 the Sherwoods toured England, and thereafter they traveled abroad frequently, spending the season in London and fashionable resorts on the Continent. By the 1870's Mrs. Sherwood's West 32nd Street residence had become a notable social center, but the expenses of maintaining it had seriously depleted her husband's resources. She had contributed verses and stories, some illustrated by her own drawings, to newspapers and magazines for years; now necessity forced her to take up the pen in earnest. Her stories and articles on manners were soon appearing in *Harper's Bazar, Appleton's Journal, Frank Leslie's Weekly,* and other periodicals of the day. Her first novel, *The Sarcasm of Destiny* (1878), aroused little interest, but *A Transplanted Rose* (1882), in which a raw Western girl is transformed into an acceptable member of New York society, was well received. Her most popular work, one which went through many editions, was *Manners and Social Usages,* first published in 1884.

By 1890 Mrs. Sherwood's financial situation had become critical, and during one of her periodic European visits her husband was forced to sell their house and furnishings. Under severe economic and personal strain, John Sherwood underwent a mental and emotional decline, the nature of which was never clearly disclosed, and died in February 1895. Despite these blows, and the exigencies of hotel living, Mrs. Sherwood continued her literary output undiminished. In 1889 she published a third novel, *Sweet-Brier,* similar in theme to her second, and in 1892 a volume of poems by "M. E. W. S." and *The Art of Entertaining.* Her memoirs, rambling catalogues of famous people encountered in a lifetime of travel and entertaining, were issued in two volumes, *An Epistle to Posterity* (1897) and *Here & There & Everywhere* (1898).

A heavy, round-faced, bejeweled woman devoted to luxury and pleasure, Mrs. Sherwood did not permit the disabling rheumatism of her later years to interfere seriously with her extravagant ways or her pursuit of celebrities. She remained, in the recollection of her grandson, the playwright Robert E. Sherwood, "a very gaudy old lady until the end" (Brown, p. 36). She died in Manhattan's Hotel Majestic of heart disease in 1903, when she was seventy-six. She had grown up a Unitarian, but after her marriage had become an Episcopalian and for many years attended New York's Church of the Ascension. She was buried in Delhi, N.Y., the Sherwoods' summer home.

Mary Elizabeth Sherwood put a considerable talent to ephemeral ends; in the judgment of her grandson's biographer, "She had a strong mind weakly used." Her one real success was her *Manners and Social Usages.* Like the popular etiquette book of her Philadelphia contemporary CLARA SOPHIA JESSUP MOORE, this is a monument to the self-consciousness of a newly developed Society in the Gilded Age: suddenly wealthy but without experience in the world of the wealthy, unsure of itself in a period when rapid growth of the economy and universal manhood suffrage offered no guarantee that even Senators would be cultivated men. In her book Mrs. Sherwood offered specific rules on the minutiae of etiquette, such as the manipulation of the fork, the requirements of drawing-room conversation, and the conventions of the calling card. She also expressed her own basic prejudices against the "adventurers" from the lower classes who strove to join the society of their betters, and her conviction that every city needed an established "reigning set . . . based on talent and money." Those of the newly rich who were troubled by the inequalities and injustices of American life were exhorted to cultivate personal kindness. The social code, asserts a character in one of her novels, "not only means elegance, but habitual and constant regard for others." In both her novels and her manuals Mrs. Sherwood stressed the view that natural virtue is simply enhanced by wealth.

Since Society in America was "in the hands of women almost exclusively," it was to them she spoke. Although she welcomed the expanded opportunities for women's education and employment, she felt uncomfortable with the "new woman" and continued to believe that "the happiest women are those who can lead the ordinary life, be amused by society, dress, and conventionalities, and who can be early married to the man of their choice, and become in their turn domestic women, good wives and mothers." In a materialistic society, it was woman's holy mission "to make man better, to temper his greed, control his avarice, soften his temper, refine his grosser nature, and teach him that there is something better than success." Mrs. Sherwood may have suggested more elaborate social forms than did such earlier arbiters of etiquette as ELIZA WARE FARRAR, ELIZA LESLIE, and LYDIA H. SIGOURNEY, but her concept of woman's role was little different from theirs.

[Mrs. Sherwood's *An Epistle to Posterity* and *Here & There & Everywhere;* Charles H. Bell, *The Bench and Bar of N.H.* (1894); *Vital Statistics of the Town of Keene, N.H.* (1905), pp. 71–72, 205, 246; Frances E. Willard and Mary A. Livermore, eds., *A Woman of the Century* (1893); *Who Was Who in America,* vol. I (1942); *Biog. Directory Am. Cong.* (1950); Frances W. Halsey, *Women Authors of Our Day in Their Homes* (1903); John Mason Brown, *The Worlds of Robert E. Sherwood* (1962), especially pp. 33–39; obituaries in *N.Y. Daily Tribune,* Feb. 12, 1895 (John Sherwood), and *N.Y. Times,* Sept. 15, 1903; death record from N.Y. City Dept. of Health.]

BARBARA A. WELTER

**SHINN, Milicent Washburn** (Apr. 15, 1858– Aug. 13, 1940), author, editor, and psychologist, was born in Niles, Calif., on the ranch where her father, James Shinn, conducted a farming and orchard-tree nursery business. Both he and her mother, Lucy Ellen (Clark) Shinn, came of old New England families; Shinn was born in Salem, Ohio, his wife in Farmington, Conn. Milicent was the third of their four children. An older brother, Charles Howard Shinn, became a well-known writer and a leader in the early Western conservation movement. A particular influence in Miss Shinn's youth was her association with her cousin and near-contemporary Edmund Clark Sanford, later a noted psychologist. After attending public school in Centerville, Calif., she went to Oakland (Calif.) High School, graduating in 1874. She entered the University of

California that fall but took a leave of absence in 1877 to teach school in order to raise money to continue her education. She returned to the university to receive her A.B. in 1880.

Even before her graduation she had joined the editorial staff of the *San Francisco Commercial Herald*. In the literary career she thus began she was greatly influenced by the poet Edward Rowland Sill, who had taught at Oakland High School when she was there and afterward at the University of California while she was an undergraduate. When the *Californian* was founded in 1880 to replace the defunct *Overland Monthly* in the intellectual life of the Pacific Coast, Miss Shinn was a regular contributor of poetry and prose, and about 1882 she became associated with Warren Cheney in that publication. In 1883, when they decided to use the old *Overland* name, the copyright owner gave it to Miss Shinn, and she became editor, serving until 1894. Sill encouraged her to take up editorial work and acted as her adviser—and an anonymous contributor—until his death in 1887. In the early years of her editorship Miss Shinn contributed both poetry and prose as well as editorial matter, and probably a good deal more anonymously. She sold her interest in the *Overland Monthly* when she gave up the editorship early in 1894, but remained a part of the literary group associated with it.

Meanwhile she had embarked on a new project, one that was to bring her a wide reputation. When in 1890 her oldest brother's wife bore a baby girl, Miss Shinn began keeping an elaborate and careful record of the physical and mental development of the infant, presumably in the pattern of the work of William Preyer, whose *Die Seele des Kindes* had been translated the year before. Her initial observations, supplemented by further ones to the third year and by fragments of infant observations made by others, were published as *Notes on the Development of a Child (University of California Publications in Education*, vols. I, 1893–99, and IV, 1907); some of her reports appeared in German translation in 1905. Entering the University of California briefly as a graduate student at the time she began her observations, Miss Shinn was continuously in residence from 1894 until December 1898, when she received the Ph.D. degree, presenting as a thesis her study of the sensory development of infants "with pedagogical applications." She was the first woman and the eleventh person to receive that degree at the university. Her work gained attention from psychologists and educated people generally in the United States and even to some extent abroad, and for some years hers were among the very few systematic observations of infants available in English. She popularized them in several articles, later made into a charming little book published in 1900, *The Biography of a Baby*, from which she was still receiving royalties a quarter of a century later. But she made no further contribution to psychology.

Around the turn of the century, while in her early forties, Dr. Shinn retired to the family ranch at Niles and lived quietly there for the rest of her life. Much of her time she spent tutoring her brother's children. She wrote very little but was visited by literary people and occasionally by scientists who remembered her work on infants. She was a member of the Congregational Church and of many societies, from the Save-the-Redwoods League and a "local anti-saloon organization" to the League of Nations Association and the American Eugenics Society. Active in the Association of Collegiate Alumnae, she helped organize its California branch and from 1895 to 1909 headed its national committee on child development. In politics she was independent and strongly in favor of woman suffrage. She was of medium height and had fine features. In her younger years an active outdoorswoman, she became increasingly frail in later life. She died of heart disease in Niles at the age of eighty-two. Her body was cremated. Neither in literature nor in science had she sustained her early promise.

[The fullest information is contained in Edgar J. Hinkel and William E. McCann, eds., *Biogs. of Calif. Authors and Indexes of Calif. Literature* (1942), I, 195–96. See also *N.Y. Times*, Aug. 15, 1940; *Woman's Who's Who of America*, 1914–15; and *Who Was Who in America*, vol. I (1942). There is no full bibliography of her writings; a few of her articles are listed in the *Readers' Guide to Periodical Literature*. There are indexes of newspaper articles and biographical articles in the Calif. State Library, Sacramento, and the Oakland Public Library has a clipping file. A few letters of Miss Shinn are in the Bancroft Library, Univ. of Calif.; many more papers are in the possession of the family. Information about the family is in Myron W. Wood, *Hist. of Alameda County, Calif.* (1883), p. 973, and in standard biographical references to Charles Howard Shinn. Other details from her writings, from records of Oakland High School and the Univ. of Calif., and from Joseph Shinn, Jr. An account of her editorial work is in Charles S. Greene, "Memories of an Editor," *Overland Monthly*, Sept. 1902. On her work with the Assoc. of Collegiate Alumnae, see Marion Talbot and Lois K. M. Rosenberry, *The Hist. of the Am. Assoc. of Univ. Women* (1931). Death record from Calif. Dept. of Public Health.]

JOHN CHYNOWETH BURNHAM

SHIRLEY, Dame. *See* CLAPP, Louise Amelia
Knapp Smith.

SHULER, Nettie Rogers (Nov. 8, 1862–Dec.
2, 1939), suffragist and clubwoman, was born
in Buffalo, N.Y., one of two daughters of Alexander and Julia Antoinette (Houghtaling)
Rogers. Her mother's American forebears
dated back to the Revolution; her father, a
clerk for the American Express Company, had
come to the United States from County Perth,
Scotland, as a small boy. Nettie (Antoinette)
Rogers was educated at Buffalo Central High
School, where she took courses in languages,
history, and art. On Mar. 31, 1887, she was
married to Frank J. Shuler (1852–1916), a native of Lockport, N.Y., and a bookkeeper. They
had one child, Marjorie (born Nov. 10, 1888),
who joined her mother in the later stages of
the suffrage campaign and afterward became
a prominent newspaperwoman on the staff of
the *Christian Science Monitor*.

In the first decade of the twentieth century
the woman's club movement was not only an
outlet for the energies of able and active-
minded women but a training ground for
many of the women who became organizers
and leaders in the struggle for suffrage. By
1908 Mrs. Shuler, then president of the Western New York Federation of Women's Clubs,
was welcoming the annual convention of the
National American Woman Suffrage Association to Buffalo, pointing out that her organization was the first in the General Federation of
Women's Clubs to admit suffrage clubs as
affiliates. The following year the Western New
York Federation passed a resolution supporting
woman suffrage, and Mrs. Shuler, along with
other leaders of the large women's organizations, was a member of a cooperating committee which presented the case for a suffrage
amendment to the state constitution at hearings before the lower house of the New York
legislature.

Although she served as president of the New
York State Federation of Women's Clubs in
1912–14, Mrs. Shuler thereafter gave her principal energies to the suffrage movement. She
led the Eighth campaign district (western New
York) for the New York Woman Suffrage Party
in the two-year campaign which culminated in
the 1915 referendum for a suffrage amendment
in New York. The referendum was lost, but
Mrs. Shuler had made her mark as an organizer. CARRIE CHAPMAN CATT, president of the
National American Woman Suffrage Association, took her out of the second—and victorious
—campaign of 1916–17 to replace HANNAH
JANE PATTERSON of Pennsylvania as the associ-

ation's corresponding secretary, a post she was
to retain until the organization went out of existence after the passage of the Nineteenth
Amendment.

During these four years (1917–21) Mrs.
Shuler demonstrated outstanding organizational ability on a national scale; her post, far
from dealing with routine correspondence, became that of alter ego to Mrs. Catt. Five feet
seven inches in height, with hair that had
turned white when she was still a young
woman, an effective speaker and—like most
suffrage leaders—possessed of apparently inexhaustible energy, she repeatedly left her desk
in the New York City office of the national
organization to participate in the crucial state
referendum campaigns, where victory gradually built up the winning bloc of votes in Congress which made the amendment's passage
possible. She helped conduct training schools
for field organizers (the curriculum included
such topics as Suffrage History and Argument;
Organization, Publicity and Press; Money Raising; and Parliamentary Law); held conferences
with field workers; addressed countless public
meetings; and testified before committees of
state legislatures. Some of the states which
gratefully recorded her services after the battle was over were Maine, Massachusetts, Maryland, Michigan, New Hampshire, Oklahoma,
Rhode Island, South Dakota, and West Virginia. In 1923 she was co-author, with Mrs.
Catt, of a history of the suffrage movement,
*Woman Suffrage and Politics*.

From 1929 to 1931 Mrs. Shuler served as
president of the New York City Federation of
Women's Clubs. A staunch Republican, she
worked for enforcement of the prohibition
law, but actively opposed passage of an equal
rights amendment to the federal constitution.
She was a member of the Daughters of the
American Revolution. Originally a Baptist, she
became a Christian Scientist, serving at one
time as second reader of the Seventh Church
of Christ, Scientist, in New York City. She died
in that city at the age of seventy-seven; her
body was cremated.

[Ida H. Harper, *The Hist. of Woman Suffrage*,
vols. V and VI (1922), including Mrs. Shuler's
chapter on the League of Women Voters (vol. V,
chap. xxii); Carrie Chapman Catt and Nettie Rogers Shuler, *Woman Suffrage and Politics* (1923);
*Woman's Who's Who of America*, 1914–15; obituaries in *N.Y. Times*, Dec. 3, 1939, *Buffalo Courier-
Express* and *Buffalo Evening News*, Dec. 4, 1939;
correspondence with Mrs. Shuler's daughter, Mrs.
F. Felix Charles; marriage record from County
Clerk, Erie County, N.Y.; information from Buffalo and Erie County Hist. Soc., Buffalo.]

ELEANOR FLEXNER

SIBLEY, Mary Easton (Jan. 1, 1800–June 20, 1878), educator, founder of Lindenwood College in Missouri, was born in New York state, probably in the town of Rome. When she was about four she was brought to St. Louis, Mo., by her parents, Rufus B. and Abby Abial (Smith) Easton. Her father, who came of an old Connecticut family that had migrated from England early in the seventeenth century, served as the first postmaster of St. Louis, was one of the first judges of the territorial court in Missouri, became the first attorney general of the State of Missouri, and acquired large landholdings. Mary was the eldest of seven girls and had four brothers. Precocious and energetic by nature, she seems to have been encouraged by her family to make full use of her talents. A long trip to attend a female seminary at Shelbyville, Ky., was only one of many journeys that she made on horseback. She is said to have been well grounded in Latin and French and to have been an accomplished musician.

At the age of fifteen, on Aug. 9, 1815, Mary Easton was married to George Champlin Sibley, eighteen years her senior, born in Massachusetts but reared and educated at Fayetteville, N.C. As a clerk in the United States Indian Bureau, Sibley had been sent to St. Louis and on up the river to build Fort Osage near the present site of Sibley in Jackson County, where he served as factor and later as Indian agent. Immediately following her marriage Mrs. Sibley set out with her husband, her library, her piano, and her household furnishings on a month-long honeymoon trip by keelboat up the Missouri River to their home at Fort Osage.

During their stay at that post the Sibleys became well known for their gracious hospitality to travelers. Mrs. Sibley, who had no children, also began to teach a younger sister who resided with them and Indian girls who came to the fort. This seems to have given her and her husband the idea of sponsoring a girls' school. After Sibley retired from government service in 1826 they settled at St. Charles, Mo., where they developed a large and beautiful estate. Within a short time they had established a school for girls in their home, moving it in 1828 to a nearby tract of land called Linden Wood. Mrs. Sibley seems to have served as principal of the school during its early years, and as a believer in a college education for women she maintained a direct interest in its welfare throughout her life. The school seems to have been suspended for a short time in the early 1840's, and this perhaps accounted for a fund-raising trip to the East, where Mrs. Sibley obtained some $4,000 from friends and acquaintances for its support. In 1853 the Sibleys helped secure a charter for Lindenwood Female College from the state legislature, and in 1856 they deeded the 120 acres of college land to trustees appointed by the St. Louis Presbytery, the college thus becoming Presbyterian in affiliation. Affectionately known to the students as Aunt Mary, Mrs. Sibley frequently toured the campus in her carriage, which the girls dubbed the "Ship of Zion."

In later life Mary Sibley organized the "Sisters of Bethany," a Protestant group whose members took vows to help the poor, the sick, and those in trouble. After her husband's death she became an ardent believer in the second advent of Christ and turned to religion as her major concern. A lifelong interest in foreign missions led her to set out at seventy-one for missionary work in Japan, but infirmities caused her to turn back after reaching California. She died at Lindenwood and was buried in the cemetery on the college grounds.

[The most complete account of Mrs. Sibley is contained in Charles T. Jones, Jr., "George Champlin Sibley: The Prairie Puritan (1782–1863)" (unpublished doctoral dissertation, Univ. of Mo., 1969). See also Lucinda de Leftwich Templin, *Two Illustrious Pioneers in the Education of Women in Mo.* (1926), on Mrs. Sibley and her husband, and sketch in *Mo. Hist. Rev.*, July 1957. There are Sibley Papers in the Mo. Hist. Soc. (St. Louis) and at Lindenwood College.]

LEWIS ATHERTON

SIDNEY, Margaret. *See* LOTHROP, Harriett Mulford Stone.

SIGOURNEY, Lydia Howard Huntley (Sept. 1, 1791–June 10, 1865), author, known at the height of her fame as "the Sweet Singer of Hartford," was born at Norwich, Conn., the only child of Ezekiel Huntley by his second wife, Zerviah Wentworth. Her father, of Scottish parentage, was the hired man in the household of Mrs. Daniel Lathrop, an aged widow, who made a great pet of the precocious little girl and had her read aloud from the Bible and Young's *Night Thoughts*. Lydia picked up an education in the local schools and through reading in Mrs. Lathrop's library. To prepare herself to teach she spent some months in Hartford female seminaries acquiring the ornamental accomplishments and then in 1811, with a friend, opened a school for young ladies in Norwich. Three years later she was invited to Hartford by Daniel Wadsworth, a wealthy relative of Mrs. Lathrop's, to conduct a school for the daughters of his friends.

He also arranged the publication by subscription of her first book, a collection called *Moral Pieces, in Prose and Verse* (1815), to help her support her parents.

Though her school was successful, Lydia gave it up to marry, on June 16, 1819, Charles Sigourney, a widower with three small children. He was a hardware merchant, later president of the Phoenix Bank, a trustee of Trinity (then Washington) College, and a warden of Christ Church. Mrs. Sigourney, reared a Congregationalist, now became an Episcopalian. After her marriage she continued writing in order to contribute to charitable causes like the temperance movement, peace societies, Greek war relief, and the work of missionaries abroad and among the Choctaws and Cherokees. In *Traits of the Aborigines of America* (1822) she turned Indian tales from Henry R. Schoolcraft and J. G. E. Heckewelder into blank verse urging conversion of the Indians to Christianity as a way to make the West safe for white settlers; her husband supplied learned notes for the work, which was published anonymously.

When Sigourney's prosperity declined, Mrs. Sigourney began to sell poems and sketches to the magazines and compiled edifying books like *Biography of Pious Persons* (2 vols., 1832). She won immediate success. After *Letters to Young Ladies* (1833), her most popular prose work, she abandoned anonymity, despite her husband's disapproval, and set out frankly to pursue literature as a trade. Within a year eight other volumes came from her pen, including *Poems* (1834), a popular collection known after the third edition as *Select Poems* (1838). Most of her verse served double duty, appearing first in newspapers and magazines, where it made her name familiar everywhere in America. Annuals and gift books both here and abroad solicited her articles, which the most punctilious parents found suitable for their daughters. Mrs. Sigourney edited one of these annuals, *The Religious Souvenir*, for 1839 and 1840, writing much of the text herself; with characteristic thrift she acquired the plates and reissued the volumes occasionally under various titles. From 1840 to 1842 the publisher Louis Godey paid her $500 a year merely to use her name on the title page of his *Lady's Book*, and the rival *Ladies' Companion* competed for contributions. Edgar Allan Poe begged her to give *Graham's Magazine* an article each month, offering compensation "at least as liberal as that of any publisher in America."

The most fertile poetic mind could not have satisfied the demand from the new periodicals springing up all over the country. Mrs. Sigourney relied on the old formulas she had used from the beginning: historical, moral, and religious. Death was always her favorite theme—the death of infants, of consumptive children, of missionaries in Burma and Liberia, of poets and lunatics, of artists and sailors, of college students and deaf-dumb-and-blind girls. Her rhyming of pious truisms made a wide appeal and established a trade that newspaper poets have carried on prosperously.

Perhaps in search of new subjects Mrs. Sigourney went abroad in 1840, calling on English literary figures like Joanna Baillie, Mrs. Mary Ann Jameson, Maria Edgeworth, and Samuel Rogers. Wordsworth received her politely at Grasmere, and Carlyle invited her to tea in Chelsea, where her affectation in dress and manners provoked a vitriolic portrait from Mrs. Carlyle's pen. In Paris she was presented at the court of Louis Philippe. On her return she gave a glowing account of her travels in *Pleasant Memories of Pleasant Lands* (1842). At this period in her life Mrs. Sigourney was a small, plump woman with flaxen hair, beautiful hands, of which she was rather vain, an effusive manner, and an unabashed interest in playing the part of a lady of letters.

Between 1840 and 1850 Mrs. Sigourney published fourteen volumes, mostly réchauffés of her earlier work. *The Voice of Flowers* (1846) gathered up most of her verses about flowers; *The Weeping Willow* (1847) collected seventy obituary poems; *Whisper to a Bride* (1850), bound in white moire silk, sought (in the author's words) "the hand of many a fair young creature as she left the paternal hearthstone." The title piece of *Pocahontas, and Other Poems* (1841), in pseudo-Spenserian stanzas modeled on those of Mrs. Felicia Hemans' *The Forest Sanctuary*, describes the baptism and marriage of the "forest-princess," "the first convert from the heathen tribes." Mrs. Sigourney's reputation reached its zenith with the publication of her *Illustrated Poems* (1849) in a series uniform with those of Bryant and Longfellow, a sumptuously bound, gilt-edged volume of 408 pages with thirteen steel engravings by the celebrated illustrator Felix O. C. Darley and a portrait of the author.

Mrs. Sigourney had two children, Mary Huntley (born in 1827) and Andrew (1831–1850), whose death of tuberculosis his mother recorded with fulsome detail in a biographical sketch, *The Faded Hope* (1853). Charles Sigourney died of apoplexy in December 1854. With his estate and the income from her writings his widow lived comfortably, enjoying the homage paid her as Hartford's most famous literary celebrity. Each year saw another volume from her pen. Few of them were new works: *Past Meridian* (1854), a treatise on old age; *The Western Home* (1854), with a poem on the Blennerhassett Conspiracy; *The Man of Uz* (1862), a poor versification of Job. The most popular of the later books was *The Daily Counsellor* (1859), offering a Bible text for each day followed by a poem.

The Civil War, which one might have expected to inspire elegiac strains, passed almost without notice from Mrs. Sigourney. Her mind turned toward the past in the autobiographical *Letters of Life* (1866), written in the "poetic" style common to her prose and verse, substituting euphemisms for ordinary words to make sugar and butter "saccharine and oleaginous matter" or the pig "a quadruped member of our establishment . . . scarcely mentionable to ears polite." Outliving her fame, she died in Hartford in 1865 and was buried there in Spring Grove Cemetery. Her formulas were never original, and other sweet singers, with whom the woods were vocal, could use them equally well. From the first the note of critical disparagement had been checked by respect for the woman rather than her work. But she did not deceive herself. "If there is any kitchen in Parnassus," she wrote, "my Muse has surely officiated there as a woman of all work and an aproned waiter." She will be remembered as one of the first American women to make a successful career of literature.

[Gordon S. Haight, *Mrs. Sigourney: The Sweet Singer of Hartford* (1930), is the only complete treatment of her life. Her own autobiography, *Letters of Life,* is partially useful. Earlier accounts include Louise J. R. Chapman in *Conn. Quart.,* Jan.–Mar. 1895, and Grace L. Collin in *New England Mag.,* Sept. 1902. Extensive collections of Mrs. Sigourney's correspondence are in the Conn. Hist. Soc., Hartford, and the Yale Univ. Library.]

GORDON S. HAIGHT

**SILL, Anna Peck** (Aug. 9, 1816–June 18, 1889), educator, founder of Rockford Female Seminary (later Rockford College) in Illinois, was born in Burlington, Otsego County, N.Y., the youngest of ten children (six boys and four girls) of Abel and Hepsibah (Peck) Sill. Her ancestry brought together austere and self-questioning New England Puritanism and nineteenth-century zeal for reform. Her father, a farmer and a descendant of John and Joanna Sill, settlers in Cambridge, Mass., in 1637, had moved west with his family from Lyme, Conn., about 1789. Anna's grandfather on her mother's side, Judge Jedediah Peck, wrote the bill creating free rural schools in New York state,

led the agitation for its acceptance, and was a prominent figure in the movement to abolish imprisonment for debt in New York. Hepsibah Sill, Anna's mother, was a woman of outstanding education for the frontier community of Burlington. She was the dominant influence in Anna's upbringing, her father having died when she was seven. Although he had preferred the Episcopal Church, Anna grew up a Congregationalist.

Her schooling was typical of education along the path of New England emigration westward. At four she attended the local rural school, walking two miles daily to equip her mind with Webster's *Spelling Book,* Morse's *Geography,* and Murray's *Grammar.* At home she acquired the frontier household skills of spinning, weaving, and wool carding. Always deeply religious, she underwent at fourteen an inward struggle to surrender to God's will; she emerged, during the revival of 1831, with a serene certainty of salvation and a sense of consecration to the service of God. At twenty she left Burlington to teach at the district school in Barre, N.Y., earning two dollars per week and eking out her wages by spinning and weaving. In 1837, in search of further education, she entered Miss Phipps' Union Seminary, Albion, N.Y., and remained there until 1843 as a pupil and teacher. For three years she headed a seminary of her own in Warsaw, N.Y., after which she took charge of the Cary Collegiate Institute of Oakfield, N.Y.

Deep questioning during these years as to whether God's providence decreed her service in foreign mission or educational work had been resolved in favor of the latter, but her urge to "labor in a more 'destitute' field" if not on "heathen soil" led her to seek to establish a school in the "wild Northwest." The opportunity opened in 1849. Two years before, a group of Congregationalists and Presbyterians, organized as the Society for the Promotion of Collegiate and Theological Education in the West, having founded Beloit College in Wisconsin, had acquired a charter for an affiliated female seminary to be established in northern Illinois. A group of citizens in Rockford, Ill., hopeful of securing the seminary for their town, invited Miss Sill to open a private girls' school in a building to be furnished rent-free by the community. There, in July 1849, she began classes.

Her teaching was deeply rooted in her faith, and initially her school had little other support. At the close of the school's second day she wrote in her diary, "To-day numbered sixty scholars. Oh, the responsibility of teachers! O Lord, aid me." In September 1850

Rockford was chosen as the seminary's site and Miss Sill's school was taken over by the society's trustees. Rockford ladies pledged $1,000 for land and other citizens of the town subscribed $5,000 for buildings. The first structure, erected in 1852, was soon overflowing. Returning to the East that same year, Miss Sill brought back sufficient donations from New York and New England to begin another building, Linden Hall. Meanwhile debate had arisen over her qualifications for appointment as principal. Her character and religious zeal were unquestioned, but there was at first some doubt about her intellectual abilities. Her appointment, however, was confirmed in June 1852.

Miss Sill modeled her school on the Mount Holyoke Seminary of MARY LYON. Initially a three-year course was offered in mental and moral philosophy, natural sciences, ancient languages, mathematics, history, and literature. The emphasis in teaching was upon Biblical and classical studies, and Miss Sill regarded conversions and calls to missionary endeavor as evidence of the efficacy of the seminary as an educational institution. In 1855 a friendly estimate of her teaching achievement was critical of the onerous regimentation of the school, of the students' parrotlike knowledge, the overloaded curriculum, and the absolutism of Miss Sill's control. Administrative changes dealing with these problems followed; they showed that Miss Sill possessed an unsuspected capacity for adaptation to changing educational needs. Her opposition to "women in public life" and to coeducation, her views as to ladylike conduct, and her beliefs as to the correct methods of stimulating missionary endeavor did not alter, but her conception of the role of Rockford Female Seminary as a teaching institution did change in response to the development of more secular educational institutions elsewhere. After the founding of Vassar, Wellesley, and Smith she began to press upon the trustees the necessity of raising Rockford Female Seminary to collegiate status with an accompanying improvement in teaching facilities and faculty standards. The seminary was made a degree-granting institution in 1882, but her campaign for improved facilities was not successful, although it was maintained unceasingly until after her retirement in 1884 and was pushed with new vigor by her successor, Martha Hillard (see MARTHA HILLARD MAC LEISH). Miss Sill remained at the college, living in Linden Hall as principal emerita until her death there from pneumonia in 1889; she was buried in Rockford's West Side Cemetery. Three years later the seminary officially became Rockford College.

In Anna Peck Sill a union of Calvinist determinism and humanitarian zeal found expression in the unhesitating activism of the pioneer. "My desire for usefulness is an *insatiable thirst*," she wrote shortly after reaching Rockford. ". . . It seems to nerve every energy of my being." Her achievement is best assessed in her own terms. She believed that the basis of an educational institution was the fusion of faculty, students, and curriculum into a meaningful pattern which would produce what she designated by the Victorian term "character," which she said was "living power." Her attempt to create a model of Christian service to the community was successful, although Rockford Female Seminary was not distinguished by intellectual originality during her administration. Among her students were Adeline Potter (mother of JULIA C. LATHROP), Elizabeth Griffin (mother of Edith and GRACE ABBOTT), JANE ADDAMS, ELLEN G. STARR, CATHARINE WAUGH MC CULLOCH. These Midwestern women transposed Miss Sill's concern with personal sin to a preoccupation with social sin, but they possessed in common the union of conscience and energy which she had striven to create. In this sense her contribution to her generation would be difficult to overestimate.

[Anna Peck Sill Letters and Scrapbook, Rockford College Archives; Emerson-Bannister Correspondence, 1846–89, and Chapin Correspondence, Beloit College Archives; *Memorials of Anna Peck Sill* (1889); Hazel Paris Cederborg, "Early Hist. of Rockford College" (unpublished master's thesis, Wellesley College, 1926); Helen L. D. Richardson, "The Beginnings of Rockford Female Seminary," part of an unpublished centenary history in the Rockford College Archives; *Profiles of the Principals of Rockford Seminary and Presidents of Rockford College* (1947).]

JILL KER CONWAY

SIMMS, Daisy Florence (Apr. 17, 1873–Jan. 6, 1923), leader in the Young Women's Christian Association, was born in Rushville, Ind., the older of the two daughters of Michael M. Simms, a farmer, and Jennie (Taylor) Simms. Her father's family had moved from Virginia to Kentucky, where he was born; her mother was a native of Homer, Ind. Educated in the Rushville schools, where she excelled as an elocutionist, Florence, as she was known, won top honors in high school, spurred by her father's promise of a college education if her record justified it. She went on to DePauw University in Indiana, from which she graduated with a Ph.B. degree in 1895. As a student she displayed a deeply religious cast of mind; she revered FRANCES E. WILLARD and was a strong believer in the causes of temperance and woman's rights.

Miss Simms had considered teaching English, but her student activity in the campus branch of the Young Women's Christian Association led instead to a career with that organization. Appointed in September 1895 a national secretary in the college department of the Y.W.C.A. American Committee, whose headquarters were in Chicago, for a time she toured Midwestern colleges for the association. In 1902, after five years as secretary of local Y.W.C.A.'s in Portland, Maine, and Binghamton, N.Y., she was chosen executive secretary of the Michigan state committee. Two years later she became one of the two secretaries of the American Committee's industrial department. When the American Committee and the International Board of the Y.W.C.A. were united under the leadership of GRACE H. DODGE in December 1906, Miss Simms moved to New York City and, with MABEL CRATTY and another Y.W.C.A. worker, rented an apartment near Columbia University. New York remained her home for the rest of her life.

Miss Dodge, a pioneer in the working girls' club movement, had already seen the importance of bridging the gap between organized churchwomen and working women. In 1909 she set up an industrial department of the unified Y.W.C.A. and appointed Florence Simms as the director. Until this time Miss Simms' concept of the needs of working women had reflected the conventional evangelical ideas of her Methodist upbringing. In her early Y.W.C.A. meetings with factory girls, she later recalled, "I went *down* to these girls. I had that feeling. I wanted to give them religion. . . . I was not concerned about the hours they worked" (Roberts, pp. 182–83). But the more liberal atmosphere prevailing in New York Y.W.C.A. circles soon converted her to the "social gospel" of Walter Rauschenbusch and others, with its emphasis on economic reform, and she became convinced that no religious work among women in industry could have meaning unless it attempted to improve the bad working conditions which cramped and impoverished their spirits. At the same time she "recoiled violently" from the prospect of labor and class conflict, and urged education and persuasion instead (*ibid.*, p. 187).

For the four years preceding the 1910 World Conference of Young Women's Christian Associations in Berlin, Miss Simms served as chairman of an international commission to gather information as to the possibilities of Y.W.C.A. work among "industrial women." Her report became the basis of a set of reso-

lutions adopted by the Berlin convention urging Y.W.C.A. leaders to seek more members from industry and to encourage the study of social and industrial problems as they affected the physical and economic needs of working women. The Y.W.C.A. national convention of the following year, again at Miss Simms' instigation, went even further, condemning "the utterly inadequate wages" received by many women, affirming the need for legislation to regulate wages and hours, and calling for the extension of Y.W.C.A. work into factories and shops.

To help implement these resolutions Miss Simms inaugurated a highly successful program to establish "industrial clubs." By 1915 there were 375 such clubs functioning in laundries, mills, factories, and stores across the country, and their number continued to increase. Though affiliated with the Y.W.C.A., they were self-governing and free to carry out programs of their own choosing within certain broad limits. Besides the religious program, which was an important part of their work, they promoted recreational activities, and held classes in citizenship, English, homemaking, and health; within a given city, they often federated to carry out a public service or aid in civic programs. In no sense trade unions, the clubs nevertheless, under Miss Simms' leadership, collaborated with the Consumers' League, the Women's Trade Union League, and other groups to secure and enforce protective legislation for working women and children, and to support the Women's and Children's bureaus of the federal Department of Labor.

During the First World War, Miss Simms' position as Y.W.C.A. industrial secretary gave her a central role in the efforts of the association's War Work Council to provide for the physical and spiritual needs of the women who poured into war industries, and to safeguard the rights of working women amid the pressures for increased production. Inspired by its wartime success, the War Work Council in 1919 appointed a special Industrial Commission, led by Miss Simms, which toured Europe to cooperate with union leaders and others in exploring the possibilities for achieving internationally acceptable labor standards for women.

Still committed to the "social gospel" in the more conservative postwar period, Miss Simms as a member of the Social Service Commission of the Federal Council of Churches of Christ helped bring about the council's adoption in 1919 of a sixteen-point program, "The Social Ideals of the Churches," a reformulation of the "social creed" it had espoused in various forms since 1908. In May 1920 the national convention of the Y.W.C.A., largely in response to pressure from Miss Simms and her industrial clubs, endorsed the program, thus committing itself unequivocally to the cause of social justice, as spelled out in clauses dealing with the abolition of child labor, minimum-wage legislation, collective bargaining, the right of workers to organize, and similar subjects. This action by the Y.W.C.A. was not taken without strong internal opposition, and it stands as a tribute to the tactical skill and personal influence of Miss Simms. Her last important achievement was to organize the first National Assembly of Industrial Girls. Held at Hot Springs, Ark., in conjunction with the Y.W.C.A. national convention of 1922, it marked the first full participation of the industrial membership in the association's affairs. Joint meetings of delegates from factories and stores with the student delegates who comprised the bulk of Y.W.C.A. membership served to bring about closer cooperation and understanding between the two groups.

A woman of warm human sympathy, restrained by a reserve based on a deep sense of individual human dignity, Florence Simms had the ability to work with people of varied social backgrounds. A dynamic speaker and a good listener, she was tall and handsome, with auburn hair which she wore coiled on top of her head. In 1912 she suffered a breakdown, from overwork, and went to Italy for a rest. After her return she never regained full health, and early in 1923, at the age of forty-nine, she died of meningitis in a hospital in Mattoon, Ill. (the home of her parents), following surgery for mastoiditis. She was buried in the nearby cemetery of Humboldt, Ill.

[Richard Roberts, *Florence Simms: A Biog.* (1926); Marion O. Robinson, *Eight Women of the YWCA* (1966); articles by Miss Simms in the *Woman's Press*, the Y.W.C.A. monthly; Nat. Board of the Y.W.C.A., *Report*, 1920, pp. 29–32, 1924, pp. 100–02; Nat. Board, Dept. of Research and Method, *Report*, 1919–20, pp. 60–69; Genevieve M. Fox, *The Industrial Awakening and the Y.W.C.A.* (1920); Grace H. Wilson, *The Religious and Educational Philosophy of the Y.W.C.A.* (1933); Mary S. Simms, *The Natural Hist. of a Social Institution—the Y.W.C.A.* (1936); obituaries in *N.Y. Times*, Jan. 7, 1923, and *Woman's Press*, Apr. 1923; death record from Ill. Dept. of Public Health.]

ELEANOR FLEXNER

**SIMMS, Ruth Hanna McCormick** (Mar. 27, 1880–Dec. 31, 1944), Congresswoman and political leader, was born in Cleveland, Ohio, the second daughter and youngest of three children of Marcus Alonzo and Charlotte Augusta (Rhodes) Hanna. Mark Hanna belonged to the fifth generation of Hannas established on American soil, a family of predominantly Scotch-Irish stock and of Quaker faith. Charlotte Rhodes was the daughter of Daniel Pomeroy Rhodes, Cleveland ironmaster, banker, and railroad president, who had come to Ohio from Vermont in the 1830's.

Ruth Hanna inherited her father's industry and ambition, his capacity for detail, and his high talent for organization. She was educated in private schools in Cleveland and, briefly (1897), at the Masters School, Dobbs Ferry, N.Y., and Miss Porter's School, Farmington, Conn. She did not attend college, disappointing many in her family; but her own preference was to learn as her father had, from experience. She was encouraged in this by being allowed to participate in his business and political activities, accompanying him as he investigated labor difficulties in the mines, attending political meetings, working at Republican campaign headquarters. In 1896 she joined him in touring the country as he managed William McKinley's presidential campaign. When Hanna went to Washington in 1898 as United States Senator, she went along as his personal secretary.

The next few years provided additional opportunities for furthering her political education. On June 10, 1903, she was married to (Joseph) Medill McCormick, who after graduating from Yale in 1900 had gone to work on the *Chicago Tribune*, of which his maternal grandfather, Joseph Medill, had been publisher. They had three children: Katherine Augusta (Katrina), born in 1913, John Medill (1916), and Ruth Elizabeth (1921). Medill McCormick and his wife shared an interest in improving social and economic conditions in Chicago, and for a time they lived at the University of Chicago Settlement. In 1912 Mrs. McCormick broke with her father's tradition of party regularity to join her husband in supporting Theodore Roosevelt, McCormick serving that year as vice-chairman of the Progressive party's national campaign committee. His election to the Illinois legislature in 1912, to the national House of Representatives in 1916, and to the United States Senate in 1918 undoubtedly owed much to his wife's active assistance.

In her own right Mrs. McCormick became a strong supporter of various progressive causes, particularly the welfare of women and children, an interest she had developed in the early 1900's as a member of the National Civic Federation. She took an active part in the National Child Welfare Association, the American Association for Labor Legislation, and the Women's Trade Union League. In 1915 she represented the Illinois Consumers' League before the state legislature in behalf of a child labor bill. She worked hard to advance the cause of woman suffrage, lobbying for a successful suffrage bill in Illinois in 1913, delivering numerous speeches, appearing before the House Judiciary Committee in 1914, and giving generous financial support. As chairman of the Congressional committee of the National American Woman Suffrage Association, Mrs. McCormick was co-author of the Shafroth-Palmer amendment placed before the Congress on Mar. 2, 1914. Conceived as a political counter to objections that a simple federal suffrage amendment would be an invasion of states' rights, the Shafroth-Palmer amendment would have required any state to hold a referendum on woman suffrage whenever 8 per cent of its legal voters so petitioned, but it met opposition within the suffrage movement and was abandoned.

In international affairs Mrs. McCormick advocated greater American military preparedness following the outbreak of World War I and founded the women's section of the Navy League. After the war she united with her husband in his irreconcilable opposition to the League of Nations. American liberties, she stated in a speech before the Republican party's national committee, would not be yielded "for any scheme of socialist or imperialist internationalism."

As a reflection of her growing stature, Mrs. McCormick was chosen early in 1919 as the first chairman of a new women's executive committee of the Republican National Committee. The next year she was one of the eight women taken into the National Committee's own executive committee, where she remained until 1924, after which she became Republican national committeewoman from Illinois. During this time she organized a statewide group of women's Republican clubs in Illinois numbering several thousand members, a following which some contemporary observers felt constituted almost a personal political machine (*Nation*, Oct. 26, 1927). Her advice to women was that they disaffiliate themselves from nonpartisan organizations and cease working primarily for women's rights.

After Medill McCormick's death, in February 1925, her political activity increased. At the Republican National Convention of 1928 she aided the presidential boom of Gov. Frank O. Lowden of Illinois. That same year she sought the Republican nomination for Con-

gressman-at-large from Illinois, declaring that her objective was not to further the cause of women. "I am no longer a suffragette or a feminist," she emphasized. "I am a politician." Nevertheless, her victory in the primary election, in which she ran first in a field of eight, was widely interpreted as a triumph for women unmatched since they had received the vote. In the general election she led all Republicans on the ticket, including Herbert Hoover, and many now considered her the ablest woman politician in the country. Extremely well informed and an above-average speaker, she impressed audiences more by her vivacity and quick wit than by grace and sophistication.

As a freshman Congresswoman, Mrs. McCormick had a negligible record. After less than two months in office she announced that she was running for the United States Senate in 1930. Her party opponent for this seat was Charles Deneen, the man who had defeated her husband's bid for reelection in 1924. After a carefully planned and well-organized campaign, in which she declared the chief issue to be her outright opposition to the World Court, as opposed to Deneen's qualified acceptance of that organization, Mrs. McCormick won the primary election by a nearly two-to-one margin. Her career now at its zenith, she prepared to meet James Hamilton Lewis, the Democratic candidate, whom Medill McCormick had defeated in 1918. In the campaign Lewis cleverly minimized the Court issue, stressing prohibition (he favored repeal) and the economic decline of the country under Republican rule. Mrs. McCormick, while continuing to emphasize her opposition to the Court, modified her previous support of prohibition and agreed to abide by a state referendum on the question. This decision brought charges of political expediency against her; a Senate investigation of her large primary campaign expenditures, which some estimates placed as high as $750,000, caused further unfavorable publicity. Laboring under these partly self-imposed difficulties, and unable to counter the "hard times" issue, she was soundly defeated by Lewis. This loss ended any further attempts to win national office, though it did not terminate her political career.

For the next several years most of her time was absorbed by other activities. On Mar. 9, 1932, she was married to Albert Gallatin Simms, a former Congressman from New Mexico, whom she had met while serving in the House. In 1926 she had acquired control of a newspaper in Rockford, Ill., as an adjunct to her political activities; by 1930 she had added a second newspaper and a radio station. She also owned a 2,500-acre dairy farm at nearby Byron. After her second marriage she developed a 250,000-acre cattle and sheep ranch at Trinchera, Colo., and founded the Sandia School for Girls at Albuquerque, N.Mex.

In 1939 Mrs. Simms returned to the political scene as co-manager of Thomas E. Dewey's preconvention campaign for the Republican nomination for president. Unsuccessful in obtaining Dewey's nomination, she threw her support after the convention to Wendell Willkie. In 1944 she again came out for Dewey, aiding in his nomination, though she did not serve on his official "strategy board." She died that December in Chicago, following an operation for pancreatitis, and was buried at Fairview Cemetery, Albuquerque, N.Mex. Mrs. Simms had no formal religious affiliation but attended Quaker and Presbyterian services. Few women in her time held so many important political positions. Although her career did not reach the heights that some had predicted, she won wide respect as a "working politician," as she described herself, and this perhaps was her greatest desire.

[Mrs. Simms' papers are in the Library of Congress. Of secondary sources, the following proved most helpful: obituaries in *N.Y. Times* and *Chicago Tribune* of Jan. 1, 1945; *Nat. Cyc. Am. Biog.*, XXXIV, 162–63; Raymond Moley, *27 Masters of Politics* (1949); Ida C. Clarke, "A Woman in the White House," *Century Mag.*, Mar. 1927; Charles A. Selden, 'The Father Complex of Alice Roosevelt Longworth and Ruth Hanna McCormick," *Ladies' Home Jour.*, Mar. 1927; William G. Shepherd, "Mark Another Hanna," *Colliers,* Mar. 15, 1930. See also Mabel W. Cameron, ed., *Biog. Cyc. Am. Women,* I (1924), 188–89; Ida H. Harper, ed., *The Hist. of Woman Suffrage,* vols. V and VI (1922); Mildred Adams in *Nation,* Oct. 26, 1927; William T. Hutchinson, *Lowden of Ill.* (2 vols., 1957).]

RALPH A. STONE

**SINCLAIR, Catherine.** *See* FORREST, Catherine Norton Sinclair.

**SKINNER, Constance Lindsay** (Dec. 7, 1877–Mar. 27, 1939), author and historian, was reared in the remote Canadian Northwest, the only child of Robert James Skinner and Annie (Lindsay) Skinner. Her father was of English ancestry; her mother's Scottish forebears included Lady Anne Lindsay, balladeer, and David Lindsay, poet and historian. In her own literary career she used Lindsay as her middle name, though on her birth record she is Constance Annie Skinner. Born in Quesnel, British Columbia, she spent her girlhood at a fur-trading post in the Peace River area, where her father was an agent for the Hudson's Bay Company. This early exposure to Indian life and rugged frontier conditions etched deep impressions upon the young girl's mind and decisively influenced all her writings. A childhood literary bent was encouraged by her parents, who supervised their daughter's early education and made it possible for her to read the classics of English literature in their extensive library. When she was fourteen the family moved to Vancouver, where she attended a private school and published stories in local newspapers.

At sixteen, for reasons of health, Constance was sent to live with an aunt in California. She was to remain in the United States the rest of her life. She pursued her precocious career in journalism by writing drama and music criticism for the *Los Angeles Times* and the *San Francisco Examiner,* spending one summer in the La Jolla ranch house of the Polish actress HELEN MODJESKA, whom she had met in connection with a newspaper interview. Upon reaching adulthood she left the West Coast and lived for three years in Chicago, where she gained more experience as a writer for the *Chicago American.* Eventually traversing the continent completely, she settled in New York City as a free-lance writer. She wrote book reviews for the *Herald Tribune* and, from 1913 onward, published in such periodicals as *Poetry*, the *North American Review,* and the *Bookman* poems which often evoked the frontier and the Indian life she had known as a girl. In 1910 her first play, *David,* had been presented in Carmel, Calif., and in 1917 another, *Good Morning, Rosamund!* was produced in New York. In a 1919 article in the *Bookman* she expressed the view that such plays dealing with patriotic themes could help "Americanize our non-reading amusement-seekers of foreign birth and foreign ideas."

Her literary work having attracted attention, Miss Skinner was asked to write two volumes dealing with frontier topics in the fifty-volume Yale University Chronicles of America series, an ambitious attempt to present American history to the general reader. Reviewers found her *Pioneers of the Old Southwest* (1919) and *Adventurers of Oregon* (1920) highly readable but rather facile and factually imprecise. "[T]he effort to maintain a swiftly moving narrative has betrayed the author into sacrificing clarity," wrote one (*Mississippi Valley Historical Review,* September 1920). Her subsequent historical works, *Adventures in the Wilderness* (a 1925 publication in Yale's Pageant of America series) and *Beaver, Kings and Cabins* (1933), received similarly mixed notices. The historian Frederick Jackson Turner, however, author of the seminal essay "The Significance of the Frontier in American History" (1893), praised her books, and the two carried on an extended correspondence. Writing of Turner's influence upon her, Miss Skinner said it had turned her thoughts "more intensely upon America, as a land and a nation unique in the world." She was hostile to the economic interpretation of American history propounded by Charles A. Beard and his adherents, and viewed her own books, with their stress on rivers, mountains, and forests, as ammunition in what she believed to be a great struggle between Beardian "Economists" and Turnerian "Geographers" for supremacy in American historiography.

As she grew older, Miss Skinner increasingly chose to treat her favorite themes in poetry and fiction. From 1925 to 1934 she produced eleven adventure stories for children, again based on frontier life. These books have been praised for their realism and "splendid vitality" (Cornelia Meigs et al., *A Critical History of Children's Literature*, 1953, pp. 501–02). In 1930 she published *Songs of the Coast Dwellers*, a collection of poems inspired by the mythic legends of the Squamish Indians of British Columbia which she recalled from girlhood. This won high praise from such critics as Louis Untermeyer and Granville Hicks, who spoke of the "delicately woven lyrics of a texture unique in our literature."

In the 1930's Miss Skinner conceived the concept of writing an ambitious work which would demonstrate the crucial historical importance of the world's great rivers. At Turner's suggestion she reduced the scope of the project to American rivers and decided that a cooperative effort utilizing many authors was more practicable. The proposal appealed to the publishers Farrar & Rinehart, who in 1935 initiated a Rivers of America series with Constance Skinner as general editor. She enthusiastically supervised the realization of her dream and in 1937 made a coast-to-coast tour promoting the series in speeches before interested groups. The first volume, *Kennebec: Cradle of Americans* by Robert P. Tristram Coffin, appeared in that year. Reflecting Miss Skinner's views, the authors of the various books in the series emphasized literary grace and popular appeal while giving secondary consideration to careful research and accuracy of detail. The series proved a commercial and popular success, more than forty volumes eventually being published.

Constance Skinner was dark and striking in appearance, a fact she attributed to a Spanish ancestor on her father's side. She never married. For most of her adult life she lived in a New York City apartment filled with frontier memorabilia. She had planned to write the Missouri River volume in the Rivers of America series, but died in 1939 in her Park Avenue apartment (of arteriosclerosis and a coronary occlusion) before she could complete it. Her ashes were placed in the Ferncliff Mausoleum at Hartsdale, N.Y. The following year the Women's National Book Association established the Constance Lindsay Skinner Award, a bronze plaque presented annually to a woman who has made "an outstanding contribution to the world of books."

Miss Skinner was not a careful scholar, and her patriotic stress on "Americanism" exposed her to the temptations of chauvinism and nativism, particularly in the fervid days of World War I. Yet in her dedicated work for the Rivers of America series and in her own best writing she was, as Henry Steele Commager wrote at her death, "inspired by a lyric affection for the land and its people."

[For important insights into Miss Skinner's thinking see her "History as Literature: and the Individual Definition," *Bookman*, Aug. 1919; "Rivers and Am. Folk," a prefatory essay appearing in the earlier volumes of the Rivers of America series; and Frederick Jackson Turner's letter to her published with an introduction by Miss Skinner in *Wis. Mag. of Hist.*, Sept. 1935, pp. 91–103. For biographical details see: Jean West Maury, "From a Fur-Trading Post to N.Y.," in *Boston Transcript*, May 6, 1933; Durward Howes, ed., *Am. Women*, 1937–38; articles in *Horn Book*, July–Aug. 1939; obituaries in *Publishers' Weekly*, Apr. 1, 1939, *Library Jour.*, Apr. 15, 1939, and *N.Y. Times*, Mar. 28, 1939. For reviews of *Songs of the Coast Dwellers* see *N.Y. World*, May 4, 1930 (Hicks); *Saturday Rev. of Literature*, May 31, 1930 (Untermeyer); *Poetry*, Aug. 1930; and *Nation*, June 18, 1930. Henry Steele Commager's tribute appears in the *N.Y. Herald Tribune* book section, Apr. 9, 1939. Birth record from Division of Vital Statistics, Victoria, B.C.; death record from N.Y. City Dept. of Health.]

PAUL S. BOYER

**SLAGLE, Eleanor Clarke** (Oct. 13, 1871–Sept. 18, 1942), leader in occupational therapy, was born in Hobart, N.Y., the younger of two children and only daughter of William John Clarke, a cooper, who had risen from enlisted to officer rank during the Civil War, and Emmaline J. (Davenport) Clarke, said to have been a descendant of the John Davenport who was one of the founders of Yale. Originally named Ella May, she later used the name Eleanor. Her brother, John Davenport Clarke, served for some years (1921–25, 1927–33) as a Republican Congressman from New York. For most of Eleanor's childhood the family lived in Stamford, N.Y.; in 1887 they moved to Delhi, where her father became sheriff of Delaware County.

Little is known of her early life and schooling. When her parents were divorced she chose to live with her father, and she apparently attended Claverack College in Columbia County, N.Y., for at least one term. She was married, probably in Chicago, to Robert E. Slagle, who is said to have been an officer of the Pullman Company; in 1897 she was living in St. Louis. There were no children, and the marriage ended in divorce. A niece later commented that "there were whole periods of her life she never mentioned."

In 1908, now in her late thirties, Mrs. Slagle entered the field of social welfare. Working at Hull House in Chicago under the guidance of JANE ADDAMS and of JULIA LATHROP, who was especially concerned with the care of the mentally ill, she was a member of the first class to take the course in "Invalid Occupation" offered by the Chicago School of Civics and Philanthropy (later the school of social work of the University of Chicago). Her fledgling interests in occupational therapy were also encouraged by the psychiatrist Adolf Meyer, who from his work in hospitals for the insane in Illinois, Massachusetts, and New York had become strongly convinced of the value of occupational therapy—manual and mental occupations suited to the individual patient's needs—in healing the mentally ill. When Dr. Meyer became the first director of the Henry Phipps Psychiatric Clinic at the Johns Hopkins Hospital in Baltimore, he called in Mrs. Slagle (1913) to help organize its occupational therapy program.

Mrs. Slagle returned to Chicago in 1915 to become the director of the Henry B. Favill School of Occupations for the training of occupational therapy aides. Two years later she set up training courses in occupational therapy at Hull House. In 1918 she became superintendent of occupational therapy for the Illinois Department of Public Welfare, and in that position organized and supervised a therapy program in the state's mental hospitals. The success of this program led to her appointment, in 1922, as director of occupational therapy for the New York State Hospital Commission (later the State Department of Mental Hygiene), a position she held until her death. Although by 1922 the value of occupational therapy in treating mental illness was well recognized and such therapy was frequently used in smaller, private hospitals, few thought

that it could be applied successfully on as large a scale as would be necessary in a state hospital system—a feat that Eleanor Slagle accomplished. Under her leadership the number of classes for patients increased, capable therapists were employed, and ward classes and occupational centers were introduced. By 1933 nearly 70,000 patients in New York's state mental hospitals were participating in such programs. Mrs. Slagle also began, in 1924, an annual institute for the chief occupational therapists of the New York state hospital system as a means of improving professional practice. Her work became the model for institutions throughout the nation, and she was frequently called upon to guide the development of similar programs elsewhere.

Mrs. Slagle was one of five persons who organized, in 1917, the National Society for the Promotion of Occupational Therapy, after 1921 renamed the American Occupational Therapy Association. She served as its secretary in 1918, vice-president in 1919, president in 1920, and from 1922 to 1937 as executive secretary. Through the organization she worked for the establishment of minimum standards of training and for the registration of occupational therapists. She also sought to make the association a counseling organization that would provide information and assistance to all institutions seeking to establish occupational therapy programs. She served as chairman of a committee on occupational therapy for the General Federation of Women's Clubs, guided Junior League activities in occupational therapy in several cities, and encouraged groups such as the League of Women Voters to help make it possible to meet the needs of the mentally ill in rehabilitation through therapy. When she retired from her association post in 1937, Mrs. Slagle was given a testimonial dinner at Atlantic City at which Mrs. Franklin D. Roosevelt paid tribute to her, Dr. Adolph Meyer referred to her as "the personification of occupational therapy," and members of the association presented her with a gift of $2,000. This she used to help buy a home in Philipse Manor, near Tarrytown, N.Y.

For the last ten years of her life Mrs. Slagle suffered from arteriosclerosis. In 1940 she sustained a back injury that left her a semi-invalid, and in September 1942 she died in her home, of a coronary thrombosis. After funeral services at Christ Episcopal Church, Philipse Manor, she was buried at Locust Hill Cemetery in Hobart, N.Y. From Mrs. Slagle's work dates the beginning of a planned and sustained program in occupational therapy for the mentally ill. Among the first to give courses for the training of occupational therapists, she became the recognized leader in a new professional field.

[Mrs. Slagle's published works include: "Training Aides for Mental Patients," *State Hospital Quart.*, Feb. 1922 (also published in *Archives of Occupational Therapy*, Feb. 1922); "A Year's Development of Occupational Therapy in N.Y. State Hospitals," *State Hospital Quart.*, Aug. 1923 (also published in *Modern Hospital*, Jan. 1924); "To Organize an 'O.T.' Department," *Occupational Therapy and Rehabilitation*, Apr. 1927; "Training of Occupational Therapists," *Psychiatric Quart.*, Jan. 1931; "Occupational Therapy Programme in the State of N.Y.," *Jour. of Mental Science*, Oct. 1934. She also compiled and edited *Games and Field Day Programs* (1933). Many of her activities are chronicled in various notes and reports of annual meetings of the Am. Occupational Therapy Assoc. appearing in *Occupational Therapy and Rehabilitation;* also useful are reports on occupational therapy in the *Modern Hospital*. A concise biographical sketch appears in Durward Howes, ed., *Am. Women*, 1939–40. Several brief and often repetitious sketches of her life and work appeared at the time of her death; see *Occupational Therapy and Rehabilitation*, Dec. 1942; *Am. Jour. of Psychiatry*, Nov. 1942; *Mental Hygiene*, Jan. 1943; *Psychiatric Quart.*, Oct. 1942; and *N.Y. Times*, Sept. 20, 1942. Mrs. Slagle's position in the development of occupational therapy is briefly mentioned in William R. Dunton's "Hist. and Development of Occupational Therapy," in Helen S. Willard and Clare S. Spackman, eds., *Principles of Occupational Therapy* (1947). Information about her family and early life was provided by a niece, Mrs. Catherine Clarke Colby of Newcastle, Maine, and by Miss Elizabeth H. McDowell, Librarian, The Cannon Free Library, Delhi, N.Y., drawing upon census records for 1870, 1875, and 1880 and soldiers' discharge records in the County Clerk's office, Delhi. Although Mrs. Slagle's death record (N.Y. State Dept. of Health) gives her birth year as 1876 and her tombstone has the year as 1868, census records list her age in 1875 as four and in 1880 as nine.]

**SLOCUM, Frances** (Mar. 4, 1773–Mar. 9, 1847), Indian captive, was born in Warwick, R.I., the third daughter and seventh of ten children of Jonathan Slocum, a farmer, and Ruth (Tripp) Slocum, and a descendant of Anthony Slocum, an English settler of Taunton, Mass., in 1637. In 1777 her Quaker parents migrated to the Wyoming Valley in Pennsylvania, settling on the present site of Wilkes-Barre. The family survived the Wyoming massacre by Tories and Indians in the summer of 1778, but on Nov. 2 three Delawares captured red-haired Frances, then five years old, and a neighbor boy; Jonathan Slo-

cum was killed by Indians six weeks later. At the close of the war Frances' brothers began a widespread search for her, visiting Indian villages from western New York to Detroit. Mrs. Slocum never reconciled herself to the girl's disappearance and at her death in 1807 charged her children to continue the search, which altogether lasted fifty-nine years.

Frances had been taken after her capture to Tioga (Athens, Pa.) and thence to an Indian village near Niagara Falls, where she was adopted by a Delaware couple and given the name of a daughter they had recently lost, Weletawash. During the last years of the Revolutionary War her Indian family lived on the Detroit River, then moved to the great Miami town of Kekionga (Fort Wayne, Ind.). About 1791 or 1792 she was married to a Delaware, but apparently the marriage was not satisfactory, for her husband moved west of the Mississippi with his people and Frances remained with her foster parents. Sometime after 1794 she married a Miami named Shepancanah, taking the Miami name of Maconaqua, or "Little Bear." The couple presently moved southwest to the Mississinewa River in Indiana, where they lived peacefully the rest of their lives. Shepancanah became war chief of his village, but deafness eventually obliged him to relinquish his leadership, and he moved his family four miles upstream to a small settlement which became known as "the Deaf Man's village." Frances gave birth to two sons, who died very young, and to two daughters who survived her: Kekesequa, born in 1800, and Ozahshinqua, born about 1809. The village was untouched either by the War of 1812 or by the ever-increasing numbers of white settlers, and Frances Slocum lived undetected by her own people. Her husband died about 1832; her daughters married and lived close by. A good manager, well esteemed by the Miamis, she had accumulated a hundred or more horses, cattle, and other livestock.

In January 1835 a visiting fur trader, George W. Ewing, noticed the whiteness of Frances Slocum's skin, questioned her (in the Miami language), and eventually learned her story. She told him all she could remember: her father's name, that he was a Quaker, that she had brothers and sisters, and that they had lived on the Susquehanna River. Only the probability that all her family were dead now induced her to speak, for she had always feared that her relatives would take her away if they knew where she was; she distrusted the whites and was devoted to her daughters and grandchildren. Ewing wrote to the postmaster at Lancaster, Pa., to learn if there were any Slocums in the vicinity, but his letter was neglected until March 1837, when it was published in the local paper. The account reached Joseph Slocum, a younger brother of Frances, in Wilkes-Barre, and, notifying his brother Isaac and sister Mary in Ohio, he set out for Peru, Ind., the town nearest to Frances' village. In September 1837 the three visited their sister with two interpreters. Frances was sixty-four, her sister four years older, her brothers two and three years younger. The meeting was painful to all, but with her daughters and son-in-law Frances accompanied her relatives to Peru for supper. The next day she talked again to them, but she refused to go back east since she was happy where she was and wanted to die where "the Great Spirit will know where to find me."

Two years later Joseph Slocum took his two daughters to visit her, and Frances was pleased and honored. One daughter described her as small, somewhat gray-haired, her eyes a bright chestnut, her face very much wrinkled and weathered; she wore several Indian earrings. Her dress consisted of "a blue calico short gown, a white Mackinaw blanket, somewhat soiled by constant wear; a fold of blue broadcloth lapped around her, red cloth leggins and buckskin moccasins." When in 1840 the Miamis agreed to give up the last of their lands in Indiana and remove to Kansas, Frances appealed to her brothers and with their aid successfully petitioned Congress to allow her to remain on the tract of land granted to her daughters under an earlier treaty. At her request her nephew George Slocum and his family went to live with her in 1846 to help manage her farm and stock. She died of pneumonia in 1847, shortly after her seventy-fourth birthday, and was buried a few yards from her cabin beside her husband and two sons. Her elder daughter died four days later, her younger daughter in 1877. Numerous grandchildren of mixed Indian, English, and French blood survived; in 1900 some of her descendants erected a stone shaft over her grave. White settlers near her referred to Frances Slocum as "the White Rose of the Miamis," and her story of courage and adaptation is a favorite in Indiana. In 1965, in preparation for a new dam on the Mississinewa River which flooded the site of the Deaf Man's village, her grave was moved a short distance to a new location on Bowman Road near the Frances Slocum State Forest.

[John Todd, *The Lost Sister of Wyoming* (1842), first told her story. The most complete and careful account is John F. Meginness, *Biog. of Frances Slocum* (1891). See also Martha Bennett Phelps, *Frances Slocum, the Lost Sister of Wyoming* (1905), by a grandniece; Otho Winger, *The Lost Sister among the Miamis* (1936); *The Journals and Indian Paintings of George Winter* (1948); and Howard H. Peckham, *Captured by Indians* (1954).]

HOWARD H. PECKHAM

**SLOWE, Lucy Diggs** (July 4, 1885–Oct. 21, 1937), teacher, school administrator, and college dean, was born in Berryville, Va., the third daughter and youngest of seven children of Henry and Fannie (Potter) Slowe. After losing her father at nine months and her mother at six years, she went to live in Lexington, Va., with a paternal aunt, Martha Slowe Price; in 1898 they moved to Baltimore, Md. Lucy entered the elementary school at approximately the fifth grade. Upon graduation, as salutatorian, from the colored high school in Baltimore in 1904, she entered Howard University, Washington, D.C., with the aid of a scholarship. During her college years she was one of the founders and vice-president of Alpha Kappa Alpha, the first sorority among Negro college women.

Following her graduation in 1908, Lucy Slowe embarked upon a career in secondary education, teaching English in high schools in Baltimore and Washington for the next eleven years, in the course of which she took a master's degree in English from Columbia University (1915). When in 1919 the Shaw Junior High School was established in Washington, the first such school in the colored division of the city system, she became its principal. Here she initiated in-service training by arranging for an extension course on education at the junior high school level to be given by Columbia University, a course which was also attended by the staff of the white junior high school.

In 1922 Miss Slowe was called to Howard University as dean of women, serving also as professor of English and of education. Guided by the points of view of such women as Professors Sarah Sturtevant, Harriet Hayes, and Esther Lloyd-Jones of Teachers College, Columbia, and Thyrsa Amos of the University of Pittsburgh, she launched a vigorous struggle to change the image of the dean of women from that of a matron, as then conceived by the heads of most Negro institutions of higher learning, to one of a specialist in the education of women. She introduced a course for deans and counselors to girls. The influence of her battle for the newer concept of deanship extended not only to women's education in other Negro schools but also to that of men, and her organization of deans and advisers to girls in Negro schools undoubtedly stimulated a similar group among male personnel workers. Thomas E. Hawkins, who became assistant to the dean of men at Howard in 1933 and later dean of men at Hampton Institute, drew particular inspiration from her.

Dean Slowe founded or assisted in the organization of the National Council of Negro Women (1935), of which she was the first secretary, and the National Association of College Women, of which she was the first president (1923–29). Patterned after the American Association of University Women (of which she was a member), the latter group through its committee on standards exerted an influence on curricular offerings in institutions seeking a place on its approved list of schools. Miss Slowe also served on the boards of several Washington welfare agencies and worked with the National Young Women's Christian Association and the Women's International League for Peace and Freedom. She was an accomplished tennis player, winning seventeen tennis cups. Long interested in music, having sung in Baltimore as a contralto in St. Francis Catholic Church and in the choir of her own church, the Madison Street Presbyterian, she inaugurated a lecture-concert series at Howard.

Lucy Slowe was an intense and unremitting worker, and over the years her health suffered. In August 1937 she contracted influenza. Failing to recover, she died that October at her Washington home of kidney disease, aged fifty-three. She was buried in Lincoln Cemetery in Washington. A stained-glass window in the Howard University Chapel honors her memory.

[*Jour. of the Nat. Assoc. of College Women*, No. 14 (1937), an issue dedicated to Dean Slowe—see especially articles by Dwight O. W. Holmes and Joanna Houston; *Jour. of the College Alumnae Club of Washington*, Memorial Edition, Jan. 1939, a special number containing writings and addresses of Dean Slowe and tributes to her (both publications available in Moorland Collection, Howard Univ.); *Negro Hist. Bull.*, Jan. 1955, pp. 90–91; Durward Howes, ed., *Am. Women*, 1935–36; interviews with friends and former associates of Dean Slowe; close personal association. A number of articles by Dean Slowe, including her presidential addresses, may be found in the *Jour. of the Nat. Assoc. of College Women*, 1924–35. Other articles by her include: "What Contributions Social Activities Fostered by the Institutions Make to the Moral and Social Development of Students in Negro Colleges," *Quart. Rev. of Higher Education among Negroes*, July 1933; "Higher Education of Negro Women," *Jour. of Negro Education*, July 1933.]

MARION THOMPSON WRIGHT

**SMEDLEY, Agnes** (1892?–May 6, 1950), author and foreign correspondent, champion of revolutionary China, was born in rural northwest Missouri, the second daughter and second of the five children of Charles H. and Sarah (Ralls) Smedley. Her father, who had only a third-grade education, was a heavy-drinking farmer and unskilled laborer. Her mother, only slightly more educated, led a life of toil as housekeeper, washerwoman, and keeper of boarders. Although Agnes Smedley was later to maintain that her early life was "healthy and securely rooted in the soil," there is little doubt that the family had to struggle for its meager existence. When she was about ten, they moved to southern Colorado, where for the next six years her father tried vainly to improve his fortunes in the region's coal-mining towns. The children went to school irregularly, and Agnes did not finish grade school. Instead she held a variety of menial jobs, as washerwoman, hired girl, and tobacco stripper in a cigar factory.

A stint as a teacher in impoverished schools in New Mexico, however, whetted her appetite for learning and independence, and soon after the death of her mother and her older sister, when Agnes was sixteen, she broke from her family. With the help of an aunt she learned stenography and worked as a secretary in Denver. After several painful experiences as a traveling book agent, she enrolled in the Normal School in Tempe, Ariz. It was during her year there (1911–12) that she met the young Swedish-American civil engineer whom she was to marry precipitously and who, after a few years, divorced her. Little is known of this marriage, but it was spent mostly in California, where she attended university classes part-time, taught in a state normal school, and was first introduced to socialist ideas by Upton Sinclair and other friends.

With the breakup of her marriage she moved to New York City, probably in the winter of 1916–17. Here she attended New York University at night and worked for a magazine during the day. She was increasingly active in socialist affairs and opposed the entry of the United States into World War I. Now in her mid-twenties, she had begun to write and to be interested in poverty as a subject, not merely as a personal experience. At this time she met and studied with Lala Laipat Rai, an exiled Indian Nationalist. On Mar. 18, 1918, she was arrested on charges that she had violated the federal Espionage Act by serving as an unregistered agent of the Indian Nationalist Party (which unbeknown to her had received some funds from German sources). Before these charges were dismissed, Miss Smedley was held in the Tombs prison in New York for several weeks, part of the time in solitary confinement.

Leaving the United States in 1919 as a stewardess on a Polish-American freighter, she soon made her way to Germany, where she spent nine difficult years of work, study, and political activity on behalf of Indian independence. She taught English at the University of Berlin, where she also did graduate work in Oriental studies, and joined with a group of Berlin physicians in establishing Germany's first state birth control clinic. Although they were never legally married, she lived in Berlin as the wife of the Indian revolutionary Virendranath Chattopadhyaya. The multiple tensions of these years drove Miss Smedley to attempt suicide, and for two years she underwent psychoanalysis. Several months of 1927 were spent in the writing of her patently autobiographical novel, *Daughter of Earth* (1929). When the alliance with Chattopadhyaya ended in 1928, she left Germany for China as special correspondent for the *Frankfurter Zeitung*, hoping to proceed from there to India.

It was in strife-torn revolutionary China, however, that Agnes Smedley's sympathies and talents found fulfillment. Here she reconciled the conflicting elements of her nature: for the first time she could be a tender woman, militantly compassionate, yet have the freedom of action of a man. Moreover, though her life was often hard, she could, by virtue of her profession as journalist, withdraw periodically from the harsh reality and transmute her private experience into compelling communication. Reaching Manchuria early in 1929, she proceeded after some months to Shanghai, which became her headquarters for periodic journalistic forays to other cities. Initially a supporter of Chiang Kai-shek's Kuomintang government, she soon came under the influence of a group of Communist and anti-Chiang intellectuals in Shanghai, notably the writers Lu Hsün and Mao Tun, with whom she collaborated in the preparation of anti-Chiang manifestos for the Western press. She now lost her *Frankfurter Zeitung* position and turned to free-lance writing, producing in *Chinese Destinies* (1933) a series of powerful vignettes of Chinese life in the early 1930's.

In the spring of 1934, after eleven months of treatment for a heart condition in a Soviet sanatorium in the Caucasus, Miss Smedley returned to New York in a fruitless search for journalistic employment. Her *China's Red Army Marches*, an enthusiastic account of the organization and growth of the Red Army and its early campaigns against the Kuomintang, based in part upon firsthand evidence, was published in New York in 1934. Back in Shanghai by late 1935, Miss Smedley interviewed veterans of the Red Army's epic "Long March" northward in 1934–35, collected medical supplies for the Communist forces, and in 1936 herself set out for the Communists' north China stronghold. After an interlude in Sian, where she made English-language broadcasts for the Communists at the time of the bizarre "Sian Incident" (December 1936) involving the capture and brief imprisonment of Chiang Kai-shek, she proceeded early in 1937 to Yenan. As one of the first Westerners to reach this Communist headquarters city, she organized clandestine visits to Yenan by her Shanghai journalistic colleagues. She also commenced a biography of the Red Army commander Chu Teh (published posthumously in 1956 as *The Great Road: The Life and Times of Chu Teh*); formed close associations with Mao Tse-tung, Chou En-lai, and others who were to figure prominently in postwar Chinese affairs; and, at Chu Teh's request, gathered from abroad a library of books on military strategy. By her own testimony she herself never joined the Communist party, feeling a profound unwillingness to "become a mere instrument in the hands of men who believed that they held the one and only key to truth" (*Battle Hymn of China*, p. 10).

With the outbreak of the Sino-Japanese war in July 1937, Agnes Smedley joined the Eighth Route Army (the renamed Red Army) on the battlefront against the Japanese. She spent the closing months of 1937 in Shansi Province, dividing her time between the headquarters of Chu Teh and that of Lin Piao, then a divisional commander. She kept her hair cropped close and wore regular Red Army fatigues, her features, handsome in a masculine way, growing more rugged through exposure to the elements. Covering hundreds of miles on foot despite a painful spinal condition, and living under circumstances of great privation, she nevertheless managed to continue her writing. Her *China Fights Back: An American Woman with the Eighth Route Army* was published in New York in 1938.

Early that year, on instructions from Chu Teh, she went south to Hankow, Chiang Kai-shek's provisional capital. Here she became a publicist and field worker for Dr. Robert K. S. Lim's Chinese Red Cross Medical Corps and a special correspondent for the *Manchester Guardian*. From October 1938 to mid-1940 she traveled in the lower Yangtze River region with units of the New Fourth

Army, a Communist guerrilla force engaged in village-level political organization in areas nominally held by the Japanese. She helped establish medical centers and delousing stations; secured Red Cross supplies where needed; lectured on international affairs to peasants and army recruits; and, when possible, filed her stories with the *Guardian*. Illness brought this period to a close, and after a summer in hospitals in Chungking and at Dr. Lim's Red Cross headquarters in Kweiyang, she was flown in September 1940 to Hong Kong for treatment of malaria and a gall-bladder condition. Partially recovered, she was soon deep in the efforts being made from Hong Kong to aid the Chinese war effort. She returned to America in the summer of 1941. Here she wrote *Battle Hymn of China* (1943), an extended account of her experiences in the Far East. Published by a well-known house (Knopf) at a time when most Americans viewed Chinese of all factions as courageous allies, *Battle Hymn of China* became Miss Smedley's most widely read book.

In terms of popular acceptance, the years 1943–44 represent the zenith of her career. She continued thereafter to write, lecture, and broadcast, but as American opinion on the subject of Chinese Communism hardened, her position became untenable. A 1949 report issued from Gen. Douglas MacArthur's Tokyo headquarters accused her of complicity in a Soviet spy ring in the Far East, and though the accusation was quickly withdrawn by the Secretary of the Army, the damage to her reputation forced Miss Smedley to seek refuge in England. She died in an Oxford nursing home in May 1950, of bronchopneumonia following a partial gastrectomy. Her request for burial in China was granted, and in an unexpected honor her ashes were placed in Peking's National Memorial Cemetery of Revolutionary Martyrs with a marble cenotaph inscribed: "To Agnes Smedley, friend of the Chinese Revolution." Fifteen years later she was still the only non-Communist foreigner buried there.

Agnes Smedley's news reports, her books, and her personal efforts on behalf of the Chinese revolution give her a unique place among the handful of Americans who played a direct part in one of the most critical decades of modern Chinese history. However partial she was to the ultimate goals of Chinese Communism, she wrote with the insight of a good journalist, and much in her books remains of value for an understanding of the events in which she participated. In the opinion of a fellow American correspondent, Theodore H. White, Miss Smedley was memorable "not so much for her judgment (which was poor), as for her great heart and selfless devotion to those causes which stirred the American left in the thirties and forties."

[Miss Smedley's *China Fights Back* and *Battle Hymn of China*, the latter including an autobiographical introduction covering her life prior to 1929, are primary sources. The "Publisher's Foreword" (by Leo Huberman and Paul M. Sweezy) to *The Great Road: The Life and Times of Chu Teh* is a partisan assessment of her contributions to contemporary historical writing about China. *Current Biog.*, 1944, includes a sketch and photograph, and Evans F. Carlson, *Twin Stars of China* (1940), contains a number of references. Hilda Selwyn-Clarke and Harold L. Ickes wrote obituaries for, respectively, the *New Statesman and Nation* (May 20, 1950) and *New Republic* (May 29, 1950). For Miss Smedley's articles in the *Nation, New Republic, Asia,* and other periodicals, see *Readers' Guide to Periodical Literature,* 1925–47. For her friendship with Upton Sinclair, see his MS. "The Red Dragon: The Story of Agnes Smedley in America and China," Sinclair Papers, Ind. Univ. Library. Theodore H. White supplied a helpful assessment, and Edgar Snow provided much useful information, including the inscription on her cenotaph. Miss Smedley's enrollment date from Ariz. State Univ., Tempe; death record from General Register Office, Somerset House, London.]

RONALD GOTTESMAN

SMITH, Abby Hadassah (June 1, 1797–July 23, 1878) and Julia Evelina (May 27, 1792–Mar. 6, 1886), Connecticut suffragists, were born in Glastonbury, where their paternal ancestors had settled in 1693. Their father, Zephaniah Hollister Smith, a graduate of Yale, had left the Congregational ministry after concluding that it was against his conscience to receive money for preaching and had established a law practice. His wife, Hannah Hadassah Hickock of South Britain, Conn., invariably described as "a remarkable woman," was an amateur poet, linguist, mathematician, and astronomer. Their five daughters, of whom Abby and Julia were the youngest, shared the parents' independence of thought and diversity of interests.

Except for a few years during which Julia and an older sister taught in EMMA WILLARD's school in Troy, N.Y., the five spinsters spent their quiet lives in the farm homestead, absorbed in perfecting their individual skills (one sister, Laurilla Aleroya, produced a quantity of creditable primitive paintings), in the work of the household, in temperance meetings and singing school, and in quiet charity to the sick and needy. Deeply religious, but taught by their father to go directly to the Bible for inspiration and instruction, they acknowledged no established doctrine, did not attend church, and refused to allow a minister to officiate at family burials. The Smiths first came into public notice in pre–Civil War days when they invited William Lloyd Garrison, barred from the Hartford churches, to hold abolitionist meetings on their front lawn. Mrs. Smith drew up and secured signatures for one of the first antislavery petitions presented before Congress by John Quincy Adams, and Julia was the local distributor for the *Charter Oak,* an antislavery newspaper.

In 1869 Abby and Julia Smith, now the sole surviving members of the family, attended a woman suffrage meeting in Hartford, and in 1873 Abby attended in New York the first meeting of the Association for the Advancement of Women. Convinced that "the women had truth on their side," the sisters soon found occasion to witness to their conviction. In November 1873, indignant over what they believed to be an inequitable property tax levied against them, they braved the male stronghold of town meeting. Abby, the more intrepid of the two, requested permission to speak, and read a spirited protest against taxation without representation, drawing analogies to the antislavery struggle and insisting that women who were required to pay taxes should have an equal voice in their levying and expenditure. When, on a second appearance five months later, she was refused the right to speak, Abby climbed on a wagon which stood outside the building and determinedly read aloud the speech she had prepared. To all subsequent bills for taxes the sisters replied that they could not feel it right to pay.

In January 1874 seven of the sisters' cherished Alderney cows were attached and sold. In June of the same year fifteen acres of the Smith pastureland, valued at $2,000, were put up for auction to cover delinquent taxes of about fifty dollars. Expecting to buy back their land as they had the cows, the sisters found the bidding closed before they could speak and the valuable acreage sold for $78.35 to a neighbor who had coveted it for years. They at once brought suit against the tax collector for violating a town law that land could not be taken before movable property for unpaid taxes. Through two years, three trials, and countless evasions and discouragements, this suit dragged through the Hartford courts. At one time, despairing of a lawyer, the two aged sisters began the study of law with the intention of conducting their own case. A lawyer was found, however, who won a final decision in their favor in November 1876.

Abby Smith's first speech had appeared in the *Hartford Courant,* and soon newspapers and magazines across the country took up the story. "The Glastonbury cows," which were twice more driven to the auction block, became famous (souvenirs made from the hair of their tails appeared in Chicago), and contributions poured in to a defense fund set up by the *Springfield Republican.* The sisters' frequent letters to the editor, written with sprightly style, disconcerting logic, and dry Yankee humor, sounded a fresh and insistent note in the woman's rights movement and attracted the notice of ISABELLA BEECHER HOOKER, LUCY STONE, and other leaders. Clearly relishing their sudden fame, the sisters accepted invitations to speak at numerous suffrage gatherings, including conventions of the National Woman Suffrage Association. In January 1878 Julia spoke at a hearing before the Senate Committee on Privileges and Elections in Washington, and in March, Abby testified in Hartford before a committee of the Connecticut legislature. In their joint appearances the sisters stood side by side on the platform, Abby, the taller, usually delivering an earnest speech written in advance, while Julia, slight and wiry, spoke more informally and with a keener awareness of the humorous aspects of their plight. The letters, speeches, and newspaper accounts pertaining to the case were later collected and published by Julia in a ninety-four-page pamphlet, *Abby Smith and Her Cows, with a Report of the Law Case Decided Contrary to Law* (1877).

Julia Smith was the scholar of the two, and in 1876, hoping to aid the suffrage cause by demonstrating what a mere woman had accomplished (and also slightly piqued by her sister's greater celebrity), she published at her own expense a translation of the Bible she had completed twenty years before. Always an earnest student of the Scriptures, she had first turned to the original Greek in 1843 to determine the authority for William Miller's prediction of the end of the world. Concluding that the King James version was in many passages unsatisfactory, she began, for her own instruction, a literal, word-by-word translation of both the Old and New Testaments. She made a translation from the Septuagint, another from the Latin Vulgate, and, still dissatisfied, taught herself Hebrew and completed two more translations from that language— in all, a labor of seven years.

Abby Hadassah Smith died at her home in 1878, aged eighty-one. A year later, on Apr. 9, 1879, Julia, now in her eighty-seventh year, married Amos Andrew Parker of Fitzwilliam,

N.H., a retired judge of eighty-six who had sought her acquaintance after reading her Bible. Moving from the Glastonbury homestead, she spent the remaining years of her life in Hartford. In 1884, at the age of ninety-one, she addressed the Connecticut Woman Suffrage Association. She died at Hartford two years later, several months after suffering a broken hip. At her request she was buried with her sisters in the family plot in Glastonbury, with only her maiden name recorded on the tombstone. The Smiths' gentle, resolute battle, in the words of a contemporary newspaper editor, had brought "into sharper relief the injustice of denying women the right to vote than any number of speeches on woman suffrage in the abstract."

[The basic source is Julia Smith's own pamphlet record of the case, *Abby Smith and Her Cows*. See also Elizabeth C. Stanton et al., *Hist. of Woman Suffrage*, vol. III (1886); Addie Stancliffe Hale, "Those Five Amazing Smith Sisters," *Hartford Courant*, May 15, 1932; Elizabeth G. Speare, "Abby, Julia, and the Cows," *Am. Heritage*, June 1957; *Woman's Jour.*, Jan. 26, Mar. 2, Apr. 20, 1878; obituaries by Lucy Stone in *ibid.*, Aug. 3, 1878, and Mar. 13, 1886; *Hartford Times*, Mar. 11, 1886; unpublished MSS. in the Glastonbury Hist. Soc., Conn. Hist. Soc., Hartford, and Conn. State Library, Hartford.]

ELIZABETH GEORGE SPEARE

SMITH, Amanda Berry (Jan. 23, 1837–Feb. 24, 1915), Protestant evangelist and missionary, described by FRANCES E. WILLARD as "the African Sybil, the Christian Saint," was born a slave in Long Green, Md. Samuel Berry, her father, and Mariam (Matthews) Berry, her mother, were held in bondage on the adjoining farms of Darby Insor and Shadrach Green. Amanda was the oldest girl among thirteen children, five of whom were born in slavery; three of her brothers later served in the Union Army during the Civil War. Well before the war, her father, through hard work and determination, purchased his own freedom and that of most of his family and moved to a farm in York County, Pa. His house there became a station on the Underground Railroad. Amanda, while still very young, began work as a maid and washerwoman. Her mother and father, both of whom could read, taught her at home; she received only a few months of formal education.

In September 1854, at the age of seventeen, she was married in Columbia, Pa., to Calvin M. Devine. Of their two children, one died in infancy; the other, Mazie, died in her twenties. Amanda Berry's marriage was not a happy one and was probably saved only by her religious

conversion in March 1856. From that time on, she stoically accepted the burdens of hard, tedious work as a domestic servant, family tragedy, and the setbacks that she encountered as a Negro woman.

In 1862 her husband enlisted in the Union Army and went south. He did not return, and a year later Amanda moved with her daughter, Mazie, to Philadelphia, where she met and married James Smith, an ordained deacon in Old Bethel African Methodist Episcopal Church. Their first child, Nell, died in infancy in 1864. A second, Thomas Henry, born in 1865, died a few weeks later in New York City, where they had moved. After several years, James Smith, a coachman by occupation, accepted a higher-paying job in New Utrecht, N.Y., leaving Amanda and a third infant, Will, in New York. Though her husband visited regularly for a while and sent some money, Amanda had to work long hours as a house servant and washerwoman in order to maintain even a minimal level of existence.

Perhaps through her attendance at the Tuesday meetings of PHOEBE PALMER, Amanda Smith had encountered the doctrine of Christian perfection, or entire sanctification, and in September 1868, at a sermon by the Methodist minister John S. Inskip, she experienced this spiritual grace for which she had prayed. The death of her husband and of her youngest child in 1869 left her free of close family ties, and she began to devote much of her time and energy to preaching in colored churches of the New York–New Jersey area. Though she sometimes met with resistance from African Methodist Episcopal pastors who felt that it was not proper for a woman to preach or conduct services, there were enough who felt otherwise.

In the summer of 1870, with the encouragement of a white employer, Mrs. Smith attended one of the "holiness" camp meetings devoted to spreading the doctrine of Christian perfection. Though diffident at first about speaking before white audiences, she quickly won respect at this and later camp meetings by her spiritual fervor, as she related her experience of sanctification. Her smooth black skin, tall, well-proportioned figure, and simple, Quakerlike dress and scoop bonnet, together with the rich contralto voice with which she would break into song when inspired, made her a person not easily forgotten. In the fall of 1870 she gave up domestic work to devote herself to evangelism.

Over the next eight years Amanda Smith became a familiar figure in the holiness movement, participating in camp meetings as far afield as Kennebunk, Maine, and Knoxville,

Tenn., and holding services in white churches in New York and other cities. In 1878 one of her associates in the work of evangelism suggested that she go to England. As always, she prayerfully sought God's will and, feeling herself directed, sailed for England. The three months she had planned to spend there stretched to over a year as she attended English holiness conferences at Keswick and, as the guest of Lord Mount Temple, at Broadlands and filled a variety of evangelistic engagements. In the fall of 1879 she went on, by invitation, to India, where for nearly two years she did evangelical and missionary work. James M. Thoburn, Methodist Episcopal Bishop of India, with whom she worked in Calcutta, found her meetings more successful than those of any other visiting evangelist and commented on her "rare degree of spiritual power," clearness of vision, and keen discernment of character. From Amanda Smith, he later testified, he learned more that was "of actual value to me as a preacher of Christian truth . . . than from any other one person I had ever met."

Mrs. Smith had inherited from her parents a concern for Africa and its spiritual needs, and at the close of 1881, following a sojourn in England, she set sail for Monrovia, Liberia. She remained in West Africa for nearly eight years, working primarily with Methodist missionaries, among them William Taylor, Methodist Episcopal Bishop of Africa, but also with those of other denominations active in Liberia and Sierre Leone. During her years in Africa she also organized temperance societies. She returned to England in November 1889, accompanied by Bob, a native Gredebo boy she had "adopted" in 1887 and whom she placed in an English school. After several months of evangelical work in England, Ireland, and Scotland, she returned to the United States in September 1890.

Back home, Amanda Smith preached for a time in churches on the Eastern seaboard. In October 1892, perhaps through her friendship with Frances Willard, she moved to Chicago, planning to write her memoirs and settle down to a more sedentary existence in the temperance community that became the Chicago suburb of Harvey. She was now fifty-five years old, and the years of hard work and travel had taken their toll in the form of a recurring backache and rheumatism. Her *Autobiography* was published in 1893. She devoted the final two decades of her life to an attempt to alleviate the suffering of black orphans in the United States. Beginning in 1895, she acquired land in Harvey and in 1899 she opened

an orphans' home there. It was initially supported from her savings, the profits from the sale of her autobiography and a newspaper she conducted, the *Helper*, and with money from large donors, but the continued need for funds led her to go back to work preaching and singing in churches—black and white. When in October 1912 she accepted the offer of a wealthy real estate man, George Sebring, to provide a house for her retirement in Sebring, Fla., the orphans' home was granted a state charter as the Amanda Smith Industrial School for Girls. From its inception the school had suffered from insufficient funds and inadequate and poorly trained staff, and state inspectors had urged its closing as early as 1905, but as the only such Protestant institution in the state accessible to colored children, it was maintained until destroyed by fire in 1918.

Amanda Smith died in Sebring, Fla., in 1915 of a paralytic stroke. She was seventy-eight years old. Her body was brought by train to Chicago, where an elaborate funeral was held at Quinn Chapel African Methodist Episcopal Church, in which leading figures of the A.M.E. Church and of Chicago's black community participated, as did white leaders from the Woman's Christian Temperance Union and the Methodist Episcopal Church. She was buried in Harvey.

Amanda Smith was a fervently religious person, desiring only to serve her God. Yet, as an ex-slave and a woman, she was conscious of the problems facing those who shared her race and sex. As an internationally famed evangelist, she helped expand the accepted role of women in both the A.M.E. and Methodist churches.

[The chief source of information is Amanda Smith's *An Autobiog.* (1893), which contains a full account of her life up to 1892 and her views on a number of contemporary questions; it includes an introduction by Bishop J. M. Thoburn. For her later life see M. H. Cadbury, *The Life of Amanda Smith* (Birmingham, England, 1916), and obituary in the *Chicago Defender*, Mar. 6, 1915. An earlier brief account is Marshall W. Taylor, *The Life, Travels, Labors, and Helpers of Mrs. Amanda Smith* (1886). The "Amanda Smith Industrial Home" folder in Box LXX of the Julius Rosenwald Papers at the Univ. of Chicago Library has data on the management and financial problems of the school. There are useful references to Mrs. Smith in William Taylor's *Story of My Life* (1896) and *The Flaming Torch in Darkest Africa* (1898); Kathleen Fitzpatrick, *Lady Henry Somerset* (1923); Alec C. Kerr, ed., *History: The City of Harvey, 1890–1962* (1962); and Allan Spear, *Black Chicago* (1967), pp. 102–03.]

JOHN H. BRACEY, JR.

SMITH, Bessie (Apr. 15, 1894–Sept. 26, 1937), blues singer, was born in Chattanooga, Tenn. Her parents, William and Laura Smith, had three other daughters and a son. Elizabeth, as she was named, grew up in extreme poverty, but little else is known about her early life; she is said to have displayed considerable dramatic talent in school plays, and at the age of eight or nine reportedly made her singing debut at Chattanooga's Ivory Theatre. At some point, perhaps as early as 1910, the blues singer GERTRUDE ("Ma") RAINEY heard Bessie sing, taught her the style of country blues, and for a time added her to her touring company. For the next few years Bessie traveled throughout the South with carnivals and tent shows, sang in waterfront dives and bistros, and later appeared on the Negro vaudeville circuit in the ghettos of such large cities as Atlanta, Birmingham, and Memphis.

Although Bessie Smith made a phonograph recording in 1921 that was never released, her real career as a recording artist began in February 1923 at the Columbia Phonograph Company under the direction of Frank Walker. Her first four sides, which included "Downhearted Blues" and "Gulf Coast Blues," had a phenomenal sale. Having signed an exclusive contract with Columbia, she bought a house in Philadelphia and brought her sisters and brother there. On June 7, 1923, she was married to Jack Gee, a Philadelphia policeman, who resigned to become her manager. They had no children and were separated in 1930.

Bessie Smith was at the height of her fame in the years from 1923 to 1930. Always an attractive woman, in her youth she was tall and slender. Later she became heavier, at times weighing more than two hundred pounds, but her warm personality and dramatic ability drew the complete attention of her listeners. The writer Carl Van Vechten, who first heard her sing in 1925 in Newark, commented that "her face was beautiful with the rich ripe beauty of southern darkness, a deep bronze brown, matching the bronze of her bare arms." She dressed strikingly; for the final performance of an engagement, she sometimes wore a regal headdress and white satin gown, dramatized by shifting colored spotlights. Billed as "Empress of the Blues," during this period she made 160 recordings, which were so popular that the proceeds reportedly saved the Columbia company from bankruptcy, and some records sold as many as 100,000 in a week's time. Meanwhile she formed her own show, which played largely to black audiences in Boston, New York, and Chicago, as well as in the larger cities of the South. She had a rich,

powerful contralto voice, perfectly controlled (she always refused the aid of the microphone), and as she gained confidence she began to write many of her own songs. Her blues had a special appeal for the Negroes of the South and the migrants to the North, for her themes were the basic ones of poverty, sex, joy and grief, and natural catastrophes. Even the commercial songs she sometimes sang she infused with her own intuitive blues feeling.

Bessie Smith's talents did not evoke the admiration of everyone in the Negro community; some regarded her as "very rough." Some accounts describe her as a ribald, violent, quarrelsome woman who squandered her money and made unreasonable demands of her employers. During much of her life she was a heavy drinker, and her song "Me and My Gin," like several of her other hits, may have had autobiographical significance. Many associates, however, remember her warmth, generosity, and unselfishness, and recall, for example, the time she canceled her professional engagements to take on the responsibility of nurse and maid at the home of Frank Walker when his young child was seriously ill.

Bessie Smith's career had already started a sharp decline by 1931, when, with the collapse of the record market owing to the depression and the advent of radio, she was dropped by Columbia. Plunged back into poverty, she returned to performing in road shows and in night clubs. In 1937 she had begun to attract the attention of white audiences and hoped to make a comeback. That September she was traveling with a minstrel show in northern Mississippi, planning soon to return north for another recording session, when she was fatally injured in an automobile accident near the village of Coahoma north of Clarksdale. A legend that grew up among musicians and jazz fans pictured her as a victim of racial intolerance, her death resulting from delay in receiving treatment because of the refusal of a white hospital to admit her. Although the story was embodied in a Broadway play, it apparently has no factual basis. A Memphis physician who happened upon the accident gave her emergency care, and she was taken in an ambulance to a Negro hospital in Clarksdale but died, probably of internal injuries, either on the way or shortly after arrival there. Her body was taken to Philadelphia for burial in Mount Lawn Cemetery.

No jazz or blues singer possessed greater native talent or exerted more influence than Bessie Smith. Such outstanding jazz musicians as Louis Armstrong, James P. Johnson, Joe Smith, Charlie Green, and Fletcher Henderson accompanied her on records, and jazzmen are nearly unanimous in choosing her as the best of all the blues singers. She expressed her sorrows and frustrations, and those of other Negroes, along with a joy of living which enabled her to endure them. The clarinetist Sidney Bechet commented that "she was the best blues singer there was, but that trouble was inside her and it wouldn't let her rest." Louis Armstrong said: "She used to thrill me at all times, the way she could phrase a note with a certain something in her voice no other blues singer could get. She had music in her soul and felt everything she did." Many of the most creative personalities of jazz music, including the singers Billie Holiday and Mahalia Jackson and the trombonist Jack Teagarden, were profoundly influenced by Bessie Smith. Her records, reissued in a complete set in 1970 for the first time, preserve her voice and musical expression for posterity.

[*Jazz Record,* Sept. 1947, contains reminiscent source material and George Avakian's Bessie Smith discography. A condensed version of Avakian's notes for Columbia's four-record *Bessie Smith Story* (CL 855–858) is printed in Martin T. Williams, ed., *The Art of Jazz* (1959). Several musicians' recollections are included in Nat Shapiro and Nat Hentoff, eds., *Hear Me Talkin' to Ya* (1955). The same editors' *The Jazz Makers* (1957) contains George Hoefer's useful sketch. The New Orleans Jazz Club's publication, the *Second Line,* July–Aug. and Sept.–Oct. 1959, has material on Bessie Smith's death. Paul Oliver's *Bessie Smith* (1961) is a brief interpretive book.]

LARRY GARA

**SMITH, Eliza Roxey Snow** (Jan. 21, 1804–Dec. 5, 1887), the "mother of Mormonism," was born in Becket, Berkshire County, Mass., the second daughter and second of seven children of Oliver and Rosetta Leonora (Pettibone) Snow. (Her middle name is sometimes spelled Roxcy or Roxcey.) Her father was a native of Massachusetts and her mother of Connecticut; both were direct descendants of early Puritan settlers of New England. In 1806 Oliver Snow emigrated with his family to Mantua, Portage County, Ohio, where he became a successful farmer. Poorly educated but mentally alert, he gave much thought to the claims of religion. By the 1820's he and his wife, previously pious Baptists, had joined the "Reformed Baptist," or Campbellite, Church, a new sect led by Alexander Campbell, Walter Scott, and Sidney Rigdon. In 1830, when the first Mormon missionaries arrived in the area of Mentor and Kirtland, Ohio, Rigdon and most of his followers were converted to the Church of Jesus Christ of Latter-day Saints.

Eliza Snow had first heard of Joseph Smith's preaching the discovery of the "golden plates" of Moroni in 1829. Two years later Smith himself, who by this time had settled in Kirtland, called at her father's house in Mantua in the course of a proselytizing mission and greatly impressed Eliza. She was still more impressed when she visited Kirtland early in 1835, soon after her mother and elder sister had joined the Mormons. She accepted baptism at the hands of the Prophet on Apr. 5, experiencing that night, it is said, a vision that unfolded her entire future in the church. The next year her brother Lorenzo joined the new church, of which he soon became a leader, serving ultimately as president (1898–1901).

Eliza's parents were liberal both in their views of education for women and in their religious tolerance, giving their children the right to examine all creeds and choose their own. While still a Campbellite, Eliza had begun the systematic study of the Bible; her approach was unusually serious for a girl of her time, age, and environment. Her parents, however, were also concerned with her formal and domestic education. She became skilled in various housewifely arts, including weaving, and she attended for some years a local "Grammatical Institution" taught by a Presbyterian clergyman, though despite frequent reports to the contrary, she did not attend Oberlin College. This well-rounded early education goes far to explain her many-sided contributions to the development of Mormonism.

While still in her teens she began writing verse, which she published in various local journals under such noms de plume as "Narcissa," "Pocahontas," "Minerva," "Tullia," and (after 1835) "A Mormon Girl." Nurtured on the tales of her Revolutionary grandfather, she occasionally exhibited her intensely patriotic republican feelings in her poems. Her verse was sentimental, didactic, sometimes turgid, and often stilted—full of *boon's, glee's, lo's,* and *melting lutes*—but well suited to her audience and her times. Essentially religious in spirit and content, at its best it reflected the strong rhythmic verse of evangelical hymns. To Mormon hymnology she contributed at least a dozen standard hymns, including "O My Father."

Eliza Snow began to influence Mormonism as early as December 1836, when she left her parental home in Mantua to live among the Mormons in Kirtland. There she boarded in the household of Joseph Smith, became governess to his children, and for a number of years was companion to his wife EMMA HALE SMITH. She also conducted a "select school for young ladies" and, having brought her patrimony into the church, contributed generously to the building of the Mormon temple that still stands in Kirtland. In the summer of 1838 she and her brother joined the Mormon exodus to Missouri, but anti-Mormon mobs soon forced the persecuted Saints to emigrate to Illinois. After temporary residence in Quincy and Lima (where she supported herself by needlework), Eliza Snow settled in the Mormon town of Nauvoo (then called Commerce), Ill., where she again taught school.

It was in Nauvoo that polygamy was introduced into the church. On June 29, 1841, Eliza Snow, who had always adored Joseph Smith and who had long been writing poems glorifying him and his prophetic mission, secretly became one of his plural wives. Within a year Mormon polygamy became public knowledge, and when it came under violent attack Eliza was one of several women who denied the charge in a sworn statement; in the isolation of Utah, however, she frequently and proudly testified to her marriage to Smith. According to a tradition in the Snow family (for which there is some evidence) she became pregnant by him early in 1844 but suffered a miscarriage as the result of a violent attack at the hands of the Prophet's jealous wife Emma. After Smith's assassination she lived in the family of Brigham Young, to whom she was sealed in marriage in 1849; she bore him no children.

Next to Emma Smith, Eliza Snow was the most popular woman in Nauvoo. During her years there she exerted a powerful influence on many of the Mormon institutions that later flowered in Utah. When the Mormon temple of Nauvoo was built, she pioneered in women's "temple work," that is, assisting in secret "endowment" rituals, doing genealogical work, and performing other tasks of religious administration. When the Mormons were driven out of Nauvoo, she went to Utah in one of the earliest pioneer companies, arriving in the fall of 1847. In 1855, before any temples were built in Utah for endowment rituals, Brigham Young made her president of the women workers in the newly built Endowment House.

Even more important for the development of Mormonism was her role in women's organizations and activities. By a revelation of March 1842 in Nauvoo, the Prophet founded the Female (later Women's) Relief Society, a charitable institution. Though Emma Smith was president, Eliza Snow as secretary was the very soul of the organization; and later, in Utah, she became general president, reorganized the society, and directed it from 1866

to her death. From her central office she set into motion or personally organized women's cooperative stores (for the sale of homemade Mormon goods), Relief Society halls, bazaars, classes in hygiene, a women's hospital (the first Mormon hospital, 1882), and a women's newspaper, together with most of the conferences that guided the work. She traveled throughout the state forwarding these projects with the zeal of a missionary.

When in 1869 Brigham Young founded the "Young Ladies' Retrenchment Association" to bring about a "retrenchment" in the dress and general manner of living of young women, he made Eliza Snow responsible for organizing it and putting it into operation. In 1878 this society became, under her leadership, the Young Ladies' Mutual Improvement Association, the basic and profoundly influential Mormon organization for women. That same year she had a hand in the formation of the Primary Association, a kind of church kindergarten, and still found time to preside at a mass meeting of 15,000 women in defense of polygamy. Two years later President John Taylor ordained her president of Latter-day Saints women's organizations throughout the world.

As "captain of Utah's woman-host" Eliza Snow was a dedicated feminist. Her interest was partly inspired by Mormon apologetics: she vigorously fought the anti-Mormon myth (inspired by polygamy) of the subjection of Mormon women, pointing out their equality of franchise in both general and church affairs; as part of these efforts she aided in the preparation and publication of Edward W. Tullidge's *Women of Mormondom* (1877). She conceived of women as protectors of virtue and of the weak, as obedient "helpmeets," whose chief virtue was fortitude and who, in Utah, had no need of woman's "rights" as such.

Dark of eye, medium in height, slender in build, Eliza Snow was always graceful and dignified. More than once the hebraizing Mormons noted approvingly the "slightly Hebrew cast" of her "exquisitely cut" features. Thoughtful and deliberate in speech and action, a sponsor of literary and musical activities, she represented the pinnacle of refinement and culture for the frontier community of Utah. She was probably most important for the example she gave as the model Mormon woman. Active until late in life, she accompanied her brother Lorenzo on a trip to Palestine in 1872–73, sending back reports in both prose and verse. In 1876 she organized an important part of Utah's exhibition at the Philadelphia Centennial celebration. Although her health failed after 1880, her mind remained clear. She died in her eighty-fourth year in her apartments in Brigham Young's "Lion House" in Salt Lake City. In accordance with her wishes, white instead of black was used at her funeral, and a long cortege accompanied her to her final resting place in the private cemetery of Brigham Young.

[Mrs. Smith's most important works are: *Biog. and Family Record of Lorenzo Snow* (1884) and *Poems, Religious, Historical and Political* (2 vols., 1856–77). Indispensable is her autobiography, written at the request of the historian H. H. Bancroft; this was published serially in the *Relief Soc. Mag.* (Salt Lake City) in 1944; the original manuscript is in the Bancroft Library, Univ. of Calif. The official organ of the Church of Jesus Christ of Latter-day Saints (Mormons), *Improvement Era*, published the two volumes of her overland diary from Nauvoo to Salt Lake City in fourteen installments in vols. XLVI (1943) and XLVII (1944). In 1875 she gathered together letters written by two companions and herself in *Correspondence of Palestine Tourists*. Mormon serials published in Utah are extremely important for fugitive verse, letters, and biographical data: *Deseret News* (including obituary of Dec. 5, 1887); *Improvement Era;* the *Relief Soc. Mag.;* the *Contributor;* the *Hist. Record;* and *Woman's Exponent*. Official biographies appear in Andrew Jenson, *L.D.S. Biog. Encyc.*, vol. I (1901); Augusta J. Crocheron, *Representative Women of Deseret* (1884); and Susa Young Gates and Leah D. Widtsoe, *Women of the "Mormon" Church* (1926). Also useful are: Edward W. Tullidge, *Women of Mormondom* (1877); Church of Jesus Christ of Latter-day Saints, General Board of the Relief Soc., *A Centenary of the Relief Soc., 1842–1942* (1942); Susa Young Gates, *Hist. of the Young Ladies' Mutual Improvement Assoc.* (1911); Fawn M. Brodie, *No Man Knows My History* (1945), a biography of Joseph Smith; George Dollinger Pyper, *Stories of L.D.S. Hymns, Their Authors and Composers* (1939); and various editions of Mormon hymnbooks.]

MARIO S. DE PILLIS

**SMITH, Elizabeth Oakes Prince** (Aug. 12, 1806–Nov. 15, 1893), author, lecturer, and reformer, was born near North Yarmouth, Maine, the younger of two daughters of David and Sophia (Blanchard) Prince and a descendant of John Prince, a Massachusetts settler of the 1630's. The Puritan influence from her father's side was softened somewhat by her Universalist and freethinking maternal grandfather, Seth Blanchard, whom she often visited, although she joined the Congregational Church at thirteen. Her father, a ship captain, was lost at sea when she was two years old, but she loved her stepfather, a wealthy merchant and widower, and welcomed the family's move

to Portland in 1814. Something of a prodigy, Elizabeth learned to read at two by listening to her sister's lessons. Her advancement was over-rapid, however, and at six she had a complete breakdown. A long period of rest and play at her grandfather's farm brought full recovery, and she was soon devouring such diverse books as Foxe's *Book of Martyrs* and Fielding's *Tom Jones*. On one occasion, to compare her own courage with that of Foxe's heroes, she fastened a large mustard plaster to her leg and silently bore the pain until she fainted.

She attended the private school of Mrs. Rachel Neal, mother of the poet and critic John Neal, and dreamed of opening a girls' school of her own. Her mother thought otherwise, however, and Elizabeth was married at sixteen, on Mar. 6, 1823, to Seba Smith, editor of the Portland *Eastern Argus*. Smith was bald, bespectacled, and thirty-one, while she herself, as she later wrote, was only a "dreamy, imaginative, undeveloped child" (Wyman, *Selections*, p. 44). Nevertheless, she managed with considerable skill a household that included several printers and apprentices and soon five sons: Appleton, Rolvin, Alvin, Sidney, and Edward. (The second child, Rolvin, died accidentally at the age of seven.) During these years she became a firm believer in greater opportunity and freedom for women. She began writing poems and sketches for local periodicals and eagerly cultivated such literary lights as Portland offered. In further demonstration of her independence of mind she joined William Ladd's American Peace Society and left the Congregational Church to become a Unitarian.

In the 1830's Seba Smith rose to unexpected celebrity with his "Major Jack Downing Letters." Written for the *Portland Courier*, of which he was then editor, these humorous, homespun comments on the Jacksonian political scene, along with their fictional author—the forerunner of such later creations as Petroleum V. Nasby and Mr. Dooley—won wide popularity. Seba Smith, however, went bankrupt following the panic of 1837 as a consequence of ill-advised land speculations, and in 1839, after a fruitless trip to Charleston, S.C., to promote a Maine-invented cotton gin, the Smiths moved to New York City.

In New York, while Seba Smith wrote "Down East" tales for various magazines, edited with little success a series of short-lived publications, and expounded his rather cranky mathematical notions in *New Elements of Geometry* (1850), his wife, under the force of circumstances, also embarked upon a literary career. *Riches without Wings,* a slight volume for children, had already appeared in 1838, and in 1843 *The Sinless Child, and Other Poems* was published, amid warm praise from Edgar Allan Poe and other critics. While producing scores of poems, sketches, and short pieces for such leading magazines as *Godey's Lady's Book, Graham's Magazine,* the *Ladies' Companion,* and the *Southern Literary Messenger,* Mrs. Smith also wrote *Stories for Children* (1847) and other juveniles; *The Western Captive* (1842), a Cooperesque adventure tale; and *Old New York,* a historical drama about Jacob Leisler which appeared briefly on Broadway in 1853. "Mrs. Seba Smith" on title pages soon gave way to "Elizabeth Oakes Smith" or to such pseudonyms as "Ernest Helfenstein" and "Oakes Smith," a name she so fancied that she had her sons' surname legally changed to Oaksmith. A minor fixture in New York literary circles, she came to know Poe, William Cullen Bryant, Horace Greeley, MARGARET FULLER, the landscape artist Thomas Cole, and others. Henry Clay, who met her during this period, found her "irresistibly fascinating. . . . Seldom has a woman in any age acquired such ascendancy by the mere force of a powerful intellect. Her smile is the play of a sunlit fountain" (Wyman, *Two American Pioneers,* p. 207).

But a New England reformist strain lurked beneath the literary facade. In 1839 she had taken her reluctant husband to hear a lecture by the radical FRANCES WRIGHT; by 1851 she was attending the Second National Woman's Rights Convention in Worcester, Mass. Though her fancy New York dress led SUSAN B. ANTHONY to deny her the presidency of the convention (Harper, I, 72), she returned to New York to write for Greeley's *New York Tribune* a series on woman's rights, soon published as *Woman and Her Needs* (1851). Though advocating political emancipation, the book's central theme is that women should be free to develop their talents to the fullest. In a later *Tribune* article (Jan. 15, 1853) she wrote: "there are thousands capable of a sphere beyond the fireside and being thus qualified, they hold a commission from God himself to go out into this broader field. . . ."

As though to illustrate this thesis (and also for economic reasons) she became in 1851 one of the earliest women to join the lyceum circuit, and for most of the decade she made annual lecture tours, speaking principally on the woman question. She also sometimes appeared with Wendell Phillips in antislavery meetings. Very feminine in appearance, with brown hair and eyes and a small mouth with full lips, she was a popular performer. Henry Thoreau, however, who as secretary of the Concord lyceum carried her handkerchief-wrapped manuscript to the lecture hall, later grumped, "My pocket exhales cologne to this moment." Neither was Thoreau impressed with her mind. "You had to substitute courtesy for sense and argument," he recalled (Wyman, *Two American Pioneers,* p. 200). She also contributed to her friend PAULINA WRIGHT DAVIS' feminist journal, *Una,* wrote pamphlets on marriage and dress reform, and in 1854 published a woman's rights novel, *Bertha and Lily.* Another novel of the same year, *The Newsboy,* grew from her work with the Young Men's Christian Union and is said to have stirred a wave of popular indignation over the condition of New York's street waifs.

In 1860 the Smiths moved to Patchogue, Long Island, where Mrs. Smith continued to lecture occasionally on the literary figures she had known and produced a series of ephemeral but lucrative "dime novels," of which *Bald Eagle* (1867) is typical. Her life during these years was not easy; two sons, Edward and Sidney, and her husband died in quick succession, the last in 1868. A lifelong interest in religion and the occult, which for a time had drawn her powerfully to the Roman Catholic faith, now grew stronger. For most of 1877 she was pastor of an independent congregation in Canastota, N.Y., near Oneida. Thereafter she settled in Hollywood, N.C., with her eldest son and his family. Continuing her interest in woman's rights, Elizabeth Oakes Smith had been in 1868 a charter member of New York's first woman's club, Sorosis; in 1878 and 1879 she represented North Carolina at the annual conventions of the National Woman Suffrage Association. In North Carolina she was also active in the temperance lodge, the Good Templars. She died in Hollywood in 1893 at the age of eighty-seven and was buried at Patchogue.

[The N.Y. Public Library has extensive papers of Elizabeth Oakes Smith, including a manuscript autobiography from which Mary Alice Wyman has published *Selections* (1924). The same author wrote the valuable *Two American Pioneers: Seba Smith and Elizabeth Oakes Smith* (1927), which includes an extensive bibliography. Also see *Old Times in North Yarmouth, Maine,* Mar. 1877, Apr. 1879, Oct. 1881, Jan. 1882; and Robert E. Riegel, *Am. Feminists* (1963). On her woman's rights work, see Elizabeth C. Stanton et al., *Hist. of Woman Suffrage,* vols. I and III (1881–86), and Ida H. Harper, *Susan B. Anthony* (1898), I, 72. On her "dime novels," see Albert Johannsen, *The House of Beadle and Adams* (1950), I, 259–61.]

ALICE FELT TYLER

SMITH, Emily James. *See* PUTNAM, Emily James Smith.

SMITH, Emma Hale (July 10, 1804–Apr. 30, 1879), prominent figure in early Mormonism, was the wife of the prophet Joseph Smith. The enigmatic character of her husband and the continuing controversy between Mormon and non-Mormon historians over the validity of his supernatural claims have served to obscure her role. The two branches of the Mormon Church treat her very differently: the Utah-based Church of Jesus Christ of Latter-day Saints largely ignores her; the Reorganized Church of Jesus Christ of Latter-Day Saints, in Missouri, accords her immense prestige. The non-Mormon historian finds an abundance of documents pertaining to her life, but they are so controversial that much of importance remains elusive.

She was born in Harmony, Pa., the seventh of eleven children. Her parents, Isaac and Elizabeth (Lewis) Hale, were simple farm people who had migrated from Vermont to Pennsylvania in search of a livelihood; her father was a zealous Methodist. Emma grew into a beautiful young woman, with enormous hazel eyes and an air of quiet dignity. She first met Joseph Smith in November 1825 when he came south from Palmyra, N.Y., and worked as a diviner, or scryer, for a farmer who was attempting to find a lost silver mine. For a time he boarded with the Hale family. Isaac Hale, at first friendly, became hostile and contemptuous of the youth's alleged magic talents. Emma, however, fell in love with him, and despite her father's opposition eloped with him to South Bainbridge, N.Y., where they were married on Jan. 18, 1827.

In succeeding years Emma Smith had to face poverty, hardship, and persecution as the wife of a man who said he talked with angels and received revelations from God. For the first year of their marriage the couple lived with Joseph's parents in Manchester, N.Y.; they then returned to Harmony to her parents' home and later lived for a time in Fayette, N.Y., with the family of David Whitmer, one of Smith's early followers. There is evidence that Emma suffered at first from inner doubts about her husband's claims, particularly in regard to the famous golden plates, from which he "translated" the *Book of Mormon*. Their hiding place, he said, had been pointed out to him by an angel; the plates contained a history of the American Indians which proved them to be descendants of ancient Hebrews. Although Emma was her husband's first scribe, he forbade her to look at the "reformed Egyp-

tian" characters in which the plates were written, permitting her only to feel them through a cloth. When the *Book of Mormon* was published in 1830, however, it included the statements of eleven witnesses who swore that they had seen the characters and "hefted" the plates. Emma's discontent at having been denied the same privilege can be deduced from the content of one of Joseph Smith's earliest revelations. "Hearken unto the voice of the Lord your God, while I speak unto you, Emma Smith," it said, ". . . thou art an elect lady whom I have called. Murmur not because of the things which thou hast not seen. . . . Continue in the spirit of meekness and beware of pride. Let thy soul delight in thy husband. . . . And except thou do this, where I am you cannot come."

It seems clear that Emma Smith eventually ceased doubting and worked devotedly in her husband's church. She edited a hymnbook, worked among the sick as a nurse and herb doctor, and later, in 1842, became president of the Female Relief Society, the leading women's organization of the Mormon Church. Greatest among her early griefs were the successive deaths of her children. Her first son died at birth in Harmony; twins born to her in 1831 also died at birth. She adopted another pair, but only one, Julia Murdock, survived. Joseph Smith III, born in 1832, was the first of her own children to survive infancy; out of nine born to her, only four lived to maturity.

In Kirtland, Ohio, where Joseph Smith and his followers moved in 1831, the church flourished. But persecutions also multiplied; the young prophet was beaten, tarred and feathered, and harried with lawsuits. The Mormons saw even worse troubles after they moved to Missouri in 1838, for they were hounded mercilessly from one community to another, and finally in 1839 driven out of the state altogether. Emma Smith was forced to flee with her children, crossing the ice of the Mississippi River on foot. Sewn into her petticoats was the manuscript of her husband's *Holy Scriptures, Translated and Corrected by the Spirit of Revelation,* published in 1867.

After settling in Nauvoo, Ill., the Mormons enjoyed a brief period of growth and prosperity. Joseph Smith's missionary system was extraordinarily successful, and converts came in thousands from all parts of the East and Great Britain. Emma Smith was now accorded great respect and affection. Her husband described her in 1842 as "the wife of my youth and the choice of my heart . . . undaunted, firm, and unwavering—unchangeable, affectionate

Emma." Nevertheless, at about this time he began secretly the practice of polygamy, and on July 12, 1843, he dictated an official revelation commanding it as a law of God.

Emma Smith in later years denied all knowledge of the polygamous activities of her husband. "There was no revelation on either polygamy or spiritual wives," she said. "He had no other wife but me." But there is much good evidence not only that she knew about some of his plural marriages but also that she had seen the revelation, which specifically commanded her to "receive all those that have been given unto my servant Joseph," and which threatened her with destruction if she did not comply. The prophet is said to have burned the revelation as a result of her pleading, but he went on to take new wives until the number reached almost fifty.

Joseph Smith was jailed in Carthage, Ill., for ordering the destruction of a printing press and newspaper of protest against polygamy, the *Nauvoo Expositor*. There, on June 27, 1844, he was murdered by a mob of anti-Mormons. Desolated by the loss, Emma found solace in her three sons, Joseph, Frederick, and Alexander, and then in David, who was born five months after his father's death. Despite the increasing bitterness of the anti-Mormon persecutions, she chose to remain in Nauvoo rather than go west with the bulk of the Mormons, who migrated to the safety of the Great Salt Lake Valley under the leadership of Brigham Young.

On Dec. 27, 1847, she was married to a non-Mormon, Lewis Crum Bidamon. She remained true to her first husband's religion, however, and reared her sons to be devout believers, although tenaciously hostile to polygamy and to Brigham Young. In 1860 Joseph Smith III became the leader of an antipolygamous Mormon group which became the Reorganized Church of Jesus Christ of Latter-Day Saints, with headquarters in Lamoni, Iowa, and later in Independence, Mo. To this church Emma Smith contributed a vital continuity with the past and a record of fortitude and devotion. She continued to live in the Mansion House in Nauvoo, and died there in 1879. She was buried in Nauvoo.

[The basic source book for the life of Emma Smith is the *Hist. of the Church of Jesus Christ of Latter-day Saints. Period I. Hist. of Joseph Smith, the Prophet, by Himself* (6 vols., 1902–12). For a modern history written from the point of view of the Reorganized Church, see Inez Smith Davis, *The Story of the Church* (3rd ed., 1943). A fictionalized biography with the same point of view is Margaret W. Gibson's *Emma Smith, the Elect Lady* (1954). For a non-Mormon account which includes much material left out of the official Mormon histories, including detailed documentation on the polygamous wives of Joseph Smith, see Fawn M. Brodie, *No Man Knows My History: The Life of Joseph Smith, the Mormon Prophet* (1945). A brief summary of Emma Smith's life may be seen in Edith Deen, *Great Women of the Christian Faith* (1959). Manuscripts and letters illuminating her story are in the library of the Reorganized Church, Independence, Mo.]

FAWN M. BRODIE

**SMITH, Erminnie Adele Platt** (Apr. 26, 1836–June 9, 1886), ethnologist, was born in Marcellus, N.Y., the ninth of ten children of Joseph Platt, a substantial farmer and Presbyterian deacon, and his wife, Ermina Dodge. Her paternal grandparents had been among the original settlers of the area in the late eighteenth century. Her mother died when Erminnie (originally Ermina) was two, and she was therefore primarily influenced by her father, a rock collector who encouraged a childhood interest in botany and geology. In 1850 she was enrolled in the Troy (N.Y.) Female Seminary, founded by EMMA WILLARD, where she showed a particular aptitude for languages. She graduated in 1853, and two years later was married to Simeon H. Smith, a wealthy Chicago lumber dealer and commission merchant. In 1866 they moved from Chicago to Jersey City, N.J., where Smith was a stockyards official and later city finance commissioner.

Mrs. Smith's early married years were given over to the rearing of four sons (their names are thought to have been Simeon, Willard, Carlton, and Eugene), but while still in Chicago she had pursued her geological interest by helping to classify and label mineral specimens being collected for display in European museums. When a Continental schooling was planned for the four boys she decided to avail herself of the opportunity to continue her own education. In Germany with them for four years, she studied crystallography and German literature at Strassburg and Heidelberg and completed a two-year mineralogy course at the School of Mines in Freiberg.

Returning to Jersey City, she turned her home into something of a mineralogical museum and began to deliver parlor lectures on geological and cultural subjects. These proved highly popular, and in 1876 she founded the Aesthetic Society, a group of women who met monthly to read and discuss papers on science, literature, and art. These gatherings, reflecting newly affluent American society's eagerness for cultural uplift, drew as many as five hundred people for such diverse fare as an evening with Matthew Arnold and the first local demonstration of the phonograph. Erminnie Smith was the president and motivating spirit, and the Aesthetic Society disbanded after her death. She was also an active member of Sorosis, the pioneer New York City woman's club, to which she was elected in 1878 and whose science programs she directed for four years. Her success as a popularizer became known in the scientific community, and, probably through a cousin, Frederic W. Putnam, curator of Harvard's Peabody Museum, she was drawn into the American Association for the Advancement of Science, before whose annual meeting in 1879 she read a monograph on jade.

At these gatherings she learned of the new science of anthropology, and particularly of American Indian ethnology, the field to which she was to devote the final years of her life. Having grown up near the Onondaga reservation, she decided to make the "Six Nations," or tribes, of the Iroquois federation her special province. In May 1880, encouraged and partially financed by Major John W. Powell of the Smithsonian Institution's Bureau of American Ethnology, and provided with advice and introductions by the aged Lewis Henry Morgan, pioneer Iroquois investigator, she began her studies on the Tuscarora reservation near Lewiston, N.Y. The first woman to engage in field ethnography, she accurately recorded a mass of legends, published in 1883 by the Bureau of American Ethnology as *Myths of the Iroquois*. A gifted and enthusiastic amateur,' she traveled each summer from 1880 to 1885 among the scattered reservations of New York and Canada, compiling a monumental Iroquois dictionary. Among the Tuscarora she was held in such affection that the appellation "Beautiful Flower" was bestowed upon her. Introducing a technique later used with success by ethnologists like ALICE CUNNINGHAM FLETCHER and Edward Sapir, she trained a succession of "native informants," one of whom, John N. B. Hewitt, a Tuscarora, became a noted ethnologist in his own right.

A faithful attendant at the annual meetings of the American Association for the Advancement of Science, where each year she read two or three papers on her Iroquois research, Mrs. Smith was in 1885 elected secretary of its anthropology section. She was also made a Fellow of the New York Academy of Sciences (the first woman so honored) and of the London Scientific Society.

Erminnie Smith was a woman of great charm, a gifted speaker and an effortless writer. Her first interest remained the Aesthetic Society, to whose monthly gatherings she de-

voted much thought and planning. She died at the age of fifty of valvular disease of the heart and a cerebral embolism. After funeral services in the Lafayette Reformed Church, of which she had been an active member, she was buried in New York Bay Cemetery, Jersey City. In 1888 a group of her friends endowed in her name at Vassar College an annual award for the best student research paper on mineralogy or geology.

[Erminnie Smith Papers, Bureau of Am. Ethnology, Smithsonian Institution, Washington, D.C.; *In Memoriam, Mrs. Erminnie A. Smith* (1890); *Echoes of the Aesthetic Soc. of Jersey City* (1882); reports of her scientific papers in *N.Y. Times*, Aug. 29 and Sept. 2, 1880; *Appletons' Cyc. Am. Biog.*, V, 563; obituary in *N.Y. Times*, June 10, 1886; biographical sketch in Mrs. A. W. Fairbanks, ed., *Emma Willard and Her Pupils* (1898); memorial tribute by Jane C. Croly (unidentified clipping, Julia Ward Howe Scrapbooks, vol. I, A-24, Schlesinger Library, Radcliffe College). Other information from: Miss Lucy Sweet, Town Historian, Marcellus, N.Y., including a record of the children of Joseph and Ermina (Dodge) Platt from a Dodge family Bible, which confirms her birth year; letters of Erminnie Smith in Lewis Henry Morgan and Henry A. Ward Papers, Univ. of Rochester; Alexander McLean, *Hist. of Jersey City* (1895), p. 371, on her husband (courtesy of N.J. Division, Newark Public Library); burial records of N.Y. Bay Cemetery; death record of Mrs. Smith from N.J. Dept. of Health. The *Annual Reports* of the Bureau of Am. Ethnology, 1881–87, contain brief reports of her investigations. Her papers before the Am. Assoc. for the Advancement of Science are in its *Proc.*, 1880–87. For a full bibliography of her scholarly work see James C. Pilling, *Bibliog. of the Iroquoian Languages* (Bureau of Am. Ethnology, *Bull.* No. 6, 1888). Her middle name is sometimes given as "Adelle."]

NANCY OESTREICH LURIE

**SMITH, Hannah Whitall** (Feb. 7, 1832–May 1, 1911), religious author, evangelist, feminist, and temperance reformer, was born in Philadelphia, Pa., the first of five children of John Mickle Whitall and Mary (Tatum) Whitall. On both sides of the family she was descended from a long line of colonial Quaker ancestors; her parents had grown up as childhood friends near Woodbury, N.J. Her father, earlier a sea captain and a moderately successful cotton merchant, eventually became a wealthy glass manufacturer, heading the firm of Whitall-Tatum & Company. Hannah received her education in the Friends' schools of Philadelphia. Reared in strictest Quaker discipline, she was shielded from exposure to art, music, and popular novels, a cultural lack that she later called a "monstrous pity" and avoided in bringing up her own children. A happy child, she idolized her father, whose pious but gay nature, some felt, was reincarnated in her.

From adolescence on, the absorbing interest of her life was the search for religious truth. At the same time she was gripped by a burning desire to preach, to become a "public character," as she confessed in her diary, and gloried in daydreams about a "young eloquent Quaker girl" who brought an admiring world to her feet. On June 25, 1851, at nineteen, she was married to Robert Pearsall Smith, a salesman in her father's business. They had seven children: a firstborn daughter, Nelly, who died at five, Franklin Whitall, born in 1854, Mary Logan Whitall (1864), Logan Pearsall (1865), Alys Pearsall (1867), Rachel Pearsall (1868), and a child who died at birth in 1873. Also a birthright Quaker, Smith joined Hannah in her spiritual quest. In 1865 he became resident manager of the Whitall-Tatum glass factories at Millville, N.J. Here he and his wife came under the influence of a little group of Methodist employees who converted them to Wesleyan "holiness" doctrines of sanctification by faith as a distinct and separate step beyond justification, or the attainment of righteousness. Becoming acquainted, apparently, with the itinerant evangelist William Edwin Boardman, Robert Smith began preaching in camp meetings and revivals and soon gave up his job to devote himself to evangelism. In 1869 he returned to Philadelphia and presently started a religious periodical, *The Christian's Pathway to Power,* to which Hannah Smith became a popular contributor, marking the beginning of her career as a religious author. Like her husband, she also did some preaching at this time, probably at Quaker meetings and at the city mission for Negroes in Philadelphia established by her father, and perhaps at camp meetings.

In 1873 Robert Smith, whose fame as a lay preacher had already crossed the Atlantic, traveled to England, where he conducted a series of religious meetings. His wife joined him early the next year, and the two were soon deeply involved with William Boardman and his wife in the interdenominational "Higher Life" movement which swept over England from 1873 to 1875. In a series of revivalistic "holiness" conferences, designed primarily for the aristocracy and the upper class of English society, they became almost at once the most conspicuous and influential leaders. Stressing a difference of life rather than a difference of belief, they conducted a nonsectarian conference at Broadlands, the country estate of Lord Mount Temple, and huge revivalistic meetings at Oxford and Brighton. Hannah's Bible readings proved especially popular; John Bright, the eminent British statesman, praised her oratorical ability. Tall, with blond hair, eloquent, and charming in her Quaker dress, she won the name "angel of the churches" and made the acquaintance of such aristocratic religionists as Lady Henry Somerset and the Duchess of Sutherland. At the height of the Smiths' success, however, their mission ended abruptly when Robert Smith was discredited by scandal. One version has it that he was accused of antinomian teachings; but his son, Logan Pearsall Smith, has stated that the trouble stemmed from his father's promiscuous proffering of St. Paul's "holy kiss" to his female disciples. Hannah, who had often warned her handsome husband that such behavior would only lead to grief, stood by him loyally, but the affair left a scar; in later life she called herself an "ignorant idiot" for marrying at nineteen and found it hard to believe a woman could find happiness in marriage (*Philadelphia Quaker,* pp. 176, 190–91n). They returned at once to America, where Smith, truly repentant but crushed, took a job in the Philadelphia office of the Whitall-Tatum Company and promptly faded out of public life. In time he lost his faith completely.

By contrast, Hannah Smith was now entering, in middle life, her most productive years. The death of her elder son, Franklin Whitall Smith, in 1872 had inspired her to write a tribute entitled *The Record of a Happy Life* (1873). The same theme of spiritual joy was developed in *The Christian's Secret of a Happy Life,* written during the enthusiasm of the Higher Life movement and published in 1875. This minor classic, in its many editions and translations, ultimately sold more than two million copies. A combination of Quaker quietism and the Wesleyan doctrine of sanctification, it preached the necessity of the soul's complete surrender to the life-giving spirit of Christ. Mrs. Smith's career as a religious author continued over the next three decades. She wrote more than a dozen books on religious subjects and a long series of booklets and tracts; the initials with which she signed her work, "H.W.S.," became world-famous. Among her ardent admirers was the philosopher William James.

In the years after 1875 Hannah Whitall Smith attained further recognition through her loyal support of many social reform movements. She stoutly championed the right of girls to attend college, helping to infuse with her feminism her niece M. CAREY THOMAS, later president of Bryn Mawr. Both of her daughters obtained college degrees. Mrs. Smith was an active partisan of the woman suffrage movement and attended many of its conventions, sometimes as a featured speaker. It was to temperance reform, however, that she gave her heart. For nearly twenty-five years she was a confidante of FRANCES WILLARD, who in her autobiography called her "my staunch sister and ally" (*Glimpses of Fifty Years*, 1889, p. 507). She took a prominent part in the foundation of the Woman's Christian Temperance Union, and in 1883 became the first superintendent of its national Evangelistic Department. A faithful worker in the Pennsylvania W.C.T.U., she received frequent invitations to give her famous Bible readings at state and national W.C.T.U. conventions. After she moved to England, she joined the British Women's Temperance Association, becoming a member of the executive committee, honorary recording secretary, and finally honorary vice-president. She was one of the important links between the temperance movements in England and America, and she accompanied the English leader Lady Henry Somerset to the United States for the first meeting of the World's W.C.T.U. in 1891.

In 1885 the Smiths traveled to England, where their daughter Mary married Benjamin Conn Costelloe, an Anglo-Irish barrister and writer. After several visits to America, Hannah and Robert Smith settled permanently in London in 1888, the year their son Logan entered Oxford. Here they lived in affluence, largely upon the income from the family bottle works and Mrs. Smith's royalties. Gone, now, were her Quaker dress and sugar-scoop bonnet. Even though she preached occasionally and continued to write devotional literature, her interests became broader and more secular. On one occasion she served as chairman of a women's trade union meeting. Most significantly, however, this transatlantic shift belatedly opened up for her a vista of the literary-intellectual world. Frequent callers in her home were such notables as Bernard Shaw, George Santayana, Bertrand Russell, the Sidney Webbs, Israel Zangwill, Roger Fry, Bernard Berenson, and William and Henry James. The main attraction in the Smith home, however, was the presence of her three grown children: Mary, who married Bernard Berenson in 1900 after the death of her first husband; Logan, who became an essayist and arbiter of the England language; and Alys, the first wife of the philosopher Bertrand Russell (who divorced her in 1921). The Smiths' daughter Rachel had died in 1879 at eleven.

Widowed in 1899, Mrs. Smith shortly after gave up all public work and devoted her last years to rearing her only two grandchildren, the Costelloe daughters, whom she held in ward while their mother was living with Berenson in Italy. With typical broadmindedness, though not without qualms, she reared them as strict Roman Catholics, fulfilling the desire of her deceased son-in-law. By the autumn of 1904 she was a wheelchair victim of arthritis or rheumatism. Her letters in the pain-racked years that followed reveal a serene person of continuing interests, buoyant spirits, and saving wit. In the decline of life she became more mystical, more of a quietist, and less positive than in her preaching days. But her mystical outlook was counterbalanced by an emphasis upon Biblical standards and reason. Her husband's downfall and her own investigations into fanatical sects warned her of the dangers of mysticism. "I would, therefore," she wrote, "always urge every seeker after the deep things of God to ignore emotions and care only for convictions" (*Religious Fanaticism*, p. 164). In 1906 she moved into her son's house at Iffley, near Oxford, where she died in 1911 at the age of seventy-nine.

A devoted mother and indulgent grandmother, she had happily combined the duties of homemaker with a remarkably varied and busy public life. Her domestic responsibilities never allowed her to give full time to reform agitation, and so she seldom held high office in the many organizations to which she belonged. But her counsel and hospitality, her oratorical and literary skills, were constantly demanded by the chief feminists of her day, and she had the distinction of being at the center of several nineteenth-century reform movements on two continents.

[A general account of the Smith family is given in Robert Allerton Parker, *The Transatlantic Smiths* (1959). Genealogical data on Mrs. Smith's Whitall ancestors appear in "The Whitall Family of Red Bank," *Bull. of the Gloucester Hist. Soc.*, Mar. 1954, and in her own *John M. Whitall: The Story of His Life* (privately printed, 1879). Miscellaneous material pertinent to her life, consisting mainly of unpublished MSS., some early diaries, and copies of letters, is included in the Logan Pearsall Smith Papers, Library of Congress. There are a number of letters from Mrs. Smith in the Frances E. Willard Papers at the national W.C.T.U. headquarters in Evanston, Ill. Helpful insights into her character and life may be found in: Logan Pearsall Smith, *Unforgotten Years* (1939), and the volume he edited, *Phila. Quaker: The Letters of Hannah Whitall Smith* (1950); Ray (Rachel Costelloe) Strachey, *A Quaker Grandmother: Hannah Whitall Smith* (1914); Frances E.

Willard, *Woman and Temperance* (1883), pp. 195–207. The work of the Smiths in the "Higher Life" movement and their theology is exhaustively treated in Benjamin Breckenridge Warfield, *Perfectionism* (1931), II, 463–558. Other major works by Mrs. Smith are *Every-day Religion; or, The Common-sense Teaching of the Bible* (1893); and *The Unselfishness of God and How I Discovered It: A Spiritual Autobiog.* (1903). A series of papers on religious sects and sectarians she had encountered over the years was edited by Ray Strachey and published posthumously as *Religious Fanaticism: Extracts from the Papers of Hannah Whitall Smith* (1928; republished in 1934 under the title *Group Movements of the Past and Experiments in Guidance*). See also obituary notices in the (London) *Times*, May 3, 1911, and *Phila. Public Ledger*, May 4, 1911.]

EARL C. KAYLOR, JR.

SMITH, Jessie Willcox (Sept. 8, 1863–May 3, 1935), painter and illustrator, was born in Philadelphia, Pa., the youngest of four children, two girls and two boys, of Charles Henry Smith, an investment broker, and Katherine DeWitt (Willcox) Smith. Her father was a native of New York, her mother of Connecticut. Educated in private schools, Miss Smith was first drawn by her love of children toward a career as a kindergarten teacher, and at sixteen she went to Cincinnati to prepare for teaching. While there, however, she attended an art class with a friend and discovered her own talent for drawing. Giving up her teaching plans, she presently entered the School of Design for Women in Philadelphia (later Moore College of Art). She continued her studies at the Pennsylvania Academy of the Fine Arts with Thomas Eakins from 1885 to 1888, also attending a portrait class taught by William Sartain at the School of Design for Women in 1886–87. After this early training she did a few drawings for *St. Nicholas* magazine, but it was not until her study with Howard Pyle at the Drexel Institute of Arts and Sciences (now Drexel University) that her style fully developed.

In 1894 Drexel Institute asked Pyle to teach a class in illustration, in which Miss Smith enrolled. In 1898 she was one of the students awarded a scholarship and admitted to the informal class Pyle conducted in an old grist mill on the Brandywine, and early in 1900, when Pyle started his own school in Wilmington, Del., she was among the few promising students whom he accepted without tuition. While at Drexel she met two fellow artists, Violet Oakley (d. 1961) and Elizabeth Shippen Green, who also went with Pyle to Wilmington. Their friendship led them to establish a studio and home together, at first in an old farmhouse at Villanova, outside Philadelphia, and later, when a fourth artist, Henrietta Cozens, joined them, in the Chestnut Hill section of Philadelphia.

Miss Smith received her first commissions—illustrations for two books about Indians—through Pyle's custom of having his students compete for the work he did not have time to do himself. After the second Indian book she requested illustrations of children for her next assignment and was rewarded with a Louisa May Alcott story. With Violet Oakley she illustrated Longfellow's *Evangeline* (1897) while both were still students of Pyle. Her work first came to national attention in 1902 in the Charleston Exposition, where she won a bronze medal. Her first major commercial success was "The Child," a calendar published for Miss Smith and Elizabeth Shippen Green in 1903. A steady and prolific worker, she was soon receiving so many commissions that her artist friends nicknamed her "the Mint." In succeeding years she amassed a large income through advertisements and illustrations for various magazines, including the *Ladies' Home Journal, Collier's, Scribner's, Harper's*, the *Century*, and *Good Housekeeping*, the last of which paid her $1,800 per cover.

She liked best, however, her illustrations for children's books. The most important were those for Robert Louis Stevenson's *A Child's Garden of Verses* (1914), Louisa May Alcott's *Little Women* (1915), Charles Kingsley's *Water Babies* (1916), George MacDonald's *At the Back of the North Wind* (1919), Johanna Spyri's *Heidi* (1922), and *The Children of Dickens* (1925). Although the children she pictured had the simplicity and innocence of her day, they were never sentimental darlings—she disliked "pinked-up" children—but flesh-and-blood youngsters, busy and unposed. When painting, she would study the child's individuality at work or play, and it was largely her ability to portray child personality that built her reputation.

Tall and handsome, with black hair and fair skin, she often served as a model for her colleague Violet Oakley. Miss Smith never married, but at various times in her career she assumed the financial responsibility for some eleven children, including the two sons and daughter of her invalid sister. She was generous also to other causes, often contributing posters to orphanages and other charities. The grace and charm of her pictures made her probably the artist best known to American women in the early twentieth century. At the same time she won critical praise and received numerous awards and prizes, among them the

Mary Smith Prize of the Pennsylvania Academy of the Fine Arts in 1903 and a silver medal for watercolor at the Panama Pacific Exposition in San Francisco in 1915. Failing eyesight and ill health marred her last years. She died at her home in Philadelphia at the age of seventy-one, of chronic interstitial nephritis, arteriosclerosis, and myocarditis. She was buried in Woodland Cemetery, Philadelphia.

[The chief sources are the *Catalogue to Memorial Exhibition of the Work of Jessie Willcox Smith* (Pa. Academy of the Fine Arts, 1935), with appreciation by Edith Emerson; and interviews with Miss Emerson, who was the artist's friend and associate. See also Miss Smith's own account in Bertha E. Mahony and Elinor Whitney, *Contemporary Illustrators of Children's Books* (1930); Bertha E. Mahony, Louise P. Latimer, and Beulah Folmsbee, *Illustrators of Children's Books, 1744–1945* (1947); Edith Emerson, "The Age of Innocence: Portraits by Jessie Willcox Smith," *Am. Mag. of Art,* July 1925; Elizabeth L. North, "Women Illustrators of Child Life," *Outlook,* Oct. 1, 1904; *Nat. Cyc. Am. Biog.,* XXVI, 473; Stanley J. Kunitz and Howard Haycraft, eds., *The Junior Book of Authors* (1940); Gertrude B. Biddle and Sarah D. Lowrie, eds., *Notable Women of Pa.* (1942); *N.Y. Times,* May 4, 1935. A niece, Mrs. Percyval Tudor-Hart of Cataraqui, Bergerville, Quebec, supplied family information. Death record from Pa. Division of Vital Statistics.]

DOROTHY GRAFLY

**SMITH, Julia Evelina.** *See* SMITH, Abby Hadassah.

**SMITH, Kate Douglas.** *See* WIGGIN, Kate Douglas.

**SMITH, Margaret Bayard** (Feb. 20, 1778–June 7, 1844), author, early chronicler of Washington society, was born in Pennsylvania at a farm on the Schuylkill River to which her father, Col. John Bubenheim Bayard, had moved his family when the British occupied Philadelphia. A prominent Philadelphia merchant of Huguenot descent and a leader in both civil and military affairs during the Revolutionary War, he was with Washington at Valley Forge during part of the winter in which Margaret was born. Her mother was his first wife, Margaret Hodge. Of their eight children who survived infancy, she was the seventh child and second daughter. The family also included the three orphaned children of Colonel Bayard's twin brother, who had married Margaret Hodge's sister. Among these double first cousins was James A. Bayard, later a noted statesman, diplomat, and Federalist leader.

When Margaret was two, her mother died; by the time she was ten she had also lost a stepmother. She was then sent to the noted Moravian boarding school at Bethlehem, Pa.; but her education really began in 1792, when her sister Jane, having married Andrew Kirkpatrick, a lawyer (later judge) in New Brunswick, N.J., took the girl to live with her. In Kirkpatrick's well-stocked library Margaret read everything from Newton on the prophecies to the plays of Sophocles, and grew up to be an erudite, attractive, lighthearted young woman. To one of her suitors, a second cousin named Samuel Harrison Smith, she described herself in 1796 as "a downright trifler and romp," accusing him of being much too solemn.

Between her and Smith, who was six years older, there were other contrasts: she was a devout Presbyterian and he an agnostic; she was a Federalist and he a Republican, a protégé of Vice-President Thomas Jefferson, who had encouraged him to start a weekly paper in Philadelphia. In spite of these differences, Margaret fell in love with Cousin Samuel. Her father reluctantly gave his consent, and after three years of an engagement marked by financial reverses, bouts with yellow fever, and other discouragements, they were married on Sept. 29, 1800. By that time Jefferson had persuaded Smith to follow the government when it moved from Philadelphia to Washington and to establish in the new capital a Jeffersonian newspaper, the *National Intelligencer.*

Arriving in Washington by stagecoach early in October 1800, the young Smiths moved into a new row of buildings at New Jersey Avenue and C Street, S.E., where Smith leased two adjoining houses, one for his newspaper plant and printers, the other for his family. The bride, serving her wedding cake to her first callers, members of the small residential society of Washington and Georgetown, was immediately popular. Handsome rather than pretty, with the long nose and deep-set eyes characteristic of the Bayards, she was warmhearted and charming. Her circle of friends widened with the arrival of members of Congress, the diplomatic corps, and, after Jefferson's inauguration in March 1801, the Madisons, Gallatins, and other officials of the new administration. Jefferson himself was an early visitor and won her heart completely.

But life in the raw little capital was not all visiting and sociability. Servants were scarce and unsatisfactory; Margaret often had to cook dinner for the printers as well as her husband, and soon had the care of a baby, Julia Harrison Smith, born late in 1801. The climate was unhealthy; she suffered severely from recurring malaria. To get away from the malarial Washington summers, Smith bought a farm, Turkey Thicket, on a hill three miles from town (now part of Catholic University). Renaming it Sidney, the Smiths after 1804 summered there, later adding fireplaces that made occasional winter residence possible. In the summer of 1807 Smith, whose health had become affected by long hours of hard work at the *Intelligencer*, engaged Joseph Gales, Jr., as his assistant on the paper and contemplated retiring to devote himself to farming and writing. His future, however, lay in the world of finance. He became president of the Bank of Washington in 1809, selling the *Intelligencer* to Gales in 1810; in 1813 he was appointed by President Madison the first Commissioner of the Revenue; and in 1828 he was made president of the Washington branch of the Bank of the United States. At that time he established his family on Fifteenth Street, N.W., between H Street and Pennsylvania Avenue in the newly fashionable Lafayette Square neighborhood, and it was there that the Smiths were most actively a part of the Washington social scene. By then they had a second daughter of marriageable age, Susan Harrison Smith (born in 1804); a son at Princeton, Jonathan Bayard Harrison Smith (born in 1810); and Anna Maria Harrison Smith (1811).

To her children, to the care of her household, and to her share of entertaining in the growing society of the young capital, Margaret Bayard Smith devoted most of the first twenty years of her life in Washington. Her propensity for writing she indulged only by long entries in her notebooks and by letters to her own and her husband's sisters. She lent her aid, however, to one public cause. At the close of the War of 1812, with most public buildings destroyed, Washington had no provision for orphans except in an institution that also housed vagrants and criminals. In 1815 Mrs. Smith joined with other public-spirited women to establish the Washington Female Orphan Asylum, which was later renamed the Washington City Orphan Asylum and accepted boys as well as girls.

In the 1820's Mrs. Smith began to write for publication. Among her earliest efforts was a two-volume novel, *A Winter in Washington, or Memoirs of the Seymour Family* (1824), supposed to have been based on real incidents. The proceeds of another novel of Washington society, *What Is Gentility?* (1828), were donated toward the construction of a new building for the orphan asylum. Mrs. Smith contributed a serial, "Who Is Happy?" (1837),

an account of presidential inaugurations, and some short stories to *Godey's Lady's Book;* essays, stories, and verse to the *National Intelligencer,* the *Southern Literary Messenger,* and *Peter Parley's Annual* (mainly between 1835 and 1837); and several biographies, including one of DOLLEY MADISON, to James Herring and James B. Longacre's *National Portrait Gallery of Distinguished Americans* (4 vols., 1834–39). Most of her writings appeared anonymously, although their authorship was generally known.

Margaret Bayard Smith's reputation rests not on these publications but on a selection from her private papers—her letters and notebooks written between 1800 and 1841—made by the historian Gaillard Hunt and published in 1906 by Charles Scribner's Sons under the title *The First Forty Years of Washington Society.* The book constitutes one of the most valuable sources for the social and political history of the United States from Jefferson's presidency to that of Jackson. It is full of illuminating sidelights on Jefferson and his family, the Madisons, the Clays, the Calhouns, and other national figures. Mrs. Smith visited Monticello and Montpelier; saw the ruins of Washington when the British burned it in 1814; observed its splendid rebuilding and growth; and appreciated keenly the fascinating variety of its society—official, diplomatic, and residential. The city and the time found in her a perceptive, talented, and lively chronicler. She died in Washington at the age of sixty-six and was buried there in Rock Creek Cemetery.

[Mrs. Smith's papers, in the Library of Congress; Gaillard Hunt, ed., *The First Forty Years of Washington Society* (1906); Constance McLaughlin Green, *Washington: Village and Capital, 1800–1878* (1962); Frank van der Linden, *The Turning Point: Jefferson's Battle for the Presidency* (1962); obituary in *Daily Nat. Intelligencer* (Washington), June 8, 1844.]

LIDA MAYO

SMITH, Nixola Greeley. *See* GREELEY-SMITH, Nixola.

SMITH, Nora Archibald. *See* WIGGIN, Kate Douglas.

SMITH, Sophia (Aug. 27, 1796–June 12, 1870), founder of Smith College, was born in Hatfield, Mass., the oldest daughter and fourth of seven children of Joseph and Lois (White) Smith. She was descended from Samuel Smith who came from England to Boston in 1634 and was among the group of settlers from Wethersfield, Conn., that founded the town of Hadley, Mass., in 1659. Joseph Smith was a prosperous farmer, prominent in town affairs, thrifty, keen, and kindly. His wife, considered a model housekeeper, had unusual artistic taste and pleasure in dress. Sophia learned household accomplishments at home, attended the Hatfield School, where at that time boys were taught in the morning and girls in the afternoon, and at fourteen spent one term at a school in Hartford, Conn. Brought up in a family where books were read aloud and discussed around the living-room lamp, she greatly enjoyed reading throughout her life. She was deeply and permanently influenced by the Rev. Joseph Lyman, pastor of the Hatfield Congregational Church, believing herself converted at the age of sixteen, although out of deference for her Unitarian father she did not join the church until 1834. Though shy and retiring by nature, she enjoyed with her family the social life of the small town, the daily drives and calls, neighborhood gatherings and formal parties, frequent long visits of house guests, and trips to Boston, New York, Newport, and Saratoga.

At forty Sophia Smith became deaf and soon was obliged to resort to the unsatisfactory trumpet hearing aid of the period. Her deafness cut her off from social intercourse and intensified the sensitive, introspective side of her nature. Joseph Smith died in 1836, leaving more than $10,000 to each of his four surviving children: Austin, Sophia, and Harriet, all of whom remained unmarried and continued to live together in the family homestead, and Joseph, who was married but died childless in 1861. The energetic Harriet managed the household and the social life of her reliant sister until she died in 1859. Austin amassed a fortune through extraordinary thrift and a talent for speculation in stocks and died unexpectedly on a business trip to New York in 1861. Thus at the age of sixty-five Sophia Smith was left, the last of her family, with the burden of an accumulated fortune.

Weighed down by the responsibility of wisely disposing of this inheritance, Sophia Smith turned for advice to her young pastor, the Rev. John Morton Greene. A graduate of Amherst College, Greene believed that education was the salvation of mankind, a faith shared by his wife, Louisa Dickinson, a graduate of Mount Holyoke Female Seminary. Although eager for guidance, Sophia Smith had a strong and independent mind and refused to be persuaded to direct her fortune to aid either of these existing local institutions.

Greene, aware of the plans for the newly chartered Vassar College, then proposed the foundation of a true college for women, comparable in academic program and standards to the best colleges for men, which would be the first such institution in New England. Miss Smith listened favorably to this proposal, remarking that she wished she might have had the advantages of such a college as a girl. Before proceeding further Greene sought guidance from expert opinion, but the educational leaders whom he consulted, including the presidents of Amherst, Harvard, Williams, and Yale, warned that the higher education of women was still a dangerous experiment. Miss Smith, who had also expressed a wish to aid "the infirm, the aged, or the unfortunate of some kind," then decided to accept another of Greene's proposals and leave the bulk of her fortune to found an institution for deaf-mutes. But seven years later, in 1868, the Clarke School for the Deaf was established in nearby Northampton through the gift of John Clarke, and Sophia Smith was obliged to select another object for her benefaction.

Greene now vigorously revived his proposal for a woman's college. This was warmly supported by Profs. William S. Tyler and Julius H. Seelye of Amherst College, who assisted him in drawing up the "Plan for a Woman's College," which was incorporated in her revised will. "It is my opinion," the will read, "that by the higher and more thoroughly Christian education of women, what are called their 'wrongs' will be redressed, their wages will be adjusted, their weight of influence in reforming the evils of society will be greatly increased; as teachers, as writers, as mothers, as members of society, their power for good will be incalculably enlarged." She did not wish, she concluded, "to render my sex any the less feminine, but to develop as fully as may be the powers of womanhood & furnish women with means of usefulness, happiness, & honor now withheld from them." In a last revision of her will, shortly before her death, she directed that the college should be located in Northampton, a larger and more accessible town than Hatfield.

Sophia Smith's uneventful life came to a close at her home in her seventy-fourth year, following a stroke. She was buried in the Hatfield Cemetery. Her bequest, history-making in providing for the foundation of a woman's college by a woman, amounted to $393,105; Smith College was chartered in 1871 and opened in 1875.

[Unpublished material in the Smith College Archives, including the Personal Journal of Sophia

Smith, Journal and Narrative of John Morton Greene, and pertinent correspondence selected by John M. Greene; *Last Will and Testament of Miss Sophia Smith, Late of Hatfield, Mass.* (1871); *Addresses at the Inauguration of Rev. L. Clark Seelye as President of Smith College* (1875); series of twelve articles on "The Early Hist. of Smith College" by John M. Greene in the *Hampshire Gazette* (Northampton), July 31, 1891–Apr. 12, 1893; *The Centennial of the Birth of Sophia Smith* (1896); *Celebration of the Quarter-Centenary of Smith College* (1900); Elizabeth Deering Hanscom and Helen French Greene, *Sophia Smith and the Beginnings of Smith College* (1925); Gladys Wookey Davis, *Miss Sophia's Legacy* (1950); *Heritage: A Play in Honor of the 75th Anniversary of the Founding of Smith College,* ed. by Hallie Flanagan Davis and George Brenden Dowell (1953).]

MARGARET STORRS GRIERSON

**SMITH, Virginia Thrall** (Aug 16, 1836–Jan. 3, 1903), Hartford city mission and charitable worker, pioneer in child care in Connecticut, was born in Bloomfield, Conn. Christened Tryphena Virginia, she was the second daughter and fourth of six children of Hiram Thrall, businessman and surveyor, and Melissa (Griswold) Thrall, whose forebears had settled in Windsor, Conn., as early as 1639. Growing up in Bloomfield, she was educated at the Suffield (Conn.) Institute, the Hartford Female Seminary, and, in 1856–57, at Mount Holyoke Seminary, South Hadley, Mass. On Dec. 31, 1857, at twenty-one, she was married to William Brown Smith (1832–1897). They settled in Hartford, where Smith engaged in various business ventures; city directories list him as proprietor of a tailor shop and later of a blacksmith shop, as a partner in a firm which made carriages, and as a commission merchant in grains. Of their six children—Oliver Cotton (born 1859), Edward Carrington (1861), Lucy Virginia (1865), Kate Richardson (1867), William Brown (1871), and Thomas Hammond (1874)—Edward, Lucy, and Kate died of diphtheria in infancy. Oliver became a physician and surgeon; William, to the family's chagrin, chose a career on the stage, where as Winchell Smith he achieved some success as actor and playwright.

During her early married life Mrs. Smith played a church organ, gave readings at small social gatherings, and wrote stories for the newspapers ("Electa Millington's Disappointment"). A kindly neighbor, she also interested herself in church and private charity. In 1876 she was chosen as city missionary, the administrative head of the Hartford City Mission, established in 1851 as a joint enterprise of the city's six Congregational churches, which dis-

pensed food, clothing, and good advice to the needy.

Always forward-looking, Mrs. Smith at once set about expanding the mission's program, adding to it many of the features of a social settlement. She started a loan fund and organized a women's sewing class and reading society, a singing school for girls, and a boys' club. In 1878 she added a volunteer corps of thirty-three charitable visitors. The next year she began sending children out of the city for country vacations. In 1881 she opened a laundry and cooking school, a girls' sewing school, and a free kindergarten. So successful did the kindergarten prove that two years later a separate Free Kindergarten Association was formed to carry on the work, and in 1885 a state law was secured authorizing the establishment of kindergartens in public schools throughout Connecticut. In 1884 Mrs. Smith established the Sister Dora Society for young working girls, later the Women's Exchange. To help with these new activities she organized in 1888 the Hartford City Mission Association, a women's auxiliary to supplement the all-male City Mission board.

Her special concern, however, was with children, and her appointment to the State Board of Charities, in July 1882—a position she held for nine years—gave her the opportunity to pursue it. Personal visits to local almshouses, of which there were then 101 in Connecticut towns, led her to estimate that within them were 2,500 children, housed indiscriminately among the senile, the insane, and the criminal. Though her figures were questioned, an official investigation soon afterward found over double that number. The law she had pressed for, establishing temporary county children's homes, was enacted in May 1883. Within her own City Mission she had also developed a program for placing unwanted children in adoptive homes. The reports she gave on placement at meetings of the National Conference of Charities and Correction, in 1885, 1886, and 1893, were listened to with respect and interest.

Her child care program, however, and her inspection of almshouses had roused the hostility of local officials, who felt her welfare program infringed on their rights. In 1892 some of these opponents seized upon a case where Mrs. Smith had arranged for the local adoption of an illegitimate baby, born at her home to a Massachusetts girl who had come there for aid and had died in childbirth. Charges of "baby-farming," of "encouraging sin," of making Hartford a dumping ground for out-of-state paupers rocked the community.

The Hartford selectmen issued a pamphlet, *Report on Baby-Farming;* John Hooker, husband of the suffragist ISABELLA BEECHER HOOKER, countered with a *Defence of Mrs. Virginia T. Smith.* Mrs. Smith's family suffered, embarrassed by the publicity, bitter at the false charges; the younger boys especially had always resented their mother's absences from home. The City Mission board, in secret session, voted to return to its original purpose: "To relieve the absolute necessities of the poor, especially whenever they can thus be brought within the influence of the means of Grace or their children be gathered into Sabbath schools" (*Hartford Courant,* Oct. 19, 1892). That December Mrs. Smith resigned her post.

Her supporters had meanwhile swung into action. The Hartford City Mission Association changed its name to the Children's Aid Society to carry on her work. A group of women led by Mrs. Francis Bacon of New Haven (see GEORGEANNA WOOLSEY) late in 1892 organized the Connecticut Children's Aid Society, with Mrs. Smith as a director and the salaried secretary; this she headed until her death. One other concern had weighed on Mrs. Smith: the problem of those handicapped children whom no one would adopt or take as boarders. In 1898, after some years of fund raising, she opened the Home for Incurables—later the Newington Hospital for Crippled Children—at Newington, Conn.

Her own health was soon failing. In November 1901 she was operated on for an abdominal tumor. Her recovery was only temporary, and a recurrence led to her death, at her Hartford home, early in 1903. Pastors of a Congregational church, the denomination of her childhood, and of a Unitarian church, whose services she attended in later life, conducted her funeral, and she was buried in Cedar Hill Cemetery, Hartford. The Children's Aid Society—now the Children's Services of Connecticut—and the Newington Hospital perpetuate her memory.

[Obituaries in Hartford newspapers, especially the *Courant,* Jan. 5, 1903; annual reports of Conn. Children's Aid Soc.; information furnished by Paul Butterworth, West Hartford, Conn., from the Thrall family Bible and other sources, and by his brother-in-law, Harrison Smith, a grandson of Mrs. Smith. On the "baby-farming" controversy, see the pamphlets cited in the text and *Hartford Courant* and *Hartford Jour.,* June 1, 7, Aug. 6, Nov. 11, 1892. Records of the City Mission Assoc. are in the Conn. State Library, Hartford. Mary K. O. Eagle, ed., *The Congress of Women* (1894), includes (pp. 178–80) a photograph of Mrs. Smith and excerpts from her address on "The Kindergar-

ten." A fuller account of her career by Barbara P. Atwood is in *New-England Galaxy,* Summer 1961.]

BARBARA P. ATWOOD

**SMITH, Zilpha Drew** (Jan. 25, 1852?–Oct. 12, 1926), social worker, was born in Pembroke, Mass., the second daughter and third of the six children of Silvanus and Judith Winsor (McLauthlin) Smith. Shortly after her birth the family moved to East Boston, where her father, an experienced carpenter and sailmaker, established a large shipyard. Both Silvanus and Judith Smith (who lived to be a hundred) were *Mayflower* descendants born in Massachusetts of seafaring and farming stock. They reflected their New England heritage in a lifelong dedication to social causes, including abolition, education, temperance, religious tolerance, and woman suffrage. To their children they transmitted not only their own sense of moral and social responsibility but also a respect for hard, honest labor and wholesome family life. As a social worker Zilpha Smith would always encourage voluntary personal service in philanthropy as a duty of citizenship, would subordinate material relief to the "uplifting" of character, and would measure philanthropic achievement by its success in strengthening family ties.

After graduating from Boston's Girls' High and Normal School in 1868, Miss Smith became a telegrapher. She received her first opportunity to display the organizing abilities, perfectionism, penchant for accuracy in detail, and analytic turn of mind which were to typify her career when she undertook to revise the index of the Probate Court of Suffolk County. This experience, combined with volunteer relief work following the disastrous Boston fire of 1872, qualified her in 1879 for the post of registrar of the newly formed Associated Charities, a consolidation of Boston's social agencies. As head of its registration bureau, or confidential exchange, she was technically responsible for maintaining a central file of all individuals served by the various agencies; in fact, she functioned as general secretary, a title formally bestowed in 1886.

Under Miss Smith's executive leadership the Boston Associated Charities became one of the most successful organizations of its type, as the "charity organization" movement spread through American cities in the late nineteenth century. The leaders of the movement hoped that a policy of investigation and registration of all cases, cooperation between agencies, discriminating relief, and volunteer "friendly visiting" would alleviate, if not eliminate, the pauperism, poverty, and class frictions of an urban-industrial society, as well as ensure the efficient management and coordination of the community's charitable resources. Charity organization, however, was merely a theory in 1879 and depended upon capable administrators like Zilpha Smith to create the machinery and apply the theory in practice.

The Boston Associated Charities, like some other such societies, combined paid and volunteer workers, provided a training program for both groups, and established a centralized form of administration tempered by considerable district autonomy. Such were Miss Smith's skills that no other agency surpassed hers in the number of volunteers enlisted or in the care devoted to training workers. The paid agent was responsible for initial investigation of applicants, district administration, and advice to volunteers and district committees. It was Miss Smith's assumption, however, that the entire machinery existed to encourage volunteer service, or the "friendly visiting" which would foster personal, face-to-face relationships between rich and poor. Poverty, she believed, was often the consequence of some moral or personal defect—indolence, ignorance, intemperance, improvidence; the educated and prosperous visitor would transmit middle-class virtues to the poor, thus ensuring their permanent rehabilitation.

Miss Smith attempted to mold the district conference or committee into an educational forum in which paid agents and volunteers traded experience, learned from each other's success or failure, and sustained each other's morale. She recognized, in effect, that the charity worker as well as the client needed help and guidance, and thus anticipated the development of supervision in casework. Miss Smith also pioneered in social work education when she established training classes for district agents and, in the 1890's, study classes for agents and volunteers. When she and Charles W. Birtwell of the Boston Children's Aid Society formed the Monday Evening Club in 1888, a social workers' discussion group, she helped set a precedent for the professional social work association of the twentieth century.

The success of the Boston Associated Charities led many charity secretaries and agents, including MARY RICHMOND in Baltimore, to turn to Miss Smith for advice, and her influence spread far beyond Boston. She was for many years active in the National Conference of Charities and Correction, and in the summer of 1900 she lectured at the newly organized New York School of Philanthropy. A lecture that she gave at this school in 1908,

"Methods Common to Social Investigations," an early exposition of the casework technique, inspired Miss Richmond's 1917 textbook on casework, *Social Diagnosis.*

Zilpha Smith resigned from the Associated Charities in 1903 (her successor was ALICE LOUISE HIGGINS LOTHROP). The next year she became associate director of the new Boston School for Social Workers, established by Harvard University and Simmons College. The development of a full year's academic training course (the New York School of Philanthropy also expanded its curriculum in 1904 to cover an academic year) represented a milestone in the evolution of professional social work. Miss Smith's responsibilities at the school included the organization of special problem classes in which case records were used to illustrate principles of investigation, diagnosis, and treatment.

Miss Smith retired in 1918. Her students at the Boston School, like her agents and volunteers at the Associated Charities, had found her an exacting, demanding, sometimes brusque teacher, but one sincerely interested in them as human beings with special aptitudes and problems. On superficial acquaintance she seemed reserved and lacking in humor. Undoubtedly she was a serious-minded, disciplined, and iron-willed woman, but she possessed deep emotional reserves which she lavished upon close friends like Mary Richmond. Intellectually Zilpha Smith was wary of generalization. She had what the Massachusetts civic leader Joseph Lee described as a "common law" mind, competent in the handling of detail or fact and thus well fitted to charity organization work with its focus upon problems of individual maladjustment. In her leisure moments she enjoyed music, drama, and literature. She found peace and solace in nature, delighting in exploring the hills and countryside of New England. She became a member of the Massachusetts Society of Mayflower Descendants in 1924. In religion she was a Unitarian. She died in Boston of arteriosclerosis at the age of seventy-four and was buried in the Mayflower Cemetery, Duxbury, Mass.

One of the outstanding administrators and educators produced by the charity organization movement, Zilpha Smith helped give the principles of that movement a pervasive influence in the world of philanthropy. Though devoted to the ideal of volunteer personal service, she nevertheless played a major role in nurturing the professionalization of social work, which ultimately subordinated the volunteer to the paid worker. She herself was among the first women to find in the charity organization movement a creative professional career.

[A scrapbook in the archives of the Simmons School of Social Work and a folder in the archives of the Family Service Assoc. of Greater Boston contain clippings and some unpublished material. The Mary Richmond Papers at the N.Y. School of Social Work include many letters by Miss Smith. The following articles by Zilpha Smith are useful for understanding her ideas: "Volunteer Visiting: The Organization Necessary to Make It Effective," Nat. Conference of Charities and Correction, *Proc.*, 1884, pp. 69–72; "How to Get and Keep Visitors," *ibid.*, 1887, pp. 156–62; "Report of the Committee on the Organization of Charity," *ibid.*, 1888, pp. 120–30; "The Education of the Friendly Visitor," *ibid.*, 1892, pp. 445–49; "Needy Families in Their Homes: Introduction," *ibid.*, 1901, pp. 284–89; "Field Work," *ibid.*, 1915, pp. 622–26; "Friendly Visitors," *Charities*, Aug. 24, 1901. For her views on broken families see her pamphlet *Deserted Wives and Deserting Husbands: A Study of 234 Families Based on the Experience of the District Committees and Agents of the Associated Charities of Boston* (1901). For her casework principles see her "Methods Common to Social Investigations," Charities Publication Committee, *Field Dept. Bull.*, May 1909. Sketches of Miss Smith's life and work can be found in: *The Family*, May 1930 (by Margaret E. Rich); *Encyc. of the Social Sciences*, XIV, 118–19 (by Jeffrey R. Brackett); the memorial volume, *A Meeting in Memory of Zilpha D. Smith* (1926); *Social Worker* (Simmons School of Social Work alumni publication), Aug. 1945; and *Who Was Who in America*, vol. I (1942). See also Frank J. Bruno, *Trends in Social Work, 1874–1956* (1957); and Roy Lubove, *The Professional Altruist* (1965). Miss Margaret Curtis, a director of the Family Service Assoc. of Greater Boston and a former student of Zilpha Smith, contributed information in an interview. Most sources, including a genealogical chart she gave to the New England Historic Genealogical Soc., give her birth year as 1852. Pembroke town records, however, list her birth date as Jan. 25, 1851.]

ROY LUBOVE

**SNOW, Eliza Roxey.** See SMITH, Eliza Roxey Snow.

**SNYDER, Alice D.** (Oct. 29, 1887–Feb. 17, 1943), professor of English, was born in Middletown, Conn., the second of three children and only daughter of the Rev. Peter Miles Snyder and Grace Evelyn (Bliss) Snyder. Her middle name, which she disliked and did not use, was Dorothea. Both her brothers had distinguished academic careers, Franklyn Bliss Snyder as president of Northwestern University and Edward Douglas Snyder as professor of English at Haverford College.

Alice was a remarkably precocious child,

although bad health caused her to miss much of her early schooling. After her fifteenth year, however, she became physically vigorous, reveled in walking, boating, and playing golf, and began to develop the unusual intellectual potentialities characteristic of her family. Her mother, a member of the class of 1877 at Vassar College, was a talented pianist, at one time taught mathematics, and displayed a dazzling conversational brilliance which Alice is said to have equaled at times. Her father, a Congregational minister, had a relatively placid and judicial temperament that balanced his wife's volatility. After graduating from Williams College in 1874, he had traveled in Europe and the Near East for three years before entering Union Theological Seminary. The family life was happy; there was much reading aloud and stimulating conversation, and the children were encouraged to amuse themselves by writing parodies and light poems.

While Alice was still a child the family moved to Burlington, Vt., and then to Rockford, Ill., where she graduated from high school in 1905. After receiving her A.B. degree from Vassar in 1909, she accepted a fellowship there in English, receiving her A.M. degree in 1911. By 1915 she had earned the Ph.D. degree, in English and philosophy, from the University of Michigan. These years of study had included teaching as well: as assistant in English at Rockford College (1909–10), as instructor in English at Vassar (1912–14), and as assistant in rhetoric at the University of Michigan (1914–15). After receiving her doctorate she returned to Vassar as a member of the English department, of which she was chairman at the time of her death.

As a teacher Miss Snyder possessed the rare gift of exacting the utmost intellectual application from her students while at the same time winning their absolute devotion. If at first they were in awe of her, they soon found that her interest in them was both genuine and kind. Moreover she carried her activities beyond the classroom. She played a leading role in the developing educational policy at Vassar College, and for many years she served on the committee of the College Entrance Examination Board.

As a scholar Miss Snyder played a major part in reawakening interest in the critical and philosophical writings of Samuel Taylor Coleridge. In her doctoral dissertation, *The Critical Principle of the Reconciliation of Opposites as Employed by Coleridge* (1918), she discussed the philosophical basis of Coleridge's ideas, as derived from the German metaphysicians;

how this metaphysical principle found expression in his aesthetic theory; and how he applied the principle to literary problems, particularly to his critical studies of Shakespeare. She centered her discussion around a passage from the *Biographia Literaria* in which Coleridge describes the imagination as a power revealing itself "in the balance or reconciliation of opposite or discordant qualities," a concept, hitherto unappreciated, that has since come to be considered the core of Coleridge's philosophical thought. In *Coleridge on Logic and Learning, with Selections from the Unpublished Manuscripts* (1929), Miss Snyder was able to include previously unpublished manuscript material, obtained from the poet's great-grandson, the Rev. Gerard H. B. Coleridge, which represented Coleridge's early attempts at a systematic treatise on logic. The book, which also discussed Coleridge as "potential" scientist, encyclopedist, and logician, has proved invaluable to students of Coleridge and prompted the British philosopher J. H. Muirhead to speak of Miss Snyder as "a pioneer in the sympathetic re-examination of these manuscripts." In 1934 she published an edition of Coleridge's *Treatise on Method* as it had originally appeared in the *Encyclopaedia Metropolitana*, which, aided by her scholarly introduction, provides further evidence of the nature of Coleridge's intellectual powers. Miss Snyder also published seventeen lesser articles on Coleridge, among them a detailed description of the only surviving manuscript of *Kubla Khan* (*Times Literary Supplement*, Aug. 2, 1934) and numerous reviews. All these papers were models of scholarship.

Miss Snyder took an active part in the Modern Language Association and the Modern Humanities Research Association, and particularly encouraged younger scholars. She was concerned with broad social issues and took a lively interest in both local and national affairs. At various periods of her life her commitments included woman suffrage, the Better Housing League, the Teachers' Union, the American Labor Party, and the National Council for American-Soviet Friendship. She was also a member of the Women's City and County Club of Poughkeepsie and the League of Women Voters.

Miss Snyder died of a heart attack at her apartment on the Vassar campus at the age of fifty-five and was buried in Watertown, N.Y. The Alice D. Snyder Fund was established at Vassar to perpetuate her ideals of literary research. She is remembered by her friends not only for the depth of her scholarship, but also for the warmth of her personality and for the influence she exerted on her students and colleagues.

[Information from records of Vassar Alumnae Office and President's Office; information supplied by Prof. Edward D. Snyder and other members of the family; personal recollections. See also Elinor Bliss Dayton and Arthur Bliss Dayton, *Bliss and Holmes Descendants* (1961); and obituary in *N.Y. Times*, Feb. 18, 1943.]

EARL LESLIE GRIGGS

**SOLOMON, Hannah Greenebaum** (Jan. 14, 1858–Dec. 7, 1942), clubwoman and welfare worker, founder of the National Council of Jewish Women, was born in Chicago, Ill., the fourth daughter and fourth of ten children of Michael and Sarah (Spiegel) Greenebaum. Both parents had emigrated from the German Palatinate, the father in 1845, the mother in 1848. Michael Greenebaum (the family name was originally Gruenebaum) soon established himself as a prosperous Chicago hardware merchant and an important figure in the city's growing Jewish community; he and his wife were prominent members of the city's first Reform congregation of Judaism. Their daughter received part of her early education at a temple school, where German and Hebrew were taught. She also attended public schools, including two years at Chicago's only public high school (the West Division High School), until, in keeping with the family's strong musical interests, she chose in 1873 to continue her education by studying piano with the noted Chicago teacher Carl Wolfsohn. On May 14, 1879, she was married to Henry Solomon, a young merchant who shared her interest in music and the arts. His support and encouragement were of great importance in her later work. They had three children, Herbert (died in 1899), Helen, and Frank, who took over the family clothing business when Henry Solomon died in 1913.

From her youth, Hannah Solomon had been a member of many of the Jewish social and cultural clubs of the city. In 1877 she and her sister Henriette (Mrs. Henry Frank) became the first Jewish members of the Chicago Woman's Club, an organization founded the year before primarily for literary purposes, though it soon added practical work; Mrs. Frank became the club's president in 1884–85. Mrs. Solomon gave up outside activities for a time while her children were young, for though she later described herself as "a confirmed woman's-rights-er," she gave a warm priority to family life.

In 1890, when preparations were begun for the World's Columbian Exposition to be held in Chicago three years later, Hannah Solomon was asked to organize a nationwide Jewish Women's Congress as an adjunct of the Exposition's Parliament of Religions. By her personal efforts she brought together many of the leading Jewish women in the United States, the first such assembly in the history of American Jewry. As she had urged, the Congress resolved itself into a permanent organization, the National Council of Jewish Women. Its purpose, as Mrs. Solomon conceived it, was to teach all Jewish women their obligations both to their religion and to the community of which they were a part. Local sections were quickly organized (fifty by 1896), which not only studied Judaism but also sponsored social service projects. More broadly, the Council gave to Jewish women the means through which they could make their influence felt with the same unity as other groups of American women who shared their concern with vital social issues. Mrs. Solomon was elected as the Council's first president and held the office until 1905, when she was made honorary president for life.

Her interests extended to other women's organizations, local and national, among them the Illinois Federation of Women's Clubs, which she helped found in 1896, and the Council of Women of the United States, which she represented, with SUSAN B. ANTHONY and MAY WRIGHT SEWALL, at a convention of the International Council of Women in Berlin in 1904.

Mrs. Solomon also took part in many philanthropic and reform projects in the Chicago area, as an outgrowth of her work with the Russian-Jewish immigrants who were crowding into Chicago in the 1890's. In 1896 she conducted a statistical survey of the immigrants in the Jewish district, tabulating the agencies and schools available to deal with their problems. The next year, with funds from the Chicago section of the National Council of Jewish Women, she established the Bureau of Personal Service, an organization designed to give much-needed guidance and legal advice to the newcomers. Since the Jewish area was near Hull House, Mrs. Solomon worked closely with JANE ADDAMS, both through the bureau and on other committees, especially those concerned with child welfare. She was one of the members of the Chicago Woman's Club who took a prominent part in establishing the Cook County (Chicago) juvenile court in 1899.

It was as an outgrowth of this interest and as a representative of the Woman's Club that Mrs. Solomon began her work with the Illinois Industrial School for Girls, in 1905.

Largely through her efforts, the school was rehabilitated and moved to healthier surroundings where, in 1907, it became the Park Ridge School for Girls. Mrs. Solomon served for many years on its board, in 1906–09 as president. As a charter member of the Women's City Club, founded in 1910, she contributed to numerous civic reforms. In 1910 she was appointed chairman of the club's committee which investigated Chicago's waste disposal system. In her autobiography Mrs. Solomon recalls conducting an inspection tour of the city dumps clad in trailing white lace and carrying an elegant parasol, an experience which came to symbolize for her both the determination and the complete lack of preparation with which she and other women of her day met their new obligations.

After retiring in the early 1920's from the strenuous activity which had dominated most of her life, Mrs. Solomon devoted her time to travel, in the United States and Europe, and to music and art. She died at her home in Chicago in her eighty-fifth year, of hemiplegia followed by bronchopneumonia. Funeral services were held at Sinai Temple, which she had attended since childhood and upon whose board of directors she had served for many years, and she was buried in Chicago's Graceland Cemetery. The public services Mrs. Solomon had performed were characteristic of a period which brought increased freedom and responsibility to American women. Although her desire for social betterment was perhaps rooted more deeply in religious convictions than that of many such women, she nevertheless followed within the Jewish community a pattern typical of the progressive reformers of her period.

[Mrs. Solomon wrote *A Sheaf of Leaves* (1911), a collection of articles and speeches, and *Fabric of My Life* (1946), an autobiography. For other biographical accounts see *Am. Hebrew*, Jan. 6, 1933; and Hyman L. Meites, ed., *Hist. of the Jews of Chicago* (1924). Briefer references are in *Nat. Cyc. Am. Biog.*, XXXVI, 390; *Who's Who in Am. Jewry*, 1939; *Universal Jewish Encyc.*, IX, 640; *Woman's Who's Who of America*, 1914–15; *Am. Jewish Year Book*, XLV (1943), 395; *N.Y. Times*, Dec. 9, 1942. See also *The First Fifty Years: A Hist. of the Nat. Council of Jewish Women* (1943).]

SYLVIA A. JOHNSON

**SOULE, Caroline Augusta White** (Sept. 3, 1824–Dec. 6, 1903), author, church worker, and Universalist minister, was born in Albany, N.Y., the third of six children of Nathaniel White, a mechanic, and Elizabeth (Mèrselis) White. Her father's ancestors had emigrated from England in the seventeenth century; he was a native of Hartford, Conn. On her mother's side Caroline was of Dutch and French descent. She was christened in her mother's Dutch Reformed Church but reared in her father's Universalist faith. Her parents, firm believers in the value of education despite their lack of means, enrolled their daughter in the Albany Female Academy when she was twelve. She graduated with high honors in July 1841, and the next April became principal of the female department of the Clinton Liberal Institute, a secondary school established by the Universalists in Clinton, N.Y. Though frail and shy, she proved a good teacher, but illness obliged her to return home after only two terms. In Albany on Aug. 28, 1843, she was married to Henry Birdsall Soule, a Universalist minister who had been a fellow teacher at the Clinton Institute, and went to live in Utica, N.Y., where her husband was then preaching. Frequent moves to new churches followed: to Boston in 1844, to Gloucester, Mass., in 1845, to Hartford, Conn., in 1846. The couple remained in Hartford until 1850, when illness forced Soule to retire temporarily. Improved by the spring of 1851, he served briefly in Granby, Conn., prior to accepting a call to Lyons, N.Y. Before his family could join him there, he died from smallpox in January 1852, leaving his twenty-seven-year-old wife with three hundred dollars, a few hundred books, and five young children. (The four whose names are recorded were Sarah, Elizabeth, Frank, and Henry Channing.)

Though Mrs. Soule had earlier contributed occasionally to newspapers, she now began to write in earnest in order to support her family. In a few months she published a life of her husband which became one of the standard Universalist biographies, and her articles began to appear in such well-known Universalist magazines as the *Rose of Sharon* and the *Ladies' Repository*. With money from her literary efforts and from teaching, she remained in Granby until 1854, when financial straits forced the family to move to a log cabin in Boonsboro, Iowa, her home for the next decade. In 1855 Abel Tompkins, a Universalist publisher of Boston, issued a collection of her moral tales, *Home Life*. Many of these, as well as her first novel, *The Pet of the Settlement* (1860), a story of the prairie land, were drawn from her own experiences. From 1856 to 1865 she was corresponding, then assistant, editor of the *Ladies' Repository*. After her last book, *Wine or Water* (1862), her writing chiefly concerned her church work.

Mrs. Soule returned to Albany in 1864, for treatment of an eye ailment, and three years later moved to New York City, where she established and edited for eleven years her own Sunday-school paper, the *Guiding Star*. In 1869 she helped organize the Woman's Centenary Aid Association, formed to assist in raising an endowment fund for the Universalist Church. This was reorganized two years later as the Woman's Centenary Association, the first national organization of churchwomen in the United States. Its purposes were to assist disabled preachers and their families, to help educate women students for the ministry, and to engage in home and foreign missionary work. As president from its founding to 1880, Mrs. Soule traveled widely, did much writing and speaking, solicited funds, and mailed out thousands of tracts. In a single year (1873) she raised over $25,000. In addition she supported the temperance cause and was active in the Association for the Advancement of Women, sponsored by Sorosis, the pioneer American woman's club, serving on the executive committees of both organizations in the early 1870's.

Mrs. Soule's schedule proved so exhausting that her health, always delicate, broke down, and in 1875 she went to England and Scotland for several months' rest. Not one to remain idle, however, she preached to Universalists in Scotland, helped them organize a Scottish Universalist Convention, participated in the dedication of their first church, and in 1878 returned to Scotland as a missionary for the Centenary Association. The next year she became minister of St. Paul's Universalist Church in Glasgow, being officially ordained in 1880. The people of her parish came to love this sensitive woman of simple tastes and friendly disposition, and she in turn formed a lasting attachment for Scotland. Save for an interim in 1882–86, when she returned to the United States to work again for the Centenary Association, she remained in Scotland the rest of her life. She retired from the ministry in 1892, but continued to live in Glasgow, characteristically lending a helping hand wherever needed. She died in Glasgow in 1903 at the age of seventy-nine and was cremated at the Glasgow crematorium. She had once remarked, "I have written everything from a sermon to a song, and done everything from making sorghum molasses in a log-cabin on a prairie to preaching three times a Sunday in the city of London" (*Appletons' Cyclopaedia of American Biography*, V, 610). In an age of limited opportunities for her sex, her life was a testimonial to the fact that woman's work need know no boundaries.

[A good collection of Mrs. Soule's letters and papers is in the N.Y. Public Library. Published material is scarce and inadequate; the best accounts are: Mrs. E. R. Hanson, *Our Woman Workers* (1882), pp. 437–51; Emily Sherwood Ragan, *Character Sketches of the Pioneers of the Woman's Centenary Association* (n.d.); Phebe A. Hanaford, *Daughters of America* (1883), pp. 661–65; *Universalist Register*, 1905, pp. 96–97. See also: *Lamb's Biog. Dict. of the U.S.*, VII, 154–55; and M. Louise Thomas, *Centenary Voices; or, A Part of the Work of the Women of the Universalist Church* (1886). For a fuller account of Mrs. Soule, see Alan Seaburg in Unitarian Hist. Soc., *Transactions*, Oct. 1967.]

ALAN SEABURG

**SOUTHWORTH, Emma Dorothy Eliza Nevitte** (Dec. 26, 1819–June 30, 1899), popular novelist, was born in Washington, D.C., the elder of the two daughters of Charles Le Compte Nevitte, an Alexandria, Va., importer of French descent, and his second wife, Susannah Wailes, of St. Mary's County, Md. Charles Nevitte's fleet of merchant ships suffered severe losses in the War of 1812, in which he served as captain of a company and received a wound from which he never fully recovered; he died when Emma was three. Some two years later her mother married Joshua L. Henshaw, a Bostonian who had come to Washington as Daniel Webster's secretary and who later opened a school. Emma remembered herself as a plain, lonely child, happiest when riding and exploring the countryside around her grandmother's home in Maryland. Her girlhood interest in Tidewater scenery and legends later furnished material for many of her novels. Though baptized in her father's Roman Catholic faith, she was reared in the Episcopal Church of her mother.

After graduating from her stepfather's academy in 1835, Emma taught school until, on Jan. 23, 1840, she was married to Frederick Hamilton Southworth, an inventor from Utica, N.Y. They moved the next year to Prairie du Chien, Wis., where Mrs. Southworth taught school in nearby Platteville until her first child, Richmond J. Southworth, was born. In 1844, when she was again pregnant, Mrs. Southworth and her husband separated, and she returned to Washington, where she gave birth to a daughter, Charlotte Emma. Although she would never talk about her unhappy marriage, the novels she wrote are full of abandoned and otherwise mistreated wives. She once considered remarrying, after her husband died, but never did so.

Mrs. Southworth taught for a time in the Washington public schools, but the $250 a year she was paid barely supported her children and herself. To supplement her income, and to take her mind off her troubles, she began to write. Her first story, published about 1846 in the *Baltimore Saturday Visiter*, brought no money, but it did attract the attention of Gamaliel Bailey, editor of Washington's *National Era*, who bought her subsequent stories and in 1849 published her first novel, *Retribution*, in serial form. Issued as a book by Harper's that same year, it was so well received that Mrs. Southworth was able to stop teaching and spend all her time writing. In the next seven years the *National Era* and the *Saturday Evening Post* published twelve of her novels serially, and T. B. Peterson of Philadelphia put them out in book form. Sales and critical praise increased with each book, yet Mrs. Southworth's personal troubles continued. She and her children were all in poor health a good part of the time. Her daughter once became so ill that her life was despaired of; Mrs. Southworth nursed the child unaided, writing one entire book at the bedside.

In 1857 Robert Bonner of the *New York Ledger* came to her rescue. In return for exclusive serial rights to her novels, he promised to pay Mrs. Southworth even if illness interrupted her work. This new security restored her health and spirits, and over the next thirty years Bonner published thirty of her novels in his magazine. The *Ledger* was the most popular story journal of its day, and "Mrs. E. D. E. N. Southworth" was long its most popular author. Her earnings eventually reached about $10,000 a year—then a princely sum for a writer. In 1850 she moved to a large house in Georgetown, D.C. Unlike her close friend HARRIET BEECHER STOWE, Mrs. Southworth was no reformer. Though she sometimes described the mistreatment of slaves, for the most part she wrote sympathetically about the antebellum South. She went to England in 1859 and spent the first two years of the Civil War abroad. After her return in 1862, however, she was an outspoken Union sympathizer and served as a volunteer nurse in a hospital near her home.

Mrs. Southworth continued to write at a prodigious rate for most of her long life. At first she wrote as many as three novels a year, working from morning to midnight, and even as she grew older she steadily produced one a year. Only after she was nearly seventy, in the last ten years of her life, did she stop writing, but her novels continued to be reprinted and widely read. In 1877 Peterson issued a uniform edition of her novels in forty-two volumes. Her literary success brought on a plague of imitators, plagiarists, and literary pirates, as well as importunities from her estranged husband, in whose name she placed one copyright in 1861.

Emma Southworth's firm face, rather sharp features, and severely styled dark hair express her inner strength and sense of moral purpose. "Writing, sewing, almsgiving, worshipping," she said, made up the routine of her life (Noel, p. 270). She joined the Swedenborgian Church in 1883 and in her later years became much interested in spiritualism. For most of her life she lived near where she had been born, except for some years, from 1876 to 1890, in Yonkers, N.Y. She died in Georgetown in 1899, in her eightieth year, and was buried in Oak Hill Cemetery, Washington, D.C.

Mrs. Southworth was the most popular of the sentimental mid-century American novelists, and she is generally considered the best writer among them. She used the creaky machinery of the Gothic romance—ghosts, abductions, trapdoors, thieves' dens, deserted houses —with freshness, and though her stories do not depart from the melodramatic conventions of her day, they are full of lively incident. Her greatest achievement was to introduce two democratic ideal types to popular fiction. In *The Hidden Hand* (1859), her most popular novel, Capitola, the heroine, suffers all the injustices against which nineteenth-century women had no legal recourse. Stolen from her widowed mother by a villainous uncle at birth, Capitola only by a lucky chance escapes degradation in the slums of New York, where there is plenty of honest work for boys but none for girls. Her guardian tyrannizes over her, and under the law she is helpless to claim her rightful—and large—inheritance. These are trials from which an earlier heroine would have had to be rescued by a hero, but Mrs. Southworth endows Capitola with bravery and boldness of spirit that make her a match for any man, and she rescues herself. Although Mrs. Southworth never joined the feminist movement, Capitola in her own way was a powerful argument against the helplessness then assumed to be inherent in female nature.

Mrs. Southworth's second ideal character, Ishmael, the hero of "Ishmael; or, In the Depths" and its sequel, "Self-Raised; or, From the Depths" (serialized in the *Ledger* in 1863–64 and later published in book form as *Self-Made*) is a prototype of the self-made man. His career demonstrates the belief that in America the virtuous could triumph over adversity and, despite low birth, wring respect from the most snobbish aristocrat. Both Capitola and Ishmael reflect and illuminate the social changes that accompanied the trans-formation of provincial, traditional antebellum America into a dynamic, socially mobile industrial society.

[The most complete study of Mrs. Southworth's life and work is Regis Louise Boyle, *Mrs. E. D. E. N. Southworth, Novelist* (1939), though it displays many of the faults of the academic dissertation. The best appreciation of her writing is in Helen Waite Papashvily, *All the Happy Endings* (1956). See also Herbert Ross Brown, *The Sentimental Novel in America, 1789–1860* (1940); Mary Noel, *Villains Galore: The Heyday of the Popular Story Weekly* (1954); Frank Luther Mott, *Golden Multitudes* (1947), chap. xxi; and Donald Gallup, "More Letters of Am. Writers," *Yale Univ. Library Gazette,* July 1962. The sketch in Frances E. Willard and Mary A. Livermore, eds., *A Woman of the Century* (1893), includes a photograph. A short contemporary biography of the author prefaces *The Haunted Homestead* (1860).]

BEATRICE K. HOFSTADTER

SPALDING, Catherine (Dec. 23, 1793–Mar. 20, 1858), Roman Catholic nun, first superior of the Sisters of Charity of Nazareth, was born in Charles County, Md., into an old Maryland family. Though there is much uncertainty on this point, her parents may have been Edward and Juliet (Boarman) Spalding. They evidently migrated to Kentucky, where Catherine and a sister, Ann, were orphaned at an early age and brought up by relatives.

In January 1813, a beautiful girl of nineteen with eyes so deep a blue that they seemed black, Catherine Spalding joined two "pious ladies of mature age" who had offered themselves to the Rev. John David to help form a sisterhood. Father David, the scholarly and ascetic assistant to Bishop Benedict J. Flaget, whose newly established diocese—the first west of the Alleghenies—stretched from Ohio to Missouri and from Tennessee to Minnesota, had been in Kentucky only a year and a half. He had already established the West's first seminary for the training of priests, at St. Thomas's, a donated farm three miles from Bardstown which served also as the bishop's headquarters. His colleague the Rev. Charles Nerinckx a few months before had founded the first sisterhood of the Bardstown see, near the Hardin's Creek settlement, under the leadership of Mother MARY RHODES. Now Father David established his novices in a tiny tenant's cabin at St. Thomas's, giving them the name Sisters of Charity and a rule modeled on that used by Mother ELIZABETH SETON's community in Maryland, the first American order of nuns, whom he had once served as spiritual adviser. Father David and Bishop Flaget for a time hoped to join their fledgling sisterhood to

Mother Seton's group, but had to abandon the plan as impractical.

In June 1813 Catherine Spalding, whose remarkable gifts of mind and spirit had been evident from the first, was chosen mother superior. She was again elected after she and three other nuns took their first vows as religious on Feb. 2, 1816. In their sparsely furnished quarters, called "Nazareth" by Father David, they suffered great poverty during these early years. Doing their own domestic and farm work, they made clothing for students at St. Thomas's Seminary, visited the sick, and catechized poor children and servants. Under Mother Catherine they opened a school in August 1814, with nine students; in 1818, to house the increasing numbers of boarding students, a brick convent was built. The next year the sisters opened a school in Bardstown, near the newly erected cathedral of the diocese. At the end of Mother Catherine's second term as superior, in 1819, Father David and the nuns urged her to continue in that office during her lifetime. But so strongly did she plead for strict adherence to the constitution, which limited the superior to two consecutive terms, that they allowed her to retire.

Mother Catherine nevertheless remained the guiding spirit of the community. Sent to Scott County, Ky., in April 1823, she helped establish a school that still survives as St. Catherine's Academy in Lexington. In September 1824 she was called back to the motherhouse to serve as superior for six more years. There she found conditions chaotic. The nuns had recently had to move to a new location (the present Nazareth, Ky.) and begin building afresh; no records of receipts or expenditures had been kept, and the order was heavily in debt. It taxed even Mother Catherine's abilities to straighten the disordered finances and place the order on a sound financial basis. Despite these handicaps the school continued to grow; in July 1825 the first public examination of the students took place before distinguished visitors, with Secretary of State Henry Clay presenting the diplomas, and by 1828 some $20,000 had been expended upon new buildings. The following year Mother Catherine obtained from the Kentucky legislature a charter giving the society and academy a legal status. In 1826 a papal rescript granting the sisterhood many spiritual advantages had been secured from Leo XII.

When her term ended in 1831 Mother Catherine went to Louisville, where she opened the first Catholic school in the city, now Presentation Academy. For the rest of her life, except for later terms as superior, Louisville remained her home. During the cholera epidemic of 1832–33 she devotedly nursed the sick and then cared for children orphaned by the plague. More than once the stocky nun arrived at the sisters' residence carrying an infant in her apron and another in her arms, while a third child toddled beside her. Out of these acts of charity grew St. Vincent's Orphan Asylum, "the most cherished of all her life works," which she established in a former tavern and persuaded wealthy citizens, both Catholic and Protestant, to support with donations of supplies. In one end of this building she opened the first Catholic infirmary in Kentucky, now St. Joseph's Hospital.

Reelected superior in 1838, she left Louisville "to take again a burden I little suited and less desired. My heart still clings to the orphans." As superior she showed both clarity of insight and depth of feeling, giving admonitions well and overlooking faults readily. During this term, however, she was troubled by a lack of harmony within the community, stemming evidently from a few dissatisfied nuns, which for a time aroused criticism from the outside. Bishop Flaget, after making an investigation, proposed radical changes which would have united the order with the Maryland Sisters of Charity in a subordinate position and placed it directly under his supervision. Mother Catherine, with her ability to strike a balance between wisdom and obedience, opposed these proposals, and in the end the sisters were allowed to retain their independence.

In 1844, at the end of this third period as superior, Mother Catherine returned to Louisville. From 1850 to 1856 she again served as superior, opening an orphan asylum at St. Thomas's Seminary in Bardstown and directing the construction at Nazareth of a French Gothic convent church which her kinsman the Rev. Martin J. Spalding, Flaget's successor as bishop, called "the gem of the diocese." She died in Louisville, of bronchitis developing from a severe cold taken on an errand of mercy, and was buried in the motherhouse cemetery at Nazareth, at her request near the grave of Bishop John David. Together they had established one of the pioneering Catholic institutions of the West.

[Archives of the Sisters of Nazareth, Nazareth, Ky.; Columba Fox, *The Life of . . . John David* (1925); Anna B. McGill, *The Sisters of Charity of Nazareth* (1917); Martin J. Spalding, *Early Catholic Missions of Ky.* (1844); J. H. Schauinger, *Cathedrals in the Wilderness* (1952). The hypothesis advanced in David Spalding, "The Mystery of

Mother Catherine Spalding's Parents," *Records of the Am. Catholic Hist. Soc. of Phila.*, Sept.–Dec. 1960, is debatable.]

J. HERMAN SCHAUINGER

**SPALDING, Eliza Hart** (Aug. 11, 1807–Jan. 7, 1851), pioneer missionary to Oregon, was born near what is now Berlin, Conn., the eldest of the three daughters and three sons of Levi and Martha (Hart) Hart. Her father is said to have been "a plain substantial farmer." Eliza was descended on both sides of the family from Stephen Hart, who migrated to America from Essex County, England, in 1652. Though her parents were not notably pious, Eliza was of a deeply religious nature, bordering at times on the mystical; in August 1826 she joined the Presbyterian Church of Holland Patent, N.Y., the Oneida County town near which the Harts had settled six years before. According to family tradition, she attended an academy conducted by the Misses Anna and Mary Chipman in Clinton, N.Y., and then taught school for a time. In 1830, through the offices of a mutual friend, Eliza began an acquaintance by letter with Henry Harmon Spalding of Prattsburg, N.Y., who had expressed a wish to correspond with a young lady. They met the next year. In 1832–33 Eliza lived and perhaps attended a girls' school in Hudson, Ohio, where Spalding was completing his studies at Western Reserve College. They were married in the college chapel on Oct. 13, 1833; Eliza was twenty-six, her husband twenty-nine. They went to live in Cincinnati, where Spalding attended Lane Theological Seminary, while his wife ran a student boardinghouse, shared her husband's courses in the Greek Testament and the Hebrew Bible, and attended the Rev. Lyman Beecher's theological lectures.

In 1835 the Spaldings received appointment from the American Board of Commissioners for Foreign Missions as missionaries to the Osage Indians in western Missouri. Their departure was delayed, however, for a visit to Eliza's home, where she gave birth to a stillborn daughter in October. In the meantime they were induced by Dr. Marcus Whitman, also under appointment by the American Board, to accompany him and his wife-to-be to the Oregon country. On an exploratory tour of the Rockies earlier that year Whitman had learned that wagons had been taken over the continental divide and had concluded that women could now be safely transported overland to Oregon, resting in the wagons when they wearied of horseback riding. The Spaldings set out for the West in February 1836.

Whitman and his bride, NARCISSA PRENTISS WHITMAN, joined them the following month in Cincinnati, and from there the party proceeded to Liberty, Mo., where they assembled their equipment. Throughout the late spring and summer of 1836 their party, under the protection of an American Fur Company caravan, crossed plain and mountain, Mrs. Spalding and Mrs. Whitman riding sidesaddle much of the way. Eliza Spalding fell ill from the steady diet of buffalo meat, but she had recovered by the time the party reached Fort Walla Walla, in present-day Washington, in September.

While the Whitmans established a mission among the Cayuse Indians at Waiilatpu, near Fort Walla Walla, the Spaldings settled among the Nez Percés at Lapwai, near present-day Lewiston, Idaho. Two additional mission stations were opened in 1838, when eight more missionaries joined the original group. During the eleven-year history of the American Board's Oregon Mission, no station was more successful than that at Lapwai, and none of the six women missionaries more effective than Mrs. Spalding. Though sharing with many Protestants of her day an intense anti-Catholicism and a conventional view of the Indians as "dark minded heathen," she was also a woman of great industry, personal courage, and interest in others. She quickly learned the language of the Nez Percés and taught in the school which she and her husband established. Under her direction, the women and girls learned to sew, spin, and weave. Gifted with a modest artistic talent, she drew pictures of Biblical scenes which Spalding used in his preaching. She is described as above medium height and slender, with blue eyes, dark hair, and heavy features. While at Lapwai, Mrs. Spalding gave birth to four children: Eliza (1837—the first white child born in what is now Idaho), Henry Hart (1839), Martha Jane (1845), and Amelia Lorene (1846).

Perhaps the most difficult feature of Mrs. Spalding's life as a missionary was the tension existing between her husband and the Whitmans. Henry Spalding had once been rejected as a suitor by Narcissa Prentiss (also a native of Prattsburg, N.Y.), and he continued to nurse resentment toward her and her husband. Relations eventually eroded so alarmingly that in 1842 the American Board decided to dismiss the Spaldings and transfer the Whitmans to another mission. Only a hasty trip east by Whitman in 1842–43 prevented this dire outcome. Mrs. Spalding seems to have avoided involvement in these conflicts, however, for even Narcissa Whitman, who made little attempt to conceal her distaste for Henry Spalding, took care to emphasize her good relations with Eliza.

Initially the Nez Percés had eagerly accepted the opportunity to learn of the white man's religion and way of life. A welcoming party of 150 Nez Percés had accompanied the Spaldings from Fort Walla Walla to Lapwai, and the Indians had enthusiastically assisted in the construction of the first mission buildings. But as more and more white settlers began to arrive in the Oregon country the Indians grew increasingly hostile. By the mid-1840's the Lapwai school was nearly deserted, vandalism was rife, and the Spaldings had several times been mortally threatened. They escaped, however, the massacre which began at Waiilatpu on Nov. 29, 1847, in which the Whitmans and twelve other missionaries were killed by a small band of Cayuse. Indeed, such was the regard in which Mrs. Spalding was held that the Nez Percés rallied to her protection, her husband being absent at the time.

But the massacre dealt a final blow to the struggling Oregon Mission, and the Spaldings soon moved to the Willamette Valley, staking a claim on the Calapooya River, near the present town of Brownsville, Oreg. Here Mrs. Spalding, whose health had long been declining, died of tuberculosis in January 1851, at the age of forty-three. Her husband, who survived to 1874, returned to the Nez Percés in his old age and led a great revival which resulted in about a thousand baptisms among that tribe and the Spokane. In September 1913 Mrs. Spalding's body was removed from Brownsville to rest beside her husband's near the old mission home at Lapwai, where a granite monument stands over the two graves. In 1936 the Lapwai site was made a state park and in 1968 it was included as one of several historical sites in Idaho to form the Nez Percé National Historical Park. A small monument at South Pass, on the continental divide in present-day Wyoming, memorializes the fact that Eliza Spalding and Narcissa Whitman passed that way on July 4, 1836, the first women of United States citizenship to cross the Rocky Mountains.

[Clifford M. Drury, *Henry Harmon Spalding* (1936) and *The First White Women over the Rockies* (3 vols., 1963–66), especially I, 173–233; Alfred Andrews, *Genealogical Hist. of Deacon Stephen Hart and His Descendants* (1875). See also bibliography of the article on Narcissa Whitman.]

CLIFFORD M. DRURY

SPENCER, Anna Carpenter Garlin (Apr. 17, 1851–Feb. 12, 1931), minister and reformer,

lecturer and writer on ethics and social problems, was born in Attleboro, Mass., the third daughter and youngest of four children of Francis Warren Garlin (the family name had originally been Garland) and Nancy Mason (Carpenter) Garlin, both of seventeenth-century New England descent. She grew up in Providence, R.I. Little is known of her father, who may have been the Francis W. Garlin listed in Providence city directories of 1844–50 as a clerk; according to a family genealogy he served in the navy during the Civil War and died in 1870. Her mother was a staunch abolitionist, and Anna's earliest memory was of her enthusiastic support of Frémont in 1856. After attending public schools and taking "private collegiate work," Anna Garlin taught (1869–71) in the Providence schools, at the same time doing some writing for the *Providence Daily Journal*. She also began to make public appearances as a speaker, growing in reputation as her powers of speech and pen developed. Though small and always modestly dressed, she had a vibrant and compelling presence, an orator's voice, and a clear expository style.

On Aug. 15, 1878, she was married to William Henry Spencer, a Unitarian minister eleven years her senior. They had two children, Fletcher Carpenter (who died soon after his birth in 1879) and Lucy (born in 1884). Mrs. Spencer's marriage doubtless encouraged the increasingly liberal trend of her religious thinking. She had in 1876 withdrawn from the Union Congregational Church of Providence over doctrinal issues, and during the next two years she preached occasionally for the city's Free Religious Society. After 1878 she sometimes delivered sermons in her husband's churches, as he occupied pastorates in Haverhill and Florence, Mass., Troy, N.Y., and Scituate, Mass. In 1891, now back in Providence, Mrs. Spencer became minister of the Bell Street Chapel, a liberal, nondenominational ethical group endowed in 1888 by James Eddy, a local philanthropist. Her ordination was a matter of public note, since she was the first woman minister in the state. Her husband led a small Unitarian group in Providence until 1893, when he retired from the ministry. Mrs. Spencer preached an active faith and frequently spoke on controversial social problems of the day. She left the Bell Street Chapel in 1902 and moved, with her husband and family, to New York City. Joining the New York Society for Ethical Culture, she became associate director in 1904. Differences with the director, Felix Adler, developed, however, and around 1912 she ceased her active association with the movement, though throughout her life she retained membership in Unitarian and other liberal religious groups.

Gradually Mrs. Spencer's social concerns took precedence over her religious activities. In Providence she had helped found the city's Society for Organizing Charity and had worked for child labor and factory inspection laws. In 1893, as a member (1891–97) of the board of control of the State Home and School for Dependent Children, she attended the International Congress of Charities, Correction, and Philanthropy at the World's Columbian Exposition in Chicago, addressing it on "The Relation of the Church to Charities" and chairing the section on dependent, neglected, and wayward children. In New York she became an associate director (1903–07) and lecturer (until 1912) at the New York School of Philanthropy, having attended the school's first summer session in 1898. For three years, 1908–11, she was a special lecturer on social service and the social aspects of education at the University of Wisconsin, at the same time directing (1910–11) the Institute of Municipal and Social Service convened in Milwaukee by the university's extension service and conducting (1908–12) the Summer School of Ethics held at Madison by the American Ethical Union.

The ideas that Mrs. Spencer had been evolving found expression in a series of magazine articles beginning in 1908. Ultimately totaling over seventy, they appeared regularly in scholarly periodicals such as the *American Journal of Sociology* and the *International Journal of Ethics,* social work publications like *Forum* and *Survey,* and general magazines, including the *Ladies' Home Journal* and *Harper's.* Though she touched on a variety of themes, from child welfare and industrial education to world peace, her central interest was always in problems of women and family relationships. Her best-known book, *Woman's Share in Social Culture* (1913), a compilation of her magazine pieces, grapples interestingly, if somewhat diffusely, with a variety of feminine subjects, including the difficulties of the married woman wage earner, the frustrations of the talented woman, and problems of spinsters and older women, as well as prostitution, divorce, and suffrage. Underlying her approach was the view (earlier formulated by CHARLOTTE PERKINS GILMAN) that women should not only seek equality in a masculine world, but should evolve entirely new ethical and social positions based on uniquely feminine traits and insights.

*The Family and Its Members* (1923) continued the campaign for a refurbished view of the family. In it Mrs. Spencer attacked as a threat to stable family life the concept of "free love" as advocated by Ellen Key and others, and challenged the view of Charlotte Perkins Gilman's *Women and Economics* that to be wholly free women had to be economically independent. While urging married women to join in the broader life of their community, she asserted that the role of breadwinner still belonged to the husband. Reflecting the pragmatic spirit of the day, she was down-to-earth in her approach. In discussing divorce, for example, she avoided moralizing and concentrated on specific questions such as the advantages of domestic relations courts, society's responsibility to the children of a broken marriage, and the need for education to render marriages more stable.

The problem of prostitution was a central one in Mrs. Spencer's thinking. Again avoiding mere exhortation, she argued that an economic problem lay at the heart of the situation and that a program was needed to retrain the women involved to social usefulness. From 1890 on she was a leader in the American Purity Alliance; this she helped develop into the American Social Hygiene Association, which held that ignorance lay at the root of many social and sexual problems. As head of its Division of Family Relations she fostered the introduction of courses on the family into high schools and colleges.

Her academic connections continued, and she became successively professor of sociology and ethics at the Meadville (Pa.) Theological School (1913–18), lecturer at the University of Chicago in 1918, and, from 1920 until her death, a special lecturer in social science at Teachers College, Columbia University, where she helped develop its consultation center.

Mrs. Spencer was active in a variety of reform movements. She was an early member of the Rhode Island Woman's Christian Temperance Union, the national W.C.T.U., and the executive committees of the state's Anti-Saloon (later Temperance) League and the Unitarian Temperance Society. An enthusiastic suffragist, she joined the Rhode Island Woman Suffrage Association at seventeen, becoming its secretary and later vice-president. She was a close friend of SUSAN B. ANTHONY and regularly attended and spoke at conventions of the National Woman Suffrage Association. A pacifist, she served on the executive committee of the National Peace and Arbitration Congress of 1907; in 1915 she became a vice-chairman of the Woman's Peace Party, formed on the initiative of CARRIE CHAPMAN CATT and JANE ADDAMS. She declined, however, to join Henry Ford's peace ship that year, finding his slogan

"Out of the trenches by Christmas" chimerical, and successfully urged Miss Addams not to take part in the venture. After the war she was a charter member of the Women's International League for Peace and Freedom, serving at one time as its president.

William H. Spencer died in 1923 after ten years of invalidism, but Anna Garlin Spencer continued active into her eightieth year, when she died in New York City of a heart attack while attending a dinner of the League of Nations Association. The funeral was held at the West Side Unitarian Church in New York, and a memorial meeting at the Ethical Culture Society was attended by representatives of organizations she had supported. She was buried at Swan Point Cemetery in Providence.

[Other writings by Mrs. Spencer include: *Bell Street Chapel Discourses* (1899); *The Hist. of the Bell Street Chapel Movement* (1903); *The Care of Dependent, Neglected and Wayward Children,* ed. with Charles W. Birtwell (1894); and "Institute of Municipal and Social Service in Milwaukee," *Survey,* Feb. 18, 1911. Biographical sources: Anna Garlin Spencer Papers in Swarthmore College Peace Collection; James G. Garland, *Garland Genealogy* (1897), p. 146; William Henry Spencer, *Spencer Family Record* (1907), pp. 41–43; *Memorial: Anna Garlin Spencer* (1931); biographical sketch in *Parting Words of Anna Garlin Spencer at Bell Street Chapel* (pamphlet, 1902); obituary in *N.Y. Times,* Feb. 13, 1931. See also: Howard B. Radest, *Toward Common Ground: The Story of the Ethical Culture Societies in the U.S.* (1969); Benjamin R. Andrews, "Anna Garlin Spencer and Education for the Family," *Jour. of Social Hygiene,* Apr. 1932; Mary Ross in *Encyc. of Social Sciences,* XIV, 294–95; Winifred and Frances Kirkland, *Girls Who Became Leaders* (1932); references to Mrs. Spencer in Susan B. Anthony and Ida H. Harper, eds., *The Hist. of Woman Suffrage,* vols. IV–VI (1902–22); *Woman's Who's Who of America,* 1914–15; *Who Was Who in America,* vol. I (1942); records of Unitarian-Universalist Assoc., Boston.]

LOUIS FILLER

SPENCER, Cornelia Ann Phillips (Mar. 20, 1825–Mar. 11, 1908), North Carolina author and educational crusader, was born in Harlem, N.Y., where her father, James Phillips, son of an Anglican minister of Nevenden, England, had established a classical school for boys in 1818. Her mother, Judith (Julia) Vermeule of Plainfield, N.J., came of a well-to-do family of Dutch colonial descent. Of their three children, Cornelia was the youngest and the only daughter. Her father became professor of mathematics at the University of North Carolina in 1826, and thereafter the family was completely identified with Chapel Hill. Professor Phillips entered the Presbyterian ministry in 1833 and until his death in 1867 combined preaching with teaching, as did Charles, his elder son and successor. Mrs. Phillips for a time ran a small girls' school.

From early childhood, when she eagerly joined her brothers in their studies, trying hard to outdo them though they were older, Cornelia Phillips exhibited unusual force of character. Under the exacting tutelage of her parents, she was taught with her brothers until they entered the university at Chapel Hill (no women were admitted until 1897); thereafter she studied on her own and bemoaned the custom which allowed her only the "crumbs from the college table." On June 20, 1855, she was married to a young lawyer, James Monroe ("Magnus") Spencer, and went to live in Clinton, Ala. There her only child, Julia James (June), was born in 1859. Upon her husband's death in 1861 she returned with her child to her father's house and began her long career as one of Chapel Hill's leading citizens.

Well aware that her grief would be helped only by hard work, Cornelia Spencer turned at first to teaching Latin and Greek to village children. The Civil War and the defeat of the South, however, soon set her active mind to appraising the weaknesses of her native state, and, first in letters, then in public print, she began analyzing North Carolina and exhorting its citizens to self-improvement. Her position was that of a proud Carolinian who wanted the state to equal the best in the Union. Her initial venture into journalism came when a former North Carolinian, the Rev. Charles Force Weems, asked her to write for his New York magazine, the *Watchman,* a series of articles describing conditions during the final weeks of the Civil War when the Northern armies marched through the state. The accounts were later collected and published as *The Last Ninety Days of the War in North Carolina* (1866). To obtain accurate material she wrote to friends and conferred with many of the state's leading men. She enjoyed a particularly close association with David Lowry Swain, president of the University of North Carolina, and with Zebulon B. Vance, the wartime governor of the state.

For the next nine years Mrs. Spencer concentrated her interests chiefly upon the need for improving educational standards in the South, and especially upon the problems of the University of North Carolina. After the war and the death of President Swain, the Reconstruction government had dismissed the entire faculty and replaced it by men chosen more for their political views than for their scholarship, and in 1871 a financial crisis forced the closing of the university. Along with other North Carolinians devoted to the cause of education, Mrs. Spencer joined in the struggle to reopen the university, a project she brilliantly supported in newspaper articles and in letters to friends and persons of influence. When on Mar. 20, 1875, the legislature voted the necessary funds, Mrs. Spencer in her delight climbed the steps to the bell tower and rang the college bell. The new president, Kemp P. Battle, like David Swain before him and George T. Winston after him, looked upon Mrs. Spencer as a close friend and trusted adviser. In 1893–94 the survival of the university was again endangered, by inadequate funds and by militant attacks from sectarian colleges, and Mrs. Spencer once more aided the defense with all the powers of her writing and her ardent personality.

A vigorous and devout member of the Presbyterian Church, Cornelia Spencer wrote regularly from 1870 to 1876 for the *North Carolina Presbyterian,* contributing a lively "Young Lady's Column" that still retains freshness and appeal. She continually emphasized the need for education. Constantly urging the girls to set themselves higher standards of excellence, she gave them pungent and often witty advice, as well as reports of what was going on in the great world outside North Carolina. No political or social controversy was beyond her range, and in her comments on the subject of woman's rights she gave her readers considerable insight into the development of her own ideas. Although she maintained a proper Southern belief in the natural inferiority of women, she confessed in 1870 her discovery that "the female reformers . . . have really an argument or two on their side," and thereafter she wrote a good deal about the widening opportunities becoming available to women.

Mrs. Spencer played an important unofficial role in establishing the university's Summer Normal School for the training of teachers, which opened in 1877, and was a tireless fund raiser and writer on its behalf. She made similar contributions to the founding (1891) of the Normal and Industrial School for Women, later the Woman's College of the University of North Carolina, at Greensboro. The educators who began to reform North Carolina's public school system in the 1890's owed much to her encouragement and help; many, indeed (like Charles D. McIver), had known her when they were in college at Chapel Hill. The student body held her in great esteem. "I remem-

ber her appearance most distinctly," wrote one student in later years, "and had a feeling that she ought to be addressed in Latin. Her personality was most extraordinary. . . . She simply radiated something invisible and inspiring; a sort of magnetic field. She could furnish an empty room by simply sitting there" (quoted in Russell, facing p. 1). She was the first person honored by the university's LL.D., in 1895.

Cornelia Spencer knew everyone in town and many in the state, and was interested in them all. She felt particular warmth for the hardworking, self-reliant farm people and had a deep concern for the welfare of the freed Negroes. Until the end of her long life she continued to comment with interest and insight not only upon the passing scene but also upon books, men, and history. For two years, 1881–82, she lived in Washington with her brother Samuel, then Solicitor General of the United States. In 1894 she left Chapel Hill for the home of her daughter, whose husband, James Lee Love, taught mathematics at Harvard. From Cambridge she continued to carry on her extensive correspondence, and there she reveled in the joys of the Harvard library. She died in Cambridge of influenza shortly before her eighty-third birthday and was buried in the village cemetery at Chapel Hill. Both the University of North Carolina and the Woman's College at Greensboro have named buildings in her honor.

[There is no adequate biography of Mrs. Spencer. Hope S. Chamberlain, *Old Days in Chapel Hill* (1926), and Phillips Russell, *The Woman Who Rang the Bell* (1949), are useful, and Louis R. Wilson has edited the *Selected Papers of Cornelia Phillips Spencer* (1953). Her diaries, journals, and copies of her letters and papers are filed in the Southern Hist. Collection of the Univ. of N.C. See also Kemp P. Battle, *Hist. of the Univ. of N.C.* (2 vols., 1907–12); Rose H. Holder, *McIver of N.C.* (1957); and Josephus Daniels, *Tar Heel Editor* (1939).]

ANNE FIROR SCOTT

**SPENCER, Lilly Martin** (Nov. 26, 1822–May 22, 1902), painter, was born at Exeter, England, to French parents who had come from Brittany. Christened Angelique Marie Martin, she was the oldest of four children. Her father, Giles Marie Martin, had once studied for the priesthood; her mother, Angelique (le Petit) Martin, had been reared in a convent; they were married in England. Giles Martin, who at the time of Lilly's birth was teaching French at the Exeter Academy, emigrated with his family to the United States in 1830. Living at first in New York City, where he had hoped to establish an academy, he moved west after the 1831–32 cholera epidemic to a farm near Marietta, Ohio. In 1833 he was appointed a teacher of French at the Marietta Collegiate Institute (later Marietta College). Although Lilly apparently had no formal schooling, she was liberally educated at home by her parents, who possessed a large personal library. They were also active in the woman's rights movement, corresponding with such leaders as LU-CRETIA MOTT, ELIZABETH CADY STANTON, and AMELIA BLOOMER.

Early recognizing Lilly's artistic talent, her parents had sent her to classes at the old Academy of Design in New York City before she was ten. In Marietta the sketches she drew on the plaster walls of the family farmhouse first attracted public notice. Encouraged by two local artists, Charles Sullivan and Sala Bosworth, who introduced her to oils, she had, by the age of eighteen, executed over fifty oil paintings, including portraits, genre scenes, and scenes inspired by literature. She held her first public exhibition at Marietta in 1841 in an effort to raise money for study; in the fall of that year she and her father took the same group of paintings downriver to Cincinnati, the art center of the West. The showing there was well received, and a local art patron, the elder Nicholas Longworth, offered to send Lilly east to study with Washington Allston and later abroad to study and copy old masters. She chose, however, to settle in Cincinnati.

Studying intermittently with artists there, Lilly Martin strove through several years of hardship to establish herself as a painter. During the first spring her father returned to Cincinnati and gave private lessons in French for a time to assist her. She was married on Aug. 26, 1844, to Benjamin Rush Spencer, an Englishman who had moved to Cincinnati after an unsuccessful business venture in Virginia. He does not seem to have prospered in any occupation, and much, if not all, of the family's support was to fall on his wife. The couple had thirteen children, of whom seven lived to maturity: Benjamin Martin, Angelo Paul, Charles F., William Henry, Flora S., Pierre A. C., and Lilly Caroline. Mrs. Spencer, less than five feet tall and, by the stereotype of the time, "frail," was, however, dynamic and ambitious. By 1846 she had won a solid local reputation as a painter of portraits and of romantic and genre works. The next year she wrote to her parents, "I mean to try to become a Michael Angelo, if I possibly can. . . . I plan to try to make my paintings have

a tendency toward Moral improvement . . . oh! A fine painting has a beautiful power over the human passions. . . ."

Successful showings of her work in New York, at the National Academy of Design and the American Art-Union, probably prompted Mrs. Spencer's move with her husband and three children to that city in 1848. The patronage of the art unions now advanced her rapidly to national renown and financial success. These institutions, which anyone might join, not only held annual exhibits but also offered members each year a graphic reproduction of a famous painting and the chance to win an original work of art as a lottery prize, thus creating an art-conscious America and a wide market. The Western Art Union in 1849 commissioned an engraving of a Lilly Spencer painting, "One of Life's Happy Hours," as its first premium for its members. The next year she did the illustrations for Mrs. ELIZABETH F. ELLET's *Women of the American Revolution*, which, reproduced in the pages of *Godey's Lady's Book*, reached a nationwide public. For the most part, however, she now abandoned "fancy and historical pieces," turning instead to anecdotal domestic scenes, often nursery incidents with her own children as models. These sentimental representations of family life, such as the popular "Shake Hands?" are characterized by a realism that sacrifices unity of composition to specific detail. Both subject matter and technique exactly suited the public taste. In the 1852 exhibition of the American Art-Union only the works of Frederick E. Church and Richard C. Woodville commanded higher prices than Mrs. Spencer's, which brought more than those of George Caleb Bingham, John James Audubon, Eastman Johnson, and William S. Mount. By the time antilottery legislation killed the art unions, she was securely established, with many commissions for paintings, from *Godey's Lady's Book* and other magazines and from firms selling reproductions. More than a million colored lithographs and etchings of her works were published, each of them bearing her name, although she received no profit beyond the purchase price of the original painting. Oddly enough, she did not sign the portraits and other works commissioned by private patrons, many of which can no longer be identified.

In 1858 the Spencers, possibly to accommodate their still growing family, moved to Newark, N.J., to a house owned by former Gov. Marcus L. Ward, a relative of Nicholas Longworth. In lieu of rent Mrs. Spencer undertook to execute two portraits of the Ward family and "one handsome fancy piece." The large portrait of the Ward children (c. 1858, now in the Newark Museum) shows the quality of her private work, noticeably finer than the paintings executed for reproduction, many of which she herself called potboilers. In the late 1860's she rented a studio in New York City to execute her most famous work, the monumental "Truth Unveiling Falsehood" (1869). Many notables of the day visited the studio to inspect the progress of the painting, which received wide publicity in the newspapers and upon completion was hailed as one of the masterpieces of the age. Although Mrs. Spencer twice refused offers of $20,000 for it, its whereabouts today is not known.

In the following years Mrs. Spencer's popularity gradually declined. She did not exhibit after 1876. In 1880 she settled in the neighborhood of Poughkeepsie, N.Y. Among her friends of this period was Col. Robert G. Ingersoll, with whose agnostic views she is said to have sympathized, and whom she painted with his two grandchildren. Other subjects during these years were Elizabeth Cady Stanton and Mrs. CAROLINE LAVINIA SCOTT HARRISON, wife of the President, both painted in a freer, more illusionistic style which places these portraits among her best works. Mrs. Spencer's husband died in 1890. In 1900, now seventy-eight, she moved back to New York City, established a studio, and began to receive old friends and new commissions. She died at her easel in the spring of 1902 and was buried beside her husband at Highland, N.Y. Virtually without professional training, Lilly Martin Spencer was an able craftsman with an unusual capacity for artistic growth. Her popular paintings, sincere, romantic, and enthusiastic, reflected the folk culture of mid-nineteenth-century America.

[The fullest account of Mrs. Spencer is Ann Byrd Schumer, "Lilly Martin Spencer: Am. Painter of the Nineteenth Century" (unpublished M.A. thesis, Ohio State Univ., 1959); see also the same author's "Aspects of Lilly Martin Spencer's Career in Newark, N.J.," N.J. Hist. Soc., Proc., Oct. 1959. Unpublished sources include letters and records of the Martin family, Campus Martius Museum, Marietta, Ohio; letters of Mrs. Spencer to the Am. Art-Union, in the N.-Y. Hist. Soc.; Frederick Sweet, "Lilly Martin Spencer" (typescript, 1946, N.Y. Public Library); and information from Mrs. Spencer's granddaughter Mrs. Lillian Spencer Gates, Rutherford, N.J. Earlier published accounts of Mrs. Spencer include: Elizabeth F. Ellet, Women Artists in All Ages and Countries (1859); N.Y. World, Sept. 22, 1901 (on the occasion of her return to N.Y.); obituaries in N.Y. Herald, May 22, 1902, and N.Y. Times, May 23, 1902.]

ANN BYRD SCHUMER

SPEYER, Ellin Leslie Prince Lowery (Oct. 14, 1849–Feb. 23, 1921), philanthropist and New York society hostess, was born in Lowell, Mass. Her paternal grandfather, John Dynely Prince (1779–1860), was an expert textile printer who in 1826 was called from his native Lancashire, England, to head the print works at the newly founded Merrimack Manufacturing Company in Lowell, a position he held until his retirement in 1855. Her father, John Dynely Prince (c. 1814–1862), was a chemist; her mother, Mary (Travers) Prince, was the daughter of John Travers of Baltimore, Md.; they had one other child, an older son. Both parents died when Ellin was young, and she was brought up by an uncle, William Riddell Travers, a wealthy New York lawyer, wit, and social leader, and his wife, the daughter of Judge Reverdy Johnson of Maryland, noted jurist and onetime minister to Great Britain. Reared in an environment of wealth and social prominence, Ellin was educated by private tutors. Little is known of her first marriage, in October 1871, to John A. Lowery of New York City, which ended with his death in 1892. On Nov. 11, 1897, she was married to James Speyer (1861–1941), born in New York City of a distinguished German-Jewish banking family and himself a noted philanthropist. Neither marriage produced any children.

Her participation in charitable activities apparently began in 1881, when she was one of the founders of the Hospital Saturday and Sunday Association (later the United Hospital Fund); she afterward served as treasurer of its women's auxiliary. In 1886 she helped establish the New York Skin and Cancer Hospital. At the outbreak of the Spanish-American War she joined Mrs. Whitelaw Reid (ELISABETH MILLS REID) in American Red Cross Auxiliary No. 3 of New York, which supplied trained nurses for war duty, and during World War I she was chairman of the mayor's committee on trained nurses for overseas work.

Besides hospital work, one of her sustained interests was in working women. In 1883 she was associated with GRACE H. DODGE and Mrs. Richard Irwin in founding a club for working girls (later named the "Irene Club"). Mrs. Speyer was its president and treasurer for thirty years. From the club grew a nationwide system of working girls' societies. In this same vein, Ellin Speyer contributed funds to the New York League of Women Workers and the Working Girls' Vacation Society, and in 1915 served as chairman of Mayor John P. Mitchel's subcommittee on unemployment among women, establishing workshops which provided employment for hundreds of jobless women. In 1906 she organized in her home the girls' branch of the Public School Athletic League. Other causes to which Mrs. Speyer gave support included St. Mary's Free Hospital for Children, the Nursery for Colored Children, and the National League on Urban Conditions among Negroes. In 1902 she and her husband gave $100,000 to Teachers College at Columbia University to found the experimental Speyer School.

Ellin Speyer's most intense single interest, however, was in animal welfare. In 1910 she founded the New York Women's League for Animals, of which she was president until her death. With the help of Mrs. Marshall Wilson, Mrs. Frederick W. Vanderbilt, and other friends, she raised funds for the Lafayette Street Hospital (for animals), which was built in 1913 and named after her death the Ellin Prince Speyer Free Hospital for Animals. She organized the "Work Horse Parade," in which medals were given for the best-cared-for horses in the New York police, fire, and street cleaning departments; found homes for discarded police department horses; and saw to it that work horses received nonslip shoes for use on icy streets. In her will she left $50,000 to her animal hospital and considerably less to charity organizations.

Apart from her good works, she was known, after her marriage to James Speyer, as a leader in New York society. In this capacity she was admired both for her gracious manners and for her conversation, which "was remarkable alike for high intelligence and for the play of humoresque fancy" (New York Times, Feb. 26, 1921). She was a member of New York's exclusive social club for women, the Colony Club. A patron of the Metropolitan Opera Company, Mrs. Speyer was a friend of Fritz Kreisler, the violinist, who played at her funeral. She died at her Fifth Avenue home of pyelonephritis and bronchial pneumonia at the age of seventy-one. After an Episcopal funeral service at the Cathedral of St. John the Divine, she was buried in Sleepy Hollow Cemetery, Tarrytown, N.Y.

[J. E. Homans, ed., Cyc. Am. Biog., X (1924), 27–30, with portrait; Nat. Cyc. Am. Biog., XXV, 164–65; N.Y. Times, Feb. 23 (obituary), 24 (funeral), 26 (editorial), and Mar. 1, 1921 (will); Vital Records of Lowell, Mass., to the End of the Year 1849 (1930), I, 311 (the source for her birth date); death record from N.Y. City Dept. of Health. Other information from death record of her father (Mass. Registrar of Vital Statistics). On her grandfather, see Old Residents' Hist. Assoc., Lowell, Mass., Contributions, II (1882), 168–70.

On James Speyer, see Who's Who in Am. Jewry, 1936, and Who Was Who in America, vol. I (1942).]

CHARLES R. HEARN

SPOFFORD, Harriet Elizabeth Prescott (Apr. 3, 1835–Aug. 14, 1921), author, was born in Calais, Maine, the eldest of five children—four of them daughters—of Sarah Jane (Bridges) and Joseph Newmarch Prescott. Descended from her father's side from John and Mary Prescott, emigrants from Yorkshire who settled in Watertown, Mass., in 1640, she came of a family distinguished through two centuries of New England history for its military heroes, sea captains, writers, clergymen, and merchants. The economic tide loosed by the War of 1812, which reversed the family fortunes and nearly ruined her shipowner grandfather, continued to run against Harriet Prescott's father, a lumber merchant and lawyer, driving him to leave his family in 1849 while he sought his fortune in Oregon. Her mother moved with the five children to Newburyport, Mass., in the vicinity of numerous Prescott relatives, and the neighborhood of Newburyport became Harriet Prescott's permanent home. Her formal schooling consisted of four years in the Putnam Free School, Newburyport, and two years in Pinkerton Academy, Derry, N.H. (1853–55), both excellent institutions in which the literary talents of the young girl were fostered.

At sixteen, while still in school, she had written a prize-winning essay analyzing Hamlet's madness. This attracted the attention of Thomas Wentworth Higginson, then a Unitarian minister in Newburyport, who gave her valuable literary counsel and encouragement. In 1856 her father returned from the West, penniless and in broken health. With the family in grave economic circumstances, Harriet turned to writing stories for the Boston weeklies, for which the pay was poor but the market steady. In 1858 she submitted a colorful and finely imaginative tale, "In a Cellar," to James Russell Lowell, editor of the newly established Atlantic Monthly, who published it (February 1859). Recognition now came swiftly to the young author. Under Higginson's sponsorship she found herself admitted to the inner circle of the Boston literati, the object of flattery and praise. In 1860 her first novel, Sir Rohan's Ghost, was published anonymously; in 1863 her first volume of short stories, The Amber Gods; and in 1864 another novel, Azarian: An Episode—all characterized by a Gothic romanticism manifested in unusual plots drawn from legend or local history, shrouded with elements of mystery or the supernatural treated realistically. With these volumes Harriet Prescott Spofford's long and uneven writing career was launched. Thereafter, almost without pause for sixty years, a succession of short stories, novels, novellas, poems, articles on the home, travel books, children's books, literary reminiscences, and critical essays streamed from her tireless pen, constituting an output surpassed by few professional writers of her day.

On Dec. 19, 1865, Harriet Prescott was married to an able young lawyer, Richard Smith Spofford, of an old Newburyport family. The marriage, culminating a long romance, was unusually happy and congenial, since Spofford shared his wife's literary and intellectual interests and gave every encouragement to her career. During the period when he was associated with Caleb Cushing in Washington, D.C., the Spoffords divided their time between the capital and Newburyport and developed a close association with Washington intellectual circles. In 1874 they bought Deer Island-in-the-Merrimack, in Amesbury, Mass., near Newburyport, and established the spacious home which became famous as the center of Mrs. Spofford's bountiful hospitality. Writing steadily all the while, she entertained her literary friends—ANNIE FIELDS, SARAH ORNE JEWETT, ROSE TERRY COOKE, LOUISE CHANDLER MOULTON, and Gail Hamilton (MARY ABIGAIL DODGE), among others—and housed many of her relatives, including her literary sister Mary Newmarch Prescott, fourteen years her junior. Here her husband died in 1888; an only son, Richard, born in 1867, had died in infancy.

Harriet Prescott Spofford's most prolific period, 1868–90, coincided with the post-bellum expansion of popular magazines. The best of her several hundred stories appeared in the *Atlantic, Scribner's,* and the *Century;* some of these were collected and published in *A Scarlet Poppy, and Other Stories* (1894) and *Old Madame and Other Tragedies* (1900). As Mrs. Spofford's readership and popularity increased, the pressure for output grew and the literary value of her work inevitably declined. By the turn of the century she was recognized as one of the most popular of women writers, though the critical estimate of her work had sunk to a low ebb. Between 1900 and 1920 the aging author turned away from romance to the familiar material of her native New England and wrote a series of realistic stories about its humble folk and their daily lives. Collected in *The Elder's People* (1920), these ranked with the very best of her earliest work and went far to reverse the critics' estimates of her literary accomplishment.

Mrs. Spofford did her best writing in the short story genre; with her ardent nature and rich imagination, she had a genuine power to create atmosphere. Her best work, however, with its insights into the effect of sin on the human conscience and a concern for what is universal in human experience, strikes a deeper note, in harmony with her Puritan heritage and her own Unitarian beliefs. Howells, in paying tribute to the New England writers of this period, placed her among the names of "second brilliancy" (*Atlantic Monthly,* November 1907), which is perhaps a fair estimate. Her biographer aptly terms her "a romantic survival," producing for a generation responding to the forces of realism a blend of romanticism and realism particularly agreeable to the popular taste.

Of her other writing, the best known of Harriet Prescott Spofford's volumes of poetry is *In Titian's Garden and Other Poems* (1897). Distinctly a minor poet, she infused her poetry with her love of nature and the sea, speaking in a highly personal, lyrical voice. Her numerous articles on the home and the history of home furnishings, her travel and personality sketches, are characterized by clarity of style, urbanity of tone, good taste, and timeliness, but have little literary interest. More important is her literary criticism, her critical gift being perhaps best revealed in the long biographic and interpretive introduction to the Aldine edition of Charlotte Brontë's *Jane Eyre* (1898), in which she shows a deep personal insight into the motivation of a talented woman. Never openly allied with the feminists, she nevertheless brought warm sympathy to the critical interpretation of such writers as the Brontës, George Eliot, and George Sand.

Harriet Prescott Spofford managed through a long life to retain the zestful charm which characterized her earliest years. A little above medium height, with a slight and graceful figure, she had "a face of intellectual beauty lighted by remarkable eyes" and a distinguished bearing. She became the center of a coterie of New England women writers who were drawn into an increasingly self-conscious alliance in the 1890's through their unanimous rejection of the naturalistic tendencies which grew out of and finally supplanted the realism of Howells and James. Of this group, Harriet Prescott Spofford was the last survivor. She died of arteriosclerosis at her Deer Island home in her eighty-seventh year, and was buried in Oak Hill Cemetery, Newburyport.

[Elizabeth K. Halbeisen, *Harriet Prescott Spofford: A Romantic Survival* (1935), is the fullest account of her life and work; it includes a bibliography of her writings. See also William Prescott, *The Prescott Memorial* (1870); Rose Terry Cooke in *Our Famous Women* (1884); obituaries in *Boston Transcript*, Aug. 15, 1921, and *N.Y. Times*, Aug. 16, 1921; death record from Mass. Registrar of Vital Statistics. Frank L. Mott, *A Hist. of Am. Magazines*, vols. II–IV (1938–57), gives some indication of Mrs. Spofford's extraordinary periodical output. For critical comments see William Dean Howells, ed., *The Great Modern Am. Stories* (1920), with "reminiscent introduction"; Fred L. Pattee, *The Development of the Am. Short Story* (1923); and Arthur H. Quinn, *Am. Fiction* (1936).]

LOUISE M. YOUNG

SPRAGUE, Kate Chase (Aug. 13, 1840–July 31, 1899), political hostess, was born in Cincinnati, Ohio, the daughter of Salmon Portland Chase and his second wife, Eliza Ann Smith. Named Catherine Jane, after Chase's first wife, who had died in childbirth, she was herself left motherless at the age of five, but gained a stepmother a year later and a half sister in 1847. That year, now seven, Kate was enrolled at the exclusive New York finishing school of Henrietta B. Haines, which she attended until 1856. When in 1852 her stepmother died, Kate and her young half sister remained the sole survivors of three wives and six children. Her father, successful in law and prominent in antislavery politics, recruited relatives to help bring up his two daughters. The elder, however, was the focus of his home life. Chase, a former teacher, visited her fairly often at school and carefully watched her progress. Intelligent, lively, and willful, Kate found herself the center of her world and acquired a sense of self-importance which shaped her life.

She early became involved in her father's political career. Chase was elected to the United States Senate in 1849 by a combination of Free Soil and Democratic votes. Six years later, having joined the new Republican party, he was elected governor of Ohio. In 1856, a prominent contender for his party's presidential nomination, he bought a house in the Ohio capital and called Kate, now fifteen, home from school to be his official hostess. She embarked on a program to make the establishment a dazzling social center, furnishing it lavishly and acquiring an elaborate wardrobe. During the winter social season she was regularly the brilliant hostess of an "evening party." When visitors discussed politics, she participated as an expert. One of them, Carl Schurz, was impressed with her beauty, charm, and political knowledge: "She was . . . tall and slender," he wrote, "and exceedingly well

formed. . . . Her little nose . . . fitted pleasingly into her face with its large, languid but . . . vivacious hazel eyes, shaded by long dark lashes, and arched over by proud eyebrows. The fine forehead was framed in waving gold-brown hair. She had something imperial in the pose of the head" (*Reminiscences*, II, 1907, p. 169). Actively managing house and grounds, even canning fruit, Kate also studied music and languages at Lewis Heyl's seminary. In 1860, as another Republican convention neared, Chase again sought the presidential nomination, this time with the active help of nineteen-year-old Kate, who wrote letters to potential supporters, tabulated their replies, and charmed politicians who visited the Chase home. Although these labors failed of their goal, they led to Chase's appointment as Secretary of the Treasury in Lincoln's cabinet.

In Washington, Chase leased a house on the corner of Sixth and E streets, and his daughter spent thousands of dollars furnishing it to her taste. By January 1862, at the beginning of the social season, Kate, at twenty-one, was the ranking active hostess in the capital, since Mrs. Lincoln was in mourning for her son and Mrs. Seward (wife of the Secretary of State) was ill. To build up her father's political following Kate staged a series of brilliant parties which became the talk of Washington. MARY TODD LINCOLN, a suspicious woman at best, sensed Kate's ambitions and disliked her. Others criticized her extravagance.

Among the many eligible bachelors who attended Kate's parties was William Sprague of Rhode Island, a wealthy industrialist who had served as governor of his state, had led a contingent of Rhode Island volunteers early in the war, and in 1863 was elected to the United States Senate. Although he was said to be intemperate and to have a fondness for women, Kate chose to marry him, perhaps because she believed his money would help realize her political ambitions for her father. The wedding took place at her home on Nov. 12, 1863, and the ceremony and reception were attended by all official Washington, including President Lincoln. After a prolonged honeymoon, Kate brought her husband back to her father's house in Washington. Sprague presently bought the house; Chase stayed on as a paying guest and Kate remained his official hostess. This arrangement was unfortunate, for it threw Sprague's deficiencies into bold relief. When she visited her husband's home state Kate had been shocked to learn that the best families of Rhode Island looked down on the Spragues, for all their wealth, as tradesmen and social inferiors. Shorter than his wife, unimpressive in manner, without influence in the Senate, Sprague was characterized by John Hay as "a small insignificant youth who bought his place."

In the next decade four children were born: William (1865), Ethel (1869), Portia (1872), and Kitty (1873). Serious discord, however, soon divided Kate and her husband. In 1866 Kate went alone to Europe, but was hastily joined by Sprague when rumors of a divorce began to circulate. Chase exerted himself to prevent a break, writing long letters to his daughter enjoining Christian forbearance. Kate's discontent was partially assuaged by the construction of Canonchet, a rambling and expensive sixty-room Victorian Gothic "summer house" at Narragansett Pier, R.I. On her European trip in 1866, and again in 1867, Kate freely bought furnishings for her dream house, including a $50,000 spiral staircase and a set of Persian soup bowls made from the dust of crushed garnets.

Her first interest, however, remained her father's career. When he discussed remarriage she firmly routed prospective brides, resolved not to be displaced as his hostess. As the 1864 election approached, Kate schemed to have her father replace Lincoln on the Republican ticket. Her husband's money financed the group which issued the notorious "Pomeroy Circular" seeking this end. After Lincoln's renomination Chase resigned his cabinet position. When Lincoln appointed him chief justice of the Supreme Court of the United States, Kate complained that he was being shelved. In 1868 a new route to the White House opened as the Democrats sought a candidate of unquestioned loyalty to counteract the party's secessionist reputation. A Chase boom developed, and when the Democratic convention met in New York City, Kate established headquarters in a nearby hotel and managed his campaign. The nomination, however, went to Horatio Seymour. Chase retired to Edgewood, an estate he had purchased near Washington, where he died in 1873.

With her father's conciliatory influence removed, Kate became completely alienated from her husband, whose drunkenness and philandering had become notorious. She had always been attractive to men, and she now began an open affair with Senator Roscoe Conkling of New York; Conkling visited her frequently at Edgewood, and she often journeyed to the Capitol to watch him on the Senate floor. In 1878 she yielded to her mother-in-law's importunities and rejoined her husband once more at Canonchet. Reconciliation

became impossible, however, when Sprague, returning unexpectedly from a trip, found Conkling with his wife. He drove the Senator from the premises with a loaded shotgun and the country buzzed with scandal. Kate went into seclusion, then fled to Europe, and at last retreated permanently to Edgewood with her daughters. She divorced her husband in 1882.

Living on at Edgewood, no longer a social luminary, Kate kept up appearances by drawing on the principal of her small inheritance and at last by selling some of Edgewood's furnishings. Old friends who saw her now, wearing false blond hair and heavy cosmetics and bedizened with jewelry, found it hard to realize that she had once been queen of Washington society. Of her children, William committed suicide in Seattle, Ethel defied convention to go on the stage, and Portia rarely saw her mother; Kate was left with her youngest daughter, Kitty, who was feebleminded. As her finances continued to worsen, she managed for a time by selling the chickens, eggs, and milk produced at Edgewood from door to door in Washington. Finally, in 1896, a group of her father's old friends created a trust fund for her support. Three years later, at the age of fifty-eight, she died at Edgewood of a liver and kidney ailment. She was buried at Spring Grove Cemetery, Cincinnati, beside her father.

[Ishbel Ross, *Proud Kate* (1953); Mary M. Phelps, *Kate Chase, Dominant Daughter* (1935); Thomas G. and Marva R. Belden, *So Fell the Angels* (1956); obituary in *N.Y. Times*, Aug. 1, 1899. See also biographies of Salmon P. Chase; and Chase's papers, in the Library of Congress and Hist. Soc. of Pa.]

WILLIAM E. BARINGER

**STANFIELD, Agnes.** *See* CLARE, Ada.

**STANFORD, Jane Eliza Lathrop** (Aug. 25, 1828–Feb. 28, 1905), philanthropist, co-founder with her husband of Stanford University, was born in Albany, N.Y., where her father had achieved a modest success as a merchant. She was the second of three daughters and the third of seven children of Dyer and Jane Ann (Shields) Lathrop. Through her father she was descended from John Lothropp of Yorkshire, England, who came to Scituate, Mass., in 1634; some of his descendants moved to Connecticut and thence to New York state. After elementary schooling she spent a year (1840–41) at the Albany Female Academy.

On Sept. 30, 1850, Jane Lathrop was married to Leland Stanford (1824–1893), an energetic and ambitious young lawyer of nearby

Watervliet, N.Y. They settled in Port Washington, Wis., where Stanford had recently begun practice, but after two years a fire destroyed his law office and library, and they returned to Albany. There Mrs. Stanford lived with her family while her husband followed his brothers to California to recoup his losses, which he did in short order. Engaging in general merchandising in the mining country, within three years he amassed a fortune of $125,000. He returned in 1855 expecting to establish himself in Albany, but the lure of California proved strong, and at his wife's urging they moved to Sacramento. Stanford quickly prospered. He entered politics, became governor of California in 1861, and soon embarked upon a career as railroad builder in which he and his associates gained tremendous fortunes. Besides leading an active social life as the mistress of a multimillionaire's ménage, Mrs. Stanford became interested in a variety of philanthropic enterprises, including the San Francisco kindergartens of Mrs. SARAH B. COOPER and a children's hospital in Albany, N.Y. With Stanford's election to the United States Senate in 1885, she became a Washington hostess as well.

The Stanfords were childless until the birth of Leland Stanford, Jr., on May 14, 1868. The parents lavished love and attention upon their only child, giving him all the advantages denied them in their childhood. But on a European tour in 1884 the boy contracted typhoid fever and died suddenly in Florence, a few weeks before his sixteenth birthday. Grief-stricken, Mrs. Stanford found comfort in her husband's determination to immortalize their son's memory by founding a university bearing his name; indeed, her absorption in the planning and developing of the university soon surpassed his. Following a formal Grant of Endowment in November 1885, plans were drawn and building commenced on the Stanfords' 7,000-acre Palo Alto farm, thirty-five miles south of San Francisco. The Leland Stanford Junior University (as it was initially called) convened its first classes in October 1891 under the presidency of David Starr Jordan, eminent naturalist and recent president of Indiana University, whom the Stanfords had selected on the advice of President Andrew D. White of Cornell.

Senator Stanford died in June 1893, leaving in his widow's hands a long series of financial problems that sorely tried her patience and abilities. When the probate court tied up the estate, including Stanford's bequests to the university, advisers urged Mrs. Stanford to close the school until the estate was settled and business had recovered from the panic of 1893. Refusing this counsel of despair, she used the slender income allowed her by the court, pared her own expenses to a minimum, and, by imposing salary reductions, was able to keep the university open. In 1894 another blow fell when the United States government filed a claim of fifteen million dollars against the Stanford estate. Mrs. Stanford conferred with Washington officials, including President Cleveland and Attorney General Richard Olney, and in 1896 the Supreme Court of the United States threw out the government's claim. By 1901 Mrs. Stanford had completed the family's endowment of the university by deeding to the trustees 100,000 acres of land and transferring to them more than $11,000,-000 in stocks, bonds, and other properties.

Before Stanford's death the structure of the university had merely been outlined, and it now fell to Mrs. Stanford, with the help of President Jordan, to give substance to these plans. Somewhat remote from the realities of academic life, and deeply influenced by spiritualism, Mrs. Stanford visualized an ideal institution, beautiful and imposing in its physical aspects and aloof from mundane concerns. In keeping with this vision she undertook in the early 1900's a building program so extensive that faculty salaries and morale suffered severely. "It is too bad that the men can't feed their families buff sandstone," one professor commented (Elliott, p. 298). The construction of a massive Memorial Church was a particularly favored project. Increasingly arbitrary with advancing years, Mrs. Stanford was able to reject President Jordan's cautious objections to her fiscal policies, since under the terms of the endowment grant she possessed wide authority to exercise all the "functions, powers, and duties" of the trustees.

Similarly she believed that professors should be "high and noble" individuals, above political partisanship (ibid., pp. 337, 341). Although she usually refrained from interfering in Jordan's handling of academic matters, a striking exception was her role in the dismissal of Edward A. Ross, a promising young economist whom Jordan had brought to Stanford in 1893. Though a popular teacher and respected scholar of exemplary character, Ross soon proved something of an enfant terrible. In 1894 he supported Eugene V. Debs' railroad strike, in 1896 he wrote and spoke for Bryan and free silver, and in 1900 he denounced Japanese immigration—a highly popular stand in labor circles. Moreover, he was sharply critical of the great railroad fortunes. In May 1900, after "reflection and prayer,"

Mrs. Stanford instructed Jordan to dismiss Ross. When the president remonstrated, she agreed to a reappointment for one year, but in November, Jordan yielded to her continuing pressure. The ensuing crisis shook Stanford severely. Ross set forth his position in a long newspaper statement, and soon editors, ministers, academic leaders, and fellow economists joined in condemning Mrs. Stanford; seven members of the university faculty resigned in protest.

Mrs. Stanford, convinced that "in no other institution [is] . . . freedom of speech . . . so thoroughly safeguarded" (*ibid.*, p. 376), was deeply hurt by the tumult. She was by nature an anxious woman, subject to frequent headaches, and the heavy burdens of her widowhood imposed a constant and growing strain. On June 1, 1903, she surrendered to the board of trustees her powers under the founding grant. The trustees promptly elected her president of the board, but believing that they needed freedom to fulfill their new responsibilities, she left for a nine-month world tour, followed in 1904 by a visit to educational institutions and childhood haunts in the East. In February 1905, while recovering from an accidental poisoning, she undertook a Pacific cruise. Later that month, at seventy-six years of age, she died suddenly of a heart attack in Honolulu. After Episcopal services there, her remains were returned to California and eventually placed along with those of her husband and son in a family mausoleum on the university campus.

[Bertha Berner, *Mrs. Leland Stanford: An Intimate Account* (1935); Orrin Leslie Elliott, *Stanford Univ.: The First Twenty-Five Years* (1937); David Starr Jordan, *The Story of a Good Woman: Jane Lathrop Stanford* (1912); *Palo Alto Times* (Special Memorial Edition), Mar. 24, 1905. See also Jordan's autobiography, *The Days of a Man* (2 vols., 1922); Edward A. Ross, *Seventy Years of It* (1936); and James C. Mohr, "Turmoil and Public Opinion: The Ross Case at Stanford," *Pacific Hist. Rev.*, Feb. 1970.]

GEORGE HARMON KNOLES

**STANTON, Elizabeth Cady** (Nov. 12, 1815–Oct. 26, 1902), woman's rights leader, was born in Johnstown, N.Y., the fourth of the six children of Daniel and Margaret (Livingston) Cady. Her father, of English ancestry, was an able lawyer who served in the state legislature, in Congress, and as a judge of the supreme court of New York. Her mother, of Scottish and Dutch descent, was the daughter of Col. James Livingston, who fought in the Revolution under Washington and was later elected to the New York legislature. As a child Eliza-

beth was fascinated by her father's law office, where she often overheard the pitiful stories of married women who came for help when deprived under the law of their property and their children. Active and intelligent, she rebelled against the view that women were mentally and legally inferior to men. When her father, grieving over the death of his only son, Eleazer, in 1826, said to Elizabeth, "Oh, my daughter, I wish you were a boy!" she resolved to prove to him that a daughter was as good and as valuable as a son (*Eighty Years and More*, p. 20). Encouraged by her Presbyterian minister, Simon Hosack (for whom she retained great affection even after she had rejected her severe religious upbringing), she studied Greek, first at home and later at the Johnstown Academy, adding Latin and mathematics as well. She also learned to emulate her male schoolmates in riding horseback and became skillful at chess and other games. Although it was her ambition to attend her brother's college, Union College in Schenectady, she was sent instead to EMMA WILLARD's famous Troy Female Seminary, graduating in 1832.

For several years thereafter Elizabeth Cady was deeply involved emotionally with Edward Bayard, who was unhappily married to her sister Tryphena. Bayard declared his love and the two saw much of each other, but she refused his pleas that they elope and turned her mind instead to other subjects. Through visits to the home of her cousin, the wealthy landowner and reformer Gerrit Smith, in nearby Peterboro, she became interested in the antislavery and temperance movements. Here she saw fugitive slaves hidden and sent to Canada and freedom, and here, too, she heard woman's rights discussed in connection with the participation of women in antislavery organizations. With Gerrit Smith's daughter Elizabeth (see ELIZABETH SMITH MILLER), she attended antislavery meetings in neighboring towns and frequently heard the stirring speeches of Henry Brewster Stanton, a journalist and reformer ten years her senior. Attracted to each other at once, they were married May 10, 1840, after Elizabeth had with difficulty overcome her father's objections to her marrying an abolitionist. After a ceremony from which the word "obey" was omitted at her insistence, they sailed immediately for England to attend the World's Anti-Slavery Convention in London, to which Henry Stanton was a delegate. Although merely an observer, Mrs. Stanton soon became involved in the controversy over the exclusion of women delegates from the convention. She expressed her protests freely, particularly to LUCRETIA MOTT, the liberal Quaker minister from Philadelphia, who was one of the rejected delegates. Her stimulating talks with Mrs. Mott aroused in her a determination to improve the legal and traditional status of women and helped free her from the bondage of the stern Presbyterianism which had haunted her childhood. The two women, forming a warm friendship, resolved to hold a woman's rights convention when they returned to the United States.

At the close of the Anti-Slavery Convention, the Stantons traveled in England, Scotland, Ireland, and France, where Henry Stanton filled lecture engagements and wrote travel articles for American newspapers. Returning home in November 1840, they settled in Johnstown for two years while Stanton studied law with Judge Cady. Here their first child, Daniel Cady, was born in 1842. Six more children followed: Henry in 1844, Gerrit Smith in 1845, Theodore in 1851, Margaret in 1852, Harriot (see HARRIOT STANTON BLATCH) in 1856, and Robert in 1859. Of her seven children, all but Daniel survived her. Late in 1842 Henry Stanton opened a law office in Boston, and when Mrs. Stanton joined him in 1843, an active and stimulating life among the abolitionists and liberal thinkers of that city awaited her. Here she met Frederick Douglass, John Greenleaf Whittier, LYDIA MARIA CHILD, ABBY KELLEY (FOSTER), and MARIA WESTON CHAPMAN, listened to Theodore Parker's sermons, and visited Brook Farm. Henry Stanton's health, however, forced a return to a drier climate, and in 1847 they moved to Seneca Falls, N.Y., where he continued his law practice and served briefly in the state senate.

After Boston, life in Seneca Falls with its routine household duties seemed dull to Mrs. Stanton. Her discussions with Lucretia Mott in London and their talk of a woman's rights convention were not forgotten. Nor had she lost her interest in freeing women from their bondage under the common law. Whenever opportunities arose, she talked with legislators on the subject and circulated petitions for a married woman's property bill. When in March 1848 a law was passed by the New York legislature granting married women the right to hold real estate in their own name, she felt she had had a small part in the victory. By this time, too, she had asked her friends to direct their letters to "Elizabeth Cady Stanton" rather than to "Mrs. Henry B. Stanton," for she felt that a woman should not submerge her identity in marriage.

In July 1848, when she learned that Lucretia Mott was visiting in nearby Waterloo, N.Y., Mrs. Stanton paid her a visit and to her delight not only found her ready to make plans for the long-delayed woman's rights convention but learned that three other Quaker ladies, Jane Hunt, Mary McClintock, and MARTHA C. WRIGHT, Lucretia Mott's sister, were also eager to cooperate. Together they issued a call for a convention to meet on July 19 at the Wesleyan Methodist Church in Seneca Falls. Using as models the antislavery and temperance conventions with which all of them were familiar, they began planning the agenda, resolutions, and a Declaration of Sentiments. Mrs. Stanton undertook the drafting of the last, using the Declaration of Independence as a model; the result, a telling variation of that historic document, declared that "men and women are created equal," and enumerated eighteen legal grievances suffered by women, including lack of the franchise and of the right to their wages, their persons, and their children. It also called attention to women's limited educational and economic opportunities and protested against the double standard of morals. At this well-attended convention, over which James Mott presided, Mrs. Stanton, in spite of the opposition of her husband and even of Lucretia Mott, proposed a resolution advocating suffrage for women. The resolution —the first public demand by women for the vote—was eloquently defended by Frederick Douglass, and was finally adopted. Reintroduced in every successive woman's rights convention, it became the rallying cry for generations of women as they campaigned for their enfranchisement.

The ridicule and denunciation directed by pulpit and press against this unprecedented gathering did not deter Mrs. Stanton and her colleagues. The convention was reconvened two weeks later in the Rochester Unitarian Church, where it reached a wider circle of interested men and women, many of whom added their signatures to the Declaration of Sentiments. Soon Mrs. Stanton began writing letters stating her views on woman's rights to Horace Greeley's *New York Tribune*, the one influential newspaper to treat the conventions with seriousness and respect. When these were published she ventured to write to other papers, correcting misstatements about the convention and its aims. Under the pseudonym "Sun Flower" she also wrote provocative articles for Amelia's Bloomer's temperance paper the *Lily*, published in Seneca Falls. For a few years in the early 1850's she wore the costume introduced by her cousin Elizabeth Smith Miller and publicized by Mrs. Bloomer. She firmly believed that less hampering clothing was essential for a freer, healthier life for women, but she ceased wearing the Bloomer costume when she realized it was making enemies for woman suffrage.

In 1851, through Mrs. Bloomer, Elizabeth Cady Stanton met SUSAN B. ANTHONY, who had come to Seneca Falls for an antislavery meeting. Thus began the historic friendship that was to have so marked an effect upon the progress of American feminism. Within a year Mrs. Stanton had impressed Miss Anthony with the importance of the ballot for women, and their half-century-long collaboration was launched. There were marked differences between the two women: the plain Miss Anthony appeared severe and devoted herself with single-minded intensity to the suffrage movement and related reforms; Mrs. Stanton was an attractive woman of catholic tastes and wide-ranging interests whose jolly disposition quickly won friends. Their association was based, perhaps, less on temperamental affinity than upon a mutual recognition of the complementary nature of their talents. Each supplied abilities the other lacked. Mrs. Stanton, an eloquent speaker and forceful writer, supplemented Miss Anthony's organizational ability and taste for campaigning. Busy with her family, Mrs. Stanton could do little traveling, but she did find time to address many educational, temperance, antislavery, and other gatherings. "We made it a matter of conscience to accept every invitation to speak on every question, in order to maintain woman's right to do so. . . . Night after night by an old-fashioned fireplace, we plotted and planned the coming agitation," she wrote (*Eighty Years*, pp. 164, 166). When in 1854 Miss Anthony and several legislators urged her to address the New York legislature on the legal disabilities of women and the need for broadening the married women's property law, she consented. To speak in the senate chamber in Albany was an unprecedented undertaking for a woman, but she made a most favorable impression, and in 1860 the legislature did grant married women the right to their wages and the guardianship of their children. During these years Mrs. Stanton wrote articles for the *New York Tribune* and for a new women's magazine, the *Una*, published by her friend PAULINA WRIGHT DAVIS of Providence, R.I. One of these articles, satirizing the trite comment "I Have All the Rights I Want," was reprinted from the *Una* and widely circulated. She also encouraged and advised Miss Anthony, often writing her speeches, drafting resolutions for their annual woman's rights conventions, composing articles and fliers, and sending vigorous letters to meetings which she

could not attend. After Miss Anthony had gathered the facts and they had discussed and evaluated them, Mrs. Stanton would put them into effective, vital prose. Judge Cady was far from happy with his daughter's activities and for a time even disinherited her, but he relented before his death in 1859. Henry Stanton, too, frequently complained about the amount of time she was spending in agitation.

Early in her career Mrs. Stanton revealed a radical turn of mind that was for fifty years to be the despair of her more cautious co-workers. "It is a settled maxim with me," she once said, "that the existing public sentiment on any subject is wrong" (*Eminent Women of the Age*, p. 360). In 1852 the members of the Woman's State Temperance Society, which Mrs. Stanton and Miss Anthony had formed because the regular New York temperance organization discriminated against women, were shocked when Mrs. Stanton, in her presidential address, announced that drunkenness should be considered a sufficient cause for divorce. Defeated for reelection the following year, she and Miss Anthony resigned and the society soon disbanded. In 1860, when more liberal divorce laws were being debated in the New York newspapers and proposed in several states, Mrs. Stanton created a sensation in that year's national woman's rights convention by offering a resolution endorsing easier divorce; she also spoke before the New York senate in support of such legislation, denouncing the law which treated a wife as a piece of personal property and therefore without redress in an unhappy marriage. Her commonsense approach to the problem is suggested in a letter of 1860: "What would we think of the chemist who should sit twenty years trying to mix oil and water, and insist upon it that his happiness depended upon the result of the experiment?" (*Elizabeth Cady Stanton*, II, 83).

The coming of the Civil War temporarily interrupted her involvement with these questions. Early in 1861 she joined Susan B. Anthony and other abolitionists on a speaking tour in western New York because she felt strongly that at this critical time it was important to press for the immediate emancipation of Negro slaves and for the right of free speech, even if it meant facing unruly mobs. By this time Henry Stanton had received a New York Custom House appointment and was writing editorials for the *New York Tribune*, and in 1862 the family moved from Seneca Falls to Brooklyn and then, a few years later, to Manhattan. Eager to make some contribution toward winning the war beyond knitting and sewing for the soldiers, Mrs. Stanton and Miss

Anthony in May 1863 organized the Women's Loyal National League, which secured over 300,000 signatures to a petition, presented to the Senate by Charles Sumner, demanding the immediate abolition of slavery by constitutional amendment. In 1864 Mrs. Stanton supported a movement to replace Abraham Lincoln on the Republican ticket with a more outspoken enemy of slavery, a step she came in time to regret.

After the war her commitment to the cause of women again came to the fore. When amendments were proposed to extend civil rights and the franchise to male Negroes, she and Miss Anthony demanded that these rights be extended to women as well. Many former colleagues refused to support this demand, declaring with Wendell Phillips, "This is the Negro's hour," and arguing that woman's rights could wait. Failing to achieve their goal in either the Fourteenth or Fifteenth amendments, Mrs. Stanton and Miss Anthony opposed both measures; as Mrs. Stanton tersely expressed it, they were determined no longer to boost the Negro over their own heads. This further alienated many of their old friends, but they were convinced that the majority of enfranchised male Negroes would swell the ranks of those opposed to woman suffrage. In 1868 they secured the introduction of a proposed Sixteenth Amendment providing that suffrage be based on citizenship irrespective of race, color, or sex, but it was ignored.

Wishing to test women's constitutional right to seek public office, Mrs. Stanton in 1866 ran for Congress as an Independent, but received only 24 of 12,000 votes cast. The following year, when both Negro and woman suffrage amendments were being referred to the voters of Kansas, she and Miss Anthony carried on a vigorous though unsuccessful campaign for the woman's amendment in all parts of that frontier state, Mrs. Stanton traveling widely with former Gov. Charles Robinson in his mule-drawn carriage. The suffragists were aided in Kansas by an eccentric reformer, George Francis Train, and after the defeat he offered to pay the expenses of Miss Anthony and Mrs. Stanton on a speaking tour en route to the East and to finance a weekly paper for them in New York. Launched in January 1868, with Miss Anthony as publisher and Mrs. Stanton as co-editor (along with Parker Pillsbury, a fellow suffragist and former abolitionist), and bearing the militant title the *Revolution,* the paper continued for a year and a half. Mrs. Stanton in her forceful editorials called for woman suffrage, jury service and wider economic opportunities for women, and more liberal divorce laws, and condemned prostitution and the Fifteenth Amendment. In 1869 she began a twenty-one-year tenure as president of the National Woman Suffrage Association, organized in that year by herself and Miss Anthony. Her poise as a presiding officer and the warmth of her personality made her the natural choice for president through the years and gave assurance, as Miss Anthony expressed it, that "the brave and true word would be spoken." Later in 1869, however, a group of more conservative suffragists, primarily New Englanders led by LUCY STONE, objecting to the secrecy with which the Stanton-Anthony group had been formed and disapproving of the *Revolution's* championing of unpopular causes and individuals (such as the notorious VICTORIA WOODHULL), formed a rival organization, the American Woman Suffrage Association.

Meanwhile Mrs. Stanton, who in 1868 had moved from New York to Tenafly, N.J., felt the need of raising money to help finance the education of her children, and in 1869 began lecturing throughout the country for the New York Lyceum Bureau. For twelve years she carried a strenuous lecture schedule, becoming one of the most popular speakers on the lyceum circuit. Her favorite lecture, and the one most in demand, was "Our Girls," in which she expressed her views on a fuller, freer life for women. Other popular subjects were "Our Boys," "Coeducation," and "Marriage and Divorce." A handsome though rather portly woman, five feet three inches tall, with rosy cheeks and neatly curled white hair, stylishly dressed in black silk, she made a most favorable impression. She was a natural orator, and her ready humor, the twinkle in her eyes, and her spontaneous friendliness, as well as the fact that she was the mother of seven children, endeared her to her audiences and aided mightily in changing public opinion regarding women's ability and place in society.

The woman's movement, however, always came first with Mrs. Stanton, and the nationwide popularity established by her lecture tours lent prestige to the cause. In 1871 she traveled with Miss Anthony to the Far West, speaking in the woman suffrage states of Wyoming and Utah and in California. In 1876 she was a principal framer of the Woman's Declaration of Rights at the Philadelphia Centennial Exposition, and two years later she persuaded Senator Aaron A. Sargent of California to introduce a federal woman suffrage amendment following the wording of the Fifteenth Amendment. This was reintroduced in every succeeding Congress until finally adopted in 1920, and Mrs. Stanton was for many years the outstanding speaker in its support at Congressional hearings. Of the stimulating messages she regularly wrote for each woman suffrage convention, two of the most popular and widely circulated were "The Degradation of Disfranchisement" (1891) and "The Solitude of Self" (1892). The latter, also delivered before the House and Senate Judiciary committees, was hailed by Susan B. Anthony as "the strongest and most unanswerable argument and appeal ever made . . . for the full freedom and franchise of women." In 1888 Mrs. Stanton, feeling that the time had come for action rather than words (and emulating an earlier effort by Miss Anthony), tried unsuccessfully to cast her ballot in Tenafly, N.J.

Throughout these years her close collaboration with Susan B. Anthony continued, though not without periodic strains as Miss Anthony made her unending demands for speeches, resolutions, and pamphlets from her older friend. "One would think I were a machine; that all I had to do was to turn a crank and thoughts on any theme would bubble up like water," she noted testily in her diary in 1896 when faced with one of Miss Anthony's perennial requests (*Elizabeth Cady Stanton*, II, 321). Such outbursts were rare, however. More common were assurances of affection. "You are entwined with much of my happy and eventful past," wrote Mrs. Stanton to her friend in 1865, "and all my future plans are based on you as a coadjutor. Yes, our work is one, we are one in aim and sympathy and we should be together" (Ida H. Harper, *Life and Work of Susan B. Anthony*, I, 1898, p. 244). In the early 1880's they spent many hours together at Tenafly, reviewing the documents and letters of the suffrage movement as they prepared the monumental *History of Woman Suffrage*, the first three volumes of which, covering the years 1848 to 1885, appeared between 1881 and 1886. "We have furnished the bricks and mortar for some future architect to rear a beautiful edifice," Mrs. Stanton wrote. (Three later volumes, the last two edited by IDA HUSTED HARPER, carried the story through 1920.) Even this collaboration was not without its frictions, however. When Mrs. Stanton, radical as usual, asserted in the preface of Volume III that "the legislature, directly representing the people, is the primary source of power, above all courts and constitutions," Miss Anthony disagreed strongly and consulted several lawyers on the point. Unabashed, Mrs. Stanton wrote her, "You have not made me take your position. I repudiate it from the bottom of my soul. It is conservative, autocrat-ic, to the last degree" (*Elizabeth Cady Stanton*, II, 163).

As she grew older, Mrs. Stanton spent a great deal of time in England with her daughter Harriot, who had married an Englishman, and in Paris with her son Theodore, a journalist. During these years she helped interest the women of England and France in the idea of an international organization of women, and through the efforts of Susan B. Anthony this finally materialized in the International Council of Women formed in Washington in 1888. Mrs. Stanton, as the woman who had called the first woman's rights convention forty years before, was the featured speaker at this meeting.

After the death of her husband in 1887, Mrs. Stanton made her home in New York City. When the two suffrage organizations merged in 1890 as the National American Woman Suffrage Association, she served the reunited group as president for two years, but she devoted more and more of her time to writing for newspapers and magazines, including the *Westminster Review, Arena, Forum, North American Review,* and CLARA B. COLBY's *Woman's Tribune*. She was now famous and widely honored, but her iconoclastic nature was to carry her into yet another controversy. As early as 1855 she had pursued her study of the works of Thomas Paine, unruffled when newspapers labeled her an "infidel," and the noted freethinker Col. Robert G. Ingersoll later became a good friend. Convinced that the church and its interpretation of the Bible were the greatest obstacles to the progress of women, and impatient with clergymen who quoted the Bible to limit woman's sphere, she undertook a thorough study of the subject. In 1885 she strongly endorsed a resolution critical of religion before the National Woman Suffrage Association, but it was tabled through the determined efforts of Miss Anthony, who felt it was divisive and diverted attention from the suffrage cause. Mrs. Stanton, however, pursued the subject. In 1895, when she was honored on her eightieth birthday by a gathering of six thousand in the Metropolitan Opera House in New York, she asserted in her address that the spheres of men and women differ only according to the capacities of the individual, and, more specifically, that women must demand an equal place in the church, including its business matters, discipline, and the formulation of creeds. That same year she published *The Woman's Bible*, to which she added a second volume in 1898. This was a commentary which analyzed the Bible's derogatory references to women and reinterpreted them in the light of other passages, as well as of reason and common sense. The work sold well, but it aroused a storm of protest from the clergy, the press, and even from many of Mrs. Stanton's woman suffrage colleagues, who, led by ANNA HOWARD SHAW, RACHEL FOSTER AVERY, CARRIE CHAPMAN CATT, and other younger women of the movement, in the 1896 convention adopted a resolution dissociating the suffrage organization from *The Woman's Bible*. In this showdown Miss Anthony spoke eloquently against the resolution, with its implied censure of her old co-worker.

In 1898, the year she turned eighty-three, Mrs. Stanton published her reminiscences, *Eighty Years and More.* She continued to promulgate her views on divorce, religion, and other subjects in newspaper and magazine articles, including regular contributions to the *New York Journal* and *American*, which featured her as "The Grand Old Woman of America." She recommended sensible, convenient clothing for women, with short skirts and pockets, as well as more physical activity. In one article she answered the question "Should women ride the bicycle?" with an emphatic "Yes." She was always a favorite with reporters, who never failed to get an interesting story from her. In her later years, although her eyesight failed, she kept abreast of the times and continued her interest in public affairs. In politics her sympathies were liberal; she opposed the Chinese exclusion bill and supported the Populist party in 1896. Her friendship with Susan B. Anthony continued, but the period of close cooperation was over. "Miss Anthony has one idea and she has no patience with anyone who has two. I cannot sit on the door just like Poe's raven and sing suffrage evermore," she confided to her close friend Clara Colby (Lutz, *Created Equal*, p. 296). She sometimes chafed at what she considered the growing conservatism of the woman suffrage movement as it reflected the thinking of the younger generation. In October 1902, at the age of eighty-six, she died in her sleep at her New York home just after writing to President Theodore Roosevelt urging him to declare himself for woman suffrage. After a private funeral service conducted by her friend the Unitarian minister Moncure D. Conway, she was buried in Woodlawn Cemetery in New York. For months afterward newspapers and magazines paid her tribute as the statesman of the woman's rights movement and the mother of woman suffrage.

Although more popular during her lifetime than Susan B. Anthony, Elizabeth Cady Stanton has not lived in the memory of the young-er generation as has Miss Anthony, who left behind her an organization which cherished and publicized her memory. Perhaps Mrs. Stanton's greatest contribution was her effort to emancipate women's minds. She was essentially a torchbearer whose liberal thinking and courageous outlook were potent factors in freeing women from the psychological barriers which hedged them in, and in pointing the way to wider interests and activities. Realizing that they could not use the ballot intelligently and effectively if they concentrated only on suffrage to the exclusion of other social issues, she urged women to reject encumbering traditions and to dare to question any edict of church or state which limited woman's sphere.

[Elizabeth Cady Stanton Papers, Library of Congress and Vassar College Library; other letters in Henry E. Huntington Library, N.Y. Public Library, Sophia Smith Collection, Smith College, and Schlesinger Library, Radcliffe College; Susan B. Anthony Scrapbooks of Press Comments relating to Elizabeth Cady Stanton, Library of Congress; Elizabeth Cady Stanton, *Eighty Years and More* (1898); Theodore Stanton and Harriot Stanton Blatch, eds., *Elizabeth Cady Stanton as Revealed in Her Letters, Diary, and Reminiscences* (2 vols., 1922); Elizabeth Cady Stanton et al., *Hist. of Woman Suffrage*, vols. I–III (1881–86); Alma Lutz, *Created Equal: A Biog. of Elizabeth Cady Stanton* (1940); Harriot Stanton Blatch and Alma Lutz, *Challenging Years: The Memoirs of Harriot Stanton Blatch* (1940); Alma Lutz, *Susan B. Anthony: Rebel, Crusader, Humanitarian* (1959); Theodore Tilton, "Mrs. Elizabeth Cady Stanton," in *Eminent Women of the Age* (1869), pp. 332–61.]

ALMA LUTZ

**STARBUCK, Mary Coffyn** (Feb. 20, 1644/45 O.S.–Nov. 13, 1717 O.S.), Quaker minister, was born in Haverhill, Mass., the third daughter and seventh of nine children of Tristram Coffyn (or Coffin) and Dionis (Stevens) Coffyn, natives of Devonshire who emigrated to New England about 1642. Tristram Coffyn, who initiated the plan to colonize the island of Nantucket, moved there with part of his family in 1660 or 1661 and subsequently became chief magistrate.

Little is known about his daughter Mary before 1701. She learned to read and write. Shortly after her father's move to Nantucket, she was married to Nathaniel Starbuck, son of another leading partner in the purchase of the island, who became a well-to-do farmer and local official. They had ten children: Mary, Elizabeth, Nathaniel, Jethro, Barnabas, Eunice, Priscilla, Hepzibah, Ann, and Paul. All but the last two are known to have lived to maturity.

Sketchy evidence indicates that after mar-

riage Mary Starbuck deserted her father's religion (Massachusetts orthodoxy) and joined
her husband and father-in-law in a predes-
tinarian baptist circle probably led by Peter
Folger, who may have baptized her about
1665. Later, she said "their Principle was,
*That such who believed once in Christ, were
always in him, without Possibility of falling
away; and whom he had once loved, he loved
to the End:* And it was a Distinction they had
given to their Church, to be called *Electarians . . ."* (John Richardson, *An Account of
the Life of That Ancient Servant of Jesus
Christ, John Richardson,* 1757, p. 97). After
Folger's death (1690) she exerted some leadership in the sect and also roused public opposition to calling a salaried orthodox minister
to the island. Though dissatisfied with the man
preaching to the Electarians at the end of the
seventeenth century, she wanted a ministry
based on "openings" of the Holy Spirit, not a
professional parson, and ultimately sought it
in still another sect.

Mary Starbuck and her eldest son started a
wave of conversions which made Quakerism
the foremost religion on Nantucket in the
eighteenth century. Her leadership in the wave,
which has been sentimentally exaggerated, is
known only from mutually inconsistent accounts (and traditions obviously derived from
them) by three Quaker missionaries, who understood little about the island and may have
revised their journals in the light of the subsequent success of their religion on it. Only
one of them found out about the Electarian
group, and he did not fully appreciate how it
had prepared the way for him; his information strongly suggests that this sect embodied
tendencies found in Puritanism elsewhere
which often led to Quakerism.

Thomas Chalkley, the first Quaker known
to have held a public meeting on Nantucket,
claimed to have started a regular meeting for
worship by converting Mary Starbuck's son
Nathaniel in 1698. Apparently he was unaware
that several Quakers had lived on the island
for many years. The second traveling Friend
who recorded his labors there, John Richardson, found young Nathaniel only a potential
convert in 1701 and quickly decided that
Mary Starbuck was the most important person he could win over. He sailed away believing he had succeeded.

Yet Thomas Story, when he arrived in July
1704, discovered that she was not attached to
any sect, although, like others in Nantucket,
intellectually convinced of most of the distinctive Quaker doctrines and beginning to
know the spirit of them. He, too, thought

Mary Starbuck the obvious potential leader,
and passed over the long-professed Friends to
ask her to start holding weekly religious meetings in her family and welcome others who
might wish to join.

She agreed to this proposal, which probably
involved little departure from the habits of the
Electarians. Off-island Friends visited in
great numbers for three years, helping the
Quaker nucleus to grow rapidly. In 1708 the
group sought and received the approval of
New England Yearly Meeting to form a meeting for discipline and business. In organization
matters the younger Nathaniel Starbuck, rather
than his mother, was the most prominent.

Mary Starbuck served as clerk of the wom-
en's meeting and became the first recognized
minister among the islanders. John Richardson
observed in 1701 that she made an impressive
and dignified figure in public and seemed
naturally to speak in an elegant manner; as no
later description survives, nothing is known
about her ministry. In religion she, rather than
her husband, led the family—and ultimately
much of the island.

Credible local tradition has it that she was
active in town as well as Quaker meeting, paying her spouse the dubious courtesy of introducing her views with a phrase such as, "My
husband and I think. . . ." Public business
was so often conducted at their home that it
earned the nickname "Parliament House."
Richardson received the impression in 1701
that she was "esteemed as a Judge" by the islanders, and that "little of Moment was done
there without her." Accordingly, he gave her
the ungainly epithet that has dogged her ever
since: "the great Woman." Less plausible is
the claim that she gave crucial advice about
the beginning of whaling in Nantucket; if she
took any part in commerce it was trading with
the Indians.

Mary Starbuck, the archetype of the strong-
minded Nantucket wife, died on the island in
1717 at the age of seventy-two. Fittingly, her
body was laid to rest in Friends' burial ground
next to the new meetinghouse built on land
donated by her son and the Nantucket proprietors.

[No significant writings by Mary Coffyn Starbuck
survive. The numerous existing biographical
sketches are brief and fanciful, except for that in
Lydia S. Hinchman, comp., *Early Settlers of Nantucket* (1896 and later editions). Alexander Starbuck, *The Hist. of Nantucket* (1924), contains the
basic genealogical and historical information, including accurate transcriptions of the pertinent
passages from the journals of Thomas Chalkley,
John Richardson, and Thomas Story. *Vital Records*

of Haverhill, Mass., vol. I (1910), and *Vital Records of Nantucket, Mass.*, vol. V (1928), supply quasi-official birth and death dates. Florence Bennett Anderson, *A Grandfather for Benjamin Franklin* (1940), offers a brilliant but not undoubtable reconstruction of the first twenty years of the Nantucket settlement. Henry B. Worth, "The First Whaling Merchant of Nantucket," Nantucket Hist. Assoc., *Proc.*, 1915, pp. 26–34, discusses the inconclusive evidence for Mary Starbuck's trading activities. H. B. Worth, "Nantucket Lands and Land Owners," Nantucket Hist. Assoc., *Bulls.*, vol. II (Bulls. 1–7, 1901–13), gives details on the Coffin and Starbuck family affairs. Robert J. Leach, "The First Two Quaker Meeting-Houses on Nantucket," Nantucket Hist. Assoc., *Proc.*, 1950, pp. 24–33; Henry J. Cadbury, "Nantucket and Its Quakers in 1722," *ibid.*, 1946, pp. 18–19; and William R. Bliss, *Quaint Nantucket* (1896), chap. iv, give important additional information on the early years of Quakerism on the island.]

SYDNEY V. JAMES

STARR, Belle (Feb. 5, 1848–Feb. 3, 1889), legendary "Bandit Queen" of the Southwest, was born either in Carthage, Mo., or on a nearby farm. Christened Myra Belle Shirley, she was the only daughter and third child of John and Elizabeth Shirley. Few facts of her life are firmly established, since her mode of existence demanded secrecy, and many legends arose after her death, but it is probable that her parents came originally from Kentucky or Tennessee. In June 1848 John Shirley took legal possession of an 800-acre government grant about ten miles northwest of Carthage, then a small town on one of the principal Western trails. Three years later, selling part of this land, he settled in Carthage itself and opened a tavern. Here Belle acquired a rudimentary education and a modest facility at the piano.

When the Civil War broke out her brother Edward became a plundering "bushwhacker" vaguely identified with William C. Quantrill's roving band of outlaws and Confederate irregulars; he was killed by Federal troops in 1863. In October of that year the town of Carthage was burned, and the Shirley family moved to Texas, settling on a farm near Scyene, ten miles east of Dallas. When Quantrill himself was shot in 1865, remnants of his gang, including the four notorious Younger brothers and their legendary cousins Jesse and Frank James, continued a career of banditry throughout the Southwest, occasionally taking refuge at the Shirley farm in Texas. Belle's remaining brother, succumbing to the pervasive lawlessness, died in a gunfight at Spring Creek, Texas, in 1867. Belle herself appears to have fallen in love with Thomas Coleman

("Cole") Younger; though they never married, she bore a child around 1869 whom she named Pearl Younger.

While her desperado friends staged a series of bank robberies and train holdups, Belle became a habitué of Dallas dance halls, saloons, and gambling casinos. Her father tried to keep her on the farm, but soon she eloped with James H. (Jim) Reed, an outlaw whom she had known as a child in Missouri. According to one romantic tale, Reed abducted Belle from her second-story room and "married" her on horseback in a mock ceremony performed by another bandit. In any event, she became his common-law wife. The couple lived briefly in Missouri and then fled to Los Angeles, Calif., after Reed killed a man in a family feud. Here Belle's second and last child, Edward Reed, was born in the early 1870's. Harried by federal agents as a counterfeiter, Reed returned with his family to Texas, where in April 1874 he led a sensational holdup of the Austin–San Antonio stage, only to be fatally shot by a deputy sheriff several months later. No evidence supports the legend that Belle participated directly in this robbery, though she was named as an accessory in the indictment.

For several years Belle continued to live a loose life in Dallas, operating a livery stable where she dealt in stolen horses, and consorting with a succession of disreputable characters. Eventually she placed her children with relatives, moved to Oklahoma, and in 1880, under tribal law, married Sam Starr, a Cherokee whose lawless family had long been intimates of the Youngers, the James brothers, and their ilk. They settled in Starr's Canadian River cabin, on the Cherokee reservation about forty miles west of Fort Smith, Ark. This remote spot, which Belle renamed Younger's Bend, was for several months the hideout of Jesse James and became a favorite retreat for numerous lesser bootleggers, horse thieves, and cattle rustlers who preyed upon the cowboys and livestock moving over the nearby Chisholm Trail to Dodge City and Abilene.

Unquestionably Belle Starr gave aid and comfort, as well as occasional legal assistance, to these outlaws. Whether she was herself the mastermind of a gang remains conjectural, although an 1883 indictment minced no words in calling her "the leader of a band of horse thieves." She and Sam Starr were convicted on this occasion by the famous "hanging judge" Isaac C. Parker of Fort Smith—the only charge on which she was ever found guilty—and, in March 1883, were sentenced to the federal penitentiary at Detroit, where they served nine months. In 1885 one John Middleton, hiding at Younger's Bend to avoid a Texas murder charge, persuaded Belle to elope with him. As they proceeded by separate routes to a pre-arranged rendezvous, however, Middleton drowned while fording a stream, and Belle returned to Sam Starr. On three occasions in 1885 and 1886 she was indicted for horse theft or robbery, but her considerable legal acumen enabled her each time to introduce delays or otherwise escape trial. One indictment charged her with participating in a post-office robbery disguised as a man. Her sole surviving photograph reveals her to have been exceedingly plain of face, but she compensated for this by fancy clothing, ornate pistols, expensive riding gear, and a confident manner. Her frequent court appearances in Fort Smith attracted considerable attention. Wrote a local reporter in 1883: "A devil-may-care expression rested on her countenance during the entire trial, and at no time did she give sign of weakening before the mass of testimony that was raised against her."

In December 1887 Sam Starr was shot and killed in a dispute, and shortly thereafter a twenty-four-year-old Cherokee, Jim July, moved into the cabin at Younger's Bend. He proved to be Belle Starr's last lover, for in February 1889, while he was making a court appearance in Fort Smith, she was shot in the back and killed near her cabin; her age was forty. Jim July accused a neighbor of having done the deed, but the court refused to indict. Belle's two children were living at Younger's Bend at the time, and local gossip fixed on young Edward Reed as the killer.

Her immediate survivors met fates similar to hers. Jim July was killed in 1890 while resisting arrest; Belle's son was shot in a saloon brawl in 1896; and her daughter became a prostitute in Arkansas, having first erected over her mother's grave at Younger's Bend a tombstone on which were carved a bell and a star, her favorite horse, and the sentimental epitaph:

> Shed not for her the bitter tear,
> Nor give the heart to vain regret;
> 'Tis but the casket that lies here,
> The gem that filled it sparkles yet.

A few months after her death an anonymous and wholly fictitious "biography," *Belle Starr, the Bandit Queen; or, The Female Jesse James,* was published in New York by Richard K. Fox of the *National Police Gazette.* It portrayed Belle as a beautiful and cultivated daughter of the Old South who had become a Civil War spy and then a bandit chief to avenge the death of her Confederate officer brother. Re-

plete with alleged extracts from her diary and letters, the book persuaded a willing public, which has persisted in the conviction that Belle Starr was a noble, misunderstood, and highly romantic lady of the Wild West.

[Burton Rascoe, *Belle Starr* (1941), is the best biography; it is the source of the quoted passages above. Ramon F. Adams, *Burs under the Saddle: A Second Look at Books and Histories of the West* (1964), methodically exposes the errors of some fifty other books in which Belle figures.]

                                        LON TINKLE

**STARR, Eliza Allen** (Aug. 29, 1824–Sept. 7, 1901), writer and lecturer on art and religion, poet, and pioneer teacher of art in the Midwest, was born in Deerfield, Mass., where her mother's family had long been established. Named Eliza Ann (she took Allen as her middle name in adulthood), she was the second of four children and elder of two daughters of Oliver and Lovina (Allen) Starr. Through her father she was descended from Dr. Comfort Starr, who emigrated to the Bay Colony about 1635. Both her father, a dyer and farmer, and her mother encouraged her early interests in drawing and literature. At the district school she learned to paint under Caroline Negus, who as the wife of Richard Hildreth, the historian, became a well-known miniature painter; at twelve she was enrolled in the Deerfield Academy. In 1845 she went to Boston to continue her studies under Mrs. Hildreth, opening a studio of her own the next year.

This period in Boston also marked the beginning of a nine-year struggle toward Catholicism. Listening to a sermon by Theodore Parker in 1845, she realized he was demolishing "every foundation-stone" of the Unitarian faith in which she had been reared. Her next three years were an unfocused search for an "authorized faith." This took on more specific direction when, in Philadelphia in 1848, she visited her cousin George Allen, onetime Episcopal clergyman, then professor of Latin and Greek at the University of Pennsylvania and a very recent Catholic convert, and through him met Bishop Francis P. Kenrick of Philadelphia, later Archbishop of Baltimore. That year, in poor health, she left Boston and taught drawing briefly in private schools in Brooklyn and Philadelphia before taking a position in 1851 as tutor in the family of a wealthy planter in Natchez, Miss., where she remained for two years. Her final conversion to Catholicism took place upon her return, and on Dec. 23, 1854, she was baptized by Bishop John B. Fitzpatrick of Boston. For some time thereafter she corresponded with Bishop Kenrick about the possibility of a religious vocation, an idea she did not abandon until 1860, and then because of the delicate health which plagued her most of her life. She did become a member of the Third Order of St. Dominic and at her death was buried in a Dominican habit sent her by the nuns.

After her conversion, fresh religious ardor infused all her work. In 1856, armed with letters of introduction from Bishops Kenrick and Fitzpatrick, she went to Chicago, where she soon established a studio in rented rooms and began a residence of forty-five years during which she made for herself a distinctive niche in the city's cultural life—at once a liberating teacher in technique and a conservative, enthusiastically religious influence on artistic taste. From the first she received support from the Chicago chancery and the patronage of the city's leading men, whose children constituted the majority of the pupils in her drawing and painting classes. By the time she moved into her own studio in 1863 she had attracted wide attention for her insistent enforcement of the dictum "never copy," which she had received from her mentor, Mrs. Hildreth; she was the first instructor in the Midwest area whose pupils worked exclusively from nature and casts, of which she built up an impressive collection.

The verse and the articles on Christian art which she published frequently in such periodicals as the *Catholic Mirror, London Monthly, Freeman's Journal,* and *Catholic World* added to her reputation. These popularizing essays were soon supplemented by public lectures begun at St. Mary's Academy near South Bend, Ind., where she founded the art department after taking refuge there with the Sisters of the Holy Cross when her studio burned down in the Chicago Fire of 1871. Miss Starr's lectures, given during the next two decades in Chicago and other cities of the Midwest and East under the general title of "The Literature of Art," were among the first in the United States to make extensive use of photographs and slides. Popular rather than technical in approach, they were, according to a contemporary account, "suggestive and inspiring, stamped with originality of thought and great tenderness of expression" (clipping, Sophia Smith Collection).

Support from wealthy friends, both Catholic and non-Catholic, financed in large part Miss Starr's European trip of 1875–77, out of which she drew the materials for her best-known work, *Pilgrims and Shrines* (2 vols., 1885). Friends also built her new studio, St. Joseph's Cottage, where she took up residence on her return and reigned over a small, intense part of Chicago's genteel art world. Her lectures helped create an audience for a number of books composed uniquely of Catholic devotion and quasi-scholarly art appreciation and often illustrated by her own etchings. Her poems were first collected and published in 1867; brought up to date, they were again issued as *Songs of a Lifetime* in 1887.

Miss Starr received a medallion from Pope Leo XIII in recognition of *The Three Archangels and the Guardian Angel in Art* (1899). She was earlier (1885) the recipient of Notre Dame University's Laetare Medal and of a special gold medal from the Catholic Congress at Chicago's World's Columbian Exposition (1893). She died at the age of seventy-seven while visiting her brother Caleb Allen Starr in Durand, Ill., and was buried in Calvary Cemetery, Chicago. ELLEN GATES STARR, co-founder of Hull House, was her niece.

[Miss Starr's other works include *Patron Saints* (1st series, 1871; 2nd series, 1881), *Isabella of Castile* (1889), *Christian Art in Our Own Age* (1891), *Three Keys to the Camera Della Segnatura of the Vatican* (1895), and *The Seven Dolors of the Blessed Virgin Mary* (1898). The most complete biographical source is James J. McGovern, *The Life and Letters of Eliza Allen Starr* (1905), an uncritical, disorganized amassing of autobiographical sketches and eclectically chosen letters. More useful is the sketch in Frances E. Willard and Mary A. Livermore, eds., *A Woman of the Century* (1893). See also Burgis P. Starr, *A Hist. of the Starr Family* (1879), in which she is correctly named Eliza Ann Starr; the "Allen" first appeared on the title page of her *Poems* in 1867. The *Chicago Tribune* obituary (Sept. 9, 1901) gives a sense of her service to the city. The library of Notre Dame Univ. has a collection of her letters, and there is a smaller one in the Sophia Smith Collection at Smith College.]

ARCHIBALD J. BYRNE

**STARR, Ellen Gates** (Mar. 19, 1859–Feb. 10, 1940), settlement worker, co-founder of Hull House, was born on a farm near Laona, Ill., the second daughter and third of four children of Caleb Allen Starr and Susan (Gates) Starr. She was a direct descendant of Comfort Starr, a physician who emigrated from Kent, England, to Boston about 1635. A branch of the family moved to Connecticut in the eighteenth century, and in 1855 Ellen's father gave up a career as a sailor to settle in Illinois. As a child Ellen attended a local one-room school and watched her grandmother dip candles and use a spinning wheel. Later the family moved to Durand, Ill., where Caleb Starr became a village businessman. The greatest childhood influence on Ellen was her aunt ELIZA ALLEN STARR, a devout convert to Catholicism and a writer and lecturer on Christian art, whom she visited frequently in Chicago.

In part through her aunt's influence, Ellen enrolled at Rockford Seminary, Rockford, Ill., in the fall of 1877. As her father could afford tuition for only one year, she spent the following year teaching in a country school in Mount Morris, Ill., and in 1879 accepted a position at Miss Kirkland's School for Girls in Chicago. Here she taught a variety of subjects, including art appreciation. A small, rather frail girl with a quick wit, a flashing smile, and a great deal of energy, she was sensitive to beauty wherever she found it. Religion had played only a minor role in the mildly Unitarian Starr household, but much of Ellen's life was spent in a quest for religious truth. She found Chicago's Church of the Unity intellectually, but not spiritually, satisfying, and in 1884 she joined a "low" Episcopal church. A few years later, influenced by the Rev. James O. S. Huntington, founder of the Anglican Order of the Holy Cross, she came to consider herself an "Anglican Catholic." She was an avid reader of Carlyle, Ruskin, and William Morris, and her religious quest was closely linked with a passionate interest in art and its fate in modern industrial society.

During these years Miss Starr shared her concern and her questioning, in frequent and earnest letters and occasional visits, with JANE ADDAMS, a close friend from Rockford days. Miss Addams, eighteen months her junior, replied in letters that were equally intense and revealed a strong emotional dependence upon her older friend. Both young women, perhaps Miss Addams more acutely, were troubled by a sense of aimlessness and futility, and in April 1888, while they were visiting Madrid in the course of a joint European trip, Jane Addams confided to Ellen Starr her dream of establishing a settlement house. Miss Starr reacted enthusiastically, and the hitherto vague plan began to assume definite shape as a joint undertaking. Together, upon their return, they searched Chicago's West Side in the early months of 1889 for an appropriate building, and together they opened Hull House that September. Unquestionably, Jane Addams was the driving force behind the venture. She conceived the idea, provided most of the money, and was the principal executive and administrator. Nevertheless, without the support and encouragement of her Rockford friend it is doubtful if she would have translated her ideas into action. Furthermore, Miss Starr's years at the fashionable Kirkland School had made her well known in Chicago society, a fact which enabled Hull House from the first to win the confidence and support of the city's wealthy and influential elements.

If Hull House helped Jane Addams overcome a sense of futility and alienation, it gave Ellen Starr the opportunity to advance the sacred cause of art. She believed, with Victorian certitude, in the ennobling power of the great paintings, sculptures, and literary creations of the past, and she was appalled by their absence from the West Side. The immigrant had lost his capacity to create folk art, and yet had no access to the treasures of classical art and literature. This situation Miss Starr set out to remedy. She sought to bring meaning into the lives of the slum dwellers by establishing reading clubs devoted to Dante, Shakespeare, and Browning, and by decorating the walls of Hull House and nearby schools with reproductions of great art. She organized art history classes and in 1894 founded and became the first president of the Chicago Public School Art Society. Her influence in this early period was great; indeed, the first large gift received by Hull House was the $5,000 contributed in 1891 by Edward Butler for an art gallery.

Like her spiritual kinsmen Ruskin and Morris, Miss Starr decried the decline of handicrafts and skilled craftsmanship, and in the late 1890's she spent fifteen months in London studying bookbinding with T. J. Cobden-Sanderson. She returned eager to teach the art to others, only to find it of little practical use to the men and women who frequented Hull House. "If I had thought it through," she remarked much later, "I would have realized that I would be using my hands to create books that only the rich could buy." At Hull House she lived simply in a small apartment near her bookbindery, supported almost entirely by a modest annual sum provided by Mary Wilmarth (mother of ANNA WILMARTH THOMPSON ICKES), one of the settlement's early benefactors. She never married.

Gradually Miss Starr became convinced that a far more radical approach was needed if artistic enjoyment were to survive in a city like Chicago. "The soul of man in the commercial and industrial struggle is in a state of siege," she wrote in 1895. "For the children of the 'degraded poor,' and the degraded rich as well, in our present mode of life, there is no artistic hope outside of [a] miracle." Noting the prevalence of sweatshops, child labor, low wages, and long hours, she concluded that the only answer was to help the oppressed achieve "a new life, a freed life," by eliminating the conditions which destroyed creativity and deadened the aesthetic response. (See her essay

"Art and Labor," in *Hull-House Maps and Papers*, 1895, especially p. 178.) She joined FLORENCE KELLEY and others of the Hull House group in the battle against child labor. She was a charter member of the Illinois branch of the National Women's Trade Union League, formed in 1903. In 1896, 1910, and again in 1915 she came to the aid of striking textile workers, organizing mass meetings, collecting money, delivering flaming speeches, protesting to the mayor and to the newspapers, bringing clothing and food to the needy, and marching in the picket lines. She was arrested for "interfering with a police officer in the discharge of his duty" during a 1914 restaurant workers' strike, but her delicate, hundred-pound frame, pince-nez, and impeccable speech persuaded the jury of the implausibility of the charge. She was a close friend of the labor leaders Sidney Hillman and Jacob Potofsky, and after the 1915 textile strike she was made an honorary life member of Hillman's Amalgamated Clothing Workers of America.

Having long thought of herself as a Christian socialist, she eventually formally joined the Socialist party, whose principles she thereafter defended with "a sort of charming fierceness" (Linn, p. 131). In 1916 she ran for alderman because, as she explained, "there was no other Socialist in the ward to go on the ticket and . . . I couldn't reasonably decline." Her sometimes sharp impatience with those who did not share her radical militancy was a source of concern to Jane Addams, who, though not shrinking from commitment, sought to preserve at Hull House a tolerant climate where all points of view might be heard with respect.

As it had for her aunt and for John Henry Newman, whom she had read and admired for years, Ellen Starr's spiritual quest culminated in her conversion to Roman Catholicism. Increasingly drawn by the beauty of the Catholic liturgy, she overcame her doubts during a visit to St. Joseph's Benedictine Abbey in Louisiana and in March 1920 was received there into the Church. Thereafter she spent much of her time writing and speaking about Catholic art and worship and her own conversion experience. She continued to be an occasional visitor at Hull House until 1929, when an operation to remove a spinal abscess left her paralyzed below the waist. In 1930 she settled at the Convent of the Holy Child in Suffern, N.Y., where in 1935 she became an oblate of the Third Order of St. Benedict. Visitors during these final years found her somewhat more serene than during her days as a labor agitator but "as passionate for divinity and salvation, as she ever was for beauty or

for justice" (Linn, p. 132). She died in 1940, at eighty, and was buried at the convent.

[Primary sources: Ellen Gates Starr Papers, Sophia Smith Collection, Smith College, including notes on her life by her niece, Josephine Starr; letters of Ellen Starr in Jane Addams Papers, Swarthmore College, and Henry Demarest Lloyd Papers, State Hist. Soc. of Wis.; articles by Miss Starr: "A By-path into the Great Roadway," *Catholic World*, May, June 1924 (on her conversion); "Two Pilgrim Experiences," *ibid.*, Sept. 1930; "Efforts to Standardize Chicago Restaurants—The Henrici Strike," *Survey*, May 23, 1914; "The Chicago Clothing Strike," *New Review*, Mar. 1916; and "Hull House Bookbindery," *Commons*, June 30, 1900. The principal secondary sources are: Jane Addams, *Twenty Years at Hull-House* (1910) and "The Art-Work Done by Hull-House, Chicago," *Forum*, July 1895; James W. Linn, *Jane Addams* (1935), especially pp. 130–32. See also: Allen F. Davis, *Spearheads for Reform* (1967); Allen F. Davis and Mary Lynn McCree, eds., *Eighty Years at Hull House* (1969); Jacob S. Potofsky, "Happy Birthday to Ellen Gates Starr," *Advance*, Apr. 1939; Matthew Josephson, *Sidney Hillman* (1952); obituaries in *N.Y. Times* and *Chicago Tribune*, Feb. 11, 1940; and sketch by Eleanor Grace Clark in *Commonweal*, Mar. 15, 1940.]

ALLEN F. DAVIS

**STEARNS, Lutie Eugenia** (Sept. 13, 1866– Dec. 25, 1943), librarian, lecturer, and reformer, was born in Stoughton, Mass., the tenth daughter and youngest of eleven children of Dr. Isaac Holden Stearns and Catherine (Guild) Stearns. Her father, whose forebears had emigrated from Nottingham, England, to Watertown, Mass., in 1630, had graduated from Columbia Medical College in Washington, D.C., shortly before the Civil War. During that conflict, in which he served as surgeon of the 22nd Massachusetts Volunteers, his wife supported the family by bleaching and braiding straw for the currently popular Tuscan hats. Following the war, in 1871, Dr. Stearns was appointed surgeon in the National Soldiers Home in Milwaukee, Wis., a post from which he resigned in 1876 to take up general practice in Milwaukee.

While Lutie was in high school in Milwaukee her father deserted the family, divorced her mother, and returned to Massachusetts. Responsibility for the support of the household then fell on Lutie's shoulders. After graduating from the Milwaukee State Normal School in 1887, she taught for two years in the city's public schools. Appalled at the paucity of reading matter available to her pupils, she instituted a classroom library and made such heavy and continuing use of the juvenile materials in the Milwaukee Public Library that she attracted the attention of the library officials, who in 1890 offered her the position of superintendent of the circulation department. In 1893 Miss Stearns met Frank A. Hutchins, founder of the Wisconsin Library Association, who shared her passionate devotion to the cause of library extension. Together they began to work for the establishment of a state library commission similar to those already in operation in several New England states. With the active aid of James H. Stout, a philanthropist and state senator, such a commission was authorized in 1895, with Miss Stearns as honorary secretary. In 1897 she resigned her Milwaukee post to become the new Free Library Commission's first paid staff member and to embark on a career which has made her a legend in Wisconsin's library history. A slight, plain woman, handicapped by a stammer—said to have been induced when an early teacher forced her to change from left- to right-handedness—and by a recurrent skin cancer which plagued her most of her life, she nevertheless traveled the length and breadth of the state by rail, boat, buggy, and sleigh, preaching the library gospel and, according to her own statement, wearing out five fur coats in the process. Less an innovator than a missionary, she concentrated on getting public and traveling libraries organized, particularly in the undeveloped northern areas of the state, and successfully aided in the establishment of 100 free libraries and 1,480 traveling libraries.

In 1914, after a serious illness and a nervous breakdown which followed the deaths of her mother and a favorite sister, she resigned from the Library Commission to devote herself to lecturing and the support of reform causes. Painstakingly writing her speeches so as to avoid those consonants which accentuated her stammer, she became a popular lecturer throughout the country, aided by her wit, her decided opinions, and her gift for turning quotable phrases. She campaigned for woman suffrage in Iowa, Missouri, and Texas as well as in Wisconsin; and she worked for state prohibition and child labor legislation. Drawing her inspiration from David Starr Jordan and the Rev. Jenkin Lloyd Jones, she also spoke widely for the cause of world peace. Shortly after World War I she left the Congregational Church and joined the Quakers. She was one of the founders of the Wisconsin Federation of Women's Clubs. From 1932 to 1935 she wrote a column for the Sunday *Milwaukee Journal* in which she expounded her views as a reformer and a political independent. Although her own writing was largely confined to her newspaper column and to professional library journals, she numbered numerous women writers among her friends, among them such fellow Wisconsinites as ZONA GALE and Edna Ferber; the latter in her autobiography described Miss Stearns as "a terrific and dimensional human being." She was also greatly influenced by her friend of long standing JANE ADDAMS. After a long illness and a period of semiretirement, Miss Stearns died of cancer at her home in Milwaukee at the age of seventy-seven. Her ashes were buried in Forest Home Cemetery, Milwaukee, next to her mother's grave.

[Archives of Wis. Free Library Commission and of State Hist. Soc. of Wis.; Lutie E. Stearns, "My Seventy-Five Years," *Wis. Mag. of Hist.*, Spring and Summer 1959, Winter 1959–60; Earl Tannenbaum, "The Library Career of Lutie Eugenia Stearns," *ibid.*, Spring 1956; "Library Hall of Fame," *Library Jour.*, Mar. 15, 1951; *Wis. Clubwoman*, May–June 1940; *Milwaukee Jour.*, Dec. 30, 1943; *Who's Who in America*, 1914–15; *Dict. of Wis. Biog.* (1960); bibliography compiled by Virginia Potter, Univ. of Wis. Library School, 1960. See also, on Dr. Isaac Stearns, Louis Frank, *Medical Hist. of Milwaukee, 1834–1914* (1915). Though Miss Stearns gives her date of graduation from normal school as 1886, records of the school confirm 1887 as the correct date.]

WILLIAM CONVERSE HAYGOOD

**STEBBINS, Emma** (Sept. 1, 1815–Oct. 24, 1882), painter and sculptor, was born in New York City, the third daughter and sixth of the nine children of John Stebbins, president of the North River Bank and a Wall Street broker, and Mary (Largin) Stebbins. Her father had been born in Ridgefield, Conn., a descendant of early colonists. Her mother, daughter of an aide to the British colonel Banastre Tarleton during the Revolutionary War, was a native of Nova Scotia. One of Emma's brothers, Henry George Stebbins, became president of the New York Stock Exchange and of the Central Park Commission and served in Congress as a War Democrat; strongly musical, he headed the New York Academy of Music and helped launch the career of the singer CLARA LOUISE KELLOGG. Emma was reared in the Episcopal Church and in comfortable and cultured surroundings. As a child she was encouraged to express herself in verse and song as well as in the pictorial arts. Her early pictures of friends drew the attention of Henry Inman, then the leading portrait painter in New York, who gave her instruction in oil painting. Her work during her girlhood, it is said, included a manuscript volume of poetry, "A Book of Prayer," which she decorated with illuminations. She also produced watercolors, crayon portraits, and studies in oil from original paintings by other artists.

By 1843 Miss Stebbins had achieved sufficient recognition as a talented amateur to be elected an associate of the National Academy of Design in New York City. Her "Portrait of a Lady" was exhibited at the Pennsylvania Academy of the Fine Arts in 1845, her "John in the Wilderness" and "French Sweep Boy" in the exhibition of 1847. In 1855 she showed two crayon portraits in the annual exhibition of the National Academy. In 1857, having decided to devote herself to art, she went abroad to Rome. There for a time she continued to create crayon portraits, but her interest soon turned to sculpture.

Advised by the well-known English sculptor John Gibson, who had also given encouragement to HARRIET HOSMER, Emma Stebbins studied with Benjamin Paul Akers, a Maine-born sculptor, painter, and author then in Rome, and with Italian masters. Her earliest work was a statuette of the Biblical Joseph, represented in boyhood; this was followed by a statue of Columbus and one entitled "Satan Descending to Tempt Mankind." One of her first commissions came from the owner of a Pennsylvania coal mine, Richard Heckscher, for representations of "Industry" and "Commerce"; she completed the first of these in 1859. Her bronze statue of Horace Mann was installed in 1865 in front of the State House in Boston. Her numerous portrait figures and busts include one of her brother John Wilson Stebbins (in the New York Mercantile Library) and a bust of the actress CHARLOTTE CUSHMAN, made in 1859–60 at the request of R. D. Shepherd and presented by his daughter to the Handel and Haydn Society of Boston. Her most famous commission was "The Angel of the Waters," her sculptured figure for the Bethesda Fountain in Central Park in New York City; unveiled in May 1873, it was greatly admired by the public and critics.

Charlotte Cushman, whom Miss Stebbins met during her first winter in Rome, became her lifelong friend and companion. They returned to New York City in 1870 and spent much of the last years of Miss Cushman's life at her villa in Newport, R.I. After the actress' death in 1876 Emma Stebbins compiled her life and letters for publication. She herself died in New York City in 1882, of "phthisis," at the age of seventy-three. She was buried in Greenwood Cemetery, Brooklyn.

[Ralph S. and Robert L. Greenlee, *The Stebbins Genealogy* (1904), I, 496–97; *Nat. Cyc. Am. Biog.*, VIII, 292; Elizabeth F. Ellet, *Women Artists in All Ages and Countries* (1859), pp. 346– 49; Emma Stebbins, *Charlotte Cushman: Her Letters and Memories of Her Life* (1878); Clara Erskine Clement and Laurence Hutton, *Artists of the Nineteenth Century and Their Works* (1879); Phebe A. Hanaford, *Daughters of America* (1883), pp. 288–89; Henry T. Tuckerman, *Book of Artists* (1867); Lorado Taft, *The Hist. of Am. Sculpture* (1903). On Henry G. Stebbins, see *Biog. Directory Am. Cong.* (1961) and *N.Y. Times*, Dec. 11, 1881. Death record from Greenwood Cemetery. There are 14 letters by Emma Stebbins in the Anne Whitney Papers, Wellesley College Library.]

WILLIAM H. GERDTS

STEIN, Gertrude (Feb. 3, 1874–July 27, 1946), author, was born in Allegheny, Pa., the youngest of the seven children of Daniel and Amelia (Keyser) Stein, both of German-Jewish descent. Her grandfather Michael Stein was a merchant in the Bavarian village of Weikersgrubben. Her father and his four brothers emigrated to the United States in 1841 and settled in Baltimore, Md., where by 1843 they had founded Stein Brothers, a large clothing establishment. In 1862, after a family quarrel, Daniel Stein and his brother Solomon moved to Allegheny, a town just across the Ohio River from Pittsburgh. Daniel brought with him from Baltimore his bride, who in the next twelve years bore Michael, two children who died in infancy, Simon, Bertha, Leo, and Gertrude Stein.

Shortly after Gertrude's birth, Daniel Stein, having broken with Solomon and his wife, took his family to Austria—first to Gemünden, then to Vienna. Two years later, restless, he returned to America, leaving Amelia and the children in Vienna until he should find a position equal to his talents and energies. In 1878 Amelia moved her brood to Paris, where they lived for a year, and where Gertrude Stein, now four, first encountered the city that was ultimately to be her home for nearly forty years.

Daniel brought his family back to America in 1879, and after some searching about settled them in Oakland, Calif., where they lived until 1892. For four years of this time they owned a large old house on a ten-acre lot; and it was this house that was always to serve as the focus for Gertrude's recollections of her California girlhood. Here she and her brother Leo, who was from the first closer to her than her other siblings, set off frequently on long excursions; and here she read Shakespeare, Wordsworth, Scott, Burns, Smollett, Richardson, Fielding, Carlyle, and—more remarkably—many bound volumes of the *Congressional Record* and Lecky's formidable *Constitutional*

*History of England.* Michael was very much older than she, and already at Harvard; both Simon and Bertha were retarded; the Oakland schools were—to her—dull; so that Gertrude was forced to fall back on her reading and her wanderings about with Leo. Their mother was, to the two younger children, a nonentity, and when she died, in 1888, she was scarcely missed. Their father they revered but avoided, and were rather frankly relieved when he died three years later. Michael returned to Oakland, disposed of his father's business interests very satisfactorily, and arranged that his brothers and sisters should have a small independent income for life.

Bertha, Leo, and Gertrude returned to Baltimore in 1892, to live with their mother's sister, Fannie Bachrach. Leo, having begun his education at the University of California, transferred to Harvard; and in 1893 the nineteen-year-old Gertrude registered as a special student at the Harvard Annex, soon to become Radcliffe College. Feeling that she had already learned as much as necessary about literature, she divided her time between Santayana's courses in the American philosophers and William James' seminars in psychology. It would be impossible to exaggerate the influence of James on Gertrude Stein. His insistence on empirical procedures, his distrust of the "intellectual method," and most especially his new theory about the "stream of consciousness" were to dominate her entire literary career. Whenever she wrote, later, about the "continuous present," the "immediate existing," or the "including everything," one senses the presence of James. Though she was afterward to deny that she had the slightest interest in automatic writing, she did in fact publish an article in a psychological journal while at Radcliffe in which she recorded her experiments in "spontaneous automatic writing." In the main, though, Gertrude became a thoroughgoing Jamesian Pragmatist at Radcliffe, and remained such throughout her life. The unconscious and the intuition (even when James himself wrote about them) never concerned her.

In 1897 she set off for the Johns Hopkins University Medical School. (She received her A.B. magna cum laude from Radcliffe in 1898.) At Johns Hopkins she performed sometimes brilliantly, sometimes sloppily, until in her fourth year she lost interest, failed an important course, and left. Leo was by this time in Italy, absorbing "Culture" from the art critic Bernard Berenson; and in the spring of 1902 she joined him there. That summer they went to London, took a flat in Bloomsbury, and divided their time between making social contacts and reading at the British Museum. Gertrude did not like England (she recorded her depression at this time in her first book, *Q.E.D.*, published posthumously, in 1950, as *Things as They Are*) and returned to America. But Leo was now in Paris, where she joined him in October 1903.

Leo, hoping to become a painter, had rented a little two-story *pavillon* with a large atelier next to it in the courtyard of 27 rue de Fleurus. Gertrude moved in, and the two (joined occasionally by their brother Michael, who had by this time come with his wife, Sarah, and son, Allan, to live in Paris) soon began exploring art galleries in search of Cézannes to collect. The dealer Ambroise Vollard had cornered most of the Cézanne market, and so became their first important contact with a world they were both to inhabit for the rest of their lives. In a very short time the two had bought not only several Cézannes, but also more than a few paintings by Renoir, Daumier, Manet, Gauguin, Derain, Rousseau, Matisse, Braque, and—most importantly—Pablo Picasso, who was to become a lifelong friend of Gertrude. By the time she was thirty-two, Gertrude Stein was conducting Paris' most important salon: literally hundreds of well-known painters (and, later, writers), hangers-on, culture snobs, and publicity seekers visited her weekly, to see and be seen, and to inspect the ever-increasing collection of paintings that covered every wall of the house. In the midst of it all sat Gertrude Stein, like (as someone remarked) "a great Jewish Buddha," calmly authoritative, arbitrating—and imposing her own views upon—every manner of aesthetic dispute.

In later years Braque, Eugene Jolas, Matisse, André Salmon, and Tristan Tzara published jointly a *Testimony against Gertrude Stein* (1935), in which they denied her understanding of their work, of Cubism, and of painting in general. According to Braque, "Miss Stein understood nothing of what went on around her"; and Salmon echoed this condemnation: "I had thought, along with all our friends, that she had really understood things. It is evident that she understood nothing, except in a superficial way." But such strictures are probably too harsh. There is, in any case, no doubt that Gertrude and Leo saw very quickly the importance of Matisse and Picasso, to name only the most famous of their enthusiasms, and greatly accelerated the rise to fame of those painters. They understood enough, at least, of the new painting to know that it was of permanent significance; and they made sure that people came to 27 rue de Fleurus to see these disturbing new works. Indeed, there are those who feel that if Gertrude Stein is to be remembered at all, it is for her championing of abstract painting, and not for her writing or for her influence on other writers.

Be that as it may, it was as a writer that Gertrude Stein wished to be known. In 1905–06, as she sat for Picasso's portrait of her, she began to translate Flaubert's *Trois Contes*. Soon she had dropped Flaubert and had begun to write her own book. Originally called *Three Histories*, and later *Three Lives*, it was a genuine literary curiosity. Today these stories of the Good Anna, Melanctha, and the Gentle Lena seem almost tame, stylistically speaking, and are often cited as evidence that Gertrude Stein could, when she chose, write intelligibly. But in their own time they were judged almost incoherent: rambling, monotonous, affectedly repetitious, almost simpleminded. In fact they were very early specimens of stream of consciousness technique, yet vastly different from the techniques of, say, Proust and Joyce, in that she had no interest at all in investigating the depths of her characters and situations. In her own time Gertrude Stein was as single-mindedly insistent on the sovereignty of surfaces as Alain Robbe-Grillet was to be in the 1960's. She wished only to be accurate, to record with precision those aspects of life that one could see and hear.

Publishers were understandably not eager to encourage Gertrude Stein, and it was not until 1909 that the Grafton Press, a "vanity" house, brought out *Three Lives*. One volunteer for proofreading chores was Alice B. Toklas, freshly arrived from California. She soon became a constant visitor at 27 rue de Fleurus, and very quickly made herself indispensable to Gertrude—so much so that within a year she had become a permanent member of the household. She served Miss Stein for the rest of her life as confidante, typist, critic, and, finally, as nurse.

Miss Toklas' first typing chore was monumental: Gertrude's magnum opus, the unreadable *The Making of Americans*, a thousand-page history of every sort of American "who ever can or is or was or will be living," in "a space of time that is always filled with moving." Most of her admirers (like Ernest Hemingway, who was to be most helpful in arranging for the publication of the book, in 1925) thought *The Making of Americans* a masterpiece; but few could finish reading it. The book was not completed until 1911, but by 1909 Gertrude Stein had already begun a continuing series of "portraits" of friends and ac-

quaintances; and it was obvious in even the earliest of these that her notions of clarity were not those of everyone else. The first paragraph of Picasso's portrait, for instance, read: "One whom some were certainly following was one who was completely charming. One whom some were certainly following was one who was charming. One whom some were following was one who was completely charming. One whom some were following was one who was certainly completely charming." This was her attempt to employ the techniques of abstract painting in the writing of literature, and about all one can say for it is that repetition of lines and colors may succeed in painting, but that repetition of lines and words in writing has a very limited effectiveness, and ultimately bores. Gertrude Stein's passion for an abstract accuracy was directed not at the word, nor at the sentence, but at the paragraph. Words themselves were, she felt, trivial—a notion that is fatal to writers.

Next came *Tender Buttons*, first published in 1914, the work which was to make her, if not famous, at least notorious in her own country, and which led wags like Clifton Fadiman to call her "the Mama of Dada" (a movement which, incidentally, she abhorred). *Tender Buttons* was a collection of—what is one to call them?—aperçus, cameos, illuminations, prose poems, on such subjects as umbrellas, petticoats, cutlets, purses, boxes. Typical of these was "Eye Glasses": "A color in shaving, a saloon is well placed in the centre of an alley." If this is "art by subtraction," as Kenneth Burke called it, then one is inclined to sympathize with B. L. Reid, who felt that Gertrude Stein had subtracted so much—had so completely abdicated her responsibility to convey anything susceptible to understanding on any level—that there was no art left.

But Gertrude Stein was nothing if not sure of herself ("Einstein was the creative philosophic mind of the century and I have been the creative literary mind of the century"), and seldom again wavered in the direction of intelligibility. Critics like Edmund Wilson mistook her for a symbolist, performing the ultimate in noncommunicative suggestion. Others saw her as a genuine primitive, a naïf who used words as children do. But she was neither a symbolist—since for her the words meant only what they said, and nothing more—nor a primitive, since her writing was the product of a completely systematic and sophisticated aesthetic: what one might call the psychological theories of William James grafted onto the Cubist concepts of Picasso and Braque.

In 1912 Leo broke with his sister, more or

less amicably, and moved to Florence, taking with him all of their Renoirs, all but one of the Matisses, and most of the Cézannes. Gertrude retained all of the Picassos. She and Miss Toklas were in England, staying at the country home of the philosopher Alfred North Whitehead, when the war broke out in August 1914. After some delay they returned to Paris briefly, then went to Mallorca, where Gertrude worked on her first plays. In 1916 they returned to France and entered the war effort: Gertrude had a Ford motor van sent from America, learned to drive it, and then, in 1917, enlisted herself and Miss Toklas as an ambulance unit in the American Fund for French Wounded.

Paris after the war was different. Old friends like Apollinaire were dead, Cubism was passing out of vogue, and Americans were everywhere. Though Gertrude Stein began again to collect painters—Juan Gris was a favorite acquisition—this period in her life was marked by her association with writers like Sherwood Anderson, F. Scott Fitzgerald, Ezra Pound (whom she disliked, possibly in part because he was less susceptible than the others to her authoritarianism), and Ernest Hemingway. The young Hemingway began as an admirer ("Gertrude was always right"), and stated often how much he had learned about writing from her; but the two eventually drifted apart —especially after Gertrude, in *The Autobiography of Alice B. Toklas*, called Hemingway "yellow." Hemingway responded in kind by mocking her in several of his works: in *Green Hills of Africa*, when Hemingway's wife speaks to him about Gertrude ("She's just jealous and malicious. You should never have helped her"); in *For Whom the Bell Tolls*, when he allows Robert Jordan to say "An onion is an onion is an onion . . . and a stone is a stein is a rock is a boulder is a pebble"; and finally in *A Moveable Feast*, when he recounts an experience at 27 rue de Fleurus full of not-so-subtle hints about the nature of the relationship between the Misses Stein and Toklas. But Hemingway did learn much from Gertrude Stein, especially, according to John Malcolm Brinnin, "the value of skillfully maneuvered repetitions, the simple power of the declarative sentence, and the necessity for saturation in an attitude within which the writer can write as a possessed and still self-possessed being, rather than as a mere reporter or analyst" (*The Third Rose*, p. 257). And, after all, it was Gertrude Stein who gave him the tag about the Lost Generation, which he used to advantage in *The Sun Also Rises*.

In the spring of 1926 Gertrude Stein lectured at Cambridge and Oxford, with conspicuous success. Her audiences, which had come expecting to see and hear a literary freak, were impressed by her regal, no-nonsense manner, and by the plausibility of what she said. This lecture was to become her essay, *Composition as Explanation* (1926), perhaps the chief expression of her literary theories. She and Miss Toklas had been for some years spending their summers in the French town of Belley when, in 1928, they rented a house in the hamlet of Bilignin, some three kilometers away. For the next seventeen years they spent every summer and fall in Bilignin, with Gertrude writing prolifically, and entertaining all sorts of visitors, while Alice B. Toklas undertook the formation of the Plain Edition, which was to make a great deal of her friend's work available to the small public which actually read it. Gertrude Stein's first commercial success came in 1933 with the publication of *The Autobiography of Alice B. Toklas,* a highly entertaining tour de force in which Miss Toklas was made to tell about her life with Gertrude in a style which was immediately recognizable as Gertrude's own. The book is sometimes coy, sometimes vicious—but always clever, and an invaluable record of their life together, of their friends and enemies, and of *la vie bohème* as they saw it.

In 1933 Virgil Thomson persuaded Gertrude Stein to allow him to set to music her opera, *Four Saints in Three Acts* (the work that contains her famous "Pigeons in the grass alas" poem); and the following year it was performed, to acclaim, with an all-Negro cast in Hartford and in New York. On the heels of this success came many invitations to lecture in America, and in October of 1934 she and Miss Toklas sailed home. Gertrude was a celebrity now, and enjoyed being one. Her lectures were well received, students loved her, and writers and politicians schemed to be seen with her. In May 1935 the two returned to France, with Gertrude even more enthusiastically American than she had been before the trip. She described the whole experience in *Everybody's Autobiography* (1937).

Late in 1937 the two ladies moved from the rue de Fleurus to a new apartment, V rue Christine, in the Faubourg St. Germain, where they remained until the summer of 1939, when the outbreak of war caught them in Bilignin. They decided to sit out the Occupation in France rather than attempt to return to America; and this they did—first in Bilignin, and then in the town of Culoz, somewhat further up the Rhône. Gertrude Stein was in her mid-sixties by now, but still she wrote constantly. Notable from this period were *Paris France*

(1940), *Ida, A Novel* (1941), and *Wars I Have Seen* (1945), in which she gave her account of the Occupation. In December 1944 she and Miss Toklas returned to Paris, where they daily found themselves besieged by hundreds of American servicemen: V rue Christine had become a shrine, and they came as pilgrims to meet and talk with the comical old heroine that Gertrude Stein had become. Gertrude, ever patriotic, enjoyed this all immensely. *Brewsie and Willie* (1946) was her tribute to the G.I.

But she was now very ill. On July 19, 1946, she was admitted to the American Hospital at Neuilly-sur-Seine, suffering from an abdominal tumor in an advanced stage of malignancy. On July 27 she underwent surgery, but was too weakened to survive. She became conscious only long enough to ask those in the room with her: "What is the answer?" When no one spoke, she said: "In that case, what is the question?" Almost immediately after this she lapsed into a coma, and that evening she died. She was buried in the cemetery of Père-Lachaise in Paris. The legend on the marker above her grave reads simply: "Gertrude Stein, San Francisco." Alice B. Toklas, who died in 1967, was buried beside her.

When one considers the many paintings, photographs, and statues done of Gertrude Stein by such artists as Picasso, Francis Picabia, Man Ray, and Jo Davidson, one is struck by how unanimously they depict her as she must indeed have been: monolithic, energetic, and shrewd. For one of the most controversial and influential women of the century these were certainly appropriate qualities. Extremists of one sort see her as a charlatan; those of another sort, as a strange amalgam of Wise Child and Great Mother. More likely, Gertrude Stein was a very intelligent and very lucky woman, who was fortunate enough to step precisely into the center of the cultural life of her century, and clever enough to make herself indispensable to those at the center.

[The Am. Literature Collection of Yale Univ. is the chief repository for MSS., letters, diaries, notebooks, and general memorabilia pertaining to Gertrude Stein. The Univ. of Calif. at Berkeley possesses the diaries of her mother. The most valuable critical and biographical studies are the following: John Malcolm Brinnin, *The Third Rose* (1959); Frederick J. Hoffman, *Gertrude Stein* (Univ. of Minn. Pamphlets on Am. Writers, No. 10, 1961); Michael J. Hoffman, *The Development of Abstractionism in the Writings of Gertrude Stein* (1966); Bravig Imbs, *Confessions of Another Young Man* (1936); Rosalind Miller, *Gertrude Stein: Form and Intelligibility* (1949); Benjamin L. Reid, *Art by Subtraction: A Dissenting Opinion of Gertrude Stein* (1958); William C. Rogers, *When This You See, Remember Me* (1948); Elizabeth Sprigge, *Gertrude Stein: Her Life and Work* (1957); Allegra Stewart, *Gertrude Stein and the Present* (1967); Donald Sutherland, *Gertrude Stein* (1951). Of the many articles about Gertrude Stein, the following are most useful: Sherwood Anderson, "The Work of Gertrude Stein," *Little Rev.,* Spring 1922; Hilary Corke, "Reflections on a Great Stone Face," *Kenyon Rev.,* Summer 1961; Oliver Evans, "The Americanization of Gertrude Stein," *Prairie Schooner,* Spring 1948; James Feibleman, "The Comedy of Literature: Gertrude Stein," *In Praise of Comedy: A Study in Its Theory and Practice* (1939), pp. 236–41; George Haines, "Gertrude Stein and Composition," *Sewanee Rev.,* Summer 1949; Alfred Kazin, "From an Italian Journal," *Partisan Rev.,* May 1948, pp. 555–57; James Laughlin, "New Words for Old: Notes on Experimental Writing," *Story,* Dec. 1936, pp. 105, 107, 110; Katherine Anne Porter, "Gertrude Stein: A Self-Portrait," *Harper's,* Dec. 1947; Laura Riding, "The New Barbarism, and Gertrude Stein," *Transition,* June 1927; Aline B. Saarinen, "The Steins in Paris," *Am. Scholar,* Autumn 1958; Carl Van Vechten, "How to Read Gertrude Stein," *Trend* (Paris), Aug. 1914; Edmund Wilson, "Gertrude Stein," in his *Axel's Castle* (1931). The two principal bibliographical studies, now out of date, are: Robert B. Haas and Donald C. Gallup, *A Catalogue of the Published and Unpublished Writings of Gertrude Stein* (1941), and Julian Sawyer, *Gertrude Stein: A Bibliog.* (1940). Also bibliographically useful are Donald C. Gallup, "The Gertrude Stein Collection," *Yale Univ. Library Gazette,* Oct. 1947; and Julian Sawyer, "Gertrude Stein: A Checklist of Critical and Miscellaneous Writings about Her Work, Life, and Personality from 1913 to 1947," *Bull. of Bibliog.,* Jan.–Apr. 1948.]

DOUGLAS DAY

**STEPHENS, Alice Barber** (July 1, 1858–July 13, 1932), illustrator, was born on a farm near Salem, N.J., the eighth of nine children of Samuel Clayton Barber and his wife, Mary Owen. Her paternal grandfather, William Barber, was an English Quaker who settled in Princeton, N.J.; her mother's family had come from Wales to Wading River, Long Island, before the American Revolution. From childhood Alice was seldom without a pencil in her hand, and when her family moved to Philadelphia, she took advantage of the opportunity, while completing her public school education, to attend the Philadelphia School of Design for Women. There she learned the art of wood engraving and at the age of fifteen began supporting herself. One of her important early commissions was a series depicting prominent women for the Philadelphia periodical *Woman's Words;* she also did engravings for *Scribner's Monthly* and *Harper's Weekly.*

Her creative instincts, however, soon sought wider scope. For several winters, beginning in 1876, she studied at the Pennsylvania Academy of the Fine Arts, where Thomas Eakins was then director. Not long afterward, she turned from wood engraving to book and magazine illustrating, using a wide variety of media: black-and-white oils, wash, charcoal, full-color oils, and watercolors. The vigor and simplicity of her style, combined with conscientious attention to detail, won her commissions for many magazines, including the Harper publications and *Century, Cosmopolitan,* and *Frank Leslie's Weekly.* The winter of 1886–87 she spent in Europe, studying in Paris at the Académie Julian and the school of Filippo Colarossi and sketching in Italy; she exhibited a pastel study and an engraving at the Paris Salon of 1887. After her return she became a regular illustrator for the *Ladies' Home Journal* and for the publishers Houghton Mifflin and Thomas Y. Crowell. For these and other publishers she illustrated books of LOUISA MAY ALCOTT, Bret Harte, Sir Arthur Conan Doyle, and MARGARET DELAND, and a special edition of Longfellow's *The Courtship of Miles Standish.*

Alice Barber was married in June 1890 to Charles Hallowell Stephens, an instructor at the Pennsylvania Academy who had begun his studies there at the same time she did. They had one son, Daniel Owen (born in 1893). During the decade following her marriage Mrs. Stephens was at the peak of her career. Besides her work as an illustrator, for which she maintained a studio on Chestnut Street in Philadelphia, she did some painting in oil; the Pennsylvania Academy awarded her the Mary Smith Prize in 1890 for her "Portrait of a Boy." In 1895 she won a medal at the Atlanta Exposition and in 1899 a gold medal at an exhibition of women's work held at Earl's Court, London, the latter for her drawings for George Eliot's *Middlemarch* and paintings for Maria Mulock Craik's *John Halifax, Gentleman.* A year later she received a bronze medal at the Paris Exposition. She prepared the illustrations for a special two-volume edition of Hawthorne's *The Marble Faun* published in 1900.

Impaired health forced Mrs. Stephens to turn down an invitation in 1899 to teach at the Pennsylvania Academy of the Fine Arts, but a fifteen-month sojourn abroad (1901–02) restored her strength. Upon her return she settled with her husband and son in Rose Valley, Pa., in a stone barn remodeled into a studio and house and named Thunder Bird. For some years she taught at the Philadelphia

School of Design for Women, and in 1904 she served on the fine arts jury for the Louisiana Purchase Exposition at St. Louis. The illustrations of her last period, which ended in 1926, were usually wash, or charcoal with a wash of one color, often varying shades of yellow, ochre, or orange. For her own enjoyment she continued to paint landscapes and a few portraits of Quakers and Pennsylvania Germans. There was a retrospective exhibition of her work in 1929 in the Plastic Club in Philadelphia, of which she was a founder.

Mrs. Stephens died at the age of seventy-four at Rose Valley, following a paralytic stroke. She was buried in West Laurel Hill Cemetery, Bala-Cynwyd, Pa. A contemporary critic, surveying the work of women illustrators, singled out Alice Barber Stephens and MARY HALLOCK FOOTE as especially distinguished for their breadth and vigor (Frank Weitenkampf, *American Graphic Art*, 1912, p. 219).

[A collection of Mrs. Stephens' original drawings is in the Art and Print Division of the Library of Congress. The Art Room of the N.Y. Public Library has a scrapbook of her illustrations from all periods. For a biographical account with an excellent portrait, see *Nat. Cyc. Am. Biog.,* XXIII, 278–79. Magazine articles on her work appeared in *Woman's Progress,* Nov. 1893; *Brush and Pencil,* Sept. 1900 (by F. B. Sheafer); *Twentieth Century Home,* Dec. 1904; *Outlook,* Oct. 1, 1904 (p. 273); and Phila. *Press,* Sept. 26, 1915. See also *Woman's Who's Who of America,* 1914–15; *Who Was Who in America,* vol. I (1942); and obituaries in *Phila. Evening Bull.,* July 14, 1932, and *Art News,* Aug. 13, 1932.]

AGNES ADDISON GILCHRIST

**STEPHENS, Ann Sophia** (Mar. 30, 1810– Aug. 20, 1886), popular author, was born in Humphreysville (later Seymour), Conn., the third daughter and third of ten children of John and Ann (Wrigley) Winterbotham, emigrants from England. Her father had come from Manchester in 1806 at the invitation of the Connecticut poet and patriot Col. David Humphreys to superintend the latter's new woolen mill and had soon become a partner in the enterprise. Her mother died when Ann was young, and she was brought up by her stepmother, her mother's sister Rachel. She was educated at a local dame school and in South Britain, Conn. "I have no idea," she wrote later, "how my literary tastes originated. My father was very intelligent and a great reader, but he took no pains to influence me, and long before I knew what authorship was, I had made up my mind to write stories and make books" (*Frank Leslie's Illustrated Newspaper,*

Aug. 16, 1856). In 1831 she was married to Edward Stephens, a young merchant of Plymouth, Mass., and moved with him to Portland, Maine. There she edited and contributed extensively to the *Portland Magazine*, a literary monthly published by her husband (October 1834–June 1836). In its columns first appeared her poem "The Polish Boy," long popular as a "recitation" in an elocutionary age.

In 1837 the Stephenses moved to New York City, where Edward secured a clerkship in the customhouse and Ann became associate editor of the *Ladies' Companion*, the first of several popular women's magazines with which she was to be connected. In December 1841 she joined the staff of *Graham's Magazine*, of which Edgar Allan Poe was at that time an editor. In addition she contributed to the *Columbian Lady's and Gentleman's Magazine*, the *Ladies' Wreath*, and *Frank Leslie's Ladies Gazette of Fashion*, which she also edited. Her longest association, however, was with *Peterson's Magazine*, the closest competitor of *Godey's Lady's Book;* in its early years (1842–53) she was listed as co-editor, and for nearly forty years she was a voluminous contributor, particularly of serials. In 1856 she began her own magazine, *Mrs. Stephens' Illustrated New Monthly* (published by her husband), but it was merged in 1858 with *Peterson's*. Though her husband had earlier published her *High Life in New York* (1843)—humorous sketches in the Down East tradition, ostensibly by "Jonathan Slick"—her first full-length clothbound novel was *Fashion and Famine* (1854), a domestic tale of city life, which was dramatized for the stage. Over the years more than twenty-five of her historical romances and domestic novels were serialized in *Peterson's Magazine* and later issued in book form.

In 1860 Irwin P. Beadle & Company paid Mrs. Stephens $250 for the right to reprint one of her early serials as the first in its series of dime novels. *Malaeska: The Indian Wife of the White Hunter*, the gaudy but sad and moral tale of an Indian princess wed to a white frontiersman, became a best seller. She followed it with six other Beadle romances between 1860 and 1864: *Myra, the Child of Adoption*, based upon the celebrated lawsuit of Mrs. MYRA CLARK GAINES; two tales of the Far West; and three Indian romances.

Tall, stout, and stately, Mrs. Stephens was a leading light in New York literary circles from the 1840's to the 1870's. Literary and political notables flocked to her receptions; she seemed determined to know all celebrities. Though she had two children, Ann, born in

1841, and Edward, in 1845, domestic responsibilities did not impede her career. Indeed, she seems to have been the financial mainstay of the family. Her husband, whom she left with the children for two years while she toured abroad (1850–52), supplemented his customhouse clerkship with intermittent publishing and newspaper ventures, only to be demoted from his government post a few years before his death in 1862.

During the Civil War Mrs. Stephens served as vice-president of the Ladies National Covenant, a society for the "suppression of extravagance," and compiled a *Pictorial History of the War for the Union* (1863). After the war her novels remained popular; a fourteen-volume uniform edition of her works was published in 1869, and a new twenty-three-volume edition was in the press at the time of her death in 1886. She died at seventy-six of nephritis at Newport, R.I., where she was visiting Charles J. Peterson, her friend and publisher. An Episcopal rector officiated at her funeral, and she was buried in Greenwood Cemetery, Brooklyn.

During an era when a great number of women found writing novels a socially acceptable and lucrative source of needed income, Mrs. Stephens followed the trend of her day in turning out domestic-sentimental tales and historical romances. The sales of her *Malaeska*, *Fashion and Famine*, and *The Old Homestead* (1855) rivaled those of such American novelists as Mrs. E. D. E. N. SOUTHWORTH and AUGUSTA JANE EVANS WILSON. In some respects, however, she surpassed her contemporaries. She was versatile and especially adept at the popular serial form; and her style, though florid, was perhaps more vigorous and not quite so verbose as that of her compeers. She was particularly skillful in combining passion-filled heroes and strong sensational plots with a decorous moral tone, and her narrative powers, especially in recounting violent events, were eminently suited to the fast-paced dime novels, to which she gave a significant impetus.

[Mrs. Stephens' birth date, usually given as 1813, is established as 1810 by her death record (City Clerk, Newport, R.I.). Scattered letters by her may be found at the Boston Public Library, Brown Univ. Library, Conn. Hist. Soc., Hist. Soc. of Pa., Huntington Library, and N.-Y. Hist. Soc.; the N.Y. Public Library has her manuscript scrapbook. For details of her life and work, see James A. Eastman, "Ann Sophia Stephens" (master's essay, Columbia Univ., 1952); Samuel Orcutt and Ambrose Beardsley, *The Hist. of the Old Town of Derby, Conn.* (1880); William C. Sharpe, *Hist. of Seymour, Conn.* (1879); Hollis A. Campbell, William C. Sharpe, and Frank G. Bassett, *Seymour,*

*Past and Present* (1902); William W. Winterbotham, *Recollections* (William W. Woodside, ed., 1950); Edgar Allan Poe, "The Literati of N.Y.," *Godey's Lady's Book*, July 1846; Albert Johannsen, *The House of Beadle and Adams* (1950); *Publishers' Weekly*, Aug. 28, 1886. See also Madeleine B. Stern, *We the Women* (1963), chap. ii.]

MADELEINE B. STERN

**STEPHENS, Kate** (Feb. 27, 1853–May 10, 1938), university professor, author, and editor, was born in Moravia, N.Y., the third of five children of Nelson Timothy Stephens, a lawyer, and Elizabeth (Rathbone) Stephens. The family moved to Lawrence, Kans., in 1868 and prospered there. Judge Stephens, as he became, was the major influence in his daughter Kate's life; he supervised her reading, exchanged thoughts with her on nature and life, and was a close companion.

She entered the junior preparatory class of the University of Kansas at the age of fifteen and graduated from the regular college course as valedictorian in 1875. In 1878 she received an M.A. in Greek. Meanwhile, however, she had lived through her greatest personal experience. Byron Caldwell Smith had joined the university staff in 1872 as a brilliant young instructor in Greek, rising the next year to full professor. In 1874 he and Miss Stephens became engaged. Illness, however, forced him to take a leave of absence, and his liberal religious views lost him his professorship; before they could be married he died in Colorado at the age of twenty-seven (May 4, 1877). Years later, Miss Stephens published Smith's love letters to her under the title *The Professor's Love-Life: Letters of Ronsby Maldclewith* (1919), which was subsequently republished, with names more forthrightly presented, as *The Love-Life of Byron Caldwell Smith* (1930).

Upon receiving her master's degree Miss Stephens became assistant professor in charge of Greek language and literature at the University of Kansas and in 1879 full professor. She was reportedly an excellent teacher, like Smith inspiring rather than pedantic. But her health deteriorated, as overwork and nervous tension were aggravated by further personal losses (her mother became an invalid and, in 1884, her father died); her imperiousness and pantheistic views roused opposition, and in 1885 Kate Stephens was dismissed from the university. Maintaining that her conduct and outlook would have been tolerated in a man, she became an active and eloquent feminist.

Moving with her mother to Cambridge, Mass., in the fall of 1885, she planned a life of study and travel. But financial losses about 1890 forced her to undertake editorial labors

for D. C. Heath & Company. As junior editor she prepared a series of readers for children. When the senior editor, Charles Eliot Norton, backed by the publishers, attempted to assume sole credit, she defended her position with spirit; later the quarrel inspired one of her controversial works: *A Curious History in Book Editing* (1927). In 1894 she moved to New York City, where she did editorial work for a number of publishers and maintained a constant stream of correspondence, magazine articles, book reviews, and letters to the newspapers. She saw few people, and those mostly at her club, the Pen and Brush. Active on numerous committees, she earned a War and Navy citation for her World War I work at the New York War Camp Community Service.

Miss Stephens' nonpolemical writings were varied and informative, reflecting a studious and thoughtful temperament, though lacking any trace of humor. *American Thumb-Prints: Mettle of Our Men and Women* (1905) dealt with early Kansas and discrimination against women in business, among other topics. *A Woman's Heart* (1906)—later republished as *Pillars of Smoke*—was fiction in the form of epistles, chiefly notable for revealing her anti-Catholic bias. *Workfellows in Social Progression* (1916) emphasized her feminist predilections, as in her essay which protested against the use of the word "female" in discussing women. *The Greek Spirit* (1914) enthusiastically read the virtues of American democracy into the ancient civilization. *Delphic Kansas* (1911) and *Life at Laurel Town in Anglo-Saxon Kansas* (1920) saluted her well-remembered homeland.

More memorable were her polemical writings, which had a spare and direct quality. A belief that her father had been deprived of credit for the founding of the University of Kansas law school brought out her most creative qualities, as in *Truths Back of the Uncle Jimmy Myth in a State University in the Middle West* (1924), which challenged the title to greatness of Dr. James Green, dean of the law school—and her brother-in-law. Her most notable campaign, however, involved Frank Harris, the erratic Irish-American editor and author, fin de siècle friend of Max Beerbohm, Oscar Wilde, and George Bernard Shaw. As a young man, Harris had lived in Lawrence for several years and briefly attended the university. Back in America during World War I, he made contact with Miss Stephens, whom he had scarcely known in Kansas, and solicited her aid in drawing a "portrait" of Byron Caldwell Smith. In the first volume of his notorious autobiography, *My Life and Loves* (1922), he presented a version of Smith, of other Lawrence personages, and of Miss Stephens herself which was irresponsible and mendacious. Years of earnest effort enabled her to prepare, and herself publish, the notable *Lies and Libels of Frank Harris* (1929), edited by Gerrit and Mary Caldwell Smith, with arguments by herself.

Miss Stephens returned to live in Lawrence in 1935, at the age of eighty-two. Having suffered ill health through much of her adult life, in old age she was hale and alert. She died in 1938 at the home of a niece in Concordia, Kans., two months after suffering a cerebral hemorrhage, and was buried in the Stephens family plot at Oak Hill Cemetery, Lawrence. Her entire estate of $30,000 was willed to the University of Kansas, part of the income providing for the Judge Stephens Lectureship of the School of Law.

[Miss Stephens' career is thoughtfully assayed in Margaret Habein, "Kate Stephens: A Study of Her Life and Writings" (Ph.D. thesis, Univ. of Kans., 1952); its bibliography includes particulars of her extensive writings, which are heavily laden with details of her life and thoughts. The Univ. of Kans. has her private papers and scrapbooks, including a manuscript study of Byron Caldwell Smith and Miss Stephens by A. I. Tobin. Tobin's book, prepared with Elmer Gertz, *Frank Harris: A Study in Black and White* (1931), treats the Smith-Stephens episode fearlessly, but with a sense of Harris' other qualities which Miss Stephens could not perceive. Miss Stephens is portrayed as "May Hutchins" in Harris' story "Gulmore, the Boss," published in *Elder Conklin and Other Stories* (1894). See also *Who Was Who in America*, vol. I (1942); *N.Y. Times*, May 13, 1938; and article on Byron Caldwell Smith in *Dict. Am. Biog.*]

LOUIS FILLER

STERN, Frances (July 3, 1873–Dec. 23, 1947), social worker and dietitian, was born in Boston, Mass., the fourth daughter and last of the seven children of Louis Stern, a dealer in boots and shoes, and Caroline (Oppenheimer) Stern. Her parents had been born in Rheinfals, Germany, her mother at Bleekastl and her father at Alberseveiler. Their Jewish orthodoxy and their sense of communal obligation early inculcated in Frances a sense of duty to her fellow men. As a young girl, with only a grammar school education, she taught at Mrs. Lina (Frank) Hecht's Sunday school of Congregation Beth Israel in Boston and, beginning in 1890, at the newly established Hebrew Industrial School in the North End. The sight of "little children with sad, pinched faces . . . wretchedly and inade-

quately clothed" set the course of her career. In 1895, with her friend Isabel Hyams, she rented the first floor and basement of a tenement in Boston's South End and opened the Louisa Alcott Club to teach homemaking to the young of this slum neighborhood. Soon realizing that the mere "desire for social betterment was not sufficient," she enrolled for further training in the Garland Kindergarten Training School in Boston, from which she graduated in 1897.

The milestone in her life, the "happy chance, with unforeseen developments," was her association with the distinguished ELLEN H. RICHARDS, instructor in sanitary chemistry at the Massachusetts Institute of Technology and a founder of the profession of home economics, with whom Miss Hyams had studied. Miss Stern's service with Mrs. Richards, as secretary and research assistant, stimulated her desire for further scientific knowledge about the relation of food to sociological problems, and toward this end she took courses at M.I.T. in food chemistry and sanitation in 1909, 1911, and 1912. After Ellen Richards' death in 1911 she undertook, the next year, to develop a visiting housekeeping program for the Boston Association for the Relief and Control of Tuberculosis, and, somewhat later, a similar program for the Boston Provident Association. From 1912 to 1915 she served as industrial health inspector for the State Board of Labor and Industries. Up to this point, she later recollected, she "had known the child in school, the mother in the home." Her experience with "the father in industry" led her to hope that a knowledge of proper diet could mitigate some of the illnesses and hardships of workers.

In 1917 Miss Stern published, with Gertrude T. Spitz, *Food for the Worker*, "to show the need for the unification of science, social work, income and nutrition." By then she had a clear vision of the need for a center in the community "where each member of the family unit would be given expert food guidance correlated with his medical treatment and with the needs of his economic and social life." Her work brought her into contact with Dr. Michael Davis, director of the Boston Dispensary, at whose request she established a Food Clinic there in 1918.

The war, however, drew her almost at once to Washington, where she worked as a member of the Division of Home Conservation of the United States Food Administration and, in the Department of Agriculture, as an investigator of the adequacy of food for the industrial worker. In 1918 she went to France for the

American Red Cross and remained as head worker for the Child and Family Welfare Association in Paris. Before coming back to the United States in 1922, she studied economics and politics as a special student at the London School of Economics.

On returning to the United States she was prepared to carry on her major lifework, the Boston Dispensary Food Clinic. Here, in a homelike setting, furnished with colorful artifacts attractive to its Russian, Italian, and Syrian clientele, she began to give outpatients individual food guidance to implement medical treatment, working out diets featuring low-cost national dishes and explaining them with a variety of visual aids. Here, too, through a Nutrition Education Department which she set up as early as 1925, she began to train American and foreign doctors, dentists, social workers, and nurses in dietetics and to explore through scientific research her intuitive insight into the impact of environmental factors on personality and health.

Beautiful and vivacious, blond and blue-eyed, Frances Stern liked elegant clothing and attractive surroundings and enjoyed a host of friends. Early in the century, when her parents had died and she had become responsible for the care of an invalid brother, she made her home a center to which came students and young business and professional people to discuss ways of improving the world about them. Always she dealt with problems both idealistically and realistically. In 1914, as a member of the Welfare Committee of the Federated Jewish Charities, she successfully urged that organization to replace old-fashioned practices with "social, preventive and charitable work" along modern lines and to subordinate factional differences to "the future welfare of the community." Her abiding concern for the community and for the individual in it tempered her faith in the ability of science alone to achieve "a varied dietary of sufficient nutritious food at the lowest possible cost." In the last analysis, she insisted, "an adequate wage or income . . . is the only economic basis on which to meet the requirements of life."

Miss Stern's busy life encompassed membership on the boards of various educational and philanthropic organizations. She was active in the American Public Health Association, the American Home Economics Association, and especially in the American Dietetic Association, of which she was one of the early members (1922) as well as the first chairman of its Social Service Section. At one time or another she taught nutrition or dietetics at the Simmons College School of Social Work, Tufts

College Medical School, Massachusetts Institute of Technology, and the State Teachers College at Framingham.

Miss Stern died at her home in Newton, Mass., in 1947 of congestive heart disease, an illness that had incapacitated her physically but had left her alert and involved to the very end in the management of the food clinic. A memorial service was held at Temple Israel, Boston, and her ashes were placed in the Chapel of Peace at the city's Forest Hills Cemetery. Her clinic, in 1943 renamed in her honor the Frances Stern Food Clinic, has since become the Frances Stern Nutrition Center.

[Sketches of Miss Stern's life appear in Barbara M. Solomon, *Pioneers in Service* (1956); in the *Boston Globe*, Dec. 25, 1947; and (by Mary Pfaffman) in the *Jour. of the Am. Dietetic Assoc.*, Feb. 1948. She also published an account of her own career, "Dietetics and the Food Clinic Development," in *Nutrition* (Quaker Oats Co.), Sept.–Oct. 1941. Her other books are: *Food and Your Body: Talks with Children* (with Mary Pfaffman, 1932), revised under the title *How to Teach Nutrition to Children* (1942); *Applied Dietetics* (1936); and, with Helen Rosenthal and Dr. Joseph Rosenthal, *Diabetic Care in Pictures* (1946). She was a frequent contributor to the *Jour. of the Am. Dietetic Assoc.* and *Mental Hygiene*. Birth and death records from Mass. Registrar of Vital Statistics; father's occupation from city directories.]

MARY F. HANDLIN

**STETSON, Augusta Emma Simmons** (Oct. 12, 1842–Oct. 12, 1928), Christian Science leader, was born in Waldoboro, Maine, the daughter of Peabody and Salome (Sprague) Simmons. She was descended from Pilgrim stock, the first American Simmons (Symonds) having come to Plymouth in 1621. In her infancy her parents moved from Waldoboro to nearby Damariscotta, where her father worked as a carpenter and architect. Notably religious, they were members of the local Methodist church, where Augusta, an accomplished musician, served as organist at the early age of fourteen. She attended the Damariscotta High School and Lincoln Academy, New Castle, Maine, excelling in the field of public speaking.

In 1864 she was married to Capt. Frederick J. Stetson, a Civil War veteran. The marriage was childless. Entering his father's shipbuilding business, Stetson moved with his wife to London, England, after which they spent some years in Bombay, India, and Akyab, British Burma. Plagued, however, by chronic ill health dating from his wartime incarceration in Libby Prison, Stetson retired from business at the age of thirty-one and returned with his wife to Boston, where both resided with her parents. To support herself and her husband, Mrs. Stetson enrolled at the Blish School of Oratory in 1882, intending to become a public lecturer.

The decisive turn in her career came early in 1884 when she attended a lecture on Christian Science by MARY BAKER EDDY. Mrs. Eddy, sensing her possibilities for leadership, persuaded Mrs. Stetson to become one of her students. After graduation from the three-week course at Mrs. Eddy's Massachusetts Metaphysical College in November 1884, Augusta Stetson went to Maine to practice her new faith. In letters to the *Christian Science Journal,* she was soon reporting a number of phenomenal healings, including broken bones, cancer, diphtheria, and tuberculosis. Impressed by her pupil's success and dynamic personality, Mrs. Eddy first appointed Mrs. Stetson one of the five preachers in her own Boston pulpit and then, in November 1886, asked her to go to New York City, where Christian Science work had previously been started but remained totally unorganized. Mrs. Stetson hesitated to leave her family and friends, but finally consented.

On Feb. 3, 1888, a group of seventeen persons in New York incorporated themselves as a Christian Science church and elected Mrs. Stetson their preacher. She was formally ordained pastor of First Church of Christ, Scientist, New York City, in October 1890, with the title of "Reverend" (after 1895, First Reader). In 1891 she organized the New York City Christian Science Institute, where she trained a cadre of practitioners who not only treated patients but also formed a core of unshakable support within the congregation. About 1899, with the new work well established, Mrs. Stetson brought her invalid husband, now suffering from rheumatism, to New York, where he resided until his death in 1901 from cerebral apoplexy.

As membership in First Church increased, the worshipers moved from its initial meeting hall over a drugstore to a succession of larger quarters until the need for a building of their own became apparent. The location chosen was 96th Street and Central Park West. A massive granite edifice was then built at a cost of more than a million dollars. Dedicated on Nov. 29, 1903, it was even larger than the Mother Church in Boston. The following year an adjoining home was built and luxuriously furnished for Mrs. Stetson at a cost of $100,-000. To her, such opulence was a demonstration of Christian Science, which she believed should find expression in wealth and beauty.

She gravitated toward the wealthy and the fashionable, and they in turn seemed attracted to her. Tall and stately, dark-haired and elegantly dressed, Augusta Stetson made a striking appearance before an audience. A gifted speaker, she delivered her sermons in a "deep, mellow intonation."

Her success as a leader gave rise to rumors that she desired to supplant Mrs. Eddy. Though she disclaimed all such reports, the Board of Directors of the Mother Church in Boston became increasingly alarmed at her mounting personal following and evidently conveyed its concern to Mrs. Eddy, now in retirement in Concord, N.H. In a ruling of 1902 thought to have been directed in part at Mrs. Stetson, Mrs. Eddy limited the tenure of all Christian Science readers to three years. Though obediently resigning her official post, Mrs. Stetson retained her dominant position at First Church. In 1908, only a direct plea from Mrs. Eddy persuaded Mrs. Stetson to abandon her plans for building a large branch of her church, in contravention of the prevailing practice of having all local churches linked only with the Mother Church.

Early in 1909 the Christian Science Board of Directors, under instructions from Mrs. Eddy, began an investigation of conditions in New York, particularly of the adulation heaped upon Mrs. Stetson by her inner circle of practitioners. Matters came to a head that autumn when the First Reader in the New York church laid before the Boston leaders evidence showing that Mrs. Stetson had carried certain Christian Science tenets to questionable lengths. It was charged that she taught her practitioners that sex and procreation were evil, that one's "real," or spiritual, self might deny what one's "human" self had said and done (in a 1901 legacy suit, it was revealed, Mrs. Stetson and several of her followers had knowingly lied under oath), and that, in the words of the Board's later findings, she had attempted "to control and to injure persons by mental means."

The Board of Directors, after calling various practitioners and officials of the New York church to Boston for questioning, in September 1909 revoked Mrs. Stetson's license as a Christian Science teacher and practitioner. Two months later, after she herself had been called before the Board, she was, by Mrs. Eddy's express wishes, dropped from membership. The deeply divided New York congregation, decisively swayed by a written appeal from Mrs. Eddy, accepted Mrs. Stetson's resignation, voted out the trustees who had supported her, and expelled fifteen of her practitioners.

Retaining her title as principal of the New

York Christian Science Institute, Mrs. Stetson continued to instruct students and to live in her home next door to First Church. She remained unwavering in her loyalty to Mrs. Eddy, who, she felt, was simply testing her faithfulness and would soon come to her rescue and reinstate her. As she waited in vain, Mrs. Stetson began to interpret her expulsion as a victory, an experience she had been forced to undergo as preparation for her role in establishing a wholly spiritual form of Christian Science, independent of material organization, which she sometimes called the "Church Triumphant." When Mary Baker Eddy died in 1910, Mrs. Stetson did not, as some had anticipated, step forward as her successor, but she did proclaim that Mrs. Eddy would return to life, even as Christ had arisen, a prediction she was to repeat as late as 1927, despite disclaimers from the Christian Science Board of Directors.

Loyally supported by a large body of students throughout the country, she now undertook an energetic campaign to spread her concept of Christian Science, while pointing out the "spiritual decline" of the Mother Church in Boston. Between 1912 and 1917 her students gave periodic receptions at New York hotels, where as many as eight hundred people gathered to hear readings from the Bible and Mrs. Eddy's works and an address by Mrs. Stetson. A series of pamphlets setting forth her views of the true Christian Science and attacking the Mother Church was followed by a thick volume of *Reminiscences, Sermons, and Correspondence* (1913) and, the next year, by *Vital Issues in Christian Science,* in which she reviewed the whole controversy.

Mrs. Stetson believed that "spiritual music" was a mighty power with which to combat "animality," and in 1918, inspired by the wartime movement for community singing, she founded the Choral Society of the New York City Christian Science Institute. Until 1926 this group of three hundred voices gave highly successful annual concerts at the Metropolitan Opera House, with Mrs. Stetson, who attended all rehearsals, seated on the stage. A new patriotic anthem, "Our America," for which she wrote the music and one of her students the words, was widely sung during the war years. Then and later Mrs. Stetson vigorously attacked "The Star-Spangled Banner" as unChristian and anti-British.

In 1920 she undertook a spectacular newspaper advertising campaign, financed by wealthy followers, to promote her religious views, beginning with the publication of four full pages of Mrs. Eddy's letters to her in the *New York Tribune.* Her major work, *Sermons Which Spiritually Interpret the Scriptures and Other Writings on Christian Science,* was published in 1924. That year she supported the publication of a short-lived magazine, the *American Standard,* written mostly by her students, whose stated purpose was to guard and foster Nordic supremacy in America. Its program merged with that of a radio station purchased for her by a student in 1925, over which, five times a week, she talked and read from the Bible and Mrs. Eddy's works. The remainder of station time was devoted to broadcasts of Christian Science music and propaganda for "the Protestant principle of traditional Americanism," which presented the Declaration of Independence, the Constitution, and the Monroe Doctrine as divinely inspired weapons against Catholicism.

Active until the summer of 1928, Augusta Stetson died that October of "general dropsy" (edema) at the age of eighty-six, at the home of a nephew in Rochester, N.Y. Her cremated remains were interred at Damariscotta, Maine. A dwindling band of friends and students sought to carry on until the day when both she and Mrs. Eddy should return in a final triumph over death and the material world.

[Altman K Swihart, *Since Mrs. Eddy* (1931), based on the extensive Stetson collection at the Union Theological Seminary in N.Y. City, contains a full bibliography. See also Ernest Sutherland Bates and John V. Dittemore, *Mary Baker Eddy* (1932); *Who Was Who in America,* vol. I (1942); *Nat. Cyc. Am. Biog.,* XVIII, 400–01; obituary in *N.Y. Times,* Oct. 13, 1928; death record of Mrs. Stetson (N.Y. State Dept. of Health), which gives her date of birth, and of her husband (N.Y. City Dept. of Health).]

ALTMAN K SWIHART

**STETSON, Charlotte Perkins.** *See* GILMAN, Charlotte Anna Perkins Stetson.

**STETTHEIMER, Florine** (Aug. 19, 1871– May 11, 1944), painter, central figure in an important art salon, was born in Rochester, N.Y., the fourth of five children and third daughter of Joseph and Rosetta (Walter) Stettheimer. Both parents came of prominent German-Jewish families. The father, a banker, left his family before the children were grown. The two eldest were to marry: Walter (whose daughter became the wife of Julius Ochs Adler, publisher of the *New York Times*) and Stella (whose son was the Hollywood producer Walter Wanger). Florine, however, with her sisters Carrie and Ettie soon formed an independent virgin cult, securely immured with their mother in an epicurean way of life. Educated by private tutors, while still adolescent they felt themselves especially "creative." Ettie wanted to write novels, which ultimately she did, under a pseudonym, "Henrie Waste"; Florine wanted to paint. Beginning in the mid-1890's she studied in New York with Kenyon Cox and Robert Henri, and later, while the Stettheimers, to conserve their resources, were living abroad, under teachers in Munich, Stuttgart, and Berlin.

World War I ended their travels among European art scenes and sent them speeding patriotically back to reestablish their home in New York. (Florine, instinctively fond of personal and aesthetic cults, adored George Washington, who rivaled Apollo in the pantheon of her idols.) The moment was altogether a crucial one for her. Very personal and proud, steeped in cultural traditions but with a taste for the unconventional, she was, behind a bland surface of high propriety, remarkably daring. She, Carrie, and Ettie now decided to lead a life of supreme leisure, half centered upon artistic pleasures, half upon artistic work. The Wall Street firm of Alfred A. Cook shrewdly handled the modest fortune remaining to them and saved it from disaster in the stock market crash of 1929.

Thus came about the Stettheimers' art salon, which was legendary in New York even in the century's teens and drew into its orbit such distinguished artists as Marcel Duchamp, Gaston Lachaise, Elie Nadelman, Georgia O'Keeffe, and (later) Pavel Tchelitchew, such authors as H. L. Mencken, Avery Hopwood, Sherwood Anderson, Joseph Hergesheimer, and Carl Van Vechten, such art critics as Leo Stein, Paul Rosenfeld, and Henry McBride. Nothing could be more serious, more haut monde, than these artistic-social drawing rooms. Yet the social strictness was leavened by an ingrained wit and humor, especially in Florine, and by the militant eccentricity of the sisters in keeping to a style of life as well as of clothes and decor which tended conspicuously, as the 1920's passed, to "date" them. They were loyal to the harem-skirt long after it went out of fashion and generally dressed like luxurious bohemians, expensively but "aesthetically," keeping old dresses as long as possible. Florine meanwhile worked at her painting. Knoedler's arranged a one-man show in 1916, with white muslin, at her direction, draping the gallery walls—the effect crowned by a reproduction of her bed canopy at home. But the show attracted little critical notice and no purchasers, and thereafter she refused to exhibit except for a painting or two in museum group shows.

When Mrs. Stettheimer died in 1937, Florine chose to live apart from Carrie and Ettie (who took adjoining apartments at the Dorset on 54th Street) and settled in large, duplex "bachelor quarters" at the Beaux Arts studios on Bryant Park. Here she climaxed her gift for creative decor with great cellophane curtains and cellophane flowers, glittering chandeliers, white furniture self-designed and bearing her initials, a fantastic boudoir all of lace, and a canopied bed somewhere between medieval orthodoxy and a Victorian dressing table. Here, too, she regularly "received," continuing also the Stettheimer tradition of cultural dinner parties. Meanwhile her reputation as an eccentric artist who did not wish to sell her work was growing. The failure of the Knoedler's show had helped induce her to give up the modern scholastic art she had been taught and to seek a more purely personal expression. She herself was wispy in figure, and her style became light, gay, gently satiric and streamlined, yet full of people and details drawn with a miniaturish, rather oriental delicacy. She began portraits of her family and friends by painting them in their own environments, as if one's home were part of one's self-creation. Her "Family Portrait No. 2," owned by the Museum of Modern Art, has the effect of showing a nunnery of gilded aristocrats (herself, Carrie, Ettie, and their mother) evoking, in their "ecstasies," the Statue of Liberty and the Chrysler Building. This was "self-taught art," but of great sophistication: worldly because mock-innocent.

Florine's style matured as fantastic and rather theatrical. In 1934 she designed the sets and costumes for the Virgil Thomson–Gertrude Stein opera, *Four Saints in Three Acts,* which had an *intime* success on Broadway. It was the first time in this country that an artist of note had worked in the theatre, and Florine's "confection of a visionary Spain," fashioned out of "cellophane, crystal, feathers, seashells, lace, and brilliant colors such as the American stage had never seen before" (Hoover and Cage, pp. 80–82), at last brought her into the professional spotlight of art; some critics had more praise for the stage designer's contribution than for the music and the words. Undoubtedly inspired by this experience, she initiated her series of large masterpieces, the "Cathedrals." Fifth Avenue, Broadway, Wall Street, and Art (represented by New York's leading museums) were the four subjects of this scenic group, which busily and breezily mixed much gaiety with elfish satire. Art dealers were now interested in her, but to no avail. By the time of her death in 1944, from cancer,

at the New York Hospital, she had relinquished her lifetime obsession of having her
paintings buried with her in a mausoleum;
over a hundred in number, they passed into
the hands of her sister Ettie. Florine Stettheimer was given an imposing memorial show
by the Museum of Modern Art in 1946. Over
twenty years later, Columbia University's plan
to establish a room for her paintings in its
Art Center gave evidence of continuing critical respect for her work. She now occupies a
unique and exquisite niche in American art.

[A collection of Florine Stettheimer's verse, *Crystal
Flowers*, was privately printed in 1949. The principal biographical source is Parker Tyler, *Florine
Stettheimer: A Life in Art* (1963). See also: Henry
McBride, *Florine Stettheimer* (Museum of Mod-
ern Art, 1946), the catalogue of her memorial
show; McBride's "The Three Miss Stettheimers,"
*Town and Country*, Dec. 1946; "Florine Stettheimer: A Reminiscence," *View*, Oct. 1945; and *New
Yorker*, Oct. 5, 1946, pp. 24–25. For contemporary
comment, see: Carl Van Vechten, "Pastiches et
Pistaches," *Reviewer*, Feb. 1922; Marsden Hart-
ley, "The Paintings of Florine Stettheimer," *Cre-
ative Art*, July 1931; Guy Pène duBois, "The Am.
Soc. of Painters, Sculptors and Gravers," *ibid.*,
Feb. 1932; Paul Rosenfeld, "The World of Flor-
ine Stettheimer," *Nation*, May 4, 1932, and "Flor-
ine Stettheimer," *Accent*, Winter 1945; Ralph
Flint, "Lily Lady Goes West," *Town and Country*,
Jan. 1943. On *Four Saints in Three Acts*, see
Kathleen Hoover and John Cage, *Virgil Thomson*
(1959); Virgil Thomson, *Virgil Thomson: An
Autobiog.* (1966); and N.Y. *Sun*, Feb. 24, 28,
Nov. 16, 1934.]

                                        PARKER TYLER

**STEVENS, Alzina Parsons** (May 27, 1849–
June 3, 1900), labor leader, journalist, and
settlement worker, was born in Parsonsfield,
Maine, a town founded by her paternal grandfather, Col. Thomas Parsons, on land received
for his service as commander of a Massachusetts regiment in the Revolutionary War.
Christened Alzina Ann, she was the seventh
and youngest child and fourth daughter of
Enoch and Louise (Page) Parsons; her father
also had a daughter by an earlier marriage.
Enoch Parsons, who served in the War of
1812, was a relatively prosperous farmer and
small manufacturer. After his death, however,
the family knew hard times, and Alzina was
forced at thirteen to go to work in a textile
factory. There she lost her right index finger
in an industrial accident; the missing finger
served as a perpetual stimulus and reminder
in her later struggles against child labor.

An unfortunate early marriage soon ended
in divorce, and though she kept her husband's
last name, she refused to talk about him even

to her closest friends, and no information about
him survives. Alzina Stevens had little formal
education, but great drive and ambition. At
eighteen she learned the printing trade and
went to work as a newspaper proofreader and
typesetter, settling eventually (1872) in Chicago where she joined Typographical Union
No. 16. In 1877 she organized and became the
first president of a women's labor group,
Working Woman's Union Number 1. About
1882 she moved to Toledo, Ohio, where she
worked for the *Toledo Bee*, first as proofreader
and compositor and then between 1885 and
1891 as correspondent and editor. Continuing
her interest in organized labor, she soon became one of the leading spirits in the Knights
of Labor in Toledo. She helped organize a
women's local assembly, the Joan of Arc Assembly, and became its first master workman
(president) and a delegate to the city-wide
District Assembly. In 1890 she was elected
district master workman (chief officer) of District Assembly 72 of the Knights of Labor,
comprising twenty-two Toledo local assemblies. She attended the Knights of Labor national conventions from 1888 through 1890. A
popular figure in the movement, she was in
1890 nominated by acclamation for director
of woman's work—an honor she declined. In
1892 she represented the labor organizations
of northwestern Ohio at the national convention of the People's (Populist) party.

That year she returned to Chicago, where
she became co-editor and proprietor, with
Lester C. Hubbard, of the *Vanguard*, a weekly
newspaper devoted to economic and industrial
reform that seems to have lasted only for a
year. She soon became a resident of Hull
House, joining JANE ADDAMS, ELLEN STARR,
JULIA LATHROP, and others of the remarkable
group of women who were leaders in the struggle for social justice. An able organizer, a
persuasive writer and speaker, Alzina Stevens
also brought to the group a background of
experience in the labor movement that none of
the others could match. Shifting her allegiance
from the declining Knights of Labor to the
American Federation of Labor, Mrs. Stevens
helped organize several new unions in Chicago
and aided in the picket line during strikes.
One of her close friends was Eugene V. Debs,
whom she shielded from newspapermen while
he drowned his sorrow in drink after the collapse of the Pullman strike in 1894. She was,
however, just as critical of those who were
sentimental in their attitude toward labor as
she was of those who opposed labor's right to
organize. When a young Hull House resident
defended a notoriously corrupt labor leader,

Mrs. Stevens informed her sharply that it was "the worst kind of snobbishness to assume that you must not have the same standards of honor for working people as you have for the well-to-do" (Hamilton, p. 62).

In 1893, under the newly passed Workshop and Factories Act, Gov. John P. Altgeld appointed Mrs. Stevens assistant factory inspector under FLORENCE KELLEY. Together the two women gathered statistics, lobbied at the state capital, and, with the help of the rest of the Hull House group, were primarily responsible for the passage of a better child labor law in 1897 and a stronger compulsory school attendance law two years later. For four years, until they were replaced by a new state administration, Mrs. Stevens joined with Mrs. Kelley in the preparation of her annual reports and in other writings, such as the study of child labor conditions published in *Hull-House Maps and Papers* in 1895. In her role as assistant factory inspector she once clashed head-on with the Chicago department store owner Marshall Field over his use of sweatshop labor.

In the late 1890's, her interest in child welfare now well known, Alzina Stevens established an informal arrangement with the police sergeant at the station nearest Hull House giving her provisional custody over many juvenile offenders. In 1899 she became the first probation officer of the newly established Cook County (Chicago) Juvenile Court. She worked alone at first, her expenses paid by the privately organized Chicago Juvenile Court Committee, but within a few months she was supervising a staff of six. In the words of Mrs. Joseph T. Bowen, Mrs. Stevens was a person of great "singleness of purpose and strength of character," and her round-faced, matronly appearance, coupled with an evident love of children, inspired trust in her young charges and enabled her to achieve a notable success during her brief service as a probation officer. She died in Chicago of diabetes in 1900 at the age of fifty-one. After a funeral at Hull House, her cremated remains were buried at Chicago's Graceland Cemetery.

[There are several Alzina Stevens letters in the Henry D. Lloyd Papers, Wis. State Hist. Soc. See also her article "Life in a Social Settlement—Hull House, Chicago," *Self Culture*, Mar. 1899, pp. 42–51. Other sources: Frances E. Willard and Mary A. Livermore, eds., *A Woman of the Century* (1893); obituaries in *Toledo Bee* and *Chicago Tribune*, June 4, 1900, the latter the best single account of her life; Henry Parsons, *Parsons Family*, II (1920), 207, on her family and forebears; biographical sketch in *Jour. of United Labor* (Phila.), Aug. 16, 1888; Dorothy Rose Blumberg, *Florence Kelley* (1966), pp. 137–38; John B. Andrews and

W. D. P. Bliss, *Hist. of Women in Trade Unions* (vol. X of *Report on Condition of Woman and Child Wage-Earners in the U.S.*, Senate Doc. No. 645, 61 Cong., 2 Sess., 1911), p. 128; Alice Henry, *The Trade Union Woman* (1915) and *Women and the Labor Movement* (1923); Jane Addams, *Twenty Years at Hull-House* (1910); Alice Hamilton, *Exploring the Dangerous Trades* (1943); Mrs. Joseph T. Bowen, "The Early Days of the Juvenile Court," *The Child, the Clinic and the Court* (1927), pp. 299–300; Henriette G. Frank and Amalie H. Jerome, comps., *Annals of the Chicago Woman's Club* (1916), pp. 181, 188–89; Allen F. Davis, *Spearheads for Reform* (1967); Allen F. Davis and Mary Lynn McCree, eds., *Eighty Years at Hull House* (1969). On Illinois child labor and school attendance legislation in the 1890's, see Edith Abbott and Sophonisba P. Breckinridge, *Truancy and Non-Attendance in the Chicago Schools* (1917), chap. v. Other information from interview with Dr. Alice Hamilton and from the Toledo Public Library, Chicago Hist. Soc., and Maine State Library, Augusta. Death certificate from Cook County Bureau of Vital Statistics.]

ALLEN F. DAVIS

**STEVENS, Georgia Lydia** (May 8, 1870– Mar. 28, 1946), musician, Roman Catholic nun, co-founder of the Pius X School of Liturgical Music, was born in Boston, Mass., the third in a family of five daughters of Helen (Granger) and Henry James Stevens. Her mother was a native of Pittsford, Vt. Her father's family had long resided in Andover, Mass., where their ancestor John Stevens, a native of Oxfordshire, England, had settled in 1638. Henry Stevens, a graduate of Harvard College, was a prominent lawyer whose clients included the Boston and Maine and other railroads. Georgia began her education at home with tutors and governesses, studying the violin from the age of seven. The Stevens family were Episcopalians, but when she was twelve Georgia was enrolled in Elmhurst, the convent school of the Society of the Sacred Heart in Providence, R.I. Two years there were followed by a period at a Mrs. Gillian's boarding school in Newport, R.I. In 1888, at eighteen, she went to Germany for musical training at the Hoch Conservatorium in Frankfurt-am-Main under the direction of Hugo Hermann. On her return to the United States she became a pupil of Charles Martin Loeffler, a leading violinist of the Boston Symphony Orchestra.

After the death of her father in 1891, Georgia Stevens turned to music as a career. She continued her own studies, gave violin lessons, and performed in concerts. Meanwhile she had kept up her ties with Elmhurst, giving concerts there, teaching violin, and playing in the chapel during services, and in 1894, at the age of twenty-four, she entered the Roman Catholic Church. Her music, her family, and charitable work among the sick and poor of South Boston occupied her time over the next twelve years.

On Dec. 23, 1906, now thirty-six, Georgia Stevens entered the Society of the Sacred Heart at Kenwood, its North American novitiate near Albany, N.Y. After two years as a novice, she taught for five years in the secondary school of the Sacred Heart academy at Roehampton, England, giving violin and cello lessons and building an orchestra. She made her final profession as a religious at Ixelles, Belgium, in August 1914, and in September of that year she returned to the United States to teach at Manhattanville, the Sacred Heart school in New York City.

There, with the generous financial support of Mrs. Justine Bayard (Cutting) Ward, Mother Stevens in 1916 founded a Chair of Liturgical Music, which shortly became the Pius X Institute and in 1931 the Pius X School of Liturgical Music of Manhattanville College of the Sacred Heart. The center was established in response to the encyclical *Motu Proprio* (1903) of Pope Pius X, which had urged a return to the authentic musical heritage of the Church—the use of Gregorian chant and sacred polyphony—and had emphasized the importance of participation by the congregation in both music and liturgy. Both Mother Stevens and Mrs. Ward realized that the success of such a directive depended on the careful preparation of the teachers and the proper training of their pupils. Until new teachers could be trained, Mother Stevens taught each day in the parish school. Later a high school was established where gifted students could obtain musical training and, beginning in 1917, summer courses for teachers were initiated.

The courses in Gregorian chant were shaped from the start according to the principles and convictions of the Benedictine monks of the Abbey of St. Pierre, Solesmes, France. In 1920 the Pius X Institute was instrumental in organizing an International Congress of Gregorian Chant in New York, where 3,500 schoolchildren trained in the Ward Method sang the *Missa de Angelis*, under the direction of Dom André Mocquereau, O.S.B., in St. Patrick's Cathedral. In the 1930's the Pius X Choir, composed of high school girls, presented a series of public concerts of Gregorian chant and classic polyphony, which received high critical approval. In 1932 Mother Stevens began the publication of the Tone and Rhythm Series, in which she incorporated her ideas and experience in the teaching of music to children.

In her frequent addresses to musical and liturgical societies she always pleaded the cause of good music and the early training of children.

Mother Stevens' talent for music was equaled by her talent for making friends, who included persons among religious and lay groups, both young and old. She possessed marked initiative, inventiveness, quickness of insight, and an understanding of essentials. Her interest in her work never flagged. She strove always to integrate the aesthetic with the spiritual significance of church music. Mother Stevens suffered a fatal heart attack at the Manhattanville convent in New York City in 1946. Her requiem mass was sung in the Manhattanville chapel by hundreds of those whom she had taught during her thirty years as director of the Pius X School, and she was buried in the cemetery of the Society of the Sacred Heart at Kenwood, Albany, N.Y. The school she developed continued to exert a strong influence on the musical and religious activity of the Catholic Church in the United States.

[The archives of Manhattanville College and personal recollections are the principal sources. Brief obituaries were published in the *Catholic World*, May 1946, and the *N.Y. Times*, Mar. 29, 1946. Information about Mother Stevens' father from the published *Reports* of the Harvard College Class of 1857.]

SISTER JOSEPHINE MORGAN
SISTER CATHERINE CARROLL

STEVENS, Lillian Marion Norton Ames (Mar. 1, 1844–Apr. 6, 1914), temperance reformer, was born at Dover, Maine, where her father, Nathaniel Ames, a native of Maine, was a teacher. Her strong-willed mother, Nancy Fowler (Parsons) Ames, was of Scottish descent. Lillian had two sisters and one brother; her brother's death in childhood prompted her first significant thoughts about religion. Ultimately she accepted her father's Universalist belief in the salvation of all souls, though she strongly supported the local church of the Baptists, her mother's denomination. After attending the local Foxcroft Academy and Westbrook Seminary near Portland, the studious girl taught school for several years. In October 1865 she was married to Michael T. Stevens, a grain and salt wholesaler, and moved to his fine family homestead in Stroudwater (later part of Portland). They had one child, Gertrude Mary.

Having grown up in a reformist home, the young matron readily joined the "woman's crusade" against saloons that swept through the Midwest and the East early in 1874. The next year she helped found and became treasurer of the new Maine Woman's Christian Temperance Union. With the approval of her husband, also a foe of alcohol, she began to substitute reform work for household duties, leaving her daughter with a governess. In 1878 Mrs. Stevens became president of the Maine W.C.T.U., a position she retained throughout her life.

As a resident of a state that had long had prohibition, Mrs. Stevens took a special interest in legal attacks on alcohol. Becoming friendly with Neal Dow of Portland, the most prominent nineteenth-century prohibitionist, she helped him in his successful campaign of 1884 to bolster the ban on liquor by writing it into the Maine constitution, speaking at meetings throughout the state in support of the pending referendum. She often lobbied at the Maine legislature for laws to enforce prohibition and to require schools to teach temperance.

During these years she supported other causes of particular interest to her sex. She helped in the management of several local institutions to aid and reform delinquent women and children, often taking neglected children temporarily into her own home. "The streets of Portland," wrote FRANCES E. WILLARD in 1883, "have not a sight more familiar, and surely none more welcome to all save evildoers, than Mrs. Stevens in her phaeton rapidly driving her spirited horse from police station to Friendly Inn; from Erring Woman's Refuge to the sheriff's office" (*Woman and Temperance*, p. 511). For several years she represented Maine at the National Conference of Charities and Correction, and she campaigned for a state women's reformatory, though success did not come until after her death. She was an ardent suffragist; and from 1891 to 1895 she served as treasurer of the National Council of Women.

Mrs. Stevens' most important work, however, came as a leader of the National Woman's Christian Temperance Union. She regularly attended its conventions and after 1880 was one of its secretaries. She became a devoted friend of its president, Frances Willard, who in 1894 in effect designated her as successor by securing her election to the new post of vice-president-at-large. After Miss Willard's death in 1898 Mrs. Stevens became president of the W.C.T.U. and, five years later, also vice-president of the World's W.C.T.U. Though troubled with poor health, she was a hardworking executive, her very features suggesting a masterful determination. She spent much time at the W.C.T.U. headquarters in

Evanston, Ill., at conventions in America and Europe, and on lecture tours. Her speeches, like her numerous articles for temperance publications, were stronger in organization and factual content than in eloquence. Yet she had the sentimentality and personal magnetism needed to sway her following.

Aided by the Frances Willard Memorial Fund, the W.C.T.U. during Mrs. Stevens' presidency underwent a rapid expansion, involving both the rejuvenation of existing local Unions and the formation of new ones; in the decade after 1900 membership climbed from 168,000 to 248,000. Mrs. Stevens loyally endorsed the "Do-Everything" policy of Miss Willard, and during her administration the W.C.T.U. backed such progressive measures as the federal Pure Food and Drug Act of 1906 and the Mann Act of 1910 and continued to cooperate with the woman suffragists. In practice, however, the organization under her direction concentrated more narrowly on the alcohol question, as typified by a successful campaign in 1901 for legislation barring the sale of alcoholic beverages on military bases. For two decades following the adoption of constitutional prohibition by Maine, Kansas, and North Dakota in the 1880's, further state prohibition campaigns had met with failure, and indeed prohibition laws had been repealed in a number of states. This stalemate was broken during Mrs. Stevens' administration when Georgia in 1907 adopted statewide prohibition, to be followed in the next five years by Oklahoma, Mississippi, North Carolina, Tennessee, and West Virginia. These successes, attributable to the burgeoning Anti-Saloon League (founded in 1893) as well as to the W.C.T.U., encouraged a shift away from "local option" efforts and made the goal of national prohibition within a decade, proclaimed by Mrs. Stevens following a successful Maine referendum in 1911, seem attainable. She now spent more and more time in Washington, lobbying, engaging in prohibitionist demonstrations, and presenting mammoth petitions to Congress. In 1914, however, before achieving her goal, she died at Portland of chronic nephritis, and it was left to her loyal lieutenant ANNA ADAMS GORDON to lead the W.C.T.U. through the final stages of the campaign. Like her friend Frances Willard, Mrs. Stevens had requested cremation, and her ashes were buried in Portland's Stroudwater Cemetery.

[The most useful general sources are the W.C.T.U.'s *Union Signal*, Apr. 16, 1914; Gertrude Stevens Leavitt and Margaret L. Sargent, *Lillian M. N. Stevens: A Life Sketch* (1921), a pamphlet; Helen E. Tyler, *Where Prayer and Purpose Meet*

(1949), a history of the W.C.T.U.; and Frances E. Willard and Mary A. Livermore, eds., *A Woman of the Century* (1893). The *Minutes* of the Nat. Woman's Christian Temperance Union, 1899–1913, contain her annual addresses; excerpts from them are available in Anna A. Gordon, comp., *What Lillian M. N. Stevens Said* (1914). See, for her home, Federal Writers' Project, *Portland City Guide* (1940); for her early prohibitionism, Annie Wittenmyer, *Hist. of the Woman's Temperance Crusade* (1882); for her religious views, Frances E. Willard, *Woman and Temperance* (1883); and for her death, Portland city records.]

FRANK L. BYRNE

STEVENS, Nettie Maria (July 7, 1861–May 4, 1912), biologist and geneticist, was born in Cavendish, Vt., the second of three children and elder of two daughters of Ephraim A. Stevens, a carpenter and sawyer, and Julia (Adams) Stevens. Aside from the fact that her father was a native of Chelmsford, Mass., nothing is known of her family background or of the first three decades of her life except that she served for a time as librarian of the Free Public Library in Chelmsford. In September 1892, at the age of thirty-one, she entered the Normal School at Westfield, Mass. (where her first name was recorded as "Addie"), and four years later transferred as an undergraduate to Stanford University in California, to prepare herself for teaching. Majoring in physiology, she received the B.A. degree in 1899 and the M.A. in 1900.

Miss Stevens must already have been interested in biological research. As an undergraduate she spent three summers in the Hopkins Seaside Laboratory at Pacific Grove, Calif., and work begun there on the life cycle of *Boveria*, a protozoan parasite of sea cucumbers, was published in 1901 in the *Proceedings* of the California Academy of Sciences. In 1900 she entered Bryn Mawr College as a graduate student in biology. In her second year a fellowship enabled her to study at the Zoological Station at Naples, Italy, and at the Zoological Institute of the University of Würzburg, Germany, under the great German biologist Theodor Boveri. In 1903 she received the Ph.D. degree from Bryn Mawr with a thesis on ciliate protozoa. Dr. Stevens continued at Bryn Mawr as research fellow in biology (1903–04), reader in experimental morphology (1904–05), and associate in experimental morphology (1905–12). In 1905 the association that maintained the "American Women's Table" at the Naples station awarded her the Ellen Richards Research Prize of $1,000, given to promote scientific research by women, for her paper "A Study of the Germ Cells of *Aphis Rosæ* and *Aphis Œnotheræ*." In 1908–09 she again spent a year working with Boveri in Würzburg.

Nettie Maria Stevens carried out research in three major areas of biology. Her earliest work was concerned with the morphology and taxonomy of ciliate protozoa. Later she became interested in cytology, particularly the histology of regenerative processes in hydroids and planarians, and in 1904, with the geneticist Thomas Hunt Morgan, she published a paper on the regenerative processes in the hydroid *Tubularia*. Hans Driesch had found that isolated blastomeres of sea urchin embryos could develop into whole organisms, but Dr. Stevens showed that this was not true of all organisms. Using developing eggs of the roundworm, *Ascaris*, she applied ultraviolet radiation to kill selected cells in the two- and four-cell stages of the embryo and demonstrated that in these earliest stages of development cells are already restricted in their potentialities for regeneration.

Dr. Stevens' most important researches dealt with chromosomes and their relation to heredity. Mendel's laws on the transmission of hereditary factors had been rediscovered in 1900, and the studies of Boveri and Walter S. Sutton on chromosome behavior had suggested that Mendel's factors might actually be associated with chromosomes. Dr. Stevens and the biologist Edmund Beecher Wilson, working independently, were the first to demonstrate that sex was determined by a particular chromosome. Dr. Stevens found that in the beetle *Tenebrio molitor* the male produced two kinds of sperm, one carrying a large (X) chromosome and the other a small (Y) chromosome. The unfertilized eggs, however, were all alike in possessing two X-chromosomes. She correctly inferred that an egg fertilized by an X-carrying sperm produced a female embryo, and that the Y-sperm produced a male. This discovery, though not universally accepted at the time, was of profound importance in genetics and the theory of sex determination. In the years following, Dr. Stevens extended her research in this field to include other species of beetle, as well as flies and plant lice. In the complex life cycle of aphids she found a perfect correlation between chromosome composition and sex. Other important contributions in this field were her discovery of supernumerary chromosomes in certain insects and of the paired state of chromosomes in somatic cells of flies and mosquitoes.

Dr. Stevens' research was characterized by precision of observation and caution in interpretation. Her writing is notable for both its clarity and its brevity. She was not only a devoted scientist but also an inspiring teacher, and once wrote to a former student: "How could you think your questions would bother me? They never will, so long as I keep my enthusiasm for biology; and that, I hope, will be as long as I live." Nettie Maria Stevens died in her fiftieth year, of carcinoma of the breast, at the Johns Hopkins Hospital in Baltimore. She was buried in Westfield, Mass.

[Nettie Stevens' most significant research papers are: "Experiments on Polarity in *Tubularia*" (with T. H. Morgan), *Jour. of Experimental Zoology*, Dec. 1904; "Studies in Spermatogenesis with Especial Reference to the 'Accessory Chromosome,'" Carnegie Institution, *Publications*, no. 36 (1905); "A Study of the Germ Cells of *Aphis Rosæ* and *Aphis Œnotheræ*," *Jour. of Experimental Zoology*, Aug. 1905; "A Study of the Germ Cells of Certain *Diptera*, with Reference to the Heterochromosomes and the Phenomena of Synapsis," *ibid.*, Mar. 1908; "Further Studies on the Chromosomes of the *Coleoptera*," *ibid.*, Jan. 1909; "The Effect of Ultraviolet Light upon the Developing Eggs of Ascaris megalocephala," *Archiv für Entwicklungsmechanik*, June 1909; "A Note on Reduction in the Maturation of Male Eggs in Aphis," *Biological Bull.*, Jan. 1910; "Heterochromosomes in the Guineapig," *ibid.*, Aug. 1911; "Supernumerary Chromosomes, and Synapsis in *Ceutophilus*," *ibid.*, Mar. 1912. Biographical sources: T. H. Morgan, "The Scientific Work of Miss N. M. Stevens," *Science*, Oct. 11, 1912; *Bryn Mawr Alumnae Quart.*, June 1912, pp. 124–25; *Am. Men of Sci.* (2nd ed., 1910); information from: Town Clerk, Cavendish, Vt.; Adams Library, Chelmsford, Mass.; Westfield State College; Stanford Univ.; and Baltimore City Health Dept. (death record).]

HANS RIS

STEVENSON, Matilda Coxe Evans (May 12, 1849–June 24, 1915), ethnologist, was the daughter of Alexander H. Evans, an attorney, and Maria Matilda (Coxe) Evans, natives, respectively, of Virginia and New Jersey. She was born in San Augustine, Texas, but shortly after her birth her parents moved to Washington, D.C. She received her formal schooling at Miss Anable's Academy in Philadelphia. On Apr. 18, 1872, the twenty-two-year-old Matilda, or Tilly, as she was commonly known throughout her life, was married to James Stevenson, a government geologist who became in 1879 executive officer of the United States Geological Survey. They had no children.

When the federal Bureau of American Ethnology was founded in 1879, James Stevenson, in addition to his other duties, was appointed by its head, Major John Wesley Powell, to report on archaeological remains and collect specimens in the Western territories. Mrs. Stevenson accompanied her husband that year

on an anthropological expedition which included the ethnologists Frank H. Cushing and J. K. Hillers. The group spent six months at Zuñi pueblo in New Mexico, and there Matilda Stevenson discovered her lifework. For a number of years she aided her husband unheralded, and although she wrote a thirty-page paper, "Zuñi and the Zuñians," which was privately printed in 1881, her research received little notice until she was commended by the British scholar Edwin B. Tylor, foremost anthropologist of the nineteenth century. After a visit to the Stevensons at Zuñi, Tylor, in an 1884 address before the Anthropological Society of Washington, noted that women could obtain data on domestic and womanly matters not readily disclosed to male researchers. Anthropologists, therefore, should not "warn the ladies off from their proceedings, but rather . . . avail themselves thankfully of their help."

Imbued with the philosophy that women had a special role to play in anthropology, Matilda Stevenson became in 1885 the founder and first president of the Women's Anthropological Society of America. Her first major publication, "Religious Life of the Zuñi Child" (in the *Fifth Annual Report* of the Bureau of American Ethnology, 1883–84), made her "the first American ethnologist to consider children worthy of notice" (Mead and Bunzel, p. 205). The selection of religion as a field of study, however, indicates that her range of interest was broadening and points toward her later work, which was without a specific female emphasis. All aspects of pueblo culture—legends, irrigation ditches, games, ethnobotany, and particularly religion—came within her purview. Eventually Mrs. Stevenson was to see the general, unqualified acceptance of women in anthropology, symbolized by the dissolution in 1899 of the Women's Anthropological Society and the transfer en masse of its members to the hitherto exclusively male Anthropological Society of Washington, and the founding, that same year, of the American Anthropological Association, which included women among its charter members.

Meanwhile Mrs. Stevenson, upon the death of her husband in 1888 of a heart condition aggravated by his strenuous explorations, was appointed to the staff of the Bureau of American Ethnology to complete work on the notes they had gathered. The following year she set out alone for Sia pueblo, New Mexico. The results of her study of this small tribe were published in the bureau's *Eleventh Annual Report* (1889–90). Although she visited and worked at many pueblos, she returned often to Zuñi, where she enjoyed a cordial and affectionate relationship. Acutely aware that the American Indian people were changing rapidly in the face of influences from the dominant culture, she stressed the need for collecting data before they were irrevocably lost. As a consequence, she sometimes sacrificed the niceties of rapport to this single-minded purpose. On one occasion she disregarded Indian warnings to stay away from Hopi ceremonies at Oraibi pueblo and was made a prisoner in a kiva there until the trader Thomas Keam rescued her.

Matilda Stevenson's major work, *The Zuñi Indians: Their Mythology, Esoteric Fraternities, and Ceremonies,* a six-hundred-page study with over a hundred illustrative plates, appeared in the *Twenty-third Annual Report* (1901–02) of the Bureau of American Ethnology, published in 1904. This was followed in the *Thirtieth Annual Report* (1908–09) by a study of the ethnobotany of the Zuñi. Over the twenty-five-year period of her acquaintance with the tribe, Mrs. Stevenson was able to observe the great changes wrought by the railroad and other encroachments of modern civilization. Although she herself had purposefully introduced the use of soap in 1879, the greater cleanliness of the village and the many new material comforts brought by trade were offset by other factors: the unifying power of the Zuñi religion was diminishing, and "the adoption of foreign ways . . . has brought with it the evils of intoxication and trickery." And though other anthropologists of her day, such as ALICE CUNNINGHAM FLETCHER, saw the acquisition of modern conveniences and ways as an entirely desirable end, Matilda Stevenson perceived that it is the integrity of a people rather than their standard of living which makes for contentment and a meaningful existence.

A person of great energy, Mrs. Stevenson collected a herbarium of over two hundred edible, medicinal, and fetishistic plants used by the Zuñi, as well as a number of their sacred masks, which she contributed to the Smithsonian Institution. Besides her contributions to the *Annual Reports* of the Bureau of American Ethnology, she published articles on aspects of Zuñi life in the *American Anthropologist* (February 1898 and July–September 1903), *Science* (Mar. 23, 1888), and the *Proceedings* of the American Association for the Advancement of Science (vol. XLI, 1892), of which she was a Fellow. She presented two papers on the Zuñi at the Chicago World's Columbian Exposition in 1893, before the International Congress of Anthropology and the Congress of Women. In 1903, utilizing Zuñi materials

she had collected, she prepared an exhibit for the Louisiana Purchase Exposition on the religious symbolism embodied in the various Zuñi arts. In her last years she made her home near San Ildefonso pueblo in the Rio Grande valley and continued her researches there, particularly among the Tewa Indians. Her health failing, she returned east in 1915 and died at the home of friends in Oxon Hill, Md., a Washington suburb, of congestive heart failure. She was buried in Bladenburg Cemetery, Washington.

Matilda Stevenson was one of a small group of pioneer ethnologists in the United States who established the tradition of impartial, participant observation and purposeful collection of data in the field. Though her associates at times found themselves in conflict with her strong personality, they had a high regard for her abilities. John Wesley Powell judged her "exceptionally thorough," and William H. Holmes, a later head of the Bureau of American Ethnology, in an obituary tribute described her "great work" on the Zuñi as "a monument to her energy, ability and perseverance." More recently Margaret Mead and Ruth L. Bunzel, though finding her less perceptive than another Zuñi ethnologist of the period, Frank H. Cushing, have praised her as "an active and industrious field worker." Her publications remain a significant contribution to knowledge and a treasure of source material for students of the pueblo cultures of the Southwest.

[William H. Holmes, "In Memoriam: Matilda Coxe Stevenson," *Am. Anthropologist,* Oct.–Dec. 1916, which includes a bibliography of her writings; clippings, MS. material, and correspondence in the Bureau of Am. Ethnology, Smithsonian Institution, Washington. See also Margaret Mead and Ruth L. Bunzel, eds., *The Golden Age of Am. Anthropology* (1960); Mary K. O. Eagle, ed., *The Congress of Women* (1894), the source for her date of birth; *Memoirs of the Internat. Congress of Anthropology* (1894); *Organization and Hist. Sketch of the Women's Anthropological Soc. of America* (1889); Jane C. Croly, *The Hist. of the Woman's Club Movement in America* (1898), pp. 341–43; *N.Y. Times* and Washington *Evening Star* of June 25, 1915; *Who's Who in America,* 1914–15; *Woman's Who's Who of America,* 1914–15; *Nat. Cyc. Am. Biog.,* XII, 556 (on her husband), and XX, 53–54. Death record from Md. Dept. of Health. A somewhat lurid account of her imprisonment by the Hopi appeared in the *Illustrated Police News,* Mar. 6, 1886.]

NANCY OSTREICH LURIE

**STEVENSON, Sarah Ann Hackett** (Feb. 2, 1841–Aug. 14, 1909), physician, was born in Buffalo Grove (later Polo), Ogle County, Ill., the younger of two daughters and fourth of seven children. Her Scotch-Irish grandfather, Charles Stevenson, had come to the United States from Ireland after the Rebellion of 1798. Her father, John Davis Stevenson, born in New York City, had moved west at an early age to Ohio and thence to New Orleans, where he became a merchant, meanwhile marrying a Philadelphia girl, Sarah T. Hackett. Because of his wife's poor health he removed in 1835 to Illinois, opening the first store in Buffalo Grove; he later became a farmer. Sarah was educated at the Mount Carroll (Ill.) Seminary and the State Normal University at Normal, Ill., from which she graduated in 1863. During her two-year course there she showed particular interest in scientific subjects. Following her graduation she taught school for four years in Bloomington, Ill., and then in the towns of Mount Morris and Sterling, serving the last school also as principal. She then went to Chicago, apparently with the intention of doing scientific writing (Hanaford, p. 545), and began the study of anatomy and physiology at the Woman's Hospital Medical College of Chicago, recently established by MARY HARRIS THOMPSON and others. She also spent a year at the South Kensington Science School in London, where she studied with Thomas Huxley; her high school text, *Boys and Girls in Biology* (1875), was based on his lectures. According to the English philanthropist and feminist Emily Faithfull, with whom she formed a close friendship, Miss Stevenson was "one of Professor Huxley's brightest pupils." Now determined, apparently, on a medical career, she returned to Chicago, completed her medical course, and graduated, M.D., in 1874 as valedictorian of her class.

After a further postgraduate sojourn abroad, visiting hospitals and clinics, Dr. Stevenson began her practice in Chicago in 1875. The next year she was chosen by the Illinois State Medical Society as one of its delegates to the American Medical Association convention in Philadelphia. Championed by Dr. William H. Byford, a leading Chicago gynecologist, and by another of her male colleagues, she was admitted to the convention, thereby becoming the A.M.A.'s first woman member, although only five years earlier it had refused even to discuss a motion for the admission of women. Dr. Stevenson was later the first woman appointed to the staff of the Cook County Hospital in Chicago (1881) and the first woman appointed to the Illinois State Board of Health (by Gov. John P. Altgeld, 1893). Joining the faculty of her alma mater (which became in 1879 the Woman's Medical College), she served as professor of physiology and histology (1875–80) and of obstetrics (1880–94). Besides carrying on a large and successful practice, she was a consulting physician to the Woman's and Provident hospitals and an attending physician at the Mary Thompson Hospital. She was one of the leaders, with LUCY L. FLOWER, in founding the Illinois Training School for Nurses (1880). "A remarkably tall, handsome woman, with a commanding presence," she was "sympathetic and womanly" as a practitioner (Faithfull, p. 113).

After the death of Mary Harris Thompson, Dr. Stevenson was the most widely known woman physician of Illinois and the Midwest. Talented, energetic, scholarly, and self-reliant, she did much by her example to advance the cause of medical education for women. Besides her high school text, she wrote a popular work, *The Physiology of Woman* (1880). An earnest Methodist in religion, she showed throughout her career a strong interest in reform and humanitarian movements. She was active in the Woman's Christian Temperance Union, serving as the first superintendent (1881–82) of its national Department of Hygiene, and as president of the staff of the National Temperance Hospital (later the Frances Willard Hospital), organized in 1886 by Chicago members of the W.C.T.U. as an institution using no medication containing alcohol. She gave generous personal support to the American Medical Missionary College in Chicago. Once she made an eloquent appeal before the Chicago Woman's Club for the admission of a Negro member. Her characteristic straightforwardness offended some, but she was nevertheless welcome in the upper circle of Chicago society. She was a member of the Twentieth Century, Fortnightly, and Chicago Woman's clubs and served as president of the last during the World's Fair year of 1893. Long identified with the "new woman" movement, she opposed the extremism of some of the woman's rights advocates.

Dr. Stevenson retired from active practice following a cerebral hemorrhage in 1903; three years later she was honored by a reception attended by fifteen hundred persons. Paralyzed after 1906, she spent the final three years of her life as a patient at St. Elizabeth's Hospital in Chicago and during her last year was in a coma; her death there, at the age of sixty-eight, was officially attributed to "exhaustion." She was buried in St. Boniface Cemetery, Chicago.

[The fullest biographical sketch, though containing some errors, is in Chicago Medical Soc., *Hist. of Medicine and Surgery, and Physicians and*

Surgeons of Chicago (1922). Other useful accounts are in Phebe A. Hanaford, *Daughters of America* (1883), pp. 543–46; *Who's Who in America*, 1899–1900; and F. M. Sperry, comp., *A Group of Distinguished Physicians and Surgeons of Chicago* (1904). On her father, see *Portrait and Biog. Album of Ogle County, Ill.* (1886), p. 750; and Newton Bateman and Paul Selby, eds., *Hist. Encyc. of Ill.*, with *Hist. of Ogle County* by Horace G. and Rebecca H. Kauffman, II (1909), 1028. Other information may be found in David J. Davis, ed., *Hist. of Medical Practice in Ill.*, vol. II 1955); Emily Faithfull, *Three Visits to America* (1884), pp. 112–13; and Samuel Unger, "A Hist. of the Nat. Woman's Christian Temperance Union" (unpublished Ph.D. dissertation, Ohio State Univ., 1933), p. 176. See also Mary I. Wood, *The Hist. of the Gen. Federation of Women's Clubs* (1912), p. 61. Important obituaries are in the *Chicago Tribune*, Aug. 15, 1909 (with photograph), and *Jour. of the Am. Medical Assoc.*, Aug. 21, 1909. Death certificate from County Clerk, Cook County. Other information from Ill. State Normal Univ., Normal, Ill., and Ill. State Hist. Library, Springfield. Though a later birth year is sometimes given, the 1850 census—of which her father was county enumerator—lists her age that year as nine.]

THOMAS NEVILLE BONNER

STEWART, Eliza Daniel (Apr. 25, 1816– Aug. 6, 1908), temperance reformer, was born at Piketon, Ohio, where her maternal grandfather, Capt. John Guthery, a Revolutionary officer, had settled before the town was founded. Her parents, James Daniel, a farmer from Virginia, and Rebecca (Guthery) Daniel, each had Scotch-Irish antecedents. Her mother died when Eliza was three and her father before she was twelve. In 1833 her older brother, who was postmaster at Piketon, secured her appointment as assistant postmaster, and it is claimed that she was the first woman to be sworn in to such a position. Educated at Piketon and at seminaries in Granville and Marietta, Ohio, she became a teacher. She was married, first to Joseph Coover of McArthur, Ohio, who died a few months after the wedding, and in 1848 to Hiram Stewart, son of Daniel Stewart, one of the most prominent farmers of Athens County. Five children born to the Stewarts died in infancy, but Mrs. Stewart mothered two stepsons by her second marriage.

As a girl she had joined the Methodist Church and become interested in various types of uplift. Much of her early married life with Stewart was spent in Athens, Ohio, where about 1858 she helped organize a lodge of the temperance order of Good Templars. At about the same time she gave her first temperance lecture at a Band of Hope meeting in Pomeroy, Ohio. With the coming of the Civil War she gathered supplies to be sent to the soldiers and visited camps in the South, earning the name "Mother Stewart" by which she was thereafter known. In 1866 the Stewarts moved to Springfield, Ohio, where the next year Eliza helped organize the city's first woman suffrage organization and was elected its president. In 1870 she participated in a pioneer prison reform conference, the National Prison Congress, at Cincinnati.

The liquor problem, however, was Mrs. Stewart's chief concern. On Jan. 22, 1872, she began her "temperance warfare" in earnest with a lecture at Springfield in which she sought to secure pledges from women in attendance that they would seek out drunkards' wives and encourage them to prosecute liquor dealers under Ohio's Adair Act. This law, passed in 1854 and amended in 1870, provided that the wife or mother of a drunkard could sue a liquor dealer for damages because of a sale to her husband or son. A few days after her lecture Mrs. Stewart helped win a case of this sort in court, herself addressing the jury. Her second such victory, in October 1873, roused the women of Springfield, and Mrs. Stewart led them in petitioning the city council for a local option ordinance against liquor. A series of weekly mass meetings followed, and calls began to come to her to "wake up the women" in other cities and towns. On Dec. 2, 1873, she organized at Osborn, Ohio, the first Woman's Temperance League, a precursor of the Woman's Christian Temperance Union.

A similar stirring was taking place almost simultaneously in other communities in Ohio and western New York. Late in December 1873 praying bands of women invaded the saloons of Fredonia and Jamestown, N.Y., and Hillsboro and Washington Court House, Ohio, the Hillsboro women under the leadership of Mrs. ELIZA JANE TRIMBLE THOMPSON. This onslaught on the saloon initiated a "Woman's Crusade" that spread through the Middle West and parts of the East during the early months of 1874. Mrs. Stewart helped lead such an attack in Springfield, and early in January she became president of a new Temperance Union in her city. In April she headed a county union, believed to be the first such organization in the country, and in June founded a state union. That November she took a prominent part in the convention at Cleveland which organized the National Woman's Christian Temperance Union. Although distrusted by some delegates as representing "the extreme radical portion of the temperance women," Mother Stewart was elected chairman of the resolutions committee after FRANCES WILLARD spoke of her in glowing terms as the acknowledged leader of the crusade (*Cleveland Daily Herald*, Nov. 19, 1874). Later (1879), as chairman of the W.C.T.U.'s committee on Southern work, she organized both white and Negro unions in the South.

On the invitation of the Good Templars, Mrs. Stewart spent about five months in Great Britain in 1876, lecturing and holding religious meetings, her work contributing to the formation of the British Women's Temperance Association and the Scottish Christian Union. Later she was a W.C.T.U. fraternal delegate to the world convention of Good Templars. In 1895 she made the opening speech at the World's W.C.T.U. convention in London and thereafter addressed temperance meetings in France, Germany, and Switzerland. With "keen, flashing" eyes and a very effective voice, she was called a "Wendell Phillips in Petticoats."

Late in life Mrs. Stewart joined the Christian Catholic Church of John Alexander Dowie in Zion City, Ill., and was by him ordained an elder. Somewhat disillusioned by what she deemed religious fanaticism, she left the community, and as an invalid she spent the last year of her life at the home of her former private secretary, Mrs. M. M. Farnsworth, in Hicksville, Ohio, where she died at the age of ninety-two. Her funeral, which followed the Methodist ritual, was held in the First Lutheran Church in Springfield, scene of one of her pioneer temperance meetings. She was buried at Ferncliff Cemetery, Springfield.

[Mrs. Stewart's own works, *Memories of the Crusade: A Thrilling Account of the Great Uprising of the Women of Ohio in 1873, against the Liquor Crime* (1888), and *The Crusader in Great Britain; or, The Hist. of the Origin and Organization of the British Women's Temperance Assoc.* (1893); Frances E. Willard, *Woman and Temperance* (1883), chap. vi; Frances E. Willard and Mary A. Livermore, eds., *A Woman of the Century* (1893); Annie Wittenmyer, *Hist. of the Woman's Temperance Crusade* (1882), pp. 301–10; Mary F. Eastman, *The Biog. of Dio Lewis* (1891), pp. 209–19; *Standard Encyc. of the Alcohol Problem*, VI (1930), 2531–32; Helen E. Tyler, *Where Prayer and Purpose Meet: The W.C.T.U. Story, 1874–1949* (1949); *Who's Who in America*, 1903–05; *A Biog. Record of Clark County* (1902); files of Springfield (Ohio) *Daily Republic*, 1873–74; *Springfield Daily News and Press Republic*, Aug. 9, 10, 1908; Springfield *Times and the Republican Gazette*, Aug. 8, 1908.]

FRANCIS P. WEISENBURGER

STEWART, Maria W. Miller (1803–Dec. 17, 1879), teacher and public speaker, was born in Hartford, Conn., of Negro parents about

whom nothing is known other than that their name was Miller. Left an orphan at the age of five, she was bound out in the family of a clergyman, with whom she lived until she was fifteen, receiving no education except what she derived from access to the family library and from attending "Sabbath schools."

On Aug. 10, 1826, Maria Miller was married in Boston to James W. Stewart of that city, about forty-four years old and described as "a light, bright Mulatto." A veteran of the War of 1812, during which he had served as a "Seaman and in other capacities" on the *Essex* and other warships and had undergone capture and imprisonment in England, Stewart was employed in fitting out whaling and fishing vessels. It was at his suggestion that his wife added the middle initial W. to her name. Stewart died on Dec. 17, 1829, leaving his widow with some means, of which she was defrauded by his executors. In 1830 she underwent conversion and a year later made a public profession of "faith in Christ," consecrating herself to God's service.

She is known for four public addresses, delivered in Boston at a time when no woman except FRANCES WRIGHT (and women in Quaker meetings) had had the temerity to speak from a public platform, and when Negro speakers were also unknown. Mrs. Stewart's addresses are religious in tone and heavily Biblical in style but are mainly devoted to exhorting free Negroes in America to educate themselves and sue for their rights. She had apparently long been concerned for the plight of her people when William Lloyd Garrison's interest in them turned her concern into "a holy zeal" for the cause. The young abolitionist printer had begun publishing the *Liberator* in January 1831. Emboldened by his remarks on the power of female influence, Mrs. Stewart came into his office shortly thereafter and submitted a manuscript containing several essays, one of which, "Religion and the Pure Principles of Morality, the Sure Foundation on Which We Must Build," he published in tract form later that year. In 1832 Garrison brought out as another tract her long religious "Meditations . . . Presented to the First African Baptist Church and Society of the City of Boston." She then composed ("while my hands are toiling for their daily sustenance") and delivered three addresses: one to the Afric-American Female Intelligence Society early in 1832; another at Franklin Hall on Sept. 21, 1832; and a third at the African Masonic Hall, Feb. 27, 1833. All were printed in the *Liberator*.

Mrs. Stewart considered the free Negro's

condition little better than that of the slave. White Americans, she pointed out, raised money to help subjugated people abroad to freedom—the Greeks, the Poles, the Irish—but refused to recognize an independent Haiti and gave Negroes at home no opportunity to rise above the condition of servants. Furthermore, having "obliged our brethren to labor; kept them in utter ignorance; . . . and raised them in degradation," and having enjoyed the profits of their labor, Americans were now saying "that we never can rise to respectability in this country" and were proposing to send them back to Africa. "But before I go, the bayonet shall pierce me through." If these colonizationists were real friends to the Negro, she declared, they would build a college with the money collected for transportation, but she feared they would rather see their money sunk in the ocean first. She therefore called upon her people to pursue knowledge on their own, "for knowledge is power," and to trust in God's eventual deliverance.

Maria Stewart made one more speech, a farewell address delivered Sept. 21, 1833. In this she announced her decision to leave Boston, "for I find it is no use for me, as an individual, to try to make myself useful among my color in this city." She had been condemned by her own people for her presumption in speaking in public, but she stoutly maintained that God had spoken before through women, and that even St. Paul, did he "but know of our wrongs and deprivations, . . . would make no objection to our pleading in public for our rights." Other critics had said, "Do not talk so much about religion," but her parting message was, "Pure religion will burst your fetters." Garrison subsequently published the collected *Productions of Mrs. Maria W. Stewart* (1835).

From Boston, Mrs. Stewart moved in 1833 to New York City, where she remedied the gaps in her education by joining a Female Literary Society and became a teacher in the public schools, first in Manhattan, then in what is now the Williamsburg section of Brooklyn. In 1852, having lost the latter position, Mrs. Stewart went south to Baltimore and began teaching Negro children, distributing circulars to obtain paying pupils. In 1861 she moved on to wartime Washington, where she was befriended by ELIZABETH KECKLEY, dressmaker and confidante of MARY TODD LINCOLN, and after much difficulty succeeded in organizing a school. After Freedmen's Hospital was established she lived and worked there as matron, or head of the housekeeping services. Now a devout Episcopalian, in 1871 she opened a

Sunday school where she gathered "poor and destitute children in the neighborhood of the hospital," as well as those who could pay, in a building costing $200, for which she had raised the money. The school was also near Howard University, from whose students she occasionally drew teachers to assist her.

In March 1879, under a new law of the previous year granting pensions to widows of the War of 1812, she succeeded in getting from Congress a monthly grant of eight dollars, retroactive to the date of the law's passage. This she used to finance the publication of a second edition of her speeches and writings, under the title *Meditations from the Pen of Mrs. Maria W. Stewart* (1879). The book was introduced by supporting letters from Garrison and others, her account of her "Sufferings during the War," and a preface in which she once more called for an end to tyranny and oppression. Mrs. Stewart died at the Freedmen's Hospital that December. Funeral services were held at St. Luke's Episcopal Church, of which she was a member.

[Her published works, above, particularly the *Meditations,* are the chief source of information about Mrs. Stewart. Other data from pension records in the Nat. Archives, Washington, D.C., including an affidavit by Mrs. Stewart dated Feb. 26, 1879. Death record from St. Luke's Episcopal Church, Washington.]

　　　　　　　　　　　　　　ELEANOR FLEXNER

**STIMSON, Julia Catherine** (May 26, 1881– Sept. 29, 1948), professional nurse, superintendent of the Army Nurse Corps, was born in Worcester, Mass., the second daughter and second of seven children of the Rev. Henry Albert Stimson and Alice Wheaton (Bartlett) Stimson, both of seventeenth-century New England descent. Her father, a well-known Congregational minister, was born in New York City; her mother, the daughter of the Rev. Samuel Colcord Bartlett, president of Dartmouth College from 1877 to 1892, was a native of Salisbury, N.H. A strong tradition of professional service ran in the family. A brother and sister of Julia became physicians, another brother a lawyer, and a sister dean and professor of history at Goucher College; all had noteworthy careers. Henry Lewis Stimson, a cousin, served in the cabinets of three presidents of the United States.

Julia's father moved to a pastorate in St. Louis in 1886 and six years later to one in New York City. After earlier education in St. Louis public schools, Julia Stimson prepared for college at the Brearley School in New York. She graduated from Vassar (B.A., 1901) and went on to graduate study in biology at Columbia University (1901–03); for a time she did medical drawing at Cornell Medical School. She was still unsettled as to her career when, on a trip to Europe, a chance meeting with Annie Warburton Goodrich (1866–1954), the dynamic superintendent of the New York Hospital Training School for Nurses in New York City, led to her decision to enter that school (Nov. 14, 1904), from which she graduated May 16, 1908. Her first position (1908–11) was as superintendent of nurses at Harlem Hospital, a New York municipal institution. Seeing the need in that underprivileged area for work with families as well as patients, she developed, in conjunction with another nurse, Florence M. Johnson, a social service department at the hospital. Her next call was to head a similar department at the hospitals (Barnes and Children's) associated with Washington University, St. Louis. Adding the duties of superintendent of nurses in 1913, she remained until 1917. During this period she completed the work for an A.M. degree (1917) in sociology, biology, and education at Washington University.

Julia Stimson's major contributions to public service and nursing, however, came through the American Red Cross and the Army Nurse Corps. A reserve Red Cross nurse since 1909, she organized a group of St. Louis nurses in March 1913 to staff an emergency hospital and do public health nursing in Hamilton, Ohio, at the time of the Ohio Valley flood. In 1914 she became a member of the National Committee on Red Cross Nursing. When in World War I the Red Cross embarked on a program of organizing, at various American hospitals, "base hospital units" to be ready for military service overseas, Julia Stimson became chief nurse of Base Hospital No. 21 at Washington University. Enlisting in the Army Nurse Corps in 1917, she accompanied her unit to France that May for duty with the British Expeditionary Forces at Rouen; her experience there she recorded, with humor and sensitivity, in a series of letters to her family that were later published under the title *Finding Themselves* (1918). Her exceptional organizational and administrative skills were soon recognized, and in April 1918, while retaining her army status, she was assigned to detached duty as chief nurse of the American Red Cross in France. Seven months later she was called back to army duty as director of the nursing service of the American Expeditionary Forces. For her war service she received, among other decorations, the Distinguished Service Medal, awarded by Gen. John J. Pershing, and a citation from the

Allied Expeditionary Forces by Field Marshal Douglas Haig.

After the Armistice, Miss Stimson remained in Europe until July 1919, when she returned to Washington, D.C., as dean of the Army School of Nursing (a post which she held until the school was closed in 1933) and acting superintendent of the Army Nurse Corps. On Dec. 30, 1919, she was given permanent appointment as superintendent. Over the next eighteen years she scored a brilliant record of accomplishments, especially in the area of personnel administration. The personnel policies and practices which she instituted, including opportunities for postgraduate study and participation in the activities of professional organizations, improved morale and nursing service and made membership in the Army Nurse Corps an attractive career. Problems which had arisen during the war—the first war in which professional nurses served under the United States Army—stimulated the nursing organizations to seek military rank for army nurses. In 1920 Congress granted nurses "relative" rank —a status which gave them authority next after medical officers in and about military hospitals but did not confer the same privileges and salary as commissioned rank—and Julia Stimson as superintendent became the first woman major in the United States Army. She resigned May 31, 1937. During World War II she was recalled to active duty for a period of six months (1942–43) to aid in the recruitment of army nurses. Her unusual facility in establishing rapport with audiences and arousing enthusiasm was never more evident than in the addresses she gave for this purpose, to widely varying groups. Full commissioned rank was granted to army nurses in 1947, and Julia C. Stimson was promoted to the rank of colonel on the retired list on Aug. 13, 1948, six weeks before her death.

Throughout her career Miss Stimson was active in the national nursing organizations, and after her retirement she devoted a large part of her time and talents to them. Among her early interests were the promotion of nursing as a career for college women, an interest which she never lost, and the introduction of student government into "training schools," as they were then called. Besides other offices, she served on the board of directors of the National League of Nursing Education and was president of the American Nurses' Association, 1938–44. Her professional writings include an early nursing text, *Nurses' Handbook of Drugs and Solutions* (1910), and several well-documented articles on the service of women nurses in early American wars, published in the *Mili-*

*tary Surgeon* (February 1926; January, February 1928) as part of a series she initiated. In other areas of interest, she was a founding member of the American Women's Association of New York and active in the League of Women Voters and the American Association of University Women. In addition to her wartime decorations, she received an honorary degree from Mount Holyoke College (1921) and the Florence Nightingale Medal of the International Red Cross (1929).

Colonel Stimson was striking in appearance, nearly six feet tall, with penetrating blue eyes and a vibrant personality. Although positive and independent in speech and action, with strong, outspoken convictions, she was understanding and sympathetic when dealing with individuals needing help. She found recreation in playing the violin and in outdoor activities. After retirement from the Army Nurse Corps she made her home in Briarcliff, N.Y., where she served on the board of trustees of the town library and of the Congregational church. Her summers were spent in Rockland, Maine. She died, after surgery, in a Poughkeepsie, N.Y., hospital, of acute circulatory collapse caused by generalized arteriosclerosis. Her ashes were privately interred, as she had requested, in the woods near her home in Briarcliff.

[Obituary and editorial, *Am. Jour. of Nursing*, Nov. 1948; *Nat. Cyc. Am. Biog.*, Current Vol. B, p. 67; *Biog. Cyc. Am. Women*, III, 218–20; Lavinia L. Dock et al., *Hist. of Am. Red Cross Nursing* (1922); Portia B. Kernodle, *The Red Cross Nurse in Action, 1882–1948* (1949); Am. Soc. of Superintendents of Training Schools for Nurses, 17th *Annual Report*, 1911; Nat. Nursing Council, *Hist. of the Council* (1951); information from family and friends of Miss Stimson, from the registrar of Washington Univ., from the Army Nurse Corps, and from personal knowledge; death record from N.Y. State Dept. of Health.]

                                        STELLA GOOSTRAY

**STODDARD, Cora Frances** (Sept. 17, 1872–May 13, 1936), temperance educator, was born in Irvington, Nebr., where her father was then farming. Her parents, Emerson Hathaway Stoddard and Julia Frances (Miller) Stoddard, natives respectively of North Brookfield and New Braintree, Mass., soon returned east and settled in East Brookfield, Mass., where both were active in temperance work, her mother as president of the local Woman's Christian Temperance Union. Cora was educated in public schools and at Wellesley College, receiving her A.B. degree in 1896. After teaching high school for a year in Middletown, Conn., she spent two years in business in East Brookfield. Moving to Boston, she became private sec-

retary in 1899 to MARY H. HUNT, director of the Department of Scientific Temperance Instruction of the National Woman's Christian Temperance Union. According to W.C.T.U.-sponsored legislation enacted in most states, the public schools were required to teach the dangers of alcohol, and Miss Stoddard assisted Mrs. Hunt in preparing and reviewing textbooks and temperance materials intended for such instruction. Mrs. Hunt had also founded the Scientific Temperance Association, which received royalties from the publishers of science textbooks that won her endorsement. When she died in 1906 the W.C.T.U., disturbed by this financial link, rejected a proposal to absorb the association. Miss Stoddard had meanwhile left the work in 1904, owing to ill health, and was in 1906 residing in Cortland, N.Y., where she held an administrative post in the local normal school. In that year, however, she returned to Boston to join a small group of interested persons in founding the Scientific Temperance Federation to perpetuate the Hunt organization. As its executive secretary for the next thirty years, she compiled statistics, prepared exhibits, wrote numerous pamphlets and magazine articles on the physiological and social effects of alcohol, and edited the quarterly *Scientific Temperance Journal*. In 1909 she was a delegate to the International Congress against Alcoholism, in London, and she attended four subsequent congresses.

In 1913 the Anti-Saloon League began to publish and distribute the *Scientific Temperance Journal* and other Scientific Temperance Federation literature, and Miss Stoddard moved into the orbit of that burgeoning organization. She now turned primarily to the production of propaganda for use in Anti-Saloon League campaigns for state and national prohibition amendments and, during World War I, the armed forces' temperance program. Although her pamphlet *Alcohol's Ledger in Industry* (1914) is a restrained and documented study of the deleterious effects of liquor on industrial efficiency and safety, her *Handbook of Modern Facts about Alcohol* (1914) is more consciously propagandistic in its use of data. It reflects the concern over immigration and urbanization characteristic of the period and views alcoholism solely as a cause, rather than a symptom, of social and personal problems.

A rapprochement with the W.C.T.U. came in 1918 when Miss Stoddard became director of its Bureau of Scientific Temperance Investigation and, four years later, of its Department of Scientific Temperance Instruction. In 1925 she assumed similar positions in the World's

W.C.T.U. With the coming of national prohibition in 1920, however, interest in school temperance instruction waned, and Miss Stoddard instead undertook to study the effects of prohibition, producing books like *Wet and Dry Years in a Decade of Massachusetts Public Records* (1922) and a number of pamphlets on such topics as the alleged correlation between prohibition and rising drug addiction. She also wrote a *History of Scientific Temperance Instruction* (n.d.), which viewed the coming of age of a temperance-educated generation as a prime factor in the adoption of the Eighteenth Amendment. She served as an associate editor of the *Standard Encyclopedia of the Alcohol Problem* (6 vols., 1924–30), prepared under Anti-Saloon League auspices.

Cora Stoddard was remembered by her associates as a gentle, devout woman. An Episcopalian when young, she later became a Congregationalist. In 1933, confined to a wheelchair by arthritis, she was forced to resign all her offices except that with the Scientific Temperance Federation, in which she continued active until her death of cancer three years later, at sixty-three, in her brother Hubert's home in Oxford, Conn. She was buried in Walnut Grove Cemetery, North Brookfield.

[Memorial issue of *Scientific Temperance Jour.*, Summer 1936; Ernest H. Cherrington, ed., *Standard Encyc. of the Alcohol Problem*, V (1929), 2379–80, VI (1930), 2535–36. For a fairly complete bibliography of her writings see *Who Was Who in America*, vol. I (1942), and *Readers' Guide to Periodical Literature*, vols. III–VI. On Mrs. Hunt's Scientific Temperance Assoc., see Norton Mezvinsky, "The White-Ribbon Reform, 1874–1920" (unpublished doctoral dissertation, Univ. of Wis., 1959), pp. 165–67, and Nat. W.C.T.U. *Minutes*, 1906. Marriage record of her parents from Mass. Registrar of Vital Statistics; death record from Conn. State Dept. of Health, Hartford.]

FREDERICK L. SCHEPMAN

STOECKEL, Ellen Battell (Mar. 10, 1851– May 5, 1939), philanthropist and patron of music, was born at Norfolk, Conn., the only child of Robbins and Ellen Ryerson (Mills) Battell. Her father was descended from early Massachusetts and Connecticut colonists; her mother was from Newark, N.J. Robbins Battell, for many years probate judge of Norfolk, served also as treasurer of the town and of its church, as the town's representative in the legislature, and as state comptroller.

Ellen Battell was the heir to a rich musical tradition. Her grandfather Joseph Battell, a prosperous merchant, and his wife, Sarah Robbins, had nurtured in their children their own love of music. Two of their offspring devoted the major part of their lives to musical activity. Ellen's aunt Irene Battell Larned, wife of Prof. William Augustus Larned of Yale, was chiefly responsible for winning a place for music in Yale's curriculum. Ellen's father was an amateur flutist; while an undergraduate at Yale he had become one of the leading singers in the chapel choir and a helpful partner to his fellow student Richard Storrs Willis of Boston in organizing Yale's first orchestra in 1839. In the 1840's with his sister Irene he built up the Litchfield County Musical Association, and although in the latter part of his life he became increasingly involved in the family's business affairs, which included iron interests in New York City as well as the real estate holdings of the Battell estate in Norfolk, his love of music never waned.

Ellen Battell's mother died a few days after the girl's birth. Growing up in close companionship with her father, Ellen received her formal schooling in the Norfolk grade schools and from private tutors. She began in early youth to study music, became an accomplished singer and pianist, and cultivated discriminating taste as a patron of art. Adding valuable paintings by such artists as Winslow Homer and George Inness to the family gallery begun by her father, she also continued to maintain the house as a mecca for music lovers by bringing in singers and instrumentalists. On Feb. 5, 1873, she was married to Frederick Peet Terry, a recent graduate of Yale. He died only a year later; their only child, Frederick Battell Terry, died at sixteen in 1890.

During her years of widowhood Mrs. Terry developed a close friendship with Carl Stoeckel, son of a German musician, Gustave Stoeckel, who had been appointed organist and instructor in sacred music at Yale in 1855 through the influence of Irene Battell Larned. The younger Stoeckel had in 1874 moved to Norfolk to become Robbins Battell's secretary and to assist in the management of the family estate. His marriage, on May 6, 1895, to Ellen Battell Terry brought together two persons of many common interests. In that same year, with the death of her father, Ellen Battell inherited the sizable Battell estate.

During the first four years of their marriage, she and her husband traveled extensively abroad and made themselves familiar with the summer festivals of Wagnerian opera at Bayreuth and with the great choral festivals which had become traditional in England. In 1899 they founded the Litchfield County Choral Union in memory of Robbins Battell. The original Litchfield County Musical Association had lapsed soon after mid-century, but the idea never died, and the new Choral Union, directed by Richmond P. Paine, shortly numbered 700 singing members from Norfolk, Winsted, Salisbury, Canaan, and Torrington. Summer festival performances, financed by Mrs. Stoeckel and organized "to honor the composer and his works under the most elevated conditions and to bring to the people of Litchfield County great music in its purest form," were first held in Norfolk in June 1899 on three successive evenings, with a supporting orchestra recruited from the New York Philharmonic Society and the Metropolitan Opera and with world-famous soloists.

In 1906 the Stoeckels erected a private auditorium seating 1,500 and accommodating on its stage a chorus of 500 and an orchestra of 100. For the following seventeen years, until 1922, the Norfolk Festivals featured specially commissioned works by the greatest American and European composers; they became the model upon which other summer music festivals in the Berkshire and Litchfield hills have since been developed. Following her husband's death in 1925, Mrs. Stoeckel continued to use the auditorium, sponsoring country-wide hymn sings in Norfolk, with an orchestra imported from New York. She died in Norfolk in 1939, two years after the final program in this series, and was buried beside Stoeckel on the family estate.

Ellen Battell Stoeckel willed the entire Battell estate, together with a liberal endowment, for the establishment of a summer school of music and art to be administered by Yale University. The Norfolk summer schools of music (opened in 1941) and art (opened in 1946) have grown and prospered, continuing the musical and cultural heritage descending from the Robbins, Battell, and Stoeckel families.

[This article is based principally on the author's forthcoming history of music at Yale. See also collected letters and obituaries of Robbins Battell, Yale Univ. Archives; Theron W. Crissey, comp., *Hist. of Norfolk, Litchfield County, Conn.* (1900); Joseph H. Vaill, comp., *Litchfield County Choral Union* (2 vols., 1912); Sydney Thompson, *The Ellen Battell Stoeckel Trust* (printed for the Norfolk Summer School of Music and Art, 1951); David S. Smith, *Gustave J. Stoeckel, Yale Pioneer in Music* (1939).]

MARSHALL BARTHOLOMEW

STOKES, Olivia Egleston Phelps (Jan. 11, 1847–Dec. 14, 1927) and **Caroline Phelps** (Dec. 4, 1854–Apr. 26, 1909), philanthropists, were born in New York City. They were, respectively, the second daughter and sixth child, and fifth daughter and last of the ten children of James Boulter Stokes and Caroline

(Phelps) Stokes. Their paternal grandfather, Thomas Stokes, had come from England to the United States in 1789, settling eventually in New York City, where James B. Stokes was born. Anson Greene Phelps, their maternal grandfather, was descended from colonial governors of Massachusetts and Connecticut (the birthplace of their mother). A brother of Olivia and Caroline, Anson Phelps Stokes, became a prominent banker and merchant and an advocate of free trade, civil service reform, and anti-imperialism. Another brother, William Earl Dodge Stokes, became a noted real estate promoter. Their nephew I. N. Phelps Stokes was an architect who possessed an unusual interest in the design and planning of low-cost tenement housing. Another nephew was James Graham Phelps Stokes, prominent Socialist and husband of the radical leader ROSE PASTOR STOKES.

Although surrounded by many of the comforts provided only by wealth—a large house, gardens, a summer home in Ansonia, Conn.— the sisters from earliest childhood were exposed to an atmosphere pervaded by evangelical Protestant piety, missionary zeal, and good works. Their father and grandfathers viewed the wealth they acquired from banking, real estate, and trade as a stewardship, or trust, to be invested in the conquest of sin and pursuit of Christian perfection on earth. Thomas Stokes, while still in England, had been active in missionary and Sunday school affairs; after coming to the United States he became involved in the establishment or administration of such agencies as the American Bible Society and the American Tract Society. His friend Anson Greene Phelps was equally absorbed in the work of these societies and such similar ones as the American Board of Commissioners for Foreign Missions, the Domestic Missionary Society, and the Marine Bible Society. As president of the New York Colonization Society he had helped establish the Republic of Liberia, whose first president was a visitor in the Stokes home during Olivia's and Caroline's childhood. Their father's philanthropies included the New York Hospital for Ruptured and Crippled Children, New York Eye and Ear Infirmary, Society for the Prevention of Cruelty to Animals, Greenwich Savings Bank, and New York Association for Improving the Condition of the Poor. Committed first and foremost to the nurture of Christian character, he developed a particular interest in the Y.M.C.A.

The Christian zeal of Mrs. Stokes was wondrous even by the standards of the family and the times. Her combination of otherworldliness and charity probably influenced the lives of the sisters most directly. A temperance and sabbatarian extremist, an abolitionist and benefactor of the Negro, who helped found and maintain the Colored Orphan Asylum of New York and supported Negro students both in the United States and in African mission schools, Mrs. Stokes reared her children with a concern for their Christian purity on earth exceeded only by her concern for the salvation of their eternal souls. Frequent prayer at home in the company of her children was supplemented by visits to missionary meetings and monthly home gatherings devoted to missionary stories. A liberal donor of Bibles, tracts, and Sunday school libraries, and a visitor to tenement families, Mrs. Stokes always emphasized the importance of personal service to the poor and unregenerate. Deeply interested in the work of the Phelps Chapel at 34th and 35th streets, she conducted a sewing class there for many years.

Mrs. Stokes and her husband cared little for temporal diversions. They visited and entertained infrequently, avoided the theatre, and prohibited it to their children. Literature at home was restricted, by and large, to devotional or inspirational material, and Mrs. Stokes was loath to permit her offspring to associate with other children unless she knew and approved of their religious training. Olivia and Caroline Phelps Stokes never questioned the doctrines they inherited. On the contrary, they shaped their lives in the image of their parents, especially their mother, who exemplified in their eyes the meekness, awareness of Christ's constant companionship, and daily dedication to serve others for His glory, to which they aspired throughout their lifetime. They were educated at home, although Caroline spent some time at Miss Porter's School in Farmington, Conn., in company with her cousin GRACE DODGE.

Their other sisters married, and Olivia and Caroline, almost identical in their outlook and tastes despite a seven-year difference in age, were left to a quiet domestic and charitable routine. For a time, probably during her late twenties, Olivia served (as secretary) on the board of the New York Young Women's Christian Association. Caroline taught Sunday school, carried on her mother's sewing class at the Phelps Chapel, and went once a week to a club for working girls. They shared a love of nature as the symbol of God's beneficence; Caroline painted in watercolors and was an expert horsewoman. There were a few close friends, such as the writers SUSAN and ANNA WARNER, of whom Olivia later wrote a memoir. Both she and Caroline read and studied and developed a modest talent for writing, Olivia publishing such inspirational works as *Pine and Cedar: Bible Verses* (1885), *Forward in the Better Life* (1915), and *Saturday Nights in Lent* (1922). Both were Presbyterians but were attracted to the Episcopal service in their later years. After the death of their parents, the sisters made several extended journeys in the company of their brother James Stokes, Jr., a founding member of the International Committee of Young Men's Christian Associations, including a trip around the world in 1896–97 on which they observed "philanthropic and Christian work" in India and elsewhere.

Everywhere they contributed generously, separately or together, to charitable or religious enterprises. Their benefactions included public baths in New York, St. Paul's Chapel at Columbia University, a new building for the Peabody Home for Aged and Infirm Women in Ansonia, Conn., a library there, an administration building, Woodbridge Hall, for Yale University, and a lunch wagon in New York City designed to lessen the allure of the saloon. They donated substantial sums to the New York Zoological Society and New York Botanical Garden, provided an open-air pulpit for the Cathedral of St. John the Divine and a chapel for Berea College in Kentucky, and supported numerous missionary causes.

Their most memorable philanthropic achievements, however, evolved from their recognition of the Negro's plight. These took place after Caroline Phelps Stokes' death. Incapacitated with rheumatism in the later years of her life, she had moved to California, where she occupied her leisure with writing *Travels of a Lady's Maid,* a novel based on her world tour which was published anonymously in 1908. She died in Redlands, Calif., the next year at the age of fifty-four. The sisters had been especially interested in opening opportunities for vocational education in the South, where they had visited a number of institutions. Caroline's bequests included large sums to Tuskegee Institute for a chapel, to Calhoun Colored School in Alabama for a chapel or other needed building, and to Hampton Institute in Virginia for an endowment fund for the education of Negroes and Indians. Most important, she bequeathed the residue of her estate to establish the Phelps-Stokes Fund, stipulating that its income be used to improve tenement housing in New York, and to educate Indians, "deserving" white students, and Negroes in Africa and the United States. Following her sister's death, Olivia Phelps Stokes became a liberal contributor to the fund, which concentrated primarily upon Negro education and the improvement of race relations. Her own bequests included $100,000 apiece to Tuskegee and Hampton institutes, and a smaller sum to establish similar facilities in Africa.

In 1901 the sisters had financed the Tuskegee, a "model" tenement house in New York City designed by I. N. Phelps Stokes and reserved for Negro occupancy. Their mother had been active in model tenement work as a stockholder in the Improved Dwellings Company of New York, and in 1896 Caroline served on the model apartment house committee of the Improved Dwellings Council, which evolved into the City and Suburban Homes Company of New York, the largest model tenement company in the United States. In 1915 Olivia donated two model tenements she had built in memory of her sister to the Phelps-Stokes Fund. Surviving Caroline by nineteen years, Olivia died of bronchial pneumonia in Washington, D.C., at eighty. She was buried in California near her sister, in Hillside Memorial Park in Redlands.

The place of Olivia and Caroline Phelps Stokes in the history of American philanthropy is related not only to their distinctive interest in Negro welfare, and the large sums of money they contributed for this purpose, but to the assumptions which guided their benefactions. They emphasized charity—the relief of immediate necessity—less than long-range goals of progress through educational opportunity and housing betterment. Admirers of JOSEPHINE SHAW LOWELL, they were undoubtedly influenced by charity organization principles which minimized the importance of relief in favor of character development and self-help. At the same time, their emphasis upon character reformation and social melioration represented a kind of secularized religious idealism directed toward social regeneration and equity. The sisters personified the combination of secular charity organization goals and Protestant religious enthusiasm which profoundly influenced the course of American philanthropy in the late nineteenth and early twentieth centuries.

[The Phelps-Stokes Fund possesses a manuscript biography by Olivia Egleston Phelps Stokes, "The Story of Caroline Phelps Stokes" (1927). Also in the fund's archives are letters written by Olivia Phelps Stokes. The Schlesinger Library, Radcliffe College, has some letters and several journals of the sisters. The following are useful for data concerning the Stokes and Phelps families: Anna Bartlett Warner, *Some Memories of James Stokes and Caroline Phelps Stokes* (privately printed, 1892); Oliver S. Phelps and Andrew T. Servin, *The Phelps Family of America* (2 vols., 1899);

Anson Phelps Stokes, *Stokes Records* (1910); and articles in the *Dict. Am. Biog.* on Anson Greene Phelps, Anson Phelps Stokes, and William Earl Dodge Stokes. See also obituaries in *N.Y. Times,* Apr. 28, 1909, Dec. 15, 1927, and *N.Y. Herald Tribune,* Dec. 15, 1927, and report of Olivia's will in *N.Y. Times,* Dec. 25, 1927. *Reports* of the Phelps-Stokes Fund issued in 1920, 1932, and 1948 contain information on the two sisters, as well as accounts of the agency's operations; see especially Olivia's biographical sketch of Caroline in the 1920 *Report.* The Rev. Anson Phelps Stokes, Jr., of Boston provided assistance in an interview.]

ROY LUBOVE

**STOKES, Rose Harriet Pastor** (July 18, 1879–June 20, 1933), Socialist and Communist leader, was born to Jewish parents, Jacob and Anna (Lewin) Wieslander, in Augustów, Russian Poland, some 130 miles northeast of Warsaw. Her father died shortly after her birth and her mother married a cigar maker named Pastor, whose name Rose took. The poverty-stricken family soon emigrated to London, where they lived in the Whitechapel ghetto. From the age of four Rose helped her mother sew bows on ladies' slippers to eke out the family income. Two years at the Bell Lane Free School for the poor, between the ages of seven and nine, comprised her formal education. When she was eleven the Pastors moved on to America and settled in Cleveland, Ohio. With six younger brothers and sisters now in the family, Rose went to work in a cigar factory. There the cigarmakers' tradition of paying someone to read aloud as they worked may have supplemented her meager schooling. She began writing poems, and in 1900, having submitted several to the Yiddish *Jewish Daily News* of New York City, was invited to become a regular contributor at $2 a week.

After her family moved in 1903 to the Bronx, Rose became an assistant editor of the *Daily News,* writing a column of advice to young women in the newspaper's English section. Five months after her arrival in New York the vivacious girl with deep-set eyes and a mass of dark hair was sent to interview James Graham Phelps Stokes, a wealthy young New Yorker whose socialist sympathies had led him to the University Settlement on New York's Lower East Side. From this meeting grew their marriage, on July 18, 1905, hailed by the popular press as a Cinderella match. After a three-month wedding trip abroad, they took an apartment in New York's Russian quarter and cultivated a circle of radical and artistic friends. They had no children.

Renewing her earlier membership in the Socialist party, Rose Stokes and her husband devoted themselves to party work, Rose in particular as a lecturer for the Intercollegiate Socialist Society, which Stokes headed from 1907 to 1917. Though she brought no remarkable intellectual clarity or organizational ability to the movement, her exuberance and contagious enthusiasm undoubtedly generated interest and attracted followers. With her authentic working-class background she was an effective leader among urban working women and was especially active in the New York restaurant and hotel workers' strike of 1912. A prolific writer, she published poems, articles, and reviews on social themes in such diverse periodicals as the *Independent, Everybody's,* the *Arena,* and the *Century.* In 1914 she collaborated with Helen Frank in translating from the Yiddish Morris Rosenfeld's *Songs of Labor and Other Poems.* Two years later (reflecting the interest in proletarian theatre being fostered by EMMA GOLDMAN's *The Social Significance of the Modern Drama*) she wrote *The Woman Who Wouldn't,* a play in which the emancipated heroine becomes a labor leader.

When the United States entered World War I in April 1917, Rose Stokes and her husband were among those who withdrew from the Socialist party in opposition to its antiwar stand. In October they helped organize in Chicago the short-lived National party, incorporating remnants of the 1912 Progressive party. For James Stokes the separation from the Socialist movement was permanent, but Rose changed her mind after the Russian Revolution of November 1917 and by the following February had announced her return to the party. In March 1918 she was indicted under the wartime Espionage Act for writing in a letter to the *Kansas City Star:* "I am for the people, while the Government is for the profiteers." The judge at her trial instructed the jury to find her guilty if her letter produced a spirit tending "naturally and logically to interfere" with military recruitment, and Mrs. Stokes was sentenced to ten years' imprisonment. Though upon appeal the conviction was reversed by a higher court in 1920, it has frequently been cited as an example of the overzealous harrying of those who opposed the war.

Mrs. Stokes gradually moved to the extreme left wing of the Socialist party and in September 1919 was among those who left it to form the Communist party. Though never in the highest echelon of Communist leadership, she was in 1922 an American delegate to the Fourth Congress of the Communist International in Moscow, where she was the reporter for the Congress' special Negro Commission (*Worker,* Mar. 10, 1923). She also supported

the American faction which favored continuation of the illegal underground apparatus, but when the Russian leaders decreed otherwise she acquiesced and was elected to the central executive committee of the newly formed Workers' party, the direct forerunner of the Communist Party of the U.S.A.

In the 1920's Mrs. Stokes walked picket lines, wrote articles for *Pravda* and the *Worker* (after 1924 the *Daily Worker*), ran for Manhattan borough president on the Communist ticket (1921), made speeches (when not banned by local authorities), exhibited paintings at a show of the Society of Independent Artists (1925), and had frequent encounters with the law, such as her arrest in 1929 while picketing in a strike of the Needle Trades Industrial Union. Her political views and those of James Stokes had diverged too far for a harmonious marriage, and when he was granted a divorce in October 1925 Rose announced that they had been "friendly enemies" for years. In 1927 she married Isaac Romaine (also known as V. J. Jerome), a language teacher and Communist theoretician.

In 1930 Mrs. Stokes (she retained the name) learned that she had cancer and retired to Westport, Conn. Communist friends, attributing her illness to a police clubbing during a 1929 pro-Haitian demonstration, raised funds to send her to Europe for medical treatment; she died in the municipal hospital at Frankfurt am Main, Germany, at the age of fifty-three. Her cremated remains were returned to New York City for a memorial service under Communist auspices at Webster Hall in Greenwich Village. Having refused alimony at the time of the divorce, she left an estate of less than $2,000; by her will this was divided among Communist friends.

[For her numerous poems and articles see *Readers' Guide to Periodical Literature,* vols. II–VII and IX. The *N.Y. Times Index,* 1913–33, reports many of her activities. See also the *Times* obituary, June 21, 1933, and reports of her memorial service and will, July 25 and Aug. 26; *Who's Who in America,* 1918–19 (for both Rose Stokes and James G. P. Stokes); *Woman's Who's Who of America,* 1914–15; *Universal Jewish Encyc.,* X, 67; *New Masses,* June 1933, pp. 23–24; *Daily Worker,* June 21, 22, 1933, and June 20, 1939. On her early New York days and marriage see *Am. Jewish Year Book,* 1904–05, p. 163; *N.Y. Tribune,* July 19, 1905; and Lillian B. Griffin, "Mrs. J. G. Phelps Stokes at Home," *Harper's Bazar,* Sept. 1906. On her socialism see David A. Shannon, *The Socialist Party of America: A Hist.* (1955), and Ray Ginger, *The Bending Cross* (1949). On her wartime espionage conviction: Zechariah Chafee, Jr., *Free Speech in the U.S.* (1941), pp. 52–53. On her Communist activities see Theodore Draper, *The Roots of Am. Communism* (1957); and, for interesting sidelights, Benjamin Gitlow, *I Confess* (1939), pp. 139–40; and Claude McKay, *A Long Way from Home* (1937), pp. 160–62. Before her death Mrs. Stokes turned over several cases of personal papers, including an autobiography, to friends in the Communist party; these have never been made public.]

DAVID A. SHANNON

**STOKOWSKI, Olga Samaroff.** *See* SAMAROFF, Olga.

**STONE, Lucinda Hinsdale** (Sept. 30, 1814–Mar. 14, 1900), educator and clubwoman, was born in Hinesburg, twelve miles south of Burlington, Vt., the ninth daughter and youngest of the twelve children of Aaron and Lucinda (Mitchell) Hinsdale, both of old New England stock. Her father, who owned a small water-powered woolen mill, died when she was not quite three, and she was brought up by her mother, an omnivorous reader and a firm believer in education for women. After district school, Lucinda attended the Hinesburg Academy and combined teaching with further study at female seminaries in Burlington and nearby Middlebury. An able student, she was laughed at for studying Greek and for her unfeminine wish to go to college. Three years as tutor to the children of a planter near Natchez, Miss., reenforced her antislavery sentiments. On June 10, 1840, at the home of a sister in Grand Rapids, Mich., she was married to the former principal of the Hinesburg Academy, James Andrus Blinn Stone, now a Baptist minister in Gloucester, Mass. They had three children: Clement Walker, Horatio Hackett, and James Helm.

After living briefly in Gloucester and in Newton, Mass., the Stones moved in 1843 to Kalamazoo, Mich., a frontier town as yet without railroad connections, where James Stone took charge of the Baptist church and of an institution recently formed by a merger of the Kalamazoo Literary Institute and the local branch, or preparatory school, of the University of Michigan, which became known as Kalamazoo College. Lucinda Stone became principal of the college's "Female Department." Here she sought, by informal and liberal methods of teaching, to develop independent thinking and useful character. Convinced that the teachers needed continued intellectual stimulus from superior minds and new ideas, she invited them to her home on Saturday evenings to meet visiting celebrities, who were often abolitionists and woman's rights leaders and included Ralph Waldo Emerson, of whom

Mrs. Stone was a lifelong admirer. These gatherings gained such fame that local women urged her to do the same for them; thus she helped organize, in 1852, the Kalamazoo Ladies' Library Association, a combined library and literary club.

The college prospered and enrollments multiplied until 1857, when registration dropped off sharply, partly because of the economic depression, but also because of orthodox Baptist opposition to the liberalism of the Stones. Borrowing from the endowment fund to cover operating deficits caused such a financial tangle that appeals for new capital were hopelessly unsuccessful. Stone resigned in 1863, followed by Mrs. Stone, who was aware of a proposal to replace her with a man. She then started her own school in her home, attracting so many girls from the college that the trustees pressed her to return and offered to reinstate her husband in his theology professorship. After their refusal, a church court convicted Stone on unproved charges of immorality and his wife was voted out of church membership. When a fire destroyed their home in 1866, Lucinda Stone, now fifty-two, turned to a new educational venture, taking a group of girls on a tour of Europe and the Near East to study art and history. Between 1867 and 1888 she conducted eight of these traveling schools, each lasting from twelve to eighteen months. Between trips, influenced by the New England Woman's Club, whose structure and program she had studied on a trip to Boston, she organized similar clubs in Kalamazoo (1873) and other Michigan cities, considering them the most effective agencies then available for educating women. Newspapers in Detroit, Port Huron, and Kalamazoo featured her weekly column, "Club Talks," which counseled her organizations and suggested study materials. Mrs. Stone was also instrumental in organizing the Michigan Women's Press Association in 1890. Widely known as the "mother of clubs," she turned to the federation movement as she approached eighty, serving as chairman of correspondence for Michigan of the General Federation of Women's Clubs and engineering the formation of the Michigan federation in 1895.

A champion of college training for women ever since her Vermont academy days, Mrs. Stone was also, as a result of her experiences with girls' schools, a staunch advocate of coeducation. The University of Michigan, founded in 1817, had never admitted women, but when one of the Stones' students, Madelon Stockwell, applied there in 1869, Mrs. Stone and her husband made an issue of her case, convinced that there was no legal obstacle. In January 1870 the regents voted to admit qualified women. Later, as executive secretary of the Women's Auxiliary Association of the university, Mrs. Stone pressed for the appointment of women to the faculty, a policy approved by the regents in 1894 and implemented two years later when Dr. ELIZA MARIA MOSHER became professor of hygiene and dean of women. Mrs. Stone had meanwhile (1890) been awarded an honorary Ph.D. degree by the university.

After her husband's death in 1888, she joined the Unitarian church of Kalamazoo, renamed the People's Church in 1894, to which the Rev. Caroline Bartlett (see CAROLINE BARTLETT CRANE) brought a vigorous social gospel. For the church Mrs. Stone organized a club for Negro men, taught a class in comparative religion, and built up the Channing Library of liberal religious thought. In 1897 she became a member of the Theosophical Society. She died in Kalamazoo at the age of eighty-five and was buried there in Mountain Home Cemetery.

[The principal sources are the Lucinda Hinsdale Stone Scrapbooks, Kalamazoo Public Library, containing correspondence, lecture notes, and clippings relating to the last twenty years of her life; and Belle McArthur Perry, *Lucinda Hinsdale Stone: Her Life Story and Reminiscences* (1902), a eulogistic account by a close friend, which includes autobiographical sketches, travel recollections, and reminiscences by pupils. See also Anson D. P. Van Buren, "Attending the University Branch at Kalamazoo in 1843," *Mich. Pioneer and Hist. Collections*, XIV (1890), 326–40, an early student's account of the Stones; Mary M. Hoyt, "Mrs. Lucinda Hinsdale Stone," *ibid.*, XXXVIII (1912), 171–76; *An Episode in the Hist. of Kalamazoo College: A Letter to Hon. J. M. Gregory, LL.D.* (1868), which presents the Stones' side of the resignations and the church trials; Frances E. Willard and Mary A. Livermore, eds., *A Woman of the Century* (1893); Jane C. Croly, *The Hist. of the Woman's Club Movement in America* (1898), pp. 678–81, 710; Mildred W. Wells, *Unity in Diversity: The Hist. of the Gen. Federation of Women's Clubs* (1953), pp. 142–43; obituary articles in Kalamazoo *Morning Gazette*, Mar. 15, 17, 18, 21, 1900; and Charles R. Starring, "Lucinda Hinsdale Stone," *Mich. Hist.*, Mar. 1958.]

                                        CHARLES R. STARRING

STONE, Lucy (Aug. 13, 1818–Oct. 18, 1893), feminist, abolitionist, and suffragist, was born of a family long established in New England, her ancestor Gregory Stone having left England in 1635 for religious liberty in Massachusetts. Her great-grandfather Jonathan Stone died in battle during the expedition against Crown Point in 1755. Her grandfather Francis Stone was a captain in the American Revolution and one of the leaders in Shays' Rebellion. Her father, also named Francis, was a well-to-do farmer and tanner; her mother, Hannah (Matthews) Stone, accepted his view that a husband ruled his family by divine right. Lucy was born on the family farm on Coy's Hill, about three miles from West Brookfield, Mass., the eighth of nine brothers and sisters and the third daughter among the seven children who survived. Even as a child she resented the assigning of women to an inferior role, expressing indignation at the preference shown an older brother despite the fact that she could learn and run faster than he. She was distressed by her mother's hard life and at the age of twelve began rising very early on Monday mornings to help her by doing the family laundry before school. She likewise resented her lack of a vote at the local Congregational church, and when she read in the Bible that men should rule women she suspected inaccuracy in translation and determined to go to college to study Greek and Hebrew, an ambition her father dismissed as utterly ridiculous for a girl. Another injustice began to prey upon her as she attended antislavery lectures and read William Lloyd Garrison's abolitionist journal, the *Liberator*.

At sixteen she ended her own schooling and began teaching district school. Her salary of a dollar a week impressed upon her the disparity between the wages paid men and women. With her earnings from teaching she studied for brief periods at Quaboag Seminary in Warren, Mass., and at Wesleyan Academy in Wilbraham, and in 1839 entered Mount Holyoke Female Seminary in South Hadley. In 1843, aged twenty-five, she enrolled at Oberlin College in Ohio, noted for its antislavery principles and its introduction of the coeducational system.

At Oberlin, Lucy Stone, fighting occasional intense headaches, studied for the next four years. Living frugally, she supported herself through housework and teaching. A brother and a sister loaned her money, and at last her father, reluctantly acknowledging her persistence, aided her as he had her brothers. Her Greek and Hebrew studies did indeed convince her that crucial passages in the Bible respecting woman's role had been misconstrued, and her special knowledge in the field later made her formidable on the platform when the subject arose. Though she had hoped to practice public speaking, she found such activities closed to women at the college and could only develop her oratorical talents secretly before a few friends. In 1847, graduating with honors, she became the first Massachusetts woman to take a college degree. She refused an invitation to write a commencement address, however, because she would not have been permitted to read it herself, owing to the prevailing belief that it was improper for women to participate in public exercises with men. (The injustice was corrected thirty-six years later when Lucy Stone was an honored speaker at Oberlin's semicentennial jubilee.) William Lloyd Garrison, who attended the 1847 commencement, wrote of Lucy Stone to his wife: "She is a very superior young woman, and has a soul as free as the air, and is preparing to go forth as a lecturer, particularly in vindication of the rights of women. Her course here has been very firm and independent, and she has caused no small uneasiness to the spirit of sectarianism in the institution" (Blackwell, p. 74).

A few months later, after her first public address, given from her brother's pulpit in Gardner, Mass., she was appointed a lecturer by the Garrison-dominated American Anti-Slavery Society, partly through the influence of ABBY KELLEY FOSTER. But before long her continuing interest in woman's rights caused trouble with the abolitionists. Inspired by Hiram Powers' statue, the "Greek Slave," she devoted an entire lecture to the position of women. To the Anti-Slavery Society's objection she replied, "I was a woman before I was an abolitionist. I must speak for the women." As a compromise it was agreed that she could lecture on woman's rights on her own responsibility all week if she would talk for the Society on weekends. This she did, making all her own arrangements, posting her own notices, and taking up collections for expenses. When one of her engagements conflicted with an antislavery concert by the Hutchinson family singers (see ABBY HUTCHINSON PATTON), they persuaded her to join forces and share receipts. Convinced by this experience that an admission fee would not damage her cause, she cleared about $7,000 in three years.

An impressive speaker, she drew large audiences. As a young woman she looked like a small pink-cheeked schoolgirl, with her smooth brown hair cut round at the neck and her clear gray eyes; but her voice was her chief asset—low and musical, yet clear and strong. She used no rhetorical tricks and little humor, but concentrated intensely on her subject, her very sincerity producing a natural eloquence that stirred her listeners. She often faced hostile audiences, but showed little fear, even when in real danger. When she and a fellow speaker, the abolitionist Stephen S. Foster,

were threatened by a mob at a celebrated meeting on Cape Cod, she urged him to escape, and when he asked who would protect her she slipped her hand about the arm of one of the rioters, saying: "This gentleman will take care of me." He not only did so, but later took up a collection of twenty dollars to pay for Foster's torn coat. The notoriety accumulated from such experiences, along with her quiet acceptance of Unitarianism, led to expulsion from her church for conduct "inconsistent with her covenant engagements."

In 1850 she led in calling the first national woman's rights convention at Worcester, Mass. Though less famous than the Seneca Falls convention of 1848, it included a more truly national representation and had a woman, PAULINA WRIGHT DAVIS, in the chair. Lucy Stone, only barely recovered from typhoid fever, made a speech at Worcester which converted SUSAN B. ANTHONY to the cause. Reported overseas, the address prompted the writing, for the *Westminster Review,* of the feminist classic "The Enfranchisement of Women," an article by John Stuart Mill embodying the thought of Harriet Taylor, soon to become his wife. In the next few years, wearing the garb associated with AMELIA BLOOMER, Lucy Stone traveled extensively, lecturing on woman suffrage in Canada, as far west as Missouri, and even in the South.

Though she had not lacked suitors, she had early decided against marriage, determined to "call no man master"; but Henry Browne Blackwell, a Cincinnati hardware merchant and abolitionist, made up his mind to test this resolution. She had met Blackwell, seven years her junior, while on a lecture tour. The pioneer women physicians ELIZABETH and EMILY BLACKWELL were his sisters, and his brother Samuel later married Antoinette L. Brown, Oberlin friend and classmate of Lucy Stone and the first woman ordained as a minister in America (see ANTOINETTE BROWN BLACKWELL). Henry Blackwell courted Lucy Stone for two years, first winning her admiration by his bravery in rescuing a fugitive slave from her owners. Gradually he won Lucy's affection and finally her consent by persuading her that she could be perfectly free within marriage and that two could advance her cause better than one. After their marriage, on May 1, 1855, she kept her own name, calling herself Mrs. Stone and thereby adding the phrase "Lucy Stoner" to the language to denote a married woman retaining her maiden name. At Blackwell's suggestion they read at the ceremony a protest against the marriage laws which received wide publicity through Thomas Wentworth Higgin-

son, the officiating minister, who had it published with his endorsement.

In 1856 Lucy Stone presided over the Seventh National Woman's Rights Convention in
New York, but domestic concerns now occupied
her attention. Though she had hoped for a
large family, the couple had only one child,
ALICE STONE BLACKWELL, born in 1857. (A premature son died shortly after birth in 1859.)
Alarmed by mishaps that befell Alice when
left with a nursemaid while she was away
lecturing, Lucy Stone determined to care for
the child herself and gave up an active career
until after the Civil War. In 1858, however,
having recently moved from Cincinnati to
Orange, N.J., she permitted some of her
household goods to be sold for taxes in protest
against her lack of the vote, a gesture which
roused public interest and entered the lore of
the woman's rights movement. She also supported the Women's Loyal National League,
established in May 1863 by ELIZABETH CADY
STANTON and Susan B. Anthony to mobilize
support for the pending Thirteenth Amendment to abolish slavery.

After the war, in 1866, Mrs. Stone helped
to organize and served on the executive committee of the American Equal Rights Association, designed to press for both Negro and
woman suffrage. The following year she resumed a full lecture schedule, taking an active
part in the unsuccessful campaigns for a state
woman suffrage amendment in Kansas and
New York, the first of many such state efforts
to which she lent her aid. She served as president of the New Jersey Woman Suffrage Association and, in 1868, while still living in
New Jersey, assisted in founding the New England Woman Suffrage Association under the
presidency of JULIA WARD HOWE, whose enthusiastic support Mrs. Stone had won for the
cause. Urged by the Massachusetts leaders,
the Blackwells the following year moved to
Boston, where Lucy Stone became the leading
spirit in the New England wing of the suffrage
movement.

The national movement had meanwhile developed the historic schism which found Mrs.
Stanton and Miss Anthony on one side and
Mrs. Stone on the other. Though exact details
of the division are obscure, it rose partly from
differences over policy and tactics, partly from
personal conflicts. When the Fifteenth Amendment, forbidding disfranchisement on account
of "race, color or previous condition of servitude," was pending, some suffragists, including
Mrs. Stone, while making every effort to
broaden the amendment to include woman
suffrage, planned to support it in any case;

others, notably Mrs. Stanton and Miss Anthony, felt that if it could not be so broadened
it must be defeated. The Stanton-Anthony
group also offended more conservative sensibilities by espousing, in the Equal Rights Association's journal, the *Revolution,* such less-
than-respectable causes as greenbackism, labor
unions, and easier divorce, and by accepting
as allies the erratic George Francis Train and,
later, the notorious VICTORIA WOODHULL. In
1869 the two factions separated, Mrs. Stanton
and Miss Anthony founding, apparently rather
secretively, the National Woman Suffrage Association (in May), and Mrs. Stone, Mrs.
Howe, and others the American Woman Suffrage Association (in November).

Lucy Stone served on the executive board
of the second group, but perhaps her greatest
contribution was in founding and largely financing its weekly newspaper, the *Woman's
Journal.* In 1872, after MARY A. LIVERMORE
had served as editor for two years, Mrs. Stone
and her husband assumed full editorial responsibility. During an unbroken existence of
forty-seven years, under the editorship of Lucy
Stone, Henry Blackwell, and later Alice Stone
Blackwell, the *Woman's Journal,* more than
any other newspaper, was the "voice of the
woman's movement." It gained a high reputation for journalistic excellence and for the
caliber of its contributors. Its progressive stand
on woman's rights did not extend into other
areas, however, and on such questions as labor
unions and strikes the *Journal's* position echoed
that of the Republican party, of which Mrs.
Stone was a loyal adherent. The editorial and
financial problems of the *Journal* were a great
strain, and she once likened the paper to "a
big baby which never grew up, and always
had to be fed." The chronic deficit was somewhat relieved in 1885 when, by the bequest of
Mrs. Eliza F. Eddy, Lucy Stone and Susan B.
Anthony each received nearly $25,000 to
further their reform efforts.

After 1887 Mrs. Stone's voice failed, and
she spoke only to small gatherings. She still
made an arresting appearance in public, however, her smooth hair now habitually covered
by a white lace cap, her posture firm despite
increased weight and painful attacks of rheumatism. Over the years her temperament mellowed somewhat, and though her earnestness
never flagged, her kindly disposition continued to win friends. Despite this apparent
calm, her inner life was far from serene. "At
all times of her life," wrote Henry Blackwell
after her death, "Lucy was subject to occasional severe nervous headaches accompanied
by days of extreme depression, during which

she sought refuge in absolute silence" (Hays, p. 160). During their married life she and her husband were frequently separated as he followed a variety of business pursuits, including land speculation in Wisconsin, publishing ventures in Chicago, and efforts to raise sorghum and sugar beets commercially in Maine and Massachusetts. The affectionate letters they exchanged often had an apologetic tone, Henry Blackwell deploring his lack of single-minded dedication to the woman's rights cause, Lucy Stone resolving to make greater efforts to be a good wife and homemaker.

In 1890 old antagonisms in the suffrage movement gave way to a desire for unity among younger workers, and the two groups were united as the National American Woman Suffrage Association. Though Lucy Stone became chairman of the executive committee, Mrs. Stanton president, and Miss Anthony vice-president of the new body, the old bitterness among them was never wholly overcome. Mrs. Stone's last lectures were delivered at the World's Columbian Exposition in Chicago in 1893. Several months later, at the age of seventy-five, she succumbed at her Dorchester, Mass., home to a stomach tumor. She had prepared for death with serenity and an unwavering concern for the woman's cause. Her funeral brought great numbers of people to do her honor. At her request, her body was cremated at Boston's Forest Hills Cemetery; an innovator to the end, she was the first person to be cremated in New England.

[Alice Stone Blackwell's *Lucy Stone, Pioneer of Woman's Rights* (1930) is both a work of love and an informed study of primary importance. Elinor Rice Hays, *Morning Star: A Biog. of Lucy Stone* (1961), is a valuable modern account which draws illuminatingly from family papers. Elizabeth C. Stanton et al., *Hist. of Woman Suffrage* (6 vols., 1881–1922), is inadequate in its treatment of Mrs. Stone but contains odds and ends of relevant material. For her background and early environment, see J. Gardner Bartlett, *Gregory Stone Genealogy* (1918), and D. H. Chamberlain, "Old Brookfield and West Brookfield," *New England Mag.*, Dec. 1899. Lillie B. Chace Wyman, "Black and White," *ibid.*, Dec. 1891, describes her connection with the case of the fugitive slave Margaret Garner, and Fredrika Bremer, *The Homes of the New World* (1853), I, 193–95, includes a vignette of her in Boston. The *Woman's Jour.*, 1870–93, offers many details about her career and personality. See also John W. Hutchinson, *Story of the Hutchinsons* (1896); and W. P. Garrison's estimate of Lucy Stone's career in the *Nation*, Oct. 26, 1893, pp. 302–03. A portrait bust by ANNE WHITNEY, commissioned by a group of friends and exhibited in the Woman's Building at the 1893 Chicago Exposition, is in the Boston Public Li-

brary. The Schlesinger Library, Radcliffe College, has a portrait in oils. Of Lucy Stone's letters, the largest collection is in the Blackwell Family Papers, Library of Congress. Others may be found in the Schlesinger Library, in the Blackwell, Olympia Brown, and Anna Howard Shaw papers.]

LOUIS FILLER

**STONEMAN, Abigail** (fl. 1760–1777), publican of colonial Rhode Island, Massachusetts, and New York, the first Newporter to marry an Englishman with a title, was probably born at Newport, R.I., sometime after 1740. Her maiden name and the dates of her birth and death are unknown, but at the time of her second marriage the *Newport Mercury* (Sept. 5, 1774) described her as "a lady descended from a respectable family, of a good genius, a very polite and genteel address, and extremely well accomplished in every branch of family economy." Mrs. Stoneman's first husband may have been Samuel Stoneman, who was lieutenant, then adjutant, of the Rhode Island regiment sent against Crown Point and Canada, 1757–60, in the French and Indian War. She must have been widowed by 1760, when she was listed alone as a member of "Mr. Vinal's [First Congregational] Meeting" (Ezra Stiles, *Literary Diary*, 1901, I, 44n), though some of the Stonemans were baptized and married in Trinity Church. While occupying "a large and commodious dwelling house" on Marlborough Street, Newport, in 1766, she was robbed of "about one hundred [Spanish] dollars, and some pieces of China" (*Newport Mercury*, Nov. 17, 1776).

Her straitened condition and possibly this loss evidently forced Mrs. Stoneman to become "a Feme sole Trader" in May 1767, when she opened "The Merchant's Coffee House" at the Sign of the King's Arms, where she also sold West India goods "for Cash." The next year she invested £1,400 (Rhode Island currency) in a house and land in Middletown, about four miles from Newport. She improved this property for the entertainment of the summer visitors, who already consisted of the families of merchants and planters from Pennsylvania and South Carolina. Mrs. Stoneman added "an elegant ballroom" to her establishment in 1769, and advertised to "furnish Entertainment for large and small companies in the genteelest manner" (*ibid.*, May 22, 1769). By October, however, she had moved over to Whitehall, which had been the seat of Bishop George Berkeley, the philosopher, during his American residence. This she renamed Vauxhall after the popular London place of entertainment.

Apparently prospering, Abigail Stoneman

decided to try her luck in Boston, and in 1770 she applied for a license to open a coffeehouse, to be known as the Royal Exchange, in King Street, only six months after "the Bloody Massacre" had taken place before its door. She had the premises repaired and "newly fitted," and advertised in the *Boston Gazette* "for constant or occasional Boarders" when she opened for business on Dec. 10. By June 1772, however, she was back in Rhode Island at her teahouse in Middletown, offering to the increasing summer influx of gentle valetudinarians "Large entertainments . . . on the shortest notice." After the season ended she offered her property for rent and moved into Newport to open the British Coffee House on New Lane. She was the only woman of Newport to receive a license to keep a tavern and sell spirituous liquors in 1772 and 1773. When the summer colony began arriving again, she returned to "her Seat" in Middletown.

Upon the departure of the summer folk in November 1774, the bustling innkeeper reopened the King's Arms in Newport near the Point-bridge. There she fitted out a good dancing room, for which she supplied music for gentlemen and their ladies to dance in the winter evenings from six to nine, save on Thursdays, when the Newport Assembly was being held. Mrs. Stoneman also provided "Board and Lodging for Gentlemen," one of whom won the affection of his hostess. On Aug. 28, 1774, at Hampton, Conn., the *Newport Mercury* announced, "was married . . . the Hon. Sir *John Treville*, Knight of Malta, Capt. of cavalry in the service of his most Christian Majesty, to Mrs. Abigail Stoneman of this Town." Thereupon the bride announced "a private sale" of her house and land in Middletown, a billiard table, and two pews (one in Mr. Hopkins' Congregational Meetinghouse and one in Trinity Church).

Before long, Newport became too hot a place for an officer who did not side with the rebels, and the knight fled with his lady to New York. It is not known precisely what happened to the couple, but either Sir John was killed in the War for Independence or, having spent most of Abigail's money, he abandoned her. She used what funds she still had to resume her old business in 1777. At Manhattan on Oct. 25, so ran the notice in *Rivington's New York Loyal Gazette:* "The London Coffee-House is this day opened next door to Mr. Francis's, at the lower end of Broad-Street, by Mrs. Treville, who formerly kept a Coffee-House in Boston and Rhode-Island—As she has sustained considerable losses during the present rebellion, and put herself

to great expence in providing every thing necessary for the accommodation of gentlemen, she flatters herself she will meet with suitable encouragement." This she must have received, for on Nov. 29 she advertised that inasmuch as she had conducted "the Assembly at Newport . . . to the general satisfaction of the polite and gay," she would open one for the gentlemen of the army and navy each Wednesday from 6 to 10 P.M. for a charge of one dollar a ticket, which included a lady. She courteously acknowledged her indebtedness to the "politeness and humanity" of the British military gentry. This genteel Tory lady from Newport deserved better of life—but the rest is silence.

[The principal sources are the newspapers: *Newport Mercury*, Aug. 12, 1765, Nov. 17, 1766, May 11, June 8, 1767, Apr. 10, June 12, Oct. 30, 1769, Oct. 29, 1770, June 29, Sept. 21, 1772, Jan. 4, Mar. 15, Apr. 26, Nov. 8, 1773, May 23, Aug. 29, Sept. 5, 1774; *Boston Gazette*, Dec. 10, 1770; *Boston Evening Post*, Dec. 17, 1770; *Boston Post-Boy*, Dec. 10, 1770; *Rivington's N.Y. Loyal Gazetter*, Oct. 25, Nov. 1, 29, Dec. 6, 1777. Fleeting references may be found in the Court Records, Newport County, R.I., and Land Evidence Book, No. 2, Middletown Town Hall.]

CARL BRIDENBAUGH

**STONEMAN, Bertha.** *See* FERGUSON, Abbie Park.

**STORER, Maria Longworth Nichols** (Mar. 20, 1849–Apr. 30, 1932), patron of music, ceramist, and Catholic convert, whose intervention in Vatican politics involved her in public controversy with Theodore Roosevelt, was born in Cincinnati, Ohio, the daughter of Joseph Longworth (1813–1883) and Ann Maria (Rives) Longworth. Her grandfather Nicholas Longworth, who had come to Cincinnati from New Jersey about 1803, had built an immense fortune in real estate. Her father managed the family estate, held many civic posts, and contributed generously to the Cincinnati art museum and other cultural and charitable causes. Her mother was the daughter of Landon Cabell Rives, a Virginia physician who removed to Cincinnati in 1829. Maria and her two older brothers were given expensive educations. At nineteen, on May 6, 1868, she was married to George Ward Nichols, eighteen years her senior, a journalist and author of New England background. They had two children: Joseph Ward, who became a physician, and Margaret Rives, who later married the Marquis de Chambrun.

Sharing with her husband an interest in music and art, Mrs. Nichols a few years after her marriage took the lead in founding the famous

Cincinnati May Music Festival, conducted by Theodore Thomas for many years beginning in 1873. She originated the idea, suggested it to Thomas, and undertook to secure the necessary backing (George P. Upton, ed., *Theodore Thomas: A Musical Autobiography*, I, 1905, pp. 78–79). Her husband, who had earlier been one of the founders of the Cincinnati School of Design, headed the Cincinnati Musical Festival Association and the College of Music of Cincinnati (1879) that grew from the stimulus of these noted concerts.

Maria Nichols and her husband made their most direct contribution to the arts following a visit to the Japanese pottery exhibit at the Philadelphia Centennial Exposition of 1876. Nichols returned to write a manual of pottery-making, while Mrs. Nichols experimented with designs and techniques. In an old schoolhouse purchased by her father she opened in 1880 Ohio's first art pottery, named Rookwood after the family estate; for ten years she worked there almost daily. With the help of an old Staffordshire potter and later a chemist, she developed and patented a glaze that gave the pottery a deep, rich tone, winning for it artistic recognition that included a gold medal at the 1889 Paris Exposition. Though for several years Rookwood Pottery operated at a considerable loss, it was a going concern by 1890 when she turned it over to an associate. She won a second gold medal at the Paris Exposition of 1900 for her decorative work in bronze.

Meanwhile, however, in 1885, her first husband had died, and on Mar. 20, 1886, she had married Bellamy Storer, a prominent Cincinnati attorney. Storer's two terms in Congress (1891–95) gave them entrée into Washington society, and his service on the House Foreign Relations Committee added to his qualifications for a diplomatic post when his friend William McKinley became president in 1897. Storer's first appointment, that year, was as minister to Belgium. An uneventful stay there was followed by selection in mid-1899 as minister to Spain. In Madrid, Mrs. Storer found herself "captivated altogether" by the Queen Regent's warm reception and led in organizing an American women's charity drive for relief of Spanish prisoners in the Philippines. She wished, however, for the greater social prestige of an embassy. She thus welcomed Storer's appointment, in September 1902, as ambassador to Austria-Hungary, though both she and her husband were convinced that first McKinley and then Theodore Roosevelt had reneged on promises to offer Berlin or Paris.

Maria Storer had entered the Catholic Church in early 1896˙ after conversion by Archbishop John Ireland, and her husband had followed in October. Like Ireland, they advocated an "American" spirit in the Church that emphasized an open relationship with Protestants, the ecumenical ideal, and hope of increased Anglo-Saxon influence at the Vatican. The Storers, seeking to help Ireland—an effective supporter of the Republican party—to the cardinalate, had in 1899 obtained a letter from their good friend Roosevelt (then governor of New York) urging President McKinley to send a request to this effect to the Pope. McKinley did so, and the next year sent the Storers to Rome to convey his wish directly. Roosevelt himself, as president, though too cautious to commit himself in writing, apparently commissioned Bellamy Storer in 1903 to make a similar representation viva voce to the Pope (Moynihan, p. 351). But Roosevelt, it appears, presently felt obligated to give a second "unofficial" endorsement, this time of Archbishop John M. Farley of New York. Meanwhile Mrs. Storer continued her zealous efforts for Ireland, making frequent trips to Rome that drew comment in the press, and freely citing Roosevelt's endorsement in her persistent wire-pulling. Alarmed, the President on Dec. 11, 1905, sent her a stinging letter of rebuke denying that he had endorsed any candidate and requesting her written promise to cease all activity in Vatican politics while her husband remained in the diplomatic service. To compound Roosevelt's discomfiture, the Papal consistory two days later chose no Americans among the new cardinals, his double endorsement having spelled defeat for both candidates. In March 1906, having received no reply from Mrs. Storer or her husband despite renewed requests, Roosevelt dismissed Storer from his post. The result was a press sensation. The Storers took their case to the public, quoting in their defense a number of Roosevelt's private letters. Mrs. Storer had meanwhile, in February, canceled plans to attend the wedding of her nephew Nicholas Longworth to the President's daughter Alice. The breach was permanent. In later years Mrs. Storer referred to the Ireland episode at length in her pamphlet *Theodore Roosevelt, the Child* (1921) and in her *In Memoriam Bellamy Storer* (1923).

Free of official responsibilities after 1906, the Storers summered in Paris and made their home on the Fenway in Boston until late in 1911, when they returned to Cincinnati. Mrs. Storer was, with her husband, active in charity organizations during these years. Before his death in 1922 she wrote a pamphlet on a miracle at Lourdes and occasional fiction for popular sale. She died at her daughter's home in Paris and was buried on the Chambrun estate at Marjevols.

[Good manuscript sources begin in the 1890's and end in 1906: Theodore Roosevelt Papers and John Hay Papers, Library of Congress, and John Ireland Papers, St. Paul Seminary, St. Paul, Minn. Important letters appear in her partly autobiographical *In Memoriam Bellamy Storer* and in Storer's pamphlet, *Letter to the President and the Members of His Cabinet, November, 1906*. Roosevelt's letter of Dec. 11, 1905, is printed in Elting E. Morison, ed., *The Letters of Theodore Roosevelt*, V (1952), 107–11; cf. *ibid.*, 180–82. See also James H. Moynihan, *The Life of Archbishop John Ireland* (1953); and Dorothy G. Wayman, ed., "Some Unpublished Correspondence between the Bellamy Storers and Cardinal O'Connell, 1908–1929," *Catholic Hist. Rev.*, July 1954. On the Rookwood Pottery, see Ohio Geological Survey, *Bull.* no. 26 (4th Series, 1923), pp. 91–94. Personal glimpses include those in Alice Roosevelt Longworth, *Crowded Hours* (1939); Clara Longworth de Chambrun, *The Making of Nicholas Longworth* (1933); and *Cincinnati: The Story of the Queen City* (1939). Both Bellamy Storer and George Nichols appear in the *Dict. Am. Biog.* The *N.Y. Times* obituary of Mrs. Storer, May 4, 1932, is inaccurate as to some dates. Her other writings include *Probation* (1910), *Sir Christopher Leighton* (1915), and *The Borodino Mystery* (1916). Information on particular points from James Rives Childs, *Reliques of the Rives* (*Ryves*) (1929), a genealogy; and from the Cincinnati Hist. Soc.]

THOMAS E. FELT

**STORMS, Jane McManus.** *See* CAZNEAU, Jane Maria Eliza McManus Storms.

**STOWE, Harriet Beecher** (June 14, 1811–July 1, 1896), author, was born in Litchfield, Conn., the seventh child and fourth daughter of the eminent Congregational minister Lyman Beecher and Roxana (Foote) Beecher. Eleven years younger than the firstborn, CATHARINE ESTHER BEECHER, Harriet Elizabeth (as she was named) was for two years the family's "baby," but in 1813 she was weaned to make way for Henry Ward, and in 1816 Charles, the last of Roxana's children, was born. Harriet's mother brooded over the household with a comfortable fecklessness about rules and money and with a radiant, meditative piety. Shy in public, she was fond of plants and of intricate embroidery, and enjoyed problems in science and metaphysics. Though in his Litchfield days Lyman Beecher was becoming noted as a revivalist and moral reformer, he found time to discipline and frolic with the children and to discuss theology with his wife, sister, and oldest daughter.

When Harriet was four Roxana died. The dominant adult influence upon the child henceforward was her father, who, she recalled, made the home "a kind of moral heaven, replete with moral oxygen—full charged with intellectual electricity." Over family apple peelings, Lyman argued the slippery points of his strategic Calvinism with his sons, or set the family reciting scenes from Scott; he liked to fiddle and to dance in his stocking feet, and he "wisht" Harriet had been a boy. Moody, flamboyant, dyspeptic, in fits of despair he would throw himself on the floor and announce that he could not go on. Yet he inspired in all his children a reposeless ambition for some large service. To the girl Harriet he seemed "the image of the Heavenly Father." Lyman held before the family the haloed memory of his lost wife, and the children—the daughters particularly—grew up within the luminescent shadow of their bereavement, knowing that their mother had achieved that selfless, delighted love of God which in their father's strenuous faith signalized the elect.

For Harriet, the maternal role was assumed by several people. Catharine, bossy and energetic, took over many household tasks, and supervised Harriet's progress with a dutiful censoriousness. At the time of Roxana's death and often thereafter, Harriet paid long visits to her mother's home at Nutplains, Conn., where she was reprimanded and regulated by her Aunt Harriet Foote and cosseted by her Episcopalian grandmother Foote. In the parsonage, Lyman's sister Esther fretted over money and tried to institute a familial system for the absent-minded Lyman and the boisterous children. Within two years, the children had a new mother, Harriet (Porter) Beecher, who bore Lyman three more children. Roxana's children never took to their stepmother, who awed them by her elegance and "superior breeding," and whose sole extravagances seemed to be the austerity of her discipline and the somberness of her faith. With no living woman with whom she could identify, Harriet turned to her busy father for spiritual guidance and to her brother Henry Ward for acceptance and play. "They are always hand in hand," their stepmother wrote. In later years, during the Beecher-Tilton scandal, the defensive, loyal Harriet wrote of Henry simply, "He is myself."

Brought up in an "uncaressing, let-alone system," Harriet became an "odd," undersized, inward child, "owling about" according to Henry, slouching and daydreaming while other people talked, according to Catharine. The household economy, Harriet later decided, tutored each child in his personal "insignificance" and "in the virtue of non-resistance." She had her best times reading in her father's study, where she silently watched him at "some holy and mysterious work" and joyfully seized upon Cotton Mather's *Magnalia*, where she found stories that made her feel "the very ground I trod on" was "consecrated by some special dealing of God's providence." At eight she began to attend the famed school of Miss SARAH PIERCE in Litchfield, where she studied until 1824, when, now thirteen, she left home to attend the female seminary recently opened by her sister Catharine in Hartford. Still shy and solitary, she applied herself, in addition to the regular curriculum, to Latin, French, and Italian, while privately composing a tragedy in blank verse depicting the conversion to Christianity of a young wastrel at the court of Nero.

For most middle-class New England children of the time, and especially for a Beecher, the knowledge of saving grace was one of the primary events by which personal autonomy was won. At home the next summer, on a Communion Sunday, she listened to her father preach on the text "I call you no longer servants but friends" and felt the assurance of Christ's saving love. For the rest of her life, the beatitude of this acceptance defined one pole of her religious experience. But the ecstasy was brief; though her father accepted her claims, by Calvinist standards the conversion had been suspiciously easy. In the fall, when Harriet returned to the Hartford Female Seminary, the authorities of this larger world—Catharine, and Dr. Joel Hawes, Harriet's Hartford pastor—doubted the adequacy of her evidences. Gentle and retiring, she had elected to define herself by love; she had bypassed the conviction of sin which should precede regeneration. She now lapsed into spiritual despondence, chronicled in lengthy letters to her brother Edward, minister at the Park Street Church in Boston. Sometimes she cried until midnight; she judged herself proud, erring, listless, "set before and behind" by sin. Like her father, for the rest of her life she had periods of paralyzing depression. She believed in God's omnipotence, yet as she considered the "great laws of Nature," "so silent, so unfeeling, so unsparing," and the human frailties subverted by God's "silent permission of evil," she discovered that stern Being who had helped to make some of Jonathan Edwards' sermons as "terrible as Dante's Hell." Harriet's Christ, on the other hand, called men to that selfless "true virtue" which had sanctified the life of Roxana Beecher. In her own affection for her children, Harriet was to discover a devotion so altruistic that she would have gladly sacrificed her salvation for them.

Within the Beecher family, grace was a private assurance wrestled from despair, but once won it constituted a public calling. Beecher anguish, Beecher doubts, Beecher grace were all put to a public service: the harvest of other souls. Lyman was determined that each of his seven sons should be ministers, and as a mother, Harriet would reenact her father's paternal campaigns. But the feminine role which might match the calling of a Christian minister was problematic. By Harriet's mid-twenties, Catharine had drawn up a feminine mission: a program for the redemption of the nation through the conversion of women to their vocation as teachers, nurses, and mothers. Woman's proper work was the Christian training of children within homes where the mother reigned with a selfless benevolence. Beginning as a teacher at the Hartford Seminary at sixteen, the younger, wool-gathering Harriet worked under her peremptory and visionary sister. Like Catharine, Harriet seemed headed for spinsterhood: shy, thin, small-boned, with the large Beecher nose, she thought of herself as homely and "humpbacked."

In 1832 the Beechers moved to Cincinnati. Lured by a vision of saving the West for evangelical Protestantism, Lyman became president of Lane Theological Seminary and pastor of the Second Presbyterian Church, and Catharine founded the Western Female Institute. Harriet taught in Catharine's school and wrote a children's geography book, the first edition of which was sold under Catharine's name. Both of them joined the city's intelligentsia in the Semi-Colon Club, where Catharine kept the "ball of conversation rolling" by her whimsical wit, and where Harriet was distressed that "there was so little that was serious and rational about the reading." Both sisters contributed sentimental or humorous bits to gift books. Though Harriet won first prize in a contest in the *Western Monthly Magazine* in 1834 for a sketch, "Uncle Lot," she was in these years frequently despondent. "About half of my time I am scarcely alive, and a great part of the rest the slave of morbid feeling and unreasonable prejudice," she wrote a friend.

But on Jan. 6, 1836, Harriet decisively changed the pattern of her life by marrying the widowed Calvin Ellis Stowe (1802–1886), another transplanted New Englander, professor of Biblical literature at Lane. Orphaned at six, Stowe had been apprenticed in a paper mill, but he put himself through Bowdoin College and Andover Theological Seminary, and by the time of his marriage to Harriet had published an *Introduction to the Criticism and Interpretation of the Bible* (1835). A stocky, nearsighted, balding man, he was scarcely a romantic figure, but the marriage was a sensible one for the self-consciously plain twenty-four-year-old woman and the scholarly, humorous widower of thirty-three. In his own way, Calvin was distinguished: he had been valedictorian of his class at Bowdoin and professor of Greek at Dartmouth College. On a trip abroad later in 1836, to purchase books for the Lane library, he traveled also as the emissary of the Ohio legislature, delegated to prepare a study of public education in Europe. Still, he needed someone to protect him against himself during his frequent fits of self-contempt. He had trouble making friends, and in his weird psychic loneliness he had from childhood found his world peopled with shifting phantoms. Sometimes distorted forms of friends or foes, sometimes elegant apparitions of the devil, these "little men" usually smiled and yet were vaguely sinister; their unpredictable arrivals left him pale and exhausted.

The early years of the marriage were not easy. Calvin regretted that he did not "know how" to be intimate; the future of Lane Seminary was uncertain, and Harriet never felt at home in the frontier city of Cincinnati; during the first seven years of marriage, she bore five children. Calvin was apt to get "the blues"; Harriet believed that instead of "sliding" into moods, people should get "to work," for it was their "duty" to be happy. With a Puritanic conscientiousness, the couple labored at their marriage, articulating their dissatisfactions (by letter during separations), searching out the reasons why they were less contented than they "ought to be." Calvin was prompt to chronicle his weaknesses—his lustfulness, his fondness for brandy, his sense that he was a "feeble, healthless thing, always ready to halt." Yet Calvin's eccentric strength lay in the flexibility which made him bend to his moroseness, his failure as a fund raiser, his obesity. He could be, as his sister-in-law noted, "very *comfortably* sick." Throughout his life, Calvin kept the menacing "little men" at bay. Though they were always smaller than the women figures, they assured him that they were his friends. In daily life Calvin handed over what worries he could to his wife; in 1844 he gave her charge of the family finances; studious and lazy, he wedged himself down in his fate.

Characteristically, Harriet proposed to make the marriage an instrument of sanctification, which would bring a second conversion to both, enabling her to become "rooted and grounded in love." "Before your ministry, before your studies, there is a work, a battle to be done *in you*," she wrote Calvin, urging him

to "*overcome*" the sin that so easily subdued him. Calvin had less stiffness of spirit. Less spiritually acquisitive than his wife, he preferred to count up daily irritations. He liked his prayers and his meals at fixed times, while she was careless about schedules. He was "naturally particular"; she was "slack." He wanted his newspapers neatly folded up, and she gave him "inexpressible torment" by "wabbling" them "into one wabble and sprawling them on the table like an old hen with his gizzards squashed out." He wished she would give as much time to the kitchen as to her garden. But he admired in his wife a "Christian purpose to amend" which he lacked.

As Mrs. Calvin Stowe, Harriet could now realize Catharine's program for women. In September 1836 she gave birth to twins, Harriet Beecher and Eliza Tyler; a son, Henry Ellis, was born in 1838. She saw her maternity as sacredly sacrificial. Yet with a household of small children, a meager income, and a critical mother-in-law, the tone of redemptive holiness was hard to sustain. She had taken, she later informed Calvin, "little comfort" in being a mother. In 1838, writing an unmarried friend, she described herself as "a mere drudge with few ideas beyond babies and housekeeping," yet she obviously felt a pawky pride in her many maternal chores. In 1840 Harriet had another son, Frederick William.

During these years she was writing intermittently, as the family's financial straits demanded. She had discovered that by dashing off a tale or a sketch she could hire a "stout German girl," and thus avoid becoming a "mere domestic slave," "shut up in my nursery." Despite the slimness of her productions, the Beecher family prized her literary talent, and in 1843 Harper & Brothers published a collection of her stories entitled *The Mayflower*. Exhilarated by this success, she laid plans for more serious effort, and wrote Calvin of her need for a room of her own within which she could compose. She was briefly concerned about the possible conflict between literary ambition and her maternal vocation; but Calvin encouraged her and did not seem worried about the children. She could mold "the mind of the West for the coming generation," he said. "God has written it in His book that you must be a literary woman, and who are we that we should contend against God?"

Destiny, however, was long deferred. A fifth pregnancy was accompanied by prolonged illness; in August 1843 a frail infant girl, Georgiana May, lay "withering" in Harriet's arms, and the thirty-two-year-old mother reflected on the harshness of God's Providence. The child survived, but Harriet was an invalid for months. In 1845, "sick of the smell of sour milk, and sour meat, and sour everything," of clothes that would not dry, and of a moldy stench everywhere, she felt as if she "never wanted to eat again." A year later, after a period of undiagnosed ill health, she escaped to New England, where she spent ten months at a fashionable "water-cure" establishment in Brattleboro, Vt. The regimen of icy baths, spinal water sprays, and prescribed walks left her greatly improved in health and spirits, though she concluded finally, as she wrote Calvin, that life "seriously considered" had "few allurements—only my children." A sixth child, Samuel Charles, born early in 1849, died in a cholera epidemic that summer. A small measure of comfort amid the anguish of this loss came with the news of an offer to Calvin Stowe of a professorship at his alma mater, Bowdoin College.

In May 1850 a shabby and worn Harriet Beecher Stowe, nearing the end of her seventh pregnancy, arrived in Brunswick, Maine, and with her children was warmly received into the comfortable and well-ordered New England home of a Bowdoin faculty colleague. Calvin arrived in July, shortly before the birth of Charles Edward Stowe. Soon, with renewed energy, Harriet was tacking down carpets and covering furniture in her Brunswick house, doing all the cooking, nursing baby Charley, and reading to her children two hours each evening (going through all of Scott's novels). To eke out Calvin's still scanty salary, she also ran a small school in her home and found time to write. Like her earlier work, her stories and sketches dispensed domestic sentiment and moral uplift according to popular stereotypes of the day and exalted the "true home" and intelligent, sensible, sympathetic womanhood.

To sound the deeper sources of her creativity, Mrs. Stowe needed a subject not so conveniently defined by standard conventions, and one which could dramatize the polarities of her psychological and religious experience. She needed, too, a special "calling," more ancient and disordering than Catharine's homemaker, closer to the "sacred woman" of the Bible, who was not only wife and mother, but also "poetess, leader, . . . prophetess." Mrs. Stowe's most serious work, like that of her father, was to be the conversion of a people through an apocalyptic warning. But such a vocation could not be commanded, and when Harriet Beecher Stowe later claimed that in the writing of *Uncle Tom's Cabin* she was only "the instrument" of God, she pointed toward the sources

beyond her conscious will that made the novel radical and urgent.

Mrs. Stowe's creative impulse sprang from a passionate reaction against the recorded sadisms of slavery. In LYDIA MARIA CHILD's *An Appeal in Favor of That Class of Americans Called Africans* (1833), in Theodore Weld's *American Slavery As It Is* (1839), in the autobiographies of fugitives like Lewis Clark and Frederick Douglass, she had at hand full documentation of the atrocities possible within the system. Slave mothers killed their babies or destroyed themselves after the sale of their children; white mistresses poured vinegar and salt in open wounds; slaves' ears were cut off, their backs and faces branded. In a letter from New Orleans, where he was working, her brother Charles had re-created the voice of a Louisiana overseer, whose words were to reappear in the mouth of Simon Legree: "Well, I tell ye this yer fist has got as hard as iron *knocking down niggers.*" When one of Harriet's Cincinnati servants had been claimed as a slave, Henry Ward and Calvin had helped the girl escape. Harriet had read Frederick Law Olmsted's detailed and sober account of his travels in the slave states; while living in Cincinnati she had briefly visited a small Kentucky plantation. But it took the Fugitive Slave Act and its aftermath to galvanize her into action. Her brothers Edward and Henry Ward were denouncing the Act from Boston and Brooklyn pulpits. Stories of hair-breadth escapes and legal reenslavements appeared in the newspapers, troubling New England consciences and quickening Harriet's childhood memories of her father's sobs and prayers for "poor, bleeding Africa" at the time of the Missouri Compromise. She wished her father would "preach on the Fugitive Slave Law, as he once preached on the slave-trade, when I was a little girl in Litchfield." But her father, now seventy-five, had retired from the ministry.

The book began in a vision: as she recalled it, the triumphant death of Tom flashed before her at a Communion service, during the same sacrament at which she as a child had come to Christ, not as "servant" but as "friend." Though Harriet Beecher Stowe could not rationally bring together her knowledge of Jehovah and her faith in Christ, she found in fiction a form which could integrate the puzzling dualities of experience within herself and within her country. To write the story of slavery, she had to bring together the fact and the significance of human cruelty: to place slavery within God's Providence. Forced to account for the evils she recorded, she devised a special form for the novel. She conceived of both fic-

tion and the Bible as essentially parables, and
in this novel that had the task of turning a nation from sin, she rewrote the "parable" which
she deciphered in the whole of the Bible: "a
paradise of innocence . . . the conflict with
principalities, powers, rulers of darkness of this
world,—and finally Paradise regained." Her no-
tations of "life among the lowly" were set within the transforming pattern of the drama of
redemption. Not only much of the book's sentimentality, but also much of its comedy, its
lyricism, and its range spring from the underlying evangelical ritual which shaped the psychic experience of many of Harriet's countrymen. She was writing the fable of sin within a
chosen country and of the wrongs permitted
by its God. Only within the framework which
had shaped her imagination since childhood
could Harriet depict the human brutality which
her country licensed and the counterbalancing
vision which made her hideous knowledge endurable.

The promise and the threat of another time
and another judgment pervade the story, and
much of the grotesque humor as well as the
moral melodrama of the novel derives from the
disparity between the given moment and life
everlasting. Mrs. Stowe's fictional record of the
inquisition by eternity becomes dense and persuasive through the voices of Negro and white,
Kentuckian and Vermonter, adult and child.
The slave trader Haley approaches the question with sly thrift. "I b'lieve in religion, and
one of these days, when I've got matters tight
and snug, I calculates to tend to my soul."
Against the cosmic hornswoggling of the
whites, the plaintive threnodies of the adult
Negroes sound a ritual chant, while their gra-
tuitous faith rebounds with comic pathos within the unyielding mystery of their pain. "Wal,
anyway," says Aunt Chloe, "thar's wrong about
it *somewhar.* . . . I can't jest make out whar't
is, but thar's wrong somewhar, I'm *clar* o'that."
The staccato Calvinist catechism of Miss
Ophelia breaks against the rhythm of Topsy's
lackadaisical agnosticism. "Do you know who
made you?" "Nobody, as I knows on. I spect I
grow'd. Don't think nobody never made me."
And through the whole novel runs the simple
liturgy of the Negro's counter-catechism to the
sophisticated skepticism of the whites. "How
do you know there's any Christ, Tom? You
never saw the Lord." "Felt Him in my soul,
Mas'r,—feel Him now!"

*Uncle Tom's Cabin* is a novel about enslave-
ment in a world where "powers and principalities," the law, the economy, even the church,
have largely become the machinery of the devil.
Character, event, and scene spring from moral

captivity, and the novel's action examines the
possible meanings of liberty within a disorder,
which fetters the white man by allowing him to
follow his will. Mrs. Stowe had no interest in
the economics of slavery. She saw it rather as a
system releasing natural impulses which easily
overpowered calculation and prudence.

As William Gilmore Simms noted, the book
is not history, but romance. The salient figures
of the epic of Negro bondage are not presented
as the likely products of slavery. Tom is a
"moral miracle" within a bestializing system.
Improbable, Tom, George, Eliza, and Topsy
define moral possibilities which point beyond
slavery to God's final Providence. In creating
her central Negro characters, Mrs. Stowe made
no use of the Negroes' dread of the North, nor
of their fixed mistrust of the white race, to
which many fugitive slaves testified. Limned
larger than life, they suggest archetypical forms
of liberty, not its psychological complexities.
Before receiving a "new heart" through the
death of angelic little Eva, Topsy embodies the
ironical liberty in sin of the elected victim of
God and society. "I 'spects, if they's to pull
every spear o' har out o' my head, it wouldn't
do no good, neither,—I's so wicked. Laws! I's
nothin' but a nigger, no ways!" More dimly
etched behind the central characters stands the
mass of Negroes, the creatures of the system,
for whom there is no freedom and only an
equivocal God. These figures illustrate the
"typical" results of slavery, as described by
contemporary Northern and Southern writers:
the shiftless, posturing houseslaves, the childish
adults, the sadistic Negro drivers.

The property system shackles whites as well
as Negroes. Beginning with the genial, debt-
ridden Shelby, forced to sell Uncle Tom, the
whites emerge as the victims of slavery. Epit-
ome of them all is the debonair Augustine St.
Clare, who constitutes a new type in the fictive
conventions of Southern plantation life. George
Tucker, James Kirke Paulding, and Mrs.
E. D. E. N. SOUTHWORTH had sketched the typical planter: prodigal, courteous, hospitable, addicted to duels, gambling, wine, and debts. St.
Clare is a more subtle figure. Fonder of the
Negroes than his abolitionist New England sister, he disbelieves in slavery as much as she
does. Ironic, generous, lazy, he resorts finally to
a self-deprecating moral laxity which corrupts
himself and his servants. Typically, he dies
without having gotten around to freeing Tom.
In his pointless, luxurious life, his loveless marriage, his hypochondriac wife, St. Clare pre-
figures Faulkner's Mr. Compson, and like him,
interests through the lucidity of his perceptions
and the debilitation of his will.

Within the nation, only one institution stands between the Last Judgment and the political corruption of the republic. From Uncle Tom's begonia-decked cabin through the spotless kitchen of the Quaker Rachel, the firelit parlor of the Birds, and little Eva St. Clare's Louisiana room with its bamboo lounge, rose damask curtains, and statue of Jesus receiving the little children, the novel specifically renders a series of domestic sanctuaries where women quietly and persistently subvert the laws of the land. Scenically the novel alternates between such enclosed havens and the more public steamboats, taverns, and markets of the Ohio and the Mississippi, where the business of the nation is transacted and where the isolatoes of America gather to drink their grog, chew tobacco, and discuss their intricate rights. "So long as your grand folks wants to buy men and women, I'm as good as they is," said Haley. " 'Taint any meaner sellin' on 'em than 't is buyin' 'em." Along the river the slaves strike out for freedom, pursued by dogs and professional slave catchers, while within the home the fugitives are fed and abetted by women. George's experience of a Quaker home converts him from belligerent doubt to faith, and the ultimate crime of slavery in the novel is not the barbaric tortures of which antislavery literature furnished an encyclopedia, but the separation of mothers and children for the more profitable use of each.

The extreme cruelties of a Simon Legree mark the moral outpost of evil, but every slave mother in the story knows the anguish of the probable sale of her child, and behind the suicide of Lucy, the alcoholism of Prue, lies an anonymous drama—not that of sexual or physical outrage, but the less lurid story of maternal loss. The recurrent pattern of this passion makes heroines of most of the novel's women. No one episode could contain this universal yet various pain, which Harriet Stowe had known at firsthand as she watched her six-month-old baby, mutely imploring her help during the cholera epidemic. "It was at his dying bed and at his grave that I learned what a poor slave mother may feel when her child is torn from her," she later wrote.

Yet the instrument of redemption in the novel finally exists not in the home, but in the communion of the powerless. Victims of society's inequity, Tom and Eva unite as they read of the splendor of the New Jerusalem and both die in the beatitude which springs from their faith. As George Sand remarked, theirs is the novel's love story. And their love, selfless and sacrificial, reaching out to a Topsy, a Miss Ophelia, a Cassy, a Sambo, or a Quimbo, redeems. The novel is peculiarly representative of nineteenth-century America in that it is structured by the mystery of conversion. Working within the world, the saintlike child Eva re-creates Miss Ophelia and Topsy by her death. Tom, who dies on Legree's plantation, must undergo a more severe ordeal before he, too, accomplishes God's work.

The "muddy, turbid" Red River leads to the ultimate testing place of the spirit, and that place is Hell. The final scenes of *Uncle Tom's Cabin* are enacted by the damned; like creatures in limbo, the spiritless, brutalized Negroes wind their way to Legree's weighing room and hand over their baskets "with crouching reluctance." God isn't here, Cassy tells Tom, "there's nothing here, but sin and long, long, long despair!" In scene, dialogue, and imagery, the novel particularizes the Inferno which slavery has legitimized and where "de debil" Legree reigns. Sambo and Quimbo, Negro drivers who enjoy beating the slaves, personify the "powers of darkness," and the "home" itself images a fatal disorder. The sitting room has a "peculiar sickening, unwholesome smell." The wallpaper is spotted by "slops of beer and wine; or garnished with chalk memorandums, and long sums footed up, as if somebody had been practising arithmetic there." Too tired to read his Bible, discovering among his fellows only apathy and insensibility, Tom briefly doubts his God. On the Red River plantation, the ordinances which from Puritan times in America had checked man's native depravity become the means of his ruin. Even the family perverts. "You can do anything with a woman, when you've got her children," says Cassy, summing up the maternal love which has driven her to prostitution and to the poisoning of her baby. The memory of his mother's love scares Legree into a morbidity in which his sole recourse is drink and cruelty; the recollection of her pious maternal devotion only confirms him in his ruin.

Like damnation, salvation lies beyond "the home." Instead of returning to his family, Uncle Tom elects to stay among the brutalized slaves whom he now can serve. Like Eva, the child who has no childhood, so Tom, the miraculous Negro, becomes the *Imago Dei*, the man of sorrows and forgiveness. Finally he converts even the vicious Sambo and Quimbo. "Sartin', we's been doin' a dreful wicked thing!" says Sambo. "Hopes Mas'r 'll have to 'count for it, and not we."

The scene depicting the death of Uncle Tom had been written in February 1851. In March, Mrs. Stowe started on a beginning to the story, which she expected to finish in three or four installments, and accepted an offer of $300 for it from Gamaliel Bailey, publisher of the Washington, D.C., antislavery newspaper *National Era*. The installments had grown to forty and another March had come before the story reached its end. It was issued in book form that month by John P. Jewett, a small Boston publisher. Almost overnight *Uncle Tom's Cabin* made Mrs. Stowe a famous and, for a time, a comparatively wealthy woman. She received a royalty of 10 per cent; after three months, her premiums amounted to $10,000.

That summer the Stowes moved to Andover, Mass., where Calvin had been appointed professor of sacred literature at Andover Theological Seminary. The book was now a national sensation, and within a year it had sold more than 300,000 copies. "How she is shaking the world with her Uncle Tom's Cabin!" the poet Longfellow recorded in his journal. "At one step she has reached the top of the stair-case up which the rest of us climb on our knees year after year." And Henry James recalled that the Jameses "lived and moved . . . with great intensity" in the novel, which proved for many "less a book than a state of vision, of feeling and of consciousness." In the American South, she was abused as a sexually driven "nigger lover," and within three years some thirty anti-Uncle Tom novels appeared.

Mrs. Stowe responded to the protests against *Uncle Tom's Cabin* by her haphazard *A Key to Uncle Tom's Cabin* (1853), which bristled with fury and miscellaneous evidence. Unlike *Uncle Tom's Cabin*, the *Key* was not relieved by any vision of love. Behind the quoted advertisements for scarred fugitives, the court decisions permitting the severe punishment of slaves, the separations of families, Mrs. Stowe could decipher only a God that hid Himself. She wrote the book in "agony of spirit," testifying against the country she loved and beseeching a God she could not comprehend, comforted only by the conviction that she was bearing a vicarious torment like that of Christ.

With the *Key* finished, she and Calvin embarked for England. On this and subsequent journeys abroad in 1856 and 1859, she was feted by English nobles and cheered by Scottish crowds; the Duchess of Sutherland gave her a gold bracelet in the form of a slave's shackles. She dined with Dickens, Thackeray, Charles Kingsley, Gladstone, and Lord Palmerston, and became the devoted friend of Lady Byron. *Sunny Memories of Foreign Lands*, an account of her travels, came out in 1854.

The next year civil warfare in Kansas turned Mrs. Stowe to writing another antislavery novel. *Dred* (1856) used the grim documentation derived from "the abyss" of research for the *Key*, and like the *Key* offered no compensating promise of transfiguration. An outlaw in the Dismal Swamp of North Carolina, preaching to a small band of Negro fugitives and orphans, Dred prophesies a Holy War; his vision springs from the Old Testament not the New; and he requires justice for his people. The novel attempted to show the debasing effects of slavery upon Southern whites: the degraded poor white, too proud to work "like a nigger"; the furtive love of a white father for his mulatto son; the intemperate, malignant planter, ruined by his power; the mealy-mouthed, compromising ministry. But for all the forays made against slavery in *Dred*, Mrs. Stowe failed to coalesce her many angers into a story. Reviewers were cool, but the public bought and read the book with enthusiasm.

Mrs. Stowe enjoyed the fame which came to her in middle age, but it did not destroy the wry modesty which issued so largely from her sense of divine election. *Dred* was her last antislavery novel. She still wrote: the family lived chiefly on the money earned by her writing and her investments, though some of these were imprudent. Her novels seemed to her a work of Christian service, and she could not shake off the need to question the sovereignty behind the universe, nor the conviction that the significant personal life sprang from the gracious tempering of the will to that power. After *Dred*, the best of her novels dramatize the individual's battle to acquiesce in a difficult world, and because she pursued her inquiry through the customs, characters, scenes, and talk of her New England girlhood, Mrs. Stowe caught something of the "din and buzz" of human life. Casting her fight with God in the terms of her past, she endowed it with the comedy of detachment and an intimate, specific understanding of people and places.

The first of these novels sprang from the loss of her firstborn son, a student at Dartmouth College, drowned in 1857 while swimming in the Connecticut River. The boy died without having been converted, and in her bereavement, in her terrified ignorance of his soul's fate, Mrs. Stowe felt that the Devil was separating her from God. Soon she decided that Christ could not betray that maternal love which imaged His own, but much of her subsequent New England fiction centered on questions of faith which Henry's death had rekindled.

*The Minister's Wooing*, which appeared serially in the *Atlantic Monthly* in 1858–59, is organized less by action than by meditation, variously comic, lyrical, satiric, and somber, upon a central perplexity: the proper stance of the individual within the apparent harshness of God's Providence. The events turn on the balked human will: Newport, R.I., parishioners hear their minister denounce the slave trade, which is the source of much of their prosperity; the unconverted fiancé of Mary Scudder disappears at sea; lacking now all "stake in self," Mary agrees to marry the middle-aged minister, Dr. Hopkins, embodiment of the austere selflessness of Edwardian Calvinism. Set against the unworldly Dr. Hopkins is the charming, Byronic Aaron Burr, who has made self-gratification the law of existence. The story of Burr's calculating affair with a married Frenchwoman is trite, but the minister's naive love and his renunciation of Mary, when the ebullient sailor unexpectedly returns, focus the theme with a kind of passionate sobriety.

With the Civil War, the inscrutable God of America's history at last announced Himself in Providence, and in the costly fighting Mrs. Stowe saw the nation's necessary atonement for its complicity in crime. Even in the wrecked life of her son Fred, whose alcoholism seemed to date from a wound at Gettysburg, she acknowledged partial payment of a nation's debt to God. The war, in its justice, was God revealed, and it was God's will "that the slave mothers, whose tears nobody regarded, should have with them a great company of weepers, North and South,—Rachels weeping for their children and refusing to be comforted. . . ." When the war was over, she was in her fifties. She was still to know much grief, but the sin which had burdened her consciousness of God and society had been paid for in blood.

Mrs. Stowe was to try only once more to tell the fable of redemption from sin. In Lady Byron's life she saw, as she wrote to her in 1857, God's strange call to a "beautiful and terrible ministry, when He suffered you to link your destiny with one so strangely gifted, so fearfully tempted." In 1869 Mrs. Stowe published an article in the *Atlantic Monthly* to defend Lady Byron, now dead, against the many current calumnious interpretations of her life. She portrayed the Byron marriage as a woman's incessant Christ-like effort to save a fallen, tormented genius, and, to ensure that "The True Story of Lady Byron's Life" would be heard, she revealed the secret Lady Byron had confided to her: that Lord Byron had committed incest. The article infuriated the English and American public even more than *Uncle Tom's Cabin* had angered the South. Accused of covert boasting, scandalmongering, and mudslinging, Mrs. Stowe responded with typical pluckiness by elaborating her case.

*Lady Byron Vindicated* (1870) set out to prove that Lady Byron was a victim of a man's world of drunken jokes, licentiousness, and a "justice" which allotted to women only the virtue of suffering. She saw the story as "the type of the old idea of woman." Had she been a man, Lady Byron might have "controlled . . . the thought of England," but instead her life was doomed to be a "silent sacrifice."

In 1864 Calvin Stowe, now sixty, retired from teaching, and the family moved to Hartford, Conn., home territory to Harriet, where she could be near her sisters Mary Beecher Perkins and ISABELLA BEECHER HOOKER. There she built Oakholm, a huge, impractical Italianate-Tudor villa. Calvin slid into the role of the scholarly husband of unreliable health. Harriet catered to his needs, intervening between him and the children, bragging about his erudition, and taking upon herself the moral guardianship of the family. She prodded Calvin into writing *Origin and History of the Books of the Bible* (1867) and used his droll knowledge of New England dialect and characters in her later fiction. In 1868 she bought a home in Mandarin, Fla., where both of them might enjoy milder winters. In the 1870's, she referred to him usually as her "old Rabbi"; she watched him "nibble" at his books and read the newspaper on their Florida verandah; she knew by then that he depended upon her "for his very life."

Between 1862 and 1884 Mrs. Stowe produced, on the average, more than a book a year. To a large extent, during the 1860's and 1870's, the family depended on "advances" on uncompleted manuscripts. Oakholm was sold at a substantial loss in 1870; the orange grove Mrs. Stowe purchased in the hope of rehabilitating her alcoholic son, Fred, decayed under his uncertain management. But she had to support her husband, her two eldest spinster daughters, her unstable son. She put the youngest boy, Charley, through Harvard and sent him to the University of Bonn. Even after Charley's marriage, she periodically sent checks to the impecunious young couple. Always short of money, Mrs. Stowe could resort with quiet conscience to what would sell. Financial duress made it psychologically easier to write hastily, carelessly, and repetitiously.

But for the most part she could not write trivially. Her didactic essays, her children's stories, her biographies, her "foreign" novel, *Agnes of Sorrento* (1862), came easily and did not amount to much. In chatty essays on the home, monitory tales for boys and girls, and novels of society she returned to Catharine's cause of idyllic domesticity, lecturing against bad air and corsets, against extravagant "crushes" in which late hours, oysters, wine, and tobacco ensured only debts, flirtations, and headaches, against the "emancipated woman," who smoked and called men "bub." She pictured the felicity which a fond, competent, and thrifty wife could create, and upbraided the mothers who preferred balls to nursing their children, and who aped European architecture, manners, and infidelities. Conventional and repetitive, the novels occasionally managed unexpected moral accents: the parasitic affection of the belle Lily in *Pink and White Tyranny* (1871) is chilling, yet pathetic; the officious Aunt Maria in *We and Our Neighbors* (1875) battles her nieces' improvident idealism from the most generous worldly motives.

The best of her later novels—*The Pearl of Orr's Island* (1862), *Oldtown Folks* (1869), *Poganuc People* (1878)—came from her recollections of the "strange world of folks" of her New England childhood. The novels fused the comedy of New England dialect and character with that seriousness of inquiry which invested Mrs. Stowe's finest work with the "poetry of ideas." Irritated by Oliver Wendell Holmes' jocular way of disposing of New England life, Mrs. Stowe determined to do justice to the somberness which underlay and heightened the drollery of Yankee experience. Characteristically, she dramatized the weird gestures of each individual as he launched himself against the universe, and by the very magnitude of his assaults upon the unknowable, each character, whether morose like Old Crab, fatly sentimental like Aunt Roxy, or "sot" in meanness like Black Hoss, achieves a grotesque dignity.

We know the people of Poganuc or Old Town through their busy, pat, or lazy self-justifications before the God to whose service they have been called. The explication of His ways constitutes the lifework of the ministry. At sewing bees and corn huskings, the Sunday sermon is critically overhauled, and every variety of temperament is tried by the ordeal of belief. The exactions of the Calvinist God haunt the brooding consciousness of the introspective and the self-critical, until they are pushed to the verge of "moral insanity." The abundant systems of divinity devised in country parsonages by assiduous Edwardians, the more aesthetic, gentle, and unreasoning forms of Episcopalianism, the glibness of deism are wrought into the habits and lives of the characters. Together they record a century in the spiritual history of New England, and at the same time magnify each human fable by the odd, lasting forms of man's spiritual desperation.

Against the serious comedy of the adult world, the New England novels set the idyllic time of childhood, during which the beliefs and stances which will govern a life are being determined. The tentative, lonely gropings of the child are counterpointed against adults "sot" in their ways, who offer the children the half-truths, the grumpiness, the tenderness, the disfigurements by which they have made their truce with life. The novels re-create the fun and the sports of childhood festivities of the late eighteenth and early nineteenth centuries: the Fourth of July, election day, nutting and huckleberrying parties, Christmas. Like George Eliot's *Mill on the Floss,* the scenes of childhood frolic, dream, rebellion, and schooling alternate with communal gatherings where the adults trade their distorted wisdom. The two worlds, one of immature and uncertain promise, the other of comic or grave resignation, set the limits of Mrs. Stowe's fictional mimesis of New England life. To her, the novels were, as she wrote of *The Pearl of Orr's Island,* "pale and colorless as real life, and sad as truth." They are loosely constructed. What drama there is springs from the interaction of worlds: the proximate destruction of Tina's capacity to love, in *Oldtown Folks,* by the dour self-righteousness of Miss Asphyxia, or the counterstory, dear to Mrs. Stowe, in which drear or rebellious adults like Miss Mehitable of *Oldtown Folks* or Old Zeph of *Poganuc People* are reborn in love by their encounter with a child.

As she grew old, Mrs. Stowe gradually gave in to the childlikeness which she had so gamely battled as daughter, crusader, wife, and mother. In the 1860's she handed over the housekeeping and the household accounts to her spinster daughters; in the 1870's she basked in Florida sunlight "like a lizard," and turned out *Palmetto-Leaves* (1873), light sketches of the pleasures of Florida. Still, until the second childhood of senility, she continued her resolute service. In 1862, when her daughters became Episcopalians, she began attending the Episcopal church, although she was never confirmed in it. It seemed to her the best system "for training immature minds like those of our negroes," and she and Calvin organized a chapel for neighboring colored people. She watched over Calvin and sustained him through "fits of the blues" which left him "helpless as a baby."

Throughout her married life, she spent much time and energy upon her children. "To them in their needs," she wrote her publisher's wife, ANNIE FIELDS, in 1868, "I *must* write *chapters* which would otherwise go into my novel." She gave her young son, beginning a ministerial career, canny Beecher advice on avoiding ticklish issues; she worried over her married daughter, Georgiana, whose acute attacks of nervous depression ended only with her death at the age of forty-four. Mrs. Stowe fought stubbornly and vainly to save her alcoholic son, Fred, and to turn his illness into an instrument of sanctification for the family. In all her troubles, she held to her faith in a God whose very severities announced a special election. "I read God's providence to us as a family," she wrote Fred's censorious sisters, "in taking away him that would have been our pride and reliance, and leaving him . . . for whom we suffer, as meant to teach us the great lesson of pitifulness to all who sin—and sinning, suffer." Even in 1880, after a period of feebleness and ill health, she planned an autobiography which would bring in money for the family, and with the aid of her youngest son, Charley, she completed the book in 1889.

Calvin had died in 1886. Around 1890, Mrs. Stowe's mind began to fail. In 1893 (her eighty-second year) she wrote Oliver Wendell Holmes of her psychic weariness. "My brain is tired out. It was a woman's brain and not a man's, and finally it gave out before the end was reached." In her last years she wandered about Hartford, harmless, vague, apparently cheerful. She would pick flowers in the conservatory of Mark Twain or, he reminisced, "softly slippered" sneak up behind people's backs and suddenly "fetch a war whoop." During church services, she might suddenly whimper painfully and convulsively. She died on July 1, 1896. The doctors diagnosed the cause as a brain congestion complicated by partial paralysis. She was buried in the cemetery of the Andover (Mass.) Theological Seminary chapel, between the graves of her husband and her son Henry.

[The most abundant and useful manuscript material is in the Beecher-Stowe Collection at the Schlesinger Library, Radcliffe College; this provides an intimate and vivid picture of Mrs. Stowe as wife and mother and an extensive record of her theological concerns and beliefs. Charles Edward Stowe's *Life of Harriet Beecher Stowe* (1889), in which Mrs. Stowe closely collaborated, conveys her self-image and her own interpretation of her life. The best biography is Forrest Wilson, *Crusader in Crinoline* (1941); based on wide research and gracefully written, it provides a detailed and persuasive picture of the places of Mrs. Stowe's life and of her times and family. The best critical analysis of her writings is Charles Foster, *The Rungless Ladder: Harriet Beecher Stowe and New England Puritanism* (1954).]

BARBARA M. CROSS

**STRANGE, Michael.** *See* TWEED, Blanche Oelrichs Thomas Barrymore.

**STRATTON, Mercy Lavinia Warren Bump** (Oct. 31, 1841–Nov. 25, 1919), midget, better known as Mrs. Tom Thumb, was born on a farm in Middleboro, Mass. Her parents, James S. and Huldah (Warren) Bump, were natives of Middleboro; her mother traced her ancestry to a *Mayflower* settler, Richard Warren. Her mother and father and two of her three sisters were all of normal size; her four brothers were six feet and over; her youngest sister, Huldah, or "Minnie," was, however, also a midget. When Lavinia was ten, and thirty-two inches tall, she stopped growing; but she was perfectly proportioned, healthy and intelligent, with dark hair and a round dimpled face. Her brothers carried their fun-loving sister to school, where she studied hard. At sixteen she became a third-grade teacher, and though her pupils towered over her, she got along well with them. An efficient little person, she could sew, knit, and cook and had a special fondness for music and poetry.

Eager for wider horizons, she shortly joined the troupe of a cousin, who exhibited her on his "floating theatre" on the Mississippi. In the summer of 1862 her renown reached P. T. Barnum. The famous showman arranged to have her appear at his American Museum in New York, shortened her name to Lavinia Warren, provided her with a stylish wardrobe, installed her at the Fifth Avenue Hotel, and introduced her to New York society. Through Barnum she met "General Tom Thumb" (Charles Sherwood Stratton, 1838–1883), an equally well-proportioned midget of forty inches who under Barnum's tutelage had developed a skill and charm as an entertainer that made him a world celebrity before his tenth birthday. Now twenty-four, he fell in love with Lavinia at first sight and won her hand over a rival midget known as Commodore Nutt. Their fashionable wedding at Grace Church in New York on Feb. 10, 1863, attended by members of Congress, governors of states, and other notables, crowded Civil War news off the front page. After a honeymoon in Washington, where President and Mrs. Lincoln received them, the General brought his bride to a mansion he had built in his native Bridgeport, Conn., and filled with delicate, tiny furniture. Soon Barnum had them touring New England, Canada, and the Midwest. Under his management they went abroad in 1864, where the Prince of Wales and Queen Victoria entertained them in London, and Napoleon III and Empress Eugénie in Paris. After the Civil War they visited the Southern states. In June 1869, with a company of thirteen, they embarked on a three-year trip around the world, first braving the perils of the American West and then crossing the Pacific to Japan, China, and Australia, touring through India to Cairo and Alexandria, and returning via Italy, where they delighted Pope Pius IX and King Victor Emmanuel.

Now wealthy, they retired from the stage in 1872 to live with Lavinia's sister Minnie and her midget husband, "Major" Edward Newell, in Middleboro. When Minnie died in childbirth, however, in 1878, Lavinia could no longer bear to remain there, and she and the General returned to show business. The year 1881 found them again under Barnum's management in the "Greatest Show on Earth." For publicity purposes Barnum hired children to pose with them from time to time, and this gave rise to the erroneous report that they had a child of their own. They were at the Newhall House in Milwaukee when it burned to the ground on the night of Jan. 10, 1883, and though both were carried to safety, the General never recovered from the shock. He died suddenly from an apoplectic stroke the following July, leaving his wife practically penniless because of his lavish spending. The next year she went on the road in a company which included two Italian midgets, to one of whom, Count Primo Magri, she was married on Apr. 6, 1885, at the Church of the Holy Trinity in New York. Lavinia, her new husband, and her brother-in-law, Baron Ernesto Magri, formed a midget opera company, appearing in vaudeville, with a circus, and in sideshows at country fairs. But the Countess never again attained her former popularity, and in 1901 she was reduced to playing one-night stands across America.

For a time the Count and Countess lived in Marion, Ohio, where their home with its diminutive furniture attracted tourists. When a flood destroyed the house they returned to Middleboro. Here they ran a little store gaily called "Primo's Pastime," and summered at Coney Island in New York. As Lavinia grew older her round cheeks sagged and her sight gradually failed, but she held her head high and retained her zest for life. She became a Christian Scientist, joined the Eastern Star and the Daughters of the American Revolution, dwelt more and more in the past, and delighted in talking about the General, who always held first place in her affections. After her death (in Middleboro, of chronic interstitial nephritis) at the age of seventy-eight, she was laid beside him in Mountain Grove Cemetery, Bridgeport, her simple headstone standing, as was perhaps fitting, in the shadow of his grander monument.

[See especially two works by Alice C. Desmond: *Barnum Presents Gen. Tom Thumb* (1954) and "Gen. Tom Thumb's Widow," *N.-Y. Hist. Soc. Quart.,* July 1954, the latter based largely on an unpublished journal of Mrs. Tom Thumb now in the possession of the N.-Y. Hist. Soc. See also P. T. Barnum, *Struggles and Triumphs* (1871), chap. xxxvii, and *N.Y. Times,* Nov. 30, 1919, Oct. 13, 1920. The Theatre Collection of Harvard Univ. has a few clippings on Mrs. Tom Thumb, including an article entitled "A Day with Mrs. Tom Thumb in Her Country Home," *Boston Sunday Globe,* Mar. 19, 1905. Her death record (under Magri) and that of her sister were obtained from the Mass. Registrar of Vital Statistics.]

ELIZABETH F. HOXIE

**STRATTON-PORTER, Gene** (Aug. 17, 1863–Dec. 6, 1924), popular novelist, was born on Hopewell Farm near Wabash, Ind., the youngest of twelve children. Christened Geneva Grace Stratton, during her teens she changed her first name to Geneve and later, at her husband's suggestion, to Gene. Her father, Mark Stratton, was fifty when she was born; her mother, Mary Schallenberger, forty-six. Stratton, whose English ancestors had come to America in the mid-eighteenth century, had been born on a farm in New Jersey; his wife was a native Pennsylvanian of Dutch ancestry. After their marriage, in 1835, they had gone to Ohio, and in 1847 they moved on to unsettled land in Indiana, where Stratton developed a large and prosperous farm. He was also a licensed Methodist minister and took great pride in his claim that he knew the Bible by heart. Geneva's mother, who became ill when the girl was five, died in 1875 after seven years of infirmity. Though her older brothers and sisters taught her to read and write, Geneva had little formal schooling in her earlier years. Most of her time she spent wandering in the woods, developing an interest in nature which was encouraged by her father. At eleven, when the family moved to Wabash, she began to attend school, completing all but the last term of high school.

On Apr. 21, 1886, she was married to Charles Darwin Porter, a druggist twenty years her senior. Porter had a good business in Geneva, Ind., but for his wife's sake he decided to move to the larger town of Decatur, commuting to work by railroad fifteen miles each way. Their only child, Jeannette, was born in 1887. Two years later the family moved to Geneva, and soon after, oil was found on farmland Porter owned. Mrs. Porter used their new wealth to build a fourteen-room house which she herself designed, the lower story built of Wisconsin cedar logs and the upper of redwood shingles from the Pacific Coast. She named it Limberlost Cabin, after the wild swamp south of the town.

About 1895, with her husband's encouragement, she began to learn how to photograph birds and animals in their natural habitat. Soon she sent her photographs with explanatory notes to *Recreation* magazine. The editor asked her to conduct a camera department, paying her with new equipment. After a year she was hired to do similar work by *Outing* magazine. Her success as a nature writer then prompted her to try her hand at fiction. She wrote her first story in secret, renting a post-office box to conceal possible rejection, but it was accepted by the *Metropolitan* magazine and published in September 1901. Now she decided to try to make a career of writing fiction. Her husband again gave her his enthusiastic support, insisting that the family eat at the village hotel to relieve her of domestic responsibilities. Her daughter, until her first marriage in 1909, typed her mother's stories from dictation.

Mrs. Porter's first book, *The Song of the Cardinal* (1903), a humanized account of bird-life somewhat in the manner of *Black Beauty,* was expanded from a short story at the suggestion of Richard Watson Gilder, editor of the *Century,* to whom she had sent the first version. The book was moderately successful, but it was her next novel, *Freckles* (1904), in which bird lore was woven together with a conventional romance, that established her tremendous popularity. She had made a unique series of photographs of the life history of vultures, from the hatching of the eggs and nurture of the young to the first flights of the fledglings. *Freckles* is based on the adventures and difficulties she had had while doing this series. Freckles, the hero of the novel, is a poor but pure-hearted youth who guards the valuable timber of the Limberlost Swamp against poachers and loves the wildness of the virgin forest. The elegant, wealthy heroine, called The Angel, was modeled on Mrs. Porter's daughter. The Angel shares Freckles' feeling for nature, and in the end all social and economic obstacles to their marriage vanish when it is revealed that he is the long-lost son and heir of a wealthy Irish lord. Mrs. Porter's daughter and biographer credits her popularity to such characters as these, who, she says, were all drawn from real life. But however factual their origin, in Mrs. Porter's romantic hands they retain little reality. In *Freckles,* as in her other books, Mrs. Porter's interest is not in human nature but in wildlife as a source of moral virtue. Even the snakes in her paradisaical swamps have a sense of fair play and rattle before they strike; but men, when they are corrupted by materialistic greed, despoil nature without warning.

In 1907 Mrs. Porter published her first book of nature lore, *What I Have Done with Birds,* but its disappointing sales made her realize that, despite the current vogue for the great outdoors, stimulated by Theodore Roosevelt's interest in conservation, nature lore alone would not sell books. From then on, she promised her publishers, she would alternate novels with natural history. Her next successful novel, *A Girl of the Limberlost* (1909), continued in the vein of *Freckles* and was written, Mrs. Porter said, "to carry to workers inside city walls, to hospital cots, to those behind prison bars, and to scholars in their libraries, my story of earth and sky." In plain, old-fashioned country homes, she goes on to say, there is a wealth of human virtue unknown to people in cities (Meehan, pp. 148–49). In *The Harvester* (1911) she urged young men to leave the city and earn their living in the woods, and also told them how to do it. *Laddie* (1913) is a romantic picture of her childhood; its hero is an older brother who was drowned when she was a child, shortly before he was to be married. Her later novels continue to praise life lived close to nature. These books earned for Mrs. Porter a popularity she shared with Harold Bell Wright, which derived from newly urbanized America's nostalgia for the country, a nostalgia that reverberated through American culture from the turn of the century until after the First World War.

When in 1913 Limberlost Swamp was reclaimed for cultivation, Mrs. Porter moved to northern Indiana and built a second "cabin," containing twenty rooms and staffed by a number of servants. In 1919 she made a trip to California, where the climate so pleased her that she moved there permanently the next year, buying a large house on the outskirts of Los Angeles. Her husband was reluctant to leave Indiana but did spend some time with her in her new home. Highly displeased with the film treatment of one of her early books, Mrs. Porter in 1922 organized her own film company and became absorbed in making movies based on her stories. To write the adaptations and direct the pictures she employed James Leo Meehan (a young man who later became the second husband of her daughter, Jeannette), but until her death she worked closely with him on the set. She believed that movies such as *A Girl of the Limberlost* (produced in 1924), suitable for showing in schools or churches, could exert a wholesome influence on family life.

Increasingly Mrs. Porter became irritated by the disparity between her popularity with the novel-reading public and her low standing with professional critics. "I am desperately tired," she wrote to a friend, ". . . of having the high-grade literary critics of this country give a second- and at times a third-class rating to my literary work because I would not write of complexes and rank materialism, which is merely another name for adultery" (Meehan, p. 234). Hoping, nevertheless, to earn critical praise, she wrote a long narrative poem, *The Fire Bird* (1922), which purports to be an Indian legend about a woman's tortured conscience, and a novel, *The White Flag* (1923), which she sought to make modern and realistic, but it proved less popular than her earlier work. In 1924 she built two large houses in California, one in Bel Air, Los Angeles, the other on Santa Catalina Island. She was fatally injured in Los Angeles that year in a collision between her car, driven by a chauffeur, and a streetcar.

During her lifetime, Mrs. Porter's books enjoyed a phenomenal popularity, second only to the novels of Scott and Dickens in their day. Her first book, *Freckles,* sold 10,000 copies in the original edition and about 1,400,000 in a cheap reprint. At the time of her death, between eight and nine million copies of her nineteen works had been sold, for which she is reported to have received some $2,000,000.

[Besides the autobiographical elements in Mrs. Porter's novel *Laddie,* the character Abram in *The Song of the Cardinal* and the hero of *The Harvester* are both modeled after her father. Her daughter has written the only full-length biography: Jeannette Porter Meehan, *The Lady of the Limberlost* (1928). See also the short biography issued by Doubleday, Page, her publishers: Eugene F. Saxton, *Gene Stratton-Porter: A Little Story of the Life and Work and Ideals of "The Bird Woman"* (1915). Flossie E. Bailey, in *Pioneer Days in the Wabash Valley* (1933), describes Mrs. Porter's family and their farm at some length. See also Harriet R. Stratton, *A Book of Strattons* (2 vols., 1908–18); Fred L. Pattee, *The New Am. Literature* (1930); Grant M. Overton, *The Women Who Make Our Novels* (1918); Frank L. Mott, *Golden Multitudes* (1947).]

BEATRICE K. HOFSTADTER

**STRONG, Harriet Williams Russell** (July 23, 1844–Sept. 16, 1929), California agriculturist, civic leader, and student of water supply problems, was born in Buffalo, N.Y., the fourth daughter among the seven children of Henry Pierpont Russell and Mary Guest (Musier) Russell. Her father's forebears had played a

prominent part in the early history of New Haven and Middletown, Conn.; the Musiers, of Huguenot origin, had settled in the Hudson River valley in the seventeenth century. Henry P. Russell found it difficult to discover a career suited to his modest talents and the financial needs of his large family. In Buffalo in the 1830's, Wisconsin in the later 1840's, California in the 1850's, and Nevada in the early 1860's he tried a variety of employments, including real estate, farming, mining, and the offices of postmaster, coroner, and acting sheriff. His chief success seems to have been as a militia officer: a lieutenant colonel in the militia of New York, a brigadier general in that of Wisconsin, and adjutant general of Nevada.

Russell moved his family to the Pacific Coast when his daughter Harriet was about eight years old, and by 1854 they had settled in the lovely but isolated American Valley, near Quincy, Plumas County, Calif., in the heart of the Sierra Nevada mountains. Harriet suffered from a persistent "affection of the spine" that caused her, in her own words, to be a "semi-invalid for many years." She used the enforced seclusion to train her mind in a number of fields, including music, art, literature, and history. Money was raised to send her to the Young Ladies' Seminary of MARY ATKINS at Benicia, Calif., for two years (1858–60). There the catalogues listed "Hattie Russell" as a pupil in music, French, and "the Higher English Branches."

Shortly after she finished at Benicia, her father was caught up in the excitement over the discovery of silver on Nevada's Comstock Lode. By the beginning of 1861 he had settled his family at Carson City, Nev., where his daughter soon found herself importuned by several suitors. After a courtship of two years, she accepted Charles Lyman Strong, nearly twice her age, one of the leading figures in Nevada. Like his fiancée's father, Strong came of old New England stock and had tried his hand at many jobs, in New York City and San Francisco, before going to the Comstock Lode in 1860 as superintendent of the Gould & Curry mine, one of the first great mines to be opened there. They were married in Virginia City on Feb. 26, 1863. Four daughters were born to them: Harriet Russell, Mary Lyman, Georgina Pierpont, and Nelle de Luce. Strong proved to be a devoted husband and father, but he was prone to overwork and worry; one year after their marriage he suffered the first of several breakdowns and had to resign his lucrative position. Thereafter the Strongs made their home at Oakland, Calif., and Charles

Strong's life alternated between periods of rest, travel, and farming, during which he regained his health, and periods of mining, during which he always overextended his nervous and physical strength. Finally in 1883, despondent over his heavy investment in a mine that proved to have been "salted," he killed himself.

His widow was left an estate that was so badly encumbered with legal difficulties and dubious partners that eight years of litigation were necessary before a settlement could be reached. In the meantime, forced to look after herself and her children, Mrs. Strong became a very different person. Just before his death her husband had sent her to Philadelphia to undergo medical treatment by the famous neurologist Dr. S. Weir Mitchell, to whom Mrs. Strong later said that she was indebted for her achievement of good health. After 1883 her vigor, dominating personality, and versatility were as notable as her previous semi-invalidism.

She turned first to agriculture. Her husband had purchased 220 acres of semiarid land in southern California from Pio Pico, the last Mexican governor of California. Located near the present city of Whittier, the property was named Rancho del Fuerte, but soon became better known as the Strong Ranch. Here, starting four years after her husband's death, Mrs. Strong ordered the planting of walnuts—a crop just coming into favor with California farmers—as well as citrus fruits, pomegranates, and pampas grass, the last used chiefly for decorative purposes and sold primarily in Germany. To make her experiment pay, Mrs. Strong studied problems in marketing as well as irrigation and flood control. In 1887 and 1894 she took out patents on designs for a sequence of storage dams, so placed that the water impounded in one would back up and help support the next higher dam. In this same period she also patented inventions of several household articles. Her successes caused her to become known as the "walnut queen" and "pampas lady" and won her election as the first woman member of the Los Angeles Chamber of Commerce; she gained national recognition by her exhibits of water storage schemes and pampas grass at the World's Columbian Exposition at Chicago in 1893. At the exposition she gave a speech on the importance of business training for women and was chosen president of a new feminist Business League of America. Yet she did not abandon her earlier interest in cultural affairs. She was a founder and the first president of the Ebell Club of Los Angeles, formed in 1894 to en-

rich cultural opportunities for women. She was active also in another Los Angeles women's group, the Friday Morning Club, and in the Ruskin Art Club, and she was vice-president of the Los Angeles Symphony Association.

During her later years Mrs. Strong was a leading advocate of flood control and water supply measures to help Los Angeles County, and she was an early proponent of federal aid to develop the Colorado River. In 1918 she appeared before a Congressional committee to urge damming the Grand Canyon. An ardent feminist and Republican, in 1920 she founded the Hamilton Club to encourage women to study public affairs. When the famous old adobe residence of Gov. Pio Pico, near Whittier, was threatened by destruction, she organized local women in a successful drive to preserve it as a historic monument. Having been converted to Christian Science, she helped found a church of that faith in Whittier. Her active life came to an end in 1929 in her eighty-sixth year, when she was killed in an automobile accident near Whittier. She was buried at Forest Lawn Memorial Park, Glendale, Calif.

[Mrs. Strong's granddaughter Mrs. John R. Mage of Pasadena, Calif., has an extensive collection of family papers that includes much about Mrs. Strong and her husband. Mrs. Mage has also supplied from memory and from her own studies of her family details that could not be found in written records. Of key importance for understanding Mrs. Strong are several articles by and about her published in the first issue (Jan. 1895) of a short-lived Boston periodical, the *Business Folio;* and an interview by Flavia Gaines Leitch in the *Los Angeles Examiner,* Apr. 1, 1923 (both with photographs). Less revealing is an interview in *Sunset,* Apr. 1911. An important appraisal of Mrs. Strong's career was given by the Los Angeles Chamber of Commerce in *Southern Calif. Business,* Nov. 1926. Her testimony before Congress and illustrated documents concerning her storage-dam patents may be found in U.S. House of Representatives, Committee on Water Power, *Hearings,* Parts 1, 2, 3, and 4, 65 Cong., 2 Sess. (Mar. 18–May 15, 1918), pp. 787–812. Her exhibits and the prizes she won are described in Calif. World's Fair Commission, *Final Report* (1894). Obituary notices were published in the *Los Angeles Times, Los Angeles Herald,* and *Whittier . (Calif.) News,* Sept. 17, 1926. During her lifetime Mrs. Strong's career was summarized in three biographical articles that were probably written after consultation with her: *Who's Who in the Pacific Southwest* (1913), p. 358; *Nat. Cyc. Am. Biog.,* XVII, 34–35; and John S. McGroarty, ed., *Hist. of Los Angeles County* (1923), III, 279–82.]

RODMAN WILSON PAUL

**STUART, Helen Campbell.** *See* CAMPBELL, Helen Stuart.

**STUART, Jessie Bonstelle.** *See* BONSTELLE, Jessie.

**STUART, Ruth McEnery** (May 21, 1849–May 6, 1917), author, was born in Marksville, La., the eldest of the eight children of James and Mary Routh (Stirling) McEnery. She was named Mary Routh McEnery but simplified her name to Ruth when she became a writer. Her maternal grandfather, Sir John Stirling, was a wealthy emigrant to Louisiana from Dundee, Scotland; her maternal grandmother, Mary Routh, came of a Welsh family which had emigrated to Virginia. Her father, born in Limerick, Ireland, counted among his forebears Irish gentry whose estates were confiscated in the years of the Puritan Commonwealth; after his family had emigrated to Virginia early in the nineteenth century, he and three of his brothers decided to settle in Louisiana. Some of his kinsmen rose to high office in the state, but James McEnery was less prosperous. When Ruth was about seven years old, he took his family to New Orleans, where for many years he was on the staff of the customhouse. How much formal education Ruth had is unknown. The family were moderate Presbyterians and not averse to reading novels, especially those of Sir Walter Scott, her father's favorite author. The young girl also came to know the motley world of the Creoles, Italians, Irish, and Negroes centering around the colorful old French Market.

The family suffered from the hard times that came with the Civil War, and evidence suggests that Miss McEnery may, for financial reasons, have been a teacher for a time at the Locquet-LeRoy Institute in New Orleans, a fashionable school for girls. She did not marry until 1879, when on Aug. 5, at the age of thirty, she became the fourth wife of Alfred Oden Stuart, a fifty-eight-year-old planter and merchant of Washington, Ark., where they made their home. In 1883, a year after the birth of their only child, Stirling McEnery, Alfred Stuart died. His fortunes had declined, and the widow's share of the estate proved insufficient to support her and her son. "When the time came when I found I must make money," she later recalled, "I did not know which way to turn. Like the majority of Southern women, I had been brought up to enjoy life, and take no thought of its serious complexities. . . ." She may have taught for a time in the New Orleans public schools, but in 1887 she decided to seek a literary career.

Bringing to her task the valuable assets of a sharp ear and an observing eye, Mrs. Stuart began to write stories for the ready market awaiting writers of the fashionable local-color school. With faithful precision she recorded the distinct dialects of the Southern poor white, the Negro, the Italian and French immigrants to New Orleans, and the Latin-Negro Creoles. She also possessed, and used, a keen sense of folk humor and an empathetic understanding of the people about whom she wrote. Her first story, "Uncle Mingo's 'Speculations,'" appeared in the *New Princeton Review* in January 1888, and was quickly followed, in the May issue of *Harper's New Monthly Magazine*, by "Lamentations of Jeremiah Johnson," both in Negro dialect. From this time on, Mrs. Stuart's pen, except for a period of depression following the accidental death of her son in 1905, was continually busy.

In 1891, in order to be nearer her publishers, she moved to New York City, her home for the rest of her life. There she became a well-known member of the "Harper Set," and for a short time was temporary editor of *Harper's Bazar*, but her reputation was not dependent on any single publisher. Numerous national magazines bid for her services, and volume after volume of her collected stories sold well, perhaps the best known and most admired of these being *In Simpkinsville: Character Tales* (1897), dialect stories of Arkansas hillbillies, and *Napoleon Jackson: The Gentleman of the Plush Rocker* (1902), a sympathetic treatment of Negro folkways.

Making use of her ready wit and her ability to speak dialect as well as write it, Mrs. Stuart began in 1893 to give readings from her works on the lecture platform. She drew audiences not only by her talents and her easy grace, but also by the novelty of being one of the few women writers to take to the platform in the tradition of such "literary comedians" as Mark Twain. Despite her support of woman suffrage, Mrs. Stuart was always feminine rather than feministic. Hiding her true age, she appeared throughout her career to be, in the words of a New York reporter who saw her in 1893, a "slender, dark-eyed middle-aged widow." She died in 1917 of bronchopneumonia in Bloomingdale Hospital, White Plains, N.Y., at the age of sixty-seven and was buried beside her son in Metairie Cemetery, New Orleans.

Mrs. Stuart's literary reputation seemed at the time of her death sufficient to ensure her a long period of fame, but the public forgot her almost at once. Although Joel Chandler Harris had told her, "You have got nearer the heart of the negro than any of us," her works did not achieve the permanence of art. Unlike MARY NOAILLES MURFREE, SARAH ORNE

JEWETT, and MARY E. WILKINS FREEMAN, or her regional contemporary KATE CHOPIN, Mrs. Stuart lacked the power to transcend a literary fashion based on stereotyped, sentimental humor and pathos. She could not conceive of the purpose of the writer extending beyond that of the entertainer. Even so, the historical value of her tales and sketches is considerable, embodying as they do significant literary myths of the genteel South.

[The best source of information is the unpublished Ph.D. dissertation by Mary Frances Fletcher, "Ruth McEnery Stuart: A Biog. and Critical Study" (La. State Univ., 1955); primarily biographical and bibliographical, it includes a record of the materials in the Stuart Collection in the Tulane Univ. Library, New Orleans. No full critical study of Mrs. Stuart's works has been written. Of considerable interest are an account of her attitudes toward writing in "Am. Authors at Home," N.Y. Mail and Express, Apr. 28, 1900; and John D. Barry's interview with her in Illustrated American, June 6, 1896. See also Edwin L. Stephens in Library of Southern Literature (1907), XI, 5145–51; Julia R. Tutwiler in Bookman, Feb. 1904; Walter L. Fleming, ed., The South in the Building of the Nation (1909), XII, 429; obituary and tributes in La. Hist. Soc., Proc. and Reports, 1917 (Publications, vol. X); obituary in N.Y. Times, May 8, 1917, and editorial, May 13, (sec. 7). Mrs. Stuart's death record (N.Y. State Dept. of Health), for which her sister provided the personal data, is the source of her date of birth.]

LEWIS P. SIMPSON

STURGIS, Caroline. See HOOPER, Ellen Sturgis.

STURGIS, Ellen. See HOOPER, Ellen Sturgis.

SULLIVAN, Anne. See MACY, Anne Sullivan.

SULLIVAN, Mary Josephine Quinn (Nov. 24, 1877–Dec. 5, 1939), art teacher and collector, one of the founders of the Museum of Modern Art in New York, was born in Indianapolis, Ind., the eldest of the two sons and six daughters of Thomas F. and Anne E. (Gleason) Quinn, Roman Catholics whose families had both emigrated from Ireland. Thomas Quinn, who settled in Indianapolis in 1857, worked first for a meat-packing company and then as a fireman, and by 1877 was farming on the outskirts of the city. The Quinns allowed their children to develop their talents freely. Mary attended the public Shortridge High School, where she studied art and helped teach drawing and kindergarten classes.

Seeking to continue her art education, Miss Quinn moved in 1899 to New York City and enrolled at the Pratt Institute. A spirited and energetic student, she completed her studies in June 1901 and took a position as drawing instructor in a school in Queens. Impressed by her work, the Board of Education sent her to observe art schools in Europe, and in 1902, traveling in France and Italy, she first became aware of Impressionist and Post-Impressionist painting. Back in the United States, she transferred to the DeWitt Clinton High School, becoming in 1909 head of its art department. Active in city-wide school affairs, she became supervisor of drawing in the elementary schools and secretary of the New York High School Teachers' Association.

In 1910, having resigned her public school position, Mary Quinn studied for several months at the Slade School of Fine Art in University College, London, and then joined the Pratt Institute faculty as an instructor of design and household arts and sciences. From this period dates her textbook, Planning and Furnishing the Home: Practical and Economical Suggestions for the Homemaker (1914). For a time during the First World War she helped give art training to occupational therapists at the Pratt Institute. She resigned from the institute staff in October 1917, shortly before her marriage.

As early as 1907 Mary Quinn had taken lodging in the home of the Theodor Dreier family in Brooklyn Heights, whose gifted daughters (see MARGARET DREIER ROBINS) were known not only for their woman suffrage and settlement-house work, but also, particularly Katherine Dreier, for their interest in modern art. She also formed close friendships with the prominent art collectors and patrons LIZZIE PLUMMER BLISS and ABBY ALDRICH ROCKEFELLER, with both of whom she frequently visited galleries. It was the influence of Miss Bliss and Miss Quinn that helped turn Mrs. Rockefeller's interests to the field of modern art. Through Lizzie Bliss, Mary Quinn met the artist Arthur B. Davies, who persuaded the two women to lend financial aid to the landmark Armory Show of 1913.

A shared interest in art also underlay her marriage, on Nov. 21, 1917, to Cornelius Joseph Sullivan, seven years her senior, a prominent New York attorney and collector of rare books and paintings. Childless, the Sullivans devoted themselves to building an art collection at their Hell Gate home overlooking the East River in Astoria, Queens, Long Island. Here they often entertained a wide circle of friends, including Irish artists, political figures, and writers. With her husband's active aid, Mrs. Sullivan began assembling her own collection about 1920. The first major works were acquired in February 1927 at the auction of the collection of John Quinn, her husband's friend and Harvard Law School classmate who had died three years before. Here they purchased Paul Cézanne's "Madame Cézanne" (1872–77), Henri de Toulouse-Lautrec's "Woman in the Garden of Mr. Forest" (1891), and George Rouault's "Crucifixion" (1896). Further works were acquired from galleries and private collections in New York and throughout Europe, including a Picasso from the Leo Stein collection and Amedeo Modigliani's "Sculptured Head of a Woman" from Leopold Zborowski, the artist's benefactor and patron. The Sullivan collection also contained such earlier works as a sixteenth-century Flemish "Madonna and Child," a still life by Jean Baptiste Simeon Chardin, Benjamin West's "Death of General Wolfe," and portraits by Gilbert Stuart, as well as an impressive sampling of silver and furniture, including a Hepplewhite mahogany tambour-top desk once owned by Degas. These works were frequently loaned to museums in the United States and abroad for exhibition.

Mary Quinn Sullivan maintained close ties with her family and was active in art affairs in Indianapolis. In 1927 she founded in that city the Gamboliers' Society, whose sixteen subscribers paid twenty-five dollars annually into a general fund from which Mrs. Sullivan purchased works of art to be contributed to the John Herron Art Institute.

It was during many gallery excursions and discussions in the 1920's that Mrs. Sullivan, Miss Bliss, and Mrs. Rockefeller, joined by Arthur Davies, formulated the idea of providing an institutional base for modern art in New York. The dispersal of the John Quinn collection and that of Davies himself, who died in 1928, made the need for a museum more pressing. By early 1929 plans had crystallized, and at a May luncheon at Mrs. Rockefeller's 54th Street home, the collector A. Conger Goodyear, a founder of the Albright-Knox Gallery in Buffalo, N.Y., agreed to become chairman of the committee of organization. Space was rented at 730 Fifth Avenue; the charter was signed by seven trustees (including Mrs. Sullivan); and in November the newly appointed director, Alfred Barr, opened to the public "Cézanne, Gauguin, Seurat, van Gogh"—the first exhibition of the Museum of Modern Art. In May 1932 the museum moved to its own quarters on 53rd Street.

An earlier venture along similar lines, the Société Anonyme, founded in 1920 by Katherine Dreier, had flourished for a time in rented rooms under the guidance of Miss Dreier and Marcel Duchamp, but, lacking secure financial backing, it collapsed during the early years of the depression. The Museum of Modern Art, however, with the active support of the Sullivans and many others, survived the difficult depression era. Cornelius Sullivan was counsel for the museum until his death in April 1932; Mary Sullivan became chairman of the extension committee and the furnishing committee for the new galleries, and also served on the membership committee. She resigned as a trustee on Oct. 17, 1933, but was elected honorary trustee for life two years later.

A new chapter of Mrs. Sullivan's career began in 1932 when she opened a gallery in an East 56th Street brownstone, where she gave one-man shows for Peter Hurd and others. Later she operated a small two-room gallery within the larger Park Avenue gallery of Lois Shaw. In 1937, perhaps owing to precarious financial circumstances, she sold her husband's collection at a Parke-Bernet auction. In the fall of 1939, in failing health, she gave up her gallery and prepared to sell her own collection of about two hundred works. On Dec. 5, the day before the sale was to open, she died at her home in Astoria of pleurisy and diabetes. A funeral was held in New York at the Church of St. Vincent Ferrer and another at St. Joan of Arc Church in Indianapolis, where she was buried in Holy Cross Cemetery.

The auction of her collection at the Parke-Bernet Galleries (Dec. 6–7, 1939), perhaps the most important since that of the Quinn collection in 1927, made available to the public a distinguished group of paintings reflecting a refined judgment which had weighed individual merit rather than mere speculative potential. At the auction, which realized a total of $148,750, Abby Aldrich Rockefeller purchased two works, a Modigliani and an André Derain, and placed them in the permanent collection of the Museum of Modern Art in memory of her long-time friend and collaborator.

[A. Conger Goodyear, *The Museum of Modern Art: The First Ten Years* (1943); Geoffrey T. Hellman, "Profile of a Museum," *Art in America*, Feb. 1964; Dwight MacDonald, "Action on West Fifty-Third Street," *New Yorker*, Dec. 12, 19, 1953; Allene Talmey, "The Museum of Modern Art: The Story of an Institution," *Vogue*, July 1945; Aline Saarinen, *The Proud Possessors* (1958); Mary Ellen Chase, *Abby Aldrich Rockefeller* (1950); Milton Brown, *The Story of the Armory Show* (1963); Benjamin L. Reid, *The Man from N.Y.: John Quinn and His Friends* (1968); sales catalogues of collections of Cornelius J. Sullivan (Parke-Bernet Galleries, Apr. 29–May 1, 1937) and of Mrs. Sullivan (Parke-Bernet, Dec. 6–7, 1939, Feb. 23–24, 1940); Lionello Venturi, "Notes on the Collection of Mrs. Cornelius J.

Sullivan," *Parnassus,* Dec. 1939; "Sullivan Prices," *Art Digest,* Dec. 15, 1939, p. 23; "Sullivan Furniture & Decorative Objects," *Art News,* Feb. 17, 1940; obituaries in *Indianapolis Times,* Dec. 6, 1939, *Indianapolis Star,* Dec. 17, 1939, *N.Y. Times,* Dec. 6, 1939, and *Art Digest,* Dec. 15, 1939; *Amherst College Biog. Record,* 1951, on Cornelius J. Sullivan; information from Ind. State Library, Indianapolis; enrollment records of Pratt Institute and of Slade School of Fine Art, Univ. College, London; interviews with Alfred Barr and Dorothy Miller, Museum of Modern Art; Antoinette Kraushaar, Kraushaar Gallery; and Mrs. Helen Appleton Read, Portraits, Inc.]

HOWARDENA D. PINDELL

SUMNER, Helen Laura. *See* WOODBURY, Helen Laura Sumner.

SURRATT, Mary Eugenia Jenkins (May 1820?–July 7, 1865), convicted as a conspirator in the assassination of Abraham Lincoln, was born on a farm near Waterloo, Prince George's County, Md., the third child and first daughter of Samuel Isaac Jenkins and his wife, whose name is unknown. Jenkins died when Mary was small, but her mother and older brothers kept the family together. She spent several years in Miss Winifred Martin's Catholic girls' school in Alexandria, Va., and became a convert to the Roman Catholic faith, of which she thereafter remained a devout adherent. When about fifteen she was married to John Harrison Surratt, a young man in his late twenties who had inherited a farm at Condon's Mill near Glensboro, Md. They had three children: Isaac Douglas, John Harrison (born 1844), and Anna Eugenia. Fire destroyed their first farm, and in 1840, after an interlude as a railroad contractor in Virginia, Surratt purchased, mostly on credit, 1,200 acres in Prince George's County. Prospering for a time, he built a tavern and store at a crossroads about ten miles southeast of Washington that became known as Surrattsville (later Clinton).

For reasons that are not clear, possibly failing health, Surratt's fortunes declined, and by 1857 the farm had been reduced to half its original acreage through sale and rental. The Civil War completed the ruin; his slaves ran away, his son Isaac went south to join the Confederate forces, and Union troops raided the farm. When Surratt died in 1862, Mrs. Surratt called her son John home from St. Charles' College near Baltimore to take over her husband's job as postmaster of Surrattsville, but in 1863 the post went to a Republican and their financial affairs reached a crisis. Renting the Surrattsville tavern, Mrs. Surratt moved to Washington and on Oct. 1, 1864, opened a boardinghouse

on H Street. The location was good, and advertising brought in a few clients.

More portentous events were stirring, however. Young John Surratt, who joined the Washington household in December, was, though barely twenty, a Confederate courier engaged in carrying secret dispatches to Richmond. Among his pro-Southern friends was the famed actor John Wilkes Booth, who had devised a chimerical plan to kidnap President Lincoln as ransom for the release of Confederate prisoners. Surratt fell in with this scheme and recruited several accomplices, young drifters set loose by the war, who occasionally visited him at the boardinghouse. Mrs. Surratt, aware that something was afoot, implored her son to confide in her, but was put off with vague talk of cotton speculations. In March an abortive kidnap attempt took place, but the collapse of the Confederacy early in April ruled out this plan. About Apr. 11, Booth concluded that his mission now was to avenge the South by assassinating President Lincoln, and so informed his friends. Several of them abandoned him at this point, including, it appears, John Surratt, who went off to Richmond.

Mrs. Surratt, ignorant of these developments, was much worried by finances. The Calvert family, from whom the Surrattsville farm had been purchased, was pressing for overdue mortgage payments, and her own tenants were in arrears. On Apr. 11, while Washington celebrated Lee's surrender, she made a debt-collecting expedition to Surrattsville, and three days later undertook a second such trip in response to a dunning letter received that day from George H. Calvert, Jr. On this occasion, as a favor to Booth, she delivered a package containing field glasses to John M. Lloyd, her Surrattsville tenant. She returned to the capital after dark, having collected nothing, and went to bed. That night, Apr. 14, at Ford's Theatre in Washington, Booth fatally wounded the President, leaped to the stage, and escaped. A second conspirator, Lewis Payne, seriously wounded Secretary of State William Seward in his home, while a third, George Atzerodt, failed to carry out the planned assassination of Vice-President Andrew Johnson. Within several hours the police arrived at the Surratt boardinghouse and searched it. Two days later War Department officers arrested Mrs. Surratt, her daughter, and the other residents for questioning. Mrs. Surratt never returned home. Held first in the Old Capitol Prison (on the site of the present Supreme Court building), she was then transferred to the Old Penitentiary (later Fort McNair) in the southwestern part of the city. Here on May 12, 1865, she, Payne, Atzerodt, and three other alleged conspirators (Booth had meanwhile died resisting capture) went on trial before a special nine-officer military commission set up by President Johnson at the urging of Secretary of War Edwin M. Stanton.

As the trial dragged through the long weeks of the Washington summer, the gray-eyed, brown-haired Mrs. Surratt, in a weakened condition related to menopause and aggravated by harsh confinement, appeared daily in the dock wearing a heavy veil which she lifted only to permit witnesses to identify her. The War Department utilized the trial to dramatize a widely held belief, shared by Stanton himself, that the assassination had been a vast Confederate conspiracy involving not only Mrs. Surratt and her son, but even Jefferson Davis. Weak or irrelevant evidence pointing in this direction was seriously considered, while evidence tending to confute it, notably Booth's diary, was withheld. The crucial fact of the existence of two distinct plots—one of kidnapping and one of assassination—was never brought out. At no time were the defendants permitted to testify in their own behalf. The two principal witnesses against Mrs. Surratt—her tenant John M. Lloyd, and Louis J. Weichman, who had boarded with her and was intimate with John Surratt, Booth, and Atzerodt —were themselves so deeply implicated that War Department officials, including Stanton, were able to frighten them into testifying with threats of execution. Two young volunteer lawyers, aided by Senator Reverdy Johnson of Maryland, attempted a defense, but the commission found all the defendants guilty and sentenced four of them, incluing Mrs. Surratt, to hang. Although five of the commissioners recommended that Mrs. Surratt's sentence be commuted to life imprisonment, their plea was apparently suppressed when the commission's findings were presented to President Johnson by Judge Advocate General Joseph Holt. On July 5, remarking that Mrs. Surratt "kept the nest that hatched the egg," Johnson ordered the executions to take place within forty-eight hours. Mrs. Surratt's lawyers, learning of the verdict through the newspapers on July 6, worked desperately through the night to obtain a writ of habeas corpus, but it was suspended by the President, acting under his war powers. On July 7, having proclaimed her innocence to a priest, Mrs. Surratt was hanged with the others in the yard of the Old Penitentiary. Her body remained in military prisons until 1869, when her daughter secured its transfer to Washington's Mount Olivet Cemetery, where it rests under a plain marker.

At the time of her execution, the belief in Mrs. Surratt's guilt was nearly universal, but doubts soon arose. In 1867 her son was acquitted in a civil trial in which the validity of both Weichman's and Lloyd's testimony was seriously challenged. Subsequent memoirs, diaries, autobiographies, and research have uniformly pointed to her innocence; the most recent historian to review the evidence has concluded: "That she was innocent of any part in the assassination is as certain as anything can be which is not subject to absolute proof" (Moore, p. 102). Indeed, the question has become not whether, but why, she was unjustly executed. Some have suggested a conspiracy involving Secretary of War Stanton, while others blame anti-Catholic prejudice, pointing out that in 1897 Thomas M. Harris, a member of the military commission, published a book entitled *Rome's Responsibility for the Assassination of Abraham Lincoln*. More likely she was the victim of popular hysteria, growing from wartime tensions, to which responsible officials themselves succumbed.

[A basic source is Ben: Perley Poore, ed., *The Conspiracy Trial for the Murder of the President* (3 vols., 1865–66); see I, 13, for a word sketch of Mrs. Surratt at the trial. Guy W. Moore, *The Case of Mrs. Surratt* (1954), contains a full bibliography. The more important earlier works include David M. DeWitt, *The Judicial Murder of Mary E. Surratt* (1895) and *The Assassination of Abraham Lincoln and Its Expiation* (1909); George S. Bryan, *The Great American Myth* (1940), a good general narrative; John W. Clampitt (one of her attorneys), "The Trial of Mrs. Surratt," *North Am. Rev.*, Sept. 1880; Rev. Jacob A. Walter (her priest), "Remarks Made before the U.S. Catholic Hist. Soc.," *Church News*, Aug. 18, 1891. Helen Jones Campbell, *The Case for Mrs. Surratt* (1943), though undocumented, is based on original research and contains some data about her early life that does not appear elsewhere. Otto Eisenschiml, *Why Was Lincoln Murdered?* (1937), sees her as victim of a Stanton plot; cf., however, Benjamin P. Thomas and Harold M. Hyman, *Stanton* (1962).]

WILLIAM E. BARINGER

**SURRIAGE, Agnes.** *See* FRANKLAND, Agnes Surriage.

**SWAIN, Clara A.** (July 18, 1834–Dec. 25, 1910), pioneer woman medical missionary to the Orient, was born in Elmira, N.Y., the tenth and youngest child of John and Clarissa (Seavey) Swain. Her father, of Irish extraction, was a native of New York state; her mother was a frail, quiet, religious woman from New Hampshire. Clara grew up in Castile, N.Y., her parents' former home in the Genesee River valley, to which they returned when she was two. As a girl she was fond of reading, frequently borrowing books from neighbors. After earlier schooling, she alternated periods of teaching and study, beginning at about the age of fifteen when she lived with a favorite aunt in Michigan and taught for a year in a local school. About 1856 another aunt in Canandaigua, N.Y., knowing of Clara's "strong desire for self-improvement," invited her to come there for a year of study in a seminary, after which she stayed on for seven years as a teacher in a public school.

But despite her fondness for children Miss Swain "did not find teaching altogether a delight" (Hoskins, p. 10). In local illnesses she had shown a talent for nursing, and it was her hope to become a doctor. She therefore welcomed, in 1865, the opportunity to begin medical training in her hometown, at the Castile Sanitarium, recently purchased by Dr. Cordelia A. Greene, one of the early women doctors, a medical graduate of 1855 from Western Reserve University. In 1866–67 and 1868–69 Clara Swain attended the Woman's Medical College of Pennsylvania, presumably returning to the sanatorium during the term of 1867–68 to fulfill the graduation requirement of two years of study with a medical practitioner. On Mar. 11, 1869, she received her medical degree, with a thesis concerning endometritis.

By this time professional education for women had reached a point where American missionary societies could at last sponsor young women doctors "to minister to the wants of the women of heathen lands," a step that had been advocated for nearly two decades by SARAH J. HALE, editor of *Godey's Lady's Book*. Dr. Swain's attraction to evangelism, beginning as early as the age of nine, when she had been moved by a powerful Methodist sermon, had been strengthened in the deeply spiritual atmosphere of Dr. Greene's sanatorium. Shortly after her graduation a call came to the Woman's Medical College from Mrs. D. W. Thomas, who with her missionary husband headed a Methodist girls' orphanage at Bareilly, India, for a "lady physician" who could teach medicine at the orphanage and attend women whose seclusion in zenanas deprived them and their children of medical care. After weighing her family ties against the attraction of such work, Dr. Swain agreed to go to Bareilly, accepting an appointment under the New England Branch of the newly formed Woman's Foreign Missionary Society of the Methodist Episcopal Church. Early in November 1869, in company with another Methodist, ISABELLA THOBURN, she sailed from New York, the first

woman medical graduate to represent the United States as a missionary to the Orient.

In January 1870 she joined the mission at Bareilly, a city of over 100,000 in northwest India. With the aid of an interpreter she began to treat patients at once. In March she inaugurated lectures in anatomy, physiology, and materia medica to a class of seventeen, including fourteen girls from the orphanage and three young married women. After several hours of classes daily, the students took turns assisting Dr. Swain at the orphanage, in the Christian village, and in the city itself, where her practice grew rapidly. Following further training, including instruction in obstetrics, thirteen members of this class passed civil examinations and were certified to practice medicine "in all ordinary diseases."

Dr. Swain's success in gaining admittance to zenanas, and her patients' devotion to their "Doctor Miss Sahiba," proved that Indian women would accept Christian women physicians. Demands for her services multiplied until she could no longer travel to all who could not visit the mission. In October 1871, when she sought to buy land from the Nawab of Rampore for a hospital and dispensary near the mission, he gave the entire estate outright, encompassing about forty acres. Here, on May 10, 1873, she opened a six-room dispensary, a native architect helping her with the plans; in less than eight months 1,600 patients were treated, each prescription accompanied by a verse from Scripture, in Hindi, Persian, and Urdu. On Jan. 1, 1874, she opened her hospital, reportedly the first for women in India. Designed so that all women could come without breaking caste or class rules, it provided seclusion for patients observing purdah and could accommodate families and even servants of those who would not stay otherwise. Patients soon came from as far away as Burma, the sick often outnumbered by their attendants and companions. In 1874, in addition to her Bareilly practice, Dr. Swain worked at Lucknow several days each month. Her letters of 1875 indicate a practice among nearly 2,000 patients, with almost 5,000 prescriptions given at the dispensary. Despite help from former students working as Bible women and medical assistants, so much responsibility left her "at times physically unfit for work." In March 1876, well after fulfilling the five years of service expected of overseas workers before furlough, she retired to Castile in the hope of regaining her health, another graduate of the Woman's Medical College taking her place. Although not yet fully restored, Dr. Swain resumed her work in Bareilly in January 1880.

Five years later, while attending the Rani of Khetri, wife of the Rajah of Rajputana, she was invited to stay on as palace physician and to open a women's dispensary. Seeing an opportunity to bring Christian influence into a province intensely hostile to Christianity, at the same time relieving the Missionary Society in America of the expense of her support, she agreed, with the provision that she be unhindered in her activities, both medical and evangelical. Except for eighteen months in America when a sister fell ill (1888–89), she lived near the royal family for over ten years, becoming a beloved friend and companion to the Rani and a "Nāni" to the children. In June 1885 the Rajah opened one room of the palace for dispensary work among women of all classes. He later built a small dispensary and house for Dr. Swain, who saw patients at both places and moved freely about the city and countryside, dispensing books, tracts, and medicines wherever she went. By her royal affiliation she spoke with authority on such matters as river drainage and female infanticide. She in turn absorbed much of the culture about her, developing a fondness for curries and for riding her own elephant to attend patients as far away as ten miles. The Rajah and Rani urged her to make her home permanently in Khetri, but after a tour of the Holy Land she retired to Castile in 1896.

During 1906–08 she paid a final visit to India, primarily for the jubilee of the founding of the first Methodist mission there in 1856. On her return to Castile, she prepared a collection of extracts from letters her family and friends had saved over a period of twenty-five years. Although lacking in medical detail, *A Glimpse of India* (1909) provides a lively account of her life in Bareilly and Khetri, revealing an abundant sense of humor, an ever-growing affection for India and its people, and a degree of respect for their social and religious customs remarkable in someone so profoundly committed to her own beliefs. With a missionary friend, Dr. Swain spent her last years in the home of Dr. Mary T. Greene, niece and successor of Dr. Cordelia Greene at the Castile Sanitarium. Her death there, at seventy-six, was attributed to malnutrition complicated by age. An imposing tablet marks her grave in the Castile cemetery, and the Clara Swain Hospital still stands in Bareilly, now greatly expanded and open to men as well as women.

[Detailed accounts of Dr. Swain's early life may be found in Mary Sparkes Wheeler, *First Decade of the Woman's Foreign Missionary Soc. of the Methodist Episcopal Church, with Sketches of Its Missionaries* (1881), and Mrs. Robert Hoskins

(Charlotte L. R.), *Clara A. Swain, M.D.: First Medical Missionary to the Women of the Orient* (31 pp., 1912). The most extensive published account, though popular and undocumented, is Dorothy Clarke Wilson, *Palace of Healing: The Story of Dr. Clara Swain* (1968). Her medical training is best understood by reading Elizabeth Putnam Gordon, *The Story of the Life and Work of Cordelia A. Greene, M.D.* (1925), and annual announcements of the Woman's Medical College, 1866–69. In addition to *A Glimpse of India,* Dr. Swain contributed a chapter, "A 'Doctor Lady's' Story," to Ross C. Houghton, *Women of the Orient* (1877), in which Houghton also describes the Bareilly mission on his visit in 1874. Full accounts of Dr. Swain's career are set in context in Mrs. J. T. Gracey, *Medical Work of the Woman's Foreign Missionary Soc., Methodist Episcopal Church* (1888); Frances J. Baker, *The Story of the Woman's Foreign Missionary Soc. of the Methodist Episcopal Church, 1869–1895* (1896); Helen Barrett Montgomery, *Western Women in Eastern Lands* (1911); and Margaret I. Balfour and Ruth Young, *The Work of Medical Women in India* (1929). Charles V. Perrill, "Twenty Years at the Clara Swain Hospital," *Northwestern Univ. Medical School Mag.,* Jan. 1964, is a recent account of the work she started in Bareilly. Her death certificate is in the N.Y. State Dept. of Health, Albany.]

PATRICIA SPAIN WARD

**SWALLOW, Ellen Henrietta.** *See* RICHARDS, Ellen Henrietta Swallow.

**SWARTZ, Maud O'Farrell** (May 3, 1879– Feb. 22, 1937), labor leader, was born in County Kildare, Ireland, the fourth of nine girls in a family of fourteen children of William J. and Sarah Matilda (Grace) O'Farrell. Though both the O'Farrells and the Graces were of the landed gentry, the circumstances of Maud's immediate family were hard. Her father was in the flour-milling business with his brothers, but he was unsuccessful and failed to provide adequately for his large brood. Assistance came regularly from his wife's family, which included William R. Grace, a prosperous merchant, founder of the Grace Steamship Company, and later mayor of New York. The O'Farrell girls, as poor relations, were sent to convent schools and expected to become governesses; Maud's schooling was in Germany and in Paris, after which she went as a governess to Italy. In 1901 she emigrated to America, arriving in New York City nearly penniless. Finding a governess's life there no better than in Europe, she left her first place and tried a variety of jobs until she settled into a position as proofreader in a foreign-language printing firm in 1902. Probably in connection with her work, she met a printer, Lee Swartz, and married him in 1905. The marriage, which had no issue, proved an unhappy one. Within a short time she separated from her husband but, because of her Catholic faith, never divorced him.

An attractive, intelligent woman, well educated for her station in life and ambitious, Maud Swartz sought broader outlets. There was, she knew, a larger world than her own; she had been befriended by a wealthy first cousin, Mrs. Alice D'Oench, had spent weekends at her home on Long Island, and had been taken occasionally to the opera. The friendship would be lifelong, but it was not a means of personal advancement. She found her outlet instead in reform. When a woman suffrage campaign opened in New York state after the 1912 presidential election, Mrs. Swartz volunteered to speak to Italian audiences. After demonstrating oratorical talents and doing yeoman's service in the unsuccessful drive, she was enlisted by one of her suffrage associates, Rose Schneiderman, a New York labor leader—and thereafter a close friend—in the work of the National Women's Trade Union League.

The league had been founded in 1903 by a combination of middle-class and working women. Gaining strength as public awareness grew of the plight of women in industry and as trade unionism expanded among women, particularly in the garment trades, the league aimed to foster women's education, to lobby for protective legislation, and, above all, to organize women into unions. Mrs. Swartz had shown no previous interest in trade unionism (despite her long employment in the printing trade, she was initiated into Typographical Union No. 6 of New York only on Oct. 12, 1913), but this now became her career. In 1916 she was chosen to spend a year at the league's training school. Immediately thereafter, she became the full-time secretary of the Women's Trade Union League of New York.

Maud Swartz soon expanded her horizons. When the International Congress of Working Women was launched in 1919, she was chosen secretary. The Congress convened in Geneva, Switzerland, in October 1921, changed its name to the International Federation of Working Women, and moved its headquarters from Washington to London, at which time she became the American vice-president, a post she held for about two years. Besides her role in these international affairs, Mrs. Swartz played a minor part on the liberal side of the controversies that divided the American labor movement in the postwar years. As the National Women's Trade Union League's delegate to the American Federation of Labor convention in 1919 she found the proceedings "rather rigid and stereotyped." She ardently supported the abortive American Labor Party in 1919, and in 1921 she worked briefly for William Z. Foster until she became aware of his Communist ties.

Mrs. Swartz had continued to earn her livelihood as secretary of the New York League. The connection ended in 1921, but in 1922 the New York body reemployed her in another capacity, as "compensation adviser," to provide, on the pattern set by the building trades unions, free aid to women seeking workmen's compensation for industrial accidents. There was a crying need for such a service. Mrs. Swartz observed that "workers are, in general, absolutely ignorant of the law, . . . are opposed by skilled men, and are often deprived of their compensation through their own ignorance." In her new work Mrs. Swartz encountered obstacles from resentful referees and insurance company representatives ("I can assure you I was very unpopular") who sought unsuccessfully to have her barred from the proceedings. The women, particularly the foreign-born, were hard to reach. At first Mrs. Swartz would merely arrive early at hearings and accost waiting women with an offer of help. She brought to the job a quick Irish wit and a keen mind, an invaluable ability in foreign languages, a growing—and soon expert—knowledge of New York compensation law, and a passionate sympathy for the helpless. Her solitary efforts became extremely valuable. In some ways this work on a restricted stage was the most noteworthy of her career.

In June 1922 Maud Swartz was elected president of the National Women's Trade Union League. Her predecessor, MARGARET DREIER ROBINS, had been president for fifteen years and a great force in the league; a woman of means, she had contributed funds and raised money from others. This kind of role Mrs. Swartz could not fill; indeed, she had been chosen for the post partly because she was a bona fida trade unionist. The result, however, was that the presidency became more a place of honor than of power. Mrs. Swartz did not leave her post as compensation adviser of the New York League. Still, hers was the public voice of the women's labor movement. She spoke before Congressional hearings and public conferences on a variety of concerns of working women in the 1920's, including now a fervent advocacy of world peace. War, she insisted, should be treated as a crime, "and anybody going to war as a criminal." But the women's trade union movement was in decline during her tenure. When she left the presidency in 1926, she noted that organizing had become much more difficult since the start of the league.

The last phase of Maud Swartz's career began with her appointment on Jan. 1, 1931, as secretary of the New York State Department of Labor under Industrial Commissioner Frances Perkins. The office, administrative rather than policy-making, had been somewhat inactive under her predecessor. The first trade unionist in the post, Mrs. Swartz endowed it with new importance by her vigor, expanding the department's activities among women workers. In keeping with her previous work, she also frequently acted as referee in compensation cases. In January 1937, while still in office, Maud O'Farrell Swartz suffered a coronary thrombosis from which she died the next month at the age of fifty-seven. A Catholic from birth, although not devout in her mature years, she received a Catholic service and was buried in St. John's Cemetery, Brooklyn, N.Y. Among those at the funeral were Frances Perkins and Eleanor Roosevelt.

[The most useful sources on Mrs. Swartz's career are the *Life and Labor Bull.*, publication of the Nat. Women's Trade Union League, and the *Annual Reports* of the N.Y. Women's Trade Union League. An interview with Miss Rose Schneiderman and correspondence with a surviving sister, Miss Annette O'Farrell, yielded valuable information on her career, family background, and personality. There are full obituaries in the *N.Y. Times* and *Herald Tribune* for Feb. 23, 1937. Specific personal facts were gleaned from Mrs. Swartz's death certificate and records of the Internat. Typographical Union. Mrs. Swartz gave an account of her work as compensation adviser in the *Am. Federationist*, Aug. 1929. See also Gladys Boone, *The Women's Trade Union Leagues* (1942), which has helpful information on Mrs. Swartz, and Alice Henry, *Women and the Labor Movement* (1923).]

DAVID BRODY

**SWEET, Winifred.** See BLACK, Winifred Sweet.

**SWISSHELM, Jane Grey Cannon** (Dec. 6, 1815–July 22, 1884), journalist and reformer, advocate of woman's rights, was born in Pittsburgh, Pa., then a frontier town, the daughter of Thomas and Mary (Scott) Cannon. Only three of the Cannon children survived childhood: Jane, an older brother, and a younger sister. Her parents, of Scotch-Irish descent, were members of a strict Covenanter branch of the Presbyterian Church. "Converted" at the age of three, Jane learned that year to read the Bible and recite the catechism. Later, at fifteen, she joined the Covenanter Church with the customary soul-searching and disturbance of spirit. Thomas Cannon, a merchant and speculator in real estate, suffered heavily in the panic of 1819 and died in 1823. His wife, with three young children to support, made straw hats, while little Jane taught lacemaking and painted on velvet and William made chairs. Jane went to school until a cough was thought to indicate the onset of tuberculosis, which had been fatal to her father and four of her brothers and sisters. Mrs. Cannon revolted against the calomel treatment that had been unavailing in the earlier cases and prescribed outdoor exercise, much rest, and a diet of milk and eggs. Jane recovered and became, at fourteen, a schoolteacher.

She was, by a contemporary account, very feminine in appearance, small and slender, with a soft voice, expressive eyes, and a "truly enchanting smile." She was quick in thought and speech, and during her five years of teaching she discovered that she had a talent for painting, in which she took great delight. On Nov. 18, 1836, at twenty, she was married, despite her mother's doubts, to James Swisshelm, a farmer's son and a devout Methodist. The marriage, though it lasted twenty years, was turbulent from the start. Swisshelm expected a degree of wifely submission that, try as she would, her own strong principles and individualistic temperament made impossible. In addition, a domineering mother-in-law controlled the family finances and activities and never ceased trying to convert Jane, hoping to make her a Methodist preacher. Swisshelm had no sympathy with his wife's artistic and literary tastes; thinking it her duty, she gave up painting, though with "a breaking heart," and then reading. After two years the couple moved to Louisville, Ky., where James Swisshelm joined a brother in business. Here the cruelties of the slavery system which Jane witnessed made a deep impression; she ever after gave the antislavery movement her passionate, if not exclusive, attention. Her husband's fortunes did not prosper; to augment their income Jane Swisshelm built up a successful business as a corset maker. In 1839, however, she abandoned the business, against her husband's wishes, to return to Pittsburgh because of the illness of her mother, for whom she cared until Mrs. Cannon's death early in 1840. Her interest in the legal plight of married women, which must already have been aroused, became fixed when her husband proposed to sue her mother's estate for the value of his wife's nursing services. She also approved the principle of woman suffrage, although she was too

individualistic to work in women's organizations and regarded most woman's rights conventions and their leaders as impractical.

After her mother's death Mrs. Swisshelm took
charge of a seminary in Butler, Pa., where she
remained about two years. At this time she
began her newspaper career by contributing
to the local paper anonymous articles opposing
capital punishment. In 1842 she went back to
her husband, whose Louisville venture had
failed, and they lived with his family on their
farm near Pittsburgh, which she named Swissvale. Swisshelm approved of his wife's journalistic efforts and urged her to sign her work,
which now included stories and poems for
Philadelphia papers and articles on slavery and
woman's rights for a Pittsburgh abolitionist
journal. Her lively style, direct attack, and
quick wit made her work popular, and in 1848,
when Pittsburgh was left without an antislavery paper, she began to publish one of her own.
In the *Saturday Visiter* (Dr. Johnson's spelling, upon which she insisted), over a period of
ten years, she vigorously defended the rights
of women, castigated all slaveowners, attacked
Daniel Webster for urging the passage of the
Fugitive Slave Law, and declared it a "crime
for a woman to become the mother of a drunkard's child." Her editorials advocating property
rights for married women are said to have
convinced the governor of the state of the need
for this reform, which passed the Pennsylvania
legislature with his support in 1848. The *Visiter* eventually had a national circulation of six
thousand and from first to last spoke with the
voice and from the heart of its editor. Financially, however, it was always in difficulties, and in 1857, her relations with her husband having at last become intolerable, Mrs.
Swisshelm gave up her editorship, left her husband, who later divorced her for desertion,
and took her only child, Mary Henrietta
("Nettie," born in 1851), to St. Cloud, Minn.,
where her sister and her family lived.

In her new home Mrs. Swisshelm accepted
a proposal that she revive and edit an almost
defunct newspaper, which now became the *St.
Cloud Visiter*. Her extreme antislavery position and her opposition to President James
Buchanan earned her the enmity of Sylvanus B.
Lowry, the Tennessee-born boss of the Democratic party in central Minnesota. The quarrel
with Lowry brought Mrs. Swisshelm both fame
and trouble. He and his cohorts destroyed her
press and type and lodged a libel suit against
her, forcing the suspension of the paper. With
community antislavery support, however, she
at once started the *St. Cloud Democrat* on the
same lines as the *Visiter* and found, besides, a

new outlet for her crusading zeal in statewide
lecture tours denouncing Lowry and advocating all of her favorite reforms. She supported
Lincoln in 1860 but condemned the mildness
of his policies. Shocked by the Sioux uprising
of 1862 in Minnesota, in which white settlers
were massacred, she toured the state demanding severe countermeasures and in January
1863 went east to urge federal action against
the Sioux, lecturing in Chicago, Philadelphia,
Brooklyn, and Washington.

In Washington, Mrs. Swisshelm was unable
to see President Lincoln but did renew an old
acquaintance with Secretary of War Edwin M.
Stanton, whose views she greatly admired; he
offered her a minor clerkship in the War Department. She then arranged to sell the St.
Cloud newspaper. Since the clerkship was not
available immediately, she sought duty as a
nurse, and until the end of the Civil War she
served in base hospitals in and near the capital, working in the War Department intermittently. Her angry letters to the St. Cloud paper
about the conditions she found in military
hospitals are as poignant as any in print. Jane
Swisshelm became a close friend of MARY TODD
LINCOLN and always defended her, and she
met and disliked DOROTHEA DIX, whom she attacked with equal vigor. After the war, in
December 1865, she started a paper called
the *Reconstructionist* to express the views of
the radical Republicans. As a result of her
condemnation of President Andrew Johnson's
policies, however, she lost her job, and the
*Reconstructionist* came to an end after little
more than a year. On Secretary Stanton's advice, she then instituted and won a suit for a
part of her dead husband's estate at Swissvale. There she made her home, more quietly
than before, for she now suffered from a heart
ailment and a digestive difficulty variously
described as an ulcerated intestine and cholera
morbus. She took some part in reform causes:
in January 1872 she made a lecture tour in
Illinois, speaking for woman suffrage, and
later that year she was a delegate to the National Prohibition party convention. She also
wrote a lively autobiography, *Half a Century*,
published in 1880. She died at Swissvale at the
age of sixty-eight and was buried in Allegheny
Cemetery in Pittsburgh.

[The principal source is Mrs. Swisshelm's autobiography; this was written largely from memory,
for she states that she never saved letters and kept
no diaries. The Carnegie Library of Pittsburgh
has a file of the *Saturday Visiter;* a few issues of
her short-lived Washington paper, the *Reconstructionist,* and the complete files of her St. Cloud
newspapers are in the Minn. Hist. Soc. Excerpts

from the last have been published, with a good biographical sketch, in Arthur J. Larsen, ed., *Crusader and Feminist: Letters of Jane Grey Swisshelm, 1858–1865* (1934). See also Margaret Farrand Thorp, *Female Persuasion* (1949), chap. iii. On her later reform activities, see her letter in the *Woman's Jour.*, Jan. 20, 1872, p. 18; and James Black, *Brief Hist. of Prohibition* (1880), p. 23. Mrs. Swisshelm's death date was verified and her place of burial supplied by the Hist. Soc. of Western Pa., Pittsburgh.]

ALICE FELT TYLER

**SZOLD, Henrietta** (Dec. 21, 1860–Feb. 13, 1945), Zionist leader, was born in Baltimore, Md., to Benjamin and Sophia (Schaar) Szold. She was the first child in a family of eight girls, two of whom died in infancy and one at the age of four. Her father had been born in Hungary to one of the few Jewish landowning families. Though he studied in Vienna and became a rabbi, his love for the land never diminished, and he instilled a similar love in his eldest daughter. In Vienna, Rabbi Szold took part in the democratic revolution of 1848. When it failed he became a political exile and returned to his native Hungary, where he tutored for a few years in the Schaar family and in 1859 married a daughter of the house, Sophia. He was then called to the United States to become rabbi of the progressive Conservative congregation, Oheb Shalom, in Baltimore.

Henrietta Szold received from her father the attention and education usually given to the firstborn son. Since German was spoken at home, she was fluent in that language from infancy, and her father taught her French and Hebrew as well. Though she never considered herself a scholar, she was sufficiently versed in Hebraic studies to be her father's devoted literary and scholarly assistant until the time of his death in 1902. Her mother taught her sewing and cooking; gardening and botany were a family hobby.

Miss Szold graduated in 1877 from Baltimore's Western Female High School, first in her class. That same year she substituted briefly as principal of the school and taught English there. Later she taught French, German, Latin, history, natural sciences, and mathematics for nearly fifteen years at the Misses Adams' School in Baltimore, a fashionable academy for girls. During this time she also taught classes for children in the religious school of her father's synagogue, conducted classes in Biblical history for adults, and was an active member of the Baltimore Botany Club. She began to write articles for the *Jewish Messenger* of New York, under the pseu-

donym "Sulamith," and she attended lectures at the newly established Johns Hopkins University and at the Peabody Institute.

After the assassination of Czar Alexander II in 1881 and the ensuing anti-Semitic "May Laws" of 1882, a rash of pogroms drove hundreds of thousands of Jews out of Poland, Lithuania, and other parts of the Russian empire, and many of them came to America. Of those who settled in Baltimore, the more learned gravitated toward the Szold family, and the Hebraists among them organized in 1888 the Isaac Bar Levison Hebrew Literary Society to continue the "enlightened" interests, oriented toward renascent modern Hebrew letters, which they had brought with them from Russia. At Miss Szold's suggestion this group also undertook to sponsor practical education in "Americanization" by providing a school, one of the first of its kind, where adult immigrants could meet at night to learn English and something of American history and customs. Miss Szold found the teachers, formed the curriculum, and raised the money for essential supplies. Opened in November 1889 in a barren loft lit only by kerosene lamps, the new school had thirty pupils the first night and so many more in the days immediately following that several new classes had to be formed. Within a decade (the school lapsed in 1898, and the city itself began night schools a few years later) some five thousand people, Christians as well as Jews, had received instruction in these classes and a pattern had been set for similar enterprises in all of the other large Northeastern cities that were also receiving masses of immigrants from Eastern Europe.

Henrietta Szold was concurrently involved in the Jewish Publication Society. This body had been founded in 1888, largely under the leadership of her friend Cyrus Adler, to publish Jewish literature in the English language for the American-Jewish community. In 1893 Adler invited Miss Szold to accept the part-time professional responsibility of editorial secretary of the society, an office she held until 1916. Among the books she had a major part in translating and editing were Heinrich Graetz's *History of the Jews*, the first two volumes of Louis Ginzberg's *The Legends of the Jews*, Moritz Lazarus' *The Ethics of Judaism*, and Nahum Slouschz's *The Renascence of Hebrew Literature*. For many years Miss Szold did most of the work of producing the standard annual of information about American Jews and the Jewish community of the world, the *American Jewish Year Book* (begun in 1899); she was its sole editor from 1904 to 1908.

After her father's death Henrietta Szold

moved with her mother in 1903 to New York City, where, while continuing her work for the Jewish Publication Society, she took courses at the Jewish Theological Seminary. She fell in love for the first time in her life, with Prof. Louis Ginzberg, who was her junior by thirteen years, and was rejected. Unable to bury her unhappiness in her work, she took a six months' leave of absence from her editorial duties and, accompanied by her mother, went abroad on vacation. The Publication Society's board of directors provided financial assistance which made it possible for that trip to include a journey to Palestine. This marked the major turning point in Miss Szold's life, for after that visit Zionist endeavor became her dominant and soon her sole commitment.

Along with her father Henrietta Szold had become interested in Zionism much earlier, at the very beginning of Zionist stirrings in the United States. Such convictions were unusual among the Jews of Central Europe who had arrived in the United States in the middle of the nineteenth century, a large majority of whom opposed Zionism and believed in assimilation. In 1893 she had joined the newly formed Hebras Zion of Baltimore, probably the first Zionist society to be organized in the United States, and in 1907 she became a member of the Hadassah Study Circle, which met to discuss Zionism and aspects of Jewish history.

During her visit to Palestine, Miss Szold was confronted by an impoverished people shockingly lacking in medical care and standards of sanitation. Legend has it that she experienced a "moment of conversion" when she saw children nearly blinded by trachoma and became convinced at that instant that her life-work should be the curing of disease in Palestine. Upon her return to the United States in 1910 Henrietta Szold became the secretary of the Federation of American Zionists; with her usual concern for efficiency she worked hard to bring order into the records of that organization. She also proposed to the women in her Hadassah Study Circle that they dedicate themselves to the support of practical medical work in Palestine, a suggestion that bore fruit when, on Feb. 24, 1912, thirty-eight women interested in the "promotion of Jewish institutions and enterprises in Palestine" met at Temple Emanu-El in New York and organized themselves as the Hadassah Chapter of Daughters of Zion. The name was changed to Hadassah at the first national convention. The body was dedicated primarily to health work in Palestine, and Miss Szold was its founding president.

As its first practical accomplishment the group in 1913 raised funds to found the Hadassah Medical Unit, consisting of two nurses who were sent to Jerusalem to work in a manner that paralleled the district nursing system among the poor in the United States. The outbreak of World War I interrupted this work. During the war years Miss Szold traveled throughout the United States organizing new chapters of Hadassah, lecturing, and writing frequently for the *Maccabean,* the organ of the American Zionist Federation. Until 1916 she continued her work for the Jewish Publication Society, but in that year two events occurred which made a radical difference in her life. The first was the death of her mother; this loss was both painful and liberating, for her decisions as to where to live and what to do could henceforth be purely personal. The second was the gaining of financial independence, on a modest scale. At the instigation of Justice Louis D. Brandeis, Judge Julian W. Mack and other leaders of the Zionist movement had provided her with a life income which was sufficient to cover her immediate needs. This enabled her to resign her post at the Jewish Publication Society and to devote herself entirely to Zionism for the rest of her life.

In 1918, at a convention in Pittsburgh, all American Zionists were united into a single body, the Zionist Organization of America, and Miss Szold became the director of its department of education. The responsibilities of this post included the publication of educational materials, the training of leaders for adult and youth groups, and the introduction of education in Zionism into Jewish summer camps. By this time, since British forces under General Allenby had in 1917 taken Palestine from the Turks, it had become possible to resume Zionist work there. Henrietta Szold now played a central role in organizing the American Zionist Medical Unit, a joint endeavor of the Zionist Organization of America, Hadassah, and the American Jewish Joint Distribution Committee. When the unit arrived in Palestine in the early fall of 1918, it consisted of forty-four persons—doctors, nurses, dentists, nutritionists, sanitary engineers, and administrators—and four hundred tons of equipment, including vehicles as well as medical supplies. In 1920 Miss Szold was sent to Palestine as the American representative on the unit's executive committee.

Arriving in May, she found the unit rent by dissatisfaction and personal conflicts. When its director, Dr. Isaac Rubinow, resigned (1922), she took over his responsibilities until a replacement arrived, while also directing the new Nurses' Training School and supervising the health program in the Jewish schools. Financial support had proven far too little for the work planned, and in 1922 Miss Szold traveled to Europe to attend an international congress of the World Zionist Organization, where she appealed for funds, with little success. That same year, however, a gift from Nathan Straus made it possible to maintain the work until the medical unit was reorganized as the Hadassah Medical Organization; it was supported thereafter by Hadassah as its major endeavor in Palestine.

Henrietta Szold returned to the United States in 1923 to see her ailing sister Rachel and resumed the active presidency of a rapidly growing Hadassah. After three years she resigned this post and was made honorary president. The next year she was elected by the World Zionist Organization as one of the three members of its Palestine Executive Committee, along with Harry Sacher and Col. Frederick H. Kisch. She therefore returned to Palestine in 1927, as supervisor of the committee's department of health and education, but she was again in America in 1930. Her seventieth birthday was elaborately celebrated by Hadassah, and in May 1930 she was given the honorary degree of Doctor of Hebrew Letters, the first such degree to be conferred on a woman, by the Jewish Institute of Religion, the rabbinical seminary which had been founded by her friend Rabbi Stephen Wise. In 1931 she was elected to the executive committee of the National Assembly of Palestinian Jewry, the Vaad Leumi. Returning to Palestine, in the next several years she was busy with the organization of social services, the broadening of the work in hygiene, the effort to rehabilitate juvenile delinquents, and the establishment of vocational schools.

Henrietta Szold still regarded herself as a resident of the United States "on loan" to Palestine, and by 1933 she was again arranging her affairs to return to America, this time permanently. Hitler's rise to power in Germany, however, made it imperative for her to stay in Palestine to help implement the plan of Recha Freier of Berlin by which German-Jewish adolescents were sent to Palestine to complete their education. Jewish leadership in Palestine now created a new agency, Youth Aliyah, which worked in cooperation with a German-Jewish youth organization to train adolescents between the ages of fifteen and seventeen and then bring them to Palestine to live in various communal settlements. This was a lifesaving effort of profound importance, for many of the young people who came as wards of Youth Aliyah were ultimately to be the sole survivors of their families.

Miss Szold was on the pier at Haifa in February 1934 when the first group of sixty-three boys and girls arrived. Although she was now in her seventies, in the next few years she made several trips to Europe to help raise funds to bring more young people out of Germany. In 1937 she went to Germany itself to coordinate the work of Youth Aliyah there. She encountered many difficulties with the British government in obtaining permission to bring more children into Palestine, but by 1948 a total of thirty thousand had arrived under the auspices of Youth Aliyah. The effort was particularly intense in the years immediately before World War II. By that time Henrietta Szold had unified the various women's welfare groups working in Palestine into one body called the League of Jewish Women (Histadruth Nashim Ivriot) and had become the first president of this body.

Miss Szold made her last visit to the United States in 1937, reporting to the Hadassah convention in October of that year. Three years later, on the occasion of her eightieth birthday, she read her will to a group of friends in Jerusalem. Her major desire was the creation of a center for research on the problems of children, for publication of the results, and for the coordination of the activities of the existing youth organizations in Palestine; she planned to leave money for its support. This institute, begun in honor of her birthday, was renamed Mosad Szold in 1945, after her death. On her eighty-first birthday the Vaad Leumi, the leadership of the Jewish community in Palestine, appointed her to plan its endeavors in child and youth care. In 1943, now in her eighty-third year, she was busy, with the help of her close associate, Hans Beyth, caring for a remarkable group of Youth Aliyah children who had left Poland, then under Nazi occupation, and made their way to Palestine after three and a half years of wandering.

Miss Szold's health had begun to fail, and war made travel from Palestine to the United States virtually impossible in 1944. On Mar. 13 of that year Boston University conferred on her the honorary degree of Doctor of Humanity, in recognition of her lifetime of service; she listened to the citation in Jerusalem in a ceremony made possible by an international radio hookup. She contracted pneumonia in August 1944, and thereafter remained an invalid. She died the following February in Jerusalem, in the Hadassah-Hebrew University Hospital, opened in 1939, which she had done much to help create. She was buried in the Jewish Cemetery on the Mount of Olives.

In the last years of her life Henrietta Szold,

who had never married, was universally regarded as the "Mother of the Yishuv," the Jewish settlement in Palestine. In person she was poised and reserved, but her great warmth and charm were always evident. Her broad sympathies included all of the inhabitants of Palestine—Jewish, Moslem, and Christian. Deeply religious herself, she was tolerant all her life of divergent faiths and convictions. Ardent Zionist though she was, she swam against the mainstream of Zionist opinion in the 1930's, for she joined with such figures as Judah Magnes, president of the Hebrew University, and Martin Buber, the renowned philosopher, in pleading for understanding with the Arabs of Palestine and for a binational political future for the country. Despite Arab riots and Jewish angers, she was not deterred from this vision to the very end of her days.

[In addition to innumerable articles about her there have been several book-length biographies of Henrietta Szold: Marvin Lowenthal, *Henrietta Szold: Life and Letters* (1942); Elma Ehrlich Levinger, *Fighting Angel: The Story of Henrietta Szold* (1946); Rose Zeitlin, *Henrietta Szold: Record of a Life* (1952); and especially Irving Fineman, *Woman of Valor: The Life of Henrietta Szold* (1961). Miss Szold figures prominently in Alexandra Lee Levin, *The Szolds of Lombard Street: A Baltimore Family, 1859–1909* (1960), and in Eli Ginzberg, *Keeper of the Law* (1966), a biography of Louis Ginzberg. See also Alexandra Lee Levin, "Henrietta Szold and the Russian Immigrant School," *Md. Hist. Mag.*, Mar. 1962. The principal collections of Henrietta Szold's papers are at Hadassah headquarters in N.Y. City, Baltimore Hebrew College, the Zionist Archives in Jerusalem, and in family hands.]

ARTHUR HERTZBERG

# T

**TAFT, Helen Herron** (June 2, 1861–May 22, 1943), wife of William Howard Taft, twenty-seventh president of the United States, was born in Cincinnati, Ohio, the fourth of eleven children of Harriet (Collins) and John Williamson Herron. Her father, a native of Pennsylvania, was a successful lawyer and an important figure in Ohio Republican circles. A lifelong friend and onetime partner of Rutherford B. Hayes, he was also a college classmate (at Miami University, Oxford, Ohio) of Benjamin Harrison, during whose administration he served as United States Attorney in Cincinnati. Mrs. Herron, who had come to Cincinnati in girlhood from Lowville in northern New York, had, in her daughter's words, "an exceedingly keen wit" and "a stimulating personality," and despite family cares "was very popular in society." Helen Herron—always known as Nellie—had her mother's quick intelligence, a somewhat outspoken tongue, and sufficient unconventionality to win a mild reputation for Bohemianism in the innocent upper-middle-class world in which she grew up. She received her education at Miss Nourse's private school in Cincinnati, which emphasized languages and literature, and devoted much time to studying music, always one of her deep interests. At seventeen, to her great excitement, she spent a week in the White House as the guest of LUCY WEBB HAYES. Though popular, Nellie Herron wearied of "frivolities" and, after teaching

school for two years, organized in the summer of 1883 a "salon" for intellectual discussion. Among the members was Will Taft, a young Cincinnati lawyer whom she had first met when she was eighteen. They were married, after a lengthy courtship, on June 19, 1886.

Perhaps the most significant aspect of Mrs. Taft's life was the active part she played in guiding her husband's career. Without her ambitions, indeed, he would probably never have become president. She always believed that he was destined for a prominent position in public life, but she had to struggle constantly against his lesser ambitions and his happiness in judicial posts. "You are my dearest and best critic," he once wrote to her, "and are worth much to me in stirring me up to best endeavor" (July 8, 1895, Taft Papers).

Mrs. Taft's aspirations for her husband received their first encouragement in 1890 when an appointment as President Harrison's Solicitor General raised him from the bench of the Cincinnati superior court to a post that would give him the "all-around professional development" she urged. But two years later Harrison made Taft a federal circuit judge. When in 1900 President McKinley appointed him head of the Philippine Commission, his wife's eagerness helped overcome his doubts about accepting. In the islands, Mrs. Taft aided her husband's efforts to conciliate the Filipinos by breaking down the color line at receptions and dinners. She was pleased when, in 1902, he twice declined President Roosevelt's offer of a Supreme Court appointment. The next year he became Roosevelt's Secretary of War; but the Supreme Court idea continued to be raised with what seemed to her "rather annoying frequency," and when in 1906 rumors were rife that Roosevelt would appoint Taft to a new vacancy, she called on the President and urged him not to do so. Convinced by this time that her husband was a likely presidential candidate for 1908, she was forced to contend against his distaste for active politics and his persistent self-doubts until Roosevelt's support thrust him into the nomination.

After the election, her "active participation" in his career at an end, Mrs. Taft plunged into her duties as First Lady, duties she immensely enjoyed. But her activities as hostess were early curtailed. In May 1909 a nervous collapse left her briefly paralyzed and for several years impaired in speech and strength, and though she could take part in receptions where she could "speak a formula of greeting," she had to avoid dinners and social reunions. Her condition added to her husband's burdens of office.

The quieter life of New Haven, where after his presidency Taft became professor of constitutional law at Yale, greatly benefited his wife's health. They returned in 1921 to Washington when President Harding fulfilled Taft's highest ambition by appointing him chief justice of the Supreme Court. These years saw the only major disagreement of their long and happy marriage, for Mrs. Taft, though keeping her views private, was an ardent opponent of prohibition, which Taft vigorously upheld. Their religious difference—she remained an Episcopalian despite Taft's Unitarianism—was of minor consequence.

Mrs. Taft retained her residence in Washington after her husband's death in 1930. She died there at the age of eighty-one, having suffered from a circulatory ailment for more than a year, and was buried beside her husband in Arlington National Cemetery. Their three children survived them: Robert Alphonso, later Senator from Ohio; Helen Herron (Mrs. Frederick J. Manning), dean of Bryn Mawr College; and Charles Phelps, lawyer, civic leader, and mayor of Cincinnati.

[William Howard Taft Papers, Library of Congress; Henry F. Pringle, *The Life and Times of William Howard Taft* (2 vols., 1939); and Mrs. Taft's somewhat random *Recollections of Full Years* (1914). See also *N.Y. Times* obituary, May 23, 1943.]

　　　　　　　　　　　　STANLEY I. KUTLER

**TAGGARD, Genevieve** (Nov. 28, 1894–Nov. 8, 1948), poet, was born in Waitsburg, Wash., the eldest of three children of James Nelson Taggard and Alta Gale (Arnold) Taggard, fruit farmers and schoolteachers. One of Genevieve's grandfathers had moved from Vermont down the Hudson and out to Illinois, the other from Virginia over the Daniel Boone Trail to the Ozarks. Both fought under General Grant, then continued west. "They went," she wrote, "looking eagerly around them for something they never found. . . . Did they think about free land when they meant free life?" When she was two years old her parents went as missionaries to the Hawaiian Islands, where her father built up a public school at Kalihiwaena near Honolulu. She ran barefoot on coral roads, thrilled at kona storms, climbed trees for mangoes, guavas, and papayas, and in schoolbooks learned Hawaiian legends before she heard of Demeter or Prometheus. She knew her father's Hawaiian, Chinese, Portuguese, and Japanese pupils better than any American children; for American tourists she developed a positive dislike. When her parents got ready to go back to Waitsburg in 1905, Genevieve strung herself a goodbye lei of ilima flowers. "Too bad you gotta be Haole [white]," a Hawaiian playmate told her, and later she wrote, "Off and on, I have thought so too, all my life." But in 1906 the family returned to Hawaii and Genevieve entered the missionary Punahou School. In its magazine, the *Oahuan*, she published her first poem, "Mitchie-Gawa," about American Indians, in October 1910.

Words were her medium of rebellion against her domineering mother with her dictum "There is only one right way," against forced music lessons and housework. Her parents were devoted members of the Disciples of Christ and allowed no books but the Bible in their home. The family again returned to Waitsburg, where her ineffectual father worked a small pear farm for his more prosperous brother and Genevieve was made painfully aware of her "sewing circle" clothes and the snubs of children who whispered that she had lived in a grass hut with cannibals. She became editor of the high school paper, *Crimson and Gray*. In 1912 her father took his family for the third time to Hawaii. Genevieve achieved highest scholastic rank in the Punahou School, was editor of the *Oahuan* in 1914, but had to leave without graduating because her father became ill and she took his place in his school. She wrote many poems and stories. Keats, she later testified, was her "first big passion"; his "luxury suited the Island radiance." Friends helped her financially to enter the University of California at Berkeley in the fall of 1914, and Genevieve worked, taking five years to graduate. She studied with the poet Witter Bynner, enrolled in Leonard Bacon's famous English 106, and in her last year was salaried editor of the *Occident,* the exceptionally fine students' literary magazine. By this time she had become a Socialist, familiar with radical-literary circles in San Francisco, and rejoiced in her emancipation: "Am I the Christian gentlewoman my mother slaved to make me? No indeed. I am a poet, a wine-bibber, a radical; a non-church-goer who will no longer sing in the church choir or lead prayer meeting with a testimonial." She was also an extremely beautiful young lady.

*Harper's Magazine* published "An Hour on a Hill" in December 1919, the first of the many poems Genevieve Taggard wrote for national magazines. Max Eastman, editor of the radical *Liberator,* published some of her poems and offered her a job on the *Freeman* in 1920. She went to New York City, but the job did not materialize and she found one in the avant-garde publishing firm of B. W. Huebsch. The next year she helped found and became a member of the editorial board of *The Measure: A Journal of Verse,* a "little magazine" that continued to appear until 1926. On Mar. 21, 1921, she was married to Robert L. Wolf, a writer who had given up his job in Washington and gone to New York to meet her after reading her poems. *For Eager Lovers* (1922), poems written during the first year of her marriage, placed Genevieve Taggard in the company of the leading lyric poets of the day; Edmund Wilson wrote that "With Child" was the only respectable poem on childbearing he could remember. Her daughter Marcia was born in 1922, and the family spent the next year in San Francisco, where Genevieve gave courses in poetry and helped edit an anthology of California poems. In 1923 they settled in New Preston, Conn. In her introduction to *May Days* (1925), an anthology of verse from the *Masses* and the *Liberator,* Miss Taggard said that artists and radicals, united in the old *Masses,* had fallen into enmity during the 1920's. She herself wished to be both a free artist and a committed radical. Wide recognition of her lyric gift came in 1928 with publication of *Travelling Standing Still,* a selection of her poems. William Rose Benét appreciated her "shy irony, the genuine mirth, the 'scorn of scorn,'" and the poet herself as "a free spirit. She was beautiful. She was feminine . . . impetuous, impatient, and meditating and lonely."

In *Circumference: Varieties of Metaphysical Verse, 1456–1928* (1929) she defined the tradition of John Donne. EMILY DICKINSON, she felt, was the first great American practitioner of Donne's kind of poetry, and in 1928 Genevieve Taggard went to southern France and began to write a life of the New England poet. In 1929, now an instructor in English at Mount Holyoke College, she finished *The Life and Mind of Emily Dickinson* (1930). A "glowing and romantic biography," in the words of one reviewer, conjectural and intuitive in approach, it proposed George Gould as Emily's mysterious lover and her father as the repressive villain. A Guggenheim award in 1931 took Genevieve Taggard to Capri and Majorca with her daughter and sister. From 1932 to 1935 she taught at Bennington College in Vermont. In 1934 she was divorced, and on Mar. 10, 1935, she was married to Kenneth Durant, an employee of Tass, the Soviet news agency. She acquired a farm, Gilfeather, at East Jamaica, Vt., a few miles south of her grandfather's town of Londonderry. Her feelings about New England were ambivalent. She called it "hysterical country" and was appalled when she saw canned woodchuck in farmers' cellars, children picking ferns for a few cents a day, and a man who worked in a furniture factory for ten cents an hour. But she entitled a poem of 1933 "Return of the Native" and spoke of "a land permanently sad, / Bearing a somber harvest. . . . / This oddly, is my land." Her life in Hawaii had turned her against racism; the New England community rather than any proletarian experience gave substance to her anticapitalism. She supported the Vermont marble workers in a strike and for a few years was active in the Teachers' Union and in left-wing literary organizations. From 1935 to 1946 she taught at Sarah Lawrence College. To her great number of friends she added students who attested to her magical personality and gift of communication.

Her efforts to make her lyric talent serve proletarian causes and to speak the workers' idiom in *Calling Western Union* (1936) were overwrought. But unlike the work of many writers at this time, hers, as Marie de L. Welch said, was "more generous with love than anger." Her *Collected Poems: 1918–1938* (1938) paired early love and nature lyrics with later social poems as if to show their unity. The melodic characteristics of her verses led Aaron Copland, Roy Harris, and Henry Leland Clarke to set them to music; in 1939 a chorus of two hundred children sang her "Prologue," to music by William Schuman, in Carnegie Hall and Lewisohn Stadium. In 1946

Genevieve Taggard retired to her farm in failing health. She died in a New York City hospital at the age of fifty-three of complications following some years of suffering from hypertension. Her ashes were scattered on a hill above Gilfeather.

[A summary account of Genevieve Taggard's life is in a Univ. of Hawaii master's thesis by Kathryn Lucille Lins, "An Interpretive Study of Selected Poetry of Genevieve Taggard" (1956). A carbon copy, with photographs, is in the Genevieve Taggard Collection, Baker Library, Dartmouth College. This collection contains copies of most of her published work, including uncollected poems in magazines, as well as reviews by her and references to her by critics and literary historians. She wrote about herself briefly in *Twentieth Century Authors* (1942), ed. by Stanley J. Kunitz and Howard Haycraft; more extensively in the anonymous "Poet Out of Pioneer," *Nation*, Jan. 19, 1927, and in "Hawaii, Washington, Vermont," *Scribner's Mag.*, Oct. 1934. Donald A. Stauffer in "The Poet as Maker," an essay in *Poets at Work* (1948), analyzed the genesis in 15 pages of worksheets of Genevieve Taggard's "The Four Songs." The Genevieve Taggard Papers in the N.Y. Public Library contain correspondence and manuscripts. A record of readings by Genevieve Taggard of her own poetry was issued by the River Press, East Jamaica, Vt., in 1953. Selections from the large number of poems she wrote on Hawaiian themes are in *Origin: Hawaii* (1947). Other volumes of her verse not mentioned in this article are: *Hawaiian Hilltop* (1923), *Words for the Chisel* (1926), *Monologue for Mothers* (1929), *Remembering Vaughan in New England* (1933), *Falcon* (1942), *Long View* (1942), *A Part of Vt.* (1945), and *Slow Music* (1946). Obituaries are in the *N.Y. Times* and *N.Y. Herald Tribune*, Nov. 9, 1948, and *Saturday Rev. of Literature*, Nov. 20, 1948.]

BASIL RAUCH

**TALBOT, Marion** (July 31, 1858–Oct. 20, 1948), university dean and professor of household administration, daughter of Emily (Fairbanks) and Israel Tisdale Talbot, was the oldest of six children, of whom only she, a sister, and two brothers survived infancy. Although born in Thun, Switzerland, while her parents were sojourning in Europe, she belonged to New England by descent and to Boston by rearing. She grew up in an atmosphere of social amenity and humanitarian enterprise, well within the direct light of the eminent Yankees; JULIA WARD HOWE and LOUISA MAY ALCOTT were parts of her familiar world. Her father was a champion of homeopathic medicine and the first dean of the medical school of Boston University. Her mother participated actively in educational reform, partly because of obstacles the daughter encountered; in 1877, to make a college preparatory course available to young women, Mrs. Talbot took the lead in securing the establishment of the public Girls' Latin School in Boston. In the absence of such an institution, Marion Talbot had attended the private Chauncy Hall School, which admitted a few girls, and the nonclassical Girls' High School. She was also taken abroad to learn modern languages and studied Latin and Greek under private tuition. Admitted to Boston University only with conditions, she graduated with a Bachelor of Arts degree in less than four years, in 1880.

Several years of travel and social life followed, but Marion Talbot was soon, apparently, seeking a more useful role. Probably on the inspiration of ELLEN H. RICHARDS, a family acquaintance, she turned to the new applied science of sanitation, in which Mrs. Richards was pioneering at the Massachusetts Institute of Technology. Enrolling there in 1881, Marion Talbot left after one term, but returned in 1884 and received the B.S. degree in 1888. Particularly concerned, like Mrs. Richards, with the application of science to the home, she thus became involved in the emerging field of domestic science, one of the two dominant interests of her career. She collaborated with Ellen Richards in editing *Home Sanitation: A Manual for Housekeepers* (1887); and in 1890 she was appointed an instructor in domestic science at Wellesley College, thanks to the efforts of her close friend ALICE FREEMAN PALMER. Previously she had taken up her other lifelong interest, the cause of the educated woman. In 1881–82 she joined her mother, Mrs. Richards, Mrs. Palmer, and several other women in organizing the Association of Collegiate Alumnae, designed to unite the then thin scattering of college women for such purposes as providing fellowships and facilities for women graduate students and defining standards for women's schools and colleges in the United States. As the first secretary of the association and as president from 1895 to 1897 Marion Talbot thus served as a founder and manager of the organization which presently became the American Association of University Women.

In 1892 President William Rainey Harper invited Alice Freeman Palmer to frame and direct the program for women at the new University of Chicago. Mrs. Palmer accepted office on the understanding that she would be in residence only three months of each year and that Miss Talbot should serve as her colleague, virtually as her deputy, on a full-time appointment. Marion Talbot thus joined the university faculty in 1892 as dean of undergraduate women and assistant professor of sanitary science (in the department of social science and anthropology). In 1899 she was appointed dean of women for the university; and in 1905, having been made an associate professor in 1895, she was promoted to a professorship in the new—and her own—department of household administration, a department that included ALICE PELOUBET NORTON and SOPHONISBA P. BRECKINRIDGE.

As dean of women Miss Talbot had responsibility for the day-to-day living of the women students of the university, a charge which she construed broadly as a commission to convert the regime demanded by convention into a part of education toward the "higher life" of society—society in both a broad and a narrow sense. She presided over the development of "houses" for women: the improvisations of the "Beatrice," an apartment house rented by the university in 1892, evolved into a system of dormitories organized as residential clubs, each with an appointed head, an apparatus of self-government, a program of hospitality, and (in the language of the time) the simple, quiet attractions of a home. The houses were supplemented by other facilities available to women living off campus; Marion Talbot led in the creation of the Woman's Union in 1901 and later of Ida Noyes Hall, a clubhouse with gymnasium and pool. Socially the university women were for Marion Talbot a distinct and single constituency. Largely because of her opposition, chapters of national sororities were not established when fraternities were. She objected firmly and unremittingly, however, to academic discrimination based on sex.

In professional writing as in administration, Marion Talbot was a pragmatist with convictions. Her first published research in Chicago was a "practical study" of diet in the women's houses, which were to her what demonstration or laboratory schools were to progressive educators. *Food as a Factor in Student Life* (1894, with Ellen Richards as co-author) set exact findings of fact in a context of normative ideas, a mode of thought characteristic of Marion Talbot's immediate professional environment, where science and reform were often combined. Her interests and experience were thoroughly fused in *The Education of Women* (1910), a study of the changed role of women in a technological society and a critique of the educational responses to this change, and in *The Modern Household* (1912), written in collaboration with her colleague Sophonisba P. Breckinridge. These books constituted the testament of Marion Talbot's maturity. She shared the belief that "the home is still 'woman's

sphere' and will always be for most women" (*The Education of Women*, p. 56); but she also thought, with colleagues on the university faculty, that the traditional household was obsolescent. Efforts to retain the home as it had been would be for the most part futile. The modern household was a complex center of consumption, rather than a primitive producer of goods, and demanded a skillful administrator, namely, the educated woman, prepared to exert the essential and far-reaching influence of the home. Such an administrator might well regard herself "as placed at the real heart of things, responsible for the conduct of that institution which is the unit of social organization" (*The Modern Household*, p. 8).

Beyond the confines of the University of Chicago, Marion Talbot took some part, under the leadership of Ellen H. Richards, in the Lake Placid conferences that led to the formation of the American Home Economics Association (1908). After her retirement in 1925 she twice served as acting president of Constantinople Woman's College in Turkey (1927–28, 1931–32). Her religious affiliation was Unitarian. She died in Chicago of chronic myocarditis at the age of ninety and was buried in that city's Oak Woods Cemetery. She had endeavored to assist the American family through a revolution that had produced the college-educated woman and (in Marion Talbot's belief) given that woman a mission.

[Papers of Marion Talbot, Univ. of Chicago Archives; Marion Talbot, *More than Lore* (1936), a volume of reminiscences; Marion Talbot and Lois K. M. Rosenberry, *The Hist. of the Am. Assoc. of Univ. Women* (1931); *Nat. Cyc. Am. Biog.*, XXXVI, 425–26; *Univ. of Chicago Mag.*, Dec. 1948, p. 16; articles on Miss Talbot's parents in *Dict. Am. Biog.*; articles on Miss Talbot in *Jour. of Home Economics*, Sept. 1925 (by Alice Peloubet Norton), and Apr. 1949 (by Frances L. Swain). Family data from Miss Talbot's niece, Mrs. L. Earle Rowe, Providence, R.I., through the courtesy of Miss Florence E. Turner, Librarian, Boston Univ. School of Medicine. Death record from Ill. Dept. of Public Health.]

RICHARD J. STORR

TALCOTT, Eliza (May 22, 1836–Nov. 1, 1911), missionary teacher and nurse in Japan, was born in Vernon, Conn., the second of five daughters of Ralph and Susan (Bell) Talcott. Her father, a pioneer woolen manufacturer of the state, was descended from one of the first settlers of Connecticut; her mother traced her ancestry to Thomas Hooker, founder of the Hartford colony. Both parents died during Eliza's youth. She attended the well-known girls' school operated by SARAH PORTER in

Farmington, Conn., where she was also briefly an assistant teacher, and later entered the Connecticut State Normal School in New Britain. Upon graduation in 1857 she taught in Miss Porter's School and in the public schools of New Britain. In 1863 she left a promising teaching career in order to nurse an invalid aunt in Plymouth, Conn.

A devout member of the Congregational Church, Miss Talcott attended the annual meeting of the American Board of Commissioners for Foreign Missions in New Haven in 1872 and heard there an urgent appeal for additional overseas workers. She immediately volunteered and received an appointment from the mission board. In March 1873 she sailed to Japan in company with Julia E. Dudley, a graduate of Rockford (Ill.) Seminary—the first single women sent by the American Board to Japan. In the city of Kobe, to which they were assigned, the two women in 1873 started classes for girls in English, singing, the Bible, and sewing that two years later became Kobe Home, a girls' boarding school, and ultimately, in 1894, Kobe College. Miss Talcott served as principal from 1875 to 1880, when she resigned as a result of disagreement within the teaching staff.

While at the school Miss Talcott had also carried on evangelistic work, and she now became an itinerant nurse and religious instructor in Okayama Prefecture. After a furlough in the United States, she went to Kyoto in 1885 as house mother and evangelistic head of the nurses' training school at another Christian college in Japan, Doshisha University. Miss Talcott remained in Kyoto until the outbreak of the Sino-Japanese War in 1894, when she went to Hiroshima to minister to war victims. She spent over a year visiting sick and wounded soldiers, both Japanese and Chinese, in the six military hospitals of that city. Her nursing experience and thorough knowledge of the Japanese language made her work very successful there—so much so that she has been called the "Florence Nightingale of Japan."

A few years later Miss Talcott became ill with cholera and returned to the United States on leave. In the summer of 1900, on her way back to Japan, she was prevailed upon to remain in the Hawaiian Islands, where she worked for two and a half years as a missionary teacher among the Japanese who had come to work in the sugar and pineapple fields. She finally arrived in Japan in December 1902. The rest of her life she devoted to an evangelistic training institution in Kobe, the Woman's Bible School. She died in Kobe after a two

weeks' illness in 1911, and her body was buried in the foreign cemetery there.

Eliza Talcott was a tall, slender woman, quietly competent, who enjoyed great influence with both the Japanese and her missionary associates. One of the latter wrote of her: "Always gentle and unassuming, she yet gave an impression of dignity which made us younger women stand a bit in awe of her" (*Missionary Herald*, January 1912, p. 12). Though her field of missionary work was broad, her chief contribution was probably in the education of Japanese young women, at Kobe College and Doshisha University.

[Contemporary information about Miss Talcott's work in Japan may be found in the *Missionary Herald* and the annual reports of the Am. Board of Commissioners for Foreign Missions; see also James H. Pettee, comp., *A Chapter of Mission Hist. in Modern Japan* (Okayama, 1895). The fullest account of Miss Talcott's early work is in Charlotte B. DeForest, *The Hist. of Kobe College* (1950). Her sister Lora E. Learned published a brief sketch of her life in the pamphlet *Eliza Talcott, the Florence Nightingale of Japan* (1917). A colleague, Susan A. Searle, wrote obituary notices in the *Missionary Herald*, Jan. 1912, and *The Christian Movement in Japan* (Yokohama), tenth annual issue, 1912. Other obituaries are in the *Japan Weekly Mail* (Yokohama), Nov. 11, 1911, and *Mission News* (Kobe), Dec. 15, 1911. Information was supplied also by Miss Mary A. Walker of the United Church Board for World Ministries and Sugi Mibai of Kobe, Japan.]

CLIFTON J. PHILLIPS

TANGUAY, Eva (Aug. 1, 1878–Jan. 11, 1947), nationally famous as "The I Don't Care Girl" of the popular stage during the period 1904–15, was born in Marbleton, Quebec, Canada. Before she had reached the age of six, however, her French-Canadian parents, Octave and Adele (Pajean) Tanguay, had uprooted Eva, her two brothers, and her sister and sought a new life within the laboring community of Holyoke, Mass. Her father died shortly after their arrival, leaving the family isolated and without support. It seemed a stroke of good fortune that the juvenile lead of the Francesca Redding Company should fall ill during a run in Holyoke and that eight-year-old Eva, who had already charmed an amateur-night audience, should be selected as a replacement in the part of Little Lord Fauntleroy. Her education all but forgotten, her mother in attendance, Eva Tanguay completed five years of touring with this company and then moved on to small parts in *The Merry World* and *My Lady*, the latter in New York in 1901.

Her career, undertaken as an escape from

the slums, became in 1903 a high road to fame and enormous wealth. In that year she achieved headline status in both *The Office Boy* (opposite Frank Daniels) and *The Chaperones*. And with her next musical comedy, *The Blond in Black*, her stage personality crystallized. In the role of the "Sambo Girl," an energetic and carefree female who boasted freely of her charms and prowess, Eva Tanguay became the darling of the audiences—and of the producers. The show was renamed *The Sambo Girl* and her part was enlarged to fit the dimensions of a new folk character.

But vaudeville even more than musical comedy provided the lustrous showcase for this exuberant personality. The traditional elements of the song-and-dance act were redesigned for the new star and a repertoire of songs was tailored for her vaudeville appearances. Among them were "I've Got to Be Crazy," "I Want Someone to Go Wild with Me," and "It's All Been Done Before but Not the Way I Do It." The newspapers touted Eva Tanguay as the highest paid of all vaudeville performers, her salary reaching as much as $3,500 for a one-week appearance, and avidly reported her chance comments, her publicity stunts, and the events of her private life.

Her stage personality was symbolically important for the actress and for her public. Her audiences came away with contradictory impressions. They said that she was vulgar, vital, wistful with a Peter Pan quality, full of electric femininity, and refreshingly independent. They remarked upon her tousled hair, her almost hysterical singing and dancing, and her ability to command the unswerving attention of her audience. Through hindsight it is possible to see how Eva Tanguay anticipated the flapper of the 1920's, especially in her unconventionality and her nervous desire to live. But there was a certain innocence beneath the surface crassness and aggressiveness, and a naive optimism shines through the lyrics of her theme song:

> You see I'm sort of independent
> Of a clever race descendent,
> My star is on the ascendent—
> That's why I don't care.
>
> I don't care
> What people say or do,
> My voice, it may sound funny
> But it's getting me the money,
> So I don't care.

Unable to dissociate herself from the public image into which she had been cast, Eva Tanguay never succeeded in creating a whole life for herself. She attempted, as she said, to express her "real self" through her costumes, and produced such sensations as the scanty, beaded affair for *Salome* (1908) and dresses made from coins and bills. She took considerable satisfaction from her fortune—the newspapers estimated it at $2,000,000—yet in 1923 she sold her elaborate house in New York, auctioned off its furnishings, and settled in modest surroundings in California. Subsequently her fortune was totally lost through a combination of generous squanderings and real estate speculation. Both her marriages failed. The first, to John Ford, a member of her traveling troupe, took place on Nov. 24, 1913, when Miss Tanguay was thirty-five, and ended in separation thirteen months later and divorce in 1917; she testified that the marriage had been undertaken on impulse during a gay interlude in Ann Arbor, Mich., and was little more than a joke. The second marriage, to her pianist, on July 22, 1927, was annulled on the ground that he had deceived her in giving his name as Allan Parado, whereas his legal name was Chandos Ksiazkewacz.

Miss Tanguay found a measure of security in her family, who testify to the warm attachment she held for them and for her few friends. She expressed resentment that the public should consider her a "harum-scarum don't care creature." In an angry retort to a critical attack upon her by the columnist Heywood Broun she voiced the frustration of a woman attempting to maintain her identity under the tremendous pressures of show business: "I have beaten your game, and it's a hard game to beat." During the 1920's Eva Tanguay made several appearances, but poor health contributed to the decline of her stage career. An operation which removed cataracts from her eyes restored her sight in 1933, but in 1937 arthritis made her a permanent invalid. For the last twenty years of her life she lived in virtual seclusion in her small home in Hollywood. There she succumbed, at sixty-eight, to a cerebral hemorrhage. She was buried at the Hollywood Mausoleum.

Eva Tanguay was one expression of a cultural revolution in American life. Belonging by background and temperament to the urbanized folk created by the Industrial Revolution, she gave voice and gesture to the restlessness and discontent of her era. Generous and impulsive in her private life, exhibitionist and ebullient on the stage, she provided an antithetical image to the respectable and provident housewife of the middle-class ideal. The boisterous enthusiasm of her song-and-dance act, as well as the extravagant figure she cut in the headlines, disrupted the dramatic and social con-

ventions of the nineteenth century and promised a fresh, restless femininity for the twentieth.

[The most comprehensive sources of information
about the well-publicized Miss Tanguay are clippings in the Harvard Theatre Collection and the
Frank Lenthall Collection (private). Among the
most useful of many newspaper articles were those
in the *N.Y. Times*, Jan. 12, 1947; *N.Y. Dramatic
Mirror*, Jan. 27, 1915; and *Boston Herald*, Sept.
25, 1932. A niece of Miss Tanguay's, Mrs. Lillian
Collins of Hollywood, Calif., generously supplied
information regarding her aunt; other information,
including the names of her parents, from death
certificate, Calif. Dept. of Public Health. A biographical compilation by Arthur J. Paske of the
Univ. of Wis. Library School was helpful. *Who's
Who in the Theatre* (4th ed., 1922) contains a
useful biographical summary. A full description of
a typical performance by Miss Tanguay may be
found in Caroline Caffin, *Vaudeville* (1914).]

ALBERT F. MC LEAN, JR.

**TAPPAN, Caroline Sturgis.** *See* HOOPER, Ellen
Sturgis.

**TAPPAN, Eva March** (Dec. 26, 1854–Jan. 29,
1930), teacher and author of children's books,
was born in Blackstone, Mass., the only child
of Edmund March Tappan, pastor of the Free
Baptist church there, and Lucretia (Logée)
Tappan, a former teacher. Tappan, a descendant of Abraham Toppan, who settled in Newbury, Mass., in 1637, was a native of Sandwich, N.H., and a Dartmouth graduate; he had
met his wife, a native of Burrillville, R.I., while
both were students at the Smithville Seminary
in North Scituate, R.I. In 1857 Tappan moved
his family to a larger pastorate in Lawrence,
Mass., but with his death three years later Mrs.
Tappan returned to the Smithville Seminary as
a resident teacher, the first of many posts she
was to hold in private schools where she could
keep her daughter with her. Eva Tappan, in
her avowedly autobiographical *Ella* (1923),
recalled her childhood in such schools, where
she was generally the youngest pupil, longing
to attend public school with children her own
age, turning in her loneliness to books, walks,
and nature, and eagerly anticipating summer
vacations with her father's family in New
Hampshire.

In 1871 she entered Vassar College, where
she was elected to Phi Beta Kappa and graduated in 1875. Still hard-pressed for money, she
remained uncomplainingly at the college for
some of her vacations. At Vassar she began to
develop her interest in writing; she was an editor of the *Vassar Miscellany* and author of her
class history, which she presented with "sparkle
and wit." It was to teaching, however, that she

first turned after graduation, going to Wheaton
Seminary (later Wheaton College) in Norton,
Mass., where she stayed for five years (1875–
80), teaching principally Latin and German.
Her next recorded post was at Raymond Academy, Camden, N.J., where she was associate
principal (1884–94). During her last year in
Camden—just across the river from Philadelphia—she began graduate study in English
literature at the University of Pennsylvania,
from which she received a master's degree in
1895 and a Ph.D. in 1896 with a dissertation
on the seventeenth-century English poet Nicholas Breton. In 1897 she accepted a position as
head of the English department at the English
High School in Worcester, Mass. A glowing
and effective teacher, she gave special attention to children of immigrant backgrounds and
to students from poor families, whom she encouraged to participate in the school plays
which she directed.

Along with her teaching she had begun to
write books for children. The first, *Charles
Lamb, the Man and the Author*, was published
in 1896. Nine more appeared before 1903,
mostly devoted to history or folktales, among
them *In the Days of Alfred the Great* (1900),
*Old Ballads in Prose* (1901), *In the Days of
Queen Elizabeth* (1902), and *Robin Hood*
(1903). Finding that her books were profitable
and that through them she could reach more
students, Miss Tappan retired from teaching
in 1904 to devote herself to writing. She continued to live in Worcester, making a home for
her mother until the latter's death in 1911.
She lived quietly, walking a great deal, attending church (she had in the 1890's shifted from
the Baptist faith to the Episcopal) and meetings of the Vassar Club of Worcester and the
Boston Authors' Club, but devoting herself
for the most part to meticulous research and
writing. During World War I she served as
assistant editor for the United States Food
Administration.

Miss Tappan's writing derived from her experience as a teacher, and many of her books
were widely used in high schools and grade
schools. New titles appeared almost every year
until 1928. Some were explicitly textbooks, of
history and of American and English literature;
some, like *The Chaucer Story Book* (1908),
were retellings of famous literary works; others,
like *American Hero Stories* (1906), provided
an introduction to biography. Her greatest gift,
perhaps, was her ability to re-create in vivid
detail the life and thought of particular periods
of history, as she did in *The Story of the Greek
People* (1908) and *When Knights Were Bold*
(1911); these social histories anticipated the

project method in education. She also translated folktales from other countries and compiled and edited sets of supplementary readers, notably *The Children's Hour,* a fifteen-volume collection of adventure and nature stories, myths, and other literature. In her own writing her research was thorough, her style simple, direct, and dramatic. Beginning her literary work at a time of renewed interest in folk and historical stories for children, as exemplified in the work of the author and illustrator Howard Pyle, Miss Tappan remained for a generation a leader in this genre.

During her last years Miss Tappan lived in increasingly quiet retirement, in part because of growing deafness. She died in Worcester at the age of seventy-five of paralysis agitans; her ashes were deposited in Bellevue Cemetery, Lawrence, Mass. She left a generous bequest to Vassar College to establish a scholarship fund for girls from Worcester County.

[Edmund March Tappan, *Words of a Man* (1914), with foreword by Eva March Tappan; Daniel L. Tappan, *Tappan-Toppan Genealogy* (1915); Charles Nutt, *Hist. of Worcester and Its People,* vol. IV (1919); *Nat. Cyc. Am. Biog.,* XXII, 161–62; Stanley J. Kunitz and Howard Haycraft, eds., *The Junior Book of Authors* (1934); *Who Was Who in America,* vol. I (1942); obituaries in Worcester newspapers; information from Vassar College Library, from Wheaton College Library, from interviews with former pupils, and from Miss Tappan's death record.]

MADELYN C. WANKMILLER

**TARBELL, Ida Minerva** (Nov. 5, 1857–Jan. 6, 1944), journalist, muckraker, lecturer, and historian, was born on a farm in Erie County, Pa., the eldest of three surviving children. Her mother, Esther Ann (McCullough) Tarbell, a schoolteacher before her marriage, came from a northwestern Pennsylvania family that counted among its ancestors Sir Walter Raleigh and Samuel Seabury, America's first Anglican bishop. Her father, Franklin Sumner Tarbell, also a Pennsylvanian by birth, had put himself through the Jamestown (N.Y.) Academy by working as a flatboat captain and a carpenter. In 1857 he went to Iowa hoping to buy a farm, but when his plans were upset by that year's financial panic, he was forced to "teach his way back" to his young family in Pennsylvania. The discovery of oil near Titusville, Pa., in 1859 gave him a fresh opportunity. Shrewdly anticipating the need for containers, he used his carpentry skills to become the first manufacturer of wooden tanks for the infant industry and soon gained a measure of financial security for his family. They moved first to Rouseville, Pa., and then to booming Titusville.

Ida's parents were devout Christians (originally Presbyterians, later Methodists), but Ida early abandoned formal religious practice, finding it in conflict with her growing interest in science and her humanistic bent, though she later wrote that she always had a conviction of divine goodness at work in the world. As a girl she fell under the spell of the woman's rights movement, some of whose leaders, including FRANCES WILLARD, were entertained in the Tarbell home. Listening to talk of marriage as an institution where women were trapped and imprisoned, she privately prayed to avoid it, and education became for her a symbol of freedom. In 1876, after attending the local public schools, she entered Allegheny College in nearby Meadville, Pa., one of only five women students, and received her A.B. degree in 1880.

At the time her major interest was biology, but after two years of teaching English, languages, mathematics, and science at the Poland (Ohio) Union Seminary, she returned to Meadville to join the staff of the *Chautauquan* magazine, where she remained for eight years (1883–91). The *Chautauquan,* an influential monthly with a wide circulation in the Middle West, was essentially a teaching supplement for the extensive program of home study courses developed by the burgeoning Chautauqua movement. Miss Tarbell wrote and edited articles which amplified and commented upon the material in the assigned textbooks. Through her work she met and corresponded with many academic luminaries, including the historian Herbert Baxter Adams and the economist Richard T. Ely.

In 1891 Ida Tarbell left the *Chautauquan* and traveled to Paris, planning, in keeping with her feminist outlook, to study the role of women in the French Revolution, particularly that of Madame Roland. Enrolling for classes at the Sorbonne and the Collège de France, she met a diverse and stimulating group of Parisians, including the historian Charles Seignobos, the socialist intellectual Lucien Herr, and H. Wickham Steed, future foreign editor of the London *Times.* To meet expenses she contributed occasional articles to American periodicals such as *Scribner's.* She thereby came to the attention of S. S. McClure, a flamboyant young publisher who was just then starting a new magazine, *McClure's.* In 1892 he sought out the young writer in Paris and urged her to contribute to his magazine, and thereafter published her feature articles reporting interviews with such eminent Frenchmen as Pasteur, Zola, Daudet, and Dumas.

Again in Paris in the spring of 1894, McClure

persuaded Miss Tarbell to return to New York and join his staff. As part of a wave of interest in Napoleon which swept France and America in the 1890's, he was about to publish a famous collection of Napoleon prints owned by Gardiner Green Hubbard of Washington, D.C., for which he needed an accompanying text. Miss Tarbell consented to supply this, and the series was eminently successful. Helping boost the circulation of *McClure's* into the hundreds of thousands, it brought her nationwide attention and cemented her commitment to journalism as a career. The publication of her articles in book form, as *A Short Life of Napoleon Bonaparte* (1895), brought sales of 100,000 copies with still further renown and remuneration. On the strength of her reputation Scribner's in 1896 published her *Life of Madame Roland.*

Ever sensitive to the trend of popular taste, McClure next became interested in Abraham Lincoln, and Miss Tarbell's articles on the martyred president, collected in 1900 as *The Life of Abraham Lincoln,* boosted *McClure's* circulation, and her own reputation, still further. (Her interest in Lincoln continued throughout her life, and she published a total of eight books on the subject, several of them for children.) In her research for this series she not only unearthed important new material, but conscientiously sought to separate fact from legend; a recent student of Lincoln historiography, Benjamin Thomas, has called her "the pioneer scientific investigator whose work foretold the revelation of Lincoln as he really was" (*Portrait for Posterity,* p. 201). In connection with her Lincoln work she persuaded Carl Schurz to write his *Reminiscences* and herself wrote with Charles A. Dana his *Recollections of the Civil War* (1898).

In 1900, seeking yet another topic to interest his readers, McClure decided to publish a series of articles on the development of the Standard Oil Trust. Because Ida Tarbell had firsthand knowledge of the Pennsylvania oil fields she was given the assignment. She spent two years in research, carefully analyzing voluminous documents and interviewing leaders in the oil industry, including Henry H. Rogers of Standard Oil, who had known her father in the early days in Titusville. She particularly studied the complex system of secret railroad-rate agreements which, she felt, had given John D. Rockefeller his decisive advantage. When the series began in *McClure's* in 1902 it was clear that Miss Tarbell's history was to be sharply critical. As a girl she had absorbed the hatred and resentment of the independent producers around Titusville toward the growing power of Standard Oil, the company which

her father had blamed for the failure of his business and the suicide of his partner. More recently, she had been influenced by Henry D. Lloyd's hostile treatment of the Standard Oil Trust in his *Wealth against Commonwealth* (1894). Thus, despite her careful research and attempted objectivity, she could not wholly conceal her deep moral outrage as she chronicled the manipulations which had marked Standard's early history. Her powerful indictment, published in book form as *The History of the Standard Oil Company* (1904), created a sensation at the time and continues to be the work upon which her reputation principally rests.

Its appearance coincided with the beginnings of a rather amorphous journalistic movement in which a number of able writers, including Lincoln Steffens and Ray Stannard Baker of *McClure's* staff, Upton Sinclair, Mark Sullivan, David Graham Phillips, Charles Edward Russell, and others, published scores of books and magazine articles exposing corruption in all phases of American life. The movement was given a name by President Theodore Roosevelt, who compared such writers to the "Man with the Muckrake" in *Pilgrim's Progress.* In 1906 Miss Tarbell, Steffens, and Baker left *McClure's* and joined forces with McClure's former associate John Phillips and others, including Finley Peter Dunne, creator of "Mr. Dooley," to purchase the *American Magazine,* which they edited cooperatively until 1915. Miss Tarbell's major contribution was a series of articles presenting an extensive study of the tariff (published in 1911 as *The Tariff in Our Times*), in which she attacked the high protective tariff as another means whereby trusts gained monopolistic control. Of this series President Wilson commented: "she has written more good sense, good plain common sense, about the tariff than any man I know of."

Despite her personal hostility toward Standard Oil, however, Ida Tarbell was fundamentally a warm friend of American business, and she had felt "chagrin" at the popular identification of her as a muckraker. In her history she had found much to praise in John D. Rockefeller—his energy, his piety, and his philanthropies. Wishing to believe in the fundamental goodness of businessmen, she spent much of her time between 1912 and 1915 visiting carefully selected factories that were trying new approaches to industrial relations and employee welfare. She became an enthusiastic advocate of Frederick W. Taylor's "scientific management" techniques for increasing workers' productivity and of Henry Ford's industrial paternalism, with its efforts, as she wrote, to "reorganize the home life of the men." The optimistic conclusions emerging from these travels appeared in her *New Ideals in Business* (1916). Two subsequent biographies of business leaders, *The Life of Elbert H. Gary* (1925) and *Owen D. Young* (1932), were wholly uncritical of their subjects. Common to all these works was the belief that a sense of social responsibility was spontaneously developing within the American business community.

With the sale of the *American Magazine* in 1915 Miss Tarbell became a lecturer on the Chautauqua circuit of the Coit-Alber Lecture Bureau. For several months each year, seven days a week, she delivered a nightly lecture in a different city. These lectures dealt with her hopes for righteousness in American business, and matters such as unemployment, the Versailles Treaty, the League of Nations (which she supported), and disarmament. She continued to lecture, except for wartime interruptions, until 1932. The fame she had acquired with *The History of the Standard Oil Company* assured large audiences and a wide market for her books, but in many respects this was a frustrating period. The physical discomforts of the lecture circuit were great, and the psychological demands heavy. She sometimes felt herself merely "a cog in the mechanism called a lecture bureau." Her published works of this period lost the note of personal involvement which had marked *The History of the Standard Oil Company*, and she herself felt that "a certain mustiness" pervaded her post–World War I writing.

She remained, however, a person of wide-ranging interests and unfailing curiosity, as is shown by the variety of her activities. She served as a member of the Woman's Committee of the United States Council of National Defense in World War I and, after the war, as a delegate to President Wilson's Industrial Conference (1919) and to President Harding's Conference on Unemployment (1921). In 1926 she sailed to Italy to report on Mussolini's fascist state for *McCall's* magazine. She interviewed Mussolini and found his efforts impressive, though she lamented the violent and totalitarian aspects of the regime. Deeply interested in problems of peace and war, Ida Tarbell as early as 1910 had traveled to California to study the peace efforts of President David Starr Jordan of Stanford University. In 1915 she was strongly urged by Henry Ford and JANE ADDAMS to join Ford's "Peace Ship" to Europe, but she declined, expressing sympathy for their aims but doubts as to their method. After the war she attended the Paris Peace Conference as a correspondent for the *Red Cross Magazine* and in 1921 was an observer and reporter at the Washington Naval Disarmament Conference.

Though Miss Tarbell's career embodied the ideal of many feminists, she did not support the demand for woman suffrage, a position which brought her into conflict with the leaders of that movement and was a source of some tension between herself and such colleagues on the Woman's Committee in World War I as ANNA HOWARD SHAW and CARRIE CHAPMAN CATT. This cooling of her earlier enthusiasm for woman's rights may reflect a resentful feeling that the impact of feminist ideals upon her impressionable childhood had robbed her of the pleasures of marriage and motherhood. In *The Business of Being a Woman* (1912) she argued that "women had a business assigned by nature and society which was of more importance than public life."

A handsome woman with great natural dignity, Ida Tarbell remained active in old age. In her mid-seventies she gave special courses on the methods of biography at several colleges. In 1939, at the age of eighty-two, she published a highly readable autobiography, *All in the Day's Work*. After giving up lecturing, she spent most of her time on the forty-acre Connecticut farm where she had lived since 1906, at first with a niece and then with her sister Sarah. She died of pneumonia in a Bridgeport, Conn., hospital at the age of eighty-six and was buried in the family plot in Woodlawn Cemetery, Titusville, Pa.

[The most important sources for Ida Tarbell are her own writings, mentioned in the text, particularly her autobiography. Victoria and Robert O. Case, *We Called It Culture* (1948), chap. i, covers the early days of the Chautauqua movement and the *Chautauquan*. Benjamin P. Thomas, *Portrait for Posterity: Lincoln and His Biographers* (1947), pp. 178–202, gives an estimate of Miss Tarbell's work on Lincoln. Her muckraker period is discussed in Louis Filler, *Crusaders for Am. Liberalism* (1939); Frank L. Mott, *A Hist. of Am. Magazines*, vols. III and IV (1938–57); David M. Chalmers, *The Social and Political Ideas of the Muckrakers* (1964) and his introduction to Miss Tarbell's *Hist. of the Standard Oil Company: Briefer Version* (1966); and Virginia Hamilton, "The Gentlewoman and the Robber Baron," *Am. Heritage*, Apr. 1970. See also the autobiographies of S. S. McClure (1914), Lincoln Steffens (1931), William Allen White (1946), and, especially, Ray Stannard Baker (*Am. Chronicle*, 1945); Peter Lyon's biography of McClure (*Success Story*, 1963); and Elmer Ellis' biography of Finley Peter Dunne (*Mr. Dooley's America*, 1941). The bulk of Ida Tarbell's papers are at Allegheny College;

several manuscripts and 1,000 letters are at Smith College, Northampton, Mass.]

DAVID M. CHALMERS

TAYLOR, Laurette (Apr. 1, 1884–Dec. 7, 1946), actress, was born in the Harlem district of New York City; christened Loretta, she was the oldest of the three children of James and Elizabeth (Dorsey) Cooney. Her Irish immigrant parents had gained a degree of comfort and security in the New World owing to the success of her mother's dressmaking establishment; her father was an unambitious harness maker. A fanciful child, given to a dream world, Loretta early responded to her mother's love of the theatre and music. Her father, though he liked to sing and read poetry in his musical voice, thought all theatrical people damned eternally and as a righteous Roman Catholic refused to enter a playhouse. His wife's ambitions for a theatrical career for her daughter and their semistealthy excursions to the neighboring Harlem Opera House therefore brought on violent family altercations.

Despite paternal disapproval, Loretta began singing and dancing lessons at the age of twelve, in addition to her studies at the public school through the eighth grade. From staging shows on the sly for neighborhood children she moved on to appearances at charity affairs and finally, in 1896, after advertising in a circular distributed to vaudeville managers, to a Lynn, Mass., nickelodeon, where she appeared as "La Belle Laurette" in a song-and-dance act with recitations. Except for a short engagement in Gloucester, Mass., soon afterward, three years passed before another opportunity called Laurette to a vaudeville bill at the Athenaeum in Boston. There she caught the attention of the playwright-producer Charles Alonzo Taylor, who offered her the role of soubrette in the road company of his melodrama King of the Opium Ring. Since Laurette's mother would not allow her to tour without a chaperone, both mother and daughter received forty-week contracts. When Taylor offered them a new contract for Child Wife, which he wrote especially for Laurette, Mrs. Cooney bowed out to care for her other children, and Laurette became Mrs. Taylor. Then seventeen, she was twenty years Taylor's junior. After the ceremony, on May 1, 1901, they went on tour with Child Wife.

During the next six years, spent mostly on the road, Laurette Taylor appeared in a succession of her husband's melodramas (in one, From Rags to Riches, she made her New York debut in the fall of 1903), played repertory from Camille to Carmen, and learned all the tasks of the theatre from handling costumes and props to managing the box office and avoiding the bill collector. As an actress she thrived on this life, but as a young bride she suffered an unhappy marriage. One of the most successful men of his craft, Taylor made fortunes with his blood-and-thunder plays, spent them with a lavish hand, and turned his handsome head toward any pretty face within eye's reach. In December 1907 Laurette finally left Taylor in Seattle, taking her two children and her theatrical ambitions to New York. With only a handful of notices and three years in Western stock to her credit, she found no doors open on Broadway. Taylor offered reconciliation in September 1908, and she appeared in his Yosemite, which she considered his chef d'oeuvre. After seeing her in the opening at Buffalo, the Shubert brothers booked the play for Washington and offered her a three-year contract. She never acted in a Taylor play again.

Laurette Taylor's first vehicle for the Shuberts was The Great John Ganton by J. Hartley Manners. After the play's short run, parts in two more weak efforts perpetuated her obscurity; then in New York in January 1910, in a small supporting role in Alias Jimmy Valentine, starring H. B. Warner, she scored a triumph. Her success brought her leading roles in other plays by Manners, and as The Girl in Waiting she reached stardom at Philadelphia that April. Tense, however, over her new-found acclaim, she fumbled so badly in Chicago that the play failed before reaching New York, and she lost star billing for her next engagement, in Daniel Frohman's production of Seven Sisters. In January 1912 she enjoyed a break from light comedy roles as Luana, a Hawaiian princess in The Bird of Paradise, and won high praise for an "authentic portrait." Her next noteworthy appearance was in Los Angeles, where she proceeded to make theatrical history in Peg o' My Heart.

Hartley Manners had written Peg o' My Heart expressly for Laurette Taylor during the summer of 1911, and with an affectionate dedication offered it to her as a betrothal present. She had divorced Taylor in 1910, and she and Manners were married in Philadelphia shortly before rehearsals for Peg o' My Heart began in 1912. Although several managers considered the play too sentimental to be successful, Oliver Morosco took it for a four-week repertory run in Los Angeles beginning May 12, 1912. Audiences paid no attention to the critics' cool notices, and Peg o' My Heart ran 101 times to standing room only. With this encouragement, Morosco chose it to open the new Cort Theatre in New York the following December. His decision subsequently earned him more than five million dollars, for *Peg* became an instantaneous success, ran through the spring of 1914, and broke previous records for continuous performances, closing after the 604th. The London production, opening at the Globe Theatre in October 1914, won equal popularity and praise for Laurette Taylor's portrayal of the simple Irish lass who conquered English snobbery. Finally, frightened by Zeppelin raids and tired of the single confining role, she returned to the United States late in 1915.

During the next nine years she appeared in a succession of her second husband's plays. Striving to free herself of light comedy roles, in November 1916 she played the mother of a nineteen-year-old son in *The Harp of Life*, a play about sex education. She had another serious part in *Out There*, a war play Manners wrote to vent his hatred for the Germans, and which caused critics to place the star second to the author for the first time. *One Night in Rome* (December 1919) received cool notices but drew large audiences nonetheless and enjoyed a five-month run in New York and a London engagement. The phenomenal success of *Peg*, which had played around the world and earned the Manners family a million dollars by 1919, led to a New York revival and tour in 1921. On Dec. 31, 1921, Laurette opened in Manners' *The National Anthem*, a play condemning the Lost Generation of the 1920's which she considered his finest work, despite its lukewarm reception from the public. After making a movie of *Peg* in the summer of 1922, Laurette Taylor undertook the role of Sarah Kantor in Fannie Hurst's *Humoresque*. Working for weeks on tour to become convincing in accent, gesture, makeup, and movement, she finally perfected the Russian-Jewish mother for the New York premiere (Feb. 27, 1923), winning unanimous praise for a masterful stage creation. Constantin Stanislavsky, the director of the Moscow Art Theatre players then in New York, after seeing Laurette as Mrs. Kantor, called her America's finest actress. The play, however, did not win public support and closed after three weeks.

Her sensibilities injured by the failure of *Humoresque*, Laurette Taylor grew restless. She began to drift away from the somewhat superficial matter of Manners' dramas, although in 1924 they collaborated on screen versions of two of his plays, hoping to raise money for their own playhouse. Now, with her reputation firmly established, she played a variety of roles, but her personal affairs became increasingly unsettled. Unhappy with her husband's dramaturgy, she had her head turned by the romantic but mercurial screen star John Gilbert and requested a divorce, which Manners refused. Beset by discontent, ambition, and uncertainty, she turned to alcohol for refuge. Although he had lost his creative impetus, Manners wrote *Delicate Justice* in the hope that Laurette could pour her energies into the old, healthy channels, but the play failed both theatrically and psychologically. A stay in a sanatorium in the spring of 1928 briefly restored her equilibrium, but this was upset again by Manners' fatal illness and death of cancer in December 1928. Her association with Manners had been strangely ironic. The marriage gave Laurette a stability and happiness she had not known before, but Manners was not a great playwright and her captivity in his roles long frustrated her talent.

For the next ten years Laurette Taylor struggled in the obscurity of alcoholism. Making repeated attempts at self-rescue, she spent her energies in writing plays, planning productions, and appearing in summer stock. Her one Broadway appearance during this period, in William Brady's production of James Barrie's two short plays *Alice-Sit-by-the Fire* and *The Old Lady Shows Her Medals* early in 1932, caused rejoicing among critics and audiences alike but ended ignominiously in Brady's withdrawal of the plays. She did not successfully conquer her personal demons until 1938. That year, in a revival of *Outward Bound*, she played the minor part of Mrs. Midget, a dowdy, self-effacing little charwoman, with unsurpassed skill, sweeping cast, critics, and audiences to new encomiums and winning the Barter Award in 1939. Waiting for the "right" play, Miss Taylor did not find another suitable role until the summer of 1944, when Eddie Dowling sent her the script of *The Glass Menagerie* by Tennessee Williams, then an unknown playwright. After opening in Chicago in December 1944, the play moved to the 48th Street Playhouse in New York on Mar. 31, 1945. Acclaimed by critics and an enthralled public, Laurette Taylor in her moving portrait of Amanda Wingfield outshone all her other achievements and, for many in the endless audiences, all others in the memory of the American theatre. Illness, poverty, and obscurity, however, had weakened her; hampered by a worsening throat ailment, she was forced to withdraw from the company in the fall of 1946. Her resurgent spirit defeated by an exhausted body, she suffered a coronary thrombosis and died that December at sixty-two, in her New York apartment. She was buried in Woodlawn Cemetery, New York City, beside Hartley Manners. Her son, Dwight Oliver Taylor, and her daughter, Marguerite (Taylor) Courtney, survived her.

Pert and pretty when a young girl, with honey-colored hair and hazel eyes, Laurette Taylor in later years battled grimly against overweight. She turned her body and mind completely to the exacting demands of the characters she portrayed. As her art matured, she brought each role to life in every detail of motion, voice, gesture, and expression; in her own words, she could "put on the pants of the part." A theatrical legend even during her lifetime, she possessed a talent which eluded analysis and description. In the judgment of Arthur Hopkins, "Her supreme gift was radiance. Even when that unforgettable face was old and ravaged, it could suddenly be illumined by beauty that is not of this earth. She was a star of celestial illumination" (quoted in Courtney, p. 288).

[Marguerite Courtney's *Laurette* (1955) is a sympathetic but candid biography. See also Laurette Taylor's memoirs, serialized in *Town and Country* in 1942; and scrapbooks, clippings, and other unclassified material in the Theatre Collection, N.Y. Public Library. Dwight Taylor's *Blood-and-Thunder* (1962) is a biography of her first husband.]

H. L. KLEINFIELD

TAYLOR, Lucy Beaman Hobbs (Mar. 14, 1833–Oct. 3, 1910), dentist, the first American woman to earn a dental degree, was born in western New York, probably in Franklin County, rather than in Ellenburg, Clinton County, as sometimes stated. She was the third daughter and seventh of the ten children of Benjamin Hobbs, a farmer, and Lucy (Beaman) Hobbs. Both her parents were New Englanders. When Lucy was ten her mother died, and her father's second wife, his sister-in-law Hannah Beaman, died two years later. For the next four years (1845–49) Lucy boarded at Franklin Academy in Malone, N.Y., where she received her formal education. After completing her studies she began a teaching career which took her to Brooklyn, Mich. There she began to study medicine under a local physician. Deciding to enter medical practice, she gave up teaching in 1859 and, upon her preceptor's advice, moved to Cincinnati, Ohio, planning to enroll in the Eclectic College of Medicine. Her application was refused because she was a woman, but Charles A. Cleaveland, professor of materia medica and therapeutics at the college, gave her private instruction. His casual suggestion that she pursue dentistry as a profession "more suitable for a woman" led

her to seek an apprenticeship with an established dentist.

Despite general amazement "that a young girl had so far forgotten her womanhood as to want to study dentistry," Dr. Jonathan Taft, dean of the Ohio College of Dental Surgery in Cincinnati, agreed to instruct her temporarily, and after three months in his office she was accepted as an apprentice by a graduate of the college, Dr. Samuel Wardle. Under Wardle's tutelage Lucy Hobbs learned the basic techniques of the still primitive profession of dentistry, including the use of anesthesia and the manufacture of artificial teeth; she also continued her studies in anatomy, physiology, and hygiene. In March 1861 she applied for admission to the Ohio College of Dental Surgery, but was refused because of her sex. She then opened her own office in Cincinnati, a degree not yet being a prerequisite for private practice. In 1862 she moved to Bellevue, Iowa, where she "aroused sufficient curiosity to make her expenses"; from 1862 to 1865 she practiced in McGregor, Iowa.

In July 1865 Lucy Hobbs was invited to a meeting of the newly formed Iowa State Dental Society, which elected her a member and appointed her a delegate to the American Dental Association's convention in Chicago. In welcoming her "to our professional pursuits, trials, aims and successes," the society also declared that "the profession of dentistry . . . has nothing in its pursuits foreign to the instincts of women" (*Dental Register,* October 1865). That same year she reapplied to the Ohio College of Dental Surgery and this time was admitted to its senior class; she was granted the degree of Doctor of Dental Surgery after four months of study (Nov. 1, 1865–Feb. 21, 1866). According to Prof. Jonathan Taft: "She was a woman of great energy and perseverance, studious in her habits, modest and unassuming; she had the respect and kind regard of every member of the class and faculty. As an operator she was not surpassed by her associates. Her opinion was asked and her assistance sought in difficult cases, almost daily by her fellow students." Her admission to the Iowa State Dental Society and her earning a dental degree aroused considerable comment within the profession, provoking both antagonism toward and endorsement of women dentists.

She next practiced briefly in Chicago, where on Apr. 24, 1867, she was married to James Myrtle Taylor, a painter in the Chicago & Northwestern Railway car shops who, after instruction from his wife, also became a dentist. The couple had no children. In November

1867 she sold her Chicago office and moved with her husband to Lawrence, Kans. There, over the next two decades, they developed one of the most extensive practices in the state, Mrs. Taylor confining her work for the most part to women and children. After her husband's death in 1886 Lucy Taylor indulged in semiretirement, devoting her time to her activities as a member of the Rebekah Lodge, Independent Order of Odd Fellows, and the Adah Chapter of the Order of the Eastern Star. She was also president of the Ladies' Republican Club of Lawrence and a supporter of the woman's rights movement. She had no church affiliation. She died in Lawrence following a cerebral hemorrhage at the age of seventy-seven and was buried there in Oak Hill Cemetery.

Although Lucy Hobbs Taylor was not the first American woman to practice dentistry, she was the first to earn a degree and the first to be admitted to a state dental association. Having helped to open the doors of dental colleges to women, she also established a precedent for her sex as a successful practitioner.

[Of prime interest is Lucy Hobbs Taylor, "The Early Women in Dentistry," published in the *Dental Register,* Jan. 1894, and elsewhere; quotations not otherwise identified are from that source. See also Elizabeth Cady Stanton et al., *Hist. of Woman Suffrage,* III (1886), 401–02, which includes a letter from Mrs. Taylor; unpublished sketches of Mrs. Taylor by Edward Bumgardner in Kans. Collection, Univ. of Kans. Libraries, and in Kans. State Hist. Soc.; and published sketches in *Bull. of the Hist. of Medicine,* May–June 1951 (by Ralph W. Edwards), *Jour. of the Ohio State Dental Assoc.,* May 1949 (by Wilbur G. Adair), and *Oral Hygiene,* May 1943 (by Edward Bumgardner). Other pertinent information may be found in: Emily Beaman Wooden, *The Beaman and Clark Genealogy* (1909), pp. 51 ff.; [Alfred T. Andreas], *Hist. of the State of Kans.* (1883), p. 345; *Portrait and Biog. Record of Leavenworth, Douglas and Franklin Counties . . . Kans.* (1899), pp. 717–18; *Dental Cosmos,* Nov. 1910, p. 1315; *Lawrence* (Kans.) *Daily Jour.,* Oct. 3, 1910. Invaluable for Mrs. Taylor's early activities, early dental practice, and reactions of critics to women dentists are files of the *Dental Register,* 1865–66. For a fuller account, see Madeleine B. Stern, *We the Women* (1963). Most sources, including cemetery records, give her birthplace as Ellenburg, N.Y. She herself, however, stated that she was born in Franklin County; and since her brother Thomas was born in Constable, Franklin County, in 1831, it is possible that the family did not move to Ellenburg until after her birth.]

MADELEINE B. STERN

**TAYLOR, Margaret Mackall Smith** (Sept. 21, 1788–Aug. 14, 1852), wife of Zachary Taylor, twelfth president of the United States, was born in Calvert County, Md., where her forebear Richard Smith, later attorney general of Maryland, had settled in 1649. She was the daughter of Walter Smith, a well-to-do planter who had served in the Revolutionary War, and Ann (Mackall) Smith. Little is known of her early life. In 1809, while visiting a married sister in Kentucky, she met Zachary Taylor, an army lieutenant four years her senior, of Virginia and Kentucky background. They were married June 21, 1810, in Jefferson County, Ky. Five daughters were born to them: Ann Mackall in 1811, Sarah Knox in 1814, Octavia Pannill in 1816, Margaret Smith in 1819, and Mary Elizabeth in 1824. Their only son, Richard, born in 1826, became a lieutenant general in the Confederate Army.

Most of Mrs. Taylor's adult life was spent amid the privations of remote army posts in what were then frontier areas of Indiana, Minnesota, Wisconsin, Florida, and Arkansas as her husband, an infantry officer, slowly rose in grade. The details of their domestic life reflect this peripatetic existence. In 1820 two of their daughters, Octavia and Margaret, died in Bayou Sara, La., while Taylor was engaged in military road construction in Mississippi; Fort Crawford, at present-day Prairie du Chien, Wis., was the setting of their daughter Ann's marriage in 1829 to Dr. Robert C. Wood, who was to be acting surgeon general of the Union Army during the Civil War, and of Sarah's romance with Lieut. Jefferson Davis, whose bride she became in 1835, shortly before her early death.

As Taylor frequently was commandant of these various posts, social activity revolved about his quarters, and Margaret Taylor gained a reputation for gracious hospitality. Of medium height, slender and erect, she was described as "stately," "gentle," and "refined." Her manner was pleasant and her voice agreeable. Zachary Taylor said of his wife in 1820, "I am confident the feminine virtues never did concentrate in a higher degree in the bosom of any woman than in hers."

In 1846, the Mexican War broke out. Winning a major-generalship and national plaudits for victories from Palo Alto to Buena Vista, Taylor became widely known by the affectionate nickname "Old Rough and Ready," which he had acquired in the Second Seminole War. Meanwhile, his wife remained in Baton Rouge, La., where Taylor had reestablished residence in 1845. Deeply religious and now a semi-invalid, she prayed for his safe return and interested herself in the local Episcopal church. In 1848 she sincerely, though never publicly, opposed Whig efforts to elevate her husband to the presidency; but with his election, she joined him in the White House. She took no part, however, in the pomp or ceremony of its social life. Receiving kinsmen and close friends in her cheery room on the second floor, she wholly relinquished the role of official hostess to her youngest daughter, Betty, who in 1848 had married Lieutenant Colonel William Wallace Smith Bliss, Taylor's adjutant general.

In July 1850, after sixteen months in office, Zachary Taylor died of acute gastroenteritis. Nine days after the funeral, the deeply grieving Mrs. Taylor left the capital. She never mentioned the White House for the duration of her life. After three months in Baltimore with her daughter and son-in-law, Dr. and Mrs. Wood, she returned to Louisiana and then went to Mississippi, where she died at East Pascagoula in 1852, at the age of sixty-three. An Episcopal funeral service was held in New Orleans. Subsequently her remains were placed beside her husband's in what is now the Zachary Taylor National Cemetery, Jefferson County, Ky.

[The most detailed factual treatment is in Holman Hamilton, *Zachary Taylor: Soldier of the Republic* (1941) and *Zachary Taylor: Soldier in the White House* (1951). See also William H. Samson, ed., *Letters of Zachary Taylor from the Battle-fields of the Mexican War* (1908), and Brainerd Dyer, *Zachary Taylor* (1946). Some family records consulted by the present author in the 1930's have since been burned; others are in the Library of Congress. Mrs. Taylor's letters are extremely rare, and no authenticated portrait or daguerreotype has been found.]

HOLMAN HAMILTON

**TEASDALE, Sara** (Aug. 8, 1884–Jan. 29, 1933), lyric poet, was born in St. Louis, Mo., the second daughter of John Warren Teasdale and Mary Elizabeth (Willard) Teasdale and the youngest, by fourteen years, of their four children. Both parents were of old American stock, strongly Baptist in heritage. The poet's father, born in 1838 in Fredericksburg, Va., had come with his parents in 1854 to St. Louis, where he later established the firm of J. W. Teasdale and Company, wholesale dealers in dried foodstuffs. Her mother, perhaps the dominant member of the family, was born in Peoria, Ill., in 1843. Among her ancestors was Major Simon Willard, who emigrated from England in 1634 and helped found the town of Concord, Mass.

Sara—originally Sarah Trevor—was a shy and sensitive child. Throughout life she remained nervously frail, needing much rest and solitude. The almost total responsiveness with which she reacted to everything took a heavy toll of her vital energies, and she was nine before she was sent to a small school near her home. Its head, Mrs. Ellen Dean Lockwood, gave her understanding and helped her overcome some of her shyness. In 1898–99 she attended the Mary Institute in St. Louis, and at eighteen she graduated from Hosmer Hall, a private day school for girls. Since childhood Sara had admired the poetry of Christina Rossetti, and at school she fell under the spell of Heine. The work of these poets, of Sappho, and, somewhat later, of A. E. Housman and a nineteenth-century English poet, A. Mary F. Robinson, were strong influences on her own work. By the time she finished school she had written much verse and her literary talent had been recognized by her teachers. During the first two years after graduation she produced a series of sonnets inspired by photographs of Eleanora Duse, whom she had never seen. Written initially for the *Wheel*, a private amateur monthly which she and a group of friends wrote, edited, illustrated, hand-printed, and bound (1904–07), these sonnets opened her first book, *Sonnets to Duse, and Other Poems*, issued in the autumn of 1907. But it was William Marion Reedy who, having seen several copies of the *Wheel*, introduced Sara Teasdale's poetry to the world by printing her sixty-eight-line monologue in blank verse, "Guenevere," in his St. Louis weekly, *Reedy's Mirror*, of May 30, 1907. The poem attracted widespread attention.

Early in 1905 Sara and her mother had undertaken a three months' tour of the Holy Land, Egypt, England, and parts of the Continent that greatly stimulated the young woman's imagination. For her mother a religious pilgrimage, the trip became for Sara an artistic one, and she emulated Ruskin in viewing and admiring Gothic edifices and Pre-Raphaelite art. In January 1911 she made her first visit of any length to New York City, a trip repeated annually for the next three years. That fall her second book was published, *Helen of Troy, and Other Poems*, containing, together with poems less impressive, six notable blank-verse monologues spoken by Helen, Beatrice, Sappho, and other famous women.

Frail, of middle height, shy and intense, with large brown eyes, auburn hair, and a mischievous sense of humor, Sara Teasdale made many friends among the literati. In February 1914 Vachel Lindsay called on her at her home in St. Louis and not long after became an ardent suitor. In the interim Sara had met a young St. Louis businessman, Ernst B. Filsinger, the son of family friends, who proposed marriage. For a time she was torn by indecision, feeling drawn to both men, but on Dec. 19 she and Filsinger were married, at St. Louis, and in 1916 they moved to New York. The marriage (which was childless) was at first a happy one, and there ensued for Sara a period of great literary productivity. In 1915 her *Rivers to the Sea* was published, in 1917 *Love Songs* (for which she received the annual prize of the Poetry Society of America), and in 1920 *Flame and Shadow,* each marking an ascending scale in her development and acclaim as a poet. During these same years she issued two anthologies: *The Answering Voice: One Hundred Love Lyrics by Women* (1917) and *Rainbow Gold* (1922), a collection for boys and girls.

Less happy days, however, lay ahead. *Dark of the Moon,* published in 1926, reveals a more somber mood and a far subtler, more complex art. Separated for long periods when business trips took Filsinger abroad, or by her own frequent illnesses and invalidism, husband and wife drifted apart. They were divorced in September 1929. From then on the isolation and loneliness, increasingly forced upon the poet by her growing need for rest and seclusion, deepened. Friends in New York, where she continued to live, did their best to see and cheer her —among them an old friend, John Hall Wheelock, and a much younger, newer one, Margaret Conklin. Vachel Lindsay, now married, who had dedicated his book *The Chinese Nightingale* to Sara Teasdale, visited her whenever he was in town. His suicide, on Dec. 5, 1931, dealt her a nearly mortal blow. In June 1932, in an effort to rouse herself, she made a second trip to England, for renewed research on her long-contemplated biography of Christina Rossetti. There she was stricken, in August, with bronchial pneumonia. Against doctor's orders, she returned to New York before complete recovery. The illness was followed by a deep depression. On the night of Jan. 29, 1933, she was found dead in her New York apartment from an overdose of barbiturates. According to her wishes, funeral services were held in Grace Episcopal Church in New York, and her ashes were buried in the family plot in Bellefontaine Cemetery, St. Louis.

In 1930 Sara Teasdale had published *Stars To-night,* containing fifteen old and ten new poems of a high order, but her smallest and most perfect collection, bearing the sardonic title *Strange Victory,* appeared in 1933 after her death. In 1937 a *Collected Poems* was issued. From the first, Sara Teasdale had revealed herself as a true lyric poet, master of a fresh and unforced melody. Personal, even confessional in character, everything she wrote bears the imprint of a spirit excruciatingly vibrant and responsive. It is the purity of the emotion, its absolute conviction, as much as its intensity, that makes it memorable. If some of the early work was marred by a certain girlish sentimentality and prettiness, this is not true of the later poems in *Flame and Shadow, Dark of the Moon,* and *Strange Victory.* There, suffering and experience have uncovered, in this gentlest of human beings, a vein of iron, an inner strength, that enables her to speak to us in the accents of great poetry.

[Margaret Haley Carpenter, *Sara Teasdale: A Biog.* (1960); Harriet Monroe, *A Poet's Life* (1938); Louis Untermeyer, *From Another World* (1939); Eleanor Ruggles, *The West-Going Heart* (1959); Jessie Rittenhouse, *My House of Life* (1934); author's conversations and correspondence with Sara Teasdale, 1913–33. For a recent appreciation of Sara Teasdale's poetry, see George B. Saul, "A Delicate Fabric of Bird Song: Verse of Sara Teasdale," *Ariz. Quart.,* Spring 1957. Sara Teasdale's diary of her first trip abroad (1905) and the letters of Vachel Lindsay to her are in the Am. Literature Collection of the Yale Univ. Library. There are 99 letters by her in the Jessie B. Rittenhouse Collection, Rollins College, Winter Park, Fla., and 34 letters and MS. poems at the Mo. Hist. Soc., St. Louis.]

JOHN HALL WHEELOCK

**TEKAKWITHA, Catherine** (1656–Apr. 17, 1680), Mohawk Indian convert to Catholicism, sometimes known as "The Lily of the Mohawks," was born either at the Mohawk "castle" (village) of the Turtle clan, Ossernenon, on the south side of the Mohawk River near present-day Auriesville, N.Y., or at the subsequent neighboring castle of Kaghnuwage (Gandaouaga); her name is also found as Tegakwita, Tegah-Kouita, or Tegakouita. Her mother, a Christian Algonquin who had been taken captive at Three Rivers, Canada, by a raiding band of Mohawk Indians, escaped slavery or death in the Mohawk country through marriage to a native warrior. Two children were born of this union, Tekakwitha and a brother. A smallpox epidemic of about 1660 carried away both parents and the boy. The orphaned Tekakwitha recovered, but her eyesight was badly impaired and her face remained pockmarked. Adopted by her paternal uncle she learned the usages and practices of the Mohawks.

Repeated forays by the Mohawk warriors against the French and their Indian allies culminated in a French counterinvasion in 1666 which devastated the Mohawk country, forcing the inhabitants of Kaghnuwage to build a new village, Caughnawaga (Gandaougue), a half-mile to the west of the present Fonda, N.Y. The Mohawks sued for peace, which the French granted on condition that the Mohawks permit Jesuit missionaries to preach the Gospel in their villages. Three missionaries arrived in 1667; they were accommodated for three days at Caughnawaga in the longhouse of Teka-kwitha's uncle, the "foremost captain" in the village, before setting out to visit the other Mohawk villages. In 1669 preparations were made for the construction of a chapel, dedicated to St. Peter, in Caughnawaga. Despite the opposition of her uncle, Tekakwitha during 1675 requested to be instructed in the Christian faith, and on Easter Sunday, Apr. 18, 1676, she received baptism in St. Peter's chapel and was given the name Catherine (rendered in the Mohawk tongue as Kateri). Many Mohawks, however, opposed the missionary effort, and Tekakwitha was subjected to threats and maltreatment because of her new faith; she was stoned, for example, for refusing to work in the corn fields on the Sabbath. She therefore determined to join a group of Christian Mohawks who had migrated to the mission of St. Francis Xavier at Sault St. Louis (Lachine Rapids) in Canada, on the south shore of the St. Lawrence River. In 1677 three Christian Indians from that mission visited relatives at Caughnawaga, one of them a relative of Tekakwitha. Taking advantage of the temporary absence of her uncle, she left the Mohawk village and returned with the visitors to Sault St. Louis.

It was at Sault St. Louis that the religious and public life of Tekakwitha developed to such a degree that she was revered by all as a saintly woman. Contemporary biographers attest that this Indian maiden exercised every virtue in an extraordinary degree. Her love of God was manifested in frequent prayer and by daily visits to the mission chapel. By exterior conduct she revealed that her mind and heart centered upon God, seeking to do always what would be more pleasing to Him. To the astonishment of the missionaries, Tekakwitha determined not to marry and confirmed that resolve by a vow of virginity with full knowledge that she would become dependent upon others for her support. Charity toward all without exception, prudence in recognizing that prayer and labor each had its appropriate time, voluntary fastings and penances: all these actions divulged in some degree the excellent religious character of Tekakwitha. Furthermore, notwithstanding physical debility, she daily assumed her full share of arduous occupations.

She died at Sault St. Louis at the age of twenty-four and was buried east of where the Portage River empties into the St. Lawrence.

Spontaneous reverence caused Christian Indians and neighboring French inhabitants of Montreal to visit the grave of Tekakwitha, where they sought her intercession with God for themselves. This reverence, continued through generations, induced the Catholic Church to authorize in 1932 an investigation of the "Cause of Catherine Tekakwitha" for possible beatification and canonization.

[Two early accounts exist in manuscript: "The Life of the Good Katharine Tegakouita, Now Known as the Holy Savage" (1685, 1695), by Claude Chauchetière, S.J.; and "The Life of Katharine Tekakwitha, First Iroquois Virgin" (1696), by Peter Cholenec, S.J.; both are in the Archives of St. Mary's College, Montreal, Canada. These and other documents assembled in *The Positio of the Hist. Section of the Sacred Congregation of Rites on the Introduction of the Cause for Beatification and Canonization . . .* [of] *Katharine Tekakwitha* have been published in English translation by the Fordham University Press (1940). For other source material see: Reuben Gold Thwaites, ed., *The Jesuit Relations and Allied Documents* (73 vols., 1896–1901); Mère Saint-Ignace, *Les Annales de l'Hôtel-Dieu de Québec, 1636–1716*, ed. by Dom Albert Jamet (1939), pp. 197–200; and P. F. X. de Charlevoix, S.J., *Hist. and General Description of New France*, translated, with notes, by John Gilmary Shea, IV (1870), 283–96. Of the secondary accounts, the most fully documented are Ellen H. Walworth, *The Life and Times of Kateri Tekakwitha, the Lily of the Mohawks* (1891 and later editions), and Daniel Sargent, *Catherine Tekakwitha* (1936).]

THOMAS GRASSMANN

**TEMPLETON, Fay** (Dec. 25, 1865–Oct. 3, 1939), actress and singer, principally known for her appearances in light opera and vaudeville, was born in Little Rock, Ark., while her parents, John and Alice (Vane) Templeton, were on tour with their troupe, the John Templeton Opera Company. Cradled in dressing rooms, carried onstage frequently as an infant, and assigned her first speaking role before she was five, she knew no other life than that of the theatre, which was her home, education, and career. At seven she played Puck in Augustin Daly's *Midsummer Night's Dream;* at nine, again for Daly, she enacted Juliet to the juvenile Bijou Heron's Romeo in the balcony scene. Other early performances foreshadowed her later success in vaudeville: she acted in *Parepa Rosa,* her father's burlesque of the popular opera star, and did an imitation of Marie Aimée, a celebrated French star of comic opera. The youthful Fay Templeton also played in such melodramas as *East Lynne*. The early 1880's found her starring in a light opera company which bore her name. Although seldom seen in New York, the "buxom, blithe, and debonair" Miss Templeton appeared frequently in theatres throughout the country in such comic operas as *The Mascot, Patience, The Pirates of Penzance,* and *Giroflé-Girofla.* During this period of growing national reputation as a star she was married, on May 20, 1883, to the minstrel show performer William H. (Billy) West, but they separated within a few months and eventually were divorced.

Some reports maintain that Fay Templeton's career blossomed on Oct. 7, 1885, when at the Fourteenth Street Theatre in New York she played Gabriel in an elaborately staged revival of Edward E. Rice's extravaganza *Evangeline.* The following year she made her London debut at the Gaiety on Dec. 23 as Fernand in *Monte Cristo, Junior.* Certainly by 1888, when she toured in Rice's *The Corsair,* the "duskily seductive Fay Templeton" was already famous for her "divine symmetry and sensuous loveliness," for costumes which occasionally caught the eyes of the censors, and for lavish living. During the next seven years her stage appearances were infrequent; much of this time she was abroad, reportedly with Howell Osborn, a wealthy New Yorker whom she was said to have secretly married in 1885. Although before and after Osborn's death in 1895 she asserted that she was legally married to him, and although she ultimately received a $20,000 bequest from his estate, her statement was never confirmed (*Boston Journal,* Feb. 7, 1907). She returned to the New York stage in E. E. Rice's *Excelsior, Jr.* in November 1895, but the fall of 1896 found her again traveling abroad.

Her fame as a vaudeville artist came after she decided to join the famous team of Weber and Fields in 1898 when they cabled her an offer of four hundred dollars a week to appear in *Hurly Burly.* "Her first youth had passed and her figure had matured," wrote Felix Isman, biographer of Weber and Fields (pp. 241–42), "but her mimic powers had grown and mellowed. In the Music Hall she won a new public and fame. . . ." She starred on her own during the 1899 season but was back with Weber and Fields in 1900 in *Fiddle-dee-dee,* in which her deep throaty contralto made famous the song "Ma Blushin' Rosie" ("Rosie, You Are Ma Posie"). In 1901 she joined them in *Hoity Toity* and the next year in *Twirly Whirly,* starring with such great names of the stage as LILLIAN RUSSELL, David Warfield, De Wolf Hopper, Sam Bernard, and William Collier. In all of these productions she contributed

to the hilarity of Weber and Fields' burlesques of currently popular plays, like "The Curl and the Judge" (from Clyde Fitch's *The Girl and the Judge*) and "The Stickiness of Gelatine" (*The Stubbornness of Geraldine*). An admirer of CISSIE LOFTUS, whom at least one critic thought she surpassed, Miss Templeton also did imitations of such stars as Lillian Russell and Ethel Barrymore. In 1903 she left Weber and Fields to star in a musical, *The Runaways.*

Her career, at its height during her years with Weber and Fields, reached another crowning point when she played the lead in George M. Cohan's musical comedy *Forty-five Minutes from Broadway.* After a rather short run and unfavorable reviews in New York, the musical was a triumph on its road tour in 1906 and returned to Broadway as a major success; Miss Templeton made one of its songs, "Mary Is a Grand Old Name," enormously popular. The final performance of this play in May 1907 was also the first of her many "farewell appearances"; she retired to Pittsburgh with her third husband, William Joshua Patterson, a wealthy contractor of that city whom she had married (at Ridley Park, Pa.) on Aug. 1, 1906. During the next twenty-six years she reappeared intermittently as Buttercup in Gilbert and Sullivan's *H.M.S. Pinafore,* a role for which her increasing avoirdupois suited her, and in vaudeville —notably with Weber and Fields in 1912 and again in 1925, when she was greeted with warm enthusiasm by audience and reviewers. She appeared very briefly in only one film, *Broadway to Hollywood,* released in 1933. In 1932 Patterson died.

In November 1933, when almost sixty-eight, Fay Templeton returned to Broadway as Aunt Minnie in the outstanding musical comedy of that year, Jerome Kern's *Roberta.* Now distinctly corpulent, she played most of the part sitting down, and her singing was cut to a few bars, but she showed her endurance and spunk in touring the United States and Canada with the show in the 1934–35 season. By March 1936 she was living in the Actors Fund Home in Englewood, N.J. Suffering from severe arthritis, she went to live in San Francisco with a cousin, Mrs. Belle Adams, early in 1937 and died there two years later, in her seventy-fourth year. By her wish, her ashes were buried at Kensico Cemetery, Valhalla, N.Y.

"They say there never was a better Buttercup," stated an editorial in the *New York Times* two days after her death. And Felix Isman believed that although the radiant personality of Lillian Russell somewhat eclipsed the memory of Miss Templeton, yet Fay "was incomparably the greater actress."

[Felix Isman, *Weber and Fields: Their Tribulations, Triumphs and Their Associates* (1924); John Parker, ed., *Who's Who in the Theatre* (9th ed., 1939); *N.Y. Times*, Sept. 4, 1898, Jan. 2, 1906, Oct. 4, 5, and 8, 1939; George C. D. Odell, *Annals of the N.Y. Stage*, vols. IX–XIII (1937–42); Lewis C. Strang, *Prima Donnas and Soubrettes* (1900); David Ewen, *The Story of America's Musical Theater* (1961); clippings in Harvard Theatre Collection.]

                                    ALBERT E. JOHNSON

**TENNEY, Tabitha Gilman** (Apr. 7, 1762–May 2, 1837), novelist, was born in Exeter, N.H., the first of the seven children of Samuel Gilman and his second wife, Lydia Robinson Giddinge. Her father was a descendant of John Gilman, who came from England to Hingham, Mass., in 1638, and soon after settled in Exeter. During the intervening generations, members of the numerous Gilman family had served the community in various ways, civil and military. Her mother was the daughter of Zebulon and Lydia (Robinson) Giddinge, also of Exeter, and on both sides a descendant of early settlers there.

Nothing is known of Tabitha Gilman's education, but her mature work suggests a cultured background, wide reading, and training beyond what a small-town schooling of that date might have afforded. In 1788, probably in September, when a marriage intention was filed, she was married to Dr. Samuel Tenney, a native of Byfield, Mass., and a resident of Exeter prior to the Revolution, during which he had served as a surgeon in a Rhode Island regiment. Upon his return to Exeter after the war, he exchanged medical practice for scientific studies and politics. He wrote scientific papers, acted as a member of the committee to frame a constitution for the state, was judge of probate, and in 1800 was elected to Congress, serving for three successive terms.

Mrs. Tenney's first publication, *The New Pleasing Instructor* (1799), which appeared eleven years after her marriage, was a book of selections from classical poets for the use of young ladies, a popular type of anthology in its day. Her chief claim to remembrance, however, is her two-volume novel, *Female Quixotism: Exhibited in the Romantic Opinions and Extravagant Adventures of Dorcasina Sheldon*, published in 1801 during her residence in Washington. This work was closely modeled on *The Female Quixote; or, The Adventures of Arabella*, written forty-nine years earlier by Charlotte Ramsay Lennox (1720–1804), an English author reputedly of American birth; something of a sensation in its day, it was still in print in 1801. Tabitha Tenney's novel had a

briefer and more limited fame, though it went through at least five editions, one as late as 1841. Her version of Mrs. Lennox's theme of false sentiment and its dangers for the unwary reader, with its more biting satire, nicely suited the taste of her time and place. There was a growing demand for books to amuse as well as instruct, and patriotism called for novels about America written by Americans. Mrs. Tenney's account of the moonstruck Dorcasina's adventures "on the beautiful banks of the Delaware" provided an absorbing story for young lady patrons of the new circulating libraries, and by satirizing its own genre it could win approval from the still larger body of moralists who feared the harmful effect of novel reading on the female character. *Female Quixotism* thus became a landmark in early fiction reading as in fiction writing.

Mrs. Tenney's satire centered not on Cervantes' *Don Quixote*, but rather on foolish young women who could be deceived by a rogue affecting courtly manners and what passed for romantic love talk. Her inventive skill in devising falsely romantic situations was considerable. Dorcasina Sheldon is foolish beyond all reasonable belief, but her extreme gullibility, which passes for helpless innocence in a world of rogues, keeps her within the interest, perhaps also within the sympathy, of the uninitiate. Her maid, Betty, is a more original creation than the mistress and might even have amused Cervantes in moments. In the end, the enlightened Dorcasina, reconciled to spinsterhood, her name changed back again to the biblical Dorcas, speaks the moral of her own tale.

After her husband's death in 1816, Tabitha Tenney returned to Exeter, where she lived for the remaining years of her life. There is no indication that she did any further writing. She died in Exeter at the age of seventy-five and was buried there in the Winter Street Graveyard.

[Charles H. Bell, *Hist. of the Town of Exeter, N.H.* (1888); Arthur Gilman, *The Gilman Family* (1869); Martha Jane Tenney, *The Tenney Family, 1638–1904* (1904); Gustavus H. Maynadier, *The First Am. Novelist?* (1904), on Charlotte Lennox; Evart A. and George L. Duyckinck, *Cyc. of Am. Literature* (1855), I, 504–06, which also prints a summary of *Female Quixotism;* death notice in *Exeter* (N.H.) *News Letter*, May 9, 1837.]

                                    OLA ELIZABETH WINSLOW

**TERHUNE, Mary Virginia Hawes** (Dec. 21, 1830–June 3, 1922), novelist and writer on household affairs, known to contemporaries as

"Marion Harland," was born in Dennisville, Amelia County, Va., the second daughter and third of nine children. Her father, Samuel Pierce Hawes, came of a distinguished New England family; born in Dorchester, Mass., he had moved to Richmond, Va., and had become a partner in a mercantile house. In Richmond he married Judith Anna Smith, daughter of a Virginia planter who traced his ancestry to the brother of Capt. John Smith of the Jamestown colony. Before Mary Virginia's birth, Samuel Hawes suffered financial reverses and took up country storekeeping, moving his family to a succession of Virginia towns. In 1844, with his fortunes restored, he returned to Richmond, where he became a magistrate and an active figure in state and local politics.

Mary Virginia was educated mostly at home. Her father, an "independent thinker" who placed a high value on education for girls as well as boys, found the local schools inadequate and engaged tutors for his children and those of a few friends; he also encouraged his daughter to use his library freely. Her mother made reading aloud a family custom and taught her to love the traditions of Southern life and to regard the role of homemaker as that offering a woman the greatest possibilities for self-fulfillment. At thirteen Mary Virginia was sent to live for a year with a cousin at Hampden-Sydney College in Prince Edward County; there, with other girls, she received instruction from a student at Union Theological Seminary, who was ordered to educate them "as if they were boys preparing for college." The following year she attended a Presbyterian school for girls in Richmond.

A precocious child, she had begun writing essays and stories before she reached her teens, hiding the manuscripts at the bottom of a trunk, and at fourteen she was contributing anonymously to a local newspaper. When the *Southern Era*, a literary weekly, in 1853 offered a prize of fifty dollars for the best serial on a temperance theme, she submitted "Kate Harper" (under the pseudonym "Marion Harland"), which won the prize. Stimulated by seeing her tale in print, she rewrote a novel which she had begun several years earlier. When a local publisher rejected the manuscript, her father arranged to have it privately printed in Richmond. Appearing in 1854 under the title *Alone*, it received enthusiastic reviews, was published in New York by J. C. Derby in 1856, and eventually sold more than a hundred thousand copies. Derby also published her second novel, *The Hidden Path* (1856).

Already a successful writer, on Sept. 2, 1856, Miss Hawes was married to Edward Payson Terhune, a Presbyterian minister from New Jersey who was temporarily occupying a parish in Richmond. In 1859 he accepted a pastorate in Newark, N.J., which remained the family home for the next eighteen years. Six children were born of the marriage: Edward (1857), Christine (1859), Alice (1863), Virginia Belle (1865), Myrtle (1869), and Albert Payson (1872). The three who survived childhood all became authors, CHRISTINE TERHUNE HERRICK and Virginia Terhune Van de Water writing of household matters and Albert Payson Terhune becoming a popular author of dog stories.

With her husband's approval, Mrs. Terhune continued her writing, while also carrying on her domestic and parish responsibilities. She taught a Bible class, superintended the infant department of the Sunday school, and was president of the Woman's Christian Association, which raised money and found jobs for the poor. She also managed the Terhune summer home, Sunnybank, in Pompton, N.J. Her third novel, *Moss-Side*, appeared in 1857, the year after her marriage, *Nemesis* in 1860, and her seventeenth novel, *Jessamine*, in 1873. Sometime during that year her health began to fail; a persistent cough and repeated hemorrhages of the lungs eventually brought a diagnosis of tuberculosis, and in 1876 Terhune resigned his pastorate and took his wife to Europe for a two-year stay, during which she fully recovered. On their return he was assigned to a parish in Springfield, Mass., and in 1884 to another in Brooklyn, N.Y. During this time she continued her writing.

In her lifetime Mrs. Terhune published a phenomenal number of works; the fiction alone includes twenty-five novels and three volumes of short stories. Most of her stories are set in the plantations of the South before the Civil War; they are similar in having a sentimental tone, a romantic plot, and an atmosphere of religious piety. Her heroines are never "emancipated" women, but glorify the domestic role. In later romances she condemned feminist agitation, insisting that to reach her fullest bloom a woman must be sheltered and adored; her sympathy, affection, and charm would then permeate the lives around her. Nevertheless, she believed that well-educated women made better homemakers and that every woman should have a trade or profession by which, if necessary, she could support herself and her children.

Sometime during her forties Mrs. Terhune shifted her literary efforts from fiction to domestic advice. In the first years of her marriage she had had to teach herself the practical routines of cooking and housekeeping, and she embodied the results of her experience in *Common Sense in the Household* (1871), which became a best seller and was translated into French, German, and Arabic. Altogether she published some twenty-five books concerned with domestic affairs, including *The Dinner Year-Book* (1878), *Eve's Daughters* (1882), and *Every Day Etiquette* (1905). She contributed articles on homemaking to numerous magazines and for a time edited two: the *Home-Maker* (1888–90) and the *Housekeeper's Weekly*. Her syndicated columns on women's affairs written for the Philadelphia *North American* (1900–10) and the *Chicago Tribune* (1911–17) were reprinted in twenty-five daily newspapers. In her lectures for the Chautauqua Association (1891–94) she spoke on such topics as "How to Grow Old Gracefully" and "The Kitchen as a Moral Agency." Although her novels had borne little relation to contemporary society, her practical advice to women showed her awareness of the social changes that followed the Civil War. Her etiquette books included chapters addressed to "Mrs. Newly Rich" and to the "Woman in Business." She praised such mechanical devices as eggbeaters and clothes wringers and urged women to overcome "the vulgar prejudice against labor-saving machines."

In addition to her household guides, Mrs. Terhune wrote more than a dozen books of travel, biography, and colonial history. *Home of the Bible* (1896) describes her journey through the Middle East in 1889. Biographical sketches of Charlotte Brontë, William Cowper, John Knox, and Hannah More appeared in 1899–1900. *The Story of Mary Washington* (1892) successfully aroused interest in erecting a monument over the grave of the first president's mother. In *Some Colonial Homesteads and Their Stories* (1897)—the first of a three-volume series—genealogy, rather than architecture, was her chief concern. She delighted in the evidence preserved in old letters and diaries of the family-centeredness of New England and Southern aristocrats. In recognition of her work, the Virginia Historical Society elected her its first woman member, and she was invited to write "The Story of Virginia" for inclusion in a volume of state histories. She maintained active memberships in the Daughters of the American Revolution, the Association for the Preservation of Virginia Antiquities, and the Pocahontas Memorial Association.

The author Kate Sanborn described Mrs. Terhune as "a bright-faced, keen-eyed, self-poised woman, with a great deal of individuality and energy," natural in manner and a

good conversationalist. Her husband died in 1907, but her remarkable vitality continued through her ninth decade. At the age of eighty-four she published *Looking Westward* (1914), a small volume presenting her philosophy of life; her last novel, *The Carringtons of High Hill*, appeared in 1919, in her eighty-ninth year. She died of old age in 1922 at her New York City home and was buried in Pompton, N.J. To her contemporaries she had been the model career woman: a successful writer who was at the same time "the helpful wife of an eminent pastor, a leader in all the benevolent work and social life of a city parish, and a most careful and responsible mother" (Bolton, p. 90).

[Mary Virginia Terhune, *Marion Harland's Autobiog.* (1910); Kate Sanborn in *Our Famous Women* (1884), chap. xxvii; Sarah K. Bolton, *Successful Women* (1888); Frances E. Willard and Mary A. Livermore, eds., *A Woman of the Century* (1893); Florine Thayer McCray, "Marion Harland at Home," *Ladies' Home Jour.*, Aug. 1887; *N.Y. Times*, June 4, 7, 1922; *Who Was Who in America*, vol. I (1942). For an early account, see Mary T. Tardy, *The Living Female Writers of the South* (1872), pp. 433–36.]

MERRIT CROSS

**TERRY, Rose.** *See* COOKE, Rose Terry.

**THANET, Octave.** *See* FRENCH, Alice.

**THAXTER, Celia Laighton** (June 29, 1835–Aug. 26, 1894), poet, was born in Portsmouth, N.H., the daughter of Thomas B. and Eliza (Rymes) Laighton, both natives of New Hampshire. An older daughter had died in infancy; two sons were born after Celia. Thomas Laighton, who came of a seagoing family, was a lumber merchant and importer; he also followed a political career that took him from a clerkship in the local customhouse to positions as postmaster and, briefly, editor of the *New Hampshire Gazette*. In 1839, after being defeated as candidate for selectman of Portsmouth, he moved with his family to White Island, smallest of the Isles of Shoals, nine miles off the coast from Portsmouth, where he became the lighthouse keeper. When he was elected to the New Hampshire state legislature in 1841 the family moved to Smutty-nose Island, where they opened their home to summer guests and thus began their first venture as innkeepers. Save for his two-year legislative term Laighton apparently never returned to the mainland.

Celia spent most of her childhood on White Island, a rocky bit of land of less than three acres, where with her two brothers she learned the ways of wind, tides, and storm and absorbed such formal education as her father was able to provide. Her memories of these experiences formed the basis of all that she wrote in later years. When she was twelve, Laighton gave up his lighthouse post and moved to Appledore, largest island of the group and one of the four which he owned. Here, in partnership with Levi Lincoln Thaxter, a young Harvard graduate who had also felt the attraction of the islands, he built Appledore House, a summer hotel which opened in 1848. Thaxter, however, proved ill suited to the actual work of managing the hotel, the partnership was dissolved, and he became tutor of the Laighton children. The hotel, prospering beyond expectation, became the summer choice of New England writers and artists and later numbered among its guests Hawthorne, Emerson, Lowell, Whittier, Mark Twain, LUCY LARCOM, SARAH ORNE JEWETT, and the painters Childe Hassam and William Morris Hunt.

On Sept. 30, 1851, Celia Laighton, just past sixteen, was married to Levi Thaxter, fifteen years her senior. She had rarely left the islands, her longest stay on the mainland occurring when she attended the Mount Washington Female Seminary in South Boston in 1849–50, probably for only one term. Thaxter had not settled upon a profession and, in fact, never overcame his indecision and restlessness, although in his later years, as a self-styled Browning scholar, he enjoyed some success with his public readings of the poetry of Robert Browning. For the first years of their marriage they lived an itinerant life, spending time in Watertown, Mass., with Thaxter's family; on Star Island in the Isles of Shoals, where he assumed the temporary post of preacher and teacher to the fishermen's children; in Newburyport, Mass.; and in Thaxter's cottage on Appledore. In the fall of 1855, while returning from the mainland, he nearly lost his life in a sailing accident during a storm; the incident gave him a dislike for the sea and the islands, and in 1856 he moved his family, which now included two sons, Karl and John, to Newtonville, Mass. There in the summer of 1858 a third son, Roland, was born. Homesick for the island life of her youth, Celia Thaxter found an outlet in writing verse, and in March 1861 the *Atlantic Monthly* published her first poem, "Land-Locked," its title supplied by James Russell Lowell, who printed it without her knowledge.

Celia Thaxter's home soon became something of a salon, her charm, wit, and gift of storytelling making her a natural hostess. She delighted in her association with Boston's literary figures and visited frequently in the home of James and ANNIE ADAMS FIELDS, where she met Charles Dickens. She developed a close friendship with Whittier, who proved a helpful guide and encouraged her to think it was her "destiny to produce poetry." Her poems appeared in the *Atlantic,* the *Independent, Scribner's, Harper's,* the *Century,* and the *New England Magazine,* and her pieces for children in *St. Nicholas* and *Our Young Folks.* Her husband was an invaluable adviser, assisting her with the publication of her *Poems* (1872) and *Among the Isles of Shoals* (1873), a collection of prose articles about life on the islands first published in the *Atlantic Monthly.*

Her personal life was shadowed by Thaxter's reluctance to return to the islands she loved. After his first serious illness, in the winter of 1868–69, he went to Florida with their two younger sons while Celia Thaxter returned to Appledore with the oldest boy. This episode was the first of a series of long separations, and eventually they led essentially separate lives. Celia Thaxter's letters, preserved in large number, detail the weariness induced by the summer labors at the hotel, the winter loneliness caused by her husband's absence, sorrow over the death of her parents, and anxiety for her eldest son, Karl, mentally ill since childhood. (Her youngest son, Roland, became a professor of botany at Harvard and a distinguished researcher in mycology.) Nevertheless, each summer's return to Appledore brought a renewal of joy. She continued to publish her poetry; an enlarged edition of her *Poems* appeared in 1874, and five additional volumes followed during her lifetime.

In 1880 the Thaxters sold their house in Newtonville, making their home on their son John's farm in Kittery Point, Maine, although Celia often spent winters in Boston or Portsmouth. In 1881 she made a brief trip to Europe with her brother Oscar, one of the happiest experiences of her life. In her later years she took up china painting, one of the enthusiasms of the hour, as a means of earning a little extra money, and devoted much of her time to her famous island garden. Noted in her youth for her classic profile, in the last years of her life she became overweight. She was never a member of any church but for a time after her mother's death was interested in spiritualism and Indian mysticism, and in her last winters attended the Unitarian church in Portsmouth. She died at Appledore of a cerebral hemorrhage in August 1894, at fifty-nine, having survived her husband by ten years, and was buried on the island hillside near her father and mother.

During her lifetime and briefly thereafter,

Celia Thaxter was one of the better-known woman poets of America. The picturesqueness of her island home added enchantment to the personal quality of her verse, and her wide acquaintance with the famous who had been summer visitors at the island lent interest to her as an individual. Her verse both in content and style owes much to the influence of Lowell and Whittier, who urged her to write ballads and approved the quatrain form and the moral tag. Her verse differs from that of other regional writers of the day in that it seldom alludes to people but deals chiefly with the sea, the rocks, the flowers, and the creatures of Appledore. Limited by the range of her own emotions and the tight frame of piety from which she almost never escaped, her poetry nevertheless expresses authentic content and emotion.

[Mary Dickson de Pizá, "Celia Thaxter, Poet of the Isles of Shoals" (unpublished Ph.D. dissertation, Univ. of Pa., 1955), and Rosamond Thaxter, *Sandpiper: The Life and Letters of Celia Thaxter* (1963), are the fullest and most recent biographical studies. See also: Oscar Laighton, *Ninety Years at the Isles of Shoals* (1930); Perry D. Westbrook, *Acres of Flint* (1951); John Albee in *New England Mag.*, Apr. 1901; M. Wilma Stubbs in *New England Quart.*, Dec. 1935; Harriet Prescott Spofford, *A Little Book of Friends* (1916); Annie Adams Fields, *Authors and Friends* (1896); *Boston Transcript*, Aug. 27, 28, 29, 1894. There are letters of Mrs. Thaxter to Annie Adams Fields and Sarah Orne Jewett in the Boston Public Library and letters to and from Whittier in the Roland Thaxter Collection, Houghton Library, Harvard. A private collection of family correspondence is in the possession of Rosamond Thaxter, Kittery Point, Maine. A selection of *Letters of Celia Thaxter* was published in 1897.]

OLA ELIZABETH WINSLOW

**THOBURN, Isabella** (Mar. 29, 1840–Sept. 1, 1901), Methodist missionary to India, was born near St. Clairsville, Ohio, the fourth of five daughters and ninth of the ten children of Matthew and Jane Lyle (Crawford) Thoburn. Her Scotch-Irish parents had emigrated to the United States from the vicinity of Belfast in 1825 and settled on a farm near St. Clairsville. Both her father, who died when she was ten, and her mother were "persons of marked character," and the children were given a devout, but not restrictive, Methodist upbringing. Isabella received her early education in the district school and at the age of fourteen entered the Wheeling Female Seminary in Wheeling, Va. (now W. Va.). After completing the prescribed course, she taught briefly in an Ohio country school and then returned to the seminary for further study she herself planned. She

also studied art for a year at the Cincinnati Academy of Design. Though she had no conscious experience of conversion, she became a member of the Methodist Church at the age of nineteen. During the Civil War she taught for a time in a public school in Wheeling, and for a year after the war in a private school in New Castle, Pa., followed by two years as preceptress in a Methodist school, Western Reserve Seminary, in West Farmington, Ohio.

In 1866 her brother James, who had gone to India as a Methodist missionary in 1859 and had become convinced that the women of that land could not be effectively reached except by women missionaries, suggested to Isabella that she join him and undertake this task. She was willing, but reluctant to work except in her own denomination, which as yet had no agency for authorizing women missionaries. When, however, the Woman's Foreign Missionary Society of the Methodist Church was formed in Boston in 1869, one of its first actions was to send Miss Thoburn to India. Accompanied by Dr. CLARA A. SWAIN, who was to engage in pioneering medical work among the women of India, she arrived in Bombay on Jan. 7, 1870, and was assigned to the city of Lucknow, where her brother was newly stationed as presiding elder of the province of Oudh.

Miss Thoburn's first task, aside from undertaking evangelistic work among women in the zenanas, was to find a suitable location for a new school for girls. Renting a room in the midst of the bustle and noise of the bazaar, she began classes in April for six Christian girls, four of them of Hindustani birth. Two months later there were seventeen pupils. After a little more than a year the Woman's Foreign Missionary Society purchased for the growing school a desirable property named Lal Bagh, or Ruby Garden, once the palace of an official of the last king of Oudh. This made it possible to add a boarding department to the school—a new departure in missionary work for that day—so as to accommodate more girls and provide them with a Christian environment. Located near both the English and the Hindustani Methodist churches, Lal Bagh served as the headquarters of Methodist women's missionary work in Lucknow, becoming a center for the missionary families in the city and province and a place of hospitality for visiting church workers and others. Miss Thoburn also found time to aid in the Lucknow mission's Sunday school classes for poor children, mostly Eurasians, and, beginning in 1872, in classes for poor Hindu girls. She also directed the work of the women evangelists known as "Bible readers." During 1874, while continuing her work in Lucknow, she also served as principal of a girls' school in the city of Cawnpore, forty-five miles to the west.

Besides devoting herself to evangelism, administration, and teaching, Miss Thoburn also mothered distraught pupils, nursed them (and others) when they fell sick with smallpox or cholera, and otherwise tended to their needs. Her disregard of self in the service of others made a profound impression upon those who came to know her. She strove always to influence the Christian workers whom she directed, and also the schoolgirls, to forget the divisions of caste and race in a common Christian spirit.

In 1880, aften ten years of service, poor health made it necessary for Miss Thoburn to take a furlough in the United States. There the months were filled with speaking engagements in various parts of the country, which left her little chance to rest. Returning to India in 1882, she continued her work as principal of the Lal Bagh school, now creating a "normal class" to prepare girls for evangelistic work in schools (such as Sunday schools for Mohammedan children) and zenanas. After two years in her second term of service her health again began to fail; she was granted another home leave in 1886, which because of her slow recovery lasted through 1890. Her Lucknow school meanwhile continued to grow. In 1887 the curriculum was widened and it became the Girls' High School; originally mainly for "native" Christians, it was now expanded to include more Eurasians and Europeans, and also non-Christians. The next step, proposed by Miss Thoburn before her departure, was the initiation, in 1887, of a collegiate department, to meet the need for higher studies for girls. Though it began with only three pupils and had no pupils at all in 1889 and 1890, this marked the start of Lucknow Woman's College.

During her second furlough Miss Thoburn became active in the new deaconess movement in the Methodist Church, which enlisted women for social service in hospitals, orphanages, and so forth. For a year she served as "house mother" of a group of Chicago deaconesses recruited by LUCY RIDER MEYER and did some teaching in Mrs. Meyer's Chicago Training School for City, Home, and Foreign Missions. Then in December 1888 she answered a call to superintend a new Methodist deaconess home in Cincinnati. When a hospital was added, she gave it her oversight. Finally, at the close of 1890, after five years away from her adopted land, she returned to India, retaining thereafter the deaconess garb.

In her third term of service Miss Thoburn was engaged in the ever-widening work of the Girls' High School (which in 1892 had 160 pupils, including 96 boarders), the heavy responsibilities of developing the college, and service in the local Hindustani Methodist church, of which she was a member. She also undertook the editorship of a semimonthly paper, the *Woman's Friend*, published in Hindi for mothers and children and containing Bible stories, news, family stories, and practical advice on household matters. The school gained a teachers' class and a kindergarten department in 1893.

In 1895 a government charter was granted for the college and a new building was begun, a venture that involved incurring a considerable debt despite an appropriation from the Woman's Foreign Missionary Society. At the suggestion of the Methodist Annual Conference of 1899, Miss Thoburn returned once again to America to assist in the fund raising. Miss Lilavati Singh, one of her ablest graduates and teachers, toured the country with her, and the two women made a deep impression on their audiences. Her mission achieved, Miss Thoburn returned to India in 1900 and resumed her work in Lucknow in the summer of 1901. Soon afterward, however, she had a sudden attack of Asiatic cholera and died at her school at the age of sixty-one. A large crowd of mourners was present at her burial in the Lucknow cemetery. Lucknow Woman's College was renamed Isabella Thoburn College in 1903 and later became the woman's college of Lucknow University.

[James M. Thoburn, *Life of Isabella Thoburn* (1903); William F. Oldham, "Isabella Thoburn," in W. F. McDowell et al., *Effective Workers in Needy Fields* (1902); Brenton T. Badley, *Visions and Victories in Hindustan* (1931), chap. xxxviii; Frances J. Baker, *The Story of the Woman's Foreign Missionary Soc. of the Methodist Episcopal Church* (1895); *Christian Advocate* (N.Y.), Oct. 17, 1901. See also Lucy Rider Meyer, *Deaconesses* (3rd ed., 1892); Christian Golder, *Hist. of the Deaconess Movement in the Christian Church* (1903), pp. 311–15, 418–25.]

JAMES H. PYKE

**THOMAS, Edith Matilda** (Aug. 12, 1854– Sept. 13, 1925), poet, was born in Chatham, Ohio, to Frederick J. and Jane Louisa (Sturges) Thomas. Her father, of Welsh ancestry, was a second-generation Ohio farmer who also taught school; her mother, descended from the English Sturges (or Sturgis) family, had come to Ohio from Connecticut, where her grandfather had fought in the Revolutionary

War. The family, which included Edith and a younger sister, lived successively in the Ohio towns of Bowling Green; Kenton, where the father died in 1861; and Geneva, where Edith attended public school and graduated, in 1872, from Geneva Normal Institute, having completed specially arranged classes in Greek. The young Miss Thomas then went to Oberlin College for one unrewarding term, taught school for two years, and took up the trade of typesetting.

The strongest influence on her early life was provided by her father's brother, James Thomas, who supplied her with books, pictures, and accounts of the world outside Ohio. He joined her mother and sister in encouraging the submission of her precocious verse to local and even New York newspapers, where it was often accepted. In 1881 he led her, armed with a scrapbook of verse clippings, into the New York drawing room of ANNE CHARLOTTE LYNCH BOTTA, whence she was referred to HELEN HUNT JACKSON, whose enthusiastic endorsement produced almost immediate literary celebrity.

With the death of her mother in 1887, Miss Thomas moved permanently to New York City, where she was able to capitalize on *Century* magazine's handsome introduction of her work. During the next twenty years the demands of the leading literary magazines constantly exceeded her supply of verses, although more than three hundred were published between 1890 and 1909. The stimulation of these years was heightened by the hospitality of Samuel Elliott, physician, essayist, and lover of poetry, who, by taking her into his family, also included her in a celebrated group of literary and creative New Yorkers: Charles A. Dana, William Winter, Parke Godwin, and many others. Here her appearance (her face—large-boned, high-cheeked, and shadow-eyed—was sufficiently spectacular to evoke a newspaper feature from a reporter who had no idea who she was), her enthusiasm ("I was drunk with New York," she later said of those days), and her wit made her a valued part of the literary community.

Her later years were considerably less exuberant. She performed editorial tasks for the *Century Dictionary* and, until two days before her death, for *Harper's*, commuting to her lonely rooms on the fringe of Harlem, becoming increasingly withdrawn, and exciting the sympathetic pity of her friends. She died there at the age of seventy-one, of a cerebral hemorrhage resulting from chronic valvular heart disease and arteriosclerosis, and was buried in New Cemetery in her native Chatham.

Miss Thomas wrote abundant and success-ful children's verse, some of it inspired by her namesake niece, and creditable prose: philosophical and nature sketches, literary criticism, and humorous *jeux*. She became a versatile professional editor. Her reputation, however, rests solely on the serious verse which she produced with remarkable consistency for nearly sixty years. Always responsive to nature, whether in Ohio or Staten Island, she drew her principal literary inspiration from the lyrics of Keats. She was a classic poet in her prosodic regularity and in her continuing attention to Greek subjects. She was romantic in her emphasis on the self, although an aura of sentiment and pathos kept her from developing a constructive romantic position. Many found her verse discouragingly impersonal, humanized only when tragedy touched her own life, as in *The Inverted Torch* sequence. Yet for all her seeming removal from contemporary concerns, she did apply her skills to mundane affairs, from Garfield's inauguration to the advent of the First World War. She was one of the first poets to capture successfully the excitement (the "ardent bulbs") of the modern city, and one of the most consistent in crying out against the inroads of the dollar sign on American culture.

This gentle Ohio spinster, seeing life through Hellenic glasses, had by 1900, according to Edmund Clarence Stedman, secured her place "among the truest living poets of our English tongue." Both Richard Henry Stoddard, writing in 1885, and Robert Underwood Johnson, writing in 1925, called her verse the best American achievement of the last thirty years. Her reputation, however, fell victim not only to changing literary fashions, but also to comparison with the heights it had reached in the 1880's and which it could not surpass.

[The most important poetry of Edith Thomas was presented in: *A New Year's Masque* (1885), *Lyrics and Sonnets* (1887), *The Inverted Torch* (1890), *Fair Shadow Land* (1893), *A Winter Swallow* (1896), *The Dancers* (1903), *Cassia* (1905), *The Guest at the Gate* (1909), *The Flower from the Ashes* (1915), and *The White Messenger* (1915). Excerpts from these volumes, together with some 80 pages of verse not previously published in volume form, appeared in Jessie B. Rittenhouse's edition of the *Selected Poems of Edith M. Thomas* (1926). Miss Thomas also prepared 11 volumes and leaflets of children's verse, the best of which are: *In Sunshine Land* (illustrated by Katherine Pyle, 1895), *In the Young World* (1896), and *Children of Christmas* (1907). Her early prose—natural and philosophical sketches—was collected in *The Round Year* (1886); later examples of this vein are in *Atlantic Monthly*, Aug. 1893, and *Critic*, Dec. 1905. Her humorous, satirical prose is represented by pieces in *Atlantic Monthly,* Feb. 1895, and *Harper's Monthly,* Oct. 1919, Dec. 1923. For samples of her literary criticism, see her article on Poe in *Harper's Weekly,* Jan. 16, 1909, and her frequent poetry reviews in *Critic,* 1902–05. The best extended treatment of her life is Jessie B. Rittenhouse's "Memoir" in the *Selected Poems.* Also illuminating are the biographical sketches by S. R. Elliott in *Critic,* June 18, 1898, and by Alice M. Day in *Our World Weekly,* Oct. 5, 1925. The *N.Y. Times* obituary, Sept. 15, 1925, is also helpful. The most extensive appraisal of Edith Thomas' verse is also by Jessie B. Rittenhouse, in *The Younger Am. Poets* (1904). Also valuable are the estimates of Richard H. Stoddard in *Book Buyer,* June 1885 and Mar. 1888; William M. Payne in *Dial,* Feb. 1888, Feb. 1891, May 1893, and Feb. 1895; William D. Howells in *Harper's Monthly,* May 1891; Edmund C. Stedman, *An Am. Anthology* (1900), p. 826; Fred L. Pattee, *A Hist. of Am. Literature since 1870* (1915); Howard W. Cook et al. in *Mentor,* June 15, 1920; and the letter of Robert U. Johnson in *N.Y. Times,* Sept. 16, 1925.]

ROBERT H. WALKER

THOMAS, Martha Carey (Jan. 2, 1857–Dec. 2, 1935), educator and feminist, was born in Baltimore, the eldest of the ten children (five boys and five girls) of James Carey Thomas and Mary (Whitall) Thomas. Originally Welsh, the Thomases had settled in Maryland in the mid-seventeenth century; the Whitalls, who were English, came to New Jersey before 1688. Both families were Quakers. The Whitalls distinguished themselves in piety and philanthropy and outranked the Thomases in wealth. James Carey Thomas, and his father before him, were physicians, and Mary Whitall Thomas achieved independent prominence among Friends for her charitable undertakings; like her sister HANNAH WHITALL SMITH, she was active in the Woman's Christian Temperance Union.

The Thomases could perform modest charities steadily, and their style of living conformed to the substantial criteria of large town house, servants, and a country estate for summers. Yet they were not truly wealthy, and they became, as they saw it, increasingly hard pressed, eventually sinking into debt. Meanwhile they maintained tokens of Quaker simplicity which crosscut the evidences of their comfortable social position. The family code enjoined plainness of dress and abstinence from the theatre and dancing; these ways excluded them from the "best" Baltimore society of the worldlier sort but, on the other hand, did not permit great financial economies. Stylized abstinence (which excluded only some categories of childhood joy) posed no impossible barrier of conscience to Carey Thomas when, later, she had the means to experience luxury.

Known as Minnie in her youth, in most respects she had a reasonably happy childhood, one which permitted her to indulge both her voracious appetite for books and her tomboy inclinations. Almost from infancy, her parents recalled, she was imperious and difficult to manage. Her mother, religiously cherishing the worth of individual personality, reasoned with her rather than seeking to curb her will; in return she received the daughter's passionate adoration. Her sterner father met with her gradually increasing resentment. Her mother had once desired a higher education, and Minnie Thomas blamed her father and her brothers and sisters for, in effect, interfering with her mother's ambitions. Yet they were a close family, one in which love between husband and wife was the constant theme, and rupture never threatened as a result of Minnie's strenuous attitudes. When she was seven, she was badly burned in a kitchen fire. The accident left her with a slight limp, in later years to become pronounced and painful. During her convalescence she was universally pampered; it was also then, her father remembered, that she began to discover the delight in indiscriminate reading which she was never to lose. Later in childhood she began self-consciously to think of women's rights as a serious issue. In this she was stimulated by her mother's own permissive views on the subject, by the example of her mother's honored standing in Quaker circles (and hence by Quaker traditions themselves), by her aunt Hannah Whitall Smith, and by the encouragement of her cousin Frank Smith, with whom she had a close early adolescent friendship.

She attended a Friends' school in Baltimore and then the Howland Institute, a Quaker boarding school near Ithaca, N.Y. A teacher at Howland influenced her to devote her life to education instead of medicine, her earlier inclination. Her appetite for learning whetted, she begged to be allowed to enter Cornell University, but her father interposed objections. Although a trustee of the new Johns Hopkins University, James Carey Thomas long retained conventional prejudices against advanced education for women. By prolonged argument and reputedly by tears in which her mother joined, Minnie Thomas won his consent. Upon entering Cornell, as a junior, she exchanged her childhood nickname for her second name, Carey. She obtained her A.B. in 1877 and then persuaded her father to support her in the far bolder step of earning a Ph.D. in Germany, after an unsatisfactory year of private study of Greek at the all-male Johns Hopkins, where she was not allowed to attend classes. At Leipzig, in company with her long-time close companion, Mary Gwinn, she was freely welcomed in the classroom, and other women students were in evidence, but neither Leipzig nor any other German university would grant the Ph.D. degree to women at that time. Therefore after three years she transferred to the University of Zurich, where in November 1882 she obtained the degree summa cum laude—the first foreigner (and woman) to do so. Her dissertation in English philology, on the medieval epic *Sir Gawayne and the Green Knight*, was to be highly regarded by specialists more than eighty years later (see Larry D. Benson in *Modern Philology*, August 1961).

Yet Germany, and her own scholarly diligence, existed for her primarily as tokens of woman's capability. She was transforming herself into an example. She admitted that the work itself was drudgery. An Anglophile, she detested German civilization. Germany connoted rigorous, painful excellence; therefore it was necessary and useful in her struggle to prove to Americans that women could achieve the same intellectual distinction as men. In contrast, her natural bent was toward "culture": the random appreciation of drama, poetry, and fiction. In these years it was this bent which she said explicitly she was "trying to suppress." Carey Thomas' basic interests were determined during her childhood, and only in a formal sense was she one of the many importers of German standards into the American academic scene. All her life she retained the ability to travel widely, yet be unaffected by her surroundings.

In 1880 Joseph W. Taylor, a Quaker physician and businessman, bequeathed the funds to found a new women's college, under Quaker auspices, to be named Bryn Mawr. Carey Thomas' father and other relatives were appointed trustees. In 1882, after her triumph at Zurich, she wrote to the trustees asking to become its president, although women's colleges then usually had male executives. Mistrusting her youthful inexperience, the trustees instead appointed her dean and professor of English. The college opened in 1885. President James E. Rhoads lacked her vigor, and, although her role in administration during the earliest years can be exaggerated, by 1892 she was acting president in all but name. When Rhoads retired in 1894 she was named his successor by the margin of a single vote among the conservative and still doubtful trustees. She remained president of Bryn Mawr College

until 1922, simultaneously serving as dean until 1908. Unlike many heads of small colleges, she had little interest in teaching; as early as 1888 she reduced her classroom duties in favor of administrative tasks, and she stopped teaching entirely around 1894. She maintained no contact with her professional field of scholarship.

Her educational views stemmed from her dominant concern that Bryn Mawr, unlike other women's colleges, must maintain standards equal to or better than the most demanding men's institutions. Thus she insisted that entrance examinations at Bryn Mawr must be as rigid as those for Harvard, and she would not permit students to be admitted by certificate, that is, by the word of informally accredited schoolmasters. The curriculum itself was designed above all to be rigorous. From the Johns Hopkins she copied Daniel Coit Gilman's "group system," whereby students might choose among a variety of parallel courses (akin to but broader than twentieth-century "majors"), which they must pursue in logical sequence. In addition students had to fulfill other requirements which, in the instance of foreign languages, were extremely demanding because Carey Thomas subjected each student to a terrifying oral examination in sight translation.

Whatever connoted dilettantism or practical vocational training outside the scholarly fields of learning was shunned at Bryn Mawr, especially in the early years. Thus Carey Thomas continued largely to "suppress" her own deeply amateurish love of cultivation. Though an art department was established and, much later, music, the ideal of liberal culture found its main expression not in the curriculum but in the Oxonian residence halls—and in speeches she made around 1910, a season when it had become respectable once again to emphasize liberal arts as a goal of higher education in Eastern American academic circles. More consistently, and because she also found it dilettantish, she vigorously opposed the "free" elective system practiced at Charles W. Eliot's Harvard. Bryn Mawr girls were not to be allowed to choose their studies at random. Instead, Carey Thomas' educational thinking combined encouragement for scholarship along Germanic lines with the older American collegiate tradition of "mental discipline," which had been marked by rigorous assumptions concerning the sharpening of mental faculties on the grindstone of Greek, Latin, and mathematics. Side by side with the "up-to-date" provision of graduate work at Bryn Mawr— which was partly to serve as bait for young instructors—she persisted in emphasizing the need for "discipline," long after such phrases had lost their currency in American academic rhetoric. It is not surprising that one of the first acts of her successor in 1922 was to revise the entire curriculum in the direction of greater student freedom. Carey Thomas' educational ideas were only partially up to date even in 1894; in large measure Bryn Mawr represented a curious survival, until 1922, of disciplinary aims abandoned nearly everywhere else by 1890.

Most of those who knew Carey Thomas agreed that her personality was far more memorable than her ideas. Vigorous and intense, she possessed a magnetism which was enhanced by her strikingly dignified beauty. She was temperamentally both partisan and autocratic; seldom did she voluntarily relinquish authority until she achieved victory or lost interest. Thus she invited either adoration or profound mistrust; few who watched her could remain neutral. Those who were loyal to her admired her impetuous driving force and her masterful stratagems, glorying even in the deceit of which she was capable; those who mistrusted her saw these qualities as defects sometimes damaging to Bryn Mawr.

Among the faculty she was more apt to win the hearts of the women than the men. Luring young scholars of promise, she was forced to see these men use Bryn Mawr as a convenient rung in the ladder of their own careers, rather than prizing it as an end in itself. (Of the entire original faculty, only one woman remained at Bryn Mawr until retirement.) Desperately concerned for the reputation of the college, Carey Thomas worsened matters by using devious schemes to keep professors from departing. Her zealous tyranny extended into almost all aspects of policy. She was often shrewd, but she was headstrong and too energetically unreflective to be consistent (her speeches abounded with "slips" which produced merriment, as when she said a third of Bryn Mawr graduates married and half of them had children). Moving in an aura of anecdote, she pushed indefatigably ahead. Yet she admired the few students who stood up to her, and she occasionally knew when to give in. In 1915, after several arbitrary dismissals, a major "revolt" occurred among professors who did not, or could not, take her humorously. Hard pressed, she announced a sudden conversion to the thinking of the newly formed American Association of University Professors and instituted "faculty self-government," not revealing her continued contempt for the idea until 1935.

Although in her curriculum Carey Thomas showed a fearful concern to avoid the stereotype of the finishing school, she did little to relieve the notion that Bryn Mawr catered to the privileged. She never outstepped the social assumptions of her upbringing, in which charity, however generous, was bestowed paternalistically, and in which pride of ancestry posed limits upon egalitarian ideas. She caricatured rather than modified the prejudices of the Eastern seaboard aristocracy in the Progressive Era. A fervent Bull Moose Progressive in 1912, she was of the group which firmly supported England in 1914 and backed the League to Enforce Peace. Moreover, she greeted Lothrop Stoddard's racial Nordicism with enthusiasm, supported the eugenics movement, backed immigration restriction, and said she hoped "the present intellectual supremacy of the white race" would continue "for centuries to come." These views affected Bryn Mawr College, making it unlike Harvard or the University of Pennsylvania in her day. Jewish instructors found it difficult to get promoted; Negroes were never sought as students until after her retirement; and she boasted that she compiled statistics on the ancestries of all her freshmen. Such hereditarian emphases form a fascinating counterpoint to her strongly environmentalist arguments on women's capabilities and her faith in education so far as sexual, not racial, handicaps were concerned. The fascination is enhanced by her later admission that in part she had so stridently insisted upon the biological equality of women because she had begun with private doubts on the matter.

Early in her career at Bryn Mawr, in 1885, Miss Thomas had joined with Mary Gwinn, MARY E. GARRETT, and other girlhood friends in founding the Bryn Mawr School for Girls in Baltimore, which offered a rigorous college preparatory course. Four years later she led the group of feminists who secured the admission of women students to the Johns Hopkins University Medical School by making this the condition of a large gift to its endowment. With the passing years, Miss Thomas' activities on behalf of women's rights became increasingly ardent; these gave her a major place in the suffrage movement during its final two decades. When, in 1906, she began active participation in the College Equal Suffrage League, it was with the tacit understanding that in this, as in everything else, she must be a leader. In 1908 she became the first president of the National College Women's Equal Suffrage League and increased her circuit speeches. This led to intensive work for the National American Woman Suffrage Association, in which, significantly, she acted as a moderating bridge between her own more conservative Eastern wing and the radical faction led by JANE ADDAMS. The illness of Mary Garrett, second of her close companions and a major donor to Bryn Mawr, who lived with Miss Thomas at the college "deanery" from 1906, interrupted her suffrage activities in 1914, and thereafter college affairs and travel much reduced the scale of her campaigning. Yet even after 1920 she could sometimes be deeply involved in feminist politics, switching her allegiance in this period to the uncompromising National Woman's Party.

Her views on women's rights and capabilities were in themselves often both radical and logical. "One man's mind," she said, "differs from another man's mind far more widely than all women's minds differ from all men's." Protective legislation for women in industry was to be opposed, because women should be allowed to compete equally without hindrance in any job. Her central argument insisted that women should enter all the occupations (once she even mentioned bridge building) and particularly that they should claim their share in the learned professions. Her egalitarianism for women was modified in two important respects, however. First, her assumptions were tinged with an explicit elitism: women's colleges should produce rare, exceptional geniuses who would do more for "human advancement" than "thousands of ordinary college graduates." Her affections were centered in these unusual women, whom she pictured as leading "a life of intellectual renunciation." Second, Carey Thomas often wandered from arguments for women's equality to arguments which assumed an unusual, militant, and implicitly distinct role for women. Reluctantly she (who never married) admitted that perhaps half of all women should take husbands, but she emphasized that even this half ought to continue their careers. She also spoke of "a wholly new sex solidarity which is inevitably destined to become a compelling force in the new world." The phrase "sex solidarity" she associated with the recent struggle for women's rights, in which men's motives were deeply distrusted. The contrast between equality and isolationism in her thinking revealed itself in her vacillating attitudes toward coeducation. Often she approved of it, with apparent conviction; yet her conception of and pride in Bryn Mawr catered to the proudly separatist strain in her outlook.

In all her vigorous activity, and with increasing abandon, she enjoyed herself immensely. The linear movement of her life was from duty toward pleasure. Religion she early abandoned in all but name (though she never became antireligious and probably remained a theist). Dutifulness persisted in her temporary submission to the drudgery of scholarship. But, as an executive, she discovered the joys of disciplining others rather than herself (she was a long-term believer in Frederick W. Taylor's program for industrial efficiency). And, after 1915, the sudden inheritance of Mary Garrett's half-million-dollar fortune caused the element of discipline to depart from her life almost entirely, except in educational speeches. Certain social enthusiasms remained: the college's Phoebe Anna Thorne experimental school, in which, unlike the Bryn Mawr curriculum, John Dewey's ideas reigned; its Summer School for Women in Industry (begun in 1921), whereby working girls were brought to the suburban countryside and given cultural uplift for eight weeks. But the later Carey Thomas is preeminently a woman who reveled in luxury, spending four hundred thousand dollars in two decades' time. Living abroad for years at a stretch, arriving in India with thirty-five trunks (and insulating herself from both natives and British), penetrating the Sahara in her private caravan, renting French villas (which she insisted must have central heating), Carey Thomas ended up one of the lonely, wealthy Americans having worldwide flings in the 1920's. Returning to Philadelphia in the depression, encamped in a hotel suite, she survived long enough to address Bryn Mawr College on its fiftieth anniversary (a college which had basically changed and where she was already often a myth or a stranger). A month later, in her seventy-ninth year, she died in Philadelphia of a coronary occlusion; her ashes were placed in the cloisters of the college library.

Her two main causes had been woman suffrage and women's education. In the first, though a latecomer, she had for a time been a leader. In the second, she had initially been an inspiration, though Bryn Mawr was to seem increasingly less significant as an experiment owing to the widening acceptance of coeducation, with which she had had nothing active to do. Her most important impact was as a pioneering example to many restless, able, career-oriented girls of her own time: the militantly individualistic, triumphantly sexless women who became conspicuous in America early in the twentieth century.

[Among Miss Thomas' more useful articles and addresses are: "A Letter from Leipzig," *Alumnus* (Phila.), Mar. 1880; "Address," in *Celebration of* the *Quarter-Centenary of Smith College* (1900), pp. 183–92; *The College Women of the Present and Future* (6-page speech, 1901); "Should the Higher Education of Women Differ from That of Men?" *Educational Rev.*, Jan. 1901; "The College," *ibid.*, Jan. 1905; "Present Tendencies in Women's College and Univ. Education," *ibid.*, Jan. 1908; "College Entrance Requirements," Assoc. of Collegiate Alumnae, *Publications*, Feb. 1901; "The Future of Women in Independent Study and Research," *ibid.*, Feb. 1903; "Education of Women," in Nicholas Murray Butler, ed., *Monographs on Education in the U.S.*, no. 7 (1900). Edith Finch, *Carey Thomas of Bryn Mawr* (1947), is the standard biography; unusually perceptive and penetrating concerning her earlier years, it is too apologetic in discussing her administration, which is better handled in Cornelia L. Meigs' history of Bryn Mawr, *What Makes a College?* (1956). On her family see Helen Thomas Flexner, *A Quaker Childhood* (1940), the reminiscences of her youngest sister. A cousin, Logan Pearsall Smith, has a few vivid sections of reminiscence about her in his *Unforgotten Years* (1938). For faculty reactions to her devious administrative ways see Alvin Johnson, *Pioneer's Progress* (1952), pp. 145–50, and Charles M. Bakewell to George H. Howison, Feb. 8, 1899 (Howison Papers, Univ. of Calif., Berkeley). A number of articles by and about Miss Thomas are in the *Bryn Mawr Alumnae Quart.* (1907–20) and *Alumnae Bull.* (since 1921). Interviews with Mrs. Louise Crenshaw and Mrs. Rustin McIntosh and correspondence with Mrs. Helen Taft Manning were helpful. An extensive collection of Miss Thomas' papers is at Bryn Mawr.]

LAURENCE R. VEYSEY

**THOMAS, Mary Frame Myers** (Oct. 28, 1816–Aug. 19, 1888), physician and suffragist, was born at the home of her maternal grandparents in Bucks County, Pa. She was the younger of two daughters of Samuel Myers, a schoolteacher, and Mary (Frame) Myers, both birthright Friends and descendants of early settlers in eastern Pennsylvania. Not long after her birth her mother died. Her father in 1818 married Paulina Iden, by whom he had five more daughters and two sons; two of the daughters, HANNAH E. MYERS LONGSHORE and Jane Viola Myers, later became pioneer women physicians in Philadelphia. The family lived at first in Silver Spring, Md., a Quaker settlement near Washington, D.C., and then in Washington itself, where Myers, an abolitionist, is said to have helped Benjamin Lundy organize the city's first antislavery meeting. In 1833 he moved to a farm near New Lisbon, Ohio, another Quaker colony. He taught his children at home, took them to the Capitol when in Washington to hear debates in Congress, and introduced them to outdoor work on the Ohio farm.

This, with attendance in local district schools, comprised Mary's early education.

In 1839 she was married to Owen Thomas (1816–1886), and for the next ten years they lived in Salem, Ohio, where three daughters were born to them: Laura, Pauline, and Julia Josephine. An address by LUCRETIA MOTT at the local Friends' Yearly Meeting in 1845 first stirred her interest in woman's rights. About 1849, not long after the birth of their youngest daughter, the Thomases moved to the vicinity of Fort Wayne, Ind. There Mrs. Thomas began the study of medicine with her husband, who had entered medical practice after private study with a preceptor. To do so, as she wrote to a friend, took "the most vigorous discipline of my mind and systematic arrangement of time," for she was determined that her husband and children should not "suffer for any comforts a wife and mother owed them" (*Woman's Journal*, Sept. 29, 1888, p. 308). In September 1853, having by steady sewing provided her family with clothes for six months in advance and having arranged for her children's care, she left for Philadelphia to enroll in the first session of the female department of Penn Medical University in Philadelphia, where her half sister Hannah Longshore was demonstrator in anatomy. Her medical education was interrupted, however, by the long illness and eventual death of her oldest daughter. After attending medical lectures at Western Reserve College in Cleveland in the winter of 1853–54 while her husband was a student there (he graduated in 1854), she resumed her studies at Penn Medical University in the spring of 1856 and received the M.D. degree in July.

Moving that year with her husband to Richmond, Ind., Dr. Mary Thomas began the practice of medicine. During the Civil War she took part in the work of the Sanitary Commission and, by direction of Gov. Oliver P. Morton, carried supplies to the front by steamer; on the return trip she nursed soldiers wounded in the battle of Vicksburg. She later served as an assistant physician with her husband, an army contract surgeon, in a hospital for refugees in Nashville, Tenn. Her husband subsequently shifted to dentistry, which he practiced until his death in 1886. Dr. Mary Thomas remained in medicine and had a distinguished career in Richmond, serving for eight years on the city board of public health and from 1867 onward as physician for the Home for Friendless Girls, which she had helped to found. As a city physician she worked particularly among Negroes, whose cause she had advocated strongly before the war. In 1875, after being rejected twice, she was admitted to the Wayne

County Medical Society; she was elected its president in 1887. She was also the first woman regularly admitted to the Indiana State Medical Society, in 1876. The next year she represented both societies as a delegate to the American Medical Association, one of its earliest women members. Through the State Medical Society, beginning in 1880, she made active efforts to secure the appointment of women physicians in the women's wards of the state hospital for the insane. She was also partly responsible for the building of the women's prison in Indianapolis (1873).

Concurrently with her work in medicine and public health, Dr. Thomas had an active part in movements for social reform. A member of the Methodist Episcopal Church and the Order of Good Templars, she was an ardent advocate of temperance, but she made her chief contribution to the cause of woman suffrage. Though unable to be present, she wrote a letter of support and encouragement to the first Indiana woman's rights conference called in 1851 by AMANDA F. WAY and others. In 1855 she was chosen vice-president and the next year president of the new Indiana Woman's Rights Society. On Jan. 19, 1859, she read a petition to the Indiana General Assembly calling for a married women's property law and a woman suffrage amendment to the state constitution. She edited the *Lily*, a woman's rights paper begun by AMELIA BLOOMER, in 1857, and in 1861 she was associate editor of the *Mayflower*, a suffrage journal in Peru, Ind.

In 1869 Dr. Mary Thomas helped reactivate the prewar woman's rights society as the Indiana Woman Suffrage Association, a state branch of LUCY STONE's American Woman Suffrage Association organized in that year. In 1877 and 1879 she again represented the state association before the Indiana legislature in seeking the ballot for women. She was a frequent speaker at national suffrage conventions and was in 1880 elected to a one-year term as president of the American Woman Suffrage Association. She was president for a time of the state suffrage association as well, but resigned in 1885 owing to failing health. She died three years later in Richmond, of dysentery. Her medical colleagues hailed her as a "faithful worker in everything that aimed to better the human race" (*Transactions* of the Indiana State Medical Society, 1889, p. 210). By her request, six women, representing the Good Templars, the Woman's Christian Temperance Union (of which she had been state superintendent of franchise), and the African Methodist Episcopal Church, were the pallbearers at her funeral, held in the Methodist

church. She was buried in Maple Hill Cemetery in Hartford, Mich., the home of her daughter Mrs. Pauline Heald. Another surviving daughter, Julia Josephine (Thomas) Irvine, a graduate of Cornell University, became professor of Greek (1890) and fourth president of Wellesley College (1894–99).

[The most accurate biographical account, though touching only her medical career, is Frederick C. Waite, "The Three Myers Sisters—Pioneer Women Physicians," *Medical Rev. of Revs.*, Mar. 1933. For her work in woman suffrage, there is material based on her reminiscences and a brief biography in Elizabeth Cady Stanton et al., *Hist. of Woman Suffrage*, I (1881), 306–10, 314; see also III (1886), 533, and IV (1902), 614. Other information, sometimes vague or conflicting, particularly about her Civil War work, can be found in: *Hist. of Wayne County, Ind.*, I (1884), 606–08; Florence M. Adkinson, "The 'Mother of Women,'" *Woman's Jour.*, Sept. 29, 1888, pp. 307–08; obituary in *ibid.*, Sept. 1, 1888, p. 278; and the sketch by her daughter Mrs. Pauline T. Heald in *Mich. Hist. Mag.*, VI (1922), 369–73. See also Indianapolis *News*, Aug. 21, 1888; and her articles and reports in the *Transactions* of the Ind. State Medical Soc., 1880–87. Other information from: Ind. State Library, Indianapolis; Morrisson-Reeves Library, Richmond, Ind.; Hartford (Mich.) Ladies' Library; Am. Medical Assoc.; and Dr. Thomas' death record (Richmond City Board of Health).]

CLIFTON J. PHILLIPS

THOMPSON, Eliza Jane Trimble (Aug. 24, 1816–Nov. 3, 1905), temperance reformer, was born in Hillsboro, Ohio, the only daughter of Allen Trimble, a rising political leader in the state, and his second wife, Rachel Woodrow. A native of Virginia, where his Scotch-Irish Presbyterian grandfather had settled in the seventeenth century, Trimble had moved with his parents to the vicinity of Lexington, Ky., and thence, in 1804, to Highland County, Ohio. The Woodrows were Quakers, also from Virginia. Eliza grew up with two older half brothers and two older brothers in a closely knit family of comfortable circumstances. Her father was a devout Methodist, and her childhood training was deeply religious, with much Bible study; as a child she was awakened every night for midnight prayer. Yet she participated actively in the everyday world, arising at daybreak to go horseback riding with her father.

The family was a prominent one, for her father was acting governor (1822) and governor (1826–30), and an uncle, William R. Trimble, was United States Senator from Ohio (1819–21). Not only was Eliza used to meeting persons of note entertained in her home, but her father's position twice caused threats to her personal safety. An apparent plot was discovered in 1822 in time to prevent her being kidnapped by someone trying to wrest a pardon from the governor for a penitentiary inmate. While she was attending Mr. Picket's private school for girls in Cincinnati, another abduction plot was thwarted, the girl being sheltered for several weeks by family friends, including the wife of Justice John McLean of the United States Supreme Court. On Sept. 21, 1837, she was married to James Henry Thompson, a lawyer from Harrodsburg, Ky., who was an active Whig and later a fervent Republican. After a brief residence in Kentucky, the couple lived for a time in Cincinnati (1838–42), then made their home in Hillsboro.

Mrs. Thompson's fame as a temperance leader came about somewhat fortuitously. Dr. Dio Lewis, the Massachusetts temperance reformer and pioneer in physical education, lectured in Hillsboro on Dec. 23, 1873. Stressing the potential influence of women in combating such evils as excessive drink, he told how his mother, forty years earlier, had secured the closing of a saloon his father patronized by her prayerful appeal to the owner. The next day a group of Hillsboro women met in the Presbyterian church and determined to launch a concerted "crusade" of this sort in their own town. Though Mrs. Thompson had not been present at the Lewis lecture, she had long been interested in temperance reform. Her father had been the first president of the Ohio Temperance Society and in 1836 had taken her to a national temperance convention at Saratoga, N.Y., where she had been the only woman present. From her Presbyterian and Quaker forebears, too, she derived an active idealism and a firm tenacity of purpose which reinforced her own Methodist zeal. Although her husband at first regarded the proposed crusade as "tomfoolery," he gave it his support after his wife became convinced through prayer that she should join the group. Elected their president, she marched the women forth to make a personal appeal to the liquor-selling druggists. On their next sortie the ladies called at a saloon, where, as if by inspiration, Mrs. Thompson knelt on the floor and led the group in prayer. Such visits continued for about three months until stopped by court injunction.

Similar groups of women had appeared almost simultaneously in Fredonia, N.Y., and Washington Court House, Ohio, and for several months the "Crusade," or "Women's War," spread rapidly, aided by widespread newspaper publicity. From it grew the Woman's National Christian Temperance Union, organized at Cleveland, Ohio, in November 1874 in a convention of temperance delegates from seventeen states, Mrs. Thompson among them. Thereafter, unlike some of the other crusade leaders—notably "Mother" ELIZA DANIEL STEWART—"Mother" Thompson played little part in temperance organizations. But as the leader of the Hillsboro crusade, traditionally the start of the campaign, she became a sort of patron saint of the movement.

The Thompsons had eight children: Allen Trimble, Anna Porter, John Henry, Joseph Trimble, Maria Doiress, Mary McArthur, Henry Burton, and John Burton. Mrs. Thompson died at the family home in Hillsboro at the age of eighty-nine, several weeks after suffering a broken hip in a fall. Her funeral was held in the Hillsboro Methodist church, and she was buried in the Hillsboro Cemetery.

["Autobiog. and Correspondence of Allen Trimble," *"Old Northwest" Genealogical Quart.*, July 1906–Jan. 1909; Eliza J. Thompson et al., *Hillsboro Crusade Sketches and Family Records* (1896); Annie Wittenmyer, *Hist. of the Woman's Temperance Crusade* (1882), chap. ii; Mary F. Eastman, *The Biog. of Dio Lewis* (1891), pp. 153–66; Mary Earhart, *Frances Willard* (1944), pp. 138–45; *Hillsboro* (Ohio) *News-Herald*, Nov. 9, 1905; David McBride, *Cemetery Inscriptions of Highland County, Ohio* (1954), p. 244. The Ohio State Museum, Columbus, has a box of Mrs. Thompson's correspondence (including letters from Frances Willard) and a scrapbook, 1875–1903; and there are 173 letters of Mrs. Thompson and her husband at the Cincinnati Hist. Soc.]

FRANCIS P. WEISENBURGER

**THOMPSON, Elizabeth Rowell** (Feb. 21, 1821–July 20, 1899), philanthropist, was born in Lyndon, Vt., the seventh of twelve children and first daughter of Samuel and Mary (Atwood) Rowell. The family Bible recorded her name as Betsy, but she was known from youth as Elizabeth. Her father, a descendant of Thomas Rowell, one of the incorporators of Salisbury, Mass., in the seventeenth century, was born in Weare, N.H.; her mother was from Dorchester, Mass. Samuel Rowell farmed with little success in a series of towns in New Hampshire and Vermont. Elizabeth received a rudimentary education in country schools and at the age of nine hired out as a housemaid, but in spite of her humble circumstances she matured into a well-read and attractive young woman. While visiting Boston in December 1843 she met Thomas Thompson, a wealthy and somewhat eccentric Harvard graduate twenty-three years her senior, who had foresaken theology for the study of art. They were married the following month. Thereafter Elizabeth Thompson shared her husband's twin vocations of art collecting and general benevolence. The couple lived in Boston until 1860, when they moved to New York City. They had no children.

Left by the death of her husband in 1869 with an annual income in excess of $50,000, Mrs. Thompson devoted her remaining three decades to a wide range of charitable objects. She subsidized needy relatives and assisted an unknown number of other individuals. She was a frequent contributor to the woman suffrage and temperance movements, and in support of the latter compiled a statistical tract entitled *The Figures of Hell* (1878). Through her concern with intemperance she also developed an interest in Loring Moody's Institute of Heredity, a forerunner of the eugenics movement. In 1878 she purchased Francis B. Carpenter's painting "The First Reading of the Emancipation Proclamation by President Lincoln to His Cabinet" for $25,000 and presented it to Congress. During the same year, when Congress refused to appropriate funds for an investigation of yellow fever in the Southern states, Elizabeth Thompson offered the government $10,000 to establish a Yellow Fever Commission. In 1879 she gave $1,000 to Bronson Alcott's new Concord (Mass.) School of Philosophy.

Her chief reputation as a philanthropist rests upon two seemingly unrelated concerns: the cooperative colonization of the West, and the support of basic scientific research. Early in the 1870's her genuine humanitarianism, reinforced by a fear of social unrest in the depression-ridden Eastern cities, prompted Mrs. Thompson to underwrite the Chicago–Colorado Colony at Longmont, near Burlington, Colo. Established in 1871, this cooperative community was designed as a safety valve to release the pent-up economic and population pressures on the Atlantic seaboard. A few years later she became an ardent patron of the English freethinker and communitarian reformer George Jacob Holyoake. In 1879 she joined with R. Heber Newton, Felix Adler, and other reform-minded American clergymen in founding the Co-operative Colony Aid Association and sponsored Holyoake's American speaking tour. She also launched the association's short lived newspaper, the *Worker*, and subsidized the Thompson Colony, a communal farming project near Salina, Kans.

Mrs. Thompson first displayed an interest in scientific research in 1873, when she made a gift of $1,000 to the American Association for the Advancement of Science and was enrolled as its first patron. She was attracted by George Holyoake's schemes for intelligent international cooperation as well as his communitarianism,

and when in 1884 the A.A.A.S. and its British counterpart proposed an International Scientific Association, she immediately offered financial aid. The next year she placed $25,000 in the hands of one of the leading advocates of the proposed association, Dr. Charles S. Minot of the Harvard Medical School, as a research fund for the new group. When the International Association failed to materialize, Minot organized the Elizabeth Thompson Science Fund under an independent board of trustees. As one of the first endowments established in the United States for "the advancement and prosecution of scientific research in its broadest sense," the fund not only provided research grants when such grants were rare, but also served as an important precedent for later philanthropists. A week after her gift was announced, Mrs. Thompson explained her varied motives: "The truths of the Bible appeal to me, but not more than the wonderful revelations in Nature, written by God's own hand. . . . Every new discovery in science, every invention, . . . awakens in me always the deepest interest. . . . I count it my privilege to . . . contribute my mite . . . for the advancement of science, the improvement of conditions, the enlargement of liberty, and the spread of peace and good will" (*New York Tribune*, Aug. 25, 1885).

She herself, as she once stated, believed "in the true spirit of religion, of all religions, for I find good in all. I am not a church member, because I could never give my assent to any creed" (Wait, p. 231). As Elizabeth Thompson advanced in years, her generous impulses increasingly clouded her judgment, and unscrupulous individuals often exploited her desire to do good. In December 1890 she suffered an attack of apoplexy, followed by paralysis, which soon left her incapable of managing her affairs. She lived her remaining years with relatives in Stamford, Conn., and died in Littleton, N.H., where she had spent her summers, at the age of seventy-eight. She left an estate of $400,000, with no public bequests.

[Elizabeth Thompson evidently left no personal papers. For published writings, see (besides her fugitive temperance tract) *Heredity. Its Relations to Human Development. Correspondence between Elizabeth Thompson and Loring Moody* (1882). The most complete and reliable genealogical account is Roland Rowell, *Biog. Sketch of Samuel Rowell and Notices of Some of His Descendants* (1898), which includes a biographical sketch of Mrs. Thompson and an excellent photograph of her in middle age. Other useful biographical accounts are: Sheridan P. Wait in *New England Mag.*, Mar. 1888; and the sketches in Frances E. Willard and Mary A. Livermore, eds., *A Woman*

*of the Century* (1893), and *Appletons' Cyc. Am.
Biog.*, VI, 90. Obituaries include *N.Y. Tribune*,
July 22, 25, 1899, *N.Y. Times*, July 22, 1899, and
*Appletons' Annual Cyc.*, 1899, p. 642. Her involvement in cooperative colonization schemes may be
traced in the *N.Y. Times*, June 6, Nov. 19, 1879;
George J. Holyoake, *Among the Americans, and A
Stranger in America* (1881) and *Travels in Search
of a Settler's Guide-Book of America and Canada*
(1884); William F. Zornow, *Kansas: A Hist. of
the Jayhawk State* (1957), p. 188; and James F.
Willard and Colin B. Goodykoontz, eds., *Experiments in Colo. Colonization, 1869–1872* (1926).
The *N.Y. Times*, Oct. 1, 1878, details her efforts
to subsidize the Yellow Fever Commission. For the
history of the Elizabeth Thompson Science Fund,
see *Science*, July 25, Sept. 19, 1884, Aug. 21,
Sept. 11, 1885; and *The Elizabeth Thompson Science Fund, 1886–1911* (pamphlet, n.d.).]

HOWARD S. MILLER

**THOMPSON, Mary Harris** (Apr. 15, 1829–
May 21, 1895), physician and surgeon, was
born near Fort Ann, Washington County, N.Y.,
the second child of a large family. Her parents,
Col. John Harris Thompson and Calista (Corbin) Thompson, were both natives of New
York state. Her paternal grandfather had come
from Dutchess County to found a sawmill and
gristmill; her father was a partner in an iron
mine. An eager student who taught herself
Latin and mathematics, Mary attended a country school for a brief period, then entered the
Troy Conference Academy, a Methodist school
at West Poultney, Vt., and later completed her
nonprofessional education at the Fort Edward
(N.Y.) Collegiate Institute. Because of her father's business reverses, she found it necessary
at both schools to earn her way by serving as
an instructor; in her spare time she studied
astronomy, chemistry, physiology, and anatomy. To prepare herself to teach the last two
subjects, she enrolled at the New England
Female Medical College in Boston, whose
standards of professional training had recently
been raised by the efforts of Dr. MARIE
ZAKRZEWSKA. Here she became so interested
in medicine that she decided to make it her
career. After attending two courses of lectures
at the college she served a year's internship
under Drs. EMILY and ELIZABETH BLACKWELL
at the New York Infirmary for Women and
Children and then returned to Boston to receive the M.D. degree in 1863. Since Philadelphia, Boston, and New York already had wom-
en physicians with whose practices she did not
wish to interfere, she decided to begin her
work in Chicago, a rapidly growing city with
both opportunity and need for her services.

Dr. Thompson arrived in Chicago on July 3,
1863, immediately following her graduation,

and spent the remainder of her life there. The
Civil War had made relief for soldiers and
their families a necessity, and she became
active in the work of the Sanitary Commission.
She soon concluded that a hospital for women
and children was needed in Chicago. Her
efforts and those of the Rev. William H. Ryder
led to a meeting of "benevolent friends of the
soldiers and the poor" from which grew the
Chicago Hospital for Women and Children; it
opened on May 8, 1865, with Dr. Thompson
as head of the medical and surgical staff. The
hospital burned in the Chicago Fire of 1871
but was rebuilt with the aid of the Relief and
Aid Society, which contributed $25,000 on the
condition that twenty-five patients a year
would be treated free of charge.

Dr. Thompson also played an important role
in organizing a women's medical college in
Chicago. Soon after her arrival she had sought
advanced training at Rush Medical College
but, like other women applicants, had been
refused admission. At Chicago's rival medical
school, the Chicago Medical College, however,
she and two other women, who were only beginning their professional training, gained admission during the 1869–70 session through
the efforts of a sympathetic faculty member,
Dr. William H. Byford. In 1870 Dr. Thompson
received her diploma, but the next year, owing
to the opposition of the male members of the
class, who complained that "certain clinical
materials and observations have been omitted
because of the presence of women," the college
reversed its policy and the two other women
were forced to leave without completing their
studies. Dr. Byford then suggested to Dr.
Thompson that a women's medical college be
established in connection with her hospital.
Thus began in 1870, under Dr. Byford's direction, the Woman's Hospital Medical College,
at which Dr. Thompson served as professor of
hygiene (1870–77) and later as clinical professor of obstetrics and gynecology. This, too,
burned in the fire, four days after the opening
of its second year. Undaunted, the students set
up temporary quarters in an old house and
continued their studies. The school was reorganized as the Woman's Medical College in
1879. In 1891 it was made a department of
Northwestern University, as the Northwestern
University Woman's Medical School. A decade
later, when all other medical colleges in Chicago had become coeducational, a separate institution for women was no longer needed and
the school was closed in 1902.

During her lifetime Dr. Thompson was the
best-known woman surgeon in the Middle
West and one of the best-known throughout

the nation. She was the first woman to perform major surgery in Chicago and was for many years the only woman so occupied. A specialist in abdominal and pelvic surgery, she devised an abdominal needle that was widely used. According to the noted surgeon Albert J. Ochsner, it was she who "convinced many of us that it was possible for a woman to be a real physician and surgeon." Dr. Thompson was an important influence in opening the way for women physicians in Chicago, where they at first met great opposition from male members of the profession. The medical journals were uniformly unsympathetic; the *Chicago Medical Examiner,* for example, for a time consistently referred to her as "Miss Doctoress Thompson." Yet by 1881–82 she had won sufficient acceptance to be elected vice-president of the Chicago Medical Society (Andreas, III, 528). Her success was the result not only of her skill but also of her personality, for she was a woman of both charm and reticence. Even-tempered and mild-mannered, she was noted for her kindness and generosity. It was said after her death that she was known as a good Samaritan "who not only gave her professional services to the poor but followed them to their homes, giving food and shelter when needed as well as wise and loving counsel. Her patients, rich and poor, were her friends for life, and knew that they could come to her at all times, always sure of a kindly welcome" (*Chicago Medical Recorder,* Feb. 15, 1905, p. 150). Energetic and determined, she was an indefatigable worker, entering little into the social life of Chicago. She was a firm believer in woman suffrage but agitated the question little beyond the circle of her immediate friends.

Dr. Thompson never married. She died in Chicago of a cerebral hemorrhage in 1895, at the age of sixty-six, and was buried in the village cemetery in her native Fort Ann. After her death the Chicago Hospital for Women and Children was renamed the Mary Thompson Hospital of Chicago, a name it bore until 1927, when it became the Women's and Children's Hospital. In 1905 the board of managers of the hospital presented a memorial bust of her by Daniel Chester French to the Art Institute of Chicago.

[The most dependable account of Mary Thompson's life and the history of her hospital are found in *Woman's Medical School, Northwestern Univ. . . . The Institution and Its Founders* (1896). Additional biographical sketches, of varying merit, are in Chicago Medical Soc., *Hist. of Medicine and Surgery, and Physicians and Surgeons of Chicago* (1922); F. M. Sperry, comp.,

*A Group of Distinguished Physicians and Surgeons of Chicago* (1904); Howard A. Kelly and Walter L. Burrage, *Dict. of Am. Medical Biog.* (1928), pp. 1205–06; and *Biog. Cyc. Am. Women,* II (1925), 176–86. The most important obituary notices are in the Minutes of the Chicago Medical Soc. for June 3, 1895; *Chicago Tribune,* May 22, 1895 (with portrait); and a pamphlet published by the Mary Thompson Hospital of Chicago, *In Memoriam: Mary Harris Thompson* (1896). Further information on the growth of her hospital is provided by the *Annual Reports* of the hospital and in a pamphlet by Edna H. Nelson, *The Women's and Children's Hospital* (1941). The history of medical education for women in Chicago and the Midwest is traced in the *Annual Announcements* of the Woman's Hospital Medical College and in Charles W. Earle, *The Demand for a Woman's Medical College in the West* (1879). A description of the unveiling of the bust of Dr. Thompson, together with tributes by prominent Chicagoans, is printed in "A Memorial to Dr. Mary Harris Thompson," *Chicago Medical Recorder,* Feb. 15, 1905. See also A. T. Andreas, *Hist. of Chicago,* III (1886), 518–20, 528; Helga Ruud, "Woman's Medical College of Chicago," in David J. Davis, ed., *Hist. of Medical Practice in Ill.,* II (1955), 441–49; and Emilia J. Giryotas, "Dr. Mary Harris Thompson," *Jour. of Am. Medical Women's Assoc.,* June 1950.]

THOMAS NEVILLE BONNER

**THOMS, Adah B. Samuels** (Jan. 12, 1863?– Feb. 21, 1943), Negro nursing leader, was born in Virginia, the daughter of Harry and Melvina Samuels. Little is known of her early life. She was educated in the elementary and normal schools of Richmond in the hope of becoming a teacher, and was later married to a Mr. or Dr. Thoms, who may have been a physician. Sometime in the 1890's she came to New York and, after studying elocution at the Cooper Union, decided to try for admission to a course in nursing. She was accepted at the Woman's Infirmary and School of Therapeutic Massage, the only Negro in a class of thirty. After graduation in 1900, she worked in New York City and in North Carolina, where she was head nurse at St. Agnes Hospital in Raleigh.

Mrs. Thoms then decided she needed further training, and in 1903 she entered the new school of nursing at the Lincoln Hospital and Home in New York City. Originally founded in 1839 by a group of public-spirited citizens concerned with the unmet health needs of the sick and indigent colored population in Manhattan, especially the lack of hospital care, this institution had moved to a new site in the Bronx in 1898. Its training school for nurses was one of a large number established in that decade of nationwide expansion in medical

care, including about ten for Negro women—
formed in response to hardening patterns of
segregation. In this group Lincoln, the only
such school in New York City at that time,
quickly became known as a leader. It was
accredited by the Board of Regents of the
University of the State of New York in 1905,
and in 1907, to meet the requirements of the
New York State Board of Nurse Examiners,
the course was extended from twenty-six
months to three years.

Adah Thoms was a dedicated student and
in her second year was made head nurse on a
surgical ward. On her graduation in 1905 she
was employed at the hospital as its operating-
room nurse and supervisor of the surgical division. The next year she was made assistant
director of nurses, a position she held for eighteen years. Often during this period she was
appointed by the board of managers as acting
director of the training school, but despite her
obvious competence, it was not then the custom to promote a Negro to a major administrative position; the school's first Negro director
was appointed in 1954. Mrs. Thoms early recognized the importance of public health nursing, and as acting director of the school in
1917 she added a course in this new field to
the curriculum, taught by a member of the
visiting-nurse service of the Henry Street Settlement, and took it herself. She also took
special courses at the New York School of
Philanthropy (later the New York School of
Social Work), Hunter College, and the New
School for Social Research.

Throughout her career Mrs. Thoms was an
active member of professional organizations.
Through these she worked in many ways to
increase educational and employment opportunities for Negro nurses, then restricted almost
entirely to hospitals and services for the care
of Negro patients. In 1908 she played a leading part in the organization of the National
Association of Colored Graduate Nurses, inviting the founding group to meet in New York
under the sponsorship of the Lincoln Hospital
alumnae association. The Association's declared
purpose was to combat discrimination within
and outside the profession, develop leadership
among Negro nurses, and advance professional
standards. She served as its first treasurer, and
from 1916 to 1923 as president. During the
latter period she strengthened the national
registry the Association had set up in New
York, campaigned for better employment opportunities for qualified Negro nurses in hospitals and public health agencies, and worked
to raise admission standards in nursing schools;
after 1920 she encouraged Negro nurses not

only to use their newly acquired right of suffrage but also to urge their patients to do likewise. Within the Association she led the dominant group which opposed merger with the
National Medical Association, believing it wiser
to work toward amalgamation with the American Nurses Association, a goal achieved in
1951, eight years after her death.

In 1912 Mrs. Thoms took part in the meeting of the International Council of Nurses at
Cologne, Germany, one of the first three Negro
delegates to this body. Their attendance led
subsequently to membership in the council
of Negro nurses from Africa, South America,
and the Caribbean. On this trip Mrs. Thoms
was able to travel widely, visiting hospitals in
Europe.

During World War I, Mrs. Thoms as president of the National Association of Colored
Graduate Nurses waged from 1917 on a continuing campaign by letter and in person with
the American Red Cross for admission of Negro
nurses to its Nursing Service, the only avenue
into the United States Army Nurse Corps.
JANE A. DELANO, chairman of the National
Committee on Red Cross Nursing Service, informed Mrs. Thoms of her organization's willingness to utilize Negro nurses both at home
and overseas, but this the Surgeon General
refused to authorize. The first Negro nurse,
Mrs. Frances Elliot Davis, a graduate of
Freedmen's Hospital School of Nursing in
Washington, D.C., was enrolled in the Red
Cross in July 1918, but no Negro was assigned
to duty until December, when, with the great
influenza epidemic surging through the United
States, eighteen qualified Negro nurses were
appointed to the Army Nurse Corps and stationed at Camp Grant, Ill., and Camp Sherman, Ohio, with full rank and pay. At neither
camp were the patients segregated, and the
Negro nurses were assigned to all services;
they were, however, forced to live in separate
facilities on the base.

Adah Thoms retired from the Lincoln Hospital in 1923. She was subsequently married
to Henry Smith, who died, however, within a
year. During her retirement she continued to
be active in the American Nurses Association,
of which she had been an early member, and
the National Organization for Public Health
Nursing, doing much to lay the groundwork
for the later (1951) integration of the National
Association of Colored Graduate Nurses into
these organizations. She also wrote *Pathfinders:
A History of the Progress of Colored Graduate
Nurses* (1929), to which LILLIAN D. WALD contributed the preface. For this history and for
her wartime efforts for the acceptance of Negro

women in the Red Cross nursing corps she was in 1936 chosen as the first recipient of the National Association's Mary Mahoney Medal (see MARY ELIZABETH MAHONEY).

In Harlem, where she made her home, Mrs. Thoms was an active board member of the Harlem Branch of the Young Women's Christian Association, the Harlem Committee of the New York Tuberculosis and Health Association, and the New York Urban League. Through these organizations, as well as St. Mark's Methodist Church and the Hope Day Nursery, the only facility at that time offering care to Negro children of working mothers, she served the city that had fascinated her on her arrival, the city she always believed had great promise for the advancement of the Negro nurse. Toward the end of her life Mrs. Thoms' sight failed, owing to diabetes, which was a contributory cause of her death from arteriosclerotic heart disease in 1943. She was buried in Woodlawn Cemetery. She had played an important role in guiding the progress of Negro women in the field of nursing, inspiring many of them to follow her example in working toward their acceptance in all areas of this profession.

[Mrs. Thoms' *Pathfinders*, including Miss Wald's biographical preface; Mabel K. Staupers, *No Time for Prejudice: A Story of the Integration of Negroes in Nursing in the U.S.* (1961); personal knowledge of Mrs. Thoms' professional life; death certificate from N.Y. City Dept. of Health (which gives her birth year as 1883). Mrs. Gwendolyn S. Bourne and Marguerette Creth Jackson, both Lincoln graduates; Mrs. A. Kellar of St. Mark's Church; and Miss Clinton Dingle, a member, with Mrs. Kellar, of the board of managers of the Y.W.C.A. and the Hope Day Nursery, were also helpful.]

MABEL KEATON STAUPERS

THORPE, Rose Alnora Hartwick (July 18, 1850–July 19, 1939), popular poet, was born in Mishawaka, Ind., where her parents, Mary Louisa (Wight) and William Morris Hartwick, were pioneer settlers. The second of five children, Rose was an imaginative and inquisitive child who relished the school readers, the religious tracts, and the word lists that were offered to her. As her father worked at his trade of tailoring—first in Indiana, later in Kansas during a period of terrible drought, and finally in Litchfield, Mich.—she turned more and more to the world of poets like Longfellow and LYDIA SIGOURNEY. She attended grammar school and high school in Litchfield (graduating in 1868) and padded out her literary education with the poetry and fiction that she found in the popular magazines of the day. When she was fifteen she discovered in *Peter-

*son's Magazine* for September 1865 a short story entitled "Love and Loyalty" that was to give her the plot for one of the most popular of all American poems of sentiment.

The *Peterson's* story, set in the English Civil War, told how Bessie, the beautiful daughter of a forester, saved her innocent Cavalier lover from execution by the Puritans as a spy. Sentenced to be shot when the curfew bell struck, Basil was given a reprieve when Bessie raced up the steps of the church tower and silenced the bell by clinging to the clapper. She then sped to Cromwell and by her personal plea won a pardon. Writing on a school slate, it is said, Rose Hartwick quickly reworked the tale into the long, regular Longfellowlike lines that she had been writing throughout her childhood. Called "Curfew Must Not Ring Tonight," it ended with Cromwell sending Bessie back to her pardoned lover:

In his brave, strong arms he clasped her, kissed the
  face upturned and white,
Whispered, "Darling, you have saved me, Curfew
  will not ring to-night."

The poem became a family and neighborhood favorite, and in 1870 she sent it to a Detroit newspaper, the *Commercial Advertiser*, which had previously printed some of her verse. It was an immediate success. Before the end of the century it was printed and reprinted throughout the country and translated abroad; there were few lyceums, schools, and pulpits that did not echo its ringing romanticism. Rose Hartwick had early reached her literary climax —though unfortunately without benefit of copyright and hence without financial return.

On Sept. 11, 1871, she was married to Edmund Carson Thorpe, a carriage maker and author of German dialect verses. They had two daughters: Lulo May (who later helped with the profuse illustrations of her mother's books) and Lillie Maud. Mrs. Thorpe continued to write verse for such publications as *Youth's Companion, St. Nicholas, Wide Awake,* and the *Detroit Free Press.* When her husband's business failed ten years after their marriage, she went to work as an editor and writer for Fleming H. Revell, the most successful religious publisher of the day. She edited and was the chief author of moralistic monthlies like *Temperance Tales, Well-Spring,* and *Words of Life,* magazines devoted to the causes of home, temperance, and Sunday school. She also turned out five books of fiction for children, beginning with *Fred's Dark Days* (1881).

After her husband was stricken with tuberculosis the family moved to San Antonio, Texas —where Mrs. Thorpe wrote "Remember the

Alamo," another popular success—and, in 1886, to California, where she lived in or near San Diego for the rest of her life. By 1912, when the best of her newspaper and magazine verse was collected in *The Poetical Works of Rose Hartwick Thorpe*, she had all but passed from the literary scene. After her husband's death in 1916, Rose Thorpe took some part in woman suffrage and Y.W.C.A. work and in the Woman's Club of San Diego. She died in San Diego of a heart attack in 1939, on the day after her eighty-ninth birthday. Her remains were cremated.

A single poem has assured Rose Thorpe the attention of students of American literary and social life. Her "Curfew Must Not Ring Tonight," with its Christian morality, its crushing optimism, and its automatic craftsmanship, is a choice example of the sentimental verse to which the middle-class reader was addicted throughout the nineteenth century.

[George Wharton James, *Rose Hartwick Thorpe and the Story of "Curfew Must Not Ring Tonight"* (1916), is the basic source of information on her life and work. Her own account of the "Curfew" story appeared in the Chicago *Inter Ocean* for June 5, 1887. See also Edgar J. Hinkel and William E. McCann, eds., *Biogs. of Calif. Authors*, vol. I (1942); *Nat. Cyc. Am. Biog.*, X, 252; *Woman's Who's Who of America*, 1914–15; and the *N.Y. Times*, July 21 (obituary) and 22 (editorial), 1939.]

CARLIN T. KINDILIEN

**THUMB, Mrs. Tom.** *See* STRATTON, Mercy Lavinia Warren Bump.

**THURBER, Jeannette Meyers** (Jan. 29, 1850–Jan. 2, 1946), patron of music, was born in New York City, the daughter of Henry and Anne Maria Coffin (Price) Meyers (or Meyer). Her mother, born in Wappingers Falls, N.Y., was of old American stock. Her father, originally from Copenhagen, Denmark, had come to New York in 1837. A devoted amateur violinist with independent means, he did much to stimulate his daughter's interest in music. She was educated privately in New York and Paris, becoming fluent in French and German and receiving a thorough grounding in music. On Sept. 15, 1869, she was married to Francis Beattie Thurber, a successful merchant in wholesale groceries, later a lawyer and a principal organizer of the National Anti-Monopoly League in 1881. They had three children, Jeannette M., Marianna Blakeman, and Francis Beattie.

Soon after her marriage, with the sympathetic backing of her husband, Mrs. Thurber became interested in improving the facilities for musical education in the United States. Her first benefactions were to provide funds for the training abroad of talented Americans, but gradually she evolved the plan of a national conservatory in which thorough musical instruction along European lines would raise the level of professional performance in the United States. Although such a conservatory would have to begin modestly with private funds, Mrs. Thurber and her adviser, Judge William G. Choate, were confident that in time the public would recognize its services with increasing support, culminating in financial grants from the national government, as in Europe. Meanwhile, as these plans matured in her mind, she supported generously the concerts for young people conducted by Theodore Thomas in 1883 and the first Wagner festival given in America, in 1884.

With opera and the newly built Metropolitan Opera House very much in the air, Mrs. Thurber began her larger project in the operatic realm. Securing a charter from New York State in 1885 for a National Conservatory of Music, she opened its first "branch," or functioning department, that December as the American School of Opera, with eighty-four pupils. To complement it she planned an opera company that would provide employment and musical opportunities for graduates of the conservatory while bringing the masterpieces of opera to the public outside the metropolitan area. But the American Opera Company, as it was named, proved a vast and overly ambitious undertaking. To meet the exacting ideals of the man engaged as musical director, Theodore Thomas, all the elements of performance—soloists, chorus, orchestra, ballet, scenery, and costumes—had to be balanced and excellent. Eschewing the star system, the operas were to be sung in English, preferably by American singers. A notable group of wealthy men, including Andrew Carnegie and August Belmont, agreed to serve as incorporators, and Mrs. Thurber gave unstintingly of her time and resources.

The company's first performance took place Jan. 4, 1886, at the Academy of Music, New York City. Artistically it reached its objectives, despite the shortcomings of some soloists; the chorus, ballet, and mise-en-scène set standards surpassing those of any group, American or foreign, that had appeared in the United States. But financially the project was a disaster. When the company failed to show a profit in its first season, the incorporators withdrew. Reorganization as the National Opera Company kept it alive through a second season, but in June 1887 the company disintegrated. Yet the man who suffered most in the debacle, Theodore Thomas, believed that the original plans had been splendidly conceived and could have succeeded had the incorporators contributed more than their names.

With the dissolution of the opera company, Mrs. Thurber concentrated on her school, now officially called the National Conservatory of Music. Located in New York City, admitting students without regard to race, it charged only nominal fees, none at all for very talented applicants. With its course of study expanded into a full curriculum of musical subjects, the conservatory was incorporated by act of Congress on Mar. 3, 1891, with power to grant diplomas and confer honorary degrees—the only school of music to be so recognized. Its first director, from 1885 to 1889, was Jacques Bouhy, a noted French baritone who had created the role of Escamillo in *Carmen*. As his successor Mrs. Thurber, appreciating the value of a world figure as director, persuaded the composer Antonin Dvořák to accept the post. During his three-year stay (1892–95) he wrote at her suggestion several compositions utilizing American folk idioms, including his Symphony No. 9, *From the New World*. The conservatory's faculty included such notables as Rafael Joseffy, Adele Margulies, CAMILLA URSO, Victor Herbert, Henry T. Finck, and James G. Huneker; the directors succeeding Dvořák were Emil Paur (1899–1902) and Vassily Safonoff (1906–09). Its excellent work in this period was recognized abroad. Mrs. Thurber continued her financial support and her active role of president, but support from the musical public and the government did not materialize, and the conservatory gradually declined. Though its act of incorporation was renewed, and though as late as 1946 attempts were made to breathe life into an institution which still existed on paper, it had, to all practical intent, ceased to function about 1920.

The critic James Huneker, who once served as Mrs. Thurber's secretary, found her striking, with "fine, dark, eloquent eyes." Apart from her musical activities, she avoided publicity and had no taste for display. Her summers were spent in the Catskills at the Onteora Club, which she and her husband had helped to organize. She was interested in the Y.W.C.A., the Woman's Exchange, and the Woman's Art School of Cooper Union, and was a member of the Presbyterian Church and the Daughters of the American Revolution. She died of a cerebral hemorrhage at the age of ninety-five in Bronxville, N.Y. Huneker summed up her career in his statement that more was accomplished "by her failures than [by] other peo-

ple's successes." Certainly she contributed more to American music than any other nonprofessional before the noted philanthropist Elizabeth Sprague Coolidge (d. 1953).

[Thurber Scrapbooks (6 vols.), N.Y. Public Library; Merton R. Aborn, "The Influence on Am. Musical Culture of Dvořák's Sojourn in America" (unpublished Ph.D. dissertation, Ind. Univ., 1965); *Nat. Cyc. Am. Biog.*, Current Vol. D, p. 216, a sketch prepared with Mrs. Thurber's approval, according to correspondence in the files of the publishers, James T. White & Co., N.Y. City; Mrs. Thurber's letters in the N.Y. *World*, Jan. 10, 27, 1887, and in the *N.Y. Times*, Jan. 1, 1928; her article "Dvořák as I Knew Him," *Etude*, Nov. 1919; article on the Nat. Conservatory in *Harper's Weekly*, Dec. 13, 1890; *N.Y. Times* editorial, Jan. 12, 1946; obituary in *Musical America*, Jan. 10, 1946; Henry T. Finck, *My Adventures in the Golden Age of Music* (1926); James G. Huneker, *Steeplejack* (1928); Rose Fay Thomas, *Memoirs of Theodore Thomas* (1911); correspondence with Mr. Francis B. Thurber, Jr.; biographical references compiled by Jorge Bruguera, Carnegie Library School, Carnegie Inst. of Technology; death record from N.Y. State Dept. of Health. Though her death record gives her maiden name as "Meyer," the sketch she approved for the *Nat. Cyc. Am. Biog.* uses the spelling "Meyers."]

DENA J. EPSTEIN

THURSBY, Emma Cecilia (Feb. 21, 1845–July 4, 1931), concert singer and teacher, was born in Williamsburgh, N.Y. (now part of Brooklyn), the second daughter and second of five children of John Barnes Thursby, a rope manufacturer, and Jane Ann (Bennett) Thursby. Emma's great-grandfather Samuel Thursby had emigrated in 1796 from Belfast, Ireland; her mother was of French and Dutch extraction, her ancestors including Huguenots who had settled in Brooklyn in 1659. The family, of comfortable means during Emma's childhood, lived in the still-quiet town of Williamsburgh, where their life centered around the Old Bushwick (Dutch) Reformed Church. Emma early showed musical talent which her parents, admirers of Jenny Lind, encouraged. She first sang publicly at the age of five in the Bushwick church; while attending Miss E. N. Duryee's primary school in Flatbush, she appeared in school concerts. In the fall of 1857 she entered the Bethlehem (Pa.) Female Seminary, where she received excellent musical training under Sylvester and Francis Wolle. Her father's failing health and financial difficulties, however, caused her to return in the spring of 1859 to Brooklyn, where she attended classes at St. Joseph's Roman Catholic Convent until her father's death and the failure of the cordage business in November 1859. She then left school and gave private music lessons, becoming the family's emotional as well as financial mainstay.

Not until the close of the Civil War did she turn from a teaching to a singing career. Because of a moral scruple against opera she confined herself at first to church work. She began as soloist in the choir of the Bedford Avenue Reformed Dutch Church in Brooklyn at an annual salary of $150 and then moved on to other posts, including three years (1868–71) at Henry Ward Beecher's famous Plymouth Church in Brooklyn, of which she became a member in 1869 and with which she maintained a close affiliation throughout Beecher's lifetime. Her local fame grew. In 1876 the Broadway Tabernacle in New York City won her from Dr. Edwin H. Chapin's Church of the Divine Paternity for an annual salary of $3,000, the highest offered an American church soloist at that time. In April 1877, however, she gave up church singing in order to devote her full time to the increasing demands of concert appearances.

Miss Thursby, who had been supplementing her income by giving singing lessons, had meanwhile resumed her own vocal studies: at first, in 1867, with Julius Meyer, a former pupil of Mendelssohn, and in 1871 with Achille Errani. Errani advised her to go to Europe, and in June of 1872 she left for Milan, where she studied with Francesco Lamperti and Antonio Sangiovanni. Her stay abroad was cut short, however, and in 1873 she returned to New York and the tutelage of Errani. In August 1875 she began lessons with Mme. Erminia Mansfield-Rudersdorff (mother of the actor Richard Mansfield), doubtless her most influential teacher, as well as an invaluable business adviser and friend. Only once, apparently, did she seriously consider marriage—in 1873, to Edward William Hitchcock, Presbyterian minister of the American church in Paris—but the demands of her career and her family's needs prevailed.

Emma Thursby had appeared in numerous concerts from 1865 to 1874, singing with such notable artists as Ole Bull, the Norwegian violinist, and the conductor Theodore Thomas. Yet not until her concert with Patrick Gilmore's 22nd Regiment Band at the Philadelphia Academy of Music on Nov. 27, 1874, did she break "the bonds of a local reputation." The following January she made an extended tour with the Gilmore band that took her to Boston, Washington, Chicago, St. Louis, Louisville, and other cities. She had also sung frequently in oratorios, beginning with her appearance in the Brooklyn Musical Association's perform-

ance of Haydn's *Creation* on Apr. 15, 1868, and continuing with the Handel and Haydn Society in Brooklyn under the direction of Leopold Damrosch and the Boston Handel and Haydn under Carl Zerrahn. As her concert work grew predominant, she sang in a joint concert with Hans von Bülow at Chickering Hall in New York on Nov. 29, 1875, and at a Harvard Musical Association symphony concert in Boston the following January. That spring she toured California, again with Gilmore; in the fall of 1876 she appeared with Mark Twain in a series of four programs for the Redpath Lyceum. Standard Thursby concert pieces were the Proch *Variations* and Mozart's aria "Mia speranza adorata," the latter earning her the reputation of "the greatest Mozartian vocalist of her day." Critics praised the clarity and delicacy of her voice and her seemingly effortless control. Her audiences were large, and noisily appreciative.

After giving up church singing, she signed a $100,000 contract with the impresario Maurice Strakosch for a series of concerts in the United States, Canada, and Europe, though the European part was not carried out. It was under other auspices, therefore, that she made her London debut at St. James's Hall on May 22, 1878. This was followed by highly successful appearances in two important concert series, the Monday Popular Concerts and the Mme. Jenny Viard-Louis Concerts, and engagements in Manchester, Brighton, and Edinburgh. She made her Paris debut at the Théâtre de Châtelet on Mar. 23, 1879, and sang at the Pasdeloup Concerts; though unknown and unpublicized, she won the unqualified esteem of the Paris musical world. Another six months in England preceded her return to the United States late in 1879. A German tour, beginning at Bad Ems in August 1880, further established her among the foremost of European concert singers. She returned in February 1881 to Paris, where she became the first American to receive the commemorative medal of the Société des Concerts of the Paris Conservatoire. For the next three years she continued extensive tours in Europe and America. In Holland, Spain, and the Scandinavian countries she drew large and enthusiastic audiences. Her success brought renewed pressure to undertake opera, but she was reluctant now to leave the security of her position as a concert singer for the heavily competitive operatic stage.

Two deaths in the family—her mother's in June 1884 and her older sister's the following January—together with the failing health of Maurice Strakosch, her manager since 1879, and her own weariness, caused her concerts to become more and more infrequent during the next decade. She made her last appearance before a large audience in December 1895, at Chicago. Thereafter she devoted herself to teaching, which she continued until 1924; her most famous pupil was the opera singer Geraldine Farrar. From 1905 to 1911 Emma Thursby was a professor at the Institute of Musical Art in New York City, directed by Frank Damrosch. She also traveled extensively, making several trips to Europe and one, in 1903, to Japan; her Fridays at home, begun in 1889, became fashionable social and musical events. As a follower of Swami Vivekananda, a Hindu monk, she promoted his lectures in New York; she also participated in Sarah J. Farmer's Green-Acre Congresses at Eliot, Maine, which undertook the comparative study of religion, philosophy, ethics, and sociology. In 1924 Miss Thursby suffered a paralytic attack which left her an invalid, although she continued to be mentally alert and active. She died of endocarditis and arteriosclerosis at her home in Gramercy Park in New York City in 1931, aged eighty-six. She was buried in the Cemetery of the Evergreens, Brooklyn.

Emma Thursby's voice, ranging from middle C to E-flat above the staff, was remarkable for its flexibility, power, and bell-like clarity. As a popular public figure, she was, perhaps, most striking in her lack of sensational qualities or activities; according to a *Chicago Times* correspondent, "altogether she looked like a sensible American girl of a type as esteemed as it is usual." In her later life she seems to have become more sophisticated, yet she never entirely lost the modesty of a sheltered childhood. A hard worker, she demanded the best of her voice, and at a time when singers were judged by and acclaimed for their European training, she built a successful career on a basis that was undeniably American.

[The principal source is Richard McC. Gipson, *The Life of Emma Thursby* (1940), a detailed biography based on a collection of Miss Thursby's diaries, letters, programs, clippings, etc., in the N.-Y. Hist. Soc. Her N.Y. and Brooklyn appearances, 1864–93, are chronicled in George C. D. Odell, *Annals of the N.Y. Stage*, vols. VII–XV (1931–49). For contemporary comment, see *Dwight's Jour. of Music*, 1877 ff., especially Mar. 31, 1877. See also references in Geraldine Farrar, *The Story of an Am. Singer* (1916), and Walter Damrosch, *My Musical Life* (1926). Death record from N.Y. City Dept. of Health.]

VIOLA L. SCOTT

**TIBBLES, Susette La Flesche** (1854–May 26, 1903), spokesman for Indian rights, was born in a primitive village of the Omaha tribe near the site of present-day Bellevue, Nebr. Her father, Joseph La Flesche (Iron Eye), was the son of a French fur trader, also Joseph La Flesche, and an Indian woman variously mentioned in family papers as a Ponca or an Omaha. Iron Eye grew up among the Sioux, then lived for a time in St. Louis with his father, whom he accompanied on trading expeditions. He thus learned French (though never English), observed many white men, and came into contact with several Indian tribes. He became closely associated with Big Elk, one of the two principal chiefs of the Omahas, who, having no heir, designated Iron Eye as his successor. Convinced that the white man had come to stay and that the Indian must adopt his ways, Iron Eye became a Christian, and as chief from 1853 to 1864 and a leader until his death in 1888 he guided the Omahas with considerable skill through their difficult transition. Following Omaha custom, he had several wives, with children by two. One, Ta-ni-ne, was an Omaha; the other, Mary (One Woman), was the daughter of an Ioway (and part Omaha-Otoe) woman, Ni-co-mi, and of Dr. John Gale, a surgeon with the United States Army. Iron Eye gave equal opportunity to both families, but the children of Mary (who had herself been brought up by the white fur trader Peter Sarpy) swung to the white man's ways, left the reservation, and married whites, whereas the children of Ta-ni-ne, though educated at Hampton Institute, mostly returned to the reservation and Indian ways. One of the latter, however—Francis La Flesche—became a protégé of the anthropologist ALICE CUNNINGHAM FLETCHER and later himself an authority on Indian culture, serving on the staff of the Bureau of American Ethnology. Of Iron Eye's children by Mary, one daughter became a teacher, one, Rosalie La Flesche Farley, managed a large and complicated stock-raising business while bringing up eight children, and one, SUSAN LA FLESCHE PICOTTE, became a physician—probably the first Indian woman to take a medical degree—and founded a hospital in the Omaha country.

Susette La Flesche was the eldest daughter and second of five children born to Iron Eye and Mary. In the year of her birth the Omahas relinquished by treaty their hunting grounds in eastern Nebraska, reserving only a small tract on the Missouri River, and it was on this reservation that the girl grew up. There, at the age of eight, she began attending a Presbyterian mission school. Her earnest desire for a good education reached the ears of the Presbyterian proprietor of a girls' seminary, the Elizabeth (N.J.) Institute, who invited her there as a student. Graduating about 1873, she returned to the Omaha reservation and became a teacher in one of the government schools.

Her career as an Indian reformer grew out of an episode that first widely stirred the American conscience on the nation's treatment of the red man. In 1877 the federal government, having inadvertently assigned the lands of the Poncas, on the Dakota–Nebraska border, to the warlike Sioux, forcibly removed the Poncas to the Indian Territory. A third of the tribe died there of illness, and when Standing Bear, the Ponca chief, set out in 1879 with a group of his followers to return to his homeland, he was pursued by the military, arrested, and ordered back to the Indian Territory. An Omaha newspaperman, Thomas Henry Tibbles, now came to the Ponca chief's defense and, by publicizing the case, helped bring about Standing Bear's release in a court decision enunciating the principle that an Indian is a person in the eyes of the law. Tibbles then began a lecture tour of the East to publicize the Ponca wrongs, taking with him Standing Bear as well as Francis and Susette La Flesche, the latter serving as Standing Bear's interpreter.

Wearing her Indian costume and using her Indian name, Inshta Theumba, or Bright Eyes, the attractive Susette seemed to Easterners the very model of an Indian princess. The group was received with special warmth in Massachusetts. Sympathetic citizens—among them Edward Everett Hale, Wendell Phillips, Alice M. Longfellow, Prof. James B. Thayer of the Harvard Law School, and the young Louis Brandeis—organized the Boston Indian Citizenship Committee and bombarded Washington with demands for change. Other reformers took up the cause, notably Senator Henry L. Dawes and the novelist HELEN HUNT JACKSON, whose interest in Indian rights was first stirred by hearing Susette and her companions in Boston in 1879. In helping to dramatize the Poncas' removal, Susette La Flesche thus contributed to the ultimate passage of the Dawes Severalty Act of 1887, which authorized the allotment of reservation land, with citizenship rights, to individual Indians.

During much of the agitation for the Dawes Act, Susette La Flesche continued to lecture on Indian affairs, at first with Standing Bear and his party and then with Thomas Tibbles, to whom she was married on July 23, 1881; they had no children. On several occasions the two testified before Congressional committees. In 1886, with the passage of the Dawes Act in sight, they embarked under the auspices of the Pond lyceum bureau for a ten-month lecture tour of England, where Bright Eyes was well received.

She gained some standing as a writer and an artist as well as a speaker. In 1881 she gave a paper before the Association for the Advancement of Women on "The Position, Occupation and Culture of Indian Women." She contributed stories to newspapers and magazines, among them St. Nicholas, and illustrated the book Oo-Mah-Ha Ta-Wa-Tha (Omaha City), by Fannie Reed Giffen (1898). In her later years she and her husband lived briefly in Washington, D.C., and then in Lincoln, Nebr., where Tibbles in 1895 edited the weekly Independent, a Populist paper. Because of Susette's poor health they moved in 1902 to a farm near Bancroft, Nebr.—the land which had been her allotment as a member of the Omaha tribe. She died there the next year at the age of forty-nine and was buried at Bancroft.

["Zylyff" (Thomas H. Tibbles), The Ponca Chiefs (1879), a pamphlet published under the auspices of the Boston Indian reformers; Ruth Odell, Helen Hunt Jackson (1939), especially pp. 153–65; Alice C. Fletcher and Francis La Flesche, The Omaha Tribe (27th Annual Report of the Bureau of Am. Ethnology, 1911), and Fletcher, Hist. Sketch of the Omaha Tribe of Indians (1885); Loring B. Priest, Uncle Sam's Stepchildren: The Reformation of U.S. Indian Policy, 1865–1887 (1942); J. Sterling Morton and Albert Watkins, Illustrated Hist. of Nebr., vol. II (1906); Addison E. Sheldon, Hist. and Stories of Nebr. (1926); Nebr. State Jour. (Lincoln), May 30, 1903; Bancroft (Nebr.) Blade, May 29, June 5, 1903; Norma Kidd Green, "Four Sisters: Daughters of Joseph La Flesche," Nebr. Hist., June 1964, and Iron Eye's Family (1969). Other information from the La Flesche Family Papers, Nebr. State Hist. Soc., and interviews with family descendants; marriage date from marriage license in Court House of Burt County, Tekamah, Nebr.]

NORMA KIDD GREEN

TIERNAN, Frances Christine Fisher (July 5, 1846–Mar. 24, 1920), Southern writer under the pen name "Christian Reid," was born at Salisbury, N.C., the first of three children of Col. Charles Frederic Fisher, of German descent, and his wife, Elizabeth Ruth Caldwell. Both her grandfathers, David Franklin Caldwell and Charles Fisher, were wealthy landowners and influential political leaders of the region. Fort Fisher at the mouth of the Cape Fear River was named for her father, a prominent newspaper editor and railroad promoter, who was killed at the first battle of Bull Run in 1861. Since their mother had died earlier, the children were cared for by a maiden aunt, Christine Fisher, a recluse and occasional author who taught them at home. The family ties were strong, though Frances broke away for a semester at Saint Mary's School in Raleigh. Originally Episcopalians, her brother Frederic and, in 1868, she and her sister Annie became Roman Catholics like their aunt, who had been converted before the Civil War.

During the postwar years the previously affluent family managed occasional visits to Baltimore and the North Carolina mountains. Frances, whose aunt had once copied down the ramblings of her niece's imagination, now often wrote stories for amusement, a pastime which the necessity for money soon turned into a profession. Modesty demanded a pseudonym, and she chose "Christian" as ambiguous regarding her sex and "Reid" as properly unassuming. Her original plan to write a novel on the Civil War was discarded when she decided such a subject was too great for her talents. *Valerie Aylmer* (1870), the first of her novels, is instead the story of a coquette and, like most of her books with a Southern setting, looks back to antebellum days, then already romanticized as an era of elegance and good manners. With an unexpected sale of eight thousand copies, it gave her encouragement and brought her effusive letters from admirers like Paul Hamilton Hayne. She settled to the task before her, writing rapidly, often turning out a chapter of twenty pages a day and making few corrections. In the next nine years she published thirteen books. Among them were *Morton House* (1871), which she always considered one of her best, and *"The Land of the Sky"; or, Adventures in Mountain By-Ways* (1876), a travel novel of the North Carolina mountains and her only book still somewhat in demand. In December 1879, having saved some money and realizing the need for fresh material, she sailed for Europe, where she visited England and Italy but spent most of her time in Paris. *Hearts of Steel* (1883) and *Armine* (1884) have European settings. By this time many of her novels were bluntly propagandizing the tenets of Catholicism, and were gradually losing popularity as a result.

In the summer of 1887 Frances Fisher met James Marquis Tiernan, a widower who had admired her writings before seeing her in the little Catholic chapel in Salisbury. A mineralogist born in Baltimore in 1835, Tiernan was in North Carolina as a colonization agent for a railroad company. His fervid courtship of the retiring forty-one-year-old novelist led to their marriage in New Orleans on Dec. 29. Most of her next ten years were spent in Mexico, where Tiernan had mining interests. *Carmela* (1891) and *The Land of the Sun* (1894) are among her novels using Mexico as a background. After

accompanying her husband on a business trip to the West Indies, she set *The Man of the Family* (1897) in Haiti and *The Chase of an Heiress* (1898) in Santo Domingo. Tiernan's illness brought the couple back to Salisbury in 1897, and he died there the following January. In 1900 Christian Reid finally essayed the war theme in *Under the Southern Cross,* a drama whose most unconventional moment came when the Southern belle refused to marry the handsome Yankee. Following several years of rest, she returned to her pen for financial reasons when Tiernan's mines ceased operations. She died of pneumonia in Salisbury in her sixty-fourth year and was buried in Chestnut Hill Cemetery there. In 1909 the University of Notre Dame had awarded her its Laetare Medal, given annually to a Catholic layman who has made a notable contribution to American life.

Christian Reid was prim and dignified in appearance and considered notoriety and undue publicity unbecoming. Her forty-five books, generally about mild flirtations and family misunderstandings, are filled with stereotyped heroines and lifeless heroes and now are mere period pieces. She once wrote: "My purpose has always been to inculcate high standards of living, to influence none to do wrongly." The decorum, nobility, and restraint of all her vast output are characteristic of genteel popular fiction during the half-century of her professional career.

[Basic references are Kate Harbes Becker, *Biog. of Christian Reid* (1941); Lou Rogers, *Tar Heel Women* (1949); *N.C. Authors: A Selective Handbook* (1952); Archibald Henderson, in *Library of Southern Literature,* XII (1907), 5369–89; Stanton Tiernan, "Some Recollections of Christian Reid," *The State* (Raleigh, N.C.), Dec. 16, 1950; Francis B. Dedmond, "The Poems of Paul Hamilton Hayne to Frances Christine Fisher," *N.C. Hist. Rev.,* Oct. 1951; *Who's Who in America,* 1920–21; obituary, *Charlotte* (N.C.) *Observer,* Mar. 25, 1920.]

RICHARD WALSER

**TIETJENS, Eunice** (July 29, 1884–Sept. 6, 1944), author, was born in Chicago, Ill., the oldest of four children of Idea Louise (Strong) and William Andrew Hammond. Of her two sisters, Louise became an Episcopal missionary to China and Elizabeth a concert cellist; her brother, Laurens, became an inventor, known especially for his Hammond electronic organ. Her family, of English descent on both sides, had lived for several generations in the Middle West. Growing up in the Chicago suburb of Evanston, Ill., Eunice attended public schools there through her thirteenth year, when her father, a banker, died. Her mother, an active woman whose interests included painting and travel, took the children to Europe for an extended period of residence and schooling which included stays in Geneva, Dresden, and Paris and, for Eunice, courses at the Collège de France and the Sorbonne and graduation from the Froebel Kindergarten Institute of Dresden. In May 1904, in Paris, she was married to Paul Tietjens, an American composer remembered for his score for the stage version of L. Frank Baum's *Wizard of Oz*. Returning to the United States within a few weeks of their marriage, they settled in New York City and became the parents of two daughters: Idea, who died as a child, and Janet, born in 1907. The couple separated in 1910 and were divorced in 1914; after the separation Eunice with her daughter rejoined her mother in Evanston.

Back in Chicago, Miss Tietjens (she retained her first husband's name throughout her professional career) at first "conducted a kindergarten in French for the scions of the wealthy," as she later put it, but quickly decided to try to become a writer. Her mother had encouraged her early attempts at verse; now young friends in the Chicago literary movement— Floyd Dell, Margery Currey, and George Cram Cook in particular—gave her help and stimulus. HARRIET MONROE, founder and editor of *Poetry* magazine, accepted several poems, and about 1913 Miss Tietjens joined her staff "as office girl and general nuisance." Her association with the magazine, in various editorial capacities, was to last throughout her life. During the earlier years she formed particularly close associations with Miss Monroe and the core of the magazine's Midwestern contributors, including Carl Sandburg, Edgar Lee Masters, Vachel Lindsay, SARA TEASDALE, and Arthur Davison Ficke.

Miss Tietjens' own poetry was to achieve its definition during a visit she and her mother made in 1916 to her sister Louise, who was stationed at Wusih, China. Edgar Lee Masters' gift of a copy of the *Bhagavad-Gita* had first aroused her interest in the Orient; this interest had grown with her introduction to Japanese art at the Panama–Pacific Exposition at San Francisco in 1915 and a stay in Japan en route to China. The half year she spent at Wusih, she wrote later, "was one of the great influences of my life"; she was deeply moved by "the strange blend of sordidness, tragedy, beauty, and humor" she saw around her, and the result was her first volume, *Profiles from China*, published in 1917. *Body and Raiment*, a collection largely of her earlier verse, appeared in 1919, but the Chinese poems marked

the form which was to dominate in her work: descriptions or short narratives in free verse turned at their end to expressions of personal value or concern. Her visit to the Orient also reinforced her taste for foreign residence and observation.

After a year back in Chicago, Miss Tietjens in the fall of 1917 left for France, having secured a job as war correspondent for the *Chicago Daily News*. Her assignments were mainly human interest stories from Paris, but she saw the war at close hand on a few trips near the front lines and in devastated areas. On her return early in 1919 she retired to a shack on the Indiana dunes with her twelve-year-old daughter, Janet, and wrote down in a novel, *Jake* (1921), "all the sense of human pain and futility that the war had roused in me." In February 1920 she was married to the playwright Cloyd Head; they had two children: Marshall, born in 1920, and a daughter who died shortly after birth. Several years of domesticity ensued, varied by a stay at the MacDowell artists' colony in Peterboro, N.H., collaboration with her daughter Janet on a children's book, *The Jaw-Breaker's Alphabet of Prehistoric Animals* (1930), and numerous literary friendships.

In 1923 the Heads set off for a year of "adventure and creative work" in Europe on a budget of fifty dollars a week. After stays in Paris, the Riviera, and Settignano, Italy, they settled in Hammamet, Tunisia, "a country which was to turn our interest permanently away from Europe and towards the Orient— and the primitive." Upon their return to the United States in the spring of 1925, Miss Tietjens and Head took a house in Rockland County, N.Y., hoping to sell a play about Arab life which they had written together. Elaborately produced that year by Norman Bel Geddes, *Arabesque* was a spectacular failure. Miss Tietjens next set to work on an anthology of Oriental verse for Alfred A. Knopf, a signal success when published in 1928. Another stay in North Africa followed, the couple returning in 1927 to Chicago, where Head became business manager of the Goodman Memorial Theatre at the Art Institute and Miss Tietjens devoted much time to writing. Two books for young people, *Boy of the Desert* (1928) and *The Romance of Antar* (1929), grew out of her North African experience; another volume of poems, *Leaves in Windy Weather*, appeared in 1929. Her romantic interest in the primitive was now fed by friendships with anthropologists and other far travelers, including the painter Robert Lee Eskridge, whom she helped to write a book about his experiences in the

South Pacific. When Cloyd Head resigned his job in 1930, therefore, the couple with their ten-year-old son traveled to Tahiti. There they lived for ten months on the island of Moorea, while Head worked on a play and Miss Tietjens wrote a children's book, *Boy of the South Seas* (1931).

After another stay in Chicago, Miss Tietjens and her husband moved in 1933 to Florida, where they taught for two years at the University of Miami, Miss Tietjens in the English department as lecturer on poetry and Head in the speech department. They settled in Coconut Grove, where she wrote her last book, an autobiography, *The World at My Shoulder* (1938). While traveling in Scandinavia in 1939 she was stricken with cancer; she died five years later in Chicago and was buried there. Miss Tietjens will not be remembered as a major poet or writer, but her verse, at its best, speaks with a direct and personal authenticity which she shares with other members of the Midwestern movement of the early century.

[Eunice Tietjens, *The World at My Shoulder* (1938); Jessica N. North in *Poetry*, Nov. 1944; *Who's Who among North Am. Authors*, 1939; *N.Y. Times*, Sept. 7, 1944; *Who Was Who in America*, vol. II (1950). A collection of Miss Tietjens' letters and MSS. is in the Newberry Library, Chicago; see Denham Sutcliffe, "New Light on the 'Chicago Writers,'" *Newberry Library Bull.*, Dec. 1950.]

BERNARD DUFFEY

**TIMOTHY, Ann** (c. 1727–Sept. 11, 1792), printer and newspaper publisher, was born Ann Donovan, probably in Charleston, S.C. She may have been a descendant or relation of Daniel Donovan, who was in South Carolina as early as 1687. In Charleston, on Dec. 8, 1745, she was married to Peter Timothy, who about this time became publisher of the *South-Carolina Gazette*, the colony's first permanent newspaper, earlier published by his father, Lewis Timothy, and his mother, ELIZABETH TIMOTHY. The early and middle years of Ann Timothy's marriage were taken up by the bearing of children (perhaps as many as fifteen, of whom seven died in infancy) and the rearing of a large family. Not until the death of her husband did she emerge as the proprietor of a successful printing and newspaper business.

Displaced by the British occupation of Charleston, the patriot Peter Timothy and his family went to Philadelphia in 1781. In the following year Timothy and two of his daughters embarked for Santo Domingo and were lost at sea. Ann Timothy returned later in 1782 to Charleston, where on July 16, 1783, like her

widowed mother-in-law forty-three years before, she resumed publication of the *Gazette of the State of South Carolina* (as Peter Timothy had renamed the paper in 1777). With the assistance of one E. Walsh, she published the newspaper (rechristened in 1785 the *State Gazette of South Carolina*) until her death in 1792. Ann Timothy was thus the second woman in South Carolina and the second woman in her family to become the publisher of a newspaper. She seems also to have resembled Elizabeth Timothy in the possession of business acumen, for, in addition to publishing the *Gazette*, she obtained the post of "Printer to the State," which she held, apparently, from 1785 on. At least fifteen imprints were issued under her name from 1783 to 1792.

Ann Timothy died in Charleston in 1792, at the age of sixty-five. Her eldest son, Peter, had died in 1770; the names of five other children are known: Sarah (unmarried), Robert, Elizabeth Anne (Mrs. Peter Valton), Frances Claudia (Mrs. Benjamin Lewis Merchant), and Benjamin Franklin. Benjamin Timothy inherited the *Gazette* and published it until his retirement from the printing business in 1802, at which time the sixty-nine-year-old South Carolina printing and newspaper dynasty came to an end.

[The most complete sketch of Peter and Ann Timothy is in Hennig Cohen's authoritative study, *The S.C. Gazette* (1953), pp. 241–48. Glimpses of Peter Timothy's family are found in Douglas C. McMurtrie, ed., *Letters of Peter Timothy, Printer of Charleston, S.C., to Benjamin Franklin* (1935). The imprints of "A. Timothy," 1783–92, are listed in Robert J. Turnbull, *Bibliog. of S.C.: 1563–1950*, I (1956), 191, 238–83, *passim*.]

RICHARD MAXWELL BROWN

**TIMOTHY, Elizabeth** (d. 1757), printer and newspaper publisher, was "born and bred" in Holland. Her maiden name is not known, but it is possible that she was of Huguenot extraction like her husband. The latter, Louis Timothée (anglicized to Lewis Timothy in 1734), was the son of a French Protestant who took refuge in Holland after the revocation of the Edict of Nantes. Nothing is known of Elizabeth Timothy's Dutch background except that she gained there a "Female Education" which included the "knowledge of Accompts."

Lewis and Elizabeth Timothy and their four young children sailed from Rotterdam in 1731, arriving in Philadelphia that September. In 1733 they moved to Charleston, S.C., where Lewis, in partnership with Benjamin Franklin, became publisher of the one-year-old weekly *South-Carolina Gazette*, the colony's first permanent newspaper. Lewis Timothy was fatally injured in an accident in December 1738; without missing an issue, his widow continued publication of the *Gazette* in the name of her eldest son, Peter, who was then about fourteen years old.

Although it was common in colonial America for the widows of deceased printers to carry on their husbands' businesses, Elizabeth Timothy was the first American woman to publish a newspaper. She managed the *Gazette* wholly on her own for at least a year or two but gradually relinquished control to her son Peter, who became sole proprietor about 1746. The newspaper suffered somewhat in quality during Elizabeth Timothy's difficult first year of publication but in time resumed its steady improvement. In addition to the newspaper, at least twenty imprints were issued during the years (1739–45) of Elizabeth Timothy's connection with the printing business. According to Benjamin Franklin, the widow was far superior to her husband in the operation of the business. Whereas Lewis Timothy had been dilatory and unsystematic in his dealings with his partner, Franklin found that Elizabeth Timothy "continu'd to account with the greatest Regularity and Exactitude every Quarter afterwards; and manag'd the Business with such Success that she not only brought up reputably a Family of Children, but at the Expiration of the Term was able to purchase of me the Printing House and establish her Son in it."

By 1747 Elizabeth Timothy was no longer connected with the management of the *Gazette* but was proprietor of a small book and stationery shop. By the following year she had left Charleston. She was back in Charleston by 1756, made her will on Apr. 12, 1757, and died in the space of a month. Her talent for business which Franklin had noted was borne out by the amount of property she left; it included three houses, a tract of land, and eight slaves.

Elizabeth Timothy had six children: Peter, Louisa (Mrs. James Richards), Charles (d. September 1739), Mary Elizabeth (Mrs. Abraham Bourquin), Joseph (d. October 1739), and Catherine (Mrs. Theodore Trezevant). Peter Timothy (c. 1725–1782) continued to publish the *South-Carolina Gazette*, gained distinction as one of the leading American printers of his generation, and was prominent in South Carolina's Revolutionary movement. After his death the *Gazette* was continued in turn by his widow, ANN TIMOTHY.

[Hennig Cohen, *The S.C. Gazette* (1953), is the leading authority on the *Gazette* and the Timothy family; it includes the most complete account of Elizabeth Timothy (pp. 238–41). The quotations above are from Benjamin Franklin's brief but pointed sketch of her in Leonard Labaree et al., eds., *The Autobiog. of Benjamin Franklin* (1964), p. 166. The *Dict. Am. Biog.* contains a useful sketch of Lewis Timothy by Douglas C. McMurtrie. The *Pa. Archives*, 2nd series, XVII (1890), 28–29, 30, 32, record the arrival of the Timothys in Philadelphia. Brief items on Elizabeth Timothy are in the *S.-C. Gazette*, Jan. 4, May 19, Nov. 11, 1739, Dec. 15, 1746, June 26, 1749, and July 8, 1756. For imprints issued by the Timothy printing shop during Elizabeth Timothy's active connection with it, see Robert J. Turnbull, *Bibliog. of S.C.: 1563–1950*, I (1956), 90–110. Frank L. Mott, *Am. Journalism* (1941), p. 25n., states that Elizabeth Timothy was the first American woman to publish a newspaper, a judgment supported, in effect, by Isaiah Thomas, *The Hist. of Printing in America* (2 vols., 1874), and Lawrence C. Wroth, *The Colonial Printer* (1938).]

RICHARD MAXWELL BROWN

**TINGLEY, Katherine Augusta Westcott** (July 6, 1847–July 11, 1929), Theosophist and founder of the Point Loma community in California, was born in Newbury, Mass., the daughter of James P. L. and Susan Ordway (Chase) Westcott, who also had two sons, one of them older than Katherine. Her father was a lumber merchant and later a hotelkeeper in nearby Newburyport, where he also served for a time as city marshal. After the Civil War, during which the family lived for a time in Alexandria, Va., Katherine briefly attended a convent school in Montreal, leaving it in 1867 to marry Richard Henry Cook, a printer. The marriage ended within two months. Little is known of her career for the next thirteen years, though there is some indication that for a time she acted with a traveling theatrical company. About 1880, now residing in New York City, she was married to George W. Parent, an investigator for the New York Elevated Railway. Before the end of the decade this union, too, was dissolved, and on Apr. 25, 1888, she was married to Philo Buchanan Tingley, a mechanical engineer in the employ of a steamship company, who was some ten years her junior. Although Tingley outlived her, he was a dim figure who played only a minor role in her career. Mrs. Tingley was childless, but for a time during these years cared for the two children of Richard Cook by a subsequent marriage.

Much drawn to charitable work, in 1887 she founded a Society of Mercy for hospital and prison visitation, and in the early 1890's the "Do-Good Mission" on Manhattan's East Side. To raise funds for these charities she sometimes gave "psychometric readings." Her association with Theosophy began in the winter of 1892–93, when she met and became a follower of William Quan Judge. With HELENA PETROVNA BLAVATSKY and Col. Henry Steele Olcott, Judge had founded the Theosophical Society in 1875. In 1895 he split from the main body of the Theosophical Society (based in Adyar, India, and led by Olcott and the British mystic Annie Besant) to found the "Theosophical Society in America" under his own presidency. His death a year later set the stage for the emergence of Mrs. Tingley. Her transmission of apparent spirit messages from Judge, together with favorable references to her found in his diary, persuaded the leaders of the Theosophical Society in America that Judge had intended her to become "Outer Head" of the Society's Esoteric Section, a more influential position than the national presidency. (The inner headship of the Esoteric Section was believed to be a mysterious brotherhood of Tibetan mahatmas.) At this turning point in her life, Mrs. Tingley struck reporters as "robust and energetic in carriage, with attractive features set off by a mass of dark hair," her voice "pleasant and softly modulated." Though less of a "primeval natural force" than the legendary Madame Blavatsky, she seemed considerably more "even and balanced" (quoted in Greenwalt, pp. 24, 29, 70).

Boldly assuming the reins, Mrs. Tingley announced a world crusade to propagandize for her brand of Theosophy and, incidentally, to strengthen her position in the struggle with Mrs. Besant and the Adyar group. (The often bitter contest between them continued down to Mrs. Tingley's death.) In 1896, with five other leading American Theosophists, Mrs. Tingley made a world tour, seeking converts in the British Isles, Europe, the Middle East, and the Orient, and visiting the famous religious and occult centers of antiquity, from the Killarney Castle in Ireland to Grecian temples, Egyptian pyramids, and Indian holy places. In Tibet, Mrs. Tingley claimed to have sought out and conferred with a mahatma, thus duplicating a Blavatsky feat and strengthening her authority over dissident factions at home. (In February 1898, after her return to the United States, she suppressed such a faction by promulgating a new constitution which gave her absolute authority for life.)

As the tour progressed, Mrs. Tingley's attention increasingly focused on her plans for a great Theosophical school and community in California. On Feb. 24, 1897, the travelers having reached the West Coast by way of Australia, a cornerstone was dedicated at a large tract of land which had been purchased on

Point Loma, a dramatic promontory overlooking San Diego Bay, some seven miles north of the city. Here, in 1900, Mrs. Tingley officially established her headquarters. A skillful and persuasive fund raiser, she gradually built up Point Loma into perhaps the most magnificent, and certainly the most exotic, of the many Utopian communities of nineteenth- and early twentieth-century America. With its Saracenic cupolas, multicolored glass domes, and Egyptian gates, this "white city" on the Pacific drew the curious from all over the world. Its basic material was wood, painted and formed to resemble marble.

From the first, Mrs. Tingley exhibited more interest in philanthropy and social reform than in the arcane lore which fascinated many Theosophists. In Britain in 1896 she had rejected the usual tea-and-lecture approach and instead organized "brotherhood suppers" for the destitute of Liverpool, Dublin, and other cities. In 1897 she founded an International Brotherhood League, whose sixfold program included work for interracial understanding and aid to workingmen, convicts, and "unfortunate women." Its first project was the establishment of a New Jersey summer resort for slum children from New York City. In 1898 the League was merged with the Theosophical Society in America to become the Universal Brotherhood and Theosophical Society. That same year Mrs. Tingley organized Theosophist volunteers into a War Relief Corps which aided Spanish–American War veterans hospitalized at Point Montauk, Long Island. A pacifist as well as an antivivisectionist and an opponent of capital punishment, she strongly opposed United States intervention in the First World War.

Mrs. Tingley was also much interested in the arts, and under her influence Point Loma became something of a cultural mecca. Classical and Shakespearean plays were performed in a Greek theatre; musical programs of high quality were given by and for the six hundred residents; and artists, poets, and writers spent time in residence. The barren point soon blossomed with flower gardens, orchards, and citrus groves. Some of the community's experiments in forestry and horticulture, especially in the growing of such fruits as the peach and the avocado, attracted much attention. A "Woman's Exchange and Mart" produced school uniforms, silk, and batik fabrics, and a printing plant turned out Theosophical literature.

The best known of Mrs. Tingley's achievements at Point Loma was the Raja Yoga school and college. Deriving its name from a Sanskrit term meaning "royal union," the school stressed a balance of the physical, mental, and spiritual faculties. Its program was highly structured, reflecting Mrs. Tingley's environmentalist theory of human development. The three hundred children lived with their sixty-odd teachers twenty-four hours a day, arising at six in the morning for calisthenics, sharing in the manual labor of the community, and participating in its dramatic and musical activities. A number of poor children, some of them destitute Cuban youngsters, were educated free of charge. In 1919 a Theosophical University at Point Loma, successor to an earlier School for the Revival of the Lost Mysteries of Antiquity, was chartered by the State of California.

Mrs. Tingley's efforts to duplicate her model community elsewhere were unsuccessful. Projected schools in Cuba, Sweden, Germany, Minnesota, and Massachusetts either never materialized or did not long survive. Furthermore, Mrs. Tingley's total absorption in the Point Loma enterprise forced her to neglect the local Theosophical lodges throughout America, most of which either shifted allegiance to the Adyar group, joined a schismatic movement (the United Lodge of Theosophists), or disbanded altogether. Even Point Loma itself was not immune from problems. In spite of her ability and her singular appeal, Mrs. Tingley's personality was so overwhelming that many of her lieutenants found her too difficult to work with and gradually left the group. The community consistently operated at a deficit, as tuition fees, residence charges, and gifts from wealthy supporters all proved insufficient to finance the ambitious schemes of the founder. Nevertheless, the Point Loma undertaking, although attacked by such varied critics as the *Los Angeles Times* and the New York Society for the Prevention of Cruelty to Children, never lost the warm support of the San Diegans, who knew it best.

In May 1929, while on a European visit, Katherine Augusta Tingley was injured in an automobile accident in Germany. She died that July at the Theosophist community in Visingsö, Sweden, at the age of eighty-two. Her cremated remains were buried partly in Visingsö and partly at Point Loma. Her successor, the brilliant but eccentric Gottfried de Purucker, was unsuccessful in persuading Annie Besant to buy some of the estate as part of an effort to reunite the divided movement, and the Point Loma colony gradually declined. In 1942 the remnant moved to Covina, Calif., and then in 1951 to Pasadena, where a few survivors still sought to renovate the world through Theosophy.

[Emmett A. Greenwalt, *The Point Loma Community in Calif.* (1955), a scholarly study, includes the fullest account of Mrs. Tingley. See also Arthur H. Nethercot, *The Last Four Lives of Annie Besant* (1963); obituary in *N.Y. Times*, July 12, 1929; *Who Was Who in America*, vol. I (1942); *Nat. Cyc. Am. Biog.*, XV, 337–38; *Vital Records of Newbury, Mass., to the End of the Year 1849*, I (1911), 539 (the authority for her birth date); John C. Chase and George W. Chamberlain, comps., *Seven Generations of the Descendants of Aguila and Thomas Chase* (1928), p. 134; R. M. Tingley, comp., *The Tingley Family* (1910), p. 410; Fred C. Floyd, *Hist. of the Fortieth (Mozart) Regiment, N.Y. Volunteers* (1909), pp. 99–100, on her father.]

ARTHUR H. NETHERCOT

**TODD, Mabel Loomis** (Nov. 10, 1856–Oct. 14, 1932), author, first editor of the poems and letters of EMILY DICKINSON, was born in Cambridge, Mass., the only child of Eben Jenks Loomis and Mary Alden (Wilder) Loomis. On her father's side she was descended from Joseph Loomis, who came to Boston in 1638 and later settled in Windsor, Conn.; on her mother's side, from John and PRISCILLA ALDEN of the Plymouth Colony. Her maternal grandfather, John Wilder, was a Congregational minister in Concord, Mass. Eben Loomis, a mathematician, astronomer, and naturalist, was for four decades senior assistant on the *American Ephemeris and Nautical Almanac*. When its office moved from Cambridge, Mass., to the Naval Observatory in Washington, D.C., in 1866, the Loomises followed. Mabel Loomis attended private schools in Cambridge and Georgetown, D.C., receiving much of her education at the Georgetown Seminary, and then spent two or three years in Boston studying music (at the New England Conservatory of Music), German, and painting. On Mar. 5, 1879, she was married to David Peck Todd, a young astronomer connected with the *Nautical Almanac* office. Their only child, Millicent, was born Feb. 5, 1880.

In 1881 Todd was appointed to the faculty of his alma mater, Amherst College. Soon after their arrival, the young couple became close friends of Austin Dickinson, treasurer of the college, and his wife, Susan, and through them became acquainted with Austin's sisters, Emily and Lavinia. On a visit in February 1882, as Mabel Todd recorded in her diary, Mrs. Dickinson read her "some strange poems by Emily Dickinson. They are full of power" (Leyda, II, 361). Mrs. Todd never met the poet recluse face to face, but Emily Dickinson sometimes invited her to play the piano and sing for her while she hovered out of sight, and sent her notes and copies of her poems to express thanks for these and other attentions paid to her and her sister Lavinia.

When, after Emily's death in May 1886, Lavinia discovered a box containing more than eight hundred of her poems, Mabel Todd, at the family's request, undertook to try editing them for publication. In the autumn of 1887 she began transcribing them, deciphering the difficult handwriting and choosing among the alternate words and phrases written around the edges. As the editing progressed, Lavinia discovered further poems. By the autumn of 1889 Mrs. Todd was ready to consult with Thomas Wentworth Higginson, whom Lavinia had persuaded to be co-editor, about the choice of poems to be published. Together they decided what textual emendations should be made to render them acceptable to current taste. Mrs. Todd generally deferred to Higginson's judgment in substituting exact rhymes for assonant ones, "correcting" the grammar, and otherwise giving the poems the polish he felt they needed, though she protested against some of the titles he wished to give them and felt that some of the textual changes were questionable. The *Poems* appeared in 1890. Encouraged by the popular response, the co-editors prepared a second series for publication in 1891. They made fewer changes in this volume, Higginson feeling that "the public ear" had been "opened" to the unusual poetry, but the general principles remained the same, and Mrs. Todd seems to have heeded them in preparing, without Higginson's aid, a third series of poems (1896). She also edited two volumes of Emily Dickinson's letters in 1894. The project came to an end when, after the death of Mrs. Todd's beloved friend Austin Dickinson in 1895, a rift developed between her and the Dickinson family.

Although Mrs. Todd is remembered chiefly for her role in bringing the poems of Emily Dickinson to the world's attention, she was a woman of many talents. Attractive and energetic, she accompanied her husband on his astronomical expeditions to Japan (1887, 1896), Tripoli (1900, 1905), the Dutch East Indies (1901), Chile (1907), and Russia (1914). On some of these trips she collected native artifacts, most notably the collection of aboriginal Ainu objects from Japan now in the Peabody Museum, Salem, Mass. Between expeditions she was busy founding and organizing the Amherst Historical Society, encouraging conservation of nature and the beautification of Amherst, serving as a director of the Massachusetts State Federation of Women's Clubs, teaching music and painting, giving piano recitals, lecturing on literature, New England history, travel, and astronomy to audiences in various parts of the country, and writing. Her books include fiction (*Footprints,* 1883), popular science (*Total Eclipses of the Sun,* 1894, long a standard work), nature writing (*A Cycle of Sunsets,* 1910), and travel (*Corona and Coronet,* 1898, an account of a trip to Japan to observe a solar eclipse, and *Tripoli the Mysterious,* 1912).

This round of activities came to a temporary halt in 1913 when Mrs. Todd suffered a cerebral hemorrhage and partial paralysis. But in Coconut Grove, Fla., her home from 1917 to 1932, she lectured, wrote articles, and fostered the local Audubon Society and the movement to establish Everglades National Park. She died of another cerebral hemorrhage at her summer home on Hog Island, Muscongus, Maine, in 1932, and was buried in Wildwood Cemetery, Amherst. She was an Episcopalian. Her Maine island became the National Audubon Society's Todd Wildlife Sanctuary, and a state forest was named for her in Massachusetts.

[Thomas H. Johnson's edition of *The Poems of Emily Dickinson,* vol. I (1955), includes an authoritative account of earlier editing (pp. xxxix–xlviii); Mrs. Todd's role is recounted more fully in Millicent Todd Bingham, *Ancestors' Brocades: The Literary Debut of Emily Dickinson* (1945). For biographical material on Mrs. Todd see: Julia Ward Howe, ed., *Representative Women of New England* (1904), pp. 276–78; *Nat. Cyc. Am. Biog.,* XXVIII, 37–38; Millicent Todd Bingham, *Mabel Loomis Todd, Her Contributions to the Town of Amherst* (privately printed, 1935); Jay Leyda, *The Years and Hours of Emily Dickinson* (1960), I, pp. lxxiii–lxxiv; obituary in *N.Y. Times,* Oct. 15, 1932. There is some autobiographical material in Mrs. Todd's writings, especially her two travel books. Her *The Thoreau Family Two Generations Ago* (Thoreau Soc. Booklet No. 13, 1958) and the foreword by Millicent Todd Bingham contain details of Loomis and Todd family history; see also *Nat. Cyc. Am. Biog.* articles on Eben J. Loomis (XL, 446) and David Peck Todd (XXVIII, 35–36). Other information from interviews and correspondence with Millicent Todd Bingham; interview with Gladys K. Gould MacKenzie; unpublished correspondence in Amherst College Library; unpublished correspondence, journals, and other papers in Yale Univ. Library.]

DAVID HIGGINS

**TODD, Marion Marsh** (March 1841–post 1913), lawyer and Greenbacker, was born in Plymouth, Chenango County, N.Y., one of seven children of Abner Kneeland Marsh and Dolly Adelia (Wales) Marsh. Both parents were New Englanders, the father a native of Shoreham, Vt., the mother of Hartford, Conn.

Abner Marsh has been described as a Universalist preacher. During Marion's early years, it is said, she was taught by her parents at home, but when the family removed to Eaton Rapids, Mich., in 1851, she attended public school. Her father died the next year. She entered the Ypsilanti (Mich.) State Normal School at an early age and at seventeen accepted a teaching position. This she held until her marriage in 1868 to Benjamin Todd of Boston, a reform-minded lawyer. Todd was a vocal advocate of larger opportunities for women in public life and urged his wife to join him in his work. Beginning shortly after their marriage, she became a public lecturer, particularly upon temperance, woman suffrage, and the necessity for political and economic reform. During this period her only child, a daughter, Lula, was born.

In the late 1870's, because of Todd's poor health, the family removed to California. There, in 1879, Mrs. Todd entered the Hastings Law College in San Francisco—newly opened to women through the efforts of CLARA SHORTRIDGE FOLTZ and LAURA DE FORCE GORDON—where she concerned herself particularly with the law of finance. During her second year, in 1880, her husband died, and in 1881 she was forced to leave without obtaining a degree. She nevertheless gained admission to the state bar in 1881, opened a law office in San Francisco, and developed a busy practice. She soon became active in reform politics as well. In September 1882 she attended the state convention of the Greenback Labor party. Elected a member of the platform committee, she played a prominent role in drafting the party's platform and was nominated for state attorney general—one of the earliest instances of a woman running for statewide office. She stumped the state in the ensuing campaign and led her party in the election, though polling a mere 1,109 votes.

Giving up her law practice in 1883, Mrs. Todd devoted her energies for the next decade to speaking, writing, and other work for the Greenback and kindred movements. She was one of the delegates who helped organize a national Anti-Monopoly party in 1883, and the next year she attended its convention and that of the Greenback party, both of which nominated the Civil War general Ben Butler for president. For several years Mrs. Todd campaigned widely for the two parties. By 1886 she was apparently living in Michigan, although she returned briefly to California that year to conclude some important law cases. Having joined the Knights of Labor, she was sent as a delegate from Michigan to its General Assembly in Richmond, Va., in 1886. The next year, along with her friend Mrs. SARAH E. V. EMERY, she helped found a new national political group, the Union Labor party, dedicated to money and railroad reform and seeking the votes of farmers and workingmen. A newspaper account of its convention described her as "quite a good-looking woman" and a "brilliant and entertaining speaker" (*Cincinnati Commercial Gazette,* Feb. 23, 1887). In 1890 she moved to Chicago to become editor of the *Express,* a weekly reform paper of national circulation. The following year she was one of the delegates to the Cincinnati conference which organized the national People's (Populist) party.

Mrs. Todd's income came almost entirely from her public lectures and from her books. Her eight published works reveal clearly her intellectual commitments and their metamorphosis. *Protective Tariff Delusions* (1886) argued the case for free trade, maintaining that through politically maneuvered programs, principally deceitful tariff laws, American labor was robbed of the full fruit of its own hard work. Next she expanded her 1890 campaign booklet, *Honest(?) John Sherman, or a Foul Record,* widely used by the People's party, into *Pizarro and John Sherman* (1891), casting the Senator as a Shylock who, unlike his Spanish predecessor, ravished not a foreign people but his own countrymen through his ruthless monetary manipulations. *Prof. Goldwin Smith and His Satellites in Congress* (1890), originally a series of pieces in the *Express,* was a devastating assault upon Smith's arguments against woman suffrage. "For women not to demand the vote," she wrote, "is not to be cultured, and for our women not to be cultured is woe unto the race of men" (p. 166).

Her most ambitious work, *Railways of Europe and America* (1893), hailed by the Populist leader Ignatius Donnelly as "just what is needed at this time," went through a second edition in 1895 and put to use her training in law and finance. Summarizing, with ambitious statistical information, the condition and methods of operation of railroads throughout the world, she argued the need for revamping the entire American structure so that "the railway system might be adapted to the country, rather than the country to it" (p. 12). In her later works she turned to the novel as a form of political and social protest, lachrymosely chronicling the tragedy of human exploitation and debauchery, which she blamed on the capitalist system, and criticizing the churches for their hypocrisy in not rising to their social responsibilities (*Rachel's Pitiful History,* 1895). Phil-

*lip: A Romance* (1900) and *Claudia* (1902) followed the same theme, though venturing also into the realm of positive alternatives in a properly ordered society.

In her later years Mrs. Todd returned to Michigan, living for some time in Eaton Rapids and moving later to Springport, where she was residing in 1914. No record of her death has been found.

[Annie L. Diggs, "The Women in the Alliance Movement," *Arena*, July 1892; Mich. Pioneer and Hist. Soc., *Hist. Collections*, XXI (1892), 99; Frances E. Willard and Mary A. Livermore, eds., *A Woman of the Century* (1893); *Who's Who in America*, 1912–13; *Woman's Who's Who of America*, 1914–15; Winifield J. David, *Hist. of Political Conventions in Calif.* (1893), pp. 451–52; Lelia J. Robinson, "Women Lawyers in the U.S.," *Green Bag*, Jan. and Apr. 1890, pp. 26–27, 181–82. Pages 42–49 of Mrs. Todd's *Rachel's Pitiful History* (Springport, Mich., 1895) summarize all her works with extended newspaper comments on each.]

PAUL L. MURPHY

**TOMPKINS, Sally Louisa** (Nov. 9, 1833–July 25, 1916), Confederate hospital worker, was born at Poplar Grove, Mathews County, Va., the third daughter and youngest of the four children of Col. Christopher Tompkins and his second wife, Maria Boothe Patterson; Tompkins also had four children by an earlier marriage. The Tompkins and Patterson families were among the most distinguished in Tidewater Virginia. Christopher Tompkins, a native of Caroline County, was in early life a master of merchant vessels engaged in the Baltic and Mediterranean trade. Later he served as justice of the peace, became a colonel of militia, and represented his district in the state legislature. His wife was the daughter of John Patterson of Poplar Grove, who had served in the Continental army and navy during the American Revolution and had been brevetted by General Washington for bravery at the battle of Monmouth when only seventeen. Sally Louisa Tompkins spent her early years at Poplar Grove, which had passed to Colonel Tompkins after Patterson's death. There hospitality was dispensed on an impressive scale to a large circle of friends and relatives, and there also Miss Tompkins became widely known for her skill in caring for the sick. Following her father's death, shortly before the outbreak of the Civil War, the family moved to Richmond.

Soon after war commenced in 1861, numerous military hospitals—both public and private—were established in Richmond, the Confederate capital. Among the first private institutions to open was the Robertson Hospital, oper-

ated by Miss Tompkins. Improvised in a residence donated by its owner, Judge John Robertson, it had a capacity of twenty-five beds, and Miss Tompkins organized a group of socially prominent women, known as the "Ladies of Robertson Hospital," as nurses. Of the permanent hospital workers, four were slaves, one of whom had looked after Miss Tompkins since childhood, and two—a carpenter and a gardener—were veterans unfit for military service. The hospital soon established a record of healing unmatched by any other institution, government or private. So well was it regarded that when in 1861, after five large military hospitals had been erected in the Richmond suburbs, the Surgeon General moved to abandon the use of private hospitals within the city, President Jefferson Davis, in an unprecedented move, commissioned Miss Tompkins a captain of cavalry (Sept. 9, 1861) so that her hospital might remain open. She refused payment for her services, however, explaining that she would not take away from those whom she felt it her duty to help. Of the 1,333 admissions at Robertson Hospital between Aug. 1, 1861, when it received its first patient, and June 13, 1865, when it discharged its last, only seventy-three deaths were reported—an amazingly low figure and one that is all the more impressive if, as was contended, the military authorities were wont to send the most critical cases to Robertson. An important factor may well have been "Captain Sally's" concern for sanitation, as she emphasized the greatest possible cleanliness.

As hospital administrator, Miss Tompkins combined rigid discipline with an abiding concern for the souls as well as the lives of her patients. According to Judge William W. Crump of Richmond, she ruled her hospital with "a stick in one hand and a Bible in the other." Unruly or restless convalescents might find their clothes locked up and themselves listening to Captain Sally reading temperance passages from the Bible. A devout Episcopalian, she knelt in prayer each night with those who could make their way to a downstairs room, and she served as spiritual adviser to all who wished such counsel. Moreover, she appears to have possessed an unusual ability to bolster the sagging morale of disabled troops.

In postwar years Miss Tompkins did occasional nursing, engaged in "quiet charities," and labored as a faithful member of Richmond's St. James Episcopal Church. Though she was not a beauty—a slight brunette with plain features, she stood about five feet tall—her presence was dignified and forceful, and she received and rejected a number of marriage proposals. She was never forgotten by those she had served; when the United Confederate Veterans met in Richmond for their annual rally in 1896, Captain Sally rented a large dwelling and kept open house. In 1905, when financial reverses, coupled with her many good works, had almost exhausted her resources, she accepted an invitation from the board of managers of Richmond's Home for Confederate Women to become their lifetime "guest." She insisted, however, that she be permitted to pay her expenses. She died there in 1916 of chronic interstitial nephritis; after funeral services at the Home, representatives from R. E. Lee Camp, United Confederate Veterans, of which she was an honorary member, accompanied the body to the Christ Episcopal Church graveyard in Kingston Parish, Mathews County, where it was interred with full military honors. In her threefold capacity as "provider, superintendent, and nurse" of the Robertson Hospital, Sally Tompkins seems to have impressed and inspired all who knew her.

[The most complete biographical account is Elizabeth Dabney Coleman's "The Captain Was a Lady," *Va. Cavalcade,* Summer 1956. The following are also helpful: "Capt. Sallie Tompkins," *Confederate Veteran,* Nov. 1916; Mary Maury Fitzgerald in *Richmond Mag.,* May 1931; obituary and editorial in *Richmond Times-Dispatch,* July 26, 1916. There are references to Miss Tompkins in Mary Boykin Chesnut, *A Diary from Dixie* (Ben Ames Williams, ed., 1949). Data on the Tompkins family was included in the *William and Mary College Quart.,* Jan. and July 1930. Captain Sally's commission is on display in Richmond's Confederate Museum, which also has her hospital's register and several account books and a collection of papers given by Miss Tompkins' cousin Mary Randolph Lane. Death record from Bureau of Vital Statistics, Va. Dept. of Health, Richmond.]

H. H. CUNNINGHAM

TOUPIN, Marie. *See* DORION, Marie.

TOWNE, Laura Matilda (May 3, 1825–Feb. 22, 1901), educator of freedmen, was born in Pittsburgh, Pa., the third daughter and fourth of seven children of John and Sarah (Robinson) Towne. Her father, a native of Methuen, Mass., was descended from William Towne, who migrated in the 1630's from England to Massachusetts Bay. John Towne's highly successful business ventures included fruit growing, the operation of steamboats between Pittsburgh and New Orleans, and trading in cotton and sugar. Laura's mother, born in Coventry, England, was a woman of remarkable talent and energy who assisted her husband in these

enterprises. Upon her death in 1833, shortly after the birth of their last child, Towne took his family to Boston, where he became superintendent of the city gas works. Returning to Pennsylvania in 1840 a wealthy man, he purchased a handsome house in Philadelphia and a country residence nearby; by his death in 1851 he had become one of the city's outstanding citizens. Laura's older brother, John Henry Towne, a well-known engineer, continued this tradition; the Towne School of Engineering of the University of Pennsylvania commemorates his large bequest.

The Townes were members of the First Unitarian Church of Philadelphia, and under the influence of its minister, William Henry Furness, young Laura became an abolitionist. She also developed an interest in homeopathic medicine and studied under Dr. Constantine Hering, the founder of several homeopathic institutions in the Philadelphia area. She probably enrolled at the short-lived eclectic institution called Penn Medical University, but there is no conclusive evidence that she received a degree. In the late 1850's Miss Towne taught at various "charity schools" in the North (Sherwood, p. 32n). The outbreak of the Civil War found her in Newport, R.I., uncertain how she might best serve the Union cause. Soon an opportunity arose that enabled her to combine her two great interests: abolition and medicine.

In November 1861, a few months after the war began, Federal forces occupied Port Royal, St. Helena, and the other coastal islands of South Carolina, the center of long-staple cotton culture and a district noted for its high concentration of slaves. Abandoned by their fleeing masters, these Negroes, numbering about ten thousand, were left without direction, short of food and prey to disease and abuse by the soldiers. The Treasury Department of the federal government, under Secretary Salmon P. Chase, a man of strong anti-slavery convictions, moved quickly both to salvage the valuable cotton crop and to meet the Negroes' needs. Edward L. Pierce, the young Boston abolitionist appointed to direct the undertaking, issued a call for doctors, teachers, and plantation superintendents. Among the earliest to come forward was Laura Matilda Towne, now thirty-six, who sailed for the islands in April 1862 under the auspices of the Port Royal Relief Committee of Philadelphia.

Like the other volunteers, Miss Towne hoped to make the Sea Islands a showcase for freedom and by the "Port Royal Experiment" to convince a reluctant North that emancipation was a desirable war aim. Beginning as secretary and housekeeper at Edward Pierce's headquarters on St. Helena Island, she was soon busily engaged in distributing clothing, practicing medicine, and teaching school. Thomas Wentworth Higginson, who recuperated from a war injury on the plantation where she lived, considered her "the most energetic [person] in the department," and wrote that she "prescribes for half the island & teaches the other half, besides keeping house beautifully & partly carrying on the plantation . . ." (to Louisa Storrow Higginson, Oct. 23, 1863, Higginson Papers).

Laura Towne's most important single achievement on St. Helena Island was the founding of the Penn School, one of the earliest and most long-lived of the freedmen's schools. With Ellen Murray, a close friend from Newport who had joined her a few months earlier, she established the school in September 1862 in a local Baptist church. In 1864, Miss Towne's Unitarianism having caused strained relations with their Baptist hosts, the two women moved into a schoolhouse of their own which had been sent in prefabricated sections by Miss Towne's Philadelphia supporters. She soon installed a bell—a symbol of her intention to follow the traditional New England educational pattern. Well educated for a woman of her time, she adhered consistently to solid academic subjects in her primary and secondary classes: arithmetic, writing, reading, geography, and even, at one point, Latin and Greek. The vocational education inculcated by Hampton Institute and Booker T. Washington's Tuskegee Institute made but small impression on the Penn School curriculum during the founder's lifetime. By 1867, recognizing that she practiced medicine "badly and very inefficiently" (*Letters and Diary*, p. 179), Laura Towne was ready to devote the rest of her life to teaching, which she found increasingly satisfying.

In subsequent decades her school was to prove of inestimable benefit to the Negroes of the Sea Islands, long providing the only secondary education available. After 1870 it also functioned as a normal school, training teachers for service elsewhere on the islands. Besides teaching, Laura Towne energetically discharged the duties of a public health officer. She also attempted, through the Band of Hope, a 1,500-member temperance society, to stamp out liquor. As an unofficial legal adviser—a function she performed surprisingly well for one untrained in law—she was influential in the struggle that eventually enabled the islanders to become the owners of the lands they had

worked all their lives. Her annual graduation ceremonies, for which former pupils gathered from far and near, served an important unifying function in the community. During most of her almost forty years on the Sea Islands, Laura Towne volunteered her services without pay, using the "dowry money" inherited from her father and money left to her by her eldest brother upon his death in 1875. Other school expenses were paid at first by the Pennsylvania Freedmen's Relief Association, then for a time after 1871 by the Benezet Society of Germantown, Pa., and finally by Miss Towne's own family, who made the Penn School a favorite object of their philanthropy.

A short, stout, plain woman with a determined, almost pugnacious, expression, Laura Towne was no gentle uplifter. "I have the reputation of being able to look after my things pretty sharply," she wrote (*ibid.*, p. 189). Though she viewed the traditional Sea Island religious "shouts" as a deplorable reversion to savagery, she was on the whole a sensitive observer who, unlike some Northern teachers who came south after the war, welcomed the decline of docility and the rise of a spirit of independence among the freedmen. A staunch Republican whose Northern sympathies remained undimmed, she had but slight contact with Southern whites on the mainland. In 1867 she purchased and renovated an abandoned St. Helena plantation, Frogmore, and here she lived with Miss Murray for the rest of her life, finding relaxation in gardening, surf bathing, occasional visits to the North, and a succession of canine pets. She died of influenza at Frogmore in 1901 at the age of seventy-five, after some years of recurring malarial attacks. Several hundred of her Sea Island neighbors followed the simple mule cart that carried her body to the Port Royal ferry, singing the spirituals their teacher had loved. She was buried in the family plot in Laurel Hill Cemetery, Philadelphia.

With the death of Miss Towne and the retirement soon after of Miss Murray, the school was renamed the Penn Normal, Industrial, and Agricultural School and came under the leadership of Miss Rossa B. Cooley (1873–1949), a Vassar graduate and teacher at Hampton Institute, who stressed the practical education Booker T. Washington advocated: home economics for the girls, agriculture for the boys. A larger school building was erected in 1904, and an industrial building in 1912. In 1948 the Penn School became a part of the (segregated) state public school system; by the 1960's it was serving as a community center devoted to adult education and civic activities.

[Laura Towne Papers, Southern Hist. Collection, Univ. of N.C., Chapel Hill; Thomas Wentworth Higginson Papers, Houghton Library, Harvard Univ.; Rupert S. Holland, ed., *Letters and Diary of Laura M. Towne* (1912); Laura M. Towne, "Pioneer Work on the Sea Islands," *Southern Workman*, July 1901; H. N. Sherwood, ed., "Jour. of Miss Susan Walker," Hist. and Philosophical Soc. of Ohio, *Quart. Publications*, Jan.–Mar. 1912; Gerald Robbins, "Laura Towne," *Jour. of Education*, Apr. 1961; Guion G. Johnson, *A Social Hist. of the Sea Islands* (1930); Willie Lee Rose, *Rehearsal for Reconstruction* (1964); information from Miss Ida J. Draeger, Librarian, Woman's Medical College of Pa. See also: Edwin E. Towne, *The Descendants of William Towne* (1901); entries on Miss Towne's brother, John Henry Towne, and her nephew, Henry Robinson Towne, in *Dict. Am. Biog.;* Rossa B. Cooley, *School Acres: An Adventure in Rural Education* (1930); Gerald Robbins, "Rossa B. Cooley and Penn School," *Jour. of Negro Education*, Winter 1964.]

WILLIE LEE ROSE

**TRACY, Hannah Maria Conant.** *See* CUTLER, Hannah Maria Conant Tracy.

**TRACY, Martha** (Apr. 10, 1876–Mar. 22, 1942), physician, dean of the Woman's Medical College of Pennsylvania, and public health administrator, was born in Plainfield, N.J., the youngest daughter and eighth of the nine children of Jeremiah Evarts Tracy and Martha Sherman (Greene) Tracy. Both her parents were descendants of Roger Sherman of Connecticut, signer of the Declaration of Independence, the Articles of Confederation, and the Constitution. Her father, born in Windsor, Vt., and a graduate of the Yale Law School, was a nephew and law partner of William M. Evarts, Secretary of State under President Hayes.

After graduating from the Plainfield Seminary for Young Ladies and Children, Martha Tracy entered Bryn Mawr College to prepare herself for a career in medicine. Although admission to most medical schools at that time required only a high school certificate, she formulated her own set of prerequisites and at Bryn Mawr studied biology under Thomas Hunt Morgan and chemistry under Elmer P. Kohler, as well as physics, mathematics, philosophy, and Greek. She served as captain of the class basketball team. A classmate recalled that "she had the gift of beauty, brown hair and very blue eyes, and a kind of 'completed' look in her finely cut features." She graduated in 1898. Illness delayed her entrance into the Woman's Medical College of Pennsylvania, from which she received her M.D. in 1904, setting a pace for her classmates as a hard worker. She then enrolled as a graduate student at

Cornell Medical College in New York. Here for three years she served as an assistant in the laboratory of experimental pathology under Dr. William B. Coley; she is credited with having helped him develop "Coley's Fluid," long used in the treatment of sarcoma. In 1907, giving up an assured future in medical research, she returned to the Woman's Medical College as associate professor of chemistry.

Dr. Tracy took a year's leave of absence in 1911 to study physiological chemistry at Yale, whose department trained most of the country's early medical biochemists. After her return, in 1913, the chemistry department of the Woman's Medical College was converted into a department of physiological chemistry, with Martha Tracy as professor. While continuing her teaching, she next undertook the study of public health and preventive medicine, having realized the importance of this field, especially for women physicians; she received the degree of Doctor of Public Hygiene from the University of Pennsylvania in 1917. That same year, after the retirement of Dr. CLARA MARSHALL, she was made dean.

During Dr. Tracy's administration the college was shaken by a series of crises which threatened to end its existence, but her faith in the need for a women's college of medicine, based on her observation at Cornell and Yale of the limited opportunities for women in coeducational schools, never wavered. During the war years she kept the college in operation despite the departure of nine senior professors, two women and seven men, for war service, and arranged public classes in sanitation and hygiene to prepare women for war work. In 1921, when the National American Woman Suffrage Association endowed the Anna Howard Shaw Chair of Preventive Medicine as a memorial to the suffrage leader, Dr. Tracy was appointed to this professorship, relinquishing her teaching in the department of physiological chemistry.

In 1921 the Woman's Medical College was faced with bankruptcy. A majority of its trustees favored merger with the University of Pennsylvania, but resigned in the face of determined opposition from Sarah Logan Wistar Starr (Mrs. James Starr, Jr.), who then became president of a reconstituted board. There followed an administrative reorganization of the college and its associated hospital, placing control over expenditures and appointments in an executive committee of trustees, which also assumed responsibility for the college's debts. Dissension, however, arose within the college over the introduction of the new business methods and culminated in 1923 when the professor of obstetrics failed of reappointment, after eighteen years of tenure. Twenty-six members of the faculty resigned in protest, and the students went on strike. Dean Tracy met this emergency with firmness, hired new faculty, and kept the college in session, and the storm was weathered.

In 1925, reflecting Dr. Tracy's determination to maintain high standards, the decision was made to abandon the old college and hospital buildings, now in bad repair, and build a modern plant in a better location. The cornerstone of a new college at East Falls, in the northern part of Philadelphia, was laid the next year and, after an energetic fund-raising campaign directed by Mrs. Starr, the college opened in its new quarters in the fall of 1930. At this time Dean Tracy relinquished her teaching duties to devote herself fully to administration. The great depression dealt the college a severe blow. Its income decreased so sharply that it could no longer pay the salaries of the required number of full-time professors, and in 1935 for the first time it lost its acceptable rating with the American Medical Association and was placed on probation for two years. Mrs. Starr, though no longer president of the trustees, now undertook to head an emergency fund campaign. In this the Pennsylvania Federation of Women's Clubs joined as a tribute to their honorary vice-president, ninety-year-old LUCRETIA LONGSHORE BLANKENBURG, whose mother, Dr. HANNAH LONGSHORE, had been one of the college's first graduates. Mrs. Blankenburg herself made an appeal by letter, and in 1937 the college was able to recover its standing. Dean Tracy now raised the entrance requirements to four years of undergraduate work.

Martha Tracy's respected standing in her profession and her sound judgment and "invincible dignity" had given the Woman's Medical College strength in a prolonged time of trouble. She had been president of the Medical Women's National Association (later the American Medical Women's Association) in 1920–21 and was for many years a member of its board. She became a Fellow of the American College of Physicians in 1923 and in 1934 the second woman elected a Fellow of the College of Physicians of Philadelphia. From 1936 to 1940 she served on the Philadelphia Board of Health. Outdoor life was her favorite recreation, and she enjoyed spending summers at her camp in the Adirondacks. In religion she was a Presbyterian. In 1940, when approaching retirement age, she resigned from the Woman's Medical College to become assistant director of public health for the City of Philadelphia. After the attack on Pearl Harbor she worked

energetically at organizing community health defense squads. Returning home at night in March 1942 from one of her many public lectures, she suffered a chill and a few days later died of pneumonia in the Woman's Medical College Hospital. A memorial service was held at the College of Physicians of Philadelphia, and burial was in the family plot at Hillside Cemetery, Plainfield, N.J.

[*Memorial Service in Honor of Dr. Martha Tracy . . . at the College of Physicians of Phila.* (1942); memoir by Catharine Macfarlane in College of Physicians of Phila., *Transactions & Studies*, Dec. 1942, with a list of Dr. Tracy's publications (briefer versions of the memoir are in *Women in Medicine* and the *Medical Woman's Jour.*, both Apr. 1942); *Dedication of the Martha Tracy Memorial Research Room* (Bryn Mawr College, 1948); Gulielma F. Alsop, *Hist. of the Woman's Medical College* (1950); *Nat. Cyc. Am. Biog.*, XXXI, 205–06; *Phila. Inquirer*, Mar. 23, 1942; Sherman W. Tracy, comp., *The Tracy Genealogy* (1936); materials in the library of the Woman's Medical College.]

GULIELMA F. ALSOP

**TRADER, Ella King Newsom** (June 1838–Jan. 20, 1919), Confederate hospital administrator, was born in Brandon, Miss., the daughter of Julia and Thomas S. N. King. She was the second child and the oldest of four daughters in a family of seven. Her father, a native of North Carolina, was the first pastor to serve the First Baptist Church of Brandon. In later years Ella recalled that he "was quite well off in this world's goods," and that her mother came of an aristocratic Georgia family. In 1849 the Kings moved to a farm in Phillips County, Ark., where on Feb. 6, 1854, Ella was married to William Frank Newsom, a physician and a transplanted Tennessean with extensive landholdings. Dr. Newsom's untimely death left her with a rather substantial fortune, and upon the outbreak of war, she decided, in memory of her husband, to dedicate herself and her means to work in the military hospitals of the Confederacy.

When the war came Mrs. Newsom was twenty-two and living in Winchester, Tenn., superintending the education of her three younger sisters at Mary Sharp College, a Baptist institution which she herself had attended. After returning her charges to their Arkansas residence, she set out for Memphis with hospital stores which she had collected and a number of her servants. There she received instruction in nursing at the City Hospital, served in the Southern Mothers' Home, and after the battle of Belmont accepted the position of matron in the Overton Hospital. In December

1861 Mrs. Newsom took her servants and a carload of supplies to Bowling Green, Ky., where she ministered to disabled Confederate troops amidst scenes bordering on chaos, for the Confederacy at this time had organized only limited hospital service. In the absence of adequate official personnel, she agreed, at the request of medical officers, to take charge of the hospital in Bowling Green, a position she held until the surrender of Forts Henry and Donelson in February 1862.

During the weeks following this twin disaster for the Confederacy—the beginning of General Grant's advance on the Western front —Mrs. Newsom organized a military hospital in Nashville's Howard High School and directed the movements of hospitalized troops from Nashville to Winchester, Tenn., and from Winchester to Atlanta. In answer to an urgent appeal for her services after the battle of Shiloh, she left Atlanta with servants and supplies and continued her ministrations in Corinth, Miss., at the Tishomingo and Corinth House hospital establishments. The latter part of 1862 found Mrs. Newsom at Chattanooga, where she had charge of the Foard Hospital. After the act of September 1862 providing for organized hospital staffs, she served in an official capacity as chief matron of Chattanooga's Academy Hospital, where she supervised "the entire domestic economy," with particular responsibility for regulating the patients' diet. Some measure of the esteem in which she was held is seen in the naming of a Chattanooga hospital, the Newsom, in her honor.

Later, as the Army of Tennessee retreated southward, Mrs. Newsom organized hospitals in Marietta, Ga. Although failing health required her to take occasional rests from hospital duties late in the war, she adhered to her original resolution until the end of the fighting and acquired a reputation for devoted service second to no other hospital worker in the Western theatre. The high respect she commanded from top-ranking officers—attributable in part perhaps to her intelligence, wealth, and social position—helped her obtain supplies and other considerations essential to the effective care of the disabled. Her gentleness and unswerving loyalty to the cause inspired hospital associates and gave her a place in the firmament of Confederate heroines as "the Florence Nightingale of the South." As to the long-range significance of her work, there can be no question that she, with other women who braved the contemporary taboo against feminine employment in the military hospitals, gave an important impetus to the subsequent development of a trained nursing profession.

Mrs. Newsom's later life was in large part a rather grim struggle for existence. In 1867 she was married to Col. William H. Trader, a former Confederate officer of Arkansas. Much of her property had been confiscated or destroyed during the war, and the 1,100-acre cotton plantation she had inherited from her first husband was apparently lost through the business misfortunes of the second. Colonel Trader's death in 1885 left her and her daughter, May, the only survivor of their several children, in an almost destitute condition. Blind in one eye and nearly deaf, Mrs. Trader moved to Asheville, N.C. The *Asheville Advance,* aware of her wartime contribution to the Confederacy, attempted unsuccessfully to raise a popular subscription to buy her a home. When, however, the election of Cleveland brought the first postwar Democratic administration into office, with a Southerner, Lucius Q. C. Lamar, as Secretary of the Interior, Mrs. Trader obtained a government post in Washington. For the next three decades, from Aug. 20, 1886, until her resignation on Jan. 10, 1916, she served in the General Land Office, the Patent Office, and the Pension Office. She died of acute bronchitis in Washington at the age of eighty and was buried there in Rock Creek Cemetery.

[There is no adequate biography, but the most complete account is Jacob Fraise Richard's *The Florence Nightingale of the Southern Army: Experiences of Mrs. Ella K. Newsom, Confederate Nurse in the Great War of 1861–65* (1914). Briefer sketches are in: Kate Cumming, *Gleanings from Southland* (1895), pp. 271–75; Matthew Page Andrews, comp., *The Women of the South in War Times* (1927), pp. 131–44; Richard B. Harwell, ed., *Kate: The Jour. of a Confederate Nurse* (1959), pp. 39–40; *Confederate Veteran,* Apr. 1898 and Oct. 1908; and *Ark. Gazette,* Jan. 22, 1919. On Confederate hospital organization, see H. H. Cunningham, *Doctors in Gray* (1958). Family data was obtained from the Rankin County, Miss., census of 1840 (courtesy of Miss. Dept. of Archives and Hist., Jackson) and from censuses of 1850 and 1860 for Phillips County, Ark., and Phillips County tax records (Ark. Hist. Commission, Little Rock). A copy of the certificate of her first marriage was supplied by the Clerk of the Circuit Court, Phillips County. Postwar employment data was furnished by the General Services Administration's Federal Records Center, St. Louis, Mo., and her death record by the Vital Statistics Section of the D.C. Dept. of Public Health.]

H. H. CUNNINGHAM

TRASK, Kate Nichols (May 30, 1853–Jan. 8, 1922), author and philanthropist, commonly known as Katrina Trask, was born in Brooklyn,

N.Y., the first of four children of George Little Nichols and his wife, Christina Mary Cole. Her father, of English origin, was a partner in a large New York City importing firm and active in Republican political circles. Her mother's parents had migrated from Holland early in the century, changing the family name from "Kool" to "Cole." A beautiful girl with literary tastes, Kate grew up accustomed to wealth and high social position. She was educated by tutors and in fashionable private schools. On Nov. 12, 1874, she was married to Spencer Trask, a prominent Wall Street banker and financier of old New England ancestry who had amassed a considerable fortune in the industrial expansion following the Civil War. A director of several railroads and president of the Edison Illuminating Company of New York, Trask, with others, planned and financed the reorganization of the *New York Times* in 1896 that placed Adolph Ochs in control, he himself becoming chairman of the newly formed publishing company.

The Trasks had four children, Alan, Christina, Spencer, and Katrina, all of whom died in infancy or childhood. It was after a period of illness and grief following the death of the last in 1888 that Mrs. Trask began to write. In 1892 at her husband's suggestion she published (anonymously) *Under King Constantine*, a group of three long love poems. The book won praise from a contemporary critic for its "spiritual loveliness" and went through five editions; with the second edition the author acknowledged her identity as "Katrina Trask," the name she used thereafter. Her books include *Free Not Bound* (1903), a novel, and *Night & Morning* (1907), a narrative in blank verse, both of which dealt with love and marriage, and *King Alfred's Jewel* (1908), a historical drama in blank verse marked by "a noble ethical spirit" (Flower, p. 264). Mrs. Trask was an ardent pacifist, and perhaps her most successful work was an antiwar play, *In the Vanguard*. First presented in the year before the outbreak of World War I, it was widely performed before women's clubs and church groups, and in its printed form went through eight editions.

Conventionally religious, essentially a romantic, Mrs. Trask through her writings expressed her conviction that spiritual goodness exerts force. By today's standards her writing seems sentimental and superficial, using emotional devices to express moral precepts and a vague wish for social reform. As a literary figure she was at home among such turn-of-the-century custodians of traditional cultural values as Henry van Dyke and Richard Henry Stod-

dard; Benjamin O. Flower, crusading editor of the *Arena* magazine, was also a friend. She and her husband frequently entertained artists and writers at Yaddo, their three-hundred-acre country estate near Saratoga Springs, N.Y., for Mrs. Trask considered the place a mystical source of creative inspiration for herself and her guests. Her eventual dedication of her estate to this purpose became her most lasting achievement.

Believing that wealth imposes obligations on its possessor, the Trasks consistently supported a number of local charities and established in Saratoga Springs the St. Christina Hospital for the treatment of crippled children. Mrs. Trask's plans for Yaddo began in the summer of 1899 when she underwent a mystical experience in which she envisioned a perpetual pilgrimage of artists coming there to "find the Sacred Fire, and light their torches at its flame" (Waite, p. 35). Since they had no children to inherit their beloved country home, she and her husband then decided to put her vision into effect after their deaths. Spencer Trask was killed in a railroad accident in 1909, and four years later Katrina Trask publicly outlined plans for the estate's future use. That year she suffered a series of heart attacks, and much of the rest of her life was spent as a semi-invalid confined to Yaddo and devoted to its physical and financial development. On Feb. 6, 1921, she was married to George Foster Peabody, a lifelong friend, former business partner of Spencer Trask, and a well-known philanthropist in his own right. She died at Yaddo less than a year later of bronchial pneumonia, at the age of sixty-eight. Following a private Episcopal service, she was buried on the estate grounds.

Four years later, in June 1926, Yaddo was opened as an artists' colony. Like the earlier MacDowell Colony at Peterborough, N.H., it was designed as a rustic retreat where creative individuals could work for short periods of time, free of expense or disturbance. Each summer a select group of serious artists, writers, and composers has continued to come to Yaddo, to live amid the elegance of its fifty-five-room Gothic mansion, vast woodlands, lakes, rose gardens, and marble statuary, and to work at what they please, thus giving a measure of substance to the romantic dream of a generous patron of the arts.

[Marjorie Peabody Waite, *Yaddo, Yesterday and Today* (1933); *N.Y. Times*, Jan. 9, 1922 (obituary and editorial); *N.Y. Herald*, Jan. 9, 1922; *Woman's Who's Who of America*, 1914–15; *Who Was Who in America*, vol. I (1942); *Nat. Cyc. Am. Biog.*, XI, 444–45 (entries for Katrina and Spencer Trask) and III, 211 (for her father); "Mrs. Trask's

Appeal against War," *Am. Rev. of Revs.*, June 1913, which includes early photos of Yaddo; B. O. Flower, "Katrina Trask: Poet of Peace," in his *Progressive Men, Women, and Movements of the Past Twenty-Five Years* (1914), pp. 259–68. See also: Margery Swett Mansfield, "Yaddo," *Poetry*, Mar. 1927; Jacob Getlar Smith, "Yaddo: A Working Community for Artists," *Am. Artist*, Mar. 1955; "Yaddo and Substance," *Time*, Sept. 5, 1938, p. 50.]

H. R. WEBER

**TRASK, Katrina.** *See* TRASK, Kate Nichols.

**TREVILLE, Abigail.** *See* STONEMAN, Abigail.

**TROUBETZKOY, Amélie Rives.** *See* RIVES, Amélie Louise.

**TROUP, Augusta Lewis** (c. 1848–Sept. 14, 1920), labor organizer and journalist, was born in New York City. Little is known of her parents, Charles and Elizabeth (Rowe) Lewis, although her death certificate indicates that they were natives, respectively, of England and New York City. Left an orphan in infancy, Augusta grew up in the Brooklyn Heights home of Isaac Baldwin Gager, a broker and commission merchant, who had the delicate child educated by private tutors. After spending several seasons in the home of one of her teachers at Cold Spring, N.Y., on the Hudson River, she returned to New York City to attend Brooklyn Heights Seminary and later to graduate, with honors, from the convent school of the Sacred Heart in Manhattanville, where she took courses in French, the classics, literature, and philosophy.

The depression of 1866–67 compelled Augusta Lewis to earn her own livelihood, although she was not yet twenty. A facile writer and talker, gifted as well with good looks and charm (ELIZABETH CADY STANTON described her as "a brunette young lady with pleasing dark eyes"), she became a reporter for the New York *Sun* and a contributor to various magazines, including the French *Courier des États-Unis*. She then took up typesetting, and after an apprenticeship on the *Era*, joined the staff of the New York *World*. She developed a high level of skill; when asked to demonstrate the newly developed Alden typesetting machine, she set up Washington Irving's "Rip Van Winkle"—24,993 ems of solid agate type—in six and a half hours. Continuing also as a reporter, she interviewed visiting celebrities, including Charles Dickens, and developed a wide acquaintance in artistic and reform circles.

"Gussie" Lewis quickly emerged as a leader among the women of her craft. When, late in 1867, the International Typographical Union went on strike against the *World*, the nonunion women typesetters remained on the job. With the settlement of the strike the following summer, most of these women were summarily fired. Miss Lewis apparently resigned in sympathy and thereafter worked for a succession of small printing firms and reform periodicals willing to treat women workers with equality. Convinced that women typesetters, too, must organize, she joined SUSAN B. ANTHONY and Elizabeth Cady Stanton, then in New York publishing their woman's rights paper, the *Revolution*, in founding the New York Working Women's Association. Organized Sept. 17, 1868, in the *Revolution*'s offices, it proposed to "act for its members, in the same manner as the associations of workingmen now regulate the wages, etc., of those belonging to them" (*Revolution*, Sept. 24, 1868, p. 181).

The aims of the working women and the suffrage leaders showed some divergence from the start. Mrs. Stanton wanted the association to support woman suffrage, but Augusta Lewis objected, arguing that to press the issue upon working women who were taking their first steps toward cooperation would jeopardize the group's very life. Miss Anthony wished at all cost to secure wider employment opportunities for women, whereas Miss Lewis was committed to the principle of union loyalty, even when it meant forfeiting a job. These two views came into conflict early in 1869 when New York printers in book and job shops went on strike. While Miss Lewis sought earnestly to keep women from scabbing, Miss Anthony urged the employers to train and hire female typesetters. Union partisans were incensed, and at the National Labor Union convention that August in Philadelphia, delegates from New York, with the support of Miss Lewis—who, it was said, had been fired by the *Revolution*'s printer for her union activity—blocked the acceptance of Miss Anthony as a delegate from the Working Women's Association.

Meanwhile Augusta Lewis had become increasingly involved in the labor movement as president of Women's Typographical Union No. 1. This was organized in October 1868 through her initiative and with the active encouragement of the strong New York Local 6 of the International Typographical Union, particularly the local's corresponding secretary, Alexander Troup, who was also secretary-treasurer of the I.T.U. In June 1869 Miss Lewis and Eva Howard, treasurer of the women's local, appeared before the national convention of the I.T.U. in Albany to request a charter for their union. The request was granted, but the tiny group, which never numbered more than forty, had a difficult time. Antiunion firms would not hire them, and they consistently refused to scab on male union members. When they did secure work, the stubborn refusal of many employers to pay women equal wages constituted a serious threat to the union scale, and their presence in the industry came to be so resented that many union foremen refused to hire them.

Rather surprisingly, in the face of such prejudice, the International Typographical Union at its convention in 1870 elected Miss Lewis corresponding secretary, a distinction which long remained unique. This position was anything but a sinecure (at a later day the job would have been more aptly titled administrative or organizing secretary), and during her one-year term she showed marked ability, overcoming hostility with tact and firmness. She was instrumental in bringing many nonunion women typesetters into the I.T.U., and her report to the convention of 1872 on conditions among both men and women employed in the printing trades displays a firsthand knowledge of the field and a mastery of its problems. Women's Typographical Union No. 1 went out of existence in 1878, and that same year the I.T.U. voted not to charter any more women's unions. The principle for which Augusta Lewis had contended was not lost, however, for the typographers soon began to admit women in full equality to their regularly established locals.

On June 12, 1874, in Cold Spring, Miss Lewis was married to Alexander Troup, now no longer an active unionist but publisher of a daily paper friendly to labor's interests, the *New Haven* (Conn.) *Union*. The couple settled in New Haven and had seven children: Alexander (who succeeded his father as publisher of the *Union*); Marie Grace; Philip (who became postmaster of New Haven); two daughters who died in infancy, Augusta Lewis and Jessie; George Bernardine (a daughter); and Elsie. Troup's paper prospered, and he became active in politics, serving on the Democratic National Committee, as federal collector of internal revenue for Connecticut and Rhode Island, and as a member of the Connecticut legislature; he died in 1908. Mrs. Troup, despite her early differences with suffrage leaders, supported the cause of woman suffrage, wrote articles for the *Union* throughout her life, and became widely identified with charitable causes in New Haven, particularly with the welfare of the city's Italian community. Several years after her death the Augusta Lewis Troup Junior High School on Edgewood Avenue was built

and named for her; a tablet in its hallway commemorates her as the "Little Mother of the Italian Colony." In religion she was a convert to Roman Catholicism. She died in New Haven in 1920 of valvular disease of the heart and was buried in that city's Evergreen Cemetery.

[*Revolution*, Sept. 24, Oct. 1, 8, 15, 1868, Feb. 4, 11, June 24, Sept. 9, 1869; N.Y. *World*, Aug. 17, 1869; George A. Stevens, *N.Y. Typographical Union No. 6* (1913), pp. 429–40; George A. Tracy, *Hist. of the Typographical Union* (1913), pp. 250–51, 253–56; obituaries in *New Haven Evening Register*, Sept. 14, and *New Haven Jour.-Courier*, Sept. 15, 1920; death certificate from State Dept. of Health, Hartford; information from Mrs. R. P. (Elsie Troup) Daignault, Woonsocket, R.I. See also article on Alexander Troup in *Nat. Cyc. Am. Biog.*, XVII, 27.]

ELEANOR FLEXNER

**TRUTH, Sojourner** (c. 1797–Nov. 26, 1883), abolitionist and reformer, was next to the youngest of the several children of James and Elizabeth (or Betsey), slaves of a wealthy Dutch patroon, Charles Hardenbergh, in Hurley, Ulster County, N.Y. Most of the incidents in her life until 1828 are distorted by a haze of hearsay and legend, but some things are fairly clear. She was named Isabella, and her first language was Dutch. After passing through the hands of several owners, she served from 1810 to 1827 in the household of John J. Dumont of New Paltz, N.Y., where she bore at least five children by a fellow slave named Thomas; of the son and three daughters who survived infancy, two girls were sold away from her. In 1827, the year before the mandatory emancipation of slaves in New York state, she fled Dumont's household and found refuge nearby with Isaac and Maria Van Wagener, whose name she took. Learning that her son Peter had been sold illegally to an Alabaman, she instituted, with the help of Quaker friends, successful legal proceedings to secure his return.

As Isabella Van Wagener, she arrived in New York City with her two youngest children, Peter and Sophia, around 1829 and secured domestic employment. A mystic who had visions and heard voices, which she identified as God's, she joined the John Street Methodist Church and, later, the African Zion Church, but she found a more satisfactory religious outlet in her attachment to Elijah Pierson, a wealthy fanatic who called himself "The Tishbite." Pierson and his wife, Sarah, had undertaken a widespread mission of conversion in New York, especially among the prostitutes of the notorious "Five Points" area. Joined by Isabella, they preached on the streets, where Isabella's tall, gaunt, masculine figure and guttural Dutch-accented voice attracted welcome attention. Isabella also assisted in the religious services of the Retrenchment Society, a cult which Pierson founded and in the name of which he supported a church and a refuge for "fallen women" called Magdalene Asylum. Sometime between 1829 and 1831, she joined the Piersons' private household, where they prayed together interminably and fasted for three days at a stretch.

When a bearded charlatan, Robert Matthews, who called himself Matthias, appeared at the Pierson home in the spring of 1832 announcing his divine mission, the three mystics were ready to receive him. This was a time of intense evangelism and of idealistic strivings for the good life, which many Americans sought in communal associations such as Oneida in New York state and Brook Farm in Massachusetts. When in 1833 Matthews established "Zion Hill" in Sing Sing, N.Y., Pierson and his family, including Isabella, were among those who turned their resources over to him and joined the household. It lasted two years amid growing rumors of moral irregularities and ended when Pierson's mysterious death brought the arrest, trial, and eventual acquittal of Matthews. Popular rumor, fanned by newspapers and a sensational pamphlet, unjustly implicated Isabella in the scandal, and she came through these troubles—which included a successful libel suit on her part—a somewhat changed woman. For eight or nine years she lived quietly in New York, maintaining a home for her two children and earning her living as a cook, maid, and laundress, and regularly attending the African Zion Church. Though she continued to have mystical experiences and what HARRIET BEECHER STOWE was to call "strange powers," she was not again noticeably influenced by them until 1843, when the voices commanded her to take the name "Sojourner Truth" and travel east to preach.

She set out alone in June 1843 and spent the summer walking through Long Island and Connecticut. Sleeping wherever shelter offered, working when she needed food, she sang and discoursed at camp meetings, in churches, on highways, and in the streets of towns. Her message was simple: God was loving, kind, and good, and all men should love one another. Though illiterate all her life, she acquired a wide Biblical knowledge and enjoyed debating with adherents of various sects, notably the Millerites, who in the 1840's anticipated the imminent return of Christ.

The winter of 1843 found her in Northampton, Mass., a member of a communal farm and silk factory, the Northampton Association of Education and Industry, founded by George W. Benson, brother-in-law of William Lloyd Garrison. Encountering the abolitionist movement for the first time, she became an enthusiastic convert. When the Association collapsed in 1846 she remained in the Benson household as both servant and guest, while making periodic speaking forays throughout the state. The abolitionist leaders recognized her unique gifts and publicized her travels in their periodicals.

Around 1850 she went west, her growing reputation having preceded her. She had a personal magnetism that drew great crowds, which were held by her homely, trenchant, seemingly random remarks, her gift for repartee, and her gospel songs. In Ohio the office of the Salem *Anti-Slavery Bugle* was her headquarters, from whence she toured Indiana, Missouri, and Kansas, at times sharing platforms with Parker Pillsbury, Frederick Douglass, and other abolitionist leaders. She maintained herself by selling the *Narrative of Sojourner Truth* (1850), written for her by Olive Gilbert. On an eastern swing in 1852–53 she spent several days in Andover, Mass., with Harriet Beecher Stowe, who spread her fame by describing her visitor (whom she called "The Libyan Sibyl") in an *Atlantic Monthly* article of April 1863. Southern sympathizers often tried to disrupt her meetings. She was clubbed in Kansas and mobbed in Missouri, where the *St. Louis Dispatch* reported, "Sojourner Truth is the name of a man now lecturing in Kansas City." The allegation was hard to shake off. Once at a woman's rights convention in Indiana she bared her breast to prove she was a woman. Having first encountered the woman's rights movement and its leaders while selling her *Narrative* at the convention held in Worcester, Mass., in 1850, she promptly added this string to her bow, speaking at woman's rights meetings in Akron, Ohio (1851), and New York City (1853). In postwar years, with the encouragement of ELIZABETH CADY STANTON and others, she continued on occasion to put in appearances at woman suffrage gatherings.

In the mid-1850's Sojourner Truth settled in Battle Creek, Mich., to which her three daughters with their families eventually migrated. When the Civil War began, she tramped through Michigan soliciting gifts of food and clothing for Negro volunteer regiments. In 1864 she traveled to Washington, D.C., where President Lincoln received her at the White House in October. That December the National

Freedmen's Relief Association appointed her "counselor to the freed people" at Freedmen's Village, Arlington Heights, Va., a position she held for about a year. This work gave her a new idea, the "Negro State"; and this became the subject of a petition she circulated widely and presented to President Grant in 1870. It urged the government, instead of supporting Negroes in refugee camps, to settle them on public land in the West. Though the idea never became popular, it seems indisputable that the voluntary migration of substantial numbers of Negroes to Kansas and Missouri in the 1870's stemmed partly from her encouragement. She visited settlements of Negroes in the Midwest and lectured them, "Be clean! Be clean! for cleanliness is godliness." But Negro audiences occupied much less of her time than white. She stumped the East from Washington to Boston and the West to Iowa, in itinerant, unplanned speaking tours during which she sold her book and photographs of herself and reiterated her message of mystic but benevolent religious sentiments, Negro rights, and woman suffrage, and her exhortations to temperance. Her audiences ranged from "small" to "good size." Newspapers still took note of her appearances, but as the years passed the stories that lauded her were sometimes mixed with ridicule.

In 1875 Sammy Banks, her grandson and constant companion, fell ill, and Sojourner Truth returned to Battle Creek, never to leave again. By her own faulty reckoning, she was nearly a century old, and her health was poor. Though her role in the reform movements of her day had been a relatively minor one, her colorful personality and background had captured the imagination of many, and yearly until her death in 1883 she had hundreds of visitors. Her funeral at the Congregational and Presbyterian Church was said to have been the largest ever held in the town. She was buried in Oak Hill Cemetery, Battle Creek.

[The fullest biographies are Arthur H. Fauset, *Sojourner Truth* (1938), and Hertha Pauli, *Her Name Was Sojourner Truth* (1962). See also: Olive Gilbert, *Narrative of Sojourner Truth* (1850 and later editions, some with addenda); Gilbert Vale, *Fanaticism, Its Source and Influence: Illustrated by the Simple Narrative of Isabella* (1835); Elizabeth C. Stanton et al., *Hist. of Woman Suffrage*, vols. I–III (1881–86)—see index under "Sojourner"; Benjamin Brawley, *Negro Builders and Heroes* (1937).]

SAUNDERS REDDING

TUBMAN, Harriet (1820?–Mar. 10, 1913), fugitive slave and rescuer of slaves, Civil War scout and nurse, was born on a plantation in Dorchester County on Maryland's Eastern Shore, one of the ten or eleven children of Benjamin Ross and Harriet Greene. Her grandparents on both sides had come in chains from Africa. She was named Araminta, but later chose the name of her mother. From an early age she was compelled to perform various duties—as maid, child's nurse, field hand, and cook—for her master or for persons who hired her services, but she was not a satisfactory servant, and there were constant complaints about her work. When she was about thirteen years of age an overseer struck her in the head with a two-pound weight and fractured her skull. The pressure on the brain caused spells of somnolence from which she suffered for the remainder of her life. Her varied childhood also included periods spent working with her father, who hired out as a woodcutter. From such work she gained the great physical stamina which stood her in good stead in later years. About 1844 she was married to a free Negro named John Tubman. There were no children.

From 1847 to 1849 Harriet Tubman worked in the household of one Anthony Thompson, physician, real estate speculator, and Methodist clergyman, whose father was the legal guardian of Harriet's master, who was not yet of age. In 1849 this youthful master died, and rumors circulated that his slaves were to be sold out of the state. Apprehensive of her fate, Harriet decided to make the break for freedom. She was successful in reaching Philadelphia, where she secured hotel employment.

Wages interested her but little, however, except to finance the schemes that had taken shape in her mind. In December 1850 she returned to Baltimore and guided her sister and two children to freedom. In 1851 she spirited a brother and his family out of slavery; later that same year she brought out a party of eleven, including another brother and his family. She had hoped to bring her husband as well, but he had remarried and declined her assistance. In all, in the decade preceding the Civil War, between intervals of employment in the North, Harriet Tubman is believed to have made some nineteen trips into Maryland. Estimates of the number of slaves she delivered have ranged from sixty to three hundred. Her most memorable excursion was in June 1857, when she returned to the Eastern Shore, hired a wagon, and brought out her aged parents. In these efforts she sometimes worked with antislavery stalwarts associated with the Underground Railroad, particularly the Quaker Thomas Garrett of Wilmington, Del., and the Negro leader William Still of Philadelphia. The latter subsequently wrote of her: "Harriet was a woman of no pretensions, indeed, a more ordinary specimen of humanity could hardly be found among the most unfortunate-looking farm hands of the South. Yet, in point of courage, shrewdness and disinterested exertions to rescue her fellowmen, by making personal visits into Maryland among the slaves, she was without her equal" (Still, p. 297).

Harriet Tubman gradually became well known among abolitionists, whose conventions she sometimes addressed; Gerrit Smith, Wendell Phillips, Frederick Douglass, and Oliver Johnson of the New York office of the American Anti-Slavery Society all knew and praised her. Many stories testify to her remarkable resourcefulness and ingenuity. To notify prospective fugitives that she would soon arrive, she at times sent cryptic messages unintelligible except to those for whom they were intended. One such message said: "[T]ell my brothers to be always watching unto prayer, and when the good old ship of Zion comes along, to be ready to step on board." Once, suspecting that pursuers were on her trail, she deliberately boarded a southbound train, confident that no one would suspect her party if it were traveling in that direction. On another occasion, when she saw a former master approaching, she turned loose several chickens that she had purchased in a local market; in her scramble to recover them, she went unrecognized. She is said to have carried a revolver for her own protection and to prod the fainthearted among the fugitives. Maryland slaveholders grudgingly acknowledged her effectiveness, and in 1858 several conventions were held on the Eastern Shore to discuss the problem of escaped slaves. At one time the rewards for her capture reached $40,000. Not all her exploits took place in the South. In April 1860 in Troy, N.Y., she was one of the leaders in a crowd that overpowered officers who had a fugitive slave in their custody, released him, and assisted him in his escape to Canada.

Shortly after her own escape, Harriet Tubman had taken up residence in St. Catharines, Ontario, and here for several years she brought those she spirited out of Maryland. Here, too, in April 1858, she counseled and encouraged John Brown, who was formulating his plan for armed action against slavery; Brown referred to her thereafter as "General Tubman." In 1858 or 1859 she moved to a small farm on the outskirts of Auburn, N.Y., which had been sold to her on liberal terms by Senator William H. Seward. This remained her home for the rest of her life.

Harriet Tubman was a deeply religious person who never doubted that her actions were guided by divine commands conveyed through omens, dreams, and warnings. Having "foreseen" the Civil War in a vision, she was not surprised when hostilities began. She wanted to serve, and early in 1862, armed with an endorsement from Gov. John A. Andrew of Massachusetts, she made her way to Beaufort, S.C., the principal town of a group of coastal islands recently seized by Federal forces. Here, together with many other civilian volunteers drawn from abolitionist ranks, she offered her services to Major General David Hunter, commander of the Department of the South, who gave her a pass to travel on all government transports. For the next three years she served in South Carolina as a spy and scout, often securing military intelligence from Negro informants residing behind Confederate lines. At the same time she worked as a nurse, and in other ways aided the freedmen who had flocked to the Federal banner, supporting herself through the sale of chickens and eggs. In the spring and summer of 1865 she worked for a time at a freedmen's hospital in Fortress Monroe, Va.

The war over, Harriet Tubman continued to serve others with little thought of self. Returning to her home, she not only cared for her aged parents, but also took in several Negro orphans and helpless old people. Thus began the Harriet Tubman Home for Indigent Aged Negroes, which continued for several years after her death. Herself illiterate and without a day of schooling, she promoted the establishment of freedmen's schools in the South. She attended suffrage meetings and is said to have taken a leading part in the growth of the African Methodist Episcopal Church in upstate New York. Her life and exploits came to the attention of the general public in 1869, when Sarah Bradford published a brief sketch, *Harriet Tubman: The Moses of Her People*, the proceeds of which were given to Mrs. Tubman to complete the payments on her farm. This was also the year in which she was married to Nelson Davis, a Civil War veteran. (John Tubman had been killed in a Maryland shooting incident two years before.)

In the late 1860's, also, she began her long fight to secure some compensation for her wartime services. Her application was supported by numerous prominent persons who knew her, including William H. Seward, now Secretary of State, but, as Sarah Bradford observes, "Red tape proved too strong even for him, and her case was rejected, because it did not come under any recognized law." In 1897 Harriet Tubman resubmitted a petition, claiming

$1,800 for "three years' service as nurse and cook in hospitals, and as commander of several men (eight or nine) as scouts during the late War of Rebellion." A Senate committee recommended that she be given $25 per month for life, but this was reduced to $20 before Congress finally enacted a private bill in her favor. In her final years the citizens of Auburn and old friends from antislavery days contributed to the support of the Harriet Tubman Home. After her death of pneumonia in March 1913, a plaque was erected to her memory in the town square, at ceremonies addressed by Booker T. Washington. In 1868 Frederick Douglass had written her: "Excepting John Brown—of sacred memory—I know of no one who has willingly encountered more perils and hardships to serve our enslaved people than you have" (Bradford, p. 135).

[Sarah H. Bradford, *Harriet Tubman: The Moses of Her People* (1886), the basic source (expanded from the sketch of 1869), was reprinted in 1961 with a sensitive introduction by Butler A. Jones. Earl Conrad, *Harriet Tubman* (1943), is a more recent, documented study. Ann Petry has written an excellent biography, *Harriet Tubman* (1955), for young people. Harriet Tubman's almost legendary work of rescuing slaves has been discussed by such pioneer writers as William Still in *The Underground Railroad* (1872), and Wilbur H. Siebert in *The Underground Railroad* (1898). Larry Gara minimizes the extent of the Underground Railroad's work in his *Liberty Line* (1961).]

JOHN HOPE FRANKLIN

**TURELL, Jane Colman** (Feb. 25, 1708–Mar. 26, 1735), poet, was born in Boston, the elder daughter and second of three children of Benjamin and Jane (Clark) Colman. Her father's parents had come to Massachusetts from England. Her mother was the daughter of Thomas Clark, a "wealthy Boston pewterer" and one of the founders of the Church in Brattle Square, or Brattle Street Church, of which Benjamin Colman was pastor. Among Boston ministers of his day Colman was remembered for more liberal views than were current among his colleagues. In his own home, however, he was a man of traditionally strict parental discipline and extravagant zeal toward his children's religious education. Thanks to his unceasing efforts his daughter Jane, who from infancy was "wonderful weak and tender," became something of a local prodigy in knowledge of the Bible and tearful concern for her soul's salvation. Before she was two years old she is said to have known her letters and to have been able to speak distinctly and relate many stories out of the Scriptures "to the Satis-

faction and Pleasure of the most Judicious." The picture of this delicate child standing on a table in her father's home and performing such feats before Gov. Joseph Dudley and "other Wise and Polite Gentlemen" provides a key toward understanding her limitations as a poet. She was a pulpit example almost from birth.

Before she was four she could "say the greater Part of the Assembly's Catechism, many of the Psalms, some hundred Lines of the best Poetry, read distinctly, and make pertinent Remarks on many things she read." Her father instructed her daily, charged her to read the Bible, pray, fear to sin, and "fix her Mind on God and heavenly Things." Her mother prayed with her and "gave her the wisest Counsels, and most faithful Warnings." No wonder perhaps that she made "laudable Progress in her Studies" and at eleven composed a hymn. "Sing on, my Bird," her father wrote in his approving letter to her; "Already you repay the Pains I took / To form you for your Maker and your Book." Under his continuing guidance she went on to paraphrase the Psalms in rhyme and write pious meditations and prayers. Before she was eighteen she had read "all the English Poetry, and polite Pieces in Prose" in his library, besides much that she had borrowed. Her subsequent "Encomium on Sir Richard Blackmore's Poetical Works" and "On the Incomparable Mr. [Edmund] Waller" indicate two of her enthusiasms. Like other budding poetesses of the hour, she also came under the spell of the English poet Elizabeth Singer Rowe, popularly known as "Philomela," with whom her father on a visit to England had once formed a warm personal friendship.

On Aug. 11, 1726, Jane Colman was married to Ebenezer Turell, a young minister who had studied with Benjamin Colman and in 1724 had been installed as pastor in Medford, Mass. At that date she was eighteen years old. During the nine years she had yet to live Medford was her home. Her extant correspondence with her father during these years shows him to have been still the dominant force in her emotional life, her continuing mentor through her religious ups and downs and sometimes her critic in her weekly attempts to write verse. For the most part she emulated English or classic poets, writing of nightingales and "fragrant Zephyrs" playing "round our Temples." Only occasionally did she begin to touch on the life she knew:

My good fat Bacon, and our homely Bread,
With which my healthful Family is fed.
Milk from the Cow, and Butter newly churn'd,
And new fresh Cheese, with Curds and Cream just
    turn'd.

Time for maturity, critical self-judgment, and perhaps greater independence was denied her. Long subject to attacks of illness and depression, she died in Medford at the age of twenty-seven and was buried there in the Salem Street Cemetery. Four children had been born to her, of whom three died in infancy. The surviving son, Samuel, outlived his mother only eighteen months, dying at six. Of her poems, a few were printed in her husband's tribute, *Reliquiae Turellae*, appended to her father's two funeral sermons in her honor and a verse tribute by the Rev. John Adams. Unfortunately her husband suppressed "some Pieces of Wit and Humour," choosing that she be represented only by "graver and better Subjects." From a twentieth-century perspective, her place in American poetry is modest indeed. In her husband's phrase, her work was only "the promised Earnest of a future Harvest."

[The basic source is the memorial volume *Reliquiae Turellae et Lachrymae Paternae* (1735), containing Benjamin Colman's two funeral sermons and Ebenezer Turell's memoirs. See also Clayton H. Chapman, "Benjamin Colman's Daughters," *New England Quart.*, June 1953, a perceptive account of the father-daughter relationship; Ebenezer Turell, *The Life and Character of the Rev. Benjamin Colman, D.D.* (1749); Clifford K. Shipton, *Sibley's Harvard Graduates*, IV (1933), 120–37, on Colman; Charles Brooks, *Hist. of the Town of Medford* (1855); *Vital Records of Medford, Mass., to the Year 1850* (1907), p. 449. Evart A. and George L. Duyckinck, *Cyc. of Am. Literature* (1855), I, 124–25, contains a few specimens of her verse. Jane Colman's birth date is recorded in *A Report of the Record Commissioners of the City of Boston: Births, 1700–1800* (1894) as Feb. 24, 1707, but this is presumably the Old Style date.]

OLA ELIZABETH WINSLOW

**TURNBULL, Julia Anna** (June 18, 1822– Sept. 11, 1887), ballerina, was born in Montreal, Canada. Her Scottish-born father, John D. Turnbull, was an actor and playwright; her mother, a native of Barker, N.Y., was also an actress. When Julia was three the family moved to Albany, N.Y., where Julia, with her two sisters, Emily and Caroline, made her debut as a child actress. Although probably not her first appearance, an important landmark in her budding career was the performance in Albany of *The Wandering Boys* in April 1828 in which, playing the part of Justin, she appeared with another child actress, Louisa Lane, later the celebrated Mrs. John Drew (see LOUISA LANE DREW). Julia Turnbull first acted in New York City at the Chatham Theatre at the age of six. In 1834 she became a regular member of the stock company at the Park Theatre, New York, where she danced between the acts of plays and appeared in juvenile roles. Meanwhile she studied ballet under the French dancer Mme. LeComte and the latter's brother, Jules Martin. She made her first appearance in a leading role in June 1839, in the ballet *The Sisters* at the Bowery Theatre. Her co-star was MARY ANN LEE, later the first American to dance *Giselle*.

When Fanny Elssler came to the United States in the following year, she engaged Julia Turnbull as a soloist in her company. For two years Julia toured the United States with the great Viennese ballerina, going with her to Havana, Cuba, and dancing roles second only to Elssler's. At this time she continued her ballet training under Elssler's partner, James Sylvain. After Elssler's departure, she danced with her former teacher, Jules Martin, in the first New York performances of Michael Balfe's opera *The Bohemian Girl* in 1844.

She next toured the United States as a solo dancer, and then joined the regular company at the Bowery Theatre, New York, where in the spring of 1847 she scored a tremendous success in the title role of the extravaganza *The Naiad Queen*. In December of the same year she danced *Giselle* with George Washington Smith, who had staged the Bowery production of the ballet. Reviewing the performance in the *New York Morning Herald* (Dec. 7, 1847), James Gordon Bennett wrote with enthusiasm of "this favorite danseuse" who, as Giselle, "excelled every other character which we have seen her in." Commenting on a later performance that season (in *Nathalie, la Laitière Suisse*) Bennett described her (Apr. 15, 1848) as "charming and distinguished" and "an artiste of first rate ability, which is conjoined with a youthful person, a fine figure, and . . . a handsome face."

In August 1848 an intense rivalry between Julia Turnbull and a beautiful and brilliant young Italian dancer, Giovanna Ciocca, precipitated a violent riot at the Bowery Theatre. Although Turnbull won a temporary victory— she was a great favorite with the regular audience at this theatre—the uproar caused her eventual withdrawal from the company. She continued her career with increasing success, however, appearing in the title role of *Esmeralda*, as the Abbess Helena in Meyerbeer's opera *Robert le Diable*, and as Fenella in Daniel F. Auber's *La Muette de Portici*. In 1850 she began to add acting roles to her repertoire, one of the first being Katharine Kloper in the farce *Lola Montez*. During the same year she won a conspicuous success as

Leoline in *The Spirit of the Fountain.* Her last New York engagement took place in August and September 1857 at the Olympic Theatre, where she starred in such comedies and melodramas as *The Loan of a Lover, The Alpine Maid, Jenny Lind, Victims,* and *The Wizard Skiff.*

After her retirement from the stage in 1857, Julia Turnbull lived quietly in Brooklyn for thirty years. Her death record lists her occupation as "dressmaker." She died in Brooklyn of "phthisis pulmonaris" (tuberculosis) and was buried there in Greenwood Cemetery. Her older sister, Caroline, enjoyed a modest career as an actress under her married name, Mrs. Henry V. Lovell, and survived her by many years, dying in 1906. Julia Turnbull was one of the earliest American ballerinas to dance such classic roles as *Giselle* and *Esmeralda.* During the 1840's, a period when ballet enjoyed enormous popularity in the United States before its late-Victorian decline, she rivaled and sometimes surpassed the European stars who toured America.

[George C. D. Odell, *Annals of the N.Y. Stage,* vols. III–VII (1928–31); Henry P. Phelps, *Players of a Century: A Record of the Albany Stage* (1880); Lillian Moore, "Mary Ann Lee, First American Giselle," *Dance Index,* May 1943, and "George Washington Smith," *ibid.,* June–Aug. 1945; death record from N.Y. City Dept. of Health (Borough of Brooklyn).]

LILLIAN MOORE

**TURNER, Eliza L. Sproat Randolph** (1826–June 20, 1903), author, suffragist, and woman's club leader, was born in Philadelphia, Pa. Little is known of her family background. Her father, who had originally been a farmer in Vermont, was apparently associated with some aspect of writing and publishing in Philadelphia. Her mother, the former Maria Lutwyche, had come from Birmingham, England, with her family in 1818. There is no record of Eliza Sproat's education, but she taught in the Philadelphia public schools for several years and was an assistant teacher at Girard College, Philadelphia, in the years 1850–52.

In 1855 she was married to Nathaniel Randolph, a wealthy Philadelphia lumber merchant and an orthodox member of the Society of Friends. He died in September 1858, leaving his young widow with a substantial estate and with a son (her only child), Nathaniel Archer Randolph, who subsequently attended the medical school of the University of Pennsylvania. During the Civil War, Mrs. Randolph was one of many volunteers who participated in relief efforts at Gettysburg after the battle.

While there she met a fellow relief worker, Joseph C. Turner, an attorney, to whom she was married in 1864. They maintained a town house in Philadelphia and a country estate, Windtryst, in Chadd's Ford, Delaware County, Pa., where Turner eventually gave up the practice of law and engaged in dairy farming, with a subsidiary retail business in Philadelphia.

Two principal interests marked Mrs. Turner's life: literature and reform. Her first published piece, a fable called "The Enchanted Lute," appeared in the *Christian Keepsake* for 1847, and during the six years before her first marriage she contributed poetry to *Sartain's* and *Graham's* magazines. She also wrote a number of prose pieces for the *National Era,* Gamaliel Bailey's antislavery journal in Washington, D.C., and other periodicals. Contemporary anthologists of women authors early found a place for Eliza L. Sproat: Rufus W. Griswold and Caroline May in 1848, Thomas B. Read in 1849, and John S. Hart in 1851. Her satire "The Rooster-Pecked Wife" was widely acclaimed as a literary contribution to the growing feminist movement. In later years she wrote articles and short stories concerned with social problems, family relationships, and particularly the status of women for local newspapers and the *Woman's Journal* of Boston. A volume of her poetry, *Out-of-Door Rhymes,* was issued by the Boston publisher James R. Osgood in 1872. One of her poems, "A Little Goose," was popular enough to be reprinted by CAROLYN WELLS in her anthology *A Book of Humorous Verse* (1920).

Mrs. Turner's interest in social reform appears to have begun in the late 1840's when she joined the Philadelphia Union of Associationists, a group dedicated to the amelioration of social problems according to the principles of the French reformer Charles Fourier. She was later active in the Philadelphia Female Anti-Slavery Society. After the Civil War she gave her principal efforts to the cause of women. In December 1869 she helped organize the Pennsylvania Woman Suffrage Association, serving as its first corresponding secretary, with MARY GREW as president. For it Mrs. Turner wrote a suffrage tract, *Four Quite New Reasons Why You Should Wish Your Wife to Vote* (1875).

Eliza Turner took an active role in the women's work of the Philadelphia Centennial Exposition of 1876. She edited and wrote articles for the *New Century for Women,* the newspaper (conducted entirely by women) that was printed and distributed at the Women's Pavilion. Her paper on "Women's Clubs," delivered at the Women's Congress held during the Exposition, gave impetus to the growing movement to establish such a club in Philadelphia. Early the next year, in large part through the efforts of the energetic Mrs. Turner, a club was established in Philadelphia and christened the New Century Club, with Sarah C. F. Hallowell, a Philadelphia newspaperwoman, as president and Mrs. Turner as corresponding secretary. Mrs. Turner served as president, 1879–81.

Although it conducted social and literary programs of a sort similar to those of the other pioneering women's clubs of this period, the New Century Club from the start stressed also "practical philanthropy," or concern for community needs. In keeping with this purpose Mrs. Turner was in 1881 appointed chairman of a committee to organize evening classes for working women and girls. So enthusiastic was the response that the project soon became a separate organization, the New Century Guild of Working Women, with Mrs. Turner as president. Under her guidance the Guild not only offered courses in such subjects as dressmaking, cooking, millinery, laundry work, telegraphy, and bookkeeping but also became a general working girls' club, with a clubhouse, library, dining room, gymnasium, and other facilities, and study groups in history, philosophy, and the like. The vocational classes were taken over in 1892 by the newly founded Drexel Institute, but the New Century Guild, like its parent organization, has continued in active existence to the present day.

In another area of social welfare, Mrs. Turner in 1875 organized the Children's Country Week Association of Philadelphia, the outgrowth of her own personal program of bringing groups of needy children from the city for summer vacations at her Chadds Ford estate and farm. She served also as a director of the Society for the Prevention of Cruelty to Animals, assisted in the organization of the Consumers' League of Philadelphia, and worked in behalf of the Philadelphia Society for Organizing Charity. Her personal interests included art, horticulture, and music. Her stated religious preference was Unitarian. Surviving her husband by eight months, Mrs. Turner died at her Chadds Ford home in 1903. She was buried in the Turner family plot in Longwood, the Friends' cemetery in Kennett Square, Pa.

[A memorial sketch in the 1903 edition of Mrs. Turner's *Out-of-Door Rhymes*, published by the New Century Club, is the fullest biographical source. For other material see: Gertrude B. Biddle and Sarah D. Lowrie, eds., *Notable Women of Pa.* (1942); and obituaries in Phila. *Public Ledger*, June 23, 1903, *Morning Republican*, June 22, 1903, and West Chester (Pa.) *Village Record*, June 25, 1903. See also John S. Hart, *The Female Prose Writers of America* (1851), pp. 409–12; Mrs. Jane C. Croly, *The Hist. of the Woman's Club Movement in America* (1898), pp. 1021–28, 1033–35; *New Century Club Hist.* (1899); Edward D. McDonald and Edward M. Hinton, *Drexel Institute of Technology* (1941); Lucretia L. Blankenburg, *The Blankenburgs of Phila.* (1928), pp. 124–25; and obituary of Joseph Turner in *West Chester Daily Local News*, Nov. 13, 1902. The Hist. Soc. of Pa. has a letter from Mrs. Turner to a Mrs. Etting about establishing a woman's club room in Phila. (Am. Poets, Gratz Collection, Case 7, Box 10) and an undated pamphlet on the goals and finances of the New Century Guild. A portrait of Mrs. Turner by the painter CECILIA BEAUX is at the New Century Guild, Phila.]

CLAIRE E. FOX

**TURNER, Florence E.** (Jan. 6, 1888?–Aug. 28, 1946), motion-picture actress, producer, and director, was born in New York City, the only child of William Clifton Turner and Frances Louise (Bowles) Turner. Her father, a painter, died when she was only a year old. Both her mother, of part Italian descent, and her grandmother were actors in local theatres in Brooklyn, N.Y., where Florence was reared. Having no one to leave her with at home, the two women took her backstage with them. By Florence's own account, a stage manager persuaded her reluctant mother to give her a walk-on role in a production of *The Romany Rye* when she was only three. Other parts followed, but her career was interrupted at eleven when she was enrolled in school. At fifteen or sixteen, without her mother's consent, she obtained a role as an extra in a Brooklyn theatre, after which she tried musical comedy and a tour in vaudeville.

In May 1907 Florence Turner found herself out of work, and another actress suggested she try motion pictures. She applied at the Vitagraph studios, which were near her home, and was hired for the lead in a 300-foot comedy, *How to Cure a Cold*. Her popularity among audiences was immediate and widespread, and in October 1907, when the Vitagraph Players were organized, she became the first actor in American film history to receive a contract. Screen acting was then still anonymous, and she was initially known to her admirers as "The Vitagraph Girl." By 1910, however, Vitagraph was bowing to the public fascination with motion-picture personalities; Florence Turner's name was first shown on the screen in May, and she soon was delighting fans by personal appearances all over New York.

Though Miss Turner was certainly not without beauty (she has been described as "dark and magnetic," with "expressive eyes"), she preferred playing comedy and character parts rather than romantic heroines. She was also an expert mime. Several times she proved her versatility by playing all the roles in a single film, as in *Jealousy* (1911), a tour de force without a single subtitle. At Vitagraph her fellow players included Maurice Costello and Wallace Reid. Among her other films for that company were *Francesca da Rimini* (1910), which she adapted, *Launcelot and Elaine* (1911), *Aunty's Romance* (1912), *How Mr. Bullington Ran the Home* (1912), and *A Tale of Two Cities* (1911). The last, in three reels, was the first multiple-reel film to be widely shown in the United States as a feature picture, rather than serially on different days.

Miss Turner was a serious and ambitious artist, and in 1913 she left Vitagraph intent on forming her own company. Vitagraph director Lawrence Trimble persuaded her to set up Turner Films, Ltd., in England. Her popularity there had always been great, and her productions (in not all of which she herself starred) were an immediate public and critical success. In 1915, in a magazine poll, she was voted England's most popular actress. Using the facilities of the Hepworth Company at Walton-on-Thames, her company turned out a small but distinguished group of films. The earliest of these were realistic, often emphasizing character over plot; the best was the immensely popular and nostalgic *My Old Dutch* (1915), directed by Trimble and co-starring the music hall favorite Albert Chevalier. Others included *Through the Valley of the Shadows* (1914) and *A Welsh Singer* (1915). Inflationary pressures, however, brought about by the war, caused a general shutdown of British production in 1916.

Having lost all her money in the British venture, Florence Turner returned to America to find herself no longer a star, although she continued to work regularly in both shorts and feature films, as actor, writer, and director, mostly for Universal and Metro-Goldwyn-Mayer. In 1920 she returned to England on what proved to be a false offer. She did obtain the lead in a series of W. W. Jacobs comedies, but British production during this period was erratic and her career foundered. She finally managed to produce, with the Hepworth Company, the two-reel comedy *Film Favourites* (1924), her last important film, in which she burlesqued some thirty leading screen personalities, including Charles Chaplin, Ben Turpin, Mae Murray, and Lillian Gish. She was unable, however, to arrange for distribution,

and her financial situation became desperate. The actress Marion Davies, hearing of her plight, brought her back to the United States to work for Miss Davies' company in 1925. Miss Turner continued to play character parts through the 1920's and smaller parts during the next two decades. For the last ten years of her life she was a member of the M-G-M stock company.

Florence Turner lived for most of her life with her mother (who died in 1944) and grandmother. Although once reported engaged to the actor Lou Tellegen, she never married. She died of cancer at the Motion Picture Country House, an actors' home, in Los Angeles. Her body was cremated, and there was no funeral.

[*"Act for the Eye Alone," Film Index,* Oct. 23, 1909 (reprint of interview in N.Y. *Sun*); autobiographical sketch in Robert Grace, *The Stage in the Twentieth Century,* III (1912), 331–42; "The New Turner Films," *Bioscope,* May 15, 1913; "The Return of Florence Turner," *Motion Picture Classic,* Feb. 1919; L. C. Moen, "Florence Turner, First Star, Returns to U.S.," *Motion Picture News,* May 24, 1924; Rachael Low, *The Hist. of the British Film, 1906–1914* (1949) and *The Hist. of the British Film, 1914–1918* (1950); Gerald D. McDonald, "Origin of the Star System," *Films in Rev.,* Nov. 1953; obituaries in *Los Angeles Times,* Aug. 29, 1946, *N.Y. Times,* Aug. 30, and *N.Y. Herald Tribune,* Aug. 31; clipping files in Theatre Collection of N.Y. Public Library at Lincoln Center and in *Los Angeles Times* library; information from Motion Picture Relief Fund (Los Angeles) and N.Y. City Dept. of Health.]

HARVEY DENEROFF

**TUTHILL, Louisa Caroline Huggins** (July 6, 1799–June 1, 1879), author, was born in New Haven, Conn., a descendant of the city's founder, Theophilus Eaton. She was the fourth daughter and the youngest of seven children of Mary (Dickerman) Huggins and Ebenezer Huggins, a prosperous merchant. Educated at seminaries for girls in New Haven and Litchfield, Conn., she began writing in her childhood, but is said to have burned her compositions and to have resolved never to become one of the literary women whom she disdained.

On Aug. 6, 1817, she was married to Cornelius Tuthill, a native of Hopewell, N.Y., who after their marriage settled in New Haven. Three years her senior, he had graduated from Yale with the expectation of becoming a lawyer, but a religious experience caused him to study instead for the ministry under President Timothy Dwight of Yale, and several months after they were married he was licensed to preach. An attack of typhus fever—the beginning of the ill health that was to plague him the rest of his life—forced him, however, to give up the pulpit. After a short term of teaching, he began a literary venture in March 1820, a semiweekly literary magazine, the *Microscope,* "Edited by a Fraternity of Gentlemen." His young wife became hostess for this group, which included Henry E. Dwight, Nathaniel Chancey, and the poet James Gates Percival. Forced to discontinue the magazine after only six months, Tuthill, following a sojourn abroad, tried his hand at a variety of pursuits, editing the *Christian Spectator* in 1822–23 and resuming the study of law. In 1823 he was elected to the state legislature, but pulmonary disease kept him from being active. He died in 1825, leaving Louisa with a widow's portion of $131.62 and four young children: Charles Henry (born 1818), Cornelia Louisa (1820), Mary Esther (1822), and Sarah Schoonmaker (1824).

Her husband's interests had brought Louisa Tuthill into a literary circle in New Haven, and he himself had encouraged her to write. He once had one of her manuscripts published anonymously, without her knowledge, and its favorable reception helped break down her reticence. Now, in her widowhood, she turned to writing both for solace and as a source of income. Her first books were issued anonymously, beginning with *James Somers: The Pilgrim's Son,* published in New Haven in 1827; for more than a decade she hesitated to sign her own name. Of the more than thirty volumes she wrote or edited, most were for children, young people, or women: tales and stories of high moral purport, and guides to manners, to housekeeping and child care, and to ,aesthetic and spiritual improvement. She was a popular author and her works went into many editions. Among the most successful were her two guides, *I Will Be a Lady: A Book for Girls* (1845) and *I Will Be a Gentleman: A Book for Boys* (1846), which by 1868 had reached their 38th and 37th editions, respectively. SARAH J. HALE of *Godey's Lady's Book* accounted for Louisa Tuthill's success in this genre by judging her "a pleasant writer" whose "cheerful spirit and hopeful philosophy give an attractive charm even to good *advice*" (*Woman's Record,* p. 804).

As counselor Mrs. Tuthill was among the more successful of the many authors of the day writing for people made uncertain of their roles by social change, mobility, and the waning of traditional institutions. One of her books, however, took her into a more distinctive field. In 1848 she published a *History of Architecture from the Earliest Times.* Utilizing the library

of the architect Ithiel Town of New Haven, she drew on the works of European writers such as Francesco Milizia and John Claudius Loudon; Town and other architects also furnished her with plans and elevations of buildings. Dedicated "To the Ladies of the United States of America, the acknowledged Arbiters of Taste," her book sought to give them examples of beautiful buildings to improve their aesthetic judgment and thereby advance the art. In content little more than a catalogue of buildings with brief descriptions, the work is notable as the first history of architecture to be published in the United States. In her later years Mrs. Tuthill became a great admirer of John Ruskin and prepared two anthologies of his writings, both emphasizing his moralistic side: *The True and the Beautiful in Nature, Art, Morals, and Religion,* which first appeared in 1859 and was reprinted many times, and *Precious Thoughts: Moral and Religious* (1866).

Having remained in New Haven until the death of her mother in 1837 and the settlement of her father's estate in 1838, Mrs. Tuthill had then moved to Hartford, where Hezekiah Huntington of the firm of H. & F. J. Huntington, music publishers, encouraged her career. After Huntington's death in 1842 she lived in Roxbury, Mass., near Boston, until 1847, when she went to Philadelphia to supervise the publication of her *History of Architecture.* At midcentury she moved to New York City and then to Princeton, N.J., where she died in 1879 in her eightieth year; her death was officially attributed to "senile debility." After a funeral in Trinity Church (Episcopal), Princeton, she was buried beside her husband in the Huggins family plot in Grove Street Cemetery, New Haven.

[Edward D. and George S. Dickerman, *Families of Dickerman Ancestry* (1897), pp. 470–71; George F. Tuttle, *The Descendants of William and Elizabeth Tuttle* (1883), pp. 165–66; Franklin B. Dexter, *Biog. Sketches of Graduates of Yale College,* VI (1912), 713–16 (on Cornelius Tuthill); John S. Hart, *The Female Prose Writers of America* (1851); Sarah J. Hale, *Woman's Record* (1853); Evert A. and George L. Duyckinck, *Cyc. of Am. Literature,* II (1855), 676; records of Trinity Church, Princeton, N.J., and Grove St. Cemetery, New Haven; death record from N.J. State Dept. of Health. Two letters from Mrs. Tuthill to publishers are at the Hist. Soc. of Pa., Phila. Her will is recorded in the Surrogate's Court, Mercer County Courthouse, Trenton, N.J.]

AGNES ADDISON GILCHRIST

**TUTWILER, Julia Strudwick** (Aug. 15, 1841– Mar. 24, 1916), educator and prison reformer, was born in Tuscaloosa, Ala., the third daughter and third of the eleven children of Henry and Julia (Ashe) Tutwiler. Her mother was the daughter of Pascal Paoli Ashe, a North Carolinian who had become steward of the University of Alabama. Her father, a Virginian of pioneer stock, probably of German Swiss descent, had graduated with the first class at the University of Virginia; he recalled attending dinners given by Thomas Jefferson and was forever a disciple of the liberal spirit that pervaded his student years. A member of the first faculty of the University of Alabama, he later became disillusioned with college teaching and in 1847 founded the influential and prosperous Greene Springs School near Havana, Ala., which he continued to head until his death in 1884. Under his "sweet, benign, tender, sun-shiny presence," students were encouraged to proceed at their own rate, and corporal punishment was forbidden. Since he was convinced that girls should be as well educated as boys, he opened the school to his own and neighbors' daughters, who attended classes with the boys and studied the same assignments.

Her father's means enabled Julia to follow her own educational bent. Despite Southern distrust of the North, for two winters on the eve of the Civil War she attended Madame Maroteau's boarding school in Philadelphia, where she developed an interest in modern languages. When the war broke out, she longed to be a nurse, but her father, sharing the prejudice, especially strong in the South, against the nursing of soldiers by unmarried young women, refused his permission, and she spent the war years teaching in his school. In January 1866 she again went north to enter the newly founded Vassar College, but left after a semester to return to teaching in Alabama. In 1873, after a year of private language classes with professors at Washington and Lee University, she went to Europe on a tour and decided to stay for further study. Hearing of the teacher-training work of the Deaconesses' Institute at Kaiserswerth, Germany, she enrolled there in August 1873. Her year at this educational and philanthropic institution, run by a Lutheran order of sisters of charity, heightened her humanitarian zeal and stirred her interest in practical education. Still uncertain about her own career, she gave some thought to becoming a professional writer. Since girlhood she had composed poems, and while in Germany she contributed to several American newspapers and magazines, including *St. Nicholas*. But by her return to America in 1876 she had settled on teaching.

Joining the faculty of the Tuscaloosa Female College, for five years Julia Tutwiler taught modern languages and English literature. In 1881, now a well-known educator, she was appointed co-principal of the Livingston (Ala.) Female Academy. For some time she had advocated better training for public school teachers. Through her urging, in considerable part, the Alabama legislature voted in 1883 an annual appropriation to establish a normal department—the Alabama Normal College for Girls—at Livingston Academy. The expanded institution became known as the Livingston Normal College. Miss Tutwiler assumed sole charge in 1890 and remained at its head for the next two decades. Her national standing was reflected in her election in 1891 as president of the department of elementary education of the National Education Association.

She had meanwhile secured another innovation in her state. In 1878 Miss Tutwiler had been sent as the representative of the *National Journal of Education* to the Paris Exposition. Her observations in France of vocational schools for girls led her to advocate similar training in the United States as early as 1880. After she waged a long campaign, the Alabama legislature in 1893 voted funds to establish an industrial school for girls, the later Alabama College, at Montevallo. She also induced the trustees at the University of Alabama to admit women, at the sophomore level in 1893 and in 1897 as freshmen.

A sensitive Southern gentlewoman, Julia Tutwiler possessed deep convictions and, where need be, the courage to act on them. For several decades, despite criticism and discouragement, she spent much of her spare time and strength in a crusade for better treatment of prisoners. Although she had observed at Kaiserswerth a reformatory program for women prisoners, her practical interest in this subject was aroused accidentally in the winter of 1879–80 when she went to the aid of a servant girl who had been jailed. Organizing the Tuscaloosa Benevolent Association to work for prison reform, she sent a fact-finding questionnaire to the jailers of every county in the state. The returns were widely publicized and led to a legislative act in 1880 to improve physical conditions in the county jails. A few years later she accepted an invitation from the Woman's Christian Temperance Union to become its state chairman of prison and jail work. A strong believer in the need for religious instruction as a step to prisoner rehabilitation, she conducted services and distributed Bibles in the jails; but she continued to press for legislative reforms. She was among the very first in Alabama to raise her voice against the pernicious but well-entrenched convict lease system. Despairing, in the mid-1880's, of winning the necessary political support for its abolition, she mobilized pressure for a series of lesser reforms, among them the establishment (1887) of the South's first prison school of any importance.

Of medium height and build, with a friendly yet assured bearing, Julia Tutwiler had a soft, well-modulated voice and keen, alert blue eyes. Although a Presbyterian, she favored the Episcopal liturgy and, in her years at Livingston, joined all the different churches there. The establishment in 1907 of full state control over Livingston Normal College led to some friction between Miss Tutwiler and the new trustees, occasioned by her informal business procedures, and in 1910, at sixty-eight, she was retired. She died in Birmingham, Ala., six years later, of cancer. By her expressed wish, her body was cremated and the remains buried beside those of her parents in the Greene Springs Cemetery near Havana, Ala. Her will left all her property in Livingston, amounting to $15,000 in 1926, as a scholarship loan fund for the "Girls of Alabama." The University of Alabama had recognized her contributions to public education by awarding her an LL.D. degree in 1906 and naming its first large women's dormitory for her. The Julia Tutwiler Prison for Women, at Wetumpka, perpetuates the memory of her prison work. Her poem "Alabama," composed in her first lonely year in Germany, has been adopted as the state song. In 1953 she was one of the first eleven persons named to the Alabama Hall of Fame.

[Although fragmentary, the best collection of manuscript and printed material on Julia Tutwiler is in the Archives of the Univ. of Ala.; this contains most of her preserved letters and a number of her poems and articles. For biographical data, see Anne G. Pannell and Dorothea E. Wyatt, *Julia S. Tutwiler and Social Progress in Ala.* (1964). Useful also is Clara L. Pitts, "Julia Strudwick Tutwiler" (unpublished doctoral dissertation, Dept. of Education, George Washington Univ., 1942).]

DOROTHEA E. WYATT

**TWEED, Blanche Oelrichs Thomas Barrymore** (Oct. 1, 1890–Nov. 5, 1950), writer and actress, better known by her pen name, "Michael Strange," was born in New York City. Christened Blanche Marie Louise Oelrichs, she was the second daughter and youngest of four children of Blanche (de Loosey) and Charles May Oelrichs. Her mother was Austrian; her father was the grandson of a German merchant who had come to America and married into the Otis family of Massachusetts. Although he held a seat on the New York Stock Exchange, he spent most of his time at America's social capital, Newport, R.I. Moving along the restless axis of Newport, New York, and Paris, young Blanche Oelrichs prepared for the one role in life awaiting a young lady of rank: marriage. Not of a placid disposition, however, she attended three schools, was expelled from two, Brearley and the Manhattanville Convent of the Sacred Heart (she early revolted against her Catholic upbringing), and concluded her education more to her satisfaction with a tutor. By the time of her marriage, on Jan. 26, 1910, to Leonard Moorhead Thomas (1878–1937) of Philadelphia, Yale graduate and recently first secretary of the American legation in Madrid, she shone among the most envied belles of Newport.

In the years following marriage, Blanche Thomas awoke to interests that gave her life a new direction. Witnessing the harsh treatment of suffragettes in England aroused her to action. She bobbed her hair before most of her sex and took an active role in the cause, climaxed in 1915 by marching in one of the woman suffrage parades up Fifth Avenue in New York City. A more profound change came with the stirrings of a literary urge. Swept by sudden inspiration one calm summer morning in 1914, as she later recalled it, she set down her first poem, and thereafter verse flowed from her pen in flood tide. Suddenly finding in dramatic literature an entirely new world, she composed several plays, rather as a mode of expression than as stage vehicles. When her first volume of poems was accepted for publication in 1916, her publisher suggested she use a pen name; she chose Michael Strange.

Her creative interests and new associations caused a rift with her husband; she divorced him in 1919 and on Aug. 5, 1920, against the advice of intimate friends, married the actor John Barrymore, then reaching the height of his fame. Having already, in 1918, adapted for Barrymore Tolstoy's *The Living Corpse* under the title *Redemption,* she now saw her own play, *Clair de Lune,* open at the Empire Theatre (Apr. 18, 1921) with Barrymore and his sister, Ethel, in the leading roles. The casting and an ambitious production could not save what one critic called "a muddled and amorphous drama," and another (Alexander Woollcott) heard as a "certain gloating magniloquence of language and a resolutely poetic aspect." Seeking practical stage experience in summer stock at Salem, Mass., in 1925, Miss Strange drew several acting offers for the coming season, but these she refused because they would exploit her notoriety as a society woman. At last a part with "an aura of poetry and mysticism" pleased her, and in 1926 she played Eleanora in Strindberg's *Easter*. She also acted Chrysothemis in Margaret Anglin's production of Sophocles' *Electra* at the Metropolitan Opera House in 1927. Her only Broadway appearance came in the title role of Edmond Rostand's *L'Aiglon* at the Cosmopolitan Theatre the same year. Other parts were scattered through the next decade, including a summer tryout in her own work, *Lord and Lady Byron,* but neither as playwright nor as actress did Michael Strange make any further appearance of note.

In 1928 she undertook a lecture tour organized by her friend ELISABETH MARBURY. Conceived as a tribute to democracy, the lecture grew into a potpourri of reminiscence called "The Stage as the Actress Sees It." From this tour grew Miss Strange's last theatrical venture, poetic readings to music. She gave her first recital at Town Hall in New York in November 1935, with selections from Poe and Dorothy Parker but with her own verse predominating. A harpist accompanied her and also played a few solo pieces. In 1936 she read poetry for a quarter-hour program over radio station WMCA and the next year, with the support of Alfred Wallenstein's orchestra, over WOR. In 1947 she rechristened the program "Great Words with Great Music," substituted a piano for the orchestra, and included among her selections excerpts from the Old and New Testaments, the Declaration of Independence, Magna Carta, the Communist Manifesto, and Thomas Wolfe, set to the tones of Wagner, Beethoven, and other classical composers.

Michael Strange's marriage to John Barrymore had given a catalytic charge to her search for self-expression. At first so closely united that they wore the same shirts, ties, and felt hats, they nevertheless suffered continued mutual jealousy, endless conflict, and long separation. Her inability to equal his artistic success troubled her as much as his weakness for women and drink; he gave her neither the peace of mind nor the artistic support she felt vital to her. They were divorced in 1928, and the following year, on May 23, 1929, she married Harrison Tweed, a prominent New York lawyer; a third divorce came in 1942. At that time she bought a house in Easton, Conn., where she lived her remaining years. She died of leukemia at Massachusetts General Hospital, Boston, and was buried in Woodlawn Cemetery, New York City. She was survived by her son, Leonard Moorhead Thomas, Jr. (born

1911), and her daughter, Diana Barrymore (christened Joan Strange Blythe). A younger son by her first marriage, Robin May Thomas (born 1915), had died in 1944.

Trapped in a world of fashion and volatile feelings, Blanche Oelrichs sought to become a distinct individual awake to the eternal values of human experience. Only late in her life did she realize "how desperately at odds I had always been with my environment." When she marched for woman suffrage, her gentlemen friends lustily cheered her daring from the windows of the Knickerbocker Club, while other intimates of her social world could not comprehend her act. Without systematic knowledge of the past, a theoretical understanding of art, or an objective sense of human endeavor, she could never fuse form and feeling for a concrete end. Her poems sharply reflect her lack of resources. Formless and intentionally flouting the metrical conventions, they occasionally convey strong emotion or evoke a vivid image through some daring metaphor. Yet commonly they grind to a blurred halt in cloying abstractions or subjective obscurity. Bound in a narrow range, she showed the same limitations in her politics, for she adopted socialism in 1932 out of a vague sense of economic injustice and endorsed the America First Committee in 1941 to strengthen American democracy at home. Considered the most beautiful woman in America by a contemporary French artist, Michael Strange touched all who knew her as a tempestuous, vibrant woman, but for a later day her career emerges as more a symbol than an achievement.

[Michael Strange's published works are: *Miscellaneous Poems* (1916); *Poems* (1919); *Clair de Lune* (1920); *Resurrecting Life* (1921), further poems; *Selected Poems* (1928); and *Who Tells Me True* (1940), an autobiography. Other information from Diana Barrymore and Gerold Frank, *Too Much, Too Soon* (1957); Gene Fowler, *Good Night, Sweet Prince: The Life & Times of John Barrymore* (1945); clipping file in Theatre Collection, N.Y. Public Library; and Yale Memorabilia Collection. Death record from Mass. Registrar of Vital Statistics.]

H. L. KLEINFIELD

**TYLER, Adeline Blanchard** (Dec. 8, 1805– Jan. 9, 1875), trained nurse and Episcopal deaconess, Civil War hospital administrator, was born at Billerica, Mass., north of Boston, the third daughter and fifth of seven children of Jeremiah Blanchard, a farmer, and Mary (Gowen) Blanchard. She was educated at a neighborhood academy and for a time taught school in Boston. In 1826 she was married to

John Tyler, an auctioneer and commission merchant on Central Wharf in Boston, a man of substance and position. He was a widower in his mid-forties with several children; she was not yet twenty-one. No children were born of this marriage.

Mrs. Tyler had been brought up as a Congregationalist, but at about the time of her marriage she became an active member of the Episcopal Church of the Advent in Boston. Here she taught Sunday school and actively engaged in charitable work. Shortly after her husband's death in 1853 she became a deaconess of the Episcopal Church, at a time when the first experiments were being made to introduce this form of social service into American Protestantism. Soon afterward she traveled in Europe and remained to study nursing at the Deaconesses' Institute in Kaiserswerth, Germany. This Lutheran institution, founded in 1836, included a hospital in which Florence Nightingale in 1851 had taken her only training. After completing her nursing course, Mrs. Tyler returned to Boston, where she resumed her charitable work and added nursing.

In 1856 she was invited by the Rev. Horace Stringfellow, rector of St. Andrew's Church in Baltimore (with the approval of Bishop William R. Whittingham), to establish and organize an infirmary in that city "as a place of refuge for the destitute sick, and also of quiet religious nursing for sick members of the church, desirous and able to pay for the advantage." Her brother John had been rector of St. Ann's Parish, Annapolis, Md., before his death in 1834, and a brother and sister were living in Baltimore. After careful consideration, Mrs. Tyler accepted the invitation, and with Miss Caroline E. Guild of Boston as her associate, she moved to Baltimore on Sept. 18, 1856. Three days later St. Andrew's Infirmary, officially the Church Infirmary of the Diocese of Maryland, was ready to receive patients, with Mrs. Tyler in charge of a staff of deaconesses. On Oct. 7, 1857, the property of the Washington Medical College in Baltimore was purchased, the constitution was changed, and St. Andrew's Infirmary became a constituent element of the Church Home and Infirmary of the City of Baltimore, Mrs. Tyler continuing as head deaconess. She supervised the preparation and furnishing of the new institution, assumed official charge on Feb. 9, 1858, and remained in this capacity until 1860, when she resigned following the appointment of a man as her superior to handle the Church Home's finances. She then took a house on Howard Street in Baltimore, where she instructed candidates for appointment as deaconess.

Soon after the outbreak of the Civil War, the next spring, the 6th Massachusetts Volunteer Infantry passed through Baltimore on Apr. 19, 1861, en route to Washington. While marching between trains, the regiment was attacked by a pro-Southern mob which killed two men and wounded a number of others. When Mrs. Tyler learned of the attack she hurried to the police station where the wounded had been taken, seeking to aid them, and though she was at first refused admittance, the authorities gave way when she threatened to notify Governor Andrew of Massachusetts. She bound the wounds of the men and had them removed to her Deaconess House, where she kept them until they were fit to be sent to their homes in Massachusetts. When news of her action reached Boston, the Commonwealth of Massachusetts through a resolution of the legislature extended her official recognition and a vote of thanks. In September 1861 she was appointed superintendent of the new Camden Street federal military hospital in Baltimore, but was soon relieved of her post when she refused to discriminate against Southern prisoners in distributing food and other supplies brought to this Union hospital for the comfort of the sick and wounded.

The next summer, while in New York City to rest and visit friends, Mrs. Tyler was called by Surgeon General William A. Hammond to the National Hospital at Chester, Pa., where as head nurse she helped improve the hospital's unsanitary conditions. In July 1863 she was transferred to the Naval School Hospital, later known as U.S. General Hospital, Division No. 1, at Annapolis, Md. In addition to being in charge of nursing, Mrs. Tyler inaugurated and systematized a special diet department. She resigned this position on May 27, 1864, on account of ill health and sailed the next month for Europe. After visits in Paris, in Baden, Germany, and with a sister in Lucerne, Switzerland, she returned to the United States in November 1865.

For a short time after her return Mrs. Tyler was associated with the "Midnight Mission" in New York City, an organization with close Episcopal ties founded in 1868 by Dr. Wolcott Richards to give shelter, guidance, and opportunities for gainful employment to "fallen women." In 1869, at the repeated urging of Dr. Francis H. Brown, founder of the new Children's Hospital in Boston, she became its "Lady Superintendent." With responsibility for all "internal concerns of the hospital," she worked tirelessly to establish it on a sound basis. Despite the Unitarianism of the founders, she introduced a strong Episcopal flavor into the hospital's religious life. She resigned in 1872 upon learning that she was suffering from breast cancer. Both the board of managers and the Ladies Aid Society of the hospital gave her generous gifts, the latter praising her "judicious love and care of the hospital" and her "wonderful management of it, in its struggling infancy." Through Mrs. Tyler's efforts a member of the Anglican Sisterhood of St. Margaret, East Grinstead, England, replaced her as superintendent, and members of this order remained active in the hospital and (after 1889) in its school of nursing for many years.

After a final visit to England Adeline Tyler spent the remainder of her life in retirement in Boston. She died of cancer at Needham, Mass., near Boston, early in 1875 and was buried in Mount Auburn Cemetery in Cambridge. In recognition of her work for the Episcopal Church she had been elected an associate of the Sisters of St. Margaret and was therefore sometimes known as Sister Adeline Tyler. In her various positions she displayed unusual organizing talents and administrative ability, while at the same time, despite a tendency to imperiousness, retaining the human sympathy and understanding that had caused one of her wartime patients to exclaim: "She's a noble woman and ought to live forever."

[Letters and other MS. materials pertaining to Mrs. Tyler in the Md. Hist. Soc., Baltimore; in the MS. collection of the Episcopal Diocese of Md., currently housed in the Peabody Institute, Baltimore; and at Children's Hospital, Boston; L. P. Brockett and Mary C. Vaughan, *Woman's Work in the Civil War* (1867); Judith Robinson, *Ensign on a Hill: The Story of the Church Home and Hospital* (1954); William F. Brand, *Life of William Rollinson Whittingham*, I (1883), 457–59; *Vital Records of Billerica, Mass., to the Year 1850* (1908), pp. 21–24; Rosamond R. Beirne, "Baltimore's Civil War Nurse," *The Sun* (Baltimore), Apr. 23, 1961; information supplied by Mrs. Beirne, of Ruxton, Md., a descendant of Mrs. Tyler, and by the Boston Public Library. Though Mrs. Tyler's first name is sometimes given as Adaline, family sources favor Adeline.]

THOMAS ROBSON HAY

**TYLER, Alice Sarah** (Apr. 27, 1859–Apr. 18, 1944), librarian, was born in Decatur, Ill. Her parents, John William Tyler, a minister of the Disciples of Christ, and Sarah (Roney) Tyler, had moved from Fayette County, Ky., to become pioneer settlers on a farm in central Illinois. Alice was the youngest of their eleven children and the last of a family of fourteen, since her father had three children by an earlier marriage. She was educated in the Decatur

schools and remained at home with her aging parents until they died, her father in 1888 and her mother in 1893. Her interest in books, reading, and libraries had begun early, and in 1887 she became library assistant in the Decatur Public Library, but only after the death of her mother did she feel free to continue her formal education. She then attended the library school at Armour Institute in Chicago (of which KATHARINE L. SHARP was director), receiving her professional certificate in 1895, at the age of thirty-six.

Upon completing the course Miss Tyler was invited by William Howard Brett, librarian of the Cleveland (Ohio) Public Library, to serve there as head cataloguer. Her gift for organization showed clearly in her early work. She was the first to ask for typewriters to improve the work of the cataloguers. The first professionally trained assistant in the Cleveland Public Library, she insisted on better quality in the selection of her staff and was active in teaching in the summer training school established at the library by Brett.

In 1900 a wider opportunity arose when Miss Tyler accepted an invitation to become secretary to the newly created Iowa State Library Commission. Her duties were to "establish new libraries, give advice . . . to all free and public school libraries in the state, and help in the development of the traveling library system." For thirteen years she devoted much of her energy to stimulating library development in the state. During this period the number of free public libraries in Iowa increased from 41 to 114, and centers receiving traveling book collections from 90 to more than 700. She outlined ways of organizing libraries in small communities and urged the use of municipal taxation as a means of supporting them. Miss Tyler also worked out a systematic plan for developing libraries in all Iowa state hospitals and other institutions. She was greatly in demand as a speaker at library dedications, library conventions, and many local citizens' meetings. A summer school for training librarians had been organized at the State University of Iowa, and, except for the summer of 1903, when she went to Europe, she served as its director from 1901 to 1912. She was a frequent contributor to state and library publications, and in 1906 she became editor of the *Bulletin* of the Iowa Library Commission (later the *Iowa Library Quarterly*).

Active in professional organizations, Alice Tyler early emerged as a figure of national importance in library circles. She was secretary of the first executive committee of the League of Library Commissions, founded in 1904, and its president in 1906–07. The American Library Association made her second vice-president in 1909–10, and in 1909 she was elected to membership in the American Library Institute, a group of one hundred library leaders chosen by the American Library Association "to contribute to library progress by conferring together."

In 1913 Miss Tyler was invited to become director of the Library School at Western Reserve University in Cleveland, and though reluctant to leave Iowa and active library service, she accepted, feeling that the training of more and better librarians was urgently needed. The school, in part an outgrowth of the summer training class at the Cleveland Public Library, had been founded in 1903. When she became director there were only nineteen regular and sixteen special students; in 1929, when she retired, the graduating class numbered seventy-six. In 1913 full college training was not required for admission, and only a certificate was given to those completing the course. Two years after assuming the directorship Miss Tyler instituted a combined four-year course with the university's College for Women which terminated in a B.S. degree, with a fifth-year B.S. in library science for those who entered with a bachelor's degree. She early encouraged young men to enroll in the program. The school was recognized as one of the fully professional arms of the university when Miss Tyler in 1925 was given the title of dean and professor of library science. Two years later it was accredited by the Board of Education of the American Library Association. Miss Tyler was an inspiring teacher, full of idealism, who at the same time, as a result of her years of practical service in Iowa, could give a down-to-earth flavor to her lectures. She seemed to know all the important people in the library world, and was able to characterize them vividly for her students. Her fine appearance, beautiful snow-white hair, and carefully selected clothes, and her ability to express herself in public made her a model for many of her students and fellow workers.

Miss Tyler served as president of the Ohio Library Association in 1916–17 and of the Association of American Library Schools in 1918–19. Her greatest professional honor was her election to the presidency of the American Library Association for the year 1920–21. She was founder and first president of the Cleveland Library Club in 1922–23. Her nonprofessional activities included long-time membership in the Daughters of the American Revolution, the Adult Education Association, the Women's City Club of Cleveland (a charter member), and the Unitarian Club. Upon her retirement, in 1929, alumni of the school contributed to a sizable fund for travel. Her years of retirement were productive and happy, giving her time to take a course in Greek civilization at Cleveland College, a taste of the higher education she had always wanted. She was in much demand as a lecturer and library consultant, and continued to contribute to library periodicals until 1938, when a broken hip limited her activity. She died in Cleveland in 1944, shortly before her eighty-fifth birthday, and was buried in Decatur, Ill.

[The principal source is Cora E. Richardson, "Alice Sarah Tyler: A Biog. Study" (unpublished master's paper, Western Reserve Univ. School of Library Science, 1951); a digest was published in Emily Miller Danton, ed., *Pioneering Leaders in Librarianship* (1953). Other sources include *John W. Tyler, 1808–1888: A Memorial of the One-Hundredth Anniversary of His Birth* (privately printed, 1908); *Who's Who in America*, 1928–29; *Who's Who in Library Service*, 1933; *Nat. Cyc. Am. Biog.*, XXXIII, 422–23; *Iowa Library Quart.*, Apr.–June 1913, July–Sept. 1913; *Cleveland News*, Apr. 18, 1944 (obituary); *Cleveland Plain Dealer*, Apr. 20, 1944 (editorial).]

HELEN M. FOCKE

**TYLER, Julia Gardiner** (May 4, 1820–July 10, 1889), second wife of John Tyler, tenth president of the United States, was born on Gardiners Island, N.Y., the first daughter and third of four children of Juliana (McLachlan) Gardiner, daughter of a wealthy Scottish brewer of New York City, and David Gardiner, a previously impecunious lawyer of good family who later (1824–28) served in the state senate. He was a direct descendant of Lion Gardiner, a professional soldier and fortifications engineer who emigrated from England to Saybrook, Conn., in 1635 and four years later became master of Manchonake (Gardiners) Island, off the eastern tip of Long Island, having purchased it from the Indians.

Reared in East Hampton, Long Island, and educated at Mme. N. D. Chagaray's fashionable institute for young ladies in New York City (1835–c. 1838), Julia Gardiner accepted the values of a family which prized social exclusiveness, proper marriage alliances, and money. Short and plump, with raven hair and dark eyes, she was known for her beauty. She was an impulsive and romantic girl whose innocent flirtations on several occasions embarrassed her conservative parents. So, too, did her lending her name and likeness to a commercial advertisement in 1839, an indiscretion which led to a rather sudden European tour.

Her reputation as a coquette was further fortified during a family visit to Washington for the 1842–43 social season, for within four months she received five marriage proposals from highly eligible suitors, including two Congressmen, one Supreme Court justice, and the President of the United States, whose first wife, LETITIA CHRISTIAN TYLER, had died in September 1842. Playing this distinguished field with skill, Julia Gardiner finally chose the President. Tyler was thirty years her senior, with three children older than she, and their courtship thus occasioned considerable gossip. It was intensified when, after several months in East Hampton, the Gardiners again returned to Washington in December 1843 and once more embarked on a social whirl. This ended abruptly, however, on Feb. 28, 1844, when Julia's father, along with the Secretary of State and six other men, was killed in a gun explosion aboard the U.S.S. *Princeton* during a presidential cruise. When the first shock of this tragedy had passed, the twenty-three-year-old Julia, perhaps finding in Tyler's mature years something of the paternal security she had lost, readily agreed to his wishes for an early marriage. Because of the continuing gossip and the fact that the Gardiners were in mourning no engagement was announced, and their secretly planned wedding, on June 26, 1844, in the Episcopal Church of the Ascension in New York City, had about it the quality of an elopement. It was the first occasion of a president marrying while in office.

Subdued for years by the invalidism of his beloved first wife, Tyler's natural sense of humor emerged again under the influence of his new bride, and the final year of his administration was infused with something of her own youthful zest and gaiety. Though First Lady for only eight months, Julia Tyler was noted for her charm as a hostess, the opulence of her receptions and balls, and her efforts, not uncommon among nineteenth-century presidential wives, to adapt European court manners and procedures to Washington social life. Owing in part to her confidential employment of a New York reporter as press agent, she received extensive and generally favorable newspaper coverage, a matter of lively concern to both her and the President. Of more permanent significance was her energetic ballroom lobbying for the annexation of Texas, a measure enacted shortly before the expiration of Tyler's term in March 1845. She also spent much time seeking patronage for her brothers and other members of the Gardiner clan.

At the end of Tyler's presidency he and his wife retired to his extensive wheat and corn plantation, Sherwood Forest, on the James River in Charles City County, Va., near Richmond. There she gave birth to seven children: David Gardiner (1846), John Alexander (1848), Julia Gardiner (1849), Lachlan (1851), Lyon Gardiner (1853), Robert Fitzwalter (1856), and Pearl (1860). Lyon Gardiner Tyler, a historian, was for many years president of the College of William and Mary in Virginia. As mistress of Sherwood Forest and its seventy slaves, Mrs. Tyler was renowned for her entertainment of the local gentry. Between her accouchements she visited the fashionable spas at Saratoga, Newport, and the Virginia springs. For these trips her wardrobe was always as extensive as it was fashionable, and Tyler was hard pressed to meet her expensive tastes. Nevertheless, their marriage remained a happy one.

Mrs. Tyler's ancestors had been slaveowners, and after her marriage she became, like her husband, an outspoken proponent of states' rights and slavery. In February 1853, shortly after the publication of *Uncle Tom's Cabin,* she attracted wide attention with a long letter in the *Southern Literary Messenger* lauding the civilizing mission of the plantation system. In 1861 she was a vigorous advocate of secession and welcomed her husband's election to the Confederate Congress. Tyler died in January 1862 at seventy-one, however, and this, together with the proximity of Sherwood Forest to the battle zone, persuaded Mrs. Tyler twice to run the sea blockade to remove six of her children to the safety of her mother's home on Staten Island, N.Y. Settled there herself in late 1863, she plunged into local pro-Confederate political activities. These antagonized her surviving brother, David Lyon Gardiner, a loyal Unionist, and the split widened into a bitter inheritance struggle after their mother's death in 1864, leading to the celebrated case of *Tyler v. Gardiner* (1864–68) and a permanent estrangement.

Although her Virginia estate had been overrun by the Union Army, Mrs. Tyler fought a successful legal and economic battle after the war to retain and restore it. The panic of 1873 and the long depression that followed compounded her financial difficulties, but careful management and unwonted economies enabled her gradually to pay off her husband's numerous creditors, meet back taxes, and educate her children. In 1872, crushed by the sudden death of her daughter Julia and still weighed down by lawsuits and debts, Mrs. Tyler, who had been reared a Presbyterian and later had become an Episcopalian, left that church to become a Roman Catholic, a decision widely heralded in the Catholic press.

During the late 1870's the ever-energetic "Mrs. Ex-President Tyler" (as she styled herself) lived in Washington and lobbied vigorously for a federal pension for presidential widows. When Congress passed such legislation in 1882, under the shock of Garfield's assassination, the annual grant of $5,000 permitted her to resume the style of living to which she was accustomed. Her last years were spent quietly and comfortably in Richmond. There the onetime "Rose of Long Island," part Gardiner, part Tyler, and part Scarlett O'Hara, died of a cerebral stroke at the age of sixty-nine. After a funeral mass at St. Peter's Cathedral, she was buried next to her husband in Hollywood Cemetery, Richmond.

[Julia Gardiner Tyler letters are scattered through the Gardiner Family Papers, Yale Univ. Library; the Tyler Family Papers, Sherwood Forest, Charles City, Va. (not open to scholars); and the John Tyler Papers, Library of Congress. Most of those in the last collection are printed in Lyon Gardiner Tyler, ed., *Letters and Times of the Tylers* (3 vols., 1884–96). The fullest biographical account is Robert Seager II, *And Tyler Too: A Biog. of John and Julia Gardiner Tyler* (1963), based on all known manuscript letters. Other useful secondary sources include: Oliver Perry Chitwood, *John Tyler: Champion of the Old South* (1939); Elizabeth Tyler Coleman, *Priscilla Cooper Tyler and the Am. Scene, 1816–1889* (1955); Margaret Gardiner, *Leaves from a Young Girl's Diary* (privately printed, 1925); Howard Gotlieb and Gail Grimes, "President Tyler and the Gardiners: A New Portrait," Yale Univ. Library *Gazette*, July 1959; Herbert C. Bradshaw, "A President's Bride at 'Sherwood Forest,'" *Va. Cavalcade*, Spring 1958; and Robert Seager II, "John Tyler: The Planter of Sherwood Forest," *ibid.*, Summer 1963. Distinctly misleading are Laura Holloway, *The Ladies of the White House* (1880), and J. J. Perling, *The President Takes a Wife* (1959). The most complete obituaries are in the *Richmond* (Va.) *Dispatch*, July 11, 12, 13, 1889, and the *Richmond* (Va.) *State*, July 11, 12, 1889.]

ROBERT SEAGER II

**TYLER, Letitia Christian** (Nov. 12, 1790–Sept. 10, 1842), first wife of President John Tyler, was born at Cedar Grove plantation, New Kent County, Va., the third of eight daughters and seventh of twelve children of Robert and Mary (Browne) Christian. Her father, a well-to-do planter, was of a family prominent in Virginia social life and Federalist politics. Little is known of Letitia's life before her first meeting, around 1808, with John Tyler, a Richmond law student of a similar plantation background. Friendship ripened into

romance, and they were married on his twenty-third birthday, Mar. 29, 1813.

That same year Tyler was reelected to the Virginia House of Delegates, and during the greater part of their married years he continued in public life. In 1825, having served two terms in Congress, he was elected governor of Virginia; two years later he returned to Washington as a Senator. Originally a Jeffersonian Republican, he found himself increasingly opposed to Jackson and at odds with party leaders in Virginia, and in 1836 he resigned his Senate seat. Throughout this time his wife and their growing family lived on a succession of four plantations in the Richmond area. In 1837 they moved to Williamsburg, where Tyler pursued a law practice and once again served in the state legislature. Letitia Tyler had joined her husband in Richmond during his terms as governor and had briefly visited him in Washington during his Senatorial career, but except for these short interludes she remained wholly apart from his public life. Of a retiring nature, she preferred to devote herself to the duties associated with plantation life and to the care of their nine children, of whom seven survived infancy: Mary (born in 1815), Robert (1816), who later achieved some distinction as an Alabama newspaper editor and political figure, John (1819), Letitia (1821), Elizabeth (1823), Alice (1827), and Tazewell (1830).

A woman of tranquil beauty and exceptionally fair complexion, Mrs. Tyler was deeply beloved by her husband and family. Though none of her own letters survive, numerous sources bear witness to her graciousness and modesty, as well as to her selfless solicitude for others and her "peculiar air of native refinement." "Her whole thought and affections are wrapped up in her husband and children," a daughter-in-law observed (Holloway, p. 319).

In 1839 she suffered a severe paralytic stroke which rendered her an invalid for the rest of her life. Consequently, when Tyler, elected vice-president on the Whig ticket in 1840, became president a few months later upon the death of William Henry Harrison, she was unequal to the heavy social burdens thus imposed. Living in seclusion at the White House, she supervised its domestic management while her daughter-in-law, PRISCILLA COOPER TYLER (Mrs. Robert Tyler), and later her daughter Letitia (Mrs. James A. Semple), stood in her place as presidential hostess. She appeared at only one social function, the White House marriage of her daughter Elizabeth early in 1842. She died that September, having suffered a second stroke, at the age of fifty-one.

Although her death came at a time of great party rancor, all newspapers, even the *National Intelligencer*, a bitter critic of the administration, paid tribute to her personal qualities. After the rites of the Protestant Episcopal Church, of which she had been a devout lifelong member, were observed in the White House, her remains were interred in the family plot at Cedar Grove. In 1844 John Tyler took a second wife, JULIA GARDINER TYLER, by whom he had seven additional children.

[Oliver Perry Chitwood, *John Tyler: Champion of the Old South* (1939); Laura C. Holloway, *The Ladies of the White House* (1880); Esther Singleton, *The Story of the White House* (2 vols., 1907); Mary Ormsbee Whitton, *First First Ladies, 1789–1865* (1948); Lyon Gardiner Tyler, *Letters and Times of the Tylers* (3 vols., 1884–96); Robert Seager II, *And Tyler Too: A Biog. of John and Julia Tyler* (1963). On the Christian family genealogy, see *William and Mary College Quart.*, Oct. 1899, pp. 127–28.]

OLIVER PERRY CHITWOOD

**TYLER, Priscilla Cooper** (June 14, 1816– Dec. 29, 1889), actress and White House hostess, was born in New York City. Christened Elizabeth Priscilla, she was the second daughter and third of the nine children of Thomas Abthorpe Cooper, for thirty years a favorite actor on the American stage, and his second wife, Mary Fairlie. Priscilla's mother, of Anglo-Dutch ancestry, had been a bright ornament of New York society, "witty and beautiful," according to JESSIE BENTON FRÉMONT. Her father, of Irish descent, had come to America at twenty from his native England, where he had been brought up by the political philosopher William Godwin, his mother's cousin. The principle of freedom with which he had been reared Cooper in turn applied to his own children, even building a separate house for them and their governess next to the family home in Bristol, Pa., where the Coopers moved when Priscilla was three. If bouts with arithmetic occasionally harried the child, this was compensated for by visitors such as Joseph Bonaparte, brother of Napoleon, and Washington Irving. To Irving, Mrs. Cooper—the "Sophy Sparkle" of his *Salmagundi* papers— wrote of Priscilla in 1830, "She is all talent— that is, in regard to sprightliness of mind, cleverness in writing, and fun and drollery in everything; but so incapable of application that she has not of what is technically called accomplishments a single one. . . . She is not beautiful, but there is something very piquant in her countenance."

Shortly after Mrs. Cooper's death in 1833 Priscilla, fulfilling a promise made to her mother, joined her father's theatrical company as leading lady in an effort to help him recover his waning popularity. Her debut at New York's Bowery Theatre in February 1834 as Virginia in Sheridan Knowles' *Virginius* was followed by other benefit performances which took her as far south as New Orleans, supporting her father in such Shakespearean roles as Juliet and Desdemona. Her audiences praised "her sunny countenance, shaded by clustering curls of golden hair," but Priscilla Cooper had no aspiration to become a great actress. When she ended her career in Albany in 1838, she was still, in the words of the *Knickerbocker Magazine* three years before, but "a bud of promise."

The next year, on Sept. 12, 1839, in St. James's Episcopal Church at Bristol, Pa., she was married to Robert Tyler, the tall, distinguished-looking eldest son of Senator John Tyler, who according to family tradition had fallen in love upon seeing her as Desdemona. Living at first in Williamsburg, Va., she helped her lawyer husband with his speeches, and though disappointed when he gave up his practice to aid his father, the Whig vice-presidential candidate in 1840, she entered wholeheartedly into the campaign. On her father-in-law's elevation to the presidency in 1841 he asked her to be official White House hostess in place of his invalid wife, LETITIA CHRISTIAN TYLER. With DOLLEY MADISON and Secretary of State Daniel Webster as guides, Priscilla rose to the occasion; and if the French minister, Chevalier de Bacourt, thought that the "little woman who seems a good fellow" was "too sweet to be interesting," Charles Dickens considered her "a very interesting, graceful and accomplished lady."

When the President's wife died and it became apparent he would remarry, Priscilla Tyler persuaded Robert to give up his post in the Land Office and resume his law practice. They moved to Philadelphia in March 1844. In 1845 Marie Fairlie, their first child, and John, their third, died, leaving only Letitia Christian, who had been born in the White House. There were six subsequent children— Grace, Thomas Cooper, Priscilla, Elizabeth, Julia Campbell, and Robert—though Thomas died in infancy. The coming of the Civil War forced Tyler, a Southern sympathizer, to flee to Virginia, where his wife joined him. While he served the Confederacy in civilian and military capacities, she shifted between Richmond and her sister Mary Grace Raoul's home near Montgomery, Ala., as the fortunes of war dictated. At the end of hostilities she settled in Montgomery, where her husband became editor of the *Advertiser*. After his death in 1877 she stayed on in Montgomery, and it was there that she died in 1889, at the age of seventy-three. Priscilla Tyler had no personal ambitions. Her contribution to her times resulted from her association with three men: her father, for whose sake she became for a brief span an actress; her husband, with whose career she identified herself; and her father-in-law, whom she served as hostess of the White House.

[This account is drawn chiefly from Elizabeth Tyler Coleman, *Priscilla Cooper Tyler and the Am. Scene, 1816–1889* (1955), which is based on the Cooper Papers in the Univ. of Ala. Library. See also Martin S. Shockley, "Priscilla Cooper in the Richmond Theatre," *Va. Mag. of Hist. and Biog.,* Apr. 1959; Joseph N. Ireland, *A Memoir of the Professional Life of Thomas Abthorpe Cooper* (1888); Thomas M. Owen, *Hist. of Ala. and Dict. of Ala. Biog.,* IV (1921), 1696–97; and Oliver Perry Chitwood, *John Tyler* (1939).]

ELIZABETH F. HOXIE

# U

**UELAND, Clara Hampson** (Oct. 10, 1860–Mar. 1, 1927), Minnesota suffragist and civic reformer, was born in Akron, Ohio, to Eliza (Osborn) and Henry Oscar Hampson. Her father was a descendant of Robert Hampson, an early English settler of Pennsylvania. He had spent his youth on the family farm, but his health was broken by the rigors of Civil War campaigns, and he died soon after peace had been restored, leaving his wife, an older child, Fred, and Clara to seek support from relatives in Minnesota. The family moved first to Faribault and then to Minneapolis, where Clara graduated from the local high school in 1878 and at eighteen became a secondary school teacher.

Photographs of her at that age and seven years later, in 1885, when, on June 19, she was married to Andreas Ueland, portray a handsome woman with "pansy black" eyes, dark hair, classic profile, and steady gaze. Her husband, son of Ole Gabriel Ueland, a farmer and long a leader in the Norwegian parliament, had arrived in the United States from Norway in 1870, at eighteen. Studying law at night in Minneapolis while working as a common laborer, he had been admitted to the bar in 1877 and by 1881 had won election as judge of probate, an office he held for five years. Ambitious and impatient, Ueland rose rapidly in legal eminence and wealth, serving as counsel to lumber and banking interests.

In the first six years of her marriage Mrs. Ueland had four daughters: Anne, Elsa, Dorothy (who died in her second year), and Brenda; four sons followed: Sigurd (born in 1893), Arnulf, Rolf, and Torvald (1902). The Uelands reared their family in a kind of idyllic freedom in a rambling frame house on four acres by Lake Calhoun on the outskirts of Minneapolis.

A visitor in the early years recalled "large, rather bare rooms and good pictures on the walls." The presence of hired girls and other servants freed Mrs. Ueland from household chores and enabled her to read, sketch, and garden. The house was full of company, the adults entertaining such prominent figures as JANE ADDAMS, CARRIE CHAPMAN CATT, John Fiske, Björnstjerne Björnson, Fridtjof Nansen, and Roald Amundsen, as well as a succession of young artists to whom Mrs. Ueland gave warm encouragement. Sundays found the family attending the Unitarian Society, where Clara and Andreas had first met.

About 1890 Mrs. Ueland was "the moving spirit" in a group of young mothers who were studying child training; a paper she delivered on the ideals of the Froebel kindergarten prompted a successful experiment with a neighborhood kindergarten in the Uelands' library. The group then formed the Minneapolis Kindergarten Association, which established three charity kindergartens and, in 1892, a training school for kindergarten teachers. Their campaign in 1897 secured the first public school kindergarten in the city.

A devoted member of the Minneapolis Society of Fine Arts from the time of its first project, a small art school in the city library building, Mrs. Ueland helped it develop into the Minneapolis Institute of Arts, of which she was for many years a trustee. She and her husband were interested in preserving and utilizing the talents of Minnesota craftsmen and craftswomen, many of whom had skills learned in the Old World. They brought back examples of modern work from their trips to Norway and Sweden, and Mrs. Ueland, as a member of the first governing board of the state art commission, established in 1903, helped organize statewide exhibits and programs of instruction. She also introduced the annual exhibit and sale of handcrafts sponsored by the Woman's Club of Minneapolis, of which she was a founder in 1907. Her interest in architecture led her to work for better homes and school buildings and for the establishment of a city planning commission.

Always concerned for the welfare of children, she led in civic and state campaigns to secure medical examinations in the public schools, school nurses, pure milk, public playgrounds, a juvenile court, mothers' pensions, and the regulation of child labor. Gradually, however, her inherent sense of equality and social justice led her to focus on the suffrage movement. Her daughter Elsa was the first president of the College Equal Suffrage League founded at the University of Minnesota in 1907. Mrs. Ueland herself organized the Minneapolis Equal Suffrage Club (later the Hennepin County suffrage association), and in 1914 she was elected president of the Minnesota Woman Suffrage Association, a post she held until the vote was won five years later. "Too much credit for the final success of woman suffrage in Minnesota can not be given to Mrs. Ueland," writes the movement's official historian. ". . . She organized the entire State, raised large sums of money each year, induced many prominent women to join in the work, carried out the instructions of the National Association to the letter, secured legislation, and not only took advantage of every opportunity for propaganda but created opportunities" (*History of Woman Suffrage*, VI, 320n.). When the Minnesota legislature ratified the Nineteenth Amendment in September 1919, Mrs. Ueland became the first president of the Minnesota League of Women Voters.

She resigned this post to take personal charge, as chairman of the League's legislative committee, of lobbying for League-sponsored bills for the protection of women workers, child welfare, and social hygiene, and of efforts for municipal charter reform. In her last years disarmament and world peace became primary concerns. She was a member of the Democratic party. In 1927, when returning by streetcar from testifying at the state capitol in support of a maximum-hours bill for women, Clara Ueland was struck by a truck as she alighted near her home and was instantly killed. She was buried in Lakewood Cemetery, Minneapolis. A memorial service was held in the capitol, at which distinguished Minnesotans paid tribute to her womanly grace, dignity, and poise, to her breadth of view and tolerance toward those who disagreed with her, and to the quiet perseverance which made her leadership so effective. Her influence is commemorated by a plaque in the capitol rotunda and in a fellowship fund at the University of Minnesota for women graduate students in the field of "government and citizenship."

[Papers of the Political Equality Club of Minneapolis (1892–1920), of the Minn. Woman Suffrage Assoc. (1894–1921), and of the Minn. League of Women Voters, in the Minn. Hist. Soc., St. Paul; Brenda Ueland's autobiography, *Me* (1939), and "The Uelands," *Am. Scandinavian Rev.*, Winter 1950; Andreas Ueland, *Recollections of an Immigrant* (1929); memorial issue of *Minn. Woman Voter*, Mar. 1927; *Woman's Who's Who of America*, 1914–15; Mabel W. Cameron, ed., *Biog. Cyc. Am. Women*, I (1924), 320; Ida H. Harper, *The Hist. of Woman Suffrage*, vol. VI (1922), chap. xxii; Marguerite N. Bell, *With Banners: A Biog. of Stella L. Wood* (1954), pp. 48–50; clipping collection, Minneapolis Public Library; interview with Brenda Ueland, who has an unpublished typescript biography of her mother, together with some private family papers.]

CLARKE A. CHAMBERS

**UNDERWOOD, Lillias Stirling Horton** (June 21, 1851–Oct. 29, 1921), physician and Presbyterian missionary to Korea, was born in Albany, N.Y., the first of four daughters of Matilda (McPherson) and James Mandeville Horton. Her father, whose ancestor Barnabas Horton had arrived in America in 1642, was descended from Dutch and English stock, her mother from English and Scottish. Both sides of the family included Revolutionary soldiers and Presbyterian clergymen. Her father was preparing for the ministry when for financial reasons he was forced to enter the hardware business in Albany. In 1867 he moved his family to Chicago, where he became a partner in a wholesale hardware firm. Lillias Horton attended the Albany Female Academy and then a public high school in Chicago.

For several years after graduation she lived at the family home in nearby Evanston and spent summers at Lake Geneva in Wisconsin, where she was an enthusiastic sportswoman. Influenced by her mother, who had wanted to be a missionary, she became actively engaged in church and charity work in the city. Her experience visiting the sick in Chicago hospitals helped her decide to study medicine in preparation for a missionary career. She entered the Woman's Medical College of Chicago (later incorporated into Northwestern University) and graduated with the M.D. degree in 1887. The next year she served as an intern in the Chicago Hospital for Women and Children. A "bright young girl of slight and graceful figure," as a visiting missionary board official described her (introduction to *Fifteen Years among the Top-knots,* p. vi), she added to her medical knowledge some practical experience as a trained nurse. Though she originally volunteered for work in India, the Presbyterian Board of Foreign Missions asked her to go to Korea, which had been opened to Westerners only five years earlier, to take charge of the women's department and the dispensary of a newly established government hospital. She was also to act as physician to Queen Min of Korea, a post created shortly before through the influence of the American ambassador, Dr. Horace N. Allen.

Lillias Horton arrived in March 1888 in the capital city of Seoul and spent most of the next thirty years in Korea. She was married on Mar. 13, 1889, to Horace Grant Underwood, a Presbyterian missionary from New Jersey who had come to Korea three years before. One of the earliest Protestant clergymen to reside in that country, he devoted some years to preparing the first grammar and dictionary of the Korean language. On their honeymoon trip into the interior, a difficult and dangerous journey that took them as far north as the Manchurian border, Mrs. Underwood traveled by sedan chair and on foot a distance of more than a thousand miles, treated more than six hundred patients, and whenever possible instructed the women in the Christian religion. This was the first of several such trips in which the Underwoods combined medical work with evangelism. After the birth of her only child, Horace Horton Underwood (later a missionary educator in Korea) in 1890, Lillias Underwood became ill and the family took a year's furlough in the United States, where they sought greater support for their mission. Returning to Korea in 1893 with funds collected at home, they remodeled a large house to establish the Frederick Underwood Shelter, to care for patients with infectious diseases. During the severe cholera epidemic in the summer of 1895, Dr. Underwood helped organize an emergency hospital; of the patients treated there, only about a third died, compared with the two-thirds who died in the city as a whole.

As medical adviser to Queen Min, Lillias Underwood was often invited to the palace and became a friend and confidante of the royal consort during a period of great political turmoil and confusion in Korea. This intimate relationship lasted until the Queen's tragic assassination by Japanese soldiers in 1895. Though they were first and last devoted missionaries, the Underwoods' close connection with the royal court sometimes involved them

in the political struggles of the period, and they were often identified with the anti-Japanese faction in Seoul. After the annexation of Korea by Japan in 1910, however, they cooperated with the new rulers of the country in order to further their evangelistic work. Because of frequent poor health, Dr. Underwood and her husband took a few extended leaves from the Korean mission, traveling in China, Japan, Europe, and America. On one such trip to the United States, in October 1916, Horace Underwood died in Atlantic City, N.J., after a long siege of Asiatic sprue. Dr. Lillias Underwood returned to Seoul, where she remained until her own death five years later, at the age of seventy. Though she had long suffered from rheumatic fever and arthritis, she succumbed to the same disease from which her husband had died. She was buried in the Foreign Cemetery outside Seoul.

Throughout her many years in Korea as physician, teacher, and royal adviser, Dr. Underwood regarded herself as primarily an evangelist, a co-worker with her missionary husband. She deplored the low status of Korean women and believed that Christianity would offer a means of bettering their position. Besides helping her husband in his scholarly work on the Korean language and in his translations of religious tracts, she published articles in religious journals in America. She wrote two books about life in her adopted country, the autobiographical *Fifteen Years among the Top-knots* (1904) and *With Tommy Tompkins in Korea* (1905), and a biography of her husband, *Underwood of Korea* (1918). This small, rather fragile-looking woman, in poor health most of the last half of her life, was a person of courage and strong will, who carried out a difficult vocation with faith and determination.

[Lillias Underwood's own books are a basic source; see also introduction by Frank F. Ellinwood in her *Fifteen Years among the Top-knots.* Details of her family background and personal life were supplied by her sister Leonore Horton Egan, and her grandson, Horace G. Underwood. The United Presbyterian Mission Library in N.Y. City has approximately 37 letters of Dr. Underwood on microfilm, covering the years 1888–1901. Information about her medical education was received from the archivist of Northwestern Univ. Obituaries are found in the *N.Y. Times,* Nov. 14, 1921, and *Missionary Rev. of the World,* Dec. 1921; see also *Who's Who in America,* 1920–21, and Winifred Mathews, *Dauntless Women* (1947), pp. 145–64. Brief references to Dr. Underwood's work may also be found in the following: Arthur J. Brown, *One Hundred Years: A Hist. of the Foreign Missionary Work of the Presbyterian Church in the U.S.A.* (1936); Fred H. Harrington, *God, Mam-*

mon, and the Japanese: Dr. Horace N. Allen and Korean-Am. Relations, 1884–1905 (1944); L. George Paik, The Hist. of Protestant Missions in Korea, 1832–1910 (Pyeng Yang, 1929); Harry A. Rhodes, ed., Hist. of the Korea Mission, Presbyterian Church U.S.A., 1884–1934 (Seoul, 1934).]

CLIFTON J. PHILLIPS

**UPTON, Harriet Taylor** (Dec. 17, 1853–Nov. 2, 1945), suffragist, Republican leader, and author, was born in Ravenna, Portage County, Ohio, the first of two children and only daughter of Harriet M. (Frazer) and Ezra Booth Taylor. Her maternal grandmother, Anna (Campbell) Frazer, had been the first white child born in the Portage area when it was still a part of Connecticut's Western Reserve. Her father, also a native of the county, was a lawyer of some renown in Ravenna and in Warren, Ohio, to which the family moved in 1861, and later a circuit court judge. In 1880 he was elected to Congress to fill the seat vacated by James A. Garfield after the latter's elevation to the presidency. Serving in the House for thirteen years, he became chairman of the Judiciary Committee and was a leader in the fight for the passage of the Sherman Anti-Trust Act in 1890.

Growing up in a warm and indulgent household, Harriet Taylor was an energetic, positive child. She was fascinated by politics and often traveled with her father on his speaking tours, closely watching the events of each election. From childhood, she later wrote, "I liked to attend any kind of a gathering of people of any age and was always interested in organized bodies." Harriet began her education in a two-room schoolhouse. At the Warren High School she particularly enjoyed the science courses and successfully opposed the rule that barred girls from the chemistry laboratory. Her father did not want her to go to college, but she continued what proved to be an excellent political education by traveling with him on his northern Ohio circuit and by serving as secretary of the Woman's Christian Temperance Union of Trumbull County. She first encountered the question of woman suffrage in her mid-twenties when she heard SUSAN B. ANTHONY speak at Warren, but at that time and for some years afterward she strongly opposed the suffrage cause because it implied that men were unjust to women, which seemed contrary to her own experience.

When Harriet's father, now a widower, moved to Washington in 1880, she accompanied him as his official hostess. On July 9, 1884, she was married to George Whitman Upton, a lawyer who came of a prominent Oregon family. He became a partner of her father, and the Uptons made their home in Warren, living in Washington while Congress was in session. Through her father Mrs. Upton developed a close and easy acquaintance with national Republican leaders and added to her already large knowledge of the American political process.

In 1888, in Washington, she again met Miss Anthony, as well as ELIZABETH CADY STANTON, LUCY STONE, and other leaders in the suffrage movement. She was drawn to Miss Anthony, but still opposed the suffrage cause (although her father had for some time been an active supporter). While gathering material for an antisuffrage article, however, she found herself converted. She joined the National American Woman Suffrage Association in 1890 and thereafter used her political skills to further the movement. She found that she took to the practical details of convention business "as a child does to candy."

Realizing the need for more aggressive action, Mrs. Upton served in 1893 on a committee which approached all members of Congress for expressions of opinion on the suffrage question. The following year she was elected treasurer of the N.A.W.S.A., a post she held until 1910. For a time (1903–09) she managed most of the day-to-day work of the association, with the aid of only a small staff, from national headquarters in Warren, Ohio. In 1907 Progress, a monthly suffrage paper which she edited from 1902 to 1910, was enlarged and made the official organ of the association. She was good at money raising and an excellent press agent; "in the dark and devious avocation of working the unsophisticated editor," commented a Baltimore newspaper in 1906, "Mrs. Upton is truly a past mistress" (quoted in History of Woman Suffrage, V, 176). A tireless worker, she also edited the reports of the national conventions, frequently testified before Congressional hearings, supervised the circulation of large quantities of suffrage literature, and traveled widely in the interests of the cause.

Harriet Upton also served for eighteen years as president of the Ohio Woman Suffrage Association, from 1899 to 1908 and again from 1911 to 1920. In this capacity she organized annual conventions, directed two unsuccessful state suffrage referendum campaigns (1912, 1914), led the 1916 campaign which secured municipal suffrage in the state, and finally managed the campaign which assured prompt ratification of the Nineteenth Amendment by the Ohio legislature. She found time, as well, for community affairs. In 1898 she was elected to the board of education of Warren, a position she held for a number of years, part of the time as president.

Mrs. Upton was a facile writer of political articles for the newspapers. In addition, though childless herself, she particularly enjoyed writing stories for children, which were published in such magazines as *St. Nicholas* and *Wide Awake*. Her interest in children also prompted the writing of her first book, *Our Early Presidents: Their Wives and Children, from Washington to Jackson* (1892). She also wrote local history. Her two-volume *A Twentieth Century History of Trumbull County, Ohio* (1909) was followed by her most consequential work, the three-volume *History of the Western Reserve* (1910). She contributed many suffrage articles to such popular publications as the *Woman's Home Companion, Harper's Bazar,* and *Outlook*. In her writing, as in her speeches, she never lost an opportunity to emphasize the role played by women in the development of state and nation, a role she felt too long neglected by historians.

Mrs. Upton was well suited for a prominent role in political affairs once women had gained the franchise, and the opportunity presented itself in 1920 when her fellow Ohioan Warren G. Harding was the Republican presidential candidate. Appointed that year as vice-chairman of the Republican National Executive Committee—one of the first women to hold so high a party post—she retained the position for four years. She used her political contacts to win government appointments for qualified women, but was herself unsuccessful when in 1924, the year after her husband's death, she became a candidate at the age of seventy for her father's old Congressional seat, only to lose in the primaries. After brief service in 1928 as assistant state campaign manager for the Republican party, she was appointed liaison officer between the Ohio Department of Public Welfare and Gov. Myers Y. Cooper. In this capacity she succeeded in effecting reforms at the Madison (Ohio) Home for Soldiers' and Sailors' Widows and at the Girls' Industrial School at Delaware, Ohio.

In appearance Harriet Taylor Upton was described by one contemporary as "the old-fashioned type of woman—fat and jolly and motherly." Her infectious good humor and droll, easygoing platform manner won the favor of audiences and made her a beloved figure among suffrage workers. In early childhood she had briefly attended a Presbyterian Sunday school, then shifted to the Episcopal Church, of which she was a lifelong communicant. She retired from public life at the close of Governor Cooper's administration in 1931 and moved to Pasadena, Calif. There she spent her remaining years and died of hypertensive heart disease at the age of ninety-one.

[Mrs. Upton's autobiographical "Random Recollections" (mimeographed, 1927[?], copy in Schlesinger Library, Radcliffe College) is a basic source. See also: Florence E. Allen and Mary Welles, *The Ohio Woman Suffrage Movement* (1952); Ruth Neely, ed., *Women of Ohio* (1939), I, 379–81; Charles B. Galbreath, *Hist. of Ohio,* vol. II (1925), to which she contributed a chapter on "The Woman Suffrage Movement in Ohio"; Harriet Taylor Upton, *Hist. of the Western Reserve,* I (1910), 195–97 (on her father); Susan B. Anthony and Ida H. Harper, *The Hist. of Woman Suffrage,* vols. IV–VI (1902–22); *N.Y. Times,* June 6, Aug. 16, 1924; Harvey Walker, *Constructive Govt. in Ohio: The Story of the Administration of Gov. Myers Y. Cooper* (1948), p. 129; *Who Was Who in America,* vol. II (1950); obituaries in *N.Y. Times, Cleveland Plain Dealer,* and *Akron Beacon Jour.,* Nov. 4, 1945. For examples of her magazine articles see *Century,* Aug. 1923; *Ladies' Home Jour.,* Aug., Oct., 1922; and *Outlook,* Jan. 23, 1924. Death record from Calif. Dept. of Health.]

PHILLIP R. SHRIVER

URSO, Camilla (June 13, 1842–Jan. 20, 1902), violinist, was born in Nantes, France, the first of five children and only daughter of Salvatore and Emelie (Girouard) Urso. Her father, a native of Palermo, Sicily, was flutist in the orchestra of the local opera house and organist of the Church of the Holy Cross; her mother, who had come to France as a child from her birthplace in Lisbon, Portugal, was a singer. Before her sixth birthday Camilla heard a violin solo in church and pleaded for instruction on the violin. Although her parents shared the general belief that this was a masculine instrument, they eventually consented, and she began lessons with Felix Simon, a violinist in the opera house orchestra. After a year of exacting study she made her first public appearance at a benefit concert in Nantes; her performance of Charles de Beriot's "Seventh Air Varié" was a great success and convinced her father that her talent required more professional instruction. Accordingly, the family moved to Paris, where after nine months of persistent application Camilla was accepted at the Conservatory of Music, despite her sex and age. Lambert Massart, with whom she began her studies, was so impressed with her talent that he offered her private lessons free of charge. Her work at the conservatory also included harmony and solfeggio. At the end of her first year her studies were interrupted by the need to replenish the family funds; granted a six months' leave from the conservatory, she toured the provincial cities of eastern France and the Rhine valley and earned enough from her concerts to carry the family through two more years in Paris. She took first place in her final examinations and, at the age of ten, was recognized in Paris as a rising young virtuoso.

Having accepted a contract for an American concert tour, Camilla Urso arrived in New York City in September 1852 accompanied by her father and aunt. When financial backing for the tour failed, the Ursos were rescued by the singer Marietta Alboni, who arranged for Camilla to appear in three concerts. These were followed by appearances in Boston, in a Philharmonic Society concert in Philadelphia, and in a series of concerts in New England cities given by the Germania Society. During these last she lived in Boston, taking private lessons in English and reading and preparing for her confirmation in the Roman Catholic Church. In the spring of 1853 she toured the Northern and Western states with the Germania Society; that fall she joined Mme. Henrietta Sontag's troupe for a series of eighteen concerts ending in New Orleans. She continued her public appearances, both on tour and in metropolitan New York, until late 1855, when she retired into private life in Nashville, Tenn. In 1862 she was married to Frédéric Luère in Paris, and returned to New York City.

Early in 1863 Camilla Urso resumed her public career, accepting an invitation from Carl Zerrahn to play before the Philharmonic Society in Boston; that season she also performed with the New York Philharmonic. During the following season (1863–64) she was engaged by Patrick S. Gilmore to play with his band at concerts in Boston and on his tour of New England. The next year she organized her own concert company, of which her husband was business manager, touring Canada until January 1865. That June she returned to Paris, where she reestablished her European reputation with her performance of Mendelssohn's Concerto in E at a Pasdeloup Concert.

Camilla Urso was now at the height of her career. The ensuing years were filled with concert appearances in the United States, France, and England, including a series of concerts in San Francisco (1869–70) and her debut at St. James's Hall in London (February 1872). She became a favorite of the Boston public and also performed frequently before New York audiences. Later tours took her farther afield, to Australia in 1879 and 1894 and to South Africa in 1895. An artist without affectation or trickery, she included in her repertoire the concerti of Beethoven, Bruch, Mendelssohn, and Rubinstein, as well as many of the currently popular bravura pieces such as the "Carnival of Venice" Variations and works by Paganini, Henri Vieuxtemps, Henri Wieniawski, and Jean Alard. Bach, Benjamin Godard, and Louis Gottschalk were also represented on her programs.

Camilla Urso had a calm dignity which she retained from childhood; of modest stature, she had dark, expressive eyes set in a round face which the critic George P. Upton remembered as "pale, serious, [and] inscrutable." Her playing, in the words of a tribute from Carl Zerrahn and the other members of the Harvard Musical Association orchestra, was characterized by "complete repose of manner; largeness of style; broad, full, and vigorous attacking of difficulties; utmost delicacy of sentiment and feeling; wonderful staccato; [and] . . . an intonation as nearly perfect as the human ear will allow," all combined with "a comprehensive mind" and "a warm musical soul vibrating to its work . . ." (quoted in Betts, p. 562). She used at various times in her career a Giuseppe Guarnerius violin (1737), an Amati, and a Miremont. Modest and retiring by nature, she mingled little in society.

In 1895 Miss Urso settled in New York City, where she gave private lessons and taught on the faculty of the National Conservatory, founded by JEANNETTE MEYERS THURBER. Her final years were spent in relative obscurity. She died in New York in 1902, at the age of fifty-nine, of appendicitis. Her funeral was held in the Church of St. Vincent de Paul in New York, and she was buried in Greenwood Cemetery, Brooklyn. She was not only the leading woman violinist of the latter half of the nineteenth century, but one of the outstanding violinists of her day of either sex.

[Charles Barnard, *Camilla: A Tale of a Violin* (1874), is the fullest source on her life to that date. See also: Mary A. Betts, "Camilla Urso," in *Eminent Women of the Age* (1869), pp. 551–65; George P. Upton, *Musical Memories* (1908); *Musical Courier*, Jan. 22, 29, 1902. For listings of some of her performances see Henry C. Lahee, *Annals of Music in America* (1922); George C. D. Odell, *Annals of the N.Y. Stage*, vols. VI–XV (1931–49); Henry E. Krehbiel, *The Philharmonic Soc. of N.Y.* (1892); Mark A. DeW. Howe, *The Boston Symphony Orchestra* (rev. ed., 1931), p. 260. Death record from N.Y. City Dept. of Health.]

ARLAN R. COOLIDGE

# V

VALENTINE, Lila Hardaway Meade (Feb. 4, 1865–July 14, 1921), Virginia educational reformer and suffragist, was born at Richmond, the second daughter and second of five children of Kate (Fontaine) and Richard Hardaway Meade. Both parents came of old Virginia families; her father was the founder of a wholesale drug firm. Though Lila Meade received the sort of education deemed necessary to train a lady for society—some tutoring at home and attendance at private schools in Richmond— this left her unsatisfied. Aware that neither convention nor finances would permit college, she undertook to educate herself, reading avidly in her father's library and developing a particular interest in the arts. But she was by no means bookish. Her letters reflect a style that is both literate and spontaneous. Tall, with dark chestnut hair and expressive brown eyes which even her pince-nez could not obscure, she combined a fine mind with wit and charm, and delighted in dancing and social functions. On Oct. 28, 1886, she was married to Benjamin Batchelder Valentine, an urbane gentleman and occasional poet of her own social class. A bank and insurance company director and vice-president of a family business firm, Valentine also had a deep sense of public responsibility.

In 1888 Mrs. Valentine had a stillborn child; she never fully recovered from subsequent surgery, suffering thereafter from periodic attacks of acute indigestion aggravated by migraine headaches. Her husband, hoping a change might help, took her along on a business trip to England in 1892. Influenced perhaps by the strong liberal currents of the Gladstone era, she returned to Virginia with an urge to awaken the social conscience of the South. Gradually she came to believe that universal education, regardless of race or sex, was the fundamental need. In April 1900, in the wake of the Richmond visit of a Boston kindergarten advocate, she joined with several other women, including MARY BRANCH MUNFORD, to found the Richmond Education Association, dedicated to the improvement of the public schools. Through this association, of which she was president until 1904, and its Richmond Training School for Kindergartners (founded in 1901), Mrs. Valentine was responsible for the introduction of kindergartens and vocational training into the city's schools and for obtaining a $600,000 municipal appropriation for a new high school. In 1902 she attended the annual conference of the Southern Education Board, a regional group with similar aims, and was instrumental in having it meet the next year in Richmond—one of the first racially integrated gatherings held in that city since the Civil War. These efforts resulted in her appointment to the executive committee of the Co-operative Educational Association of Virginia, a citizens' organization established in 1904 to raise the standards of public schools throughout the state.

In the course of her work with the schools Mrs. Valentine observed the poor health of many of the pupils and realized the need for public health facilities. Learning of a group of volunteer nurses who were teaching hygiene to indigent patients, she gathered a group of interested women to hear them explain their work. From this gathering, in 1902, sprang the Instructive Visiting Nurse Association of Richmond. As its president in 1904 she set up an Anti-Tuberculosis Auxiliary which led the first concentrated campaign against tuberculosis in Virginia. Among its achievements were the establishment of a dispensary, clinics, and Pine Camp, a tuberculosis hospital.

Lila Valentine worked at top capacity, never sparing herself. When her health broke in 1904, doctors insisted that she retire from public life for several years. On a second visit to England in 1905 she found woman suffrage a burning issue. Giving the subject serious consideration for perhaps the first time, she gradually came to believe that political questions which "nearly concern the home and the child . . . belong peculiarly to women," and that women should therefore have a voice in deciding them. When the Equal Suffrage League of Virginia was organized in 1909, Lila Valentine became president—chosen, so ELLEN GLASGOW, one of the founders, reports, because she was the "only woman who combined the requisite courage and intelligence" with "the inexhaustible patience of which victors and martyrs are made." As its president for eleven years, she worked vainly for a state suffrage amendment. In 1912 she addressed the Virginia House of Delegates; in one year alone (1913) she made over a hundred speeches throughout the state. Conservative opponents sought to discredit her because of her work for Negro education, her membership in such groups as the National Child Labor Committee and the American Association for Labor Legislation, and her willingness to address the Central Labor Council of Richmond. She was resourceful, however; on one occasion she made an unexpected appearance before the Virginia Road Builders' Association, assuring them the women of Virginia would surely vote for more and better roads if only they were granted

504

suffrage. She was also active in the National American Woman Suffrage Association, serving on its Congressional committee in 1916 and lecturing in other states, including West Virginia, Pennsylvania, New Jersey, and the Carolinas. Unlike some Southern "states' rights" suffragists, she supported the federal woman suffrage amendment and worked, again unsuccessfully, for its ratification in Virginia.

The death in June 1919 of her husband, always a firm supporter of her suffrage and other reform work, was a severe blow, and for some months Lila Meade Valentine lived in retirement with two sisters in Maine. The woman's cause continued to engage her, however, and, realizing that the suffrage amendment would soon be ratified, she turned her attention to what she thought was women's alarming ignorance of politics. At her request, the University of Virginia in April 1920 held a three-day conference on government; and, to reach a wider audience, she urged the addition of civics to the curriculum of the public schools. Her health had failed once more, however, and this time she did not recover. She died in 1921 at St. Luke's Hospital, Richmond, following an operation for an intestinal obstruction, at the age of fifty-six. An Episcopalian in religion, she was buried in Hollywood Cemetery at Richmond. A plaque in the state capitol commemorates her work.

[The largest collections of the letters of Lila Meade Valentine are in the Valentine Papers at the Valentine Museum, Richmond—founded by Mrs. Valentine's father-in-law—and the Woman Suffrage MSS. at the Va. State Library, Richmond. Richmond newspapers, 1900–21, are an important source, particularly the *Times-Dispatch, News-Leader,* and *Evening Jour.;* these carried detailed accounts of Mrs. Valentine's activities, and she wrote articles for them as well as many letters to their editors. See also Samuel Chiles Mitchell, *An Aftermath of Appomattox* (mimeographed, 1954); Ellen Glasgow, *The Woman Within* (1954), pp. 185–86; *Woman's Who's Who of America,* 1914–15; various references in Ida H. Harper, *The Hist. of Woman Suffrage,* vols. V and VI (1922); and Lloyd C. Taylor, Jr., "Lila Meade Valentine: The FFV as Reformer," *Va. Mag. of Hist. and Biog.,* Oct. 1962. Death record from Va. Dept. of Health.]

LLOYD C. TAYLOR, JR.

**VAN ALSTYNE, Frances Jane Crosby.** *See* CROSBY, Fanny.

**VAN BUREN, Hannah Hoes** (Mar. 8, 1783– Feb. 5, 1819), wife of Martin Van Buren, eighth president of the United States, was born in Kinderhook, N.Y., the daughter of Maria

(Quackenboss) and John Dircksen Hoes, both of Dutch descent. Her maiden name (pronounced "Hoose") was originally spelled "Goes" but was changed probably because of mispronunciation by English-speaking people. Documentary evidence of her life is extremely fragmentary, owing to her own propensity for anonymity, her early death, and the fact that her husband apparently erased her from the record to preserve the privacy of his family life. In the vast collection of manuscripts Van Buren arranged for safekeeping and which are now located in the Library of Congress there are no letters written to her or by her. Moreover, in his long, sprawling, and very valuable *Autobiography,* Van Buren does not refer to her or mention her name.

Hannah Hoes was reared in Kinderhook, where her family—one of the first patentees of the community—had lived for several generations. It was a typical Dutch farming region, located to the east of the Hudson River, just a few miles south of Albany. Like her husband, Hannah spoke both Dutch and English and worshiped at the Dutch Reformed church. She knew Van Buren from earliest childhood, and later her brother married one of his sisters. There was in fact considerable intermarriage between the Hoes, Van Buren, and Van Alen families in the Kinderhook community. Hannah and Martin themselves were first cousins once removed, she being the granddaughter of his mother's brother.

On Feb. 21, 1807, the young couple left Kinderhook, crossed the Hudson River to Catskill, and at the Haxtun House, owned by Hannah's brother-in-law, Judge Moses Cantine, were married by the Rev. Peter Labagh. Their first child, Abraham, was born in Kinderhook on Nov. 27, 1807, later graduated from West Point, and married Angelica Singleton of South Carolina, who served as White House hostess during Van Buren's administration (1837–41). The family moved in 1808 to Hudson, seat of Columbia County, when Van Buren was appointed its surrogate. There the second and third sons, John and Martin, Jr., were born in 1810 and 1812 respectively. John R. Irelan, an early biographer of Van Buren, states that another child was born in Hudson but died shortly after birth.

Hannah Van Buren has been described as a small, attractive woman, almost doll-like in appearance, amiable, her temper "uncommonly mild and sweet" and her manner altogether gentle and unassuming. She was also extremely shy. As her husband rose to prominence as a leader of the state Republican party, maneuvering himself from surrogate to attorney general and winning successive elections as state senator, Hannah drew further into the background. For many years she was chronically ill, probably with tuberculosis, and after the family moved to Albany her health rapidly declined. With the birth of her fourth son, Smith Thompson, in 1818, her condition grew critical. At length, informed by her physician that she had only a few days to live, she summoned her children to her bedside and with great composure bade them farewell. She died in Albany early in 1819 at the age of thirty-five. A member of the Second Presbyterian Church in Albany, she was buried at first in its cemetery, but in 1855 her body was moved by her husband to Kinderhook. From all indications her marriage was a happy one. Van Buren himself never remarried, though his gallantries provoked many rumors of marriage.

Hannah Van Buren's early death had political significance ten years later. Van Buren, then Secretary of State in President Andrew Jackson's administration, escaped the repercussions and embarrassment which the other cabinet officers suffered when their wives ostracized Mrs. MARGARET (Peggy) O'NEALE EATON, the wife of the Secretary of War. His gentlemanly behavior toward Mrs. Eaton during the unpleasantness earned him the gratitude of Jackson and helped clear his way to the presidency.

[There are several brief references to Hannah Van Buren in letters written between Benjamin F. Butler (Van Buren's law partner) and his wife in the Butler Papers, N.Y. State Library, Albany. The Albany *Argus*, Feb. 8, 1819, carries a brief obituary notice. Mary O. Whitton, *First First Ladies, 1789–1865* (1948), and Laura C. Holloway, *The Ladies of the White House* (1880), summarize most of what is generally known about Hannah Van Buren. George E. McCracken, "The Ancestry of President Martin Van Buren," *Am. Genealogist*, Apr. 1959, and Frank J. Conkling, "Martin Van Buren, with a Sketch of the Van Buren Family in America," *N.Y. Genealogical and Biog. Record*, July 1897, provide vital statistics. Also useful are John R. Irelan, *Hist. of the Life, Administration, and Times of Martin Van Buren* (1887–vol. VIII of his *The Republic*); *The Autobiog. of Martin Van Buren* (John C. Fitzpatrick, ed., 1920); Edward M. Shepard, *Martin Van Buren* (1888); Holmes Alexander, *The Am. Talleyrand* (1935); and Denis T. Lynch, *An Epoch and a Man: Martin Van Buren and His Times* (1929).]

ROBERT V. REMINI

VANCE, Clara. *See* DENISON, Mary Ann Andrews.

VAN COTT, Margaret Ann Newton (Mar. 25, 1830–Aug. 29, 1914), Methodist evangelist, better known as Maggie Van Cott, was born in New York City. Her father, William K. Newton, a well-to-do real estate broker of English ancestry, at one time managed the estates of Peter Lorillard and John Jacob Astor. Her mother, Rachel A. (Primrose) Newton, was of Scottish ancestry. Maggie, the eldest of four children, was confirmed in the Episcopal faith of her family in 1841. After completing a high school education, she was married to Peter P. Van Cott of Williamsburgh, Long Island, on Jan. 23, 1848. He owned a dry goods store in New York City and later entered the wholesale drug business. They had two children, Rachel, who died in infancy, and Sarah Ellen Conselyea. Peter Van Cott became chronically ill after 1850, and for the remainder of his life his wife managed his business affairs with considerable efficiency and skill.

Always active in church affairs, Mrs. Van Cott had a conversion experience in 1857 or 1858 which deepened her religious convictions and led her to attend prayer meetings at the Duane Street Methodist Episcopal Church in New York. Here she found a pietistic fervor more compatible with her temperament, and shortly after her husband's death in 1866 she joined the Methodist Episcopal Church. That same year she began to lead prayer meetings and Bible study groups at the interdenominational mission founded by Mrs. PHOEBE PALMER at Five Points in the city's slum district. Her successful soul winning at this mission brought an invitation from a Methodist pastor of her acquaintance in Durham, N.Y., to conduct a series of revival meetings for his church in February 1868. Similar invitations followed from other pastors. Her initial reluctance to preach was overcome by the numerous conversions at "the anxious bench" which from the beginning attended her sermons. In September 1868 she received an "Exhorter's License" and on Mar. 6, 1869, the quarterly conference of Stone Ridge, Ellenville, N.Y., granted her a "Local Preacher's License" after due examination. She thus became the first woman licensed to preach in the Methodist Episcopal Church in the United States.

Although many Methodists, lay and clerical, disapproved of a "lady preacher," Maggie Van Cott's popular success as an evangelist overcame all opposition, and for the remainder of her life she continued to conduct revival meetings in Methodist churches throughout the United States. In many cities she obtained the cooperation of other denominations as well. To attract crowds, she advertised special meetings for mothers, for "old veterans," and for children. She also specialized in "Praise Meetings," "Silent Meetings," and "Love Feasts." At the conclusion of each revival she organized prayer bands of converts and church members to keep up the revival spirit. Mrs. Van Cott traveled from three thousand to seven thousand miles annually for over thirty years, leading an average of two thousand "seekers" to the altar each year. In 1872 Bishop Gilbert Haven, the editor of *Zion's Herald*, stated: "She is without doubt today the most popular, most laborious, and most successful preacher in the Methodist Episcopal Church." At the time of her retirement in 1902 she had reputedly converted seventy-five thousand persons, about half of whom, according to her estimate, joined the Methodist Church. She never remarried and for a time eked out the small income received from the free-will offerings taken at her meetings by lecturing on the Redpath lyceum circuit. In 1901 the presiding elders of the New York Conference raised $5,000 by public subscription to assist her in her old age.

Mrs. Van Cott was described as "a stout lady with a rosy, pleasant face which looks out with exceedingly good nature from beneath two matronly rows of black, glossy curls." She had a reputation for sartorial elegance and for "the dramatic fire of the true and natural actress." Lacking theological training, she preached exhortatory rather than doctrinal sermons. Some Methodists welcomed a handsome woman revivalist as a means of offsetting the lure of actresses and the heretical female lecturers of the era, but her career was not the result of any specific policy along these lines by the Methodist Episcopal Church, and few women have been licensed since her day. She died of cancer at her home in Catskill, N.Y., at the age of eighty-four and was buried in nearby Cairo.

[Apparently Mrs. Van Cott published nothing of her own. However, she collaborated closely with the Rev. John Onesimus Foster in *The Life and Labours of Mrs. Maggie Newton Van Cott* (1872); this was republished in 1883, slightly revised and enlarged, as *The Harvest and the Reaper: Reminiscences of Revival Work of Mrs. Maggie N. Van Cott*, with Foster's name omitted from the title page. Though eulogistic and lacking in dates, the book provides a good account of her early life. Brief mention of her career is made in William F. P. Noble, *1776–1876: A Century of Gospel Work* (1876), and Phineas C. Headley, *Evangelists in the Church* (1875). There is no adequate account of her work after 1883, but occasional mention of her revivals can be found in the Methodist *Christian Advocate* of N.Y. (e.g., Jan.

24, 1901, p. 145; Apr. 11, 1901, p. 583; Aug. 14, 1902, p. 1315) and in local newspapers of the places where she conducted meetings. Obituary notices: *N.Y. Tribune*, Sept. 1, 1914; *Boston Transcript*, Aug. 31, 1914; *Christian Advocate* (N.Y.), Sept. 3, 1914, pp. 26–27. Death record from N.Y. State Dept. of Health. See also William G. McLoughlin, *Modern Revivalism* (1959).]

WILLIAM G. MC LOUGHLIN

VAN DEMAN, Esther Boise (Oct. 1, 1862–May 3, 1937), Roman archaeologist, was born in South Salem, Ohio, the second daughter of Joseph and Martha (Millspaugh) Van Deman. She was the youngest of her father's six children, including two sons by an earlier marriage. Joseph Van Deman farmed the land which his father, born in Virginia of German origin, had received for his services in the Revolutionary War. Esther's mother, of Dutch and Scottish ancestry, trained her children in her Presbyterian faith. Both parents believed in the value of education, and they also encouraged Esther's interest in music, for which she showed considerable talent as a child. She attended the South Salem Academy, where she was an excellent student, and considered music as a possible career. In the 1870's the family moved to live with her married sister in Sterling, Kans. Esther, a vivacious young woman with light hair, blue eyes, a fair complexion, and an independent spirit, had throughout her life a strong affection for all her family, but although she was engaged three times she could never bring herself to sacrifice her personal independence sufficiently to marry.

Her interest in the classics developed when, at twenty-four, she went to college. In the fall of 1887 she entered the University of Michigan, and although she left after her first year and did not return until the spring of 1889, she received her A.B. degree in 1891 and an A.M. in 1892. From 1892 to 1906 she alternated study with college teaching. She was a stimulating teacher and took pleasure in classroom work, but she found research more sympathetic and rewarding. Administrative rules and restrictions seemed to her irksome and intolerable, and her outspokenness usually caused her to fall afoul of college administrations. After graduate work at Bryn Mawr College (1892–93), she taught Latin at Wellesley College (1893–95) and the Bryn Mawr School in Baltimore (1895–96) and then began graduate study at the University of Chicago which led to a Ph.D. in 1898. Three years of teaching Latin at Mount Holyoke College followed. Her work abroad began in 1901 when she won a fellowship to the American School of Classical Studies in Rome; she returned to the United

States as associate professor of Latin and archaeology at Goucher College in 1903. In 1906 she went back to Rome as a fellow of the Carnegie Institution of Washington. Appointed to the Institution's staff (1910–30), she continued to live and work in Rome until her death, with only brief interruptions. She returned to America during the early part of the First World War and again in 1917 when a severe nervous collapse sent her to a sanatorium; in 1924–25, when she held the Charles Eliot Norton lectureship of the Archaeological Institute of America; from 1925 to 1930, when she was Carnegie Research Professor of Roman Archaeology at the University of Michigan; and, finally, in 1936 to receive an honorary degree from Michigan.

During her thirty years in Rome, Miss Van Deman became the authority on ancient Roman building construction and established criteria for its dating which, with minor changes, remain standard. Not only was she the first woman Roman field archaeologist, but in her investigation of the fundamental problems of the chronology of building materials and methods of construction she laid the foundations for serious study of Roman architecture. Her interest in this subject began in 1907. While listening to a lecture in the Atrium Vestae in Rome, she noticed a difference between the bricks blocking up a doorway and those of the wall and became convinced that the composition and size of bricks and mortar would provide evidence for dating. When literary sources confirmed her observations at the Atrium Vestae, she determined to apply her method of identification to other buildings and constructions and published the results in several articles. She then returned to a study of Roman aqueducts, which had never received detailed attention. Her resulting monograph is a model of investigation, record, and interpretation, but it consumed so much time that only two years remained for what she considered her lifework, the perfection of methods of dating brick and concrete construction. Realizing that she would be unable to complete this study, she concentrated on arranging her notes for her colleague Marion E. Blake, whom she had selected to carry it on. Illness beset her late in 1936, and the following May, at seventy-four, she died in Rome of cancer. She was buried in the Protestant Cemetery in Rome, where her grave is fittingly marked by a pile of brick and concrete.

Miss Van Deman's outstanding qualities were loyalty to her family, particularly to a blind brother and his two blind daughters, whom she supported at the cost of her personal pleasures, and to her friends, whom she believed in to the point of finding excuses for any faults. She was also known for her generosity and kindness, particularly to promising young students. If she felt herself wronged, however, she could be a vociferous enemy. In the long years of association with the American Academy in Rome she freely shared her encyclopedic knowledge and her own discoveries with others genuinely concerned with the work she loved so ardently. Her research, as much through her students as through her own publications, forms the cornerstone of our understanding of Roman building.

[Miss Van Deman's most important published works are: *The Atrium Vestae* (1909); "Methods of Determining the Date of Roman Concrete Monuments," *Am. Jour. of Archaeology,* Apr.–June 1912; and *The Building of the Roman Aqueducts* (1934). Biographical information from *Am. Jour. of Archaeology,* Apr.–June 1937 (which includes a bibliography of her writings), from many conversations with her colleague Marion E. Blake, and from personal acquaintance in her last year. Information about her enrollment at the Univ. of Mich. was supplied by Mrs. Alison T. Myers, Alumnae Secretary.]

LUCY SHOE MERITT

**VANDERBILT, Alva Erskine Smith.** *See* BELMONT, Alva Erskine Smith Vanderbilt.

**VAN LEW, Elizabeth L.** (Oct. 17, 1818–Sept. 25, 1900), Virginia Unionist and Federal agent during the Civil War, was born in Richmond to John and Elizabeth (Baker) Van Lew. There are said to have been three children in the family, but apparently only Elizabeth and a younger brother survived. Their father, of colonial Dutch descent, was a native of Jamaica, Long Island, N.Y., who had moved as a young man to Richmond and had become a wealthy hardware merchant. The mother was a daughter of Hilary Baker, at one time mayor of Philadelphia. Elizabeth was educated in Philadelphia, but much of her intellectual stimulation came from her home. John Van Lew, a prominent Whig, freely entertained the leaders of Virginia society and distinguished visitors in his mansion on Church Hill. After his death in 1843 his son carried on the family business, and the Van Lews, members of historic St. John's Church (Episcopal), enjoyed all the advantages of wealth and social position.

Long before the Civil War it was public knowledge that Elizabeth Van Lew held strong antislavery views. Her fellow townsmen assumed she had picked them up while at school in Philadelphia, but they seem to have been shared by her quiet mother, to whom Elizabeth was always very close. The Swedish traveler Fredrika Bremer, visiting Richmond in 1851, was immediately drawn to the two ladies; "intellect, kindness, and refinement of feeling," she wrote, "were evident in their gentle countenances." Elizabeth, "a pleasing, pale blonde," showed her a tobacco factory where, observing the hard lot and sad faces of the slave workers, "Good Miss Van L. could not refrain from weeping." As the 1850's passed, the Van Lews freed their house servants; one, Mary Elizabeth Bowser, was sent north for an education. Reportedly they also purchased and then freed members of their servants' families in other households.

When the war came, Elizabeth Van Lew remained openly loyal to the Union. Securing admission to Libby Prison, where captured Federal officers were quartered during most of the war, she and her mother carried in food, books, and clothing. She is said to have helped prisoners escape, apparently hiding them in a secret chamber in her house, and to have obtained at Libby military information which she transmitted to the Union forces. Because of her social standing she was able to operate without much interference. It is known that her contacts extended into the Southern government—even into the White House of the Confederacy, where she had placed Mary Elizabeth Bowser as a domestic.

Elizabeth Van Lew's most daring exploit involved the secret removal of the body of Col. Ulric Dahlgren, killed during Kilpatrick's raid on Richmond at the end of February 1864. According to report, Federal authorities, largely because of intelligence furnished by her, had become aware of Confederate intentions to move large numbers of prisoners to the far South; to liberate these men, a raid on Richmond was planned under Gen. Judson Kilpatrick and Colonel Dahlgren. The Colonel ran into an ambush and was killed; the Confederates then charged that they had found on his body papers proving that he intended to set fire to Richmond and assassinate members of the government, including President Davis. Dahlgren's body was publicly insulted, wrapped in a coarse garment, and given a secret, degrading burial. Convinced that the papers were forgeries, Elizabeth Van Lew decided to spirit away the Colonel's remains for eventual delivery to Adm. John A. Dahlgren, his father. After her agents had discovered the grave, the body was removed, hidden in a wagon under a bed of young peach trees, and secretly taken to a farm in the country,

where it was decently reburied. In view of the public indignation against the raider, discovery would have entailed the most serious consequences.

When the Union Army approached Richmond later in 1864, Elizabeth Van Lew's intelligence work reached its peak. Disarming suspicion by deliberately affecting such peculiarities of dress and behavior that she came to be known as "Crazy Bet," she maintained five relay stations between the city and Federal headquarters downriver. Her servants carried messages hidden in the soles of their work shoes, and so excellent was her system of communication that Federal commanders, it is said, received fresh flowers from her garden on the day after she had cut them. By means of a secret code which she carried in her watch, she delivered information of great value to the Union Army. "For a long time she represented all that was left of the U.S. Government in the city of Richmond," wrote the head of the secret service of the Army of the Potomac. As soon as the Confederates had evacuated the city on Apr. 2, 1865, Miss Van Lew raised a huge American flag over her house—the first Stars and Stripes seen in Richmond since 1861. Then she hurried to the deserted government offices to collect documents for the Federal authorities. General Grant, who had provided her with a special guard to shield her from her fellow townsmen, visited her upon his arrival and personally expressed his gratitude.

Shortly after Grant was inaugurated as president, he appointed Miss Van Lew postmistress of Richmond, an office which she capably discharged despite community hostility. Deprived of her position in 1877 after President Hayes' election, she secured a clerical appointment in the Post Office Department at Washington, but resigned when she was reassigned during Cleveland's administration.

In her late sixties Miss Van Lew returned to Richmond. Impoverished by her expenditures during the war, shunned by her neighbors, and traduced by Richmond society, she was a virtual outcast. Her mother had died in 1875. In the old mansion she led a lonely life with a faithful niece and forty cats. Only after the family of Col. Paul Revere of Boston, whom she had aided in Libby Prison, raised a purse for her was she relieved of the most pressing financial worries. She spent the last years of her life fighting for woman's rights by consistently protesting against her tax assessments on the classic grounds of no taxation without representation. Alone after her niece's death in 1889, she died in her home at eighty-two and was buried in Shockhoe Hill Cemetery in Richmond. Massachusetts sympathizers erected a monument over her grave.

[The Van Lew Papers in the N.Y. Public Library constitute the most complete collection of documents. Published accounts include: James H. Bailey, "Crazy Bet, Union Spy," *Va. Cavalcade,* Spring 1952; Richard P. Weinert, "Federal Spies in Richmond," *Civil War Times Illustrated,* Feb. 1965; and sketches in William G. Beymer, *On Hazardous Service* (1912), James D. Horan, *Desperate Women* (1952), and Harnett T. Kane, *Spies for the Blue and Gray* (1954). See also Fredrika Bremer, *The Homes of the New World* (1853), II, 509–10; Mary W. Scott, *Houses of Old Richmond* (1941); and Clifford L. Dowdey, *Experiment in Rebellion* (1946).]

H. L. TREFOUSSE

VAN RENSSELAER, Maria Van Cortlandt (July 20, 1645–Jan. 24, 1688/89), administrator of the Dutch patroonship of Rensselaerswyck, was born in New Amsterdam (later New York City), the third of seven children of Oloffe Stevense Van Cortlandt and his wife, Anna (Annetje, Anneken) Loockermans. Her father, founder of the Van Cortlandt clan in America, was a merchant and city official under both the Dutch and the English regimes; he was listed in 1674 as the city's fourth wealthiest man. Her mother was a sister of another wealthy merchant of the city, Govert Loockermans. On July 12, 1662, Maria married Jeremias, third son of Kiliaen Van Rensselaer, first patroon, or proprietor, of Rensselaerswyck, the family's landed estate near Albany. Jeremias had come to New Netherland as director of the patroonship. He died on Oct. 12, 1674, leaving four sons and two daughters. Since his children were minors and no other Van Rensselaer was in the colony, the burden of administering the vast Rensselaerswyck property—approximately twenty-four miles square—fell to his widow, Maria; she was assisted by her brother Stephanus Van Cortlandt, later a prominent colonial official and landowner.

Maria Van Rensselaer faced many problems in handling this property, but as was typical of the Dutch *huisvrouw,* she was a capable businesswoman. A visiting Labadist missionary, Jasper Danckaerts, reported finding her, in 1680, "polite, quite well-informed, and of good life and disposition. . . . We went to look at several of her mills at work, which she had there on an ever-running stream, gristmills, sawmills, and others." One of the most important tasks to which Maria fell heir was that of gaining a clear title to the property after the English conquest of the colony in 1664, the Dutch reconquest in 1673, and the final English reconquest in 1674. The Van Rensselaers constantly sought a reaffirmation of their title and finally achieved it in November 1685. "You well know yourself," Maria complained to her brother-in-law in the Netherlands in 1680, "how it went, first upon the arrival of the English, then upon the arrival of the Dutch, and then again upon the arrival of the English, and how, whenever any one of importance came from New York, he had to be entertained to keep up the dignity of the colony." Maria's control of the property was interrupted briefly by the arrival from the Netherlands of Jeremias' younger brother, the Rev. Nicholas Van Rensselaer, in 1675. He immediately petitioned for the directorship, but was opposed by Maria and her brother for fear that her children's interests would suffer. A compromise was reached, however, when Nicholas became director, Maria treasurer, and Stephanus Van Cortlandt bookkeeper.

Nicholas' death in November 1678 once again placed the full burden of management on Maria's shoulders. Her brother Stephanus was named director, but his residence in New York City precluded any active role for him. Her health was now failing—lame after her last childbirth, she used crutches for the rest of her life—and she was plagued by mounting debts. But as manager she negotiated with tenants and prospective purchasers of farms, appeased the demands of the Dutch members of the family for cash remittances from the estate, and fought the efforts of Robert Livingston, who had married the widow of Nicholas, to press his claim for Nicholas' share of the estate by forcing a partition of the property among the numerous heirs. Livingston, an official at Albany and founder of a family influential in New York history, continued to harass Maria and the Dutch Van Rensselaers until 1685, when a settlement was finally agreed upon.

Because Jeremias had made no provision before his death for his children, this also became Maria's responsibility. She sent her eldest son, Kiliaen, as an apprentice to a New York City silversmith; he became so adept at this trade that his uncles subsidized his study in Boston under Jeremiah Dummer. The next two children, Anna and Hendrick, were sent to live with Maria's parents in New York City, while the three youngest—Maria, Johannes, and Jeremias—remained with her. Before her death, Maria Van Rensselaer twice achieved her major ambition: securing control of Rensselaerswyck to her children. The first time occurred when her daughter Anna married the Dutch heir to the patroonship, Kiliaen, son of Johannes Van

Rensselaer. When he died in 1687 without leaving any heirs, Maria's eldest son, Kiliaen, succeeded to the patroonship. Moreover, all of her children married well. Kiliaen married his cousin Maria Van Cortlandt; Hendrick married Catherine Van Brugh. Anna's second husband was William Nicoll, a leading lawyer and politician, and Maria married Peter Schuyler, mayor of Albany and later president of the governor's council.

Maria Van Cortlandt Van Rensselaer died at the age of forty-three apparently at Albany. She had gained for her children the richest land patent in the colony and alliances with many powerful clans, thereby firmly establishing one of the most important families of early New York.

[Arnold J. F. Van Laer, ed., *Correspondence of Maria Van Rensselaer, 1669–1689* (1935), contains all of her known writings. There are references to her in the same editor's *Minutes of the Court of Albany, Rensselaerswyck and Schenectady*, vols. II and III (1928–32). Her activities figure largely in Samuel G. Nissenson's *The Patroon's Domain* (1937), a thorough scholarly study of Rensselaerswyck through the settlement of the patroonship on Maria's eldest son. Chap. ii of Lawrence H. Leder's *Robert Livingston, 1654–1728, and the Politics of Colonial N.Y.* (1961) is devoted largely to the struggle between Maria and Livingston for control of the estate. See also Bartlett B. James and J. Franklin Jameson, eds., *Jour. of Jasper Danckaerts, 1679–1680* (1913).]

LAWRENCE H. LEDER

**VAN RENSSELAER, Mariana Alley Griswold** (Feb. 21, 1851–Jan. 20, 1934), writer, art critic, and historian, better known as Mrs. Schuyler Van Rensselaer, was born in New York City, the first daughter and second of seven children of George and Lydia (Alley) Griswold. Her paternal grandfather, George Griswold, had arrived in New York in 1794 from Old Lyme, Conn., which had been settled by a Griswold forebear in 1664. With his brother he founded the great shipping firm of N. L. & G. Griswold and engaged in the Canton tea trade. Later his interests spread to real estate and finance; for many years he was a leader of the business community in political affairs. Both sets of Mariana's grandparents lived in Washington Square, and her father, George Griswold, Jr., who succeeded to business and civic leadership, built a new house for his bride on lower Fifth Avenue.

Mariana Griswold was educated privately by tutors and in Europe, where the family spent several years in Dresden. There, on Apr. 14, 1873, she was married to Schuyler Van Rensselaer of New York, a descendant of the patroons of Rensselaerswyck, who after graduating from Harvard and the School of Mines at Freiburg, Saxony, had become a mining and metallurgical engineer. For the next eleven years they made their home in New Brunswick, N.J., visiting Europe twice and traveling frequently in the United States. In 1875 a son, George Griswold, was born, and in the following year Mrs. Van Rensselaer published a poem in *Harper's Magazine* and the first of many articles on art in the *American Architect and Building News;* her *Book of American Figure Painters* was published in 1886. The reviews of art exhibitions in New York and other cities which she wrote between 1878 and 1887 reveal a taste educated particularly by the works of Corot and the Barbizon school of landscape painters. Her concern for pictorial idealism led her to consider the early work of Winslow Homer crude, but she was a remarkably good judge of her major American contemporaries, Inness, Eakins, Ryder, Whistler, and Sargent. She could recommend even works of Manet and Degas "for those who can consent to see with the eyes of a peculiarly endowed painter instead of with their own."

After her husband's early death in 1884, Mrs. Van Rensselaer moved to New York City, settling with her mother in the trim old house at 9 West 10th Street which she was to occupy for the remainder of her life. In the same year she began her first important work of architectural criticism, "Recent American Architecture," which appeared in nine installments in the *Century Magazine*, the principal outlet for her writing in the 1880's and '90's. Late in 1884 she left for Europe, where, with Joseph Pennell, the graphic artist, she visited twelve English cathedrals and prepared a series of articles which appeared in the *Century* between 1887 and 1892; these formed the core of her most popular book, *English Cathedrals* (1892). Her *Henry Hobson Richardson and His Works* (1888) was an admirable study of an important contemporary architect and for many years the standard work. In 1889 she began in *Garden and Forest* an extended study, "The Art of Gardening: A Historical Sketch," which ranged from earliest times to the Middle Ages, and published *Six Portraits*, revised versions of essays on Renaissance and modern artists which had been written for magazines. That summer she spent five weeks in Paris, primarily studying contemporary painting at the International Exposition. Under Richardson's inspiration, she explored Romanesque churches in the South and West of France which she later described in the *Century*. She admired immensely the buildings and grounds of the World's Fair of 1893 in Chicago. From the first her sympathies were with those who wished to adapt Renaissance architectural forms to modern needs. *Art Out of Doors* (1893), a widely read introduction to landscape gardening, is her last important work on the visual arts.

Her son, George, a Harvard student, died suddenly in the spring of 1894. From about this time, partly influenced by her friend Richard Watson Gilder, editor of the *Century,* Mrs. Van Rensselaer became increasingly interested in the social problems of New York City. Between 1894 and 1898 she taught a class in literature at the University Settlement, and she was president of its women's auxiliary, 1896–98. She served on a committee which provided reproductions of works of art for the schools and for two years was a school inspector. From 1899 until 1906 she was president of the Public Education Association of New York City, organized to work for progressive reform in the city schools. During this period she wrote a group of stories dealing in considerable part with immigrants and New York slums that was collected in her *One Man Who Was Content* (1897). Her pamphlet, *Shall We Ask for the Suffrage?* (1894), argued against women voting because she believed that they should concentrate upon their families and on educational and intellectual matters, leaving business and public affairs to men; she also feared that uneducated lower-class women would be exploited by politicians.

Moved by the reviving interest in America's colonial past, Mrs. Van Rensselaer published in 1909 a two-volume *History of the City of New York in the Seventeenth Century* which presented in graceful prose the results of a careful study of the available documents and showed a broad knowledge of colonial history. The work was well received, but although she had planned to carry it on from 1689 to 1789, there is no evidence that she continued her historical studies. In her middle fifties she began to write poetry for the first time in many years; the conventionally romantic *Poems* (1910), however, is the least interesting of her works. During World War I she was president of the American Fund for the French Wounded, and between 1916 and 1923 she wrote a number of popular essays on art. At seventy she published a charming volume of poems for youngsters, *Many Children* (1921), patterned on the works of Robert Louis Stevenson, whom she admired extravagantly. Columbia University made her an honorary Doctor of Literature in 1910, and the American Academy of Arts and Letters awarded her a

gold medal "for distinction in literature" in 1923. She was an honorary member of the American Institute of Architects (1890) and the Society of Landscape Architects. A woman of impressive bearing and wide sympathies, Mrs. Van Rensselaer entertained at tea for many years, engaging in animated discussions of books and pictures and other matters of general human concern. She died at her New York home at the age of eighty-two of arteriosclerosis; burial was at Greenwood Cemetery, Brooklyn.

Few contemporary American women had the breadth of culture of Mrs. Van Rensselaer. Few had her educational advantages and few were able to use their leisure so productively. Her interests extended beyond literature and art; she could write perceptively about the acting of Sarah Bernhardt and knowingly of *Parsifal* at Bayreuth. As a woman and an amateur she was sometimes diffident in expressing her own judgments, yet she had enough confidence in herself to reject the moralistic critical principles of Ruskin and Charles Eastlake, then dominant in the English-speaking world, and to argue, as against their structural puritanism, that architecture required only "that structure be indicated sufficiently to *satisfy the eye.*" Mrs. Van Rensselaer took pride in her concise, smoothly moving expository prose. She once delighted Stevenson by telling of making twenty revisions in order to be sure that her writing was as good as she could make it. She always wrote for a general audience, and many of her books and articles depend heavily upon the scholarship of others. But all her writings are shaped by her personal style and by her taste and intelligence. Her study of Richardson and her history of New York remain impressive and important works.

[Glenn E. Griswold, *The Griswold Family: England-America* (1943), and Florence Van Rensselaer, *The Van Rensselaers in Holland and in America* (1956); *Who Was Who in America,* vol. I (1942); obituaries in *N.Y. Herald Tribune* and *N.Y. Times,* Jan. 21, 1934; letters about her in the *Times* of Jan. 26 (by Joseph B. Gilder) and Feb. 8, 1934; death record from N.Y. City Dept. of Health (the source for her birth date). On her father and grandfather see Joseph A. Scoville, *The Old Merchants of N.Y. City,* Second Series (1865); and Robert G. Albion, *The Rise of N.Y. Port* (1939). Her husband's career is covered in the published *Reports* of the Harvard Class of 1867. Both the Griswold and Van Rensselaer genealogies and Mrs. Van Rensselaer's death record give her first name as "Marianna"; she herself evidently preferred a single *n.* A relief portrait by the sculptor Augustus Saint-Gaudens is in the Fogg Museum at Harvard Univ.; it is reproduced in the *Harvard Library Bull.*, Oct. 1970.]

JAMES EARLY

**VAN RENSSELAER, Martha** (June 21, 1864–May 26, 1932), home economist, was born in Randolph, Cattaraugus County, N.Y., of Dutch and Welsh extraction. One of five children, she was the second daughter of Henry Killian Van Rensselaer and his second wife, Arvilla A. Owen. Martha's father was a storekeeper and later an insurance agent. A strict Methodist and an active Republican, he held various local political posts and was for some years a trustee of Randolph's coeducational Chamberlain Institute, a Methodist-controlled school. Her mother, a former schoolteacher who ran a boardinghouse and was active in church, temperance, and suffrage affairs, deeply influenced the young girl's outlook. Through her, Martha realized both woman's "tremendous power" in the home and the community and her need for "stimulation and assistance of an educational nature" (typescript autobiographical sketch, c. 1924). Though of modest circumstances, the Van Rensselaers were conscious of their family heritage, and Martha later recalled her home as a center of "refinement and culture" in the depressed farming region in which Randolph was situated. An industrious student despite a tomboy disposition, she graduated from Chamberlain Institute in 1884.

For the next ten years, while teaching at Chamberlain and at other public and private schools in the area, Martha Van Rensselaer participated in woman's club activities, lectured at teachers' institutes, and faithfully attended the Chautauqua Summer School, where from 1894 to 1903 she worked as secretary and instructor for the New York State Department of Public Instruction. Sometime before 1892 she rejected a long-time suitor, a struggling and consumptive medical student who intended to settle in the West. Preferring administration to teaching, in 1893 she won election as one of the two school commissioners of Cattaraugus County, having been nominated by a convention of the Woman's Christian Temperance Union. She won again in 1896 with bipartisan support, but failed to gain a third term in 1899.

As school commissioner she had encouraged the agricultural extension program of Cornell University, including ANNA BOTSFORD COMSTOCK's efforts to stimulate interest in farming through nature study, but in her visits to rural homes she had realized that little of this activity was reaching the farm wife. In 1900, therefore, she readily accepted an invitation from Liberty Hyde Bailey, professor of horticulture at Cornell, to organize an extension program for farmers' wives to complement one he had recently initiated for farmers. Bailey, who was ambitious to establish a college of agriculture at Cornell, doubtless recognized a valuable ally in Miss Van Rensselaer, who already had a rural following in western New York as well as valuable contacts in the legislature. Thus began the work which occupied the remaining thirty-two years of her life and which grew into the New York State College of Home Economics at Cornell University.

In January 1901 the first bulletin of the "Farmers' Wives' Reading Course," entitled *Saving Steps,* was distributed to some 5,000 women who had signed up for the course. Within a few years enrollment had grown to over 20,000, and a number of local study clubs had been organized. The bulletins, issued about five times a year, covered such wide-ranging subjects as sanitation, interior decorating, nutrition, reading programs, dressmaking, and child care, and were widely popular. Though fully immersed in this work, "Miss Van," with her usual zest and no false pride, also ran an Ithaca boardinghouse for students and instructors to eke out a beginning annual salary of $350.

Home economics instruction on a resident and accredited basis began at Cornell in 1903, the year Liberty Hyde Bailey became dean of the College of Agriculture. Miss Van Rensselaer at his suggestion offered a course in homemaking that year, and early in 1906 she conducted a more ambitious winter course for which visiting experts and Cornell faculty members served as lecturers. In 1907 a department of home economics was formed within the College of Agriculture, with Miss Van Rensselaer and Flora Rose, a graduate of Kansas State Agricultural College and a lecturer in the winter course, as co-chairmen. The first regular course offerings were in the 1908–09 academic year. In 1909, after several years of part-time study, Miss Van Rensselaer received her A.B. degree from Cornell, and in October 1911, by faculty vote, she and Miss Rose were promoted to professorial rank. Working together in an association "rare in its charm and devotion" (Albert R. Mann in *Journal of Home Economics,* September 1932), the two women shared administrative responsibility, Miss Rose concentrating on resident teaching and research, Miss Van Rensselaer on administration and extension work. An "aggressive and power-conscious administrator," in the judgment of a later historian of the college (Colman, p. 188), Miss Van Rensselaer effectively used the support of Bailey and his successor, Albert R. Mann, together with her own practical sense, political acumen, humor, and magnetic personality, to advance the interests of her fledgling department. By 1917 its program included not only a four-year home economics course leading to a degree, but also monthly bulletins, some two hundred Cornell Study Clubs, extension courses, junior work in the public schools, and assistance in organizing Cornell's annual Farm and Home Week. In 1919 the Cornell trustees changed its rank within the College of Agriculture from a department to a school, and on Feb. 24, 1925, after a five-year struggle by Miss Van Rensselaer, Gov. Alfred E. Smith signed a bill creating the New York State College of Home Economics, with Miss Rose and Miss Van Rensselaer as co-directors. In 1929–30, with the backing of Gov. Franklin D. Roosevelt and his wife, nearly one million dollars in state funds were allocated for a new home economics building at Cornell, appropriately named Martha Van Rensselaer Hall.

In related pursuits, Martha Van Rensselaer directed the Home Conservation Division of the United States Food Administration during the First World War and in 1923 served in Belgium with the American Relief Commission, for which she was made a chevalier of the Order of the Crown. She was also president of the American Home Economics Association (1914–16), homemaking editor of *Delineator* magazine for six years beginning in 1920, chairman of the home economics section of the Association of Land-Grant Colleges and Universities (1928–29), and assistant director of the White House Conference on Child Health and Protection which met in 1930. Active to the end, she died of cancer in St. Luke's Hospital in New York City in 1932, in her sixty-eighth year. After services in Ithaca, she was buried in the Randolph (N.Y.) Cemetery.

[Flora Rose, "A Page of Modern Education, Forty Years of Home Economics at Cornell Univ.," N.Y. State College of Home Economics, *Fifteenth Annual Report,* 1940, pp. 63–145; Caroline M. Percival, *Martha Van Rensselaer* (Ithaca, 1957), a 26-page biographical sketch with anecdotes and reminiscences; memorial articles by Katherine Glover, Liberty Hyde Bailey, Albert Russell Mann, and others in *Jour. of Home Economics,* Sept. 1932; annual registers and reports of Cornell Univ.; bulletins of the "Farmers' Wives' Reading Course." Local newspapers, including the *Cattaraugus Union* and the *Randolph Register & Weekly Courant,* are valuable for the pre-1900 period, and the *Ithaca Jour. News* contains frequent references to Miss Van Rensselaer's activities after 1900. Rele-

vant MS. sources at Cornell for the period 1907–32 include the records of the Board of Trustees and the papers of Flora Rose, Liberty Hyde Bailey, Beverly T. Galloway, Albert R. Mann, John W. Spencer, Jacob G. Schurman, Livingston Farrand, and of Miss Van Rensselaer herself. The last include family letters, 1888–1900; her 1903 letter book; and a number of brief, handwritten autobiographical sketches and reminiscences which are invaluable for the pre-1903 period. See also Gould P. Colman, *Education & Agriculture: A Hist. of the N.Y. State College of Agriculture at Cornell Univ.* (1963).]

EDITH M. FOX

**VAN RENSSELAER, Mrs. Schuyler.** *See* VAN RENSSELAER, Mariana Griswold.

**VAN VORST, Marie Louise** (Nov. 23, 1867– Dec. 16, 1936), author and reformer, was born in New York City of seventeenth-century Dutch descent, her father, Hooper Cumming Van Vorst, being a founder of the Holland Society of New York. A native of Schenectady, N.Y., and a graduate of Union College, he practiced law in New York City, served on the city's superior court, and contributed to the movement which overthrew the Tweed Ring; he was also an active Presbyterian layman. Marie's mother, Josephine (Treat) Van Vorst, was his second wife. Marie was educated, for the most part, by private tutors. Although she harbored affection for her parents and her two brothers, to all of whom she dedicated books, her closest association was with her sister-in-law, Bessie (McGinnis) Van Vorst (1873– 1928), the wife of her brother John. About the turn of the century, these two independent women—the younger recently widowed—took up residence in France and turned to writing. Marie had already published verse and prose in magazines; Bessie, correspondence in the New York *Evening Post.* In 1901 they collaborated on a successful light novel, *Bagsby's Daughter.* Marie, however—influenced possibly by such fictional efforts to cope with the social question as MARY E. WILKINS FREEMAN's *The Portion of Labor* (1901)—next wrote a novel, *Philip Longstreth* (1902), about a young man who devotes himself to ameliorating the conditions of the poor, despite the opposion of his wealthy family and associates. Although its artistic faults were manifest, this novel, too, was well received and focused the attention of the two women on the labor problem.

They now determined to experience the lot of women workers themselves. Returning temporarily to the United States, they carried out their plans with courage and resourcefulness.

Marie, as "Bell Ballard," worked in a Lynn, Mass., shoe factory and in Southern cotton mills, where she became especially aware of the child labor problem. Bessie, under the name "Esther Kelly," secured employment in several establishments including a Pittsburgh pickle factory and a knitting mill near Buffalo. They reported their findings in *The Woman Who Toils: Being the Experiences of Two Ladies as Factory Girls* (1903). In clear, unequivocal prose, Bessie Van Vorst described the difficult working conditions and mean living she had observed and their bad effects on women and young girls. In her chapter "The Meaning of It All" she called for a more humane attitude toward women in general and particularly the young. Marie Van Vorst disclaimed solutions for the painful scenes she had witnessed. A feature of her writing was the interest she evinced in local inflections and colloquialisms, which added touches of realism to her prose. *The Woman Who Toils*, published with a prefatory letter by President Theodore Roosevelt, was a landmark in social investigation and reportage. The President ignored the child labor problem and underscored the need for men to work and women to be good wives and mothers, rather than wage earners; but his patronage helped attract attention to the book and to the need for further studies in the subject, as well as for social legislation.

Though Bessie Van Vorst published a later study of child labor in the woolen and cotton mills of Alabama and New Hampshire that helped stir reform sentiment (*The Cry of the Children*, 1908), it was Marie Van Vorst who became the better-known writer. Following the success of *The Woman Who Toils*, she wrote a novel, *Amanda of the Mill* (1905), set in the Blue Ridge Mountains, which sought to portray accurately both Southern factory conditions and the local dialect. It was treated seriously by critics, despite its weaknesses in character portrayal and narrative structure. A major assignment from *Harper's Monthly* in 1906–09 sent her to Europe and Africa to prepare articles on "Rivers of the World," including the Seine, Tiber, and Nile. Other articles on art, travel, and social questions were substantial contributions to contemporary writing. The stream of fiction and verse she contributed to magazines and collected in books, including some fifteen later novels, was much thinner in quality. Her attitude toward her own work varied. Some of her romances may have given her satisfaction, but she also drove herself to write for money.

The coming of World War I, however, roused all her energetic concern for the fate of her adopted home, France. In 1914 she volunteered for service with the American Ambulance (field hospital) at Neuilly, returning the next year to the United States to lecture on her experiences and stir Americans to the need to support France's efforts. Her *War Letters of an American Woman* (1916) was her best book since *The Woman Who Toils*. Composed of letters to her friends and relatives, it provided a vivid record of her thoughts and experiences and of life behind the French lines. In 1918, after visiting the Italian front, she headed a commission sent to America by the Supreme Command to coordinate war relief for Italy.

Meanwhile, on Oct. 16, 1916, she had married Count Gaetano Cagiati of Rome in a ceremony in the Cathedral of Notre Dame in Paris; they adopted a son, Frederick John. As an ardent champion of woman's rights, however, she continued to preserve a considerable freedom of movement. In 1922 she began to paint, and she attained some standing in the field, exhibiting at the Sterner Galleries in New York. She died in Florence, Italy, of pneumonia at the age of sixty-nine and was given burial there.

[Sources of information respecting Marie Van Vorst are extremely meager and unsatisfying in detail. Her *War Letters* offers the best available insight into her ideas and personal associations; and many of her articles include details about her activities. Several articles contain biographical information, as in the *Bookman*, May 1902, pp. 214–15, and the *Critic*, Jan. 1902, pp. 10–11. See also *N.Y. Times*, Jan. 15, Oct. 18, 1916, Mar. 25, 1918, May 27, 1923 (sec. 8), Dec. 18, 1936; and various issues of *Who's Who in America*. On her father, see *Nat. Cyc. Am. Biog.*, XIII, 393, and James W. Brooks, *Hist. of the Court of Common Pleas of the City and County of N.Y.* (1896), pp. 95–96.]

LOUIS FILLER

VAN WAGENER, Isabella. *See* TRUTH, Sojourner.

VAN ZANDT, Marie (Oct. 8, 1858–Dec. 31, 1919), opera singer, was born in New York, most probably in Brooklyn. She was the second daughter and youngest of three children of James Rose Van Zandt, a Brooklyn clerk of Dutch extraction, and his wife, Jennie, daughter of an English-born magician, Antonio Blitz. By 1863 Marie's mother, Jennie Van Zandt, had become a successful concert singer in Brooklyn, and shortly thereafter, under the name of Madame Vanzini, she launched an operatic career that took her to Paris, to La

Scala in Milan, and to the Carl Rosa Company in London. She appeared in America with companies headed by Euphrosyne Parepa-Rosa and CLARA LOUISE KELLOGG and was hailed by the *New York Tribune* as "one of the best light sopranos available for the American stage."

Marie's childhood, like many of the important aspects of her life, is partly veiled in confusion. She herself claimed a childhood, and sometimes birth, in Texas amidst the "tattooed Indians." It seems clear, however, that she accompanied her mother to Europe at an early age and was placed in an English convent school for what little formal education she received. Her musical training began reportedly with the encouragement of the great ADELINA PATTI. Her first teacher was her mother, who abandoned her own career in order to promote that of her daughter. She soon brought Marie to Milan and the renowned vocal teacher Francisco Lamperti.

Marie Van Zandt made her operatic debut in Turin early in 1879, when she was twenty, performing the role of Zerlina in *Don Giovanni*. In May 1879 she made her first London appearance, as Amina in *La Sonnambula* at Her Majesty's Theatre, at that time managed by Col. James H. Mapleson, who was later to earn fame in America as the director of the Academy of Music in New York. Much more important to her career, which was mainly spent in France, was her Paris debut the following year, on Mar. 20, 1880. She sang Philine (or, by some accounts, the title role) in Ambroise Thomas' *Mignon* at the Opéra-Comique with such success that she was given a five-year contract by the company. At this time she added to her repertoire the title role in Meyerbeer's *Dinorah*. Her fame was so rapid that she became, according to one biographer, the "spoiled child of the Paris Opéra-Comique."

The highlight of Marie Van Zandt's career took place on Apr. 14, 1883, when she achieved a lasting place in the annals of opera by creating the title role in Léo Delibes' *Lakmé*, an opera reportedly written for her and definitely performed under the composer's coaching. In retrospect, the French music critic Henri de Curzon wrote of the impression she made as Lakmé: "That engaging expression, a little wild and with a grace both innocent and passionate, that voice now large and moving, now brilliant with clear lightness . . . no one since has been able to forget her." The low point of her career followed soon afterward, on Nov. 8, 1884, during the first performance at the Opéra-Comique of Rossini's *Il Barbiere di Siviglia* when she temporarily lost her voice. Friends blamed the incident on nervousness and overwork; the less sympathetic suggested that she was drunk. Whatever the cause, she was unable to continue after the first act, and the composer Charles Gounod did not help the soprano's reputation when he personally led Cécile Mézeray onstage to replace her, thereby abetting the cabals that had been formed in Paris against the American soprano who had achieved such sudden fame. The press and public were alike hostile, and Marie Van Zandt withdrew from the stage for three months. Her return resulted in riots that necessitated police protection for the singer. More than musical passion produced this early example of anti-Americanism. Some have blamed a rival soprano, for there was an intense competition between Marie and another American, EMMA NEVADA, both sharing a similar repertoire. Others have claimed that the riots were politically inspired and were even led by a prefect of police in order to turn public attention away from a certain unpopular politician. Marie Van Zandt obtained immediate release from her contract.

The popularity she had lost in Paris she subsequently regained in St. Petersburg at the Imperial Theatre and in Moscow. This temporary break in her allegiance to France also brought her to England, where she sang Amina at Covent Garden in June 1889, and to America, though only for one season. She made her debut at Chicago's Auditorium Theatre on Nov. 13, 1891, as Amina. Her first appearance at the Metropolitan Opera House in New York was in the same role on Dec. 21, 1891. During the 1891–92 season, both in New York and on tour, she sang her accustomed roles, which now also included Lady Harriet in Friedrich von Flotow's *Martha* and Ophelia in Thomas' *Hamlet*. The size of the Metropolitan may well have limited her effectiveness, as the following comment by the theatre historian George C. D. Odell suggests: "She was a small, graceful woman, too small, in fact, for that large stage, and she had a pretty, light voice and she sang nicely."

The remainder of Marie Van Zandt's career was spent in Europe. During the 1896–97 season she made a highly successful return to the Opéra-Comique. On Apr. 27, 1898, at the mayoralty of the Champs Elysées district, she was married to Mikhail Petrovitch de Tscherinoff, a Russian state councilor and a professor at the Imperial Academy of Moscow. Marriage brought her retirement from the stage and some years of residency in Moscow. The soprano died at her home in Cannes, France, in 1919, an exile from America and, because of revolution, from her husband's country.

Marie Van Zandt possessed a voice of more than two octaves in compass, with excellent execution, though little volume or power. Bernard Shaw, as a music critic in 1885, praised "the remarkable natural talent of Mlle Van Zandt, whose sole extraordinary qualification is an agile soprano voice with a range that includes E natural in *alt*." Since her custom was to sing directly to the audience and to ignore the other members of the cast, she was noted for spectacular vocalization rather than for any acting talent.

[Oscar Thompson, *The Am. Singer* (1937); Henry C. Lahee, *Famous Singers of To-day and Yesterday* (1898); Harold Rosenthal, *Two Centuries of Opera at Covent Garden* (1958), pp. 203, 232; William H. Seltsam, *Metropolitan Opera Annals* (1947); *Grove's Dict. of Music and Musicians* (5th ed., 1954); Wallace Brockway and Herbert Weinstock, *The World of Opera* (1962); Henri de Curzon, *Léo Delibes* (1926); Bernard Shaw, *How to Become a Musical Critic* (Dan H. Laurence, ed., 1960); George C. D. Odell, *Annals of the N.Y. Stage*, XV (1949), 116–18; clippings in Harvard Theatre Collection; death record from city of Cannes. On her parents and family background see: Howard S. F. Randolph, comp., "The Van Zandt Family of N.Y.," *N.Y. Genealogical and Biog. Record*, Apr. 1931; *Dict. Am. Biog.* and Brooklyn census records of 1855 on Antonio Blitz; Brooklyn city directories, 1854–61, on Blitz and James R. Van Zandt; references to Jennie Van Zandt in Odell, *Annals* (above), vols. VII, IX, and X (1931–38).]

ARTHUR REGAN


**VAUTRIN, Minnie** (Sept. 27, 1886–May 14, 1941), missionary educator in China, was born at Secor, Ill., twenty-five miles east of Peoria, the daughter of Edmond Louis Vautrin, who had come to the United States from France, and his wife, Pauline (Lohr) Vautrin. She had one brother, Louis. Minnie Vautrin graduated from the Secor High School and Illinois State Normal University at Normal, Ill., receiving its diploma in 1907. After three years as a teacher of mathematics in the Le Roy (Ill.) High School, she entered the University of Illinois, from which she received her A.B. in science in 1912 as salutatorian of the class.

Miss Vautrin's missionary vocation came to her suddenly. In March 1912, toward the end of her senior year, she attended a meeting sponsored by the missionary movement of her church, the Disciples of Christ. Hearing there that the denomination's school for girls at Luchow, China, would be closed unless a capable teacher with administrative ability were recruited to take direction of it, she volunteered for the post and was accepted. That

August Miss Vautrin sailed for China and, after two years in language study at Nanking, assumed the principalship. Her spare time she spent in evangelistic work. The school prospered under her direction, growing in quality and enrollment, and a high school department was added to the existing middle school. Devoting her furloughs to advanced study, she enrolled at Teachers College, Columbia University, in 1918–19 and there received the M.A. degree. She later (1925–26 and 1931–32) studied in the department of education at the University of Chicago.

When Miss Vautrin returned to China after her first furlough, in 1919, she was assigned to the faculty of Ginling College, the union (interdenominational) Protestant college for women at Nanking, as head of a new department of education, designed to provide teachers for Central China. She also served as acting president for the next year and a half, a difficult period when students in Chinese colleges and universities were restless and demonstrative under the growing spirit of nationalism. Her ideal for her students was mastery of theory and methods, on the one hand, and of subject matter on the other. By extensive visiting of schools in Central China, Miss Vautrin developed a close relationship with them which made possible the effective placement of Ginling graduates. President Matilda C. Thurston (d. 1958) of Ginling attested to her excellence as a teacher and to her influence in attracting students to the field of education and then in fostering their self-confidence and professional zeal.

Nanking was a primary target of the Kuomintang army in its northward march in 1927. With the antiforeign left wing in control when the city was taken, several Westerners were killed and property was looted. Western consular officials removed the foreign members of the Ginling faculty to Shanghai, but Miss Vautrin and several other women returned to Nanking to reopen the college in the autumn. The new nationalist government's requirements for higher education at this time brought Dr. Wu Yi-fang to the presidency of Ginling, and during the remainder of her teaching career Miss Vautrin worked closely with her. She also inaugurated, in 1931, a program of neighborhood social service work that became close to her heart, beginning with a short-term day school for local women.

Though Minnie Vautrin made a substantial contribution to the higher education of women and the training of teachers in China, her fame in America and Europe came through her protection and care of refugees during the capture and sack of Nanking by the Japanese army in 1937. When war broke out with the Japanese attack at Lukouch'iao on July 7, she was at Tsingtao. She managed to return immediately to Nanking, and remained on the Ginling campus through the bombing and invasion of the city. Dr. Wu on her departure left in charge an emergency committee of three teachers with Miss Vautrin as chairman. Even before the city fell on Dec. 13, refugee women and children began to crowd into the college grounds, and during the ensuing reign of terror, which lasted a month, their numbers reached nearly ten thousand. Miss Vautrin personally patrolled the campus, faced and turned away invading parties of soldiers, rescued individuals, distributed rice, and comforted the refugees. All other refugee camps were closed on Feb. 4, 1938, with assurance that women and girls would be protected by the police; but no such protection was provided, and large numbers again sought admission to Ginling. As late as the middle of March a census revealed that there were still 3,310 there. Miss Vautrin established Bible classes and other activities for the refugees. She saw to the burying of the dead and the reception of newborn babies. She had amazing success in tracing missing husbands and sons. Industrial or crafts classes were provided for women who had lost their husbands, so that they might support themselves.

Miss Vautrin bore the burden of these duties, but she could not endure the suffering of the people. Especially she brooded over the many persons she was unable to save. In the spring of 1940 she became despondent and suffered a breakdown, and it was necessary to send her to the United States under the care of a colleague. She appeared to recover for a time, but again declined and took her own life at Indianapolis, Ind., in May 1941. She was buried at Shepherd, Mich., the home of her brother.

[*They Went to China: Biogs. of Missionaries of the Disciples of Christ* (1948), p. 41; Mrs. Lawrence Thurston and Ruth M. Chester, *Ginling College* (1955). The Archives of Ginling College (microfilm at Harvard College Library) include a typescript of Miss Vautrin's diary, Aug. 12, 1937–Apr. 14, 1940; part of this was published in *The Classmate* (Cincinnati), Apr. 30 and May 17, 1938.]

R. PIERCE BEAVER

**VICTOR, Frances Auretta Fuller** (May 23, 1826–Nov. 14, 1902), author and historian, was born in Rome, N.Y., the eldest of five daughters of Adonijah and Lucy A. (Williams) Fuller. When Frances was four the family

started west, spending some time in Erie, Pa., and eventually settling in 1839 in Wooster, Ohio, where Frances and her talented sister Metta Victoria (see METTA VICTORIA FULLER VICTOR), five years her junior, attended a female seminary. In their teens and early twenties both Frances and Metta published poems and tales locally as well as in the New York *Home Journal,* and in 1848 Frances' first book, *Anizetta, the Guajira: or the Creole of Cuba,* a melodramatic romance, appeared in Boston. That same year the two sisters moved to New York City, where they were encouraged by N. P. Willis, Rufus W. Griswold, and other editors and critics. In 1851 they published jointly *Poems of Sentiment and Imagination,* which displayed more of the first quality than of the second.

Frances Fuller's ambitious plans for a literary career, however, had already received a setback when her father died in 1850, and she soon rejoined her family, who moved to St. Clair, Mich. There she was married, on June 16, 1853, to Jackson Barritt of Pontiac, Mich. A period of homesteading near Omaha ended in the breakup of the marriage, though she did not obtain a divorce until March 1862. Meanwhile she had joined her sister Metta in New York, where Metta's husband, Orville James Victor, was editing the recently inaugurated Beadle's Dime Novels. For this series Frances wrote *East and West; or, The Beauty of Willard's Mill* (1862) and *The Land Claim: A Tale of the Upper Missouri* (1862), both treating Nebraska farm life with some realism.

In May 1862 Frances married her sister's brother-in-law, Henry Clay Victor, a navy engineer. A year later his assignments took them to the Pacific Coast, where Mrs. Victor, who had no children by either of her marriages, went to work in San Francisco while her husband was on sea duty. Writing under the name "Florence Fane," she was a regular contributor to the *Golden Era,* a literary weekly, and the *San Francisco Bulletin.* Late in 1864, after Victor's health caused him to resign from the navy, the two moved to Oregon, where Mrs. Victor turned to local history while her husband restlessly moved from one project to another. History, she discovered, was her forte. She interviewed many pioneers, searched through family papers and archives, and made her twin goals thoroughness and objectivity. By the time she was widowed in 1875, when her husband drowned in the wreck of the *Pacific,* she had written an excellent account of the mountain man Joe Meek (*The River of the West,* 1870), a travel book entitled *All Over Oregon and Washington* (1872), a temperance tract called *The Women's War with Whisky* (1874), and, for the *Overland Monthly* and other Western magazines, most of the stories and poems she was to collect in *The New Penelope* (1877). She had also spent some time in New York and worked in San Francisco as columnist for the *Call-Bulletin* under the name "Dorothy D."

In 1878 the historical promoter Hubert Howe Bancroft, recognizing Frances Victor's knowledge of the Pacific Northwest, offered her a position on his staff helping to prepare his ambitious *History of the Pacific States.* Tempted by the security and access to materials, she accepted and remained with Bancroft in San Francisco until the twenty-eight-volume project was completed in 1890. Though Bancroft claimed authorship of the entire *History*, it is now clearly established that Mrs. Victor wrote all of the two volumes on Oregon; the volume on Washington, Idaho, and Montana; that on Nevada, Colorado, and Wyoming; and considerable portions of the volumes on California, the Northwest Coast, and British Columbia.

Mrs. Victor returned to Oregon in 1890, living out the rest of her seventy-six years in Salem and Portland in very modest circumstances. There she revised her early travel book under the title *Atlantis Arisen* (1891), was commissioned by the legislature to study the native Indians and produced *The Early Indian Wars of Oregon* (1894), and in 1900 issued an additional volume of poems. She died in Portland. The funeral was held in the Unitarian church to which she belonged, and she was buried in Riverview Cemetery.

Frances Fuller Victor's poems, conventionally romantic and didactic, today seem uninspired, with one or two exceptions. Her short stories, influenced by her friend Bret Harte, are successful principally in giving glimpses of the hard lot of women on the frontier. Her history, however, is carefully documented and clearly expressed, and remains basic to later studies in the fields which she covered.

[Principal sources are Hazel E. Mills in *Pacific Northwest Quart.*, Oct. 1954; William A. Morris, "The Origin and Authorship of the Bancroft Pacific States Publications," *Oreg. Hist. Soc. Quart.*, Dec. 1903; William T. Coggeshall, *The Poets and Poetry of the West* (1860); H. H. Bancroft, *Literary Industries* (1890); and Alfred Powers, *A Hist. of Oreg. Literature* (1935). Information was also provided by Hazel E. Mills, Wash. State Library, Olympia, who is writing a biography. Frances Fuller Victor's papers and MSS. are in the Oreg. Hist. Soc. Library and the Bancroft Library, Univ. of Calif.]

FRANKLIN WALKER

VICTOR, Metta Victoria Fuller (Mar. 2, 1831–June 26, 1885), popular author, was born in Erie, Pa., where her family had recently arrived from upstate New York. The third of five daughters of Adonijah and Lucy (Williams) Fuller, she was descended on her father's side from a family that included several original settlers of the Plymouth colony. The Fullers moved again in 1839 to Wooster, Ohio, where for some years Metta attended a female seminary. She began to write when she was ten; when she was thirteen a local paper printed one of her stories. Two years later a Boston firm published her full-length romance, *The Last Days of Tul,* a story of Maya Indian civilization. At the same time her work began to appear in the New York *Home Journal* under the pen name "Singing Sybil," and in 1852 a number of her pieces were collected in a volume, *Fresh Leaves from Western Woods.*

Having won this small renown, Metta, together with her older sister Frances (see FRANCES FULLER VICTOR), also a writer, moved to New York and joined the coterie of female literati centered around Rufus Wilmot Griswold, the eccentric New York editor and friend of Edgar Allan Poe. Griswold included several verses by the "Sisters of the West" in his 1848 anthology, *The Female Poets of America,* and in 1851 brought out a volume of their joint efforts, *Poems of Sentiment and Imagination.* Metta's success, however, soon came to surpass that of Frances, as she turned from lyric flights to more topical subjects. Her temperance novel of 1851, *The Senator's Son, or, The Maine Law: A Last Refuge,* went through a number of editions in both America and England. *Fashionable Dissipations* (1854) was followed by *Mormon Wives* (1856), a fictional attack on polygamy and enthusiastic religion.

Although reports of Metta's marriage to a Dr. Morse appeared in the March and July 1851 issues of the *Western Literary Messenger,* it is uncertain whether such a marriage actually took place, or what became of it if it did. In any event, in July 1856 she was married to Orville James Victor, a friend of Rufus Griswold and lately associate editor of a newspaper in his native Sandusky, Ohio. In the month of their marriage Orville Victor was made editor of the *Cosmopolitan Art Journal,* a newly established quarterly. The couple worked together on this magazine in Sandusky for two years and then moved it to New York City, where Orville Victor added the editorship of the *United States Journal.* Although she bore nine children—Lillian (1857), Alice (1859), Bertha (1860), Winthrop (1861), Lucy (1863), Guy (1865), Metta (1866),

and the twins Vivia and Florence (1872)—
Mrs. Victor continued to assist her husband
with his editorial duties, contributed to a
variety of leading periodicals, and in January
1859 began to edit the *Home,* a monthly magazine published by Beadle and Adams. The
following year she took over the editorship of
the *Cosmopolitan Art Journal* from her husband.

The *Home* ceased publication only a year
and a half after Mrs. Victor became its editor,
but her association with Beadle and Adams
continued for the rest of her career; it was
firmly cemented in 1861, when her husband
was made Beadle's general editor, a position
he retained for thirty-six years. Mrs. Victor
wrote a popular *Dime Cook-Book* for the firm
early in 1859, and her 1860 romance, *Alice
Wilde, the Raftsman's Daughter,* was a very
early representative of the new Beadle genre,
the "dime novel." In all, she was to publish
nearly a hundred titles in various Beadle series,
many of them pseudonymously. By far the most
popular of these was Dime Novel No. 33,
*Maum Guinea, and Her Plantation "Children"*
(1861), a "slave romance" about life in antebellum Louisiana that won praise from adherents to the antislavery cause.

Mrs. Victor also continued to write for other
publishers. Most of this work was in a lighter
vein. A number of satirical sketches of love
and manners she had contributed to *Godey's
Lady's Book* and the *Cosmopolitan Art Journal*
were collected (again pseudonymously) as
*Miss Slimmens' Window* (1859). After the
Civil War, when the immense popularity of
the dime novel slowly tapered off, she turned
more exclusively to this lighter style. A number of full-length works, originally serialized
in a variety of newspapers and magazines, were
published in book form, anonymously on the
whole, during these years, among them *The
Dead Letter* (1866), *The Blunders of a Bashful Man* (1875), *Passing the Portal* (1876),
and *A Bad Boy's Diary* (1880).

Mrs. Victor around 1870 reportedly was
able to command a price of $25,000 for a group
of stories. Her choice of literary subjects, and
the styles with which she treated them, at
every point reflected and exploited the changing sensibility of her public. Before 1850 she
produced prose and verse suitable for women's
magazines and gift books. During the 1850's,
when the waxing impulse to reform bespoke
pressing doubts and tensions in the public
mind, she produced reform novels, centered
around ambitious and promising characters
who fell prey to the temptations of money and
power, drink, or lust. After the Civil War the

moral urgency of her tone was transformed
into satire and then whimsy, and she turned
to gentler themes, evocations of childhood and
innocence.

The Victors had moved at the end of the
Civil War to a large house in Hohokus, N.J.
It was there that Metta Victor died in 1885,
at fifty-four, a victim of cancer. Although many
of her books were reprinted well into the
1890's, an obituary writer at the time of her
death found her "comparatively unknown to
the present generation." Survived by her husband and eight of her children, if not by her
popularity, she was buried in Valleau Cemetery, Hohokus.

[Contemporary accounts of Mrs. Victor are in the
*Cosmopolitan Art Jour.,* Mar. 1857, the *Home,* Dec.
1858, and William T. Coggeshall, *The Poets and
Poetry of the West* (1860). The best recent study
can be found in vol. II of Albert Johannsen, *The
House of Beadle and Adams* (1950), which also
contains a biography of Orville Victor. Information about the various magazines for which Mrs.
Victor worked and wrote, and about the mid-
nineteenth-century magazine world generally, can
be found in Frank L. Mott, *A Hist. of Am. Magazines* (5 vols., 1930–68).]

WILLIAM R. TAYLOR

**VILLARD, Fanny Garrison** (Dec. 16, 1844–
July 5, 1928), philanthropist, suffragist, and
pacifist, was the fourth of seven children and
only daughter of the famous abolitionist William Lloyd Garrison and Helen Eliza (Benson)
Villard. Though christened Helen Frances, she
always used Fanny as her given name. Born
in Boston, she grew up at the height of her
father's crusading activities. After completing
her education at the Winthrop School in Boston, she helped support the family by teaching
piano. On Jan. 3, 1866, she was married to
Henry Villard, a German immigrant, at that
time a newspaper correspondent, who beginning in the 1870's became a financier, president of the Northern Pacific Railroad, and
co-founder of the Edison General Electric Company. His business success provided his wife
with the leisure and wealth to lead a life of
philanthropy and public service, and his deep
interest in politics, which led him in 1881 to
purchase the New York *Evening Post* and the
*Nation,* two leading journals of Mugwump
reform, brought her into frequent contact with
national political leaders.

During the first decade of their marriage the
Villards were largely occupied with extensive
business travels in the United States and Europe and with the rearing of their four children: Helen, Oswald Garrison, Harold Garrison, and Henry Hilgard (who died at seven).

But in 1878, two years after the family settled permanently in New York City, Mrs. Villard took up her first charity: the Diet Kitchen Association, which provided nutritional foods and, later, certified milk to the sick in New York's slums. It remained a lifelong interest; she served as president of the association from 1898 to 1922. Meanwhile, in the 1880's, she became an active worker for three other projects: the New York Infirmary for Women and Children, the Woman's Exchange, and the Riverside Rest Association. To each she gave not only substantial financial support but also generous amounts of her own time and abilities as an adviser, executive board member, and fund raiser. Interested also in education, she concentrated her efforts on providing better opportunities for two deprived groups, women and Negroes. Mrs. Villard was one of those who spearheaded the establishment of Barnard College, the women's college associated with Columbia University, and she helped raise the funds needed to set up the American College for Women in Constantinople and the Harvard Annex, later Radcliffe College. Her work in Negro education consisted mainly of financial support for several Negro schools in both New York and the South, particularly Hampton Institute in Virginia.

Such philanthropic work continued to occupy Mrs. Villard for the rest of her life. During the early years of the twentieth century she became a financial supporter and active worker for several other charitable and educational institutions in New York City, including the Consumers' League, the Household Economics Association, the Working Woman's Protective Association, the Columbus Hill Day Nursery, a Froebel kindergarten for Negro children, and the National Association for the Advancement of Colored People. But after the turn of the century, there was a decided shift of her interests toward the political realm. In part this was owing to the death of her husband in 1900, which increased her time available for public affairs, and to the rise of her son Oswald as the outspoken, liberal editor of the New York *Evening Post*. But, even more, it reflected a change in her personal view of society and its needs. Initially convinced that urban problems of poverty and vice stemmed from the moral weaknesses of individuals, she had sought to reform society by rehabilitating such individuals, both physically and spiritually. But a quarter century of charity work, particularly after her presidency of the Diet Kitchen Association brought her into more intimate contact with other social agencies and their findings, convinced Mrs. Villard, like

many of her contemporaries, that the remedy lay deeper. The reforms urged by the Progressive movement struck her as well-meaning but inadequate; seeking a more fundamental and more obviously moral change, she believed that the American woman, with her innate moral superiority, must enter and redeem American politics.

Fanny Garrison Villard had long believed in the justice of woman suffrage; her father, indeed, had championed the cause during her childhood. But it was not until about 1906 that she actively joined the movement. The main scene of her work was New York, and much of her time was devoted to organization. She served for several years on the executive board of the New York State Woman Suffrage Association and filled also the important posts of auditor and chairman of the legislative committee. In New York City she belonged to three different suffrage societies and served as president of one, the William Lloyd Garrison Equal Suffrage Club. Her chief public contribution was an untiring stream of speeches. She spoke whenever and wherever she was asked: before the legislative hearings of three states, on the debate platform against the "antis," to suffrage groups, and, in what proved the severest test of all for a dignified woman of sixty-six, to street crowds assembled for a suffrage parade. Her message was always the same: the great promise which suffrage held for the "welfare and moral uplift of both men and women" (MS. speech, "Address at Yonkers").

During these same years Mrs. Villard took up the second great public cause of her life, the peace movement. She had inherited a belief in total nonresistance from her father, and in the years before 1914 she occasionally participated in meetings and demonstrations for peace. But it was the outbreak of World War I and her fear of United States involvement that enlisted her full efforts, particularly after the victory of the New York suffrage referendum in 1917. Her peace activities were similar to her suffrage work: organizational duties, speeches, conventions, parades, and petitions to the president and other national leaders urging strict American neutrality. Just after the outbreak of the war, Mrs. Villard organized and led a peace parade down Fifth Avenue. In 1915 she helped set up the national Woman's Peace Party under the presidency of JANE ADDAMS and served as chairman of its New York state branch. An uncompromising pacifist, she refused to countenance any military preparations by the United States or to concede that any belligerent act by either England or Germany could justify American entrance into the war; as a result she left the executive board of the Woman's Peace Party in 1916. She spent the period of United States belligerency aiding conscientious objectors and subscribing to refugee relief programs. In 1919 she founded her own Woman's Peace Society in New York City, dedicated to the achievement of a lasting peace based on her abiding principles of total disarmament and nonresistance.

Unusually attractive in her youth, Mrs. Villard retained throughout her life a warm-hearted and winsome charm. Though she was "certain of the triumph of every cause to which she gave her devotion" (in the words of her son), she was not "a bigot or narrowly puritanical." She continued her work into the 1920's, though feeling keenly the idealist's disillusion. Never much concerned with religion, she belonged to no congregation. She died of heart disease at the age of eighty-three at her country estate in Dobbs Ferry, N.Y., and was buried in the nearby Sleepy Hollow Cemetery.

[Mrs. Villard's diary and the great bulk of her correspondence are in the Villard Papers at Harvard Univ. She wrote one book, *William Lloyd Garrison on Non-Resistance* (1924), and contributed to the family biography of her father, *William Lloyd Garrison, 1805–1879* (4 vols., 1889). There is useful material in Henry Villard's *Memoirs* (2 vols., 1904) and especially in Oswald Garrison Villard's autobiography, *Fighting Years* (1939). The best sources on Mrs. Villard's suffrage work are memoirs of suffrage leaders with whom she worked: Carrie Chapman Catt and Nettie Rogers Shuler, *Woman Suffrage and Politics* (1923); and Anna Howard Shaw, *The Story of a Pioneer* (1915). The primary references for her peace work are the *Yearbook* of the Woman's Peace Party (1916 ff.) and the two accounts by Jane Addams of the woman's peace movement: *The Second Twenty Years at Hull-House* (1930) and *Peace and Bread in Time of War* (1922). Mrs. Villard's obituary was carried in the July 6, 1928, editions of the *N.Y. Times* and the *N.Y. Evening Post*.]

ANN GORMAN CONDON

VINCENT, Mrs. James R. *See* VINCENT, Mary Ann Farlow.

VINCENT, Mary Ann Farlow (Sept. 18, 1818–Sept. 4, 1887), actress, better known as Mrs. J. R. Vincent, was reportedly born in Portsmouth, England, where her father, John Farlow, was in the employ of the British navy. Becoming an orphan at the age of four, she was brought up by her grandmother and an aunt in Portsmouth. Though totally lacking in stage experience, she successfully made her theatrical debut on Apr. 25, 1835, at the theatre in Cowes, Isle of Wight, as the cham-

bermaid Lucy in George Colman's *The Review, or the Wags of Windsor*. She continued acting at Cowes and in August, while still only sixteen, was married to James R. Vincent, a fellow actor. With him she toured Ireland, Scotland, and England, including two seasons at the Theatre Royal, Liverpool. Showing great versatility from the start, especially in character roles, before reaching the age of nineteen she gave "a well considered interpretation" of the Nurse in *Romeo and Juliet*. After negotiations with William Pelby of the old National Theatre, Boston, the Vincents sailed from Liverpool on Oct. 21, 1846, and gave their first American performance on Nov. 11 in John B. Buckstone's *Popping the Question*, becoming members of the Boston company. James Vincent committed suicide on June 11, 1850, but his wife remained with the National until the theatre burned down on Apr. 22, 1852.

On May 10, 1852, Mrs. Vincent appeared at the Boston Museum as Mrs. Pontifex in *Naval Engagements*, thus beginning her long association with that theatre, a beloved Boston institution. On Dec. 16, 1854, she was married to John Wilson, a Boston expressman, eleven years her junior; the union proved an unhappy one, ending with Wilson's desertion in 1866 and later in divorce. In 1861–62, because of a disagreement with the manager, Mrs. Vincent left the Museum for a season. After playing briefly at the Howard Athenaeum in Boston, she accepted an engagement in Baltimore with Lucille Western's company. While there she was the original Corney Carlyle in *East Lynne*. She also appeared in Washington, where President Lincoln is said to have greatly admired her acting. The next season she was back at the Boston Museum, where she remained until her death.

Mrs. Vincent's high reputation was founded on a wide repertoire, amounting to well over four hundred roles, in plays ranging from the French melodrama *Article 47* and Dion Boucicault's *The Colleen Bawn* to the classical comedy of Goldsmith and Sheridan. Mrs. Candour was one of her most admired characterizations. She won acclaim in Shakespeare, as Audrey in *As You Like It*, Portia in *The Merchant of Venice*, Emilia in *Othello*, Gertrude in *Hamlet*, and many other parts. Though she never reached the high eminence of a JULIA DEAN or a MARY ANDERSON, few could surpass her as a comedienne in character and old-lady roles. As Prof. George P. Baker of Harvard recalled her, "The round, jolly figure, the cheery face, the tripping walk, the odd, gasping little voice, were instinct with fun." Yet her fun "came from the brain, from her keen appreciation of the part and of the situations." She brought a penetrating intelligence to her craft, yet conveyed an effect of complete naturalness.

On Apr. 25, 1885, the Boston Museum celebrated her fiftieth anniversary on the stage by presenting gala performances of *She Stoops to Conquer* and *The Rivals,* on the afternoon and evening of the same day, with Mrs. Vincent as Mrs. Hardcastle and Mrs. Malaprop, two of her notable interpretations. Her last performance took place some two years later, on Aug. 31, 1887, in *The Dominie's Daughter.* She was taken ill that night and died at her Boston home of an apoplectic stroke several days later. After funeral services at St. Paul's Episcopal Church, Boston, of which she had been a loyal member, she was buried in Mount Auburn Cemetery, Cambridge.

In an age of perambulating players Mrs. Vincent, like her fellow star at the Boston Museum, William Warren, was exceptional in her preference for staying near home. Boston came to love "the dear old lady" for her merry personality and her good works as well as for her acting. For many years she supplemented her income by letting rooms and by renting costumes and properties for amateur theatricals, with Harvard's Hasty Pudding Club performers among her regular customers. At all times she harbored a formidable family of pets—a dog, a parrot, numerous canaries, and a quintet of cats named after prominent members of the Museum company. Her devotion to animals exceeded even her love for the theatre: when she once failed to show up backstage just before a performance, messengers sent out after her found her shouting vehemently and waving her umbrella at a teamster who was driving a lame horse. To people, too, her kindnesses and charities, which left her perpetually impoverished, were legion. The actor E. A. Sothern, whom she had befriended as a young performer, started a Christmas fund of a hundred dollars that she could dispense at pleasure and have replenished whenever necessary. After her death, admirers of Mrs. Vincent, with the approbation and cooperation of Bishop Phillips Brooks of Boston's Trinity Church, started a campaign to build a hospital in her honor; it was dedicated in 1891 as the Vincent Memorial Hospital. The Vincent Club, an organization of young women drawn largely from Boston society, was formed to raise funds for the hospital's support, appropriately turning to theatrical performances for this purpose.

[Most of the available biographical information about Mrs. Vincent is contained in two booklets: *Fiftieth Anniversary of the First Appearance on the Stage of Mrs. J. R. Vincent* (1885) and James B. Richardson, *Mrs. James R. Vincent: A Memorial Address Delivered at a Meeting of the Managers of the Vincent Memorial Hospital* (1911). Personal reminiscences appear in Catherine Mary Reignolds-Winslow, *Yesterdays with Actors* (1887); Kate Ryan, *Old Boston Museum Days* (1915); and Edward H. Sothern, *The Melancholy Tale of "Me"* (1916). One may consult also T. Allston Brown, *Hist. of the Am. Stage* (1870), and a sketch by George Pierce Baker in Frederic E. McKay and Charles E. L. Wingate, eds., *Famous Am. Actors of To-day* (1896). There are numerous clippings about Mrs. Vincent in the Theatre Collection, Houghton Library, Harvard. Records of James Vincent's death and of Mrs. Vincent's second marriage were secured from the Mass. Registrar of Vital Statistics.]

EDMOND M. GAGEY

# W

**WAITE, Catharine Van Valkenburg** (Jan. 30, 1829–Nov. 9, 1913), suffragist, lawyer, and legal journalist, was born in Dumfries, Ontario, Canada, the elder child and only daughter of Joseph and Margaret (Page) Van Valkenburg. Her father, presumably a farmer, had come from Holland; her mother was a Canadian by birth. Little is known of Catharine's early schooling. When she was about seventeen the family migrated to Iowa, settling eventually in Fort Madison. In 1849, following a year of teaching near her home, she enrolled in the "female department" of Knox College in Galesburg, Ill. She completed her college work with a year at Oberlin College, graduating from the literary course there in 1853.

On Apr. 26, 1854, Catharine Van Valkenburg was married to Charles Burlingame Waite, a Chicago lawyer five years her senior who had also attended Knox College. A native of western New York, Waite had published an antislavery newspaper in Rock Island, Ill., before gaining admission to the bar. Of their six children, five reached maturity: Lucy, who became a physician, Jessie, Margaret, Joseph, and Charles. In addition to her domestic duties,

Mrs. Waite taught briefly (1857–59) in Chicago's Union Park Seminary. In 1859, when the family moved to Hyde Park, a Chicago suburb, she established the Hyde Park Seminary, a girls' school which she conducted intermittently until 1871.

In 1862 Charles Waite was appointed an associate justice of the supreme court of Utah Territory by President Abraham Lincoln, an old friend and former colleague in the Illinois bar. The Waites reached Salt Lake City after an adventurous journey by rail and covered wagon. According to Mrs. Waite's later account, they were initially received with cordiality and marks of honor, but this attitude changed to one of hostility after the arrival of federal troops in the territory in the fall of 1862, and after the publication in a Boston paper of "spicy" letters criticizing polygamy by the judge's sister, who had accompanied them. In 1863, after holding one term of court, "at which there was not a single case on the docket," Waite resigned his post. He and his wife then spent several years in Idaho, chiefly in Idaho City, where Waite practiced law and dabbled in politics. Upon their return to Chicago in 1866, Mrs. Waite published *The Mormon Prophet and His Harem,* to call public attention to the "dangerous character" of the "religious monarchy . . . growing up in the midst of the Republic." As popular feeling against polygamy rose, Mrs. Waite recast the book in more personal form, recounting lurid tales which she claimed to have heard from "plural women" who secretly visited her house. This version was published as *Adventures in the Far West; and Life among the Mormons* in 1882, the year in which Congress outlawed polygamy by the Edmunds Act.

Back in Hyde Park, Catharine Waite had applied for admission to Rush Medical College of Chicago but had been refused. She reopened her seminary and began to devote herself to woman suffrage. As early as 1855 she had advocated this cause, and in 1869 she and her husband joined with James and MYRA BRADWELL, MARY A. LIVERMORE, and others, to found the Illinois Woman Suffrage Association. Elected president in 1871, Mrs. Waite called for the creation of "a society for woman suffrage in every county and town in the State" and, giving up her seminary, toured Illinois in an effort to realize this goal. The 1869 split in the national suffrage movement did not arouse violent antagonisms in Illinois, but it did divide the state leaders, most of whom allied themselves with LUCY STONE's conservative American Woman Suffrage Association.

Mrs. Waite, however, remained loyal to the older National Woman Suffrage Association of SUSAN B. ANTHONY and ELIZABETH CADY STANTON, primarily because of a close personal friendship with the two leaders. In 1871, in one of a series of nationwide tests of women's rights under the Fourteenth and Fifteenth amendments, Mrs. Waite attempted to vote in a Hyde Park election. Her application was rejected, and her husband's effort to overturn the decision in the courts also failed. This marked the virtual end of her public suffrage activities, though she continued to serve as legislative adviser of the state organization until 1890, when she yielded this post to CATHARINE WAUGH MC CULLOCH.

As the years passed, Charles Waite, a confirmed agnostic and freethinker, spent less and less time at his law practice in order to devote himself to his *History of the Christian Religion to the Year 200,* based on several years' research in the Library of Congress. The book was published in 1881 by C. V. Waite and Co., the small family publishing firm managed by his wife. Several other works on religious and sociological subjects followed. In 1884 he departed for a three-year European tour, during which time he studied government, manners, and social customs.

Meanwhile, Mrs. Waite ably managed their Chicago real estate interests, including several apartment buildings. Having read law informally since the Utah period, she enrolled in 1885 in the Union College of Law in Chicago (later the Northwestern University Law School). She was admitted to the bar upon her graduation in June 1886, but never actively practiced; instead, that November, she inaugurated the quarterly *Chicago Law Times,* which she published for three years. More reformist in tone than Myra Bradwell's *Chicago Legal News,* the *Law Times* included biographical data on women lawyers and discussed the legal rights of women, as well as legal aspects of insanity, abortion, and divorce. In 1888 Mrs. Waite was elected president of the International Woman's Bar Association, organized in Washington under the auspices of the International Council of Women.

With the termination of the *Law Times* in 1889, Mrs. Waite once more devoted herself to private interests. After his return to Chicago, her husband remained deeply immersed in the free-thought movement as president of local societies and, after 1892, of the American Secular Union, formerly the National Liberal League. In his later years he took up linguistics, and in 1903 he and Mrs. Waite jointly issued

*Homophonic Conversations* (1903), a language-study aid. He died in 1909, and four years later, at the age of eighty-four, Catharine Waite herself succumbed to a heart ailment, at the home of her daughter Lucy in Park Ridge, Ill. A memorial service was held by the Chicago Society of Rationalism, and her cremated remains were interred in Graceland Cemetery, Chicago.

[Catharine Waugh McCulloch, "Biog. of Catharine Van Valkenburg Waite," typescript in Dillon Collection, Schlesinger Library, Radcliffe College; *Bench and Bar of Chicago* (1883), pp. 240–43; Frances E. Willard and Mary A. Livermore, eds., *A Woman of the Century* (1893); *Appletons' Cyc. Am. Biog.*, VI, 317; Elizabeth C. Stanton et al., *Hist. of Woman Suffrage*, vols. II–V (1881–1922); *Semi-Centennial Register of the Officers and Alumni of Oberlin College* (1883); *Gen. Catalogue of Oberlin College, 1833–1908* (1909); Frances J. Hosford, *Father Shipherd's Magna Carta* (1937), p. 133; files of *Chicago Law Times*, 1886–89, the *Revolution*, 1870–71, and *Woman's Jour.*; *Chicago Tribune*, Nov. 11, 14, 16, 1913. A fuller treatment will appear in the author's forthcoming study, "Women, the Bench, and the Bar."]

DOROTHY THOMAS

**WALCOTT, Mary Morris Vaux** (July 31, 1860–Aug. 22, 1940), artist and naturalist, was born in Philadelphia, Pa., the eldest of three children and only daughter of George and Sarah Humphreys (Morris) Vaux, both descended from distinguished Pennsylvania Quaker families. Mary's father was a wealthy man of affairs who in later life devoted most of his energies to causes of the Society of Friends. Her brother George, Jr., achieved prominence as an attorney in Philadelphia and was appointed by President Theodore Roosevelt to the United States Board of Indian Commissioners, serving as chairman during most of his membership. Her younger brother, William, was an architect.

Mary Vaux graduated from the Friends Select School of Philadelphia in 1879. That same year her mother died, leaving her with the responsibility of keeping house for her father and brothers on the old family estate in Bryn Mawr. During the following years she managed not only the household but also the dairy farm on the estate, breeding fine Guernsey cows and experimenting in horticulture. The Vauxs regularly spent summer vacations in the Canadian Rockies. Influenced by her uncle William Sansom Vaux, an amateur mineralogist, Miss Vaux and her brothers became interested in glaciers and made measurements of flow during successive summers; George

accumulated an extensive rock and mineral collection, and the family became active in the Academy of Natural Sciences of Philadelphia. Beginning in 1887, Mary Vaux returned to western Canada almost every summer of her life and became an ardent mountain climber. In 1900, at the age of forty, she became the first woman to climb Mount Stephen in British Columbia, and she reportedly celebrated her seventy-seventh birthday by riding twenty miles in the mountains. Mount Mary Vaux (elevation 10,881 feet) in British Columbia was named for her.

Since childhood Miss Vaux had shown considerable artistic ability and had found pleasure in painting. One summer in British Columbia a local botanist persuaded her to turn briefly from landscapes to paint a rare alpine arnica; thereafter she concentrated on painting wild flowers, her search for new specimens taking her over many trails and to many peaks in the Rockies, often on horseback. Her watercolor kit was always with her, and she often painted flowers in situ.

During the summer of 1913 Miss Vaux met Charles Doolittle Walcott (1850–1927), secretary of the Smithsonian Institution in Washington, D.C., and a noted geologist and invertebrate paleontologist, who was engaged in research in the Canadian Rockies. The next year, on June 30, Miss Vaux, fifty-three, and Dr. Walcott, a widower of sixty-four, were married. In Washington, D.C., they led a busy public life, entertaining frequently. Mrs. Walcott also assisted her husband in many projects related to his work, including the formation of the Freer Gallery of oriental art. A tall, graceful woman, with merry blue eyes and a quiet smile, she was strong-willed and self-reliant, and known for her ready sympathy and generosity. The Walcotts continued to spend their summers in the Canadian Rockies, Mrs. Walcott pursuing her wild-flower painting, with her husband's strong encouragement.

In 1925 the Smithsonian Institution announced the publication of Mary Vaux Walcott's five-volume *North American Wild Flowers*. This work contained reproductions of 400 watercolors with her brief descriptions of each, giving information not only about the plant itself but about the circumstances of painting it. Included were plants from all parts of North America, specimens found in lawns and gardens as well as in the less accessible nooks and crannies of Canadian mountains. *North American Wild Flowers* was a triumph not only for Mrs. Walcott, who was soon acclaimed by some as the "Audubon" of American wild flowers, but also for the artisans of papermaking and color printing. The success of the first limited, de luxe edition of 500 copies, sold at cost for $500 each, enabled the Smithsonian to offer subsequently a library edition of 2,500 copies at $100 a copy.

Mrs. Walcott was asked to lecture before many groups, among them the Royal Society of Canada. In 1926 she joined the Society of Woman Geographers, founded the previous year; she was elected its second national president in 1933, serving two terms. After her brother George's death in 1927, Mrs. Walcott was appointed by President Coolidge to fill his vacancy on the Board of Indian Commissioners, and was reappointed by President Hoover, serving to 1932. Throughout her life she was active in the Society of Friends; for years she served as clerk of the Twelfth Street Meeting in Philadelphia, and in Washington she became the driving spirit in the building of the Florida Avenue Friends Meeting House, dedicated in 1930. In 1935, at the age of seventy-five, she contributed fifteen paintings to *Illustrations of North American Pitcher-plants,* published by the Smithsonian with the text by the botanist Edgar T. Wherry and notes on insect visitors by the entomologist Frank Morton Jones.

Shortly after her eightieth birthday Mrs. Walcott died of a heart attack while visiting friends at St. Andrews, New Brunswick, Canada. She was buried in Rock Creek Cemetery, Washington, D.C. Her estate was bequeathed to the Smithsonian Institution to augment the fund established by her husband during his lifetime for support of scientific research. The accumulated income from her published works was used to establish the Mary Walcott Fund for Publications in Botany. Her contribution to the popular wild-flower literature of North America is classic, and she took full advantage of her position as wife of the Smithsonian's secretary to promote public understanding of scientific research, especially in the field of botany.

[Obituaries in *Science,* Oct. 25, 1940 (by Helen Walcott Younger), *Bull. of the Soc. of Woman Geographers,* Sept. 1940 (by Frances Carpenter Huntington), and Washington *Evening Star,* Aug. 23, 1940; feature articles about her in *ibid.,* Jan. 15, Feb. 26, 1939, *Washington Times,* Dec. 17, 1938, and Baltimore *Sun,* Feb. 3, 1935; *Am. Men of Science* (6th ed., 1938); clippings and other material in miscellaneous files of Smithsonian Institution; unpublished biographical sketch in files of Friends Meeting House, Washington; information from George Vaux of Bryn Mawr, Pa., a nephew; interviews by Elaine R. Shetler with Drs. Paul Conger and Waldo Schmitt of the Smithsonian Institution and Miss Alice Boyer, librarian of the Friends Meeting House.]

STANWYN G. SHETLER

**WALD, Lillian D.** (Mar. 10, 1867–Sept. 1, 1940), public health nurse, settlement leader, and social reformer, was born in Cincinnati, Ohio, the second daughter and third of four children of Max D. and Minnie (Schwarz) Wald. The "D." in her father's name, and presumably that in her own, was simply an initial. The Walds and Schwarzes, descendants of many generations of rabbis, merchants, and professional men in Poland and Germany, had come to America shortly after the revolutions of 1848 in search of economic opportunity and a freer political and social atmosphere. For the most part their hopes were abundantly realized. Max Wald prospered as a dealer in optical goods. His business took the family from Cincinnati to Dayton and eventually to Rochester, N.Y., which Lillian regarded as her hometown. Her girlhood was so happy that in later years she described herself as a spoiled child. Her mother was amiable, beautiful, and generous; her father quiet, thoughtful, and practical; her grandfather Schwarz indulgent. In this secure and kindly environment Lillian Wald grew up loving music and books, confident of her own abilities, trusting the goodness of human nature, and prepared to enjoy life.

She attended Miss Cruttenden's English–French Boarding and Day School in Rochester and at sixteen applied for admission to Vassar College, but was refused on the ground that she was too young. According to her own account, she had "the advantages of what might be called a good education, knowing Latin, and able to speak both French and German." She had the additional assets of health and beauty, and for several years she enjoyed an active social life. In 1889, at twenty-one, she wrote: "My life hitherto has been—I presume—a type of modern American young womanhood, days devoted to society, study and housekeeping duties. . . . This does not satisfy me now. I feel the need of serious, definite work." The activity she chose was nursing. In August 1889 she entered the New York Hospital training school for nurses. After graduating in 1891, she spent an unhappy year as a nurse at the New York Juvenile Asylum and then, to supplement what she felt had been inadequate training, enrolled in the Woman's Medical College in New York. Early in 1893, while attending medical school, she accepted an invitation to organize home nursing classes for immigrant families on the Lower East Side.

One morning that March she was called from her classroom to tend a sick woman in a crumbling tenement house. This experience, Lillian Wald's baptism of fire, impelled her to leave medical school and take up what proved to be a lifework as a public health nurse. With a friend, Mary Brewster, she moved to the East Side, at first to temporary quarters at the College Settlement and then, in September, to the top floor of a tenement house on Jefferson Street. The two young women resolved "to live in the neighborhood as nurses, identify ourselves with it socially, and . . . contribute to it our citizenship." Mrs. Solomon Loeb and her son-in-law, the banker and philanthropist Jacob H. Schiff, provided financial backing. The tenement apartment soon proved too small, and in 1895, through Schiff's generosity, Miss Wald was able to establish the "Nurses' Settlement" in a permanent home at 265 Henry Street. Soon eleven residents were living at the new house, nine of them trained nurses, including Lavinia L. Dock (d. 1956), later a leader in the nursing profession. By 1913 the Henry Street Visiting Nurses Service comprised ninety-two nurses, organized into specialized staffs, who were making 200,000 visits annually from the East Side headquarters and from branches in upper Manhattan and the Bronx. In addition to home care, they maintained first aid stations and convalescent facilities and made follow-up calls on patients released from hospitals.

The Henry Street idea spread rapidly, similar programs were set up across the country, and a new profession, public health nursing, was born. At its heart lay Miss Wald's conviction that many persons not ill enough to require hospitalization, but whose circumstances were such that they might otherwise receive no medical attention, were in need of home care. She had early determined that the service should be fully professional and independent of religious or official ties, and that fees should be charged "on terms most considerate of the dignity and independence of the patient." Many extensions of public health nursing were also pioneered by Miss Wald. In 1902 she offered a Henry Street nurse, Lina L. Rogers, for a month-long demonstration which induced the New York City Board of Health to establish the first public school nursing program in the United States. At her suggestion a nursing program for industrial policyholders was begun by the Metropolitan Life Insurance Company. She was a prime mover in the establishment, in 1910, of a department of nursing and health at Teachers College of Columbia University, under the chairmanship of MARY ADELAIDE

NUTTING. Two years later the American Red Cross, again at her initiative, set up a program which grew into the Town and Country Nursing Service. Recognized as the founder and leading spirit in the movement, Miss Wald was in 1912 chosen the first president of the National Organization for Public Health Nursing, a professional association in whose creation she played a leading part.

Lillian Wald's influence was felt in the social settlement movement no less than in nursing. She had moved to the East Side in 1893 without knowing of JANE ADDAMS' pioneering work in Chicago, but Henry Street very quickly outgrew its exclusively medical orientation to take on the attributes of a full-scale settlement house. Indeed, as early as the depression winter of 1893–94, when she served on a committee organized by JOSEPHINE SHAW LOWELL, founder of New York's Charity Organization Society, to provide work relief for the unemployed, Miss Wald had learned that to help the urban poor, with their complex social, economic, and physical needs, required planning and organization no less than a loving heart. Soon the Nurses' Settlement had become the Henry Street Settlement, a neighborhood center for civic, educational, social, and philanthropic work. By 1913 it occupied seven houses on Henry Street and two uptown branches. The unique combination of nursing and general settlement activities assured a close integration into neighborhood life and made Henry Street a powerful force for community betterment and reform. Special attention was given to vocational guidance and training, and a system of scholarships permitting talented boys and girls to remain in school until sixteen was set up. Miss Wald took a leading role in civic campaigns to eradicate tuberculosis, improve housing, and establish more parks and playgrounds. She supported and encouraged the pioneering work of Elizabeth Farrell, a Henry Street resident, in the development of ungraded public school classes for retarded children.

Miss Wald, who never married, was particularly touched by the needs of children, and moved to the forefront of the child welfare movement. In 1904 she, together with FLORENCE KELLEY (director of the National Consumers' League and a Henry Street resident from 1899 to 1924) and others, founded the National Child Labor Committee, an outgrowth of a similar state committee established two years earlier. For many years, as a member of both the state and national committees, she worked for legislation outlawing child labor. A suggestion first made by Miss Wald to President Theodore Roosevelt in 1905 bore fruit seven years later in the establishment of the federal Children's Bureau, with JULIA LATHROP as its chief. "It was an awakening for me to realize that when I was working in the interests of those babies . . . I was really in politics," Miss Wald later recalled (Duffus, pp. 81–82).

Despite a growing involvement in public affairs, she held fast to her purpose of closely identifying herself with those among whom she lived. Characteristically, the twentieth anniversary celebration of Henry Street Settlement featured a pageant honoring past and present inhabitants of the street. To Jacob Riis it symbolized the rebirth of "the whole crowded, suffering, once-forgotten East Side." Miss Wald genuinely loved her neighborhood, and was enthusiastic over "the really lovely things that go on down here." Fortunately—since Henry Street was dependent entirely on voluntary contributions and, even after a successful endowment campaign in 1913, was always in need of money—she was able to communicate this enthusiasm, and hence was a gifted fund raiser. "It costs five thousand dollars to sit next to her at dinner," one friend observed. Her winning appearance also aided these efforts. A newspaper reporter once described her as tall and well-proportioned with an "oval face crowned by dark wavy hair simply parted over a smooth, broad brow; eyes so large and brown and soft that they seem to look at you almost timidly" (quoted in *ibid.*, p. 89).

At the outbreak of the First World War, Miss Wald was forty-seven years old. Like many social workers, she looked upon war as a "hideous wrong," a complete negation of her ideals of social progress and human brotherhood. For a time she hoped that neutral nations might end the conflict by mediation, and as president of the American Union against Militarism, which with Jane Addams, Florence Kelley, and others she had helped to organize in 1914, she sought by letter and petition to win the Wilson administration to this view. When the United States entered the conflict, Miss Wald turned her attention to wartime encroachments on civil liberties. She also served as head of the committee on home nursing of the Council of National Defense, while her Henry Street nurses, whose roster more than doubled between 1913 and 1918, rendered invaluable service in caring for sick children and victims of pneumonia and influenza. As chairman of the Nurses' Emergency Council during the influenza epidemic of 1918, Miss Wald directed recruitment of volunteer nurses and coordinated the efforts of public and private nursing agencies. She had never worked

harder and, as she wrote to a friend, she had never felt better.

After the war Miss Wald was a founder of the League of Free Nations Association, an outgrowth of the American Union against Militarism and forerunner of the Foreign Policy Association. Henry Street remained her major interest, however, as its program expanded to serve a changing East Side. A Neighborhood Playhouse, given by Alice and IRENE LEWISOHN in 1915, became in the 1920's a leading experimental theatre, while a music school, incorporated in 1927, rounded out the settlement's cultural activities. The Visiting Nurses Service grew apace, and by 1929 over 250 nurses were taking part. On the national level, Miss Wald continued, despite the less favorable postwar climate, to work for child welfare legislation. Her personal political preferences were determined by her social concerns. At times the decision was perplexing. In 1912 she deplored Woodrow Wilson's temporizing on woman suffrage but at length supported the Democratic ticket as offering the best prospects for reform. In 1928 she backed Alfred E. Smith, feeling that his sympathetic interest in social welfare outweighed his hostility to prohibition, which she firmly favored. She experienced no such turmoil over the candidacies of Franklin D. Roosevelt, however. She had close ties with Mrs. Roosevelt and Frances Perkins, and Adolf A. Berle, Jr., Henry W. Morgenthau, Jr., Sidney Hillman, and other New Dealers were former residents of Henry Street Settlement. In 1936 she was co-chairman of the Good Neighbor League, which rallied independent voters for the Democratic ticket. Warned that her political activity might alienate potential contributors to Henry Street, she replied: "I have been myself all these years and I have not seen that being myself injured or affected the settlement."

By this time her own day-to-day association with Henry Street had come to a close. In the mid-1920's her health had begun to break, and thereafter she was periodically incapacitated by anemia and heart trouble. Although travel had long been one of her few luxuries— she took a world tour in 1910, visited Russia in 1924 and Mexico in 1925 with Jane Addams, and made frequent trips to Europe—her journeys now grew less frequent. The stress of the depression placed heavy demands on her strength, and in 1933 she resigned as head worker at Henry Street Settlement, shortly after its fortieth anniversary, and retired to Westport, Conn. She had published an anecdotal autobiography, *The House on Henry Street,* in 1915; a sequel, *Windows on Henry*

*Street,* appeared in 1934. She died in Westport in 1940 after a long illness brought on by a cerebral hemorrhage. Her ashes were interred in the family plot in Rochester, N.Y.

Lillian Wald's most distinctive contribution lies in the field of public health nursing, yet her importance far transcended the limits of a single profession. Responding pragmatically to the problems around her, she made Henry Street Settlement the cradle and catalyst of many apparently simple ideas of far-reaching significance. Belonging to a generation that produced many eminent social workers, she ranks among the greatest. In contrast to some, including even her friend Florence Kelley, who could be abrasive on occasion, Miss Wald invariably maintained warm personal relations with her opponents. That she is remembered less well than her contemporary Jane Addams may perhaps be attributed to Miss Addams' ability to abstract from her experiences a broad philanthropic philosophy, set forth in a series of books which, taken together, constitute a major rationalization and summation of the social reform and settlement movements. For those, however, who passed within Lillian Wald's personal orbit, her realistic understanding of the complexity of individual and community life, combined with her ebullience, optimism, and unselfconscious tolerance, gave her an influence at least as great at that of the more introspective founder of Hull House. As Lavinia Dock has written: "People just naturally turned their best natures to her scrutiny and developed what she perceived in them, when it had been dormant and unseen . . . before" (*ibid.,* p. 347). She brought kindness, vision, ability, and initiative to her work, making it not a battle but a joyous experience.

[Lillian Wald's papers are in the N.Y. Public Library and at Columbia Univ.; her letters and reports to Jacob H. Schiff are in the Schiff papers in the Am. Jewish Archives, Cincinnati. The best biography is R. L. Duffus, *Lillian Wald, Neighbor and Crusader* (1938). See also Miss Wald's *The House on Henry Street* and *Windows on Henry Street;* Helena Huntington Smith's profile in the *New Yorker,* Dec. 14, 1929; George W. Alger's reminiscences of Miss Wald in *Survey Graphic,* Oct. 1940; obituaries in the *N.Y. Times* and *Herald Tribune,* Sept. 2, 1940, and account of memorial service in the *Times,* Dec. 2, 1940. Her early conception of public health nursing was set forth in two articles in the *Am. Jour. of Nursing,* Oct. 1900 and May 1902; her foreword to Marguerite Wales, *The Public Health Nurse in Action* (1941), states her mature views on the subject. A valuable account of the Henry Street Settlement appeared in *Charities and the Commons,* Apr. 7, 1906. Yssabella Waters, *Visiting Nursing in the U.S.* (1909), M. Adelaide Nutting and Lavinia Dock, *A Hist. of Nursing,* vol. III (1912), and Mary M. Roberts, *Am. Nursing* (1955), examine Miss Wald's contributions to nursing. Her work as a settlement leader is touched upon in Robert A. Woods and Albert J. Kennedy, *The Settlement Horizon: A National Estimate* (1922); and their *Handbook of Settlements* (1911) contains a useful bibliography of articles pertaining to Henry Street. See the N.Y. *Times,* Mar. 11, 1937, for seventieth birthday tributes and Miss Wald's moving response. Her career is well evaluated in the *Social Service Rev.,* Dec. 1940, and *Am. Jour. of Public Health,* Nov. 1940.]

ROBERT H. BREMNER

**WALKER, Madame C. J.** *See* WALKER, Sarah Breedlove.

**WALKER, Edyth** (Mar. 27, 1867–Feb. 19, 1950), opera singer and teacher, was born in Hopewell, N.Y., between Geneva and Canandaigua, the third daughter and youngest of six children of Marquis de Lafayette Walker and Mary (Purdy) Walker. She was christened Minnie Edith, which she later changed to Mary Edyth. Her father, a carpenter and later a landscape gardener, was a native of Canandaigua, her mother of Westmoreland, N.Y., near Rome. The family early moved to Geneva and, when Edyth was about twelve, to Rome. There she graduated from the Rome Free Academy in 1884. For several years she taught school in Rome. She had, however, strong musical leanings, although her family gave her little encouragement to pursue them; as early as the age of fourteen she had reportedly been contralto soloist in a Hopewell church. The gift of $1,000 from a Rome physician who had heard her sing enabled her to go to Germany in 1889 to study at the Dresden Conservatory with Anna Aglaia Orgeni, a prominent Hungarian-born coloratura soprano. She continued at the conservatory for several years, augmenting her funds by giving lessons in singing and in English. She received further support from the wealthy New Yorker William K. Vanderbilt, to whom she appealed for a loan while he was in Vienna, enclosing credentials from Mme. Orgeni. Vanderbilt, it is said, sent her $1,000 with the word that the only return he wanted was to hear her sing when she had become successful.

Miss Walker's first European appearance was in a concert at the famous Gewandhaus in Leipzig. Her opera debut followed on Nov. 11, 1894, at the Royal Opera in Berlin as Fidès in *Le Prophète.* After a year in Berlin she went to the Imperial Opera in Vienna, where from 1898 to 1903 she was the leading mezzo-soprano of the Vienna Opera, singing all the principal roles of its repertoire under Gustav Mahler's conductorship and making guest appearances also in other Central European opera houses. Her performance of a leading role in the Austrian premiere of Wilhelm Kienzl's *Der Evangelimann* on Jan. 11, 1896, it is said, greatly impressed Emperor Francis Joseph, who bestowed upon her the rank of Kammersängerin. Her career with the Vienna Opera ended in 1903 when she broke her contract after a violent dispute with Mahler. She then accepted an engagement with the Metropolitan Opera in New York.

Edyth Walker made her Metropolitan debut on Nov. 30, 1903, as Amneris in *Aïda*, with Enrico Caruso as Radames. Henry E. Krehbiel's review for the *New-York Tribune* described her as "comely, familiar with the conventions of stage deportment, and the possessor of a voice of lovely quality, though not of great volume"; Krehbiel also found decided charm in her singing. One of her memorable achievements while at the Metropolitan was her singing of Leonora in *La Favorita* on Nov. 29, 1905. Other roles which she sang during her three years in New York included Fidès in *Le Prophète*, Azucena in *Il Trovatore*, Siebel in *Faust*, Nancy in *Martha*, La Cieca in *La Gioconda*, the Page in *Les Huguenots*, Orlofsky in *Die Fledermaus*, and, in the Wagnerian repertoire, Ortrud, Brangäne, Fricka, and the Brünnhilde of *Die Walküre*. She left the Metropolitan in 1906, according to one report because she wished to sing soprano roles exclusively. She made no further public appearances in America; a contract signed with the Chicago Opera in 1914 was canceled owing to the outbreak of World War I.

Returning to Europe, Miss Walker was for several years a member of the Hamburg and Berlin operas, appearing in both soprano and mezzo-soprano roles. In 1908 she sang Kundry in *Parsifal* at the Wagner Festival at Bayreuth. At Covent Garden in London she sang Isolde in May 1908 and, in February 1910, headed the cast of the English premiere of Richard Strauss' *Elektra*. From 1912 to 1917 she appeared with the Munich Opera; in the latter year she quietly decided to retire.

After living for some years at Scheveningen in Holland, Edyth Walker went to Paris, where she taught at the American Conservatory in Fontainebleau from 1933 to 1936. She then returned to New York City and spent her remaining years in teaching. Among her pupils were Blanche Thebom and Irene Dalis, who both became leading singers at the Metropolitan. One of her students has described her as

possessing a vibrant, dominating personality which, along with her talents, musicianship, and confidence, was a great source of inspiration. Besides her singing, she was, in private life, an expert cellist. Never marrying, she lived for her art and never sought extraneous publicity. She died in her New York City apartment at the age of eighty-two, four weeks after a heart attack. A Christian Scientist in religion, she left her principal estate to that church. Known especially for her Wagnerian roles, Edyth Walker was one of the earliest Americans to achieve an operatic success in Germany.

[Oscar Thompson, *The Am. Singer* (1937); obituaries in *N.Y. Herald Tribune* and *N.Y. Times;* music reviews in *N.-Y. Tribune;* Gustav Kobbé, *Complete Opera Book* (rev. ed., 1954); William H. Seltsam, *Metropolitan Opera Annals* (1947); Harold Rosenthal, *Two Centuries of Opera at Covent Garden* (1958); Anthony Wright, "Am. Artists at Covent Garden," *Opera News*, Mar. 30, 1953; death record from N.Y. City Dept. of Health. Information about Miss Walker's family background and early life was supplied by Miss Kathleen Dowling, Jervis Library, Rome, N.Y., and Mr. Harold C. Walker of Rome. The writer is also indebted to Irene Dalis for information and personal reminiscences.]

FRANCIS D. PERKINS

**WALKER, Maggie Lena** (July 15, 1867–Dec. 15, 1934), Negro insurance and banking executive, was born and spent her entire life in Richmond, Va. Her mother, Elizabeth Draper, formerly a kitchen slave, was assistant cook in the household of ELIZABETH VAN LEW, a wealthy Richmond spinster and Union sympathizer; her father, according to family tradition, was a Northern abolitionist author, Ecles Cuthbert. Elizabeth Draper later married William Mitchell, a butler in the Van Lew household, by whom she had a son, John. Mitchell became headwaiter at the St. Charles Hotel, but his early death left his widow the task of rearing two young children. Living in a small cottage, she took in laundry while Maggie delivered the clothes, did the marketing, and cared for her brother.

Maggie's school career began at the public Lancaster School. The teachers, two Southern white women whose families had been impoverished by the Civil War, took great interest in their pupils, and Maggie developed rapidly. Joining the First African Baptist Church at eleven, she began teaching Sunday school during her adolescence. After graduating from Richmond's Armstrong Normal School in 1883, she taught for three years at the Lancaster School. While teaching she became an agent for the Woman's Union, an insurance company, and took business courses in accounting and salesmanship. On Sept. 14, 1886, she was married to Armstead Walker, Jr., a building contractor several years her senior. They had three children: Russell Ecles Talmage, a second son who died in infancy, and Melvin DeWitt.

Mrs. Walker was meanwhile becoming increasingly active in what was to be her life's work. As a girl she had joined the Grand United Order of St. Luke, a Negro fraternal society and cooperative insurance venture founded in Baltimore in 1867 by an ex-slave, Miss Mary Prout, to assure sick care and a proper burial to members. Elected to a minor office at the age of seventeen, Maggie Mitchell received a series of promotions and in May 1899 became executive secretary-treasurer of the renamed Independent Order of St. Luke, with headquarters in Richmond. This was the era when American Negroes, segregated from the mainstream of society, were rallying to the creed of self-help and racial solidarity espoused by Booker T. Washington and others. The times were thus favorable, and under the impetus of its new leader's vision, drive, and managerial ability, the order quickly moved from near-bankruptcy into a period of rapid growth, doubling its membership within the first year. In twenty-five years the organization grew from 57 local chapters to 1,500, from some 3,400 members to over 50,000, from an indebtedness of some $400 to assets of nearly $400,000, and from a single clerk working in antiquated quarters to a staff of fifty in a modern four-story office building.

In 1902 Mrs. Walker began publishing the *St. Luke Herald,* a news sheet which reported on the order's affairs, published inspirational sketches of members, and tirelessly preached the gospel of thrift. At her initiative, in 1903 the order established the St. Luke Penny Savings Bank with herself as president. This stable and successful financial institution absorbed the other Negro banks of Richmond in 1929–30 to become the Consolidated Bank and Trust Company. Mrs. Walker relinquished the presidency at this time, but served as chairman of the board of directors until her death. Her only misconceived venture was the St. Luke Emporium, a short-lived Richmond department store founded in the early 1900's.

A large, olive-skinned woman with a round, kindly face and an unassuming manner, Maggie Walker was a respected and beloved figure in Richmond. In 1924 she was honored by the Order of St. Luke with a great twenty-fifth anniversary gathering at the City Auditorium. Possessing a social conscience as well as business ability, she was careful to nurture the religious and fraternal aspects of the organization. Local chapters were based in the churches, a juvenile department taught habits of thrift and hygiene to children, and at the Richmond headquarters the working day invariably began with devotions. As founder (1912) and president of the Richmond Council of Colored Women, Mrs. Walker led this group in raising thousands of dollars to assist the Virginia Industrial School for Colored Girls founded by JANIE PORTER BARRETT, the Negro tuberculosis sanatorium at Burkeville, and a Negro community center and visiting-nurse program in Richmond. She served also on the boards of numerous civic and educational institutions.

These years of business success and philanthropic effort were not without personal sorrow. In 1915 her son Russell accidentally killed his father, and the deaths of her mother and of Russell himself in 1922 and 1923 further reduced the family circle. Having suffered an incapacitating fall in 1907, Maggie Lena Walker was ultimately reduced to a state of paraplegia which necessitated the use of an elevator in her home, a wheelchair in her office, and a chauffeur-driven automobile. She died in her sixty-eighth year, of diabetic gangrene, and after funeral services at the First African Baptist Church was buried in Evergreen Cemetery, Richmond. The Virginia Union University of Richmond had awarded her an honorary degree in 1925, and in her native city a street, a theatre, and a high school bear her name. Her successor as executive secretary-treasurer of the Independent Order of St. Luke, Hattie N. F. Walker, the widow of her elder son, inherited a strong organization with chapters in fourteen states, a fully owned home office, and a record of over $3,000,000 in paid claims —and this notwithstanding the fact that changed economic and social conditions had by the 1930's considerably reduced the role of small-scale fraternal insurance cooperatives like the one to whose success Maggie Walker had contributed so largely.

[Wendell P. Dabney, *Maggie L. Walker and the I. O. of St. Luke* (1927); Sadie I. Daniel, *Women Builders* (1931), pp. 28–52; Mary White Ovington, *Portraits in Color* (1927), pp. 127–34; Benjamin G. Brawley, *Negro Builders and Heroes* (1937), pp. 267–72; Lily H. Hammond, *In the Vanguard of a Race* (1922), pp. 108–18; *Who's Who in Colored America,* 1928–29; August Meier, *Negro Thought in America* (1963), chap. viii; *Norfolk* (Va.) *Jour. and Guide,* Dec. 29, 1934; death record from Va. Bureau of Vital Statistics; information from Mrs. Eloise W. Shelton, Richmond, Va.; Mrs. Hattie N. F. Walker, Richmond; and Dr. Maggie Laura Walker, Chicago.]

SADIE DANIEL ST. CLAIR

WALKER, Mary Edwards (Nov. 26, 1832–
Feb. 21, 1919), Civil War medical worker,
dress reformer, and eccentric, was born in
Oswego Town near Oswego, N.Y., the daughter of Vesta (Whitcomb) Walker, a cousin of
the agnostic lecturer Robert G. Ingersoll, and
Alvah Walker, farmer, Methodist, self-taught
student of medicine, and, like his wife, a descendant of early New England settlers. Mary
had four older sisters (including Luna and
Aurora Borealis) and a younger brother. After
studying in the local common school, she attended Falley Seminary, Fulton, N.Y., for two
winter terms (1850–52) and, after teaching
briefly, entered Syracuse Medical College in
December 1853. Graduating in 1855, she practiced for a few months in Columbus, Ohio, and
then returned to Rome, N.Y. Small and slender,
assertive but not unattractive, she was married
in November to Albert Miller of Rome, a fellow
medical student. Though she never adopted his
name, the two practiced medicine together in
Rome for several years.

As a girl Mary Walker had scorned confining female clothing, and when the "bloomer"
vogue flourished briefly in the early 1850's
(see AMELIA JENKS BLOOMER) she adopted the
new costume with alacrity. In January 1857
she joined LYDIA SAYER HASBROUCK of Middletown, N.Y., and others in a dress reform convention and began contributing regularly to
Mrs. Hasbrouck's reformist periodical, the
Sibyl. In 1859 occurred a painful separation
from her husband, occasioned by his unfaith-
fulness and possibly by conjugal incompatibility. She unsuccessfully sought a divorce in
Iowa the following year; eventually, in 1869,
she won a New York decree. During the Iowa
interlude she briefly attended the Bowen Collegiate Institute in Hopkinton, but was suspended when she refused to resign from the
hitherto all-male debating society.

When the Civil War broke out, Mary Walker
journeyed to Washington and, while vainly
seeking appointment as an army surgeon,
served as an unpaid volunteer in the Patent
Office Hospital and helped organize the Wom-
en's Relief Association, to aid women visiting
relatives stationed in the capital. She continued
her work in 1862, with time off for visits to
Oswego and to New York City, where she
stayed long enough to earn a degree from the
New York Hygeio-Therapeutic College. That
autumn she ventured into the Virginia battle
zone and, though still without official standing,
rendered assistance at tent hospitals in War-
renton and Fredericksburg. In September 1863
she went to Tennessee and at last won appointment as an assistant surgeon from Gen.

George H. Thomas, despite sharp protests from
the medical director of the Army of the Cumberland and from the men of the 52nd Ohio
Regiment, encamped near Gordon's Mills,
Tenn., to which she was assigned. She wore
the same uniform as that of her fellow officers.
She often passed through Confederate lines
to minister to the medical needs of the civilian
populace, and while on such a foray in April
1864 she was captured and transported to
Richmond, where she was imprisoned for several months. In August she was freed in a
prisoner exchange and returned to Washington. Given a contract as an "acting assistant
surgeon" later that year, she rendered brief
service as supervisor of a hospital for women
prisoners in Louisville, Ky., and then as head
of an orphanage in Clarksville, Tenn. Her imperious ways and tactlessness, however, antagonized both her subordinates and the local
citizenry; early in 1865 she was ordered to
Washington and shortly thereafter she left the
government's service. Later in the year she
received the Congressional Medal of Honor
for Meritorious Service, a recognition then
rather freely bestowed.

As a Civil War celebrity Dr. Walker enjoyed
a brief fame in the immediate postwar years.
In 1866 the dwindling adherents of the National Dress Reform Association elected her
president, and in the same year she met with
some success on an English lecture tour. Returning to the United States in 1867, she lived
for a few years with a young Washington
teacher and would-be attorney, BELVA LOCK-
WOOD, and for a time the two women jointly
promoted various feminist causes, particularly
woman suffrage. Mary Walker was active in
the Central Women's Suffrage Bureau of Washington and made occasional appearances at
Congressional hearings. In 1869, on a lecture
tour of the Midwest, she participated in a Cincinnati suffrage convention attended by LUCY
STONE and SUSAN B. ANTHONY, and in 1872 she
made an unsuccessful effort to vote in Oswego
Town. She rapidly alienated the suffragists,
however, because of her growing eccentricity
and because, having persuaded herself that
women already possessed the right to vote
under the federal Constitution, she rejected as
"trash" the proposed suffrage amendment.
Though the suffragists were quite ready to
publicize and magnify her war service to aid
the feminist cause, she herself became an increasingly unwelcome gadfly at suffrage gatherings. By 1907, when she set down her suffrage views in a pamphlet called Crowning
Constitutional Argument, she was virtually
without influence. Her medical proficiency was

often challenged, and she enjoyed no standing in that profession; apparently she did not practice after the war. Her unremitting efforts to secure a pension for her war duty were only partially successful. She also sought to return to government service and in 1882 was given a job in the mail room of the Pension Office. She was dismissed the following year, however, for alleged insubordination.

Only dress reform remained, but this turned into eccentricity when she adopted as her regular garb not only trousers but a masculine jacket, shirt, stiff wing collar, bow tie, and top hat. Cut off even from those sympathetic to this reform, she became increasingly an object of ridicule. She had earlier turned to writing and had produced *Hit* (1871), a rambling autobiographical and speculative work, and *Unmasked, or the Science of Immorality* (1878), which with its extended discussion of various sexual matters, including a chapter on "hermaphrodites," perhaps provides a clue to her own confused and unhappy personality. In 1887 she made the first of several Midwestern tours in a dime museum sideshow. She spent most of her time after 1890 in Oswego Town, where the family farm had come into her hands. Here she was thought a harmless eccentric, though her behavior at times was less than benign, as in 1891 when she undertook an elaborate campaign to implicate her hired man in a New Hampshire murder, apparently in an effort to collect the $5,000 reward.

Old age brought no tranquillity. She was forever involved in litigation with relatives and tenants, and a vague plan to turn her farm into a training school for young ladies came to nothing. In 1917 the federal Board of Medal Awards, as part of a general review, declared that her Civil War citation had been unwarranted and officially withdrew it. She continued to wear her Medal of Honor, however, representing as it did a fading period when her life had held some dignity and meaning. In the same year came a final heady burst of publicity when she sent a long telegram to Kaiser Wilhelm offering her Oswego farm as a peace conference site. Now alone and poverty-stricken, she was largely ignored even by her relatives. A fall from the Capitol steps in Washington in 1917 hastened her death two years later, at eighty-six, in the home of a neighbor. Following simple ceremonies she was buried in her black frock suit in the family plot in the Oswego Town rural cemetery.

[The basic source is Charles McCool Snyder, *Dr. Mary Walker: The Little Lady in Pants* (1962), which draws upon unpublished material in Oswego and elsewhere. On her suffrage views see House Judiciary Committee, *Hearings,* No. 1, "Woman Suffrage," by Dr. Mary E. Walker, 62 Cong., 2 Sess. (1912). For a good example of the feminist glorification of her wartime career see the sketch in Frances E. Willard and Mary A. Livermore, eds., *A Woman of the Century* (1893). Also see articles on her in *Medical Woman's Jour.,* Oct. 1946, and *Phila. Medicine,* Mar. 18, 1944.]

LOUIS FILLER

**WALKER, Sarah Breedlove** (Dec. 23, 1867– May 25, 1919), pioneer Negro businesswoman and millionaire, better known as Madame C. J. Walker, was born near Delta in northeast Louisiana, the daughter of farmers, Owen and Minerva Breedlove. Orphaned in early childhood, she became dependent upon her married sister. At the age of fourteen, and now living in Vicksburg, Miss., she was married to a Mr. McWilliams and bore a daughter, A'Lelia. Six years later she was widowed and moved to St. Louis, where for eighteen years she supported herself and her daughter by working as a washerwoman.

In 1905 she hit upon—or, as she told it, dreamed—the formula for a preparation to improve the appearance of the hair of Negro women. Mixing her soaps and ointments in washtubs and kitchen utensils, and adapting and modifying hairdressing techniques already in existence, she arrived at what was to become known as "The Walker Method," or "The Walker System." Its elements were a shampoo, a pomade "hair-grower," vigorous brushing, and the application of heated iron combs to the hair. The "method" transformed stubborn, lusterless hair into shining smoothness. Encouraged by the St. Louis success of her products and method, she moved by 1906 to Denver, Colo., where her brother had already gone; there she was married to Charles J. Walker, a newspaperman. Proceeding from door to door, she demonstrated her method. She rapidly gained not only clients but also agent-operators; she called them "hair culturists," "scalp specialists," and "beauty culturists" as against "hair-straighteners," a term used by others. She herself concentrated on instruction in her methods and on manufacture of her products. After about a year she established a business and manufacturing headquarters in Denver and traveled extensively through the South and East, giving lecture-demonstrations in Negro homes, clubs, and churches. So successful were these that in 1908 she organized a second office in Pittsburgh, which her daughter, A'Lelia, managed. In 1910 Madame Walker transferred both offices to Indianapolis, building a plant there to serve as the center of the Walker enterprises.

The Madame C. J. Walker Manufacturing Company, of which she was president and sole owner, came to provide employment for some three thousand persons. Her principal employees were the women who, in the years that preceded the great national growth of beauty shops in the United States, carried her treatments to the home. Known as "Walker Agents," they became familiar figures throughout the United States and the Caribbean as they made their "house calls," dressed in characteristic white shirtwaists tucked into long black skirts and carrying the black satchels containing the preparations and apparatus necessary for dressing hair. The most important of the preparations was Madame C. J. Walker's Hair Grower. Sales of this pomade and of some sixteen other products, many packaged in tin containers whose covers bore her portrait, together with extensive advertising (mainly in Negro newspapers and magazines) and her own frequent instructional tours, made Madame Walker one of the best-known Negroes in the country. Her fame also spread to Europe, where, in the 1920's, the Walker System coiffure of the Negro dancer Josephine Baker so fascinated Parisians that a French company produced a comparable pomade and called it "Baker-Fix." In the United States, Madame Walker's activities were emulated by other Negro women, the most successful of whom were Mrs. Annie M. Turnbo Malone, with her "Poro System" and her "Poro Colleges" in St. Louis and Chicago, and Madame Sarah Spencer Washington, with her "Apex System" centered in Atlantic City. One editorialist commented in 1919 that it was a "noteworthy fact that the largest and most lucrative business enterprises conducted by colored people in America have been launched by women—namely Madame Walker and Mrs. Malone."

Madame Walker's philanthropies included sizable contributions to the programs of the National Association for the Advancement of Colored People, to homes for the aged in St. Louis and Indianapolis, to the Young Men's Christian Association of Indianapolis, and to the needy of Indianapolis, especially at Christmas. She maintained scholarships for young women at Tuskegee Institute and contributed to Palmer Memorial Institute, a private secondary school for Negroes at Sedalia, N.C., founded by her friend Charlotte Hawkins Brown. Even her business took on something of a note of uplift. Beginning in 1913 she organized her agents into "Walker Clubs," and she gave cash prizes to the clubs that did the largest amount of community philanthropic work. She required her agents to sign contracts specifying not only the exclusive use of her company's products and methods, but binding them also to a hygienic regimen which anticipated the practices later incorporated into state cosmetology laws. In frequent visits and communications to her agents she preached "cleanliness and loveliness" as assets and as aids to self-respect and racial advance. An editorial of 1919 in *Crisis*, the magazine of the National Association for the Advancement of Colored People, judged that in her lifetime Madame Walker "revolutionized the personal habits and appearance of millions of human beings."

Madame Walker's own personal life was revolutionized by the success of her endeavors. Her material possessions reached a value of a million dollars and came to include extensive real estate holdings. In 1914 she moved to New York City and built a town house at 108–110 West 136th Street. Here, in the years after her death, her daughter, now Mrs. A'Lelia Walker Robinson Wilson Kennedy, was to preside over a salon known as "The Dark Tower" where talented Negro authors, musicians, and artists met influential white intellectuals, particularly publishers, critics, and potential patrons, thus helping to stimulate the "Harlem Renaissance" in the arts during the 1920's. In 1917 Madame Walker built Villa Lewaro, an Italianate country home designed by the Negro architect Vertner Tandy, at Irvington-on-Hudson, N.Y. The villa, which cost about $250,000, was named by the noted tenor Enrico Caruso, who combined the initial syllables of A'Lelia Walker Robinson's name.

Warned by physicians at the Kellogg Clinic at Battle Creek, Mich., that her hypertension required a reduction of her activities, Madame Walker nevertheless continued her busy schedule. She became ill while in St. Louis and was removed to New York, where she died of chronic interstitial nephritis at Villa Lewaro in 1919. Funeral services were conducted at the villa by the pastor of her church, the Mother Zion African Methodist Episcopal Zion Church of New York, and she was buried at Woodlawn Cemetery in the Bronx. The bulk of her million-dollar estate, including the ownership of the Walker enterprise, was left to her daughter. A trust fund provided for the establishment of an industrial and mission school in Africa, and bequests were made to Negro orphans and old folks' homes, to Young Women's Christian Association branches, and to private secondary and collegiate institutions.

[Materials on Madame Walker's life are often fragmentary bits which require careful testing and which sometimes crumble when tested. Especially helpful, therefore, were an interview in Indianapolis with Robert Lee Brockenburr, attorney and counselor to Madame Walker, and his article in the *Southern Workman*, Feb. 1918. Sari Price Patton, social secretary to A'Lelia Walker, furnished helpful information in an interview. Many other persons who had seen and heard Madame Walker and who had known various Walker Agents also provided information. Except for a few inaccuracies, the short biographical sketches in *The Nat. Cyc. of the Colored Race* (1919), pp. 263–65, and *Who's Who of the Colored Race* (1915), and the longer, more journalistic "Life Story of Madame C. J. Walker," serialized in the *Pittsburgh Courier*, Mar 8, 15, 22, 1952, were of help. *Louisiana: A Guide to the State* (1941) was helpful in locating Madame Walker's birthplace. Long obituaries appeared on May 26, 1919, in the *N.Y. Times*, the *N.Y. Sun*, the *Indianapolis News*, and the *St. Louis Post-Dispatch;* on May 27, 1919, in the *St. Louis Republic;* and in the *N.Y. Age*, May 31, June 7, 14, 1919. J. L. Nichols and William H. Crogman, *Progress of a Race* (1920), provided a few unique details on pp. 202, 442–44, as did George Schuyler in the *Messenger*, Aug. 1924, pp. 251–66. Claude McKay gives three perceptive pages (pp. 97–99) in *Harlem: Negro Metropolis* (1940) to a discussion of Madame Walker's impact; see also Roi Ottley's *New World A-Coming* (1943), pp. 170–73, and his *Black Odyssey: The Story of the Negro in America* (1948), pp. 241–43, 256. The editorials in the *Crisis*, July 1919, and in the *African Methodist Episcopal Church Rev.*, July 1919, are excellent as contemporary judgments of Madame Walker's significance. *The Madame C. J. Walker Beauty Manual* (1928) contains a short "official" sketch which reports the date of her death erroneously. For photographs of Madame Walker, her homes, and her factories, see *Ebony*, Feb. 1956, and *N.Y. Times* magazine section, Sept. 2, 1917; for a description of Villa Lewaro see *N.Y. Times*, Nov. 29, 30, 1930. The Schomburg Collection of the N.Y. Public Library and the Moorland Collection at Howard Univ. were most helpful. Death record from N.Y. State Dept. of Health.]

WALTER FISHER

**WALLACE, Zerelda Gray Sanders** (Aug. 6, 1817–Mar. 19, 1901), temperance and suffrage leader, was born in Millersburg, Bourbon County, Ky., the eldest of the five daughters of John H. and Polly C. (Gray) Sanders, respectively of South Carolina and Virginia descent. In 1830 Sanders, a physician, moved his family to Indianapolis, Ind., where his practice flourished. Zerelda's formal education beyond grammar school was limited to two years in a Versailles, Ky., boarding school (1828–30), but she read widely and profited by conversations with her father, a man of catholic interests, and later by her husband's practice of reading aloud in the evenings. At nineteen, on Dec. 26, 1836, she was married to David Wallace, lieutenant governor of Indiana and a widower of thirty-

seven with three young sons. They had six children of their own, of whom three—Mary, Agnes, and David—survived childhood. When Wallace, an ardent Whig, was elected governor (1837–41) and then Congressman (1841–43), social as well as domestic duties fell to his young wife. After his death in 1859 she was forced for a time to take in boarders to make ends meet, but a rise in property values later gave her an assured income.

Though a prominent and respected citizen of Indianapolis, Mrs. Wallace evinced little interest in public life or reform causes prior to 1873. She was deeply religious, however—a charter member of the Indianapolis Christian Church (Campbellite)—and when in that year a wave of temperance enthusiasm swept the Midwest she felt a call to join the crusade against the saloon. In November 1874 she attended the convention at Cleveland where delegates from seventeen states organized the National Woman's Christian Temperance Union. One of the better-known women present, Mrs. Wallace was placed on two important committees, Resolutions and Plan-of-work. Back in Indiana she promptly organized the state W.C.T.U., serving as its president until 1877 and again from 1879 to 1883.

In 1875, when a temperance memorial she read before the Indiana legislature was ignored despite the signatures of ten thousand women, she concluded that the crusade against liquor would be severely handicapped so long as women remained voteless. At the national W.C.T.U. convention in Cincinnati that year she presented a resolution endorsing the principle that women as well as men should vote on prohibition questions; because of her personal prestige it was approved, although proponents of woman suffrage were at that time still a minority within the W.C.T.U. In 1878 she joined with MAY WRIGHT SEWALL to organize the Indianapolis Equal Suffrage Society and became its first president. Though already affiliated with a state suffrage society which had been formed in 1869 by supporters of LUCY STONE's American Woman Suffrage Association, Mrs. Wallace was a founder in 1887 of the Indiana Woman Suffrage Association, a group loyal to the National Woman Suffrage Association of SUSAN B. ANTHONY, and was for three years its vice-president-at-large, under her co-worker HELEN MAR GOUGAR. Little interested in suffrage for its own sake, viewing it rather as "the most potent means for all moral and social reforms" (*History of Woman Suffrage*, III, 156), she was most at home as head, from 1883 to 1888, of the Franchise (or suffrage) Department of the national W.C.T.U. In 1881 she and Mrs. Gougar lobbied effectively in the Indiana legislature for both woman suffrage and prohibition amendments to the state constitution, but despite their exertions the amendments were never brought up for the requisite second vote. More successful was an 1886 campaign in Kansas for municipal suffrage in which the two women joined.

Zerelda Wallace's talents were inspirational rather than administrative, and it was as a temperance and suffrage lecturer that she became widely known in the 1880's. Her lectures, often two hours in length, were popular. "I never make a note before talking," she said, "but depend on circumstances to afford me a suggestion for my beginning" (*Indianapolis News,* Mar. 19, 1901). Though she was plain in appearance, her rugged features were said to suggest strength of purpose to her audiences. One of her last major appearances was before the International Council of Women in Washington in 1888, where she spoke, characteristically, on "The Moral Power of the Ballot." Despite a serious illness four years later, she continued to speak occasionally.

Mrs. Wallace gained some celebrity when her stepson Gen. Lew Wallace, author of the best-selling novel *Ben Hur* (1880), identified her as the original of the character of Ben Hur's mother, a highly appealing figure. Increasingly feeble after 1898, though mentally alert to the end, she spent her final years at the home of her daughter Agnes (Mrs. John H. Steiner) in Cataract, Owen County, Ind. She died there of a bronchial ailment in 1901, at the age of eighty-three. Funeral services at the Indianapolis Christian Church were followed by burial in Crown Hill Cemetery, Indianapolis, beside her husband.

[Ind. Women's Biog. Assoc., *Women of Ind.* (1941); extensive obituaries in *Indianapolis News,* Mar. 19, 1901, and *Indianapolis Jour.,* Mar. 20, 1901; *Lew Wallace: An Autobiog.* (2 vols., 1906); Elizabeth C. Stanton et al., *Hist. of Woman Suffrage,* vols. III–V (1886–1922); Frances E. Willard, *Woman and Temperance* (1883) and *Glimpses of Fifty Years* (1889); Frances E. Willard and Mary A. Livermore, eds., *A Woman of the Century* (1893); *Woman's Jour.,* Oct. 29, 1892; various Indiana histories, including Jacob P. Dunn, *Ind. and Indianans* (1919), II, 1059–60; information supplied by Miss Louise Wood, Ind. State Library.]

PAUL S. BOYER

**WALTER, Cornelia Wells** (June 7, 1813?–Jan. 31, 1898), early woman journalist, was born in Boston, Mass., the daughter of Lynde Walter, a merchant, and Ann (Minshull) Walter. On her father's side she was descended

from Thomas Walter, who came from Lancaster, England, in 1679 and whose son Nehemiah married Sarah, daughter of Increase Mather. Cornelia's grandfather the Rev. William Walter, a graduate of Harvard and an Anglican clergyman, emigrated to Nova Scotia during the Revolution as a loyalist but returned to Boston in 1792 to become rector of Christ Church. Her brother Lynde Minshull Walter, some fourteen years older than she, with whom she lived on Belknap (now Joy) Street, was the founder and first editor of the *Boston Transcript*. During his long illness Cornelia served as his secretary; on his death in 1842 Henry W. Dutton, senior proprietor of the paper, offered her the position her brother had held, at five hundred dollars a year. A sense of duty prompted acceptance.

Cornelia Walter conducted most of her work from her home, for, though a woman of unusual beauty, warmth, and dignity, she was by nature retiring. Endowed with a fine mind, a concise but flowing style, and a fearless pen, she improved the quality of the *Transcript* and won the praise of contemporaries who had been at first antagonistic toward the idea of a female editor. Her columns faithfully reflected the literary and social life of Boston. Emerson and Lowell proved too modern for her taste, but it was Edgar Allan Poe—that "wandering specimen of the Literary Snob"—who really roused her ire. He in turn satirically characterized "Miss Walter of the Transcript" as "that most beguiling of all little divinities." Though opposed to woman suffrage, she supported higher education for her sex. She was intensely religious and challenged the unorthodox doctrines of Theodore Parker, as well as Asa Gray's pronouncement that the earth had not been formed in six days. Less interested in politics, she was nevertheless firm in her convictions, taking a stand against the annexation of Texas and the Mexican War. In the presidential campaign of 1844 she supported Henry Clay against James Polk.

Marriage, however, brought her editorship to an end after five years. On Sept. 1, 1847, she resigned her post and on Sept. 22 was married to William Bordman Richards, a Boston dealer in iron and steel. Thereafter she devoted herself to her husband and children and to presiding as hostess over her Marlborough Street home, although she continued to contribute occasionally to the *Transcript*. In addition to her newspaper articles she published *Mount Auburn Illustrated* (1847), a history and description of the famous cemetery in nearby Cambridge.

Joseph Chamberlin in his account of the *Boston Transcript* credits her with five children.

A daughter, Annie, is known to have died at three, and a son, Walter, born in 1853, at six months; his twin brother, William Reuben, and another daughter, Elise Bordman, born in 1848, survived their parents. Cornelia Walter Richards' husband died in 1877. Living on for two more decades, she died at her Boston home in 1898 at the age of eighty-four, apparently from a cerebral hemorrhage. She was cremated, and in 1911 her remains were buried in Forest Hills Cemetery, Jamaica Plain, near Boston.

[Joseph E. Chamberlin, *The Boston Transcript* (1930), and Ishbel Ross, *Ladies of the Press* (1936), pp. 481–82, contain brief accounts of Cornelia Walter. For ancestry, see notice of her son William in *Fiftieth Anniversary Report* of the Harvard Class of 1874 and *Am. Ancestry*, VII (1892), 191–92, under William R. Richards. See also William A. Hovey, comp., *A Golden Anniversary: The Transcript's Fiftieth Birthday* (privately printed, 1880), p. 8, and obituary in *Boston Transcript*, Jan. 31, 1898. The latter gives her age at death as "nearly eighty-five"; her death certificate (in the office of the Mass. Registrar of Vital Statistics) also supports 1813 as her year of birth, though her gravestone has 1814.]

ELIZABETH F. HOXIE

**WALTON, Octavia.** See LE VERT, Octavia Walton.

**WALWORTH, Ellen Hardin** (Oct. 20, 1832– June 23, 1915), clubwoman and author, was born in the first brick house erected in Jacksonville, Ill., the eldest of the four children of John J. and Sarah Ellen (Smith) Hardin, recent settlers from Kentucky. Her grandfather Martin D. Hardin had been a prominent figure in Kentucky politics, serving for a time as United States Senator. Her father was a lawyer, a Whig member of Congress (1843–45), and an officer in the Mexican War; he was killed at the battle of Buena Vista in 1847. Ellen was educated at Jacksonville Academy and also read extensively in the classics of English literature and history which were available in the family library. When in 1851 her widowed mother married Reuben Hyde Walworth, the last chancellor of New York State, Ellen moved to his home, Pine Grove, in Saratoga Springs, N.Y. There a year later, on July 29, 1852, she was married to a stepbrother, Mansfield Tracy Walworth, a lawyer by training who became a prolific minor novelist. Though reared as a Presbyterian, Ellen became a Roman Catholic like many other members of the Walworth family, who had been converted by another of her stepbrothers, the Rev. Clarence Augustus Walworth, prominent Catholic priest and missionary.

During the first nine years of their marriage the couple lived at Pine Grove and had six children in rapid succession: Francis Hardin; John J. and Mary Elizabeth, both of whom died young; Ellen Hardin; Clara Teresa; and Mansfield Tracy. Two others were born later, Reubena Hyde and, lastly, Sarah Margaret, who died in childhood. Walworth, however, proved an unstable person of increasingly violent temper, frequently breaking furniture in his rages and even physically assaulting his wife. In 1861 she left him and went with her children to live on a farm near Louisville, Ky. For a time the two were reconciled, but in 1868, after another separation, she went to Washington and secured a government clerkship. Then, having lost her position, she tried living with her husband again, this time in New York City. But their quarrels resumed until, a few days after he had bruised her during her eighth pregnancy, she left him permanently in January 1871, returned to Saratoga, and in April secured what she referred to as a "limited divorce."

To support herself and the children Mrs. Walworth opened a girls' boarding school in the family homestead, which she operated for some fifteen years (converting it during the summers into a hotel) until ill health in the later 1880's caused her to return to the milder climate of Washington, where she again secured a government job. Meanwhile Walworth had begun bombarding her with abusive and threatening letters, many of which were intercepted by their elder son, Frank. Eventually these so disturbed the son that on June 3, 1873, he shot his father to death in a New York City hotel room. When after a sensational trial Frank was sentenced to life imprisonment, his mother devoted herself to securing his release, which she achieved in 1877 on the ground of insanity. As part of this campaign Mrs. Walworth took up the study of law.

Such an episode would have driven many women into permanent seclusion. Mrs. Walworth, however, as if pride or therapy dictated more rather than fewer public appearances, now engaged in an amazing number of activities. These revealed both the possibilities and perhaps also the limitations of what was available to well-bred, restless, intelligent women in the late nineteenth century. Joining numerous artistic, scientific, educational, historical, genealogical, and patriotic organizations, both local and national, often pioneering as the first woman member, she showed, in the words of a friend, "real vigor and aggression of character, though . . . never aggression in the manner of its pursuit." Some of these groups were of the sort usually considered appropriate for women going into club life. Thus in Saratoga she was president of the Shakespeare Club for a decade from the mid-1870's to mid-1880's and a founder and president of the Art and Science Field Club. She was a vice-president of the Society of Decorative Art in New York City and a vice-president of the Society of American Authors. She helped organize an exhibition for the Women's Pavilion at the Philadelphia Centennial Exposition. But scientific interests took her into the American Association for the Advancement of Science (especially its geological section) as early as 1876, when it was almost unknown for a woman to be active in this organization. When a New York law of 1880 at last made women eligible to serve on boards of education, she and two others, winning an election in Saratoga, became the first women in the state to hold such positions. To make her work on the board more effective she undertook the study of parliamentary procedure. She gave instruction in this subject, increasingly important to women as they became active in club life, to groups in Saratoga and New York City and in 1897 published a pamphlet on *Parliamentary Rules.*

American history became another interest. On the school board she encouraged its study. In 1876 she was active in raising funds for the restoration of Mount Vernon. In the same year, with a "calm and 'lady-like' invasion of this hitherto exclusively masculine domain," she began an eighteen-year service as the only woman trustee of the Saratoga Monument Association. As chairman of its committee on tablets she did research on every episode of the Revolutionary battle of Saratoga and then traced down descendants of participants to secure funds for marking the sites. In 1877 she published a visitors' guidebook for Saratoga and in 1891 a history of the association. She also delivered or published papers for several of the historical societies to which she belonged. In a speech at the Chicago World's Fair of 1893 she was one of the first to urge the establishment of a National Archives.

These concerns made it natural for Mrs. Walworth to have a hand in founding the Daughters of the American Revolution—one of the three women that organization recognizes as its official founders. (See article on FLORA ADAMS DARLING.) When the new society, after an initial meeting held in her Washington home in August 1890, was formally organized that October, she became its first secretary general, and in 1892 the first editor of its journal, the *American Monthly Magazine.* For a quarter of a century she was a prominent figure at national meetings of the D.A.R. During the Spanish-American War, as director general of the Women's National War Relief Association, she served wounded soldiers, first at Fortress Monroe and then at Montauk. She also became an honorary member of the Military Surgeons' Association of America. In later years she divided her time between Saratoga and the home of her surviving son and daughter in Glencarlyn, Va.

In her youth Mrs. Walworth was considered a beauty and when older was described as "queenly." Though declaring herself consciously working for "the advancement of women" and "always a Suffragist," she never joined any of the groups supporting woman's rights. She displayed a strong Mugwump dislike of professional politicians, moneymaking, and speculation, which she contrasted with the tradition of public and professional service her family represented. In conversation she is said to have displayed a sense of humor, which helped her through her trials, though she deliberately suppressed it in her writing. She died in Georgetown University Hospital in Washington of an obstruction caused by gallstones and was buried in the Catholic section of Old Greenridge Cemetery in Saratoga Springs.

[Clarence A. Walworth, *The Walworths of America* (1897); Reginald Wellington Walworth, *Walworth-Walsworth Genealogy* (1962); *Who's Who in America,* 1914–15; *Biog. Dict. of America,* vol. X (1906); obituaries in *Evening Star* (Washington), June 23, 1915, and in *Washington Post* and *N.Y. Times,* June 24, 1915. Most of these, as well as sketches by friends, as in the *Am. Monthly Mag.,* July 1893, and *Americana,* Oct. 1935, omit the divorce, murder, and trial, which are covered fully in the *N.Y. Times,* June 4–July 14, 1873. For her husband, see *Nat. Cyc. Am. Biog.,* V, 359. There is a Walworth Memorial Museum in Congress Park, Saratoga Springs.]

WALLACE EVAN DAVIES

WARD, Elizabeth Stuart Phelps (Aug. 31, 1844–Jan. 28, 1911), author, was born in Boston, Mass., the eldest of the three children and only daughter of the Rev. Austin Phelps, pastor of the Pine Street Congregational Church, and his first wife, ELIZABETH STUART PHELPS, a popular writer of didactic fiction. Baptized Mary Gray Phelps, the child was called Lily by her family. The ancestors of both parents had migrated from Britain to Connecticut in the seventeenth century. Both grandfathers were ministers; Moses Stuart, her maternal grandfather, was professor of sacred literature at the Andover Theological Seminary and one of American Protestantism's most distinguished scholars. Her father was called to the Andover seminary in 1848 as professor of sacred rhetoric and homiletics and held that chair with distinction for thirty years. Though his numerous devotional and homiletic works had considerable influence in his day, an Andover professor's salary was small, and his wife, who had long suffered from what was then called a cerebral disease, had to struggle not only against ill health but with petty economies and the conflicting demands of her writing and a growing family. In 1852 she published her fourth book, bore her third child, and before the year was out, died.

Mrs. Phelps' death filled her eight-year-old daughter with a resentful sense of deprivation she never outgrew. Her mother, she wrote at the age of fifty in her autobiography, had died "at the first blossom of her very positive and widely-promising success. . . . She lived one of those rich and piteous lives such as only gifted women know; torn by the civil war of the dual nature which can be given to women only" (*Chapters from a Life*, pp. 11–12). After her mother died she chose to be called by her name. In 1854 her father married her mother's sister Mary, who had tuberculosis and died eighteen months later; in 1858, when Elizabeth was thirteen, he married Mary Ann Johnson, who bore him two sons. Phelps watched over his daughter's education with care. She attended Abbott Academy, a private girls' school in Andover, and then Mrs. Edwards' School, conducted by an Andover faculty wife, which offered the same curriculum as men's colleges of the day except for Greek and trigonometry. Her religious training was thorough and orthodox, and she studied a little theology with an Andover professor. The stern Calvinist eschatology, however, was somewhat softened by the example of her father, who was at once severe in doctrine and tender to his children. She grew up loving God, respecting hard work and the scholarly life, and disdaining worldliness.

The Civil War disrupted her quiet life. An Andover student whom she apparently loved died in battle in October 1862; before she left school the next year she had decided never to marry. Her father, who had become president of the seminary in 1860, was sinking into a state of invalidism. Loathing domestic tasks, Elizabeth Phelps determined to become a writer. At sixteen she had read Elizabeth Barrett Browning's *Aurora Leigh*, which had deeply impressed her and, along with her mother's example, had confirmed her literary aspirations, despite her family's disapproval. Mrs. Browning upheld the sanctity of the poet's

individual insight and urged that it was his task to represent the age, not to lose himself in high-flown imagery. However vaporish and overwrought her work often was, Elizabeth Phelps always practiced these precepts: her subjects were contemporary, her heroines were simple New England girls, and her plots followed the course of ordinary events. Her first story had been published in the *Youth's Companion* when she was thirteen, and she followed it with other juvenile fiction for Sunday school readers; her first adult story appeared in *Harper's* in 1864. But these small literary successes neither exempted her from irksome household duties nor entitled her to a quiet place in which to work. When in 1864 she began the book that was to make her famous and independent, *The Gates Ajar*, she had to do her writing wrapped in an old fur cape of her mother's in her unheated bedroom, in the attic, or in the barn. When *The Gates Ajar* appeared in 1868, however, its success was immediate, and her family acknowledged her triumph by giving her for her own use a summerhouse which had been her mother's study.

*The Gates Ajar* is a barely fictionalized argument that heaven will contain all that is loveliest and best on earth. This idea is expounded in a series of conversations between Mary Cabot and her aunt, Mrs. Forceythe. Mary has been embittered by the death of her beloved brother, but her aunt, recently widowed, firmly believes she will take up life with her husband, exactly as it was on earth, when they meet in heaven. Though Miss Phelps was often accused of spiritualism, *The Gates Ajar* does not suggest any earthly communication between the living and the dead. Mrs. Forceythe's style of argument is, rather, that if the Bible tells us there will be harps in heaven, why should we not also hope for pianos? She quotes proof texts much as orthodox theologians did and adds bits and pieces of fiction and theology. She insists that her opinions are not at all unorthodox, but simply spell out the hints of heaven given in the Bible.

The book was a best seller in America and in Britain and was translated into at least four languages. Although it was attacked both as bad literature and as heretical theology, Elizabeth Phelps was gratified, like many another popular author, by a deluge of letters from grateful readers thanking her for the comfort she gave them. Her book's unprecedented success has been ascribed to the consolation it offered to the vast numbers of those bereaved by the Civil War, but this explanation hardly accounts for its sales abroad. A more adequate explanation may be found in the state of popular religion when the volume was published. Under the pressure of the evangelical drive to convert the entire world, the sternly just God of Calvin had given way to a more merciful, more forgiving deity, who would receive every man into heaven, no matter what his sins, as long as he sincerely repented of them. Even Andover, the citadel of orthodoxy, was unable in its own ranks to maintain belief in the Puritan God. The popularity of *The Gates Ajar* indicates how urgently Christians everywhere felt the need to reconcile a liberal, merciful God with their orthodox faith in the literal truth of the Bible.

Through the rest of her life Miss Phelps continued to write prolifically, publishing a total of fifty-seven books, besides fiction, poetry, and articles for magazines. She kept a devoted audience, but the success of *The Gates Ajar* was not repeated, even by its two sequels. The sad plight of factory girls, whom she had seen while she was teaching Sunday school in a mill town near Andover, inspired her second novel, *Hedged In* (1870), in which she defended fallen women. This bold choice of theme, however, was largely vitiated by the sentimentality of her treatment. In the early 1870's she espoused woman's rights and published a series of articles in the *Independent* magazine advocating dress reform, suffrage, and wider employment for women, and protesting the frustration of confinement to domesticity. The heroine of *The Story of Avis* (1877) was modeled after the mother Elizabeth Phelps idealized and reflects her despair of successfully combining a career with marriage, a problem she dealt with again in *Doctor Zay* (1882). Miss Phelps also worked for the temperance cause and for several summers in the 1870's lectured on temperance to the fishermen of Gloucester, where she had built a summer home. Her own preference among her novels was for *A Singular Life* (1895); the hero of this novel, a young minister, devotes his life to temperance work in a fishing town. In her last years she took up the cause of antivivisection, producing several tracts thinly disguised as fiction.

On Oct. 20, 1888, at forty-four, Miss Phelps was married to Herbert Dickinson Ward, twenty-seven years old, a writer and the son of an old friend (the editor and orientalist William Hayes Ward). She and her husband collaborated on three Biblical romances, but the marriage was never happy. There were no children. They built a house in Newton Center, Mass., where she attended the First Baptist Church, and spent their summers in Gloucester. Mrs. Ward suffered increasingly from nervous ill health and chronic insomnia and was an invalid for years before her death. She died at her home in Newton at the age of sixty-six of myocardial degeneration; in accordance with the detailed instructions she left for her funeral, her body was cremated and the ashes buried in Newton Cemetery.

[Mrs. Ward's memoir of her father, *Austin Phelps* (1891), gives a picture of the family background. Her autobiography, *Chapters from a Life* (1896), is more valuable as a record of her feelings than for the facts of her life, for which see Mary Angela Bennett's somewhat pietistic biography, *Elizabeth Stuart Phelps* (1939). See also Oliver S. Phelps and Andrew T. Servin, *The Phelps Family of America* (1899), vol. II; the sketch by Elizabeth T. Spring in *Our Famous Women* (1884); Francis W. Halsey, ed. *Women Authors of Our Day in Their Homes* (1903); Helen Sootin Smith's introduction to the John Harvard Library edition of *The Gates Ajar* (1964); and Margaret Wyman (Langworthy), "Women in the Am. Realistic Novel, 1860–1893" (unpublished Ph.D. dissertation, Radcliffe College, 1950). Death record from Mass. Registrar of Vital Statistics.]

BEATRICE K. HOFSTADTER

**WARD, Mrs. H. O.** *See* MOORE, Clara Sophia Jessup.

**WARD, Hortense Sparks Malsch** (July 20, 1872–Dec. 5, 1944), Texas lawyer and reformer, was born near the present Simpsonville in Matagorda County, Texas, the oldest survivor of eleven children of Frederick Sparks (originally Funk) and his wife, Louisa Marie La Bauve. Her father, a stock raiser and deputy hide inspector, was an immigrant from Germany; her mother was of an old French ranching family from Louisiana. In 1883 Sparks moved with his wife and children to the new town of Edna, Jackson County, where he ran a saloon and was deputy sheriff. After attendance at Edna public schools, Hortense spent four years at the Nazareth Academy in Victoria, Texas, operated by the French Sisters of the Incarnate Word and Blessed Sacrament, and was graduated in 1890.

Following a brief stint of teaching in Edna, she was married there, on Jan. 4, 1891, to Albert Malsch (1864–1915), a tinner. Three daughters—Mary Louise, Margurite, and Hortense—were born within nine years. In the summer of 1903 Mrs. Malsch went to Houston, where she studied stenography and began work for the Wolf Cigar Company, her husband and family joining her in Houston that fall. She was more energetic and ambitious than Malsch, and after a period of discord he left her; they were divorced in Houston on May 11, 1906.

Meanwhile she had become a public stenographer and notary, sharing an office with a firm of lawyers, Hogg, Gill & Jones. Becoming interested in the law, she began to study it by correspondence course. For two years she was court reporter of one of the county courts. On Aug. 12, 1909, she was married in Houston to a lawyer, William Henry Ward (1880–1939), with whom she completed her legal preparation. She was admitted to the bar in Galveston on Aug. 30, 1910, after having been the first woman to pass the bar examination administered by the supreme judicial districts of Texas. Shortly afterward she joined her husband in the Houston law firm of Ward & Ward, limited to civil practice. Her husband, who was later to serve twice as county judge, was a trial lawyer and an expert on real estate law. Mrs. Ward never appeared in court, but confined herself to briefing and consultation. When she was admitted to practice before the Supreme Court of the United States on Feb. 24, 1915, she was said to be the first Texas woman so admitted. In 1920 she ran for the Democratic nomination to the judgeship of the court in which she had been reporter, but was defeated.

In 1912 Mrs. Ward wrote an article in a Houston newspaper pointing out the need for a married women's property law. The magazine *Delineator*, then concerned with equal rights for women, publicized her campaign; it also printed and distributed a pamphlet she had written, *Property Rights of Married Women in Texas.* When a bill on the subject came before the Texas legislature in 1913, Mrs. Ward successfully wrote and lobbied in its support; the new law was widely known as the Hortense Ward Act. She also lobbied for workmen's compensation and a fifty-four-hour week for women in industry (both passed in 1913), as well as for prohibition, a woman's division in the state department of labor, a domestic relations court, and authorization for married women to serve as officers of corporations. During World War I and afterward she was president of the Harris County (Houston) Equal Suffrage Association. In 1918 she was largely responsible for the legislature's passing the women's primary law permitting Texas women to vote in party primaries.

For years she was active in politics. She opposed James Ferguson as governor because of disparaging remarks he had made against higher education for women. In 1924, however, she supported the campaign of his wife, Mrs. Miriam Ferguson, for the governorship because of the latter's opposition to the Ku Klux Klan. Indeed, that same year Mrs. Ward went to Maine to support the unsuccessful campaign of the anti-Klan candidate for governor, William R. Pattangall. She campaigned for Oscar Underwood for the Democratic nomination for the presidency in 1924 and for Al Smith's election in 1928. In her various legal and political crusades she sought to bring about ends without focusing undue attention on herself.

In 1925, when all justices of the supreme court of Texas disqualified themselves from hearing the case of *Johnson v. Darr,* involving a fraternal order, the Woodmen of the World, of which they were all members, the governor of Texas appointed a special supreme court with Mrs. Ward as chief justice and two other woman attorneys as justices; their three individual opinions (114 *Tex.* 516, 272 S.W. 1098) are cited occasionally on equitable and naked legal titles. For a short time in 1925 Mrs. Ward was acting judge of the corporation court of the city of Houston.

Hortense Ward was an able and earnest woman, with a quick mind and quick way of speaking. Feminine in tastes, she liked to wear frilly clothes, to sew for her grandchildren, and to cook. Throughout her life she was a Roman Catholic. When a grandson, Stanton Ward Hinkley (born Anderson), was orphaned, she took him into her home and reared him. Following her husband's death and because of arthritis in one knee, Mrs. Ward closed her law office in 1939 and thereafter consulted only with old friends and clients. She died in Houston in 1944, of myocardial degeneration, at the age of seventy-two; her remains were buried in Hollywood Cemetery. She left an estate of $65,000, much of it in oil royalties.

[*Houston Chronicle and Herald,* Aug. 18, 1910; *Houston Chronicle,* Dec. 5, 7, 1944; *Houston Post,* July 27, 1920, Dec. 6, 1944; *Woman Citizen,* June 26, 1920, p. 115; *Woman's Who's Who of America,* 1914–15; Leila Clark Wynn, "A Hist. of the Civil Courts in Texas," *Southwestern Hist. Quart.,* July 1956; Hortense Ward, "Shall Women Have Adequate Laws?" *Texas Mag.,* Jan. 1913; William Hard, "Will Texas Do Better by Its Married Women?" *Delineator,* Nov. 1912; divorce record from District Clerk, Harris County, Texas.]

ANDREW FOREST MUIR

**WARD, Nancy** (c. 1738–1822), Cherokee leader, legendary "Pocahontas of the West," was probably born at Chota, a Cherokee village on the Little Tennessee River near the present reconstruction of Fort Loudoun in Monroe County, Tenn. Her father is said to have been a Delaware Indian who, following the custom in the matriarchal Cherokee society, had become a member of the Wolf clan when he married Tame Doe, the sister of Atta-kulla-kulla (Little Carpenter), civil chief of the Cherokee Nation. Nancy (an anglicized version of her Indian name, Nanye'hi), was married at an early age to Kingfisher of the Deer clan, by whom she had a son, Fivekiller, and a daughter, Catharine.

She first won notice in 1775 when her husband was killed during the battle of Taliwa (near present-day Canton, Ga.), a skirmish in the long rivalry between the Cherokees and the Creeks. At once taking his place in the battle line, she helped secure a decisive Cherokee victory. In recognition of her valor, she was chosen Agi-ga-u-e, or "Beloved Woman" of her tribe. In this capacity she headed the influential Woman's Council, made up of a representative from each Cherokee clan, and sat as a member of the Council of Chiefs.

Her second husband was Bryant (or Brian) Ward, a white trader, by whom she had a daughter, Elizabeth. Ward left the Cherokee Nation sometime prior to 1760, when the suddenly hostile Cherokees destroyed Fort Loudoun and massacred its British garrison. Although Ward returned to his home in South Carolina and married a white woman, there is evidence that Nancy occasionally visited him and his white wife and was well received. Influenced perhaps by these associations, as well as by her uncle, Atta-kulla-kulla, usually a friend of the English, Nancy Ward seems to have maintained a steady friendship for the white settlers who were gradually establishing themselves along the Holston and Watauga river valleys of eastern Tennessee.

This friendship had important results during the American Revolution. In July 1776 Nancy Ward is credited with having sent a secret warning to John Sevier, a leader of the Tennessee settlers, of a planned pro-British Cherokee attack. When one settler, Mrs. William Bean, was captured by Cherokee warriors, Nancy Ward personally intervened to save her from death at the stake (Ramsey, p. 157). Such was Nancy Ward's repute among the settlers that in October 1776, when the Cherokee villages were devastated by colonial troops, Chota was spared. Four years later, when another Cherokee uprising was imminent, she again sent a timely warning to the settlers, using as intermediary Isaac Thomas, a local trader. A countering raid was at once organized; as the expedition approached the Cherokee territory —according to the report later sent to Thomas Jefferson, governor of Virginia—"the famous Indian Woman Nancy Ward came to Camp, . . . gave us various intelligence, and made an overture in behalf of some of the Cheifs [sic] for Peace" (Jefferson Papers, IV, 361). Despite her efforts the Cherokee villages were pillaged, but again Nancy Ward and her family were given preferential treatment. At the subsequent peace negotiations conducted by John Sevier, Nancy Ward spoke for the now defeated Cherokees, again urging friendship rather than war. Throughout this difficult period she presumably acted on the conviction that the effort to drive out the white man altogether was futile, and that the Cherokees' best hope lay in winning his good will. In 1785, at the talks preceding the Treaty of Hopewell, she again pleaded eloquently for a "chain of friendship" linking the two races.

Evidently a striking person, Nancy Ward was described by one settler in 1772 as "queenly and commanding" and her residence as outfitted in "barbaric splendor" (Hale and Merritt, I, 59). While sheltering Mrs. Bean after her rescue in 1776, she had learned from her how to make butter and cheese, and soon afterward she introduced dairying among the Cherokees, herself buying the first cattle. In postwar years she sought further to strengthen the economy of her people by cattle raising and more intensive farming. At the same time she sought to stem the advancing white tide. Though too ill to be present, she sent a vigorous message to the Cherokee Council of May 1817 urging the tribe not to part with any more of its land. But other forces were stronger than her aged voice. That year a new republican government supplanted the old hierarchy among the Cherokees, and by the Hiwassee Purchase of 1819 they gave up all land north of the Hiwassee River. Thus forced to leave Chota, Nancy Ward opened a small inn overlooking the Ocoee River in the southeastern corner of Tennessee, near the present town of Benton. She died there in 1822 and was buried on a nearby hill, in a grave later marked by a Tennessee D.A.R. chapter bearing her name. Thirteen years after her death the Cherokees surrendered all claim to their historic homeland and were transported to new territories in the Southwest.

Whatever Nancy Ward's achievements in life, a body of regional legend subsequently grew up around her name. Stories illustrating her friendship for the white settlers were repeated by several nineteenth-century Tennessee historians, and were brought to national attention in Theodore Roosevelt's The Winning of the West (1905). E. Sterling King's The Wild Rose of Cherokee; or, Nancy Ward, "The Pocahontas of the West" (1895), a highly imaginative novel, was long a staple of children's reading in the Smoky Mountain areas. She also figured in local folklore as "Granny" Ward, the aged Indian prophetess. At her death, so her great-grandson reported, a light rose from her body and flew away toward Chota.

[Ben Harris McClary, "Nancy Ward," *Tenn. Hist. Quart.*, Dec. 1962, cites the known sources of information. These include Annie Walker Burns, comp., *Military and Genealogical Record of the Famous Indian Woman of Tenn.: Nancy Ward* (1957), a mimeographed and very diverse collection; Carolyn Thomas Foreman, *Indian Women Chiefs* (1954), pp. 72–83; J. D. Clemmer Scrapbooks, microfilm in Tenn. State Archives and elsewhere; James G. M. Ramsey, *The Annals of Tenn.* (1853), pp. 144, 151, 157, 161, 273; Will T. Hale and Dixon L. Merritt, *A Hist. of Tenn.* (1913), I, 59; Samuel C. Williams, *Tenn. during the Revolutionary War* (1944); Julian P. Boyd, ed., *The Papers of Thomas Jefferson*, IV (1951), 361.]

BEN HARRIS MC CLARY

WARNER, Anna Bartlett. *See* WARNER, Susan Bogert.

WARNER, Susan Bogert (July 11, 1819–Mar. 17, 1885) and Anna Bartlett (Aug. 31, 1827– Jan. 15, 1915), authors, were born in New York City, the daughters of Henry Whiting Warner, a prosperous lawyer, and Anna (Bartlett) Warner, of a Jamaica, Long Island, family of means. Susan was born after the death of the Warners' first child and survived a succeeding sister and brother; Anna was the last in the family. The mother died when the girls were quite young, and they were brought up by their father's sister, who shared their home. Educated privately, they received instruction in music and Italian from tutors; their father, a man of literary leanings fostered by his three years at Union College, himself supervised their study of history, literature, and the classics. He was a native of Canaan, Columbia County, N.Y., where his Warner and Whiting forebears had long been leading citizens. As young girls Susan and Anna often visited in Canaan, acquiring a feeling for rural life that found expression in much of their work.

Their home, however, throughout their writing career, was neither New York City nor Canaan, but Constitution Island, a rockbound and wooded retreat in the Hudson River opposite West Point. Roughly a mile square and projecting into the Hudson close to its eastern shore, the island had been an important Revolutionary outpost, and ruins of an old fort and other military works still exist. Attracted by its historical associations and by its proximity to the military academy, where his brother was chaplain, Henry Warner had bought the place

in 1836. He had intended to use it, and the house that stood on it, as a warm-weather resort, but when severe losses in the panic of 1837 forced him to abandon his expensive home in the city, the family found year-around refuge on Constitution Island. There the girls learned to do their own cooking and gardening, to cut their own firewood, and to row their boat to the mainland for mail and supplies. As hard times continued, the Warners at length were obliged to part with their most valuable possessions at public sale. It was as a result of this crowning misfortune that the sisters turned to writing.

Separated in age by eight years and differing in interests, they had not been especially close during childhood. Susan, bookish and, as she said, "a constitutional coward," found Anna's enthusiastic romps over the island's often rough terrain too much for her own nervous, uneasy temperament. The family's financial crisis affected Susan more than it did Anna: at the verge of young womanhood and just beginning to develop a love of society, Susan reacted sensitively to the dropping away of former friends and to straitened circumstances. But hardship brought the sisters closer together and, with their simultaneous joining of the Presbyterian Church, established the basis of their subsequent interdependence and inseparability. Susan, however, seems to have remained the dominant personality, never completely relinquishing the position she had long held as the much-adored only child.

An early passion for reading and a knack for weaving stories for Anna and various young cousins provided Susan's preparation for authorship; a suggestion from her aunt and a dire need of money precipitated it. Her first book, *The Wide, Wide World*, after being refused by a number of publishers (a Harper's editor wrote the word "Fudge" on one of its pages), was published by Putnam in 1851. It was first issued as "by Elizabeth Wetherell," but Susan soon dropped the pseudonym. A sentimental tale of a motherless girl who learns Christian forbearance and love despite numerous trials and cruel treatment, this novel like all of her fiction has a rural background and a marked religious flavor. Produced in an era when public taste favored the sentimental and moralistic, *The Wide, Wide World* was for years extremely popular both in the United States and abroad and, according to contemporary records, was the first book by an American to achieve a million sales. It was followed by *Queechy* (1852), a celebrated though less widely sold novel in similar vein, and *The Law and the Testimony* (1853), an exclusively religious work based on passages from the Bible. *The Hills of the Shatemuc*, another novel, following in 1856, sold ten thousand copies the day of its appearance. From then until the author's death nearly thirty years later, every year saw the publication of at least one Susan Warner book, some years of two or three. Except for half a dozen on Biblical subjects, all were fiction, and all were of considerable length, taking their place beside the books of Fanny Fern (see SARA PAYSON WILLIS PARTON) and Mrs. E. D. E. N. SOUTHWORTH on Victorian parlor tables.

Anna Warner collaborated with her sister on several books of children's stories, written primarily for quick financial return, and also wrote independently. About a year before Susan began work on *The Wide, Wide World*, Anna invented an educational game called "Robinson Crusoe's Farm," played with colored cards. The animal pictures on the cards, drawn by Anna, were painted in watercolors by both sisters, and the game was sold for years through the George P. Putnam store. Anna's first novel, *Dollars and Cents*, the somewhat humorous story of a once-prosperous family obliged to give up a city home and adapt itself to life in rural surroundings, came out in 1852, almost simultaneously with *Queechy*. Her later books—some twenty-five in number—included, besides children's fiction, a few on religious subjects and at least three on the growing of flowers and vegetables, some illustrated with her own line drawings.

Gardening was her great pleasure, and she hoarded her small funds carefully to buy seeds. *Gardening by Myself*, which first appeared in 1872, gives a charming and unsentimental account, detailed month by month, of the planning, preparing, and tending of her island garden. The first book written by an American woman urging that women do the actual work of gardening themselves, it was reprinted fifty years later. Anna Warner also wrote verse and the words of several hymns, the best known being "Jesus Loves Me, This I Know" and "Jesus Bids Us Shine." Although never as popular as her sister's writing, Anna's shows a lighter touch and greater versatility. In 1909 she published her last book, a biography of Susan.

For all their ceaseless energy and continuous output, the Warner sisters never grew rich. Susan's earnings from *The Wide, Wide World* were far from commensurate with the book's sales. She received considerable royalties from its publication in New York, but the book was widely pirated abroad, owing to the lack of copyright protection. In England, where it was especially popular, sales within a decade reached 100,000, but except for an advance from one publisher, none of the more than twenty London firms that printed and sold *The Wide, Wide World* paid the author a cent. The same was true of French, German, Spanish, Italian, and Russian editions. Although Susan's later books needed no further promotion than the line "by the author of *The Wide, Wide World*" to be assured of large sales, the sisters' constant need for immediate funds often caused them to sell their manuscripts outright, thus foregoing all royalties.

Aside from their writing, Susan and Anna Warner are remembered for their Bible classes for West Point cadets, conducted for years, first by Susan and later by Anna. An outgrowth of Susan's intensive Bible study, these were weekly sessions. An hour of serious reading and discussion would be followed by tea and gingerbread and an opportunity for the boys to roam over Constitution Island; in winter the classes were held in the Academy chapel. Attendance was of course voluntary, but the classes became a fixture of West Point life. For Susan, this was simply a continuation of her active participation in church work, begun with distributing religious tracts and teaching Sunday school while still a young woman, later carried on in various Bible-reading groups, and finding expression in her purely religious books. She herself remained a Presbyterian; her sister Anna, more interested in applied Christianity than in dogma, it is said, "classed herself a Methodist" (Putnam, "The Warner Sisters," p. 32).

Susan Warner died in Highland Falls, N.Y., at the age of sixty-five. Anna, surviving by thirty years, continued her life alone on the island much as before, taking over the Bible classes, writing, tending her garden, and visiting with friends. She had been offered large sums for Constitution Island from commercial developers, but it had always been the sisters' wish that the property should eventually become a part of the West Point reservation. After bills appropriating a relatively modest $175,000 for its acquisition repeatedly failed to pass Congress, the island was purchased for this amount by Mrs. Russell Sage (see MARGARET OLIVIA SLOCUM SAGE), who presented it to the government in her own and Miss Warner's name. President Theodore Roosevelt accepted the gift in 1908.

Anna Warner died seven years later at Highland Falls. Many former cadets returned to West Point for her funeral at the Academy. Both sisters are buried in the government cemetery at West Point, their graves atop a grassy knoll which overlooks their island home. A twentieth-century reader will find in their novels not only an excess of teary sentimentality and moral preachment but also some excellent rural realism, with touches of unforced, effective humor, and descriptive passages of real beauty.

[The principal sources are Anna Bartlett Warner, *Susan Warner* (1909), and Olivia E. Stokes, *Letters and Memories of Susan and Anna Bartlett Warner* (1925). See also Grace Overmyer, "Hudson River Bluestockings—The Warner Sisters of Constitution Island," *N.Y. Hist.*, Apr. 1959; George Haven Putnam, *A Memoir of George Palmer Putnam* (1903), and his "The Warner Sisters" in the *Fourth Report and Year Book of the Martelaer's Rock Assoc.*, 1920–23, pp. 16–33; Buckner Hollingsworth, *Her Garden Was Her Delight* (1962).]

GRACE OVERMYER

**WARREN, Ann Brunton.** *See* MERRY, Ann Brunton.

**WARREN, Lavinia.** *See* STRATTON, Mercy Lavinia Warren Bump.

**WARREN, Mercy Otis** (Sept. 14, 1728 O.S.–Oct. 19, 1814), poet, patriot, and historian, was born in Barnstable, Mass., the first daughter and third of the thirteen children of James and Mary (Allyne) Otis. Her mother was a great-granddaughter of Edward Dotey, who had come to the New World as a servant on board the *Mayflower*. A great-great-grandfather, John Otis, had settled in Hingham, Mass., early in the seventeenth century. By the eighteenth century the family had become established in Barnstable, on Cape Cod. Mercy's father drew a comfortable income as a farmer, merchant, and lawyer and served as judge of the county court of common pleas and as colonel of the militia. The Otises saw to it that their sons were prepared for college, but the daughters were given no formal education. Mercy was, however, sometimes allowed to sit in on her brothers' lessons while they were being tutored by their uncle, the local minister, and she browsed through her uncle's library. As the daughter of one of the leaders of the county, she was exposed to frequent political discussions.

On Nov. 14, 1754, at the age of twenty-six, she was married to James Warren of Plymouth, a merchant and farmer and a Harvard graduate whose background was much like her own. They had five sons, James (born in 1757), Winslow (1759), Charles (1762), Henry (1764), and George (1766). As the American colonies came into increasing conflict with the home government, her relatives' activities drew Mercy Warren closer to public affairs. Her

father was a justice of the peace, her husband a member of the Massachusetts legislature, and her brother James a king's advocate and then, after resigning his royal appointment, the leading spokesman against writs of assistance. Before long Mrs. Warren found that her home in Plymouth was a meeting place of leading opponents of royal policy within Massachusetts, including, besides her husband and brother, such men as John Adams and Samuel Adams. Her own contribution was to write for the revolutionary cause. She had composed poems as early as 1759, and she now turned to political satire.

Mercy Otis Warren couched her satiric thrusts in dramatic form, though they were written to be read, not performed. Her first play, *The Adulateur*, appeared anonymously in two installments in the Boston newspaper the *Massachusetts Spy* during 1772 and, with additions apparently written by someone else, was reprinted separately the following year. In it Thomas Hutchinson, royal governor of Massachusetts, was depicted in the guise of Rapatio, the ruler of the mythical country of Servia, who hoped to crush "the ardent love of liberty in Servia's free-born sons." Soon afterward appeared *The Defeat*, again with "Rapatio" as villain. In her next play, *The Group*, published in Boston in 1775, Massachusetts Tories, as evil as ever, were disguised under such names as Judge Meagre, Brigadier Hateall, Sir Spendall, and Hum Humbug. *The Blockheads* (1776) and *The Motley Assembly* (1779) were probably also written by Mrs. Warren, though the evidence of authorship is not definite. In 1790 she published *Poems, Dramatic and Miscellaneous*, a collection that included two verse dramas, *The Sack of Rome* and *The Ladies of Castile*—each a tract on behalf of human liberty—in which the characters are handled with more subtlety and warmth than in her political satires. On the whole, although Mrs. Warren's plays possess no remarkable literary merit, they are striking testimony to the imagination and skill of a woman who never traveled farther away from Plymouth than to Boston and Providence and who probably never saw a play performed on the stage.

During and after the Revolution, the Warrens suffered something of a political decline. James Warren lost his seat in the legislature in 1780, and their sons failed to obtain political preferment despite Mrs. Warren's active intercession with their old friend John Adams and other persons in power. Late in that decade both James and Mercy Warren were accused by political conservatives of having been sympathetic to Shays' Rebellion, the uprising of western Massachusetts farmers, and even of having supported it. Nowhere in her letters which have survived does Mrs. Warren voice any support for the rebellion; her son Henry served with the government troops sent to suppress it, and she later, in the final volume of her history of the American Revolution, sharply criticized the insurgents. The accusations against Mrs. Warren were probably an attempt to discredit her because of her spirited opposition to the ratification of the federal Constitution during the winter of 1787–88, as expressed in her *Observations on the New Constitution* (1788). Federalist Boston was still further antagonized by her defense of the French Revolution, in the preface which she wrote in 1791 for the American edition of her friend Mrs. Catharine Macaulay Graham's attack upon Edmund Burke.

During these years Mrs. Warren continued the writing of her major literary work, the three-volume *History of the Rise, Progress and Termination of the American Revolution* (1805), which she had begun in the late 1770's. Although no less reliable than other histories written during the same era, the work is now useful chiefly for its vigorous personal opinions of people and events she had known firsthand. It reflects the viewpoint of a Massachusetts Jeffersonian Republican who had more confidence in the ability of the people to govern themselves than did most of her Federalist friends. Publication of her history brought into the open the rupture in the friendship between Mrs. Warren and John Adams which had begun with the divergence of their political views and her anger at his failure to assist the Warrens' political fortunes. Her accusations in her *History* that Adams had "forgotten the principles of the American revolution" and that he was guilty of "pride of talents and much ambition" piqued the ex-president, and several heated letters were exchanged between them. Eventually, in 1812, Elbridge Gerry succeeded in effecting a reconciliation. Adams still somewhat regretted, however, that he and his wife, Abigail, had been among the first to encourage Mrs. Warren to write her account. "History," he complained to Gerry, "is not the Province of the Ladies."

Mercy Otis Warren was something of a feminist by the standards of her time. Political or legal rights for women were not an issue in her day, but she deplored the fact that women were not generally given formal education and felt that they could well participate in many activities customarily restricted to men. On one occasion she advised a friend that women should accept "the Appointed Subordination," not because of any inherent inferiority, but "perhaps for the sake of Order in Families."

In relatively good health to the end of her long life, Mrs. Warren continued to correspond with her political and literary friends, and visitors reported that her conversation was still vigorous, her mind active. She died in Plymouth, Mass., where she had spent most of her married life, at the age of eighty-six, having survived her husband by six years. Her remains lie at Burial Hill, Plymouth.

[The largest body of manuscript material is at the Mass. Hist. Soc.: the Mercy Otis Warren Papers and Mercy Otis Warren Letter-Book, and letters scattered through other collections. Important published collections of her letters are: "Correspondence between John Adams and Mercy Warren Relating to Her 'Hist. of the Am. Revolution,' July–Aug., 1807," Mass. Hist. Soc., *Collections*, 5th ser., IV (1878), 315–511; and *Warren-Adams Letters* (*ibid.*, vols. LXXII and LXXIII, 1917–25). A portrait by John Singleton Copley hangs in the Museum of Fine Arts, Boston. Full-length biographies, neither of them adequate, are Alice Brown, *Mercy Warren* (1896), and Katharine Anthony, *First Lady of the Revolution: The Life of Mercy Otis Warren* (1958). Maud M. Hutcheson provides a brief account of Mrs. Warren's life in *William and Mary Quart.*, July 1953. See also the following articles: Worthington C. Ford, "Mrs. Warren's 'The Group,'" Mass. Hist. Soc., *Proc.*, LXII (1930), 15–22; Charles Warren, "Elbridge Gerry, James Warren, Mercy Warren and the Ratification of the Federal Constitution in Mass.," *ibid.*, LXIV (1932), 143–64. For a recent analysis of Mrs. Warren's *History*, see William R. Smith, *History as Argument: Three Patriot Historians of the Am. Revolution* (1966).]

ROBERT A. FEER

**WASHBURN, Margaret Floy** (July 25, 1871–Oct. 29, 1939), psychologist, was born in New York City, the only child of Francis and Elizabeth Floy (Davis) Washburn. Her ancestry, mostly colonial, included New York Dutch, Quakers from Westchester County and Long Island, Marylanders, and a single Connecticut Yankee. Her maternal great-grandfather, Michael Floy, had come from Devonshire, England, about 1800. Settling in New York, he built the comfortable frame house on 125th Street in which Margaret was born; his success as a florist and nurseryman later enabled his great-granddaughter to pursue her undergraduate and graduate training free of financial worry. Margaret's father, a native of New York City, had followed his father into the Methodist ministry. In 1878 he shifted to the Episcopal Church, moving his family to parishes first in Walden, N.Y., and then in Kingston. Growing up without brothers and sisters, Margaret enjoyed, as she later recalled, the privilege of uninterrupted leisure for reading and thinking. She learned to read long before she began school at the age of seven. Three years later, at Kingston, she was by mistake put in a class a year beyond her proper grade, worked desperately, and came through successfully to enter the local Ulster Academy at the age of twelve. She went to Vassar at sixteen and graduated with the A.B. degree in 1891.

At Vassar she experienced various excitements, of which the curricular ones were chemistry, biology, and philosophy and the extracurricular the emergence of a love of poetry and the discovery of attitudes of religious freedom. Though out of family loyalty she continued for some years an Episcopal affiliation, she became in fact an agnostic, though not a militant one. Drawn to an intellectual career, she sought to combine her two curricular loves of science and philosophy by choosing psychology, which then partook of both. James McKeen Cattell, trained in the new experimental psychology by Wilhelm Wundt at Leipzig, had in 1891 come to Columbia University to found a psychological laboratory, and Miss Washburn applied to work with him. It took Columbia's trustees a semester to decide to allow a woman to become a "hearer" under Cattell; admission as a full-fledged graduate student was not even considered. Cattell himself received her gladly and treated her as he did the men, but advised her to go the next year to work under E. B. Titchener at Cornell, where a woman could not only be admitted but could receive a scholarship.

Her arrival at Cornell coincided with the coming of Titchener, fresh from Wundt's laboratory. They were almost contemporaries, and she felt none of the awe of him that his later students felt or that she had felt for Cattell. During her three years she came to know and admire the Cornell philosophers, while she finished under Titchener a thesis dealing with the influence of visual imagery on tactual judgments of distance and direction—a study which the great and fastidious Wundt honored by accepting for his journal. Thus she gained the Ph.D. in 1894.

After six years at neighboring Wells College as professor of psychology, philosophy, and ethics, Miss Washburn returned to Cornell for two years (1900–02) as warden of Sage College, the large women's dormitory, during which time she also gave courses in social psychology and animal psychology. Next came a year at the University of Cincinnati, and then a call to Vassar, where, after five years (1903–08) as associate professor, she served as pro-

fessor of psychology until her retirement in 1937. Her clear, incisive mind made her classroom lectures effective and popular.

The same quality of mind was reflected in her extensive writings. Her complete bibliography contains about two hundred entries, including notes and book reviews, three score of them original articles under her own name and seventy with joint authorship. The latter constitute the *Studies from the Psychological Laboratory of Vassar College*, for which the problem and the design of research were fixed by Miss Washburn, the experimentation put through by one or more advanced students, and the article written up by Miss Washburn. This well-known series, which includes studies in individual differences, in the color vision of animals, and in the aesthetic preferences of students for different colors and of poets and scientists for different speech sounds, constitutes Miss Washburn's principal contribution in experimental research.

Her most important publication, the one that kept her name for three decades constantly before the psychological community, was *The Animal Mind* (1908; 4th ed., 1936). This compendium and analysis of the large literature of animal psychology reflected her own love of animals and her intense interest in their behavior and what it might imply of conscious experience on their part. Besides her own writing, she served from 1925 onward as one of the four co-editors who took over the *American Journal of Psychology* after Titchener's sudden resignation as editor.

In the realm of psychological theory, Miss Washburn was a dualist who believed that motor phenomena play an essential role in psychology. With her training in philosophy and her love for that field, with her background in introspective psychology induced by Titchener, it was natural for her to believe that mind and matter, the conscious processes and the actual behavior of an organism, are two different kinds of events, neither of which can be reduced to the other. She noted, however, that human beings and all other animals are fundamentally locomotor organisms which react to their perceptions by moving, actually or incipiently. Psychology, she believed, must not exclude movement from its basic data, as Titchener and the Wundtians in Germany had done, nor dare it exclude consciousness and deal only with behavior, as the American behaviorists proposed to do. She presented her theory in her only book besides the animal compendium, *Movement and Mental Imagery* (1916), and reinforced it in two important papers in 1928 and in her contribution to Carl

Murchison's *The Psychologies of 1930* (1930). She established no school, but her thought represents a positive neutralism as against the two warring camps of introspectionism (only consciousness for psychology) and behaviorism (only behavior for psychology).

In manner Miss Washburn was direct and frank, but her criticism was blunted sometimes by a gracious diplomacy, sometimes by a friendly humor. She was reserved but not shy, with a few devoted friends, a host of admirers, and some others who feared her a little. She disliked sanctimony and could not tolerate insincerity. She believed so thoroughly in the equality of women that she refused to join women's societies and never gave active support to such causes as the suffrage movement. She felt deeply that women's education should be the same as that for men; it was only under a mild protest that she taught at a women's rather than a coeducational college.

Many honors came to Miss Washburn. She was elected president of the American Psychological Association in 1921 and vice-president of the American Association for the Advancement of Science in 1927. She became a charter member of the select Society of Experimental Psychologists when it was reorganized in 1929, Titchener's death having removed the opposition to the admission of women. In 1927 a special issue of the *American Journal of Psychology* commemorated the third of a century since the awarding of her doctorate. She was elected to the National Academy of Sciences in 1931, the second woman to be included in that top-level group of eminent scientists. (The first, elected in 1925, was the distinguished anatomist Florence Rena Sabin, 1871–1953.) In March 1937 Miss Washburn suffered a cerebral hemorrhage. She died two years later in Poughkeepsie, N.Y., and was buried in the rural cemetery at White Plains, N.Y. In the history of her field she stands out as one of the leaders of the second generation of American psychologists, those trained by men of the first generation who had studied in Germany, many of them at Leipzig under Wundt.

[The best source of information up to 1932 is Miss Washburn's autobiographical sketch in Carl Murchison, ed., *A Hist. of Psychology in Autobiog.*, II (1932), 333–58. For an excellent summary of her life see Robert S. Woodworth in Nat. Academy of Sciences, *Biog. Memoirs*, vol. XXV (1949), which includes a bibliography of her more important titles; for fuller bibliographies see Helen K. Mull in *Am. Jour. of Psychology*, vol. XXXIX (Washburn Commemorative Vol., 1927), and Polyxenie Kambouropoulou in *ibid.*, Jan. 1940. Other biographical sketches are by Karl M. Dallenbach in *ibid.*, Jan. 1940, and W. B. Pillsbury in *Psychologi-*

*cal Rev.*, Mar. 1940; and there are tributes by Grace H. Macurdy, Herbert S. Langfeld, Henry N. MacCracken, and Elizabeth M. Hincks in *Vassar Alumnae Mag.*, Jan. 1940. See also Mabel F. Martin, "The Psychological Contributions of Margaret Floy Washburn," *Am. Jour. of Psychology*, Jan. 1940; and, on her ancestry, *Nat. Cyc. Am. Biog.*, XXX, 248.]

EDWIN G. BORING

**WASHINGTON, Martha Dandridge Custis** (June 2, 1731–May 22, 1802), wife of George Washington, was born at Chestnut Grove plantation on the Pamunkey River in New Kent County, Va., the oldest of eight children of John and Frances (Jones) Dandridge. Her father was the son of an immigrant merchant, presumably from England; her mother was a granddaughter of the Rev. Rowland Jones, who came to Virginia from England as the first rector of Bruton Parish Church, Williamsburg. Although the Dandridges were of moderate means, Martha grew up among the wealthy and cultivated plantation families of the Pamunkey Valley, learning the nuances as well as the amenities of Tidewater Virginia life. As was customary, her education, except in the domestic arts, was minimal. In 1749, at eighteen, she was married to Daniel Parke Custis, twenty years her senior, son of the eccentric Col. John Custis of Williamsburg.

The elder Custis died that same year, leaving a large, if incredibly complicated, estate that enabled Daniel and Martha Custis to live opulently at the Custis plantation on the Pamunkey. Four children were born to them: Daniel and Frances, both of whom died in infancy; John, or "Jackie"; and Martha, nicknamed "Patsy." In July 1757, however, Daniel Custis died intestate, and to his widow fell the task of administering his affairs. Although litigation over the tangled inheritance lasted for years, Martha Custis at twenty-six was a very wealthy woman. In addition to her dower right—a third of the net product of the Custis lands and slaves—she received over $33,000 in cash and assumed guardianship of her two minor children, upon whom the balance of the estate devolved.

Young George Washington, plantation owner and commander of Virginia forces in the French and Indian War, was not unmindful of Mrs. Custis' circumstances when, in the spring of 1758, he began to court the attractive widow. After a meeting at the home of a friend he paid her a visit, and their betrothal soon followed. Evidence suggests that Washington was more drawn to another young lady, Sally Fairfax, the wife of his friend George William Fairfax, but he and Martha Custis were married in an Anglican ceremony at her home on Jan. 6, 1759. Mrs. Washington and her children moved to Mount Vernon, Washington's Potomac plantation, where, as was the custom, she assumed full management of the household and the domestic servants, creating much of the warm hospitality for which Mount Vernon became famous.

Although the ample Custis fortune, now under Washington's trusteeship, did much to ease the way for him, the marriage was marked by a growing mutual consideration and deep attachment. The couple were childless, but Washington was deeply fond of his stepchildren. Mrs. Washington was an indulgent, apprehensive mother who scarcely could bear separation from her children, and her husband shared this concern—justifiably, as it proved, for young Martha died at seventeen of epilepsy in 1773. Less than a year later John precipitously left King's College in New York to marry Eleanor Calvert of Maryland.

Meanwhile, the colonies' struggle with Great Britain had reached a crisis, and in 1775 Washington was chosen by Congress to command the American forces. He wrote to his wife from Philadelphia on June 18, justifying his acceptance as a response to duty; this and a subsequent letter of the same summer are all that survive of their correspondence. That December, making her first trip out of Virginia, Martha Washington joined her husband at his headquarters in Cambridge, Mass., and in subsequent years she made the difficult journey from Mount Vernon to his winter quarters in Morristown, N.J., Valley Forge, Pa., and Newburgh, N.Y., where her cheerful presence and the steadying sight of her constant sewing did much to encourage both the Commander and the troops. MERCY WARREN, visiting her in Cambridge, found her complacent, affable, and unaffected, well suited "to soften the hours of private life, or to sweeten the cares of the Hero, and smooth the rugged paths of War" (Wharton, p. 100). In November 1781, shortly after the battle of Yorktown, Martha Washington's twenty-seven-year-old son, John, died of "camp fever." The Washingtons took the two youngest of his four children, George Washington Parke Custis and Eleanor Parke Custis, to rear as their own at Mount Vernon. (George Washington Custis' daughter, Mary Anne Randolph Custis, in 1831 was to marry Robert E. Lee.)

At the close of the war the General returned to his estate for five tranquil years, disrupted only by the heavy burden of entertaining the steady stream of guests, many of them strangers, who passed through Mount Vernon. When

the presidency began to be spoken of, Mrs. Washington wrote somewhat wistfully, "I had anticipated that . . . we should be suffered to grow old together, in solitude and tranquility" (ibid., p. 183). She bowed to the inevitable, however, having "learned from experience that the greater part of our happiness or misery depends on our dispositions and not on our circumstances" (ibid., pp. 203–04).

A month after Washington's inauguration as president of the United States, in 1789, she joined him in New York, the nation's first capital, and assumed management of their Broadway residence. Thoroughly domestic by nature, her interests seldom straying beyond family, friends, and household routine, she bowed without relish to the social demands now placed upon her by the Federalist concept of the presidency as a highly dignified, almost regal, office. "I live a very dull life here . . . ," she wrote to a Virginia relative, "indeed I think I am more like a state prisoner than anything else . . ." (ibid., pp. 205–06). In another letter she wryly noted the fact that she "who had much rather be at home, should occupy a place with which a great many younger and gayer women would be extremely pleased" (ibid., p. 203). Besides the President's strictly formal semiweekly levees (to which only gentlemen were invited) and the Thursday state dinners, Mrs. Washington gave a weekly Friday evening reception. All persons of respectability had access to these "drawing rooms" without special invitation, for this function was designed to demonstrate that the new government was republican as well as aristocratic. Formal dress was required, but the tone was that of a pleasant, if self-conscious, informality, the President mingling with the callers while "Lady Washington," as she was often styled, remained seated to receive the bows of arriving and departing guests, with ABIGAIL ADAMS, wife of the Vice-President, seated at her right.

When the seat of government was moved to Philadelphia in 1790, the social ritual grew even more ostentatious. The Washingtons moved into the brick town house of Robert Morris on High (later Market) Street, which was enlarged and redecorated for the presidential entourage, now including a resplendent cream-colored carriage, drawn by six horses, with four servants and two gentlemen outriders in attendance. Mrs. Washington often used this conveyance for social calls, which she never failed to return promptly on the third day. Although the First Lady herself always dressed quietly, if richly, the more elegant Philadelphia dames brought an air of increased grandeur to the levees, and charges by the opposition press that this was too much opulence for a republican government grew more insistent. Mrs. Washington endured this criticism as part of the world of politics in which she was but little interested and which she was powerless to alter. Though not physically prepossessing—the plumpness of her youth had increased with the years, giving her a "portly double chin"—and not gifted with the keen wit or analytical mind of her successor and frequent companion Abigail Adams, she was nevertheless genuinely kind and sympathetic, and guests who found Washington somewhat aloof were grateful for her warmth and graciousness.

With the conclusion of a second presidential term in 1797 the Washingtons returned for the last time to Mount Vernon, where Martha resumed her familiar domestic life, "steady as a clock, busy as a bee, and cheerful as a cricket," as she wrote to a friend (*ibid.*, p. 265). Their peaceful retirement together ended on Dec. 14, 1799, when Washington died after a short illness. According to his will Martha Washington was given practical control and lifetime use of the entire estate—estimated at nearly $600,000—but she left its management to others, particularly her granddaughter Eleanor and the latter's husband, Lawrence Lewis, retiring to an attic room where she devoted herself to needlework. She was displeased as the formal presidential court she had helped establish gave way to the more casual Jeffersonian style and, in a rare lapse from discretion, made "pointed and sometimes very sarcastic" comments to a party of visiting Federalists about "the new order of things" (*ibid.*, p. 284). Martha Washington died of a prolonged "severe fever" in 1802, shortly before her seventy-first birthday. She lies buried at Mount Vernon beside her husband, in the tomb enclosure he had planned.

[Douglas Southall Freeman's *George Washington*, vols. I–VI (1948–54), and the concluding vol. VII (1957) by John A. Carroll and Mary W. Ashworth cover all sources and authorities on the Washington family known to the authors. See also Bernhard Knollenberg, *George Washington: The Va. Period, 1732–1775* (1964). Anne Hollingsworth Wharton, *Martha Washington* (1897), is still useful. Other pertinent references include: William S. Baker, *Washington after the Revolution* (1898); Gilbert Chinard, ed., *George Washington as the French Knew Him* (1940); George W. P. Custis, *Recollections and Private Memoirs* (1860); Stephen Decatur, Jr., *Private Affairs of George Washington, from the Records and Accounts of Tobias Lear, Esquire, His Secretary* (1933); John C. Fitzpatrick, ed., *The Last Will and Testament of George Washington . . . [and] of Martha Washington* (1939); Benson J. Lossing, *Mount Vernon and Its*

*Associations* (1859); Meade Minnigerode, *Some Am. Ladies* (1926); William D. Hoyt, Jr., "Self-Portrait: Eliza Custis, 1808," *Va. Mag. of Hist. and Biog.*, Apr. 1945.]

MARY WELLS ASHWORTH

**WATERBURY, Lucy McGill.** *See* PEABODY, Lucy Whitehead McGill Waterbury.

**WATERS, Clara Erskine Clement** (Aug. 28, 1834–Feb. 20, 1916), art historian and world traveler, was a New Englander born in St. Louis, Mo., during the temporary residence there of her parents. She was the eldest of three children and only daughter of John Erskine, described in a town history as "an enterprising business man in various parts of the world" (Ballou, p. 735) and on his death record simply as "gentleman." Her mother was Harriet Bethiah (Godfrey) Erskine. During her second year the family settled in Milford, Mass., for generations the home of her mother's family, and here she was to spend much of her childhood. Her father, born in Claremont, N.H., served as town clerk and justice of the peace in Milford for part of this period, but the Erskines also traveled a good deal, and Clara is often considered to have grown up in the Boston-Cambridge area. As became the daughter of a well-to-do New Englander, she was privately tutored. She early revealed her propensity for reading and study, as well as some aptitude for composition.

On Aug. 3, 1852, shortly before her eighteenth birthday, she was married in Milford to a promising young businessman, James Hazen Clement, who was soon to expand his already profitable investments in a stage line and shoe factory into a fortune that included bank holdings and a ranch in Texas. By this marriage there were born four sons and one daughter, of whom Hazen, Erskine, and Hope were living at the time of their father's death in 1881. The family resided in Newton, Mass., during the years of child rearing. There Clara Clement formed a close friendship with Mrs. Isabella Williamson Greene, wife of the rector of Grace Church (Episcopal), whom she memorialized in a small volume of prose (1872), describing the life and character of this woman of "beautiful piety," as well as her social activities among polite circles in Washington and Europe.

Travel and writing occupied Mrs. Waters even during the years when her children were growing to maturity. A visit to Palestine and Turkey in 1868 gave rise to her first book, *A Simple Story of What One of Your Lady Friends Saw in the East* (privately printed, 1869). To meet a need which she had felt in her travels, she next wrote three art handbooks, published during the 1870's and republished in edition after edition for two decades: *A Handbook of Legendary and Mythological Art* (1871); *Painters, Sculptors, Architects, Engravers, and Their Works* (1874); and, with Laurence Hutton, *Artists of the Nineteenth Century and Their Works* (1879). These books, particularly the last, reveal the solid learning and research which lay beneath her later more popular and impressionistic writings. Her versatility and range were manifested in the production of a novel, *Eleanor Maitland* (1881), and a biography of the actress CHARLOTTE CUSHMAN (1882).

On May 20, 1882, in the year following the death of her first husband, she was married to Edwin Forbes Waters, a respected and active citizen of Newton, an owner for many years of the *Boston Daily Advertiser,* and the author of a book on governmental reform. In the years that followed she made numerous trips abroad, including one around the world in 1883–84, was noted for her entertainments in Boston, and lived for a while in Italy. She made two tours of the Holy Land, traveled in every European country except Russia, and during her last journey, at the age of sixty-six, climbed the Great Pyramid.

Books flowed from her pen. In the 1880's she published a history of art "for beginners and students"; *A Handbook of Christian Symbols and Stories of the Saints as Illustrated in Art* (1886); and *Stories of Art and Artists* (1887). During the early 1890's she wrote four books on foreign cities: Venice (*The Queen of the Adriatic,* 1893), *Naples* (1894), Rome (*The Eternal City,* 1896), and *Constantinople* (1896). There followed *Angels in Art* (1898), *Saints in Art* (1899), *Heroines of the Bible in Art* (1900), and *Women in the Fine Arts* (1904). In addition she translated Renan's *Lectures,* Carl von Lutzow's book on Italian art, and a novel, *Dosia's Daughter* by Henri Gréville.

During her later years Mrs. Waters was a member of Trinity Church (Episcopal) in Boston and a patron of several local charities, founding a free hospital for women and aiding the Children's Hospital. For the last few years of her life she retired to a country home in Newburyport, Mass. She died of chronic myocarditis at the age of eighty-one in Brookline, Mass., at the home of her son Hazen Clement, and was buried at Mount Auburn Cemetery in Cambridge.

Clara Clement Waters was representative of late nineteenth-century literary culture in New England. Like those bright, wealthy, and genteel ladies in the novels of Henry James, she strove to be one of those upon whom nothing is lost. For her active mind and relentless pen, Boston and its environs were convenient starting points for the perusal of the world, for the cultivation of the art treasures of the past, and for forays into the exotic lands of the Mediterranean and the Orient. Back to a busy and practical America she brought her matronly visions of the high values implicit in Renaissance and late medieval painting. To a native land more attuned to masculine vigor than to delicacy and sensitivity she brought her politely feminist versions of the lives of women painters and of Biblical heroines as they had appeared in painting through the ages. To a mercantile world where art treasures had become tokens of conspicuous consumption, she brought a serious and appreciative interest in the aesthetic and moral elements of the art so freely bought and so handsomely displayed in American museums. Her style, in life as well as in writing, was breadth, clarity, and earnestness; and her mission to translate the historic past of Europe into palatably idealized terms for her countrymen paralleled in many ways the efforts of better-known literary contemporaries.

[Besides her own books, see: obituary in *Boston Transcript,* Feb. 21, 1916; Frances E. Willard and Mary A. Livermore, eds., *A Woman of the Century* (1893); Adin Ballou, *Hist. of the Town of Milford* (1882); records of her two marriages and her death, and also of her father's death (July 5, 1861), in office of Mass. Registrar of Vital Statistics.]

ALBERT F. MC LEAN, JR.

**WATKINS, Frances Ellen.** *See* HARPER, Frances Ellen Watkins.

**WATTEVILLE, Henrietta Benigna Justine Zinzendorf von** (Dec. 28, 1725–May 11, 1789), educator, a key figure in the beginnings of Moravian Seminary and College for Women, Bethlehem, Pa., was born in Berthelsdorf, Saxony. She was the first daughter and second of twelve children, of whom only four reached maturity, of Count Nicolaus Ludwig von Zinzendorf by his wife, Countess Erdmuthe Dorothea von Reuss. Her father, founder of the Renewed Moravian Church, was of an old family of the Austrian nobility that had migrated to Germany; her mother was of the nobility of Thuringia. Reared in the eighteenth-century Moravian Church, Benigna lived and achieved as a devout Pietist.

Her father's banishment from Saxony when she was eleven marked the beginning for her of a much-traveled life. With him she came to America for the first time in December 1741 for a stay of fourteen months, chiefly in the newly established Moravian communities of Pennsylvania. On May 4, 1742, at her father's suggestion, the sixteen-year-old countess, with two assistants, opened a girls' school in the Ashmead house in Germantown. Here twenty-five pupils were instructed in reading, writing, religion, and the household arts in what was probably the first boarding school for girls in the thirteen colonies. Seven weeks later the school moved to Bethlehem and in 1745 to nearby Nazareth, returning permanently in 1749 to Bethlehem, the center of the Moravian Church in America. In the summer of 1742 Benigna Zinzendorf interrupted her teaching to accompany her father on two of his three trips among the Indians of Pennsylvania and New York, preparatory to establishing missions among them. The Zinzendorfs returned to Europe the following winter. In 1746 Benigna was married to Baron Johann von Watteville (de Watteville), a Moravian clergyman and her father's secretary, in a ceremony performed by Zinzendorf at the new Moravian settlement in Zeist, Holland. Consecrated a bishop the following year, Watteville, aided by his capable wife, became an outstanding leader of his church. The couple came to America on church business in September 1748 and remained a year. On this visit Benigna de Watteville had a hand in the return of the girls' school to Bethlehem, its consolidation with schools in the outlying Moravian congregations, and the enlargement of its curriculum. Thirty-five years later, en route to America a third time, she was shipwrecked with her husband on the rocks off Barbuda in the Leeward Islands in February 1784. Reaching Bethlehem in June, they remained for three years. Again Countess Benigna was on hand to help direct a reorganization of the girls' seminary, which in 1785, now opened to pupils from outside the Moravian Church, became a largely new institution, known for many years as the Bethlehem Female Seminary.

The Moravian philosophy of education was the rearing of children in a controlled Christian environment under consecrated teachers. Because of the worldwide mission commitments of the Church, many parents were abroad, with their children left behind in the care of the home community. Moravian teachers, therefore, tried as nearly as possible to serve as substitute parents. Both as a parent and as a devout church member, Benigna de Watteville kept this ideal in mind. She had four children of her own: Johann Ludwig (born 1752), Anna

Dorothea Elizabeth (1754), Maria Justine (1762), and Johann Christian Friederich (1766). The older son died while a missionary in Tranquebar, India, in 1780, and the younger son died at nineteen as a student at Herrnhut, the church headquarters on his grandfather's Berthelsdorf estates. The younger daughter, who never married, served as a worker in the church. The older daughter married Hans Christian Alexander von Schweinitz (later changed to de Schweinitz) in Bethlehem, Pa., in 1779. One of their children was the distinguished American botanist Louis David de Schweinitz, and de Schweinitz descendants have for four generations been prominent in American educational and professional life. Benigna de Watteville died in the place of her birth at the age of sixty-three, a year after her husband. The Bethlehem seminary, incorporated in 1863 as the Moravian Seminary for Young Ladies, became in 1913 Moravian Seminary and College for Women and in 1953 a part of the coeducational Moravian College at Bethlehem.

[Memoir in *Nachrichten ans der Brüder-gemeine*, 1873, part 9, p. 782; references in standard Moravian historical works, especially Joseph M. Levering, *A Hist. of Bethlehem, Pa.* (1903), J. Taylor Hamilton, *A Hist. of the Church Known as the Moravian Church* (1900), and William C. Reichel, ed., *Memorials of the Moravian Church* (1870); Mabel Haller, *Early Moravian Education in Pa.* (1953); John R. Weinlick, *Count Zinzendorf* (1956); MS. diaries, reports of synods, and letters in Moravian Archives, Bethlehem, Pa.]

JOHN R. WEINLICK

**WAY, Amanda M.** (July 10, 1828–Feb. 24, 1914), temperance and suffrage reformer, Methodist and Quaker preacher, was born in Winchester, Ind., the first daughter and second of eight children of Matthew and Hannah (Martin) Way. On her father's side she was descended from Quaker pioneers who came to the Whitewater valley in Randolph County, Ind., from South Carolina in the early spring of 1817, crossing the Ohio River on the ice at Cincinnati. Her great-uncle Henry H. Way of Newport, Ind., was a well-known physician associated with Levi Coffin in the Underground Railroad and in the separation of the antislavery Friends from the Indiana Yearly Meeting in 1843. Amanda received her education in the public schools and at Randolph Seminary in Winchester. After graduation she taught school for a time, but in order to support her widowed mother and a sister's orphaned children she took up millinery and dressmaking and operated a tailor shop. She never married.

She began her career as a social reformer in 1851, when at an antislavery meeting in Greensboro, Henry County, Ind., she offered a resolution calling for a state woman's rights convention. The convention met in October of the same year at Dublin, Wayne County, and elected Miss Way vice-president of the newly formed Indiana Woman's Rights Society. For the next nine years she was a leading figure in the society, serving as president in 1855. In 1859 she assisted Mrs. Sarah E. Underhill in editing an Indianapolis newspaper, the *Woman's Tribune*. Meanwhile Amanda Way was active in the state temperance movement. In 1854 she organized a "Woman's Temperance Army" in Winchester, anticipating the later Woman's Crusade of the 1870's in its work of closing saloons. She was also a lecturer and organizer for a temperance lodge, the Independent Order of Good Templars, and was the first woman to be elected Grand Worthy Chief Templar. The Civil War brought a temporary halt to both the woman's rights and the temperance causes. When four of her brothers joined the Union Army in 1861, Miss Way became a nurse and served on battlefields and in hospitals for most of the war.

In 1869 Amanda Way was a delegate to the convention which organized the National Prohibition party (James Black, *Brief History of Prohibition and of the Prohibition Reform Party*, 1880, p. 7). That same year she reactivated the woman's rights movement in Indiana by issuing a call for a state convention at which the prewar society was reorganized as the Indiana Woman Suffrage Association, a branch of LUCY STONE's American Woman Suffrage Association. In January 1871 Miss Way was granted a hearing by the state legislature and read a memorial from the state society asking for an amendment to the Indiana constitution permitting women to vote. Later the same year the Richmond district of the North Indiana Conference of the Methodist Episcopal Church licensed her as a local preacher. A birthright Quaker, she had become a Methodist some years before and now entered energetically upon an itinerant ministry in the churches of Indiana and Kansas, to which state she moved in 1872. In Kansas she continued her interest in temperance and woman's rights and lectured for both causes. She played some part in helping secure the prohibition amendment to the Kansas constitution in 1880 and was a founder and first president of the Woman's Christian Temperance Union in that state. Although her church and temperance activities tended to monopolize her energies at this time, she remained a suffragist and in 1880 was a Kansas delegate to a Chicago convention called by the National Woman Suffrage Association to exert pressure on the Republican National Convention meeting in that city. In 1905 Miss Way, seventy-seven years old and one of the last survivors of the pre–Civil War era of woman's rights, briefly addressed the National American Woman Suffrage Association convention in Portland, Oreg., on her early years in the movement.

When the General Conference of the Methodist Episcopal Church in 1880 confirmed the action of previous conferences in discontinuing the licensing of women as local preachers, Amanda Way returned to the Society of Friends, which she served as a pastor for the rest of her life. Around the turn of the century she left Kansas for the Far West. After a short stay in Idaho, she made her home in southern California, the last few years in Whittier, where she was a minister in the Quaker monthly meeting. A quiet, modest woman, she neither sought nor received wide acclaim; yet in an age when women were just beginning to appear on the public platform, Amanda Way was an indefatigable lecturer on behalf of antislavery, woman's rights, and temperance in the Middle West. For approximately the last half of her life she apparently found the gospel ministry a more congenial occupation. A strong, vigorous woman, whose health failed only near the end of her long life, she died in Whittier, Calif., in her eighty-sixth year and was buried in the Whittier Cemetery.

[Biographical information about Amanda Way is meager. The following contain short sketches of varying degrees of accuracy: obituaries in the *Whittier* (Calif.) *News*, Feb. 27, 1914, and the *Pacific Friend*, XXI (1914), 14–15; article by Grace Julian Clarke in *Indianapolis Star*, Feb. 4, 1923; B. F. Austin, ed., *The Temperance Leaders of America* (1896); Ernest H. Cherrington, ed., *Standard Encyc. of the Alcohol Problem*, VI (1930), 2811; Elizabeth C. Stanton et al., *Hist. of Woman Suffrage*, I (1881), 306–12. See also *ibid.*, III (1886), 175–76n, 533, 538–39, 709n, V (1922), 132, VI (1922), 31; William A. Mitchell, *Linn County, Kans.: A Hist.* (1928), pp. 250–51, 311–12, 388; Ebenezer Tucker, *Hist. of Randolph County, Ind., with Illustrations and Biog. Memoirs* (1882), pp. 38–39, 55, 340–41, 344. The library of Whittier College, Whittier, Calif., and the Ind. State Library were helpful in supplying information.]

CLIFTON J. PHILLIPS

**WEBER, Lois** (June 13, 1881–Nov. 13, 1939), motion-picture director, writer, and actress, was born in Allegheny, Pa. (now a part of Pittsburgh). Christened Florence Lois, she was the second daughter of George Weber, an upholsterer and decorator, and Mary Matilda (Snaman) Weber. Her forefathers, Pennsylvania Germans, had pioneered in the settlement of western Pennsylvania; many were preachers, and the Weber home was one of strict religious observance.

Lois Weber early exhibited musical talent. She took part in church and school entertainments, sang in the church choir, and played the piano with considerable skill. She began her public career at the age of sixteen when she toured as a concert pianist; her enthusiasm was short-lived, however, and she returned to her home, where she joined the Church Army, singing at its rescue mission, on the streets, and in houses of the red-light district. She next aspired to a career as an opera singer and left home—without her parents' consent—to study voice in New York City, financing her lessons by playing for her teacher's other students.

Her first stage work was as a soubrette in the Zig Zag Company, which toured New England and Pennsylvania before going into bankruptcy. In August 1904 she was engaged for one of the three touring companies of the play *Why Girls Leave Home;* she "sang two very pretty songs very effectively," a reviewer reported, "and won considerable applause" (*Boston Globe*, Sept. 27, 1904). At this time she met Wendell Phillips Smalley, stage manager of the company and son of George Washburn Smalley, a Boston lawyer and journalist, and Phoebe (Garnaut) Smalley, adopted daughter of the abolitionist Wendell Phillips. They were married in Chicago several months later, at the home of an uncle of Miss Weber's. There were no children. During the next five years they played together whenever possible, usually in repertory and stock.

The desire to avoid separation led Lois Weber and her husband into the motion-picture industry, where for more than a decade they signed joint contracts. They made their debut in a series of experimental "talking" films —two decades before the successful coming of sound—for the Gaumont Company; Miss Weber wrote the brief scenarios and the dialogue, which was recorded on phonograph records and synchronized with the action. This was followed by a brief association with the newly formed Reliance Company in the fall of 1910. Early in 1911 the Smalleys joined Rex, one of the satellite companies of the New York Motion Picture Corporation, which in 1912 became a subsidiary of Universal Pictures. At Rex, Miss Weber acted, assisted her husband in directing, wrote the stories and subtitles, designed sets, collected props, spotted locations, cut the film, and if necessary turned the camera and developed the negative.

After an eight-month interval (1914–15) with the Bosworth Company, during which they made a series of impressive features (released by Paramount) which greatly advanced their reputation, they returned to Universal. By this time Miss Weber was established as a director in her own right. With her husband, she set up her own studio, Lois Weber Productions, in 1917, but continued to release chiefly through Universal, with which company she thereafter remained associated, save for a brief interim of directing for DeMille Pictures Corporation in 1927. Studio officials respected and admired both her business sense and her artistic taste. "She knows the motion-picture business as few people know it," said Universal's president, Carl Laemmle, "and can drive herself as hard as anyone I have ever known" (*Liberty*, May 14, 1927, p. 31). Highly successful in developing young actresses, Miss Weber directed Lois Wilson and Esther Ralston in their first screen appearances, discovered Claire Windsor, and did much to advance the careers of Mildred Harris and Billie Dove.

The first and for many years the only consistently successful American woman to direct motion pictures, Lois Weber was of medium height, dark-haired, compactly built, and decisive in manner, with energy and endurance that carried her through the long hours and heavy pressure of film directing. In 1916 she made *The Dumb Girl of Portici,* starring Anna Pavlova, in which her handling of the dancing, the masses of people, and the melodramatic story were (in the words of Julian Johnson) "testimonials of the finest female imagination in filmland." Among her most popular successes were *Jewel* (1915) and *For Husbands Only* (1918), but more typical of her work were pictures dealing with controversial social and moral problems: *Hypocrites* (1914), *Scandal* (1915), *Idle Wives* (1916), *Where Are My Children?* (1916), *Shoes* (1916, possibly the finest film she made), *The Price of a Good Time* (1917), and *What Do Men Want?* (1921). Some of Miss Weber's films encountered censorship (particularly the tremendously popular *Where Are My Children?* a dramatic plea for birth control), but they were intelligently done and free from cheap sensationalism. Eager to awaken mankind to tolerance and brotherly love through films, she felt that motion pictures could speak to everyone, reaching more people than any other medium. "The boundary lines of ignorance and poverty are taken down," she wrote, "and the intellectual reservations of centuries are thrown open to new settlers." Through films she crusaded for an enlightened moral code based on knowledge.

Miss Weber and Phillips Smalley were divorced June 23, 1922; in poor health at this time, she shortly afterward suffered a nervous breakdown. Except for *A Chapter in Her Life*, released in 1923, she made no other films until after her second marriage, in 1926, to Capt. Harry Gantz, a retired army officer. Gantz is credited with bringing her out of a retirement which was more nearly a despondent withdrawal from public life. This marriage also ended in divorce, but it led her back to the screen as the director of *The Marriage Clause* (1926), *Sensation Seekers* (1926), and *The Angel of Broadway* (1927). In 1933 she returned to Universal to interview and test screen aspirants, and in 1934, after a seven-year interval, made her last film, *White Heat*. After a long illness caused by a gastric ulcer, she died from a gastric hemorrhage at Good Samaritan Hospital in Los Angeles in 1939, at the age of fifty-eight. Her ashes were placed in the Los Angeles Crematory.

Though never an idolized favorite as a film actress, Lois Weber was intelligent and effective in her portrayals. A prolific writer, she either wrote or adapted all but seven of the hundreds of films she produced. As a director she stamped her work with her own style and personal conviction.

[Much has been written about Lois Weber, but most of it is in the tangled tales of popular publications. Some information will be found in Alice M. Williamson, *Alice in Movieland* (1927); Carolyn Lowrey, *The First One Hundred Noted Men and Women of the Screen* (1920); Miss Weber's "How I Became a Motion Picture Director," *Paramount Mag.*, Feb. 1915; Bertha H. Smith, "A Perpetual Leading Lady," *Sunset*, Mar. 1914; Charles S. Dunning, "The Gate Women Don't Crash," *Liberty*, May 14, 1927; H. H. Van Loan, "Lois the Wizard," *Motion Picture Mag.*, July 1916; feature article in *Boston Globe*, Sept. 12, 1926; and *Who Was Who in America*, vol. I (1942). Other references, all presenting some problems for the biographer, include: *Universal Weekly*, Oct. 4, 1913, Jan. 10, 1914; *Motion Picture Mag.*, May 1915, May 1918; *Moving Picture World*, Apr. 3, 1915; *Photoplay*, Oct. 1917; *Cinema Art*, Dec. 1926, Jan. 1927; *The Star*, June 8, 1921; *Motion Picture Classic*, May 1923; *Overland Monthly*, Sept. 1916. Miss Weber's sister, Ethel Weber Howland, supplied personal information.]

GERALD D. MC DONALD

**WEBSTER, Jean** (July 24, 1876–June 11, 1916), author, christened Alice Jane Chandler Webster, was born at Fredonia, N.Y., the eldest of the three children and only daughter of Annie (Moffett) and Charles Luther Webster. Her early facility in writing was probably stimulated by her childhood environment. Her maternal grandmother was Mark Twain's older sister Pamela (Clemens) Moffett, and her father (formerly a civil engineer and real estate agent) was Mark Twain's partner and publisher, in which capacity he issued, along with *Huckleberry Finn* and other books, General Grant's phenomenally successful *Personal Memoirs*. His health broken by overwork, Charles Webster retired in 1887 and died in 1891, at the age of forty.

Alice, who adopted the name Jean in boarding school, attended the Lady Jane Grey School at Binghamton, N.Y., and graduated from Vassar College in 1901. The poet ADE-LAIDE CRAPSEY was a classmate and became her lifelong friend. During her boarding school days Jean Webster began writing to her parents the delightful letters that led directly to her novels and short stories. At Vassar she earned money by contributing a weekly column to the *Poughkeepsie Sunday Courier*, and she published many stories in the *Vassar Miscellany*. While still an undergraduate she began writing the Patty stories, using Adelaide Crapsey, it is thought, as her model; in 1903 they were collected and published in book form under the title *When Patty Went to College*.

After graduation Miss Webster became a free-lance writer in New York and later made several trips to Europe. While living as a guest in a convent one winter in the Sabine Mountains of Italy, she wrote *The Wheat Princess* (1905), her favorite among her books. Here also she wrote *Jerry, Junior* (1907), tales of trips she made by donkey among the people of the mountains. In 1906–07 her travels included a journey around the world. Upon her return to New York, she settled in Greenwich Village. Along with her writing she pursued an interest in aiding the unfortunate that had begun in college, when she had visited institutions for the destitute and delinquent while studying economics. Because of her love of children, she took a special interest in the improvement of orphan asylums, an interest that was to find reflection in her writing. She served, too, on committees for prison reform and was a familiar figure at Sing Sing, where she worked with convicts, some of whom became her devoted friends.

On Sept. 7, 1915, at thirty-nine, Jean Webster was married to Glenn Ford McKinney, a lawyer, and settled in an apartment overlooking Central Park. She died the following summer in New York's Sloane Hospital for Women, a few hours after the birth of a daughter, of complications resulting from the presence of uterine fibroids. The child, Jean Webster Mc-Kinney, survived. A room in the Girls' Service League and a bed in the New York Orthopedic Hospital near White Plains were endowed in Jean Webster's memory.

Of her nine books, the most popular was *Daddy-Long-Legs* (1912), the story of Judy, a foundling who spends her first seventeen years in the dulling routine of an orphan asylum and first experiences the joys of learning when she is sent to college through the generosity of a wealthy, anonymous bachelor. Originally serialized in the *Ladies' Home Journal*, the book became a best seller and was widely translated. In 1914 Miss Webster wrote a stage adaptation which enjoyed an extensive run at the Gaiety Theatre in New York, with Ruth Chatterton as the star, and was produced by road companies throughout the United States. A film version by Mary Pickford followed in 1919. In its various forms *Daddy-Long-Legs* stirred concern for the plight of orphans, particularly for the narrow and limited training provided by custodial institutions, and a committee of the New York State Charities Aid Association began organizing auxiliary groups in colleges which would each assume responsibility for the education of at least one orphan. A sequel, *Dear Enemy* (1914), was also popular. Other books by Miss Webster that attracted interest were *The Four Pools of Mystery* (1908), published anonymously, *Much Ado about Peter* (1909), and *Just Patty* (1911).

Jean Webster was a skilled craftsman who gave much care to achieving a direct and lucid style. She wrote lengthy first drafts, then cut and pruned ruthlessly, sometimes taking months for revision. Her writing was notably more sophisticated and less sentimental than that of some of the other women writers of the period, such as ALICE HEGAN RICE (*Mrs. Wiggs of the Cabbage Patch*) and GENE STRATTON-PORTER (*Girl of the Limberlost*). So simple and absorbing are the stories that her books are often classed as juveniles; yet adults, too, have enjoyed her tales, which are animated by a sober, mature purpose and illumined by a strong sense of reality, warm humor, and sharp wit.

[Obituaries in *Century Mag.*, Nov. 1916, *Vassar Quart.*, Nov. 1916, and *N.Y. Times*, June 12, 1916; other items in *N.Y. Times*: Jean Webster, "The Vassar Literary," Mar. 21, 1915 (autobiographical sketch), news story on her plan for college groups to adopt orphans, Nov. 9, 1914, and interview, Dec. 13, 1914; Channing Pollock in *Green Book Mag.*, Dec. 1914; *Woman's Who's Who of America*, 1914–15; Stanley J. Kunitz and Howard Hay-craft, eds., *The Junior Book of Authors* (1934) and *Twentieth Century Authors* (1942); family information from Darwin R. Barker Library, Fredonia, N.Y.; death record from N.Y. City Dept. of Health.]

RACHEL SALISBURY

**WEED, Ella** (Jan. 27, 1853–Jan. 10, 1894), educator, a leading figure in the formative years of Barnard College, was born in Newburgh, N.Y., the first daughter and first of four children of Jonathan Noyes Weed, a banker, and Elizabeth Merritt (Goodsell) Weed. Her father, whose ancestors had long been resident in the area, was prominent in Newburgh business and civic life and in the Trinity Methodist Church. Her maternal grandfather taught school and her mother was active in charitable work. Ella Weed attended Miss Mackay's School in Newburgh and Vassar College. Her contributions to the *Vassar Miscellany* helped establish its high reputation among contemporary college periodicals, and she graduated with honors in 1873. Beginning in 1875 she taught at a girls' school in Springfield, Ohio, where she specialized in preparing students for entrance to Vassar. Returning to Newburgh in 1882 at the behest of her family, she combined a needed rest with teaching at Miss Mackay's. In 1884 she became head of the day school at the fashionable Anne Brown School in New York City.

On the strength of the reputation she had established at Miss Brown's, Ella Weed's assistance was sought in 1888 by Annie Nathan Meyer (1867–1951), a young New Yorker then spearheading a movement to establish a female annex at Columbia University. Before her marriage Mrs. Meyer had briefly been a student in the Collegiate Course for Women established five years earlier by the Columbia trustees in response to pleas for the opening of higher education in New York to women. She considered the course unjust, however, for it required that women prepare themselves independently, without access to the lectures available to men, in courses for which they were expected to meet the same standards and pass identical examinations. Ella Weed's readiness to assist Mrs. Meyer furthered the cause of those who wished to abandon the Collegiate Course in favor of an annex. Through her contacts at the Anne Brown School, Miss Weed enjoyed an acquaintance with the socially prominent, and her advice helped determine the names of influential New Yorkers whose signatures were to prove effective on a petition to the Columbia trustees. Thus Barnard College was launched in 1889 as a financially independent and physically separate institution whose students were to receive their instruction from visiting members of the Columbia faculty and whose degrees were to be granted by Columbia.

While continuing to teach at the Anne Brown School, Miss Weed became a member of Barnard's first board of trustees and was made chairman of the academic committee; under the nominal leadership of the Rev. Arthur Brooks, chairman of the board, she performed all the academic duties of dean. In addition she worked skillfully at the ongoing task of public relations and fund raising for the new college, suggesting the devoted George A. Plimpton to succeed Jacob Schiff in the crucial role of treasurer, and submitting names of potential donors. She met successfully a variety of challenges, ranging from the supervision of the college's first quarters at 343 Madison Avenue to the negotiations with Columbia faculty giving instruction at Barnard. It was not long before Ella Weed had set the tone and established the standards that enabled the new institution to gain early recognition as a leading women's college.

Miss Weed's educational philosophy deplored the prevailing finishing-school character of women's education. Her policies at Barnard were the practical expression of her belief that women could gain full intellectual standing only if their education were equal to men's in rigor. In spite of the scarcity of preparatory training for women in Greek, Miss Weed insisted on Greek for entrance to Barnard, matching an identical entrance requirement at Columbia College. Her vigorous adherence to the principle of breadth before specialization led to Barnard's refusal of special students in all but the sciences, in contrast to the greater leniency at the Harvard Annex. Miss Weed declined to open Barnard with a full four classes, believing that in the formative years of the college it was unwise to admit transfer students and feeling that the quality of the college could more accurately be reflected by graduates trained solely at Barnard. She also resisted pressures to admit mature women with poor preparation who wished to avail themselves of a local opportunity for higher education. In a further effort to ensure equal standards, she insisted that Columbia have supervisory power over all instruction at Barnard. Her diplomatic skill won the cooperation of Columbia's male faculty and administration.

Though not a beautiful woman, Miss Weed had a winning manner and good-humored industry that endeared her to many, and her faith in individuals could inspire seemingly unpromising students with a zeal for learning. She was convinced that women should be equipped with the tools to realize their abilities fully, but she did not urge them toward extreme positions. Her devotion to the cause of women's education kept her from developing her own considerable literary talents. Aside from a satirical novel, *A Foolish Virgin* (1883), depicting the adventures of a Vassar-trained heroine who tries to disguise her good sense and her good education in order to meet accepted standards for female behavior, her only other book was the posthumous *Pearls Strung by Ella Weed* (1898), brief selections from her favorite authors. Ella Weed's work came to a premature end. Shortly before her forty-first birthday she died in New York City of "nervous prostration" attributed to overwork in summer educational ventures. She was buried in Cedar Hill Cemetery in Newburgh.

[John J. Nutt, comp., *Newburgh: Her Institutions, Industries and Leading Citizens* (1891), and records of the Cedar Hill Cemetery in Newburgh are sources for family background. Miss Weed's contribution as class prophet to the Vassar Class Day Book of 1873 and her own two books reflect her literary tastes and talents. An obituary article in the *Outlook*, Jan. 27, 1894 (p. 177), and a letter in the 1927 *Brown Record*, the Alumnae Annual of the Anne Brown School, contain firsthand reminiscences. MSS. in the Barnard College Archives, articles in the *Columbia Univ. Quart.*, by Emily James Smith Putnam in June 1900 and by Nicholas Murray Butler in June 1915, and Barnard histories, especially Annie Nathan Meyer, *Barnard Beginnings* (1935), and Marian Churchill White, *A Hist. of Barnard College* (1954), give descriptions of her personality and assess her role in the women's college movement.]

ANNETTE K. BAXTER

**WEEKS, Helen C.** *See* CAMPBELL, Helen Stuart.

**WEIR, Irene** (Jan. 15, 1862–Mar. 22, 1944), painter, art teacher, and writer on art, was born in St. Louis, Mo., the daughter of Walter and Annie Field (Andrews) Weir. Her father, a graduate of Trinity College in Hartford, Conn., was a teacher in St. Louis but early in adult life suffered an accident and was for many years incapacitated. Of Scottish descent, the Weir family was distinguished by the large number of its members who devoted their lives to the teaching and practice of the fine arts. Irene's grandfather Robert Walter Weir (1803–1889) was a painter and for forty-two years teacher of art at the United States Military Academy, West Point. An uncle, Julian Alden Weir (1852–1919), was a prominent artist and a leader of the New York art world; another, John Ferguson Weir (1841–1926), was a painter who directed the School of Fine Arts at Yale University for over forty years. In her biography of the patriarch Robert Weir (not published until 1947, after her death), she spoke of the family legacy of God-fearing hard work and force of individual will which lent to the artists' love of beauty a special quality of practical vigor.

Little is known of Irene Weir's early life and schooling until she was nearly twenty. In 1881–82 she was enrolled at the Yale School of Fine Arts (which in 1906 awarded her the degree of B.F.A.), and later she studied under the direction of her uncle J. Alden Weir, John H. Twachtman, and Joseph Pennell. She made two early trips to Europe, probably in the period following her year at Yale, to study in the galleries of France, Italy, Spain, Holland, and England. She began her teaching career as drawing instructor in the grammar and high schools of New Haven, Conn., where she remained from 1887 to 1890. She then served for three years as director of the Slater Museum School of Art in Norwich, Conn. In December 1892 and January 1893 she lived briefly at the newly opened Denison House settlement in Boston before taking up her work as instructor and then director of art instruction in the public schools of Brookline, Mass. In 1905 she published a historical survey, *The Greek Painters' Art*, which was favorably received by the critics. She left her Brookline post in 1910 and moved to New York City, where she taught in the fine arts department of the Ethical Culture School. Later she founded and became director (1917–29) of the School of Design and Liberal Arts, which offered courses in drawing and painting with Kimon Nicolaides as critic, as well as training in crafts, interior decoration, the teaching of art in settlement houses and summer camps, fashion illustration, and commercial design. During this interval she again traveled to Europe and studied at the École des Beaux Arts Américaine in Fontainbleau, receiving the diploma in 1923.

Irene Weir's own painting followed the family pattern of cosmopolitan independence, and vigor underlies all her work: oil painting, watercolor, etching, drawing, and poster illustration. This strength is evident in her posters of the 1890's, in her paintings of flowers and landscapes, and especially in her penetrating portraits, which remind one of the work of Thomas Eakins and George Bellows, and in the bold, sweeping murals she executed in the late 1920's. In her mature paintings the expressionist richness of her palette is stabilized by solid, precise forms and strong organization. A French critic writing in 1930 characterized her work as suggestive of both Puvis de Chavannes and Raoul Dufy. Her best paintings include: "Garden of the Hesperides" (Women's University Club, New York City), "Emigrants" and "Steerage" (Huntingdon College, Montgomery, Ala.); portraits of Robert W. Weir (West Point), Annie Field Weir, and Madame Curie (Memorial Hospital, New York City); and two murals, "Child of Bethlehem" (Washington Cathedral) and "Mother and Babe with Jesus" (West Side Prison, New York City). The paintings of her later years are notable for their religious intensity, reflecting her Episcopal faith. In addition to the New York galleries, her work was exhibited at the Brooklyn Museum, the Corcoran Gallery in Washington, D.C., and in London.

As an art critic and teacher Miss Weir remained receptive to the best of the new currents in painting, while retaining the broad historical perspective characteristic of the Weirs; her views are well expressed in an article in *Parnassus* (May 1930), "A Cursive Review of Recent Museum Activities Outside New York." Her services to the art world included terms as a director of the Art Alliance of America and the Salons of America. She was an active member of artists' organizations: Independent Artists of America, National Society of Etchers, Founders Group of the Museum of Fine Arts (Houston, Texas), and the London Lyceum Club. In addition to her teaching duties she lectured at museums, colleges, and universities, including Princeton, Vassar, and the Boston Museum of Fine Arts.

Miss Weir never married. In her retirement she lived in Katonah, N.Y., where she remained active well into her seventies, lecturing occasionally to local clubs. She died in a nursing home in Yorktown Heights, N.Y., of cardiovascular disease in 1944, at the age of eighty-two, and was buried in Zion Hill Cemetery, Hartford, Conn. Her career rounded out well over a hundred years of family practice of painting and of distinguished service to the arts in America.

[Other writings by Irene Weir include articles in *Art News, Parnassus,* and *Art Digest* and, with Elizabeth Stone, *Outlines of Courses in Design, Representation and Color for High School Classes* (1910). Biographical information from: Yale Univ., *Obituary Record of Graduates,* 1943–44; Mabel W. Cameron, ed., *Biog. Cyc. Am. Women,* I (1924), 333–34; records of Denison House (Schlesinger Library, Radcliffe College); letter of Miss Weir to Prof. John H. Niemeyer, Feb. 12, 1906, in John F. Weir Papers, Yale Univ.; *Who Was Who in Amer-*

*ica,* vol. II (1950); obituaries in *N.Y. Times* and *N.Y. Herald Tribune,* Mar. 23, 1944; death record from N.Y. State Dept. of Health (which gives her date of birth). Information about her father from St. Louis city directory, 1864 (courtesy of St. Louis Public Library), and from Trinity College. For clippings and photos of paintings see folder in Arts Division, N.Y. Public Library.]

LAWRENCE W. CHISOLM

**WELD, Angelina Grimké.** *See* GRIMKÉ, Sarah Moore.

**WELLS, Carolyn** (June 18, 1862–Mar. 26, 1942), author, was born in Rahway, N.J., the oldest of four children of William Edmund and Anna Potter (Woodruff) Wells. She came, as she put it in her autobiography, of "a good sort . . . [of] stern and rock-bound ancestors." The able and prominent Thomas Wells, the earliest of her English forebears to come to America, was elected first treasurer of the Connecticut colony and later (1656) its fourth governor. On her mother's side ("a mild lot") she traced a line back through the early settlers of New Jersey to the English family of Thomas Woodrove. Her parents she remembered as "the very ultramarine of blue Presbyterians," but the affectionate portraits she draws of her family suggest a mellow Protestant household. Her father's real estate and insurance business provided his two daughters and two sons with a pleasant middle-class home that apparently was marred only by a single tragedy: a scarlet fever attack left her younger sister dead at the age of three and Carolyn Wells with a deafness that would worsen over the years.

"A jack-in-the-box brain surrounded by books": thus did Carolyn Wells image her mind and background. A precocious child, she mastered the alphabet at eighteen months, read fluently at three years, and wrote her first book at six. Getting her education "in chunks," she attended the Rahway public schools (she was valedictorian of her high school class), spent three summers at the Sauveur School of Languages in Amherst, Mass., where she studied Shakespeare under the noted literary scholar William J. Rolfe, and read widely in a "beautiful" and heavily endowed library when she worked as a young woman for the Rahway Library Association. The librarianship is an important key to her subsequent literary work. "I do not say," she wrote, "that I am highly educated, but I know a lot." The flow of books that Carolyn Wells first let loose in 1895 is more than anything else the product of a bright and good-humored librarian.

Rolfe, like Carolyn Wells a devotee of charades and puzzles, encouraged her during an Amherst summer to gather her locally famous charades and bring them out as her first book. This collection—*At the Sign of the Sphinx*—appeared in 1896 ("it didn't seem like a book to me; it just seemed a list of puzzles"); it was followed by a book of children's jingles, a story for girls, and a book of verses for grownups. When *A Nonsense Anthology,* still her best-known single work, was published in 1902, eight books had (as she put it) "happened." Early reviewers marked a new humorist—a talented young woman whose light touch, vivacious fancy, and sense of rhythm found many admirers in the literary marketplace. Later reviewers would acknowledge a warm and gracious wit and marvel at the woman's literary statistics: over 170 separate titles, more than twelve million words, by the time of her death:

> As all the signs would indicate
> Is Carolyn Wells a syndicate?

Of this extensive list, eighty-one were mystery and detective stories (most of them reporting the exploits of her most famous, and most conventional, detective, Fleming Stone), which she sent to the publishers on a schedule of three a year. "Carolyn Wells has done for the mystery story what Planck did for physics, what Copernicus did for astronomy, what Freud did for psychology," wrote a contemporary admirer. Carolyn Wells laughed at this hyperbole and recalled the details of her apprenticeship as a mystery story writer: her love of puzzles, her study of Poe and Collins and Doyle, her quick mastery of the formula detective story. Like the professional she was in all facets of her work, Carolyn Wells had adapted her talents to the requirements of the going market.

Even more characteristic of her interests and skills were the anthologies that appeared in the early years of this century: *A Parody Anthology* (1904), *A Satire Anthology* (1905), and *A Whimsey Anthology* (1906). A product, she said, of her library days, these books (none of them distinguished for their critical introductions or editing) are notable only as almost unique compilations in their day. Of her varied accomplishments, she herself perhaps took most pride in her reputation as a humorist and writer of nonsense verse. Inspired by Lewis Carroll, she regarded Oliver Herford and Gelett Burgess as her direct masters, and Burgess, through lengthy correspondence, gave her much practical criticism and help in this field. Her light verse and humorous articles appeared in most of the famous "little magazines" of the period: the *Lark* (edited by Burgess), the *Chap Book,* the *Philistine, Bibelot, Yellow Book,* and the *Lotus.* Her stories for young girls—notably the "Patty" and "Betty" collections—were popular in the new century's first decade but are quite forgotten today.

While her productions continued to appear with startling regularity, Carolyn Wells moved in an ever-widening circle of famous friends. She traveled abroad, especially to England, where she was invited to contribute to *Punch.* Her literary interests were not entirely of the moment: a rare-book enthusiast, she assembled collections of Whitman, Emerson, Longfellow, and Poe that were admired by bibliophiles. (She published, with Albert Goldsmith, a bibliography of Walt Whitman in 1922.) On Apr. 2, 1918, at fifty-five, she was married to Hadwin Houghton of the Boston publishing family, at the time the superintendent of a varnish manufacturing company; their marriage ended with his death the following year. Afterward she made her home in New York City, in a hotel overlooking Central Park. For some years a sufferer from general arteriosclerosis, she died in her eightieth year in a New York hospital after sustaining a fractured leg and wrist. She was buried in the Rahway (N.J.) Cemetery.

"All my life I have looked forward, steadily forward, and never back. I mean never back with regret for mistaken deeds, for errors of judgment, for making a fool of myself." Such personal statements—and they are recurrent ones throughout her reminiscences—come close to this woman's core. By nature a realist, a stoic, she allowed small reflection of personal grief in her work. The early death of her husband and the fearful operations to cure her deafness were not the stuff of her books. The books "happened" because editors and publishers recognized a professional writer whose wide reading and quick mind were readily available for the day's market. Her work is now in the footnotes of American literary history rather than in the hands of American readers. True enough, she was a "literary factory," but she was also a notable woman: a healthy humorist who poked fun at both the conservatives and the faddists of the day. The vitality and good humor and self-control that brought her friends aplenty are remarkable in any individual; in the still-masculine literary scene of the new century, they add up to a valid index of the changing role of the woman writer.

[Besides those already cited, her principal works are: *The Jingle Book* (1899); *Patty Fairfield* (1901); *The Clue* (1909); *A Chain of Evidence* (1912); *The Technique of the Mystery Story* (1913); *Faulkner's Folly* (1917); *The Book of Humorous Verse* (1920); *Ptomaine Street* (1921); *An Outline of Humor* (1923); *The Omnibus Fleming Stone* (1932); *Who Killed Caldwell?* (1942); and *Murder Will In* (1942). Biographical sources include her autobiography, *The Rest of My Life* (1937); articles in *Nat. Cyc. Am. Biog.,* XIII, 213–14, *Christian Science Monitor Mag.,* Oct. 21, 1939, *Publishers' Weekly,* July 22, 1939, and *Scholastic,* Apr. 15, 1940; obituaries in *N.Y. Herald Tribune* and *N.Y. Times* of Mar. 27, 1942; and death record from N.Y. City Dept. of Health (the source for her date of birth). A biographical outline and bibliography compiled by E. Doris Miglautsch, Univ. of Wis. Library School, was helpful. Information on William E. Wells from Rahway Free Public Library and N.J. Registrar of Vital Statistics.]

CARLIN T. KINDILIEN

**WELLS, Charlotte Fowler** (Aug. 14, 1814– June 4, 1901), phrenologist and publisher, was born in Cohocton, Steuben County, N.Y., of old New England stock, the fourth in a family of eight children of Horace and Martha (Howe) Fowler. Her father was probably a farmer and was a leader in his community. Growing up in a stimulating home, all the Fowler children developed marked originality of thought and a receptivity to new social and intellectual currents. Charlotte attended the district school near her home and, for two winters (a total of six months), Franklin Academy at nearby Prattsburg, N.Y., but her formal education was supplemented at home and by self-instruction. Before she was twenty she began a career in teaching, which remained a lifelong interest.

In the early 1830's she became engrossed in what was becoming an American fad, phrenology. This Austrian science which taught that there were physiological and especially cranial determinants of character was being given a typically American interpretation, adding to it the practical corollary that once character was determined by cranial examination it could be changed. Charlotte's brothers Orson Squire Fowler and Lorenzo Niles Fowler were the first and the most important popularizers of "practical phrenology," a task to which they dedicated themselves with evangelical fervor. Phrenology for them became the basis of reform in many realms: the treatment of the insane, education, personal adjustment, marriage, and sex. In 1835 the Fowler brothers left the lecture circuit to establish a permanent phrenological center in New York City, which soon expanded into a museum, a lecture-booking bureau, and a publishing house. Charlotte joined the enterprise in 1837, at her brothers' request. Thereafter, for more than sixty years there was no aspect of practical phrenology in which she did not play a major part. She taught the first regular class in phrenology in America. She gave character readings. In the family's burgeoning publishing activities she was variously proofreader, writer, business manager, editor, and, at times, all of these combined.

On Oct. 13, 1844, she was married to Samuel Robert Wells (1820–1875), a New Englander who had been won over to phrenology when the Fowler brothers lectured in Boston in 1843 and, giving up an earlier plan to become a doctor, had joined them as assistant. After the marriage he became a partner in the family business. The firm—now Fowlers & Wells—entered into a period of rapid expansion and success. As a publishing concern, in addition to bringing out numerous editions of works from the voluminous pens of the Fowlers and other practical phrenologists, it became the main outlet for a diverse body of books and pamphlets on health, diet, the water cure, sex, marriage, architecture, Spiritualism, and mesmerism. Orson and Lorenzo gradually devoted more and more of their time to writing and lecturing and in 1855 finally sold their interests in the firm to Charlotte and her husband. Together the Wellses carried on the work of the firm and of the American Institute of Phrenology, which they were instrumental in founding; they were the mainstays of phrenology in America. Their productive partnership and happy (though childless) marriage ended with Wells' death in 1875. From that time until 1884, when the enterprise was incorporated, Charlotte Fowler Wells carried on as sole proprietor, and thereafter as president of the new Fowlers and Wells Company.

Mrs. Wells was a proponent of equal rights for women; it was in her office that the organizational meetings for the New York Medical College for Women took place (see CLEMENCE SOPHIA LOZIER), and from its founding in 1863 until her death she was a member of the board of trustees. Her home in West Orange, N.J., and her office at the Phrenological Institute served as gathering places for many who sought advice, a sympathetic listener, or financial aid. She was an early believer in Spiritualism, a religion which in the 1850's provided its followers with a faith justified in terms of science and the promise of universal social reform; during this period she served as medium of the influential New York Circle. She was quick to accept technological innovations, being one of the first to make serious use of the typewriter in her business.

An active, energetic woman, short and plump, at the age of eighty she was still reading without glasses and writing a series of articles for the *Phrenological Journal* on the pioneers of the movement. In 1896 a serious fall deprived her of the sight of one eye, but she recovered and went on to give a series of lectures at the American Institute of Phrenology in 1897–98. She died three years later at her home in West Orange, N.J., at the age of eighty-six, of "degeneration of the heart." She was buried in Rosedale Cemetery in Orange.

[Charlotte Fowler Wells MS., consisting of 42 miscellaneous items on phrenology and Spiritualism, and Fowler-Wells Papers, both at Cornell Univ. Collection of Regional History; files of *Phrenological Jour.*, especially Sept. 1894, p. 113, Dec. 1895, p. 293, July 1897, p. 39, and obituary by Mrs. Wells' niece, Jessie Fowler, July 1901; Frances E. Willard and Mary A. Livermore, eds., *A Woman of the Century* (1893). For an example of her writings, see Charlotte F. Wells, *Some Account of the Life and Labors of Dr. Francis Joseph Gall* (1896). On phrenology, see John D. Davies, *Phrenology: Fad and Science* (1956), and Carl Carmer in the *New Yorker*, Feb. 13, 1937. Death record from N.J. State Dept. of Health.]

ERNEST ISAACS

WELLS, Emmeline Blanche Woodward (Feb. 29, 1828–Apr. 25, 1921), leader of Mormon women and Utah feminist, was born and grew up in Petersham, Worcester County, Mass., at that time a particularly religious New England hill town. She was the fifth of seven daughters and seventh of nine children of David and Deiadama (Hare) Woodward. Her forebears on both her father's and mother's side were English, the Woodward family having settled near Boston in 1630. The Hares had strong literary interests, and Deiadama Woodward is said to have been an enthusiastic advocate of woman's rights as early as the 1840's. When Emmeline was four her father died; there is no evidence that her mother ever remarried.

Emmeline did well in school and graduated very early from both the local grammar school and the "select school for girls" in nearby New Salem, where she boarded with a married sister. Returning home in the early spring of 1842, she found that her mother, formerly a pious Congregationalist, had been converted to the Mormon faith by missionaries of the new Church of Jesus Christ of Latter-day Saints. After attending a few missionary meetings, Emmeline herself embraced the new religion on Mar. 1. As she and six other converts entered the waters of baptism, the orthodox ministers and other local anti-Mormons stood at the water's edge and heckled them as victims of "delusion."

Completing her studies at the select school, she received her teaching certificate in 1843, at the age of fifteen, and began teaching in a country school at Orange, Mass. On July 29 of that year she was married to James Harvey Harris, son of the presiding elder of the local branch of the Mormon church. The couple left for the Mormon city of Nauvoo, Ill., in April 1844, arriving there about a month later; they were thus able to meet Joseph Smith, the Prophet, before his murder in June. In the period of apostasy that followed, Harris' parents left the church; and on Nov. 16, soon after the death of her month-old son, Eugene Henri Harris, Emmeline's husband deserted her.

In the winter of 1844–45 she was "taught the principle of celestial marriage" (plural wives) by Presiding Bishop Newel K. Whitney and his wife, Elizabeth Ann, a leading member of the church who was known as "Mother Whitney." When Emmeline accepted this principle, Bishop Whitney proposed marriage, and Brigham Young performed the ceremony in February 1845, with Mother Whitney as witness. With her new family, Emmeline Whitney joined the exodus of the Mormons from Nauvoo early in 1846, reaching the Salt Lake Valley in 1848. Here, in 1850, Bishop Whitney died, leaving her with two daughters: Isabel Modelena (born 1848) and Melvina Caroline (1850). On Oct. 10, 1852, Emmeline Whitney became the seventh wife of Daniel Hanmer Wells (1814–1891), a general in the Mormon "Nauvoo Legion," a close friend and neighbor of Brigham Young, and a high officer in the church who was frequently left in charge in Young's absence. She bore Wells three daughters: Emmeline (1853), Elizabeth Ann (1859), and Louisa Martha (1862).

After the birth of her last child, Emmeline Wells devoted her energies increasingly to church work, journalism, and the suffrage movement. Through Mother Whitney, she was drawn into the work of the Relief Society, an organization of Mormon women founded by Joseph Smith. Beginning in 1873 she made periodic contributions to the society's bimonthly organ, the *Woman's Exponent,* founded in 1872 under the editorship of Louise L. Greene. In 1875 she became associate editor and in 1877 editor, a position she retained for nearly forty years until 1914, when the paper was superseded by the *Relief Society Magazine.* Under Mrs. Wells' editorship the *Exponent* featured Relief Society news, travel notes, church items, poetry, and a smattering of general news. She not only wrote the editorials, but as "E.W.," "Aunt Em," and "Blanche

Beechwood" produced a variety of articles, poems, and features, including a long series on "Good Manners." She became increasingly involved in all aspects of the work of the Relief Society and frequently traveled with ELIZA R. SNOW SMITH and others on society work, taking a particularly active part in setting up young ladies' and primary (children's) associations. In 1876 Brigham Young made her president of the Central Grain Committee of the Relief Society, to oversee the storing of grain by women against a possible day of famine. In 1892 she became general secretary of the Relief Society and in 1910 was made president of this fifty-thousand-member body.

As editor and administrator Mrs. Wells came to exert great influence within the Mormon community, and she used it to promote female suffrage and woman's rights. As early as 1870, at Brigham Young's suggestion, the territorial legislature had given women the vote, apparently to bolster Mormon political power as against the growing non-Mormon element, then largely made up of single men. Women, however, were still banned from public office—a fact which kept Mrs. Wells from becoming Salt Lake City's treasurer in 1878, despite a county convention's unanimous endorsement. Even the right to vote was threatened in the 1880's when Congress, having banned polygamy in the territories by the Edmunds Act of 1882, moved to repeal Utah's woman suffrage provision as well. Plunging into the heated controversy, Mrs. Wells printed suffrage articles, editorials, and letters in every issue of the *Exponent.* In 1885 and 1886 she spent months in Washington with other Utah lobbyists presenting to leading Senators the Mormon view on the suffrage question and combating the campaign of the Methodist lobbyist Mrs. ANGELIA F. NEWMAN to have Congress establish an "industrial home" for Utah women "freed" from plural marriages. Her efforts were unavailing, however; the industrial home proposal was adopted by Congress in 1886 and the repeal of woman suffrage in 1887.

On Jan. 10, 1889, a group of women led by Mrs. Wells and Emily Sophia Richards formed the Woman Suffrage Association of Utah, demanding the return of the franchise they had exercised for seventeen years. Mrs. Wells and her associates lobbied vigorously at the Utah constitutional convention of 1895, which approved by a wide margin a woman suffrage clause that became operative when Utah achieved statehood in 1896. Mrs. Wells was nominated that year for the legislature as a Republican, but withdrew under protest when a question arose as to the eligibility of women to hold office at this time. As head of the Utah Woman's Republican League she continued to work for the Republican party for many years.

Her manifold activities in Utah had early brought her to the attention of the national feminist leaders. In 1874 she was made vice-president for Utah of the National Woman Suffrage Association, and from 1879 onward she was a regular attendant at its national conventions, becoming a close friend of SUSAN B. ANTHONY and ELIZABETH CADY STANTON and, in 1895, a member of CARRIE CHAPMAN CATT's influential Organization Committee. She was also a life member of MAY WRIGHT SEWALL's National Council of Women, first attending its convention in 1891. In 1899, making her initial trip abroad, she was a delegate to the meeting of the International Council of Women in London.

"Aunt Em" was widely known and much beloved among the Latter-day Saints. Her small face, kindly features, and simply arranged white hair belied a manner that was "frank and outspoken, almost to bluntness," and a warm temper. Those who wrote of her were invariably struck by her executive ability and energy. "Work is her most congenial atmosphere, her very breath of life," noted one (Whitney, IV, 590). She belonged to the Pacific Coast Women's Press Association; founded the Utah Women's Press Club in 1891; served as secretary of the Deseret (Utah) Hospital Association; and was a charter member of the state society of the Daughters of the American Revolution. Despite her many duties she loved to compose poetry. The verses that appeared in the pages of the *Woman's Exponent* and of her *Musings and Memories* (1896) praised nature, religion, and the home in the sentimental and pious style of the period. At the request of the Mormon hymn writer Evan Stephens, she wrote the words for one of the most popular Mormon songs, "Our Mountain Home So Dear."

Emmeline Wells was one of a group of gifted Mormon women who did much to dispel the suspicion of Mormonism that was rife in nineteenth-century America, fanned by the polygamy question. In the columns of the *Woman's Exponent,* in her Washington lobbying, and in her appearances before various national bodies she sought constantly to refute exaggerated rumors and present a more balanced view of her religion. Her address before the National Council of Women in 1895, "Forty Years in the Valley of the Great Salt Lake," was widely reprinted, and a similar speech before the National American Woman Suffrage Association the same year at Atlanta was the occasion of a tearful embrace on the podium with Susan B. Anthony. Mrs. Wells sensed the propaganda value inherent in the Chicago World's Fair of 1893 and labored to bring the Mormon and non-Mormon leaders of Utah together to prepare an effective exhibit. She delivered a lecture on "Western Women in Journalism" at the fair, and edited for it *Charities and Philanthropies: Woman's Work in Utah* (1893).

She grew old full of honor. In 1912 Brigham Young University gave her an honorary degree, and in the same year she was chosen to unveil the Mormon seagull monument in Salt Lake City. At the end of her life she lived in the imposing Hotel Utah, built on the site where, in 1848, she had made her first home in a wagon, in which her first daughter had been born. Many dignitaries from throughout the world visited her, and her keen memory was a valuable source of information for those interested in the early years of Mormonism. Her death, of heart failure, in Salt Lake City in 1921 at the age of ninety-three evoked profound mourning. Eulogized as a "veritable mother in Israel," she was buried in the City Cemetery as flags flew at half-staff for a woman for the first time in Utah. In 1928, the centenary of her birth, a marble bust was placed in the rotunda of the Utah state capitol.

[In addition to her own writings and published lectures, see: Andrew Jenson, *Latter-day Saint Biog. Encyc.*, II (1914), 731–34; Orson F. Whitney, *Hist. of Utah* (1904), IV, 586–90; Augusta J. Crocheron, *Representative Women of Deseret* (1884); Susa Y. Gates and Leah D. Widtsoe, *Women of the "Mormon" Church* (1926); Noble Warrum, ed., *Utah since Statehood*, III (1919), 1066–67; Bryant S. Hinckley, *Daniel Hanmer Wells* (1942); *Improvement Era* (the Church magazine), Nov. 1901, pp. 43–48, June 1921, pp. 718–21, May 1937, pp. 296–97; *A Centenary of the Relief Soc., 1842–1942* (1942); chapters on Utah in Elizabeth C. Stanton et al., *Hist. of Woman Suffrage*, vols. IV and VI (1902, 1922); *Sunset*, May 1916; and obituaries in *Deseret News*, Apr. 25, 1921, and *N.Y. Times*, Apr. 27, 1921. There are letters and other MSS. in the Church Historian's Office, the Utah Genealogical Soc., and the Utah State Hist. Soc., all in Salt Lake City, and the Huntington Library, San Marino, Calif. The most complete file of the *Woman's Exponent* outside Utah is in Widener Library, Harvard Univ.]

MARIO S. DE PILLIS

WELLS, Kate Gannett (Apr. 6, 1838–Dec. 13, 1911), reformer and antisuffragist, was born in London, England, of American parents. Christened Catherine Boott Gannett, she was the only daughter and first of three children of Anna (Tilden) and Ezra Stiles Gannett. One of her brothers, William Channing Gannett, became a prominent Unitarian minister in Rochester, N.Y.—and, unlike his sister, a supporter of woman suffrage. Ezra Gannett, who was abroad convalescing from a nervous breakdown under the care of a Dr. Boott at the time of his daughter's birth, was the colleague and successor of the Rev. William Ellery Channing at Federal Street (later Arlington Street) Church (Unitarian) in Boston. He was a grandson of President Ezra Stiles of Yale College and a descendant of Mary Chilton, one of the first generation of English migrants to New England; his wife was a native Bostonian.

On Gannett's return to pastoral duties in 1838, his family took up residence at Bumstead Place in downtown Boston. Her mother's death when Kate was a schoolgirl of eight knit her closely to her father and to his career as patron and counselor of a big city congregation. Life at Bumstead Place—austere, well ordered, earnest, bustling with high thoughts and good works—would prompt her main concerns as an adult. From her father she gained an ethic of service, but also a certain conservative Unitarian distaste for militance, aggressiveness, equalitarian fanaticism. Her social philanthropy and her opposition to woman suffrage sprang from a common cluster of values, and these were rooted in the home. On June 11, 1863, she was married to Samuel Wells, a prospering young Boston lawyer; thereafter she was known to her Back Bay community as Kate Gannett Wells. Marriage brought children (Stiles Gannett, Samuel, and Louisa Appleton), a summer place at Campobello, and the affluent leisure which underwrote her long semipublic career from the 1870's until her death.

Believing it futile for women to war against their female social function, Mrs. Wells strove toward peculiarly feminine goals. An early and continuing interest was the Massachusetts Moral Education Association to combat prostitution. Locating the causes of the evil in low wages, alcoholism, and the overcrowded loneliness of the city, she felt the surest cure lay not in laws or social agencies, but in aroused public opinion, the moral education of the young, and, above all, personal benevolence among fellow women. ("When each holds another up then there will be no occasion for falling.") She was active in the New England Women's Club and participated also in club work at the national level, as secretary (1882) and for some years a director of the Association for the Advancement of Women. Most of her causes, ranging from the peace movement to the Massachusetts Emergency and Hygiene Association, which under her leadership in the 1890's sought to instill better health practices among working class families and to provide summer playgrounds for children, stemmed from her untiring involvement in the interlocking directorate of the Boston club world. Her home was a constant center for teas, receptions, and discussions; the reformer Edwin Mead fondly recalled holding classes there in the 1880's on Aristotle.

Kate Gannett Wells drew the line at woman suffrage. Though frowning on the self-conscious, assertive mannishness of its advocates, she maintained a cool detachment toward their activities until 1884, when she entered the lists (along with Francis Parkman and Louis Brandeis) as a remonstrant against the annual woman suffrage petition presented to the Massachusetts legislature. From that point on she was one of the leading "antis" in the state. She acknowledged female political activism as an ideal future possibility. But she feared its immediate consequence would be to compound the difficulties of assimilating immigrants to good citizenship, and to foster ignorant demands for state paternalism. "Once let the great mass of uneducated women be added to the great mass of already uneducated men voters," she remarked in an oft-quoted statement, "and the State will slowly but surely be shaken under the varying demands made upon it for bread, work, money, leisure and all kinds of laws to favor all kinds of persons" (*Woman's Journal*, Feb. 16, 1884, p. 53). Ironically, a chief obstacle to woman suffrage in Massachusetts was the opposition of Catholic urban Democrats, who feared nativist hostility and proscriptive measures in the realm of prohibition and education as possible results of female voting. Mrs. Wells' diffident approach to the grimy world of politics brought her into an odd coalition hardly of her own making.

A leader since the 1870's in the Woman's Education Association of Boston, Mrs. Wells was in 1874 elected to the Boston School Committee for the year 1875. In 1888 she was appointed to the first of three eight-year terms on the Massachusetts State Board of Education. Her major interest as a board member was to foster improvements in state programs of teacher education. She lavished loving attention on the normal schools of Massachusetts, and particularly on the Normal Art School in Boston, whose staff and students became her personal concern. Convinced that the essential function of the state in education was to encourage quality and enthusiasm rather than enforce restrictive pedagogical formulas, she once speculated perceptively about the possible need for an American Molière to satirize trends in modern educational theory. In 1902 Wells Hall at the Framingham (Mass.) Normal School was named in her honor.

Mrs. Wells wrote numerous articles for the *North American Review, Atlantic Monthly,* and *New England Magazine,* frequently addressing herself to the problems of women in their emergence to modern self-awareness. Among several books her best was *About People* (1885), the collected views of a serene Unitarian gentlewoman on mundane relations among husbands, wives, servants, and children —that subtle society of the home whose importance she constantly stressed.

By the turn of the century, at a time when the older Boston she represented was fast disappearing, Mrs. Wells was acknowledged one of the first ladies of her city. In her unfailing grace and good humor she retained even the respect of militant feminists. She died in her seventy-fourth year at her Back Bay residence of acute gastritis and was buried among her kinsmen in Mount Auburn Cemetery in Cambridge. Her passing deprived proper Boston of a public possession.

[Mrs. Wells' impact is best assessed from obituary notices and eulogies in the *Boston Transcript,* Dec. 13–15, 1911. She is listed in *Who Was Who in America,* vol. I (1942). The best source for her early life is the biography of her father by her brother, William C. Gannett, *Ezra Stiles Gannett* (1875); on her brother's liberalism see William H. Pease, "The Gannetts of Rochester," *Rochester Hist.,* Oct. 1955. Her views on woman suffrage are concisely stated in the *Woman's Jour.,* Feb. 16, 1884. Her organizational activities are touched on in: *ibid.,* May 2, 1891, p. 142 (on the Mass. Emergency and Hygiene Assoc.); Lillie B. C. and Arthur C. Wyman, *Elizabeth Buffum Chace* (1914); Elizabeth M. Herlihy, ed., *Fifty Years of Boston* (1932); and Arthur Mann, *Yankee Reformers in the Urban Age* (1954). Death record from Mass. Registrar of Vital Statistics.]

GEOFFREY BLODGETT

**WELLS-BARNETT, Ida Bell** (July 16, 1862–Mar. 25, 1931), journalist, lecturer, and clubwoman, was born in Holly Springs, Miss., of slave parents, the oldest in a family of four boys and four girls. Her mother, Lizzie Bell, the child of a slave mother and an Indian father, had come from Virginia; sold for the first time at the age of seven, she belonged to a succession of owners, of whom the last, a Holly Springs carpenter named Bolling, proved the kindest. While working for him as cook she met and married James Wells, who had been apprenticed by his master—his acknowledged father—to Bolling to learn the carpenter-

ing trade. After Ida's parents became freedmen, her mother continued to work as cook and her father as carpenter.

Ida Wells was educated at Rust University, a freedmen's high school and industrial school established in Holly Springs in 1866. When her parents and three of their children died in an epidemic of yellow fever she became the family mainstay. Though only fourteen, she let down her skirts, put up her hair, and, claiming to be eighteen, got a position teaching in a rural school at twenty-five dollars a month. In 1884 she moved to Memphis, Tenn., where she taught at first in a nearby rural school and then in the city's Negro schools. Meanwhile she pursued her own education, attending summer classes at Fisk University. While traveling on the Chesapeake & Ohio Railroad about this time, she refused to comply with a conductor's demand that she leave her seat for one in a coach reserved for colored passengers and was forcibly removed. She sued the railroad and won her case in the circuit court, but the decision was reversed by the Tennessee supreme court in April 1887.

Encouraged by the Rev. William J. Simmons, president of the National Baptist Convention and a leader of the Negro Press Association, Ida Wells began to write articles for some of the small newspapers then springing up under Negro ownership, using the pen name "Iola." Because she criticized the inadequate schools available to Negro children, the Memphis school board failed to renew her contract in 1891. Thereafter she gave her full time to journalism, buying a one-third interest in the *Memphis Free Speech.* By 1892 she had become half-owner.

That year occurred an event that drastically changed the course of Miss Wells' life. On Mar. 9 three Memphis men, all friends of hers, were lynched. Denouncing the crime in the *Free Speech,* she charged that it had been committed not on the familiar pretext of defending Southern white womanhood but because the victims had been offering successful competition to white storekeepers. Urging the Negro people of Memphis to seek new homes in the West, she began to investigate other lynchings and to publish the facts as she determined them. On May 27, 1892, while she was on a visit to Philadelphia and New York, the offices of the paper were mobbed and destroyed, and it became impossible for her to return to Memphis.

That autumn, after a brief stint as a staff writer for the *New York Age,* Miss Wells launched a one-woman crusade against lynching. A large, handsome woman with powerful, flashing eyes, she lectured in Boston, New York, and elsewhere, founding antilynching societies and Negro woman's clubs. On two visits to Great Britain (1893 and 1894) she aroused much interest in her cause and was instrumental in the founding of an antilynching committee and a society to combat racial segregation. Her concern for her race was not limited to the lynching issue. In 1893, for example, she edited a pamphlet for distribution to visitors to the World's Columbian Exposition in Chicago, protesting the virtual exclusion of Negroes from a meaningful role in the exposition.

On June 27, 1895, Ida Wells was married in Chicago to the widower Ferdinand Lee Barnett, a Negro lawyer, sometime Republican politician, founder and editor of the Chicago *Conservator*, and, beginning in 1896, an assistant state's attorney. They had four children: Charles A., Herman K., Ida B. Wells, and Alfreda. Barnett fully shared his wife's interests, and in 1895 she published *A Red Record*, an account of three years' lynchings in the South, with a preface by Frederick Douglass. She was a member of a delegation that called on President William McKinley in 1898 to demand action in the case of a Negro postmaster who had been lynched in South Carolina.

While rearing her family, Mrs. Wells-Barnett did less traveling and speaking away from home, but she took a keen interest in the welfare of Chicago's Negro population, then mounting with heavy immigration from the Southern states. As early as 1893 she had organized a Negro woman's club in Chicago (it adopted the name "Ida B. Wells Club"), and as its lifelong president she initiated such projects for the Negro community as a kindergarten and an orchestra. In 1910 she took the initiative in founding the Negro Fellowship League, which for several years maintained a social center, reading rooms, and a dormitory for newly arrived Negro men and helped them find work. Actively aided by her husband, Mrs. Wells-Barnett interested herself in many cases requiring legal assistance, serving from 1913 to 1916 as a probation officer for the Chicago municipal court. A particularly noteworthy display of personal courage and initiative was her visit to East St. Louis, Ill., following the race riots of 1918, to seek legal aid for the Negro victims of mob assault. On July 7, 1919, in a somber letter to the *Chicago Tribune*, she warned that Chicago faced a similar explosion, and implored the city "to set the wheels of justice in motion before it is too late." The disastrous racial upheaval in Chicago in which nearly forty people were killed and hundreds injured occurred within a few weeks.

An uncompromising militant—in contrast to her fellow Chicagoan FANNIE BARRIER WILLIAMS—Mrs. Wells-Barnett distrusted the help of whites in the Negro cause. This placed her in direct opposition to Booker T. Washington, whose doctrine of compromise and accommodation she attacked in speeches before the National Afro-American Council and elsewhere. An ally of W. E. B. Du Bois, she served as secretary of the Council from 1898 to 1902, when Washington's forces took control. Although she was a participant in the famous Niagara meeting which led to the founding of the National Association for the Advancement of Colored People in 1910, she stood apart from the association after its inception, feeling that it was not sufficiently outspoken.

On the other hand, Mrs. Wells-Barnett worked with white women in the suffrage and women's movements. She founded what was said to be the first Negro woman suffrage organization, the Alpha Suffrage Club of Chicago. Twice she marched in suffrage parades: in Washington in 1913, on the eve of Wilson's inauguration, and, leading her club members, in the famous Chicago parade of June 1916 when five thousand suffragists marched in a torrential rain to the Republican National Convention to demand a suffrage plank in the platform. She worked with JANE ADDAMS in a successful attempt to block the setting up of separate schools for Negro children in Chicago. She was one of the founders and for years a director of the Cook County League of Women's Clubs.

In religion Ida Wells-Barnett was successively a member of Bethel African Methodist Episcopal Church, Grace Presbyterian Church, and, in later life, of the Chicago Metropolitan Church. She died in Chicago of uremia in her sixty-ninth year and was buried there in Oakwood Cemetery. The Ida B. Wells housing project in Chicago, dedicated in 1940, perpetuates her name.

[MS. autobiography in the possession of Mrs. Wells-Barnett's daughter, Mrs. Alfreda Duster of Chicago (since published as *Crusade for Justice,* 1970); articles by Mrs. Wells-Barnett in *N.Y. Age, Chicago Inter Ocean,* Chicago *Conservator,* and *Independent; The Reason Why the Colored American Is Not in the World's Columbian Exposition* (1893), a booklet prepared by Mrs. Wells-Barnett and Frederick Douglass; Allan H. Spear, *Black Chicago* (1967); August Meier, *Negro Thought in America, 1880–1915* (1963); Arna Bontemps and Jack Conroy, *They Seek a City* (1945), pp. 77–82; Mrs. N. F. Mossell, *The Work of the Afro-*

*American Woman* (2nd ed., 1908), pp. 32–46; Herbert Aptheker, *A Documentary Hist. of the Negro People in the U.S.* (1951); Emma Lou Thornbrough, "The Nat. Afro-Am. League," *Jour. of Southern Hist.*, Nov. 1961; Elliott M. Rudwick and August Meier, "Black Man in the 'White City': Negroes and the Columbian Exposition, 1893," *Phylon*, Fourth Quarter (Winter), 1965.]

ELEANOR FLEXNER

**WELSH, Lilian** (Mar. 6, 1858–Feb. 23, 1938), physician and educator, was born in Columbia, Pa., the fourth daughter and fourth of six children of Thomas and Annie Eunice (Young) Welsh, natives, respectively, of Columbia and the neighboring town of Wrightsville. Her father, after serving in the Mexican War, became a merchant and canalboat owner until the firing on Fort Sumter, when he rejoined the army, rising by 1863 to brigadier general; he died that year of illness contracted in the siege of Vicksburg.

Lilian Welsh's first career was in education. After graduating from the Columbia High School (1873) and the State Normal School at Millersville, Pa. (1875), she taught in Columbia and at the Normal School, becoming principal of the Columbia High School in 1881. Five years later, however, prompted by her deep interest in chemistry, she resigned to enter the Woman's Medical College of Pennsylvania in Philadelphia. After receiving the M.D. degree in 1889, she planned to teach physiological chemistry and spent a year and a half of graduate study in this field at the University of Zurich, where she took courses also in the new subjects of histology and bacteriology. When the hoped-for teaching position failed to materialize, she became in 1890 a physician at the State Hospital for the Insane in Norristown, Pa. In 1892 she went to Baltimore, Md., to begin private practice with Dr. MARY SHERWOOD, whom she had met at Zurich. There was still a widespread prejudice against women doctors, and the practice did not flourish, but the two physicians enjoyed opportunities for informal study at the Johns Hopkins Hospital and during their early years of professional activity came to see clearly that their real interests lay in the field of preventive medicine.

In 1894 Dr. Welsh began a thirty-year association with the Woman's College of Baltimore (later Goucher College), then in its first decade. The original faculty plan included a physician to carry on preventive health work among the students, and it was to this post that she was appointed, her longer official title eventually being shortened to professor of physiology and hygiene. Her program, then an innovation for

a woman's college, was twofold: a physical examination for each incoming student, followed by assignment to gymnastic classes; and a required sophomore hygiene course which gave a basic grounding in physiology and bacteriology and stressed not only personal but public hygiene—the application of the principles of hygiene to the health problems of the modern community. Beginning her work at a time when sex matters were not discussed freely and when physical exercise and athletics for women were considered dangerous, Dr. Welsh encountered some opposition, particularly to the required physical examination. She was, however, a forceful teacher, determined not to spare her students any unpleasant truth necessary for their well-being. "Outspoken, kindly, and caustic, and full of a delightful humor," in the words of Dr. Florence Sabin, she scorned dishonesty and sham, and her "peppery" tongue was remembered by two generations of Goucher girls.

Soon after arriving in Baltimore, Dr. Welsh became associated with the Evening Dispensary for Working Women and Girls, a private charitable organization recently founded by Drs. KATE CAMPBELL Hurd (later HURD-MEAD) and Alice Hall. In 1893 Dr. Welsh and Dr. Sherwood took over the dispensary and continued to direct it until it closed in 1910. Besides its benevolent purpose, the dispensary gave an opportunity for women physicians to practice, and a number of outstanding women, such as the surgeon ELIZABETH HURDON, gained experience there. The dispensary was responsible for the first distribution of pure milk to sick babies in Baltimore and for pioneer work in obstetrics, emphasizing prenatal care and postnatal supervision of mother and child. It employed the first visiting nurse in Baltimore and early organized a social service department. Its introduction of public health instruction in homes and of talks before women's organizations was an important contribution to medical sociology.

Educational opportunities for women in America were still meager when Dr. Welsh began her medical career, and she identified herself with all efforts to promote a wider range of useful activities for her sex. In Baltimore she found an unusually receptive environment, for a group of Baltimore women led by MARY E. GARRETT had just campaigned successfully to secure the admission of women to the Johns Hopkins University Medical School. Seeking to secure the same privileges in other graduate departments of the university, many of the same group organized in 1897 the Baltimore Association for the Promotion of the University

Education of Women, with Dr. Welsh as secretary. They achieved their goal in 1908.

As a member of the National American Woman Suffrage Association, Dr. Welsh marched in street parades, including the famous one in Washington on the day before President Wilson's first inauguration. She was a charter member of Baltimore women's organizations such as the Arundell Club (1894) and its offshoot the Arundell Good Government Club, as well as a leader in city and state public health activities. For three months in 1897 she served on the Baltimore school board, under a reform mayor. Following the death in 1935 of her close friend Dr. Mary Sherwood, with whom she had lived for many years, Dr. Welsh returned to her family home in Columbia, Pa. She died there three years later, in her eightieth year, of encephalitis lethargica. By her request, her body was cremated; burial was at Mount Bethel Cemetery, Columbia.

[The principal sources are Dr. Welsh's *Reminiscences of Thirty Years in Baltimore* (1925) and the memorial pamphlet, *A Tribute to Lilian Welsh* (Goucher College, 1938). See also *Jour. Am. Medical Women's Assoc.*, Dec. 1947, and obituary in *Columbia* (Pa.) *News*, Feb. 24, 1938. Information about her father and his family from *Biog. Annals of Lancaster County, Pa.* (1903); from Mrs. Jessie C. Criswell, Columbia (Pa.) Public Library; and from federal census schedules. Death record from Pa. State Dept. of Health.]

GENEVIEVE MILLER

WERLEIN, Elizabeth Thomas (Jan. 28, 1883–Apr. 24, 1946), leader in preserving the French Quarter of New Orleans, was born in Bay City, Mich., the elder of the two children and only daughter of Henry Thomas, a dynamite manufacturer, by his first wife, Marie Louise Felton Smith. Her father was a native of the Genesee valley of New York, her mother a Canadian of English descent; both were Episcopalians. Mrs. Thomas died when Elizabeth was very young; by her father's subsequent remarriage she had a half sister. Elizabeth attended public schools in Bay City and the Liggett School in Detroit, where she began the study of voice. After further study at the Detroit Conservatory of Music, she went in 1903 to Paris, where she entered Miss White's School and cultivated her dramatic soprano voice by lessons with Antonio Baldelli and Jean de Reszke, Wagnerian tenor and teacher.

For a time Elizabeth Thomas seems to have considered a professional career in music, but social life and romance intervened. Gifted, and striking in appearance, tall (five feet eleven inches) and blond, she became a popular member of the international set. She hunted big game in Africa with European friends. She was received by the Empress Eugénie, widow of Napoleon III; called upon the Emperor Franz Josef in Vienna; and, having become engaged to a Russian prince, visited his family in St. Petersburg. In 1906, the engagement broken, she went to England, where at a private recital she sang the Wagnerian role of Brünnhilde. With other members of fashionable society, including Frank Hedges Butler, president of the London Aero Club, and Viscount Charles Yorke Royston, now her fiancé, she was a balloon enthusiast and in 1908 ballooned to Belgium in an outfit specially designed by Worth of Paris. She was also one of the first women to fly in a plane, with the pilot Pierre Labaudie.

Soon after, on what was planned as a brief trip home, she visited New Orleans friends and with them went by steamboat up the Mississippi to a house party at Belle Grove plantation in Louisiana. Here she met Philip Werlein III, a New Orleans music publisher and musical instrument dealer who was also a civic and social leader active in the state Democratic party. They were married Aug. 4, 1908, in Bay City, and made their home in New Orleans. Elizabeth Werlein quickly adapted to her new surroundings, her vitality overflowing into philanthropic and civic activities. She opened and maintained sewing classes for underprivileged girls at Kingsley House, the social settlement headed by ELEANOR MC MAIN. She was secretary-treasurer (1915–18) and for many years a board member of the New Orleans Philharmonic Society. She entertained friends and figures of the world of music, including the opera singer Nellie Melba, who convalesced in the Werlein home following a stage accident. To all this was added the rearing of four children: Betty, Lorraine, Evelyn, and Philip.

Her husband died of influenza in February 1917, and Mrs. Werlein, still in her early thirties, immersed herself in war work, serving as chairman of the Woman's Committee of the New Orleans Liberty Loan drives, financial chairman of the Woman's Division of the Council of National Defense for New Orleans, and head of the "Landing Fields in Louisiana" Committee; for the last activity she was in 1919 awarded her "wings" by the Aero Club of New York. Turning to still more varied pursuits after the war, she founded (1919) and headed the New Orleans Red Cross canteen; was elected first president of the state League of Women Voters in 1920; was president of the Orleans Club in 1930 and of the Quarante Club in 1940–41; assisted in the restoration of paintings at the Louisiana State Museum in the mid-1930's; and in 1932 headed the Professional Women's Committee of the Roosevelt National Campaign Committee. Her only salaried position in these years was as public relations director for a Southern chain of motion-picture theatres (1924–30), assisting the campaign of the Motion Picture Producers and Distributors Association to forestall legislative censorship by publicizing the industry's efforts at self-censorship.

But her absorbing interest during these years was the Vieux Carré, the French Quarter of New Orleans. She made her home in the district, and supported such organizations as Le Petit Salon, Le Petit Théâtre du Vieux Carré, and Le Quartier Club. Familiar with the European architectural tradition, she was charmed by the old French and Spanish buildings and distressed that the area was rapidly becoming a slum. As early as 1910 she published a booklet of photographs, *The Wrought Iron Railings of Le Vieux Carré, New Orleans,* only to learn to her dismay that some of the iron work pictured had been removed before its publication. In the 1920's business and civic leaders, their interest sparked by Mrs. Werlein, Mrs. James Oscar Nixon, and others, began the restoration of some French Quarter mansions, but the neighborhood took another downward turn as the sprinkling of Prohibition-era speakeasies gave way to increasing numbers of night clubs, bars, and brothels.

To combat this situation, Mrs. Werlein in 1930 organized and became first president of the Vieux Carré Property Owners Association, and thereafter she spearheaded its campaign for the enactment and enforcement of zoning regulations and stricter building codes. Her swift and articulate reactions to threats to the physical and moral character of the Vieux Carré eventually overcame public apathy, won respect and cooperation from city and state officials, and helped preserve historic New Orleans as a national heritage. So great was her influence that few changes could be made in the Vieux Carré without her approval; when such were attempted she did not hesitate to turn to the courts. In recognition of her efforts the American Institute of Architects in 1942 made her an honorary member. She died at her home of cancer in 1946, at the age of sixty-three, and after cremation was buried in Metairie Cemetery in New Orleans. At her death the *New Orleans Times-Picayune* wrote: "The vigor of her leadership and the breadth of her logic were indispensable in the movement to retain the distinctive architectural character of the Vieux Carré."

[*New Orleans Item,* Nov. 4, 1932, Mar. 16, 1945, Apr. 24, 25, 1946; *New Orleans Times-Picayune,* Aug. 6, 1942, Apr. 25, 1946; *Who Was Who in America,* vol. II (1950); Robert Tallant, *The Romantic New Orleanians* (1950), pp. 319–20; *La. Almanac and Fact Book,* 1962; information from Lorraine Werlein Moore and Betty Werlein Carter; death record from New Orleans Dept. of Health, the source for her birth year.]

WILLIAM G. WIEGAND

**WEST, Lillie.** See LESLIE, Amy.

**WESTLEY, Helen** (Mar. 28, 1875–Dec. 12, 1942), actress, was born Henrietta Remsen Meserole Manney in Brooklyn, N.Y., the younger of two children and only daughter of Charles Palmer Manney, a drugstore proprietor, and Henrietta (Meserole) Manney. Through her father, a native of Matawan, N.J., she traced her lineage to the Huguenots; through her mother, born in Greenpoint (later part of Brooklyn), N.Y., she was of Dutch descent. Deciding on a stage career in childhood, Henrietta Manney studied at the Brooklyn School of Oratory, Emerson College of Oratory in Boston (1894–95), and the American Academy of Dramatic Art in New York. She got her start in the touring stock company of Rose Stahl, and it was with Miss Stahl that she made her New York debut at the Star Theatre, Sept. 13, 1897, in the three-act comedy *The Captain of the Nonsuch,* in which she was billed as "Helen Ransom." After trouping in vaudeville and acting in various stock companies, she was married on Oct. 31, 1900, at the Marble Collegiate Church (Dutch Reformed) in New York, to the actor Jack Westley (John Wesley Wilson Conroy). They had one child, Ethel. Until about 1912, when she separated from her husband, she gave up the stage for domesticity.

Having settled in downtown New York, Helen Westley was a member of Greenwich Village's famous Liberal Club (which included Sinclair Lewis, Theodore Dreiser, SUSAN GLASPELL, George Cram Cook, and Lawrence Langner) when, in 1915, she, Langner, and others organized the Washington Square Players. In their first offering of one-act plays on Feb. 19 at the Bandbox Theatre she appeared as the Oyster in *Another Interior,* an irreverent spoof of Maeterlinck's *Interior.* She afterward acted with the group in *The Sea Gull* (1916) and other plays. Late in 1918, after several Broadway engagements, she was one of the players who formed the Theatre Guild, and during the next fifteen years she was a dynamic member of its board of directors. In the Guild's first production, at the Garrick Theatre on Apr. 19, 1919, she portrayed Doña Sirena in

*The Bonds of Interest,* and thereafter she appeared in at least one Guild offering each season. She was essentially a character actress, even in her youth, often depicting shrewish, sometimes malevolent women. Among her roles were the lion tamer Zinida in *He Who Gets Slapped* (1922), Mrs. Zero in Elmer Rice's *The Adding Machine* (1923), Ftatateeta in Shaw's *Caesar and Cleopatra* (1925), Mama in *The Guardsman* (1924), Babka in *The Goat Song* and Mrs. Higgins in *Pygmalion* (1926), Mrs. Amos Evans in Eugene O'Neill's *Strange Interlude* and Lady Britomart Undershaft in *Major Barbara* (1928), and Frau Lucher in *Reunion in Vienna* and Aunt Eller in *Green Grow the Lilacs* (1931).

Helen Westley left the New York stage for Hollywood in 1934 to launch a successful film career as Mrs. Morris, a retired star, in *Moulin Rouge.* During the next seven years she returned to the stage only once, to play Grandma in *The Primrose Path* at the Biltmore Theatre in 1939. Her films, numbering nearly thirty, included *The House of Rothschild* and *Death Takes a Holiday* (1934), *Roberta* (1935), *Showboat* (1936), *Heidi* (1937), *Rebecca of Sunnybrook Farm* and *Alexander's Ragtime Band* (1938), *Sunny* (1940), and *My Favorite Spy,* completed early in the year of her death.

"Helen Westley looked like an actress, far more so than most of them do, in private real life," wrote Theresa Helburn, director of the Theatre Guild. "She had a theatrical appearance and manner, and dressed rather like a *femme fatale*—coal-black hair and black, slinky dresses, a little like Charles Addams's young witch. Under that dramatic façade she was a forthright person, honest, outspoken and uninhibited." Lawrence Langner remembered her as "one of the most refreshing personalities in the theatre, as well as one of its most talented character actresses. But what made Helen Westley invaluable to . . . the Theatre Guild, was her simple, direct enthusiasm for the greatest plays, her incisive mind . . . , her dislike of mediocrity, and her unwillingness to sacrifice art for money. . . ." She withdrew from the Guild's directorial board during its twenty-fourth season (1941–42). Ill with cardiovascular disease, she died of a coronary thrombosis at Jacques Lane Farm, Franklin Township, N.J., in December 1942, at the age of sixty-seven. Her body was cremated.

[Walter Prichard Eaton, *The Theatre Guild: The First Ten Years* (1929); Theresa Helburn, *A Wayward Quest* (1960); Lawrence Langner, *The Magic Curtain* (1951); Carol Bird in *Theatre Mag.,* Aug. 1922; profile in *New Yorker,* Mar. 27, 1926; newspaper stories and interviews, including *N.Y. World-Telegram,* Mar. 24, 1930 (by Ward Morehouse), and Aug. 18, 1931, *N.Y. Times,* Dec. 12, 13, 1937; John Parker, ed., *Who's Who in the Theatre* (8th ed., 1936); information from MS. "Genealogy of the Meserole Family of Greenpoint" and from family Bible, both at the Long Island Hist. Soc., Brooklyn, and from registrar of Emerson College, Boston; death record from N.J. State Dept. of Health.]

PAT M. RYAN

**WETHERELL, Elizabeth.** *See* WARNER, Susan Bogert.

**WETHERELL, Emma Abbott.** *See* ABBOTT, Emma.

**WHARTON, Edith Newbold Jones** (Jan. 24, 1862–Aug. 11, 1937), novelist, was born in New York City, the only daughter of George Frederic and Lucretia Stevens (Rhinelander) Jones. Since her two brothers were considerably older, she grew up much as an only child. Both of her parents came of families that had settled early in the American colonies. Her New York ancestors included not only the Rhinelanders but also Schermerhorns, Pendletons, and Gallatins; her maternal great-grandfather, Gen. Ebenezer Stevens, had been born in Boston and had fought at Yorktown under Lafayette. Edith thus grew up in a long-established, homogeneous society that spent its winters in New York City and its summers in Newport, R.I., or on Long Island, was Episcopalian or Dutch Reformed in religion, and distrusted sophistication, art, newcomers, and excess of any sort. The wealth of these families, largely derived from municipal real estate, was not comparable to the mammoth new fortunes then being made in railroads, steel, and oil. Throughout her life Mrs. Wharton regarded the possessors of these new fortunes with some suspicion, but the drama of their conflict with and ultimate domination over the world of her Knickerbocker childhood later provided a rich source of material for her fiction.

The economic depression that came at the end of the Civil War so reduced the family's income that, when Edith was three, her father took his wife and daughter to Europe (his sons were in college), where for the next six years they lived in Italy, France, and Germany. He taught Edith to read, encouraged her love of books, and in each country they visited provided tutors so that she gained a command of the language. When the family returned to New York she continued, with a governess, the perfunctory education then thought suitable for girls of her class, and at the age of seventeen made her debut. Her intellectual interests, however, had developed at an early age, and she took full advantage of the cultural opportunities offered by her father's library. At the age of sixteen she wrote and had privately printed a volume of poetry. Although her society provided little stimulus to artistic appreciation and accorded small respect to artists and writers, she learned to cultivate her mind and taste while at the same time conforming outwardly to the pattern expected of her. This may explain why, in later years, her demeanor and speech so often suggested discipline and formality to those who met her.

Around 1880 Edith again went to Italy with her parents, but a year or two later, after her father's death, she returned to New York. On Apr. 29, 1885, at the age of twenty-three, she was married to Edward Robbins Wharton, a wealthy Boston banker thirteen years her senior. Now retired from business, Wharton was a sensitive, intelligent man with a ready wit, who, however, shared few of his wife's interests except her enjoyment of social functions, travel, and country life. They had no children, and for several years they led a conventionally idle existence in New York, Boston, and Newport, going to Europe each February. Published fragments of her diary reveal how Mrs. Wharton learned to create a world of the imagination to compensate for her "moral solitude." Edmund Wilson has suggested that it was to escape the tensions of an incompatible marriage, and upon the advice of the neurologist (and novelist) Dr. S. Weir Mitchell, that Edith Wharton took up writing.

She herself placed "the slow, stammering beginnings" of her literary life after the Whartons' return in 1888 from a yacht tour of the Aegean, a trip that she later regarded as "the greatest step forward in my making." Now, suddenly, she began to write again, for the first time since her girlhood. Occasional verses and stories submitted to *Scribner's*, *Harper's*, and the *Century* were accepted and published, but writing remained a minor interest until after the buying of Land's End, a house in Newport. In consulting with Ogden Codman, Jr., the Boston architect who supervised its remodeling and landscaping, she discovered that she and Codman shared strong convictions on the principles that ought to be followed in the design and furnishing of houses. They incorporated their ideas in *The Decoration of Houses* (1897), which sold well; the book had a pronounced effect on styles of interior decoration, and was essentially a protest against the bad taste of the period and a plea for a return to classical values. Mrs. Wharton gave herself wider scope for these ideas when, in 1899, she and her hus-

band sold the Newport house and built a large mansion, The Mount, near Lenox, Mass., where for the next ten years they spent their summers, going to Europe for the winters. At The Mount, Mrs. Wharton "lived and gardened and wrote contentedly."

Her first books after *The Decoration of Houses* were two collections of her stories, *The Greater Inclination* (1899) and *Crucial Instances* (1901). These are bright, clever, rather brittle tales. They deal frequently, like those of Henry James, with artists and writers and seem thin in comparison with some of her later work, but they show her already in full command of the firm, crisp, easily flowing style that was to make her prose as lucid and polished as any in American fiction. Although her stories won immediate critical approval, she did not publish a novel until *The Valley of Decision* (1902), when she was forty. She made up for a late start, however, by thenceforth averaging more than a book a year for the rest of her life. *The Valley of Decision*, a historical novel, captures the spirit and color of the Italian eighteenth century remarkably well, but the characters seem somewhat pallid against the splendor of the background.

*The House of Mirth* (1905) opens Edith Wharton's major period, which was to last until 1920. Her first novel of manners, it was an immediate critical and popular success. Many authors had taken the contemporary New York social scene as their model, but none had seen it so intimately or with such a clear, dispassionate eye. She thoroughly understood the society in which she had grown up, and she had met and closely observed the "intruders" who had changed the brownstone fronts of Fifth Avenue into a fantastic jumble of derivative palaces. Lily Bart, the heroine, belongs to both worlds; she is related by birth to the old New York, but likes to play with the new. She wants and needs a great deal of money, but has too much fineness of feeling to marry for it. She is destroyed less by her principles than by her fastidiousness. In the end she loses both worlds, the old because she smokes and gambles and is seen alone with married men, and the new because she cannot play their cutthroat game. What her creator seems to be saying is that Lily cannot afford to be a lady. The drama of the novel lies in the ultimate uniting of the worlds against her, almost as if they had made their truce over her stricken figure. For Mrs. Wharton knew that the old and the new societies were only superficially different; what they had in common was a worship of money and a sullen distrust of the discriminating taste of Lily Bart. The latter's creator had too much intelligence to misconceive her heroine's plight as a tragedy. She understood that the corruption of the easily corruptible was merely pathos.

Mrs. Wharton's clear eye and a sense of humor that was merciless to the least pretentiousness made her an admirable novelist of manners in the great school of Thackeray. She is often compared to Henry James, whom she knew well and admired. But although they shared an interest in Americans in Europe, and although one or two of her works, notably *The Reef* (1912), clearly show James' influence, she never followed his subtle, speculative bent, and she mistrusted the whole approach of his last period. She is closer in spirit to George Eliot and, in the United States, to ELLEN GLASGOW. She had an exact knowledge of the disciplines to which the worldly submit themselves and of the ways in which they disguise and preserve their crasser satisfactions. She was direct and to the point, never devious and involved. But she suffered from two disadvantages. Her heroes have a tendency to be selfish, fatuous dilettantes, a pattern of which their author seems curiously unaware, possibly because of her lifelong devotion to Walter Berry, a cultivated international lawyer who gave her the intellectual companionship that her husband was unable to supply, but whom many of her friends regarded as a dry and snobbish egotist. Her other disadvantage, and one that was ultimately to depreciate much of her fiction, was an overemphasis on the importance of "good taste" and a steadily growing hostility to what she considered the vulgarities of American commercial civilization. This begins to appear as early as *The Custom of the Country* (1913), where the reader is made uncomfortably aware of her contempt for the Spraggs.

All the books of her middle period are of a very high caliber. *Madame de Treymes* (1907) and *The Reef* are polished, brilliant Jamesian tales of Americans abroad. *The Fruit of the Tree* (1907) is an interesting, if not wholly successful, attempt at a novel of reform. *Tales of Men and Ghosts* (1910) shows Mrs. Wharton's great skill with the eerie, a talent that she never lost, and *Ethan Frome* (1911) and *Summer* (1917) prove that her powers of observation were by no means limited to the rich and cultivated. The former, a bleak, stark, unforgettable tale of a doomed triangle in a freezing Massachusetts winter, sometimes threatens to preempt all of its author's niche in the history of American letters. *Xingu* (1916) is probably her finest compilation of short stories.

Her two handicaps as a writer are happily missing in her most famous novel, *The Age of Innocence* (1920), a Pulitzer Prize winner, which she wrote in a mood of nostalgia, born of the destructiveness of the World War, for what had once seemed to her the stuffy world of her childhood. Set in the 1870's, the story is free of her strictures of contemporary society and, because the theme is the redemption of a prig by love and self-sacrifice, Newland Archer becomes the most sympathetic of her heroes. But even better than the characters are the backgrounds. The era is invoked in a series of glittering slides: the shabby red and gold boxes of the Academy of Music, the small bright lawns and big bright sea of Newport, the ferns in Wardian cases, the camellias over seats of gold and black bamboo. As Edmund Wilson put it, Mrs. Wharton was not only the pioneer but the poet of interior decoration.

Early in these years of creativity, the strains of Mrs. Wharton's personal life increased. Her husband had shown growing signs of irritability and mental imbalance, and in 1910 they sold their house in Lenox and moved to France; shortly thereafter he suffered a nervous collapse and had to be placed in a sanatorium, at Kreuzlingen on Lake Constance. In 1913 she divorced him. In France, Edith Wharton found a happier fusion of the intellectual and worldly lives than had seemed to exist at home. Having means of her own, in addition to the proceeds from her books, like a Jamesian heroine she was able to enjoy for a time immunity from financial worries. She owned two beautiful, perfectly maintained homes in France, one at St. Brice-sous-forêt, just outside Paris, and the other at Hyères, on the Riviera. She traveled widely in Europe, enjoyed the friendship of many distinguished men of letters, such as Henry James, Paul Bourget, Howard Sturges, and Percy Lubbock, and was a frequent visitor at Bernard Berenson's villa, I Tatti, near Florence. If she seemed a reserved, formal, even to some a formidable person, she delighted her intimates with her wit and gaiety and warmth. She was a perfectionist in everything: in her speech, in her gardens and interiors, in her sightseeing, in her friendships, in all she read and saw and heard. During the First World War she did much work for refugees and the wounded, at one time feeding and housing six hundred war orphans at her own expense. For this France made her a chevalier (and later an officer) of the Legion of Honor, and Belgium made her a chevalier of the Order of Leopold.

The postwar years marked a fairly steady decline in Mrs. Wharton's writing talent. An ocean now lay between the artist and her subject matter, an ocean that she crossed only once after the war, to receive an honorary degree at Yale (1923). She seemed to feel in these years that she had at last localized the source of the vulgarity that had conquered the modern world; she believed that it lay in the American Middle West, an area she had never visited, but which, she felt, the novels of Sinclair Lewis, whom she greatly admired, portrayed accurately. Her books begin to be shrill with denunciations of stereotyped characters that are increasingly difficult to recognize. Perhaps because she was now writing for the larger public of the American women's magazines, needing their substantial payments to help support her expensive way of life, even her style begins to show traces of slickness. *The Glimpses of the Moon* (1922), *Twilight Sleep* (1927), and *The Children* (1928) are trivial, oddly heartless books, deficient in the very taste that had become their author's god. *Hudson River Bracketed* (1929) and its sequel, *The Gods Arrive* (1932), are better novels because of the sympathetic creation of a young American writer, Vance Weston, with whose problems Mrs. Wharton was familiar less as a fellow American than as a fellow novelist. But the old hard, bright style was recaptured only when she returned to the city of her childhood and of family memories, as she did in the four novelettes of her *Old New York* (1924).

Mrs. Wharton died at St. Brice at the age of seventy-five, of an apoplectic stroke, and was buried in the Protestant Cemetery at Versailles, next to the grave of Walter Berry. Among other tokens of recognition from her contemporaries, she had been made a member of the National Institute of Arts and Letters in 1930, and four years later of the American Academy of Arts and Letters. She left an unfinished novel, *The Buccaneers* (published in 1938), which was also set in the world of her childhood.

[No full-scale biography of Edith Wharton has been written, possibly because her papers, at Yale Univ., were closed until 1968. The principal published biographical sources are her autobiography, *A Backward Glance* (1934), and Percy Lubbock, *Portrait of Edith Wharton* (1947). Biographical and critical studies include: Edward K. Browne, *Edith Wharton: Étude Critique* (1935); essays by Edmund Wilson in his *The Wound and the Bow* (1941) and *Classics and Commercials* (1950); Blake Nevius, *Edith Wharton: A Study of Her Fiction* (1953); Wayne Andrews' introduction to *The Best Short Stories of Edith Wharton* (1958); Louis Auchincloss, *Edith Wharton* (Univ. of Minn. Pamphlets on Am. Writers, 1961), included also in his *Pioneers & Caretakers* (1965); Irving Howe, "The Achievement of Edith Wharton," *Encounter*, July 1962; Patricia R. Plante, "Edith Wharton: A Prophet without Due Honor," *Midwest Rev.*, 1962; Millicent Bell, *Edith Wharton & Henry James* (1965); Peter M. Buitenhuis, "Edith Wharton and the First World War," *Am. Quart.*, Fall 1966.]

LOUIS AUCHINCLOSS

**WHEATLEY, Phillis** (c. 1753–Dec. 5, 1784), Negro poet, was bought directly off a slave ship in Boston by John Wheatley, a wealthy merchant tailor, and his wife, who wanted a girl who could be trained as her personal servant. Neither the time nor the place of Phillis' birth is known, but since she was losing her first teeth when she was purchased in 1761, she was judged to be between seven and eight years old, and since she spoke no language the Wheatleys could identify, it was assumed that she was born in Africa.

Recognizing her unusual precosity and struck by her genteel demeanor, the Wheatleys gave the girl advantages denied to the other slaves of the household. Indeed, though nominally a slave, Phillis was in fact free. She performed only the lightest of chores, such as might be expected of a daughter in an affluent home; she ate with the family and had her own room. The Wheatleys' twin children, Mary and Nathaniel, who were ten years older than Phillis, taught the girl, with such success that within sixteen months of her arrival she had "attained the English Language . . . to such a Degree as to read any, the most difficult Parts, of the Sacred Writings." One of her earliest verses, "To the University of Cambridge, in New England," composed when she had just entered her teens, celebrates learning, virtue, and redemption through Christ—the three principal themes of all her subsequent writing. Alexander Pope was her favorite author, and her first published work, "An Elegiac Poem, on the Death of the Celebrated Divine . . . George Whitefield" (1770), shows his strong neoclassical influence. In that same year Phillis was admitted to membership in the Old South Meeting House, where the Wheatleys, an uncommonly religious family, stood sponsors.

In a period when it was generally believed that Negroes lacked all but the most elemental capacities, Phillis' talent was thought to be unusual, as in a sense it was, and though her poetry, measured by objective standards, was at best mediocre, it was cited as proof of the antislavery argument that people of her race could profit by education. During the late 1760's and the early '70's she drew much attention. Every guest of the Wheatleys—"clergymen and other individuals of high standing in society"—wanted to see the young Negro poet, who "even aspired to mastery of Latin," and she herself was frequently the guest of persons of "wealth and distinction." For some of these she wrote memorial or other occasional verse. Indeed, excepting two or three reflective pieces, such as "On Virtue," and one or two on classical themes, such as "Niobe in Distress for Her Children Slain by Apollo," nearly all of Phillis Wheatley's scant output of verse is occasional.

But it was not her talent only that won approval. Even Thomas Jefferson, who thought her poetry too inconsequential for criticism, would have esteemed her modesty, her poise, and her wit in conversation. These were the attributes that endeared her to many Bostonians. These same qualities made her a favorite with influential people abroad, when, her health failing in 1773, the family physician advised sea air, and the Wheatleys sent her to England in company with their son.

The high point of Phillis Wheatley's life, this visit to England was both a literary and a personal triumph. She was the guest of the Countess of Huntingdon, a patron who had already seen to the printing of Phillis' poem on George Whitefield. It was probably the Countess, too, who completed arrangements for the publication of Phillis' only book, for the volume, *Poems on Various Subjects, Religious and Moral*, issued in London later that year, was dedicated to her. So as to leave no doubt as to the genuineness of its authorship, a foreword attesting to Phillis' talent was signed by eighteen prominent Massachusetts men, including the wealthy merchant John Hancock and the governor of the colony.

But none who met the young poet in England doubted her personal attractiveness. Lord Dartmouth exclaimed over her. Brook Watson, Lord Mayor of London, presented her with a folio edition of *Paradise Lost*. She was urged to stay to be presented at court. Meantime, however, Mrs. Wheatley had fallen ill at home in Boston, and Phillis knew where her duty lay. After a little more than five weeks in England, she returned to America in September 1773.

The fatal illness of her mistress, who died in 1774, marked the beginning of the dissolution of the life the Negro poet knew. Mary Wheatley had married in 1771, and when John Wheatley died and Nathaniel remained abroad, family ties frayed to snapping. The Wheatley coterie melted away, and the public found other attractions. There was one brief renewal of interest: a poem that Phillis had written to Gen. George Washington was published in the *Pennsylvania Magazine* for April 1776, and sometime later, at his invitation, Phillis visited the General's headquarters in Cambridge.

Left alone in the precarious times of the Revolutionary War, Phillis was victimized by the persuasive tongue of a free Negro named John Peters, who was described as a "complaisant and agreeable" gentleman. He "kept a shop, wore a wig, carried a cane, and felt himself superior to all kinds of labor." Phillis married him in April 1778. He seems to have wandered away, returned, and wandered away again. Two of the three children she bore him soon died. Phillis was reduced to working in a cheap lodging house to support herself and her remaining child, and her health, never robust, gave way altogether. She and her child died in Boston on Dec. 5, 1784. They had been buried in an unmarked grave before her former friends and patrons read of her death in the Boston *Independent Chronicle* for Dec. 9.

Occasional later editions of her *Poems on Various Subjects*, beginning with the first American edition in 1786, helped revive the memory of Phillis Wheatley, but it was not until 1834, at the time of the beginnings of organized abolitionist activity, when Margaretta M. Odell, a distant relative of the Wheatleys, published a "Memoir" in a new edition of the *Poems*, that the first Negro woman poet in America attained the curious, small, but permanent place she holds in the history of American letters.

[*Memoir and Poems of Phillis Wheatley* (1834), including the Margaretta Odell memoir; Benjamin Brawley, *The Negro in Literature and Art in the U.S.* (1918) and *Early Negro Am. Writers* (1935); Charles F. Heartman, *Phillis Wheatley (Phillis Peters): A Critical Attempt and a Bibliog. of Her Writings* (1915) and Heartman's edition of her *Poems and Letters* (1915); Daniel A. Payne, *Recollections of Seventy Years* (1888); George W. Williams, *Hist. of the Negro Race in America from 1619 to 1880* (1883). See also Julian D. Mason, Jr.'s introduction to his edition of *The Poems of Phillis Wheatley* (1966); and Robert C. Kuncio, "Some Unpublished Poems of Phillis Wheatley," *New England Quart.*, June 1970.]

SAUNDERS REDDING

**WHEELER, Candace Thurber** (Mar. 24, 1827–Aug. 5, 1923), pioneer in American textile design and interior decoration, was born in Delhi, Delaware County, N.Y., the second daughter and third of eight children of Abner Gilman Thurber, dairy farmer and dealer in furs, and Lucy (Dunham) Thurber. Her ancestors on both sides had settled in the Plymouth Colony in the seventeenth century. Her father, an abolitionist and Presbyterian deacon, supervised her early education, encouraging her skill at drawing, her love of nature, and her appreciation of poetry. She continued her studies at Delaware Academy in Delhi, while her mother, a capable housewife renowned for her beautiful handspun linens, initiated her into the household arts and taught her to spin, knit, sew, and weave; Candace remembered her home as the center of a "lively creative interest."

On June 28, 1844, at seventeen, she was married to Thomas M. Wheeler, ten years her senior, the brother-in-law of the Thurbers' pastor and at the time bookkeeper in a New York City mercantile firm. The Wheelers had four children: Candace (born in 1845), James Cooper (1853), Dora (1856), and Dunham (1861). The first ten years of their marriage were spent in Brooklyn, N.Y., then only a village. Wheeler had strong literary interests, and in the small art world of that day he and his wife soon made friends among the younger writers and painters. Their country home, Nestledown, built near Jamaica, Long Island, in 1854, became a gathering place for such artists as Frederick E. Church, Sanford Gifford, Albert Bierstadt, and Eastman Johnson, who encouraged Mrs. Wheeler, with her interest in drawing and her instinct for color, to take up painting. In the fall of 1865 the Wheelers went abroad for a leisurely year's sojourn in Germany, Italy, and France, visiting the art galleries and mingling in artistic society. Wheeler returned the following November to New York, leaving his family in Dresden, where the children were placed in school and Mrs. Wheeler devoted herself to studying German and art. That winter in the studio of a Dresden professor of painting seemed to her later to have been "the beginning of preparation for work in the world." Other family trips abroad followed.

The death in June 1876 of her eldest daughter, Mrs. Lewis A. Stimson (mother of Henry L. Stimson, later Secretary of War), proved a turning point in Mrs. Wheeler's life. To alleviate her grief she devoted herself to a charitable project that gave direction to her interest in art while utilizing the household skills she had learned as a child. Attending the Centennial Exposition in Philadelphia that summer, she was attracted by the exhibit of the English school of art needlework at Kensington, established to provide a profitable outlet for the labors of "decayed gentlewomen." Mrs. Wheeler had herself been aware of the plight of "women of education and refinement" who lacked means of support, and in 1877 she started a movement to organize a similar institution in the United States, the Society of Decorative Art of New York City, which she

served as vice-president and corresponding secretary. Besides exhibiting and selling a variety of handicrafts, the society established classes in embroidery and china painting. Though the society prospered, Mrs. Wheeler left it the next year to help Mrs. William Choate found the Women's Exchange, to market not merely decorative objects but articles of all kinds produced by women.

In 1879 a larger opportunity arose when the New York painter and glassmaker Louis Comfort Tiffany invited Mrs. Wheeler to join him and two other artists—Samuel Colman and Lockwood de Forest—in an interior-decorating firm which would seek to supply the demands of an America newly awakened to the arts. For the Associated Artists (as the Tiffany firm was named), Mrs. Wheeler created textiles and embroideries for such important commissions as the decoration of the Union League Club in New York, Mark Twain's home in Hartford, and the White House, which was renovated at the beginning of the Arthur administration.

Feeling that her textile department could now be maintained as a separate enterprise, Mrs. Wheeler left Tiffany in 1883 to found her own Associated Artists, a New York firm made up entirely of women. A leading assistant was her daughter Dora, who had studied under the painter William M. Chase and in Paris. Mrs. Wheeler designed and arranged for the manufacture of a number of new fabrics—printed linens, silks, brocades, damasks, velvets—experimenting with rich colors and textures. Her insistence on the appropriateness of a design to its setting led her to create a Scottish thistle pattern for Andrew Carnegie, a design of bells, wheels, and drifting smoke for a railroad parlor car. A particular desire was to create modern American tapestries. She experimented with different stitches and took out British and American patents on the new techniques she developed. Her firm's tapestries—in effect, paintings in embroidery—included "Gleaner" (sketched by the painter Rosina Emmet, one of her associates), "The Peacock Girl," and, in keeping with her emphasis on American themes, "Hilda" and "Hester Prynne," from Hawthorne's *The Marble Faun* and *The Scarlet Letter*, "Evangeline" and "Minnehaha," after Longfellow, and a Zuñi Indian girl.

Meanwhile Mrs. Wheeler also worked on the advisory council of the Woman's Art School of Cooper Union and lectured at the New York Institute for Artist-Artisans. For the Chicago World's Columbian Exposition of 1893 she was named director of the exhibit of women's work in the applied arts and also color director of the Woman's Building, whose library she decorated using vivid shades of blue and green to harmonize with the view of sky and water from its window. Writing of the women's exhibit, Mrs. Wheeler declared, "Fifteen years ago, no American manufacturer thought of buying an American design for his carpet, or wall-paper, or textile. . . . To-day the manufacturers all agree that the most popular designs they can furnish are made by our native designers, who are, to a very large extent, women." The change was in large part her doing.

Shortly before 1900, now in her early seventies, Mrs. Wheeler handed her firm of Associated Artists over to her architect son Dunham and devoted herself to writing articles and books on the applied and decorative arts. Her works include an important essay, "Interior Decoration as a Profession for Women" (*Outlook*, Apr. 6, 20, 1895), as well as *Principles of Home Decoration* (1903), the autobiographical *Yesterdays in a Busy Life* (1918), and *The Development of Embroidery in America* (1921).

Mrs. Wheeler summered in Onteora in the Catskills, where her husband and her brother Francis B. Thurber had formed the Catskill Mountain Camp and Cottage Company, a colony that attracted Mark Twain, John Burroughs, and Frank Stockton, as well as MARY MAPES DODGE, SUSAN COOLIDGE, JEANNETTE WATSON GILDER, and MARIANA GRISWOLD VAN RENSSELAER. After the death of her husband in 1895 Candace Wheeler built a winter home in Thomasville, Ga. Still writing and painting, she lived to the age of ninety-six. She died in the New York apartment of her daughter Dora Wheeler Keith and was buried in Prospect Cemetery, Jamaica, Long Island. Although much of the work she had created in textiles and in fabrics proved evanescent, Candace Wheeler was a "potent influence for high taste," and played a small but effective part in the development of Art Nouveau. Most important, she opened a new field for women in American design, in textile branches of applied art, and in interior decoration.

[Candace Wheeler's autobiography, *Yesterdays in a Busy Life*; *Biog. Cyc. Am. Women*, II (1925), 186–90; Sarah K. Bolton, *Successful Women* (1888), chap. ix; "Some Work of the 'Associated Artists,' " *Harper's Monthly*, Aug. 1884; *Woman's Who's Who of America*, 1914–15; *N.Y. Times*, Aug. 6, 8, 1923. For a fuller account and extensive references see Madeleine B. Stern, *We the Women* (1963). The letters of Mrs. Wheeler to her grandson Henry L. Stimson (Stimson Papers, Yale Univ.) cast interesting light on her later life. Examples of her work in textiles and embroideries are to be found in the Textile Study Room of the Metropolitan Museum of Art, N.Y. City, the Cleve-

land Museum of Art, and the Wellesley College Art Museum.]

MADELEINE B. STERN

**WHEELER, Ella.** *See* WILCOX, Ella Wheeler.

**WHEELER, Ruth** (Aug. 5, 1877–Sept. 29, 1948), home economist, nutritionist, and dietitian, was born in Plains, Pa., the eldest of four children, two girls and two boys, of Jared Ward Wheeler and Martha Jane (Evans) Wheeler. Her father, the manager of a wholesale provision house, was descended from a Connecticut family that had settled in Wayne County, Pa., in 1814. Her mother was the daughter of a Welsh Congregational minister, the Rev. Evan Benjamin Evans of Pottsville, Pa., who studied medicine so that he could help the poor and suffering in his churches. Ruth Wheeler had her earliest education from her mother and could read well at the age of five. She attended the public school and high school at West Pittston, Pa., to which the family moved in 1882. At seventeen she entered Vassar College (despite poor preparation in Latin and algebra, which she had to make up); she graduated, A.B., in 1899. Six years of high school science teaching followed, at first in West Pittston, where she also taught German, and then for three years in Saratoga Springs, N.Y. From 1905 to 1910 she taught chemistry at Pratt Institute in Brooklyn, N.Y.

During her high school teaching Miss Wheeler was drawn to the developing field of home economics, perhaps sensing the opportunity it offered, through the study of nutrition, for able, science-minded young women. When the American Home Economics Association was founded in December 1908 she was a charter member. In the fall of 1910 she enrolled in the graduate school of Yale University to study in the laboratory of physiological chemistry established by Prof. Russell H. Chittenden. She received her Ph.D. in 1913 with a dissertation on "Feeding Experiments with Mice." Meanwhile, in 1912, she had joined the faculty of the department of household science at the University of Illinois, where she taught nutrition for six years. She then accepted an appointment (1918) as professor of home economics at Goucher College, Baltimore, Md.; during her three years there she made this a strong and popular department.

World War I brought a sudden urgency to problems of food and nutrition, with the need for food conservation and for maintaining the health of the population through good diet. Ruth Wheeler used all her knowledge to help the war endeavor and was appointed in 1917 chairman of the national committee on nutrition of the American Red Cross; she continued to head the Red Cross nutrition service until 1932. Among those professionally concerned with food and nutrition in 1917 were the nation's scattered dietitians, who were then mostly attached to hospitals, planning and supervising diets for the sick. At a conference of dietitians that fall the American Dietetic Association was organized, with Miss Wheeler participating; she became a member of the first executive committee. Her vision and her willingness to try new ideas gave important guidance to the new association. She served as its president in 1924–26, successfully establishing, despite a meager bank balance and the forebodings of some members, the association's *Journal*.

Meanwhile Miss Wheeler had in 1921 become professor and head of the newly formed department of nutrition in the College of Medicine of the State University of Iowa and chief dietitian for the University Hospitals, responsible for food service to patients and personnel. At Iowa she inaugurated professional training of dietitians by establishing the first one-year dietetic internship course leading to a master's degree. Her emphasis was on teaching, research, and food service, and her professional idealism was transmitted to students and colleagues alike.

In 1926 she returned to her alma mater, Vassar, as professor of physiology and nutrition. Here she also directed (1928–42) the Vassar Summer Institute of Euthenics, an experimental program in adult education which through courses for parents, teachers, and social workers in such subjects as child psychology, education, and household technology sought to promote "the improvement of human relations." During her Vassar years she served as consultant in nutrition (1926–30) to the Presbyterian Hospital in New York City and published her *American Red Cross Textbook on Food and Nutrition* (1927).

Ruth Wheeler was a petite person, with hair prematurely white almost from her college days. Her erect posture and light step conveyed her spirit of active alertness. "What one remembers most about her," a student recalls, "is her smile, not a perfunctory one, but always expressing a genuine feeling of friendliness." She loved the out-of-doors and could name most of the flowers and recognize birds by their call. An active Episcopalian, she taught Sunday school classes and sang in the choir; while in Iowa City, at the request of the bishop, she prepared a class of university students for confirmation when the local church was without a rector. She retired from the Vassar faculty in 1944. Four years later, at the age of seventy-one, she died in Poughkeepsie, N.Y., of an intestinal obstruction. Her ashes were buried in the Poughkeepsie Rural Cemetery.

[Nelda Ross in *Jour. of Am. Dietetic Assoc.*, Dec. 1948; Anna Boller Beach in *ibid.*, Dec. 1957; Yale Univ., *Obituary Record of Graduates*, 1948–49; *Am. Men of Science* (7th ed., 1944); *Who Was Who in America*, vol. II (1950); Mary I. Barber, ed., *Hist. of the Am. Dietetic Assoc.* (1959); Anna H. Knipp and Thaddeus P. Thomas, *The Hist. of Goucher College* (1938), pp. 415–16; family data from a sister, Helen W. Wheeler, San Francisco, Calif. For representative articles by Miss Wheeler, see *Jour. of Home Economics*, vols. VII, VIII, XIV, and XV (1915–23); and her opening editorial and presidential address in the Dec. 1925 issue of the *Jour. of the Am. Dietetic Assoc.* On the Vassar Institute of Euthenics, see *School and Society*, Mar. 29, 1930, pp. 433–34; and *Jour. of Adult Education*, Oct. 1932, pp. 455–56.]

ELIZABETH NEIGE TODHUNTER

**WHEELOCK, Lucy** (Feb. 1, 1857–Oct. 2, 1946), kindergarten educator, founder of Wheelock College in Boston, was born in Cambridge, Vt., the second daughter and second of six children of Edwin and Laura (Pierce) Wheelock. Her father, a descendant (through his mother) of John Adams and a graduate of the University of Vermont, was minister of the Congregational church in his native Cambridge. Lucy attended the Underhill (Vt.) Academy for a year, and then transferred to the public high school in Reading, Mass., where she lived with family friends, and graduated in 1874. She taught for a time in a village school at Cambridge, Vt., and in 1876 entered the Chauncy Hall School in Boston as a special student, to prepare herself to enter Wellesley College. When she saw the school's kindergarten in operation one day, however, she felt as though "the gates of heaven were opened and I had a glimpse of the kingdom where peace and love reign." After asking the advice of ELIZABETH PEABODY, founder of Boston's first kindergarten, she abandoned her plans for college and in 1878 enrolled at the Kindergarten Training School conducted by Mrs. Ella Snelling Hatch, at which Miss Peabody was one of the lecturers.

After receiving her diploma in 1879, Miss Wheelock became a teacher in the kindergarten of the Chauncy Hall School; the ten years she spent with children there were among the happiest of her life. In 1888, when kindergartens were first made an integral part of the public school system in Boston, Chauncy Hall inaugurated a one-year training course for teachers under Miss Wheelock's direction. Within a few years the course was drawing students from all over the country, and in 1893 it was lengthened to two years. Enrollment continued to increase, and in 1896 she left Chauncy Hall to establish her own Wheelock Kindergarten Training School, in rented quarters in Boston. The first of its permanent buildings was erected in 1914. From the beginning the school prospered. In 1899 its curriculum was expanded to include the training of teachers for the primary grades, and in 1926 to include preparation for teaching in nursery schools.

Lucy Wheelock had meanwhile become a leader in the nationwide kindergarten movement. In 1892 she was elected a member of a committee of the National Education Association to consider the formation of a national kindergarten organization, and she became the second president (1895–99) of the resulting International Kindergarten Union. In the same year a major controversy developed among leaders in the movement, and continued for more than a decade, over proposed modifications of the traditional methods prescribed by the founder of the kindergarten, Friedrich Froebel. Appointed to the Committee of Nineteen to study the areas of dissension, Miss Wheelock served as chairman for five years (1905–09) and helped edit the final report, *The Kindergarten*, published in 1913. Three principal factions had emerged: a conservative majority, represented by SUSAN BLOW, who opposed any alteration of the Froebelian method; a smaller group of liberals, represented by PATTY SMITH HILL, who advocated adopting more flexible routines that would allow a child much freedom in the choice of activities and play materials; and a small minority who wished to compromise between the two extremes. With ELIZABETH HARRISON, Miss Wheelock subscribed to the minority position that favored a gradual, considered evolution of the Froebelian system. Herself a devoted follower of Froebel's philosophy, she organized and led a pilgrimage of some seventy American kindergarten teachers to Froebel's home in Germany in the summer of 1911.

In 1899 Miss Wheelock was appointed to the committee on education of the National Congress of Mothers (later the National Congress of Parents and Teachers) and in 1908 became its chairman. She was also chairman of a committee on cooperation between the National Congress of Mothers and the International Kindergarten Union (1916) and a similar committee of the Kindergarten Union and the National Education Association (1913–18). An appealing and persuasive speaker, small, wiry, and energetic, she visited eight Southern states in 1916 as one of a team traveling on a "Mother's Crusade" to promote the kindergarten movement. Besides many articles in educational journals, she was the co-author, with Elizabeth Colson, of *Talks to Mothers* (1920). Early in her career she translated from the German a group of Swiss stories for children by Johanna Spyri which were published as *Red-Letter Stories* (1884) and *Swiss Stories for Children* (1887).

Miss Wheelock was always interested in extending the kindergarten system to the children of the poor. In 1895 she helped organize a free kindergarten at Hope Chapel, sponsored by Boston's Old South Church, in what was then a Negro section of the city. She served on the board of directors of the Ruggles Street Neighborhood House in Roxbury and of the House of Good Will in East Boston. At the request of Robert A. Woods, founder of South End House, a Boston social settlement, she helped organize a kindergarten there under the auspices of the Wheelock School. She early became active in Sunday school work, superintending a large primary class in Boston's Berkeley Temple, lecturing frequently to Sunday school institutes, and publishing a weekly column of "Hints to Teachers" in the *Congregationalist*. Other interests are reflected in her membership in the Woman's Educational and Industrial Union, the Twentieth Century Club of Boston, and the Woman's Republican Club. In 1929 she served on the Educational Committee of the League of Nations.

Miss Wheelock remained owner and director of the Wheelock School until 1939, when, at the time of her retirement, it was incorporated as a nonprofit institution. In 1941 it became Wheelock College. Five years later, at the age of eighty-nine, Lucy Wheelock died at her Boston home of a coronary thrombosis. Her remains were cremated.

[Lucy Wheelock, "My Life Story" (unpublished MS. in possession of her niece, Mrs. Horace B. Reed of Newton, Mass.) and "Miss Peabody as I Knew Her," in Committee of Nineteen, *Pioneers of the Kindergarten in America* (1924); Winifred E. Bain, *Leadership in Childhood Education* (1964), a history of Wheelock College; Thomas Cushing, *Hist. Sketch of Chauncy-Hall School . . . 1828 to 1894* (1895), pp. 67–69; Frances E. Willard and Mary A. Livermore, eds., *A Woman of the Century* (1893); *Nat. Cyc. Am. Biog.*, XXXIX, 119; *Yearbooks* of the Internat. Kindergarten Union, 1895–96 to 1918; *Who Was Who in America*, vol. II (1950); death record from Mass. Registrar of Vital Statistics.]

ABIGAIL A. ELIOT

WHIFFEN, Blanche Galton (Mar. 12, 1845–
Nov. 25, 1936), actress, was born in London,
England, the daughter of Joseph West Galton,
a secretary in the London general post office,
and his wife, Mary Ann Pyne, an accomplished
singer and piano teacher and one of the three
well-known musical Pyne sisters. After the
death of her father when Blanche was about
six, her mother could scarcely make ends meet.
Her aunts Louisa and Susan, however, saw
to it that Blanche, her two brothers (a third
died in infancy), and her younger sister Susan
never suffered from want. They sent Blanche
to boarding schools in Gravesend, Kent, and
in London, among them one conducted by a
Mrs. Chapman, sister-in-law of the actor
Charles Kean, son of Edmund Kean. Thanks
to Mrs. Chapman, she witnessed fine theatrical
performances, which strengthened the shy
child's desire to become an actress. After attending a convent in Saint-Omer, France,
Blanche returned to London to live with her
aunts. Following their wish, she trained to
become a pianist, but extreme nervousness,
which caused her hands to tremble, interfered
with her public performances. She then revealed her desire to go on the stage, and
though her aunts discouraged her—perhaps because she was, in her own words, "the ugly
duckling" who "never became a swan"—she
was not daunted. In 1865, while serving as
chaperone for her sister Susan, then appearing
with the Pyne and Harrison English Opera
Company at the Royalty Theatre, London, she
was allowed to play the Fairy in a burlesque,
*Turko the Terrible.* Her family, though not at
all impressed with her talents, allowed her to
go on tour. Thomas Whiffen, musician and
actor, later joined the company, and on July
11, 1868, he and Blanche Galton were married in St. Andrew's Church, London. True to
her Anglican background, Mrs. Whiffen remained an Episcopalian throughout her life.

Shortly after her marriage the troupe, including the Whiffens and Blanche's sister
Susan, with her mother as manager, went to
America, where as the "Galton Opera Company" they had been engaged to appear at
Wood's Museum on Broadway. They opened
(Aug. 31, 1868) with Offenbach's *Marriage
by Lanterns,* Blanche singing contralto. They
next joined Horace Lingard and his wife at
New York's Theatre Comique. When one of
the numerous theatre fires of the day cut short
this venture, the Galton company went on the
road. In Philadelphia, Mrs. Whiffen remained
behind to give birth to a daughter, Mary
Blanche. Then followed in quick succession
Susan's marriage and withdrawal from the

stage, the death of Mary Blanche, and the
disbanding of the troupe. The Whiffens returned to New York in search of engagements,
which eventually took them from Maine
through the pioneering West to California, on
arduous one-night stands, sometimes with the
Lingards, sometimes under the management of
John Templeton, father of FAY TEMPLETON.

Back in New York, Blanche Galton (as she
was known) at the last minute stepped into
the role of Buttercup in the first American performance of Gilbert and Sullivan's *H.M.S.
Pinafore* (January 1879). This success was
followed by another in 1880—this time on the
legitimate instead of the operatic stage—when
Steele Mackaye, manager of the Madison
Square Theatre, engaged the Whiffens for his
drama *Hazel Kirke.* It ran for 486 nights in
New York alone, Mrs. Whiffen playing the role
of the heroine's mother. The Madison Square
stock company, with which she continued,
proved a milestone in her career: at thirty-five
she began specializing in old women's parts
and dropped her maiden name for that of Mrs.
Thomas Whiffen.

In 1887 she joined Daniel Frohman's new
Lyceum Theatre stock company, of which she
remained a stalwart member for more than a
decade. She left in 1897 to return to England,
where her husband had gone to recuperate
from typhoid and where he died two weeks
after her arrival. The next year she rejoined the
Frohman company as Mrs. Mossop in the first
American production of Sir Arthur Wing
Pinero's *Trelawney of the Wells.* In 1900 she
left Daniel Frohman to spend a few seasons
in his brother Charles' Empire Theatre company. In 1906–07 she supported Henry Miller
and Margaret Anglin (d. 1958) in Miller's
impressive production of William Vaughn
Moody's *The Great Divide.* For two more
decades Mrs. Whiffen continued her career as
a character actress, appearing regularly on
Broadway and occasionally on tour, until in
1928, at eighty-three, illness forced her withdrawal from the cast of *Just Fancy*—her last
play.

Blanche Galton Whiffen, a "delightful and
finished" actress, supporter of eminent stars,
never aimed at stellar rank herself; her chief
desire was expressed in the title of her memoirs,
*Keeping Off the Shelf.* Though only five feet
tall, fragile, blue-eyed, and in later years white-
haired, she had a metallic strength which
served her well as a trouper. Her whimsicality
and charm, endearing her to both audiences
and fellow actors, helped win her the title of
"the grand old lady of the American stage."
Among her favorite roles in the more than four

hundred she played in her sixty-three-year career were those of Mrs. Carter Stafford in *Just Suppose* (1920), Mrs. Bradley in *The Goose Hangs High* (1924), and Sister Genevieve in *The Two Orphans* (1926). She spent her last years in her Blue Ridge mountain home in Montvale, Va., with her two children who had survived infancy: Thomas, an actor turned farmer, and Peggy, also a retired actress. She died there of bronchial pneumonia at the age of ninety-one. Her body was cremated in Washington and the ashes were sent to England.

[For Mrs. Whiffen's own account of her career, see *Keeping Off the Shelf* (1928). Her outlook on life is expressed in Catherine Robertson, "Is It Luck or Pluck?" *Theatre Mag.*, Apr. 1921, and in Keene Sumner, "A Wonderful Old Lady Who Has Been on the Stage 57 Years," *American Mag.*, Oct. 1922, which includes a photograph. Philip Hale pays tribute to her in the *Boston Herald*, Nov. 28, 1928; and the *N.Y. Times*, Mar. 13, 1935, describes a celebration in her honor. Obituaries are in the *N.Y. Times, N.Y. Herald Tribune, Boston Globe,* and *Boston Transcript,* all of Nov. 27, 1936. George C. D. Odell, *Annals of the N.Y. Stage,* vols. VIII–XV (1936–49), chronicles her appearances in that city to 1894. Death record from Va. Dept. of Health.]

ELIZABETH F. HOXIE

**WHITCHER, Frances Miriam Berry** (Nov. 1, 1811–Jan. 4, 1852), author and humorist, was born in Whitesboro, N.Y., where her father, Lewis Berry, owned a tavern; originally from New Jersey, he had moved to the upper Hudson Valley and thence, in 1802, to Oneida County, settling in Whitesboro by 1807. He and his wife, Elizabeth Wells of Cambridge, N.Y., had fifteen children, of whom Miriam, as she was known, was the eleventh. While still very young the girl showed a precocious gift for drawing caricatured likenesses and writing satirical verses and parodies. Early subjects of her caricatures were her first schoolteacher, a sharp old maid, and the callow youths of the village academy where she completed her education. A teacher in Utica gave her supplementary lessons in French. Though she had no training in art, she possessed enough natural talent to draw illustrations for the sketches she later published. Her satiric gifts, however, were not appreciated by her family or neighbors, who remonstrated and scolded, so that she grew up in loneliness and developed a reserve that was sometimes taken for haughtiness. She was a tall, dignified woman, with dark hair and expressive dark eyes.

Her first published writing grew out of her membership in the Maeonian Circle, a local social and literary association. The story she

read there of the "Widow Spriggins" was printed in part in a weekly paper in Rome, N.Y., edited by a personal friend. An extravagant burlesque of the sentimental novel, specifically of Regina Maria Roche's *The Children of the Abbey,* it was presented as an extended monologue in colloquial dialect. Misspellings and malapropisms heightened the incongruity of situation, in the tradition of rustic humor recently developed by Seba Smith and Augustus Baldwin Longstreet in their sketches satirizing the affectations of country girls with aspirations to gentility and sophistication.

In 1846 Miriam Berry sent some rambling monologues in the same style, ostensibly written down by "The Widow Bedott" and signed with the pseudonym "Frank," to the editor of *Neal's Saturday Gazette,* published in Philadelphia. Joseph C. Neal, a well-known humorist himself, immediately printed the stories and encouraged Miss Berry to continue the series. The stories, which owe some debts of plot and characterization to Frances Trollope's *The Widow Barnaby,* proved extremely popular and attracted the attention of Louis Godey, who printed a related series by Miss Berry entitled "Aunt Magwire's Experience" in *Godey's Lady's Book* in 1847–49. Meanwhile, on Jan. 6, 1847, Miriam Berry was married to the Rev. Benjamin W. Whitcher, an Episcopal clergyman, and moved with him to his pastorate in Elmira, N.Y. As her sketches continued to appear, she was bitterly assailed by local residents who fancied themselves her models.

The Bedott papers are chiefly concerned with the hatchet-faced, slandering Widow—her attempts to catch a "consort," her poetic pretensions and "perductions"—and with her more amiable sister, Aunt Magwire. The latter's monologues depict female hypocrisy, gossiping proclivities, and social competitiveness in a society where everyone was as good as everyone else and aspired to be better, and where a Sewing Society, planned for benevolent works, turned into a battleground of personal pride and prejudice and was effectively scuttled by the vulgar rich woman who dominated the village. The two brief references in the stories to woman's rights ridicule such an advocate as "Samanthy Hokum, a wonderful tall, slab-sided, coarse lookin' critter," who "hild that the men hadent no bizness to monopolize everything, and trammil the female sect," and describe the absurdity of a "Professor" who believes in equal rights and churns the butter while his wife splits wood. Miriam Berry belonged to her generation in finding such views nonsensical. She was no social innovator, but she was the first American woman to write a highly popular series of humorous sketches in the tradition of the Yankee yarn-spinner. Like her predecessors, she favored rural simplicity and satirized the materialism and false sophistication of growing urban centers. Her characterization and dialect were so successful that in 1879 "Petroleum V. Nasby" (David Ross Locke) dramatized them in *The Widow Bedott, or a Hunt for a Husband,* a popular vehicle of the actor Neil Burgess.

In Elmira, Mrs. Whitcher began another series in less colloquial style, called "Letters from Timberville," and the first chapters of "Mary Elmer," a serious and pious novel that she had long wished to write but did not live to finish. She had published hymns and devotional poems in *Neal's Saturday Gazette* and the Utica (N.Y.) *Gospel Messenger.* She was a sincerely devout woman, brought up in the dominant Calvinism of her village, where she had joined the First Presbyterian Church after Charles G. Finney's revival meeting in 1832. Later shifting to the Episcopal Church, she found it more congenial and of much consolation in her last years, when she developed tuberculosis after the birth of a daughter, Alice Miriam, in 1849. She returned to Whitesboro in 1850 and died there two years later at the age of forty. She was buried in Whitesboro's Grandview Cemetery. As a measure of her popularity, a posthumous collection of her sketches, *The Widow Bedott Papers* (1856), is said to have sold 100,000 copies within a decade (James D. Hart, *The Popular Book,* 1950, p. 142).

[Alice B. Neal's introduction to *The Widow Bedott Papers* gives some account of Mrs. Whitcher. A second collected volume of Mrs. Whitcher's stories, *Widow Spriggins, Mary Elmer, and Other Sketches* (1867), includes a memoir by Mrs. M. L. Ward Whitcher, Benjamin Whitcher's second wife. Other information from: Kate Berry Potter, "Passages in the Life of the Author of Aunt Maguire's Letters, Bedott Papers, etc.," *Godey's Lady's Book,* July, Aug. 1853; Thomas F. O'Donnell, "The Regional Fiction of Upper State N.Y." (unpublished Ph.D. dissertation, Syracuse Univ., 1957); D. E. Wager, "The Whitestown Centennial," Oneida Hist. Soc., *Transactions,* 1881–84; Margaret Wyman, "Women in the Am. Realistic Novel, 1860–1893" (unpublished Ph.D. dissertation, Radcliffe College, 1950), pp. 293, 296–98; correspondence with the Dunham Public Library, Whitesboro, N.Y., with the Oneida Hist. Soc., Utica, N.Y., and with Professor O'Donnell. Though Mrs. Whitcher's year of birth is sometimes given as 1814, the memoir by Mrs. M. L. Ward Whitcher makes it 1811; her gravestone, according to Professor O'Donnell, gives her age as thirty-nine years.]

MARGARET WYMAN LANGWORTHY

WHITE, Alma Bridwell (June 16, 1862–June 26, 1946), founder and bishop of the Pillar of Fire Church, was born in Kinniconick, Lewis County, Ky. Christened Mollie Alma, she was the fifth daughter and seventh of the eleven children of William Moncure Bridwell and Mary Ann (Harrison) Bridwell, natives respectively of Virginia and Kentucky. According to her autobiography, the income from the tannery and farm owned by her father was barely adequate to support the large family. She recalled as a child being required to take her turn at the tanning vats and to work in the fields. To escape such drudgery she determined to become a teacher. Although her parents possessed little education themselves, they encouraged her ambition. After attending the district school and, briefly, the Vanceburg (Ky.) Seminary, she secured her first teaching post at the age of seventeen. The next year, when the family moved to Millersburg, Ky., she enrolled for a year in the Millersburg Female College. In 1882 she accepted a job in the frontier settlement of Bannack, Mont., the home of an aunt. Her teaching career terminated on Dec. 21, 1887, when she was married to Kent White, a young Virginian then studying for the Methodist ministry at the University of Denver.

Evidently teaching was abandoned with few regrets, for she claimed that religion rather than education had always been her primary interest. At sixteen, while attending a Methodist revival where outbursts of enthusiasm were encouraged, she had been converted and had felt a strong conviction that the Lord was calling her to preach the gospel. Since, however, few Protestant denominations ordained women, she was advised by her pastor to marry a minister and make her contribution through him. White was sympathetic with his wife's desire to share in his work: in his Colorado pastorates he allowed her to lead the hymns and prayers and occasionally to preach. From all accounts, she made a dramatic impact on congregations. A tall, stout woman with a powerful contralto voice, she enhanced her appearance by wearing a simple dark costume with a high collar and a long full skirt. She stated that she never prepared her sermons in advance but chose a text and waited for the "heavenly dynamite" to explode. She could bring people to their knees, sobbing in an agony of contrition, or make them skip about the aisles, singing and shouting with joy. After she experienced the "second blessing," or sanctification, in 1893, the conviction of a divine mission became so strong that she was no longer content with merely assisting her husband; instead, she took the lead in organizing and conducting a series of revival meetings.

This evangelical work evoked a storm of protest from the Methodist hierarchy. In part, the opposition stemmed from disapproval of female preachers. Equally important was the fact that the major Protestant denominations in the United States had, in the years following the Civil War, become increasingly conservative and formal. Clergymen regarded outbursts of religious enthusiasm such as Mrs. White delighted in stimulating—which had been characteristic of Baptist and Methodist camp meetings in an earlier era—as not quite respectable. Like other zealous fundamentalists who banded together at this time in pentecostal, or "holiness," associations, Alma White refused to discourage enthusiasm, for the emotion-charged atmosphere of the revival meeting seemed to her the most effective way of bringing sinners to their knees. Her personal traits must also have provoked the antagonism of church leaders. Never prone to humility or indecision, she was, as her own statements reveal, strong-willed and outspoken, desiring dictatorial power over her converts and unwilling to listen to advice or criticism from any source. Convinced that she was carrying out the will of God, she denounced all who opposed her as agents of Satan.

When forbidden to continue preaching from Methodist pulpits, Alma White persuaded her husband to resign his pastorate; together they traveled about the country during the next few years conducting revivals without denominational sanction. Eager to retain spiritual supervision over her converts, she followed the example of other fundamentalists and, in 1901 in Denver, organized an independent sect, calling it at first the Methodist Pentecostal Union and, after 1917, the Pillar of Fire Church. In 1907 a generous gift of land in Zarephath, N.J., made it seem desirable to move her headquarters from Denver to the East Coast. She did not claim to be the founder of a new religion; rather, she insisted that she was adhering to the "pure" doctrines of Methodism as she divined that they had been set forth by John Wesley. Such tenets as the necessity of conversion *and* sanctification, the efficacy of enthusiasm, faith healing, and the ordination of both men and women were stressed. That she was successful in combining fundamentalist beliefs with modern techniques of organization and communication is demonstrated by the sect's steady growth. According to the 1936 census of religious bodies, membership increased over a thirty-year period from 230 to 4,044; and the number of congregations grew

from three to forty-six. In addition, the value of church-owned property was estimated in 1936 at nearly four million dollars.

As senior bishop (the first woman bishop of any Christian church) and president of the board of trustees, Mrs. White directed all Pillar of Fire activities. She conducted hundreds of revival meetings, often preaching three or four times a day. A tireless traveler (she crossed the Atlantic fifty-eight times and, in a single year, traveled fifty thousand miles by rail), she established congregations in such distant cities as Los Angeles, Calif., and London, England. Purchase of two radio stations—one in Denver and one in New Jersey—permitted her sermons to reach a large audience. Her many books and pamphlets, as well as the seven magazines she edited, were published on printing presses owned by the sect and were widely distributed by a corps of missionaries. She also established seven schools, in which study of the Bible was combined with training in such vocational skills as carpentry and typesetting, and, in 1921, Alma White College in New Jersey, which was authorized by the state to grant degrees in arts and sciences.

Other members of the White family were also active in the denomination. Her two children, Arthur Kent (born 1889) and Ray Bridwell (1892), were ordained as ministers; the former became senior bishop after his mother's death. Her husband assisted in church affairs until 1909, but he then became increasingly antagonistic both toward the sect and toward his wife. Sent to London in 1910 to oversee activities there, he resigned from the church and made his home in England from 1922 until a few months before his death in 1940. The fact that he joined the Apostolic Faith movement, a rival pentecostal sect, suggests that doctrinal differences may have provoked friction. In her autobiography, however, Mrs. White quotes passages allegedly taken from his journal which are calculated to prove that he resented his subordinate role in Pillar of Fire affairs.

In addition to church work, Mrs. White found time to write more than two hundred hymns and to publish several volumes of poetry. Two radio dramas in which she denounced the evils of drink were performed in Denver in 1939. When the Ku Klux Klan was reconstituted as a national organization after World War I with a creed of white supremacy, Protestantism, and "pure" Americanism, Mrs. White hailed it as "the greatest moral and political movement of the generation." Although barred from actual membership because of her sex, she aided the cause by lecturing and writing. In her book *The Ku Klux Klan in Prophecy* (1925), she reexamined various Biblical passages to prove that the Klan was sanctioned by God; by means of the "divine illumination and prophetic vision" which she claimed to possess, it was revealed to her that many heroes of the Old and New Testaments—the Apostles and the Good Samaritan, for example—were actually Klansmen. In the 1928 presidential campaign she drew cartoons for the Klan to use in its attack on the Democratic candidate, Al Smith, a Catholic who favored repeal of prohibition.

At seventy Alma White took up oil painting and in six years produced some three hundred mountain landscapes. According to a critic who viewed her third New York exhibition, her canvases combined "a simple direct approach with vigor of brush work and a certain folk art spirit." She died at Zarephath in 1946 at the age of eighty-four of arteriosclerotic heart disease. Her remains were flown to Denver, where, after funeral services in Alma Temple, she was buried in Fairmont Cemetery. Her success in creating a dynamic religious organization is evidence not only of a powerful personality, but also of the willingness of Americans to experiment in matters of religion, to break away from established institutions, and to trust in the divine inspiration of self-proclaimed leaders.

[Alma B. White, *The Story of My Life* (5 vols., 1919–30), and *Looking Back from Beulah* (1902), a short account of her life and the founding of the sect; Arthur Kent White, *Some White Family History* (1948); Elmer T. Clark, *The Small Sects in America* (1937); Charles W. Ferguson, *The Confusion of Tongues: A Review of Modern Isms* (1928), which discusses Mrs. White's contributions to the Ku Klux Klan; *N.Y. Times*, June 2, 1940, sec. 9 (on her art exhibition); *Time*, Dec. 18, 1939, p. 40 (on her radio dramas); *Nat. Cyc. Am. Biog.*, XXXV, 151–53 (on Mrs. White, her husband, and her son Ray); *Who Was Who in America*, vol. II (1950); death record, N.J. State Dept. of Health.]

MERRIT CROSS

**WHITE, Anna** (Jan. 21, 1831–Dec. 16, 1910), Shaker eldress and reformer, was born in Brooklyn, N.Y., to Robert and Hannah (Gibbs) White; of their five children who survived infancy, Anna was the next to youngest and the third daughter. On her father's side she was descended from Elder John White, who landed in Boston in 1632 and later was in the Rev. Thomas Hooker's company when he settled Hartford. Her paternal grandfather was Calvin White, a graduate of Yale, who became successively a Presbyterian, an Episcopal clergyman, and a Roman Catholic. An uncle, Chandler White, was associated with Cyrus Field in the promotion of the Atlantic cable; a cousin, Richard Grant White (father of Stanford White, the architect), was a well-known critic and Shakespearean scholar. Anna's mother was a Quaker. Her father joined the Society of Friends when Anna was a child, and she was brought up in that faith. One of her earliest memories was of a Quaker meeting where, listening fascinated to an antislavery address by LUCRETIA MOTT, she was disturbed when the speaker was "abruptly silenced by the guardians of Quaker orthodoxy." When she was two the family moved to a farm in Shrewsbury, N.J. In her early teens she was sent to Mansion Square Seminary, a Friends' boarding school in Poughkeepsie, N.Y. She returned at eighteen to New York City, where her father had a hardware business. Here she learned the trade of tailoring, and under the tutelage of her mother was trained also in "systematic benevolence to the poor."

It was through her father that Anna learned about the Shakers. Robert White had business relations with the Hancock, Mass., community of that sect and on occasion took his daughter with him on his visits, where she was deeply affected by the Shaker songs, the lively meetings, and the beauty of the Berkshire hills. White, drawn to the ideal of Christian perfection, subsequently joined the Shaker community at New Lebanon, N.Y., though he seems to have remained a novitiate member, retaining his ties with wife and family. After a long struggle with her conscience, and in spite of the pleas of unsympathetic relatives—a rich bachelor uncle warned that he would disinherit her—Anna entered the community on Sept. 16, 1849. Her father had put no undue pressure on his daughter, but both were independent spirits. "I covet for thee, my daughter," he wrote, "an independence of all save the approbation of thy own conscience."

The rest of Anna White's life was spent at the New Lebanon community as a member of the North "Family" (one of the units into which each community was divided). Here she met the venerable Ruth Landon (successor to Mother LUCY WRIGHT), who had seen Mother ANN LEE. She also came under the intellectual influence of Elder Frederick Evans and the fine spiritual leadership of Eldress Antoinette Doolittle. In 1865 she was appointed associate eldress, with particular responsibility for the care of girls. After the death of Eldress Antoinette in 1887 she became first eldress of the North Family, a position she held with distinction until her death in 1910. She died at the

New Lebanon community and was buried in the cemetery of the North Family there.

Hers was an unusual devotion to a cause. Never neglecting her duties at home, she took an active interest in reforms in the outside world, a policy favored at this time by one faction within the Shakers. In the 1890's, at the time of the Dreyfus Case, she penned for a group of French women "The Shaker Sisters' Plea for Dreyfus." An active worker in the cause of international disarmament, in keeping with the Shakers' long-held pacifist principles, she was appointed a vice-president of the Alliance of Women for Peace, a work in which she was associated with Princess Wiszniewska, daughter of Victor Hugo. She was also a member of the National American Woman Suffrage Association and a vice-president of the National Council of Women of the United States. In behalf of these interests she spoke before the Universal Peace Union in Mystic, Conn. (1899), the Equal Rights Club of Hartford (1903), and a conference in the New Lebanon meetinghouse (1905), where resolutions on arbitration, later forwarded to The Hague, were adopted; Anna herself brought them to the personal attention of President Theodore Roosevelt.

Among Eldress Anna's varied interests were Shaker songs and history. She compiled two books of Shaker music, which included some of her own "gifts of song." Her most ambitious work, in which Eldress Leila S. Taylor ably collaborated, was *Shakerism: Its Meaning and Message* (1904), the only published history of the movement by a member of the society. She also took an interest in vegetarianism, in spiritualism (the Shakers believed in communication with the world of departed spirits), and in Christian Science, through which, it is said, she was once healed of a serious illness (*Christian Science Journal*, December 1907). Her portraits suggest a dignified, self-possessed woman, with a strong, expressive face and clear, keen eyes. "So gentle and sweet yet strong was her voice," wrote one who was present at the Roosevelt interview, "that everybody in the room . . . gazed in amazement." In Shaker parlance, Anna White was a "true Believer."

[Quotations are from Leila S. Taylor, *A Memorial to Eldress Anna White and Elder Daniel Offord* (1912). Other publications by Eldress Anna include: *Original Shaker Music* (1884, 1893); *Affectionately Inscribed to the Memory of Eldress Antoinette Doolittle* (1887); *Woman's Mission* (n.d.); *Voices from Mount Lebanon* (1899); and *The Motherhood of God* (1903).]

EDWARD DEMING ANDREWS

**WHITE, Eliza Orne** (Aug. 2, 1856–Jan. 23, 1947), author of children's books, was born in Keene, N.H.; she was the only child of William Orne and Margaret Eliot (Harding) White to survive infancy. Her father was a son of Daniel Appleton White, judge of the probate court in Salem, Mass., and Eliza (Orne) White, daughter of a prominent Salem merchant of the early eighteenth century; a graduate of Harvard and the Harvard Divinity School, he was for many years a Unitarian minister in Keene. Her mother, born in Barre, N.Y., was a daughter of the famous self-taught portrait painter Chester Harding. Brought up in Boston, Mrs. White had attended ELIZABETH PEABODY's school and had known in her youth such literary figures as James Russell Lowell and Edward Everett Hale. One of her close friends throughout her life was LUCRETIA PEABODY HALE, author of *The Peterkin Papers*, who regularly spent two weeks every summer with the Whites during Eliza's childhood.

Of her birthplace, Eliza Orne White later said, "It was just the right sort of a place for a little girl to live in who was to write stories for other little girls when she grew up, for there were all the things to be found there that children most like" (Kunitz and Haycraft, p. 380). Memories of an exceptionally happy childhood were with her always, and are reflected in her books: family picnics; outdoor games; pet kittens and pigeons; walks with her father through the beautiful country around Keene; listening to him read aloud *The Iliad*, *The Odyssey*, *The Faerie Queene*, and the novels of Scott and Dickens; going to Boston with her father to hear Dickens; and her mother's quietness and strength, her delightful, often surprising humor. When Eliza was nine the Whites adopted a baby girl, Rose, an event she remembered as the realization of her fondest wish. She was "always making up stories," she later recalled, and "began to write them as soon as I could hold a pencil." When at eleven she composed with a friend a series of historical romances in the manner of Sir Walter Scott her mother had them bound like real books.

She attended the public schools of Keene, but her high school years were interrupted by eye trouble, and in her senior year a severe attack of typhoid fever kept her from graduating. At seventeen she went for a year to a small boarding and day school in Roxbury, Mass., kept by Miss Louisa Hall. At twenty she traveled for a year with her family, in the British Isles and on the Continent. Soon after their return her father gave up his parish in Keene, and the family moved in 1881 to the house at 222 High Street in Brookline, Mass., which was to remain Miss White's home until her death. During the early years in Brookline she particularly enjoyed symphony concerts and the theatre. She was a member of the Woman's Alliance of the First Parish Church (Unitarian) in Brookline and visited a needy family for Boston's Associated Charities.

But she increasingly turned her attention to writing. Although she had continued to write since her early attempts at historical romances, not until 1890 did she publish her first book, *Miss Brooks*, a novel for adults. During the next twenty-five years she published eight other novels and collections of short stories for adults; these won qualified praise from the critics, who found Miss White's delineation of New England characters and settings excellent and her quiet humor charming, but her plots somewhat eventless.

Her real talent, however, lay in writing books for children. The first, *When Molly Was Six*, appeared in 1894 and was followed over the years by twenty-eight others. Chiefly written for the ages from six to ten, these stories were set in New England and, with the exception of three cat stories and a fantasy, were vivid depictions of childhood. Miss White's most distinctive quality as a writer was her ability to create natural children and grownups in everyday situations and relationships, often based on her own childhood experiences. She became blind about 1915 and deaf soon afterward, but continued to write with unabated vigor, typing out her manuscripts and retaining the "calm strength and naturalness" that had long marked her character. Her last book, *When Esther Was a Little Girl* (1944), published when she was eighty-eight, was based on her own childhood in Keene. She died at her Brookline home of arteriosclerosis at the age of ninety.

[Bertha Mahony Miller, "Eliza Orne White and Her Books for Children," *Horn Book Mag.*, Apr. 1955; autobiographical sketch in Stanley J. Kunitz and Howard Haycraft, eds., *The Junior Book of Authors* (1934); Eliza Orne White, ed., *William Orne White: A Record of Ninety Years* (1917); Margaret E. White, comp., *After Noontide*, with a sketch of the compiler's life by Eliza Orne White (1907); Eliza Orne White, "Lucretia P. Hale," *Horn Book Mag.*, Sept.–Oct. 1940; *Woman's Who's Who of America*, 1914–15; death record from Mass. Registrar of Vital Statistics.]

RUTH HILL VIGUERS

**WHITE, Ellen Gould Harmon** (Nov. 26, 1827–July 16, 1915), co-founder of the Seventh-Day Adventist Church, was born at Gorham, Maine, to Robert and Eunice (Gould) Harmon. Her father was descended from John

Harmon, in 1667 a servant in Kittery, Maine, and later a freeholder. He was a hatter, and as was the custom in the age of homespun, his entire family assisted him in his work, including Ellen, who with her twin sister Elizabeth was the youngest of the eight children. Sometime before 1836 the Harmons moved to Portland, where Ellen attended the Brackett Street School until her education was cut short by an injury that almost took her life. At the age of nine she was struck by a large stone hurled by an older schoolgirl. When she recovered consciousness three weeks later, she found her face sadly disfigured and her nerves shattered. Every attempt to resume her schoolwork ended in frustration; she could neither fix her eyes on a page nor manage a pen. Her formal education ended in 1839, when she briefly attended the Westbrook Seminary and Female College in Portland.

The Harmon family were devout Methodists, and Ellen experienced her first religious awakening at a Methodist camp meeting in the summer of 1840. After a period of anxious questioning, she was baptized on June 26, 1842. At about this time the Adventist excitement was stirring Portland. William Miller, the Baptist farmer-preacher from western New York, had lectured in Portland in 1840 and again in 1842, predicting the personal return of Christ to earth "about 1843." The Harmons accepted Miller's message enthusiastically, and as a consequence were expelled from the Methodist Church. Many Millerites, when their expectations failed of realization, returned to their former churches or lost faith altogether; others groped for new directions. In December 1844, in a small women's prayer group, Ellen Harmon appeared to fall into a trance, and upon recovering reported having seen a vision of the Advent people "far above the dark world" on their pilgrimage to the City of God. This was the first of an estimated two thousand visions which she claimed to have received during her lifetime.

Frail of health though she was, unable at times to speak above a whisper, and weighing less than eighty pounds, she began to relate her experiences to interested listeners, and thus took up the itinerant ministry that was to occupy her life. In 1845, only eighteen years old, she ranged as far afield as New Bedford, Mass. Everywhere she shared her revelations with discouraged Millerites, reinterpreting the nature of the Advent hope and declaring that Christ's return was still imminent though of indeterminate date. Soon she was advocating observance of the seventh-day Sabbath, an interpretation of the Decalogue urged upon her by Joseph Bates, an Adventist sea captain, and confirmed to her in a vision on Apr. 7, 1847. Besides these two distinctive emphases, her religious beliefs were largely those of revivalistic pietism in antebellum New England.

On Aug. 30, 1846, at Portland, she was married to James Springer White (1821–1881), a young Adventist preacher, like herself of uncertain health, who had briefly taught school. They had four children: Henry Nichols (1847), James Edson (1849), William Clarence (1854), and John Herbert (1860). The first died at sixteen and the last in infancy, but the other two became diligent workers in Seventh-Day Adventism, William serving as his mother's assistant after his father's death in 1881.

Moving from place to place as they devoted their meager resources to spreading the Advent message, the Whites by 1849 were living in Rocky Hill, Conn. There Ellen encouraged her husband to begin publishing a small paper. Called *Present Truth,* this was to grow into the *Advent Review and Sabbath Herald,* the denomination's official organ. In 1851 Mrs. White issued a sixty-four-page work entitled *A Sketch of the Christian Experience and Views of Ellen G. White,* combining autobiography with exhortation and offering glowing accounts of her early visions. In 1854 she produced a *Supplement to the Experience and Views of Ellen G. White.* These were the earliest of some fifty books, scores of pamphlets, and 4,600 articles published during her lifetime. Doubtless mindful of the years when she could not hold a pen, she labored incessantly under a compulsion to "write, write, write; I feel that I must, and not delay" (Letter 11, 1884, quoted in A. L. White, p. 109).

From 1852 to 1855 the Whites lived at Rochester, N.Y.; they then moved to Battle Creek, Mich., which was to become the base of Adventist operations for the next half-century. The religious movement of which, after the death of William Miller in 1849, the Whites were becoming the cohesive center had never effected any kind of organization beyond scattered local groups, nor had it taken a formal name. But at a meeting in Battle Creek in 1860 a representative group chose the name "Seventh-Day Adventists," incorporated a publishing house, and projected a plan of denominational organization which was fulfilled in the formation of a General Conference in 1863. In this formative period Ellen White, speaking from the authority of her visions, guided the crucial decisions. Although she made no claim to be a prophetess, and always advocated "thorough and continuous searching of the Scriptures," it was largely her interpretation of

the Scriptures which determined Seventh-Day Adventist orthodoxy; and unquestioned acceptance of Mrs. White's visions and their divine origin remains a fundamental, if implicit, principle of the Church. There were, of course, some Adventists who rejected her authority, and these eventually drifted off to other denominations.

In a time of such religious figures as Joseph Smith and his *Book of Mormon* and MARGARET FOX and her sisters with their claim to communicate with the spirit world, there were those who took a skeptical view of Ellen White's claims. Some dismissed her visions as self-induced hysteria; others pointed to more mundane sources for her alleged revelations. Yet she apparently made no attempt to evade unbelievers, some purported visions occurring in their presence. In the description of a believer: "As the power of God came upon her, she uttered in thrilling tones, fading away as in distance, the thrice repeated shout, 'GLORY, glory, glory!' She initially lost all strength, and then received an access of strength, manifested in such feats as holding a heavy family Bible aloft in one hand for some time, while turning the pages with her other hand to the texts she correctly quoted without seeing. In all this manifestation, no breath was discernible, even by the closest tests [candles, mirrors, etc.], though she spoke audibly" (Spalding, *There Shines a Light,* p. 37). Some of her visions dealt with secret sins of Adventist preachers; these she communicated privately to the individuals involved, hoping to evoke repentance and amendment, though occasionally the result was permanent alienation. More general instructions she published as *Testimonies for the Church,* which began as a sixteen-page pamphlet in 1855 and ended as nine large volumes.

Ellen White's career reflected the reform temper of the times. Her views on health, education, and temperance became an integral part of her religious instruction. Frequent bouts with illness, both her own and her family's, convinced her that good health was not only essential to useful living but also a responsibility of Christian stewardship. Between 1848 and 1863 she formed increasingly strong convictions against tea and coffee, drugs, and flesh foods; and she stressed the importance of exercise, fresh air, and "the judicious use of water." She was instrumental in establishing the Western Health Reform Institute in Battle Creek in 1866, which, under Dr. John Harvey Kellogg, a protégé of the Whites, became the famed Battle Creek Sanitarium, prototype of similar institutions to be founded by Seventh-

Day Adventists throughout the world and pioneer in the development of appetizing grain foods. Impressed by the healthful advantages of the unconstricted "Bloomer" costume for women, she promoted for a while (c. 1865) an adaptation of it among Adventist women.

Mrs. White also shared the enthusiasm of educational reformers, adopting the "modern" viewpoint that education should be child-centered rather than subject-centered. Formal schooling, she believed, should be practical as well as cultural and should be open to all, regardless of social status or economic background. To give expression to these ideals, Battle Creek College was founded in 1874 with James White as president. Mrs. White's educational philosophy reached its most mature expression in the book *Education*, published in 1903 and reprinted many times. Under her inspiration Seventh-Day Adventists have developed an educational complex reaching all the way from graded church schools to graduate professional institutions, the most famous of which is the College of Medical Evangelists at Loma Linda, Calif., opened in 1906.

During the pre–Civil War years Mrs. White joined other Northern evangelicals in opposing Negro slavery. She counseled Adventists not to obey the Fugitive Slave Law, and (with help from the Quakers) Battle Creek became a busy station on the Underground Railroad. After the war, however, Mrs. White was somewhat out of step with advocates of social and economic reforms. She was sensitive to many of the human problems in the burgeoning cities and industrial centers, but she thought the best solution lay in returning to an agrarian economy along pastoral patterns indicated by the Old Testament. She attracted her largest audiences in public lectures on temperance. Twenty thousand people gathered at a camp meeting in Groveland, Mass., to hear her deliver two temperance lectures in August 1876. While Barnum's Great Menagerie and Circus was entertaining Battle Creek in 1877, she addressed five thousand people in a nearby tent for ninety minutes on the perils of alcohol. She cooperated with the Woman's Christian Temperance Union but never joined, primarily because she objected to its advocacy of Sunday legislation, which she opposed in the name of religious liberty, since the Adventists observed their Sabbath on Saturday. On the issue of military service she advised Adventist draftees to apply for noncombatant duty.

After the death of her husband in 1881, Mrs. White became even more active in the expanding affairs of Seventh-Day Adventism. From 1881 to 1885 she maintained a home at Healds-

burg, Calif. The next two years she traveled extensively in Europe, visiting Adventist institutions and lecturing on temperance. Returning to the United States, she lived in Battle Creek until 1891, when the General Conference designated her as a pioneer missionary to Australia, a place to which a vision of 1875 had pointed as ready for the Adventist message. She spent a decade there, evangelizing in the major cities, establishing a school at Cooranbong (now Avondale College), and writing some 15,000 pages of letters and testimonies. Upon her return to the United States in 1900 she set to work immediately on the problem of denominational reorganization. For some years she had felt a growing uneasiness over the increasing centralization in Battle Creek and that city's bustling commercialism; and she feared that control of church institutions might slip into unsympathetic hands. In 1901 the college moved to Berrien Springs, Mich. (where it remains as Andrews University). When the printing house burned in 1902, Mrs. White cried, "Get out of Battle Creek!" The next year denominational headquarters, along with the *Review and Herald*, removed to Takoma Park, a suburb of Washington, D.C., and in response to Mrs. White's urging administrative procedures were overhauled. The Sanitarium alone remained in Battle Creek; and with a growing alienation between the church and Dr. Kellogg, Adventist influence on its operation gradually declined.

The aging leader had purchased a comfortable home near St. Helena, Calif., and here she spent most of her time after 1903. She traveled to Washington for the 1909 meeting of the General Conference, and in spite of her advanced years delivered nine major addresses. She died at St. Helena in 1915, at eighty-seven, five months after suffering a fractured hip in a fall at her home. Four thousand persons attended funeral services at the Dime Tabernacle in Battle Creek, and she was buried there beside her husband in the Oak Hill Cemetery.

[Ellen G. White's enormous literary corpus remains, by provision of her will, in the custody of the White Estate, housed at General Conference headquarters in Takoma Park, Md. There are 54 books currently in print, some of them in as many as 83 languages; see *Comprehensive Index to the Writings of Ellen G. White* (3 vols., 1962–63). There are in addition some 30,000 pages of letters, diaries, and other unpublished materials from which White Publications continues to print new volumes. No critical biography of Ellen White exists, and few writers outside the Seventh-Day Adventist Church have treated her career. Of denominational literature—like most such writing, hagiographic—Arthur W. Spalding, *There Shines a Light* (1953), is the best short biography. The same author's *Origin and Hist. of the Seventh-Day Adventists* (4 vols., 1961–62), is replete with details of her life. Special themes (e.g., visions, preaching, writing) are treated in Arthur L. White, *Ellen G. White: Messenger to the Remnant* (1969). Dudley M. Canright, *Life of Mrs. E. G. White, Seventh-Day Adventist Prophet; Her False Claims Refuted* (1919), is a hostile account by an ex-Adventist. Equally negative is Guy H. Winslow, "Ellen Gould White and Seventh-Day Adventism" (Ph.D. dissertation, Clark Univ., 1933), which argues that Mrs. White was manipulated by men ambitious to extend their own authority over the new denomination. Detractors' charges were answered by Francis D. Nichol, *Ellen G. White and Her Critics* (1951). Details on Mrs. White's public ministry may be found in Horace J. Shaw, "A Rhetorical Analysis of the Speaking of Mrs. Ellen G. White" (Ph.D. dissertation, Mich. State Univ., 1959). The denominational position on her alleged prophetic gifts and the use of her writings is in T. Housel Jemison, *A Prophet Among You* (1955). On the relation of Mrs. White to the Adventist denomination, particularly the reorganization of 1901–03, see Carl D. Anderson, "The Hist. and Evolution of Seventh-Day Adventist Church Organization" (Ph.D. dissertation, American Univ., 1960). Edward M. Cadwallader has written "Principles of Education in the Writings of Ellen G. White" (Ph.D. dissertation, Univ. of Nebr., 1949). An account of dietary reforms and medical work launched by Mrs. White and her followers is in Dores E. Robinson, *The Story of Our Health Message* (1943). Gerald Carson, *Cornflake Crusade* (1957), is a lively, somewhat journalistic history of the Battle Creek food idea. For the general cultural context out of which American Adventism arose, see Whitney R. Cross, *The Burned-Over District* (1950). A derogatory account of the Millerite movement is Clara E. Sears, *Days of Delusion* (1924); the Adventist version is Francis D. Nichol, *The Midnight Cry* (1944).]

C. C. GOEN

**WHITE, Helen Magill** (Nov. 28, 1853–Oct. 28, 1944), educator, first American woman to earn the Ph.D. degree, was born, the eldest of six children, in Providence, R.I., where her father, Edward Hicks Magill, a Quaker with a Bucks County, Pa., farm background, headed the classical department of the Providence High School. Believing in coeducation and equal rights, Magill, supported by his wife, Sarah Warner Beans, educated his five strong-willed daughters as college teachers. (Their son died young.) After her father became submaster of the Boston Public Latin School, Helen, a child prodigy, was enrolled as the only girl pupil. In 1869, not yet sixteen, she entered the recently founded Swarthmore College, of which her father shortly afterward became president. She graduated in 1873 as salutatorian and second among the six members of her class—the first class to graduate. For two more years she read at Swarthmore in classics, then continued her study at Boston University, where she wrote a dissertation on Greek drama and received the Ph.D. degree in Greek in 1877. For further classical training she went to Cambridge University in England; her four years there (1877–81) she remembered as the happiest of her life. Living first at Norwich House and then at Newnham College, where in her second year she won a scholarship, she took the classical tripos, or honors examination, in 1881 and placed in the third of three classes, a considerable achievement in view of the fact that her preparation was by no means equal to that of the English students.

After her return she became principal of a private school in Johnstown, Pa. A great opportunity opened to her a year later, in 1883. On the recommendation of the Boston author and clergyman Edward Everett Hale, she was given a contract to organize and direct a nonsectarian school for some forty girls, the Howard Collegiate Institute at West Bridgewater, Mass., with authority to select teachers and to conduct college courses. Her father invested in a laboratory and gymnasium, while she—although she had earlier analyzed the weakness of such a procedure at Swarthmore—employed two of her sisters as teachers instead of seeking more prominent educators. Her administration was sufficiently successful to require a new building for additional students, but in 1887 she resigned her post. This was partly because of family troubles, partly because of antagonism she had aroused among the trustees by her too vigorous campaign for better sewerage. She then gratefully accepted a teaching position at Evelyn College, a short-lived women's annex to Princeton University.

In September 1887, while attending a meeting of the American Social Science Association to read a paper on her Newnham experiences, Helen Magill met Andrew Dickson White (1832–1918), whose distinguished presidency of Cornell University had recently come to a close. White commented privately in his diary on her paper: "Perfect manner & exquisite voice—altogether a triumph for this little Quakeress—daughter of my college mate Magill—of which I am proud." He shortly invited her and her father for a weekend at Cornell, advising Magill that his daughter should consider applying for the position of "Directoress" of Sage College for Women at Cornell. Now convinced that a comparatively young person should not combine administrative and academic responsibilities, and fearful of a repetition of her Bridgewater experience, she decided against the post. Illness and depression kept her at home until she took a position teaching physical geography in the Brooklyn (N.Y.) High School. "I feel," she wrote to White, "rather like a some what self-willed carriage horse put onto the horse cars for the first time" (Mar. 21, 1889). The erudite, argumentative Quakeress who loved fine music and the good things of life had at thirty-five reached the end of a professional career of great promise. Judging herself, she wrote (to White, May 15, 1888): "but it makes me miserable sometimes to think what I might have already done, if I had produced more and criticized less."

Meanwhile, however, her friendship with White, a widower since 1887, was ripening into the affection that led to their marriage on Sept. 10, 1890. During White's subsequent career as minister to Russia (1892–94) and ambassador to Germany (1897–1903) she was presented at both courts. She enjoyed the cultural and social life of Germany, where her husband had had close attachments for many years. A brilliant conversationalist, Mrs. White could entertain the Kaiser in discussions of architecture, sculpture, music, and literature. In these years she gradually lost the equal rights convictions of her Quaker youth, began to doubt the value of universal suffrage, and, in 1913, protesting against the militancy of English women, took an active stand against woman suffrage. Although she occasionally raised her voice on national and local issues, her abiding interest was in music. Of her two children, only a daughter, Karin Andreevna, survived infancy. Following the death of her husband in 1918, Mrs. White lived abroad and in Ithaca, N.Y., then retired to Kittery Point, Maine, where she died at the age of ninety.

[The Andrew D. White Papers and Diaries, the George Lincoln Burr Papers, and other MSS. in the Cornell Univ. Archives; the Edward Hicks Magill Papers and alumni records in the Friends Hist. Library of Swarthmore College; the William Fairfield Warren Papers and alumni records in the Boston Univ. Archives; information from Registrar of roll records, Newnham College, Cambridge, England; contemporary newspapers; Helen Magill's unsigned letter in the "Contributors' Club," *Atlantic Monthly*, Nov. 1878; Walter C. Eells, "Earned Doctorates for Women in the Nineteenth Century," *AAUP Bull.* (Am. Assoc. of Univ. Professors), Winter 1956. Edward H. Magill's *Sixty-Five Years in the Life of a Teacher, 1841–1906* (1907) and his writings on education also proved useful.]

EDITH M. FOX

WHITE, Pearl (Mar. 4, 1889–Aug. 4, 1938), motion-picture actress, was born in Green Ridge, near Sedalia, Mo. The third daughter and youngest of five children of Lizzie G. (House) and Edward Gilman White, she was named Pearl Fay White. Because in later life she enjoyed producing variously embroidered versions of her family background, reliable information on her early years is scanty. She was of English and Scottish (and also at times laid claim to Irish and Spanish) ancestry, her forebears having settled in New England in colonial times. Her father, a farmer, moved his family to Springfield, Mo., where he went into the real estate and insurance business and for a time served as deputy assessor of Greene County. Pearl left the public high school in Springfield sometime in her sophomore year and began playing small parts in the local Diemer Theatre stock company, until her father objected. In 1907, now eighteen and legally of age, she left home to join a traveling theatrical company. Though the economic panic of that year, combined with growing competition from the motion pictures, bore heavily on the live theatre of melodrama throughout the country, Pearl White persisted in her stage career until, in early 1910, difficulties with her voice caused her to join the recently formed Powers Film Company in the Bronx, New York City.

In the still young movie industry, she was soon playing starring roles and winning praise for both her acting and her beauty. In 1911, after a few months with the Lubin Company in Philadelphia, she signed with the American branch of the French firm Pathé Frères at its studio in New Jersey, where she starred opposite Henry B. Walthall, among others. Toward the end of 1912, she started making half- or split-reel slapstick comedies, such as *Her Dressmaker's Bill* and *Caught in the Act*, for the Crystal Film Company (for release by Universal). Turned out at the rate of about one a week, they were so successful that they were lengthened to a full reel the next year. The heavy schedule exhausted her and she took an extended European vacation. When she returned after seven months she was persuaded, by a promise of wide publicity and a salary of $250 a week, to star in a serial, *The Perils of Pauline* (1914), whose twenty episodes were directed by Louis Gasnier and Donald MacKenzie for the Eclectic Film Company (a subsidiary of Pathé).

Deriving their form from the serialized fiction appearing in newspapers, the first film serials, including *The Perils of Pauline*, were made up of self-contained episodes (usually about fifteen in all) with the emphasis on action, mystery, and danger to the protagonist. Soon producers found they could sustain interest by using the cliff-hanger device, in which the hero or heroine is left in mortal peril at the end of each episode, with the outcome revealed only at the beginning of the following week's segment. The fifth such movie serial made in the United States, and the best remembered, *The Perils of Pauline* was sponsored by the Hearst newspapers, which provided advertising by printing the story of each "Peril" simultaneously with the release of the film. Its phenomenal success was followed by *The Exploits of Elaine* (1914–15), which confirmed Pearl White as a major film star and earned its producers over a million dollars in profits, and *The New Exploits of Elaine* and *The Romance of Elaine* (both 1915). Her other serials included *The Iron Claw* (1916), *Pearl of the Army* (1916–17), *The Fatal Ring* (1917), *The House of Hate* (1918), *The Lightning Raider* (1919), and *The Black Secret* (1919–20).

The principal stars of the early serials were women, and the most popular was Pearl White, who gained international fame. That women were the protagonists in these stories of adventure may perhaps have reflected the current rise of the emancipated "new woman," but the basic appeal of the serials was the simple thrill of safely experiencing a sense of danger. Typical of the plots is that of *The Perils of Pauline*, where Pearl (in a blond wig) plays a wealthy young heiress who spurns marriage in favor of a writing career, but is put in constant danger of losing her life by her deceased father's secretary, who is after her fortune. Noted for her physical prowess and agility, she was in fact rarely called upon to perform stunts requiring acrobatic skill. A spinal injury sustained during the production of *The Perils of Pauline*, which was said to have contributed to her early death, was the consequence not of stunting but of a fall down a flight of stairs.

After World War I, as audiences became more sophisticated and the full-length feature film became the dominant form, serials lost their widespread popularity. Pearl White longed to play regular dramatic parts, but the three features she made for Pathé were failures. She nevertheless signed in 1919 with the Fox Film Corporation, for which she made ten features over the next two years. Although they received some critical approval, these, too, were not a commercial success, and she returned to Pathé to make one more serial, *Plunder* (1923). The pain from her spinal injury, failing eyesight, and the shock of the death of a stunt man who was doubling for her caused

her to leave New York after the film's completion and go to France for a rest. Except for three visits to the United States, she spent the remainder of her life there. In Paris she made her last film, *Terror* (released in the United States as *Perils of Paris*), a melodrama done in a style reminiscent of her early serials. She is said to have made a screen test when sound movies were introduced, but her voice apparently did not record well.

Pearl White was married twice: on Oct. 12, 1907, to Victor C. Sutherland, an actor in the stock company she had joined, who later became prominent on Broadway; and, about 1919 —five years after her first marriage was ended by divorce—to another actor, Wallace McCutcheon. They, too, were divorced, in 1921; she had no children. Having earned an estimated $2,000,000 since 1914, Miss White had managed her money wisely. She had a home in Paris and a villa in Rambouillet, kept a successful racing stable, and was one of a fashionable group who commuted between Cairo, Biarritz, the Riviera, and other resorts. She died of a liver ailment at the age of forty-nine at the American Hospital in Paris. She had become a convert to Roman Catholicism, and it was with the rites of that church that she was buried in the Passy Cemetery. One of the most famous of the early film stars, her name linked imperishably with the serial in its heyday, Pearl White was noted for her good looks and her physical agility rather than for sex appeal or acting talent. She has come to symbolize a brief but significant era in the history of the film and of popular taste in entertainment.

[Theodore M. Banta, *Sayre Family* (1901), records her genealogy. Her autobiography, *Just Me* (1919), covering her career to 1914, is unreliable. Wallace E. Davies, "Truth about Pearl White," *Films in Rev.*, Nov. 1959, is the best biographical source. See also: Kalton C. Lahue, *Continued Next Week: A Hist. of the Moving Picture Serial* (1964); obituaries in *N.Y. Times, N.Y. Herald Tribune,* and *Los Angeles Times,* Aug. 5, 1938; clipping files in Theatre Collection, N.Y. Public Library at Lincoln Center.]

HARVEY DENEROFF

**WHITE, Sue Shelton** (May 25, 1887–May 6, 1943), suffragist, lawyer, and government official, was born in Henderson, a small town in the cotton country of Tennessee. She was the younger daughter and second of three children of James Shelton White and Mary Calista (Swain) White, the latter a native of Kentucky. The White family, which claimed descent from the Jeffersons and Marshalls of Revolutionary Virginia, had experienced financial difficulties since the Civil War. Sue's father, a lawyer six days a week and a Methodist minister on the seventh, died when she was nine; from him "Miss Sue" derived a strong sense of Christian idealism as well as an avid interest in the law. After her mother's death four years later, she was reared by an aunt, but looked to her older sister, Lucy, for guidance. Her education, aside from home tutoring, included two years (1900–02) at Georgia Robertson Christian College, a normal school in Henderson; a year (1902–03) at a private school in Hernando, Miss.; an additional year at the Robertson school, where she took the teacher training course; and a year (1904–05) at the West Tennessee Business College in Dyer.

Her first job was as a stenographer in Jackson, Tenn., but when in 1907 her sister Lucy gave up her position as a court reporter in Jackson, Sue White took it over. This post, which she held for eleven years, enabled her to widen her political contacts by serving as private secretary to members of the state supreme court. Her interest in the law and politics led her to an active role in the woman suffrage movement and to several public appointments. As recording secretary of the state suffrage association after 1913, she helped set up local units. A good leader and organizer, during World War I she was made chairman of industrial registration in the Tennessee Division of the Woman's Committee of the United States Council of National Defense. When the Tennessee Commission for the Blind was created in 1918, she was named its executive secretary and served for one year.

Somewhat surprisingly in view of her background, Sue White soon found her way into the suffrage movement's militant wing, the National Woman's Party. This resulted in part from a friendship with MAUD YOUNGER formed when Miss Younger toured Tennessee in 1917, but perhaps equally from a sense of frustration at finding herself lodged just below the first level of leadership in the existing state suffrage hierarchy. She herself justified her acceptance (in June 1918) of the chairmanship of the state branch of the Woman's Party by the belief, which proved to be mistaken, that the National American Woman Suffrage Association proposed to write off the South in its 1918 efforts. Aware of being a member of a distinct minority within the state suffrage forces, she sought as state chairman to ignore the bitter hostility that existed between the National Association and the National Woman's Party and, maintaining close liaison with the leaders of the regular Tennessee suffrage association, to use her organization to supplement rather than to compete with its efforts. As chief propagandist for the militant suffragists in the South and as editor for a time in 1919 of the *Suffragist*, official publication of the Woman's Party, she depicted the party's demonstrations as merely dramatic presentations of issues raised by all suffragists. Following the 1918 elections she did, however, join the militant suffragists for their final demonstrations in Washington; imprisoned for five days for dropping a caricature of President Wilson into the flames on Feb. 9, 1919, she was one of twenty-six released militants who toured the country in their prison garb to dramatize the women's cause. During her period of suffrage activity, Miss White also drafted and eventually helped drive through the Tennessee legislature the state's first married woman's property act, a mother's pension law, and an old-age pension act.

With Tennessee's ratification of the Nineteenth Amendment in 1920, Miss White went to Washington as clerk, then secretary, to Senator Kenneth D. McKellar, who had been active in the Tennessee suffrage fight. Her papers indicate that she lost this position in 1926 because of her criticisms of the federal Women's Bureau, whose championship of protective legislation for women was opposed by the National Woman's Party. While in Washington she took evening classes at the Washington College of Law and received a law degree in 1923. Upon her return to Tennessee she practiced law in Jackson (1926–30). But politics and the Democratic party, and the welfare of women with regard to each, remained her prime concerns. In 1924 she was denied a position on the state Democratic Executive Committee, despite her tireless efforts as an organizer, probably because of the stigma of her suffrage radicalism. Four years later, when the National Woman's Party moved to support Hoover's presidential candidacy, Miss White's insistence that the party first secure Hoover's unqualified endorsement of the proposed Equal Rights Amendment, which she had helped draft in 1923, led to her resignation from her official positions within the party; she allowed her membership to lapse completely the following year.

A lifelong Democrat, Miss White, at the behest of Mrs. Eleanor Roosevelt, helped organize a Tennessee Business and Professional Women's League for Al Smith in the 1928 presidential election. She was active during the campaign with the Midwestern division of the Democratic National Committee, through which she met Mary W. ("Molly") Dewson, minimum-wage champion and Democratic leader. After Smith's defeat, Sue White aided Nellie Tayloe Ross, former governor of Wyoming, in organizing Democratic women across the country by precinct units. When Mrs. Ross was called to Washington as vice-chairman of the Democratic National Committee to direct women's activities at national headquarters, she summoned Miss White as her executive assistant. Although Rose Schneiderman, president of the National Women's Trade Union League, protested this appointment to Mrs. Roosevelt, citing Miss White's association with the Woman's Party and its opposition to protective industrial legislation for women, the Tennessean was in 1930 appointed executive secretary of the women's division of the Democratic party. In this post, until the close of 1933, she was active with Mrs. Roosevelt, Mrs. Ross, and Miss Dewson in organizing the sizable women's vote that contributed to the "Roosevelt Revolution" of 1932.

During the New Deal era Sue White held a succession of government posts. From January 1934 to September 1935 she was assistant chairman of the Consumers' Advisory Board of the National Recovery Administration and assistant director of the Consumers' Division of the National Emergency Council, serving under MARY HARRIMAN RUMSEY until the latter's death late in 1934. Her specific duties lay in organizing over a hundred local consumers' councils throughout the country. When the Supreme Court declared the N.R.A. unconstitutional in 1935, she moved to the legal staff of the newly created Social Security Board. Appointed an attorney for the board in 1936, she won several advancements and in 1938 was made principal attorney and assistant to the board's general counsel, Jack B. Tate, a good friend and fellow Tennessean. Serving the Social Security Board and its successor, the Federal Security Agency, until her death, she "contributed largely" in Tate's judgment, "to laying the foundations of the Social Security program as it is today" ("Personal Recollections of Sue Shelton White . . . by Some of Her Friends and Associates," White Papers). She died of cancer in Alexandria, Va., in 1943, in her fifty-sixth year, at the home she had shared for six years with Florence A. Armstrong, a government economist.

Only five feet three inches tall, Sue Shelton White was a vivid, colorful, and often controversial figure, "at home with the most idealistic social worker fresh from college and with the most cynical politician." A "sharp wit and naturally caustic tongue" were tempered by a sensitive understanding of human nature (Lucy Howorth and Jack B. Tate, in "Personal Recollections," White Papers). Though she achieved some fame as a militant suffragist, it was as an

organizer, administrator, and politician in the early years of the New Deal that she made her most memorable contribution.

[The well-annotated Sue Shelton White Papers are in the Schlesinger Library, Radcliffe College. James P. Louis, "Sue Shelton White and the Woman Suffrage Movement in Tenn., 1913–20," *Tenn. Hist. Quart.*, June 1963, is an attempt to present the events and issues of the later stages of the suffrage movement through the eyes of a responsible militant. Miss White also receives mention in Inez Haynes Irwin, *The Story of the Woman's Party* (1921), and Doris Stevens, *Jailed for Freedom* (1920). See also Durward Howes, ed., *Am. Women,* 1935–36; and obituaries in *Equal Rights,* July–Aug. 1943, *Democratic Digest,* May 1943, *N.Y. Times,* May 8, 1943, *Evening Star* (Washington, D.C.), May 7, 1943, and *Washington Post,* May 7, 1943.]

JAMES P. LOUIS

WHITING, Lilian (Oct. 3, 1847–Apr. 30, 1942), journalist and author, originally Emily Lillian Whiting, was born in Niagara County, N.Y., according to the best evidence in the town of Olcott, though she later gave her birthplace as Niagara Falls. She was the only daughter and oldest of the three children of Lorenzo Dow Whiting and Lucretia Calistia (Clement) Whiting. Both parents were New York state natives of New England descent, her father's ancestors including Cotton Mather, the seventeenth-century Puritan divine, her mother's a succession of Episcopal clergy. Shortly after her birth the family moved to Bureau County in northern Illinois, where her father, earlier a schoolteacher and justice of the peace, farmed land near Tiskilwa. Becoming a leader in the Granger movement, he served for eighteen years (1868–86) as a Republican member of the state legislature, where he led in efforts to restrict the railroads and develop waterways; a county history describes him as " 'Liberal' in religion."

Educated by private tutors and by her parents in a home abounding in books, especially the modern English classics, Lilian Whiting early turned toward writing as a career, starting as editor of a local paper in Tiskilwa. In 1876 she ventured to a journalistic post in St. Louis, Mo., where she came under the influence of an extraordinary group of idealist philosophers, notably William T. Harris and Henry C. Brokmeyer, who strengthened the mystic and visionary temperament inherited from her mother. In 1879 Murat Halstead, editor of the *Cincinnati Commercial,* favorably impressed with two articles Miss Whiting had written on MARGARET FULLER, gave her a post on his paper. A year later she went to Boston, where Col. Roland

Worthington, proprietor of the *Traveler*, employed her as art critic at ten dollars a week and, in 1885, as literary editor. Her first local assignment was to interview the author, lecturer, and actress KATE FIELD, for whom she formed a lasting attachment. Leaving the *Traveler* in 1890, she edited the *Boston Budget*, a weekly home journal for which she wrote editorials, book reviews, and a "Beau Monde" column until 1893, after which she became a free-lance writer. Among other periodicals, she contributed to *Harper's*, the *Arena*, and the *Independent*. Her column "Crumbs of Boston Culture" in the *New York Graphic* and her series in the *Chicago Inter Ocean* and the *New Orleans Times-Democrat* on Boston and its people did much to spread the fame of that "literary Mecca" which she loved to the point of idealization.

Idealization may well be the key to her character. A small, "sunny-haired" woman, she looked at the world through large blue eyes which descried the best in everything. Her first books, three volumes of essays on *The World Beautiful* (1894–96), emphasizing the spiritual over the physical, ran through fourteen editions. People found comfort in such homely philosophy as "A successful life lies . . . in the quality of the daily life," and "If one would accomplish anything in the world worth doing, he must have sufficient confidence in himself to take risks." Her poems, *From Dreamland Sent* (1895), praised by JULIA WARD HOWE for their "sweetness and charm," similarly voiced faith and courage. Among her other friends were MARY A. LIVERMORE (who declared, "You are a sort of breath of life to me") and MARGARET DELAND ("If you . . . could come over and sit by my fireside for a while, I should be very grateful").

A "lightning-flash vision" in 1895, which sent Miss Whiting off to Italy the following year, resulted in *A Study of Elizabeth Barrett Browning* (1899). This was the first of eighteen annual sojourns in Europe. In other volumes she celebrated the charms of Florence, of Athens, of Paris, and of London. Psychical experiences in connection with the death of Kate Field turned Lilian Whiting to Spiritualism and the writing of *After Her Death* (1897), *Kate Field* (1899), and *The Spiritual Significance* (1900). To the end of her life she contributed to the *National Spiritualist* (Chicago). She also studied other religious cults, seeking to adopt the best tenets of each. In the early 1900's she was sometimes nicknamed "The Bab," after the founder of Bahaism. She took an interest in the Theosophical Society of KATHERINE TINGLEY and wrote two pamphlets about her. She also

did perhaps as much as any other writer to popularize the principles of the New Thought movement. That she remained an Episcopalian and staunch supporter of Trinity Church, Boston, may seem a paradox; but her nature—unconventional, impulsive, yet genuine, serene—is a study in contradictions. Some deemed her a "born critic," a writer of "keen and brilliant" editorials; others thought her neither "critical nor selective." A dweller in the clouds, she came down to earth to help the needy, to address an occasional ethical or literary group, to champion woman suffrage.

As the years passed and the friends she had written about in her *Boston Days* (1902) faded from the scene, the stooped, gay little figure, considered by many an eccentric, became a familiar sight in the Back Bay section of Boston. Always young in heart, she wished to remain young in years and sometimes admitted, "I never told the truth about my age but once, when I got my first passport to go to Europe! I have regretted it ever since." For years she listed her birth date in *Who's Who in America* as 1859. At ninety-four she died of a coronary thrombosis at the Hotel Copley Plaza, Boston, to which she had moved during World War II when the government took over the Brunswick Hotel, her home for over forty years. By her request her ashes rest beside those of Kate Field in Mount Auburn Cemetery, Cambridge, Mass.

[Especially valuable is the 18-page *Memorial* (Nantucket, Mass., 1942) of Miss Whiting by Dr. William E. Gardner, assistant minister of Trinity Church at the time of her death and the executor of her will, which appends a list of her books. For a nineteenth-century impression, see Marco Tiempo in *Arena*, Apr. 1899. See also B. O. Flower, *Progressive Men, Women, and Movements of the Past Twenty-Five Years* (1914), pp. 179–80. Her own book *The Golden Road* (1918) is semiautobiographical. Biographical accounts appear in Frances E. Willard and Mary A. Livermore, eds., *A Woman of the Century* (1893), which contains some inaccuracies, and *Nat. Cyc. Am. Biog.*, IX, 261. The Boston Public Library has a collection of letters written to her. The Mass. Registrar of Vital Statistics has her death record. Obituaries are in the *N.Y. Times*, the *Boston Globe*, and the *Boston Herald*, May 1, 1942. The Ill. State Hist. Library, Springfield, supplied a copy of the 1870 federal census listing for the Whiting family and other information about Lorenzo Whiting; the best account of his career is in *Voters and Tax-payers of Bureau County, Ill.* (1877), pp. 260–61.]

ELIZABETH F. HOXIE

**WHITING, Sarah Frances** (Aug. 23, 1847–Sept. 12, 1927), physicist and astronomer, was born at Wyoming, N.Y., the daughter of Joel and Elizabeth Lee (Comstock) Whiting. Her mother's forebears included seventeenth-century settlers of Connecticut and Long Island; the Whitings were pioneers in Vermont. Her father, a graduate of Hamilton College, was principal and teacher in a series of academies in New York state. Miss Whiting's interest in experimental science began in childhood when she assisted her father in preparing demonstrations for his classes in physics, then called natural philosophy. These were the years when the recently discovered wonders of electric currents and of electromagnetic effects were dramatically displayed before students. A precocious child, she was already well advanced in Greek, Latin, and mathematics through the tutelage of her father, who taught these subjects also, before she entered Ingham University at LeRoy, N.Y. After graduating, A.B., in 1865, she taught classics and mathematics at Ingham and later at the Brooklyn Heights Seminary for girls. While in Brooklyn, taking advantage of the unusual opportunities of New York City, she attended scientific lectures and visited laboratories and exhibitions of new equipment. She became known as an enthusiastic and effective teacher who showed great ingenuity in improvising apparatus for her lectures and shared with her students her excitement over new discoveries.

When in 1875 Henry F. Durant, founder of the new Wellesley College, was seeking a teacher of physics for his all-female faculty, his choice fell on Miss Whiting, for among the few women of that time trained in physics none equaled her reputation. Durant, knowing that the laboratory method of teaching physics had recently been initiated at the Massachusetts Institute of Technology, had arranged that his appointee attend classes there preparatory to establishing a similar laboratory at Wellesley. Thus for two years after her appointment as professor of physics in 1876, Miss Whiting was a guest in the physics classes of Prof. Edward C. Pickering. After visiting other New England colleges to study their methods, and herself purchasing and installing the necessary equipment (though treated courteously, she sometimes "found it nerve-racking to be in places where women were really not expected to be, and to do things which women had not done before"), she opened, in 1878, the second undergraduate teaching laboratory of physics in America. Physics soon became one of the outstanding offerings at Wellesley.

In 1879 Miss Whiting was invited by Pickering, now director of the Harvard Observatory, to view some of the new applications of physics to astronomy, including the use of the spectroscope in the investigation of stellar spectra. While in Brooklyn she had attended lectures by the famous British physicist John Tyndall on recent developments in light and optical instruments and had learned something of the astonishing revelations of the spectroscope. Spurred by Pickering's discoveries, Miss Whiting decided in 1880 to introduce at Wellesley a course in astronomy, listed at first as "applied physics." For two decades she taught astronomy with only a celestial globe and a 4-inch portable telescope. The need for a college observatory was eventually met by the generous gift of her friend Mrs. John C. Whitin, a Wellesley trustee. The Whitin Observatory, completed in 1900 from plans drawn up by Miss Whiting and enlarged in 1906, housed a 12-inch refracting telescope with spectroscope and photometer attachment, a transit instrument, and the usual accessories. In addition there was a spectroscopic laboratory with a Rowland concave grating spectroscope. This made it possible for Miss Whiting and her advanced students to compare solar and stellar spectra with those of laboratory sources and to contribute to this fast-developing field.

Meanwhile Miss Whiting had spent her sabbatical years abroad. In 1888–89 she visited scientists and laboratories in Germany and England, where a woman physics teacher was a curiosity, and studied at the University of Berlin. In 1896–97, when Edinburgh University was opened to women, she enrolled for study there with a leading physicist, Peter Guthrie Tait. She brought back to her students knowledge of the tremendous advances of this era, the beginnings of modern physics. Throughout her teaching years she prepared many women for careers in physics and astronomy, notably the Harvard astronomer ANNIE J. CANNON. She was a teacher rather than a researcher, and her publications dealt mainly with teaching methods.

Miss Whiting lived on the Wellesley campus with an unmarried sister, at first in college dormitories, where she was a gracious hostess, then in Observatory House, built adjacent to the observatory in 1906 by Mrs. Whitin. A devout Congregationalist, she was a strong supporter of the Wellesley College Christian Association and its active missionary programs. She sought to inspire her students (in the words of Miss Cannon) "to become not only good scholars, but women of influence in their communities." In 1905 she received an honorary degree from Tufts College. Miss Whiting retired from the physics department in 1912 to devote herself solely to astronomy. Retiring as director of the Whitin Observatory in 1916, she spent her last years with her sister in Wilbraham, Mass. She died there in 1927 at the age of eighty, of arteriosclerosis and nephritis.

[Obituary articles by Annie J. Cannon in *Popular Astronomy*, Dec. 1927, and *Science*, Nov. 4, 1927; *Biog. Cyc. Am. Women*, III (1928), 251–54; *Am. Men of Science* (4th ed., 1927); *Who Was Who in America*, vol. I (1942); Florence Converse, *Wellesley College* (1939); Alice Payne Hackett, *Wellesley* (1949); death record from Mass. Registrar of Vital Statistics.]

GLADYS A. ANSLOW

WHITMAN, Narcissa Prentiss (Mar. 14, 1808– Nov. 29, 1847), missionary to the Indians of the American Northwest, was born at Prattsburg, N.Y., the third of nine children and first of five daughters of Stephen and Clarissa (Ward) Prentiss, both Presbyterians of early New England stock. Her father, a landowner, sometime carpenter, and operator of mills and a distillery, also served briefly as associate justice of the Steuben County Court.

A winsome child with expressive eyes, dutiful Narcissa was her parents' favorite. The Prentiss children all participated in family devotions, and for Narcissa the results were lasting. A winter revival in 1818–19 impelled her to join the Presbyterian Church "on a confession of faith" (June 6, 1819), and in January 1824 a further religious experience moved her to pledge her life to missionary endeavor. In 1827 she was in the first class of girls admitted to Prattsburg's Franklin Academy, a Presbyterian-sponsored secondary school. Here she was courted by the shy and awkward Henry Harmon Spalding, whose proposal of marriage she rejected. The vivacious, popular Narcissa may also have attended EMMA WILLARD's Troy (N.Y.) Female Seminary. For several years, while "awaiting the leading of Providence," she taught district school in Prattsburg, where her pupils long remembered her interest in science, and conducted an infant school in nearby Bath. In 1834 the Prentiss family moved to Amity (later Belmont), N.Y.

In the fall of 1834 the Rev. Samuel Parker, a Massachusetts-born Congregationalist inspired by a wish to carry Christianity to Indians in the Far West, was visiting churches in New York state, appealing for funds and recruits. Parker had received an appointment from the American Board of Commissioners for Foreign Missions, a joint missionary society of the Congregational, Presbyterian, and Dutch Reformed churches. In Wheeler, N.Y., a town near Prattsburg, he enlisted Dr. Marcus Whitman, thirty-

two years old, a physician and Presbyterian elder. Narcissa Prentiss heard Parker speak in the Presbyterian church at Angelica, N.Y., near her home, and offered her services, but the board was unwilling to commission "unmarried females." Before Whitman left with Parker in February 1835 for an exploratory trip to the West, he spent a weekend in Amity, proposed to Narcissa Prentiss (whom he may have known earlier) and was accepted. Narcissa received appointment from the board the following month. Whitman returned in December, having gone as far as the summer fur-trading rendezvous on the Green River in present-day Wyoming. He brought back the news that Capt. Benjamin Bonneville (not yet immortalized by Washington Irving) had taken wagons over the Rockies. Where wagons could go, he was convinced that women could go also, traveling in the wagons when they tired of walking or riding sidesaddle; he and Miss Prentiss, now twenty-seven, were married on Feb. 18, 1836, in the church at Angelica. Setting out on the long journey, the bride is said to have remarked, "We had to make love somewhat abruptly, and must do our courtship now that we are married" (Drury, *First White Women*, I, 30).

When several prospective associates drew back, Whitman had accepted as colleagues in the Oregon venture Henry Spalding and his wife, ELIZA HART SPALDING—hardly the happiest choice, for Spalding remained bitter over Narcissa's rejection of him and nursed a spiteful jealousy toward her husband. Nevertheless, early in 1836 Whitman led his party to Liberty, Mo., where two wagons were loaded. After delays occasioned by the reluctance of a brigade captain to escort white women beyond the frontier, the missionaries joined a westering caravan of the American Fur Company for a four-month trip which has been vividly preserved in the pages of Mrs. Whitman's journal. The effect of the two ladies' presence on trappers and packers in a land with no women other than Indian squaws was profound. The mountain man Joseph Meek, who observed Mrs. Whitman at the fur rendezvous on the Green River in July, was much impressed by her "womanly influence," and later recalled that while the leaders paid court to her, the bashful trappers promenaded before her tent, touching their beaverskin caps whenever they could catch her eye (Frances Fuller Victor, *The River of the West*, 1871, pp. 207–08). Beyond the Green River the Whitman party traveled with a brigade of the Hudson's Bay Company. Though their two wagons had dwindled to a single two-wheeled cart, they reached

Fort Walla Walla on the Columbia River on Sept. 1, 1836.

Despite warnings from other Indians against Cayuse treachery, the Whitmans decided to establish their mission among that tribe at Waiilatpu—"the Place of the Rye Grass"—near Fort Walla Walla. The Spaldings settled some 125 miles away at Lapwai, among the Nez Percés. From the first, Mrs. Whitman played an indispensable role in the mission venture. While her husband conducted services, practiced medicine, erected mission buildings and a gristmill, and showed the men the fundamentals of irrigation and the domestication of stock, his wife—an "indefatigable instructress" according to one associate—taught in the mission school. She also supervised the domestic economy at Waiilatpu, by far the largest and most elaborately furnished of the Oregon missions. Her only child, Alice Clarissa, was born on Mar. 14, 1837. (Over the years the Whitmans took in eleven foster children, including, in 1844, the seven Sager children, whose parents had perished on the Oregon Trail and whose legal guardians they became.) Initially, Mrs. Whitman—"a large, well-formed woman, fair complexioned, with beautiful auburn hair, nose rather large, and large gray eyes" (contemporary description quoted in Drury, *First White Women*, I, 152)—seemed to flourish in this new and challenging environment; "We never had greater encouragement about the Indians than at the present time," she wrote soon after the mission's establishment. Further encouragement was provided in 1838 by the arrival of two new missionary couples who established stations among the Flatheads and the Nez Percés.

But the bright prospect soon darkened. On June 23, 1839, two-year-old Alice Clarissa Whitman was accidentally drowned, an event which plunged Narcissa Whitman into a prolonged period of despondency aggravated by the failing eyesight which eventually brought her near blindness. Added to this were the difficulties of missionary life. Language and cultural barriers were great, and the Indians were less eager to receive the Gospel than the Whitmans had been led to believe. Within a few years Mrs. Whitman's visions of dedicated service faded before the reality of daily, intimate contact with the "uncivilized," flea-ridden Indians who roamed at will through her well-appointed house. In time, her attitude toward those among whom she lived came to verge on outright repugnance.

The situation was worsened by internal dissension in the missionary community, much of it the result of Spalding's jealousy of Whitman.

In 1842 the American Board, having received disturbing reports of affairs in Oregon, decided to close both Waiilatpu and Lapwai, dismiss the Spaldings, and transfer the Whitmans. This news, reaching Oregon in September, mobilized all of Marcus Whitman's obstinate will; he resolved to convey to the board in person his conviction that to abandon Waiilatpu would virtually destroy the Protestant cause along the Columbia River. Heedless of approaching winter, he started for the East early in October. He returned the following summer, having secured a reversal of the board's decision, but for Mrs. Whitman the months of loneliness merely worsened an already serious emotional situation. A missionary associate (the Rev. H. K. W. Perkins) left a perceptive, yet sympathetic, analysis of Mrs. Whitman's predicament. "That she felt a deep interest in the welfare of the natives," he wrote in 1849, "no one who was at all acquainted with her could doubt. But the affection was manifested under false views of Indian character. Her carriage towards them was always considered *haughty*. It was the common remark among them that Mrs. Whitman was 'very proud.' . . . No doubt she really seemed so. It was her *misfortune*, not her *fault*. She was adapted to a different destiny. She wanted something exalted—communion with mind. . . . She loved company, society, excitement & ought always to have enjoyed it. The self-denial that took her away from it was suicidal. . . . She was not a *missionary* but a *woman*, . . . [a] highly gifted, polished American lady. And such she died" (*ibid.*, I, 155–56).

The cooling enthusiasm which Mrs. Whitman noticed in the Cayuse congregation in the mid-1840's was owing in part to Roman Catholic competition, but an even more important factor was the Indians' apprehension over the rising tide of white immigration. "The poor Indians are amazed at the overwhelming numbers of Americans coming into the country," Mrs. Whitman wrote in July 1847. "They seem not to know what to make of it" (*ibid.*, I, 160). Moreover, Waiilatpu had by this time become practically a way station on the Oregon Trail, and to the suspicious Cayuse the links between the Whitmans and the influx of white settlers seemed clear. But despite the difficult situation, underscored by actual threats, the Whitmans could not well leave. To abandon their field would have seemed to betray the trust of devout supporters in the East and to cast doubt upon the divine providence which had led them to Waiilatpu. Moreover, the medical services of Whitman were proving invaluable to immigrant caravans; the Whitmans were giving more attention to needy white settlers than to the Indians.

Indian disaffection reached a peak late in 1847, when white immigrants brought an epidemic of measles to Oregon. White children responded well to Dr. Whitman's medicine and Narcissa Whitman's nursing, but the Indian children, lacking any immunity, died in great numbers. The Cayuse had always associated Whitman's medical work with witchcraft, and now their worst suspicions seemed confirmed: their children lay dead from a white witch-doctor's poison. By late November they could hold their rage no longer. On Nov. 29, 1847, a small band of Cayuse warriors, employing gun and tomahawk, murdered fourteen whites at Waiilatpu, including Marcus and Narcissa Whitman. They also took forty-seven prisoners, mostly recent immigrants.

News of the massacre, carried east by the faithful Joseph Meek—Mrs. Whitman's admirer since the Green River fur rendezvous of 1836—so aroused public opinion that Congress in 1848 created the Oregon Territory and sent a governor to administer the area that would subsequently become the states of Oregon and Washington. A century later Congress established near Walla Walla, Wash., the Whitman National Monument, where each year multitudes visit the graves of Narcissa Whitman and her husband. For her, the long journey westward in 1836 had seemed merely a trying but unavoidable prelude to a long-dreamed-of missionary career. In retrospect, however, the overland trek itself—whereby Narcissa Whitman and Eliza Spalding became the first white American women to cross the Continental Divide, blazing the trail for the countless thousands who followed—seems the dramatic culmination of her life, the rest a frustrating anticlimax moving toward a disastrous end.

[There are extensive MS. sources on the Whitmans and their party. The principal collections are listed in the "Sources and Acknowledgments" of Clifford M. Drury's *First White Women over the Rockies* (3 vols. 1963–66), which reprints a number of items. The same author's *Marcus Whitman, M.D.* (1937) includes a schedule of letters, published and unpublished, of Dr. and Mrs. Whitman along with the location of the originals (Appendix 1), as well as 17 eyewitness accounts of the massacre and captivity (Appendix 5). For biographical information see Drury's books, above, and his *Henry Harmon Spalding* (1936) and *Elkanah and Mary Walker* (1940). Other books on the Whitmans include: Opal Sweazea Allen, *Narcissa Whitman* (1959); Nard Jones, *The Great Command* (1959); Jeanette Eaton, *Narcissa Whitman* (1941); and Marvin M. Richardson, *The Whitman Mission* (1940). There are many references to the Whit-

mans in histories of the Oregon Trail and of the settlements of the Pacific Northwest; see, e.g., Bernard De Voto, *Across the Wide Missouri* (1947), and Le Roy R. and Anne W. Hafen, eds., *To the Rockies and Oreg.* (1955).]

THURMAN WILKINS

**WHITMAN, Sarah Helen Power** (Jan. 19, 1803–June 27, 1878), poet, essayist, and spiritualist, was born in Providence, R.I. She was the second of five children of Nicholas and Anna (Marsh) Power, though only she, an older sister, and a younger one survived infancy. Both parents were of Rhode Island background, Nicholas Power's earliest American progenitor, also named Nicholas, having come to the colony in 1638, after fleeing turmoil in Ireland. Sarah's notoriously handsome and adventurous father, after receiving two degrees from Rhode Island College (later Brown University), had established a prosperous mercantile business in Providence. Reduced to bankruptcy by the War of 1812, he sailed for North Carolina and then on to the West Indies, was captured by the British, and on release elected to remain away from his family for a period of nineteen years. This virtual abandonment plus ensuing legal and economic difficulties made his wife extremely cautious with regard to suitors when her daughters reached a marriageable age.

Sarah received some rudimentary education during her early years and read Shakespearean fantasies and Gothic lore. Sent for a time to the home of an aunt, Mrs. Cornelius Bogert, at Jamaica, Long Island, she attended a Quaker school, was drilled in posture and etiquette, resisted the entreaties of her beloved cousin, Anna Bartlett Warner (mother of the future author of *The Wide, Wide World,* SUSAN BOGERT WARNER), to avoid novels and poetry, and began an avid reading of Byron. Returning to Providence, she briefly attended a school for young ladies, began a study of French, German, and Italian literature, and tried her hand at writing verse. In 1824 she became engaged to a wellborn young Bostonian, John Winslow Whitman, who wrote morbid poetry and prose under the pseudonym "Ichabod" and co-edited successively the *Boston Spectator and Ladies' Album* and the *Bachelors' Journal.* He apparently was responsible for Sarah's first known publications, which appeared in the former periodical under the signature "Helen." Whitman was a dreamer, an amateur inventor, and an improvident lawyer. He was also witty and charming, and Sarah regarded him with genuine affection. After their marriage on July 10, 1828, at Jamaica, Long Island, they made their home in Boston, but on Whitman's death in

1833, Sarah, as a childless widow, returned to Providence to live with her mother and her youngest and only surviving sister, Susan Anna.

Life with her husband had brought Sarah Whitman into personal contact with prominent Boston literati, including John Neal and SARAH JOSEPHA HALE, and it had exposed her to the intellectual ferment of Boston Unitarianism. She now quickly absorbed the new concepts of Transcendentalism. Under the pseudonym "Egeria" she published critical essays lauding and defending Shelley, Emerson, and Goethe; and, joining literary coteries, she formed intimate associations with many of the liberal intellects of New England. She took an active interest in Bronson Alcott's progressive educational theories, Fourierism, woman's rights, manhood suffrage, the Dorr Rebellion, and especially in each new specter of metaphysical science. Accepting the mesmeric theories of Charles Poyen, she passed them on to Dr. Robert Collyer, who later credited her with his success in the use of animal magnetism as an anesthetic in surgery. Meanwhile, she continued to publish verse, primarily in ladies' magazines, gift books, and popular anthologies. By now a serious and recognized writer of both poetry and prose, and an advanced Transcendentalist, Mrs. Whitman in 1848 playfully invited the attention of the poet Edgar Allan Poe with an anonymous valentine poem (published that March in the New York Home Journal) that reached him through the literary hostess Anne Charlotte Lynch (see ANNE CHARLOTTE LYNCH BOTTA); and he in turn eventually honored her with the second of his poems entitled "To Helen." In November of the same year, after a frantic literary courtship which placed much emphasis on an occult affinity, Sarah Whitman in a moment of stress and under specified conditions consented to become Poe's bride. In December their engagement was terminated through the efforts of Mrs. Whitman's mother and solicitous friends and through the reluctance of both parties to risk such a union.

Sarah Whitman's interests henceforth were varied. Assuming the role of a literary priestess, she offered advice to aspiring as well as established writers, notable among whom were George William Curtis and John Hay, and in 1853 she published a collection of her own verse under the title Hours of Life, and Other Poems. Moreover, for almost thirty years she continued to contribute to periodicals and newspapers on a wide range of subjects, many of them dealing with civic and social reform or with Poe and spiritualism. She was acclaimed by Rhode Island woman suffrage leaders as the first literary woman of reputation to endorse their cause (she became a vice-president of the state suffrage association on its formation in 1868), and she achieved signal recognition as a champion of spiritualism. Convinced of her own ability, to a limited extent, to communicate with disembodied spirits, she held seances, associated with popular mediums, and accepted as genuine many of the questionable manifestations accompanying the rapidly spreading movement; but as time passed she became more interested in intellectual and scientific investigations of the subject. Yet the role for which she is best known today is that of a defender of Poe. Stung by printed calumnies, especially those of the Rev. Rufus W. Griswold, which involved herself as well as Poe, she published in 1860 a scholarly brochure, Edgar Poe and His Critics; and by corresponding laboriously and generously with each aspiring Poe biographer, she became one of the chief sources of information concerning the poet's life and character, notably for the British biographer John H. Ingram.

Endowed with a mass of brown hair, dreamy blue eyes, and nobly chiseled features, Mrs. Whitman took a feminine pride in her appearance and sought always to obscure any sign of encroaching age. But she was first of all an intellectual. Her critical essays are scholarly; her poetry, which ranges from the humorous and the sentimental to the metaphysical, in general surpasses that of her American feminine contemporaries; and her journalistic correspondence, which combines wit, humor, and seriousness, casts an informative light upon nineteenth-century America. Her eventual philosophy embraced doctrines of personal identity, perfectability, and universal salvation, and above all asserted the right of every man to moral and intellectual freedom. Proud to the point of vanity of her rebellious Irish ancestry, she boasted especially of her descent from Nicholas Power, who had assisted Roger Williams in establishing in Rhode Island "the first government which claimed no authority over the conscience." Declaring her motto to be "Break all bonds," she even dared to excuse or defend certain friends involved in the scandals of divorce and "free love." In her will she left an appreciable sum to the Providence Association for the Benefit of Colored Children, and double the amount to the Rhode Island Society for the Prevention of Cruelty to Animals; and she defied convention further by arranging that only a few intimate friends be invited to her funeral and by forbidding a public announcement of her death until after her interment. She died at Providence, where she was buried in the Old North Burial Ground.

[Caroline Ticknor, *Poe's Helen* (1916); John W. Ostrom, ed., *The Letters of Edgar Allan Poe* (1948); all standard biographies of Edgar Allan Poe; MSS. at the Univ. of Va. and Brown Univ. and in the Lilly Library of Indiana Univ.; John G. Varner, "Sarah Helen Whitman, Seeress of Providence" (unpublished doctoral dissertation, Univ. of Va., 1940).]

JOHN GRIER VARNER

**WHITNEY, Adeline Dutton Train** (Sept. 15, 1824–Mar. 21, 1906), writer of popular didactic fiction and verse, brought excellent social credentials to the literary marketplace. Born in Boston, she was by ancestry, education, and marriage well equipped according to genteel standards to pronounce on contemporary mores and morals. The daughter of Enoch Train—a pioneer Boston merchant and shipowner (the sailing packet *Flying Cloud* was designed for his fleet)—and his first wife, Adeline Dutton of New Hampshire, she was a descendant of John Traine, who came to Massachusetts in 1635 and settled in Watertown. She attended Sunday school regularly, at first in Lyman Beecher's Congregational church and then, after her father's second marriage, in 1836, in the Unitarian church of her stepmother; in later life she became an Episcopalian. For four years between the ages of thirteen and eighteen she was one of the "happy scholars" of George B. Emerson, who kept a well-known private school for girls in Boston. She spent one intervening year at a school directed by Miss Margarette Dwight in Northampton, Mass., but it was the Boston schoolmaster whom she later remembered as most influencing her life and work. The study of Latin, she observed in her *Friendly Letters to Girl Friends* (1896), gave her the discipline she needed for her household chores, especially "the preparatory processes of cookery."

After her marriage on Nov. 7, 1843, to Seth Dunbar Whitney, a trader in wool and leather whose forty years outbalanced her nineteen, she moved to her husband's hometown of Milton, Mass. There were four children: Mary Adeline, born in 1844, Theodore Train (1846), Marie Caroline (1848), who died in infancy, and Caroline Leslie (1853). The Whitneys traveled in Europe and spent one year in the western United States, but for the rest of her life Mrs. Whitney's world centered in Milton. "My history," she said, "is simply that of my book-writing, and the management of my household . . ." (Teele, p. 553). Once her children were off to school, she remembered her delight in the literary sentiments of the English authors Elizabeth Gaskell and Maria Edgeworth and set out to add her contribution to the tradition of home and heart. First venturing with instructive articles in local newspapers, she hit her stride during the Civil War years when her *Boys at Chequasset* (1862) and *Faith Gartney's Girlhood* (1863) were quick successes, the latter novel going into twenty editions.

Mrs. Whitney's work, spanning almost half a century, is a clear reflector of the moral and sentimental eddies that clogged the literary streams in Victorian America. Her first book, *Mother Goose for Grown Folks* (1859), struck the note her audience wanted to hear:

> Minding the lesson he received
> In boyhood, from his mother,
> Whose cheery word, for many a bump,
> Was, Up and take another!

She tried her hand at a variety of carriers for her homilies during the 1860's, and then found her focal theme in four stories: *A Summer in Leslie Goldthwaite's Life* (1866), *We Girls* (1870), *Real Folks* (1871), and *The Other Girls* (1873). When these four were issued as the Real Folks Series, more than ten thousand copies were sold in the first season. Real folks —the idyll of hearth and home—was to be Mrs. Whitney's core message in her remaining work. Taking no part in public affairs and disapproving of the suffrage movement in all its forms, she calmly urged her "girls" to be satisfied with "the dear fireside places," the true center of a woman's world.

Mrs. Whitney continued to present her collection of moral and social definitions in her published "letters" with their commentaries on clothes, work, and marriage; in her collections of verse: *Pansies* (1872), *Holy Tides* (1886), *Daffodils* (1887), and *White Memories* (1893); and in her many stories for girls (the last, *Biddy's Episodes*, came out in 1904). Though fond of fashioning long chains of abstract words and dependent clauses, she was capable in her fiction of telling a good story, using simple, homely detail and a touch of dry Yankee humor. Surviving her husband by sixteen years, she died in Milton of pneumonia at the age of eighty-one and was buried in the family plot in Milton Cemetery. She was doubtless mourned by many readers who hoped that Mrs. Whitney's pictures of "simple, lovely, perfect *homes*" peopled by "nice, agreeable, natural young people" were more typical than they suspected. HARRIET BEECHER STOWE praised her work, John Greenleaf Whittier was a friend and admirer, thousands of young American women read and apparently relished her words. That is Adeline Whitney's significance to her own time and to students of

American taste in matters literary and sentimental.

[Mrs. Whitney's other publications include *Square Pegs, A Novel* (1899) and an antisuffrage pamphlet, *The Law of Woman-Life* (n.d.). Harriet Beecher Stowe has a chapter on Adeline Whitney in *Our Famous Women* (1884). There are also sketches in Frederick C. Pierce, *Whitney: The Descendants of John Whitney* (1895), and Julia Ward Howe, ed., *Representative Women of New England* (1904); and articles by Florine Thayer McCray in *Ladies' Home Jour.*, Oct. 1888, and by Elinor Whitney Field in *Horn Book,* June 1953. See also the brief autobiographical statement in A. K. Teele, ed., *The Hist. of Milton, Mass.* (1887), pp. 552–53. For a recent evaluation, see Cornelia Meigs, ed., *A Critical Hist. of Children's Literature* (1953), pp. 221–22. Death and marriage data from Mass. Registrar of Vital Statistics.]

CARLIN T. KINDILIEN

**WHITNEY, Anne** (Sept. 2, 1821–Jan. 23, 1915), sculptor, was born in Watertown, Mass., the second daughter and youngest of the seven children of Nathaniel Ruggles Whitney, Jr., and Sarah or Sally (Stone) Whitney, both direct descendants of Watertown settlers of 1635. Before Anne was twelve the family moved to East Cambridge, where her father was "justice of the peace and quorum" from 1839 to 1859, but they returned in 1850 to a section of Watertown that later became the town of Belmont. Well read and "advanced liberal thinkers," the Whitneys were members of the Unitarian church in Watertown and ardent abolitionists, though they took pride in supporting moderate rather than extreme measures of reform.

As a child Anne showed an eager intellect and artistic talent which her parents recognized and encouraged. She was educated largely by private tutors save for a year (1834–35) at Mrs. Samuel Little's "Select School for Young Ladies" in Bucksport, Maine. From 1847 to 1849 she conducted a small private school in Salem, Mass. This teaching interlude was followed in 1850 by a sea trip to New Orleans to visit cousins. She had early begun to write poetry, and in 1859 she finally found a publisher for a volume of her *Poems.*

According to legend, Anne Whitney originally discovered her interest in sculpture when a watering pot overturned in a greenhouse and she found herself modeling in sand. About 1855 she started making portrait busts, chiefly of members of the family, and in 1858 she began serious work. After spending a year in New York and Philadelphia, modeling, drawing, and studying anatomy at a Brooklyn hos-

pital, she entered her first exhibit in 1860, at the National Academy of Design in New York, showing a marble bust of a child, Laura Brown (now in the National Collection of Fine Arts). She had planned to go to Italy—then the mecca for American sculptors—but the Civil War intervened, and for the next six years she worked instead at the family home in Belmont, in "the shanty," the studio given her by her youngest brother, Edward, a successful shipping broker and financial head of the family. She also rented a series of studios in Boston, one, in 1862, next to that of the sculptor William Rimmer, with whom she studied privately. Her chief works of this period reflect her persistent concern with social justice. Her first life-size marble, a representation of Lady Godiva undertaking her mission to free the peasants from oppressive taxation, and the colossal "Africa," symbolizing a race rising from bondage, were exhibited in Boston and in New York in 1864 and 1865.

Miss Whitney finally reached Rome in 1867. There she lived and worked for four years, save for extensive summer travels and four months in 1870 when the city was under siege by the revolutionary forces of Garibaldi, during which she returned to the United States for a visit. The condition of the Roman peasants inspired her first new work abroad, her "Roma," an ancient beggar woman, conceived as a symbol of the city's spiritual destitution before the final unification of Italy. Completed in 1869, it was exhibited in London, Boston, and Philadelphia. Her "Toussaint L'Ouverture," one of her several sculptures of Negroes, was exhibited in Boston after her return from Europe. While abroad she went twice to Munich to draw and study and to visit the famous bronze foundry there. She was well acquainted with her fellow artists in the American colonies at Rome and Florence, including HARRIET HOSMER and EDMONIA LEWIS, but took only a limited part in the social activity that surrounded her.

In 1873, soon after her return from Rome, Miss Whitney won the commission for a full-length statue of Samuel Adams, one of the two figures Massachusetts was contributing to the new Statuary Hall in the national Capitol in Washington. To supervise the cutting of the marble, she made her third trip to Europe in 1875, spending several months in Paris, where she studied the new school of French sculpture. This experience was reflected in her "Le Modèle" (now at the Boston Museum of Fine Arts). In September 1876 she bought a house at 92 Mt. Vernon Street in Boston, where she lived and worked for nearly two decades. During these years she executed her statue "Leif Ericson," erected on the Commonwealth Avenue mall in Boston in 1887, and a number of portrait busts, her subjects including several Harvard professors, President ALICE FREEMAN PALMER of Wellesley, and such figures of reform as William Lloyd Garrison (who pronounced it his best likeness), LUCY STONE, HARRIET BEECHER STOWE, MARY A. LIVERMORE, and FRANCES WILLARD. Her colossal marble of Harriet Martineau, the renowned English economist and agnostic, commissioned in 1878 by the Boston abolitionist MARIA WESTON CHAPMAN as a symbol of emancipated woman, was placed at Wellesley College, where it was destroyed by fire in 1914.

Still vigorous in her seventies, Miss Whitney remodeled a plaster "Leif Ericson" (now in the Smithsonian Institution) and a larger "Roma" for the Columbian Exposition in Chicago in 1893, where she also exhibited several marble busts. In October 1893 she moved to an apartment at the top of the Charlesgate Hotel on Beacon Street. The final sculpture of her career was executed from a model she had made in 1875, when she had won first place in an anonymous competition for a memorial to Charles Sumner, only to be denied the commission after the judges discovered that she was a woman. The injustice continued to rankle until, at the age of eighty, she completed the seated "Sumner" (1902) which overlooks Harvard Square in Cambridge, Mass.

A small, dynamic figure, with flashing brown eyes and, in later life, white hair worn short, Anne Whitney was a thorough Bostonian by breeding and inclination. Wholly free of sentimentality in the age of its abundance, she was known for her satiric wit. Except through her art she was not a crusader, but she supported movements for abolition and woman's rights, the education of the Negro and the blind, and forest conservation. From an early age she had vacationed in the White Mountains in New Hampshire, and in 1882 she purchased a farm at Shelburne, where for thirty years she spent her summers, taking long walks, managing the farm, and reading poetry aloud on the veranda of the house overlooking Mounts Washington, Madison, and Adams. Here, as in Boston and abroad, her constant companion was Abby Adeline Manning of Brooklyn, an amateur painter who from 1860 had devoted her life to her older, more talented friend. Miss Whitney lived to the age of ninety-three. She died in Boston of cancer and was buried in Mount Auburn Cemetery in Cambridge. More than a hundred of her sculptures, of well over fifty subjects, have been catalogued. Perhaps because of her dislike for

publicity in any form, she was less well known nationally than her fellow Bostonian Harriet Hosmer. She ranks, however, as one of the distinguished women sculptors of Victorian America.

[The Anne Whitney Papers, Wellesley College Library, are the major source; they include some 3,000 letters by and to Miss Whitney, as well as scrapbooks and the diaries of Miss Manning, 1883–1904. Seven of Miss Whitney's sculptures and two paintings of her are also at Wellesley College. Contemporary accounts include: Mary A. Livermore in *Our Famous Women* (1884), chap. xxix; Frances E. Willard and Mary A. Livermore, eds., *A Woman of the Century* (1893); obituaries in *Am. Art Annual*, vol. XII (1915), and *Boston Herald*, Jan. 25, 1915, and editorial in *Boston Transcript*, Jan. 25. On her family background see Frederick C. Pierce, *Whitney: The Descendants of John Whitney* (1895), and J. Gardner Bartlett, *Simon Stone Genealogy* (1926). For a modern estimate see Margaret Farrand Thorp, *The Literary Sculptors* (1965). A catalogue of Anne Whitney's work by Elizabeth Rogers Payne appeared in *Art Quart.*, Autumn 1962; this will be revised in Mrs. Payne's forthcoming biography. Mrs. Hugh S. Hince, great-grandniece of Anne Whitney's mother and the present owner of Whitney Farm, Shelburne, N.H., supplied information in interviews.]

ELIZABETH ROGERS PAYNE

WHITNEY, Gertrude Vanderbilt (Jan. 9, 1875–Apr. 18, 1942), sculptor and art patron, founder of the Whitney Museum of American Art, was born in New York City, the second daughter and fourth of seven children of Cornelius and Alice Claypoole (Gwynne) Vanderbilt. A great-granddaughter of Commodore Cornelius Vanderbilt, who amassed the first great American private fortune, she was brought up in an atmosphere of luxury and social prominence, spending most of her youth in New York and in Newport, R.I. She was educated by private tutors both at home and in Europe and attended the Brearley School in New York. Her father, a railroad director and financier, was also an art patron and collector. Gertrude's own interest in art began during her girlhood, when she showed some talent as a watercolorist and draftsman.

On Aug. 25, 1896, she was married in Newport to Harry Payne Whitney, a sportsman and international polo player, the son of William C. Whitney, financier and Secretary of the Navy under President Cleveland. The couple maintained a country estate at Westbury, Long Island, and a town house on Fifth Avenue. Three children were born to them: a son, Cornelius Vanderbilt Whitney, and two daughters, Flora Payne and Barbara.

Shortly after her marriage Mrs. Whitney began to devote herself to sculpture. She received her early training from Hendrik Christian Andersen and studied later under James Earle Fraser and, in Paris, under Andrew O'Connor, both of whom excelled in monumental academic work. Her first public commission was for a life-size figure, "Aspiration," shown at the Buffalo Exposition of 1901; in 1904 she was represented by a statue at the St. Louis World's Fair. Fearing that the use of her own name would invite "inaccurate and prejudiced judgments," she exhibited under an assumed name until, in 1910, her statue "Paganism Immortal" won a distinguished rating at the National Academy of Design. In the midst of numerous family and social obligations, and despite the amused skepticism of her friends and of fellow artists, Mrs. Whitney worked diligently to attain technical mastery of her art and to overcome her lack of the long studio apprenticeship by which professional sculptors of the time were trained. During these early years she produced a number of smaller pieces, treating the human figure directly but in an idealized and romantic manner.

Finding it necessary to maintain a studio away from home, Mrs. Whitney moved her work in 1907 to Greenwich Village. Here her charm and seriousness of purpose won for her the welcome companionship of other artists and brought greater self-assurance about her work. The following year she won the sculpture award in a competition given by the Architectural League of New York for the best design, made in cooperation with an architect and a mural painter, for an outdoor swimming pool and pavilion.

These years also marked Mrs. Whitney's first realization of her role as patron of contemporary American art. When in 1908 "The Eight," a group of younger artists led by Robert Henri, rebelling against the conservatism of the National Academy, held an exhibit at the Macbeth Gallery, Mrs. Whitney purchased four of the seven canvases sold. Moved by the plight of these and other young artists, she began to provide exhibit space in her studio. From this developed the Whitney Studio, established in an adjoining building in 1914. It soon became a rallying place for liberal painters and sculptors, whose informal gatherings developed in 1918 into the Whitney Studio Club. In 1928 the club, now large and unwieldy, was replaced by the Whitney Studio Galleries, which exhibited and sold works by younger artists who had no dealers. Meanwhile, Mrs. Whitney had built up impressive personal holdings in contemporary American art. Concluding, however, that "the fame of an artist is not as much increased by having his work in a private collection as it is by having it in a public collection," she offered her entire collection, in 1929, to the Metropolitan Museum of Art, together with an endowment sufficient to erect a new wing to house it. This offer was rejected, and in 1931 she established the Whitney Museum of American Art, appointing Mrs. JULIANA FORCE, since 1914 her assistant and gifted collaborator, as the first director. The new museum, in expanded quarters on West Eighth Street, functioned in an informal and personal manner, reflecting Gertrude Whitney's warm relationships with the artists who exhibited there, and she continued to make private benefactions, assisting young artists with their studio rent or financing a year or two of study in Paris.

Mrs. Whitney's own work was meanwhile making increasing demands on her time and talent. Working in the secluded gardens of her husband's Long Island estate, she completed in 1912 the terra-cotta Aztec fountain for the patio of the Pan American Union Building in Washington, D.C. From these years also dates a marble fountain composed of three male caryatids supporting an overflowing basin, which won her the bronze medal for sculpture at the San Francisco Exposition of 1915. Much of her major work, particularly of the 1920's and '30's, was done in the studio she maintained in Paris. There she met the French sculptor Auguste Rodin, who, although not her teacher, exerted a profound influence on her work, most readily seen in the idealized figures of her "Titanic Memorial," on the banks of the Potomac in Washington, D.C. In this noble statue are found her most exalted personal and aesthetic ideas; its symbolism, that of the Resurrection—"And the Sea Shall Give up Its Dead"—is readily understood.

The First World War radically changed the character of Mrs. Whitney's sculpture. In the autumn of 1914 she established at Juilly, France, a hospital for wounded soldiers which she administered personally until the spring of 1915. This experience convinced her that suffering and heroism were not abstractions to be treated symbolically but terrible realities which demanded direct expression in art if they were to be realized at all. Upon her return home she immediately went to work on a large number of statues of soldiers, depicted either in the pitch of battle or as shattered survivors. These impassioned studies formed the basis for her larger war memorials during the 1920's, beginning with two panels for the Victory Arch in New York City. Her Washington Heights

Memorial at 168th Street and Broadway won the New York Society of Architects' Medal for the most meritorious work of 1922. In 1926 she designed a large memorial for the harbor of St. Nazaire, France, commemorating the landing there of the first American Expeditionary Forces on June 26, 1917.

In a different vein entirely she produced an equestrian statue of Buffalo Bill, recapturing the adventurousness of the old scout, which was placed at Cody, Wyo. Her most heroic conception is the Columbus Monument (1929), dominating the port of Palos in Spain, which rises 114 feet and is crowned by a symbolic representation of the explorer.

During the years following her husband's death in 1930 Mrs. Whitney's health began to fail, and, lacking the strength to work on a large scale, she confined her sculpture mostly to smaller pieces. Her last two important works were the monument to Peter Stuyvesant, standing in Stuyvesant Square, New York, and the "Spirit of Flight," designed for the New York World's Fair of 1939–40. The tranquillity of these final years was broken in 1934–35 by a prolonged and highly publicized court contest in which she won the custody of her niece Gloria Vanderbilt, daughter of Gloria (Morgan) Vanderbilt, who was judged an unfit mother. These final years brought Mrs. Whitney the last of four honorary degrees (from New York University, 1922; Tufts, 1924; Rutgers, 1934; and Russell Sage College, 1940) and election as an Associate of the National Academy of Design (1940). She died in a New York City hospital in 1942, at the age of sixty-seven, reportedly of a heart condition. After Episcopal services, she was buried in Woodlawn Cemetery, New York.

Gertrude Vanderbilt Whitney's sculpture was traditional in character. For her the human figure was the principal vehicle of ideas, containing all possible intimations of human thought and feeling. In rendering it, her personal vision was for the heroic, the tender, the tragic, and the aspiring. These qualities found their most characteristic expression in her public monuments. Her principal gift to the arts, however, was her generous support of young American artists, in an era when they sought to free themselves from the domination of traditional standards, and her founding of what has become a major museum. Her belief in the work of her contemporaries, as well as her belief in the potentialities of American art at a time when public taste was primarily directed to European art and the old masters, was of inestimable value in turning the tide of neglect.

[*Memorial Exhibition: Gertrude Vanderbilt Whitney* (Whitney Museum, 1943), with preface and personal appreciation by Juliana Force; *Juliana Force and Am. Art* (Whitney Museum, 1949); obituary in *N.Y. Times*, Apr. 18, 1942; *Biog. Cyc. Am. Women*, I (1924), 94–97; *Nat. Cyc. Am. Biog.*, XVII, 149; "Richest U.S. Women," *Fortune*, Nov. 1936; Forbes Watson, "The Growth of the Whitney Museum," *Mag. of Art*, Oct. 1939; John T. McGovern, *Diogenes Discovers Us* (1933), pp. 257–74; *Art Digest*, Oct. 1, 1939; *Who Was Who in America*, vol. II (1950); editorial tributes in N.Y. newspapers and art magazines at the time of her death.]

STUART PRESTON

**WHITNEY, Mary Watson** (Sept. 11, 1847–Jan. 20, 1921), astronomer, was born in Waltham, Mass., to Mary Watson (Crehore) and Samuel Buttrick Whitney. Her father, a successful dealer in real estate, was descended from John Whitney, who came to the New World in 1635; her mother, a reserved, intellectual woman, was also of colonial stock. Mary was the elder of two daughters and the second child in a family of five (a third daughter had died in infancy). An able student, especially in mathematics, and eager for higher education, she welcomed news of the projected Vassar College and determined to go there. After graduating from the Waltham High School and spending an intervening year at a Swedenborgian academy in Waltham, she entered Vassar College with advanced standing in 1865, the year it opened. In the words of a classmate, "She was preeminent not only in mathematics and physical science but also won distinction in every other department of her college work." She chose, however, to major in astronomy, under the direction of MARIA MITCHELL, the first woman astronomer in America, the first director of the Vassar College Observatory, and a great teacher who gave her students a broad understanding of a wider universe.

After her graduation in 1868 the recent death of her father and older brother called Miss Whitney back to Waltham to aid her mother. For a while she taught in Auburndale, Mass., but she spent all her spare time in astronomical and mathematical study. In August 1869, armed with her new 3-inch Alvan Clark telescope, she joined Maria Mitchell and a group of her former students at Burlington, Iowa, to observe a solar eclipse. At the urging of Miss Mitchell, Benjamin Peirce, the eminent Harvard mathematician, invited Miss Whitney to attend his course on quaternions in 1869–70. Since Harvard was not officially open to women, she had at first to wait outside the college gates for Professor Peirce to escort her personally to the classroom. Later she joined

William Byerly and James Mills Peirce (both future Harvard professors) in a postgraduate course in celestial mechanics that Benjamin Peirce had agreed to give if three sufficiently qualified students could be found. In 1870 she worked for several months with Truman H. Safford at the Dearborn Observatory in Chicago. She received a master's degree from Vassar in 1872. The opportunity to study abroad came in 1873 when her sister Adaline, after graduating from Vassar, entered the school of medicine at the University of Zurich. The Whitney family spent the next three years in Zurich, and Mary studied mathematics and celestial mechanics at the university. On her return home in 1876, unable at first to find a job suited to her talents and training, she took a position in the Waltham High School. In 1881 she returned to Vassar as Maria Mitchell's private assistant. When Miss Mitchell retired in 1888, Miss Whitney succeeded her as professor of astronomy and director of the Vassar College Observatory.

During her years on the Vassar faculty Mary Whitney earned a reputation as a fine teacher. Wishing to prove, as well, the competence of her sex for scientific investigation, she undertook a program of research. This included the determination of the longitude of the new Smith College Observatory and the observation of double stars, asteroids, and comets. Her observation of Nova Aurigae led to a study of other variable stars. In 1896 she made an arrangement with Columbia University for the measurement and reduction of a collection of photographic plates of star clusters made by Lewis Rutherfurd—among the earliest such photographs taken in America—and also of some plates of the north polar region of the sky taken at Helsingfors (Helsinki, Finland). As a result of this program, students trained at Vassar were soon in demand in the leading observatories in America. "In discovering such talents and in giving them preliminary training," wrote her successor, Caroline E. Furness, "Miss Whitney made a greater contribution to astronomy than she had any conception of."

Through all these years Miss Whitney pushed the cause of women's education. In 1871 she helped found the Vassar Alumnae Association and became its first president. She was a member of the Association for the Advancement of Women and was particularly active on its science committee, seeking to overcome the widespread prejudice against women in science. Yet, at the same time, she worked for the advance of scientific understanding at all levels. She was a charter member of the American Astronomical Society

(1899). In 1907 she became president of the newly founded Maria Mitchell Association of Nantucket, which, as a living memorial to the island's great astronomer, sought to instill "a knowledge and a love of science among the young people of Nantucket."

Handsome in youth and in later life, Miss Whitney impressed her contemporaries by her serenity and balance. Her intellectual qualities were combined with a sense of humor and a warm interest in others. She enjoyed reading and found Emerson, Herbert Spencer, Wordsworth, and Josiah Royce especially to her liking. In religion she was a Unitarian. Partial paralysis (hemiplegia) forced Miss Whitney to retire from Vassar in 1910, at the age of sixty-two. She died of pneumonia at her home in Waltham early in 1921 and was buried at Grove Hill Cemetery, Waltham. Shortly before her death she said, "I hope when I get to Heaven I shall not find the women playing second fiddle."

[The long memoir by Caroline E. Furness in *Popular Astronomy*, Dec. 1922 and Jan. 1923, is the principal source. See also: *Woman's Who's Who of America*, 1914–15; Frederick C. Pierce, *Whitney: The Descendants of John Whitney* (1895); C. F. Crehore, *A Genealogy of the Crehore Family* (1887); Mary W. Whitney, "Life and Work of Maria Mitchell, LL.D.," *Papers Read before the Assoc. for the Advancement of Women*, 1890, pp. 12–28.]

HELEN WRIGHT

**WHITTELSEY, Abigail Goodrich** (Nov. 29, 1788–July 16, 1858), editor of magazines for mothers, was born in Ridgefield, Conn., the third daughter and third child of the Rev. Samuel and Elizabeth (Ely) Goodrich. On her father's side she was a descendant of William Goodrich, who migrated from England about 1636, settling first in Watertown, Mass., and a few years later in Wethersfield, Conn. Her maternal grandfather, Col. John Ely of Saybrook, Conn., was a physician who served in the Revolutionary War. Samuel Goodrich, as was customary in New England in that period, supplemented his meager salary as pastor of the Congregational church of Ridgefield by farming forty acres of land and by tutoring boys for college. The best known of his ten children was the sixth, Samuel Griswold, who, usually under the name of "Peter Parley," wrote or edited more than a hundred books. His *Recollections of a Lifetime* (2 vols., 1856) describes the family's life: work in the house and on the farm, contact with the world outside through visiting ministers and relatives and through books acquired whenever possible and read with eagerness by every member of the family, and school days in a "weather-beaten little shed."

Abigail Goodrich was married to the Rev. Samuel Whittelsey (1775–1842) on Nov. 10, 1808, and went with him to New Preston, Conn., where for ten years he was the pastor of the Congregational church and where four of their seven children were born: Samuel Goodrich (1809); an unnamed son who died shortly after birth (1811); Charles Chauncey (1812), who died at the age of six; and Elizabeth (1815). In 1818 the resident superintendency of the Connecticut Asylum for the Education and Instruction of Deaf and Dumb Persons in Hartford (later the American School for the Deaf), of which John Cotton Smith, a cousin of Mrs. Whittelsey's mother, was president, was "entrusted to the Rev. Samuel Whittelsey [sic] and his lady" (Second Report of the Asylum, May 16, 1818, pp. 7–8). Two more children, Henry Martyn (1821) and Charles Augustus (1823), were born in Hartford, and the seventh, Emily Chauncey, a year after the family moved in 1824 to Canandaigua, N.Y., where Whittelsey became the head of the Ontario Female Seminary and his wife served as matron. Four years later they established a similar school in Utica, N.Y.

In Utica, Mrs. Whittelsey became interested in the Maternal Association which had been organized there in 1824. When that association undertook to found a periodical directed to mothers—reportedly the first in the United States—she was chosen as editor. The initial issue of the *Mother's Magazine* appeared in January 1833, with the avowed purpose of awakening mothers to their responsibility, setting forth the "proper government" and physical care of children, promoting better schools, giving attention to the needs of poor children, orphans, and "the offspring of missionaries," and encouraging the growth of Maternal Associations elsewhere. A year later, when the Whittelseys moved to New York City, the magazine went with them. It grew in popularity, claiming a circulation of 10,000 in 1837. Samuel Whittelsey died in 1842, but Mrs. Whittelsey continued the publication with the aid of a brother-in-law, the Rev. Darius Mead, editor of the *Christian Parlor Magazine*. In 1848 there was a new proprietor, Myron Finch, whose aims seem to have been largely commercial, and Mrs. Whittelsey broke with him when he decided to buy a competitive magazine, the *Mother's Journal,* and combine the two. In 1850 she started *Mrs. Whittelsey's Magazine for Mothers*, which, with the aid of her son Henry, she edited for two years. All of these publications were highly moralistic

and religious in tone, yet the articles and the letters to the editor on such matters as discipline, diet, education, and children's interests and capacities seem both sensible and practical.

A contemporary editor, SARAH JOSEPHA HALE, described Abigail Whittelsey as an attractive woman, "gentle and persuasive" in conversation, with a "genial, warm" personality and sound judgment. Her last years were spent in the home of her son-in-law and younger daughter, the Rev. and Mrs. Lucius Curtis, in Colchester, Conn., where she died. She was buried in Maple Cemetery, Berlin, Conn.

[Sarah Josepha Hale, *Woman's Record* (1853); Charles B. Whittelsey, *Genealogy of the Whittelsey-Whittlesey Family* (1898; 2nd ed., 1941); *Memorial of the Whittelsey Family in the U.S.* (1855); Lafayette W. Case, *The Goodrich Family in America* (1889); George L. Rockwell, *The Hist. of Ridgefield, Conn.* (1927); *Hartford* (Conn.) *Courant,* July 18, 1858.]

ALICE FELT TYLER

**WIGGIN, Kate Douglas Smith** (Sept. 28, 1856–Aug. 24, 1923), author and kindergarten educator, was born in Philadelphia, Pa., the elder of the two daughters of Robert Noah Smith, a lawyer, and Helen Elizabeth (Dyer) Smith, descendants of distinguished New England families of English and Welsh ancestry. Her sister, Nora Archibald Smith (1859–1934), also followed a career in kindergarten education. Their father, who had attended Brown University, died when the two girls were very young, and their mother moved the family to Portland, Maine, where Kate attended a "dame school." After her mother's marriage some three years later to Albion Bradbury, a distant cousin and a physician, Kate spent the rest of her childhood in the rural community of Hollis, Maine, in happy companionship with her sister and her half brother, Philip. She studied for a time at home under the "capable, slightly impatient, somewhat sporadic" direction of her stepfather, briefly attended the district school, spent a year as a boarder at the Gorham (Maine) Female Seminary and a winter term at Morison Academy in Baltimore, Md., and completed her somewhat spotty education by a few months' stay at Abbott Academy in Andover, Mass. The family practice of reading aloud encouraged her early interest in books, and she especially admired the novels of Scott and Dickens.

In 1873 the family moved to Santa Barbara, Calif., where Kate's stepfather, suffering from lung disease, hoped to recover his health. His death three years later left the family in financial straits when, in the collapse of the land boom that had followed the Civil War, his investments lost most of their value. Faced with the need to earn money, Kate wrote a story, "Half a Dozen Housekeepers," and submitted it to *St. Nicholas* magazine. Although the story was accepted at once, she had no ideas for further writing. She thought of teaching, but lacked the necessary preparation. At this juncture Mrs. CAROLINE M. SEVERANCE suggested that she enroll in the kindergarten normal training class which EMMA MARWEDEL was opening in Los Angeles. To provide tuition, Kate's family mortgaged their last property, and Mrs. Severance offered her room and board in her own home. With a warm personality, an intense love for children, and unusual talent in both dramatics and music, Kate proved to be "a natural born kindergartner." Upon completing the course at Miss Marwedel's in 1877, she returned to Santa Barbara to take charge of a private kindergarten that was being opened by Santa Barbara College.

When the Public Kindergarten Society of San Francisco was formed in the summer of 1878, Kate Smith through Miss Marwedel's influence was invited to head its free kindergarten—the first in California. This was located on Silver Street in "the wretchedest of slums," and her charges she later described as "street Arabs of the wildest type," but under her guidance they quickly became exemplary. To perfect her training, she spent three months in the East in the summer of 1880 working with SUSAN BLOW and ELIZABETH PEABODY, among others. On her return she inaugurated a teacher training school in conjunction with the Silver Street kindergarten. Her sister Nora, a graduate of Santa Barbara College who had taught in a private school at Magdalena, Sonora, Mexico, and had served as principal of the girls' department of the Tucson, Ariz., public schools, joined the first class. The following year Nora Smith took over the kindergarten when Kate was married, on Dec. 28, 1881, to Samuel Bradley Wiggin, a young Boston lawyer and childhood friend who had followed her to San Francisco "hopeful that a legal career might open to him in the West." They had no children.

After her marriage Mrs. Wiggin continued some work at the Silver Street training school, giving three lectures a week. To raise money for the kindergarten she wrote *The Story of Patsy*, based on her own experiences with neglected children and privately printed in 1883. Kate Wiggin continued her interest in the movement after she and her husband moved to New York City in 1884. She visited the important kindergarten training schools in the East, carrying her observations west with her when she returned to San Francisco every spring for the Silver Street training school's final lectures and commencement exercises. She also wrote a second book to raise money for the kindergarten, *The Birds' Christmas Carol*, printed in San Francisco in 1887. Reissued commercially by Houghton Mifflin in 1889 (along with *The Story of Patsy*), it had an enormous success and remained one of her most popular works.

In the spring of 1889 Samuel Wiggin died suddenly. Exhausted, dispirited, and burdened with financial responsibilities, Mrs. Wiggin went to Maine for the summer. Even before her husband's death she had begun to consider changing the direction of her life, and during her weeks at Quillcote, the family home at Hollis, she began writing a book for children, *Timothy's Quest*, though poor health prevented her from finishing it. Still in low spirits, she went abroad with friends in the spring of 1890, traveling mostly in England and Germany, and finished the tale while she was in London. After her return to New York in November 1890, she divided her time between writing and giving public readings from her books, for the benefit of children's charities. She suffered periodically from illness and exhaustion, and for the rest of her life took rest cures as frequently as her income would permit, sometimes staying at Quillcote, where her mother and sister were now living, and making frequent trips to Europe. Out of her early travels grew a number of popular books for adults, including *A Cathedral Courtship* (1893), *Penelope's Progress* (1898), and *Penelope's English Experiences* (1900). While on her way to England in the spring of 1894, she met George Christopher Riggs, an ebullient New York manufacturer and importer whose business interests often took him abroad. They were married on Mar. 30, 1895, in New York City; his interest and pride in her work were "a sustaining force" throughout their life together.

Mrs. Wiggin wrote several books in collaboration with her sister. *The Republic of Childhood* (3 vols., 1895–96) set forth Froebelian kindergarten principles and practices, and they also completed *The Story Hour* (1890), a collection of stories (mostly their own), and *Golden Numbers: A Book of Verse for Youth*. Kate Wiggin had always taught her pupils in the kindergarten training school to be careful of tone and enunciation in telling stories, so that the children would recognize "the possibilities of language and its inner meaning." Herself a superb storyteller, she captured the attention of her listeners and later her readers with the power and directness of her narratives.

Perhaps her most popular book was *Rebecca of Sunnybrook Farm* (1903), the story of a fatherless little girl who goes to live with her two maiden aunts in a New England village and maintains an unquenchable joie de vivre in the face of their often harsh and unsympathetic treatment. Sentimental by present-day standards, the book became an immediate best seller. Mrs. Wiggin converted it into a play which opened in New York in 1910 and had a long run both in the United States and abroad; a screen version later starred Mary Pickford. Another popular novel, *Mother Carey's Chickens* (1911), was also dramatized. In 1904 Bowdoin College in Maine granted Kate Wiggin an honorary Litt.D. Houghton Mifflin collected her *Writings* in ten volumes in 1917. Her autobiography, *My Garden of Memory*, appeared after her death.

In the spring of 1923 Mrs. Wiggin went to England as a New York delegate to the Dickens Fellowship. She was ill when she arrived, and entered a nursing home at Harrow, where she died at sixty-six, of bronchial pneumonia. At her own request, her ashes were brought to the United States and scattered upon the Saco River near her home in Maine.

[Kate Douglas Wiggin, *My Garden of Memory* (1923); Nora A. Smith, *Kate Douglas Wiggin as Her Sister Knew Her* (1925); Helen F. Benner, *Kate Douglas Wiggin's Country of Childhood* (1956); Committee of Nineteen, *Pioneers of the Kindergarten in America* (1924); Doyce B. Nunis, Jr., "Kate Douglas Wiggin: Pioneer in Calif. Kindergarten Education," *Calif. Hist. Soc. Quart.*, Dec. 1962; sketch by Calvin Winter in *Bookman*, Nov. 1910; reminiscences of Mrs. Wiggin by Roderick Stebbins, *ibid.*, June 1924, and Lucy Ward Stebbins, *Horn Book*, Nov.–Dec. 1950; *Boston Transcript*, Aug. 24, 1923; *N.Y. Times*, Aug. 25, Sept. 13, 1923. See also, on Nora Archibald Smith, *Nat. Cyc. Am. Biog.*, XXVI, 400, and *N.Y. Times*, Feb. 2, 1934.]

DOYCE B. NUNIS, JR.

**WIGNELL, Ann Brunton.** *See* MERRY, Ann Brunton.

**WILCOX, Ella Wheeler** (Nov. 5, 1850–Oct. 30, 1919), poet and journalist, was born in Johnstown Center, near Janesville, Wis., the second daughter and youngest of four children of Sarah (Pratt) and Marcus Hartwell Wheeler. Her father, a teacher of deportment, music, and dancing, had moved west from Thetford, Vt., shortly before her birth. Settling eventually near Windsor, Wis., he managed to keep his family precariously balanced on the near side of poverty by combining farming and teaching. Ella's mother, a rather sensitive New England woman, sought a literary refuge from this mundane existence by reading and committing to memory large amounts of romantic poetry. She seemed to sense a possible escape for her youngest child in this field and made much of Ella's early ventures in writing.

From the age of eight until she was fourteen, Ella submitted to the discipline of the local public school, but her heart was more in the romantic melodramas of May Agnes Fleming and Mrs. E. D. E. N. SOUTHWORTH than in her multiplication tables. Inspired by these writers, she produced an eleven-chapter "novel," bound in kitchen wallpaper, when she was nine. Her active career began at fourteen when the family's subscription to the New York *Mercury* ran out and she successfully submitted some prose sketches to the periodical to earn a renewal. Shortly thereafter *Waverley Magazine* and *Leslie's Weekly* accepted poems which she sent them, and she quit school to devote her time to writing. Although her successes at this stage were few, she was obsessed by her dream of escaping the stifling pattern of family poverty through authorship. Her parents managed in 1867 to send her to the University of Wisconsin in nearby Madison, but she stayed only one year.

In 1872 Ella Wheeler responded to sentiment engendered by the Good Templars, a temperance organization to which the family belonged, with *Drops of Water*, a collection of temperance poems which won a small audience. The following year saw the publication of *Shells*, a volume of optimistic religious and moral verses which presaged much of her future work. Her poems also began to appear in newspapers and periodicals in increasing numbers. During this period Ella helped support the Wheeler household at Windsor, now swelled by the families of her older brothers and sister who had failed at farming.

Beginning to gain a minor name for herself, she was hired by a Milwaukee firm to edit and partially write the literary column in its trade journal. The job lasted only a few months, but during her stay in Milwaukee she met the local literati and experienced her first (and later characteristic) dissatisfaction with any group in which she was not the center of attention. The publication of *Maurine* (1876), a long and stickily sentimental verse narrative, widened her reading audience, but real fame did not arrive until 1883, when a Chicago firm refused to publish a collection of her more emotional love poems, claiming that they were immoral.

The poems themselves, despite references to the "Impassioned tide that sweeps through throbbing veins" and the "convulsive rapture of a kiss," were hardly sensational, and most of them had previously appeared in newspapers and periodicals, but the title, *Poems of Passion*, had an illicit ring to mid-Victorian ears. Newspapers all over the country picked up the story of the poet whose verses, even in the eyes of the "Scarlet City by the Lake," seemed to "out-Swinburne Swinburne and out-Whitman Whitman." Another Chicago publisher, quick to grasp the commercial value of this flood of notoriety, published the volume before the year was out. In its first two years it sold sixty thousand copies, and Ella Wheeler's reputation was made.

Meanwhile she had found a real romance in her own life. An earlier semiromantic correspondence with the Hoosier poet James Whitcomb Riley had ended in instant mutual dislike when they finally met, and the "Poetess of Passion" had had no other attachments. But correspondence with Robert Marius Wilcox, an executive of the firm which later became the International Silver Company, who had glimpsed her in Milwaukee, led to several meetings and finally to a mutually satisfying relationship which lasted the rest of their lives. They were married in Milwaukee on May 2, 1884, and after a summer on Long Island Sound settled in Meriden, Conn. Their only child, a son born in 1887, died a few hours after birth.

That fall the Wilcoxes moved to New York City. Here Ella formed a friendship with Mrs. Frank Leslie (SEE MIRIAM FLORENCE FOLLINE LESLIE), which continued until it became obvious to both women that only one of them at a time could be the star of Mrs. Leslie's salon of second-rank intellectuals. Thereafter Ella Wilcox and her husband spent increasing time at the summer home they had built in 1891 at Short Beach, Conn.; it became their year-round home in 1906 after Robert Wilcox retired. Here Ella ruled absolute as queen of a world keyed to writing, hospitality, and the literary circles of New York—a world suited to her theatrical appearance and personality. Mrs. Wilcox was by this time writing a syndicated column of prose and poetry for various yellow-sheet newspapers, as well as regularly issuing volumes of her poetry. As one of her assignments she was sent to England to cover the death of Queen Victoria and produced a poem, "The Queen's Last Ride," which ultimately brought her almost as large a following in that country as she had at home.

Robert Wilcox's death of pneumonia at Short Beach in May 1916 marked a new phase in Mrs. Wilcox's life. She and her husband had long been interested in Spiritualism and Theosophy, and had studied under the Hindu mystic Swami Vivekananda in the 1890's as part of an attempt to reach their dead infant son. Now she began an all-out effort to communicate with the spirit of her husband, keeping the readers of her newspaper column informed of her progress. She soon announced the success of these endeavors, and in late 1916, believing that Robert had told her to do so, she began a series of tours of Allied army camps in France. Reading her poetry and giving lectures on the sexual problems confronting young men away from home, she exhorted the boys to "come back clean." After a nervous breakdown early in 1919, she entered a nursing home in Bath, England, and subsequently returned to her home at Short Beach. She died there three months later, of cancer. After a Spiritualistic funeral service, read by her poet friend Edwin Markham, her ashes were sealed with those of her husband in a niche in the granite ledge near their home.

Impulsive and energetic, caught up in a quest for personal recognition, Ella Wheeler Wilcox remained to the end (in the words of her biographer) "a pure phenomenon of democracy." Rejecting all literary advice, she continued to turn out the lilting verse that came to her all too readily. She reached a broad audience: the nameless multitude who felt something profound in lines like "Laugh, and the world laughs with you; / Weep, and you weep alone." She comforted and was loved by thousands of persons who would never have understood her own deeply masked sense of chagrin at being belittled or ignored by critics of serious literature, critics who did not agree with her maxim that art is created by "heart." If her art is measured by the size and appreciation of her audience, she is, as her biographer suggests, not a minor poet, but a bad major one.

[Besides her autobiography, *The Worlds and I* (1918), and Jenny Ballou's full-scale biographical treatment in *Period Piece: Ella Wheeler Wilcox and Her Times* (1940), the following sources contain useful information: Ella W. Wilcox, *The Story of a Literary Career* (1905); Neal Brown, *Critical Confessions* (1899), pp. 171–200; Charles H. Towne, *Adventures in Editing* (1926), pp. 93–98; M. P. Wheeler, *Evolution of Ella Wheeler Wilcox and Other Wheelers* (1921); *Nat. Cyc. Am. Biog.*, XI, 278; interview in *Lippincott's Monthly Mag.*, May 1886; articles about Mrs. Wilcox in *Cosmopolitan*, Nov. 1888, *Bookman*, Jan. 1920 (by Theodosia Garrison), *Am. Mercury*, Aug. 1934 (by Miriam Allen de Ford), and *Harper's Mag.*, Mar. 1952 (by

Naomi Lewis); obituaries in *Literary Digest,* Nov. 22, 1919, and in *N.Y. Times,* London *Times,* and N.Y. *Sun,* Oct. 31, 1919; death record from Conn. State Dept. of Health. Though 1853 and 1855 have been given for her birth year, the federal census listing of the Wheeler family in June 1860 (courtesy of State Hist. Soc. of Wis.) lists her age as nine. There are Ella Wheeler Wilcox papers at the State Hist. Soc. of Wis., Columbia Univ., and the N.Y. Public Library.]

JULIAN T. BAIRD, JR.

**WILKINS, Mary Eleanor.** See FREEMAN, Mary Eleanor Wilkins.

**WILKINSON, Jemima** (Nov. 29, 1752–July 1, 1819), religious leader, founder of a pioneer community in western New York, was born in Cumberland, R.I., the fourth of six daughters and eighth of twelve children of Jeremiah and Amey (Whipple) Wilkinson. She was of the fourth generation of her family in America, descended from Lawrence Wilkinson, an early freeman and colonial leader, who settled in Rhode Island about 1650. Her father, a successful farmer and orchardist, was a first cousin of Stephen Hopkins, several times governor of the colony and a signer of the Declaration of Independence, and of Esek Hopkins, first commander of the American navy. An older brother, Jeremiah, was a noted inventor in Cumberland. The Wilkinsons were Quakers.

Little dependable information exists about Jemima's childhood. The traditional account that pictures her as excessively lazy, with a genius for shifting her work to her sisters and a passion for fine clothes and gay company, cannot be supported by contemporary evidence. Undoubtedly an important influence on her development was the death of her mother, worn out by childbearing, when Jemima was only twelve or thirteen. Deeply interested in religious ideas, the girl read the standard works of Quaker theology and history and so thoroughly absorbed the King James version of the Bible that scriptural phrases became an integral part of her spoken and written language. She was caught up in the religious excitement that accompanied George Whitefield's last visit to New England and, in August 1776, was dismissed from the Society of Friends for attending meetings of a New Light Baptist group in Cumberland.

In October 1776 the twenty-three-year-old woman became ill with a fever; the doctor who attended her later testified that the fever was "translated to the head." In the course of this illness she had a vision that convinced her that she had died and had been sent back from the dead to preach to a sinful and dying world.

From the time of her quick recovery she refused to recognize the name of Jemima Wilkinson, calling herself instead the Publick Universal Friend; and for more than forty years she firmly adhered to her role as an agent of the Lord.

She began her ministry in southern New England. During the years of the American Revolution she traveled and preached in Rhode Island, eastern Massachusetts, and Connecticut, and after 1782 she made four visits of increasing duration to the vicinity of Philadelphia. Everywhere she attracted followers—both men and women—many of them persons of wealth and social distinction. Most important of these was Judge William Potter of South Kingstown, R.I., who freed his slaves because of her teaching and gave up his political career; he also built a fourteen-room addition to his already spacious mansion for the Universal Friend to use as her headquarters in New England. A wealthy farmer, David Wagener, of Worcester, Pa., was another convert, whose home she used while in Pennsylvania. Meetinghouses were built for her in East Greenwich, R.I., and New Milford, Conn. Although these were held by trustees in the name of a society of Universal Friends, the Universal Friends was a personal following of Jemima Wilkinson rather than an organized church or sect. Membership apparently was contingent solely upon acceptance of her requirement that "Ye cannot be my friends except ye do whatsoever I command you." The only printed guide for her followers was a small pamphlet entitled *The Universal Friend's Advice to Those of the Same Religious Society,* first published for her in Philadelphia in 1784 and later reprinted, after her death, in Penn Yan, N.Y., in 1821 and 1833. This consisted almost entirely of seemingly unrelated quotations from the Bible.

As the Publick Universal Friend, Jemima Wilkinson preached no new or original theological concepts. Repent and forsake evil was the essence of her message; prepare for a future judgment, and "Do unto all men as you would be willing they should do unto you." Nearly all of the practices she advocated, such as the use of plain language and clothing, opposition to war and violence and to Negro slavery, were standard Quaker beliefs. Celibacy was enjoined in the spirit of St. Paul as a higher state of grace which she herself practiced and urged, although married couples who joined her society continued to live together and marriages took place among her followers. In this she was much less rigid than her contemporary ANN LEE, founder of the Shakers, with whom she was often compared. There is no indication that the two women ever had any contact with each other, and the similarities between them probably stem from their common debt to Quakerism. The Universal Friend's attraction was based, therefore, not on novelty of doctrine but on the emotional impact of her personality and the aura of mysticism that surrounded her. She apparently did little to discourage those of her followers who believed her to be a Messiah capable of performing miracles, although by her frequent denial of divine powers and her ambiguous description of her mission she avoided offending those who did not see in her the second coming of Christ. Several attempts at faith healing were recorded during her early ministry in New England, and she made prophecies and interpreted dreams throughout her life.

By all accounts an attractive woman, Jemima Wilkinson was described in her forties as "of middle stature, well made, of a florid countenance," with "fine teeth, and beautiful eyes. . . . Her black hair was cut short, carefully combed, and divided into three ringlets" (François, Duc de La Rochefoucauld-Liancourt, *Travels through the United States of North America*, 1799, I, 112). Her manner of dress, however, was decidedly masculine. She customarily wore a flowing black robe patterned after a clergyman's garb. Her followers referred to her, not as "she" or "her" but as "the Friend."

She conceived the idea of a settlement where the faithful could be free from the temptations of the "wicked world" as early as the winter of 1785–86, when scouts were sent to explore the Genesee country of western New York, publicized by the veterans of Gen. John Sullivan's expedition during the Revolution. In 1788 followers of the Universal Friend began to clear the land on the west side of Seneca Lake, the first important American outpost in this area. The "Friend's Settlement" already had a population of two hundred and sixty when the Universal Friend herself arrived two years later. Though the land was purchased by a common fund, common ownership of property was never practiced; each contributor was to receive title to a tract of land proportionate to his investment. In practice this proved difficult to arrange, and disputes over land titles caused the defection of some important members, including Judge William Potter and his son. Jemima Wilkinson moved a few miles farther west in 1794 to the vicinity of Crooked Lake (now Keuka Lake), where, with many of the faithful, she established Jerusalem township. She herself owned no land but lived modestly on the proceeds of an estate held in trust for her by a follower. Her home was always open

to offer hospitality to travelers in the wilderness and to the Indians, with whom she had a cordial relationship. Not the least of her significance is the role she played in encouraging the settlement of western New York.

A whole body of folklore, much of it hostile, has grown up around the personality of this unusual woman. Many of the stories alleging sexual immoralities and messianic pretensions were undoubtedly circulated to discredit her role as a woman preacher and to counteract her effectiveness as a religious leader. The folk image in New England depicts a conscious charlatan who cleverly deceived her followers; in contrast, the descendants of her followers in Yates County, N.Y., the site of her last home, remember her as an earnest, kindly woman who devoted herself to educating, doctoring, and preaching to her flock. During the last few years of her life she suffered from dropsy, and she succumbed to that illness in her sixty-seventh year at her home in Jerusalem township. Her body was placed in a stone vault in the cellar of her house but later was buried in an unmarked grave by two of her followers. According to tradition, the secret of its location is handed down in the families of those who buried her. Two of her disciples attempted to carry on the society after her death, but the group gradually disintegrated and within two decades had all but disappeared.

[Papers of Jemima Wilkinson and members of her society owned by the late Arnold Potter of Penn Yan, N.Y., were microfilmed by the Regional Hist. Collection of Cornell Univ.; other manuscript material is in the R.I. Hist. Soc. The only full biography is Herbert A. Wisbey, Jr., *Pioneer Prophetess: Jemima Wilkinson, the Publick Universal Friend* (1964). Useful articles are Robert P. St. John, "Jemima Wilkinson," in N.Y. State Hist. Assoc., *Quart. Jour.*, Apr. 1930, which includes an extensive bibliography; and the unsigned article on Jemima Wilkinson (by Edward E. Hale?) in *Lend a Hand* (Boston), Feb. 1893. Charles L. Marlin, "The Preaching of Jemima Wilkinson: Public Universal Friend" (unpublished master's essay, Indiana Univ., 1961), contains an interesting thesis. Books with helpful information include Stafford C. Cleveland, *Hist. and Directory of Yates County* (1873); and Israel Wilkinson, *Memoirs of the Wilkinson Family in America* (1869). Abner Brownell, *Enthusiastical Errors, Transcribed and Detected* (New London, 1783), is an early description by a former follower. David Hudson's *Hist. of Jemima Wilkinson* (Geneva, N.Y., 1821) was inspired by malice and self-interest and is inaccurate as to fact.]

HERBERT A. WISBEY, JR.

**WILLARD, Emma Hart** (Feb. 23, 1787–Apr. 15, 1870), educator, was born on a farm at

Berlin, Conn. The daughter of Samuel and Lydia (Hinsdale) Hart, she was the sixteenth of her father's seventeen children, ninth of the ten her mother bore as Samuel Hart's second wife. The American progenitor of her father's family, Stephen Hart, had left England for America in the first quarter of the seventeenth century, becoming an original proprietor of the town of Hartford, Conn., and later a pioneer settler of Farmington, Conn. Her mother was descended from Robert Hinsdale, who settled in 1637 in Dedham, Mass., and thirty years later was one of the original proprietors of Deerfield, Mass. Both Emma and her younger sister, ALMIRA HART LINCOLN PHELPS, achieved distinction as educators.

As a child, Emma was taught the usual lessons of early American farm life, including the inferiority of women. If life was simple, it was also rationalized by custom and tradition: wool gathered from sheep on the Hart farm was divided into three parts according to quality, the best for the father, the next best for the men, and the poorest for the women. Yet Emma's childhood was not a series of routine experiences: her father was a political liberal, a Jeffersonian in a region where political orthodoxy leaned to the Federalist persuasion. He encouraged her to disregard the accepted view that a girl should train herself for a life of intellectual inferiority. He discussed Locke, Berkeley, and others with her, and by the time she was fourteen he was calling her from domestic duties with her mother to listen to an essay he had written or to engage in philosophical discussion.

In 1800, the year she turned thirteen, she taught herself geometry, and in 1802 she took the significant step of enrolling at the Berlin Academy. This act was in a sense a declaration of independence, for she had earlier regarded formal education for a farm girl as a foolish attempt to acquire knowledge unsuited to one's means and potential role in life. Two years later she was teaching the younger children of Berlin; in 1805 older boys and girls became her students in classes conducted in her father's house; and in 1806 she took charge of the Berlin Academy during the winter term. During these years she also attended classes at schools in Hartford. Clearly a natural appetite for teaching and learning had been encouraged: soon she was exploring both the possibilities for herself as a teacher and the prospects of education for women beyond the confines of her immediate community.

In the spring of 1807 she was employed as an assistant at the academy in Westfield, Mass., and that summer she went to Middlebury, Vt.,

to become preceptress of the female academy there. She was now in her twenty-first year, a pretty blue-eyed girl with high coloring and fair hair—experienced, knowledgeable, something of an innovator in temperament but in no sense a revolutionary. Her opportunities had been limited, but an incident arising from denominational rivalries during her second year at the Middlebury academy apparently gave her an opportunity to show her quality: neither orthodox nor agnostic, Emma was not one to allow denominational jealousy to define the life of her school. In this episode she was effectively supported by one of the leading men of the community, Dr. John Willard, a physician and, like herself, a friend of female education, a Republican, and a liberal in religion. They were married on Aug. 10, 1809, when Emma was twenty-two. Dr. Willard, then fifty, brought to their marriage status, experience, and four children from two previous marriages. Their only child, John Hart Willard, was born in 1810.

John Willard, her husband's nephew, lived in the Willard home while attending nearby Middlebury College. Her acquaintance with this young man and his books ignited in Emma a sense of the intellectual deprivation that was the lot of American women. When Dr. Willard suffered financial reverses, she opened, in 1814, a school in her own home, the Middlebury Female Seminary, intended to remedy some of young women's educational disadvantages. Denied the privilege of attending classes and examinations at Middlebury College, she taught herself the nonornamental subjects so that she might make them available to her own students. The school served as a testing ground, proving to Emma's satisfaction that she could teach and that young women could master the various subjects that were thought to be the peculiar property of men and men's colleges. She may have disarmed much of the public, then and later, by calling her schools female seminaries, but certainly what she aspired to do was to make available to young women the classical and scientific studies that were of a collegiate order.

Her success in Middlebury enlarged her vision, and she now proposed to seize the greater opportunities she recognized in the neighboring state of New York. Describing herself as aspiring to "a new and happy era in the history of her sex, and . . . of her country, and of mankind," she sought to enlist Gov. DeWitt Clinton and the New York legislature in support of a program of state-aided schools for girls. Her campaign, although unsuccessful, produced a notable pamphlet that possessed all the best qualities of a lawyer's brief. It was a model propaganda document, passionate but controlled, and it justified Emma Willard's own assessment of herself as "not a visionary enthusiast, who has speculated in solitude without practical knowledge of her subject." *An Address to the Public; Particularly to the Members of the Legislature of New-York, Proposing a Plan for Improving Female Education* (1819) received the warm approval of James Monroe, John Adams, and Thomas Jefferson, but it did not open the coffers of the state. It was, nevertheless, an important document of its time, comparable in the history of women's education to those characteristic papers of the period with which John Quincy Adams, Ralph Waldo Emerson, and Henry Clay were defining other areas of American experience and aspiration.

In moving from Middlebury to Waterford, N.Y., in order to open an academy there in 1819, she was clearly intending to make herself and her work more visible to the legislature. The decision of the Troy (N.Y.) Common Council to raise by taxation $4,000 for a female academy encouraged her to move there and open her Troy Female Seminary in September 1821. Troy was then a small factory town and inland port on the Hudson, but Mrs. Willard early sensed what the opening of the Erie Canal in 1825 would mean to her school as an importer of students and an exporter of young women ready to be teachers. Before the first normal school was founded in the United States, her seminary turned out two hundred teachers. Its success was apparent before the first public high schools for girls were opened in New York and Boston in 1826. With the encouragement of the scientist Amos Eaton, with whom she studied, Mrs. Willard introduced science courses more advanced than those available at many men's colleges. Sixteen years before MARY LYON opened her seminary at South Hadley, Mass., Mrs. Willard was establishing a serious course of study for women that was vigorous and deserving of respect.

Francis J. Grund, a Viennese immigrant who wrote one of the classic studies of American society, caught the spirit of the school and its founder in his *Aristocracy in America* (1839). In Grund's account, one of Mrs. Willard's pupils, "a fashionable young lady" whose mother has asked her to "tell the gentleman all you have learnt," dutifully responds: "We had reading, writing, spelling, arithmetic, grammar, geography, history, maps, the globe, algebra, geometry, trigonometry, astronomy, natural philosophy, chemistry, botany, physiology, mineralogy, geology, and zoology in the morning; and dancing, drawing, painting, French, Ital-

ian, Spanish and German in the afternoon. Greek and the higher branches of mathematics, were only studied by the *tall* girls." But *all* the girls, as the mother was quick to point out, were subjected to the moral guidance of Emma Willard, received "a little polish," associated with daughters of "the first families," and were made knowledgeable as well as conversant on subjects that had been traditionally beyond the province of women.

By 1831 the seminary had an enrollment of more than a hundred boarding students and more than two hundred day students. The school made money, as did many of the textbooks that Mrs. Willard wrote, based on her own studies and on the new courses of instruction offered in her school, particularly in geography and history. (She also wrote poems, but with the exception of the well-known "Rocked in the Cradle of the Deep," none was memorable.) In these years she established a pattern of life and learning that became characteristic of the American boarding school for girls: a nonsectarian but pervading Protestantism; weekly talks by the headmistress on manners and behavior; an element of self-help encouraged by an absence of maids to make beds and by elective instruction in baking; small rooms with roommates; monitors and a system of demerits; and simple dress. The curriculum made room for both classical and newer subjects of a collegiate nature, but Mrs. Willard did not believe in the same education for boys and girls. Most girls could look forward to marriage and motherhood, and for them the management of a household and the early instruction of children would be important. Although she established the desirability and the capacity of women to undertake serious intellectual work, she encouraged her students to recognize that in women's beauty, grace, and manners was a great source of power for good.

The fame and wealth Emma Willard's work had brought her had allowed her to develop a courtly manner, a kindness, graciousness, and dignity that made her something of a queen, American style. Her students spread not only her fame but her style as well. As they moved to careers in teaching all over the United States, they helped define much of the quality of life and the intellectual tone of middle- and upper-class American society in the nineteenth century. Unlike Mary Lyon, Mrs. Willard did not focus her attention essentially on the needs of young girls who could not afford education, nor did she share the overwhelming sense of Christian mission that characterized the founder of Mount Holyoke. But it should not be forgotten that she made the Troy Female Seminary a private enterprise only after the state legislature had failed to respond to her arguments for a system of public support. In consequence, she shaped a school in harmony with the age and with the aspirations of the rising families of wealth who were ready to share with their daughters the liberating possibilities of American life.

After the death, in 1825, of Dr. Willard, who had been school physician and business manager, Emma Willard had taken full charge of the school, and by 1838 she was ready to turn over its management to her daughter-in-law, Sarah Lucretia Hudson, and her son, John Hart Willard. She followed her retirement from the Troy Female Seminary with a decision so wrong that skeptics of female education must have found their reservations confirmed. On Sept. 17 she married Christopher Yates, an Albany physician of plausible manner and good reputation, who turned out to be a gambler, agnostic, and fortune hunter. Two hours after the wedding ceremony he called on his wife to pay for the wedding dinner. In Boston, where they settled, he made life miserable for her, publishing attacks on her and demanding funds. After nine months she left him, and in 1843 she was granted a divorce by the legislature of Connecticut, where she was then living and assisting Henry Barnard in improving the common schools.

In 1844 she returned to Troy to be near the seminary. She spent the rest of her life busily —as adviser, teacher, speaker, friend of good causes, stimulus to the formation of educational societies. She traveled extensively abroad and in the United States. Although she was a reformer in education for women and even used the successful Greek revolution of 1832 as an opportunity to advance the cause of female education in Greece (see FRANCES MULLIGAN HILL), she closed her mind to women's political rights. In over a score of books and pamphlets, however, she proved the right of women to intellectual equality. Emma Willard died at Troy in 1870, in her eighty-fourth year, and was buried in Oakwood Cemetery overlooking the city. In 1895 the Troy Female Seminary was renamed the Emma Willard School.

[Alma Lutz, *Emma Willard: Daughter of Democracy* (1929), is a definitive biography with an excellent bibliography. Thomas Woody, *A Hist. of Women's Education in the U.S.* (1929), remains the standard account of its subject.]

FREDERICK RUDOLPH

WILLARD, Frances Elizabeth Caroline (Sept. 28, 1839–Feb. 17, 1898), temperance leader and feminist, was born in Churchville, N.Y.,

fifteen miles west of Rochester, the daughter of Mary Thompson (Hill) Willard and Josiah Flint Willard, a farmer and cabinetmaker. She was the fourth of five children, of whom three, including an older brother and a younger sister, survived infancy. The patriarch of the Willard family in America, Simon Willard, had come to Massachusetts from England in 1634, winning renown as a fur trader and Indian fighter and a founder of the town of Concord. His descendants included a president of Harvard College, but the branch of the family from which Josiah Willard sprang was comprised of a long line of New England and New York farmers. Frances' maternal ancestors were also New Englanders of English origins.

When she was two, the family migrated to Ohio, where her father, who aspired to be a minister, enrolled in the preparatory school of Oberlin College; her mother, eager for an education, also took courses. In 1845, however, Willard developed symptoms of tuberculosis. Advised by his doctor to return to an outdoor life, he took his family the next year by covered wagon to Janesville, Wisconsin Territory, and settled on a farm which under his skilled husbandry soon covered a thousand acres. Frances grew up on this sparsely settled frontier. Local Methodists had built a church, with which the Willards, previously Congregationalists, cast their lot, but the circuit rider preached infrequently; there were no schools, and for months at a time the Willard children saw no one outside the family. Frances shared her brother's outdoor activities and lived the life of a tomboy, wearing her hair short and insisting on being called "Frank." She resented her father's harsh discipline and despite his opposition yearned for an education. When she was nine Josiah Willard was elected to the legislature, and while he was in Madison that winter attending its sessions, Mrs. Willard gave the daughters their first schooling. This was continued sporadically by a Janesville girl who had been to Eastern schools, by a visiting aunt, and in the district school which her father, at Frances' insistence, secured for the neighborhood when she was fifteen. For one winter, she attended a "select school" for girls in Janesville. In 1856, when she was seventeen, her brother cast his first vote, leaving her with a lasting feeling of resentment that she could not share in the ritual of election day, "which was thought to be a sacred time at our house" (Earhart, p. 37).

Early in 1857 her father consented to her attending Milwaukee Female College, a Congregational institution where her aunt was teaching, but after one happy term there he

transferred her to the new North Western Female College in Evanston, Ill., north of Chicago, an inferior school but Methodist-affili-
ated. She graduated from this institution in
1859 as a "Laureate of Science," having had
altogether less than four years of formal education. Her parents had moved to Evanston
(Josiah Willard having entered a partnership
with a Chicago broker), and this remained
Frances Willard's home for the rest of her life.

At loose ends after her graduation but determined to be independent, she became a
country schoolteacher in Harlem, Ill., in 1860,
transferring after one term to a preparatory
school in Kankakee. These were but the first
of a number of teaching positions she held in
the next several years, most of them in Methodist schools, including the North Western Female College (1862) and the Pittsburgh (Pa.)
Female College (1863–64). In 1865–66 she
served as secretary of the American Methodist
Ladies Centenary Association, directing the
raising of funds for a new theological school
dormitory and winning wide recognition within the denomination. After a period of teaching in an Evanston private school, she moved to
the Genesee Wesleyan Seminary, Lima, N.Y.,
where she was preceptress in 1866–67. The
next winter she helped nurse her father
through his final illness; he died of tuberculosis
in January 1868.

During these years her life was unsettled
and disturbed. "I am more sick of it than my
best friends can tell," she wrote in her journal
in 1860 (Earhart, p. 53). Mercurial and
moody, she possessed an intense capacity for
affection which had been thwarted throughout
her childhood. She longed for understanding
companionship and found comfort in romantic
links with other girls in the schools where she
studied and taught. Surviving letters record
the history of these youthful "crushes," a succession of undying loves, anguished separations, and tearful reconciliations. In these relationships "Frank" assumed the dominant role;
as she noted in her journal in 1860, "I am the
one relied on, the one who fights the battles,
or would if there were any to fight" (Earhart,
p. 83). She was much moved by reading William R. Alger's *The Friendships of Women*
(1868). In her relationships with young men
she was hampered by a paralyzing shyness,
but in 1861 she became engaged to Charles
Henry Fowler, pastor of a Chicago Methodist
church and a friend and theological school
classmate of her brother. The circumstances
under which this engagement ended after several months are unclear. Fowler, who was to
become president of Northwestern University

and later a bishop, was a somewhat dominating man, and his insensitivity was certainly a
factor; she had been deeply distressed by his
announced intention of going to China as a
missionary, only to be told that he had merely
been "testing her love." A few months after
the breaking of the engagement, she was desolated by the death, from tuberculosis, of
her sister, Mary. She sought relief by writing
a biography lauding her sister's goodness and
purity. This work won the interest of a Methodist bishop who arranged for its publication
in 1864 as *Nineteen Beautiful Years*.

While teaching at the Genesee seminary,
Frances Willard had formed a close friendship
with Kate Jackson of Paterson, N.J. Kate's
father was wealthy, and in 1868 the two young
ladies departed for two years of travel, at his
expense, to Europe, Russia, Egypt, the Holy
Land, Constantinople, and Greece. Frances
was an indefatigable sightseer, enthusiastically attended lectures and studied languages
in Berlin, Paris, and Rome, and became acquainted with art and music. To earn money for
her personal expenses she wrote weekly articles for the local papers at home. The trip
opened up a new world, and gave her poise,
graciousness, and fresh intellectual interests.
It was an elixir to her spirits. Inspired with an
eager, restless desire to achieve, she now began
to plan a career of service "among the class that
I have always loved and that has loved me always—the girls of my native land and my
times" (Earhart, p. 93). She had "dimly felt"
that this should be her vocation ever since, at
eighteen, she had happened upon John Stuart
Mill's essay "The Enfranchisement of Women."
The writings of MARGARET FULLER had further
aroused her interest in feminism, and during
the Civil War she had been inspired by newspaper accounts of ANNA DICKINSON's speeches
and in fantasy had pictured herself swaying
crowds from the lecture platform.

In 1870 the travelers returned, and settled
in Evanston with Mrs. Willard. The following
year Frances Willard was named president of
the Evanston College for Ladies, a Methodist
institution being planned by Mrs. Mary F.
Haskin and others. The new college, which
opened in September 1871, was closely linked
to Northwestern University, where the girls
took most of their academic work, and Miss
Willard's duties were primarily those of social
supervision. But late in 1872 a new president
assumed office at the university—Charles Fowler, Miss Willard's former fiancé. Fowler was
eager to extend Northwestern's authority over
its female students, and was perhaps also victim of a certain impulse to harass the former

object of his affections. Acrimonious disputes soon arose over the extent of Miss Willard's authority, particularly over those women students who enrolled directly at Northwestern. At the same time the College for Ladies faltered financially, as the disastrous Chicago Fire of October 1871 sharply diminished contributions and undermined a planned building program, and in the summer of 1873 it was wholly absorbed by Northwestern.

Miss Willard, retained as dean of women and professor of English and art, was not at first entirely displeased by this development, which brought an increased salary and affiliation with an institution of some academic standing. An invitation to participate in the founding of the Association for the Advancement of Women, in New York City in October 1873, was a welcome honor. Miss Willard, as a prominent educator, was elected a vice-president of the new organization, sponsored by the pioneer New York woman's club, Sorosis, to provide a voice for moderate feminism at a time when the suffrage movement seemed marked by radicalism and eccentricity.

The situation at Northwestern, however, did not improve. The friction with Fowler was intensified, and during the academic year 1873–74 Miss Willard's authority was challenged in a variety of petty and exasperating ways. At last, in June 1874, she resigned, never again to hold an academic position. The Evanston College for Ladies had not evolved, as she had hoped, into an independent, coordinate institution within the university but had merely served as a prelude to the introduction of full coeducation at Northwestern. At thirty-five Frances Willard found herself adrift, with no savings, and deeply unhappy.

But the movement through which she was to realize her ambitions was already under way. In a day with little public regulation of the manufacture and sale of liquor, popular sentiment for temperance reform had been building up, particularly in the Midwest. Feeling was strong in the Protestant churches, and in December 1873 praying bands of women spontaneously began an antisaloon crusade in several Ohio and western New York towns. This spread through the Midwest and into the East; in about six months some three thousand saloons are said to have been closed. The next summer Chicago women who were organizing a temperance group following the crusade in that city asked Frances Willard to be their leader, and in October, at a convention in Bloomington, Ill., which formed a statewide women's temperance organization, Miss Willard was chosen secretary. She was a delegate

the next month to the Cleveland convention that founded the National Woman's Christian Temperance Union and was chosen its corresponding secretary.

It was soon apparent to her W.C.T.U. associates that Miss Willard's interest in temperance was but one expression of a desire to advance the cause of women and promote reform in many fields. In 1876 the Illinois union, swayed by her eloquence, unanimously adopted her resolution looking forward to "that day when the mothers, and daughters of America shall have a voice in the decision by which . . . the rum-shop is opened or shut beside their homes." Her speech on a similar prosuffrage resolution at the national convention, however, was greeted with silence, and the conservative first president of the W.C.T.U., Mrs. ANNIE WITTENMYER, supported the chairman in her declaration that "we do not propose to trail our skirts through the mire of politics." The young Westerner's first attempt to commit the national organization to woman suffrage was thus defeated, but Miss Willard had joined the issue and entered the contest for leadership. Meanwhile, as corresponding secretary in charge of all organization work, she was becoming personally acquainted with the leaders of state and local unions and was finding herself in demand as a speaker.

Early in 1877 she resigned her post with the Chicago union—her only source of income—for a position with the famous evangelist Dwight L. Moody as director of women's meetings, with freedom to carry on her W.C.T.U. work. She found his orthodoxy constricting, and in September returned to Evanston, bringing with her the young ANNA A. GORDON, whom she had met in Moody's Boston crusade and who was to become her lifelong secretary, aide, and confidante. That year Frances Willard resigned as national corresponding secretary of the W.C.T.U., relations with Mrs. Wittenmyer having become strained. She was now free to speak out for suffrage and spent a happy year lecturing across the country on "women and service" to rapt audiences.

In 1878 she was chosen president of the Illinois W.C.T.U. Aware that significant victories for temperance would come only through new laws, she conceived the idea of a huge petition asking that women of the state be given the vote on liquor questions. In a state-wide campaign organized with Anna Gordon's assistance, the names of more than a hundred thousand women were secured, and the "Home Protection" petition was presented to the state legislature in March 1879. Frances Willard lobbied vigorously in Springfield for it and secured substantial support, including the backing of the Illinois Grange. In the end the petition died in committee, but its effect was clearly seen in the spring elections, when a large majority of Illinois towns voted for local option. The campaign became a model for W.C.T.U. action in other states.

Meanwhile, though the national union continued cool to the suffrage idea, Miss Willard as head of its publications committee (1876–79) used the W.C.T.U. journal, *Our Union*, to promote her views. The sputtering criticism from Eastern conservatives that resulted was easily contained by her oratory, which won her new followers at every national convention. In 1879 she was elected president of the national W.C.T.U., a position she held for the remaining twenty years of her life.

Under her leadership the Union quickly adopted new objectives and new methods. Hitherto a praying society dedicated to temperance, it soon became a strong women's movement, solidly rooted in the Midwest, which promoted not only "temperance"—total abstinence and legal prohibition—but also a broad range of other causes. Frances Willard strengthened the local base of the organization by requiring that representation in the national convention be apportioned according to paid membership. Under her direction the annual convention became a stirring spectacle. Delegates from all over the country gathered in a hall gay with banners, flags, flowers, and music. Strict parliamentary procedure was maintained, and Frances Willard presided for hours on end with unfailing humor and self-control. On convention Sunday, it became the custom for churches in the host city to invite noted members of the Union to speak from their pulpits, and this dramatic evidence of the support of organized religion had a wide impact in the community. Miss Willard also established the practice of exchanging fraternal delegates between the W.C.T.U. and kindred societies, which brought further endorsement.

Between conventions Frances Willard undertook long speaking tours which drew crowds and made headline news everywhere. For ten years she traveled between fifteen and twenty thousand miles annually—introducing the W.C.T.U. into the South in 1881, to every state and territory in the West in 1883. Each season included a stay at the Lake Chautauqua (N.Y.) summer assembly, where she was one of the most popular speakers. She had, in fact, become a nationally famous personage. Her delicate features, close-cropped hair, and small pince-nez were familiar to millions, as

was her ability to sway audiences. "Her voice was clear and melodious and strong with a peculiar quality of blended defiance and deference, of tenderness and intrepidity that gave it an indescribable charm," a contemporary recalled (Earhart, p. 383). These triumphs were achieved despite constant anxiety over personal finances, for Miss Willard had both her mother and Anna Gordon to support, and until 1886 lecture fees remained her only source of income. In that year the national W.C.T.U. voted her a salary of $1,800, together with an allowance for clerical help and a salary for Miss Gordon. Miss Willard's salary was subsequently increased to $2,400. The success of her autobiography, *Glimpses of Fifty Years*, published in 1889, gave her financial security.

Frances Willard thought of the W.C.T.U. as a school to interest women in life beyond the family circle, so that they might take a more active and useful part in society. To encourage the timid, she tied the home to her cause and to her organization. The famous slogan "For God and Home and Native Land," which she had first devised for the Chicago union, was adopted by the national W.C.T.U. in 1876. The organization's badge, chosen the next year, was a bow of white ribbon symbolizing the purity of the home, and "Home Protection" was always to be the Union's rallying cry.

Before Miss Willard's presidency, the Union's activities had been supervised by standing committees. For these she substituted national superintendents, each in charge of a department, and this structure was repeated in the state and local organizations. The national convention in 1880 endorsed "the ballot for woman as a weapon for the protection of her home," and in 1882 a Department of Franchise was organized to distribute suffrage literature and encourage state unions to work for the vote. Under the direction first of ZERELDA WALLACE and then of ANNA HOWARD SHAW, this became the W.C.T.U.'s leading department. Miss Willard herself was a member of the American Woman Suffrage Association, led by LUCY STONE, and preferred its strategy of working at the state and local level. She was on good terms, however, with the leaders of the opposing National Woman Suffrage Association and boldly introduced SUSAN B. ANTHONY to the W.C.T.U. convention of 1881, thus precipitating a walkout of some conservative members.

Through eloquent addresses and a careful step-by-step approach, Frances Willard won her followers to the other causes she found significant. She accurately summarized her strategy in her handbook *Do Everything* (1895): "Every question of practical philanthropy or reform has its temperance aspect, and with that we are to deal" (p. vii). By 1889 thirty-nine W.C.T.U. departments had been formed. Each worked to educate the public and at the same time served as a pressure group to secure reform legislation. MARY H. HUNT headed the Department of Scientific Temperance Instruction, HANNAH J. BAILEY the Department of Peace and Arbitration. Other areas covered were labor reform, "social purity" (concerned with prostitution and the legal age of consent), health and hygiene, advice to young mothers, city welfare work, prison reform and the employment of police matrons, and work among Negroes. State organizations in the W.C.T.U. were autonomous, and the Southern states maintained separate unions for whites and blacks; there was apparently no discrimination at the national conventions.

Work on such a broad front was inevitably at times superficial, and doubtless for many members the W.C.T.U. continued merely to represent hostility to liquor. But some goals were achieved—legislation raising the age of consent, for example—and the publicity given to various causes made the path easier for other reform groups. In 1886 Miss Willard warmly praised the Knights of Labor, and for a time thereafter the two organizations exchanged fraternal delegates at their conventions.

Frances Willard's visit to San Francisco in 1883 led the W.C.T.U. into work on an international scale. Appalled by the opium addicts she saw in the city's Chinatown, she persuaded the W.C.T.U. to send to the Far East Mrs. MARY CLEMENT LEAVITT, the first of several temperance missionaries who set up Temperance Unions abroad and circulated the so-called "Polyglot Petition" through which some seven million women in various countries called on their leaders to take action against alcohol and narcotic drugs. From this evolved the World's W.C.T.U., which held its first convention in Boston in 1891, electing Miss Willard president. Delegates from twenty-one countries, said to represent a membership of nearly two million women, attended the fourth convention of the World's W.C.T.U., held in Toronto in 1897.

Occasionally Frances Willard lent her time to other organizations. In 1887 she was one of the first women—five in all—elected by local church conferences as delegates to the Methodist General Conference, only to be denied their seats by a small majority led by Bishop Charles H. Fowler. The next year she was a leader in the International Council of Women, a Washington gathering called by the suffragists to commemorate the Seneca Falls convention of 1848 and designed to unify the woman's movement by drawing together representatives of a wide variety of organizations. She headed the committee that drafted plans for permanent National and International Councils of Women, serving as the first president of the National Council (1888–90). In 1888, too, she was elected a vice-president of the Universal Peace Union, and the following year she helped found the General Federation of Women's Clubs. But it was the W.C.T.U. that dominated Frances Willard's life. "As I have long believed," she said in 1885, "it is God's way out of the wilderness for half the human race. In its glowing crucible, the dross of sectional enmity is being rapidly dissolved; the trifling occupations, the narrow aims, the paralyzing indolence of women are barriers burned away. . . ."

Probably the most controversial aspect of Miss Willard's career was her persistent attempt to bring the weight of the American W.C.T.U. to bear in party politics. In 1880 she had endorsed the Republican candidate for the presidency, James A. Garfield, believing that she had his pledge to support prohibition and woman suffrage. Disappointed the next year by his seeming repudiation of his pledge, she summoned a group of men and women prohibitionists to a conference which organized a "Home Protection" party. The leverage she was able to exert through this group induced the Prohibition party in 1882 to endorse woman suffrage and brought about a merger of the two parties and their names. Miss Willard hoped that the Prohibition–Home Protection party label would make politics more palatable to the women of the W.C.T.U. Most of them, however, shrank from the idea of a party alliance, and of the few who did not, some, like Mrs. J. ELLEN FOSTER of Iowa, a staunch Republican, preferred another party. Many Prohibitionists, on the other hand, objected to the suffrage plank in their platform, and in 1884 the party voted to resume its old name, the National Prohibition party. Miss Willard nevertheless continued to play an influential part in Prohibitionist councils. By 1884 her skillful appeals had converted the majority of the W.C.T.U. to "gospel politics," and the Union's support of the Prohibitionists, continued throughout Miss Willard's lifetime, did much to make that party a recognized political force.

By the 1890's Frances Willard had new political hopes. With sympathetic interest she watched the steps by which the gathering forces of agrarian unrest, represented by the Farmers' Alliances, joined with elements of the Knights of Labor and others to form a People's party. Envisioning its growth into a powerful national reform party in which women would take an active role, she conferred with Populist leaders in advance of a convention planned for St. Louis in February 1892. Her plan was to secure a Populist commitment to prohibition and woman suffrage and to bring the Prohibition party into the Populist fold. At St. Louis, however, the Prohibitionists, influenced by the Indiana leader HELEN GOUGAR, rebelled against Miss Willard's leadership, and with her political base lost, her grand design collapsed. This was a severe disappointment and a bitter personal defeat. She took part in one more effort, in March 1895, to unify the forces of reform, but the next year the free silver issue overrode all others, and she did not again attempt political combat. She had nevertheless been responsible for awakening the interest of thousands of women in political affairs.

In August 1892, shaken by the events at St. Louis and by the death of her mother, Frances Willard sought rest and solace in England with a friend, Lady Henry Somerset, for whom she had formed a strong attachment at the World's W.C.T.U. convention in 1891. A divorcée who lived a secluded life at Eastnor Castle in Herefordshire, Lady Henry was a devout Methodist and president of the British Women's Temperance Association. From the summer of 1892 until the end of 1896 Miss Willard spent only about sixteen months in the United States, residing the balance of the time with her English friend, writing, and attempting, with but little success, to win British temperance women to her "do everything" program. This interlude abroad profoundly influenced her own thinking. As early as 1889 she had made frequent contributions to *Dawn*, the Christian Socialist journal of the Episcopal minister W. D. P. Bliss, and now in England she joined the Fabian Society of Beatrice and Sidney Webb. Her W.C.T.U. presidential addresses of 1893 and 1894 were given over to espousals of socialism and the view that poverty was the prime cause of intemperance. More surprising to her followers, she abandoned a cardinal W.C.T.U. tenet and accepted Lady Henry's view that education, rather than prohibition, was the preferable solution to the liquor problem.

The long rest, however, only partially restored her spirits, and there were indications of a growing restlessness within the W.C.T.U. Miss Willard's increasingly unorthodox views

and prolonged absences, added to the long-standing dissatisfaction with her emphasis on politics, caused some grumbling. Many members felt that the organization should concentrate on the temperance issue. Growing problems of the Union clearly needed her closer attention, especially three Chicago ventures, the Woman's Temple and Woman's Temperance Publishing Association (see MATILDA BRADLEY CARSE) and the National Temperance Hospital. Dissatisfaction erupted at the national convention of 1897, the most acrimonious meeting over which she had ever presided. The rank and file, however, remained loyal, and Frances Willard was reelected president by a vote of 387 to 19.

As the century drew to a close, her health failed, sapped by chronic anemia. Much of the year following her final return from England was spent in a pilgrimage to ancestral shrines and childhood homes and at Dr. Cordelia A. Greene's sanatorium in Castile, N.Y. She died in a New York City hotel early in 1898 at the age of fifty-eight, of "grippe" and anemia. Funeral services were held in the Broadway Tabernacle, New York City, where two thousand people packed the auditorium. In Chicago, twenty thousand were estimated to have filed past her casket as the body lay in state for six hours at the Woman's Temple. After a second service at Evanston's First Methodist Church, she was buried in the family plot in Chicago's Rosehill Cemetery.

After Frances Willard's death the Woman's Christian Temperance Union sharply modified the "do everything" policy and ignored the heresies of her later years to concentrate on the issues of prohibition and total abstinence. Simultaneously, a cultlike worship of her memory produced an idealized myth of her life and thought, typified by such books as Anna Gordon's *The Beautiful Life of Frances E. Willard* (1898), which gives little hint of the complexities of her personality. In 1905 the State of Illinois placed her statue (by HELEN FARNSWORTH MEARS) in the national Capitol at Washington. Though her dream of an inclusive women's reformist organization had not been wholly realized, Frances Willard had succeeded for twenty years in holding the loyalty and confidence of a generation of conservative women initially largely indifferent to other reforms. By stressing the familiar themes of home, family, and temperance, she had gradually led them into many new channels of public activity.

[Mary Earhart (Dillon), *Frances Willard: From Prayers to Politics* (1944), contains a complete bibliography of Miss Willard's writings. Of these, in addition to her autobiography, see *Woman and Temperance* (1883), sketches of early W.C.T.U. leaders; *How to Win* (1886); *Woman in the Pulpit* (1889); *A Great Mother* (1894); and *A Woman of the Century* (1893), a biographical compendium of American women co-edited by Miss Willard and MARY A. LIVERMORE. The secondary works tend to be uncritical, but some, such as Ray Strachey, *Frances Willard: Her Life and Work* (1912), have value. There is considerable unpublished source material in the Willard Memorial Library, Nat. W.C.T.U. Headquarters, Evanston, Ill. Date and cause of death from records of N.Y. City Dept. of Health.]

MARY EARHART DILLON

WILLIAMS, Elizabeth Sprague (Aug. 31, 1869–Aug. 19, 1922), social worker, was born in Buffalo, N.Y., where her father's family had moved in the 1830's. She was the second daughter and last of the seven children of Frank and Olive (French) Williams, both natives of Connecticut. Her mother had been a schoolteacher before her marriage. Her father was a successful businessman who began as a civil engineer and surveyor and ended his career as a coal-mine owner. One of Miss Williams' brothers, Frank, achieved distinction as a Buffalo lawyer and civic leader and another, Herbert, as a pathologist.

Elizabeth Williams became interested in the social settlement movement while a student at Smith College. After graduating with a B.S. degree in 1891, she returned to Buffalo, where she established a library and children's classes. These activities eventually led to a settlement supported by the Unitarian congregation to which she belonged. Miss Williams left for New York City in the mid-1890's and acquired an A.M. degree from Columbia University in 1896. She took additional courses in the social sciences for the next year or two, supplementing her theoretical preparation for social service with practical experience as a resident of the College Settlement on Rivington Street. In the fall of 1898 she succeeded Mary M. Kingsbury (later Mrs. V. G. Simkhovitch, d. 1951) as head worker there.

Miss Williams remained in this position until 1919. During the two decades of her leadership the College Settlement immersed itself in reform crusades of the Progressive era. She encouraged residents to participate in such groups as the Charity Organization Society, the Consumers' League, the Public Education Association, the Outdoor Recreation League, the Committee on Amusements and Vacation Resources of Working Girls, and the Manhattan Trade School for Girls. In an effort to improve housing conditions and public health in the con-

gested Lower East Side, the College Settlement assisted the tenement-house committee of the Charity Organization Society in preparing its influential Tenement House Exhibition of 1900, and Miss Williams testified before a hearing called by the New York State Tenement House Commission that November. A few years later the College Settlement cooperated again with the Charity Organization Society in sponsoring a Tuberculosis Exhibit. No social crusade aroused Miss Williams' personal enthusiasm more than expanding educational facilities for the immigrant population. She regarded the public school as central to any Americanization program because it transmitted American values and ideals and also provided the educational opportunities through which immigrant children would enter the mainstream of national life. Interested particularly in trade or vocational training, Miss Williams reflected that broadened conception of the public school curriculum which linked the settlement and progressive-education movements in the early twentieth century. She served for a time as a member of her local school board.

Another strong influence for Americanization, in Elizabeth Williams' view, was settlement-sponsored group work. No settlement leader surpassed her in emphasizing the need for supervised club activity as an alternative to the dance halls, saloons, street gangs, and similar temptations which ensnared tenement youth. She interpreted the College Settlement's literary, social, and athletic clubs as miniature self-governing republics in which immigrant children and young adults acquired the self-control, discipline, and cooperative ethos indispensable for responsible citizenship in a democratic society. Mount Ivy, the College Settlement's summer farm and camp in Rockland County, N.Y., served the same ends. An object of Miss Williams' special affection and attention, it offered in her estimation an opportunity for club members to experience a simple, natural, cooperative existence that contrasted sharply with the artificiality and "overstimulation and sophistication of New York life."

Slim and slight in physical stature, Elizabeth Williams possessed a winsome personality and a maternal sensitivity which especially endeared her to children. Disturbed over the suffering of the young in the war-torn Balkans, she resigned her settlement post in 1919 and left for Serbia to establish an orphanage at Veles, near the Albanian border. She secured an American locomotive for the railroad that carried supplies to the town; after she returned to the United States in 1921, bringing an orphan she had adopted, the train's arrival in Veles is said to have reminded the children of their "Mother Elizabeth." The Serbian government assumed responsibility for the orphanage after her departure, and Miss Williams received a posthumous royal decoration for her services. She died of cancer in New York City in 1922, shortly before her fifty-third birthday, and was buried in Forest Lawn Cemetery, Buffalo.

No single dramatic contribution distinguishes Elizabeth Williams from her contemporaries among settlement and social reform leaders. Her persistent and self-conscious emphasis, however, upon club life as a shaper of character and citizenship illustrates with unusual clarity the settlement origins of what would later be known as social group work. Under Miss Williams' direction the College Settlement became not only a powerful influence for health, housing, sanitation, recreation, education, and labor reform in New York, but also an experimental laboratory for intensive work with small groups. Her contributions outside of New York City included the organization of the Lackawanna (N.Y.) Social Center in 1911 and a role in the negotiations leading to the formation of the National Federation of Settlements in the same year.

[The *Reports* of the College Settlements Assoc. from 1898 to 1919 constitute the best guide to the work of the N.Y. College Settlement under Elizabeth Williams' leadership and also provide insight into her understanding of the settlement movement's mission and function. Useful for biographical data are: *Who Was Who in America*, vol. I (1942); the "Alumnae Biog. Register Issue" (Nov. 1935) of the *Bull.* of Smith College; Jean Fine Spahr, "Elizabeth Williams: In Memoriam," *Smith Alumnae Quart.*, Nov. 1922; and obituary in *Buffalo* (N.Y.) *Express*, Aug. 21, 1922. Information on family background was supplied by Miss Alice J. Pickup, Librarian of the Buffalo and Erie County Hist. Soc., and Miss Olive Williams, a niece.]

ROY LUBOVE

**WILLIAMS, Fannie Barrier** (Feb. 12, 1855–Mar. 4, 1944), lecturer and clubwoman, was born in Brockport, N.Y., a small town near Rochester, one of three children, two daughters and a son. Hers was for many years the only Negro family in town. Her father, Anthony J. Barrier, a native of Philadelphia, had migrated to Brockport as a boy; her mother, Harriet (Prince) Barrier, was a native of Cherburne, N.Y. A barber and sometime coal merchant, Barrier was a homeowner, a respected member of the community, and a leader in the local Baptist church. Fannie attended the local

schools and the State Normal School at Brockport, graduating from the academic and classical course in 1870. She then taught school for some years in the South and in Washington, D.C. Having grown up in an environment free of overt prejudice or discrimination, she found conditions in the South "shattering" to her "cherished ideals." "I have never quite recovered," she wrote years later, "from the shock and pain of my first bitter realization that to be a colored woman is to be discredited, mistrusted and often meanly hated" (*Independent,* July 14, 1904, pp. 91–92). Sometime during these years she studied at the New England Conservatory of Music in Boston and the School of Fine Arts in Washington, D.C.

She was married in Brockport in 1887 to a young honors graduate of Washington's Columbian Law School, S. Laing Williams, a native of Georgia. They settled in Chicago, Ill., where Mrs. Williams helped her husband establish his law practice. She worked to secure a measure of recognition for Negroes at the World's Columbian Exposition planned for Chicago in 1893, and in May of that year, still relatively unknown, she spoke before the World's Congress of Representative Women at the exposition; her subject was "The Intellectual Progress of the Colored Women of the United States since the Emancipation Proclamation." This speech, together with one before the World's Parliament of Religions in September, brought local and national recognition. In the following year she became the center of a cause célèbre when her name was proposed for membership in the Chicago Woman's Club. After a year of controversy within the club and in the public press, she was admitted in 1895 as the "only colored member." As a result of this unsought notoriety Mrs. Williams became a popular speaker, in demand by church and club groups throughout the country. A talented musician as well as a winning personality, she frequently combined her lecture with a concert. Petite, light of skin, and vivacious in conversation, she once retained her seat in the first-class (white) coach of a Southern train by coolly informing the dubious conductor: "Je suis française." "I quieted my conscience," she wrote of this incident, "by recalling that there was quite a strain of French blood in my ancestry, and too that their barbarous laws did not allow a lady to be both comfortable and honest" (*ibid.*, p. 95).

Mrs. Williams, who had no children, was active in social welfare work in Chicago. She helped found two interracial benevolent institutions: the Provident Hospital, with its Training School for Nurses (1891), and the Frederick Douglass Center (1905), a settlement project. She was corresponding secretary of the board of directors of the Phyllis Wheatley Home Association and an active member of the Rev. Jenkin Lloyd Jones' All Souls Church (Unitarian) and its social welfare adjunct, the Abraham Lincoln Center.

Mrs. Williams early took up the cause of Negro women, whom she declared to be the "least known and most ill-favored class of women in the country." She received a steady stream of letters asking her help in finding employment. Quietly and with some success she urged employers to hire qualified Negro women applicants for positions of responsibility, pointing out that many were qualified for stenographic and clerical jobs from which their color alone barred them. In speeches and articles she urged Negro women to organize as white women did and focus their attention on race problems which particularly concerned their sex, in such areas as employment, child welfare, the family, education, and religion. She believed that the woman's club movement —representing (as she wrote in 1900) "a new intelligence against an old ignorance"—could be a means of arousing Negro women from what she called their "do-nothing, unsympathetic and discouraged condition." She was a moving spirit in the National League of Colored Women, formed in 1893; in its successor, the National Association of Colored Women; and in the Illinois Woman's Alliance.

After 1900 Fannie Williams took a strong stand in support of Booker T. Washington and his "heroic" efforts to train Negroes for existing opportunities through practical education. While conceding that "industrial education" was a narrow approach, she believed that its scope could be broadened by drawing in science and the arts to complement the practical instruction. Like Washington, she argued that the hope of Negro advancement was "practically dependent . . . upon the dominant race," and like him she played down the issue of social discrimination. In her address to the World's Congress of Representative Women (two years before Washington's famed "Atlanta Compromise") she declared: "[T]he colored people are in no way responsible for the social equality nonsense. . . . [E]quality before the law . . . is totally different from social equality."

Her championing of the ideas of the Tuskegee educator was perhaps not entirely disinterested. S. Laing Williams was Booker T. Washington's principal Chicago contact, and Mrs. Williams' most enthusiastic endorsements of Washington's position came when her husband was seeking a federal position through Washington's extensive patronage connections. (In 1908 he won appointment as an assistant United States district attorney.) This close identification with Booker T. Washington earned the Williamses the enmity of those Chicago Negro leaders—including Williams' onetime law partner Ferdinand Barnett and his wife IDA WELLS-BARNETT—who favored a more militant stand.

Laing Williams died in 1921. In 1924 Mrs. Williams became the first woman and the first Negro to serve on the Chicago Library Board. At the end of her term, in 1926, she retired to the family home in Brockport to live with her sister. Suffering increasingly the physical and mental disabilities of advanced age, she died of arteriosclerosis at the age of eighty-nine, and was buried in the Barrier family plot in Brockport's High Street Cemetery.

Fannie Barrier Williams was one of the earliest Negro leaders to identify residential segregation and limited employment opportunities as the two most critical areas of interracial relations. Segregated housing, she argued, demoralized and undermined family life, bred disease and crime, corrupted the political process, and denied to Negroes the economic, cultural, and health advantages available to whites. Employment prejudice blocked Negro advancement, stifled ambition, and perpetuated the stereotype of the Negro as incompetent and shiftless. An eloquent speaker and writer, a leader who saw beyond racial boundaries, in 1904 she reaffirmed her belief in "human love and justice," though she admitted that "progress is painful and my faith is often strained to the breaking point."

[Besides the important article "A Northern Negro's Autobiog.," *Independent*, July 14, 1904, Mrs. Williams' writings include: her addresses of 1893, as published in May Wright Sewall, ed., *The World's Cong. of Representative Women* (1894), II, 696–711, and John H. Barrows, ed., *The World's Parliament of Religions* (1893), II, 1114–15; "Opportunities and Responsibilities of Colored Women," in John T. Haley, comp., *Afro-Am. Encyc.* (1895), pp. 141–61; "Club Movement among Negro Women," in John W. Gibson and William H. Crogman, *Progress of a Race* (1902); "Industrial Education," *Colored American*, July 1904; "Social Bonds in the 'Black Belt' of Chicago," *Charities*, Oct. 7, 1905; "The Frederick Douglass Center," *Southern Workman*, June 1906. Biographical information from: Mrs. N. F. Mossell, *Work of the Afro-Am. Woman* (2nd ed., 1908), pp. 109–12; Elizabeth Lindsay Davis, *Lifting as They Climb* (1933), pp. 266–67; obituaries in *Chicago Tribune*, Mar. 8, 1944, *Chicago Defender*, Mar. 11, 1944, *Brockport* (N.Y.) *Republic-Democrat*, Mar. 9, 1944, and *N.Y. Times*, Mar.

8, 1944; local tax rolls, Village of Brockport, and various items in Seymour Museum, Brockport; interview with Miss Gertrude Page of Brockport, a second cousin of Mrs. Williams; death record from N.Y. State Dept. of Health (the source for her date of birth). Allan H. Spear, *Black Chicago* (1967), is an important secondary source. See also N.Y. State Teachers College, Brockport, *Semicentennial* (1917); and Charlotte E. Martin, *The Story of Brockport . . . 1829–1929* (1929?), pp. 21, 86–87.]

LESLIE H. FISHEL, JR.

**WILLIAMS, Mary Wilhelmine** (May 14, 1878–Mar. 10, 1944), historian, was born on an isolated farm in Stanislaus County, Calif. Her mother, Caroline Madsen, was a native of Bornholm, Denmark; her father, born in Dalecarlia, Sweden, was christened Carl Wilhelm Salander but changed his name to Charles Williams after emigrating to the United States. The large family, which included at least four daughters and two sons, was poor, and since the father forbade other expenditures until all debts were paid, they had few luxuries.

The courage and determination that later characterized Miss Williams are evident in the pattern of her early life. She attended local schools through the eighth grade and resumed her education only after an interval of several years, probably because of lack of money. At eighteen she entered the San Jose (Calif.) State Normal School, graduating in 1901. After a further interruption of three years, during which time she taught school, she enrolled in Stanford University. By carrying a heavy course load and taking summer classes at the University of California she obtained her A.B. degree at Stanford in three years, and the following year, 1908, her A.M. Although financial responsibilities made it necessary for her to return to public school teaching from 1908 to 1911, she had resolved to become a historian, and during the summers of these years she studied at the University of Chicago. To gather material for her doctoral dissertation, she traveled to Europe in 1911–12, doing research at the Public Record Office in London. She then returned to Stanford, where she served as instructor in history and received her Ph.D. in 1914. Her dissertation, *Anglo-American Isthmian Diplomacy, 1815–1915* (1916), based on the hitherto little-used records she had found in London and in the State Department files in Washington, won the Justin Winsor Prize of the American Historical Association. After a year (1914–15) as instructor in history at Wellesley College, she was called to Goucher College in Baltimore as assistant professor. There she remained until her retirement in 1940, becoming associate professor in 1919 and professor in 1920.

As a teacher Miss Williams is remembered for her complete and outspoken honesty, her exacting standards of scholarship, her insistence upon absolute mastery of subject matter, and her encouragement of students in carrying out independent research. At Goucher she added to the number of courses offered in American and Latin American history and in 1916–17 organized the first collegiate course in Canadian history given in the United States. A Viking in appearance, endowed with a marked sense of humor as well as unusual strength of character, she was a staunch feminist. Her courses included a history of the struggle for woman's rights, from which grew the articles on several leaders of the movement that she contributed to the *Dictionary of American Biography*.

Deeply interested in her teaching and in her students as individuals, Miss Williams still remained an active scholar throughout her teaching career. Her first publications after her doctoral dissertation resulted from a trip to her ancestral homeland: *Cousin-Hunting in Scandinavia* (1916), a travel account designed to acquaint Americans with the people of their "grandmother land," the land most closely related to England; and *Social Scandinavia in the Viking Age* (1920). Her major interest, however, remained Latin American history. A pioneer Latin Americanist among historians, and one who helped develop this field, she served on the board of editors of the *Hispanic American Historical Review* (1927–33) and, in the American Historical Association, as secretary of the Conference on Latin American History (1928–34). She also served on the association's executive council (1922–26). Besides many articles and reviews in the professional journals, Miss Williams wrote an account of John Middleton Clayton, signer of the Clayton-Bulwer Treaty for an Isthmian canal, which appeared in Volume VI (1928) of *American Secretaries of State and Their Diplomacy*. She also published *The People and Politics of Latin America* (1930), a general survey for college students which remained a standard work for nearly two decades; and a biography, *Dom Pedro the Magnanimous, Second Emperor of Brazil* (1937), the first study of this ruler to appear in English.

In 1918–19 the government of Honduras retained Miss Williams as a cartographic, geographic, and historical expert in connection with its boundary disputes with Guatemala and Nicaragua. In 1926–27, on behalf of the American Association of University Women, she traveled through fifteen Latin American countries to survey their facilities for higher education for women. The aviator Charles A. Lindbergh came to Goucher to consult with her in 1928 while planning his tour of South America. As an established authority, she was appointed by the State Department to serve on a number of committees dealing with problems of Latin America. In 1940 she received a decoration from the Dominican government in recognition of her work for inter-American understanding—a decoration that she wore with pride at that year's commencement exercises at Goucher.

Although a dedicated scholar, Miss Williams was not content with the cloister but was always active politically. She campaigned vigorously in behalf of peace and equal rights for women, wrote for both causes in magazines and newspapers, and expressed her convictions to her Senators in person. She helped found the Baltimore branch of the Women's International League for Peace and Freedom in 1923, and served as state chairman, 1934–36; she was also active locally in the National Woman's Party. In religion she was a Unitarian. Following her retirement in 1940 she settled in Palo Alto, Calif. She died there of a stroke in 1944, at the age of sixty-five; her ashes were buried in Alta Mesa Cemetery, Palo Alto. She left instructions that her grave be marked with her name and the words "Teacher, Historian, Pacifist, Feminist"—nouns that clearly define the scope of her life's work.

[The records of the Office of the President, Goucher College, contain correspondence, biographical and bibliographical data compiled by Miss Williams herself, and two major obituaries: *Palo Alto* (Calif.) *Times,* Mar. 11, 1944, and *Hispanic Am. Hist. Rev.,* Aug. 1944. See also *Who Was Who in America,* vol. II (1950). Prof. Ola E. Winslow, a former colleague, supplied reminiscences.]

RHODA M. DORSEY

WILLING, Jennie Fowler (Jan. 22, 1834–Oct. 6, 1916), Methodist local preacher, church worker, and temperance reformer, was born in Burford, Canada West (later Ontario), to Horatio and Harriet (Ryan) Fowler. Her mother was the daughter of the Rev. Henry Ryan, an Irishman whose prodigious labors in the wilderness had helped found Canadian Methodism; her father, of Connecticut ancestry, was a Canadian patriot who lost his property in the rebellion of 1837. After taking refuge with relatives in New York, Horatio Fowler in 1842 moved his family to a farm near Newark, Ill. There Jennie grew up, with at least two brothers, one of whom, Charles

Henry (1837–1908), was once briefly engaged to FRANCES E. WILLARD and later became president of Northwestern University and a bishop in the Methodist Episcopal Church. Because of delicate health, Jennie completed only a few months of formal schooling, but her natural curiosity, as well as her mother's example of reading informative books, spurred her on to a program of self-education so that at the age of fifteen she was able to begin teaching in the village school.

At nineteen Jennie was married to William C. Willing, four years her senior; they had no children. Leaving the law to enter the Methodist ministry, Willing held several pastorates in his native New York state. He then transferred to the Rock River Conference in northern Illinois, where he moved from one town to another, serving as presiding elder in both the Joliet and Chicago districts. Always he encouraged his wife to broaden her interests and activities. "You and I are partners," he once told her, "with equal rights and ownership." He arranged a local preacher's license for her, turning over to her all but nominal control of one Methodist charge. Over the years, she continued to preach on occasion, sometimes conducting revival meetings. Jennie Willing was also one of the early leaders of the suffrage movement in Illinois, being chosen recording secretary of the Chicago convention that formed the Illinois State Suffrage Association in 1869 (Elizabeth Cady Stanton et al., *History of Woman Suffrage,* III, 1886, p. 569n.).

Since girlhood Mrs. Willing had written essays, some of which appeared in church periodicals. Her published books and pamphlets, which eventually numbered nearly a score, as well as her many articles and stories, stressed themes of uplift, self-help, and Christian conduct of life. One article, "Helpmeets," appearing in the Methodist magazine for women, the *Ladies' Repository,* was sharply criticized for speaking of parsonage life as a "cross" and for being "strong and mannish" and "offensive to a refined taste." Her writings also attracted the attention of Methodist women who held advanced views. In 1872 the Evanston (Ill.) College for Ladies, of which Frances Willard was then president, awarded her an honorary A.M. degree. Two years later Jennie Willing was appointed professor of English language and literature at Illinois Wesleyan University in Bloomington, Ill. Her husband was given a law professorship there, and the two evidently commuted to Bloomington each week from Joliet, Ill., their home at that time.

Meanwhile, Mrs. Willing's interests had taken a new direction. During the winter of

1868 Mr. and Mrs. Edwin W. Parker, missionaries just returned from India, visited the Willings and other Methodist leaders in various parts of the United States. These visits led to the formation, in Boston on Mar. 30, 1869, of the Woman's Foreign Missionary Society of the Methodist Episcopal Church to support the denomination's missions. That June, Mrs. Willing organized an auxiliary in Rockford, Ill. (where the Willings were then living), and when provision was made for regional branches, she organized the Northwestern Branch in Chicago in March 1870 and the Western Branch in St. Louis in April. She "went through the territory like a whirlwind," the society's most recent historian has recorded, traveling widely to encourage the organization of local societies and young women's auxiliaries. For fourteen years, as corresponding secretary of the Northwestern Branch, she attended the annual meetings of the society's general executive committee. Through the columns of its paper, the *Heathen Woman's Friend*, she rejoiced at every evidence of success and offered sound advice on how to be useful as president, treasurer, or corresponding secretary of a local missionary society.

Mrs. Willing's second major cause was intemperance, "the other serpent," as she described slavery's successor. In the spring of 1874, as the Woman's Crusade against liquor selling spread through the Midwest, she helped organize a campaign for stricter license laws in Bloomington, giving eloquent public lectures in the evenings after her classes. That summer, while attending a training course for Sunday school teachers at Chautauqua Lake in New York, she and her friend EMILY HUNTINGTON MILLER met another temperance reformer, MARTHA MC CLELLAN BROWN. With the encouragement of the Rev. John H. Vincent, the three women made plans for a national women's temperance meeting, which convened on Nov. 18, 1874, at Cleveland, Ohio. On this occasion, with Mrs. Willing as temporary chairman, delegates from seventeen states officially organized the Woman's Christian Temperance Union, elected ANNIE L. WITTENMYER as their first president, and established a monthly paper, *Our Union*, with Jennie Willing as its first editor (June 1875–January 1876). For several years, beginning in the fall of 1874, she also served as president of the Illinois W.C.T.U. Because of the press of other duties she declined prohibitionist nomination that year for the post of state superintendent of public instruction.

Internal conflict over the exact role of the Woman's Foreign Missionary Society in the Methodist church structure led Mrs. Willing eventually to transfer her efforts to the cause of home missions, a field she had first explored in 1875, when she petitioned the church's Freedmen's Aid Society for the election of women to their board of managers. When the Woman's Home Missionary Society was formed after the 1880 Methodist General Conference, Mrs. Willing became general organizer and was a frequent contributor to its new magazine, *Woman's Home Missions*. In 1889 her husband moved to a charge in New York City, and Mrs. Willing turned her attention to the problems of immigrant girls. Continuing her work after her husband's death in 1894, she founded the New York Evangelistic Training School (1895), with settlement work as part of its program. Her last contribution to the *Christian Advocate*, the church's national magazine, a few months before her death, placed responsibility for the World War on "The European Sabbath." She died in New York City in 1916 at the age of eighty-two, leaving her estate to be divided equally between the Woman's Christian Temperance Union and the Evangelistic Training Schools of the Methodist Episcopal Church. At least two of her books of advice for young men were reprinted after her death.

Mrs. Willing's portraits, made during her forties and later, show a strong but pleasant face and sweet smile which must have characterized her many personal contacts. Contemporaries referred to her "rare culture of manner and of utterance," as well as her "clear brain, steady purpose, and consecrated heart." Although she held no important executive posts, she was a devoted and able promoter of the genteel causes of late nineteenth-century American Methodism.

[For general biographical data: Frances E. Willard, *Woman and Temperance* (1883), pp. 147–53; Frances E. Willard and Mary A. Livermore, eds., *A Woman of the Century* (1893); Ernest H. Cherrington, ed., *Standard Encyc. of the Alcohol Problem*, VI (1930), 2855–56; obituary in *Christian Advocate* (N.Y.), Nov. 9, 1916; *N.Y. Times*, Oct. 7, 27, 1916. Mrs. Willing's "Our Mother," *Ladies' Repository* (Cincinnati), Sept. 1873, gives impressions of her family background. For her brother Charles, see *Dict. Am. Biog.* For her husband, see obituary in *Christian Advocate* (N.Y.), Dec. 20, 1894; memoir in *Minutes* of the Annual Conferences of the Methodist Episcopal Church, Spring Conferences, 1895, p. 123; and Mrs. Willing's *A Prince of the Realm: Lessons from the Life of Rev. W. C. Willing, D.D.* (1895). For the Willings' professorships, see Elmo S. Watson, *The Ill. Wesleyan Story, 1850–1950* (1950). On Mrs. Willing and the Woman's Foreign Missionary Soc., see Frances J. Baker, *The Story of the Woman's Foreign Missionary Soc. of the Methodist Episcopal*

*Church* (rev. ed., 1898); the later history by Mary Isham, *Valorous Ventures* (1936); files of the *Heathen Woman's Friend*, 1869–84; and Theodore L. Agnew, "Reflections on the Woman's Foreign Missionary Movement in Late 19th-Century Am. Methodism," *Methodist Hist.*, Jan. 1968. For her home mission work, see files of *Woman's Home Missions*, 1884–1902 (e.g., Mrs. Willing's "How to Organize an Auxiliary," Jan. 1902); J. T. Gracey, "Woman's Home Missionary Soc., Art. I—Crucial Period," *Methodist Rev.*, Sept. 1887; and Laura E. (Mrs. T. L.) Tomkinson, *Twenty Years' Hist. of the Woman's Home Missionary Soc. of the Methodist Episcopal Church, 1880–1900* (1903). On her W.C.T.U. work, there is material in the Frances E. Willard Papers (Nat. W.C.T.U. headquarters, Evanston, Ill.); the *Minutes* of the Nat. W.C.T.U., 1874–77; and files of *Our Union*. See also the general biographical references, above; Mary Earhart, *Frances Willard* (1944); and Helen E. Tyler, *Where Prayer and Purpose Meet: The WCTU Story* (1949).]

THEODORE L. AGNEW

**WILLIS, Olympia Brown.** *See* BROWN, Olympia.

**WILLIS, Sara Payson.** *See* PARTON, Sara Payson Willis.

**WILMARTH, Mary Jane Hawes.** *See* ICKES, Anna Wilmarth Thompson.

**WILSON, Augusta Jane Evans** (May 8, 1835–May 9, 1909), novelist, the eldest of eight children of Matt Ryan Evans and Sarah Skrine (Howard) Evans, was born at Wynnton, on the outskirts of Columbus, Ga. Her mother was descended from Nehemiah Howard, a wealthy planter of pre–Revolutionary South Carolina, and her father was distantly related to eminent branches of the Crenshaw and Calhoun families of that state. Matt Evans, with his brother, had opened a general store in Columbus several months after the founding of that frontier town on the Chattahoochee River; by the year of Augusta's birth he had begun construction of a mansion, later named Sherwood Hall, which the family occupied in 1836. His prosperity was short-lived, however, for in the early 1840's floods, Indian depredations, and the commercial panic brought him to bankruptcy, and in 1845 he and his family set out for Texas in a covered wagon. They remained in Houston several months, then moved to Galveston and later to San Antonio. After four unsettled years they returned to Mobile, Ala., where poverty still plagued them. The tensions and uncertainties of Augusta's childhood help explain her preoccupation as a novelist with the theme of a strong-minded woman who is forced to combat privations and insecurity.

A precocious child, she read widely but had little formal education, though her mother found time during their Texas years to teach her children at home. Augusta always adored her mother and declared her "the one to whom I owe everything." At fifteen the serious young girl began writing a novel about a group of emigrants to Texas caught up in the Texas War of Independence. Published anonymously in 1855 by Harper (probably with a subsidy from a wealthy uncle), *Inez: A Tale of the Alamo* sacrificed the dramatic and historical possibilities of its plot to sentimental moralizing and anti-Catholic propaganda, which the author hoped would counteract the stigma still attached to the reading of novels.

Her youthful tilt against Catholicism led Augusta Evans into a frenzied but honest examination of her own religious belief, the Methodist fundamentalism her mother had taught her. By extensive reading of such authors as Carlyle, Emerson, and Kant she became convinced of the fallibility of human reason, and she allayed her own agonies of doubt by a renewed faith in the necessity of God and a determination to combat skepticism and reveal morality in her future novels. A similar crisis of doubt forms the major problem of her second novel, *Beulah*, published by Derby and Jackson in 1859. Called by a rival Southern novelist, Marion Harland (MARY VIRGINIA TERHUNE), "the best work of fiction ever published by a Southern writer," the book reached a printing of 22,000 copies within nine months and brought her the first prosperity she had known since childhood.

Her trips north in 1859 to arrange for publication of her second novel had made her aware of the dangers threatening the South. Uncompromising on matters of right and wrong, and believing firmly in the morality of the Southern cause, Miss Evans late in 1860 broke her engagement to James Reed Spalding, earnest young editor of the New York *World* and a dedicated supporter of Lincoln, whom she had met the year before. Turning her energies to the Confederate cause, she organized a hospital at an army camp near Mobile, three times followed soldier-relatives to the very edge of battlefields, and corresponded with some of the most prominent Confederate leaders on matters of military strategy and appointments. During this period she published anonymous propaganda articles in a Mobile newspaper, and her third novel, *Macaria; or, Altars of Sacrifice*, published in Richmond in 1864, was a persuasive defense of Confederate policy intended to lift the morale of the South. It contained accounts of the battles at Manassas taken directly from reports by Gen. P. G. T. Beauregard, who had visited the Evans family in Mobile. Many passages were written on wrapping paper as she nursed wounded soldiers, and the publishers printed the book on crude paper with a binding of wallpaper-covered boards. So effective was its argument that a Federal general is said to have banned it among his troops and to have burned all available copies. *Macaria* was smuggled to New York via blockade-runner and reprinted there, bringing profits which, secured by friends, supported the author through immediate postwar stringencies.

After the war the Evans family sheltered their old friend Gen. Robert Toombs when he was a fugitive in the spring of 1865. Augusta Evans led the drive to secure burial of Mobile's war dead in Magnolia Cemetery and to erect a Confederate memorial monument, but she wasted no time in mourning a cause she realized was lost forever and gave up her idea of writing a Confederate history, knowing that a novel would sell better. *St. Elmo,* her best-known work, appeared in December 1866 and enjoyed a phenomenal popularity in the nineteenth century, exceeded only by such favorites as *Uncle Tom's Cabin* and *Ben Hur.* The predominantly feminine novel-reading audience was undoubtedly fascinated by the Byronic hero, reclaimed from sin by the heroine's cautious affection and ardent prayers. Adapted for the stage, the story was produced many times between 1909 and 1915, and a silent film version in 1923 added to its popularity.

Meanwhile, a nursing mission to the home of a wealthy neighbor, Col. Lorenzo Madison Wilson, financier and owner of a Mobile street railway company, had started a friendship that ripened to affection. Although Wilson was twenty-seven years Augusta's elder, a widower with grown children, they were married on Dec. 2, 1868. Believing that any woman should put her domestic duties first, she assumed management of Ashland, her husband's estate, with its servants, gardens, and five greenhouses, and cared for an adolescent stepdaughter. She was accustomed to budgeting her time and working on a strict schedule, and thus managed to write four hours a day until she finished *Vashti,* her fifth novel, which appeared in October 1869. Its popularity did not approach that of *St. Elmo,* but it added to her royalties, which averaged more than $10,000 a year for thirty years. By 1870 her health demanded a slower pace. She and her husband traveled widely seeking relief from the violent attacks of hay fever and from the insomnia which had troubled her from the time she began writing.

Always a careful writer, she now produced only a few hundred words a month. In 1875 she published *Infelice,* closer to melodrama than the earlier novels. *At the Mercy of Tiberius* (1887) contains realistic details, some good dialect humor, and the beginnings of an excellent murder mystery, smothered by didacticism. *A Speckled Bird* (1902) opposed woman suffrage and labor unions, and *Devota* (1907), her last work, written as a short story but published in book form, was embellished by sophisticated discussions of child delinquency and the evils of the Populist movement.

After her husband's death in 1891, Mrs. Wilson moved to her sister's home in Mobile and later occupied a large Victorian town house. During the last fifteen years of her life her brother Howard was her constant companion, and his death in 1908 was a severe blow. She suffered a fatal heart attack at her home the next year, the day after her seventy-fourth birthday, and was buried in Magnolia Cemetery in Mobile. Her work has interested later generations primarily as an example of what made a best seller in nineteenth-century America.

[For a full-scale treatment, see William P. Fidler, *Augusta Evans Wilson, 1835–1909: A Biog.* (1951). Primary sources: letters in the Univ. of Ala. Library and in the Curry Papers, Library of Congress; files on Augusta Evans Wilson and her father in Ala. Dept. of Archives and Hist., Montgomery; family letters and recollections furnished by a niece, Miss Lily Bragg of Mobile; recollections of the Wilson family furnished by Miss Mary Gaillard, Mobile; files of Mobile *Advertiser* and *Register*.]

WILLIAM P. FIDLER

**WILSON, Ellen Louise Axson** (May 15, 1860– Aug. 6, 1914), first wife of Woodrow Wilson, twenty-eighth president of the United States, was born in Savannah, Ga., the first of four children of the Rev. Samuel Edward Axson and Margaret Jane (Hoyt) Axson. Both of her grandfathers were, like her father, Presbyterian ministers: Isaac Stockton Keith Axson in Savannah and Nathan Hoyt in Athens, Ga. Ellen Axson grew up in Presbyterian manses in Beech Island, S.C., McPhersonville, S.C., Madison, Ga., and Rome, Ga. The last town she considered her home, since she lived there from 1865 to 1883. Nothing is known about her early education. She graduated from the Rome (Ga.) Female College in 1876 and studied at the Art Students' League in New York City in 1882 and 1884–85.

Ellen Axson met her future husband in Rome, Ga., on Apr. 8, 1883. Wilson, then a fledgling lawyer in Atlanta, had gone to Rome to effect the division of an uncle's estate. He fell in love with Ellen almost at first sight and returned to Rome about May 27 for a visit that lasted until the end of June. Afraid to propose because he thought she would refuse him, he pressed his courtship by correspondence during the balance of the summer. In mid-September both happened by sheer coincidence to be in Asheville, N.C., on the same day, and Wilson glimpsed Ellen in a hotel window. Resolved not to miss this opportunity, for he was about to go to Baltimore for graduate study at the Johns Hopkins University, he proposed that weekend, and Ellen, dazed and tongue-tied, accepted.

They saw each other only infrequently over the next two years, while Wilson studied at Johns Hopkins and Ellen lived at home and, during her year of art study, in New York. Their daily letters of this period are among the greatest love letters in the English language. Ellen's are also extremely revealing of her philosophy, religious beliefs, and literary and cultural interests. Troubled by religious doubts, she read Hegel and Kant to reinforce her faith. She was well versed in most branches of English and American literature, particularly in the English Romantic and Victorian poets. The two were married on June 24, 1885, at the Savannah home of Ellen's grandfather Axson, who performed the ceremony together with Wilson's father, also a Presbyterian minister.

For the next three years the couple lived in Bryn Mawr, Pa., while Wilson taught at the new Bryn Mawr College for women. They moved in 1888 to Wesleyan University in Middletown, Conn., and in 1890 to Princeton, N.J., where Wilson held a professorship at Princeton University before becoming its president. Ellen gave most of her time during these years to her husband and to her three daughters—Margaret, born in 1886, Jessie Woodrow (1887), and Eleanor Randolph (1889). Mrs. Wilson educated her children at home before they went to preparatory schools and personally oversaw their religious instruction. As she began to find some leisure time in the early 1890's, she worked in a volunteer women's employment society in Princeton. In 1895–96 she sketched the plans for the house that she and her husband built the following year. About this time she took up painting again, an avocation that she would follow for the remainder of her life. From 1902 to 1910 she presided over the president's house at Princeton, whose graduates long remembered the warmth of her hospitality.

Life changed drastically for Mrs. Wilson in 1910 with her husband's entry into politics and his election as governor of New Jersey. Though she shared the Victorian ideal of the woman as helpmate and homemaker, she took an active interest in her husband's political career and gave him vital assistance in his fight for the Democratic presidential nomination in 1912. It was she who personally arranged for her husband to meet the Democratic leader, William Jennings Bryan, in March 1911.

One of Mrs. Wilson's early official acts after Woodrow Wilson had been elected president was to announce that there would be no inaugural ball, a decision indicative of her modest style as First Lady. Spurning the company of Washington's social elite, she presided over the White House with quiet dignity but continued to devote herself to her husband and family, using her free time for humanitarian work. She visited Washington's crowded alley slums, often with food and clothing in hand, and worked quietly among Congressmen for enactment of a measure to provide decent housing for Negroes. She toured governmental departments and had rest rooms for women workers installed where there were none. And one might have found her any day at a meeting of social workers, as a member of the Board of Associated Charities, listening patiently to a case worker describe the plight of a needy family.

Mrs. Wilson fell in her room on Mar. 1, 1914. Although no one yet knew it, she was suffering from tuberculosis of the kidneys and Bright's disease. Rallies alternated with declines as the disease ran its fatal course during the following months. That May saw the White House wedding of her daughter Eleanor to William Gibbs McAdoo, Wilson's Secretary of the Treasury. Ellen Wilson died in Washington that August, at the age of fifty-four, but not before she knew that Congress had approved her bill for alley clearance. She was buried in Myrtle Hill Cemetery in Rome, Ga. The lonely Wilson on Dec. 18, 1915, married Edith Bolling Galt (1872–1961).

Ellen Axson Wilson had been incomparably the greatest influence in the life and career of Woodrow Wilson during the crucial formative years of his young manhood as well as during his years of maturity. Her love made him a whole man and perfected his personality, for he was utterly dependent upon love and understanding for the realization of his own powers. In addition, she was a wise counselor to her sometimes impetuous husband, who on several critical occasions profited from her counsel of patience and self-restraint.

[The chief source of knowledge of Ellen Axson Wilson is her correspondence with Woodrow Wilson, amounting to some 2,500 letters, all of which are in the Wilson Collection at Princeton Univ. All of these letters—and numerous other letters by and about Mrs. Wilson—are being published in Arthur S. Link et al., eds., *The Papers of Woodrow Wilson* (1966– ). Eleanor Wilson McAdoo, *The Priceless Gift* (1962), prints a selection of the letters between her parents. Mrs. McAdoo's *The Woodrow Wilsons* (1937) is an affectionate family memoir. "McGregor" (A. J. McKelway), "The Social Activities of the White House," *Harper's Weekly*, Apr. 25, 1914, and Mrs. Ernest P. Bicknell, "The Home-Maker of the White House," *Survey*, Oct. 3, 1914, are excellent pen portraits of Mrs. Wilson as First Lady.]

ARTHUR S. LINK

**WILSON, Helen Hopekirk.** *See* HOPEKIRK, Helen.

**WILSON, Ida Lewis.** *See* LEWIS, Ida.

**WILSON, Sarah** (b. 1750), adventuress, self-styled "Marchioness de Waldegrave," was born in a little Staffordshire village in England. Dissatisfied with her humdrum existence, she went while still in her teens to seek her fortune in London. There she secured employment as a servant with Caroline Vernon, a maid of honor to Queen Charlotte. One evening in the spring of 1771 she slipped into the Queen's boudoir and stole a gown, a diamond necklace, and a miniature of the Queen. When she yielded to temptation a second time that night, however, she was discovered. Tried and found guilty of burglary, she was sentenced to death, but on the intervention of her mistress and the Queen, the verdict was commuted to indentured service in the American colonies.

When the convict ship arrived at Maryland in the autumn of 1771, Sarah was bought by William Devall of Bush Creek, Frederick County. Not one to endure servitude, she shortly escaped. Capitalizing upon the jewelry, the gown, and the Queen's picture—which had somehow eluded the authorities—she traveled up and down the colonies under the assumed name of Susanna (or Sophia) Carolina Matilda, Marchioness de Waldegrave, sister of the Queen of England. For eighteen months she visited in Virginia, North and South Carolina, and Georgia, displaying the miniature of "her sister" the Queen, winning the hospitality of people of the first rank of society, and promising government posts or commissions in the army to her hosts in return for the necessary fees. Among her victims were the Pages of Rosewell, the Rev. James Horrocks of Williamsburg, Va., and Samuel Cornell of New

Bern, N.C., who introduced her to the governor of that colony.

Meanwhile William Devall had hired Michael Dalton, an attorney, to track Sarah down and had offered a reward for her return. An advertisement in the *Virginia Gazette*, June 3, 1773, and other papers described her as having a "blemish in her right eye, black roll'd hair, stoops in her shoulders." From this point on, surviving accounts differ. One has her avoiding capture, making her way via Philadelphia, New York, and Newport to Boston (where she landed in January 1774) and thence to Portsmouth and Newcastle, N.H., returning to Newport (where the *Mercury* printed a notice of her arrival and departure for New York in July 1775), and then disappearing from view. Another says she was apprehended in 1773 but escaped from her master a second time in 1775, wended her way north, and eventually became the wife of Capt. William Talbot of the British army. In either case her later history is unknown.

Under different circumstances Sarah Wilson might have attained repute in a legitimate field. Certainly she had gifts as an actress and must have possessed charm and wit. As it was, she had to be content with the encomium of that Boston printer who described her as "the most surprizing genius of the female sex that was ever obliged to visit America" (as reported in the *Providence Gazette*, Jan. 22, 1774).

[For a brief factual account of Sarah Wilson see Carl Bridenbaugh, *Cities in Revolt* (1955), pp. 345–46, and for a longer and more imaginative one, Neville Williams, *Knaves and Fools* (1959), pp. 1–9. An account, part fiction, part fact, may also be found in Alice Morse Earle, *Colonial Dames and Good Wives* (1895), pp. 165–72.]

ELIZABETH F. HOXIE

**WINNEMUCCA, Sarah** (c. 1844–Oct. 16, 1891), Indian leader, was born among the Piute tribe at the Humboldt Sink in what is now Nevada, at a time when only a few white trappers and explorers had penetrated the barren Great Basin plateau. Her Indian name was Thoc-me-tony, or "Shell-Flower." She was the second daughter of Winnemucca II, the Piute chief, and fourth, apparently, of his nine children. Her grandfather Winnemucca I, better known as Captain Truckee, is said to have guided Capt. John C. Frémont across the Sierra Nevada to California in the winter of 1845–46. In 1850, impressed by the white man's ways, he took a number of his people, including his granddaughter, to work for a time on a ranch in the San Joaquin Valley. With her gift for languages Shell-Flower learned Spanish as well as English. Her facility with English increased after her return to Nevada, when she spent about a year in the home of Major William Ormsby, a stage company agent living in the new Mormon trading post of Genoa, as his daughter's companion. Here she assumed the name Sarah and became a nominal Christian without losing her primitive beliefs, which centered on a "Spirit Father." In 1860, at her grandfather's dying request, she was sent to school at St. Mary's Convent in San Jose, Calif. Her formal education, however, ended abruptly after three weeks when objections from wealthy parents to the presence of an Indian child forced the nuns to send her home.

The influx of white settlers into western Nevada and the first clash with the Indians (the Piute war of 1860) brought the establishment of a Piute reservation at Pyramid Lake (north of the later town of Reno). There began the griefs of Sarah's people at the hands of corrupt Indian agents, who at best did nothing to help the Piutes adjust to the white man's ways, and at worst exploited them, leaving them starving and destitute. In 1865 worse trouble erupted when the Piutes stole some white men's cattle. In retaliation, soldiers from a nearby army post marched against the Indian camp while the warriors were off on a hunt, killed women, children, and old men, set fire to the reed huts, and were even said to have hurled small children into the flames. "I had one baby brother killed there," Sarah wrote. A manhunt flourished for a year; Sarah's mother died during this time, and then her sister, while her own hatred for the Indian agents, whom she regarded as the authors of their disasters, grew obsessive. Without resources, many of the Piutes, in preference to further fighting, flocked to military posts for the rations the army issued them; and as Sarah knew five languages, counting three Indian tongues, she served for several years (c. 1868–71) as post interpreter at Camp McDermitt in northeastern Nevada. In 1871, by most reports, she was married to Lieut. E. C. Bartlett, but left him within a year because of his intemperance; she later married an Indian husband, whom she also left for gross abuse.

In 1872 the luck of the Piutes changed with the establishment of the Malheur Reservation in southeastern Oregon and the appointment of Samuel Parrish, the only Indian agent Sarah ever completely trusted. Accompanying her father and others of her tribe to the new reservation, she became Parrish's interpreter in 1875 and later assisted at the agency school. The next year, however, Parrish was replaced by the unpopular and less generous Major William V.

Rinehart, who banished Sarah from the agency when she reported his conduct. She soon learned that most of the other Piutes were fleeing the reservation, some joining the Bannocks, an Idaho tribe, who were more and more discontented with their treatment and ready for the warpath.

When the Bannock war broke out in June 1878, Sarah offered her services to the army. Although she had no use for civilian Indian agents, she felt, as did many of her people, that the army treated the Indians fairly and could be relied on. In turn, the military trusted her; she was requested to ask several Piute men to scout the hostile country. They refused, afraid; but when she heard that her own father was a member of a Piute band forced against its will to join the Bannocks she volunteered to go herself. Traveling without sleep, she followed Bannock trails for over a hundred miles, "through the roughest part of Idaho," into eastern Oregon, to where her father's lodges stood encircled by the hostile Indian camp; she spirited away her father and a number of his followers and brought the troops much needed information. She then served as Gen. Oliver O. Howard's guide, scout, and interpreter during the campaign.

As early as 1870, when she had visited Gen. John M. Schofield in San Francisco, Sarah Winnemucca had voiced her people's protest over the wrongs committed against them. After the Bannock war she lectured in San Francisco, appealing especially on behalf of those Piutes who had not fought but were nonetheless exiled with the hostile Indians to the Yakima Reservation in Washington Territory. One spectator described her as "nearly beautiful," of medium height, with old-gold skin and expressive eyes; she spoke "in good English" and with "such persuasion and conviction . . . that many people were moved to tears" (Haine, pp. 153–54). The press responded warmly to her vehement indictment of the Indian agents, and her talks received wide notice. Retaliation by the so-called "Indian Ring" ran to slander; her opponents suborned testimony which branded her as a liar and a "drunken prostitute," but she would not be silenced. That winter she received an invitation to come to Washington with her father and others at government expense, and there in January 1880 she pleaded the Indians' cause before Secretary of the Interior Carl Schurz and President Rutherford B. Hayes. The Secretary authorized the Piutes' return to Malheur, where they were promised individual allotments of land; but the Yakima agent refused to release those in his charge, fearing their passage southward would arouse white settlers and provoke bloodshed. Though many gradually drifted south, Chief Winnemucca refused to lead his own band back to Malheur while any Piutes remained at Yakima.

At General Howard's invitation Sarah next went to Vancouver (Wash.) Barracks, where she taught a school of Indian children for a year. She was now courted by Lieut. L. H. Hopkins, to whom she was married late in 1881, and who later went east with her for the lecture tour she planned in the interest of her people. None had received the "land in severalty" promised by Secretary Schurz, and the Malheur reserve had been allowed to revert to the public domain, for the benefit seemingly of white stockgrowers. Introductions from such patrons as General Howard ensured her warm welcome in Boston, where ELIZABETH PEABODY and MARY PEABODY MANN took up her cause. Sponsored by such respected reformers, she spoke in Massachusetts, Rhode Island, Connecticut, New York, Pennsylvania, and Maryland. Out of the lectures grew a quaint volume, *Life among the Piutes,* privately printed in 1883, after Mrs. Mann had tidied up the manuscript. Written with difficulty, often marred by confused development and inaccuracies of detail, sometimes, in faulty understanding, blaming the agents for things they could not help, the book was nevertheless honest, free from willful misrepresentation, vivid, and full of naive charm. Its sale at Sarah's lectures helped defray the expenses of the tour. She managed now to secure thousands of signatures to a petition calling on the government to grant lands in severalty to the Piutes, and in 1884 Congress passed such a bill; but the Secretary of the Interior declined to execute it.

Meanwhile Leland Stanford, the California railroad builder, had given Sarah's brother an undeveloped ranch near Lovelock, Nev., and there she opened a school for Piute children. She taught for three years with remarkable success, though half paralyzed with rheumatism and shaken with recurrent fevers. In 1886 her husband died of tuberculosis; then, exhausted by her struggles, Sarah retired to a married sister's home in Monida, Mont., where she spent her last years in failing health, herself a victim of consumption, and died before the age of fifty. White men often called her "the Princess," and the Piutes, "Mother"; both were well-merited titles, for she had fought against gigantic odds for the welfare of her people. Outwardly a failure, she remained important for the magnitude of what she had attempted; and at her death she was called "the most famous Indian woman of the Pacific Coast." General Howard concluded that her name "should have a place beside the name of Pocahontas in the history of our country."

[Her own *Life among the Piutes* remains the fullest account of Sarah Winnemucca's life, although George F. Brimlow is at work on a book-length biography. See also a reminiscent sketch by her in the *Californian,* Sept. 1882, and a letter in the appendix of Helen Hunt Jackson, *A Century of Dishonor* (1885). Pertinent archival materials are filed among the records of the Bureau of Indian Affairs in the Nat. Archives (see in particular Special File No. 286). Two pamphlets by Elizabeth Peabody have primary importance: *Sarah Winnemucca's Practical Solution of the Indian Problem* (1886) and *The Second Report of the Model School of Sarah Winnemucca* (1887). Gen. O. O. Howard incorporated sympathetic memories of her in *My Life and Personal Experiences among Our Hostile Indians* (1907) and in *Famous Indian Chiefs I Have Known* (1908), as well as in *St. Nicholas* for July 1908, supplemented there by a sketch by Charles E. S. Wood. See also William Wright ("Dan De Quille"), *Hist. of the Big Bonanza* (1877); and the memoirs of Jean J. F. Haine in *Calif. Hist. Soc. Quart.,* June 1959, pp. 153–55. Newspaper references include *Sacramento* (Calif.) *Record Union,* Jan. 16, 1875; San Francisco *Alta California,* Nov. 26, Dec. 4, 7, 24, 1879; *San Francisco Chronicle,* Nov. 23, 1879; *San Francisco Morning Call,* Nov. 22, 1879, Oct. 18, 1883, Oct. 3, Dec. 8, 1884, Jan. 22, Feb. 4, 11, 22, 1885, Feb. 23, Apr. 1, 1886; *Va. City* (Nev.) *Territorial Enterprise,* Jan. 14, 1875; and an obituary in the *Helena* (Mont.) *Daily Herald,* Nov. 4, 1891. Other newspaper items were provided by the Nev. Hist. Soc. Secondary sources include: George F. Brimlow, "The Life of Sarah Winnemucca: The Formative Years," *Oreg. Hist. Quart.,* June 1952, and two books by Brimlow, *The Bannock Indian War of 1878* (1938) and *Harney County, Oreg., and Its Range Land* (1951); Katharine C. Turner, *Red Men Calling on the Great White Father* (1951), chap. xii; Sam P. Davis, *The Hist. of Nev.* (2 vols., 1913); Royal R. Arnold, *Indian Wars of Idaho* (1932); Otto L. Hein, *Memories of Long Ago* (1925); Frederick W. Hodge, *Handbook of Am. Indians,* Part II (1910); J. F. Santee, "Egan of the Piutes," *Wash. Hist. Quart.,* Jan. 1935; Robert Heizer, "Notes on Some Paviotso Personalities and Material Culture," *Nev. State Museum, Anthropological Papers,* no. 2 (1960); Lalla Scott, *Karnee: A Paiute Narrative* (1966).]

THURMAN WILKINS

**WINSER, Beatrice** (Mar. 11, 1869–Sept. 14, 1947), librarian and museum director, was born in Newark, N.J., the eldest of three children of Henry Jacob and Edith (Cox) Winser. Her father, a journalist, was a native of Bermuda; her mother was a daughter of Dr. Henry G. Cox, a Bermudian who became a prominent physician in New York City. Two months after the birth of his daughter Beatrice, Henry Winser left an editorial position on the *New York Times* to become United States consul general at the court of the Duke of Saxe-Coburg, a post he held for twelve years. On his return he served as assistant editor of the New York *Commercial Advertiser* and then as managing editor of the *Newark Advertiser*.

During her childhood years in Germany, Miss Winser learned French and German and developed an interest in books. In 1888 she enrolled in the newly established Columbia University Library School, and the following year she joined the staff of the Newark Public Library as a cataloguer of French and German books. She became assistant librarian in 1894, serving first under Frank P. Hill and then under the dynamic John Cotton Dana, who was appointed librarian in 1902. A crusader who believed that education was a stronger force for social reform than either the law or the ministry, Dana was convinced that the wide circulation of books among both adults and children would help provide that education. Stimulated by his enthusiasm, Miss Winser became an energetic and able assistant. She strongly supported his advocacy of the open-shelf system; working together, they made it their business to "put into the hands of all the people they could reach all the books they could read." On Dana's death in 1929 she succeeded him as librarian.

Miss Winser's second great interest was the Newark Museum, founded in 1909 by Dana as the outgrowth of an exhibit of Japanese art at the Newark Library. The museum rapidly expanded to include exhibits and books in the fields of industry and science as well as art. Miss Winser shared Dana's belief that museums should be "the handmaidens of our schools," and she gave particular attention to the Junior Museum Club, where children were encouraged to develop their individual interests, such as the collecting of rocks, insects, or birds. She assumed many of the duties of managing the new institution, in 1915 becoming assistant director and assistant secretary and, the following year, a member of the board of trustees. After Dana's death she was chosen director and secretary and continued to maintain a close working relationship between the museum and the library. Among the exhibits held during her museum directorship were: "American Primitive Painting" (1930) and "American Folk Sculpture" (1931), which gave early impetus to the appreciation of American folk art; "Aviation" (1932), on a Newark industry; and "Three Southern Neighbors: Ecuador, Bolivia, Peru" (1941), to promote the current

good-neighbor policy. During the depression years she inaugurated Sunday concerts and an arts workshop for adults.

In 1915 Miss Winser was appointed to the Newark Board of Education, the first woman ever to serve on a governing board of the city. A few months later she offered a specific proposal to reorganize the system in such a way as to give broader powers and more responsibility to the superintendent of schools and to diminish the authority of the board itself. When the plan was defeated and her chief opponent became president of the board, she resigned as a matter of principle.

Miss Winser was a charter member of the New Jersey Library Association, founded in 1890, and served as its president for the years 1907–08 and 1921–22. In the American Library Association she was a member of the Council of Fifty (1909–12, 1930) and second vice-president (1931). In 1918 she became a member of the women's committee of the New Jersey College for Women (later Douglass College). She resigned as head of the Newark Public Library in 1942, charging that the trustees were interfering with its administrative functions and hoping that this dramatic step would help guarantee the future of the library as the kind of free public institution she and Dana had built. She stayed on, however, as head of the museum until a few months before her death.

An energetic woman with a "strong voice, hearty laugh, [and] quick sympathy," Miss Winser was an effective agent in establishing the Newark Library and Museum as integral parts of the complex industrial city. Although she seldom involved herself in national issues, she opposed federal aid to libraries lest it lead to political control, opposed prohibition, and took a firm stand against the censorship of foreign books by customs officials. When in 1937 the University of Newark (later part of Rutgers—The State University of New Jersey) conferred on her the honorary degree of Doctor of Laws, the citation characterized her as "an ideal public servant and a luminous personality." She died at her home in Newark of arteriosclerotic heart disease in 1947, at seventy-eight. After Episcopal services at the Trinity Cathedral in Newark, she was buried in the family plot in Greenwood Cemetery, Brooklyn, N.Y.

[Newark Museum, *Beatrice Winser, 1869–1947* (booklet, 1948); Newark Public Library, *This Is to Be a People's Library* (1963); *Who Was Who in America*, vol. II (1950); information from Newark Museum and Library files. See also Beatrice Winser, ed., *John Cotton Dana* (1930), and Chalmers

Hadley, *John Cotton Dana* (1943); *N.Y. Times,* Apr. 27, 1947 (tribute by Edward Alden Jewell), Sept. 16, 1947 (obituary), Sept. 18, 1947 (editorial). Death record from N.J. State Dept. of Health. On her father and grandfather, see *Appletons' Cyc. Am. Biog.*]

KATHERINE COFFEY

**WINSLOW, Catherine Mary Reignolds.** *See* REIGNOLDS, Catherine Mary.

**WINTER, Alice Vivian Ames** (Nov. 28, 1865–Apr. 5, 1944), woman's club leader and author, was born in Albany, N.Y., the first of the two daughters of Charles Gordon Ames and his second wife, FANNY BAKER AMES. A half brother, the only child of her father's first marriage, completed the family. As the daughter of a Unitarian clergyman, Alice spent her early years on California mission fields and in the Philadelphia and Boston areas. Her childhood environment offered unusual opportunities for the development of a sense of social responsibility. Her father preached and practiced a religion of service and believed in the equality of the sexes; her mother was active in various church and woman suffrage organizations and was a pioneer in the charity organization movement. Family friends included leading reformers of the day. An aspiring artist, Alice for a time studied at the Pennsylvania Academy of the Fine Arts. She did not pursue this career, but art remained a lifelong avocation. Graduating from Wellesley College in 1886, she received an M.A. in 1889 in political science and Greek and thereafter taught for two years (1890–92) in Mrs. Shaw's School in Boston as principal of the upper department.

On June 25, 1892, Alice Ames was married in Boston to Thomas Gerald Winter, a twenty-nine-year-old English-born Canadian whom she had met while vacationing in the Canadian Rockies. The young couple settled in Minneapolis, Minn., where Winter became president of a grain firm. They had two children: Charles Gilbert, born in 1893, and Edith Ames (1895). The household also included an orphaned niece and nephew from Winter's side of the family.

While still a young mother, Mrs. Winter became interested, through Mrs. CLARA UE-LAND, in the kindergarten movement. During the 1890's, as president of the Minneapolis Kindergarten Association, she led a successful campaign for the inclusion of kindergartens in the public schools. She also did some writing, publishing two unexceptional romantic novels, *The Prize to the Hardy* (1905) and *Jewel Weed* (1906), which expressed faith in the common man. Grief-stricken by the accidental death of her son in 1907, Alice Winter turned for relief to further activities outside the home. She was the first president (1907–15) of the Woman's Club of Minneapolis. She also served on the Minneapolis Playground Commission and the Minnesota Child Labor Committee and founded a college woman's club. In World War I, her leadership abilities now well recognized, she directed the Minneapolis chapter of the American Red Cross and served as head of the woman's committee of the Minnesota Council of National Defense.

Mrs. Winter first achieved national prominence as a leader of the General Federation of Women's Clubs. Attending her first convention in 1914, she rose in its ranks with unusual rapidity, advancing from the chairmanship of the Department of Literature (1916) and of the Americanization Division (1919) to become, in 1920, president of the organization. During Mrs. Winter's four-year administration the General Federation, despite a growing undercurrent of conservatism among its members, continued to support such reform measures as the Child Labor Amendment, the Sheppard-Towner Act for federal aid to maternal and infant health, and a federal amendment to authorize a uniform marriage and divorce law. It established an important and active Indian Welfare Committee in 1921 at the urging of GERTRUDE SIMMONS BONNIN, and in 1922, on Mrs. Winter's recommendation, an International Relations Committee. Having assumed office just as the final victory for woman suffrage was achieved, Mrs. Winter worked to strengthen the federation's legislative (lobbying) department. She also helped establish in 1920 the Women's Joint Congressional Committee, a clearinghouse through which women's groups could work together for common legislative goals.

With a warm and dynamic personality, poise, and a sense of humor, Mrs. Winter was a popular and able president. Tactful but firm, she inspired confidence and cooperation. To revitalize the organization, which had stagnated during the war, she visited clubs in every state in the Union, urging increased vigor and effectiveness. As a result, club and individual membership multiplied rapidly, and the General Federation was able to purchase a national headquarters building in Washington, D.C., and for the first time to publish its own periodical. In 1921, recognizing Mrs. Winter's club leadership and Republican sympathies, and aware of the widespread concern among women for peace, President Harding appointed her to the advisory committee for the Washington Conference of 1921–22 on naval disarmament.

Since early in the century Mrs. Winter had often written for women's periodicals, and she continued to do so upon her retirement as president of the General Federation of Women's Clubs. For four years (1924–28) she was a contributing editor of the *Ladies' Home Journal*. In 1927, as the author of two more books, *The Business of Being a Club Woman* (1925) and *The Heritage of Women* (1927), she organized and became first president of the Minnesota branch of the League of American Pen Women. She was a member of the American Association of University Women and the Daughters of the American Revolution.

In 1929, as a result of a New York conference between representatives of the film industry and community leaders concerned about the moral tone and social effects of many Hollywood films, Mrs. Winter was appointed by the Motion Picture Producers and Distributors of America to act as liaison between organized women and the industry. Moving with her husband to Pasadena, Calif., she held this post until her retirement in 1942. The University of Southern California honored her with a Litt.D. degree in 1938. In 1944, at seventy-eight, Mrs. Winter succumbed in Pasadena to a heart ailment. Her husband had died ten years before. Her ashes were buried in Lakewood Cemetery, Minneapolis.

[The Gen. Federation of Women's Clubs Archives in Washington, D.C., contain records of Mrs. Winter's administration, MS. biographical sketches, press releases, and a letter of reminiscences by her. In addition to her books mentioned above, she edited *Charles Gordon Ames: A Spiritual Autobiog.* (1913), to which she appended an epilogue expressive of her spiritual heritage. For her numerous articles see *Readers' Guide to Periodical Literature*, 1900–37. The most helpful biographical account is Lillian E. Taaffe, "Alice Ames Winter," *Woman Citizen*, May 31, 1924. See also Mildred W. Wells, *Unity in Diversity: The Hist. of the Gen. Federation of Women's Clubs* (1953); Marguerite N. Bell, *With Banners: A Biog. of Stella L. Woods* (1954), on Mrs. Winter's kindergarten activities; Alice Ames Winter, "And So to Hollywood," *Woman's Jour.*, Mar. 1930, on her motion-picture post and its background; *Woman's Who's Who of America*, 1914–15; *Who Was Who in America*, vol. II (1950), on Mrs. Winter, and vol. I (1942), on her husband; obituary in *Los Angeles Times*, Apr. 6, 1944. Verification of certain facts came from: federal census schedules of 1880 (Nat. Archives); marriage record, City Registrar's office, Boston, Mass.; death certificate, Calif. Dept. of Public Health (the source for her day of birth); and information from Wellesley College, Univ. of Southern California, and Lakewood Cemetery Assoc., Minneapolis. Also helpful were the recollections of Mrs. Stephen J. Nicholas,

Executive Secretary of the Gen. Federation of Women's Clubs.]

DOROTHY E. JOHNSON

**WINTHROP, Margaret** (c. 1591–June 14, 1647), wife of John Winthrop, first governor of the Massachusetts Bay Colony, was the fourth child and second daughter of Sir John and Lady Anne (Egerton) Tyndal of Great Maplestead, Essex, England. Her father was one of the masters of chancery; her mother was the daughter of Thomas Egerton of Suffolk and the widow of William Deane of Deaneshall.

Nothing is known of Margaret Tyndal's early life and education. She was married to John Winthrop on Apr. 29, 1618, and moved to his father's home, Groton Manor in Suffolk. She was his third wife. At the time of her marriage she was twenty-seven years old, four years younger than her husband. Adam Winthrop, father of John, was still lord of the manor, and his unmarried daughter Lucy was still a member of the household. As the new wife and mistress of the manor, Margaret Winthrop was charged with the care of her husband's four children by his two former marriages, ranging in age from twelve to three. Within three years she had two children of her own, Stephen and Adam. In addition to nursery cares, household duties were heavy. Visitors were numerous, markets remote, and roads suitable for horseback travel only; the manor had to be sufficient unto itself for all its varied needs. Superintendence of such a household was the best preparation she could have had for the more straitened, but in some ways less difficult, pioneer life in New England.

During many months of the twelve years before 1630, when John Winthrop sailed with the vanguard of the Massachusetts Bay Colony, his position as attorney at the Court of Wards and Liveries kept him at his chambers in London. His visits to Groton Manor were brief and infrequent, especially after plans for emigration were under way. It was during this long period of enforced separation that the letters which are Margaret Winthrop's chief claim to remembrance as an individual were written. "Puritan Letters" they have been entitled in their modern reprinting, and fittingly enough. On both sides love to God came first, love of husband and wife second. In Margaret Winthrop's words, "I have many reasons to make me love thee, whereof I will name two, first because thou lovest God, and secondly because that thou lovest me." Religious feeling exalted their mutual love and dignified it. The word *Puritan* gains a new dimension as these letters interpret its meaning in personal terms; the minutiae of daily life in Groton Manor and London are only incidental.

After her husband had left England, Margaret Winthrop remained at Groton for more than a year until he could make suitable preparation for her coming. Only a few brief notes are preserved for this period. She arrived in Boston Nov. 4, 1631, in the good ship *Lyon,* which brought a cargo of much-needed supplies for the winter. Her baby daughter, Anne, had died on the voyage. Her first impressions of the New World would have been of hospitality at the landing in Boston, when "Most of the people of the near plantations, came to welcome them." "The like joy and manifestations of love had never been seen in New England," John Winthrop wrote in his *Journal.* One week later, on Nov. 11, "We kept a day of thanksgiving at Boston."

Margaret Winthrop had sixteen years of pioneer experience as the first lady of the colony during her husband's long service as governor and assistant. She took no recorded part in the political or religious controversies which repeatedly found center at the Winthrop home in Boston, but to judge from the strength of her convictions, the steadiness of her faith, and her serenity of outlook, as revealed in her letters, doubtless only the record of her share is lacking. In one letter, dated "Sad Boston, 1637," while the ANNE HUTCHINSON disturbance was at its height, she confessed to being "unfit for any thinge, wonderinge what the Lord meanes by all these troubles among us." She found in herself a "fierce spirit, unwilling to submit to the will of God," and yet in the next sentence could say, God's will be done. She did not know how to say otherwise.

She died after one day's illness in midsummer 1647, apparently of influenza. In her husband's words, she "left this world for a better, being about fifty-six years of age: a woman of singular virtue, prudence, modesty and piety, and especially beloved and honoured of all the country." There is no portrait of that "lovely countenance" that he had so "much delighted in and beheld with so great contente." Her burial place is not marked, but supposedly she rests beside her husband in King's Chapel Churchyard in Boston. Four of her eight children survived her, Stephen, Adam, Deane, and Samuel.

[The published volumes of *The Winthrop Papers* (1929–   ) supersede earlier compilations, including *Some Old Puritan Love-Letters—John and Margaret Winthrop,* ed. by Joseph H. Twichell (1893), and Joseph J. Muskett, *Evidences of the Winthrops of Groton* (1894–96; also in his *Suffolk Manorial Families,* vol. I, 1900). See also: John Winthrop, *The Hist. of New England,* ed. by James Savage (2 vols., 1825); Alice Morse Earle, *Margaret Winthrop* (1895); Robert C. Winthrop, *Life and Letters of John Winthrop* (2 vols., 1869); and Edmund S. Morgan's biography of Winthrop, *The Puritan Dilemma* (1958). On the cause of her death, see Ernest Caulfield, "The Pursuit of a Pestilence," Am. Antiquarian Soc., *Proc.,* LX (1950), 26.]

OLA ELIZABETH WINSLOW

**WISCHNEWETZKY, Florence Kelley.** *See* KELLEY, Florence.

**WISE, Louise Waterman** (July 17, 1874–Dec. 10, 1947), charitable worker and Zionist, wife of Rabbi Stephen S. Wise, was born in New York City, the third child and second daughter of German-Jewish immigrants, Julius and Justine (Mayer) Waterman. Her father, a skilled craftsman, had come during the 1840's from Bayreuth to New Haven, Conn., following his brother Sigmund, who became one of the first professors of German at Yale. After starting a hoop-skirt factory and achieving success in business, Julius Waterman sent to Germany for his fiancée, a woman unusually well educated for the time; shortly before Louise's birth the family moved to New York. Known in her childhood as "Quicksilver" because of her gay spirits, Louise was educated at a finishing school, Comstock, where she mastered French and German and received some training in music and art. Although her parents held membership in Temple Emanu-El, as enlightened "liberals" they placed little emphasis on the Jewish tradition and allowed their daughter to attend an Episcopal Sunday school.

After the sudden death of her mother in 1890, Louise Waterman suffered a period of depression, in which she turned for solace to literature, reading widely in the great books of several cultures. The poems and essays of Ralph Waldo Emerson, with their counsel of rebellion against the chains of custom, strongly attracted her, and about the same time she came under the influence of Felix Adler, founder of the Ethical Culture Society and a passionate moralist. Adler induced her, over the objections of her family, to work in the settlement houses of the New York slums and conduct art classes for the underprivileged.

Louise Waterman first met her future husband in January 1899, when, on the death of a cousin, she was asked to summon the family's rabbi, Stephen Samuel Wise. They were married on Nov. 14, 1900, although her family had strongly opposed the match on the grounds that Wise was Austro-Hungarian rather than Bavarian; that he was poor and a rabbi, rather than a lawyer or banker; and that he was a Zionist. Thus began forty-seven years of close companionship, in which Louise Wise lent constant support to her husband in his stormy career. In turn Stephen Wise supplied the Jewish background that had been lacking in his wife's early life.

From 1900 to 1906 the family lived in Portland, Oreg., where Wise was the rabbi of Temple Beth Israel. Here Mrs. Wise organized (1902) the Free Nurses Association, a pioneer social service agency which provided free medical attention and nursing care for young mothers among the poor. Her own two children were born in Portland—James Waterman (1901), who became a writer, and Justine (1903), who became a lawyer and a judge of the domestic relations court in New York City.

In 1905 Stephen Wise was offered the pulpit of New York City's Temple Emanu-El, known as the Cathedral Synagogue of the country. When he learned that his work would be subject to the control of a board of trustees he refused, but brought his family back to New York and in 1907 established the Free Synagogue. The rest of his career was a crusade for clean government in state and city, for social justice, including an end to child labor, for understanding between Jew and Christian, and for the building of a Jewish homeland. Thoroughly sympathizing with these goals, Louise Wise was also busy with her own efforts to help those who could not help themselves. In 1909 she led a movement to provide better ventilation for the poorly designed classrooms in some of the public school buildings of New York. Learning by chance that orphaned Jewish children were regularly placed in asylums, since no agency existed to provide for their adoption by Jewish families, in 1916 she founded the Child Adoption Committee of the Free Synagogue. She enlisted the help of Jewish physicians and nurses and undertook the difficult task of gaining custody of such children, removing them from institutions, accepting applications for adoption, and trying to place each child in a suitable family.

Her Zionist sympathies were strengthened by her experience in Europe in 1919. Accompanying her husband to the Paris Peace Conference, where he served on the delegation attempting to secure minority rights for Jews in Eastern Europe and to obtain an international agreement that would permit the formation of a Jewish state in Palestine, Mrs. Wise met representative Jews from all the countries of Europe and heard their accounts of suffer-

ing. Four years later, after a visit to Palestine, she gave both money and encouragement to HENRIETTA SZOLD's work for children there.

The stresses of these years were lessened by quiet vacations at Camp Willamette, the summer home that the Wises built in 1908 on an island in Lake Placid in the Adirondacks. As her children grew older, Louise Wise returned to some of her earlier interests. In the 1920's she enrolled at the Art Students' League in New York to study painting, and produced portraits, as well as canvases which expressed her passion against injustice, such as "Orphanage," "Flight from Belgium," and "Sacrifice of Abraham." Her work was widely exhibited and is preserved in several museums, including that at Tel Aviv. She also translated from the French important books relating to Judaism, including Aimé Pallière's The Unknown Sanctuary (1928) and Edmond Fleg's My Palestine (1933) and Why I Am a Jew (1934).

The danger represented by Hitler and Nazism became apparent to Stephen and Louise Wise very early in the 1930's. Mrs. Wise was moved to speak publicly, although she disliked doing so. In 1931 she created the Women's Division of the American Jewish Congress, one of whose primary aims was to alert the public to the dangers of fascism and anti-Semitism, abroad and at home. In 1933, under the auspices of the Women's Division, she established the Congress House for Refugees, on West 68th Street in New York, to provide temporary homes for refugees from Central and Eastern Europe. Two more houses were added, in 1935 and 1936; the three homes gave shelter to some three thousand refugees before the outbreak of World War II. During the war Mrs. Wise converted them into Defense Houses to serve as hostels for Allied servicemen, no matter what their religion. She herself traveled throughout the United States to raise funds to send medical aid to the wounded civilians of Britain and Russia and to care for children evacuated from London during the Blitz.

At the close of the war, though in failing health, she went with her husband to Europe seeking ways to aid those European Jews who had survived the holocaust. Most wished to find a home in Palestine, but the British government blocked immigration there. When, therefore, in July 1946 the British Foreign Office offered Louise Wise the Order of the British Empire in recognition of her wartime services, she refused to accept the decoration. She died of pneumonia at her home in New York City in December 1947 and after services at the Free Synagogue was buried in Westchester Hills Cemetery. She had lived to see the United Nations call for the establishment of an independent Jewish state in Palestine, which became a reality in 1948. Stephen Wise survived her by less than two years, dying in 1949.

[James Waterman Wise, *Legend of Louise: The Life Story of Mrs. Stephen S. Wise* (1949); *Challenging Years: The Autobiog. of Stephen Wise* (1949); Justine Wise Polier and James Waterman Wise, eds., *The Personal Letters of Stephen Wise* (1956). See also *Who's Who in Am. Jewry*, 1938–39; *N.Y. Times*, Dec. 11, 13, 1947.]

ARTHUR HERTZBERG

**WITTENMYER, Annie Turner** (Aug. 26, 1827–Feb. 2, 1900), Civil War relief worker, leader in church and charitable work, and first president of the Woman's Christian Temperance Union, was born at Sandy Springs, Ohio, a small town on the Ohio River, one of the older children of a moderately large family which included four brothers. Her father, John G. Turner, of English descent, had moved from his native Maryland to Kentucky; her mother, Elizabeth (Smith) Turner, was a Kentuckian of Scottish and Scotch-Irish ancestry. Annie spent some of her early years in Kentucky but reportedly received her final schooling at a seminary in Ohio. In 1847 she was married to William Wittenmyer of Jacksonville, Ohio, an older man and a wealthy merchant. All but one of their five children died in infancy. The family moved in 1850 to Keokuk, Iowa, where Mrs. Wittenmyer helped organize a Methodist church and established a free school for poor children. Shortly before the outbreak of the Civil War, her husband died.

When troops began collecting at her Mississippi River town, Annie Wittenmyer turned to comforting the sick and became secretary of the Soldiers' Aid Society of Keokuk. In late April 1861 she entrusted her surviving child, Charles Albert, to the care of her mother and a married sister and went to visit the Iowa troops encamped a short distance downriver. The report she sent back to Keokuk on the need for hospital supplies was publicized in the press and inspired women in other Iowa towns to form aid societies and send shipments to her; by late summer her Keokuk society had formally assumed the role of forwarding agent for relief supplies from the whole state. Mrs. Wittenmyer also visited the front to nurse the wounded and came under fire at Vicksburg and other battles. Paying her own expenses at first, she soon received support from the Keokuk Soldiers' Aid Society and in September 1862, under a new state law, became one of several women appointed as paid "State Sanitary Agents."

Her work as a relief agent, cooperating with the Western Sanitary Commission of St. Louis, brought her into conflict with an all-male Iowa Army Sanitary Commission affiliated with the United States Sanitary Commission of New York. In October 1863, at a convention called at Muscatine, Iowa, to discuss the rivalry over relief, Mrs. Wittenmyer fought off efforts to merge the women's work with the men's under the United States Sanitary Commission, and became president of an independent Iowa State Sanitary Commission. But a month later another convention reorganized the state's relief effort under the auspices of Mrs. Wittenmyer's rivals, and when the legislature met early in 1864, her opponents introduced a bill to repeal the law authorizing her appointment, charging that she had been extravagant in her expenses and had sold donated supplies to hospitals. She was able to refute the charges, and her friends in the legislature blocked the repeal bill, but in May 1864 she resigned her position.

Mrs. Wittenmyer had already arranged to continue in another way her work with the wounded. She had conceived a plan for special diet kitchens attached to hospitals to provide patients with alternatives to army rations. In January 1864 she had won support for her proposal from another relief group, the United States Christian Commission, which thereafter supplied her with money and special foods. Her first kitchen at Nashville proved so successful that similar kitchens under her direction were set up in other army hospitals. To manage them, Mrs. Wittenmyer recruited some one hundred gentlewomen who, she stressed, were not to be cooks or servants. The ladies supervised soldiers detailed for the physical work and made sure that the food actually reached the patients. Mrs. Wittenmyer frequently enjoined these pioneer dietitians to Christian conduct and deference to the male hospital officials, and she ultimately saw her kitchens become an accepted part of the military hospital system.

Beginning in 1863 Annie Wittenmyer had been prominent in a movement to care for the children of Iowa's dead soldiers, and in October 1865, on a trip to Washington, she persuaded the government to turn over to the Iowa Orphans' Home Association some new barracks at Davenport and a large quantity of hospital supplies. Within the Methodist denomination, Mrs. Wittenmyer played a leading part in establishing in 1868 the Ladies' and Pastors' Christian Union, through which women, under the guidance of their local pastors, would visit and aid the sick and needy; she lectured widely in behalf of the new organization and in 1871 became its corresponding secretary. About this time she moved to Philadelphia, where for eleven years she published as her own enterprise a successful periodical, the *Christian Woman*. She also began to write books, among them the exhortatory *Woman's Work for Jesus* (1871) and *Women of the Reformation* (1884). In addition she wrote a number of hymns. In 1872, inspired by the interest of Bishop Mathew Simpson, who had seen the work of deaconess orders in Germany and felt that the Ladies' and Pastors' Union might introduce this form of charitable work into American Methodism, Mrs. Wittenmyer visited the Lutheran deaconess centers at Kaiserswerth, Germany. Another cause, however, soon absorbed her energies, and the inauguration of Methodist deaconess work fell to others (see LUCY RIDER MEYER and JANE MARIE BANCROFT ROBINSON).

When the "Woman's Crusade" against alcohol swept the Midwest in the winter of 1873–74, Annie Wittenmyer quickly joined the movement. In November 1874 she lent her prestige as a leader of Methodist churchwomen to the meeting at Cleveland which organized the National Woman's Christian Temperance Union; she was elected the W.C.T.U.'s first president. During the following year she and the organization's corresponding secretary, FRANCES E. WILLARD, made extensive lecture tours to stimulate the formation of local unions, and Mrs. Wittenmyer secured the establishment of the W.C.T.U.'s first official journal, *Our Union*. In 1875 and 1878 she presented to Congress bulky petitions calling for investigation of the liquor traffic and enactment of a federal prohibition amendment. In her *History of the Woman's Temperance Crusade* (1878) she repeatedly demonstrated her belief that the W.C.T.U. was leading a divinely inspired "Gospel Temperance Movement" against a liquor traffic dominated by "a low class of foreigners."

Mrs. Wittenmyer's concept of the W.C.T.U.'s work brought her into increasing conflict with a group of Western women, led by the young, ambitious Frances Willard, who wanted the organization also to embrace other causes, including woman's rights. At the conventions of 1877 and 1878 President Wittenmyer won reelection despite strong support for Miss Willard, but she lost to her in 1879. During her five-year presidency more than a thousand local unions, encompassing some twenty-six thousand members, had been formed. Despite the W.C.T.U.'s subsequent commitment to woman suffrage, Mrs. Wittenmyer remained active in the Pennsylvania and national unions,

but she joined J. ELLEN FOSTER and others who vainly opposed Miss Willard's policy of having the W.C.T.U. endorse the Prohibition party. When some of these opponents split off and organized the Non-Partisan Woman's Christian Temperance Union in 1890, Annie Wittenmyer gave them moral support; she was president of the dissident group, 1896–98.

By this time the aging Mrs. Wittenmyer had returned to a cause associated with the Civil War. In 1889–90 she was president of the Woman's Relief Corps, the women's auxiliary of the Grand Army of the Republic. During her presidency she began a successful movement to establish in Ohio a National W.R.C. Home for ex-nurses and for the widows and mothers of veterans. She served as a director of this institution and of a similar one in Pennsylvania. In 1892 her lobbying helped induce Congress to pass a bill to pension former war nurses, and in 1898 she herself received a special pension. Frequently lecturing for the W.R.C., she also contributed to and helped edit veterans' publications. She reminisced about her wartime experiences in *Under the Guns* (1895). This last book indicated that her intense patriotism had a strongly nativist cast, although within the W.R.C. she opposed the introduction of racial segregation.

After the late 1880's Annie Wittenmyer lived with her son in Sanatoga, Pa. Her seventieth birthday brought congratulations and gifts from many parts of the nation. Three years later she died at her home of cardiac asthma, a few hours after delivering a lecture at nearby Pottstown; she was buried in Edgewood Cemetery, Sanatoga. Having inherited from her husband a substantial estate, Mrs. Wittenmyer experienced a degree of independence relatively unusual for a woman of her day. The handsome, prematurely white-haired widow became a pioneer in urging the members of her sex to participate in relief and reform work on a nationwide scale. Highly articulate and literate, she combined strong qualities of leadership with a preference for a persuasive approach to gain concessions from male leaders. Her piety, her sentimentality, and her coolness toward woman suffrage appealed to moderates of both sexes.

[The most useful general sketches of Mrs. Wittenmyer's life are: an anonymous one in *Annals of Iowa*, Jan. 1900, especially strong on her ancestry; Ruth A. Gallaher in *Iowa Jour. of Hist. and Politics*, Oct. 1931, the best source on her activities in Iowa; and the generally accurate articles in the *Nat. Cyc. Am. Biog.*, XII, 363–64, and in Ernest H. Cherrington, ed., *Standard Encyc. of the Alcohol Problem*, VI (1930), 2888–89. Frances E. Willard and Mary A. Livermore, eds., *A Woman of the Century* (1893), is inadequate on the subject's role in temperance, but Miss Willard's earlier *Woman and Temperance* (1883) partially supplies this lack. Excessively laudatory are several articles about her in the W.C.T.U. journal, the *Union Signal,* and Lucy Shelton Stewart, *Lest We Forget: Annie Wittenmyer . . . An Address Given before a Meeting of Temperance Women in Evanston, Ill., Aug. 20, 1915* (1916). For more details on aspects of Mrs. Wittenmyer's wartime services, see her own *Under the Guns* (1895); John S. Newberry, *The U.S. Sanitary Commission in the Valley of the Mississippi* (1871); and Lemuel Moss, *Annals of the U.S. Christian Commission* (1868). The account of Mrs. Wittenmyer in L. P. Brockett and Mary C. Vaughan, *Woman's Work in the Civil War* (1867), is incomplete and not wholly accurate. On her Methodist charitable work, see Christian Golder, *Hist. of the Deaconess Movement in the Christian Church* (1903), pp. 306–11. The *Minutes* of both the Nat. W.C.T.U. and the Non-Partisan W.C.T.U. contain much on her temperance activities. See also her own *Hist. of the Woman's Temperance Crusade* (1878); Helen E. Tyler, *Where Prayer and Purpose Meet* (1949); and Mary Earhart, *Frances Willard* (1944). Wallace E. Davies, *Patriotism on Parade* (1955), has information on Annie Wittenmyer and the Woman's Relief Corps. Her death record is on file at the Orphans' Court of Montgomery County, Norristown, Pa. According to the Gallaher article cited above, there are 8 volumes of letters written to Mrs. Wittenmyer while she was Iowa Sanitary Agent in the "War Correspondence" files at the State Hist. Dept., Des Moines, Iowa.]

FRANK L. BYRNE

**WITTPENN, Caroline Bayard Stevens** (Nov. 21, 1859–Dec. 4, 1932), New Jersey welfare worker, was born to Edwin Augustus and Martha Bayard (Dod) Stevens at Castle Point, the family estate in Hoboken, N.J. Her paternal grandfather, John Stevens, had purchased this site, which included almost all of present-day Hoboken, in 1784, after having served as treasurer of the revolutionary government of New Jersey, and it was for the development of the estate that he undertook his famous efforts to improve and apply steam engines in ferryboats and railways. His four sons, continuing these interests, became leading figures in the Camden and Amboy Railroad, which in their generation dominated transportation between New York and Philadelphia. Even before her grandfather's death, Caroline's father was recognized as the "balance wheel" among these energetic and enterprising men, manager of the family fortune, heir to its estate. She was born when he was sixty, the third of his seven children by his second wife and the only daughter (two children of a previous marriage

were already grown). In this masculine household she drew very close to her mother, who was much younger than her father and long survived his death in 1868. Martha Stevens was the child of a Princeton professor known for theological conservatism and brilliant conversation; he was, however, poor by Stevens standards, and it is said that Mrs. Stevens' well-known sympathy with the needy, as well as her pervasive piety, was a result of this background.

Caroline was educated by private tutors and for a time at Bonchurch, a small girls' school on the Isle of Wight which occasionally admitted students "from America or the colonies." By this and other means she made many English friends, and her adult love of home, garden, pets, and fox hunting, as well as her Episcopal faith, was decidedly English in spirit. In June 1879 she was married to Archibald Alexander, of a well-known Princeton family, who taught philosophy at Columbia University; the following year she bore him a namesake. They made their home in Hoboken, and Mrs. Alexander busied herself in charitable affairs in the little town, still mostly owned by her family but now a populous annex of New York and Jersey City.

Her public career began at about the time of her separation from her husband, in 1895. Though its cause is unclear, this break was complete, bitter, and painful to her. She undertook probation work for the Hudson County Court, which had jurisdiction over Jersey City and its suburbs; her work was with girls and women, while her youngest brother, Richard, helped male offenders. She thus saw the problems of the underprivileged in a new way, and the ability, zeal, means, and influence she brought to her work quickly made her a leading personage. She helped revitalize the State Charities Aid Association, assisted the campaign to get children out of almshouses and to establish juvenile courts, and even interested herself in the state inspection of weights and measures, to the end of giving housewives fair value in their purchases. In 1903 she served on a state commission which reopened an old battle for a separate women's reformatory; she was a member of another commission which, reporting on causes of dependency and crime, took the same position in 1908. When the state established Clinton Farms reformatory, in 1913, she became president of its board of managers and its effective guide and partisan for two decades.

Meanwhile other attachments led her into public life. Her son, a graduate of Princeton and New York University Law School, was close to Woodrow Wilson; in 1906, 1908, and 1910 young Alexander was in the state legislature, where he worked for a women's reformatory, among other measures, before his promising career ended with death from typhoid fever in 1912. Always a partisan of Woodrow Wilson, Mrs. Alexander was Wilson's adviser, during his governorship of New Jersey, on state welfare problems, and during his presidency she became the first Democratic National Committeewoman for her state.

On Jan. 6, 1915, Mrs. Alexander was married to H. Otto Wittpenn, who had been county supervisor during her early years as probation officer; she had supported his rapid rise to mayor of Jersey City, which office he held for four terms. Though she had not heard of or from Alexander for many years, in observance of canon law she did not remarry until he was presumed dead by her bishop. Wittpenn, forty-three at the time of their marriage, was Democratic candidate for governor in 1916 and later naval officer of the Port of New York, but his political career ended when he broke with the Hudson County Democratic organization, already coming under the control of Frank Hague. He was more successful as a businessman, looking after his own manufacturing and banking interests as well as his wife's. Their happy marriage lasted until his death in 1931.

During World War I, Mrs. Wittpenn was women's chairman of the several Liberty Loan drives in New Jersey. In 1918 she was appointed to the recently organized board of control of the New Jersey Department of Institutions and Agencies, which undertook a reorganization of the state's charitable and correctional institutions; except for the years 1926–29 she served in this capacity until her death. During these years she was also president of the Board of Children's Guardians and of Clinton Farms; a member of boards managing state institutions for retarded women and epileptics; and active in probation work. She was president of the New Jersey Conference of Social Welfare in 1926; in 1929 President Hoover appointed her to the International Prison Commission. Shortly after a public celebration of her seventy-third birthday, at which she was called "the best-loved woman in New Jersey," she became ill and died of pneumonia at Castle Point, Hoboken. A thousand people and representatives of sixty organizations attended her funeral; she was buried in Hoboken Cemetery, North Bergen.

By all accounts Mrs. Wittpenn was a beautiful and charming woman. She sometimes carried a portable altar on her travels and made an occasional retreat, but she was never dour;

she was a feminist and suffragist but not inclined toward speechmaking or parading. She was a founder of the Colony Club of New York and active in the Cosmopolitan Club, but in her work she easily made friends in all classes. Beginning in the spirit of noblesse oblige, she presently attained a rare professional expertise and zeal for correctional and welfare programs. In this way the advantages and sorrows of her life were fruitfully combined.

[Archibald D. Turnbull, *John Stevens* (1928); John E. Watkins, *Biog. Sketches of John Stevens, Robert L. Stevens, Edwin A. Stevens* (1892); clipping files, *Jersey Jour.* (Jersey City) and *Newark* (N.J.) *News; Welfare Reporter* (N.J. Dept. of Institutions and Agencies), Aug. 1947; obituaries in *Jersey Jour.* and *N.Y. Times,* Dec. 5, 1932; conversations with Archibald S. Alexander, Bernardsville, N.J., her grandson; James Leiby, *Charity and Correction in N.J.* (1967).]

JAMES LEIBY

WIXOM, Emma. *See* NEVADA, Emma.

WOERISHOFFER, Emma Carola (August 1885–Sept. 11, 1911), social worker and philanthropist, was born in New York City, the younger of two daughters of Charles Frederick and Anna (Uhl) Woerishoffer. From her German-born father, a prominent Wall Street financier who died the year after her birth, she inherited a fortune of well over a million dollars. Her maternal grandmother, ANNA UHL OTTENDORFER, and her step-grandfather, Oswald Ottendorfer, for many years edited and managed the *New-Yorker Staats-Zeitung,* a liberal German-language daily. Ottendorfer was active in reform Democratic politics, while his wife contributed to medical and other philanthropic causes. From this background Carola, as she was called, developed an early interest in philanthropy and social service.

In 1903, after attending New York's fashionable Brearley School, she entered Bryn Mawr College, whose president, M. CAREY THOMAS, she had admired since childhood. At Bryn Mawr she elected a course of study—philosophy, economics, politics, psychology, and languages—that reflected her determination to prepare for a career in social work. Like Miss Woerishoffer's later associates, her college classmates were both intimidated and fascinated by her forcible and impetuous personality. On one occasion, to resolve a dispute about the safety of the college's fire nets, she jumped from the top of her dormitory into a net held by fearful friends below.

Upon her graduation in 1907 she entered at once the exciting reformist milieu of lower

Manhattan, as a part-time resident and member of the board of managers of Greenwich House, a neighborhood settlement founded by Mary Kingsbury Simkhovitch (d. 1951). She soon became active in a number of social welfare and labor organizations, bringing to each a unique combination of passionate intensity and personal diffidence. She took pains to remain out of the public eye, and as a consequence much of her work was anonymous. Typical was her financial backing of the "Congestion Exhibit" which a committee composed of Mrs. Simkhovitch, FLORENCE KELLEY, and others held in the American Museum of Natural History in 1908, to open the eyes of New Yorkers to the overcrowded housing conditions in their city, and her continued underwriting of the committee's crusade for reform legislation. In the summer of 1909 she performed a remarkable piece of research in the laundry industry of the city. For four months, without revealing her identity, she worked fifteen hours a day as a laundress in a dozen different establishments, sharing and observing the wretched conditions under which the girls labored. She reported her findings to the Consumers' League of New York City and to a state commission then investigating the need for employers' liability legislation.

She joined the then weak and little-known New York Women's Trade Union League in 1908, serving as treasurer, executive committee member, and president of its "label shop," where goods made under approved conditions were sold. Late in 1909 thousands of women shirtwaist makers went on strike, and many were jailed. The courts demanded real estate as security for bail, but the league had none. At this point Miss Woerishoffer appeared in court, put up a $75,000 property as bond, and declared she would remain in court until the strike was settled. Later she contributed $10,000 to inaugurate a permanent strike fund to meet such emergencies. Newspapers were eager to print articles about the rich girl with a social conscience, but she refused permission and threatened to cut off information about the strike if they violated her wishes. The technique worked.

She soon came to believe that strikes were at best stopgap measures. Convinced that real improvement of working conditions depended on effective government regulation, she agreed to serve on the executive committee of the New York State Association for Labor Legislation, and when the state government's Department of Labor created a Bureau of Industries and Immigration in 1910, she became a special investigator for the bureau and gave large sums

to supplement its appropriation. Pragmatically willing to explore any avenue of reform, she joined the board of the Taylor Iron and Steel Company of High Bridge, N.J., because of her interest in its plans to organize a model industrial village. Amid her varied welfare activities, she found time, too, for service as a district leader of the New York Woman Suffrage Party. A small-faced, dark-eyed young woman, with a mass of dark hair, she scorned convention and had an intense physical vitality. She loved exercise; during the summer of 1909, while working long hours in sweltering laundries, she regularly arose at 6 A.M. for an hour of basketball at Greenwich House before reporting for work.

Her duties with the New York Department of Labor included the investigation of immigrant labor camps throughout the state, and in September 1911, in the course of such an inspection tour, the automobile she was driving overturned on a rain-slick road near Cannonsville, N.Y., pinning her beneath it. She died in Cannonsville the following morning, her promising career of public service cut short at the age of twenty-six. On Oct. 30 a memorial meeting was held at Greenwich House, where many of New York's social work leaders paid tribute to her.

In the manner of early twentieth-century Progressives, Carola Woerishoffer used a variety of techniques to strike at social injustice. Her most far-reaching philanthropy was a bequest of $750,000 to her alma mater, Bryn Mawr College. The money was put into an endowment fund in her name and part of the income used to found in 1915 the Carola Woerishoffer Graduate Department of Social Economy and Social Research (see SUSAN M. KINGSBURY), the first professional school of its kind to be connected with a college or university.

[The most useful source is *Carola Woerishoffer: Her Life and Work*, published in 1912 by the Class of 1907 of Bryn Mawr College. It contains the proceedings of the memorial meeting at Greenwich House as well as editorials, resolutions, and tributes from her acquaintances. Obituaries appeared in the N.Y. *Times* and other papers for Sept. 12, 1911, and the *Times* on Sept. 15 published an editorial. Of special importance are Ida M. Tarbell's "A Noble Life: The Story of Carola Woerishoffer," *American Mag.*, July 1912, and Vladimir G. Simkhovitch's obituary in *Survey*, Sept. 30, 1911. Also pertinent are Mary K. Simkhovitch, *Neighborhood: My Story of Greenwich House* (1938); Cornelia Meigs, *What Makes a College? A Hist. of Bryn Mawr* (1956); *Bryn Mawr Alumnae Quart.*, Nov. 1911; and N.Y. State Dept. of Labor, Bureau of Industries and Immigration, *First Annual Report*, 1911. On her family background, see Lyman Horace Weeks, ed., *Prominent Families of N.Y.* (1897), p. 437, and Henry Hall, ed., *America's Successful Men of Affairs*, I (1895), 489–92. The Alumnae Assoc. of Bryn Mawr College provided information from its files. Death record from N.Y. State Dept. of Health.]

RODERICK W. NASH

WOLFE, Catharine Lorillard (Mar. 8, 1828–Apr. 4, 1887), philanthropist, was born in New York City, the second and only surviving child of John David Wolfe and Dorothea Ann (Lorillard) Wolfe. Both parents were descendants of early eighteenth-century German immigrants to New York. Her father acquired a substantial fortune in commerce, particularly the hardware trade, and real estate speculation. Her mother was a member of the Lorillard family, manufacturers of tobacco and snuff. CATHERINE WOLFE BRUCE, the patron of astronomy, was a first cousin. Catharine Wolfe was educated at home by private tutors and on trips abroad with her parents. Fond of social life and travel, distinguished by the elegance of her dress and figure, she was generally believed to have had a romance in her youth, though she never married. After the death of her mother in 1866, she allied herself closely with the interests of her father, who had retired early from business to devote himself to philanthropic projects. Upon his death in 1872 she received a large inheritance which, added to the Lorillard wealth left by her mother, made her the possessor of a fortune estimated at $12,000,000. Miss Wolfe dedicated the rest of her life to charitable causes, particularly those that had been aided by her father.

Deeply devoted to the Protestant Episcopal Church, like both her parents, Miss Wolfe made some of her largest gifts to Grace Church in New York, of which she was a member. She provided $250,000 to build the church's chantry and reredos and at her death left it an endowment of $350,000. She founded Grace House, containing reading and lecture rooms for the poor. Her other religious philanthropies included funds for a central building for the Episcopal diocese of New York and building funds for the American chapels in Paris and Rome; gifts to church schools west of the Mississippi River and the seminary in Alexandria, Egypt; the Wolfe Fund for aged and infirm Episcopal clergy; gifts to St. Philip's, a Negro church, the Italian Mission on Mulberry Street, and St. Luke's Hospital (Episcopal), all in New York City; and $65,000 to St. Johnland Hospital on Long Island.

In other areas of philanthropy, Miss Wolfe gave $100,000 for the endowment of Union College at Schenectady, N.Y., which her father had aided. She was a principal contributor to the building and maintenance of the Newsboys' Lodging House of the Children's Aid Society in New York City, and she provided a thirteen-acre site at Fordham, N.Y., which had been part of the Jacob Lorillard estate, for the Home for Incurables. She also purchased Dr. John C. Jay's library of rare books on conchology and his collection of shells and presented them to the American Museum of Natural History, of which her father had been president at the time of his death. She left the museum an endowment fund of $200,000.

In two areas Miss Wolfe established her own pattern of philanthropy. She contributed funds to the American School of Classical Studies in Athens, Greece, and financed the first American archaeological expedition to Babylonia (Iraq), led by William Hayes Ward, the Orientalist and Biblical student, in the winter of 1884–85. The work of this exploratory group provided the basis for the University of Pennsylvania's successful excavation, beginning the year after Miss Wolfe's death, of the ancient city of Nippur. Secondly, she commissioned a cousin, John Wolfe, to help her make a collection of European paintings, which she gave by her will to the Metropolitan Museum of Art in New York. The collection, assembled from 1872 until her death, consisted of 120 paintings and twenty-two watercolors by nineteenth-century artists, mainly of the French Academic, Munich, and Düsseldorf schools. A contemporary critic described it as "eminently a popular collection" (Rowlands, p. 13). Miss Wolfe, however, was unique among wealthy American collectors of her time in emphasizing contemporary art rather than old masters. The collection was valued at half a million dollars in 1887. A special feature of the bequest was an accompanying sum of $200,000 for the upkeep of the collection and for the purchase of modern paintings of "figure, landscape and genre subjects" (*New York Tribune*, Apr. 9, 1887). The bequest marked the first million-dollar year in the history of an American art museum and the first time a donor had provided an endowment to help meet the future costs of a gift.

Catharine Wolfe's total gifts before her death aggregated approximately four million dollars: an average of $100,000 a year for the first decade, and $250,000 annually in the last years of her life. She did not seek publicity, but contemporaries agreed that she had a strong personality, could be brusque and curt when her wishes were not carried out to the letter, and would refuse an application for money with "cold sternness" if she thought the object unworthy. With "jet black hair" and "a brow well proportioned and intellectual" (*ibid.*, Apr. 5, 1887), Miss Wolfe also possessed great charm. Her house on Madison Avenue was crowded with pictures, statuary, and bric-a-brac, and her summer home, Vinland, at Newport, R.I., was decorated by notable artists. The lawn was laid out by Frederick Law Olmsted, and the house contained a frieze by Walter Kane and a stained-glass window by Sir Edward Burne-Jones, both with subject matter from Longfellow's "Skeleton in Armor."

Catharine Wolfe became ill after her return from Newport in the autumn of 1886 and died in her New York home of Bright's disease (apparently common in the Lorillard family), complicated by pneumonia, at the age of fifty-nine. She was buried in the Wolfe family plot in Greenwood Cemetery, Brooklyn. Hailed at her death as "one of the wisest stewards of wealth" New York had known (*Churchman,* Apr. 9, 1887), Catharine Wolfe was notable as one of the first Americans to extend that stewardship to include artistic and scientific causes.

[*N.Y. Times,* Apr. 5 (an extensive obituary) and 9, 1887; *N.Y. Tribune,* Apr. 5 (obituary), 7, 9, 17, 1887; Sarah K. Bolton, *Famous Givers and Their Gifts* (1896), pp. 323–25; Walter Rowlands, "The Miss Wolfe Collection," *Art Jour.* (London), Jan. 1889—which reproduces the portrait of her by Alexandre Cabanel. See also Walter W. Spooner, *Historic Families of America* (1907), I, 282–83; Frances E. Willard and Mary A. Livermore, eds., *A Woman of the Century* (1893); and, for contemporary tributes, *Churchman* (N.Y.), Apr. 9, 1887, pp. 398–99, and William R. Huntington, *The Religious Use of Wealth* (19 pp., 1887), a memorial sermon. On her father see *Dict. Am. Biog.* and Evert A. Duyckinck, *A Memorial of John David Wolfe* (1872).]

DANIEL M. FOX

WOLLSTEIN, Martha (Nov. 21, 1868–Sept. 30, 1939), pathologist and medical researcher, was born in New York City to Louis and Minna (Cohn) Wollstein. Little is known about her family or early life, save that her parents, who were born in Germany, were Jewish and had one other child, a son named Isaac. In 1886 she entered the Woman's Medical College of the New York Infirmary, founded twenty-one years earlier by Drs. ELIZABETH and EMILY BLACKWELL to make medical education of a high standard available to women. The early years of both the college and the infirmary, its associated hospital, had been precarious, but by 1886 both institutions were on a firm financial basis, with an excellent faculty, including MARY PUTNAM JACOBI, and new quar-

ters in a large building on East 15th Street, where some thirty thousand patients a year were treated. Martha Wollstein received her medical degree from this bustling medical center in 1889. A decade later the college was absorbed by the Cornell University Medical School, which then made provision to accept women students. Throughout her life Dr. Wollstein had a keen appreciation of the revolution in medical education of which she had been a part; in 1908 she wrote one of the first historical accounts of women's medical education in the United States.

In 1890 Dr. Wollstein joined the Babies Hospital in New York City as an intern, and two years later she was appointed pathologist there. The hospital was then relatively new, but under the direction of Luther Emmett Holt as house physician it was becoming one of the important centers of pediatric care in the nation. Initially, Dr. Wollstein concentrated her studies on malaria, tuberculosis, and typhoid fever. From time to time she also assisted Holt as a bacteriologist, as for example in a study of brain abscess in infants. She did little experimental pathology at first, simply because there were no facilities, but in 1896 Christian Herter, one of the pioneers in biological chemistry in the United States, privately financed the construction of a pathological laboratory at the Babies Hospital, and in 1903 Dr. Wollstein made her first major contribution as a pediatric pathologist, on the subject of infant diarrhea.

The cause of this condition had long puzzled physicians, who generally ascribed it to poor feeding practice, but in 1902 Charles Duval, pathologist to the Tulane Medical School in New Orleans, discovered Shiga bacilli in the stools of some infants suffering from diarrhea. He also related the diarrheas he had found in infants to an ongoing outbreak of dysentery among adults. Dr. Wollstein confirmed Duval's work when she discovered a related dysentery bacillus in the stools of thirty-seven infants suffering from diarrhea in New York. The bacillus Dr. Wollstein had discovered had been isolated by the distinguished pathologist Simon Flexner several years before, while studying dysentery in the Philippines; her study attracted his attention, and in 1904 an expanded version was published as a special monograph of the Rockefeller Institute, of which Flexner was the director. Two years later she joined the institute's staff as an assistant, while continuing her work at the Babies Hospital.

Dr. Wollstein served at first in Flexner's laboratory. In 1907 she joined him in the first experimental analysis of polio in the United

States, an attempt to transmit polio to monkeys using the cerebrospinal fluid of human polio victims. The experiments failed. The following year she made one of the early studies of the character of the cerebrospinal fluid in polio victims during the initial stages of the disease. Though there were again no significant findings, these studies prepared the way for more successful research by Flexner and others on the pathological characteristics of polio in man and monkeys.

At the Rockefeller Institute, Dr. Wollstein also worked closely, in 1910 and for several years thereafter, with the distinguished physiologist Samuel Meltzer in an experimental study of pneumonia. By means of intrabronchial insufflation of pneumococcus, streptococcus, and other bacteria, they sought to discover whether different bacteria caused differing types of pneumonias. But the experiments contributed little to the ultimate solution of the treatment of pneumonia; this was to develop from research carried on contemporaneously at the Rockefeller Institute Hospital under the direction of Oswald T. Avery.

Not all of Dr. Wollstein's investigations, however, ended in a cul-de-sac. One of her notable successes occurred in the field of meningitis research. Although Flexner had developed an immune serum for treatment of the disease as early as 1907, such treatment continued to present many difficulties, and epidemics of cerebrospinal meningitis in army camps during the First World War stimulated new work on serum therapy. In 1918 Dr. Wollstein, in collaboration with Harold Amoss (who had earlier worked with Flexner on polio), not only developed a new method for the rapid preparation of antimeningitis serum but also devised criteria for the standardization of such sera—research which ultimately led to the preparation of potent polyvalent sera against meningitis.

At the same time she was engaged in research on mumps. By the end of the nineteenth century many European investigators attributed the cause of this ancient disease to bacteria, and some even indicted a gram-positive diplococcus as the infecting agent. In 1913 Charles Nicolle of the Pasteur Institute of Tunis hinted that the disease might well be caused by a virus. Dr. Wollstein in 1918 attempted to extend Nicolle's research. Using filtrated mouth washings taken from mumps patients, she succeeded in transmitting the disease from humans to cats and ultimately from cat to cat. Although her research indicated the viral nature of mumps it did not prove it, nor did she make claims that she had reproduced mumps in ani-

mals. It was not until 1934 that Ernest Goodpasture and Claud Johnson succeeded in transmitting mumps experimentally to monkeys and isolating and identifying the virus which caused the disease.

Martha Wollstein never achieved membership in the Rockefeller Institute. This, however, is no indication of her merit as an investigator. Though it was relatively easy for a woman to be appointed to the institute during its early years, few advanced very far in rank; the only woman to achieve full membership during the first fifty years of the institute's existence was Florence Sabin (d. 1953). There can be little doubt that Dr. Wollstein was a careful and imaginative investigator. She was, for example, the first scientist at the Rockefeller Institute to recognize the importance of the bacteriophage discovered by Felix d'Herelle in 1917, and in 1920, a year before she left the institute, she began the arduous task of classifying different varieties of phage, a work subsequently developed by Jacob Bronfenbrenner.

From 1921 on, Dr. Wollstein devoted herself to pediatric pathology at the Babies Hospital, concentrating on problems of congenital anomalies, leukemia in children, hemolytic jaundice, tuberculosis, and influenzal meningitis. It was here that she made her greatest contribution, in the careful pathological studies which helped sharpen the diagnostic acumen of generations of physicians who used the hospital's facilities during the forty-three years of her tenure. Her services were prized and appreciated by three distinguished pediatric chiefs: Holt, Herbert Wilcox, and Rustin McIntosh. She was appointed head of the pediatric section of the New York Academy of Medicine in 1928 and in 1930 was made a member of the American Pediatric Society, the first woman so honored.

Martha Wollstein never married. Her colleagues seldom got to know her as a person. Many considered her difficult to work with; few bothered to pierce the protective shell of this intellectually gifted, shy, and lonely woman. Following her retirement in 1935, she moved to Grand Rapids, Mich. She returned to New York in 1939 to enter the Mount Sinai Hospital as a patient and died there that September. She was buried in Beth-El Cemetery, Brooklyn. Her death, like her life, was hardly noticed. A handful of colleagues attended her funeral, and obituary notices were brief —at best a paltry witness to the achievement of this distinguished pioneer in pediatric pathology.

[Of Dr. Wollstein's 80 scientific papers, the following were most useful in the preparation of this article: "The Hist. of Women in Medicine," *Wom-*

an's Medical Jour., Apr. 1908; "A Biological Study of the Cerebro-spinal Fluid in Anterior Polio-myelitis," Jour. of Experimental Medicine, July 8, 1908; "The Development of Experimental Pneu-monia under Direct Observation of the Lungs in the Living Animal" (with S. J. Meltzer), Soc. of Experimental Biology and Medicine, Proc., vol. X (1913); "The Pulmonary Reaction to B. Pyoca-neus" (with S. J. Meltzer), ibid., vol. XI (1914); "Pneumonic Lesions Caused by B. Megatherium" (with S. J. Meltzer), Jour. of Experimental Medi-cine, Nov. 1, 1913; "A Method for the Rapid Prep-aration of Antimeningitis Serum" (with Harold L. Amoss), ibid., Mar. 1, 1916; "An Experimental Study of Parotitis (Mumps)," Jour. Am. Medical Assoc., Aug. 24, 1918; "A Further Study of Ex-perimental Parotitis," Jour. of Experimental Med-icine, Oct. 1, 1918; "A Study of Tuberculosis in Infants and Young Children" (with Ralph C. Spence), Am. Jour. of Diseases of Children, Jan. 1921; "Brain Tumors in Young Children" (with F. H. Bartlett), ibid., Apr. 1923; "Studies on the Phenomenon of d'Herelle with Bacillus Dysen-teriae," Jour. of Experimental Medicine, Nov. 1, 1921; "Lymphatic Leukemia in Infancy with the Report of a Case" (with F. H. Bartlett), Am. Jour. of Medical Science, June 1925; "Familial Hemolytic Anemia of Childhood—Von Jaksch" (with Katherine V. Kreidel), Am. Jour. of Dis-eases of Children, Jan. 1930. There are references to her work in the unpublished "Reports to the Board of Scientific Directors" of the Rockefeller Institute for Medical Research, 1907–20. Bio-graphical sources are scant: Am. Men of Science (6th ed., 1938); obituaries in N.Y. Times, Oct. 1, 1939, and Jour. Am. Medical Assoc., Dec. 2, 1939 (the latter also in Medical Woman's Jour., Mar. 1940); death record from N.Y. City Dept. of Health. See also: Kate Campbell Hurd-Mead, Medical Women of America (1933); Rustin Mc-Intosh and Harold Faber, Hist. of the Am. Pedi-atric Soc. (1966); George W. Corner, A Hist. of the Rockefeller Institute for Medical Research (1964). A biographical report and bibliography compiled by Brenda Crudge, Columbia Library School, was helpful.]

SAUL BENISON

WOOD, Edith Elmer (Sept. 24, 1871–Apr. 29, 1945), housing economist, was born in Portsmouth, N.H., the older of two children and only daughter of Horace and Adele (Wiley) Elmer. Both parents, descended from early colonial English stock, were natives of New Jersey. Her maternal grandfather, John Wiley, was a prominent South Jersey physician, inter-ested in civic improvements, who had been a regimental surgeon in the Union Army during the Civil War. Her father, also a Civil War veteran, was a naval officer and graduate of Annapolis. Because of his military assignments, Edith as a child lived a cosmopolitan existence in the United States and abroad. She was edu-

cated by tutors and governesses and at Smith College, where she received the B.L. degree in 1890. On June 24, 1893, she was married to Albert Norton Wood, like her father a naval officer. Their four children were Horace Elmer (who died in early childhood), Thurston Elmer, Horace Elmer II, and Albert Elmer.

During the years following her marriage, as she accompanied her husband on various for-eign assignments, Mrs. Wood wrote genteel fic-tion and travel literature that gave little hint of her later concern with housing problems. In 1906, however, while living in Puerto Rico, she abruptly terminated her literary efforts and became involved in a public health crusade. A servant in her household had contracted tuber-culosis, and the realization that there were no facilities on the island to care for the girl en-couraged Mrs. Wood to found the Anti-Tuber-culosis League of Puerto Rico. She became its president, and two years later she attended an International Congress on Tuberculosis in Washington, D.C. In that city, a few years later, she found that public health and the prevention of tuberculosis were closely related to housing conditions. From 1913 to 1915 she investigated Washington's housing problems and fought to eliminate the congested Negro alley slums with their "almost unbelievable" tuberculosis death rate.

Realizing the handicap of her lack of formal training in housing or social economy, Mrs. Wood in 1915 moved with her family to New York City and at the age of forty-four enrolled in Columbia University's graduate school. Her husband, who had retired from the navy, was recalled to duty in 1917 and stationed in Phila-delphia, but Edith Wood had by that time finished her course work. She took an M.A. degree in 1917 with a thesis on "Constructive Housing Legislation and Its Lesson for the United States," a study of European programs in the government financing and construction of low-income housing. In the same year she received a diploma from the New York School of Philanthropy, and in 1919 the Ph.D. Her dissertation, published that year, was on The Housing of the Unskilled Wage Earner: Amer-ica's Next Problem. While a student at Colum-bia, Mrs. Wood prepared for the Bureau of Municipal Research an administrative study of the New York Tenement House Depart-ment's Vacation Bureau, served as adviser in housing legislation to the Women's Municipal League of Boston (1917–19), and in 1917 began a twelve-year tenure as chairman of the national committee on housing of the American Association of University Women.

After leaving Columbia, Mrs. Wood quickly

emerged as one of the nation's outstanding housing authorities. She excelled as educator, publicist, historian, and economist. Through her books and articles, her position with the A.A.U.W., and the courses she taught at Columbia, she struggled to arouse a widespread public interest in America's housing problems. The heart of her message was that private enterprise alone could not supply the nation's needs. For the next quarter century she stressed the distinction between "constructive" and "restrictive" housing legislation, arguing that although minimum legal standards of light, air, ventilation, sanitation, and fire protection were indispensable, they in no way guaranteed an adequate supply of good housing at rents the lower-income groups could afford. Indeed, high standards of regulation might intensify the housing problem if they reduced speculative profits and thus discouraged building. In short, the restrictive codes had to be supplemented by "constructive" legislation. For middle-income groups, this would make possible low-interest government loans to individuals or to limited-dividend housing associations, and for the poor, low-rent municipal housing.

Mrs. Wood impatiently dismissed the arguments of economic conservatives that housing was not within the government's province and that government aid threatened to pauperize its beneficiaries. She asserted that housing, which in her opinion was basic to the welfare of the nation, must be regarded as a kind of public utility and thus a community responsibility in the congested, interdependent urban society of the twentieth century. Government aid to housing, she believed, no more threatened the character of the poor than did the free public school or the postal system. The test for government intervention was not abstract economics or morality but social need. Drawing upon her phenomenal grasp of the details of "constructive" European housing practice, particularly in England, Germany, Belgium, and Holland, she insisted that housing progress in Europe since the 1890's was a product of government financing and construction, and that America could succeed in clearing her slums and housing her people properly only if she emulated the Old World example.

Although Mrs. Wood did not play a significant role in the drafting and enactment of the public housing program of President Franklin D. Roosevelt, she was intimately involved as a publicist and an adviser to the new housing agencies. She served as consultant to the housing division of the Public Works Administration (1933–37) and its successor, the United States Housing Authority (1938–42). She advanced the cause of public housing as an officer of the National Public Housing Conference (1932–45) and served on the executive committee of the New Jersey State Housing Authority (1934–35). As an officer of the Regional Planning Association of America and the International Housing Association, Mrs. Wood promoted not only housing reform, but also zoning and city and regional planning, here and abroad. In recognition of her services, Smith College awarded her an honorary LL.D. degree in 1940. From 1919 onward she and her family had made their home at Cape May Court House, N.J. Mrs. Wood died in Greystone Park, N.J., of a cerebral hemorrhage in 1945 and was buried in the Naval Academy Cemetery at Annapolis, Md. Although she had no formal religious affiliation, she preferred the Episcopal service.

In contrast to her youthful romantic fiction, Mrs. Wood's housing publications were the product of a disciplined, precise, and realistic mind. More important than the fact that she was America's first woman housing economist was her uncompromising devotion to the principle of "constructive" legislation. She was among the first to revolt against America's almost exclusively "restrictive" housing program, and was probably the most influential interpreter of European government efforts in this field. Those Americans who were swayed by her writings in the 1920's did not need the shock of the depression to convince them of the need for a positive housing program.

[There are dozens of boxes of Mrs. Wood's papers stored at the architecture library of Columbia Univ., including personal and professional correspondence and pamphlets and articles on housing collected over several decades. The most convenient source for her thoughts on "constructive" legislation and the significance of European programs are her doctoral dissertation, above, and her *Housing Progress in Western Europe* (1923) and *Recent Trends in Am. Housing* (1931). Good examples of her early fiction are *Her Provincial Cousin: A Story of Brittany* (1893) and *Shoulder Straps and Sun-Bonnets* (1901). Short summaries of her life and work can be found in *Who Was Who in America*, vol. II (1950), and in the *Cape May Court House* (N.J.) *Gazette*, May 4, 1945. Mrs. Wood's son, Prof. Albert Elmer Wood of Amherst College, supplied information concerning family background, and Charles Abrams, the late N.Y. housing expert, discussed his memories of Mrs. Wood in an interview.]

ROY LUBOVE

WOOD, Mrs. John. *See* WOOD, Matilda Charlotte Vining.

WOOD, Julia Amanda Sargent (Apr. 13, 1825–Mar. 9, 1903), author, pioneer Minnesota newspaper editor, and Catholic novelist, was born in New London, N.H., the twelfth of fourteen children of Ezekiel Sargent, of whom eight were by his first wife and six (including one daughter older than Julia) by his second, Emily Everett (Adams) Sargent. Julia's father, who according to a town historian "possessed considerable property, and was influential in town affairs," gave his daughter an unusually extensive education for a girl of her era, at the New London Literary and Scientific Institution, at Colby Academy, and at the Charlestown (Mass.) Seminary, where she studied art, French, and Italian. In 1849 she was married to William Henry Wood (1817–1870), a lawyer eight years her senior whose brother had earlier married her sister Emily. Wood, also born in New Hampshire, had moved west with his parents to Tecumseh, Mich., at the age of fourteen, although he returned east to graduate from Union College in 1843. They were married in Covington, Ky., where he had gone to edit a newspaper for the presidential campaign of 1848. In 1851 they moved to the recently established Minnesota Territory, settling at Sauk Rapids, then little more than a fur-trading post.

Wood practiced law in Sauk Rapids, where he soon became district attorney for Benton County and a member of the first state legislature. He also edited and later purchased the *Sauk Rapids Frontiersman* (founded 1855), which he renamed in January 1859 the *New Era*, installing his wife as editor. They published the *New Era* until June 1863. JANE GREY SWISSHELM, then a fellow Minnesota journalist, described her colleague in 1860 as "exceedingly prepossessing, of medium height, with fair and ruddy complexion, dark masses of brown hair and large hazel eyes beaming with intelligence. In manner she is diffident almost to bashfulness, yet graceful, [and] ladylike. . . . She appears to be one of the few literary women who are happy in their domestic relations, and who have not fled to the pen to get away from the pressing consciousness of some crushing misery" (*St. Cloud Visiter*, Jan. 14, 1858). But unlike Mrs. Swisshelm, Mrs. Wood did not plead for woman's rights, and the *New Era* did not come out against slavery.

Mrs. Wood had contributed to local newspapers as early as the age of fourteen. After her marriage, writing under the pen name "Minnie Mary Lee," she published articles, poems, and stories in both the *Frontiersman* and the *New Era*. Many of them were reprinted in such Eastern periodicals as *Arthur's*

*Home Magazine* and *Peterson's*, to which she also contributed directly. Chief among her early articles is her "Life in the Woods" (*New Era*, Mar. 1, 15, 29, 1860), an account of her own pioneer experiences in Minnesota. This has historical value and is still readable, but most of her poems seem little better than doggerel to twentieth-century taste, and her stories are conventionally sentimental, though her pen name was well known in the mid-nineteenth century.

In 1868 Mrs. Wood began to turn from her earlier Protestant faith (presumably Congregational) toward Catholicism, and shortly after her husband's death, despite concern about alienating her friends, she entered that church. Her conversion, by her own account, grew out of the reading of Catholic literature, at first out of curiosity, that she had discovered accidentally in her maid's possession, particularly the Rev. Isaac Hecker's *Aspirations of Nature* (1857). In 1872 there appeared the first of her several novels on Catholic themes: *The Heart of Myrrha Lake*, a thinly disguised autobiography. At least seven more novels followed, including *Hubert's Wife* (1875), *The Brown House at Duffield: A Story of Life without and within the Fold* (1876), *Strayed from the Fold* (1878), and *From Error to Truth* (1890), all essentially tracts in which the hero and heroine have to overcome a difference of faith, giving the author an opportunity to set forth Catholic dogma.

Mrs. Wood had five children: Willie Percy (born 1852), Arthur De Lacy (1855), Grace Mary Eldred (1858), Harry P. (1861), and Julia May (1863), of whom the first and third died in infancy. The two surviving sons continued the family tradition of journalism, establishing, with Mrs. Wood's assistance, newspapers in Sauk Rapids and Two Harbors, and ultimately a chain of some thirty-two papers in Minnesota, the Dakotas, Michigan, and Wisconsin. Mrs. Wood spent her final years among the Benedictine nuns in St. Cloud, Minn. She died there at St. Raphael Hospital and was buried in the cemetery at Sauk Rapids.

[The Minn. Hist. Soc. has files of the Woods' newspapers and copies or brief descriptions of nearly all of Mrs. Wood's publications. Sister Grace McDonald has published a brief biography in *Mid-America*, Jan. 1935, and supplied other data for this sketch. On the family genealogy see Myra Belle Lord, *A Hist. of the Town of New London, Merrimack County, N.H.* (1899), pp. 139–41, 526. See also brief references in Warren Upham, *Minn. Biogs., 1655–1912* (Minn. Hist. Soc., *Collections*, vol. XIV, 1912), pp. xviii, 876–78; Mrs. W. J. Arnold, ed., *Poets and Poetry of*

Minn. (1864); *Northwestern Chronicle,* Sept. 4, 1869; and obituaries in St. Cloud *Daily Times* and *Jour. Press,* Mar. 10, 1903. The Wood family papers are at the Minn. Hist. Soc., which also has copies of Mrs. Wood's novels].

GRACE LEE NUTE

WOOD, Mary Elizabeth (Aug. 22, 1861–May 1, 1931), Episcopal missionary and librarian in China, was born in the township of Elba, N.Y., near Batavia, one of seven children of Edward Farmer Wood and Mary Jane (Humphrey) Wood. Both parents were of English ancestry and New England stock. Soon after Mary's birth the family moved to Batavia, where Wood became an express agent. Miss Wood attended private and public schools, including the Batavia High School. As a girl she took special charge of her youngest brother, Robert Edward, whom she trained with a strict hand, directing his education and prescribing books for him to read. When the Richmond Library in Batavia was founded in 1889 she became its first librarian.

Ten years later a visit to her brother Robert, now an Episcopal missionary in Wuchang, China, opened a new field to Miss Wood. At his suggestion, she took charge of an elementary English class at the mission's Boone School to relieve a shortage of teachers. She was to spend the rest of her life in China, receiving appointment by the Episcopal mission board as a lay missionary in 1904. Her drills in grammar and introduction to English literature were long remembered, but teaching did not entirely satisfy her, and two developments convinced her that she could be of wider service. A collegiate department was established at Boone in 1903, and the next year the Manchu government abolished the old Chinese system of classical examinations in favor of modern schools to introduce Western learning. Both innovations emphasized the need for libraries.

Soliciting funds and books from friends, women's auxiliaries, and church periodical clubs in the United States, Miss Wood built up a small library at Boone. On her first furlough in America, after an absence of seven years, she devoted time and energy to raising money for a separate library building. Many prominent people contributed to the cause, among them Seth Low, former president of Columbia University, and OLIVIA PHELPS STOKES, and the library building was opened in 1910. During succeeding furloughs she took library courses at Pratt Institute in Brooklyn, N.Y., and Simmons College in Boston to equip herself further for her lifework.

Miss Wood had hoped to make the Boone

Library a public as well as a college institution, reaching the people of the three neighboring cities of Wuchang, Hankow, and Hanyang, but this proved a difficult task. Her repeated efforts to bring students from outside schools to Boone for reading largely failed, owing to the long hours and fixed rules of the government schools and Boone's location far from the center of the city. Miss Wood then attempted an experiment that proved more successful. Branches of the Boone Library were established at several institutions in Wuchang and Hankow, both church and secular. Traveling libraries were sent not only to schools, but also to factories and other large institutions, like the Hanyang Iron and Steel Works. Some ventured to faraway places along the Yangtze River; a few went to north China; and one journeyed as far as Peking. These libraries usually consisted of a hundred or more books, sometimes all Chinese, sometimes all English, sometimes a combination. When Miss Wood introduced university extension lectures at Boone, many outside students came to browse among the books in the Boone Library.

As the work grew, Miss Wood felt keenly the need of technically trained Chinese assistants. In 1915 she sent Samuel T. Y. Seng to the United States to attend the library school of the New York Public Library (now the School of Library Service at Columbia University), and three years later another student, Thomas C. S. Hu. With their help Miss Wood started a library school at Boone in 1920, thus introducing professional education for librarians into China. The first six students graduated in 1922; by 1949 the Boone Library School had trained nearly five hundred. Several graduates came to America for further instruction, some returning to China as leading librarians, others remaining to serve with distinction in university and other libraries in the United States.

In 1923 Miss Wood took another step of national consequence. At the suggestion of Dr. David Yu, graduate of Boone College and general secretary of the Chinese Y.M.C.A., she initiated a petition, signed by some 150 Chinese leaders, asking that the United States remit an unassigned portion of the indemnity imposed after the Boxer Rebellion of 1899–1900 to be used for public library development in China. To support the petition she journeyed to Washington in 1924 and interviewed more than five hundred Senators and Congressmen. Some thought had already been given in Congress to remission, but Miss Wood's "unselfish zeal, . . . tact and good sense" (in the words of Senator William Cabell Bruce) were a major factor in securing passage of such a bill, though with the broader provision that the money be used for "educational and other cultural activities in China." The administration of the fund (which ultimately totaled $12,000,000) was entrusted to a special board, the China Foundation for the Promotion of Education and Culture, which included representatives of both countries. Among its various educational and scientific projects, the foundation allocated a large sum to establish the National Library of Peiping (Peking) and gave three annual grants to the Boone Library School for scholarships and general expenses. Miss Wood was also influential in having the American Library Association send a former president, Arthur E. Bostwick, librarian of the St. Louis Public Library, to China in 1925 to arouse interest among the Chinese people in public libraries. During Bostwick's lecture tour the Library Association of China was organized at Peking in 1926.

When in 1924 British and American mission groups in central China joined forces to found a union college—Huachung (Central China) University—located on the Boone campus and incorporating Boone College, the Boone Library School was at first taken into the new institution. Miss Wood and her colleagues, however, retained considerable autonomy. Friction arose over administrative policies, and in 1930 the Boone Library School withdrew from the university. Miss Wood, though failing in health, devoted her last years to raising an endowment for the school under the control of a board in the United States; this was later known as the Mary Elizabeth Wood Foundation. Under the Communist government of China the school was absorbed in 1950 by the National Wuhan University. In 1970 it was one of two professional library schools affiliated with universities, the other being at the National University of Peking.

Elizabeth Wood—tall, thin, upright of carriage—was not only a friend of the educated middle class, but also of the poor, whom she aided materially. Though she raised thousands of dollars for the library cause in China, she spent almost nothing on herself. Her clothes she picked up in church rummage sales. Like most American missionaries to China at this time, she was not educated in the Chinese language and literature; she could speak Chinese, but scarcely read it. Nevertheless, her labors for China's welfare won her the gratitude of the Chinese people. In a letter to the *New York Times* after her death, Dr. Fan Yuanlien, former Minister of Education of the Republic of China and later director of the China Foundation, described her as "the best friend

of the library movement in China." In the spring of 1931 many of her admirers were planning a triple anniversary celebration in honor of her coming to China, the building of the Boone Library, and the founding of the Library School, when she died of a heart attack in Wuchang. She was cremated in the Japanese crematory in Hankow and her ashes returned for burial in the Batavia Cemetery.

[Memorial number of *Boone Library School Quart.*, Sept. 1931; Marion DeC. Ward in *Library Jour.*, June 1, 1931; obituaries in *N.Y. Times* and Batavia (N.Y.) *Daily News*, May 2, 1931; *Literary Digest*, June 27, 1931; Mary Elizabeth Wood, *The Boxer Indemnity and the Library Movement in China* (Hankow, 1924?); Boone Univ., *China's First Library School* (Wuchang, 1928); Arthur E. Bostwick, *A Life with Men and Books* (1939); *A Summary Report of the Activities of the China Foundation for the Promotion of Education and Culture from 1925 to 1945* (1946); John L. Coe, *Huachung Univ.* (1962); information from Richmond Memorial Library, Batavia, N.Y.; MS. materials in the author's possession and personal acquaintance as a member of the first graduating class at the Boone Library School. The Mission Archives at the Nat. Council of the Protestant Episcopal Church, N.Y. City, contain materials on the school.]

A. KAIMING CHIU

**WOOD, Matilda Charlotte Vining** (Nov. 6, 1831–Jan. 11, 1915), actress and theatre manager, better known as Mrs. John Wood, was born in Liverpool, England, of theatrical parents. Her father, Henry Vining, was one of nine children of Charles Vining, silversmith, all of whom had stage careers; her mother, whose maiden name was Quantrell, was also an actress. One of her cousins was Fanny Elizabeth Vining, later the wife of the American actor E. L. Davenport and mother of the actress FANNY DAVENPORT.

Matilda Vining made her stage debut in 1841 and for the next twelve years acted in provincial English theatres. In May 1854, having married a fellow actor, John Wood, she signed a contract to come to America with her husband for the first season of the Boston Theatre in Boston, Mass. Wood was to act in low comedy roles, Mrs. Wood to play a "singing chambermaid." They made their American debuts on Sept. 11, 1854, as, respectively, Bob Acres in *The Rivals* and Gertrude in J. R. Planché's vaudeville, *The Loan of a Lover*. During their three seasons in the Boston Theatre company, mainly in farces and burlesques, Mrs. Wood began to outshine her husband. They first appeared in New York on Sept. 4, 1856, at the Academy of Music for one performance in Planché's fairy extravaganza, *The Invisible Prince;* and Mrs. Wood acted at Wallack's Theatre from Dec. 25, 1856, to Jan. 21, 1857.

In September 1857 the couple set out for San Francisco, playing in St. Louis and New Orleans en route. They opened in Maguire's Opera House on Jan. 18, 1858, and then toured the Pacific circuit, returning to San Francisco for a final week in May. Mrs. Wood now separated from her husband (who died in Victoria, British Columbia, on May 28, 1863) and the next season performed without him. In January 1859 she briefly managed the Forrest Theatre in Sacramento, Calif., and in March the American Theatre in San Francisco. According to Walter M. Leman, who acted with her at this time: "No more popular actress ever visited the Pacific Coast; her songs were whistled and sung in the streets. . . ."

Returning to New York, Mrs. Wood appeared at the Winter Garden in September 1859 in a company headed by Joseph Jefferson. For the next four years she acted in New York, Boston, Philadelphia, and New Orleans. In New York, on Oct. 8, 1863, she began three seasons as actress-manager of her own Olympic Theatre (which formerly had borne the name of her predecessor as manager, LAURA KEENE), with a company which included William E. Davidge, Charles Wyndham, James H. Stoddart, James Lewis, and Mrs. G. H. Gilbert (see ANNE HARTLEY GILBERT) and a repertoire largely of farce, burlesque, and extravaganza. "She was immensely popular," wrote Stoddart, "and much liked and respected by her company. While she managed the Olympic it was conducted in a thoroughly artistic way; she was a power in herself . . . and spared no expense. . . ."

In the summer of 1866 Mrs. Wood returned to England, and thereafter, except for an American tour of nine months in 1872–73, she distinguished herself as actress and manager in London, appearing at most of the important theatres there until her retirement in 1905. She managed the St. James Theatre, 1869–79, and was co-manager with Arthur Chudleigh of the New Royal Court Theatre from 1888 to 1891. At the old Court Theatre she created important roles in A. W. Pinero's *The Magistrate* (1885), *The Schoolmistress* (1886), and *Dandy Dick* (1887). Her last appearance was at the Drury Lane Theatre (1905) in *The Prodigal Son.* In religion she was a Christian Scientist in later years. She died at the age of eighty-three in her home, Dilkoosha, at Birchington-on-Sea, on the Isle of Thanet in Kent, and was buried there. Her only child, Florence,

also an actress, married Ralph Lumley, a playwright, in 1890.

Mrs. Wood was not beautiful, but she had a petite figure, a piquant face, and such warmth, vivacity, and high spirits that she charmed audiences everywhere. Laurence Hutton considered her one of the best burlesque actresses to appear in America. Bernard Shaw admired her Mrs. Malaprop. William Winter called her "that most dazzling of female comedians, that incarnation of frolic."

[F. Jerome Hart and John Parker, eds., *The Green Room Book* (1907); Charles E. Pascoe, ed., *The Dramatic List* (1880); obituary in London *Times*, Jan. 14, 1915; J. M. Bullock, "Hereditary Theatrical Families," in John Parker, ed., *Who's Who in the Theatre* (11th ed., 1952); T. Allston Brown, *A Hist. of the N.Y. Stage* (1903), vol. II, especially pp. 146–55; George C. D. Odell, *Annals of the N.Y. Stage*, vols. VI–IX (1931–37); files of the *Spirit of the Times* and *Wilkes' Spirit of the Times*, Sept. 1854–Aug. 1866; Eugene Tompkins and Quincy Kilby, comps., *The Hist. of the Boston Theatre, 1854–1901* (1908); George R. MacMinn, *The Theater of the Golden Era in Calif.* (1941); John H. Barnes, *Forty Years on the Stage* (1914); Walter M. Leman, *Memories of an Old Actor* (1886); James H. Stoddart, *Recollections of a Player* (1902); William Winter, *Vagrant Memories* (1915).]

BARNARD HEWITT

**WOOD, Sally Sayward Barrell Keating** (Oct. 1, 1759–Jan. 6, 1855), novelist, the ablest of the American women to continue the style of sentimental fiction established by Mrs. SUSANNA HASWELL ROWSON, was born in York, Maine, at the home of her maternal grandfather. Her father, Nathaniel Barrell, who at the time of her birth was serving as a lieutenant in General Wolfe's victorious army at Quebec, was descended from one of Boston's oldest families; he was a leading merchant in his native Portsmouth, N.H., and remained a loyal subject of King George through the American Revolution. Her mother, Sally (Sayward) Barrell, was the only child of Judge Jonathan Sayward, a man who had risen from the status of laborer to a position of wealth and eminence in the Pisquataqua region second only to that of Sir William Pepperell. Sayward's positions of trust included command of the sloop *Sea Flower* in the Louisbourg campaign, representative to the Massachusetts General Court, and judge of probate for York County. His Toryism during the Revolution caused a decline in his wealth and political influence, but he remained a substantial and respected citizen in York until his death in 1797.

The oldest of eleven children, Sally (sometimes called Sarah) spent most of her early life in her grandfather's mansion at York, imbibing the atmosphere of that unique seaboard aristocracy—often loyalist in politics, moderately Anglican or at least of a relaxed Puritan temper in religion, and rather gay and worldly in social tone. In contrast to her father and grandfather, she approved the American Revolution, though one can deduce from her later attendance at the Unitarian Church and at St. Paul's Episcopal Church in Portland, from her thoroughly conservative views on woman's role, and from her position in the top level of Portland society in the 1820's that she was not a radical democrat.

On Nov. 23, 1778, she was married to Richard Keating, a clerk in Judge Sayward's office. This happy match, which produced two daughters and a son, was prematurely ended by Keating's death from a fever in June 1783. Sally Keating then settled down at York to twenty-one years of widowhood and the trials of rearing her children alone. In this period she wrote four novels. All were published anonymously; in the preface to the first the author reported "that not one social, or one domestic duty, have ever been sacrificed or postponed by her pen; . . . a favorite implement, it has soothed many *melancholy*, and sweetened many *bitter* hours." In this first novel, *Julia and the Illuminated Baron* (1800), she joined with the New England clergy in their current tirade against the perils of the fanatical secularism of the French Revolution, as represented by the supposed secret society of the Illuminati. Her moralizing was enlivened by scenes of Gothic horror and the spice of the conventional seduction story as she hinted at the orgies of the hedonistic devotees of the Enlightenment. She selected a target closer to home in *Dorval; or the Speculator* (1801), in which she shrewdly implied that the whole system of paper money with its apparently arbitrary inflation and contraction in the Revolutionary era was unjust. In *Ferdinand and Elmira: A Russian Story* (1804) she wrote a Gothic romance in the style of the English author Ann Radcliffe; this book revealed more than her others her inability to create plausible characters and her consequent reliance on a mechanical plot. Her central message was contained in *Amelia; or the Influence of Virtue* (1802): that female virtue is the key to personal fulfillment and social stability. The humble slave of a profligate husband, Amelia accepts his bastard offspring and the taunts of his mistress without a whimper, finding the idea of divorce so degrading that death would be preferable. For "Amelia was not a disciple

of Mary Woolstonecraft [*sic*], she was not a woman of fashion, nor a woman of spirit. She was an old-fashioned wife, and she meant to obey her husband: she meant to do her duty in the strictest sense of the word."

Mrs. Keating's years of widowhood ended with her marriage, on Oct. 28, 1804, to Gen. Abiel Wood, a well-to-do citizen of Wiscasset, Maine. After his death in 1811 she moved to Portland, where as "Madam Wood" she was a local celebrity, often given the place of honor at social gatherings. In 1827, in her sixty-eighth year, her *Tales of the Night* was published in Portland. It was in many ways her best work, for here she stuck more closely to writing about what she knew: the climate and scenery of Maine and the manners of the people. About 1830 she moved to New York City to be near her son, Richard Keating, a sea captain; upon his death in 1833 she returned to Maine to live with a granddaughter in Kennebunk. Still alert mentally, she was described in her nineties as "a delightful companion to her great great grandchildren." She died in Kennebunk at the age of ninety-five.

Always modest about her literary ability, Mrs. Wood was said to have destroyed her manuscripts and given up writing upon first reading a novel by Scott. But her purposes had never been mainly artistic. In the preface to her first book she had expressed the hope that "if it cannot obtain the praise of the literati, it will not offend the moralist . . . [since] the motive which induced its publication, was a wish to do good, or at least to guard against evil."

[William Goold, "Madam Wood," Maine Hist. Soc., *Collections and Proc.*, 2nd ser., I (1890), 401–08; Henry E. Dunnack, *The Maine Book* (1920), pp. 140–46; Charles E. Banks, *Hist. of York, Maine* (1931), I, 375, 389–401; Charles A. Sayward, *The Sayward Family* (1890); Wilbur D. Spencer, *Maine Immortals* (1932), pp. 313–16; obituary in *Eastern Argus* (Portland), Jan. 9, 1855.]

RICHARD D. BIRDSALL

WOODBURY, Helen Laura Sumner (Mar. 12, 1876–Mar. 10, 1933), labor historian and government official, was born in Sheboygan, Wis., the only daughter and second child of George True Sumner and Katharine Eudora (Marsh) Sumner, natives, respectively, of Maine and Wisconsin. She was descended from William Sumner, who settled in Dorchester, Mass., in 1636; her maternal grandfather, Jerome Luther Marsh, was an early newspaper editor in southwestern Wisconsin and Colorado. Helen moved with her family to Durango, Colo., when she was five, and to Denver eight years later. Her youth also included six months' homesteading on a ranch in the Montezuma Valley of Colorado. Her father, a lawyer, served as district attorney in Sheboygan and judge in Durango.

Helen Sumner entered Wellesley College from the East Denver High School and was awarded a bachelor of arts degree in 1898 after three years of study. The Wellesley faculty of the 1890's included Vida D. Scudder (d. 1954) and KATHARINE LEE BATES in literature, KATHARINE COMAN in economics and history, Emily Greene Balch (d. 1961) in economics, and MARY WHITON CALKINS in psychology and philosophy—all activists on emerging social and economic questions. Miss Sumner's involvement began with a novel defending free silver during the Bryan campaign, *The White Slave or, "The Cross of Gold"* (1896), and service with the College Settlements Association.

Graduate study at the University of Wisconsin starting in February 1902 deepened her commitment to the rights of labor and to social justice. Prof. Richard T. Ely, for whom she was secretary, and his associate John R. Commons, who named her honorary fellow in political economy in 1904–06, deeply influenced her life and her professional work; she also studied American history with Frederick Jackson Turner and Ulrich B. Phillips. She contributed a chapter to Commons' *Trade Unionism and Labor Problems* (1905) and collaborated with another of her professors, Thomas S. Adams, an Ely associate, in an undergraduate textbook on *Labor Problems* (1905). In September 1906 she interrupted her graduate studies for a fifteen-month field investigation of woman suffrage in Colorado, financed by the Collegiate Equal Suffrage League of New York State; back in Madison, she wrote a model report, *Equal Suffrage* (1909), in six months. Later, in 1913, she marched in suffrage parades in Washington.

Her work for the doctorate brought her into closer association with Professor Commons. As his collaborator in the American Bureau of Industrial Research at the University of Wisconsin she helped edit *A Documentary History of American Industrial Society* (11 vols., 1910–11), especially volumes V and VI on the labor movement from 1820 to 1840. Her exhaustive investigations in primary sources for early American labor history also yielded "The Labor Movement in America, 1827–1837," the dissertation with which she received the Ph.D. in political economy and American history in 1908. In revised form, this constituted a major segment of the *History of Labour in the United States* (2 vols., 1918), written by Commons and a group of his protégés—the first scholarly study of the subject. Helen Sumner thus became part of the Commons group which dominated the study of American labor problems for decades, sharing writing and editorial duties with such figures as Selig Perlman, David J. Saposs, John B. Andrews, Ira Cross, and H. E. Hoagland. Also incorporated into the Commons volumes was the substance of her pioneer "History of Women in Industry in the United States," sponsored by the United States Bureau of Labor Statistics and published as volume IX (1910) of its monumental *Report on Condition of Woman and Child Wage-Earners in the United States.*

Between 1909 and 1913 Helen Sumner did not readily find permanent employment commensurate with her professional training and her outstanding record as investigator and labor scholar. Experience as a correspondence instructor at Wisconsin in 1907–08 had not attracted her to teaching. Early in 1910 she confided to Commons her ambition to write the history of industrial democracy in the United States: "I have been looking forward to that for years, and shall never be satisfied until I have realized my dreams. And nothing would please me more than to have the opportunity of working with you as we worked from 1905 to 1906 when we laid the foundation for the whole study of labor history. I look back upon that year as, in many respects, the most profitable of my life. My ambition, however, is to *be* . . . an author" (letter of Apr. 3, 1910, Commons Papers). But Commons could only offer marginal, temporary employment on his labor history.

Living with her widowed mother in Washington, D.C., after 1909, Miss Sumner engaged in contract studies for federal bureaus and similar scholarly projects. A research mission to Europe for the Bureau of Labor Statistics during 1910 produced *Industrial Courts in France, Germany, and Switzerland* (Bureau Bulletin No. 98). Her enthusiastic advocacy of American experimentation with such courts is found in articles in the *Review of Reviews* (October 1911) and *New Republic* (Sept. 18, 1915). Early in 1913 she joined JULIA LATHROP in the newly created Children's Bureau. She was promoted from expert in the industrial division to assistant chief of the bureau in 1915, but, wishing no responsibility for enforcement of the federal child labor law in 1917, she stayed on primarily as investigator. With Ella A. Merritt she compiled relevant state statutes for *Child Labor Legislation in the United States* (1915). To a Children's Bureau series on Administration of Child Labor Laws she contributed, with Ethel E. Hanks, case studies of the *Employment Certificate System* in Connecticut (Part 1, 1915) and in New York (Part 2, 1917), and an analysis of law enforcement in *Standards Applicable to the Administration of Employment-Certificate Systems* (1924). Such documented studies reflected the cautious strategy of Miss Lathrop toward the politically dangerous child labor problem.

Helen Sumner also directed and wrote for the Children's Bureau a sophisticated study of *The Working Children of Boston: A Study of Child Labor under a Modern System of Legal Regulation* (1922). Her statistical collaborator was the economist Robert Morse Woodbury, a Cornell University Ph.D. of 1915 who had joined the bureau in 1918. Following their marriage on Nov. 25, 1918, she resigned as director of bureau investigations and thereafter served on contract only. She had no children. Both she and her husband joined the staff of the Institute of Economics (Brookings Institution) in 1924; they retired in 1926. When Woodbury was appointed associate editor of *Social Science Abstracts* in 1928 they moved to New York City.

Throughout her writing and her life Helen Sumner Woodbury maintained a faith, deepened if not acquired through her association with Commons and other pragmatists at the University of Wisconsin, in the value of empirical investigation and in man's potential for improving society through knowledge and application of facts. An early ideological commitment in Colorado and Wisconsin to socialism and the Intercollegiate Socialist Society survived as membership in the League for Industrial Democracy, but her studies and her work experience gradually modified her views. She was especially attracted by the utilitarian philosophy of James MacKaye (author of *The Economy of Happiness,* 1906). A personal warmth shone through her scholarly demeanor, but her major influence flowed directly from her pioneer research and writing itself—twelve volumes and many articles on American labor history, labor problems, and the labor of women and children. Mrs. Woodbury died at her New York home of heart disease shortly before her fifty-seventh birthday. She was buried in Washington's Rock Creek Cemetery.

[Biographical details from *N.Y. Times*, Mar. 12, 1933; *Who's Who in America*, 1912–13 to 1932–33; Univ. of Wis. Archives; and correspondence with Robert Morse Woodbury. On her family, see William S. Appleton, *Record of the Descendants of William Sumner of Dorchester, Mass.* (1879),

p. 155. Mrs. Woodbury's own books and articles provide the best insights into her work and thought. Some of her many addresses to professional audiences have been published: see, e.g., Nat. Education Assoc., *Jour. of Proc.,* 1914, pp. 572–77, and *Jour. of Sociologic Medicine,* Apr. 1917. Her many periodical articles include two in the *Masses* in 1912. The State Hist. Soc. of Wis. has a collection of Mrs. Woodbury's papers, including correspondence, MSS., clipping files, and pamphlets. See also the Commons and Ely papers at the same repository; her correspondence with Commons between 1906 and 1918 reveals their collaborative methods.]

FREDERICK I. OLSON

**WOODHULL, Victoria Claflin** (Sept. 23, 1838–June 10, 1927), and her sister **Tennessee Celeste CLAFLIN** (Oct. 26, 1845–Jan. 18, 1923), unconventional reformers whose antics jolted Victorian America, were born in the tiny town of Homer, Ohio, into the clan of Reuben Buckman Claflin and Roxanna (Hummel) Claflin. Both parents were of obscure origins. Buck Claflin was a one-eyed backcountry drifter whose family had moved from Massachusetts to Pennsylvania while he was still a boy. Around 1825 he married Roxanna, a fierce, odd girl who was probably the daughter of a tavernkeeper at Hummel's Wharf on the Susquehanna. Sometime thereafter the couple moved to central Ohio and raised a squalid, swarming family. Of their ten children, Victoria was the seventh and Tennessee the ninth.

In 1849 a fire in Buck Claflin's freshly insured gristmill prompted the Claflins' hasty departure from Homer at the insistence of suspicious local citizens. A period of wandering ensued, during which they settled briefly in Mount Gilead, Ohio. In these rootless circumstances the girls' schooling was rude and intermittent. But more vivid influences abounded. Spiritualism raged in those years into the Middle West and profoundly affected the Claflins' fortunes. Victoria, a beautiful, sensitive girl, was swept by trances from early childhood, and the more earthy Tennessee soon became an able practitioner of the séance. A pooling of family talents produced a Claflin traveling medicine show featuring an elixir of life with Tennessee's picture on the bottle, brother Hebern posing as a cancer doctor, and the sisters offering a variety of psychic remedies for the credulous and comfort-hungry.

In 1853, at age fifteen, Victoria was married to Canning Woodhull, a physician, an apparently respectable but feckless man who was no match for her energies. Over the course of their twelve-year marriage she bore him two children—Byron, a mental defective, and Zula

Maud, who accompanied her mother through-out her subsequent career. Shortly after her marriage Victoria journeyed with her husband to California, where she dabbled briefly in the theatre. Reunion with the Claflins followed this excursion, and thereafter Victoria and Tennessee were a team; Dr. Woodhull, who had taken to drink, eventually drifted away. Charges of fraud, blackmail, and prostitution punctuated the sisters' travels through the Middle West; when one of Tennessee's patients died in Ottawa, Ill., in 1864, she fled to escape a manslaughter indictment. Two years later Tennessee secretly married a gambler named John Bartels, of whom little was heard thereafter. Meanwhile Victoria had met a dashing Civil War veteran, Col. James Harvey Blood, in a clairvoyant consultation in St. Louis. The two promptly became lovers, divorced their respective mates, and secured a marriage license on July 14, 1866, though there is no record that a ceremony was performed and Victoria continued to use her first husband's name. It was Colonel Blood who initiated Victoria into the constellation of reform causes surrounding nineteenth-century spiritualism. A free-lance intellectual faddist, embracing enthusiasms from mystic socialism through free love to greenbackism, he was her faithful mentor and companion over the turbulent decade to come.

By her later account it was in a Pittsburgh hotel room in the summer of 1868 that the spirit of Demosthenes appeared to Victoria Woodhull and instructed her to go to New York City. The impulse was sufficient to move the entire entourage—sisters, parents, Colonel Blood—to Manhattan. The promise of a ribald past was now to be fulfilled. Soon after their arrival the sisters arranged an interview with the railroad promoter Cornelius Vanderbilt. The Commodore, whose wife had just died, was aging but vigorous, keenly devoted to mystic wisdom, and lonely. The ministrations of Tennessee appealed. She afterward claimed to have extracted a promise of marriage from him, but the Vanderbilt family carefully steered him to a more suitable rematch. In any event it seems clear that Vanderbilt was the silent partner in the sisters' bizarre new career in financial speculation. After initial success in real estate ventures and a small share in the profits of Black Friday in September 1869, Victoria and Tennessee (who now styled herself Tennie C.) set up shop in two parlors of the Hoffman House in January 1870 and announced the brokerage firm of Woodhull, Claflin & Company open for business. Business thrived. Soon the "Bewitching Brokers" had moved to more elegant offices at 44 Broad Street in the heart of the financial district. Their quarters swarmed with the curious and skeptical, and while the men of Wall Street scoffed or fumed over their brazen stratagems, the sisters unquestionably prospered at their new calling. Vanderbilt's tips doubtless guided their speculations in his New York and Harlem Railroad, but native shrewdness ensured their survival in the city. The mansion they maintained on Murray Hill, spilling over with the Claflin coterie, was sufficient testimony to their achievement.

Having mastered the business world of the Gilded Age on its own terms, Victoria Woodhull now sailed blithely into politics, that other masculine preserve. Fresh inspiration had entered her life in the person of Stephen Pearl Andrews. A fifty-eight-year-old aberrant philosopher, Andrews carried the baggage of a long career in radical reform. College-trained in law and medicine, a disciple of Swedenborg and Fourier, a skilled linguist who had invented a universal language of his own, and a veteran of the abolition cause, he converted Victoria to his climactic vision. This was Pantarchy—the perfect state, where free love reigned among individuals while children and property were managed in common. Victoria Woodhull had long since concluded that the marriage tie was a degrading form of female bondage, and she proved an eager spokesman for Andrews' notions. Under her name they were delivered to the world as *Origin, Tendencies and Principles of Government*, first printed as articles in the *New York Herald* in 1870 and published as a book a year later.

On Apr. 2, 1870, flushed with notoriety and intent on her assertion of female competence, Victoria Woodhull declared herself a candidate for president of the United States. Six weeks later the first issue of *Woodhull & Claflin's Weekly* appeared to elaborate her program. Edited chiefly by Andrews and Colonel Blood during its intermittent six-year history, the *Weekly* was strident, eccentric, and outraging. Short skirts, free love, legalized prostitution; tax, housing, and dietary reform; world government and thinly veiled blackmail competed in its columns for attention. Sordid tales of Wall Street fraud made the *Weekly* an early pioneer in muckraking. When Section Twelve of Marx's International Workingmen's Association was organized in New York in 1871, Victoria and Tennessee cheerfully assumed its leadership, and the Communist Manifesto was published in English in their journal for the first time in America.

Meanwhile Victoria's interest in running for

the presidency had brought the woman suffrage movement to her attention. Having had no previous connection with this cause, she made a frontal attack. On Jan. 11, 1871, she delivered a memorial to the Judiciary Committee of the House of Representatives urging Congress to legalize woman suffrage under the Fourteenth Amendment. It was understood that Congressman Benjamin F. Butler of Massachusetts, a suffrage sympathizer, helped in the preparation of her address, which was the first important public speech of her career. Although the committee tabled her memorial, it served her immediate purpose. Leaders of the National Woman Suffrage Association, convening in Washington at the time, went to hear the Woodhull memorial and were impressed by Victoria's becoming appearance and modest behavior. She was invited to address their convention as well, and charmed many who had been apprehensive over stories of "The Woodhull." Tough-minded SUSAN B. ANTHONY was accustomed to discount attacks on the reputations of women with radical views, and ELIZABETH CADY STANTON, a lifelong crusader against the double standard of morality, joined her in forcefully defending the new recruit against hostile critics.

In befriending Victoria Woodhull, the suffragists risked more than they intended. Not only did her entry into the field deepen the wedge between the National Woman Suffrage Association and LUCY STONE's more conservative American Woman Suffrage Association, but Mrs. Woodhull quickly became a headstrong contender for leadership in the movement. The 1871 meeting of the national association in New York was labeled the Woodhull Convention when Victoria, by now an accomplished orator, delivered a ringing revolutionary appeal: "We mean treason; we mean secession. . . . We are plotting revolution; we will . . . [overthrow] this bogus Republic and plant a government of righteousness in its stead . . ." (*Speech of Victoria C. Woodhull on the Great Political Issue of Constitutional Equality . . . Together with Her Secession Speech,* 1871). A year later, with Mrs. Stanton's approval, she published a manifesto in her *Weekly* over the names of the N.W.S.A. leadership calling on its convention to form a new People's party to enter the presidential race of 1872. Miss Anthony now recognized the threat of disaster. Having concluded that Victoria Woodhull was dominated by *"men spirits"* and that she sought to "run our craft into her port and none other," she repudiated the Woodhull manifesto and came to New York to battle at close quarters. The upshot was

that Miss Anthony reasserted command of the N.W.S.A. and Victoria Woodhull held her own convention, which on May 10, 1872, acclaimed her the presidential nominee of the "Equal Rights" party. The Negro leader Frederick Douglass was named as her running mate, but ignored the honor, preferring Grant.

By election day Victoria Woodhull was in jail, engulfed in the flaring melodrama of the Beecher-Tilton adultery case. Her own domestic arrangements had been complicated when the ailing Dr. Woodhull reappeared to share her home with Colonel Blood, and in May 1871 scandalmongers seized this pretext to assail her for harboring two husbands. In an open letter Victoria Woodhull defended her practices and hurled back a charge of concubinage and hypocrisy in high places. Her target was the powerful preacher of Brooklyn's Plymouth Church, Henry Ward Beecher (whose sister HARRIET BEECHER STOWE had recently caricatured Victoria in her novel *My Wife and I,* although another sister, ISABELLA BEECHER HOOKER, remained Victoria's loyal friend). Having learned from Mrs. Stanton the tale of Beecher's liaison with Elizabeth Tilton, one of his parishioners and the wife of the editor Theodore Tilton, Mrs. Woodhull demanded from Beecher a candid profession of his conduct, in effect an endorsement of her own views. Beecher maintained official silence, dismissing Victoria and Tennessee as "two prostitutes." For his part Theodore Tilton tried strenuously to mollify Victoria by taking her into his confidence and writing a flattering biography of her. But Victoria was unappeased.

Her troubles were accumulating. Attacked in the press and by Beecher's friends, rebuffed by the suffragists, expelled from the International (in March 1872) for the eccentricities of her Section Twelve, abandoned by Vanderbilt, she had had to give up her Murray Hill mansion and suspend publication of her bankrupt *Weekly* in the summer of 1872. In a cool rage she spilled the whole story of Beecher and Mrs. Tilton in a speech before the National Association of Spiritualists in Boston. When newspapers refused to publicize her charges, she printed them in a special issue of her *Weekly* (revived for the occasion) on Nov. 2, 1872. Within hours she and her sister were arrested and jailed under a federal statute, applied to them at the behest of the inventive moralist Anthony Comstock, for passing obscenity through the mails. Seven months of litigation followed, during which Ben Butler publicly denied the relevance of the statute in question to Victoria's case. Free speech seemed at issue, and the sisters won considerable sympathy before they were acquitted. But the entire episode, including Beecher's own acquittal in the later Beecher-Tilton trial, essentially ended Victoria Woodhull's American career.

Suffering a siege of poor health, no longer a sensation on the lecture circuit, she began to moderate her shrill insistence on public vindication and veered toward respectability. Religious symbolism now veiled her views on sex. She abandoned her spiritualist associations, divorced Colonel Blood for adultery (1876), and in the last published issue of her *Weekly* defined marriage as "a divine provision." When Commodore Vanderbilt died in 1877, leaving the lion's share of his fortune to his son William, the rest of the family contested the will, citing the Commodore's spiritualism as evidence of incompetence. At this juncture Victoria and Tennessee quietly departed for England; rumors flew that their journey was subsidized by William Vanderbilt to forestall the sisters' testimony.

Soon Victoria was lecturing again. A London address, "The Human Body the Temple of God," found an eager listener in John Biddulph Martin, of Martin's Bank, London. He professed his love, and after overcoming six years' opposition from his genteel parents they were married on Oct. 31, 1883. Victoria set to work improving her genealogy and disowning her past to meet the needs of her new station, and even went to the trouble of suing the British Museum for holding pamphlets about her part in the Beecher scandal. Not to be outdone, Tennessee Claflin married Francis Cook, head of a large London dry goods firm, in October 1885, and when Cook became a baronet a year later she assumed the title Lady Cook. The sisters' activism remained unstifled, if muted. With the help of her daughter Zula Maud, Victoria published the *Humanitarian*, a journal devoted to eugenics, from 1892 to 1901. Both sisters returned frequently to the United States to refight old battles. Surviving their husbands, they lived on amid affluence and assorted good works. Tennessee died in London in her seventy-eighth year and was buried at West Norwood Cemetery. Victoria lived to the age of eighty-eight and died in her sleep at her home at Bredon's Norton, Tewkesbury. Her body was cremated.

From the moment of their first notoriety, the sisters' lives were obscured in a swirl of yellow journalism, tortured apologetics, and well-spiced hearsay. Only their physical attractiveness seems undisputed. Tennessee was the gayer and less complicated of the two, a pretty, uninhibited hoyden. It was Victoria, with her fine features and contained expression, who

possessed the rarer beauty and a presence which was urgent if not profound. Strong-willed and impressionable, she had stormed the domestic and public conventions of a society which badly needed heretics. She fell well short of prophecy. But she and her sister had made life interesting for many, and perilous for a few.

[The primary sources are scattered and unsatisfactory. Emanie Sachs, *"The Terrible Siren": Victoria Woodhull (1838–1927)* (1928), rambling, impressionistic, and perceptive, remains the best biography. Theodore Tilton's dime tract, *Victoria C. Woodhull* (1871), is an unreliable curio. A brief sketch and excellent bibliography appear in Madeleine B. Stern, *We the Women* (1963). Irving Wallace offers a balanced appraisal of Mrs. Woodhull in *The Square Pegs* (1957). Two recent book-length treatments are Johanna Johnston, *Mrs. Satan: The Incredible Saga of Victoria C. Woodhull* (1967), and M. M. Marberry, *Vicky: A Biog. of Victoria C. Woodhull* (1967). *Woodhull & Claflin's Weekly* is assayed in Frank L. Mott, *A Hist. of Am. Magazines*, III (1938), 443–53. Mrs. Woodhull's militant views on marriage are vividly conveyed in a published lecture, *Tried as by Fire* (1874). Other publications include: *The Origin, Tendencies and Principles of Government* (1871), *Stirpiculture, or the Scientific Propagation of the Human Race* (1888), *Garden of Eden: Allegorical Meaning Revealed* (1889), and *Humanitarian Money: The Unsolved Riddle* (1892). Obituary information may be found in the *N.Y. Times*, Jan. 20, Mar. 22, 1923, June 11, Aug. 17, 1927, and the London *Times*, Jan. 20, 1923, and June 11, 1927.]

GEOFFREY BLODGETT

**WOODROW, Nancy Mann Waddel** (1866?–Sept. 7, 1935), author, better known as Mrs. Wilson Woodrow, was born in Chillicothe, Ohio, one of nine children of William and Jane S. (McCoy) Waddle (she later used the spelling Waddel). One of her paternal great-grandfathers had emigrated from Ireland in 1787, settling first in Pennsylvania and later in Virginia. John Waddle, her grandfather, became one of the early merchants of Chillicothe. Her father, a physician, developed a large practice there and later became a trustee of Ohio University, his alma mater.

Little is known of Nancy Waddel's early life. She apparently received no formal education but was tutored in any subject in which she developed an interest. Regarding her earliest efforts at writing verse, she once observed that with eight brothers and sisters she had no lack of adverse criticism. In 1896 she became assistant editor of the *Chillicothe Daily News*. She resigned the position after her marriage, on Aug. 4, 1897, to James Wilson Woodrow, a mining engineer and prospector who was a distant cousin of Woodrow Wilson, later president of the United States. For the next three years Mrs. Woodrow accompanied her husband on prospecting trips through the mountains of Colorado and the deserts of Arizona, gathering much of the material she was later to use in stories and novels. Life in mining and lumber camps fascinated her, particularly the vitality and self-sufficiency of the women.

About 1900 she moved to New York City and launched upon a writing career that lasted almost to the end of her life. At this point or shortly thereafter she apparently separated from her husband (*Scioto Gazette*, Chillicothe, Ohio, Sept. 7, 1935). Despite her inexperience, she encountered little difficulty in selling her first stories and articles. Her initial success had a stimulating effect, and during her most productive period (1902–13) she contributed a prodigious number of articles (both serious and humorous), short stories, and verse to more than seventeen magazines of the day, including *McClure's, Cosmopolitan, Life, Harper's, American*, and *Good Housekeeping*. She also found time to write a play and thirteen novels. She wrote almost exclusively under the name Mrs. Wilson Woodrow, with the exception of a serial, "A Leaf in the Current," published in *Metropolitan Magazine* under the pseudonym "Jane Wade." Her career closely paralleled that of her brother Charles Carey Waddell (1868–1932), a prolific writer of mystery stories who came to New York about the same time, and they collaborated on at least one story. A sister, Eleanor Waddel, was also a writer and an editor of *Vogue Magazine*.

Editors to whom Mrs. Woodrow submitted her early stories and novels of life in Western mining and lumber settlements were impressed by the "virility" of her writing and were inclined to believe the author was actually a man using a woman's pseudonym. Although there is a definite strain of masculine forcefulness and vigor in her style, the emphasis is actually on the heroine as the real embodiment of strength and ingenuity, who finally defers to the hero more from convention than from necessity. In thus presenting a "New Woman," allowed to realize her capabilities to the fullest extent without radically disrupting a man-centered society, Mrs. Woodrow differed both from the sentimental women novelists of the period and from the ardent feminists who sought radical social changes. Later, when she turned to writing mysteries, her story pattern remained the same.

Mrs. Woodrow was at her best in the short story and in the quick, incisive delineation of character. She also showed definite ability as a humorist, perhaps most evident in a series of satires on popular novels written for *Life* magazine in 1905–06. Though her humorous writing was generally designed to expose absurdities in social customs of the period, other articles such as "The Splendid Years" (*Sunset*, January 1920), were a serious attempt to present a way out of the restrictions placed on women by society. She died in New York City in 1935 of a coronary occlusion and chronic nephritis, and was buried in Grandview Cemetery in Chillicothe.

[Among Mrs. Woodrow's writings are the novels *The New Missioner* (1907), *The Silver Butterfly* (1908), *The Black Pearl* (1912), and *Swallowed Up* (1922); the following articles in *Life:* "The Beautiful Gentleman" (Oct. 26, 1905), "The Scrambler" (Dec. 9, 1905), and "Mausoleum of Laughter" (Jan. 18, 1906); and a play, "The Universal Impulse," *Smart Set*, June 1911. Biographical sources: obituaries in *N.Y. Times* and *N.Y. Herald Tribune*, Sept. 8, 1935, and *Publishers' Weekly*, Sept. 14, 1935; *Who Was Who in America*, vol. I (1942); *Bookman*, Dec. 1912, p. 365; *Reader*, Feb. 1906, p. 310; Gelett Burgess, ed., *My Maiden Effort* (1921), p. 279; *The Biog. Cyc. and Portrait Gallery with an Hist. Sketch of the State of Ohio*, II (1884), 368–69 (on William Waddle); information from Chillicothe Public Library, including an obituary from the *Chillicothe News-Advertiser*, Sept. 7, 1935, which gives her birth year as 1866; death record from N.Y. City Dept. of Health, which gives her age as sixty-five.]

THOMAS JOHNSRUD

**WOODROW, Mrs. Wilson.** *See* WOODROW, Nancy Mann Waddel.

**WOODS, Katharine Pearson** (Jan. 28, 1853–Feb. 19, 1923), author, teacher, and social service worker, was born in Wheeling, Va. (now W.Va.), the eldest of three daughters of Alexander Quarrier Woods and Josephine Augusta (McCabe) Woods. She grew up in Baltimore, Md., to which the family moved in 1856. Her father, descended from an early Huguenot emigrant to Virginia, Alexander Quarrier, was a tobacco merchant; he enlisted in the Confederate Army during the Civil War and died of pneumonia in 1863. Her mother's family, Irish Protestants, had been eminent in colonial Pennsylvania, from which a Revolutionary ancestor had moved to Virginia. There the McCabes became prominent in literature and education. For several years after her father's death Miss Woods lived in the rectory of her talented grandfather, the Rev. James Dabney McCabe of St. James' Episcopal Church, West River, Md. A literary atmosphere prevailed there (an uncle, James Dabney McCabe, Jr., was an author), and she indulged her precocious taste for reading and reflection.

The Woods family returned in 1867 to Baltimore, where Katharine studied with her mother and in a private seminary. In 1874 she became a postulant with the All Saints Sisters of the Poor at Mount Calvary Episcopal Church, and although she withdrew because of frail health, the deep religious experience awakened an urge for social betterment that found expression in charitable work and in her literary career. For ten years (1876–86) she taught in girls' schools, for a time in Wheeling, W.Va., where she also worked among the poor. In 1884 she published a sympathetic account of a strike in Wheeling and two short stories dealing with the nail workers there. Back in Baltimore by 1888, she joined the Knights of Labor. Her concern for the working classes was broadened by reading Edward Bellamy's *Looking Backward* (1888) and by her acquaintance with Richard T. Ely, professor of economics at the Johns Hopkins University and an advocate of Christian socialism. Bellamy and Ely helped arouse public interest in her secretly written and anonymously published first novel, *Metzerott, Shoemaker* (1889). Reflecting her life among the German working people of Wheeling, it set the character of her social novels, advocating a more just relation between capital and labor through Christian cooperation. Considered by many as her best work, it was a literary sensation and became required reading in sociology courses at some colleges and universities.

A similar theme prevails in Miss Woods' *A Web of Gold* (1890). Her *From Dusk to Dawn* (1892) anticipated the Emmanuel Movement for faith healing, which won her ardent support. Later she turned to the popular vein of religious fiction derived from early Christian history in *John: A Tale of King Messiah* (1896) and *The Son of Ingar* (1897). The family's sentimental tie with Virginia inspired *The True Story of Captain John Smith* (1901), a frank effort to redeem his reputation. Over the years she also published many poems and short stories in magazines. Her novels, all strongly moral and religious, were widely read and helped promote interest in social reformation. Less convincing is her religious fiction, which is on uncertain ground where it departs imaginatively from the Biblical narratives. Her verse displays a deep appreciation of natural beauty and the power of love, but does not give her high rank as a poet.

The bulk of Miss Woods' significant writing was done in the twelve years 1889–1901.

Thereafter she lived mostly in Baltimore, serving the community in charitable activities connected with the Episcopal Church. A paper she read at the Woman's Literary Club is said to have brought about "Baltimore's awakening to the question of woman suffrage" (*Woman's Journal*, May 2, 1891, p. 142). In 1893–94, under a fellowship from the College Settlements Association, she made a study of factory working conditions in Philadelphia and Boston that was issued by the American Statistical Association in its *Quarterly Publications* (December 1895), one of a number of articles she wrote on current social problems. In 1895 she was head resident of the Hartford (Conn.) Social Settlement. Between 1903 and 1906 she worked as a missionary among the mountain folk of North Carolina, and from 1907 to 1912 she taught kindergarten in Baltimore.

Miss Woods' influence radiated from her personality quite as much as from her writings. She is affectionately remembered as "tiny," refined, soft-spoken and retiring, with a keen sense of humor, abundant energy, and firm character. She was loved by everyone, and especially by children. All were impressed by the spiritual quality of her countenance, with its deep and tender gray eyes. Early in February 1923 a severe cold turned into pneumonia, and after a few days she died at her home. She was buried in Greenmount Cemetery, Baltimore.

[The fullest and most objective account of Miss Woods is in the *Library of Southern Literature*, XIII (1907), 5979–99, which includes a biographical sketch by Fannie K. Reiche and selections from her writings. See also Hester Crawford Dorsey, "The Author of 'Metzerott, Shoemaker,'" *Lippincott's Monthly Mag.*, Sept. 1890; *Woman's Who's Who of America*, 1914–15; *Who Was Who in America*, vol. I (1942); Robert A. Woods and Albert J. Kennedy, eds., *Handbook of Settlements* (1911), p. 27. Information was received also from Mother Virginia, Superior of All Saints Sisters, Catonsville, Md., and from Rebecca· E. (Mrs. Charles E.) Woollen, the wife of Miss Woods' nephew. Miss Woods published an article on Edward Bellamy in *Bookman*, July 1898.]

NELSON R. BURR

**WOODWARD-MOORE, Annie Aubertine.** See MOORE, Annie Aubertine Woodward.

**WOOLLEY, Helen Bradford Thompson** (Nov. 6, 1874–Dec. 24, 1947), psychologist, was born in Chicago, Ill., the daughter of David Wallace Thompson, a shoe manufacturer, and Isabella Perkins (Faxon) Thompson. After attending Englewood High School she entered the University of Chicago, where she concentrated in philosophy and neurology, receiving the Ph.B degree in 1897 and the Ph.D., summa cum laude, in 1900. Her doctoral dissertation, "Psychological Norms in Men and Women," written under the direction of James R. Angell, was published in 1903 (both under that title and as *The Mental Traits of Sex*). After a year of study in Paris and Berlin on a fellowship of the Association of Collegiate Alumnae (later the American Association of University Women), she became an instructor at Mount Holyoke College and, in 1902, director of its psychological laboratory and professor of psychology. She left this post in 1905 and on Aug. 8, in Yokohama, Japan, was married to Dr. Paul Gerhardt Woolley, director of the Serum Laboratory in Manila, Philippine Islands, whom she had known at the University of Chicago. Their two children were Eleanor Faxon (born in 1907) and Charlotte Gerhardt (1914).

In Manila, Mrs. Woolley worked as experimental psychologist in the Philippines Bureau of Education, but in April 1906 she moved to Bangkok, where her husband headed Siam's new serum laboratory and in 1907 became chief inspector of health. The Woolleys returned to the United States in 1908, and after a year at the University of Nebraska, where Paul Woolley served as associate professor of pathology, settled at the University of Cincinnati, where he became professor of pathology and (1910–13) dean of the medical college. Helen Woolley now resumed her faculty role, serving as instructor in philosophy (1909–11).

Early in 1911 Mrs. Woolley was appointed director of the new Bureau for the Investigation of Working Children, founded through the efforts of the Cincinnati social economist M. Edith Campbell (1875–1962) following enactment of the 1910 Ohio child labor law, which made possible extensive comparisons of working and school children. From this project developed the Cincinnati Vocation Bureau, which in 1914 became an integral part of the Cincinnati public school system. Directed by Mrs. Woolley, it included a pioneering psychological laboratory. The bureau's five-year follow-up study of the mental and physical characteristics of more than 750 children who had left school to go to work at the age of fourteen, as compared with those of an equal number who remained in school, provided a store of challenging facts. Mrs. Woolley drew upon this material for articles, speeches (before national groups of educators, social workers, and vocational guidance personnel), special reports (including a psychological monograph, *Mental and Physical Measurements of Working Children*, written with Charlotte Rust Fischer,

1914), and related studies (in 1921 of the feebleminded; in 1923 of school failures). Mrs. Woolley's full report of the investigation was published in 1926 as *An Experimental Study of Children at Work and in School between the Ages of Fourteen and Eighteen Years* (1926). She drew upon her experience also when she and Miss Campbell, working with the state superintendent of public instruction, drafted and helped lobby through to passage a revised compulsory school attendance and child labor law for Ohio—the Bing Law of 1921, a model of its kind.

During World War I, while her husband served in the army, Mrs. Woolley was active on several committees of the Ohio branch of the Council of National Defense and helped organize a scholarship fund (the later Cincinnati Scholarship Foundation) which became a part of the first Cincinnati War Chest. An influential leader, she was elected president of the National Vocational Guidance Association in 1921 and, that same year, served on the boards of the Cincinnati Community Chest and the Woman's City Club. In person a small, slender, attractive brunette and in her work a cautious, open-minded scientist, Mrs. Woolley was nonetheless a fearless fighter when causes she embraced were threatened. In 1921 she led the exodus from a professional meeting in a leading hotel when the admission of a Negro member was questioned. Long a member of the Ohio Woman Suffrage Association, in 1919 she was chairman of the Woman's Suffrage Committee of Greater Cincinnati during the final, successful stage of the fight for ratification of the federal amendment.

In the fall of 1921 the Woolley family moved to Detroit, Mich., where Paul Woolley had become affiliated with the Detroit College of Medicine. Before leaving Cincinnati, Helen Woolley was tendered a farewell civic dinner arranged by the Woman's City Club, and an annual scholarship was established in her honor. In Detroit she was appointed the psychologist on the staff of the Merrill-Palmer School, recently established under the bequest of LIZZIE MERRILL PALMER, and in 1922 she became associate director. One of her first responsibilities was organizing a nursery school—one of the first in the country—to serve as a laboratory for the study of child development and the education of teachers. She also gave courses to both undergraduate and graduate students in child psychology and child guidance, and supervised graduate research.

Dr. Woolley's own investigations during her years at the Merrill-Palmer School centered in two areas: the personality development and the mental development of children. Her studies of the development of personality were based on her unusual ability to observe behavior and to interpret motivations in children, originally stimulated by her observations of her own two daughters. Her first publication in this field, "Personality Studies of the Three-Year-Olds" (*Journal of Experimental Psychology,* December 1922), was followed by three classic case studies of children in the Merrill-Palmer nursery school: "Agnes: A Dominant Personality in the Making" and "Peter: The Beginnings of a Juvenile Court Problem" (*Pedagogical Seminary and Journal of Genetic Psychology,* December 1925 and March 1926) and *David: A Study of the Experience of a Nursery School in Training a Child Adopted from an Institution* (Child Welfare League of America, *Case Studies,* no. 2, 1925).

At the time Dr. Woolley came to Detroit, she was one of the few psychologists in the United States who had made experimental studies of mental abilities. At the Merrill-Palmer School she became interested in the possible effect on mental ability of an optimum environment like the nursery school, and made preliminary studies of the changes in three-year-olds over the span of a year. With Elizabeth Cleveland, a graduate student at the University of Michigan, she worked on the standardization of four performance tests based on Montessori apparatus; this was the beginning of the Merrill-Palmer Scale of Mental Tests. The work with Miss Cleveland stimulated a friendship that led to other joint professional projects and gave emotional support to Helen Woolley in later years, particularly after 1924, when Paul Woolley separated from his wife and moved to California.

During these years (1921–26) Mrs. Woolley contributed significantly to the broader child development movement that was then gaining momentum in the United States. An excellent speaker, much in demand among women's groups, educational institutions, and scientific societies, she also wrote in a clear, straightforward style, contributing not only to scientific journals but to such magazines as *Mother and Child, Child Study,* and the *New Republic.* She thereby stimulated interest in child development among both professionals and laymen. As vice-president (1923–25) of the American Association of University Women and chairman of its committee on educational policies, she helped institute a program within its branches for the study of elementary education and of the preschool child, in the hope that women college graduates might provide community leadership for the improvement of

schools and the welfare of preschool children, as well as supervise more adequately the development of their own children. Largely through her efforts, the association received a five-year grant from the Laura Spelman Rockefeller Memorial Fund to finance this study program.

In 1925, now fifty and at the height of her career, Mrs. Woolley accepted an invitation to go to New York as professor of education at Teachers College, Columbia University, and director of the Institute of Child Welfare Research, which had been recently established at the college by a grant from the Laura Spelman Rockefeller Memorial Fund. By the end of her first year there, the institute had moved to a building of its own, two nursery schools had been organized, and the educational clinic had revised its program to center research on various phases in the life of the preschool child and in the closely related field of parental education.

Living alone in New York, with her daughters away at school, Mrs. Woolley found the impersonal atmosphere of a large university difficult. When she learned that the separation from her husband would be permanent (he remained in California and died there in 1932), she became ill, and in 1926 was given leave from the university. Nearly two years later, in the fall of 1928, she resumed her duties, having meanwhile visited a number of research centers in Europe. But the difficulties of adjusting to changes which had taken place during her absence brought on renewed feelings of insecurity, and in the fall of 1929, at Mrs. Woolley's request, Lois Hayden Meek was appointed associate director of the institute to take over some of the administrative responsibilities. With this help, Mrs. Woolley continued teaching during the next academic year, but she had lost her ability to work effectively, and in February 1930 the college asked her to resign. Gradually her professional career ended, and she spent the remaining years of her life under the care of her daughter Eleanor. She died at her daughter's home in Havertown, Pa., late in 1947, of a disecting aortic aneurysm, the result of hypertensive cardiovascular disease. Cremation followed at West Laurel Hill Cemetery, Philadelphia. Her religious affiliation had been with the Presbyterian Church.

Helen Thompson Woolley was not only a gifted psychologist but also a woman with a strong social goal: to better the lives of women and children through improvements in family life, education, welfare, and social legislation. In her work she exemplified the movement of the 1920's, led by Lawrence K. Frank, which sought to bring together different disciplines concerned with the study of children in order to perceive the child as a whole. Her last major publication, the chapter on "Eating, Sleeping and Elimination" in *A Handbook of Child Psychology* (1931), edited by Carl Murchison, integrated material from nutrition, physical growth, pediatrics, education, and psychiatry, as well as psychology. The child development movement was permanently enriched by her pioneering contributions.

[The account of Mrs. Woolley's life through her Cincinnati years was written by Mrs. Zapoleon, the rest by Dr. Stolz. The principal sources for the first part of the article are (besides Mrs. Woolley's own writings): information from the Univ. of Chicago Archives and the Chicago Hist. Soc. (father's occupation); Martin Fischer's biographies of *Christian R. Holmes* (1937) and *William B. Wherry* (1938); and the author's research for a biography of M. Edith Campbell. The sources for the second part of the article are: information from archives of Merrill-Palmer Institute and of the Am. Assoc. of Univ. Women; Elizabeth Cleveland, *Training the Toddler* (1925); reports of the Institute of Child Welfare Research (later the Child Development Institute) as published in Teachers College, *Report of the Dean*, 1925–30; Lawrence A. Cremin et al., *A Hist. of Teachers College, Columbia Univ.* (1954); author's correspondence with Mrs. Woolley and with Prof. Mabel Carney; personal acquaintance; death record from Pa. Dept. of Health. Published biographical information is meager. See Cedric Fowler, "They Train the Young Idea," *New Outlook*, Feb. 1935, p. 35; Ruth W. Tryon, *Investment in Creative Scholarship* (1957), p. 52; *Who Was Who in America*, vol. I (1942), on Paul Woolley, and vol. III (1960); Durward Howes, ed., *Am. Women*, 1939–40; *Am. Men of Science* (7th ed., 1944); obituary in *Educational Forum*, May 1948).]

MARGUERITE W. ZAPOLEON
LOIS MEEK STOLZ

**WOOLLEY, Mary Emma** (July 13, 1863–Sept. 5, 1947), college president, was born at her mother's family home in South Norwalk, Conn. Her ancestors were English; with the exception of her paternal grandfather, who migrated from Jamaica, they had lived in New England for several generations. She was the first child of Joseph Judah Woolley, a Congregational minister, and his second wife, Mary Augusta (Ferris) Woolley, a former schoolteacher. She had two brothers; a sister died in infancy. When May, as she was called, was eight, her father left his pastorate in Meriden, Conn., for one in Pawtucket, R.I. There his interest in helping factory workers, whether Protestant or not, contributed to a split in his

church. His daughter, who resembled him in many ways, recalled that "his belief in the social mission of the church was far in advance of his day." A chaplain in the Civil and Spanish-American wars, he instilled in her a lasting pacifism.

Mary Woolley had her first formal education at Mrs. Fannie Augur's in Meriden, a tiny school fostered by her father. In Pawtucket she attended successively Miss Bliss', Mrs. Lord's, and Mrs. Davis' schools. She next studied at Providence High School, but withdrew in the spring of 1882 because of her father's church difficulties and at his insistence entered Wheaton Seminary, Norton, Mass., that fall. Though not yet a college, Wheaton had, she recalled, "a vitality of intellectual life any college might envy." After graduating in 1884, she returned as a member of the faculty from 1885 to 1890 (except for the 1886–87 term).

A two-month tour of Europe in the summer of 1890, with a group largely from Smith College, enlarged Mary Woolley's educational ideals. Inspired by the scholarly work in English women's colleges, she determined to go to Oxford. Her father, however, related her plans to E. Benjamin Andrews, president of Brown University, who was eager to give women the privileges of his institution, and at his invitation she entered Brown in the fall of 1891, the first of her sex to do so. She participated as a "guest" in classes with men (notably Hebrew under James Richard Jewett, history under J. Franklin Jameson, and philosophy under Andrews) before joining the separate courses for women opened later that fall.

A handsome woman with dark hair and dark eyes, rosy cheeks, and a conspicuously erect bearing, Miss Woolley was the natural leader of her sister students. She set an example of dignity and conscientious study, stressing their responsibility for the future of women's education at Brown. Elected in her senior year to the editorial board of the college magazine, she recalled "nothing but the utmost courtesy from any student." In 1894 she and Anne Tillinghast Weeden received the first A.B.'s given by Brown to women. Miss Woolley remained a fourth year, working chiefly under Jameson and winning the A.M. Her only works of formal scholarship, three scrupulously "scientific" historical articles, appeared during the 1890's.

In 1895 she became instructor in Biblical history and literature at Wellesley College, in 1896 associate professor, and in 1899 professor. Besides teaching required Biblical courses she introduced electives in church history. Quickly recognized as a gifted teacher and public speaker, she proved her administrative talents as department chairman and head of a large dormitory. In December 1899, when she was planning a year's leave for graduate study, she received two offers: the deanship of what had now become the Women's College at Brown and the presidency of Mount Holyoke College. She accepted the position at Mount Holyoke and was formally elected early in 1900, although she did not assume her new duties until Jan. 1, 1901, having meanwhile spent three months abroad, chiefly in Great Britain, studying educational problems.

Although her predecessor, ELIZABETH STORRS MEAD, had raised academic standards in keeping with the rechartering of Mount Holyoke as a college in 1888, the institution still tended to cling to the program of its founder, MARY LYON. Miss Woolley's inaugural on May 15, 1901, showed that she treasured Mary Lyon's educational principles: stressing character as well as intellect, making thinkers not encyclopedias, preparing women for lives of service, building on a Christian foundation. But her arrival as one of the youngest college presidents in the country gave promise of a transforming leadership.

She went at once to the heart of the college's problem and began building a strong faculty, drawing on leading graduate schools. Gradually she won higher salaries (that for professor reaching $1,600 by 1910 and $5,000 by 1931). In 1905 the college became one of the first to join the Carnegie Foundation pension program. Fellowships aided young faculty members seeking to complete their training, and sabbaticals were established in 1925. The faculty began to be drawn from both sexes, though a steady increase in the number of men was not notable until after 1926. Miss Woolley recognized accomplishment by sending appreciative letters and by listing publications in her annual reports. By 1911 the college had ninety faculty members, double the number in 1901, thirty-four of them with Ph.D.'s. A Phi Beta Kappa chapter had been established in 1905.

Looking on differences of opinion as evidence of a healthy college, Miss Woolley gave a large measure of freedom to the instructional staff, most of whom were devoted to her. She presided deftly at monthly faculty meetings, using humor to ease tension. Sometimes she allayed clashes by reorganizing departments. When necessary, however, she did not shrink from causing pain. On one occasion she wrote: "It is not fair to save the feelings of one or two people at the expense of the students, other members of the staff and the college. . . . [T]he question must be considered im-

personally and 'in the large'" (Marks, p. 67).

In curricular matters, she cooperated with changes that usually originated with faculty or students. Under Mrs. Mead one-sixth of the student's program had been made free electives; the proportion was increased in 1905 and 1916. Honors work was introduced in 1923 and general examinations for seniors in their majors a year later. After 1930 greater concentration and more electives were allowed. Perhaps nowhere did Miss Woolley better demonstrate her loyalty to the liberal arts than in her steady resistance to trustee suggestions for the introduction of home economics.

During the 1920's graduate work expanded, and by 1931 Mount Holyoke had thirty-seven graduate students. In 1935 a novel master's program for prospective secondary school teachers began, stressing both teacher-training and subject-matter preparation. The proportion of Mount Holyoke graduates pursuing scholarly careers reached its height during Miss Woolley's presidency and was second only to Bryn Mawr among women's colleges (Newcomer, pp. 195–99).

She led many of the reforms that changed nearly every aspect of student life. Her tenure began with an important step away from religious exclusiveness (withdrawal of students from the local Congregational church in favor of services on the campus with visiting ministers) and ended with another (the replacement of the Y.W.C.A. by a "Fellowship of Faiths"). The trend toward "practical religion" —from the establishment of a College Settlements Association chapter in 1902 to the many chapel talks on social problems during the 1930's—also suited the president's inclinations. She communicated much of her religious faith in talks at chapel and vespers, which her charismatic presence made memorable.

Miss Woolley heightened student awareness of the contemporary world—often along her own Progressive line of vision—by bringing in outside speakers and inspiring new organizations. Notable changes in the students' immediate environment during her early years included the abolition of secret societies in 1910 and of required housekeeping chores in 1914, and the establishment of an honor system for both social and academic matters in 1916–17. Her interest in student health quickly led to an increased physical education requirement with new stress on outdoor exercise and later to her advocacy of youth hosteling. As one who emphasized the right of women to self-government, she could hardly have been disconcerted to find the ideal applied to student government, as it was in the "Mount Holyoke College

Community," launched in 1922. Only in the matter of smoking did she conspicuously oppose student opinion; when the "Community" abolished antismoking rules, the matter was removed from its jurisdiction. Keenly aware of the changing nature of the student body, which had doubled by 1925, she looked on the passing of the "militancy" of early college women as a normal development and welcomed the disappearance of "the more puerile types of sex-consciousness and 'school spirit' in colleges."

Although she recognized the importance of endowment—and succeeded in increasing Mount Holyoke's from half a million to nearly five million dollars—she found little enjoyment in this phase of her work and remarked that fund drives were wasteful of the energies of president and faculty. During her years in office sixteen major buildings were added to the college plant.

Miss Woolley's educational labors extended far beyond Mount Holyoke. She became the first woman senator of Phi Beta Kappa in 1907; served as chairman of the College Entrance Examination Board, 1924–27; and took a leading part in cooperative efforts by women's colleges to raise funds and set standards. She visited China in 1921–22 to survey education for the Foreign Missions Conference of North America, but resigned a similar assignment in 1931 because of complaints over her frequent absences from Mount Holyoke. Under President Herbert Hoover she participated in federal conferences on education and child care. It was often her influence which brought accommodation out of conflict in the committee work which such undertakings involved.

Miss Woolley seemed tireless in her support of "good causes," leading many and lending her prestige to others by accepting honorary posts. She was on the advisory council of the American Association for Labor Legislation and stressed the responsibility of women not to purchase "bargains" made in sweatshops. She was chairman of the Women's Cooperating Commission of the Federal Council of Churches and, in 1936, honorary moderator of the General Council of the Congregational-Christian Churches. A vice-chairman of the American Civil Liberties Union, she supported defense activities in the celebrated Sacco-Vanzetti case, opposed legislation requiring teachers' oaths, and refused to consider censorship a proper method of preventing international animosity. At one time she was blacklisted by the Massachusetts D.A.R., although she belonged to the Pawtucket, R.I., chapter. Politically she considered herself an independent Republican.

In the suffrage struggle, Mary Woolley was called "convincing, rather than militant." In 1906 she addressed the first "College Evening" of the National American Woman Suffrage Association, honoring SUSAN B. ANTHONY, and in 1908 she was a leader in the formation of the National College Women's Equal Suffrage League. The women's organization to which she contributed most was the American Association of University Women, of which she was president, 1927–33, later heading its international relations committee.

Her activities on behalf of internationalism and peace began well before World War I. She was a vice-president of the American Peace Society and addressed the Peace Congress of Women held in 1907 to protest military display at the Jamestown Exposition. Although with other leading women in March 1917 she offered her services to President Woodrow Wilson in case of war, she never played the chauvinist; even in October 1917 she could comment favorably on the thoroughness of German education. She worked for American entry into the League of Nations and for student exchange programs.

The most publicized undertaking of her career came when President Hoover—under pressure from women's organizations—appointed her a delegate to the Conference on Reduction and Limitation of Armaments which met in 1932 in Geneva. Ray Lyman Wilbur, with whom she had worked at the 1925 and 1927 conferences of the Institute of Pacific Relations, recommended her as "steady and reasonable, although inclined to the pacifist side." She was hailed as the first woman to represent the country at an important diplomatic conference, and her departure was preceded by a mass meeting and a banquet in New York sponsored by the Women's International League for Peace and Freedom and other women's societies. Not a participant in the special negotiations among delegates of the major powers, she never exaggerated her role, calling it only an entering wedge for women in diplomacy. It was at her insistence, however, that the many petitions submitted to the conference were presented before the full assembly, and she kept in touch with American and international women's groups. In May she privately sent samples of recent petitions to Hoover, fearing that "politicians" were keeping public opinion from him. When in June the "Hoover plan" arrived, calling for abolition of offensive weapons and a one-third reduction of armies, she was enthusiastic. In later years she condemned the cool reactions of France and Britain.

After her return, her reputation at a new

high, she wrote and spoke frequently on peace. She tried to combat the pessimism which followed the conference, admitting that it had not overcome "human nature" but stressing the wide support given the Beneš Resolution. She became chairman of the Peoples Mandate to End War, and in 1936 and 1937 represented it in interviews with President Roosevelt. Besides disarmament, she recommended economic sanctions as an alternative to war. By 1940, however, though she hoped the United States might stay out of the war, she felt that aid to Hitler's opponents was justified.

Although she had once stated that she intended to retire at seventy, Mount Holyoke alumnae successfully petitioned Miss Woolley to remain in office until after the centennial celebration of 1937. Her decision to stay disappointed certain trustees, and rumors and complaints began circulating. Those which she herself tracked down involved her frequent absences, unwise investment of college funds, financial favoritism among departments, and the influence of her close friend Jeannette Marks, professor of English literature. Her age was probably also held against her, though she bore her years remarkably well. Her closing months at the college were further embittered by the trustees' choice of a man (Roswell Gray Ham) as her successor. She had frequently asked that the tradition of women presidents be continued, a desire shared by a majority of the faculty. It was a matter of principle, not personalities, she maintained: choosing a man, with the implication that no qualified woman could be found, undermined the aims of an institution dedicated to preparing women for leadership. She did nothing to halt the public agitation of alumnae who sought reconsideration of what they called a "railroaded" election, and after retirement she never returned to the campus.

In her last years she continued active, especially as a speaker. During World War II she organized the Committee on the Participation of Women in Post-War Policy (later Women in World Affairs). Perhaps influenced by the more vigorous feminism of Miss Marks, whose Westport, N.Y., home she (and her beloved collies) now shared, Miss Woolley joined the National Woman's Party and endorsed the proposed Equal Rights Amendment to the federal Constitution. On Sept. 30, 1944, she suffered a cerebral hemorrhage which left her partly paralyzed, though able to dictate letters. She died at Westport three years later of another hemorrhage and was buried in Hillside Cemetery, Wilton, Conn.

Influenced by the essay "Homo Sum" by Jane Harrison, the English classicist, Miss Woolley often repeated that women must be considered first of all as human beings. She wanted full equality in rights and responsibilities and felt that women had characteristics which enabled them to be of special service, particularly in interpersonal relations and in the cause of peace. These beliefs inspired her work for the higher education of women, a field where, with her brilliant administrative abilities, she made her greatest contribution. Despite the frustrations of her later years, she maintained to the end that she was an optimist, believing that "some day there will be 'a Kingdom of God on earth.' The last thing for us to do, is to stop working for it!"

[Although Miss Woolley's personal papers are not at present available for scholarly use, many extracts appear in Jeannette Marks' *Life and Letters of Mary Emma Woolley* (1955), a work emotional in tone, presenting its subject as a martyr for woman's rights. A few letters by and about Miss Woolley are in the Treasure Room of the Mount Holyoke College Library; the College History Collection in the library's Cleveland Room includes most of her articles, her annual reports, clippings about her speeches and other activities, and a typed bibliography of her writings. Her Kappa Delta Pi lecture, *Internationalism and Disarmament*, was published in 1935. Arthur C. Cole's *A Hundred Years of Mount Holyoke College* (1940) is full and fair on Miss Woolley's contribution. A more intimate view of her character and work appears in Frances Lester Warner, *On a New England Campus* (1937), chap. ii. Other sources of information were: Jeannette Marks, "What It Means to Be President of a Woman's College," *Harper's Bazar*, June 1913; Eunice Fuller Barnard, "Armed with Faith, She Strikes at Arms," *N.Y. Times Mag.*, Jan. 3, 1932; obituary in *N.Y. Times*, Sept. 6, 1947; Mabel Newcomer, *A Century of Higher Education for Am. Women* (1959); and interviews and correspondence with colleagues of Miss Woolley.]

HUGH HAWKINS

**WOOLMAN, Mary Raphael Schenck** (Apr. 26, 1860–Aug. 1, 1940), home economist, textile specialist, and vocational educator, was born in Camden, N.J., the elder of two daughters of Martha (McKeen) and John Vorhees Schenck. Her mother, from Philadelphia, was of Scotch-Irish descent. Her father, a physician, was a descendant of Jan Schenck, a Dutch settler at Flatlands, Long Island, in 1650. Long established in East Jersey, the Schencks were prominent in politics and in the medical profession; Mary's paternal grandfather, Ferdinand Schureman Schenck, also a physician, was a Jacksonian Congressman from New Jersey in the 1830's and for twelve years a judge of the

New Jersey court of errors and appeals. Mary was educated at the private school of a Philadelphia Quaker, Mary Anna Longstreth, graduating in 1878. On Oct. 18, 1883, in Camden's First Presbyterian Church, she was married to Franklin Conrad Woolman, a lawyer of Burlington, N.J.

In 1891 the Woolmans moved to New York City. They were joined by Mrs. Woolman's mother and sister, who after the death of John Schenck had been forced by financial difficulties to sell their Camden home. Franklin Woolman was a semi-invalid, and to help with family support Mrs. Woolman took employment as a copy editor while seeking a position as a teacher of languages, which she had studied during a year of college work (1883–84) at the University of Pennsylvania. By chance, however, her interests were turned in a different direction. Among the fellow lodgers at the boardinghouse where she and her family were living were several faculty members of Columbia University's new Teachers College. One of these, Franklin Baker, asked her to criticize a book on sewing instruction that had been written for the college. Her reaction to the book was so unfavorable that she was asked to write down her own views on the subject. Departing from the English fancywork exercises then in vogue, Mrs. Woolman stressed the making of utilitarian articles, the selection of textiles and materials, and figuring the cost of garments, together with teaching methods founded on child psychology. So well received were her ideas that, despite her lack of a college degree, she was appointed an assistant in domestic science at Teachers College in 1892 and an instructor of sewing the following year. Although now in her thirties, she continued her education while serving on the faculty, receiving a diploma from Teachers College in 1895 and a B.S. degree in 1897. In the latter year she was made adjunct professor of household arts education and in 1903 professor, one of the first women to achieve this rank at Columbia. At Teachers College she organized a department of domestic art and introduced the study of textiles. Active also in the New York Association of Sewing Schools, a group organized to encourage the teaching of sewing in the schools, she frequently lectured in other cities, urging the value of vocational training for girls.

In 1901 a group of New York residents proposed the establishment of a privately supported school to train girls for employment in the factories and workrooms of the city. Mrs. Woolman, who was vitally interested in this project, was granted half-time off from her work at Teachers College to organize and direct it. The school, known as the Manhattan Trade School for Girls, opened in November 1902. Although originally aimed at training girls for the needle trades, the offerings were soon expanded to include a variety of vocational programs. Mary Woolman divided her time between the college and the trade school for eight years; in 1910, when the Manhattan Trade School for Girls was incorporated into the city school system, she returned full time to the Teachers College faculty. Through her interest in the welfare of young girls, Mrs. Woolman also become associated with the group, led by Luther Halsey Gulick, that founded the Camp Fire Girls. She was elected the first chairman of the committee on organization in 1911, and the following year she served on the first board of electors of the new organization.

In 1912 Mrs. Woolman left Teachers College and moved to Boston to become acting head of the home economics department of Simmons College and president of the Women's Educational and Industrial Union in Boston. By accepting the two positions, she was able to utilize the resources of the Educational and Industrial Union to give practical experience in vocational education to Simmons undergraduates. In 1914, with this program well established, Mrs. Woolman resigned both offices. The remaining years of her career were spent in a variety of activities. From 1915 to 1917 she was educational lecturer for the Retail Trade Board of the Boston Chamber of Commerce; during World War I she organized the Clothing Information Bureau in Boston and served as a textile specialist for the Department of Agriculture, with an office in Amherst, Mass. Later (1923–28) she was textile specialist for the General Federation of Women's Clubs. During these years she also lectured at a number of colleges and universities. Periodically after 1914 Mrs. Woolman took summer courses at various universities, and in 1921 and 1926 she enrolled at Radcliffe College in order to study aspects of the textile industry with the Harvard economist Thomas Nixon Carver. With Carver and Ellen B. McGowan she was co-author of *Textile Problems for the Consumer* (1935).

One of the pioneers in home economics education, Mary Woolman was a member of the Lake Placid Conference on Home Economics and a founding member of the American Home Economics Association in the winter of 1908–09. She worked throughout her career to improve the quality of education in this field and to achieve greater protection for the consumer.

More significant, however, were her efforts in behalf of vocational education. By her work she helped modify methods of instruction and broaden the scope of vocational education, while through her writing and lecturing she became an influential publicist for the whole movement. Although best known for her work for women, she was also committed to the cause of Negro education, with special interest in Hampton and Tuskegee institutes. An active member of the National Society for the Promotion of Industrial Education (later the American Vocational Association), she served on several survey committees and lobbied energetically for the passage of the Smith-Hughes Act (1917) authorizing federal aid for vocational education. In 1917–18 she served as vice-president of the National Education Association. In recognition of her efforts the National Institute of Social Sciences awarded her its gold medal in 1926.

A vigorous woman, Mrs. Woolman loved the out-of-doors and was an enthusiastic traveler. She visited Europe many times, studying vocational education in England and on the Continent and such domestic arts and crafts as spinning, dyeing, and weaving. A member of the Episcopal Church through most of her adult life, she became a Unitarian in her later years. She remained active, writing and working in various organizations, until about five years before her death, when a serious automobile accident resulted in permanent invalidism. She died of arteriosclerosis at her home in Newton, Mass., at the age of eighty and was buried in Evergreen Cemetery in Camden, N.J. She had been a widow for many years.

[Mary Schenck Woolman's other writings include: *A Sewing Course* (1900); *A Sewing Course for Teachers* (1907); *The Making of a Trade School* (1910); *Textiles* (1913), with Ellen B. McGowan; and *Clothing: Choice, Care, Cost* (1920). For her life and career, see: memorial articles by Anna M. Cooley and Ellen B. McGowan in *Jour. of Home Economics*, Nov. 1940; *Who's Who in America*, 1906–07 to 1938–39; *Woman's Who's Who of America*, 1914–15; *Biog. Cyc. Am. Women*, II (1925), 98–103; *Encyc. Am. Biog.*, n.s., vol. II (1934); Helen Buckler et al., *Wo-He-Lo: The Story of the Camp Fire Girls, 1910–1960* (1961); *Jour. of the Nat. Inst. of Social Sciences*, XI (1926), 51–60. For ancestry and family background, see *Am. Ancestry*, vol. IV (1889); and George R. Prowell, *The Hist. of Camden County, N.J.* (1886). Other information from records of Radcliffe College and Teachers College, Columbia Univ. Marriage record from N.J. Registrar of Vital Statistics; death certificate from Mass. Registrar of Vital Statistics.]

ROBERT J. FRIDLINGTON

**WOOLSEY, Abby Howland** (July 16, 1828–Apr. 7, 1893), **Jane Stuart** (Feb. 7, 1830–July 9, 1891), and **Georgeanna Muirson** (Nov. 5, 1833–Jan. 27, 1906), Civil War relief and hospital workers who were also active in postwar hospital, charitable, and educational work, were the eldest, second, and fourth daughters, respectively, of Charles William and Jane Eliza (Newton) Woolsey. The family included four other daughters—Mary Elizabeth Watts, Eliza Newton, Harriet Roosevelt, and Caroline Carson—and one son, Charles William, the youngest child. Their father, head of a prosperous sugar refining business in East Boston, Mass., had been born in New York City but reared in England, where his merchant father had moved during the War of 1812; he was a descendant of George Woolsey, who had emigrated from England to Dutch New Amsterdam early in the seventeenth century. Their mother, a descendant of John Newton of Hull, England, who had settled in Westmoreland County, Va., in 1660, was the daughter of William Newton, a merchant in Alexandria, Va. Theodore Dwight Woolsey, president of Yale College from 1846 to 1871, was their uncle; their cousins included SARAH CHAUNCEY WOOLSEY, author of children's books under the pseudonym "Susan Coolidge," and William Henry Aspinwall, New York merchant and philanthropist.

Although the three sisters were born in different places—Abby in Alexandria, Va., Jane on board the ship *Fanny* on the run from Norwich, Conn., to New York City, and Georgeanna (christened George Anna) in Brooklyn, N.Y.—their early years were spent in Boston, where the Woolseys lived on fashionable Sheafe Street and the girls attended the Misses Murdock's School. After their father's death in the fire on the Long Island Sound steamer *Lexington* on Jan. 13, 1840, the family moved to 17 Rutgers Place in New York City, later establishing itself at 8 Brevoort Place. In New York the Woolsey daughters attended the Rutgers Female Institute, followed by a year of finishing school—Abby and Jane at Pelham Priory in New Rochelle, N.Y., kept by the Woolseys' English friends the Boltons, Georgeanna at the Misses Anable's Young Ladies Seminary in Philadelphia—and various European excursions. Presbyterian churchgoers, their politics formed by Horace Greeley's *New York Tribune*, the Woolseys were firm abolitionists, despite the fact that Mrs. Woolsey had come from a slaveholding family. To Abby especially, who had witnessed a slave auction in the spring of 1859, the main objective of the Civil War was the abolition of slavery.

With the fall of Fort Sumter, the whole family plunged into the Union effort. On Apr. 25, 1861, Abby was one of the group of fifty or sixty socially prominent women who attended the meeting at Dr. ELIZABETH BLACKWELL's New York Infirmary for Women and Children which led to the formation of the Woman's Central Association of Relief of New York, an important forerunner and later an integral part of the United States Sanitary Commission. No. 8 Brevoort Place became a headquarters for bandage making, sewing, and the collection of hospital equipment; bundles awaiting shipment frequently filled the front entry. Thoughout the war the furnishing of supplies was Abby's primary concern; through her nursing sisters she kept track of what was most needed and often bought with her own funds large quantities of air beds, havelocks, shirts, socks, bolts of unbleached cotton, and handkerchiefs.

Georgeanna was among the hundred applicants selected by the Woman's Central Association for their qualities of leadership and given a thirty-day training program in nursing at New York hospitals. When her sister Eliza's husband, Joseph Howland, went to Washington in June with the 16th New York Volunteers, Georgeanna and Eliza followed him. Acting as informal agents of the Woman's Central Association of Relief, they visited and nursed in hospitals, bringing supplies and delicacies provided by "family and friends and societies at home." At the request of Dr. Blackwell, they also received nurses sent by the Woman's Central Association, assisting them to secure passes and government ambulances for transportation and reporting on their services. Their financial independence and influential social position made the sisters particularly successful in cutting through the red tape and chaos of the first months of the war before the usefulness of the Sanitary Commission and its branches was fully recognized by officialdom. Together with Abby at home, Georgeanna and Eliza also helped bring about the appointment by President Lincoln of the first hospital chaplains.

At the request of Frederick Law Olmsted, secretary of the Sanitary Commission, Georgeanna and Eliza in April 1862 joined the commission's newly formed hospital transport service as "nurses at large." With Christine Kean Griffin, Caroline E. Lane, and KATHARINE PRESCOTT WORMELEY, for three months they fitted up the ships used for carrying sick and wounded soldiers from the Peninsular campaign, prepared food, dressed wounds, and generally made themselves useful. In July, when the service was turned over to the army's

medical department, they returned to New York. That September, Georgeanna went for five months to assist Miss Wormeley at the United States General Hospital in Portsmouth Grove near Newport, R.I., with her cousin Sarah and her sister Jane. Jane had spent the greater part of 1862 helping Abby in the distribution of supplies, as well as visiting and nursing soldiers in the Park Barracks Hospital and the hospital of the New England Relief Association in New York City. After her work at Portsmouth Grove she went briefly (August 1863) to Hammond General Hospital at Point Lookout, Md., with Georgeanna and from there to Fairfax Theological Seminary Hospital, near Alexandria, where she and Georgeanna were placed in charge of the nursing and dietary departments. Jane stayed at Fairfax until the end of the war; her activities there are recorded in her privately printed *Hospital Days* (1868).

Georgeanna, in addition to her work at Point Lookout and Fairfax in 1863, also spent three weeks at Gettysburg. Having heard—erroneously—that her brother was wounded, she and her mother arrived just after the battle and remained to take charge of a feeding station and lodge for the wounded soldiers slowly being transported to Baltimore. Later that summer, before going to Maryland, she wrote for the Sanitary Commission *Three Weeks at Gettysburg*, designed, as she put it, "to 'fire the hearts' of the sewing circles" (*Letters of a Family*, II, 534). Abby attended to the details of printing. In May 1864, having an understanding with the Sanitary Commission that she "was to be called on at any time for hospital service at the front" (*ibid.*, p. 582), Georgeanna left Fairfax to go first to Belle Plain on the Potomac and then to Fredericksburg in May 1864 to set up relief stations for the wounded from the battle of the Wilderness; early in June, after the death of her sister Mary, she returned to New York. Her Civil War hospital nursing ended in the fall of 1864 after she helped organize a regular army hospital at Beverly, N.J., with her sister Caroline and ABBY HOPPER GIBBONS, the Quaker abolitionist.

The Woolsey sisters' experiences are well chronicled in Georgeanna and Eliza's two-volume *Letters of a Family during the War for the Union* (1899). They were united by close affection and usually worked in pairs; yet each emerges as a distinct personality, contributing according to her own talents. All wrote well, Jane's writing in particular having a poetic quality. Abby seems to have been of a serious, somewhat melancholy nature. Jane possessed a quick wit; in frail health throughout her life, she was more ethereal, with an "illuminated face, . . . wonderful eyes, . . . wonderful smile, [and] fragile form," yet capable of long periods of sustained effort. Georgeanna, dark-eyed and dignified in bearing, was in many ways the sprightliest—energetic and resource-ful, with a notable sense of humor.

After the war Jane Woolsey volunteered to teach at Hampton Normal and Agricultural In-stitute in Virginia, founded by her friend Gen. Samuel Chapman Armstrong; from 1869 to 1872 she was director of the girls' industries there. At the end of this period she accepted the position of resident directress of the new Presbyterian Hospital in New York City, where with Abby, who was appointed acting clerk at the same time, she effected the hospital's original organization. Setting and attaining high standards, Jane developed "a fairly effi-cient corps of nurses" (Delavan, p. 103), al-though no training school for nurses was yet envisioned; she also established drug, kitchen, supply, and other departments and attended to the many details of coordinating a complex sys-tem (*ibid.*, p. 65). Both sisters resigned in 1876 after four years of volunteer service. Jane's health—already impaired by her war work—had given way after a serious contro-versy with some members of the medical staff who were reluctant to accept a woman direc-tor, though she received constant support from the board of managers. Jane Woolsey had earlier been an advisory member of the New York State Charities Aid Association, founded in 1872 by LOUISA LEE SCHUYLER, and she now became a regular member, serving on the "Centennial Committee" and contributing gen-erously from her own funds. She spent many of her remaining years as an invalid, suffering from a series of ailments; she died of septice-mia at the age of sixty-one in Matteawan, N.Y., at the home of her sister Eliza Howland. She was buried in the family plot at Dosoris, near Glen Cove, Long Island.

Abby Woolsey, in addition to her work at Presbyterian Hospital, which included acting as executive officer during Jane's temporary absences, was an original member of the State Charities Aid Association. For twelve years a member of the board of managers, first chair-man of the association's library committee and its librarian, Abby continued her interest in hospital work as a member of the committee on hospitals, serving also on the committees for the insane and on hospital construction. As an influential member of the special committee appointed to visit public hospitals in New York City, and of the ensuing committee which drafted a plan for nurses' training, she was in-

strumental in the founding (1873) of the Bellevue Hospital Training School for Nurses, the first in this country to be developed accord-ing to Florence Nightingale's principles. Along with such others as ELIZABETH C. HOBSON, she was a member of the school's first managing committee and of its first board of managers after its incorporation in February 1874. The Charities Aid Association, however, regarded Abby's reports as her most valuable service, especially *A Century of Nursing* (1876), which outlined historically the prevailing systems of nursing as she herself had observed them in several European countries and included her plan for the organization of a school of nurs-ing. Her other reports include several hand-books on hospital subjects and a survey of *Lunacy Legislation in England* (1884). Her writing, revealing capable organization, exten-sive research, and knowledge of several lan-guages, was indicative of the thoroughness and efficiency of all her work. She died at sixty-one of nephritis and heart disease at her home in New York City and was buried at Dosoris.

A year after the war, on June 7, 1866, Georgeanna Woolsey was married to Dr. Fran-cis Bacon, professor of surgery at the Yale Medical School. A son of the Rev. Leonard Bacon, famous antislavery preacher, he came of a prominent New Haven family; DELIA SALTER BACON was his aunt and ALICE MABEL BACON his half sister. For the next forty years Georgeanna took an active part in numerous projects in the New Haven community. With her husband she was one of the principal founders of the Connecticut Training School for Nurses, established in the New Haven Hospital in June 1873—one of the earliest schools on the Nightingale plan. As a member of its executive committee she played an im-portant role in determining its policies and practices; she was also an active member of the visiting committee, which personally super-vised the school's operations and patient care in the hospital. Her *Hand Book of Nursing for Family and General Use*, published by the school in 1879, had a wide circulation among hospitals, nursing schools, and the public.

From 1883 to 1893 Georgeanna Bacon was a member of the State Board of Charities of Connecticut, in which capacity she made many visits to almshouses, state prisons, reformatory schools, insane asylums, and children's homes in New Haven and New London counties. Though she had no children of her own, she worked constantly for children's welfare, be-coming a founder (1892) and corporator (1896) of the Connecticut Children's Aid So-ciety. She and her husband established, and until her death directed, Playridge, a country home in Woodmont, Conn., which offered special care to crippled children sponsored by the society. Georgeanna Woolsey Bacon died of a heart ailment at her home in New Haven in 1906 and was buried in the Bacon family plot in Grove Street Cemetery there.

[For the Woolseys' ancestry, see Eliza Newton Woolsey Howland, *Family Records* (1900), and John Ross Delafield, "Woolsey Family of Great Yarmouth and N.Y.," in his *Delafield: The Family Hist.*, vol. II (1945). On the sisters' wartime activities, see, in addition to their own books: L. P. Brockett and Mary C. Vaughan, *Woman's Work in the Civil War* (1867); Katharine Prescott Wormeley, *The U.S. Sanitary Commission* (1863) and *The Other Side of War* (1889); and Frederick Law Olmsted, *Hospital Transports* (1863). On their postwar work, see Robert J. Carlisle, *An Account of Bellevue Hospital* (1893); John S. Billings and Henry M. Hurd, eds., *Hospitals, Dispensaries, and Nursing* (1894), pp. 513–26; Elizabeth C. Hobson, *Recollections of a Happy Life* (1916); M. Adelaide Nutting and Lavinia L. Dock, *A Hist. of Nursing*, II (1907), chap. ix; Edith A. Talbot, *Samuel Chapman Armstrong* (1904); David B. Delavan, *Early Days of the Presbyterian Hospital* (1926); Albert R. Lamb, *The Presbyterian Hospital and the Columbia Presbyterian Medical Center, 1868–1943* (1955); *Annual Reports* of the N.Y. State Charities Aid Assoc., 1874–92, of the Conn. State Board of Charities, 1884–90, and of the Conn. Training School for Nurses, 1875–1907; Georgeanna Woolsey Bacon, "Conn. Training School," *Trained Nurse and Hospital Rev.*, Oct. 1895; Margaret Stack, "Résumé of the Hist. of the Conn. Training School for Nurses," *Am. Jour. of Nursing*, July 1923; unpublished records of the Conn. Training School (Cushing Library, Yale Univ.); Hartford *Courant*, Jan. 5, 1903; *New Haven Morning Jour.*, Jan. 29, 1906. Death records from the health departments of N.Y. State, N.Y. City, and Conn. Sources in family hands include Georgeanna Woolsey's "Hist. of the Woolsey Family," a large MS. volume; diaries of Abby Woolsey, 1849–51; Georgeanna Woolsey's wartime journal, Sept. 25, 1861–July 14, 1862 (2 MS. vols.); and various newspaper clippings. A fuller treatment will appear in the author's forthcoming book-length study, *The Woolsey Sisters of N.Y.*]

ANNE L. AUSTIN

**WOOLSEY, Sarah Chauncey** (Jan. 29, 1835– Apr. 9, 1905), author, known by the pen name "Susan Coolidge," was born in Cleveland, Ohio, the oldest of five children, four of them girls. Her father, John Mumford Woolsey, whose distinguished ancestors included Timothy Dwight, clergyman, author, and college president, and Jonathan Edwards, the eminent colonial divine, was a graduate of Yale. Beginning a business career with his father, a New

York hardware merchant, he had moved in 1830 to Cleveland, where he was a land agent and "capitalist" until his retirement in 1852. He and his wife, Jane (Andrews) Woolsey, who came from Wallingford, Conn., brought up their close-knit family in a large house with enough land for a rollicking out-of-door life, which Sarah later described with loving care in *What Katy Did* (1872). She loved to read and from an early age enjoyed telling and writing stories. Tall, quick-witted, and impulsive like the Katy of her stories, she was a good student, although she "retained only that which interested her," chiefly history and literature. Her formal education and that of her sisters was completed at the Select Family School for Young Ladies in Hanover, N.H., often called "The Nunnery," the name Sarah gave it in *What Katy Did at School* (1873).

When Sarah was twenty the Woolsey family moved to New Haven, Conn., where her uncle Theodore Dwight Woolsey was president of Yale. During the Civil War she devoted her energies to hospital work, finding it "a very developing and vivid experience." At this time she began her lifelong friendship with the author "H.H." (HELEN HUNT JACKSON), who described her, thinly disguised, in "Joe Hale's Red Stockings" (*Scribner's Monthly Magazine,* January 1878)—a memoir of Civil War days and of their work together in the linen room of the Government Hospital in New Haven, "mending, mending, mending." During the second year of the war Sarah worked with her cousins JANE and GEORGEANNA WOOLSEY as an assistant superintendent at Lowell General Hospital in Portsmouth Grove, R.I., under the direction of her friend KATHARINE P. WORMELEY. After John Woolsey's death (1870) and some months of travel abroad, the family followed "H.H." to Newport, R.I., and built The Jungle, a high-ceilinged, book-lined home, where except for vacations, some European travel, and a transcontinental trip with Helen Hunt, Sarah was to live for the rest of her life.

In 1870 Miss Woolsey, who previously had published only a few magazine articles, began writing in earnest. While vacationing with Helen Hunt in Bethlehem, N.H., she jotted down the outline for *The New-Year's Bargain,* a group of twelve stories for children published the next year by Roberts Brothers. From then on she wrote steadily as Susan Coolidge, a name taken in fun because a younger sister, Jane, had published stories as "Margaret Coolidge." Her pieces often appeared first in *St. Nicholas* magazine. Besides her collections of stories, there were several novels for children, of which the five volumes about "Katy" were the enduring favorites. The Katy books, depicting the lives of the six motherless Carr children from childhood to marriage, blended imaginary episodes with the real-life experiences of the Woolsey children so thoroughly that even Sarah herself could not always separate the two. Her portraits of both children and adults are clearly drawn, and though morals are often pointed, they are never insisted upon. Katy, the eldest child and central character—imaginative, willful, high-spirited—is based on Sarah Woolsey herself. Her schoolgirl friend "Rose Red," heroine of *What Katy Did at School*, is a composite portrait of two classmates, daughters of the Massachusetts lawyer Joseph Choate. Amy Cruse, in *The Victorians and Their Books* (1935), credits Susan Coolidge with starting a veritable revolution in school stories, which had previously been strongly didactic, and writes: "Into this correct company came dancing merry, mischievous Rose Red and her companions . . . a class of schoolgirl heroine whose popularity has never waned."

For thirty-five years Sarah Woolsey's books appeared steadily, eagerly awaited and enjoying good sales. Besides the fiction for children, she often wrote for adults, producing three volumes of poetry (a fourth combined the material previously published in the first two volumes) and frequently contributing stories, verses, and travel articles to the *Outlook*, *Scribner's*, and *Woman's Home Companion*. She also translated Théophile Gautier's *My Household of Pets* (1882) and brought out scholarly editions of the *Autobiography and Correspondence of Mrs. Delany* (1879), *The Diary and Letters of Frances Burney, Mme. d'Arblay* (1880), and the *Letters of Jane Austen* (1892). Her skill and discretion as an editor were highly valued by Roberts Brothers and their successors, Little, Brown & Company, for whom she worked for years as a manuscript reader.

Despite her extensive and varied literary output, Sarah Woolsey never found it the "most absorbing part" of her life and seldom spoke of her work. She had many talents, wrote easily, talked well, and enjoyed cooking, gardening, and painting. In the late 1880's Sarah and Dora, the two unmarried Woolsey sisters, built a summer home at Onteora, N.Y., in the Catskills, though they continued summer visits with a married sister on Mount Desert Island in Maine. On trips to Boston, Sarah frequently stayed in the home of the artist Sarah Wyman Whitman, where she saw SARAH ORNE JEWETT and William James, who once described Miss Woolsey, with her large frame and sprightly

manner, as "a cross between an elephant and a butterfly." Her last years went by with modest wealth, pleasant things to do, and the leisure in which to do them. She died in her Newport home of a heart condition in her seventy-first year. She was buried on Dosoris Island at Glen Cove, Long Island, on land where the first Woolsey to come to America had settled in 1623.

[Biographical introduction by her sister Elizabeth Woolsey Gilman to Susan Coolidge's *Last Verses* (1906); Franklin B. Dexter, *Biog. Sketches of the Graduates of Yale College*, VI (1912), 614, on her father; Gertrude Van Rensselaer Wickham, *The Pioneer Families of Cleveland* (1914); Frances C. Darling, "Susan Coolidge," *Horn Book Mag.*, June 1959; obituaries in *N.Y. Times*, Apr. 10, 1905, and *Outlook*, Apr. 15, 1905, p. 924; L. P. Brockett and Mary C. Vaughan, *Woman's Work in the Civil War* (1867), pp. 322, 342; Helen Hunt Jackson, *Bits of Travel at Home* (1878); Ruth Odell, *Helen Hunt Jackson* (1939); Paulina C. Drown, *Mrs. Bell* (1931); Raymond L. Kilgour, *Messrs. Roberts Brothers, Publishers* (1952); letters in Little, Brown & Co. files, the Galatea Collection of the Boston Public Library, and Yale Univ. Library; talks with Miss Edith Woolsey (a first cousin) and others.]

FRANCES C. DARLING

WOOLSON, Abba Louisa Goold (Apr. 30, 1838–Feb. 6, 1921), teacher, author, and dress reformer, was born in Windham, Maine, near Portland, the second daughter and second of seven children of William and Nabby Tukey (Clark) Goold. Her father, descended from an early eighteenth-century settler at Kittery, Maine, rose from tailor's apprentice to merchant tailor in Portland, served three terms in the state legislature, and pursued an active interest in local history as corresponding secretary of the Maine Historical Society and author of *Portland in the Past* (1886). Abba attended Portland public schools and graduated as valedictorian of her class from the Portland High School for Girls in 1856, gaining there a proficiency in French and Latin to which she was later to add a knowledge of German, Greek, Italian, and Spanish. On Aug. 14 of that year she was married to the principal of the school, Moses Woolson, seventeen years her senior, a native of Concord, N.H., and a graduate of Waterville (later Colby) College. They had no children.

Immediately following her marriage Mrs. Woolson launched both her teaching and her literary career, the former at the Portland High School, the latter with a sonnet in the New York *Home Journal* and with contributions to the *Portland Transcript*. In 1862 she and her husband moved to Cincinnati, Ohio, where Abba Woolson taught literature in the Mount Auburn Young Ladies' Institute while her husband served as principal of the Woodward High School. Three years later they returned to New England, Woolson having accepted the principalship of the high school at Concord, N.H. His wife, described by a local historian as "a woman of rare gifts and an excellent teacher" (Lyford, II, 1267), assisted him there in 1866–67. In the latter year Moses Woolson was appointed a submaster in the English High School in Boston, Mass., but he resigned after six years to open a private school at Concord, N.H. He later (1887) returned to Boston.

During their first sojourn in Boston, Mrs. Woolson contributed frequently to the *Boston Journal*. Several of her essays in that magazine were brought together and published in 1873 as *Woman in American Society*, with a foreword by John Greenleaf Whittier. The *Christian Register* (Apr. 5, 1873) commented that though Mrs. Woolson "evidently sympathizes with the Women's Rights party . . . she has none of the complaint and wail over the degradation of woman which burdens so much of the argument of her party," and described the book as "good in style, good in thought, good in its practical purpose, its shrewd sense, its exquisite humor, its delicate sarcasm, its honesty and its earnestness." The essays portray a young lady's evolution from "The School-Girl" to "The Queen of the Home." Mrs. Woolson deplored the lack of opportunity for independence upon leaving school, the necessity of marrying for support, and the life of frivolity and display prescribed by society to win a husband. She pointed out the effects of such a life upon health, especially emphasizing the evils of the fashionable dress of the day—"complicated, voluminous, and burdensome; flimsy in texture, calculated to impede the bodily movements in every part, and scarcely endurable save in a state of indolent repose." The Bloomer costume, she contended, had been "hooted out of existence" not only because it was too radical a change and lacked beauty, but because it emanated from an American woman and not from Paris. She herself looked with favor on loose-flowing garments and "the short walking-skirt."

In 1873 Abba Woolson was chairman of a committee of the New England Women's Club to consider the subject of dress. The end result was *Dress-Reform*, which she edited in 1874, a book consisting of five lectures originally delivered in Boston and repeated in other cities, the first four by woman physicians (among

them MARY J. SAFFORD), the last by Mrs. Woolson herself. Its purpose was to stress the "physical discomfort and disease" caused by corsets and other contricting forms of dress, and to suggest healthful and attractive substitutes, for the design of which detailed directions were given in an appendix. The *Christian Register* in its issue of Dec. 26, 1874, strongly recommended the book.

Of Mrs. Woolson's later writings, *Browsing among Books*, containing essays on varied subjects including "Smoking" and "The Morality of Amusements," appeared in 1881, and *George Eliot and Her Heroines* in 1886. In addition to her talks on women, Mrs. Woolson lectured on English literature and on Spain, which she visited in 1883–84 and 1891–92. She founded the Castilian Club in Boston in 1887 and was its president for many years. She was also a founder (1872) and president of the Massachusetts Moral Education Association, which sought to prevent prostitution, and president of the Massachusetts Society for the University Education of Women. Moses Woolson died in 1896. Abba Woolson survived him for a quarter century. She died in Portland, of arteriosclerosis, in her eighty-third year. She was buried, as her husband had been at his request, in the Goold family tomb in Windham, Maine.

[*Nat. Cyc. Am. Biog.*, IX (1907 ed.), 533–34; Frances E. Willard and Mary A. Livermore, eds., *A Woman of the Century* (1893); Laura C. Holloway, *The Woman's Story* (1889), pp. 311–13; Stanley J. Kunitz and Howard Haycraft, eds., *Am. Authors, 1600–1900* (1938); James O. Lyford, ed., *Hist. of Concord, N.H.* (1903), II, 1074–75; Nathan Goold, "Moses Woolson," *Portland Sunday Times*, Mar. 11, 1906; Julia A. Sprague, comp., *Hist. of the New England Women's Club* (1894), pp. 19–20, 34; obituary in *Boston Transcript*, Feb. 7, 1921; death record from City Clerk, Portland, Maine; information about William Goold and his children from Maine Hist. Soc., Portland.]

ELIZABETH F. HOXIE

**WOOLSON, Constance Fenimore** (Mar. 5, 1840–Jan. 24, 1894), author, was born in Claremont, N.H., to Charles Jarvis Woolson, a stove manufacturer, and Hannah Cooper (Pomeroy) Woolson. She was the sixth daughter and sixth of nine children, but within a few weeks of her birth the three older sisters nearest her age died of scarlet fever. In her infancy the family moved to Cleveland, Ohio, where Woolson reestablished himself in business and became a successful promoter of the Cleveland Savings Bank. The children were brought up in an atmosphere of cultured intelligence and Episcopal faith. Their mother was a niece of the author James Fenimore Cooper, and the Cooper relationship unquestionably influenced Constance's youthful imagination.

Constance attended Miss Hayden's school in Cleveland and the Cleveland Female Seminary, and in 1858 graduated at the head of her class from Mme. Chegaray's finishing school in New York. Summers were spent with her family on Mackinac Island at the head of Lake Michigan. Wide reading, a lifelong habit of taking long walks in the country, and the family's love of travel furthered her informal education. She had a fine contralto voice, and music remained a major passion until deafness restricted her enjoyment of it. During the Civil War she served as a volunteer nurse, and fancied herself in love with a childhood friend turned colonel.

Upon her father's death in 1869 the Cleveland household was broken up. Constance accompanied her mother on travels in the East and South, frequently spending the summer in New York state and the winter and early spring at St. Augustine, Fla., with visits in Virginia, Tennessee, and the Carolinas. Her widowed sister Clara Benedict and Clara's daughter Clare were often with them. Miss Woolson's professional career began in 1870 with a few travel and descriptive sketches, followed by short stories of the Great Lakes region, somewhat in the Bret Harte manner. These early local-color stories appeared in leading magazines such as *Harper's* and *Putnam's;* the best of them were collected in *Castle Nowhere: Lake-Country Sketches* (1875). She wrote, too, of the Ohio Valley, and of the area around Cooperstown, N.Y.

As she grew familiar with the South, this region became another literary resource. She is credited with being perhaps the first Northern writer to treat the postwar South honestly and sympathetically, without sentimentality. *Rodman the Keeper: Southern Sketches* (1886) contains some of her finest Southern tales, which reflect an artistic balance of interest in regional description and character development. In both Northern and Southern stories appear such recurrent themes as duty, frustration, suffering, and renunciation. Her first novel, *Anne,* completed in 1879, was published in book form in 1882 after serialization in *Harper's.* This rambling, episodic narrative, which includes a vivid picture of life on Mackinac Island, becomes a mystery thriller. It proved the most popular of her longer works, selling more than 57,000 copies.

After her mother's death in 1879, Miss Woolson went abroad with her sister and niece and lived in Europe for the remaining fourteen years of her life. In Florence in the spring of 1880 she met the author Henry James, with whom she formed a close and lasting friendship. Arranging her travels according to the seasons, she usually visited Switzerland and Germany in the summer, staying in Florence and Venice during the remainder of the year. She lived in England in 1883–86 and 1890–92, chiefly in London, Warwickshire, and Oxford, and made a winter trip in 1889–90 to Greece and Egypt. A hard worker, she devoted much of the day to writing and revising, but allowed time also for walks. James paid her occasional visits, and when she spent several years (1886–89) in villas at Bellosguardo, overlooking Florence, he joined her for a time, subletting apartments from her. Her generous devotion to James was repaid by his kindly appreciation of her qualities. After her death he wrote to a friend: "I had known Miss Woolson for many years and was extremely attached to her—she was the gentlest and tenderest of women, and full of intelligence and sympathy" (Edel, III, 359).

During her years in Europe, Constance Woolson produced four novels, all serialized in *Harper's* and then published by Harper & Brothers in book form. In general they are carefully localized (in America, except for part of one novel), with plot and characters coordinated with environment, though the plots tend to be loose. *For the Major* (1883), a novelette, is one of her best pieces, an unusual psychological study, compact and forceful. *East Angels* (1886) contains a noteworthy picture of Florida and a careful representation of a narrow facet of society. The excessively melodramatic action of *Jupiter Lights* (1889) takes place on a Georgia island and on the shore of Lake Superior. Her final novel, *Horace Chase* (1894), is a rather didactic work with a male protagonist. Miss Woolson's last short stories, set in Europe, are generally disappointing: settings are more decorative than integral, and the characters—chiefly American expatriates—are not strongly individualized. These stories, however, illustrate the development of her art toward the Jamesian manner of less overt action and more psychological analysis. Two collections of stories and one of travel sketches appeared after her death: *The Front Yard, and Other Italian Stories* (1895), *Dorothy, and Other Italian Stories* (1896), and *Mentone, Cairo and Corfu* (1896).

Miss Woolson always regarded herself primarily as a realist; realism to her meant an accurately delineated landscape and, even more important, faithful characterization. Yet her preference for unusual and remote scenes, exceptional characters (she was particularly successful with self-sacrificing heroines, including sympathetically portrayed spinsters), and exciting, mystifying plots makes her work inherently romantic despite its realism in detail. The decline of public interest in local color and the nineteenth-century gentility pervading her fiction probably hastened Constance Woolson's literary eclipse.

Class-conscious and conservative in taste and manners, Miss Woolson carried no feminist banners, but believed woman's place was essentially private and domestic, though certainly not cloistered. In temperament she was energetic, independent, and alertly observant of people, places, and events. She was an avid reader, not only of American and English writers, but also of Continental authors, notably French and Russian. Possessing an unusual capacity for sympathy with the suffering of others, she herself was subject to both physical illness and severe mental depression, a state she considered an inevitable part of the creative spirit. Although a self-styled introvert, she had many friends. In the summer of 1893 a bout of influenza weakened her health. Traveling to Venice, she took an apartment and completed work on *Horace Chase*. Here in January 1894 she contracted a second case of influenza, which apparently gave way to typhoid fever. On Jan. 24, while her nurse was out of the room, she either fell or threw herself out of her upper-floor window and died a few hours later without regaining consciousness. Henry James supposed that she had committed suicide out of depression brought on by her illness, but no one witnessed the scene. She was buried in the Protestant Cemetery in Rome.

[*Five Generations* (3 vols., 1929–30), a compilation of family letters, journals, etc., edited by Clare Benedict, Miss Woolson's niece, is the principal primary source. A few MS. notebooks of Miss Woolson are among the personal memorabilia in Woolson House at Rollins College, Winter Park, Fla.; and there are 16 letters (4 to James) in the Houghton Library, Harvard Univ. For full-length studies, see John D. Kern, *Constance Fenimore Woolson: Literary Pioneer* (1934); Stella C. Gray, "The Literary Achievement of Constance Fenimore Woolson" (unpublished doctoral dissertation, Univ. of Wis., 1957); and Rayburn S. Moore, *Constance Fenimore Woolson* (1963). Leon Edel discusses her relationship with Henry James in vols. II and III (1962) of his biography of James; see in addition James' chapter on Miss Woolson in his *Partial Portraits* (1888). Also of interest are the following: Alexander Cowie, *The Rise of the Am. Novel* (1948), pp. 568–78; Jay B. Hubbell, ed., "Some New Letters of Constance Fenimore Woolson," *New England Quart.*, Dec. 1941;

Fred L. Pattee, "Constance Fenimore Woolson and the South," *South Atlantic Quart.*, Apr. 1939; Lyon N. Richardson in *ibid.*, Jan. 1940, and in William Coyle, ed., *Ohio Authors and Their Books* (1962); Henry M. Alden in *Harper's Weekly*, Feb. 3, 10, 1894; *N.Y. Times*, Jan. 25, 27, 28, Feb. 1, 1894.]

STELLA CLIFFORD GRAY

**WORKMAN, Fanny Bullock** (Jan. 8, 1859– Jan. 22, 1925), traveler, mountain climber, and explorer of the Himalayas, was born in Worcester, Mass., the second daughter and youngest of three children of Alexander Hamilton Bullock and Elvira (Hazard) Bullock. Her maternal grandfather, Augustus George Hazard, was a wealthy Connecticut merchant and manufacturer of gunpowder. Her father, a native of Royalston, near Worcester, and a graduate of Amherst College, followed a political career that made him the Republican governor of Massachusetts in the years 1866–68. Fanny Bullock was educated by tutors and at Miss Graham's finishing school in New York City, and then spent two years at schools in Paris and Dresden. Returning to Worcester when she was twenty, she met William Hunter Workman, a prominent physician there. They were married on June 16, 1881. Their only child, Rachel, born in 1884, was later a graduate of London University and a geologist, who married Sir Alexander MacRobert of Aberdeenshire, Scotland.

The Workmans began traveling in 1886, taking trips to Norway, Sweden, and Germany. Three years later Dr. Workman gave up his practice and resigned from his medical posts in Worcester because of ill health, and they spent the nine following years in Europe, with headquarters in Germany. They enjoyed concerts and art galleries, and Mrs. Bullock Workman (as she preferred to be known), as an ardent Wagnerite, visited Bayreuth for five seasons. She had been introduced to mountaineering by her husband in the White Mountains of New Hampshire, and she now did her first serious climbing, making such classic Alpine ascents as the Matterhorn, Mont Blanc, and the Zinal Rothorn.

In the mid-1890's the Workmans started traveling extensively in the Mediterranean region: North Africa, Egypt, Palestine, and Greece. Adopting the currently popular sport of bicycling, they made trips through Algeria and Spain, averaging forty to fifty miles a day and more than once finding themselves in situations not wholly safe for unarmed foreigners. They told of their experiences in the first of the many books on which they were to collaborate: *Algerian Memories* (1895) and

*Sketches Awheel in Modern Iberia* (1897), the latter being one of at least nine bicycle travel books published in the United States that year. In 1897–99 the Workmans ventured farther afield, bicycling 1,800 miles in Ceylon, 1,500 in Java, Sumatra, and Cochin China (later South Vietnam), and 14,000 through India. They recorded their observations of the art, architecture, and peoples of the East in *Through Town and Jungle* (1904).

In the summer of 1899, when Mrs. Bullock Workman was forty and Dr. Workman fifty-two, they entered the northwest Himalayas to explore the Karakorum range, and thus began their real lifework. They were to make seven expeditions to these previously unmapped and almost unknown regions. Besides mapping and photographing, they made many scientific observations and kept exact records. They listed altitudes measured with both aneroid and boiling-point thermometers; studied the structure of ice and snow, and glacier movement; made detailed meteorological observations, including maximum and minimum sun and shade temperatures; and observed and recorded the physiological effects of high-altitude living.

Just to organize and run this sort of expedition—aside from the work of exploration and research—would be even today a major undertaking. The party must be completely self-contained, to travel for long periods and unknown distances in wild, barren country, mostly on rock, snow, and ice, with the added handicaps of cold and altitude. A small army of temperamental porters must be kept well and contented and working efficiently. Year after year, without the modern aids of airplanes and radio contacts, of dehydrated foods, light windproof clothing, and other special equipment, these two seasoned travelers ran successful expeditions. In making preparations they alternated responsibilities. One year Dr. Workman would take charge of the general planning and organization, Mrs. Bullock Workman giving her attention to photography and scientific research projects. Another year they would reverse tasks. In an affectionate double dedication in one of their books, Mrs. Bullock Workman pays tribute to her husband's "skill in planning the long route . . . and attention to detail," and Dr. Workman praises her "courage, endurance and enthusiasm . . . in hardship and danger."

On their first expedition in 1899 they followed the great Biafo Glacier in Baltistan, reaching the Hispar Pass at its head (17,500 feet). Two snow peaks above the Skoro Glacier were ascended on the return trip. Expeditions in 1902 and 1903 to northern Baltistan explored the Chogo Lungma Glacier and its branch glaciers, regions previously unvisited. Many weeks were passed in snow and ice above 15,000 feet—or at about the height of the summit of Mont Blanc. On the 1903 trip Mrs. Bullock Workman climbed Mt. Koser Gunga (21,000 feet), setting an altitude record for women, and Dr. Workman, now fifty-six, climbed with two Italian guides over 23,000 feet, a world record for men at that date.

In 1906 a camp was pitched at 21,300 feet, and Mrs. Bullock Workman reached an altitude of 23,300 feet on the second highest of the Nun Kun peaks. This established a record for women which was not broken until 1934. (In 1908 ANNIE SMITH PECK climbed Huascarán in the Andes, a mountain then not yet accurately measured. Miss Peck's own estimate, and that of her Swiss guides, made it about 24,000 feet. "Another woman mountain climber claims to have surpassed my height," wrote Mrs. Bullock Workman in *Travel* magazine. "A careful triangulation is being undertaken." She sent a team of French scientists, who found Huascarán to be a mere 21,812 feet.)

In 1908 the Workmans ascended the Hispar Glacier to reach Hispar Pass, and then descended the great Biafo Glacier, making a total ice journey of seventy-four miles. In 1911 the couple were active on the glaciers around Masherbrum, among peaks later popular with mid-twentieth-century mountaineers. They investigated the upper half of the Siachen (Rose) Glacier, "the largest and most complicated Himalayan glacier, fifty miles long," and on a return expedition in 1912 explored its source in two snow passes of about 20,000 feet on the Indus-Turkestan watershed. On the way back they crossed an 18,000-foot snow pass and made the first descent of the Kalberg Glacier.

The accounts of the Workmans' experiences and observations on these expeditions are contained in five thick volumes illustrated with fine photographs: *In the Ice World of the Himalaya* (1900), *Ice-bound Heights of the Mustagh* (1908), *Peaks and Glaciers of·Nun Kun* (1909), *The Call of the Snowy Hispar* (1910), and *Two Summers in the Ice Wilds of Eastern Karakorum* (1917). Though some place names have been changed since these books were published, and a few minor errors have been detected, they remain outstanding reference works for the Karakorum region.

Mrs. Bullock Workman, who was fluent in French, German, and Italian, lectured extensively before learned societies and Alpine clubs in Europe and America. She was a Fellow of the Royal Geographical Society and a member of the Royal Asiatic Society. She is said to have been the first American woman to lecture before the Sorbonne. Her other honors included the highest medals of ten European geographical societies. She spent her latter years, including the World War I period, in France, dying in Cannes at the age of sixty-six after a long illness. She was cremated, and her ashes were buried in the Rural Cemetery in Worcester. Dr. Workman died in Newton, Mass., in 1937.

A feminist and a suffragist (she once carried a "Votes for Women" banner into the Himalayas), Mrs. Bullock Workman was always deeply interested in the higher education of women. In her will she bequeathed a total of $125,000 to four leading women's colleges: Bryn Mawr, Radcliffe, Smith, and Wellesley. For herself, she felt that she met considerable "sex antagonism" from men scientists and mountaineers. In a formal photograph she appears as an imposing figure in a large hat and a feather boa, with a calm, pleasantly determined expression. In mountain photographs she looks solid and businesslike in a jacket and very full climbing skirt.

J. P. Farrar of the Alpine Club of London described Fanny Bullock Workman in the *Alpine Journal*'s obituary as "a woman of determination and energy, a valiant and indefatigable lady . . . with the doctor her devoted companion and supporter." She was "a doughty fighter," he said, ". . . involved at times in warm paper arguments," though these were "based on facts which it was difficult to controvert." Those who got to know her well, the *Alpine Journal* concluded, "could not fail to recognize her warmness of heart, her enthusiasm, her humour, her buoyant delight in doing." Her husband's long eulogy of her ends, "She was a firm friend and a loyal wife."

[The best accounts of Mrs. Bullock Workman are the obituaries in the *Alpine Jour.* (London), May 1925, and *Appalachia* (Appalachian Mountain Club), June 1925, the latter by her husband; see also obituaries of Dr. Workman in *Alpine Jour.*, Nov. 1938, *Am. Alpine Jour.*, 1938, and *Himalayan Jour.*, 1939, pp. 212–13. For a more critical view of Mrs. Bullock Workman see Dorothy Middleton, *Victorian Lady Travellers* (1965); and Kenneth Mason, *Abode of Snow* (1955). Other sources include: clippings in "Workman Brochures," Montagnier's Mountaineering Pamphlets (vol. I, nos. 21, 28), and Montagnier's Magazine Articles, in Am. Alpine Club library, N.Y. City; and memories of acquaintances. See also: *Woman's Who's Who of America*, 1914–15; *Who Was Who in America*, vol. I (1942); articles on Mrs. Bullock Workman in *Encyc. Britannica* and *Encyc. Americana* and on her husband in *Nat. Cyc. Am. Biog.*, Current Vol. C, p. 541; *N.Y. Times*, Jan. 27, Feb. 4, 1925. On her family background, see Mass. Hist. Soc., *Proc.*, June 1887, for a memoir of her father, and *Dict. Am. Biog.* on her grandfather. On her controversy with Miss Peck, see their letters in *Scientific American*, Feb. 12, 26, 1910; Mrs. Bullock Workman's article in *Travel*, Mar. 1911, and Société Générale d'Études, *Détermination de l'Altitude du Mont Huascarán* (1909).]

ELIZABETH KNOWLTON

**WORMELEY, Katharine Prescott** (Jan. 14, 1830–Aug. 4, 1908), Civil War relief and hospital worker, author, translator, and charitable leader, was born in Ipswich, Suffolk, England, the second of three daughters and third of four children of Caroline (Preble) and Ralph Randolph Wormeley. Her older sister, Mary Elizabeth Wormeley Latimer (1822–1904), became an author of some repute, most noted for her series of popular histories. Their mother, daughter of an East India merchant in Boston and niece of Commodore Edward Preble of the United States Navy, was "a lady in every motion, thought, and instinct" and, although reserved, held her children's affection and respect. Their father, a sixth-generation Virginian and a great-nephew of Edmund Randolph, Attorney General in Washington's cabinet, had been taken to England in childhood; he became a British subject and served in the Royal Navy, rising to the rank of rear admiral. His active service, however, apparently largely ceased after 1814: liberal in his political views, he openly endorsed the incipient reform movement in England and thus jeopardized his career.

The Wormeleys nonetheless lived comfortably, and their daughters were reared gently. Trained in the social graces of the time, they were taught a sense of social responsibility prompted by Ralph Wormeley's abhorrence of poverty and sympathy for the poor and dependent. In 1836 the family moved to London, where they lived until 1847, with the exception of three years (1839–42) spent in France and Switzerland. After a year in Paris, they sailed in 1848 for the United States for a prolonged visit, which became permanent after Admiral Wormeley's death in 1852. Wintering in either Boston or Washington, they spent the milder months in Newport, R.I.

At the outbreak of the Civil War, Katharine Wormeley was among the first to participate in relief work in Newport. That July she was instrumental in forming a local Women's Union Aid Society, which she headed until April 1862. Concerned with the financial plight of soldiers' families, she secured from the quartermaster general a government clothing contract which provided employment for soldiers' wives and daughters; under her supervision, the women turned out some fifty thousand shirts in the winter of 1861–62. In May 1862 Miss Wormeley joined the hospital transport service of the United States Sanitary Commission, serving on hospital ships which plied the York and Pamunkey rivers on the Virginia peninsula, searching out and caring for the sick and wounded. Her work with the service, which continued until July when it was adopted by the army as part of the medical program, is documented by her letters of those two months, published in 1889 under the title *The Other Side of War*. She returned home physically exhausted in August.

The next month, at the urging of the surgeon general, she accepted the position of "lady superintendent" of Lowell General Hospital, then being organized in Portsmouth Grove, R.I., near Newport. In charge of the female nurses, the diet kitchen, the linen department, and the laundry, she was aided by several assistant superintendents, including SARAH, JANE, and GEORGEANNA WOOLSEY, the last of whom had also worked with Katharine Wormeley in the hospital transport service. "Miss Wormeley, our chief," Jane Woolsey wrote in 1863, "is clever, spirited and energetic in the highest degree—a cultivated woman, with friends and correspondents among the best literary men here and in England, . . . a great capacity for business and not a single grain of mock-sentiment about her . . ." (Georgeanna Bacon and Eliza Woolsey Howland, *Letters of a Family during the War for the Union, 1861–1865*, 1899, II, 501). But her health finally gave way, and in September 1863 she resigned and went home to Newport. That December she wrote *The United States Sanitary Commission: A Sketch of Its Purpose and Work* for the Boston Sanitary Fair; its sales earned some hundreds of dollars for the needs of the commission.

After the war Miss Wormeley turned her attention to charity work in Newport. She was the principal founder, in 1879, of the Newport Charity Organization Society, of which she was the initial secretary and general agent, a member of the governing "board of reference" for some fifteen years, and a district visitor. In connection with the society she maintained classes in sewing and domestic work for the poor women of the city. In 1887 she established a girls' industrial school, offering classes in cooking, sewing, dressmaking, and household work. She directed and supported the school until 1890, when it was made a part of the public school system. Adept at persuading others to help carry out her projects, she introduced many new features into Newport social

work and accomplished much that less determined workers thought impossible.

During the 1880's and '90's Miss Wormeley also occupied herself in translating the work of French authors, notably Honoré de Balzac, whose *La Comédie Humaine* she translated in forty volumes (1885–96). In 1892 she published *A Memoir of Honoré de Balzac;* she also translated works by Molière, Alphonse Daudet, Paul Bourget, and the Duc de Saint-Simon. An accomplished French scholar, she conveyed the spirit of the writing as well as the meaning. Katharine Wormeley lived for the last fifteen years of her life in Jackson, N.H., where she died of pneumonia after fracturing a hip in a fall. She was buried, after cremation, in the family plot in Island Cemetery in Newport.

[Besides Miss Wormeley's own *The Other Side of War*, there is material on her Civil War work in L. P. Brockett and Mary C. Vaughan, *Woman's Work in the Civil War* (1867), pp. 318–23. Information about her early life may be found in the account of her father written by Miss Wormeley and her sisters, Elizabeth Wormeley Latimer and Ariana Randolph Wormeley Curtis, *Recollections of Ralph Randolph Wormeley* (privately printed, 1879). See also George H. Preble, *Genealogical Sketch of the First Three Generations of Prebles in America* (1868), pp. 154–59; obituaries in *Newport* (R.I.) *Daily News* and *N.Y. Times* of Aug. 6, 1908, and the *Dial*, Aug. 16, 1908; *Nat. Cyc. Am. Biog.*, VIII, 366–67; *Annual Report* of Newport School Committee, 1889–90, pp. 53–54. Helpful material concerning her charity work in Newport, R.I., was supplied by the Newport Hist. Soc. Death record from N.H. Bureau of Vital Statistics.]

ANN TOWNSEND ZWART

**WRIGHT, Frances** (Sept. 6, 1795–Dec. 13, 1852), writer and reformer, was born in Dundee, Scotland, the elder daughter and second of three children of James and Camilla (Campbell) Wright. Her father, a graduate of Trinity College in Dublin and a warm admirer of the American patriot and freethinker Thomas Paine, was a linen merchant by trade. Fanny never experienced a normal family life; when she was two years old her parents died, and her brother was killed while she was still a young girl. She and her sister, Camilla, two years her junior, became extremely close. They were reared by a succession of Campbell relatives in London and (after 1806) in the Devonshire village of Dawlish.

When Frances was twenty-one, she and Camilla went to live with James Milne, a great-uncle who taught moral philosophy at Glasgow College. Repelled by the stuffiness of her maternal relatives, Frances welcomed the intellectual opportunities afforded by this new environment. She read widely in the college library, concentrating particularly (if her own later accounts may be credited) on books about the United States, a country in which her interest had been aroused by a reading of Carlo Botta's *Storia della Guerra dell'Independenza degli Stati Uniti d'America.* Her reformist cast of mind and her facility with the pen were early evident. Among her youthful literary productions were *Altorf,* a play celebrating Swiss independence, and *A Few Days in Athens* (published in 1822), a utopian tract cast in the form of a historical fantasy. Enchanted by the poetry of Byron, she also produced a sheaf of undistinguished romantic verse. Her personal life was not happy; a broken engagement plunged her into deep gloom and gave rise to the conviction that the "passionate side" of her nature was somehow deficient.

In August 1818, accompanied only by her sister, the twenty-two-year-old Frances embarked from Liverpool for a visit to America. The two settled first in New York City, where Frances, taking advantage of letters of introduction supplied by Scottish friends, tried to establish herself as a dramatist. *Altorf* was published and staged early in 1819, with James Wallack in the title role, but it closed after three performances. Frustrated as a playwright, she spent the summer touring the northeastern United States with Camilla. In May 1820, after a winter in Philadelphia, the pair returned to Britain.

Frances Wright had faithfully recorded her travels in a series of long, self-consciously literary letters to a Glasgow friend, Mrs. Rabina Craig Millar, and upon her return she determined to publish this correspondence. The result was *Views of Society and Manners in America* (1821), one of the most celebrated travel memoirs of the early nineteenth century. The few earlier accounts of the United States, by Europeans traveling on specific military, diplomatic, ecclesiastical, or commercial missions, had been terse and restricted in outlook. The end of the Napoleonic wars and improvements in sea transport opened the way for the more casual tourist, however, and Frances Wright was among the first to turn this new accessibility to literary advantage.

Miss Wright's view of America, unlike that of many of her peripatetic compatriots of later decades, is unabashedly enthusiastic. Landscapes and vistas are invariably "pleasing" or "smiling." The traveling citizenry as casually encountered in stagecoaches and inns prove intelligent, whole-souled, patriotic, and remarkably articulate. A Congressional wrangle over

the tariff impresses her as "worthy of the Roman Senate in its best days," and the Pennsylvania penal code wins the unlikely adjective "beautiful." Far from being repelled by the new nation's rusticity, she saw it as a guarantor of righteousness. Describing with approval the muddy streets and half-finished public buildings of Washington, she muses with foreboding about a future day when "the road to the senate house shall lead through streets adorned with temples and palaces . . . and when the rulers of the republic . . . shall roll in chariots . . . through a sumptuous metropolis, rich in arts and bankrupt in virtue" (*Views,* p. 261).

In contrast to Alexis de Tocqueville's analytical work of several years later, *Democracy in America,* Frances Wright's book is the leisurely and anecdotal travelogue of a still immature young woman overwhelmed by the sublimity of Niagara Falls and eager to record, at great length, the melodramatic tale of a recent steamboat disaster on Lake Champlain. The book is, nevertheless, written from a staunchly libertarian and secular viewpoint, and frequently uses the happy state of affairs in America as a bludgeon with which to attack backward conditions prevailing in the Old World. "The prejudices still to be found in Europe . . . which would confine . . . female conversation to the last new publication, new bonnet, and *pas seul,*" she writes, "are entirely unknown here. The women are assuming their place as thinking beings . . ." (*ibid.,* p. 218).

Predictably, readers on the western side of the Atlantic were generally pleased by the book's perceptiveness, although the *North American Review* and other conservative organs expressed annoyance at its equating the rise of the Republican party with the emergence of the true American character. In England, the Tory press dismissed Miss Wright's "ridiculous and extravagant panegyric," though reformers like Jeremy Bentham were enthusiastic.

In addition to its literary fruit, Frances Wright's American visit restored her capacity for emotional involvement. The trip, she wrote, "thawed my heart and filled it with hopes which I had not thought it could know again" (*ibid.,* p. 261). In September 1821 she went to France for an extended visit with the Marquis de Lafayette, who had been deeply moved by her book, and the two lovers of America formed a strong attachment. Returning to London in 1822, she became an enthusiastic participant in Lafayette's clandestine intrigues in support of various revolutionary movements and had a brief, intense romance with a young Spanish conspirator. In 1824, when Lafayette was planning a farewell visit to his adopted country, he urged Miss Wright to accompany him. Aware that their friendship had aroused gossip and family dissension, she in turn suggested that he marry or legally adopt her. In the end he avoided either alternative, but she followed him to America, sailing with Camilla in a separate vessel. As the beloved general moved triumphantly about the country, Frances Wright followed discreetly in his wake. The arrangement proved unsatisfactory for all concerned, however, and by the time Lafayette embarked for France in 1825 their relationship had cooled.

In any event, Miss Wright had decided definitely to cast her lot with America, where the "pestilence" of Negro slavery—described in her book (p. 267) as "odious beyond all that the imagination can conceive"—had come to dominate her thinking. In 1825, after viewing the slave system firsthand on a voyage up the Mississippi, she published in Baltimore *A Plan for the Gradual Abolition of Slavery in the United States without Danger of Loss to the Citizens of the South,* a pamphlet in which she urged Congress to set aside large tracts of public land on which slaves would labor, the profits from their work to go to their owners toward their eventual emancipation. The national leaders to whom she advanced her proposal were vaguely encouraging ("Your prospectus has its aspects of promise," wrote Jefferson politely), and Miss Wright determined to found in the South a model settlement along the lines she envisioned. She was confirmed in this plan by a visit to the communal settlement recently established at New Harmony, Ind., by Robert Owen.

In December 1825 she purchased 640 acres on the Wolf River thirteen miles east of Chickasaw Bluffs (now Memphis), Tenn. She called her plantation Nashoba, the Chickasaw word for "wolf." Although various eminent men, including Lafayette, were listed as trustees of the venture, Nashoba was in reality a one-woman undertaking in which Miss Wright was joined by a small group of associates, among them her sister, an eccentric Scottish overseer named James Richardson, and a mulatto schoolteacher from New Orleans with her several children. A number of Negro slaves were purchased, given pledges of eventual emancipation, and set to work. Slaveholders were invited to cooperate in the experiment, but the only one who did was a South Carolinian who made the long journey to deposit at Nashoba a pregnant slave, Lucky, with her five small children.

The project never prospered. About a hundred acres were cleared by dint of exhausting effort, but crops were meager and debt chronic. Fanny Wright found refuge and inspiration in frequent visits to New Harmony, and in May 1827, broken in health, she sailed for Europe in the company of Robert Dale Owen, son of New Harmony's founder. In her absence affairs at Nashoba went from bad to worse. Benjamin Lundy's abolitionist newspaper, the *Genius of Universal Emancipation,* in August printed lengthy extracts from the plantation's manuscript journal, as furnished by James Richardson, and soon a scandalized nation was discussing Fanny Wright's colony, where "free love" was openly practiced by Richardson and endorsed by others, including Camilla Wright.

Although distressed by Richardson's indiscretion, Frances Wright did not repudiate his views. She sailed for America in November to salvage what remained of her project, accompanied by Mrs. Frances Trollope, a London friend whose husband was planning a business venture in Cincinnati. Reaching Nashoba in January 1828, they found the place a ruin. "Desolation was the only feeling—the only word that presented itself," wrote Mrs. Trollope, hastening on to Ohio. The rude cabins were roofless; the only food was rice and pork; rain offered the only safe water supply. Incredibly, Frances Wright showed no evidence of dismay. "I never heard or read of any enthusiasm approaching her's," marveled Mrs. Trollope, "except in some few instances, in ages past, of religious fanaticism" (*Domestic Manners of the Americans,* 1832, p. 44).

Not only did Miss Wright retain faith in the wisdom of her undertaking, but she chose this moment for a full and complete statement of her views. In a widely circulated article first published in the *Memphis Advocate,* she proceeded from a restatement of her compensated-emancipation plan to a wholesale attack on racially segregated schools, organized religion, racial taboos in sex relations, and marriage. "Let us enquire," she wrote defiantly, "—not if a mother be a wife, or a father a husband, but if parents can supply, to the creatures they have brought into being, all things requisite to make existence a blessing." The reverberations from this new thunderbolt sealed Nashoba's fate. "[C]o-operation has well nigh killed us all," wrote Miss Wright in a rare moment of gloom. James Richardson had long since departed with his mulatto mistress; the other free members of the colony had drifted away; and in April 1828 even faithful Camilla and her husband (despite Camilla's brave principles, she and Richeson Whitby, another Nashoba resident, had been legally married the preceding December) departed for New Harmony. Left alone with some thirty Negro slaves, Frances Wright did not forget her pledge to them. Though she followed Camilla to New Harmony in June, she returned late the next year and, at great personal expense and discomfort, transported the slaves to Haiti, effected their emancipation, and made arrangements for their housing and employment.

Nashoba represented a critical turning point in Frances Wright's life. Once accepted and popular, she was now driven to the fringes of American life, shunned and feared by the conventional and pious majority. A venture undertaken with high expectations had collapsed amid hostility and ridicule, costing her more than half her fortune. Still in her early thirties, she nevertheless began, without apparent misgivings, a fresh chapter in her remarkable career. Indeed, as she later recorded, "she felt herself better equipped for her next adventure in the field of social service than ever before in her life."

One lesson she had learned was that it was in the centers of population, and not in isolated utopian colonies, that social reform must be pursued. In the summer of 1828, while living at New Harmony and helping edit the *New-Harmony Gazette,* she learned that a religious revival was sweeping the city of Cincinnati. Taking up "the cause of insulted reason and outraged humanity," she instituted a series of anticlerical lectures there. In 1829 she expanded her itinerary to include most of the major cities of the East and Midwest. Her addresses condemned organized religion as the chief obstacle to human happiness, barring the way to a free, unbiased pursuit of knowledge. She made an impressive appearance on the platform, her tall figure clothed in simple white muslin, her sole text a copy of the Declaration of Independence which she dramatically flourished from time to time. Her features, "noble" or "masculine" depending on the sympathies of the observer, were dominated by piercing blue eyes and a massive forehead beneath short, curly chestnut hair. Her platform manner was invariably calm and dignified, but in a period when most American ladies (as Mrs. Trollope observed) were "guarded by a sevenfold shield of habitual insignificance," the unprecedented appearance of a woman on the lecture circuit—and with a message so radical—"caused an effect that can hardly be described" (*Domestic Manners,* p. 72). New York City, despite hostile newspaper coverage, proved particularly receptive to her ideas. The reaction of the ten-year-old Walt Whitman, whose carpenter father was a staunch Fanny Wright enthusiast, was typical. Young Whitman attended her every lecture and years later described Miss Wright as "one of the few characters to excite in me a wholesale respect and love" (Horace Traubel, *With Walt Whitman in Camden,* 1908, II , 445).

Deciding to settle in New York, Miss Wright purchased a small East River farm some six miles from the city and established residence with Camilla (now separated from her husband), Camilla's small son, and Robert Dale Owen, Frances' frequent companion during this period. Early in 1829 she bought a small church on Broome Street near the Bowery and transformed it into a "Hall of Science." Here she lectured regularly, and here she and Owen edited and published the *Free Enquirer,* a periodical which had succeeded the *New-Harmony Gazette* in October 1828 and was transferred to New York early in 1829. In her speaking and writing she ranged over her favorite topics and several new ones. She condemned capital punishment and demanded improvements in the status of women, including equal education, legal rights for married women, liberal divorce laws, and birth control. Her identification with the last reform provided fresh ammunition for those determined to keep alive the scandal of Nashoba, and the newspapers outdid themselves in pillorying "The Great Red Harlot of Infidelity."

Her central interest, however, was shifting to education. She and Owen had come to believe that America's great need was for a national system of free state boarding schools, financed by a graduated property tax, where all children from two to sixteen would be taught industrial skills, along with the traditional subjects, and rigidly shielded from religious indoctrination. Despite her dependence on a kind of abstract logic reminiscent of a Swiftian satire (the proposal, she explained in her *Address on the State of the Public Mind,* would benefit "the industrious classes" by relieving them of "the charge of their families"), she won considerable support for the scheme. At a time when barely half the children of New York City attended school, she argued with some cogency that the premature entry into the labor market of thousands of young people was closely linked to the unemployment that plagued the city.

These educational proposals presupposed political action, and Frances Wright became a central figure in the working-class political movement which now emerged in New York. Workingmen in the city began to organize in April 1829. That summer, an Association for the Protection of Industry and for the Promotion of National Education was founded at a mass meeting of *Free Enquirer* readers. Though Frances Wright and Owen disliked the demand of Thomas Skidmore, spokesman for the workingmen, for a redistribution of property, the two groups in October pooled their strength sufficiently to win a seat in the legislature in the state elections. Frances Wright, having departed on her mission to Haiti in September, took little overt part in these developments, though the opposition was quick to dub the amorphous protest movement of workingmen and reformers "the Fanny Wright party."

In July 1830, a few weeks after her return from the Caribbean, she sailed for Europe. Her purpose was both to give the ailing Camilla a change of scene and to remove herself from New York, where her differences with "the crude schemes and ill digested arguments of Thomas Skidmore" (as she wrote in her *Parting Address . . . to the People of New-York, 1830*, p. 15) had become acute. The sisters settled in Paris, where, a few months later, Camilla died. Thirty-five years old and deprived of her lifelong companion, Frances Wright turned to Guillaume Sylvan Casimir Phiquepal D'Arusmont, a French physician and reformer some sixteen years her senior whom she had first met when he was teaching at New Harmony. Their marriage, on July 22, 1831, occurred shortly after the birth of their first child, a girl who did not long survive. A second daughter, Frances Sylva, was born Apr. 14, 1832. These Paris years were among the most placid of Frances Wright's life. The Positivist doctrine espoused by her friend and neighbor Auguste Comte won her allegiance, but except for a brief London lecture appearance in 1833 she remained out of the public eye.

In her absence her New York undertakings crumbled. The national education movement collapsed; the Hall of Science became a Methodist chapel; and the *Free Enquirer* expired in 1835, having survived that long only through the efforts of Robert Dale Owen. Late that year, Frances Wright, with her husband and daughter, returned to America to look after investments there. Settling in Cincinnati, she was soon back on the lecture platform, and in the presidential election of 1836 she spoke for the Democratic ticket, attacking the Bank of the United States and arousing once again the ire of Whig editors. In the midterm elections of 1838 she campaigned for the Democrats in New York. She also offered a new series of lectures, in which she took a historical—and Comtean—view of the evils of contemporary society. This proved to be the end of her public career. Disappointed with her scanty audi-

ences, she sailed in the spring of 1839 for another stay in France.

Over the next decade Frances Wright made five more Atlantic crossings in a vain effort to untangle her personal and financial affairs. A visit to Britain, where she had inherited some property, was the inspiration for her final book, *England, the Civilizer* (1848), a feverish, disjointed forecast of a global federation justly governed and united in peace. In October 1850, after repeated separations and much acrimony and legal wrangling, she and D'Arusmont were divorced in Cincinnati, Sylva remaining in her father's custody. Only two years later, in December 1852, Frances Wright died at the age of fifty-seven, having never recovered from a broken hip suffered in a fall on the ice the previous winter. She was buried in Cincinnati's Spring Grove Cemetery.

Her death went largely unnoticed. In the three decades since the appearance of her first and best-known work, her reputation had been severely tarnished. A self-described "moral observer," Frances Wright had moved from a largely uncritical view of America to a jaundiced attitude toward all society, including that of the United States, as "a complicated system of errors" (*Address on the State of the Public Mind*, pp. 3, 9). From such a perspective, she was able to identify and illuminate a remarkable number of the social issues that would agitate the national conscience for a century and more after her death. At once brilliant and erratic, she often appeared to lose interest in problems which did not readily yield to the panaceas she devised, leaving to others the long battles in whose opening skirmishes she fought with imagination and vigor.

[Unless otherwise attributed, quotations above are from A. J. G. Perkins and Theresa Wolfson, *Frances Wright, Free Enquirer* (1939). Also of value is the earlier biography by William O. Waterman, *Frances Wright* (1924). One of her useful published speeches is *Address on the State of the Public Mind* (1829); other speeches are reproduced in *Course of Popular Lectures* (1829; new and expanded edition, 1836). The quotations from her *Views of Society and Manners in America* are from the John Harvard Library edition of 1963, edited by Paul R. Baker. Further sources of value include *Biog., Notes, and Political Letters of Frances Wright D'Arusmont* (1844); reminiscences by Robert Dale Owen in *Atlantic Monthly*, Oct. 1873, and Elizabeth Oakes Smith in *Revolution*, Apr. 29, 1869, pp. 258–59; Lillian O'Connor, *Pioneer Women Orators* (1954); Richard W. Leopold, *Robert Dale Owen* (1940); Frank L. Mott, *A Hist. of Am. Magazines*, I (1957), 536–38; Arthur E. Bestor, Jr., ed., *Education and Reform at New Harmony* (1948); Arthur M. Schlesinger,

Jr., *The Age of Jackson* (1945); and Walter E. Hugins, *Jacksonian Democracy and the Working Class: A Study of the N.Y. Workingmen's Movement, 1829–37* (1960). Scattered letters of Frances Wright may be found in the library of the Working Men's Institute at New Harmony; the Robert Owen Papers at the Univ. of Ill.; the Lafayette Papers at the Univ. of Chicago; and the Percy Bysshe Shelley Papers at Duke Univ. Files of the *Free Enquirer* for the period of her editorship are at Rutgers Univ. and Cornell.]

PAUL S. BOYER

WRIGHT, Laura Maria Sheldon (July 10, 1809–Jan. 21, 1886), missionary to the Seneca Indians in western New York, was born at St. Johnsbury, Vt., near the town of Barnet, of which her grandfather Willard Stevens had been a pioneer settler in 1763. The tenth of twelve children, seven boys and five girls, of Solomon and Dorothy (Stevens) Sheldon, she was brought up, from the age of seven, by a married sister in Barnet. She made her first identification with Indians at the age of eight when she crossed a gorge on a plank to visit an encampment on the opposite bank, frightening her family. At ten she was holding prayer meetings for her playmates. These two concerns—Indians and Christian duty—were to govern her life. To prepare herself to be useful, Laura learned to make every moment count, to read and reflect at odd moments, and to write with precision. At seventeen she was able to spend a year at the Young Ladies' School in St. Johnsbury. For the next six years she taught school at Barnet and at nearby Newbury.

It was through the Rev. Clark Perry, with whose family she boarded in Newbury, that Miss Sheldon met his Dartmouth classmate, the Rev. Asher Wright. Six years her senior, Wright was a native of Hanover, N.H., and a graduate of Andover Theological Seminary. In 1831 (the year of his ordination) he had gone with his young bride, Martha Edgerton, to the wilderness of western New York as a missionary, under the American Board of Commissioners for Foreign Missions, to the Seneca Indians. His wife, however, died two months after their arrival. Perry then encouraged Wright to ask permission to correspond with Miss Sheldon, who in a long and pragmatic reply decided: "I can only say I can have no objections to commencing a correspondence with the proposed end in view. . . . But still I am quite sure I can never fully supply the place of your amiable Martha." A year passed before Wright could take leave, travel the long path from the Buffalo Creek Reservation to Barnet, Vt., and meet his correspondent. They were married at Barnet on Jan. 21, 1833, and left the next day

for the return trip by stage. In fifteen days and nights of midwinter travel the dedicated pair ignored the cold by drilling on Seneca vocabulary and sentences, so that Laura Wright arrived in Buffalo prepared to greet her Iroquois hosts in their own language.

In his second wife Asher Wright found a missionary colleague and helpmate who could reach into the realm of Iroquois women and touch their children, a world that in this matrilineal society a man could not possibly explore. Her linguistic facility, combined with a willingness to learn, her striking physical appearance—she was tall, with jet black hair and dark eyes—her rare composure, and her compassion won the respect and affection of the Indians, with whom she was to abide for fifty-three years. Late in life she wrote: "You know the Indians cannot be driven; they will follow if they can be made to believe that you really love them. They will not bear scolding." She learned not to criticize them openly and to appeal to their subtle role-directed humor. As "Auntie Wright" she would become legendary among them.

The Seneca Mission House at Buffalo Creek, where the Wrights took up residence on Feb. 5, 1833, was a two-story log building furnished with straight-back chairs and beds. The family fare consisted mainly of bread, pork, and potatoes, which was becoming the standard reservation diet. A substantial number of the Senecas then lived within walking distance, but to reach outlying settlements the Wrights traveled on horseback, fording streams or crossing on logs, carrying in their saddlebags food and medicine, scripture and notebook. Western New York was then still one vast forest, but game was already scarce and Seneca hunters took to farming reluctantly, since gardening was women's work. They were now completely dependent on the traders for cloth, flour, kettles, guns, and tools; their gradual civilization awaited the introduction of useful arts and literacy.

The Wrights taught the Indians to read and write by reducing Seneca to a written and printed language. Asher Wright devised a system of phonetic orthography that accounts for the vowels and consonants, including the glottal stop; and his developed structural sense comprehended the prenominal system, although Mrs. Wright admitted that they never quite mastered the verb. They both became accomplished speakers, so that Wright was able to preach without an interpreter, and Mrs. Wright could explain the "Jesus Way" to old people and minister to the medical and spiritual needs of their children. They soon began to produce teaching materials in both languages, translating hymns, prayers, and books of the Bible. Mrs. Wright prepared the first of their bilingual schoolbooks, a small paper-covered primer issued in Boston in 1836. This was followed by a speller (1842) and a bilingual journal (1841–50), both printed at the mission itself, where Wright set up a press equipped with special fonts of type to accommodate Seneca phonetics. The enlarged Seneca hymnal in Wright's orthography, first printed in 1843, is still in use.

Evidence abounds that with the Wrights' help the Indians were improving their lands and finding solutions to their own problems. But the builders of Buffalo, then the frontier port on the Great Lakes, and the promoters of the Ogden Land Company regarded them as an obstacle to progress. Through the "Seven Years' Trouble" (1837–45) the Wrights struggled to help the Senecas keep their land. In the end they lost the Buffalo Creek Reservation, but Asher Wright, it is said, secured the "Compromise Treaty" (1842) which saved the Allegany and Cattaraugus reservations. To the latter the Buffalo Senecas, bitterly resentful against the white people, Christianity, and even their own chiefs, withdrew. Soon afterward the chiefs were overthrown, and in 1848 a republican Seneca Nation came into being that was dominated by Wright's students.

During these difficult years Seneca families suffered from deprivation and disease. Hungry people came daily to beg for food and medicine at the mission, which the Wrights had in 1845 reestablished on the flat near Cattaraugus Creek. Laura Wright saw to it that the mission family shared what it had. In September 1847 typhoid struck, carrying off seventy in six months. When Laura Wright, who had no children of her own, took in the orphans of this epidemic she honored an ancient virtue of the Seneca people which they immediately sensed and sanctioned. She could now walk into the homes of Christian and pagan Indian alike. In 1854 the Wrights, finding on the Cattaraugus Reservation alone some fifty children orphaned and in extreme want, solicited the aid of Philip E. Thomas, a wealthy Quaker merchant of Baltimore, and with the approval of the council of the Seneca Nation founded the Thomas Asylum for Orphan and Destitute Indian Children, of which they became co-directors. During these years Laura Wright was the mainstay of the mission, rescuing a child from infanticide, accepting another left on the railroad track, persuading a widowed husband to entrust his flock to her, and performing similar acts of mercy.

Not the least of the barriers to Christianization was intemperance. Laura Wright founded the Iroquois Temperance League, which came about through an accident to one Peter Twenty-canoes, of notable lineage but frequently drunk, who fell one day on a borrowed scythe while inebriated and cut off his nose. Mrs. Wright restored his dignity with adhesive plaster, which enabled the jubilant man to walk among his fellows sporting a variety of shapes and sizes of noses which, appealing to Seneca humor, converted a calamity into an asset. Mrs. Wright was less certain of their success in inculcating the idea of work, which was foreign to Iroquois culture. Late in her life she is quoted as having said: "We have preached to them faithfully, we have sent away many young men and women to be trained intellectually, we have looked carefully after their souls; but with all the training of heart and head, that training by which the daily bread must be provided has been neglected." Her plan for industrial education enjoyed only partial success.

After Asher Wright's death in 1875 Mrs. Wright moved from the Mission House to the home of Nicholson H. Parker, a member of a distinguished Seneca family who had assisted Wright at the press and served for many years as the government interpreter. It was here that "Auntie Wright" died of pneumonia in 1886, in her seventy-seventh year. "In the house and all about it," wrote her brother Henry, were "groups of bereaved Indians in tears." She was buried with her husband in the Mission Cemetery at Iroquois, N.Y. In the 1930's old Senecas still spoke of Asher and Laura Wright with reverence.

[There are letters of Laura Wright in the Papers of the Am. Board of Commissioners for Foreign Missions, Houghton Library, Harvard Univ. The principal published source is Mrs. Harriet S. Caswell, *Our Life among the Iroquois Indians* (1892), written by a member of the mission staff. On the Seneca Mission at Buffalo Creek, see Henry R. Howland in Buffalo Hist. Soc., *Publications*, VI (1903), 125–61; and William N. Fenton, "Toward the Gradual Civilization of the Indian Natives: The Missionary and Linguistic Work of Asher Wright (1803–1875)," Am. Philosophical Soc., *Proc.*, C (1956), 567–81. For the Seneca Mission Press, see Asher Wright in James C. Pilling, *Bibliog. of the Iroquoian Languages* (1888); for the Parker family, Arthur C. Parker, *The Life of Gen. Ely S. Parker* (Buffalo Hist. Soc., *Publications*, vol. XXIII, 1919).]

WILLIAM N. FENTON

WRIGHT, Lucy (Feb. 5, 1760–Feb. 7, 1821), Shaker leader, the dominant figure during the period of the society's greatest growth, was a worthy successor to its founder, ANN LEE. Modest, discreet, serene, she was nevertheless a born executive, talented, practical, strong-willed. Little is known of her life before her conversion. She was born in Pittsfield, Mass., the daughter of John and Mary (Robbins) Wright. Her parents had some means, and she received whatever educational advantages were available in a settlement that was not incorporated as a town until 1761. Her mother died when she was about eighteen years old. At nineteen she was married to Elizur Goodrich, a young merchant in the neighboring town of Richmond.

Soon after their marriage the couple became deeply affected by the enthusiasm generated by a New Light Baptist revival. When this work failed to fulfill its promise, Elizur Goodrich eagerly accepted the millennial gospel which the Shakers were beginning to preach at Watervliet, N.Y. "Burdened for the soul of his beautiful young wife," he tried to persuade her to join him. But Lucy was a prudent spirit, not given to hasty action. That she was sympathetic, however, is evidenced by the fact that in August 1780, when Ann Lee was confined to the Poughkeepsie jail, Lucy sent her "presents for her comfort and convenience." During the period (1781–83) when Mother Ann was on her mission journey into New England, Lucy Wright remained at Watervliet. She was with the prophetess at Harvard, Mass., however, and became a Shaker during that period. Faithful to the rule of celibacy, she and Goodrich quitted their "fleshly relations" and lived in separate men's and women's orders, Lucy thereafter using only her maiden name. She lived at Watervliet; her husband became an itinerant preacher and finally settled at New Lebanon, N.Y.

In 1787, after the deaths of Mother Ann and Father James Whittaker, Father Joseph Meacham (their successor) selected Lucy Wright as the "first leading character in the female line." He thus presaged the dual order based on the equality of the sexes that became characteristic of Shaker society. Under the joint administration of Father Joseph and Mother Lucy, the Believers were gathered together at the mother church in New Lebanon, forming a common-propertied, socioreligious organization which was copied by the ten other Shaker communities in New York and New England. By this decision the Shakers were transformed from a loosely organized body of followers into an association of monasticlike communities, industrious and self-supporting.

On Meacham's death in 1796, Mother Lucy assumed the leadership of the central ministry,

assisted by one or two "elder brothers" and in the female line by Rebecca Kendal and Ruth Hammond and especially by Ruth Landon. Under her administration the decision was made, in 1804, to send out the mission which eventually led to the establishment of seven Shaker societies in Kentucky, Ohio, and Indiana. And it was Lucy Wright who authorized the publication of the basic theological work of the sect, Benjamin S. Youngs' *The Testimony of Christ's Second Appearing* (1808).

One of Lucy's great interests was the mode of worship. Dissatisfied with the early solemn, wordless hymns, the stereotyped dances, the repetitive shaking and whirling "gifts," she brought greater order, variety, and vitality to the exercises. Little "extra" songs with words, sung "promiscuously," were added, together with lively dances, "union marches," and symbolic gesturing with the hands—innovations which made the meetings more animated and meaningful. Another interest was education. With the assistance of Seth Y. Wells, she instituted schools in the Children's Order which eventually achieved an established reputation in the outside world.

In a contemporary manuscript Lucy Wright is described as a strong, "handsome" woman of medium height, with dark brown hair, fair complexion, and dark eyes which were "clear and penetrating yet mild and placid." Her countenance was open and serene, her manner modest, but frank and "affable." She died at Watervliet at the age of sixty-one and was buried there beside the grave of Ann Lee. In the hearts of the Shakers she was a noble embodiment of that mother spirit which was such a pervasive influence in the movement.

[Anna White and Leila S. Taylor, *Shakerism, Its Meaning and Message* (1904); Edward D. Andrews, *The People Called Shakers: A Search for the Perfect Society* (1953); manuscript records in Edward Deming Andrews Memorial Shaker Collection, Winterthur Museum, Winterthur, Del.]

EDWARD DEMING ANDREWS

**WRIGHT, Mabel Osgood** (Jan. 26, 1859–July 16, 1934), nature writer, bird protectionist, and novelist, was born in New York City, the last of three children, all girls. Her father, the Rev. Samuel Osgood, born in Charlestown, Mass., was a descendant of John Osgood, one of the founders of Andover, Mass. A graduate of Harvard and the Harvard Divinity School and a "Channing Unitarian," he was for two decades pastor of New York's Church of the Messiah, until in 1870 he took orders in the Episcopal Church. Professionally he was known for his translations of religious works—German theology was his special interest—and for essays, biographies, and sermons. Socially and culturally he was part of the New York group centered on the author William Cullen Bryant. His wife, Ellen Haswell Murdock, a descendant of Richard Russell of Charlestown, Mass., was related to SUSANNA HASWELL ROWSON, author of *Charlotte Temple.*

Mabel Osgood was educated at home and in a private school at "Number One Fifth Avenue" in New York. Visits to the country in girlhood apparently developed an interest in nature. On Sept. 25, 1884, she was married to James Osborne Wright (1852–1920), and after a long visit to his native England the couple settled in Fairfield, Conn., Wright commuting from there to his New York business in rare books. Though evidence is uncertain, they probably had no children. Mrs. Wright's first printed work, apart from a few verses, was an essay, "A New England May Day," in the New York *Evening Post* in 1893. This and other newspaper pieces were collected as *The Friendship of Nature* (1894), her first book (published, as were all that followed, by Macmillan). A year later came *Birdcraft*, subtitled *A Field Book of Two Hundred Song, Game, and Water Birds.*

These books represent two major aspects of her creative work in nature study. In the words of the renowned ornithologist and author Frank M. Chapman, the first "records a loving intimacy with birds and flowers and seasons," the second stands out as "one of the first and most successful of the modern bird manuals." Both the love of nature and the accurate description of it preoccupied Mrs. Wright throughout her career in nature study, leading logically to a third concern, the wish to protect the natural heritage. In the pursuit of these ends, Mrs. Wright went on to write *Citizen Bird* (with the noted naturalist Elliott Coues, 1897) and *Gray Lady and the Birds* (1907), several books on plants and mammals, nature stories and fables for children, and numerous articles. From its inception she was associated with Chapman's magazine *Bird-Lore,* serving in the executive or school departments from 1899 to 1910, then as a contributing editor until her death.

Helping to found the Connecticut Audubon Society in 1898, Mrs. Wright was elected president and served for many years; she was a director of the National Association of Audubon Societies from 1905 to 1928. She was made an associate member of the American Ornithologists' Union in 1895 and a full member in 1901. She pioneered in bird protection by planning and constructing Birdcraft Sanctuary on a tract of wasteland near her Connecticut home. When she wrote in 1917 that over the preceding two decades "a great awakening to the value and beauty of bird life has swept the land," Mrs. Wright was noting a development for which she herself could take much credit.

Although she is mainly remembered as a nature writer, she seems to have set more store by the romances she penned, under her own name or the pseudonym "Barbara," in the early years of the twentieth century. Between *The Garden of a Commuter's Wife* (1901) and *The Stranger at the Gate* (1913) there were ten such works, half of them conventional novels, the others freer in form, combining fictional episodes with letters, diary entries, passages of autobiography and social criticism, and pieces on nature study or gardening. Though widely reviewed and often reprinted, they failed to win her a secure literary reputation. As a rule her fictional range was narrow, limited geographically to lower New England and Manhattan, socially to the better classes (an occasional villain or "low" person excepted), and emotionally to the domestic, pious, and sentimental. Furthermore, her command of character and plot was uncertain and her use of dialogue frequently inept.

But two aspects of her fiction reward study. Often woven into her romantic tales is a critical appraisal of changing social patterns—the urban world of the 1860's and '70's giving way to one dominated by the "new magnates" whose money was fast remaking metropolitan society, or the rural quietude of lower Connecticut disappearing with the advent of suburbanites who brought their city tensions with them. A second theme is even more insistently examined: the "new woman," whose appearance Mrs. Wright dates from the Civil War and "the general necessity . . . for the woman's stepping into the man's empty shoes, so that the labor horizon for all time widened for all women." This new woman also pursues new educational, social, religious, and even sexual horizons, seeking "what she calls 'recognition' and 'identity' . . . outside the protecting walls of her natural affections!" Mrs. Wright, herself something of a career woman, nevertheless displays an interesting ambivalence, with sympathy and awareness on the one hand, and shrill attacks on feminism and careerism on the other. Nearly always she resolves the problem in conventional and even saccharine terms of marriage to a proper male—or, failing that, virtual madness, as with Ivory Steele, the intransigent heroine of *The Woman Errant* (1904).

*My New York* (1926) is also a book of social commentary, autobiographical in form and valedictory in mood. Tone is here as important as fact, the implied as revealing as the stated. Mrs. Wright's numerous references to her father, his moral and religious imperatives and his paternal stance and outlook, suggest several esteemed and authoritative males in her romances, and the general atmosphere of gentility and moral probity of the Osgood household similarly reappears in her fiction. Curiously, she makes almost no reference in this account to her early nature study or to her thirty years of work in natural history and conservation. In 1934, in Fairfield, she succumbed to a heart ailment (hypertensive myocardial disease with angina) at the age of seventy-five. She was buried in Oaklawn Cemetery, Fairfield.

[Besides Mrs. Wright's overtly autobiographical *My New York* (which as a personal record is vague and sometimes ambiguous and seems more contrived than candid), there are numerous bits of semiautobiography scattered through her romances. There are also references *passim* in her contributions to *Bird-Lore* through the issue of July–Aug. 1934. Other sources: *Who Was Who in America*, vol. I (1942); *Nat. Cyc. Am. Biog.*, XII, 545; Joseph Adelman, *Famous Women* (1926), p. 284 (which gives 1851 as the year of her birth); Eben Putnam, ed., *A Genealogy of the Descendants of John, Christopher and William Osgood* (1894), pp. 293–94; obituaries in *Bird-Lore*, July–Aug. 1934, the *Auk*, Oct. 1934, *N.Y. Times*, July 18, 1934, and, for James Osborne Wright, May 28, 1920; death record from Conn. State Dept. of Health.]

                                    ROBERT H. WELKER

**WRIGHT, Martha Coffin Pelham** (Dec. 25, 1806–Jan. 4, 1875), woman's rights leader, was born in Boston, Mass., the youngest of eight children, seven of them girls; she was a sister of the famous LUCRETIA COFFIN MOTT. Her father, Thomas Coffin, and her mother, Anna (Folger) Coffin, were descendants of two of the original settlers of Nantucket Island in 1662, Tristram Coffyn and Peter Folger. Thomas Coffin, a merchant and ship captain, had moved his family and business from Nantucket to Boston in 1804. Persuaded, however, that Philadelphia offered a more congenial climate for the practice of the family's Quaker religion, he removed to that city in 1809 and there operated a small factory. He suffered severe financial reverses during the War of 1812 and died soon afterward, but Martha's widowed mother resourcefully supported her large family by various enterprises, including a small shop and a boardinghouse. Martha, who loved the theatre and other frivolities, was frequently the object of her sister Lucretia's reformist impulses. Once, when Lucretia gave her a white

handkerchief to replace a gaudy red one, Martha passed off the incident with characteristic humor: "I have no objections as long as the expense is not mine, to being friendified to their heart's content" (Cromwell, p. 43).

On Nov. 18, 1824, after three years at the Kimberton Boarding School near Philadelphia, Martha Coffin, ignoring her mother's wishes, was married to a family boarder, Peter Pelham, an army captain from Maysville, Ky., and moved with him to Florida. On his death two years later she returned to Philadelphia with their daughter, Marianna, born in August 1825. Because of marrying out of meeting she had been expelled from the Society of Friends, and as she grew older, although possessing the characteristic Quaker traits of dignity, kindness, and simplicity, she came to have little regard for organized religion; indeed, she was considered an "infidel" by more pious neighbors. "As to the teachings of the pulpit or the Bible," she wrote in 1872, "they come only from fallible mortals like ourselves, & their opinion is worth just as much as yours or mine . . . *less* if it seems less rational" (quoted in Riegel, p. 26).

After a brief engagement to Julius Catlin, a brother of the painter George Catlin, was ended for lack of financial means, Martha Pelham moved in 1827 with her mother to Aurora, N.Y., and taught in a school which Mrs. Coffin had opened. There, in 1829, she was married to a lawyer from Philadelphia, David Wright (1805–1897). They lived in Aurora until 1839, and then for many years in Auburn, N.Y. They had six children: Eliza, born in 1830, Matthew Tallman (1832), Ellen (1840), who married William Lloyd Garrison, Jr., William Pelham (1842), who was severely wounded at Gettysburg, Frank (1844), and Charles (1848), who died in infancy. The two Wright daughters became suffragists, and Eliza's son Thomas Mott Osborne a noted prison reformer. Mrs. Wright's daughter by her earlier marriage, Marianna Pelham, married a first cousin, Thomas Mott, the son of James and Lucretia Mott.

Martha Wright's career in reform began in 1848 when she joined her sister Lucretia Mott and ELIZABETH CADY STANTON in planning the first woman's rights convention in America, held in Seneca Falls, N.Y., that July. From that year until her death Mrs. Wright, warmly supported by her husband, was active in the movement. She was a secretary of the larger 1852 woman's rights convention in Syracuse, N.Y., vice-president of the 1854 gathering in Philadelphia, and in 1855 was elected president of three separate conventions—in Cincinnati, Saratoga, and Albany. An active member of the New York State Woman's Rights Committee, she presided over the tenth national woman's rights convention in New York City in 1860. Perhaps more important, however, was her advisory role. Her good friends SUSAN B. ANTHONY and Elizabeth Cady Stanton frequently consulted her, and her incisive wit, shrewd practicality, impatience with unnecessary flamboyance, and commitment to results proved invaluable.

When a program of action for the woman's rights movement was first being developed, Martha Wright advocated the realistic pacing of demands, working first for property and marriage rights at the state level, and later for national suffrage legislation. With her sister, she was among those who argued for a curtailment of feminist agitation during the Civil War so that women could work for the elimination of slavery. This reflected both her strong abolitionist sentiments and her belief that the country would look more favorably upon an organization which had supported the Union cause. Though this hope was not realized, the plan had some plausibility; indeed, a similar approach during World War I did hasten public acceptance of suffrage. Mrs. Wright remained loyal to Miss Anthony and Mrs. Stanton when the woman's movement divided after the war, joining them in founding the American Equal Rights Association in 1866 and the National Woman Suffrage Association in 1869. "Her home was my home," wrote the grief-stricken Susan B. Anthony when her long-time friend and supporter died (Harper, I, 467).

Though taller than Lucretia Mott, Martha Wright, with her dark hair and penetrating dark eyes, resembled her more famous sister. Very close despite a thirteen-year age difference, the two women exchanged many letters on literature, religion, and politics. Mrs. Wright on occasion urged her sister to curtail her more active public life to safeguard her health, but she sometimes chafed under her own constricting domestic duties: "I dread the care of the furnace—of the house—of the cow—of the children" (Cromwell, p. 201). She composed poetry, short stories, and sketches, but aside from a few magazine articles on women's rights, the bulk of her writing was confined to a family audience. Her years of work for woman's rights were recognized in 1874 with her election as president of the National Woman Suffrage Association. She died the following year of pneumonia, at the age of sixty-eight, while visiting her daughter in Boston, and was buried in Auburn, N.Y.

[Martha Wright's papers, including diaries, 1,500 letters, and an unpublished biographical sketch by Eliza Wright Osborne, are a part of the Garrison Family Papers in the Sophia Smith Collection at Smith College. Biographical information is available in the several published studies of Lucretia Mott, especially Anna Davis Hallowell, *James and Lucretia Mott, Life and Letters* (1884), and Otelia Cromwell, *Lucretia Mott* (1958). See also Elizabeth C. Stanton et al., *Hist. of Woman Suffrage* (6 vols., 1881–1922); Ida H. Harper, *Life and Work of Susan B. Anthony*, vol. I (1898); and Robert E. Riegel, *Am. Feminists* (1963). An obituary and editorial tribute are in the *Woman's Jour.*, Jan. 9, 1875.]

PAUL MESSBARGER

**WRIGHT, Patience Lovell** (1725–Mar. 23, 1786), sculptor in wax, was born in Bordentown, N.J., the fifth daughter of John and Patience (Townsend) Lovell. Her father's family, originally from Massachusetts, had long been settled at Oyster Bay, Long Island (where the painter Robert Feke was a distant cousin), but had moved early in the eighteenth century to New Jersey. John Lovell was a prosperous farmer and a Quaker of firm and individualistic principles, whose singular mode of life, Patience later claimed, included not only strict vegetarianism, but also the insistence that his whole family, including a son and six daughters, dress in pure white from head to foot. This regimen perhaps had a part in inclining his children to mix colors, paint pictures, and model figures in dough or clay. It may also have hastened Patience's flight to Philadephia in her early twenties. There, on Mar. 20, 1748, she was married to Joseph Wright, a cooper whose family had similarly migrated from Oyster Bay to Bordentown. Little is known of her life for the next twenty-one years, but her husband's death on May 7, 1769, left her with five children, of whom the eldest, Mary (Mrs. Benjamin Van Cleef), and the youngest, Sarah, born in her widowhood, died a few years later. There remained Elizabeth, Joseph (born in 1756), and Phoebe (born in 1761).

Thrown on her own resources, Patience Wright began a career as a modeler in wax, a medium in which she soon displayed considerable talent. By 1772, aided by her sister Rachel (Mrs. James Wells), she had created a traveling waxwork exhibit of a sort previously unknown. Other workers in wax had attempted only manikinlike criminal, historical, and allegorical characters, but Mrs. Wright chose living and well-known personages. Her skill in reproducing their features accurately and rapidly, together with her colorful and forceful personality, won the friendship and patronage of many of her key subjects, and her wax show attracted favorable comment in Charleston, Philadelphia, and New York. A fire in June 1771 which destroyed much of the New York exhibit may have been a factor in Mrs. Wright's determination to move to England.

With letters of reference from important Americans, she sailed in February 1772; her children followed sometime later. In London her friend Benjamin Franklin introduced her to various eminent persons, including the historian Catherine Macaulay, the political leader John Sawbridge, and the painter Benjamin West. She was soon ensconced in rooms in Pall Mall surrounded by wax likenesses of these persons and of assorted dukes, scholars, actors, and radicals. Her technique far outshone that of her only London competitor, a Mrs. Salmon, and the novelty of her art was matched by her amusing and incessant conversation. As her letters make plain, she lacked formal education, but this was offset by her ebullient, intuitive vigor of mind. Cultivating her reputation as a bohemian eccentric, she used profanity with gusto; she struck the proper ABIGAIL ADAMS as slatternly in appearance and overfamiliar in manner. English society, however, was delighted with the "American Sibyl." Even the King and Queen, it is said, enjoyed receiving her advice, addressed to them bluntly as "George" and "Charlotte."

Patience Wright was fascinated by politics, and she made good use of her friendships with British and colonial leaders. Though a firm American patriot, she enjoyed intrigue for its own sake. In the deepening American crisis of 1773–74 she passed along to William Pitt (Lord Chatham) political gossip which he seems to have valued, though it was somewhat incoherently mingled with her adulation of him as America's "guardian Angel." With the outbreak of war she came to view Benjamin Franklin in this exalted role, but her letters to Franklin in Paris do not substantiate the claim that they contained strategic intelligence picked up in London among the ladies of her acquaintance. She is said to have sent secret communications to members of Congress (Pasquin, p. 92), and an anonymous letter of 1785 in the Franklin Papers quotes John Hancock as having commended her efforts. One unsubstantiated but credible legend is that these communications were concealed in the wax effigies of Lord North and others which she sent to her sister Mrs. Wells, then operating a wax museum in Philadelphia. It is, in any case, well established that she opened her London house to American prisoners of war, one of whom, Ebenezer Platt, married her daughter Elizabeth in

1777; both died a few years later while traveling in America with a waxwork exhibition. In 1780 her remaining daughter, Phoebe, became the wife of the portraitist John Hoppner, and in that same year her son Joseph made his own artistic debut at the Royal Academy with a portrait of his mother modeling a wax head. Only when the portrait was hung did shocked spectators note that the head was that of Charles I, and that two onlookers upon whom Mrs. Wright was casting a significant glance were George III and Queen Charlotte.

While this scandal was echoing in the news, Patience Wright bustled off to Paris to introduce her art to the French and to interest Franklin in the schemes for fomenting rebellion in England and Ireland in which she and one Major Peter Labilliere, "Christian Patriot and Citizen of the World," were now deeply involved. Here she met the young American merchant Elkanah Watson, who has left a description of her as she hailed him, a stranger but a fellow American, from her hotel window: "In two minutes, she came blustering down stairs, with the familiarity of an old acquaintance. We were soon on the most excellent terms. . . . She was a tall and athletic figure; and walked with a firm, bold step; as erect as an Indian. Her complexion was somewhat sallow; her cheekbones, high; her face, furrowed; and her olive eyes keen, piercing and expressive. Her sharp glance was appalling; it had almost the wildness of a maniac's. The vigor and originality of her conversation corresponded with her manners and appearance. She would utter language, in her incessant volubility, as if unconscious to whom directed, that would put her hearers to the blush. She apparently possessed the utmost simplicity of heart and character" (*Men and Times of the Revolution*, p. 137).

Unable to open an exhibition in Paris, where Philippe Curtius (uncle of the famous Madame Tussaud) had preempted the market, Mrs. Wright returned to England in 1781, consoled for the failure of her revolutionary schemes by the victorious conclusion of the war. One of her last major efforts was a reproduction in wax of the meeting of the peace commissioners. Her popularity in London having waned, she yearned again for her native land, averring that she could not be "content to have her bons Laid in London." Laid in London they were, however, following her sudden death there in 1786, after a fall. Her sister Rachel, living in semiretirement at Bordentown with a company of thirty-three wax figures, survived her by ten years.

A vivid if minor figure, Patience Lovell

Wright mingled considerable commercial vulgarization and ballyhoo with her art, yet within her limited range she was unexcelled; apart from masthead and tombstone craftsmen, she ranks as America's first professional sculptor. Together with other American artists resident in London—Copley, West, Stuart—she profited by the eighteenth century's trend toward naturalism. And, like Franklin, she consciously encouraged the idealized European image of the New World, particularly the notion that both her open personality and her lifelike art were natural products of a country where Quaker simplicity and arcadian equality reigned supreme. Several extant bas-reliefs are attributed to her. The one work clearly known to be hers is a full-length effigy of Lord Chatham, now preserved in a somewhat damaged condition among the wax figures in Westminster Abbey.

[Manuscript sources include: Benjamin Franklin Papers, Am. Philosophical Soc., Phila.; Henry Laurens Papers, S.C. Hist. Soc., Charleston; Lord Chatham Papers, Public Records Office, London. Mrs. Wright's will is in the N.Y. County Surrogate Court records. For the wills of her daughter Elizabeth Platt and her sister Rachel Wells see *N.J. Archives*, vols. XXXVII and XXXVIII (1942, 1944). Pertinent letters are printed in Lyman H. Butterfield, ed., *The Adams Papers: Adams Family Correspondence*, II (1963), 235–36; Charles F. Adams, *Letters of Mrs. Adams* (1848), pp. 177–78; Mrs. Paget Toynbee, ed., *Letters of Horace Walpole* (1904), VIII, 237, XI, 169; Julian P. Boyd et al., eds., *The Papers of Thomas Jefferson*, VIII (1953), 380–81, IX (1954), 101–02; Leonard W. Labaree et al., eds., *The Papers of Benjamin Franklin* (1959– ). Contemporary references include: [Philip Thicknesse,] *The New Prose Bath Guide, for the Year 1778* (1778); *London Chronicle*, July 4–7, 1772, p. 24; *Morning Chronicle and London Advertiser*, May 7, 1776; *London Courant*, May 3, 1780; *European Mag. and London Rev.*, Mar. 1786, p. 210; *London Mag.*, Nov. 1775, pp. 555–56. Later accounts include: Anthony Pasquin [John Williams], *Memoirs of the Royal Academicians* (1796), p. 154; William Dunlap, *A Hist. of the Rise and Progress of the Arts of Design in the U.S.* (1918 edition, edited by Frank W. Bayley and Charles E. Goodspeed), I, 150–56; Elkanah Watson, *Men and Times of the Revolution* (2nd ed., 1856), pp. 137–43; Howard D. Perrine, *The Wright Family of Oysterbay, L.I.* (1923); Charles H. Hart in *Connoisseur*, Sept. 1907; Friends Hist. Soc., *Jour.*, Jan. 1923; Parker Lesley in *Art in America*, Oct. 1936; Rita S. Gottesman, comp., *The Arts and Crafts in N.Y., 1726–1776* (1938) and *1777–1799* (1954); William T. Whitley, *Artists and Their Friends in England, 1700 to 1799* (1928), II, 55–59; L. E. Tanner and J. L. Nevinson, "On Some Later Funeral Effigies in Westminster Abbey," *Archaeologia*, vol. LXXXV (1935); Lewis Einstein, *Divided Loyalties* (1933), on her wartime role; John C. Long, *Mr. Pitt and America's Birthright* (1940); Charles C. Sellers, *Benjamin Franklin in Portraiture* (1962).]

CHARLES COLEMAN SELLERS

**WRIGHT, Sophie Bell** (June 5, 1866–June 10, 1912), educator and welfare worker, was born and spent her life in New Orleans. Her parents, both children of wealthy planters, had grown up in the luxury of the antebellum South, her mother, Mary (Bell) Wright, at Oak Bluff plantation in Franklin, La. Her father, William Haliday Wright, the son of Scottish immigrants, had served during the Civil War in the Confederate Army and Navy. But the war left the family plantations in ruin and her father without a means of livelihood. As a further hardship, Sophie, the third of the Wrights' seven children, fell at the age of three and seriously injured her back and hips. For six years she was strapped to a chair, unable to move; at the age of nine, with great perseverance, she began to get about on crutches. Sophie did not become bitter, for her mother, a devout Presbyterian, taught her to accept her condition as the work of God. Educated at first by her father—to whom she afterward credited her proficiency in mathematics—she later added five years of formal instruction at the Franklin Elementary School and the Girls' Central High School, from which she graduated in 1880. Determined to become self-supporting and to assist her family, the frail young fifteen-year-old the next year opened a "Day School for Girls" in her parents' home.

Sophie Wright's day school grew and prospered. Feeling the need for further training as her students advanced, she enrolled in the Peabody Normal Seminary in New Orleans. Here she taught mathematics in exchange for instruction in foreign languages, conducting her own school in the mornings and studying and teaching in the afternoons. In 1883 her school was formally chartered as the Home Institute, a "Classical School for Young Ladies and Children." Expanded in 1885 with boarding as well as day facilities, it soon became recognized as one of the city's better private schools.

Increasingly, however, a new project came to absorb Sophie Wright's energies. In 1884 she had agreed to assist a destitute young circus performer seeking a school where he could prepare for a civil service examination. Each night he came to the Home Institute for instruction. Soon other young men joined him. Thus before she realized it Sophie Wright was conducting a free night school for men and boys, and by the end of the year it had become, an established institution. The only criteria for admission were that the applicants be employed during the day and that they be too poor to pay. As the classes expanded she enlisted volunteer teachers. Needing more space, she borrowed the funds to buy a larger house, to which she moved both the Institute and the Free Night School, her profits from the former supporting the latter. In 1897 a benefaction from two New Orleans citizens—her first outside support—enabled her to buy proper equipment for the Night School, which in a year increased its enrollment from 300 to 1,000 (it ultimately grew to over 1,500). The warmth and personal force of this tiny woman—capable, despite her crutches and steel harness, of chastising an unruly pupil—enriched the lives of thousands of workingmen and boys and won her in time the city's esteem. In 1903, at a mass gathering in a public park, she was awarded the *New Orleans Picayune* loving cup for outstanding service to the community, a group of admirers at the same time raising $10,000 to pay off the mortgage on her school. Six years later, the city board of education having opened its own free night schools, Sophie Wright brought her own memorable institution to a close.

She continued to teach at the Home Institute and to participate, as she had long done, in a variety of charitable and civic activities. Her executive ability found outlet in the Louisiana Woman's Club, of which she was president in 1897–98. An effective public speaker, direct and appealing in manner, she assisted other New Orleanians in their unsuccessful attempt to obtain state aid for Sophie Newcomb College for Women in 1906, and she worked with the legislative committee of the Louisiana Nurses Association in 1912 to obtain passage of a bill raising the educational standards for nurses in the state. (She was, however, opposed to woman suffrage.) She was an active member of such groups as the United Daughters of the Confederacy, the Woman's Christian Temperance Union, the Prison Reform Association, and the State Congress of Mothers. But she gave particular time and energy, as secretary and in 1906 as president, to the Louisiana branch of the International Order of the King's Daughters and Sons, a nonsectarian religious organization for social service. With this group she worked to provide vacations for needy women and children at its summer camp, Rest-Awhile, and to secure public baths and playgrounds. And with the King's Daughters' assistance, she raised the necessary funds to build an annex for crippled children—the first in Louisiana—at the New Orleans Home for Incurables.

Although this pale and sad-eyed woman bore her personal sufferings stoically, it was obvious by 1907 that Sophie Wright, New Orleans' "First Citizen," was seriously ill. But she recovered in that year from pneumonia and two paralytic strokes and for five years carried on her work despite increasing weakness. In 1911 the city named a new girls' high school after her. She died in New Orleans in 1912, at forty-six, of valvular disease of the heart. With the entire city in mourning, she was buried in the family tomb in the Metairie Cemetery. Two of her sisters, Jennie and Mary, carried on the Home Institute.

[The best source is Viola Mary Walker, "Sophie Bell Wright, Her Life and Work" (unpublished M.A. thesis, Tulane Univ., 1939). For her family and childhood, see Alcée Fortier, *Louisiana*, vol. III (1914); Amelia S. Pasteur, ed., *New Orleans Society Reference*, 1904–07. General biographical material includes *Nat. Cyc. Am. Biog.*, X, 51; *Literary Digest*, June 29, 1912; John L. Mathews in *Everybody's Mag.*, July 1906; Helen C. Bennett, *Am. Women in Civic Work* (1915); *New Orleans Daily States*, June 10–12, 1912; and *New Orleans Times-Picayune*, June 11–12, 1912, July 21, 1946. For information on Sophie Wright's work at the Free Night School, see the monthly magazine published by its students, *Progress: "Help the Helping Hand,"* vols. III–V (1905–08). Data on her efforts in behalf of Newcomb College and nursing legislation can be found in Marcus M. Wilkerson, *Thomas Duckett Boyd* (1935), and *Hist. of La. State Nurses' Assoc. Silver Jubilee, 1904–1929* (n.d.). On her club work, see Jane C. Croly, *The Hist. of the Woman's Club Movement in America* (1898), p. 515; and *Womans Era* magazine (New Orleans), 1910–11. The Howard-Tilton Library, Tulane Univ., has a Sophie Wright Scrapbook, and useful details were found in various manuscript holdings of the La. Hist. Assoc. Collection in the same library. Death record from New Orleans City Health Dept.]

L. E. ZIMMERMAN

WRIGHT, Susanna (Aug. 4, 1697–Dec. 1, 1784), colonial frontierswoman and poet, was the oldest daughter of John and Patience (Gibson) Wright, Quakers, of Warrington, later of Manchester, England. Her birth is entered in the Lancashire Quaker register, followed by the birth records of three sisters and three brothers; a fourth brother, James, was born in America. Her father had been educated for the practice of medicine, but he chose to combine the vocation of a bodice maker with that of a Quaker minister. His devotion to his spiritual calling was apparently detrimental to his worldly prosperity, a fact which may have accounted for his decision in 1714 to start over again in America. On Mar. 16, 1713/14, he obtained from Hartshaw Monthly Meeting of Friends a certificate of good standing which he presented to Chester Meeting in Pennsylvania three months later, on June 9. Susanna is said to have remained in England to complete her education, but she presently joined her family in Chester, where her father had established himself as a shopkeeper.

In 1727, or early in 1728, John Wright and his family moved again, this time to the banks of the Susquehanna, on the farthest frontier of settlement in Pennsylvania, where the former bodice maker operated the ferry (two canoes lashed together) which became the main gateway into the Great Valley. As head of her father's large household (her mother having died in 1722), Susanna Wright lived for twenty years at Hempfield, the Wright homestead; after 1745 she moved into a larger house bequeathed to her by another pioneer settler, Samuel Blunston, and assumed responsibility for her brother James' family. She never married, though there is a persistent legend of an unconsummated love affair with Blunston, a legend to which his bequest of a life interest in his house and lands lends credibility. Here, at Wright's Ferry (later Columbia), she lived two concurrent lives, both of extraordinary fullness: the arduous practical life of an American frontierswoman, replete with anxieties and hard work, and the intellectual and aesthetic life of an eighteenth-century bluestocking, artist, and poet.

Her household duties were always heavy, for John Wright was often away from home, representing Lancaster County in the provincial assembly or presiding over the county court. Since the Wrights, father and son, controlled the ferry, their home was the resort of every westward-bound fur trader, prospective settler, or traveler. Important guests from Philadelphia, arriving on official business, were invariably charmed by "Suzey's" generous hospitality, her witty conversation. She carried on the domestic manufactures common to every backcountry household, but specialized in producing silk from cocoons raised in her own mulberry trees. Robert Proud, the historian, saw fifteen hundred silkworms "at work under her direction," and heard her claim that with proper encouragement she could raise a million. In 1771, when the nonimportation movement created a flurry of domestic textile production, she won a premium of £10 offered in Philadelphia for the largest number of cocoons raised by one individual. A court dress spun from her silk was presented to

Queen Charlotte of England by Benjamin Franklin.

Susanna Wright's facility with the pen created a demand for her services as a scrivener. She often wrote out deeds, wills, and indentures for her unlettered neighbors, thus serving her community as a kind of unpaid legal counselor; after Blunston's death she is said to have been commissioned as prothonotary. As the local settlers came to know and respect her judgment, they regularly brought their disputes over land and cattle before her for arbitration; thus she sat as a kind of extrajudicial magistrate. Drawing perhaps on her father's half-forgotten medical lore, she functioned also as an amateur physician and apothecary, distilling simples and compounding medicinal herbs, which she prescribed and dispensed gratis to her neighbors. She always lived on friendly terms with the nearby Indians; after the bloody massacre of the Conestogas by the Paxton Boys in 1763, she is said to have entered the pamphlet war with a defense of the peaceful victims in answer to the Rev. Thomas Barton of Lancaster.

When not engaged in reeling silk or listening to her neighbors' troubles, she sought refuge in her "large and well-chosen" library. At eighty-seven she told Benjamin Rush "that she still retained her relish for books—that 'she could not live without them.'" Her friends in Philadelphia—James Logan, Benjamin Franklin, Charles and Isaac Norris—kept her supplied with the latest publications. Fluent in French, conversant with Italian and Latin, knowledgeable in natural philosophy, she was one of the few persons, and perhaps the only woman, in the colony who could hold her own in conversation or correspondence with the learned James Logan, who always referred to her as "Philomel" in tribute to her talent for poetry. Unfortunately, only a few of her poems have survived; they smack of the contemporary "graveyard school" but possess a certain refreshing simplicity of language and rhythm. Of her skill in drawing, often mentioned by contemporaries, no examples are known to exist.

In her last years many visitors came to see "the celebrated Susanna Wright." At seventy-five she was described as having "all the vivacity of a woman of forty," though "remarkably plain in her dress and manner of living," as became a Quaker. "She was small," a younger woman recalled many years later, "and had never been handsome, but had a penetrating, sensible countenance, and was truly polite and courteous in her address and behavior." She died in her eighty-eighth year and was buried in the Quaker burying ground at Columbia. In her long life at Wright's Ferry, she had watched the Pennsylvania frontier slowly creep westward, seen civilization gradually come to the Susquehanna country. She had been in the vanguard of both processes—a hardy, resourceful pioneer woman, a remarkable exemplar of culture on a moving frontier.

[The vital facts concerning the Wright family in England and their migration to and in America are documented in the Quaker meeting records; no records exist, however, for the uniquely independent meeting at Wright's Ferry. Most of the details of Susanna Wright's life derive ultimately from the recollections of younger contemporaries as set down in Samuel Hazard's *Register of Pa.,* Sept. 17, 1831, pp. 177–78, and Mar. 10, 1832, p. 145; and Samuel I. Knapp's *Female Biog.* (1836), pp. 484–87. The Library Company of Phila. has a few of her poems in MS. and a piece of her homespun silk. Her surviving correspondence is chiefly at the Hist. Soc. of Pa., in the Logan, Norris, and Pemberton papers; for her correspondence with Franklin see Leonard W. Labaree et al., eds., *The Papers of Benjamin Franklin* (1959– ). Her "Directions for the Management of Silk-Worms" was printed in the *Phila. Medical and Physical Jour.,* I, pt. 1 (1804), 103–07. See also Marion Wallace Reninger, "Susanna Wright," Lancaster County Hist. Soc., *Jour.,* Oct. 1959, and references to her in *ibid.,* Jan. 1957, pp. 3–10, and in the Soc.'s *Papers,* LII (1948), 216–17, and in *Pa. Mag. of Hist. and Biog.,* Oct. 1950, p. 455.]

FREDERICK B. TOLLES

WYLIE, Elinor Morton Hoyt (Sept. 7, 1885– Dec. 16, 1928), poet and novelist, was born in Somerville, N.J., the eldest of five children of Philadelphia parents, Henry Martyn Hoyt and Anne (McMichael) Hoyt. She grew up, as Carl Van Doren put it, "among minds and manners," in a family that was socially well placed and distinguished by public service. Her father, a graduate of Yale, was a lawyer and afterward Solicitor General of the United States. Her great-grandfather Morton McMichael had been mayor of Philadelphia; her grandfather Henry Martyn Hoyt, Sr., had been governor of Pennsylvania. Taken from Somerville to Rosemont, a suburb of Philadelphia, at the age of two, Elinor lived there until she was twelve, when the family moved to Washington, D.C. She attended Miss Baldwin's School in Bryn Mawr, Pa., and, in Washington, Mrs. Flint's School and the Holton-Arms School, from which she graduated in 1904; she also studied drawing at the Corcoran Gallery. With her Grandfather McMichael and her sister Constance, she spent the summer of 1903 in London and Paris. The first half of her life, with its unruffled gentility, must have been stifling

to her independent spirit, but few of her family or friends were prepared for the defiance of conventions which characterized the second.

In 1905, when she was twenty, Elinor Wylie was married to Philip Hichborn, an admiral's son whose family was as socially prominent as her own. The marriage ended after five years when Elinor left her husband (who committed suicide two years later) and her young son, Philip, to elope with a married man seventeen years her senior, Horace Wylie, a graduate of Yale and a Washington lawyer. Since all the families involved were well known, the elopement, in December 1910, raised a much-publicized scandal. Wylie's wife refused to grant him a divorce, and the couple went to live in England, attempting, but failing to achieve, anonymity as Mr. and Mrs. Horace Waring. At the start of the First World War they returned to the United States, residing first in Boston and later in Augusta, Ga. They were legally married on Aug. 7, 1916. In 1919 they returned to Washington, where Horace Wylie obtained a position in a government bureau.

It was in Washington that Elinor Wylie began to take herself seriously as a writer. There she met Sinclair Lewis and William Rose Benét (who was editing a journal for the Department of Commerce), Edmund Wilson, John Dos Passos, and John Peale Bishop. Through them she was introduced to a world that did not hold her past against her and whose interest gave her the needed assurance to submit her poems for publication. Although her first book of poems, *Incidental Numbers,* had been privately printed, anonymously, in London in 1912 (curiously, the same year in which Philip Hichborn's posthumous collection of stories appeared), it was nine years before she tried a commercial publisher. In 1921 Harcourt, Brace issued *Nets to Catch the Wind,* and Elinor Wylie found herself the subject of much popular and critical attention. Mrs. Wylie offered both technical polish and human interest to a reading public intolerant of the allusive rhythms of Pound and Eliot. The readers of the *Saturday Review of Literature* were not interested in impersonal, difficult verse. In poems like "The Eagle and the Mole," Mrs. Wylie must have seemed like another EMILY DICKINSON, a sensitive soul who suffered because she chose her own society; one who, out of intensely felt experience, confronted life with courage and dignity.

Avoid the reeking herd,
Shun the polluted flock,
Live like that stoic bird,
The eagle of the rock. . . .

If you would keep your soul
From spotted sight or sound,
Live like the velvet mole;
Go burrow underground.

And there hold intercourse
With roots of trees and stones,
With rivers at their source,
And disembodied bones.

From "a brilliant amateur, who had produced a few striking poems and started a novel or two, but who had never worked with much application," she now became, in Edmund Wilson's judgment, "one of the most steadily industrious and most productive writers of my acquaintance." In the next seven years Elinor Wylie completed three volumes of verse and four novels. The novels, particularly *The Orphan Angel* (1926; a Book-of-the-Month Club selection), which reflected her passionate interest in the personality of Shelley, demanded extensive historical research. The settings ranged from baroque palaces in Venice to English country houses to the Middle West in American frontier days. She expended great energy on her work, but her vitality, as Wilson writes, "triumphed and flourished at the cost of desperate nervous strain. Though she had sometimes enjoyed fairly long periods of tranquility, comfort and leisure, her life had been broken up by a series of displacements and emotional dislocations which might have destroyed a weaker nature," and her well-being hence was always "precarious."

A domestic history that seemed shocking to Washington seemed dramatic to New York, and on the strength of the reception of *Nets to Catch the Wind*, Elinor Wylie moved to that city and into the literary world which found her personal beauty and her talk so engaging. She was striking in appearance, with hazel eyes, her tawny hair bobbed and waved, her clothes understated and elegant; she had the grand manner and a sharp tongue, and was completely at ease in the lounge of the Algonquin Hotel with the staff of the *New Yorker*, or in her West 9th Street apartment, where she indulged her passion for everything silver—clothes as well as objets d'art—and surrounded herself with good porcelain and books in fine bindings. Taste was another of her defenses from the world. Her decision to leave Washington and live in New York meant a separation from Horace Wylie and, two years later, a divorce, although they continued to be friends. On Oct. 5, 1923, Elinor Wylie was married to William Rose Benét, then editor of the *Saturday Review of Literature*. Beginning with the summer of 1926 she spent long periods of time in England, and in 1928 took a house in Chelsea. She confided to Carl Van Doren there that during this period in England she had found someone she fully loved "for the first time." After a stroke that left her partly paralyzed, she returned to her husband in New York in time to read the proofs of her last volume of poems, *Angels and Earthly Creatures* (1929). She died suddenly in New York in December 1928 after another stroke, and was buried in Woodlawn Cemetery.

Elinor Wylie's work today holds little critical interest; the poems include far too many references to goldfish, moonbeams, and snowflakes for modern taste, and her novels are almost unreadable. An exception must be made for *The Venetian Glass Nephew* (1925), a fantasy aptly characterized by R. P. Blackmur as a "fable for frigidity"; it is as if Hawthorne's "The Birthmark" were rewritten by an aesthete. Nevertheless, Mrs. Wylie has had her distinguished admirers, including William Butler Yeats. What so attracted her early readers was her skill, but her technical facility kept her, as Allen Tate observed, "from ever quite knowing what was her own impulse" and what she had merely assimilated from others: "It is this feature of her work that explains her brilliant moments and in the end her lack of style. . . ." In spite of her admiration for the metaphysical poetry of John Donne and for the Romantic tradition of Shelley, Mrs. Wylie made only superficial use of these poets. Her friends, such as Carl Van Doren, Carl Van Vechten, and William Rose Benét, probably influenced by her vivid personality, made exaggerated claims for her achievement, but in a period which saw the flowering of such poetic talent as that of Wallace Stevens, Marianne Moore, Hart Crane, and William Carlos Williams, Mrs. Wylie cannot be numbered among the most gifted. She was a minor poet, but was never indifferent to her craft. It is a pity that she so indulged her fancy. She built too many pagodas. When she confronted the actual landscape, only suggesting the emotional hurt which drew her to it, she could make memorable poetry.

[Except for *Nets to Catch the Wind*, all of Elinor Wylie's work was published by Alfred Knopf. Besides those mentioned above, her other volumes of poetry include *Black Armour* (1923) and *Trivial Breath* (1928). The *Collected Poems* were published in 1932; *Last Poems*, ed. by Jane D. Wise, in 1943. The selection from her verse included in F. O. Matthiessen's *Oxford Book of Am. Verse* (1950) is admirable. The Yale Univ. Library has a collection of her letters and MSS. The best critical articles are those of Edmund Wilson (in *The Shores of Light*, 1952), James Branch Cabell (*Va. Quart. Rev.*, July 1930), Allen Tate (*New Re-*

*public,* Sept. 7, 1932), and Morton D. Zabel (*Poetry,* Aug. 1932). The best of many personal reminiscences is Carl Van Doren's "Elinor Wylie: A Portrait from Memory," *Harper's,* Sept. 1936. This and Nancy Hoyt's biography of her sister, *Elinor Wylie* (1935), are the principal sources for the biographical information above. Particular details were supplied by the Holton-Arms School, by the marriage record of Elinor and Horace Wiley (Mass. Registrar of Vital Statistics), and by the *N.Y. Times,* Dec. 19, 1928.]

FRANCIS MURPHY

# Y

**YALE, Caroline Ardelia** (Sept. 29, 1848–July 2, 1933), educator of the deaf, was born in Charlotte, Vt., the third daughter and youngest of five children of William Lyman Yale, a prosperous farmer, and Ardelia (Strong) Yale. Her parents were of Welsh and English descent, their forebears having moved to the Lake Champlain valley from Connecticut, where her paternal ancestor, Thomas Yale, had settled in 1637.

On their isolated farm the Yales led a rich family life, infused with the Congregational faith, with much reading aloud by the mother, prayers and singing led by the father, frequent visits from relatives, and lessons in the upstairs schoolroom with a view over the lake and the Adirondacks. William Yale encouraged independence in his children, girls as well as boys; his wife, though an invalid, stood at the center of the home, in close touch with the concerns of her husband and children, supervising the latter's tutoring under a series of teachers, usually Mount Holyoke Seminary graduates, who came to live at the farm. To give their children more advantages, the Yales moved to the town of Williston, Vt., when Caroline was ten. Here her father took an active part in church and community affairs, and Caroline attended the local academy which he helped found. Doctors frowned on further study for the frail girl, but her mother encouraged her to plan an active life, and the parents sent her in 1866 to Mount Holyoke. After two years she was needed at home, but she taught for a time in the local Vermont schools.

In 1870, at twenty-two, Caroline Yale went to teach at the Clarke Institution for Deaf Mutes (later renamed the Clarke School for the Deaf) in Northampton, Mass. The school had been founded three years earlier by HARRIET BURBANK ROGERS, with the purpose of teaching deaf children to speak and to read the lips, and of educating them with these tools of communication. "From the first," Miss Yale later recalled, "there was a fascination about the work which was irresistible." Before the end of her second year she had given up plans to return to Mount Holyoke in order to stay with her new career. Her life from that time was devoted, in the words of her Northampton neighbor, President William Allan Neilson of Smith College, "with extraordinary singleness of purpose" to the school, which she served from 1873 as associate principal, then, from 1886 until her retirement in 1922, as principal; she continued to direct the teacher training program from 1922 until her death in 1933 at the age of eighty-four.

To the Clarke School, Miss Yale brought an alert, experimental turn of mind. In its early years, beginning under Miss Rogers, the school used Alexander Melville Bell's "Visible Speech," a system of phonetic symbols, each representing the physiological formation (the position of the mouth, tongue, and so forth) of a particular sound. In 1882, however, it was decided to substitute the characters of the English alphabet. The problem was to make the twenty-six letters represent the more than forty elementary sounds of the English language. In collaboration with Alice C. Worcester, one of the Clarke teachers, Miss Yale devised the widely used "Northampton Vowel and Consonant Charts," which sought to make the letters "mark themselves" for pronunciation, to the greatest possible extent, by their position in words and their connection with other letters. Her pamphlet, *Formation and Development of Elementary English Sounds* (1892), explained the use of the charts, which came in time to be employed not only for the teaching of the deaf but in the so-called phonovisual method of teaching reading to children of normal hearing.

Another of Miss Yale's innovations which had wide influence was the teacher education department she established at the Clarke School in 1889. Through the student teachers she trained, the visitors who came from all parts of the world to observe the school's work, and her participation in professional meetings, she helped shape the whole trend of education for deaf children in the United States. It was largely through her influence and that of the Clarke School that the teaching of speech was introduced before her death into nearly every school for the deaf in America, where previously the use of signs and finger spelling had been the only method of communication. She was one of the founders, in 1890, of the American Association to Promote the Teaching of Speech to the Deaf and for some years one of its directors.

Within the Northampton community, Miss Yale was for several years a member of the faculty of Smith College, where she lectured on phonetics in the department of spoken English. She served for twenty-five years on the Northampton School Committee and was a trustee of the Northampton Hospital for the Insane. Honorary degrees were conferred on her by Illinois Wesleyan University (1896), Smith College (1910), and Mount Holyoke College (1927). Active to the last in her work, she died at her home on the Clarke School grounds in 1933, of bronchial pneumonia. Her ashes were buried in Charlotte.

Miss Yale possessed a special combination of mind and spirit. Her serenity, charm of manner, and beautiful speaking voice, together with her wisdom, tact, and courage, won the respect and admiration even of those who differed from her in method. The children with whom she labored were inspired to regard their handicap as only a hurdle to be leaped. Her steadfast goal, often achieved with remarkable success, was to prepare deaf boys and girls to take their place in the society of people with normal hearing.

[Caroline A. Yale's autobiography, *Years of Building* (1931); Clarke School *Annual Reports;* personal papers of Miss Rogers and Miss Yale at the Clarke School; *Nat. Cyc. Am. Biog.,* XXXI, 265; obituary in *Volta Rev.,* Sept. 1933; Lucille D. Schoolfield and Josephine B. Timberlake, *The Phonovisual Method* (1962); death record from Mass. Registrar of Vital Statistics.]

                                                        MARY E. NUMBERS

**YARROS, Rachelle Slobodinsky** (May 18, 1869–Mar. 17, 1946), physician and reformer, was born at Berdechev near Kiev, Russia, the daughter of Joachim and Bernice Slobodinsky. Her family was well-to-do, but at eighteen, having received a preliminary education in Russian schools, she joined a subversive political society and was obliged to flee from the Czarist police to the United States. Arriving in New York in the late 1880's, she supported herself at first by working at a sewing machine in a sweatshop. Moving to Boston, she met a fellow countryman, the journalist and philosophical anarchist Victor S. Yarros, to whom she was married on July 18, 1894. They had no children of their own but eventually adopted a daughter, Elise Donaldson.

Even before their marriage Yarros had urged her to continue her education, and in 1890 Rachelle Slobodinsky entered the College of Physicians and Surgeons in Boston, the first woman admitted. After a year she enrolled in the Woman's Medical College of Pennsylvania, receiving the M.D. degree in 1893. She interned for a year at the New England Hospital for Women and Children in Boston, and then took postdoctoral work in pediatrics at the New York Infirmary for Women and Children and at the Michael Reese Hospital in Chicago. In 1895 she began an obstetrical and gynecological practice in Chicago while her husband followed a career in journalism and the law.

Establishing herself in the medical profession, Rachelle Yarros in 1897 was appointed instructor in clinical obstetrics in the "College of Physicians and Surgeons," a clinical staff associated on a part-time, unsalaried basis with the medical school of the University of Illinois. Advanced to an associate professorship five years later, she continued in this post until 1926. She was a Fellow of the American College of Surgeons, an associate director of the Chicago Lying-In Hospital, and for a time president of the West Side Branch of the Chicago Medical Society. In 1908, in addition to her other activities, she became director of an obstetrical dispensary on Chicago's West Side.

From 1907 to 1927 Dr. Yarros and her husband lived at Hull House, Chicago's famous social settlement. Her marriage and her residence there, acting upon her own youthful radicalism, produced a remarkable broadening of her social and political interests. She became convinced that it was impossible to treat the diseases of the body without treating the social conditions which often bred them. The women's disorders in which she specialized were often bound up, she discovered, with promiscuity, ignorance, and excessive childbearing.

This conviction found expression in a reform career which gradually supplanted her medical practice. The two causes with which she became most closely identified were social hygiene and birth control. The social hygiene movement, an effort to eradicate prostitution and venereal disease through education and legislation, won her enthusiastic support from the first. A founder of the American Social Hygiene Association in 1914, she became vice-president of the Illinois Social Hygiene League when it was created a year later. She directed social hygiene programs for the Chicago Health Department and the Illinois Board of Health, headed the social hygiene committee of the General Federation of Women's Clubs, served as special consultant to the venereal diseases division of the United States Public Health Service, and in the 1920's lectured widely to Y.W.C.A. groups on the subject. Her leadership in this field was recognized in 1926 when the University of Illinois medical school appointed her to a special professorship in social hygiene on its clinical staff, a post she held until her retirement in 1939.

The rising birth rate, in Dr. Yarros' opinion, was the source of "all kinds of social ills and disorders," and about 1915 she persuaded the Chicago Woman's Club (to which she belonged) to establish a birth control committee. From this there soon evolved the Illinois Birth Control League, of which she was director for many years. In 1923, at the urging of Margaret Sanger (d. 1966), she opened in a thickly populated Chicago neighborhood the nation's second birth control clinic.

But these reforms in turn depended not merely on the spread of technical information but on a changed attitude toward sex, especially among women; and, beyond that, on a general redefinition of woman's place in the world. To this end Dr. Yarros published her book, *Modern Woman and Sex* (1933; reissued in 1938 as *Sex Problems in Modern Society*). Juvenile delinquency and the liberalization of divorce laws were among the many other causes to which she was drawn. There seemed no end to the chain of social amelioration; one reform depended on another; all were equally relevant.

Such versatility was characteristic of the first generation of professional women; the very question of their pursuing careers at all was a burning social issue which made indifference to similar issues impossible. Mrs. Yarros took it as axiomatic that "the physician is also a citizen," that he should "not be ignorant of economics, of political science, of history, of philosophical ethics, of literature," and that he would as a matter of course "sympathize with labor, with victims of exploitation and industrial autocracy, with the juvenile and adult delinquents—products of slums." A religious agnostic, in politics she was a socialist who later became "a half-apologetic pragmatist." Unlike other Russian émigrés, she admired the Soviet Union, to which she and her husband made visits in 1930, 1936, and 1939. She was particularly impressed with the vereological institute at Moscow—"the kind of institution I have dreamed of for many years"—and with the measures by which the Bolsheviks had "practically done away with commercialized prostitution." Although uneasy about evidences of increasing police control, she did not linger over the darker side of life in Stalinist Russia. "My friends," she once wrote, ". . . like to think of me as an optimist, a believer in life and in the joy of life. . . ."

After suffering a heart attack in 1939, Rachelle Yarros lived for two years in Winter Park, Fla., and then moved to La Jolla, Calif., in 1941. She died in San Diego, Calif., of congestive heart failure and coronary heart disease; her remains were cremated. Her husband survived her.

[Of Rachelle Yarros' numerous published articles, the following are particularly valuable for insights into her life and thought: "Birth Control and Its Relation to Health and Welfare," *Medical Woman's Jour.*, Oct. 1925; "Birth Control and Democracy," *World Democracy*, Sept. 1925; "Training and Guidance in Recreation," *Jour. of Social Hygiene*, Feb. 1929; "Social Hygiene Observations in Soviet Russia," *ibid.*, Nov. 1930; "Moscow Revisited," *ibid.*, Apr. 1937; and "An Open Letter," *ibid.*, Mar. 1943. See also the biographical sketch by William F. Snow and obituary in *ibid.*, Mar. 1941 and Oct. 1946; *Woman's Who's Who in America*, 1914–15; *Nat. Cyc. Am. Biog.*, XXXV, 168; Margaret Sanger, *An Autobiog.* (1938), p. 361; Victor S. Yarros, "Jane Addams, Humanitarian," *Character*, Sept.–Oct. 1935. For her teaching positions, see Board of Trustees of the Univ. of Ill., *Report*, 1898–1940. Dr. Yarros' death certificate, supplied by the Calif. Dept. of Public Health, records her birth date as May 15, 1869; all other sources give May 18. Her marriage certificate, on file in the Manhattan Marriage License Bureau, records her mother's name as Augusta. On Victor Yarros, see James Martin, *Men against the State* (1953), pp. 232–37. A biographical outline prepared in 1960 by Elizabeth A. Devine, Univ. of Wis. Library School, was helpful.]

CHRISTOPHER LASCH

**YAW, Ellen Beach** (Sept. 14, 1868–Sept. 9, 1947), singer, sometimes called "Lark Ellen," was born in Boston, N.Y., some twenty miles south of Buffalo. She was the youngest of five children of Ambrose Spencer Yaw, descendant of a French Huguenot family originally named Ghneau, and Mary Jane (Beach) Yaw, of Welsh and English ancestry. Her father, who died when she was nine, was a manufacturer of cowbells; he had a strong voice of considerable range. Her mother was an accomplished pianist. While still a child, Ellen Yaw began to imitate the songs of birds, to pick out melodies at the piano, and to sing at churches and local concerts. She attended the nearby Hamburg (N.Y.) Academy, then transferred to Griffith's Institute at Springville, N.Y., to study typing and shorthand. Moving west soon afterward, perhaps with her mother, at fourteen she became secretary to a lawyer in Morris, Minn. There she gave shorthand lessons in the evenings in order to raise money for voice study. She began her vocal training under a Minneapolis teacher, Charles Whitmore, and then, after further study in Minneapolis and in Boston, Mass., went to New York City to work with Mme. Theodore Bjorksten (later Mme. Hervor Torpadie), her principal teacher. As early as November 1888 she sang on a concert program in Brooklyn, and on Apr. 15, 1891, she appeared at Steinway Hall (Odell, XIV, 182, 705).

Ellen Yaw first became widely known in 1894 when, in order to finance European study, she signed up for the first of a series of American tours under the management of Victor Thrane. She had already discovered that she could reach the unusually high note of E above high C, and though some critics were to complain that these high notes were little more than squeaks, Thrane now advertised her as having the highest vocal range in history; skeptics came to her concerts armed with pitch pipes and tuning forks. In 1895 she made her first European tour, performed in London, then toured Switzerland and the Rhine countries. On Jan. 22, 1896, she appeared at Carnegie Hall in New York, where music critics, expecting a humbug because of the sensational advertising, were pleased to hear a thoroughly trained voice full of color and character and especially good in the middle register.

In 1899 Sir Arthur Sullivan composed for Ellen Yaw the leading soprano role in the comic opera *The Rose of Persia,* which opened at the Savoy Theatre in London on Nov. 29, was a brilliant success, and ran for over two hundred nights. Impressed with her performance, an English patron, Lady Valerie Meux, arranged for her to study under the foremost teacher in Paris, Mathilde Marchesi. While in Paris, Miss Yaw sang for Massenet and Saint-Saëns and at the Opéra-Comique. After three years of intensive study she sang in Nice and in Rome, gave a private concert for the Shah of Persia, and toured England, Italy, and Switzerland. In 1907 she made her debut in grand opera in Rome, in the title role in *Lucia;* the following year she made her first appearance with the Metropolitan Opera in New York in the same role. She remained with the Metro-

politan for only one season, though she continued to tour in Europe until 1912. Popular with her audiences, she was tall and slender, with fair hair and wide blue eyes, a "dainty, flower-like face," and a simple, unaffected manner. Although known originally for her unique vocal range, it was the vibrant and beautiful voice Ellen Yaw developed within a normal range which gave her a place with the other twentieth-century American sopranos who have been welcomed by the musical world of Europe.

Her two marriages did not interrupt her career. Her first husband, Vere Goldthwaite, a Boston lawyer whom she met on board ship in 1899 and to whom she was married on Mar. 21, 1907, died in 1912. The following year she met Franklin Cannon, a pianist and teacher fifteen years her junior; they were married on Aug. 22, 1920. Cannon wrote arrangements for several songs Miss Yaw composed to display her high notes, and accompanied her on American tours during the 1920's. When she retired to her estate in West Covina, Calif., in 1931, he returned to New York to continue his career, and in 1935 she quietly obtained a divorce.

Ellen Beach Yaw had first settled in southern California with her mother in the early 1890's. In later years she became the center of a group of music enthusiasts which included the composer Mary Carr Moore, her cousin. In 1934 she opened the Lark Ellen Bowl at West Covina and in 1939 organized an open-air studio of singing. Each year she performed a benefit concert for her favorite charity, the Los Angeles Newsboys Home, which took the name Lark Ellen Home for Boys in her honor. In later life she was a Christian Scientist in religion. She continued to give recitals for charities and for close friends until the year before her death, and to make phonograph records, as she had since 1899. She died in West Covina of yellow jaundice shortly before her seventy-ninth birthday and was buried at Rose Hills Memorial Park near Whittier, Calif.

[Antonio Altamirano in *Record Collector,* Dec. 1955; Paul Jacquelin in *Opera News,* Mar. 31, 1958; Stephen Fasset in *Hobbies,* Apr. 1947 and Jan. 1948; Durward Howes, ed., *Am. Women,* 1939–40; *Nat. Cyc. Am. Biog.,* XIII, 246; interview in *Strand Mag.,* July 1899; George C. D. Odell, *Annals of the N.Y. Stage,* vols. XIV and XV (1945–49); *The Times* (London), Nov. 30, 1899; *N.Y. Times,* Jan. 22, 1896, Mar. 22, 1908, Aug. 23, 1920, Sept. 10, 1947; *Los Angeles Times,* Aug. 23, 1920, Oct. 1, 1935, Sept. 10, 1947. Other information from: Hamburg (N.Y.) Hist. Soc.; Mr. Charles B. Bradley, town historian, Boston, N.Y.; Dr. Paul Jacquelin of Los Angeles; Mass. Registrar of Vital Statistics; and records of Rose Hills Memorial Park. Miss Yaw contributed a series of articles, "To Girls Who Want to Sing," to *Delineator* (Jan.–Apr. 1909). Her unpublished memoirs, "Flight of the Lark," in the possession of Antonio Altamirano, Montebello, Calif., who is editing them for publication, were not available for this study.]

JOAN M. JENSEN

YOUNG, Ann Eliza Webb (Sept. 13, 1844–post 1908), lecturer and writer against Mormon polygamy, "twenty-seventh wife" of Brigham Young, was born at the Mormon settlement of Nauvoo, Ill., a few weeks after the murder of Joseph Smith, the founder and first prophet of the Church of Jesus Christ of Latterday Saints. She was the youngest of the six children and only surviving daughter of Chauncey Gilbert Webb, an expert wagonmaker, and his wife Eliza Churchill, a former schoolteacher. Both natives of New York state, and early converts to Mormonism, the Webbs had met and married in the Mormon center of Kirtland, Ohio. When Eliza was not yet two, in January 1846, her father took a second and younger wife, although the practice of polygamy was not made publicly official until 1852. By this marriage he eventually had eleven children. Chauncey Webb made many of the wagons for the great Mormon migration westward from Nauvoo and himself left for Utah with his family in the spring of 1846, arriving in Salt Lake City in September 1848. When Ann Eliza was twelve her father married three other wives, one of whom he subsequently divorced. His eldest daughter matured with an evergrowing consciousness of her mother's bitter hostility to the whole system of polygamy.

A brother of the Mormon leader Brigham Young had converted Mrs. Eliza Webb to the faith before her marriage, and Young himself continued to be paternally interested in the Webb family. He became enamored of Ann Eliza, a striking beauty, when she was sixteen, but she vowed she would never be his plural wife. Piqued by her resistance, he persuaded her to become an actress in the Salt Lake Theatre and to live with his daughters in the celebrated Lion House, where he kept many of his wives and children. On Apr. 4, 1863, aged eighteen, she was married to James Leech Dee, an English convert who was a plasterer by trade and an amateur actor. She bore him two sons, Edward Wesley in 1864 and Leonard Lorenzo in 1865. When the marriage proved unhappy, Brigham Young assisted her in getting a civil divorce, on Dec. 23, 1865. Three and a half years later, after a tempestuous

courtship, which included, she said, a threat to bankrupt her brother, she was married to the Mormon leader in a secret ceremony in the Endowment House in Salt Lake City on Apr. 7, 1869. She was twenty-four, Brigham Young sixty-eight. Ann Eliza called herself his nineteenth and last wife. Research by recent scholars in the church's Genealogical Archives in Salt Lake City indicates that Young married at least seventy women, but many of these were "spiritual wives," whom he married without the intention of exercising his connubial privileges. Ann Eliza's biographer, making an effort to distinguish between "real" and "spiritual" wives, concludes that Ann Eliza Webb was number twenty-seven, the last of the "real" wives, but this is mere speculation.

When Ann Eliza upon her marriage refused to live in the Lion House, Young built her a separate home, a privilege he accorded few of his wives. After the first year she felt herself mistreated and largely abandoned. Contradictory stories handed down to Young's descendants make it impossible to ascertain if she was a difficult and denying wife, or if her complaints of being neglected were justified. She took in non-Mormon boarders to supplement her meager income and won the sympathy of one of them, Major James Burton Pond, a newspaperman for the non-Mormon *Salt Lake Tribune*. Encouraged by Pond, by the Rev. and Mrs. C. C. Stratton of the Methodist Episcopal Church, and by Judge James B. McKean, High Justice of Utah, she decided to sue for divorce. On July 15, 1873, after four years of childless marriage, she left her home to live in a Salt Lake City hotel. Four days later she filed for divorce, asking $200,000 as a settlement and $20,000 for attorney fees.

The news caused a sensation in the American press. She was besieged by reporters and by offers for lectures against polygamy. In her interviews she attacked Young with much frankness and passionately denounced polygamy. Brigham Young branded her an adulteress and offered her a $15,000 settlement with freedom to leave the territory. She turned down the settlement and in November, leaving her sons with her parents, fled secretly to Wyoming, where under the guidance of Major Pond she began the lecture tour that quickly made her one of the most famous women in America.

In contrast with the sensational nature of her subject, she looked and dressed like a lady and acted with extreme prudence. Traveling always with a chaperone, she survived press insinuations that Pond was actually her lover and won sympathetic audiences all over America. On Apr. 14, 1874, in Washington, D.C., she spoke before a large group that included many Congressmen and their wives; President and Mrs. Ulysses S. Grant attended her second lecture soon afterward. Her fulminations against polygamy played no small role in securing the passage a few weeks later of the Poland Bill, the first federal antipolygamy legislation. In July she courageously returned to Salt Lake City, lecturing there and in the smaller Mormon towns. Her parents were excommunicated for defending her, but her father was eventually restored to fellowship. Her mother, however, left Utah forever and moved east, settling with her daughter and her two grandsons in Lockport, N.Y., where she had a sister. In 1875 Ann Eliza was converted to the Methodist faith.

The divorce action dragged on with intermittent legal fencing for four years. Brigham Young used as a defense that he had only one legal wife, that the ceremony with Ann Eliza had been "a celestial marriage," "a kind of mutual arrangement according to faith." Judge McKean ruled on Feb. 25, 1875, that she had been Young's legal wife and granted her $3,000 to cover the court costs and $500 a month alimony, retroactive to the date of her separation. This amounted to $9,500, payable in twenty days. When Young refused to pay anything but the court costs, he was found guilty of contempt of court, fined $25, and imprisoned for one day in the federal penitentiary. Later he was held in house arrest for five months for nonpayment of alimony and finally freed after paying $3,600. Judge McKean's decision, however, had embarrassed federal legislators trying to outlaw polygamy, and the court fight continued. A final decision, in April 1877, annulled the alimony ruling and held that the marriage had never been legal in the first place. Brigham Young, who by now was beginning to win some national sympathy, died in August 1877 at the age of seventy-six.

In 1876 Ann Eliza Young published her 600-page *Wife No. 19, or The Story of a Life in Bondage*, an impassioned account of the humiliations in her own life and in those of other polygamous women. Her exposé of the Mormon temple mysteries, "blood atonement," and the Mountain Meadows Massacre was entirely secondhand, but her account of life among the wives of Brigham Young, though laced with resentment, is an invaluable source book for students of Mormon history. She continued her highly successful lecture tours until the passage of the punitive Edmunds Bill in 1882 outlawed polygamy and outdated her message. The Mormon church officially abandoned the practice in 1890.

In ten years of lecturing Ann Eliza Young had won a·modest financial security, but despite her fame she had paid heavy penalties in poor health and loneliness. On May 19, 1883, now thirty-eight, she was married to Moses R. Denning, some sixteen years her senior, a wealthy lumber and coal dealer of Manistee, Mich., who had heard her lecture two years before and had divorced his wife to capture the still handsome ex-wife of the Mormon prophet. This, her third marriage, lasted nine years. During this period she became deeply interested in Christian Science. She and Denning were divorced in January 1893; the record of the trial suggested that a deep-seated sexual hostility may well have been a decisive complicating factor in all her marriages.

For a time she stayed on in Manistee, then moved in 1897 to Denver and in 1902 to El Paso, Texas, where she lived for several years with dwindling resources. In 1908 she published a revised version of *Wife No. 19* with a new title, *Life in Mormon Bondage*, but the polygamy issue was now moribund and the book failed to sell. Following its publication she vanished. Her two sons had died of tuberculosis in early maturity. Scattered rumors put her in a dozen different cities, but the most determined research on the part of her recent biographer, Irving Wallace, failed to disclose either the date or place of her death. A courageous but basically unhappy and hostile woman, she had been more responsible than any other individual for the nationwide agitation against the Mormon institution of polygamy and the resulting federal laws proscribing it.

[There is only one full-scale biography of Ann Eliza Young, Irving Wallace's excellent *The Twenty-Seventh Wife* (1961); unfortunately, it is not completely documented and has no index. Her own books, *Wife No. 19* and *Life in Mormon Bondage*, are basic source material. See also the sketch in Helen Beal Woodward, *The Bold Women* (1953); *Portrait and Biog. Record of Northern Mich.* (1895); James B. Pond, *Eccentricities of Genius* (1900); and Charles F. Horner, *The Life of James Redpath* (1926). For sympathetic accounts of the home life of Brigham Young, see the books written by his daughters: Susa Young Gates, *The Life Story of Brigham Young* (1930), and Clarissa Young Spencer, *One Who Was Valiant* (1940).]

FAWN M. BRODIE

YOUNG, Ella Flagg (Jan. 15, 1845–Oct. 26, 1918), educator and school administrator, was born in Buffalo, N.Y., the second daughter and youngest of three children of Theodore and Jane (Reed) Flagg. Her parents were Presbyterians of Scottish descent, practical-minded and liberal in their religious beliefs. Frail as a child, Ella Flagg did not attend the early grades of elementary school but spent her time at gardening and outdoor exercise. When her father, a skilled sheet-metal worker, moved his family to Chicago in 1858, she attended grammar school for a short time and then was admitted to the Chicago High School. At fifteen she entered the Chicago Normal School, graduating two years later in 1862.

With her appointment that year to teach in a primary school, Miss Flagg began a career in Chicago education that was to cover more than half a century of rapid expansion and change in the city and its schools. Recognized for her teaching ability and her quick mind, she was promoted to a head assistantship the next year, and in 1865 she became the first principal of the practice school of the Chicago Normal School. In 1868 she was married to William Young, a Chicago merchant, who died the following year. Her mother and brother had died before her marriage, and when her father and sister died shortly after her husband, Mrs. Young gave herself over fully to her educational work. Resigning her principalship at the Normal School in 1871, she gained experience and administrative skill over the next two decades first as a high school teacher and then as a grammar school principal. During these years she formulated the ideas which she espoused throughout her career—that teachers should be more thoroughly trained and have a larger role in planning school policy, and that the school should function as an instrument of society rather than be an enclave in it.

Appointed assistant superintendent of the Chicago schools in 1887, Mrs. Young sought to secure more adequate training for the teaching force and to broaden the curriculum by introducing drawing, commercial subjects, manual arts, and home economics into the elementary and secondary grades. She helped organize teachers' councils to develop an effective voice for teachers in administrative decisions and brought such noted figures as William James and John Dewey to speak before them. When policy changes threatened to render her councils inoperative, she resigned her post in 1899 and took a position as associate professor of pedagogy at the University of Chicago, where she had been studying part-time under Dewey since 1895. In 1900 she received her doctorate from the university and was appointed professor of education there.

For the next few years Ella Young was a close associate of Dewey in his educational studies, and he came to regard her as "the wis-

est person in school matters with whom he has come in contact in any way" (Jane M. Dewey in P. A. Schilpp, ed., *The Philosophy of John Dewey*, 1939, p. 29). Mrs. Young and Dewey collaborated on the six-volume University of Chicago Contributions to Education series (1901–02), each of them writing three volumes; Mrs. Young's doctoral dissertation, *Isolation in the School* (1900), was reprinted as the first. The series widely influenced American educational thought. Her collaboration with Dewey was even closer in her capacity as supervisor of instruction at Dewey's laboratory school at the university. Benefiting from her practical experience, Dewey later wrote: "What I chiefly got from Mrs. Young was . . . the translation of philosophic conceptions into their empirical equivalents" (McManis, p. 120).

When a dispute over the laboratory school caused Dewey to leave the University of Chicago in 1904 (see ALICE CHIPMAN DEWEY), Mrs. Young also resigned her position. She became principal of the Chicago Normal School in 1905 and began again to apply her ideas to the city's public schools. In 1909 she was appointed by the Chicago Board of Education as superintendent of schools, the first woman to head a major school system in the United States. She directed an elaborate program of curriculum revision, introducing vocational courses, physical training, and (until vetoed by the board) sex education. She worked for higher teachers' salaries and greater participation of teachers in school administration. Her teachers' councils and her respect for the integrity and rights of the teaching staff especially endeared her to the Chicago Teachers' Federation, whose leader, MARGARET HALEY, proved a steadfast ally throughout Mrs. Young's career. In 1910 Ella Young became the first woman president of the National Education Association.

Facing Board of Education opposition to her policies and her administrative independence, Mrs. Young anticipated a move to block her reappointment by resigning as superintendent in July 1913. She resumed her post under assurance that she would be retained, but at the December vote of the board she failed of a majority, and on Dec. 10 she again resigned. A women's delegation led by JANE ADDAMS, charging a political attempt to gain control of the schools, called on the mayor to protest the board's action, and two thousand newly enfranchised women held a rally for Mrs. Young. The mayor accepted resignations from four board members, and on Dec. 23 Mrs. Young was returned to her post. The controversy and continued opposition from the board, however, hampered her effectiveness, and she resigned at the end of 1915. In 1917 she became chairman of the Woman's Liberty Loan Committee. While traveling in its service the next year, she contracted influenza and died of pneumonia in Washington, D.C., at the age of seventy-three. She was buried in Rosehill Cemetery, Chicago.

Ella Flagg Young was active in women's organizations and supported the suffrage cause, but nothing took precedence over her work in education. In her final report as superintendent, she singled out as her administration's "distinctive contribution" to Chicago education the creation of "a fine courage and mentality active in the Educational Division helping to forward the modern movement that broke away from hide bound method, based on narrow, logically consistent, educational psychology" (*Annual Report* of the Board of Education, 1915, p. 37). She was one of the leading administrators and a significant theorist of the progressive era in American education. Though she pioneered in instituting vocational classes in the public schools, she always believed children should learn to appreciate the "delights of genuine scholarship." She did not oppose an academic curriculum, but rather archaic methods which failed to take cognizance of the mind and natural tendencies of the child and of his existing environment. She favored teaching methods that encouraged students to think independently and cultivated in them a sense of responsibility. Mrs. Young had a strong faith in the intellectual capacity of all persons; she strove to provide freedom of thought and expression for both teachers and children as a means of strengthening democracy in the nation.

[Mrs. Young's early life and career are covered extensively but uncritically in a defense of her policies written after her resignation as superintendent: John T. McManis, *Ella Flagg Young and a Half-Century of the Chicago Schools* (1916). See also George S. Counts, *School and Society in Chicago* (1928); *Nat. Cyc. Am. Biog.*, XIX, 26; and obituaries in *Chicago Tribune*, Oct. 27, 1918, and Nat. Education Assoc., *Proc. and Addresses*, 1918, p. 685. For more informal impressions, see Helen C. Bennett, *Am. Women in Civic Work* (1915); and Edward Wagenknecht, *Chicago* (1964). Along with *Isolation in the School, Ethics in the School* (1902), and *Some Types of Modern Educational Theory* (1902), Mrs. Young's monographs in the Univ. of Chicago Contributions to Education series, she prepared many other articles and papers, some of which may be found in the *Proc. and Addresses* of the Nat. Education Assoc. from 1887 to 1917. Her reports as superintendent are in the *Annual Reports* of the Board of Education, 1910–15. There are

Ella Flagg Young papers at Ill. State Normal Univ., Normal, Ill.]

JUDY SURATT

**YOUNGER, Maud** (Jan. 10, 1870–June 25, 1936), suffragist and labor reformer, was born in San Francisco, Calif., to William John Younger and Annie Maria (Lane) Younger, both pioneer settlers in the city. Her father, a highly successful dentist, had come there with his Scottish parents in 1848; her mother was a native of New Orleans. She died when Maud was twelve, leaving to her four daughters and one son a substantial fortune inherited from their maternal grandfather. This independent income might have made Maud Younger a mere socialite. But though she followed traditional patterns for a time, attending private schools, playing the organ in the family's Episcopal church, and interspersing social life in San Francisco with visits abroad (her father settled in Paris in 1900 and became a fashionable practitioner), she eventually broke sharply with convention.

In 1901, while on her way to Europe, she stopped in New York City and asked to stay at the College Settlement. This pioneer among the settlement houses had been established in the heart of New York's crowded and impoverished East Side by a group of graduates from the early women's colleges. Miss Younger expected to stay a week and "see the slums"; she remained five years, emerging from the experience an ardent advocate of trade unionism, protective legislation for women, and woman suffrage. She learned what the life of working women was like by taking a job as a waitress in a chain of New York restaurants, a discovery she vividly described in *McClure's Magazine* in 1907. Having joined the Waitresses' Union, she repeated her experiment when she returned to San Francisco in 1908. There being no union for waitresses in her home city, she took the lead in organizing one, and although she became known as "the millionaire waitress," her fellow workers showed their confidence by electing her president of their local and for three terms delegate to the Central Trades and Labor Council. In 1911 she took an active role in securing a state eight-hour law for women. Through her union connections she was able to get the measure endorsed by the California State Federation of Labor, and she helped push it through the legislature by gathering statistics, organizing testimony at hearings on the bill by waitresses, laundry workers, and factory workers, and lobbying among the legislators.

That same year saw the statewide campaign

for a woman suffrage amendment to the California constitution, resulting in a victory that impelled the entire national suffrage movement to new levels of activity. Maud Younger won wide publicity for the cause by driving a team of six horses drawing a suffrage float down San Francisco's Market Street in the Labor Day parade. Her most significant contributions, however, were speaking on behalf of the amendment all over the state and organizing a Wage Earners' Equal Suffrage League, which served as the working women's arm of the campaign. This Miss Younger represented on the five-member Central Campaign Committee.

In 1912 she was back in the East and deeply involved in the "White Goods Strike" launched by the International Ladies' Garment Workers Union to rid New York of subcontracting in the dress and shirtwaist-making trades. Her activity, according to one account, extended "from 6 a.m. on the picket lines till the closing hours of the Women's Night Court," where the women had difficulty getting a fair hearing and securing bail. During this period Miss Younger was also getting her first taste of Congressional work, helping the National Women's Trade Union League secure passage of protective legislation for women workers in the District of Columbia.

Her wide experience made Maud Younger an ideal lieutenant to Alice Paul, leader of the Congressional Union, the more militant wing of the suffrage movement, when in 1913 the union began an all-out effort to secure passage of a federal suffrage amendment. Although small of stature—she was only five feet three inches tall—Miss Younger was a vivid and compelling speaker. She delivered the keynote speech at the founding convention of the National Woman's Party (successor to the Congressional Union) in Chicago on June 5, 1916, and the memorial oration for INEZ MILHOLLAND BOISSEVAIN on Christmas Day of the same year. In 1917 the Woman's Party sent her all over the country to publicize the case of the women who, having been arrested for picketing the White House on behalf of suffrage, protested the brutality of their prison treatment by going on hunger strikes.

When it came to working with Congress, Maud Younger's wit and high spirits stood her in good stead. She headed the National Woman's Party's Congressional committee, whose work and famous "card index" she later described in colorful detail in a series of articles in *McCall's Magazine*. Probably the most important distinction between her and Mrs. Maud

Wood Park (1871–1955), her opposite number in the more orthodox National American Woman Suffrage Association, arose from the different tactics of the two groups. Mrs. Park made every effort to win the confidence and friendship of members of Congress; Miss Younger and her organization put more emphasis on pressure, from the members' constituents and through demonstrations and public meetings.

Her father's serious illness in Paris called Miss Younger from Washington early in January 1920, and not until late that year, after tending to family business in San Francisco following his death, did she return, driving alone by car—a slow and adventurous cross-country trip over muddy roads soaked by autumn rains. For several years thereafter she continued her efforts on behalf of working women through the Women's Trade Union League and the National Consumers' League, and as a member of the advisory committee of the federal Women's Bureau. But in 1923 she broke with all three groups when she helped initiate the proposed Equal Rights Amendment to the Constitution, insisting, in contravention to those who felt that such an amendment would threaten existing protective legislation, that in no other way could the position of women be fully equalized with that of men in all walks of life. As Congressional chairman of the National Woman's Party she made the Equal Rights Amendment the major effort of her last years. Maud Younger died of cancer at her ranch in Los Gatos, Calif., in 1936, in her sixty-seventh year. Her body was cremated, and the ashes scattered.

[Maud Younger, "The Diary of an Amateur Waitress: An Industrial Problem from the Worker's Point of View," *McClure's Mag.*, Mar., Apr. 1907, "Taking Orders—A Day as a Waitress in a San Francisco Restaurant," *Sunset Mag.*, Oct. 1908, and "Revelations of a Woman Lobbyist," *McCall's Mag.*, Sept., Oct., Nov. 1919; Vera Edmondson, "Feminist and Laborite," *Sunset Mag.*, June 1915; Inez Haynes Irwin, *The Story of the Woman's Party* (1921) and "Adventures of Yesterday" (unpublished autobiographical MS., Schlesinger Library, Radcliffe College), chap. viii; obituary, *N.Y. Times*, June 28, 1936; Nat. Woman's Party Papers, presently in the Library of Congress (Special Correspondence, Woman's Party Leaders, Tray 29, Box 3); death record from Calif. Dept. of Public Health. On her father and his family, see Daughters of the Am. Revolution of Calif., *Records of the Families of Calif. Pioneers*, XI (1942), 499–502; *Nat. Cyc. Am. Biog.*, XX, 250–51.]

ELEANOR FLEXNER

# Z

ZACHRY, Caroline Beaumont (Apr. 20, 1894–Feb. 22, 1945), educational psychologist, was born in New York City, the daughter of two transplanted Southern aristocrats, James Greer Zachry and Elise Clarkson (Thompson) Zachry; her parents later had another daughter and a son. Caroline's maternal grandfather, Hugh Smith Thompson, was a distinguished South Carolina educator and public official who served as governor of his state, as Assistant Secretary of the Treasury under President Grover Cleveland, and on the federal Civil Service Commission before coming to New York as comptroller of the New York Life Insurance Company. Charles Zachry, her paternal grandfather, had been a brigadier general in the Confederate Army. Her father, a native of Georgia, about 1890 had begun a law practice in New York that lasted for forty years.

Educated chiefly in New York City, Caroline Zachry attended the Spence School for girls from 1908 to 1914, graduating at the bottom of her class. For the next ten years she combined teaching with study at Teachers College, Columbia University, where she received the B.S. degree in 1924; for two years she also taught in the college's experimental Lincoln School. Continuing at Teachers College, she received a master's degree in 1925, with a thesis on the teaching of English in the junior high school, and a Ph.D. in 1929, with a dissertation on the personality adjustment of schoolchildren. Both were directed by William Heard Kilpatrick, professor of the philosophy of education, who remained a devoted friend and adviser throughout her life.

As her dissertation subject reveals, Miss Zachry in the mid-1920's became deeply interested in psychology and its message for the teacher. Early in the 1930's she studied in Vienna under the famous psychiatrist Carl Jung, an experience which profoundly influenced her intellectual development. (Although not a psychiatrist, she became a Fellow of the American Orthopsychiatric Association.) Her educational interest quickly shifted from new methods of teaching traditional subject matter to a much deeper examination of the psychological forces determining the development of the schoolchild. She had been only moderately successful as a teacher at the Lincoln School, but following her psychological baptism she found much greater success in working with prospective and practicing teachers. In 1926 she became head of the English department at the New Jersey State Teachers College in Upper Montclair, but after a year she shifted to the psychology department, and from 1930 to 1934 she directed the college's Mental Hygiene Institute.

Miss Zachry gained a wider audience as administrator and spokesman of several projects seeking a revision of traditional methods of schooling to bring them into accord with newly revealed psychological principles. From 1934 to 1939 she directed a study of adolescence for the Commission on Secondary School Curriculum of the Progressive Education Association, publishing the results in *Emotion and Conduct in Adolescence* (1940), her best-known work. She then became director of the Institute for the Study of Personality Development—founded, under the sponsorship of the Progressive Education Association, largely through her efforts—which after her death was renamed the Caroline B. Zachry Institute of Human Development. For several years (1940–42) she directed the association's summer workshop for teachers and laymen at Vassar College.

In 1942 she left the Institute to accept appointment by her friend Mayor Fiorello La Guardia as director of the Bureau of Child Guidance of the New York City Board of Education. But her early death cut off her work after three years. She died of cancer at the age of fifty in New York City and was buried in Kensico Cemetery, Valhalla, N.Y. Although she never married, Miss Zachry adopted two children in the late 1930's, Stephen Beaumont and Nancy Greer. She was a lifelong member of St. Thomas's Episcopal Church in New York.

In her *Emotion and Conduct in Adolescence*, Miss Zachry expressed her conviction that "the chief duty of the school is to give the help young people need in order to make socially constructive adjustments in the course of their growth—that is, the school is mainly concerned with their social development." In accepting her Board of Education post she commented: "We have spent so much time taking the child apart; it is time to put him back together"—a statement which may have reflected a premonitory awareness of the excesses of an overly psychological or child-centered approach to education. Whatever the shortcomings of such an approach, Caroline Zachry achieved considerable renown in the psychologically oriented faction of the progressive education movement. Two of her colleagues in educational reform, Sidonie Matsner Gruenberg of the Child Study Association and ELISABETH IRWIN, founder of the Little Red School House, considered her work seminal in its field, and Dr. Benjamin Spock, the widely read writer on child care, has credited Miss Zachry with the "broadest, deepest influence" on his thinking (*Ladies' Home Journal*, March 1960, p. 138).

[Other books by Miss Zachry include: *Personality Adjustments of School Children* (1929); *Reorganizing Secondary Education*, with Vivian T. Thayer and Ruth Kotinsky (1939); and, with several other progressive educators, *Democracy and the Curriculum* (1939). For biographical data, see *N.Y. Times* obituary, Feb. 24, 1945; *Who's Who in America Monthly Supplement*, Sept. 1943; *Am. Men of Science* (7th ed., 1944). For her background, see *Dict. Am. Biog.* on Hugh Smith Thompson and *N.Y. Times* obit. of James Greer Zachry, Aug. 31, 1930. Interviews with Prof. William H. Kilpatrick, Mrs. Sidonie Gruenberg, Mrs. Evelyn Stiefel, and Miss Zachry's brother, Greer Zachry, all in N.Y. City, provided valuable information. Other data from records of Teachers College and of Montclair State College, the former N.J. State Teachers College.]

PATRICIA ALBJERG GRAHAM

**ZAKRZEWSKA, Marie Elizabeth** (Sept. 6, 1829–May 12, 1902), pioneering physician, was born in Berlin, Germany, the oldest of the five daughters and one son of Martin Ludwig Zakrzewski and his wife, Frederika C. W. Urban. Marie's father, of a Polish landed family, was a Prussian army pensioner, having been dismissed for his liberal views; her mother counted among her immediate ancestors gypsies of the Lombardi tribe. At the age of eight, after three years in primary school, Marie Zakrzewska (pronounced Zak-*shef*-ska) was enrolled in a school for young girls. A good student, but lonely and unpopular, she left after six years, at her father's insistence, to learn housework like other German girls.

Marie now spent most of her time reading medical works. Several years before, her mother, to help support the growing family, had entered the school for midwives at the Charité hospital in Berlin; for several months Marie had lived with her at the hospital, developing a keen interest in medicine. Soon she was assisting her mother, and at age eighteen she applied for admission to the midwives' school. Though refused at first as too young, she came under the favorable notice of a professor, Dr. Joseph Hermann Schmidt, who two years later secured her admission, took her as his private pupil, and during her second year made her his teaching assistant. She graduated in 1851; in May of the following year Dr. Schmidt, though ailing and despite strenuous opposition, succeeded in having her installed as chief midwife and professor in the hospital's school for midwives, only a few hours before his death. Miss Zakrzewska was a successful

teacher and midwife, but opposition and intrigue against her proved too strong, and after six months she resigned. A year later she emigrated with a younger sister to the United States, having heard of the new Female Medical College in Philadelphia and expecting to find in America greater freedom for women to practice medicine.

The two girls arrived in New York in May, and were joined by a third sister in September. For nearly a year they lived on the proceeds of a small knitting enterprise. Then, in May 1854, Marie was introduced to Dr. ELIZABETH BLACKWELL, who was immediately impressed by her visitor's character and potentialities and took her on as a pupil. Dr Blackwell persuaded Marie that she must learn English and get an M.D. degree, and gained admission for her to the medical department of Western Reserve College (commonly known as the Cleveland Medical College), from which EMILY BLACKWELL had recently graduated. One of four women in a class of about two hundred, Miss Zakrzewska matriculated in October 1854. She was welcomed on her arrival in Cleveland by Mrs. CAROLINE M. SEVERANCE, who assisted her financially and became a lifelong friend, and she was cordially received by the dean, Dr. John J. Delamater. Other students and most townspeople, however, treated her coldly. In March 1856 she received her M.D. degree. Returning to New York, she could not even rent rooms, so great was the prejudice against women physicians. She finally opened an office that April in Elizabeth Blackwell's back parlor.

Dr. Blackwell and Dr. Zakrzewska were both eager to start a small hospital where women doctors and students might have the opportunity to practice and learn denied them elsewhere. To this project Dr. Zakrzewska now devoted herself, seeking funds in Boston, Philadelphia, and New York, wherever advanced ideas were discussed. On May 1, 1857, the New York Infirmary for Women and Children opened, the country's first hospital staffed by women. For two years Dr. Zakrzewska served as resident physician and general manager, sharing with the Blackwell sisters the care of a growing number of dispensary and bed patients. By 1859 the institution seemed firmly established, its success in no small measure owing to the solid practical ability and hard work of Dr. Zakrzewska.

In that year she accepted an offer from the New England Female Medical College of Boston to be professor of obstetrics and diseases of women and children and resident physician of a projected new hospital. Samuel Gregory, a would-be medical reformer who considered "man-midwives" an affront to decency, had founded the college in 1848, primarily to train female practitioners who could give parturient women skilled attendance. Gregory's pamphlets were insulting to regular physicians, he knew nothing about medical education, and his school had a weak faculty of dubious backgrounds. Dr. Zakrzewska's inaugural address strongly urged the importance of a good general education and the role of science in medicine. Her views were well above the American average; Gregory's were below. Inevitably the two quarreled, and in 1862, increasingly dissatisfied with the school's low standards and its perpetual state of financial crisis under Gregory's control, she resigned.

With the advice and support of a board of lady managers Dr. Zakrzewska had built up the clinical department of the New England Female Medical College into a small hospital and dispensary for women. When Gregory closed this hospital and disbanded its board upon her departure, many of these women and several of the college trustees backed Dr. Zakrzewska in founding a new institution, the New England Hospital for Women and Children. Opened July 1, 1862, it was incorporated in March 1863. Its three stated purposes were: to provide women with medical aid from competent physicians of their own sex; to provide educated women with an opportunity for practical study in medicine; and to train nurses. With Dr. Zakrzewska freed of the association with Gregory, a few of Boston's leaders in medicine gave consistent encouragement. Most of her support, however, came from outside the profession, particularly from those active in the woman's rights movement. Though not without struggles, the ten-bed hospital grew steadily. In 1864 it moved to larger quarters and in 1872, after a successful fund-raising campaign, to a new site in Roxbury, where the original main building, later named in honor of Dr. Zakrzewska, still stands.

The job of resident physician, initially handled by Dr. Zakrzewska, was soon taken over by Dr. LUCY SEWALL and later by other younger women doctors. Dr. Zakrzewska was attending physician until 1887, and then advisory physician. Though ably supported by a board of directors including Lucy Goddard, EDNAH D. CHENEY, and Samuel E. Sewall, she played the leading role in guiding the hospital's development. Because of the prevailing prejudice, Dr. Zakrzewska felt it all the more necessary to give women physicians the best possible training, including hospital experience. This in her opinion was the New England

Hospital's most important program. She limited the staff to women, not because she was against coeducation in medicine but because almost no other hospitals admitted women physicians. Herself well trained and dedicated to her profession, she perceived that neither sentimental sympathy nor a desire for status was an adequate motive for a woman to enter it, but only a talent for practice combined with an interest in scientific investigation. At first some women without degrees studied medicine at the hospital, but after 1881 all resident students were required to be M.D.'s. Many of the ablest women doctors of the time completed their training with an internship at the New England Hospital for Women and Children, where Marie Zakrzewska inspired them with an intense loyalty to her and to the institution. To her more than to any other person, in the opinion of Ednah D. Cheney, was due the success of women in medicine in America.

Intelligent, persuasive, and persevering, if somewhat opinionated and quick-tempered, Dr. Zakrzewska had deep human sympathies and a special understanding of the problems of the poor. In her early days in Boston she took on a heavy burden of charity cases, both out of principle and from a desire to establish herself professionally. At first she made her calls on foot, often to distant parts of the city, but in 1865 she acquired a horse and buggy "to uphold the professional etiquette and dignity of a woman physician" (quoted in *Marie Elizabeth Zakrzewska*, p. 17). In time she acquired a substantial private practice. She was plain of appearance, with a generous mouth and prominent nose, but advancing years softened her features and lent dignity to her bearing.

Though most of her energies were devoted to her hospital and medical practice, Marie Zakrzewska was from time to time drawn into other reforms, including the antislavery crusade. While still a student she had met Theodore Parker, William Lloyd Garrison, and Wendell Phillips, who later became her close friends. She supported woman suffrage and was one of the first members of the New England Women's Club, where she gave a number of lectures on hygiene and related topics. For many years, until his death in 1880, the German radical journalist Karl Heinzen and his wife lived with her in Roxbury. Later she shared her home with Julia A. Sprague, a devoted friend. Essentially a freethinker in religion, Dr. Zakrzewska in her early years had "a bitter contempt for the church and professed Christians" (C. Annette Buckel in *Woman's Journal*, Nov. 8, 1902). More tolerant as she grew older, she still explicitly denied any belief in an afterlife. She retired in 1899, having suffered for several years from arteriosclerosis and heart disease, and died three years later of apoplexy at her home in Jamaica Plain, Boston. In lieu of a conventional funeral service, friends gathered at the chapel of Forest Hills Cemetery, where her ashes were interred, to hear a paper she had written for the occasion.

[Nearly all accounts of Dr. Zakrzewska's life to 1859 are based on the autobiographical *A Practical Illustration of "Woman's Right to Labor,"* ed. by Caroline H. Dall (1860). This is carried forward in the other chief biographical account, Agnes C. Vietor, ed., *A Woman's Quest: The Life of Marie E. Zakrzewska, M.D.* (1924). The New England Hospital for Women and Children published an able brief sketch, *Marie Elizabeth Zakrzewska: A Memoir* (1903). See also Dr. Zakrzewska's *Introductory Lecture Delivered . . . before the New England Female Medical College* (1859) and "Report of One Hundred and Eighty-seven Cases of Midwifery in Private Practice," *Boston Medical and Surgical Jour.,* CXXI (1889), 557–60; Frederick C. Waite, *Western Reserve Univ. Centennial Hist. of the School of Medicine* (1946) and *Hist. of the New England Female Medical College, 1848–1874* (1950); Ednah Dow Cheney, *Reminiscences* (1902); Carl Wittke, *Against the Current: The Life of Karl Heinzen* (1945); annual reports of the New England Female Medical College and the New England Hospital for Women and Children; Emma L. Call in Julia Ward Howe, ed., *Representative Women of New England* (1904); obituary in *Woman's Jour.,* May 17, 1902; "Memorial Meeting for Dr. Zakrzewska," *ibid.,* Nov. 8, 1902, pp. 356–57; death record from Mass. Registrar of Vital Statistics.]

JOHN B. BLAKE

**ZANE, Elizabeth** (1766?–1831?), frontier heroine, better known as Betty Zane, is said to have saved a besieged fort in one of the final Indian attacks of the Revolutionary War by carrying gunpowder to replenish the defenders' exhausted supply. Very little about her is known with certainty. She was probably born in Hardy County, on the south branch of the Potomac River in present West Virginia, although Berkeley County, in the same state, has also been given as her place of birth. Her father, William Zane, was a grandson of Robert Zane, who had migrated from Ireland to New Jersey in 1677. The Zanes were of Quaker stock, but William married outside the Society of Friends, which perhaps induced him to move to the Virginia frontier. Of his four sons and one daughter, Elizabeth seems to have been the youngest. Her brother Ebenezer founded the town of Wheeling, Va. (now W. Va.), to

which three of the brothers moved in 1769. Here a fort was built in 1774, first called Fincastle but renamed Fort Henry in 1776. The fort was twice attacked during the American Revolution, in 1777 and again in 1782, both times by Indians under the authority of the British. Though some sources suggest that the "gunpowder exploit" of Betty Zane occurred in the earlier year, most place it in 1782, when the attack lasted nearly three days.

Betty, so the story goes, had recently returned from Philadelphia, where she had been staying with relatives and attending school, and was living with her brother Col. Ebenezer Zane. Colonel Zane had built and fortified a house, containing a powder magazine, forty or fifty yards from the fort; it had been rebuilt after being burned by Indians in 1781. Then, on Sept. 11, 1782, with only brief warning, the Indians attacked again. So swiftly did the enemy arrive that there was barely time for the inhabitants to seek refuge, and only a part of the powder from Colonel Zane's house was removed to the fort. Zane, with four or five others, remained to guard the house. In the usual version of the story, the powder supply in Fort Henry ran desperately low and it was necessary to replenish it from Colonel Zane's magazine if the fort were to be saved. Several persons volunteered for the hazardous enterprise, among them Betty Zane. "You have not one man to spare," she is reputed to have said when told that a man could run faster than she. Shedding surplus clothing, she darted from the fort to her brother's house. The Indians, watching her in amazement, exclaimed "Squaw, squaw" and did not fire. When she arrived at the house, Colonel Zane emptied a keg of powder into a tablecloth which he fastened around her waist. When Betty once more appeared before the Indians, they opened fire. Bullet after bullet whizzed past her, and although one tore a hole in her dress, she managed to reach the gate of the fort unharmed. With the added supply of powder the little group within the walls held off the Indians until help arrived.

Evidence to substantiate the legend is sketchy. The story was apparently written down by Betty's nephew Noah Zane, Ebenezer's son, who intended to prepare a biography of the family. When he abandoned this project he turned his notes over to Alexander S. Withers, who apparently drew on them for his *Chronicles of Border Warfare* (1831); the notes themselves were later scattered and lost. Using Withers as their source, most later writers have repeated the story; eventually it was told, with romantic embellishments, by a descendant, Zane Grey, in his novel *Betty Zane* (1903).

Not all historians are agreed about the authenticity of the legend. Some attack it on the grounds of improbability, suggesting that at best Betty Zane must have been one of the group in Ebenezer Zane's house and that she ran only from the house to the fort. In 1849 a supposed eyewitness, Mrs. Lydia (Boggs) Cruger, gave a wholly different version; by her deposition, made at the age of eighty-four, Elizabeth Zane was still in school in Philadelphia when the attack occurred, and it was another girl, Molly Scott, who carried powder—not to the fort, but from the fort to the Zane house (De Hass, pp. 280–81). But a grandson of Molly insisted that Molly herself had always credited the exploit to Betty Zane (Galbreath, p. 586).

Little else is known of Elizabeth Zane. Her first husband was John (or Henry) McGloughlin (McGlaughlin, McLaughlin), by whom she had five daughters—Mary, Rebecca, Nancy, Catherine, and Hannah. Sometime after his death she married Jacob (or John) Clark, by whom she had two children, Catherine and Ebenezer; they lived on a farm west of Martins Ferry, Ohio, not far from Wheeling. At her death, which her son Ebenezer placed as "not . . . later than 1831," she was "about 65 years old" (Wilbur C. Brockunier to Lyman C. Draper, Jan. 19, 1891, Draper Manuscripts). She was buried in the Walnut Grove Cemetery in Martins Ferry, where a statue commemorating her exploit was erected in 1928.

[The bibliography on the sieges of Fort Henry and the gunpowder exploit is fairly extensive. The most important material is in the Draper Manuscripts, 4ZZ6–23, in the State. Hist. Soc. of Wis. This collection contains letters from Wilbur C. Brockunier of Wheeling (a great-grandson of Col. Ebenezer Zane) to Lyman C. Draper, comments and bibliographical notes made by Draper, newspaper clippings, and copies of articles on Fort Henry which appeared in the *Southern Literary Messenger* and *Western Messenger*. Other sources of information are: Wills De Hass, *Hist. of the Early Settlement and Indian Wars of Western Va.* (1851); Alexander S. Withers, *Chronicles of Border Warfare* (Reuben G. Thwaites, ed., 1895); Benson J. Lossing, *The Pictorial Field-Book of the Revolution* (2 vols., 1860); Charles McKnight, *Our Western Border* (1875); Consul W. Butterfield, *Hist. of the Girtys* (1890); Consul W. Butterfield, ed., *Washington-Irvine Correspondence* (1882); Lucullus V. McWhorter, *The Border Settlers of Northwestern Va. from 1768 to 1795* (1915). See also: C. B. Galbreath, "Unveiling of Memorial to Elizabeth Zane," *Ohio Archaeological and Hist. Quart.*, July 1928 (which gives a later death date); William H. Egle, *Some Pa. Women during the War of the Revolution* (1898); Gibson L. Cranmer, ed., *Hist. of Wheeling City and Ohio County, W. Va., and Representative Citizens* (1902); Gibson L. Cranmer, *Hist. of the Upper Ohio Valley* (1890); Henry Howe, *Hist. Collections of Va.* (1845); J. H. Newton et al., *Hist. of the Pan-Handle* (1879); Charles A. Wingerter, ed., *Hist. of Greater Wheeling and Vicinity* (2 vols., 1912). For information on the Zane family, see: *Pa. Mag. of Hist. and Biog.*, Apr. 1888, pp. 123–25; Samuel Kercheval, *A Hist. of the Valley of Va.* (1850); John G. Patterson, "Ebenezer Zane, Frontiersman" (M.A. thesis, Univ. of Va., 1939) and "Ebenezer Zane, Frontiersman," *W. Va. Hist.*, Oct. 1950.]

ELIZABETH COMETTI

ZEISLER, Fannie Bloomfield (July 16, 1863–Aug. 20, 1927), concert pianist, was born in Bielitz, Austrian Silesia, the youngest of three children and only daughter of Jewish parents, Solomon and Bertha (Jaeger) Blumenfeld. (She anglicized the family name as early as 1883.) Of her two brothers, Maurice Bloomfield (1855–1928) became a distinguished philologist and professor of Sanskrit at Johns Hopkins University. Moritz Rosenthal (1862–1946), also famous as a virtuoso pianist, was a cousin. Solomon Blumenfeld emigrated to America in 1866, locating first in Appleton, Wis., where his wife and children joined him the next year. About 1869 they settled in Chicago. For many years the father and mother maintained a dry goods business, which was sustained in later years with the help of their other son, Sigmund. Fannie was educated at home and also, according to one account, in the public schools and at the Dearborn Seminary in Chicago.

Maurice Bloomfield was reportedly his sister's first piano teacher. Fannie later studied with Bernhard Ziehn, whose highly regarded theoretical writings would suggest that she received unusually sound training in the fundamentals of music. An often-repeated story dating from this period recalls the girl of eight, after the Chicago Fire of 1871, practicing at the family piano in the street while workmen busily cleared the ruined city. In 1873 the conductor and impresario Carl Wolfsohn came to Chicago. Wolfsohn quickly became a leader in Chicago's musical life, and Fannie was one of his first pupils. After a year of study with Wolfsohn, she made an inconspicuous debut on Feb. 26, 1875, aged eleven, at one of his Beethoven Society concerts, performing Beethoven's F-major Andante. Several other local performances under Wolfsohn's auspices followed over the next three years.

The celebrated Russian pianist Annette Essipoff while in Chicago during her tour of 1877 heard Fannie perform and encouraged her to study with her own mentor, the master teacher Theodor Leschetizky. Five years of study with Leschetizky in Vienna followed, culminating in several public performances there. Returning to Chicago in 1883, Fannie Bloomfield performed the first movement of a Henselt concerto at one of the Beethoven Society concerts on Jan. 11, 1884; she gave a full concert, assisted by Wolfsohn, at Chicago's Hershey Hall on Apr. 30. Her New York debut on Jan. 30, 1885, under the direction of Frank Van der Stucken, was particularly well received and helped establish her growing American reputation. With the fall term of 1884 she joined the faculty of Chicago's School of Lyric and Dramatic Art. Her long and successful teaching career, later carried on at her home one day a week, followed the pattern of individual lessons conducted in the presence of a critical group of fellow students.

On Oct. 18, 1885, Fannie Bloomfield was married to Sigmund Zeisler (1860–1931), a prominent young Chicago lawyer. The Zeisler family, distantly related to the Blumenfelds, had also come from Bielitz. Sigmund had helped work his way through law school by writing music criticism for a Chicago German newspaper; he was soon to establish a reputation of his own as a defender of the Chicago anarchists following the Haymarket Riot. Active in Democratic politics in the sound money and anti-imperialist movements of 1896 and 1900 and a founder of the Municipal Voters League, he was noted as an orator and as a leader of Chicago's intellectual and liberal community. The informal receptions held at the Zeislers' Woodlawn Avenue home on the last Wednesday evening of every month became a feature of the city's cultural life. The couple had three sons: Leonard Bloomfield, born in 1886, Paul Bloomfield (1897), and Ernest Bloomfield (1899). Mrs. Zeisler liked to use tools, and for relaxation at home is said to have enjoyed carpentry and upholstering.

Fannie Bloomfield Zeisler carefully fitted her concert career around her responsibilities to family and students, scheduling long practice hours, especially before a tour, grouping her appearances and repertoire whenever possible, and measuring and apportioning the full capacity of her time and energies with rigorous discipline. In the fall and winter of 1888–89 she worked again with Leschetizky in Vienna. As with most European-trained American musicians of this period, her initial reputation was based on her reception abroad. Established in the front rank of the world's concert pianists

by the 1890's, she concertized extensively over the next twenty years, gradually cutting down her appearances thereafter. Her six European tours began with one in the fall of 1893 that took her to Berlin, Leipzig, Dresden, and Vienna, but was uncompleted because of illness. A second tour the next fall was a completion and extension of the first. The third in 1898 was devoted largely to England, but also included notable appearances at the Lower Rhine Music Festival in Cologne. The fourth in 1902 included a major success at the Concerts Lamoureux in Paris. The fifth took place in 1911–12 and the last in the spring of 1914, although Mrs. Zeisler visited Europe often in later years.

Concertizing in America also required strenuous tours, involving long hours on the train, making difficult connections, and appearing under unexpected hardships. Illness prevented her from performing during 1905–06, but in other seasons she appeared with orchestras in Boston, New York, Philadelphia, Pittsburgh, Cincinnati, Chicago, St. Louis, and Minneapolis, and performed chamber music with the Popper, Bohemian, and Hubay quartets. A highlight of Mrs. Zeisler's American career was the pleasant, dialectically reasoned paper on "Women in Music" which she delivered in July 1890 at the Detroit meetings of the august and male-dominated Music Teachers' National Association. She also performed the Chopin F-minor Concerto for the group, with an orchestra directed by Theodore Thomas. (Thomas soon afterward settled in Chicago to found the Chicago Symphony Orchestra, with which Mrs. Zeisler appeared as soloist over nineteen seasons.) In 1896 in San Francisco she gained additional fame by giving eight programs, all entirely different, within eighteen days.

Among the culminating events of her career were two Chicago concerts. At the first, on Feb. 3, 1920, at Orchestra Hall, her program consisted of three concertos, by Mozart, Chopin, and Tchaikovsky, the sparkling scherzo of the Litolff concerto serving as an encore. On Feb. 25, 1925, a special evening honored fifty years of concertizing. It included concertos of Chopin and Schumann in which she was accompanied by the Chicago Symphony Orchestra under Frederick Stock, these works preceded by the little Beethoven andante with which her career had begun. This performance, proceeds from which were devoted to the Fannie Bloomfield Zeisler Musicians' Relief Fund, which she had founded, proved to be her farewell concert. Mrs. Zeisler suffered a disabling heart illness in the fall of 1926. She died the following summer at sixty-four, at her home in the Cooper-Carlton Hotel in Chicago. By her wishes her body was cremated, at Oakwoods Cemetery in Chicago.

The Austrian critic Eduard Hanslick reportedly called Fannie Bloomfield Zeisler a "powerful master of the keyboard," and spoke of her "fiery temperament and a technique which is developed in the most minute detail. Her delicacy in the finest florid work is as marvelous as her fascinating energy in forte passages." Other reviewers usually praised these same qualities, citing also the beauty and fullness of her tone and the clarity and finish of her passage-work. Her performances were credited with that rare quality of reflecting the individuality of the music itself rather than that of the performer. Her large tone and her successful conception of the powerful and massive masterworks of the piano literature were often contrasted with her frailty and slightness of physique. Her repertoire consisted largely of standard classics in preference to new and experimental works, although in later years she often included a group of short compositions by women composers. Her intense devotion to the highest standards of musical performance, successfully achieved in spite of limited physical resources and diligent attention to family and students, belongs to a heroic tradition of keyboard virtuosity.

[For Mrs. Zeisler's paper on "Women in Music," see Music Teachers' Nat. Assoc., *Official Report of Annual Meeting*, 1890, pp. 38–44. For biographical material, see W. S. B. Matthews, "A Great Pianist at Home," *Music*, Nov. 1895; and obituaries by Rossetter Cole in *Chicago Tribune*, Aug. 21, 1927, and Music Teachers' Nat. Assoc., *Papers and Proc.*, 1927, pp. 76–83. See also *Woman's Who's Who of America*, 1914–15; *Who Was Who in America*, vol. I (1942); *Nat. Cyc. Am. Biog.*, XIV, 192–93; and the *Dict. Am. Biog.* sketch of her husband. Miscellaneous contemporary references were found in: scrapbooks of Frederick Grant Gleason (Newberry Library, Chicago), including reviews, clippings, and programs, among them an 1884 announcement of the School of Lyric and Dramatic Art; and files of the *Am. Art Jour.* and of Chicago newspapers, especially the *Tribune* and *Daily News*. Death record from Ill. Dept. of Public Health. Paul B. Zeisler provided personal recollections. Critical reactions can be found in Henry C. Lahee, *Famous Pianists of Today and Yesterday* (1901), pp. 321–24; Richard Aldrich, *Concert Life in N.Y., 1902–1923* (1941); and Walter Niemann, *Meister des Klaviers* (1921), p. 213. Some correspondence and papers are in family hands, including an unpublished biography of Mrs. Zeisler by her husband, of which the Music Division of the Library of Congress has a microfilm.]

DONALD W. KRUMMEL

**ZINZENDORF, Benigna.** *See* WATTEVILLE, Henrietta Benigna Justine Zinzendorf von.

# CLASSIFIED LIST
## OF SELECTED BIOGRAPHIES

### Abolitionists

Cary, Mary Ann Shadd
Chace, Elizabeth Buffum
Chandler, Elizabeth Margaret
Chapman, Maria Weston
Child, Lydia Maria Francis
Cowles, Betsey Mix
Craft, Ellen
Crandall, Prudence
Douglass, Sarah Mapps Douglass
Follen, Eliza Lee Cabot
Foster, Abigail Kelley
Gage, Frances Dana Barker
Gibbons, Abigail Hopper
Grew, Mary
Griffing, Josephine Sophia White
Grimké, Angelina Emily
Grimké, Charlotte L. Forten
Grimké, Sarah Moore
Haviland, Laura Smith
Holley, Sallie
Howland, Emily
Hutchinson, Abigail Jemima
Jones, Jane Elizabeth Hitchcock
Mott, Lucretia Coffin
Pugh, Sarah
Remond, Sarah Parker
Stone, Lucy
Truth, Sojourner
Tubman, Harriet
Wright, Frances

### Actresses and Theatre Managers

Allen, Viola Emily
Anderson, Mary
Arthur, Julia
Barrymore, Georgiana Emma Drew
Bateman, Kate Josephine
Bates, Blanche Lyon
Bayes, Nora
Bonstelle, Jessie
Booth, Agnes
Brady, Alice
Cahill, Marie
Carter, Caroline Louise Dudley
Cayvan, Georgia Eva
Chapman, Caroline
Clare, Ada
Clark, Marguerite
Claxton, Kate
Cline, Maggie
Coghlan, Rose
Cowl, Jane
Crabtree, Lotta
Crews, Laura Hope
Crosman, Henrietta Foster
Cushman, Charlotte Saunders
Davenport, Fanny Lily Gypsy
Dean, Julia
De Wolfe, Elsie
Drake, Frances Ann Denny
Dressler, Marie
Drew, Louisa Lane
Duff, Mary Ann Dyke
Eagels, Jeanne
Elliott, Gertrude
Elliott, Maxine
Ellsler, Effie
Eytinge, Rose
Fisher, Clara
Fiske, Minnie Maddern
Florence, Malvina Pray
Forrest, Catherine Norton Sinclair
Fox, Della
Frederick, Pauline
Gilbert, Anne Jane Hartley
Guinan, Mary Louise Cecilia
Hallam, Mrs. Lewis
Held, Anna
Herne, Chrystal Katharine
Heron, Matilda Agnes
Howard, Caroline Emily Fox
Howard, Cordelia
Irwin, May
Janauschek, Francesca Romana Magdalena

709

Kalich, Bertha
Keene, Laura
Kemble, Frances Anne
Loftus, Cissie
Logan, Olive
Lord, Pauline
McClendon, Rose
Marlowe, Julia
Menken, Adah Isaacs
Merry, Ann Brunton
Miller, Marilyn
Mills, Florence
Mitchell, Maggie
Modjeska, Helena
Montez, Lola
Morgan, Helen
Morris, Clara
Mowatt, Anna Cora Ogden
Nazimova, Alla
Perry, Antoinette
Phillipps, Adelaide
Poe, Elizabeth Arnold Hopkins
Rehan, Ada
Reignolds, Catherine Mary
Robertson, Agnes Kelly
Robson, May
Rowson, Susanna Haswell
Russell, Annie
Russell, Lillian
Shaw, Mary G.
Tanguay, Eva
Taylor, Laurette
Templeton, Fay
Tweed, Blanche Oelrichs Thomas Barrymore
Tyler, Priscilla Cooper
Vincent, Mary Ann Farlow
Westley, Helen
Whiffen, Blanche Galton
Wood, Matilda Charlotte Vining

*See also* Film Actresses and Directors

## Anthropologists and Folklorists

Benedict, Ruth Fulton
Converse, Harriet Maxwell
Curtis, Natalie
Eckstorm, Fannie Pearson Hardy
Fletcher, Alice Cunningham
Garrison, Lucy McKim
Moore, Annie Aubertine Woodward
Nuttall, Zelia Maria Magdalena
Parsons, Elsie Clews
Smith, Erminnie Adele Platt
Stevenson, Matilda Coxe Evans

## Architects and Interior Decorators

Bethune, Louise Blanchard
De Wolfe, Elsie

Murdock, Louise Caldwell
Nichols, Minerva Parker
Wharton, Edith Newbold Jones
Wheeler, Candace Thurber

## Art Collectors and Patrons

Bliss, Lizzie Plummer
Cone, Claribel
Cone, Etta
Cooke, Anna Charlotte Rice
Evans, Anne
Force, Juliana Rieser
Gardner, Isabella Stewart
Greene, Belle da Costa
Havemeyer, Louisine Waldron Elder
Murdock, Louise Caldwell
Palmer, Bertha Honoré
Rockefeller, Abby Greene Aldrich
Rogers, Grace Rainey
Stein, Gertrude
Sullivan, Mary Josephine Quinn
Whitney, Gertrude Vanderbilt
Wolfe, Catharine Lorillard

## Art Critics and Historians

Cary, Elisabeth Luther
Gardner, Helen
Mechlin, Leila
Pennell, Elizabeth Robins
Van Rensselaer, Mariana Alley Griswold
Waters, Clara Erskine Clement

## Art Educators

Brown, Alice Van Vechten
Levy, Florence Nightingale
Prang, Mary Amelia Dana Hicks
Sartain, Emily
Starr, Eliza Allen
Weir, Irene

## Astronomers

Cannon, Annie Jump
Fleming, Williamina Paton Stevens
Leavitt, Henrietta Swan
Mitchell, Maria
Whiting, Sarah Frances
Whitney, Mary Watson

## Authors (by literary period)

*1607–1820*

Bleecker, Ann Eliza
Bradstreet, Anne
Ferguson, Elizabeth Graeme

Foster, Hannah Webster
Morton, Sarah Wentworth Apthorp
Murray, Judith Sargent
Rowson, Susanna Haswell
Tenney, Tabitha Gilman
Turell, Jane Colman
Warren, Mercy Otis
Wheatley, Phillis
Wood, Sally Sayward Barrell Keating

## 1821–1860

Bacon, Delia Salter
Botta, Anne Charlotte Lynch
Brooks, Maria Gowen
Cary, Alice
Cary, Phoebe
Child, Lydia Maria Francis
Clapp, Louise Amelia Knapp Smith
Clare, Ada
Cooper, Susan Augusta Fenimore
Crosby, Fanny
Cummins, Maria Susanna
Davidson, Lucretia Maria
Davidson, Margaret Miller
Eastman, Mary Henderson
Ellet, Elizabeth Fries Lummis
Farley, Harriet
Farrar, Eliza Ware Rotch
Fuller, Margaret
Gilman, Caroline Howard
Hale, Sarah Josepha Buell
Harper, Frances Ellen Watkins
Haven, Emily Bradley Neal
Hentz, Caroline Lee Whiting
Hooper, Ellen Sturgis
Howe, Julia Ward
Judson, Emily Chubbuck
Kinzie, Juliette Augusta Magill
Kirkland, Caroline Matilda Stansbury
Leslie, Eliza
Le Vert, Octavia Celeste Walton
Lippincott, Sara Jane Clarke
Lowell, Maria White
McCord, Louisa Susannah Cheves
McIntosh, Maria Jane
Moïse, Penina
Mowatt, Anna Cora Ogden
Osgood, Frances Sargent Locke
Parton, Sara Payson Willis
Peabody, Elizabeth Palmer
Pike, Mary Hayden Green
Prentiss, Elizabeth Payson
Ripley, Sophia Willard Dana
Sadlier, Mary Anne Madden
Sawyer, Caroline Mehitable Fisher
Sedgwick, Catharine Maria
Sigourney, Lydia Howard Huntley
Smith, Elizabeth Oakes Prince
Smith, Margaret Bayard

Southworth, Emma Dorothy Eliza Nevitte
Stephens, Ann Sophia
Stowe, Harriet Beecher
Tappan, Caroline Sturgis
Turner, Eliza L. Sproat Randolph
Tuthill, Louisa Caroline Huggins
Victor, Frances Auretta Fuller
Victor, Metta Victoria Fuller
Warner, Susan Bogert
Warner, Anna Bartlett
Whitcher, Frances Miriam Berry
Whitman, Sarah Helen Power
Wilson, Augusta Jane Evans

## 1861–1900

Allen, Elizabeth Anne Chase Akers
Andrews, Eliza Frances
Bacon, Alice Mabel
Barr, Amelia Edith Huddleston
Bolton, Sarah Tittle Barrett
Brown, Alice
Bryan, Mary Edwards
Catherwood, Mary Hartwell
Cheney, Ednah Dow Littlehale
Chopin, Kate O'Flaherty
Clarke, Mary Bayard Devereux
Cooke, Rose Terry
Coolbrith, Ina Donna
Crosby, Fanny
Davis, Mollie Evelyn Moore
Davis, Rebecca Blaine Harding
Deland, Margaret
Denison, Mary Ann Andrews
Diaz, Abby Morton
Dickinson, Emily
Dodge, Mary Abigail
Dorsey, Sarah Anne Ellis
Dupuy, Eliza Ann
Elliott, Maud Howe
Elliott, Sarah Barnwell
Fields, Annie Adams
Foote, Mary Anna Hallock
Freeman, Mary Eleanor Wilkins
French, Alice
Gilder, Jeannette Leonard
Green, Anna Katharine
Greene, Sarah Pratt McLean
Guiney, Louise Imogen
Hale, Lucretia Peabody
Hale, Susan
Hanaford, Phebe Ann Coffin
Harper, Frances Ellen Watkins
Harrison, Constance Cary
Holley, Marietta
Holmes, Mary Jane Hawes
Howard, Blanche Willis
Jackson, Helen Maria Fiske Hunt
James, Alice
Jewett, Sarah Orne

King, Grace Elizabeth
Larcom, Lucy
Lazarus, Emma
Libbey, Laura Jean
McCrackin, Josephine Woempner Clifford
McDowell, Katharine Sherwood Bonner
Magruder, Julia
Miller, Emily Clark Huntington
Moore, Annie Aubertine Woodward
Moore, Clara Sophia Jessup
Moulton, Louise Chandler
Murfree, Mary Noailles
Nelson, Alice Dunbar
Pennell, Elizabeth Robins
Piatt, Sarah Morgan Bryan
Prentiss, Elizabeth Payson
Preston, Margaret Junkin
Reese, Lizette Woodworth
Rives, Amélie Louise
Sadlier, Mary Anne Madden
Sherwood, Katharine Margaret Brownlee
Sherwood, Mary Elizabeth Wilson
Smith, Hannah Whitall
Southworth, Emma Dorothy Eliza Nevitte
Spencer, Cornelia Ann Phillips
Spofford, Harriet Elizabeth Prescott
Stowe, Harriet Beecher
Stuart, Ruth McEnery
Terhune, Mary Virginia Hawes
Thaxter, Celia Laighton
Thomas, Edith Matilda
Thorpe, Rose Alnora Hartwick
Tiernan, Frances Christine Fisher
Todd, Mabel Loomis
Victor, Metta Victoria Fuller
Ward, Elizabeth Stuart Phelps
Whiting, Lilian
Whitney, Adeline Dutton Train
Wiggin, Kate Douglas Smith
Wilcox, Ella Wheeler
Wilson, Augusta Jane Evans
Wood, Julia Amanda Sargent
Woods, Katharine Pearson
Woolsey, Sarah Chauncey
Woolson, Constance Fenimore

## 1900–1950

Andrews, Mary Raymond Shipman
Antin, Mary
Atherton, Gertrude Franklin Horn
Austin, Mary Hunter
Bates, Katharine Lee
Branch, Anna Hempstead
Brown, Alice
Cather, Willa Sibert
Clarke, Helen Archibald
Coates, Florence Van Leer Earle Nicholson
Crapsey, Adelaide

Elliott, Maud Howe
Field, Rachel Lyman
Follett, Mary Parker
Gale, Zona
Gerould, Katharine Elizabeth Fullerton
Gilder, Jeannette Leonard
Glasgow, Ellen Anderson Gholson
Glaspell, Susan Keating
Harris, Corra May White
Hill, Grace Livingston
Johnston, Mary
Lowell, Amy
Mackenzie, Jean Kenyon
Martin, George Madden
Mayo, Katherine
Millay, Edna St. Vincent
Miller, Alice Duer
Mitchell, Margaret Munnerlyn
Monroe, Harriet
Nelson, Alice Dunbar
Newman, Frances
O'Neill, Rose Cecil
Peabody, Josephine Preston
Porter, Charlotte Endymion
Pryor, Sara Agnes Rice
Putnam, Emily James Smith
Reed, Myrtle
Reese, Lizette Woodworth
Repplier, Agnes
Rice, Alice Caldwell Hegan
Rickert, Edith
Ridge, Lola
Rittenhouse, Jessie Bell
Rives, Amélie Louise
Roberts, Elizabeth Madox
Rourke, Constance Mayfield
Sampter, Jessie Ethel
Sedgwick, Anne Douglas
Skinner, Constance Lindsay
Stein, Gertrude
Stephens, Kate
Stratton-Porter, Gene
Taggard, Genevieve
Tarbell, Ida Minerva
Teasdale, Sara
Thomas, Edith Matilda
Tietjens, Eunice
Trask, Kate Nichols
Tweed, Blanche Oelrichs Thomas Barrymore
Van Vorst, Marie Louise
Webster, Jean
Wells, Carolyn
Wharton, Edith Newbold Jones
Wiggin, Kate Douglas Smith
Woodrow, Nancy Mann Waddel
Wright, Mabel Osgood
Wylie, Elinor Morton Hoyt

*See also* Children's Authors

## Biologists

Clapp, Cornelia Maria
Eigenmann, Rosa Smith
Hyde, Ida Henrietta
Rathbun, Mary Jane
Stevens, Nettie Maria

## Botanists and Horticulturists

Andrews, Eliza Frances
Bodley, Rachel Littler
Brandegee, Mary Katharine Layne Curran
Britton, Elizabeth Gertrude Knight
Colden, Jane
Furbish, Kate
King, Louisa Boyd Yeomans
Logan, Martha Daniell
Mexia, Ynes Enriquetta Julietta
Phelps, Almira Hart Lincoln
Pinckney, Elizabeth Lucas
Pringle, Elizabeth Waties Allston
Sessions, Kate Olivia
Shattuck, Lydia White
Strong, Harriet Williams Russell
Warner, Anna Bartlett

## Businesswomen

*See* Entrepreneurs

## Chemists and Physicists

Bodley, Rachel Littler
Hahn, Dorothy Anna
Maltby, Margaret Eliza
Richards, Ellen Henrietta Swallow
Whiting, Sarah Frances

## Children's Authors

Alcott, Louisa May
Alden, Isabella Macdonald
Andrews, Jane
Bianco, Margery Williams
Brown, Abbie Farwell
Burnett, Frances Eliza Hodgson
Clarke, Rebecca Sophia
Dodge, Mary Elizabeth Mapes
Field, Rachel Lyman
Finley, Martha
Follen, Eliza Lee Cabot
Gág, Wanda Hazel
Hale, Lucretia Peabody
Johnston, Annie Fellows
Leslie, Eliza
Lothrop, Harriett Mulford Stone

Miller, Emily Clark Huntington
Miller, Olive Thorne
Perkins, Lucy Fitch
Porter, Eleanor Hodgman
Prentiss, Elizabeth Payson
Rice, Alice Caldwell Hegan
Richards, Laura Elizabeth Howe
Tappan, Eva March
White, Eliza Orne
Wiggin, Kate Douglas Smith
Woolsey, Sarah Chauncey

## Circus Performers

Leitzel, Lillian
Oakley, Annie
Stratton, Mercy Lavinia Warren Bump

## Civil War Figures

Andrews, Eliza Frances
Barton, Clara
Bickerdyke, Mary Ann Ball
Boyd, Belle
Bradley, Amy Morris
Buckel, Cloe Annette
Carroll, Anna Ella
Chesnut, Mary Boykin Miller
Clay-Clopton, Virginia Caroline Tunstall
Collins, Ellen
Comstock, Elizabeth Leslie Rous
Cumming, Kate
Davis, Varina Anne Howell
Dickinson, Anna Elizabeth
Dix, Dorothea Lynde
Edmonds, Sarah Emma Evelyn
Fowle, Elida Barker Rumsey
Frietschie, Barbara Hauer
Gage, Frances Dana Barker
Gibbons, Abigail Hopper
Gillespie, Mother Angela
Gilson, Helen Louise
Greenhow, Rose O'Neal
Grimké, Charlotte L. Forten
Hancock, Cornelia
Hoge, Jane Currie Blaikie
Hopkins, Juliet Ann Opie
Livermore, Mary Ashton Rice
McCord, Louisa Susannah Cheves
May, Abigail Williams
O'Connell, Sister Anthony
Parsons, Emily Elizabeth
Pember, Phoebe Yates Levy
Pickens, Lucy Petway Holcombe
Porter, Eliza Emily Chappell
Pryor, Sarah Agnes Rice
Safford, Mary Jane
Schofield, Martha

Schuyler, Louisa Lee
Surratt, Mary Eugenia Jenkins
Tompkins, Sally Louisa
Towne, Laura Matilda
Trader, Ella King Newsom
Tubman, Harriet
Tyler, Adeline Blanchard
Van Lew, Elizabeth L.
Walker, Mary Edwards
Wittenmyer, Annie Turner
Woolsey, Abby Howland
Woolsey, Georgeanna
Woolsey, Jane Stuart
Wormeley, Katharine Prescott

## Classicists

Dohan, Edith Hayward Hall
Hawes, Harriet Ann Boyd
King, Lida Shaw
Kober, Alice Elizabeth
Leach, Abby
Macurdy, Grace Harriet
Van Deman, Esther Boise
White, Helen Magill

## College Administrators

Agassiz, Elizabeth Cabot Cary
Butler, Mother Marie Joseph
Douglass, Mabel Smith
Elliott, Harriet Wiseman
Frame, Alice Seymour Browne
Gulick, Alice Winfield Gordon
Gulliver, Julia Henrietta
Hazard, Caroline
Hebard, Grace Raymond
Irwin, Agnes
Kellas, Eliza
King, Lida Shaw
McGroarty, Sister Julia
Mead, Elizabeth Storrs Billings
Mills, Susan Lincoln Tolman
Morgan, Mary Kimball
Mortimer, Mary
Mosher, Eliza Maria
Palmer, Alice Elvira Freeman
Patrick, Mary Mills
Pendleton, Ellen Fitz
Putnam, Emily James Smith
Reinhardt, Aurelia Isabel Henry
Sabin, Ellen Clara
Slowe, Lucy Diggs
Talbot, Marion
Thomas, Martha Carey
Weed, Ella
Woolley, Mary Emma

## Composers

Beach, Amy Marcy Cheney
Bond, Carrie Jacobs

## Dancers

Bonfanti, Marie
Douvillier, Suzanne Theodore Vaillande
Duncan, Isadora
Fuller, Loie
Lee, Mary Ann
Maywood, Augusta
Morlacchi, Giuseppina
Turnbull, Julia Anna

## Editors

*See* Magazine Editors

## Educational Reformers

Beecher, Catharine Esther
Bethune, Joanna Graham
Birney, Alice Josephine McLellan
Colton, Elizabeth Avery
Crocker, Lucretia
Dodge, Grace Hoadley
Flower, Lucy Louisa Coues
Grant, Zilpah Polly
Hallowell, Anna
Hatcher, Orie Latham
Hemenway, Mary Porter Tileston
Irwin, Elisabeth Antoinette
Lyon, Mary
Munford, Mary Cooke Branch
Parrish, Celestia Susannah
Shaw, Pauline Agassiz
Spencer, Cornelia Ann Phillips
Thomas, Martha Carey
Valentine, Lila Hardaway Meade
Willard, Emma Hart
Wright, Frances
Zachry, Caroline Beaumont

## Educators

*See* College Administrators; Educational Reformers; Educators of the Handicapped; Kindergartners; Religious Educators; School Founders and Administrators

## Educators of the Handicapped

Fuller, Sarah
Garrett, Emma

Garrett, Mary Smith
Holt, Winifred
Macy, Anne Sullivan
Rogers, Harriet Burbank
Yale, Caroline Ardelia

## Entrepreneurs

Aitken, Jane
Alexander, Mary Spratt Provoost
Ayer, Harriet Hubbard
Boit, Elizabeth Eaton
Bradford, Cornelia Smith
Brent, Margaret
Demorest, Ellen Louise Curtis
Driscoll, Clara
Estaugh, Elizabeth Haddon
Follett, Mary Parker
Franklin, Ann Smith
Gleason, Kate
Goddard, Mary Katherine
Goddard, Sarah Updike
Green, Anne Catherine Hoof
Green, Hetty Howland Robinson
Haughery, Margaret Gaffney
Knox, Rose Markward
LaForge, Margaret Getchell
Lukens, Rebecca Webb Pennock
McCormick, Nettie Fowler
Marbury, Elisabeth
Moody, Lady Deborah
Nicholson, Eliza Jane Poitevent Holbrook
Ottendorfer, Anna Sartorius Uhl
Patterson, Eleanor Medill
Patterson, Hannah Jane
Pelham, Mary Singleton Copley
Penn, Hannah Callowhill
Perkins, Elizabeth Peck
Philipse, Margaret Hardenbrook
Pinckney, Elizabeth Lucas
Pinkham, Lydia Estes
Pringle, Elizabeth Waties Allston
Seymour, Mary Foot
Stoneman, Abigail
Timothy, Ann
Timothy, Elizabeth
Van Rensselaer, Maria Van Cortlandt
Walker, Maggie Lena
Walker, Sarah Breedlove
Wells, Charlotte Fowler

## Explorers and Travelers

Adams, Harriet Chalmers
Knight, Sarah Kemble
Mexia, Ynes Enriquetta Julietta
Peck, Annie Smith
Royall, Anne Newport

Royce, Sarah Eleanor Bayliss
Workman, Fanny Bullock

## Feminists

Anneke, Mathilde Franziska Giesler
Anthony, Susan Brownell
Blackwell, Alice Stone
Blackwell, Antoinette Louisa Brown
Bloomer, Amelia Jenks
Cowles, Betsey Mix
Crocker, Hannah Mather
Croly, Jane Cunningham
Cutler, Hannah Maria Conant Tracy
Dall, Caroline Wells Healey
Davis, Paulina Kellogg Wright
Diaz, Abby Morton
Dorr, Rheta Childe
Eastman, Crystal
Farnham, Eliza Wood Burhans
Ferrin, Mary Upton
Foster, Abigail Kelley
Fuller, Margaret
Gage, Frances Dana Parker
Gardener, Helen Hamilton
Gilman, Charlotte Anna Perkins Stetson
Goldman, Emma
Grimké, Angelina Emily
Grimké, Sarah Moore
Hale, Sarah Josepha Buell
Hanaford, Phebe Ann Coffin
Hasbrouck, Lydia Sayer
Hunt, Harriott Kezia
Hutchinson, Abigail Jemima
Jones, Jane Elizabeth Hitchcock
Kennedy, Kate
McDowell, Anne Elizabeth
Miller, Elizabeth Smith
Mott, Lucretia Coffin
Murray, Judith Sargent
Nichols, Clarina Irene Howard
Nichols, Mary Sargeant Neal Gove
Owens-Adair, Bethenia Angelina
Packard, Elizabeth Parsons Ware
Parsons, Elsie Clews
Rose, Ernestine Louise Siismondi Potowski
Schwimmer, Rosika
Smith, Abby Hadassah
Smith, Elizabeth Oakes Prince
Smith, Julia Evelina
Spencer, Anna Garlin
Stanton, Elizabeth Cady
Stephens, Kate
Stone, Lucy
Swisshelm, Jane Grey Cannon
Thomas, Martha Carey
Walker, Mary Edwards
Ward, Elizabeth Stuart Phelps

Ward, Hortense Sparks Malsch
Warren, Mercy Otis
Wells, Emmeline Blanche Woodward
Willard, Frances Elizabeth Caroline
Wright, Martha Coffin Pelham
Woodhull, Victoria Claflin
Woolson, Abba Goold

*See also* Suffragists

## Film Actresses and Directors

Brady, Alice
Clark, Marguerite
Crews, Laura Hope
Dressler, Marie
Frederick, Pauline
Guinan, Mary Louise Cecilia
Harlow, Jean
Lawrence, Florence
Lombard, Carole
Moore, Grace
Nazimova, Alla
Normand, Mabel Ethelreid
Robson, May
Turner, Florence E.
Weber, Lois
White, Pearl

## Geographer and Geologist

Bascom, Florence
Semple, Ellen Churchill

## Hawaiian Nobility

Bishop, Bernice Pauahi
Emma
Kaahumanu
Kapiolani
Liliuokalani

## Health Reform Advocates

Baker, Sara Josephine
Bissell, Emily Perkins
Blackwell, Elizabeth
Breckinridge, Madeline McDowell
Crane, Caroline Julia Bartlett
Daniel, Annie Sturges
Davis, Katharine Bement
Davis, Paulina Kellogg Wright
Dennett, Mary Coffin Ware
Dix, Dorothea Lynde
Fowler, Lydia Folger
Gantt, Love Rosa Hirschmann
Hunt, Harriot Kezia

Jones, Jane Elizabeth Hitchcock
Lakey, Alice
Mosher, Eliza Maria
Nichols, Mary Sargeant Neal Gove
Packard, Elizabeth Parsons Ware
Slagle, Eleanor Clarke
Stern, Frances
Valentine, Lila Hardaway Meade
Wells, Charlotte Fowler
Yarros, Rachelle Slobodinsky

## Heroines

Alden, Priscilla
Burk, Martha Cannary
Corbin, Margaret Cochran
Corey, Martha
Dare, Virginia
Darragh, Lydia Barrington
Duston, Hannah
Frankland, Agnes Surriage
Frietschie, Barbara Hauer
Hart, Nancy
Lewis, Ida
McCauley, Mary Ludwig Hays
McCrea, Jane
Nurse, Rebecca
Pocahontas
Ross, Betsy
Sacajawea
Sampson, Deborah
Tubman, Harriet
Zane, Elizabeth

## Historians

Abel, Annie Heloise
Adams, Hannah
Barnes, Mary Downing Sheldon
Booth, Mary Louise
Caulkins, Frances Manwaring
Coman, Katharine
Earle, Alice Morse
Ellet, Elizabeth Fries Lummis
Gardner, Helen
Hemenway, Abby Maria
Hurd-Mead, Kate Campbell
Kellogg, Louise Phelps
Kinzie, Juliette Augusta Magill
Lamb, Martha Joanna Reade Nash
Logan, Deborah Norris
Neilson, Nellie
Nuttall, Zelia Maria Magdalena
Salmon, Lucy Maynard
Skinner, Constance Lindsay
Tarbell, Ida Minerva
Van Rensselaer, Mariana Alley Griswold
Victor, Frances Auretta Fuller

Warren, Mercy Otis
Waters, Clara Erskine Clement
Williams, Mary Wilhelmine
Woodbury, Helen Laura Sumner

## Historical Preservationists

Cunningham, Ann Pamela
Driscoll, Clara
Werlein, Elizebeth Thomas

## Home Economists

Atwater, Helen Woodward
Bevier, Isabel
Campbell, Helen Stuart
Corson, Juliet
Farmer, Fannie Merritt
Herrick, Christine Terhune
Huntington, Emily
Kander, Lizzie Black
Lincoln, Mary Johnson Bailey
Marlatt, Abby Lillian
Norton, Alice Peloubet
Parloa, Maria
Randolph, Mary Randolph
Richards, Ellen Henrietta Swallow
Rorer, Sarah Tyson Heston
Rose, Mary Davies Swartz
Stern, Frances
Talbot, Marion
Terhune, Mary Virginia Hawes
Van Rensselaer, Martha
Wheeler, Ruth
Woolman, Mary Raphael Schenck

## Illustrators

Alexander, Francesca
Comstock, Anna Botsford
Foote, Mary Anna Hallock
Gág, Wanda Hazel
Hokinson, Helen Elna
McMein, Neysa
O'Neill, Rose Cecil
Preston, May Wilson
Smith, Jessie Willcox
Stephens, Alice Barber

## Indian Captives

Duston, Hannah
Jemison, Mary
Kelly, Fanny Wiggins
Oatman, Olive Ann
Parker, Cynthia Ann

Rowlandson, Mary White
Slocum, Frances

## Indian Reform Advocates

Bonney, Mary Lucinda
Bonnin, Gertrude Simmons
Converse, Harriet Maxwell
Fletcher, Alice Cunningham
Ickes, Anna Wilmarth Thompson
Jackson, Helen Maria Fiske Hunt
Quinton, Amelia Stone
Robertson, Alice Mary
Sanders, Elizabeth Elkins
Tibbles, Susette La Flesche
Winnemucca, Sarah

## Indian Women

Bonnin, Gertrude Simmons
Brant, Mary
Davis, Alice Brown
Dorion, Marie
Francis, Milly
Lawson, Roberta Campbell
Montour, Madame
Musgrove, Mary
Picotte, Susan La Flesche
Pocahontas
Sacajawea
Tekakwitha, Catherine
Tibbles, Susette La Flesche
Ward, Nancy
Winnemucca, Sarah

## Inventors

Jones, Amanda Theodosia
Knight, Margaret E.
Masters, Sybilla

## Kindergartners

Blaker, Eliza Ann Cooper
Blow, Susan Elizabeth
Bryan, Anna E.
Cooper, Sarah Brown Ingersoll
Hallowell, Anna
Harrison, Elizabeth
Hill, Patty Smith
Kraus-Boelté, Maria
Laws, Annie
Mann, Mary Tyler Peabody
Marwedel, Emma Jacobina Christiana
Peabody, Elizabeth Palmer
Putnam, Alice Harvey Whiting

Schurz, Margarethe Meyer
Shaw, Pauline Agassiz
Wheelock, Lucy
Wiggin, Kate Douglas Smith

## Labor Leaders

Bagley, Sarah G.
Barry, Leonora Marie Kearney
Bellanca, Dorothy Jacobs
Collins, Jennie
Haley, Margaret Angela
Jones, Mary Harris
Kennedy, Kate
Nestor, Agnes
O'Reilly, Leonora
O'Sullivan, Mary Kenney
Rodgers, Elizabeth Flynn
Stevens, Alzina Parsons
Swartz, Maud O'Farrell
Troup, Augusta Lewis

## Labor Reformers

Barnum, Gertrude
Edson, Katherine Philips
Evans, Elizabeth Glendower
Gillespie, Mabel Edna
Henrotin, Ellen Martin
Henry, Alice
Ickes, Anna Wilmarth Thompson
Kehew, Mary Morton Kimball
Kelley, Florence
McCreery, Maria Maud Leonard
McDowell, Mary Eliza
Marot, Helen
Robins, Margaret Dreier
Simms, Daisy Florence
Ward, Hortense Sparks Malsch
Woerishoffer, Emma Carola
Younger, Maud

## Lawyers

Bittenbender, Ada Matilda Cole
Boissevain, Inez Milholland
Bradwell, Myra Colby
Couzins, Phoebe Wilson
Foltz, Clara Shortridge
Foster, Judith Ellen Horton
Gillett, Emma Millinda
Gordon, Laura de Force
Kilgore, Carrie Burnham
La Follette, Belle Case
Lockwood, Belva Ann Bennett McNall
McCullough, Catharine Gouger Waugh
Mansfield, Arabella

Mussey, Ellen Spencer
Ray, Charlotte E.
Ricker, Marilla Marks Young
Todd, Marion Marsh
Waite, Catharine Van Valkenburg
Ward, Hortense Sparks Malsch
White, Sue Shelton

## Lecturers and Orators

Adams, Harriet Chalmers
Bacon, Delia Salter
Baldwin, Maria Louise
Barry, Leonora Marie Kearney
Brown, Hallie Quinn
Davis, Mary Fenn
Davis, Pauline Kellogg Wright
Dickinson, Anna Elizabeth
Diggs, Annie LePorte
Emery, Sarah Elizabeth Van De Vort
Farnham, Eliza Wood Burhans
Field, Kate
Follett, Mary Parker
Foster, Abigail Kelley
Fuller, Margaret
Gage, Frances Dana Barker
Gilman, Charlotte Anna Perkins Stetson
Goldman, Emma
Gougar, Helen Mar Jackson
Harper, Frances Ellen Watkins
Jones, Jane Elizabeth Hitchcock
Lease, Mary Elizabeth Clyens
Lippincott, Sara Jane Clarke
Livermore, Mary Ashton Rice
Logan, Olive
Morgan, Anna
Newman, Angelia Louise French Thurston
Peck, Annie Smith
Rose, Ernestine Louise Siismondi Potowski
Sanford, Maria Louise
Shaw, Anna Howard
Smith, Elizabeth Oakes Prince
Spencer, Anna Carpenter Garlin
Stanton, Elizabeth Cady
Starr, Eliza Allen
Stearns, Lutie Eugenia
Stewart, Maria W. Miller
Tarbell, Ida Minerva
Todd, Marion Marsh
Wells-Barnett, Ida Bell
Williams, Fannie Barrier
Wright, Frances
Young, Ann Eliza Webb

## Librarians

Ahern, Mary Eileen
Askew, Sarah Byrd

Bogle, Sarah Comly Norris
Fairchild, Mary Salome Cutler
Flexner, Jennie Maas
Greene, Belle da Costa
Hazeltine, Mary Emogene
Hewins, Caroline Maria
Isom, Mary Frances
Kroeger, Alice Bertha
Plummer, Mary Wright
Rathbone, Josephine Adams
Sharp, Katharine Lucinda
Stearns, Lutie Eugenia
Tyler, Alice Sarah
Winser, Beatrice
Wood, Mary Elizabeth

## Literary Scholars

Bates, Katharine Lee
Donnelly, Lucy Martin
Folger, Emily Clara Jordan
Reynolds, Myra
Rickert, Edith
Snyder, Alice D.

## Magazine Editors

Booth, Mary Louise
Bryan, Mary Edwards
Clarke, Helen Archibald
Clarke, Mary Bayard Devereux
Croly, Jane Cunningham
Dodge, Mary Elizabeth Mapes
Farley, Harriet
Gilder, Jeannette Leonard
Hale, Sarah Josepha Buell
Lane, Gerrtude Battles
Larcom, Lucy
Leslie, Eliza
Leslie, Miriam Florence Folline
Monroe, Harriet
Porter, Charlotte Endymion
Sangster, Margaret Elizabeth Munson
Sawyer, Caroline Mehitable Fisher
Shinn, Milicent Washburn
Wells, Emmeline Blanche Woodward
Whittelsey, Abigail Goodrich

## Mathematician

Scott, Charlotte Angas

## Ministers and Evangelists

Avery, Martha Gallison Moore
Barnard, Hannah Jenkins

Blackwell, Antoinette Louisa Brown
Brown, Olympia
Chapin, Augusta Jane
Comstock, Elizabeth Leslie Rous
Crane, Caroline Julia Bartlett
Dyer, Mary
Eastman, Annis Bertha Ford
Fisher, Mary
Gurney, Eliza Paul Kirkbride
Hanaford, Phebe Ann Coffin
Hume, Sophia Wigington
Jones, Rebecca
Jones, Sybil
Livermore, Harriet
McPherson, Aimee Semple
Mott, Lucretia Coffin
Palmer, Phoebe Worrall
Shaw, Anna Howard
Smith, Amanda Berry
Smith, Hannah Whitall
Soule, Caroline Augusta White
Spencer, Anna Carpenter Garlin
Starbuck, Mary Coffyn
Van Cott, Margaret Ann Newton
Way, Amanda M.
Willing, Jennie Fowler

## Missionaries

Bridgman, Eliza Jane Gillett
Cabrini, Saint Frances Xavier
Coppin, Fanny Marion Jackson
Denton, Mary Florence
Duchesne, Rose Philippine
Farrar, Cynthia
Fiske, Fidelia
Frame, Alice Seymour Browne
Fulton, Mary Hannah
Gulick, Alice Winfield Gordon
Hayden, Mother Mary Bridget
Haygood, Laura Askew
Hill, Frances Maria Mulligan
Jones, Sybil
Judson, Ann Hasseltine
Judson, Emily Chubbuck
Judson, Sarah Hall Boardman
Kugler, Anna Sarah
McBeth, Susan Law
Mackenzie, Jean Kenyon
Mills, Susan Lincoln Tolman
Miner, Sarah Luella
Moon, Lottie Digges
Newell, Harriet Atwood
Patrick, Mary Mills
Peabody, Lucy Whitehead McGill Waterbury
Reed, Mary
Robertson, Ann Eliza Worcester
Russell, Mother Mary Baptist

Spalding, Eliza Hart
Swain, Clara A.
Talcott, Eliza
Thoburn, Isabella
Underwood, Lillias Stirling Horton
Vautrin, Minnie
Whitman, Narcissa Prentiss
Wood, Mary Elizabeth
Wright, Laura Maria Sheldon

## Missionary Society Leaders

Bennett, Belle Harris
Bennett, Mary Katharine Jones
Coleman, Alice Blanchard Merriam
Doremus, Sarah Platt Haines
MacLeish, Martha Hillard
Meyer, Lucy Jane Rider
Montgomery, Helen Barrett
Newman, Angelia Louise French Thurston
Peabody, Lucy Whitehead McGill Waterbury
Robinson, Jane Marie Bancroft
Willing, Jennie Fowler
Wittenmyer, Annie Turner

## Mormon Women

Smith, Eliza Roxey Snow
Smith, Emma Hale
Wells, Emmeline Blanche Woodward
Young, Ann Eliza Webb

## Music Educators and Patrons

Hackley, Emma Azalia Smith
Hughes, Adella Prentiss
Mannes, Clara Damrosch
Stevens, Georgia Lydia
Stoeckel, Ellen Battell
Storer, Maria Longworth Nichols
Thurber, Jeannette Meyers

## Musicians

See Composers; Performing Musicians

## Naturalists

Bailey, Florence Augusta Merriam
Comstock, Anna Botsford
Doubleday, Neltje Blanchan De Graff
Eckstorm, Fannie Pearson Hardy
Martin, Maria
Miller, Olive Thorne
Shattuck, Lydia White
Walcott, Mary Morris Vaux
Wright, Mabel Osgood

## Negro Women

Baldwin, Maria Louise
Barrett, Janie Porter
Bowles, Eva del Vakia
Brown, Hallie Quinn
Cary, Mary Ann Shadd
Coppin, Fanny Marion Jackson
Craft, Ellen
Douglass, Sarah Mapps Douglass
Garnet, Sarah J. Smith Thompson
Greenfield, Elizabeth Taylor
Grimké, Charlotte L. Forten
Hackley, Emma Azalia Smith
Harper, Frances Ellen Watkins
Hunton, Addie D. Waites
Jones, Matilda Sissieretta Joyner
Keckley, Elizabeth
Laney, Lucy Craft
Lewis, Edmonia
McClendon, Rose
Mahoney, Mary Eliza
Matthews, Victoria Earle
Mills, Florence
Moten, Lucy Ella
Nelson, Alice Dunbar
Pleasant, Mary Ellen
Ray, Charlotte E.
Rainey, Gertrude Pridgett
Remond, Sarah Parker
Ruffin, Josephine St. Pierre
Slowe, Lucy Diggs
Smith, Amanda Berry
Smith, Bessie
Stewart, Maria W. Miller
Thoms, Adah B. Samuels
Truth, Sojourner
Tubman, Harriet
Walker, Maggie Lena
Walker, Sarah Breedlove
Wells-Barnett, Ida Bell
Wheatley, Phillis
Williams, Fannie Barrier

## Newspaperwomen

Allen, Elizabeth Anne Chase Akers
Ames, Mary E. Clemmer
Ayer, Harriet Hubbard
Black, Winifred Sweet
Bradford, Cornelia Smith
Briggs, Emily Pomona Edson
Cary, Elisabeth Luther
Cary, Mary Ann Shadd
Croly, Jane Cunningham
Dorr, Rheta Childe
Felton, Rebecca Ann Latimer
Field, Kate
Franklin, Ann Smith

Gilder, Jeannette Leonard
Goddard, Mary Katherine
Goddard, Sarah Updike
Greeley-Smith, Nixola
Green, Anne Catherine Hoof
Hamm, Margherita Arlina
Harper, Ida A. Husted
Henry, Alice
Jordan, Elizabeth Garver
Kelly, Florence Finch
Leslie, Amy
Leslie, Annie Louise Brown
Loeb, Sophie Irene Simon
McDowell, Anne Elizabeth
Manning, Marie
Mechlin, Leila
Meloney, Marie Mattingly
Nicholson, Eliza Jane Poitevent Holbrook
Ottendorfer, Anna Sartorius Uhl
Rind, Clementina
Royall, Anne Newport
Scripps, Ellen Browning
Seaman, Elizabeth Cochrane
Sherwood, Katharine Margaret Brownlee
Smedley, Agnes
Swisshelm, Jane Grey Cannon
Timothy, Ann
Timothy, Elizabeth
Walter, Cornelia Wells
Wells-Barnett, Ida Bell
Wood, Julia Amanda Sargent

## Nurses

Crandall, Ella Phillips
Delano, Jane Arminda
Dempsey, Sister Mary Joseph
Fedde, Sister Elizabeth
Mahoney, Mary Eliza
Maxwell, Anna Caroline
Nutting, Mary Adelaide
Palmer, Sophia French
Powell, Louise Mathilde
Richards, Linda
Robb, Isabel Adams Hampton
Stimson, Julia Catherine
Thoms, Adah B. Samuels
Tyler, Adeline Blanchard
Wald, Lillian D.

## Painters

Beaux, Cecilia
Bridges, Fidelia
Brownscombe, Jennie Augusta
Cassatt, Mary
Fuller, Lucia Fairchild
Goldthwaite, Anne Wilson
Goodridge, Sarah

Greatorex, Eliza Pratt
Hale, Susan
Hall, Anne
Hardy, Anna Eliza
Hawthorne, Sophia Amelia Peabody
Johnston, Henrietta
Knowlton, Helen Mary
Martin, Maria
Peale, Anna Claypoole
Peale, Margaretta Angelica
Peale, Sarah Miriam
Pinney, Eunice Griswold
Rand, Ellen Gertrude Emmet
Sartain, Emily
Spencer, Lilly Martin
Stettheimer, Florine
Walcott, Mary Morris Vaux
Weir, Irene

*See also* Printmakers

## Peace Advocates

Addams, Jane
Andrews, Fannie Fern Phillips
Bailey, Hannah Clark Johnston
Catt, Carrie Clinton Lane Chapman
Dennett, Mary Coffin Ware
Dudley, Helena Stuart
Eastman, Crystal
Hooper, Jessie Annette Jack
Lockwood, Belva Ann Bennett McNall
Mead, Lucia True Ames
O'Day, Caroline Love Goodwin
Schwimmer, Rosika
Villard, Fanny Garrison
White, Anna
Woolley, Mary Emma

## Performing Musicians

Abbott, Emma
Bishop, Anna Rivière
Braslau, Sophie
Carreño, Teresa
Cary, Annie Louise
de Cisneros, Eleonora
de Lussan, Zélie
Fay, Amy
Fox, Della May
Greenfield, Elizabeth Taylor
Gluck, Alma
Hackley, Emma Azalia Smith
Hauk, Minnie
Homer, Louise Dilworth Beatty
Hopekirk, Helen
Jones, Matilda Sissieretta Joyner
Juch, Emma Johanna Antonia
Kellogg, Clara Louise

Kronold, Selma
Mannes, Clara Damrosch
Moore, Grace
Morgan, Helen
Nevada, Emma
Nielsen, Alice
Nordica, Lillian
Patti, Adelina
Phillipps, Adelaide
Powell, Maud
Rainey, Gertrude Pridgett
Rider-Kelsey, Corinne
Rivé-King, Julie
Samaroff, Olga
Sanderson, Sibyl Swift
Schumann-Heink, Ernestine
Sembrich, Marcella
Smith, Bessie
Thursby, Emma Cecilia
Urso, Camilla
Van Zandt, Marie
Walker, Edyth
Yaw, Ellen Beach
Zeisler, Fannie Bloomfield

## Philanthropists

Anderson, Elizabeth Milbank
Bishop, Bernice Pauahi
Bliss, Lizzie Plummer
Booth, Ellen Warren Scripps
Bruce, Catherine Wolfe
Caldwell, Mary Gwendolin
Carnegie, Louise Whitfield
Cheney, Ednah Dow Littlehale
Cole, Anna Virginia Russell
Collins, Ellen
Cone, Claribel
Cone, Etta
Dodge, Grace Hoadley
Draper, Mary Anna Palmer
Driscoll, Clara
Eustis, Dorothy Leib Harrison Wood
Fuld, Carrie Bamberger Frank
Garrett, Mary Elizabeth
Greene, Catherine Littlefield
Harkness, Anna M. Richardson
Harkness, Mary Emma Stillman
Harriman, Mary Williamson Averell
Haughery, Margaret Gaffney
Havemeyer, Louisine Waldron Elder
Hearst, Phoebe Apperson
Hemenway, Mary Porter Tileston
Holt, Winifred
Howland, Emily
Jeanes, Anna Thomas
Jenkins, Helen Hartley
Ladd, Kate Macy
Lewisohn, Irene

McCormick, Edith Rockefeller
McCormick, Nettie Fowler
Newcomb, Josephine Louise Le Monnier
Ottendorfer, Anna Sartorius Uhl
Palmer, Lizzie Pitts Merrill
Perkins, Elizabeth Peck
Peter, Sarah Anne Worthington King
Rand, Caroline Amanda Sherfey
Reid, Elisabeth Mills
Rockefeller, Abby Greene Aldrich
Rogers, Grace Rainey
Sage, Margaret Olivia Slocum
Scripps, Ellen Browning
Shaw, Pauline Agassiz
Smith, Sophia
Speyer, Ellin Leslie Prince Lowery
Stanford, Jane Eliza Lathrop
Stoeckel, Ellen Battell
Stokes, Caroline Phelps
Stokes, Olivia Egleston Phelps
Thompson, Elizabeth Rowell
Thurber, Jeannette Meyers
Trask, Kate Nichols
Villard, Fanny Garrison
Walker, Sarah Breedlove
Woerishoffer, Emma Carola
Wolfe, Catharine Lorillard

## Philosophers

Calkins, Mary Whiton
Gulliver, Julia Henrietta
Ladd-Franklin, Christine

## Photographer

Käsebier, Gertrude Stanton

## Physicians

Baker, Sara Josephine
Barrows, Katharine Isabel Hayes Chapin
Bennett, Alice
Blackwell, Elizabeth
Blackwell, Emily
Bodley, Rachel Littler
Broomall, Anna Elizabeth
Brown, Charlotte Amanda Blake
Brunswick, Ruth Jane Mack
Buckel, Cloe Annette
Cleveland, Emeline Horton
Cone, Claribel
Cutler, Hannah Maria Conant Tracy
Daniel, Annie Sturges
De Witt, Lydia Maria Adams
Dimock, Susan
Dolley, Sarah Read Adamson
Fearn, Anne Walter

Fowler, Lydia Folger
Fulton, Mary Hannah
Gantt, Love Rosa Hirschmann
Hunt, Harriot Kezia
Hurd-Mead, Kate Campbell
Hurdon, Elizabeth
Jacobi, Mary Corinna Putnam
Kugler, Anne Sarah
Longshore, Hannah E. Myers
Lozier, Clemence Sophia Harned
McGee, Anita Newcomb
Marshall, Clara
Mayo, Sara Tew
Mergler, Marie Josepha
Mosher, Eliza Maria
Owens-Adair, Bethenia Angelina
Picotte, Susan La Flesche
Preston, Ann
Remond, Sarah Parker
Ripley, Martha George Rogers
Robbins, Jane Elizabeth
Safford, Mary Jane
Sewall, Lucy Ellen
Sherwood, Mary
Stevenson, Sarah Ann Hackett
Swain, Clara A.
Taylor, Lucy Beaman Hobbs
Thomas, Mary Frame Myers
Thompson, Mary Harris
Tracy, Martha
Underwood, Lillias Stirling Horton
Welsh, Lilian
Wollstein, Martha
Yarros, Rachelle Slobodinsky
Zakrzewska, Marie Elizabeth

## Political Figures

### Advisers and Appointees

Abbott, Grace
Berkeley, Lady Frances
Berry, Harriet Morehead
Brent, Margaret
Cunningham, Kate Richards O'Hare
Edson, Katherine Philips
Elliott, Harriet Wiseman
Felton, Rebecca Ann Latimer
Frémont, Jessie Ann Benton
Gardener, Helen Hamilton
La Follette, Belle Case
Lathrop, Julia Clifford
Logan, Mary Simmerson Cunningham
Moskowitz, Belle Lindner Israels
Patterson, Hannah Jane
Rumsey, Mary Harriman
Shaw, Anna Howard
White, Sue Shelton

### Congresswomen and Senators

Caraway, Hattie Ophelia Wyatt
Felton, Rebecca Ann Latimer
Huck, Winnifred Sprague Mason
Kahn, Florence Prag
Langley, Katherine Gudger
O'Day, Caroline Love Goodwin
Robertson, Alice Mary
Simms, Ruth Hanna McCormick

### Other Elected Officials

Barnard, Kate
Ickes, Anna Wilmarth Thompson
Kearney, Belle
Kempfer, Hannah Jensen
Kryszak, Mary Olszewski
Landes, Bertha Ethel Knight

### Party Workers

Brown, Hallie Quinn
Cunningham, Kate Richards O'Hare
Diggs, Annie LePorte
Driscoll, Clara
Edson, Katherine Philips
Emery, Sarah Elizabeth Van De Vort
Foltz, Clara Shortridge
Foster, Judith Ellen Horton
Hay, Mary Garrett
Lease, Mary Elizabeth Clyens
Nelson, Alice Dunbar
Todd, Marion Marsh
Upton, Harriet Taylor
Ward, Hortense Sparks Malsch
White, Sue Shelton

### Propagandists

Carroll, Anna Ella
Cazneau, Jane Maria Eliza McManus Storms
Emery, Sarah Elizabeth Van De Vort
Frémont, Jessie Ann Benton
Greenhow, Rose O'Neal
Holley, Mary Phelps Austin
Todd, Marion Marsh

## Printmakers

Comstock, Anna Botsford
Moran, Mary Nimmo
Palmer, Frances Flora Bond
Sartain, Emily

## Prison Reformers

Barrows, Katharine Isabel Hayes Chapin
Booth, Maud Ballington

Comstock, Elizabeth Leslie Rous
Cunningham, Kate Richards O'Hare
Davis, Katharine Bement
Falconer, Martha Platt
Farnham, Eliza Wood Burhans
Felton, Rebecca Ann Latimer
Foltz, Clara Shortridge
Gibbons, Abigail Hopper
Gilbert, Linda
Hall, Emma Amelia
Hodder, Jessie Donaldson
Johnson, Ellen Cheney
Tutwiler, Julia Strudwick
Wittpen, Caroline Bayard

## Psychologists

Calkins, Mary Whiton
Downey, June Etta
Follett, Mary Parker
Hollingworth, Leta Anna Stetter
Ladd-Franklin, Christine
Martin, Lillien Jane
Shinn, Milicent Washburn
Washburn, Margaret Floy
Woolley, Helen Bradford Thompson
Zachry, Caroline Beaumont

## Religious Educators

Bethune, Joanna Graham
Bishop, Harriet E.
Brownson, Josephine Van Dyke
Butler, Mother Marie Joseph
Case, Adelaide Teague
Connelly, Cornelia Augusta
Gillespie, Mother Angela
Gratz, Rebecca
Hardey, Mother Mary Aloysia
McGroarty, Sister Julia
Morgan, Mary Kimball
Polyblank, Ellen Albertina
Rhodes, Mary
Rogers, Elizabeth Ann
Seton, Elizabeth Ann Bayley
Stevens, Georgia Lydia
Watteville, Henrietta Benigna Justine Zinzendorf von

## Religious Founders and Leaders

Ayres, Anne
Blavatsky, Helena Petrovna Hahn
Booth, Evangeline Cory
Booth, Maud Ballington
Cabrini, Saint Frances Xavier
Cannon, Harriet Starr

Connelly, Cornelia Augusta
Davis, Mary Fenn
Dickinson, Frances
Duchesne, Rose Philippine
Eddy, Mary Baker
Fillmore, Myrtle Page
Fox, Ann Leah, Margaret, and Catherine
Gestefeld, Ursula Newell
Gillespie, Mother Angela
Hardey, Mother Mary Aloysia
Heck, Barbara Ruckle
Heinemann, Barbara
Hopkins, Emma Curtis
Hutchinson, Anne
Lathrop, Mother Mary Alphonsa
Lee, Ann
McPherson, Aimee Semple
Matthews, Ann Teresa
Rhodes, Mary
Riepp, Mother Benedicta
Russell, Mother Mary Baptist
Seton, Elizabeth Ann Bayley
Spalding, Catherine
Stetson, Augusta Emma Simmons
Szold, Henrietta
Tingley, Katherine Augusta Westcott
White, Alma Bridwell
White, Anna
White, Ellen Gould Harmon
Wilkinson, Jemima
Wright, Lucy

*See also* Ministers and Evangelists; Missionaries

## School Founders and Administrators

Andrews, Jane
Anneke, Mathilde Franziska Giesler
Atkins, Mary
Baldwin, Maria Louise
Barrett, Janie Porter
Beecher, Catharine Esther
Berry, Martha McChesney
Bliss, Anna Elvira
Bonney, Mary Lucinda
Brackett, Anna Callender
Bradley, Amy Morris
Bridgman, Eliza Jane Gillet
Butler, Mother Marie Joseph
Coppin, Fanny Marion Jackson
Cowles, Betsey Mix
Crandall, Prudence
Dickey, Sarah Ann
Dorsey, Susan Almira Miller
Duchesne, Rose Philippine
Ferguson, Abbie Park
Gillespie, Mother Angela
Grant, Zilpah Polly

Griffith, Emily
Gulick, Alice Winfield Gordon
Hancock, Cornelia
Hardey, Mother Mary Aloysia
Hayden, Mother Mary Bridget
Haygood, Laura Askew
Hill, Frances Maria Mulligan
Holley, Sallie
Howland, Emily
Irwin, Agnes
Irwin, Elisabeth Antoinette
Kellas, Eliza
Laney, Lucy Craft
Lyon, Mary
MacLeish, Martha Hillard
Mills, Susan Lincoln Tolman
Miner, Myrtilla
Miner, Sarah Luella
Morgan, Anna
Morgan, Mary Kimball
Mortimer, Mary
Moten, Lucy Ella
Packard, Sophia B.
Parrish, Celestia Susannah
Phelps, Almira Hart Lincoln
Pierce, Sarah
Polyblank, Ellen Albertina
Porter, Sarah
Richman, Julia
Robertson, Alice Mary
Rogers, Elizabeth Ann
Rowson, Susanna Haswell
Rutherford, Mildred Lewis
Schofield, Martha
Sewall, May Eliza Wright
Sibley, Mary Easton
Sill, Anna Peck
Stone, Lucinda Hinsdale
Towne, Laura Matilda
Tutwiler, Julia Strudwick
Watteville, Henrietta Benigna Justine Zinzendorf von
White, Helen Magill
Willard, Emma Hart
Wright, Sophie Bell
Young, Ella Flagg

## Sculptors

Eberle, Mary Abastenia St. Leger
Hosmer, Harriet Goodhue
Lewis, Edmonia
Mears, Helen Farnsworth
Ney, Elisabet
Ream, Vinnie
Scudder, Janet
Stebbins, Emma
Whitney, Anne

Whitney, Gertrude Vanderbilt
Wright, Patience Lovell

## Settlement House Leaders

Abbott, Grace
Addams, Jane
Barnum, Gertrude
Bradford, Cornelia Foster
Branch, Anna Hempstead
Dudley, Helena Stuart
Kander, Lizzie Black
Kelley, Florence
Lathrop, Julia Clifford
Lewisohn, Irene
McDowell, Mary Eliza
McMain, Eleanor Laura
Pettit, Katherine
Robbins, Jane Elizabeth
Starr, Ellen Gates
Stevens, Alzina Parsons
Wald, Lillian D.
Williams, Elizabeth Sprague

## Social and Civic Reformers

Bacon, Albion Fellows
Barnard, Kate
Bissell, Emily Perkins
Blankenburg, Lucretia Longshore
Breckinridge, Madeline McDowell
Breckinridge, Sophonisba Preston
Campbell, Helen Stuart
Collins, Ellen
Coman, Katharine
Cotten, Sallie Sims Southall
Crane, Caroline Julia Bartlett
Daniel, Annie Sturges
Davis, Katharine Bement
Decker, Sarah Sophia Chase Platt
de Graffenried, Mary Clare
Diaz, Abby Morton
Diggs, Annie LePorte
Eastman, Crystal
Edson, Katherine Philips
Einstein, Hannah Bachman
Eliot, Charlotte Champe Stearns
Evans, Elizabeth Glendower
Flower, Lucy Louisa Coues
Fuller, Minnie Ursula Oliver Scott Rutherford
Garrett, Mary Smith
Gilman, Charlotte Anna Perkins Stetson
Gilman, Elisabeth
Goldmark, Josephine Clara
Gordon, Jean Margaret
Gordon, Kate M.
Haley, Margaret Angela

Hancock, Cornelia
Harper, Frances Ellen Watkins
Henrotin, Ellen Martin
Iams, Lucy Virginia Dorsey
Ingham, Mary Hall
Jacobs, Pattie Ruffner
Kehew, Mary Morton Kimball
Kelley, Florence
Kingsbury, Susan Myra
Lakey, Alice
Landes, Bertha Ethel Knight
Lathrop, Julia Clifford
Laws, Annie
Loeb, Sophie Irene Simon
Low, Juliette Magill Kinzie Gordon
Lowell, Josephine Shaw
Martin, George Madden
May, Abigail Williams
Montgomery, Helen Barrett
Moskowitz, Belle Lindner Israels
Mumford, Mary Eno Bassett
Munford, Mary Cooke Branch
Mussey, Ellen Spencer
Nathan, Maud
O'Day, Caroline Love Goodwin
Schoff, Hannah Kent
Schuyler, Louisa Lee
Solomon, Hannah Greenebaum
Spencer, Anna Carpenter Garlin
Stevens, Alzina Parsons
Stokes, Caroline Phelps
Stokes, Olivia Egleston Phelps
Turner, Eliza L. Sproat Randolph
Ueland, Clara Hampson
Valentine, Lila Hardaway Meade
Van Vorst, Marie Louise
Wells, Kate Gannett
Williams, Fannie Barrier
Wittpen, Caroline Bayard Stevens
Woerishoffer, Emma Carola
Wood, Edith Elmer

*See also* Health Reform Advocates; Labor Reformers; Settlement House Leaders

## Social Economists

Goldmark, Josephine Clara
Kingsbury, Susan Myra
Peixotto, Jessica Blanche
Wood, Edith Elmer
Woodbury, Helen Laura Sumner

## Social Leaders

Adams, Marian Hooper
Astor, Caroline Webster Schermerhorn

Belmont, Alva Erskine Smith Vanderbilt
Bingham, Anne Willing
Botta, Anne Charlotte Lynch
Burr, Theodosia
Caldwell, Mary Gwendolin
Churchill, Jennie Jerome
Clay-Clopton, Virginia Caroline Tunstall
Cole, Anna Virginia Russell
Curzon, Mary Victoria Leiter
Davis, Mollie Evelyn Moore
De Wolfe, Elsie
Douglas, Adèle Cutts
Fields, Annie Adams
Fish, Marian Graves Anthon
Franks, Rebecca
Gardner, Isabella Stewart
Graeme, Elizabeth Ferguson
Greene, Catherine Littlefield
Greenhow, Rose O'Neal
Harrison, Constance Cary
Johnston, Harriet Lane
Jumel, Eliza
King, Grace Elizabeth
Le Vert, Octavia Celeste Walton
McCormick, Edith Rockefeller
McLean, Evalyn Walsh
Madison, Dolley Payne Todd
Moulton, Louise Chandler
Palmer, Bertha Honoré
Pickens, Lucy Petway Holcombe
Pryor, Sara Agnes Rice
Reid, Elisabeth Mills
Schuyler, Catherine Van Rensselaer
Sherwood, Mary Elizabeth Wilson
Smith, Margaret Bayard
Speyer, Ellin Leslie Prince Lowery
Sprague, Kate Chase
Tweed Blanche Oelrichs Thomas Barrymore
Tyler, Priscilla Cooper
Werlein, Elizebeth Thomas

## Social Workers

Breckinridge, Sophonisba Preston
Dinwiddie, Emily Wayland
Glenn, Mary Willcox Brown
Kingsbury, Susan Myra
Lothrop, Alice Louise Higgins
Pratt, Anna Beach
Regan, Agnes Gertrude
Richmond, Mary Ellen
Smith, Zilpha Drew

## Socialists and Radicals

Avery, Martha Gallison Moore
Cunningham, Kate Richards O'Hare
Evans, Elizabeth Glendower

Gilman, Elisabeth
Goldman, Emma
Herron, Carrie Rand
Kelley, Florence
McCreery, Maria Maud Leonard
Marot, Helen
Rand, Caroline Amanda Sherfey
Ridge, Lola
Smedley, Agnes
Starr, Ellen Gates
Stokes, Rose Harriet Pastor
Wright, Frances

## Suffragists

Anneke, Mathilde Franziska Giesler
Anthony, Susan Brownell
Avery, Rachel G. Foster
Belmont, Alva Erskine Smith Vanderbilt
Bissell, Emily Perkins
Bittenbender, Ada Matilda Cole
Blackwell, Alice Stone
Blackwell, Antoinette Louisa Brown
Blake, Lillie Devereux
Blankenburg, Lucretia Longshore
Blatch, Harriot Eaton Stanton
Bloomer, Amelia Jenks
Boissevain, Inez Milholland
Breckinridge, Madeline McDowell
Brown, Olympia
Catt, Carrie Clinton Lane Chapman
Chace, Elizabeth Buffum
Cheney, Ednah Dow Littlehale
Clarke, Grace Giddings
Clay, Laura
Clay-Clopton, Virginia Caroline Tunstall
Colby, Clara Dorothy Bewick
Couzins, Phoebe Wilson
Cutler, Hannah Maria Conant Tracy
Davis, Katharine Bement
Davis, Mary Fenn
Davis, Paulina Kellogg Wright
Dennett, Mary Coffin Ware
Dodge, Josephine Marshall Jewell
Duniway, Abigail Jane Scott
Elliott, Sarah Barnwell
Foltz, Clara Shortridge
Fuller, Minnie Ursula Oliver Scott Rutherford
Gage, Matilda Joslyn
Gardener, Helen Hamilton
Gordon, Jean Margaret
Gordon, Kate M.
Gordon, Laura de Force
Gougar, Helen Mar Jackson
Grew, Mary
Griffing, Josephine Sophia White
Harper, Ida A. Husted
Havemeyer, Louisine Waldron Elder

Hay, Mary Garrett
Hebard, Grace Raymond
Hooker, Isabella Beecher
Hooper, Jessie Annette Jack
Howe, Julia Ward
Howland, Emily
Ingham, Mary Hall
Jacobs, Pattie Ruffner
Kearney, Belle
Laidlaw, Harriet Burton
Leslie, Miriam Florence Folline
Livermore, Mary Ashton Rice
Lockwood, Belva Ann Bennett McNall
McCreery, Maria Maud Leonard
McCulloch, Catharine Gouger Waugh
May, Abigail Williams
Merrick, Caroline Elizabeth Thomas
Minor, Virginia Louisa
Morris, Esther Hobart McQuigg Slack
Nathan, Maud
Patterson, Hannah Jane
Ricker, Marilla Marks Young
Robinson, Harriet Jane Hanson
Severance, Caroline Maria Seymour
Sewall, May Eliza Wright
Shaw, Anna Howard
Shuler, Nettie Rogers
Smith, Abby Hadassah
Smith, Julia Evelina
Stanton, Elizabeth Cady
Stone, Lucy
Thomas, Martha Carey
Thomas, Mary Frame Myers
Turner, Eliza L. Sproat Randolph
Ueland, Clara Hampson
Upton, Harriet Taylor
Valentine, Lila Hardaway Meade
Villard, Fanny Garrison
Waite, Catharine Van Valkenburg
Wallace, Zerelda Gray Sanders
Way, Amanda M.
Wells, Emmeline Blanche Woodward
Wells, Kate Gannett
Wells-Barnett, Ida Bell
White, Sue Shelton
Woodhull, Victoria Claflin
Younger, Maud

## Temperance Advocates

Bailey, Hannah Clark Johnston
Bateham, Josephine Abiah Penfield Cushman
Bittenbender, Ada Matilda Cole
Bloomer, Amelia Jenks
Brown, Martha McClellan
Carse, Matilda Bradley
Chapin, Sarah Flournoy Moore
Colman, Julia

Comstock, Elizabeth Leslie Rous
Foster, Judith Ellen Horton
Fowler, Lydia Folger
Fuller, Minnie Ursula Oliver Scott Rutherford
Gage, Frances Dana Barker
Gordon, Anna Adams
Gougar, Helen Mar Jackson
Harper, Frances Ellen Watkins
Hay, Mary Garrett
Hunt, Mary Hannah Hanchett
Kearney, Belle
Leavitt, Mary Greenleaf Clement
Livermore, Mary Ashton Rice
Merrick, Caroline Elizabeth Thomas
Miller, Emily Clark Huntington
Nation, Carry Amelia Moore
Smith, Hannah Whitall
Stevens, Lillian Marion Norton Ames
Stewart, Eliza Daniel
Stoddard, Cora Frances
Thompson, Eliza Jane Trimble
Wallace, Zerelda Gray Sanders
Way, Amanda M.
Willard, Frances Elizabeth Caroline
Willing, Jennie Fowler
Wittenmyer, Annie Turner

## Translators

Booth, Mary Louise
Conant, Hannah O'Brien Chaplin
Hapgood, Isabel Florence
Moore, Annie Aubertine Woodward
Wormeley, Katharine Prescott

## Welfare Work Leaders

Ames, Fanny Baker
Barrett, Janie Porter
Barrett, Kate Harwood Waller
Barton, Clara
Bayer, Adèle Parmentier
Bethune, Joanna Graham
Boardman, Mabel Thorp
Booth, Evangeline Cory
Booth, Maud Ballington
Bowles, Eva del Vakia
Cannon, Harriet Starr
Collins, Jennie
Cratty, Mabel
Cushman, Vera Charlotte Scott
Dodge, Grace Hoadley
Dodge, Josephine Marshall Jewell
Doremus, Sarah Platt Haines
Fedde, Sister Elizabeth
Fields, Annie Adams
Flower, Lucy Louisa Coues

Graham, Isabella Marshall
Gratz, Rebecca
Griffing, Josephine Sophia White
Hamilton, Elizabeth Schuyler
Haughery, Margaret Gaffney
Haviland, Laura Smith
Henrotin, Ellen Martin
Hobson, Elizabeth Christophers Kimball
Hoge, Jane Currie Blaikie
Huntington, Emily
Hunton, Addie D. Waites
Jacobs, Frances Wisebart
Lathrop, Mother Mary Alphonsa
Lowell, Josephine Shaw
Matthews, Victoria Earle
Meyer, Lucy Jane Rider
O'Connell, Sister Anthony
Palmer, Phoebe Worrall
Peter, Sarah Anne Worthington King
Prior, Margaret Barrett Allen
Ripley, Martha George Rogers
Robinson, Jane Marie Bancroft
Rumsey, Mary Harriman
Russell, Mother Mary Baptist
Sampter, Jessie Ethel
Schuyler, Louisa Lee
Simms, Daisy Florence
Smith, Virginia Thrall
Solomon, Hannah Greenebaum
Szold, Henrietta
Wells, Kate Gannett
Wise, Louise Waterman
Wittenmyer, Annie Turner
Wittpen, Caroline Bayard Stevens
Wright, Sophie Bell

*See also* Social Workers

## Wives of the Presidents

Adams, Abigail Smith
Adams, Louisa Catherine Johnson
Arthur, Ellen Lewis Herndon
Cleveland, Frances Folsom
Fillmore, Abigail Powers
Garfield, Lucretia Rudolph
Harding, Florence Kling
Harrison, Anna Symmes
Harrison, Caroline Lavinia Scott
Harrison, Mary Scott Dimmick
Hayes, Lucy Ware Webb
Hoover, Lou Henry
Jackson, Rachel Donelson Robards
Jefferson, Martha Wayles Skelton
Johnson, Eliza McCardle
Lincoln, Mary Ann Todd
McKinley, Ida Saxton
Madison, Dolley Payne Todd

Monroe, Elizabeth Kortright
Pierce, Jane Means Appleton
Polk, Sarah Childress
Roosevelt, Alice Hathaway Lee
Roosevelt, Edith Kermit Carow
Taft, Helen Herron
Taylor, Margaret Mackall Smith
Tyler, Julia Gardiner
Tyler, Letitia Christian
Van Buren, Hannah Hoes
Washington, Martha Dandridge Curtis
Wilson, Ellen Louise Axson

## Women's Club Leaders

Birney, Alice Josephine McLellan
Blankenburg, Lucretia Longshore
Brown, Hallie Quinn
Clarke, Grace Giddings
Cotten, Sallie Sims Southall
Croly, Jane Cunningham
Cunningham, Ann Pamela
Darling, Flora Adams
Decker, Sarah Sophia Chase Platt
Demorest, Ellen Louise Curtis
Doyle, Sarah Elizabeth

Driscoll, Clara
Garnet, Sarah J. Smith Thompson
Harper, Frances Ellen Watkins
Henrotin, Ellen Martin
Howe, Julia Ward
King, Louisa Boyd Yeomans
Lakey, Alice
Landes, Bertha Ethel Knight
Laws, Annie
Lawson, Roberta Campbell
Matthews, Victoria Earle
May, Abigail Williams
Mumford, Mary Eno Bassett
Robinson, Harriet Jane Hanson
Ruffin, Josephine St. Pierre
Severance, Carolina Maria Seymour
Sewall, May Eliza Wright
Sherman, Mary Belle King
Sherwood, Katharine Margaret Brownlee
Shuler, Nettie Rogers
Solomon, Hannah Greenebaum
Stone, Lucinda Hinsdale
Turner, Eliza L. Sproat Randolph
Walworth, Ellen Hardin
Wells-Barnett, Ida Bell
Williams, Fannie Barrier
Winter, Alice Vivian Ames